HISTORY

The Agrarian History of England and Wales: Volume IV 1500 to 1640

Editor: JOAN THIRSK
Reader in Economic History, University of Oxford

General Editor of the series: H. P. R. FINBERG
Professor of History, University of Leicester

The first volume to be published of an important new project—a complete social and economic history of rural England and Wales from the beginning of systematic agriculture in the Neolithic period to the present time. The series will include much new research into original sources, and will become the standard work on the subject.

THE
AGRARIAN HISTORY OF
ENGLAND AND WALES

GENERAL EDITOR

H. P. R. FINBERG, M.A., D.LITT., F.S.A., F.R.HIST.S.

"The people in the old time (as Cato, a man of great wisdom and a teacher of husbandry doth witness) as oft as they would give a man the name of an honest man, they would call him a good husband, comprehending in that name as much commendation as they could give him."

(GERVASE MARKHAM, *The Whole Art of Husbandry*, 1631)

"In which discourse as the rustical people and plain clouted shoes shall happily find some variety of soil in sundry places where their ordinary dung doth fail them, so those which are ingenious may gather philosophical matter enough to stir up their sharp wits to a higher contemplation of Nature then the bare letter doth impoort."

(HUGH PLATT, *The Jewell House of Art and Nature* 1594)

IV. 1500–1640

THE
AGRARIAN HISTORY OF
ENGLAND AND WALES

VOLUME IV 1500–1640

EDITED BY

JOAN THIRSK

Reader in Economic History, University of Oxford

CAMBRIDGE
AT THE UNIVERSITY PRESS

1966

Published by the Syndics of the Cambridge University Press
Bentley House, 200 Euston Road, London N.W.1
American Branch: 32 East 57th Street, New York, N.Y. 10022
West African Office: P.M.B. 5181, Ibadan, Nigeria

Printed in Great Britain
at the University Printing House, Cambridge
(Brooke Crutchley, University Printer)

Library of Congress Catalogue
Card Number:

PREFACE

In 1883 Frederic Seebohm published his *English Village Community*, a book which, as Maitland, its chief critic, remarked, "made an epoch" in the writing of agrarian history. At that time the *History of Agriculture and Prices in England, 1259–1793*, by J. E. Thorold Rogers, was still in progress; the seventh and last volume appeared in 1887. These two master-works laid the foundations for all subsequent study of the English rural past.

Debate on the origins of the manor, initiated by Seebohm, was fruitfully continued by Vinogradoff and Maitland. Enclosures of common land, and the social effects of enclosure, were examined by G. Slater (*The English Peasantry and the Enclosure of the Common Fields*, 1907), A. H. Johnson (*The Disappearance of the Small Landowner*, 1909), and E. C. K. Gonner (*Common Land and Inclosure*, 1912). In 1911 John and Barbara Hammond published *The Village Labourer*, a concentrated and impassioned study of the effects of parliamentary enclosure on the rural proletariat. A year later R. H. Tawney's *Agrarian Problem in the Sixteenth Century* pushed the investigation further back, and R. E. Prothero (later Lord Ernle) brought out the first attempt at a comprehensive survey, *English Farming Past and Present*. Finally the American historian H. L. Gray made a detailed study of English field systems in a book of that name, published in 1915.

All these books are still read and are likely to remain standard works. As Dr Thirsk has remarked (AHR, CXI, 1955, p. 67), they "made their appearance during an agricultural depression, in the midst of earnest, anxious discussion about the future of agriculture, which taxed the historian with questions about the past." But the war of 1914 brought a renewal of prosperity to our farmers, the discussion lost urgency, and the study of agrarian history languished for several decades. When it was taken up again, historians turned their attention to detailed local studies and no longer attempted to produce surveys on a national scale. They were encouraged in this approach by the growth of public interest in local history and by the opening of archive repositories in many counties, where immense new accumulations of documentary material invited study.

After the interruption of another war, interest revived, and a number of new monographs appeared. Scholars were now at work in sufficient numbers to encourage the foundation of a new society and a new periodical. The British Agricultural History Society held its inaugural meeting in April 1953. Since then its membership has grown continually, and its journal, the *Agricultural History Review*, has provided a medium for the publication of important original work. Encouraged by the success of these ventures, some of us began to dream of something on a more ambitious scale. At a meeting held in London on the 14th of January 1956 under the presidency of the late R. H. Tawney plans were laid for the project which now bears its first-fruit with the publication of this volume. The conduct of the undertaking was entrusted to a General Editor, assisted by an Advisory Committee of scholars from eleven universities. None of those who took part in the inaugural discussion harboured any illusions about the magnitude of the task. A complete social and economic history of rural England and Wales, from the beginnings of systematic agriculture in the neolithic period down to a terminal point in the twentieth century, would require at least seven volumes and could only be conceived as an effort of co-operative scholarship extending over many years. A vast amount of new research would have to be undertaken if the History were to be more than a synthesis of existing knowledge revealing almost equally large tracts of ignorance. It was decided that each volume should have its own editor, that the volumes should not necessarily follow a uniform plan, and that the fourth volume, covering the sixteenth and part of the seventeenth centuries, should be the first to be put in hand.

The concept of agrarian history, *Agrargeschichte*, is perhaps more familiar to German than to English readers. Objection has been taken in some quarters to its use in the title of this work, but semantic and lexicographical authority does not support the objection. According to the *Oxford English Dictionary*, agrarian means, in general, 'pertaining to land'. Two other, more specific, senses are: 'relating to, or connected with, landed property', and 'of, relating to, or connected with, cultivated land, or its cultivation'. No other single word so fully covers a work dealing with arable and pastoral husbandry, the marketing of produce, housing, the distribution of landownership, and the structure of rural society.

No academic body has taken the History under its wing to the extent of providing it with permanent headquarters, but the Trustees of the Nuffield Foundation generously made two grants towards the expenses of research. For this encouragement and help the editors and contributors are deeply grateful.

Notwithstanding the long preparation and sustained efforts of Dr Thirsk and her contributors, there are gaps in this volume which the editors regret, and there are doubtless errors of which they are unaware. There can be no finality in any work of historical research. In this connection a remark once made by R. H. Worth, in his time the patriarch of the Devonshire Association, is apposite. "One always writes too soon; but if one puts it off, one may not write at all."

H. P. R. FINBERG

ADVISORY COMMITTEE

FOR THE AGRARIAN HISTORY OF ENGLAND AND WALES

1956

Chairman: R. H. Tawney, LITT.D., F.B.A., *Professor Emeritus of Economic History, University of London*

M. W. Beresford, M.A., *Reader in Economic History, University of Leeds*

E. G. Bowen, M.A., *Gregynog Professor of Geography and Anthropology, University College of Wales (Aberystwyth)*

J. D. Chambers, B.A., PH.D., *Reader in Economic and Social History, University of Nottingham*

H. C. Darby, O.B.E., M.A., PH.D., *Professor of Geography, University College, London*

H. P. R. Finberg, M.A., F.S.A., *Head of the Department of English Local History, University College, Leicester, editor of the Agricultural History Review*

Alexander Hay, *General Secretary of the Association of Agriculture*

J. W. Y. Higgs, M.A., *Lecturer in the History of Agriculture and Keeper of the Museum of English Rural Life, University of Reading*

R. H. Hilton, D.PHIL., *Lecturer in History, University of Birmingham*

W. G. Hoskins, M.A., PH.D., *Reader in Economic History, University of Oxford*

H. C. Pawson, M.B.E., M.SC., *Professor and Assistant Director of the Department of Agriculture, King's College, Newcastle upon Tyne*

Stuart Piggott, B.LITT., F.B.A., F.S.A., *Abercromby Professor of Prehistoric Archaeology, University of Edinburgh*

M. M. Postan, M.SC., M.A., *Professor of Economic History, University of Cambridge; editor of the Economic History Review*

C. E. Stevens, M.A., B.LITT., *Fellow of Magdalen College, and Lecturer in Ancient History, University of Oxford*

(Mrs) I. Joan Thirsk, B.A., PH.D., *Senior Research Fellow in Agrarian History, University College, Leicester*

Edgar Thomas, B.LITT., B.SC., *Professor of Agricultural Economics, University of Reading*

Sir James A. Scott Watson, C.B.E., LL.D., D.SC., *President of the British Agricultural History Society; formerly Chief Scientific and Agricultural Advisor to the Ministry of Agriculture and Fisheries*

Edith H. Whetham, M.A., *Gilbey Lecturer in Agricultural Economics and History, University of Cambridge*

David Williams, M.A., *Sir John Williams Professor of Welsh History, University College of Wales (Aberystwyth)*

ADVISORY COMMITTEE

FOR THE AGRARIAN HISTORY OF ENGLAND AND WALES

1966

Chairman: The Rt. Hon. the Lord Rennell of Rodd

M. W. Beresford, M.A., *Professor of Economic History, University of Leeds*

E. G. Bowen, M.A., *Gregynog Professor of Geography and Anthropology, University College of Wales (Aberystwyth)*

W. H. Chaloner, M.A., PH.D., *Reader in Modern Economic History, University of Manchester*

J. D. Chambers, B.A., PH.D., *sometime Professor of Economic History, University of Nottingham*

H. C. Darby, O.B.E., M.A., PH.D., *Professor of Geography, University of Cambridge*

H. P. R. Finberg, M.A., D.LITT., F.S.A., *Professor Emeritus of English Local History, University of Leicester*

Alexander Hay, *sometime General Secretary of the Association of Agriculture*

J. W. Y. Higgs, M.A., *Lecturer in the History of Agriculture, Fellow of Exeter College, University of Oxford*

R. H. Hilton, B.A., D.PHIL., *Professor of Medieval Social History, University of Birmingham*

W. G. Hoskins, M.A., PH.D., *Hatton Professor of English History, University of Leicester*

A. H. John, B.SC., PH.D., *Professor of Economic History, London School of Economics*

G. E. Mingay, B.A., PH.D., *Reader in Economic History, University of Kent at Canterbury*

Sir Thomas Neame, *Royal Agricultural Society of England*

H. C. Pawson, M.B.E., M.SC., *Emeritus Professor of Agriculture, King's College, Newcastle*

Stuart Piggott, B.LITT., D.LITT.HON., F.B.A., F.S.A., *Abercromby Professor of Prehistoric Archaeology, University of Edinburgh*

M. M. Postan, M.SC., M.A., F.B.A., *sometime Professor of Economic History, University of Cambridge*

C. E. Stevens, M.A., B.LITT., *Fellow of Magdalen College, Lecturer in Ancient History, University of Oxford*

(Mrs) I. Joan Thirsk, M.A., PH.D., *Reader in Economic History, University of Oxford*

Edgar Thomas, B.LITT., B.SC., *Professor of Agricultural Economics, University of Reading*

F. M. L. Thompson, M.A., D.PHIL., *Reader in Economic History, University College, London*

Edith H. Whetham, M.A., *sometime Gilbey Lecturer in Agricultural Economics and History, University of Cambridge*

Glanmor Williams, J.P., M.A., D.LITT., *Professor of History, University College of Swansea*

CONTENTS

CHAPTER I

The Farming Regions of England

By JOAN THIRSK, B.A., PH.D., F.R.HIST.S., Reader in Economic History, University of Oxford

CHAPTER II

The Farming Regions of Wales

By FRANK EMERY, B.LITT., M.A., Fellow of St Peter's College, Oxfotd; University Lecturer in Historical Geography

CHAPTER III

Farming Techniques

By JOAN THIRSK

CHAPTER IV

Enclosing and Engrossing

By JOAN THIRSK

CHAPTER V

Landlords in England

By GORDON BATHO, M.A., F.R.HIST.S., Lecturer in Education,
University of Sheffield

CHAPTER VI

Landlords in Wales

By GLANMOR WILLIAMS, M.A., D.LITT. (WALES), F.R.HIST.S.,
Professor of History, University College of Swansea

CHAPTER VII

Farm Labourers

By ALAN EVERITT, M.A., PH.D., Research Fellow in Urban History,
University of Leicester

CHAPTER VIII

The Marketing of Agricultural Produce

By ALAN EVERITT

CHAPTER IX

Agricultural Prices, Farm Profits, and Rents

By PETER BOWDEN, B.A., PH.D., Senior Research Fellow,
Business Research Unit, University of Durham

CHAPTER X

Rural Housing in England

By M. W. BARLEY, M.A., F.S.A., Senior Lecturer in Archaeology,
University of Nottingham

CHAPTER XI

Rural Housing in Wales

By PETER SMITH, B.A., F.S.A., member of staff of the Royal Commission
on Ancient Monuments in Wales and Monmouthshire

Statistical Appendix

By Peter Bowden

PLATES

Between pages oo *and* oo

ACKNOWLEDGEMENTS

We are grateful to the following for permission to use their photographs: Messrs B. T. Batsford for Plates V and VI *b*; the Royal Commission on Historical Monuments (England) for Plates VI *a*, XI *a* and *b*, XII *b*, and XVI; the National Monuments Record for Plates VII, IX *b*, X, XIII *a* and *b*, XIV *a* and *b*, and XV *b*; Mr E. W. Parkin for Plate VIII *a*; Mr F. H. Crossley for Plate VIII *b*; the Essex County Record Office for Plate XV *a*; the Royal Commission on Ancient Monuments and Mr H. Brooksby for Plates XVII *a*, *b*, and *c*, XVIII *a* and *b*, XIX *a*, XXI *a*, and XXII *a* and *b*; the Royal Commission on Ancient Monuments also for Plates XXIII *a* and *b*; and Mr D. B. Hagne for Plate XXIII *b*.

TEXT-FIGURES

TABLES

STATISTICAL APPENDIX

A. Price of agricultural commodities: annual averages

B. Price of agricultural commodities: decennial averages

INTRODUCTION

It is not easy to see familiar places in the countryside, and imagine how they looked in the age of the Tudors. Journeys were impeded by obstacles that have now disappeared; the farmer was hindered by infertile or waterlogged soils which have since been so transformed by the labours of man that it is difficult to believe the unlovely descriptions given them by contemporaries. Who would recognize in the harsh, monotonously repeated phrases of a seventeenth-century surveyor describing furzy, bushy, and barren pasture an account of the orchard country of Worcestershire, or believe that Staffordshire could once have been described as "for the most part barren, one fourth being heath and waste, and another fourth being chases and parks"? Can anyone embarking nowadays on the journey from Oxford to Cambridge appreciate the complaints of an Elizabethan traveller at the "villainous, boggy, and wild country," "very little inhabited," and "nearly a waste" which he encountered at the start of his tour?[1]

No wayfarer in England expected an easy passage all the way, even when he confined himself to the well-trodden thoroughfares of the Home Counties. But having seen the worst as well as the best, the barren mountain sides and the marshy vales as well as the fair cornfields and the sweet downland pastures, what overall impression did he form of England and Wales? The most dispassionate views, perhaps, were expressed by foreigners. They came as diplomats, as merchants, or as young men completing their education. And although some travelled no further north than Theobalds, nor further west than Oxford, some did venture far afield, and one at least went to Scotland.

Surprising though it may at first seem, the foreigner saw England first and foremost as a country of woodland and pasture, parks and chases. Nicander Nucius, travelling through the kingdom in 1545–6, described it as "diversified with fruitful hills and plains, and abound-[ing] with marshes and well-timbered oak forests." The French scholar, Estienne Perlin, writing in 1558, portrayed the same scene, but in more imaginative prose. "The country is well wooded and shady, for the fields are all enclosed with hedges, oak trees, and several others sorts of trees, to such an extent that in travelling you think you are in a con-

---

[1] *The Parliamentary Survey of the Lands and Possessions of the Dean and Chapter of Worcester*, ed. T. Cave and R. A. Wilson, Worcs. Hist. Soc., 1924, pp. 40–54; SP 14, 113, 17; W. B. Rye, *England as seen by Foreigners*, p. 31.

tinuous wood." Again to the same purpose, but with Germanic precision, wrote Paul Hentzner, a native of Brandenburg, in 1598. "The soil is fruitful and abounds with cattle, which inclines the people rather to feeding than ploughing, so that near a third part of the land is left uncultivated for grazing." Finally, in a compendium of hints written some time before 1606 to assist the Frenchman, Loiseau de Tourval, during his travels in England, these facts about Britain were driven home by a direct comparison. "The face of the countryside bears some resemblance to that of Brittany and Normandy, differing in one thing only from all the other countries of the world, that there is none which uses so much land for pasture as this."[1]

In this country of grassland and forest, then, the attention of foreigners was fixed, not upon the arable crops, but upon the cattle and horses, the pigs "larger than in any other country," and the multitudes of sheep. On these topics they all dilated in astonishment. "Of such animals as are tame and domesticated with us," exclaimed Nicander Nucius, "there are almost too many to be enumerated, so many horses and those of noble breed too, and so many oxen, and so many flocks of sheep, that wonder arises in the beholders on account of the multitude of them." He sang a refrain which was taken up by every roving reporter from the Continent. Frederick, duke of Württemberg, may stand as chorus master for all the rest. In one of his few passages describing the countryside in 1592, he wrote of the land between London and Oxford that it was "in some places very fertile, in others very boggy and mossy, and such immense numbers of sheep are bred on it round about that it is astonishing. There is besides a superabundance of fine oxen and other good cattle."[2]

Once convinced that pasture and woodland predominated, that stock claimed more attention than crops, foreign travellers were moved to generalize about the character of the English countryman. According to Andreas Franciscus, who visted England from Italy in 1497, the farmer was slow and lazy, and did not bother to plant more wheat than was necessary for his own consumption, preferring to use his ground for sheep. The Mantuan, Litolfi, thought him lazier still: no peasant, male or female, walked if he could possibly help it; he rode on horseback, and "miserable must that man be who follows his cart on foot."

---

[1] *The Second Book of the Travels of Nicander Nucius of Corcyra*, ed. J. A. Cramer, Camden Soc., XVII, 1841, p. 18; *Description des Royaumes d'Angleterre et d'Écosse composée par Estienne Perlin, Paris, 1558*, ed. R. Gough, London, 1775, p. 25; Rye, *op. cit.*, p. 109. See also Italian comments to like effect—E. Gurney Salter, *Tudor England through Venetian Eyes*, 1930, pp. 70–2; Georges Ascoli, *La Grande-Bretagne devant l'Opinion Française au XVIIe Siècle*, Paris, 1930, Travaux et Mémoires de l'Université de Lille, NS, Fascicule 13, I, p. 290.

[2] Nicander Nucius, *op. cit.*, p. 18; Rye, *op. cit.*, p. 30.

It was no surprise to him that England was commonly known as "the land of comforts."[1]

Others writers encountered the parks and chases, observed the deer and the hares—in the vicinity of Windsor, the duke of Württemberg counted upwards of sixty deer parks—and drew their own conclusions about the pleasure-loving ways of the gentry. The English preferred the delights of hunting to the hard work of cultivating their land. So concluded Emanuel van Meteren, an Antwerp merchant, who travelled through England and Ireland in 1575. They were not as industrious as the Netherlanders or the French.[2]

The foreigner did not, of course, entirely fail to see the ploughed fields and their crops. Lupuld von Wedel, riding northward in 1584, saw oats and barley standing in the fields of Alnwick fourteen days after the feast of St Bartholomew. Thomas Platter commended the corn crops and orchards along the roads in the immediate vicinity of London. Paul Hentzner witnessed a harvest home near Eton.

"As we were returning to our inn we happened to meet some country people celebrating their harvest home; their last load of corn they crown with flowers, having besides an image richly dressed, by which, perhaps, they would signify Ceres; this they keep moving about, while men and women, men- and maidservants riding through the streets in the cart, shout as loud as they can till they arrive at the barn. The farmers here do not bind up their corn in sheaves as they do with us but directly as they have reaped or mowed it, put it into carts and convey it to their barns."

Colourful passages like this, however, were few and far between. In the eys of the stranger they did not depict the most characteristic scenes in the English countryside.[3]

How correct were the foreigner's impressions? They were one-sided, perhaps, but was not the Englishman's view of his country with its obstinate emphasis on the valiant husbandman equally one-sided? The ploughman bent over his plough, or the sower sowing his seed—these were the conventional figures symbolizing agriculture—but did they not reflect aspirations rather than convey a picture of reality? There had been a time when England, and much of Wales too, had been almost completely covered by trees, and although this was ancient history, the forests were still extensive and reminded the Englishman at every turn

[1] C. V. Malfatti, transl., *Two Italian Accounts of Tudor England*, 1953, p. 41; Cal. SP Ven. VI, 3, App. p. 1672.

[2] Rye, *op. cit.*, pp. 14–15, 70. See also E. Gurney Salter, *op. cit.*, p. 70.

[3] W. Robson Scott, *German Travellers in England, 1400–1800*, 1953, p. 44; Clare Williams, *Thomas Platter's Travels in England, 1599*, 1937, pp. 183, 108.

of the former condition of the countryside. Nor were they a peculiar feature of the thinly-populated and less cultivated counties of northern and western England. Hertfordshire, wrote John Norden, was "most inclined to woods and coppices." Certain districts of Essex were "for the most part woods and woody grounds and forests, as the most part of Essex in time past hath been." A traveller from the east Midlands could make a journey to Southampton riding almost the whole way through woodland country. Rockingham, Salcey, and Whittlewood forests took him through Northamptonshire, and Bernwood and Shotover forests through Buckinghamshire. Then, escaping for a while the shadow of the trees, he had to traverse the wet, low-lying country along the Thames valley, only to enter Windsor Forest, Alice Holt, and Bere forests, and so to arrive at Southampton. By another route, the cloth merchants who made regular journeys from Kendal to Southampton to fill the holds of Italian merchantmen with northern cloth could have driven their pack-laden horses through ten forests between Cheshire and their destination—through Macclesfield, Cannock, Kinver, Feckenham, Wychwood, Savernake, Chute, Buckholt, and the New Forest. None of these forests was an impenetrable jungle of trees, of course; there were wide stretches of open pasture in all the forests. But their limits were not difficult to recognize. Cornfields did not open many views into the distance, for the woodlanders got their living from pasturage and forestry.[1]

The forest which occupied so considerable a proportion of southern and central England thinned out further north, and from the foothills of the Pennines in Staffordshire and Derbyshire to the Scottish border, throughout most of north Wales, even in parts of the south-western counties of Cornwall, Devon, and west Somerset, many a farmer from his stone, cob or timber-framed farmstead, with its small cornfields and precious meadows, looked out upon a bleak landscape of moorland, and barren rock. Here too a ploughed field was like an oasis in a desert, but an oasis which made no fair promises to posterity. "Cold and barren land" were the dispirited words used by the tenants of the vaccary of Accrington in Lancashire to describe their estates, "but by manuring, marling, and tilling, they and every vaccary will yield a certain grain called oats, but after such manuring, etc., in short time it will grow to heath, ling, moss, and rushes."[2]

The traveller who chose to avoid the main roads and frequent

[1] John Norden, *Speculum Britanniae. An Historical and Chorographical Description of Middlesex and Hertfordshire*, 1723, p. 1; *Speculi Britanniae Pars: An Historical and Chorographical Description of the County of Essex by John Norden*, 1594, ed. Sir Henry Ellis, Camden Soc., IX, 1840, p. 9.

[2] Lancs. RO, DD Ta, 216.

instead the tracks of the drovers could have travelled for several days in such a countryside. But in practice he kept to the well-worn routes within easy reach of villages, and hence within sight of cultivated land. Is it any wonder, then, that our native topographers, who readily admitted the existence of mountain and moorland, passed them over quickly in order to regale their readers with more congenial descriptions of the fertile vales where cornfields greeted the eye at every turn? Westmorland, William Camden told his readers, had a name meaning "an uncultivated tract lying towards the west," but, he hastened to add, "the south part of the county [the barony of Kendal] is in the valleys pretty fruitful, though not without its bare stony rocks." The remainder of his remarks on the county was concerned with its towns and castles. Of Cumberland, he wrote, "After swelling rocks and the crowding mountains, big (as it were) with metals (between which are lakes stored with all sorts of wild fowl) you come to rich hills clothed with flocks of sheep and below them are spread out pleasant large plains which are tolerably fruitful." He was on sympathetic ground again. Only once did Camden shrink from the sight of a truly desolate landscape without directing the reader forthwich to cast his gaze upon the fruitful valleys. He was describing Richmondshire where it meets Lancashire: "the prospect among the hills is so wild, solitary, so unsightly, and all things so still, that the borderers have called some brooks that run here *Hellbecks*, that is to say *Hell* or *Stygian* rivulets... Here is safe living in this tract for goats, deer, and stags..."[1]

In the south-west of England no one could close his eyes to the sight and extent of Bodmin Moor, Dartmoor, and Exmoor, nor fail to notice elsewhere the large areas of poor soil, unimproved as yet by the farmer. Here the topographer mingled brief and realistic descriptions with optimistic exhortations. Cornwall "is for the most part mountainous: in the bottoms 'tis of itself pretty fruitful; but they make it incredibly rich with a sort of seaweed called *Orewood* and a fat kind of sea-sand." Devon, he admitted, had a soil that was in some places poor and lean. But it "makes a good return to the husbandman, if he has skill in husbandry, a mind to labour, and a good purse to bestow upon it."[2]

Yet again in Wales, Camden did his best to cheer the Welshman by conjuring up a vision of virtue rewarded. The eastern part of Monmouthshire, abounded with pastures and woods, the western was somewhat mountainous and rocky. Yet let no one despair. The soil was still "not unserviceable to the industrious husbandman." Denbighshire possessed fruitful vale land, but it also carried a burden on its western

[1] *Camden's Britannia*, ed. Edmund Gibson, 1695, pp. 806, 819, 759.
[2] *Ibid.*, pp. 2, 26.

side. Nevertheless, "the diligence and industry of the husbandmen hath long since begun to conquer the barrenness of the land on the sides of these mountains as well as other places of Wales."[1]

On every page of Camden's work, poetry fought with truth to tell a tale that was substantially correct, and yet garnished with intent to stir the listless husbandman into effort, to plough the heath and fell the woods. His exhortations exerted their influence not only upon the farmer but upon most other topographers. The only English writer of this period who saw his native land as did the foreigner was William Harrison. He did not boast an extensive first-hand knowledge of the kingdom, but did claim "an especial eye unto the truth of things." Moreover, as he discloses in his *Description of Britain*, he had an acquaintance with other countries of Europe (whether through books, through his wife, born of French parents, or through his own travels, we cannot say) which broadened his mind and prompted many a comparison between Britain and "the main." For him, as for the foreigner, then, Britain was a grass-growing country, its soil "more inclined to feeding and grazing than profitable for tillage, and bearing of corn, by reason whereof the country is wonderfully replenished with neat and all kind of cattle; and such store is there also of the same in every place that the fourth part of the land is scarcely manured for the provision and maintenance of grain."[2]

Perhaps then the foreigner was not greatly misled in his view of England. It might not be strictly true to say that the whole country was devoted to pasturage, but much of it was. It might not be flattering to the Englishman to be told that his country abounded with marshes and forests, well-timbered with oaks, but certainly many river valleys were waterlogged in wet years, some of the fens were inundated throughout the winter, and the forests were still extensive, even though their owners did not agree that they were well-timbered.

How then are the divergent views of foreigners and most English writers to be explained? Mainly by the fact that they catered for different audiences. The stranger appraised his subject in a cool and distant manner, and through his greater familiarity with Germany, France, the Netherlands, Italy, and even Poland, he judged England by Continental standards. The patriotic antiquaries of Tudor England were only acquainted with their own island, and were intent upon extolling the virtues of the English countryside to their fellow countrymen. They won their attention and sympathy by pampering their unspoken prejudices. The assumption was commonplace that the test of a country's worthiness was the abundance of its cornfields; corn-

[1] *Camden's Britannia,* ed. Edmund Gibson, 1695, pp. 594, 679.
[2] *Elizabethan England by William Harrison,* ed. F. J. Furnivall, pp. xii, 130–1.

fields, indeed, were the passport to salvation, while pasture and meadow were necessary adjuncts, but were not evidence of the soil's natural fertility or the inhabitants' industry. "So long as they [the cottagers in Rockingham Forest] may be permitted to live in such idleness upon their stock of cattle, they will bend themselves to no kind of labour," wrote a surveyor of the forest in Elizabeth's reign, and by this definition of labour he summarily surrendered half the kingdom at least into the hands of the indolent. It was prejudice, but not irrational prejudice. A green landscape too often consisted of common pastures, heaths, and woodlands, that were still relatively untouched by the hand of the improver. And when improvement was the order of the day, often the farmer's first move was to introduce the plough. Not surprisingly, then, the furrows that followed the ploughshare were deemed the only reliable sign of agricultural progress.[1]

Foreigners too, as their diaries bear witness, were not altogether untainted by the same prejudices. They were familiar with the notion that cornfields signified industry. But first-hand experience of Britain obliged them to recognize that the reverse was not always true: pastures did not necessarily signify sloth. They all admitted that the more substantial English peasant—the only ones the foreigner encountered—enjoyed a high standard of living. He ate a great deal of meat, particularly mutton and beef, and of excellent quality, "very properly cooked and roasted." The proof of this predilection lay in the large number of butchers' shops in the towns: the Mantuan traveller, Litolfi, thought there were more butchers in London than in any two of the chief towns of Lombardy. Moreover, the Englishman enjoyed various other meats as delicacies: swans, seabirds, deer, and rabbits. More than this, his pastures supported so many milch kine that milk, butter, and cheese were unwontedly plentiful. Thomas Platter, riding between Canterbury and Sittingbourne in 1599, was astonished when he stopped for refreshment and was offered tankards of milk instead of beer.[2]

The material comfort of the houses and inns matched the Englishman's sumptuous table. "Lodgings are excellent," wrote the Italian Ambassador, Barbaro, in Edward VI's reign, "a sure sign of the country's wealth," and those who entered farmers' houses—again mostly those of the more substantial husbandmen and yeomen—did not gainsay him. Farmhouses impressed with their size as well as their comfortable and, in hot summers, sweet-smelling interiors: chamber

[1] Northants. RO, Westmorland, Apethorpe Collection, 4, XVI, 5. See also *infra*, p. .

[2] Nicander Nucius, *op. cit.*, pp. 16, 19–20; C. V. Malfatti, *op. cit.*, p. 37; E. Gurney Salter, *op. cit.*, p. 120; Rye, *op cit.*, p. 70; Clare Williams, *op. cit.*, p. 150.

floors were cooled with a sprinkling of water and then strewn with sedge; parlours were decorated with green boughs, fresh herbs, and vine leaves. By the end of the sixteenth century, farmers' beds were usually covered with tapestry, and their tables adorned with silver. "He must be a poor peasant, indeed, who does not possess silver-gilt salt cellars, silver cups and spoons," wrote Lupuld von Wedel in 1584, echoing, perhaps consciously, the words of William Harrison, but adding also an original touch of his own: "many a peasant here keeps greater state and a better table than the nobility in Germany." No stranger's curiosity, of course, was compelling enough to take him into the tiny huts of the poor. But it is significant that rural poverty was not so obtrusive as to deserve comment.[1]

These impressions of England and Wales, collected by those who had greater experience across the Channel, correct some of our one-sided notions about this kingdom in the period 1500–1640, and confirm and enrich others. Since foreigners saw more green than gold in the summer landscape, since shepherds and neat herds seemed ubiquitous, we may be at fault in insisting so much upon England's nucleated villages and common fields—the habitat of the ploughman. Another lesson lies in the evident admiration with which the European traveller observed the grazing skills of the peasant. Little of his learning was bookish, often he was illiterate. Yet to the foreigner he appeared inordinately clever, living so well by the laziest of occupations—pasture farming. But was it in truth a sluggard's job? "Grazing in my view is much more of an art than a science," writes the present-day connoisseur of grassland management, André Voisin, and fears to shock his readers by declaring that scientific methods in the last two hundred years have done little to improve upon the traditional lore of the shepherd. The sixteenth-century farmer may have had an advantage that neither the foreigner of his time nor we today can fully appreciate—an eye that was not yet dulled by the reading of overmuch print, but sharpened rather by centuries of experience.[2]

Finally, we are taught by foreign observers to assess England and Wales as a whole, and not to regard the Midlands or Middlesex as the mirror of the kingdom. Camden, it is true, reflected the spirit of the age when he rallied men to the plough. But East Anglia's corn growers were not the nation, nor were the common fields of the east Midlands the only landscape.

In the chapters that follow a fresh attempt is made, with the aid of

[1] E. Gurney Salter, *op. cit.*, p. 72; Rye, *op. cit.*, pp.   , 110; W. Robson Scott, *op. cit.*, p. 48.
[2] André Voisin, 'Grazing is an Art', *Agriculture*, LXVI, 1959, p. 163; *ibid.*, *Grass Productivity*, 1959, p. 25.

contemporary archives, to see England and Wales as a whole. The accuracy of the foreigner's description of the countryside—as a generalization, no more—is borne out in the study of farming systems in both countries. His impressions of luxury and comfort in many a peasant house and household prove correct. The Englishman's preference for meat appears understandable enough in the light of our knowledge of land use at this period. But, of course, there is much more to be told of all classes and all facets of rural life than that contained in the accounts of travellers and topographers. The gentry had other interests than hunting. The peasant was not always a contented and prosperous freeholder; sometimes he was landless; more often he was a tenant under a lord, whether gentleman, ecclesiastic, or one of his own class; and the relationship of tenant and lord was of supreme importance in determining, or disturbing, social peace in the countryside.

In this volume a number of historians and one historical geographer attempt to interpret and generalize, but at the same time to convey some impression of the infinite variety of social forms and economic activity that lie beneath their generalizations. As Polydore Vergil reminded his readers in one of the first descriptions of Britain from a foreign pen, England and Wales is divided into several parts. England south of the Humber is different from England to the north; Wales is another kingdom, and Cornwall yet another. And all differ among themselves.[1]

[1] *Polydore Vergil's English History*, ed. Sir Hen. Ellis, Camden Soc. XXXVI, 1846, pp. 1, 4–5.

ABBREVIATIONS

Agric. Hist.	*Agricultural History.*
AHR	*Agricultural History Review.*
Amer. Hist. Rev.	*American Historical Review.*
AO	Archives Office.
Arch. Aeliana	*Archaeologia Aeliana.*
Arch. Camb.	*Archaeologia Cambrensis.*
Arch. Cant.	*Archaeologia Cantiana.*
Arch. J.	*Archaeological Journal.*
B.Acad.	British Academy.
BM	British Museum.
Bull. BCS	*Bulletin of the Board of Celtic Studies.*
Bull. IHR	*Bulletin of the Institute of Historical Research.*
Bull. JRL	*Bulletin of the John Rylands Library.*
C	Proceedings in the Court of Chancery, Public Record Office.
CP 40	Court of Common Pleas, Plea Rolls, Public Record Office.
CPR	Calendar of Patent Rolls.
CSPD	Calendar of State Papers Domestic.
E	Exchequer Records, Public Record Office.
E 134	Exchequer, Depositions.
E 159	Exchequer, King's Remembrancer, Memoranda Rolls.
E 164	Exchequer, King's Remembrancer, Miscellaneous Books.
E 178	Exchequer, Special Commissions.
E 315	Exchequer, Augmentations Office, Miscellaneous Books.
E 318	Exchequer, Augmentations Office, Particulars for Grants.
E 321	Exchequer, Augmentations Office, Proceedings.

EcHR	*Economic History Review.*
EHR	*English Historical Review.*
EPNS	English Place-Name Society.
HMC	Historical Manuscripts Commission.
Hist. Mon. C	Historical Monuments Commission.
JMH	*Journal of Modern History.*
LP	Letters and Papers of Henry VIII.
Mont. Coll.	Montgomeryshire Collections.
NQ	*Notes and Queries.*
PRO	Public Record Office.
R.C.A.M.	Royal Commission on Ancient Monuments.
Req. 2	Court of Requests, Public Record Office.
RHS	Royal Historical Society.
RO	Record Office.
Roy. Inst. Cornwall	*Royal Institution of Cornwall.*
SP	State Papers Domestic.
VCH	Victoria County History.
Yorks. Bull.	*Yorkshire Bulletin of Economic and Social Research.*

I Types of plough illustrated in one of the best seventeenth-century books of husbandry: Walter Blith, *The English Improver Improved or the Survey of Husbandry Surveyed, Discovering the improveableness of all Lands*, 1653.

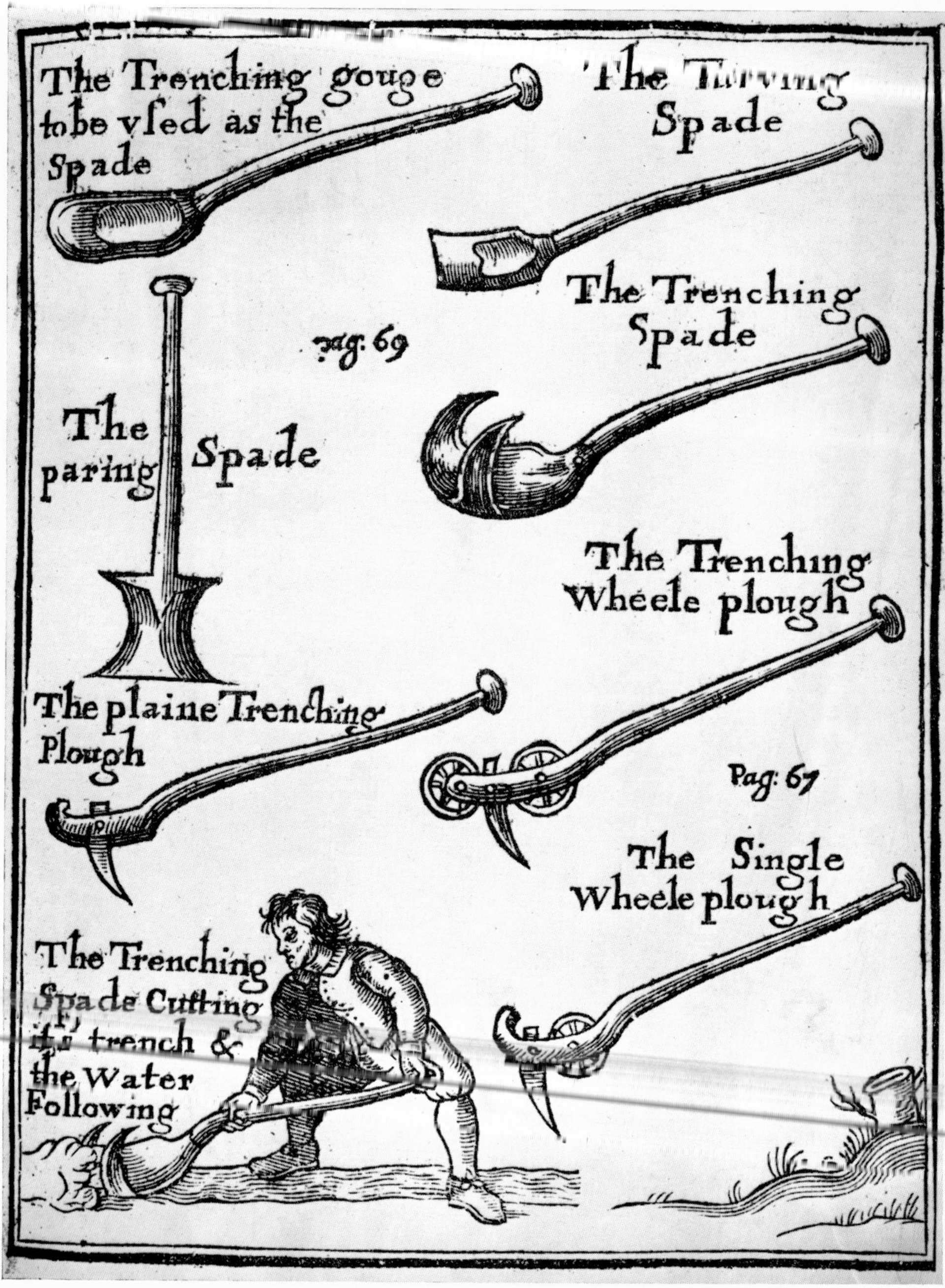

The Trenching gouge to be vfed as the Spade

The Turving Spade

pag: 69

The Trenching Spade

The paring Spade

The Trenching Wheele plough

The plaine Trenching Plough

Pag: 67

The Single Wheele plough

The Trenching Spade Cutting its trench & the Water Following

II Farm tools from Walter Blith, *The English Improver Improved*, 1653.

1 *Auena Vesca.*
Common Otes.

2 *Auena Nuda.*
Naked Otes.

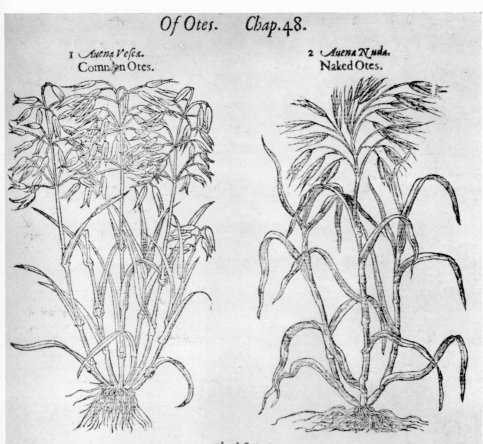

✱ *The description.*

1   A *Vena Vesca*, common Otes, is called *Vesca à Vescendo*, bicauseit is vsed in many countries to make sundry sorts of bread, as in Lancashire, where it is their chiefest bread corne for Iannocks, Hauer cakes, Tharffe cakes, and those which are called generally Oten cakes; and for the most part they call the graine Hauer, whereof they do likewise make drink for want of Barly.

2   *Auena Nuda* is like vnto the common Otes, differing in that, that these naked Otes immediately as they be threshed without helpe of a mill become Otemeale fit for our vse. In consideration whereof in Northfolke and Southfolke they are called vnhulled and naked Otes. Some of those good huswiues that delight not to haue store of any thing but from hand to mouth, according to our English prouerbe, may (whiles their pot doth seath) go to the barne, and rub foorth with their hands sufficient for that present time, not willing to prouide for to morrow, according as the Scripture speaketh, but let the next day bring with it.

✱ *Tho*

III   Common and naked oats from John Gerarde, *The Herball or
General Historie of Plantes,* 1597.

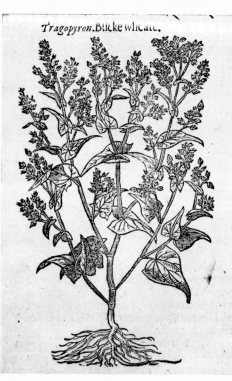

Tragopyron. Bucke wheate.

❋ The description.

BVcke Wheate may very well be placed among the kindes of graine or corne, for that oftentimes in time of necessitie bread is made thereof, mixed among other graine. It hath round fat stalks somwhat crested, smooth and reddish, which is deuided in many armes or branches, whereupon do grow smooth and soft leaues, in shape like those of Iuie or Basill; whereof *Taber montanus* called it *Ocymum Cereale :* the flowers be small, white and clustered togither in one or moe tufts or vmbels, slightly dasht ouer heere and there with a florish of light carnation colour. The seedes or graines are of a dead or darke blackish colour, triangled or three square like the seede of blacke Bindeweede, called of the ancient Herbarists *Malacocissos.* The roote is small and threddie.

❋ The place.

It prospereth verie well in any ground be it neuer so drie or barren, where it is commonly sowen to serue as it were in steede of a dunging: It quickly commeth vp and is very soone ripe,

ripe, it is very common in and about the Namptwiche in Cheshire, where they sowe it aswell for foode for their cattell, pullen and such like, as to the vse aforesaid. It groweth likewise in Lancashire and some parts of our south countrey, about London in Middlesex, as also in Kent and Essex.

❋ The time.

This base kinde of graine is sowen in Aprill and the beginning of Maie, and is ripe in the beginning of August.

❋ The names.

Buckwheat is called of the high Almaines Heydenkorn : of the base Almaines Buckenweidt, that is to say, *Hirci Triticum,* or Goates wheate. Of some *Fagi Triticum,* Beech wheate. In Greeke .... in Latine *Fago-Triticum :* taken from the fashion of the seede or fruit of the Beech tree. It is called also *Fegopyrum* and *Tragopyron :* in English French wheate, Bullimong and Bucke wheate : In French *Dragee aux cheueaux.*

❋ The nature.

Bucke wheate nourisheth lesse than wheate, rie, barlie, or otes; yet more than either Mill or Panicke.

❋ The vertues.

Bread made of the meale of Bucke wheat is of easie digestion, it speedily passeth through the bel- A ly, but yeeldeth little nourishment.

IV   Buckwheat from John Gerarde, *The Herball or General Historie of Plantes,* 1597.

V   The Gatehouse of Layer Marney, Essex, which contains in all thirty-nine chambers.

VI   (a) The surviving part of Horham Hall, Thaxted, Essex, one of the three houses built by Sir John Cuttes, Under Treasurer of England. (b) The Gatehouse of Butley Priory, Suffolk, converted into a house.

VII   Upwell Rectory, Norfolk, built early in the sixteenth century.

VIII (*a*) Elham, Kent: a house of 1614 with a continuous jetty and (originally) range of windows upstairs. (b) Chorley Hall, Cheshire: a medieval house improved *c.* 1560 by raising the hall roof (to make an upper storey) and adding a parlour wing (right).

IX (*a*) Lower Old Hall, Norland, Halifax, Yorks., built in 1634 by a yeoman clothier. (*b*) Clock House, Little Stonham, Suffolk, showing the chamber with fire place inserted over the hall of a medieval house.

X   An aisled barn at Rogate, Sussex.

XI (*a*) A cruck barn at Park House, Heversham, Westmorland. (*b*) A Dartmoor long-house: Lower Tor, Widecombe in the Moor, Devon.

XII (a) The old vicarage, Thorverton, Devon, built c. 1531 with the hall chimney on the front of the house (now three cottages). (b) Brick chimneys at the Meeting House, West Hanningfield, Essex.

XIII (*a*) The storeyed porch of the Old Manor House, Evenley, Northants. (*b*) High Combe Farm, Rampisham, Dorset, with three rooms on the ground floor: kitchen (nearest camera), hall and parlour.

XIV (a) Wootton Lodge, Staffs., built c. 1610 with the services in the basement, and probably designed by Robert Smythson. (b) Lodge Park, Sherborne, Glos., built c. 1650 by the Dutton family for the New Park.

XV (a) Part of a map of matching, Essex, 1609, with careful representation of houses. (b) Rectory Farm, Britford, Wilts., a compact and symmetrical design with central chimney stack.

XVI The fireplace in Mapperton House, Dorset, with plaster overmantel (dated 1604) and ceiling and panelled walls.

XVII   Tower and hall. (*a*) Gwydir, Trewydir, Caerns, is a tower of *c.* 1520, the nucleus of a large courtyard house; see Fig. 32 *b*. (*b*) Candleston Castle, Merthyr-mawr, Glam., is a rare example of a tower complete with hall and barmkin. (*c*) Brithdir-mawr, Cilcain, Flints., 1589, illustrates the late survival of the hall plan; the dormers are a seventeenth-century addition to an inserted first floor. See Figs. 33.

XVIII Regisnal houses type A. (*a*) Bod-llosged, Ffestiniog, Mer. (*b*) Plas-ucha, Llanfair D.C. Rural, Denbs.; note the tall chinneys and lateral fireplace, very characteristic of north-east Wales; the house is probably a reconstructed hall-house.

XIX Regional houses type B. The entry to each house is through the lower room, in (a) a kitchen, in (b) a byre. Which is the primary form of the plan is in dispute. (a) Sutton, Ogmore, Glam. (b) Hafod–uchaf, Lower Lledrod, Cards.

XX Regional houses type C. The entry is by a vestibule alongside a back-to-back fireplace which stands where the cross-passage would have been in the medieval house. (*a*) Talgarth, Trefeglwys, Mont., is a 'gentleman's' house of 1660–70. See Fig. 45*b*. Note the ornate treatment of the end walls characteristic of mid-seventeenth-century work. (*b*) Ystradfaelog, Trefeglwys, Mont.; a Yoeman's house but with a similar plan.

XXI Large traditional plan houses with wings. (*a*) Pentrehobyn, Mold Rural, Flints., was probably built in 1640 as an entity; see Fig. 51 *c*. (*b*) Penarth, Newton, Mont., is a late sixteenth-century reconstruction of a medieval hall. Both retain the off-centred 'cross-passage' entry.

XXII Smaller houses showing Renaissance influence. (*a*) Fferm, Hope, Flints.; the porch
(probably 1596) has been added to a slightly older cross-passage house. (*b*) Dolau Gwyn,
Towny, Mer.; the porch and most of the house date from 1628, the projecting wing was
added in 1656.

XXIII Large houses showing Renaissance influence. (a) Treowen, Wonastow, Mon.; a porch probably dating from 1627 has been placed in front of a slightly earlier house, which, although double pile in plan, retains a cross-passage; see Fig. 53. (b) Plas-teg, Hope, Flints., built in 1610, is a typical house of a successful courtier, in this case Sir John Trevor, surveyor of the Queen's Ships; see Fig. 50.

XXIV Houses with regional and Renaissance features. Two seventeenth-century type C central-chimney regional houses (cf. Plate XX) but with storeyed porch, and rear kitchen instead of service room at end of hall. (*a*) Plasau-duon, Carno, Mont. (*b*) Glanhafren, Newton, Mont.

CHAPTER I

THE FARMING REGIONS OF ENGLAND

The variety of England's scenery is a commonplace to the Englishman, yet his textbooks of economic history have not so far taken full account of the significance of this variety in ordering men's work and shaping their societies. The conventional notions about farming and the structure of rural communities still rest upon the convenient generalization that England was composed largely of nucleated villages, populated by corn-and-stock peasants, who farmed their land in common fields and pastures. It is an assumption that ignores the clear evidence of the eye in the hills of highland England and in the forests that still survive, though in a shrunken form, in the lowlands.

Some recent work on the agrarian economy of different counties has produced information in sufficient detail to dissipate illusions about the uniformity of English farming and English rural society. It may always be difficult to make progress in this field for earlier periods of history, but the student of the sixteenth and early seventeenth centuries cannot complain of lack of records.

It is appropriate then to begin a fresh study of agrarian history in the Tudor and early Stuart periods with a narrative that dwells not upon the many changes that took place in this century and a half—for change normally dominates our discussions—but which dwells rather upon the more permanent features of rural life. This entails an enumeration of the basic farming systems of England's different regions—many of which systems survived even this period of agrarian upheaval—and an analysis of the types of community associated with each. These things may justly be regarded as part of the more permanent fabric of economic and social life. But permanence is a relative term, and one of the conclusions of this study is the realization that not all farming systems and not all societies were equally stable. We may feel certain that in some regions the conditions of life at the beginning of the sixteenth century were an ancient story; in others we cannot rid ourselves of the suspicion that some alteration in the framework of rural life had recently wrought significant changes in the structure of society and the uses of its land. We cannot, however, pursue these problems back into the Middle Ages.

The task of describing, even in outline, the economies of England's many regions is large, and it is undertaken here in the full knowledge

I

that it ignores much detail with which the historian of small localities is familiar, and which he deems important. At the same time, it is clear that only a survey which is wide in scope brings enough examples together to show significant recurrences in types of farming and types of community. And at a certain stage in the accumulation of local knowledge some generalizations, based upon the recurrent patterns that emerge from this analysis, are a necessary prelude to further fruitful research.

A. THE STRUCTURE OF REGIONS

It is impossible to understand the economic and social structure of England's regions in the sixteenth century without first taking account of the physical environment which men could modify but could not change. In the sixteenth and early seventeenth centuries men made war upon the forests, moors, and fens with a zeal which they had not felt for some three hundred years. They cleared woods and drained wet, low-lying land to make new pastures, they turned old pastures into cornland, old cornland into grass. Even on the least promising soils, many a hopeful, energetic farmer hacked out an acre or two of scrub to make a sweeter pasture which later generations have surrendered to bracken. In some places the desire of men at this period to improve their environment seemed to admit of no obstacles. In fact, however, the geography of England imposed strict limitations. Beneath the man-made landscape, and underlying all the institutions of society which differentiated neighbouring communities and united widely separated ones, nature had laid a foundation which men were forced to accept. She had cleft England in twain and imposed a division upon the kingdom which had the deepest significance for its economic and social development. To the inhabitants of the north and west of England belonged a land dominated by mountains and moors, where soils are poor and thin, the valleys and plains few and far between, where the whole countryside lies athwart the path of rain-carrying winds, affording a cool, wet climate. Except in certain favoured districts, the sixteenth-century farmer, like his forebears and successors, had to accept this as grass-growing country, and to specialize in animal production. The south and east of England, in contrast, was blessed with a different kind of country and climate. It is an undulating low-land, with smaller hills, gentler slopes, a richer deeper soil, and a drier climate. It can grow corn as well as grass, and so allows the farmer a wider choice of alternatives in his farming. This was the country of mixed farming in the sixteenth century. The peasant might sometimes keep as many cattle or sheep as his neighbour in the highlands, but he kept them not as an end in themselves but rather as an aid in working and fertilizing his ploughland.

The most obvious distinction between the highlands and the lowlands of England at this period, therefore, lay in these two contrasted kinds of farming. In the grass-growing uplands, where the principal asset was stock, men either specialized in rearing sheep and cattle, or fattening them, in dairying, pig-keeping, or horse-breeding or did a little of each. In the lowlands, the farmer could grow both corn and grass and vary the proportions of arable and pasture, according to the condition of his land, the place of stock in his system of husbandry, and the state of the market. He might grow corn for the town and keep animals chiefly for the sake of maintaining fertility in the corn fields, as did the sheep-corn farmers on the downlands, wolds, and brecklands of East Anglia; he might grow much the same acreage of arable crops but use most of them for feeding animals for the butcher, like some Hertfordshire and Leicestershire farmers; or he might fatten for the butcher, but feed his animals mostly on grass, growing a smaller amount of corn, for his own needs, and sometimes also for the market, as did the marshland farmers of Yorkshire, Lincolnshire, and Essex. Many different combinations were possible, depending upon the different emphasis placed on grass and corn and on the different types of stock. The mixed farmer had many, though not, of course, unlimited opportunities for adapting his routine to his particular situation. And he could often change his system in minor ways without great difficulty to meet new economic circumstances.[1]

The farming specialization of the grass-growing north and west on the one hand, and the corn *and* grass-growing south and east on the other was greatly emphasized by economic trends in the sixteenth century. A rising population in both town and countryside increased the demand for food and the demand for land. Few farmers were so completely self-sufficient on their farms that they could ignore the market entirely. Hence, each half of England found itself exerting greater efforts to produce the food which it could grow well, and which best served the needs of the nearest market. In specializing in one direction, each region gradually placed itself in greater dependence than before upon other regions for some item of food or ingredient of its farming. The whole country was drawn more firmly than ever before into a dovetailed system of agricultural production. The highland farmer bred cattle and sheep, kept some sheep for their wool, but sold most of the rest of his young stock for fattening to the lowland

[1] Footnote references in this section have been reduced to a minimum since the points made here are elaborated, and full references given, in the following regional sections of this chapter.

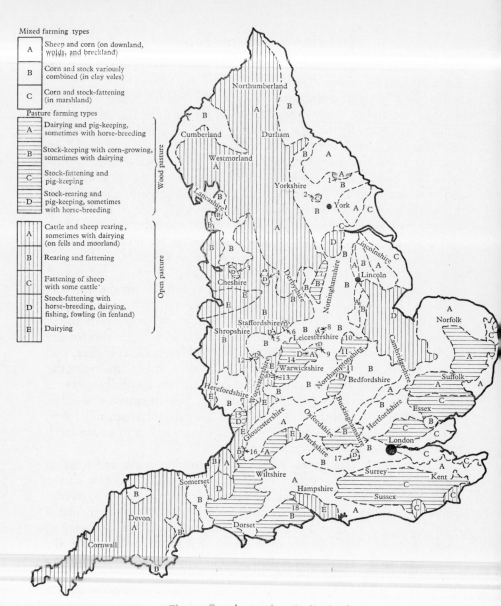

Mixed farming types

A	Sheep and corn (on downland, wolds, and breckland)
B	Corn and stock variously combined (in clay vales)
C	Corn and stock-fattening (in marshland)

Pasture farming types

Wood pasture

A	Dairying and pig-keeping, sometimes with horse-breeding
B	Stock-keeping with corn-growing, sometimes with dairying
C	Stock-fattening and pig-keeping
D	Stock-rearing and pig-keeping, sometimes with horse-breeding

Open pasture

A	Cattle and sheep rearing, sometimes with dairying (on fells and moorland)
B	Rearing and fattening
C	Fattening of sheep with some cattle
D	Stock-fattening with horse-breeding, dairying, fishing, fowling (in fenland)
E	Dairying

Fig. 1. Farming regions in England.

This is a very tentative map of farming regions in England in the sixteenth and early seventeenth centuries. The boundaries between the regions are the most tentative of all, and will certainly require amendment in the light of more detailed local investigation. Not all royal forests are indicated on the map since it has not been possible to identify all their boundaries with certainty. All, however, belong in the category of wood-pasture regions, and most lie within or on the fringe of regions of open pasture. The Warwickshire Arden is depicted as a wood-pasture region undergoing change from stock-rearing, etc., (D) to dairying etc. (A). The forests are numbered as follows: 1, Pickering Forest; 2, Galtres Forest; 3, Delamere Forest; 4, Macclesfield Forest; 5, Cannock Forest; 6, Needwood Forest; 7, Sherwood Forest; 8, Charnwood Forest; 9, Leicester Forest; 10, Leighfield or Rutland Forest; 11, Rockingham, Whittlewood, and Salcey Forests, Northamptonshire; 12, Kinver Forest; 13, Feckenham Forest; 14, Forest of Arden; 15, Forest of Dean; 16, Kingswood Forest; 17, Windsor Forest; 18, New Forest.

grazier. This was the régime throughout most of the four northern counties, in north and east Lancashire, on the hills and moors of Devon and Cornwall, and in west Somerset. In the west Midlands, this programme included a good deal more cattle fattening and some dairying. Farmers grew as much corn as they could for their own needs, but their harvest of oats and bigg or barley was small and in bad years they relied on the lowlands to supply their deficiencies. The lowland farmer, on the other hand, grew corn or fattened meat for the butcher and relied upon the highlands for many of his store animals. As markets expanded in the course of this period, much farm produce moved along the internal trade routes of the kingdom, from the north and west to the south and east. Fat cattle and stores followed the drovers from as far north as Cumberland and Westmorland to the Midlands, Lincolnshire, East Anglia, and thence south to Hertfordshire and Essex, while from Wales and the Welsh border a similar procession trudged through the southern counties to be sold *en route* or to be finished on the pastures of Kent and Essex. In a less bounteous flow, the corn that was not needed in the lowlands passed by coastal vessel from the south and east, from East Anglia and Kent, for example, to the north and west. The position of London in relation to the rest of the kingdom seemed to account for the direction of agricultural traffic, but in fact much of the produce so directed never reached the capital, but went to feed industrial towns in the Midlands, and to furnish vessels anchored in the harbours of the south and east coast ports. The trend was inevitable in view of the different specialities of highland and lowland England. London's need for food was greatest and most insistent, but to many farmers it was not more compelling than that of other towns.

In its main farming types, therefore, England was split in two. Taking into account the historical evidence as well as the geographical differences, a line drawn between Teesmouth in the north-east and Weymouth in the south-west defines the two halves most accurately. It places the counties of Cornwall, Devon, Somerset, west Dorset, Gloucestershire, Herefordshire, Worcestershire, Shropshire, Staffordshire, Derbyshire, Cheshire, Lancashire, West Yorkshire, Durham, Northumberland, Cumberland, and Westmorland in the pastoral zone, and all other counties of England in the lowland zone of mixed husbandry.

In its field systems and customs of land cultivation, England was again split in twain. Some communities farmed their land on a co-operative basis, cultivating their arable in open commonable fields, pasturing their beasts in common flocks and herds, and submitting themselves to a multitude of common rules of cultivation. In other districts farms were enclosed, and farmers followed what system they pleased on their arable land, and on all, or some, of their pastures, though it was not unusual to find some pastures, even in enclosed country, grazed in common.

By the sixteenth century the enclosure movement was making great headway all over the country. But since it provoked different responses in different parts of the country, it behoves us to look again at the various common-field systems and notice that they were fundamentally of two kinds. The type made most familiar by the textbooks was centred upon two, three, or four large arable fields surrounded by common pastures and waste which were used as a reserve for increasing the arable as population increased. In other words, the pasture served the arable: it fed the animals which ploughed the fields and fertilized the crops. This system was most characteristic of common-field areas in lowland England. In highland England the arable fields were more often small, they might be few or numerous—one, five, six, seven, and more fields were just as usual as two, three, and four fields. And since the farming was pastoral, the pastures were not continually being nibbled away to increase the cornland until a dangerous pasture shortage threatened. The pasture was ample and was the mainstay of the farming system; the arable was subsidiary. Enclosure by agreement in this type of common-field community was sanctioned by ancient custom and continued to be permitted throughout this period. Hence, although it is impossible to draw an accurate map showing enclosed and common-field areas in England in the sixteenth century, it is possible to make a more valuable generalization. The highland zone consisted for the most part of land which was either completely enclosed by the beginning of the sixteenth century, or, if the land was worth enclosing at this time, could and often did undergo painless enclosure. In lowland England where common fields were subject to a system of mixed husbandry, where common grazing rights were highly prized because the pasture steadily diminished as the arable was enlarged, enclosure constituted, at the beginning at least, a painful and socially disturbing reorganization of land and ways of living.

How then does one explain the fact that some areas of lowland England had managed to achieve enclosure early, before 1500? The answer seems to be that they were exceptional regions, practising pasture farming, and possessing a settlement pattern as well as other features of social organization more usually associated with the highland zone. Kent, Essex, and Suffolk, three of the counties most often cited as examples of early enclosure, illustrate this point most readily. Contrary to the assumption on which the old generalizations were based, the field arrangements and farming system were not uniform within each county. In Suffolk, only the wood-pasture region in the central sector of the county was enclosed early, and the corn-growing brecklands to east and west contained many common fields, some of which lingered into the eighteenth century. In Essex, similarly, common fields remained at the end of the Tudor period in the corn-growing district of the north-west, though they had disappeared (if they had ever existed) from the pastoral, meat-producing and dairying, districts in the rest of the county. Only in Kent had common fields disappeared everywhere, and here it is doubtful whether the system had ever been practised at all.[1]

An earlier generation of historians, observing the differences between the enclosed and common-field areas of England, defined them by counties and so drove themselves into a political or racial explanation for the different systems. It is possible that other factors were of greater importance. Indeed, the fact that the three regions in lowland England which never had common fields or else painlessly enclosed them in the Middle Ages were also areas with little arable land prompts the hypothesis that common fields and co-operative husbandry were best suited to, and survived longest, in areas of mixed husbandry, whereas they either never came into existence, or met an early death, in pastoral areas. This proposition stands up well when tested in highland England. All the pastoral areas of highland England were either enclosed from the beginning, or having entered upon a system of communal cultivation in arable fields and meadows did not allow those rules to hinder them from carrying out enclosure when they wished. Shropshire is an excellent example of a cattle-rearing, meat-producing county, generally regarded by Tudor writers as wholly enclosed. In fact, as scholars have recently shown, it possessed many common-field communities. Yet it managed to achieve much enclosure in this period without disturbance or resentment, by means of a multitude of friendly exchange agreements. The dairying, grassland regions of Wiltshire, similarly, achieved easy enclosure by agreement in the sixteenth and seventeenth centuries. So did the Arden, or northern half of Warwickshire: it was a cattle-breeding, and later a dairying, district with many old enclosures, and some common fields which underwent enclosure in this period. The juxtaposed region of Felden, or champion Warwickshire, south of the Avon, on the other hand, pursued a system of mixed farming, had large acreages of ploughland in the sixteenth century, and preserved many common fields until the age of parliamentary enclosure.

[1] M. R. Postgate, 'The Field Systems of Breckland', AHR, x, 1962, pp. 83–6; F. Hull, *Agriculture and Rural Society in Essex, 1560–1640*, London Ph.D. thesis, 1950; A. R. H. Baker, *The Field Systems of Kent*, London Ph.D. thesis, 1963.

Just as the lowland half of England had its exceptional regions where pasture farming was carried on in closes or in small and steadily dwindling common fields, so highland England had its exceptional islands of mixed husbandry which were almost always associated with large common fields. Felden Warwickshire, already mentioned, was one such region. The coastal lands of Cumberland constituted another, the eastern plain of Durham, a most prosperous and highly organized region of mixed husbandry, serving a hungry market by the end of the sixteenth century, was another. Much of Herefordshire also falls into this category, for it was deemed the corn barn of the west Midlands in the sixteenth century; parts of Somerset and Devon were veritable orchards and granaries for provisioning not only the population of the west country but coastal vessels riding in their harbours as well. In short, the more fertile, sheltered valleys, plains, and coastal lowlands of highland England were nearly always districts of mixed farming with a considerable number of common fields. Drawn on a map of highland England, however, they constituted but small islands in a sea of pasture farms.

The social framework of community life in upland and lowland England was as distinct as the farming arrangements. Common fields were associated with nucleated villages in the lowlands, and with nucleated villages or, at least, small hamlets in the highlands. Nucleated villages were usually associated with a highly organized manorial community, except in those cases where an absentee landlord by his neglect allowed his estate to be carelessly administered, or where, through the sale of a manor and the parcelling of its demesnes, the whole manorial structure fell asunder. This occurred at Wigston Magna in Leicestershire, for example, in the sixteenth century and gave Dr Hoskins the opportunity of tracing the far-reaching consequences of the dismemberment of Wigston's manors on the later development of the township. But this course of events was far less usual in the lowlands, whence he took his example, than in the highlands.[1]

In the pastoral districts of England, the more typical unit of settlement was either the hamlet or the single farmstead having little working association with its neighbours except sometimes in the use of common grazing grounds. Manorial control was more difficult to exercise since the centres of settlement were many, and farming matters demanding communal regulation were so few as to afford little occasion for bringing the community together. If the common grazings were enclosed as well as the ploughland, as was the case in many parts of Kent, for example, the need for discipline in farming matters disappeared almost entirely, leaving the manor court to deal with little

[1] W. G. Hoskins, *The Midland Peasant*.

more than the cleaning of ditches and the clearing of footpaths and cart tracks.[1]

Thus many communities in pastoral regions were not firmly held together by manorial discipline so much as by their loyalty to kinsmen, whether to the large clan or small family. These loyalties controlled the younger generation, and governed the distribution of land among descendants. In Redesdale in Northumberland the clan was still the recognized social group with commanding authority over its members at the beginning of the seventeenth century. In most other parts of highland England, however, where communities were less isolated from external influences, the clan had been forgotten, but the family often exerted a stronger authority than the manorial lord. Family estates of all classes below that of the squire and gentry were liable to be broken up into a number of parcels in every successive generation, and manorial lords were either unable or unwilling to intervene. In some places the disintegration of estates began to pose serious economic problems for the community by the end of the sixteenth century, and forced some manorial lords to intervene to arrest the trend. This action was taken by the Crown in Furness, Lancashire, when it forbade the subdivision of estates below a certain size. On other manors the circumstances in which the custom of partible inheritance was brought to an end is unknown. But we shall not be far wrong if we assume varying pressure by the lord and varying degrees of willingness on the part of tenants in their own interests to prevent excessive partition of the land.

Since customs of inheritance and their effects on the distribution of land have not yet been properly investigated for any part of England, it is impossible to say very much about their influence in shaping different types of local community. But one cautious generalization seems to be justified, namely, that the custom of partible inheritance was more widely practised in highland England at the beginning of the sixteenth century than in the lowlands. And where it survived in the lowlands, as in Kent, for example, it was associated with a pattern of settlement and a social framework reminiscent of the highlands, in which the family was a powerful agent of social control and discipline.

As for the economic effects of partible inheritance, here again we venture upon almost uncharted territory. The inhabitants of Dentdale and Garsdale in the North Riding of Yorkshire thought that the custom had had a decisive effect in reducing their holdings to an uneconomic size, and was the fundamental cause of their economic problems in the early seventeenth century. The same explanation was given for a

[1] The types of settlement associated with different types of farming were noticed by William Harrison. See *Elizabethan England by William Harrison*, ed. F. J. Furnivall, p. 20.

similar problem of overpopulation in Redesdale and Tyndale, Northumberland, in the mid-sixteenth century. A recent study of Halifax
parish has underlined the part played by partible inheritance in multi-
plying the number and reducing the size of manorial holdings in the
sixteenth and seventeenth centuries. Dr Tupling observed its effects in
the course of a century and a half (1500–1660) upon tenants' holdings in
Rossendale in Lancashire. Finally, since it is generally agreed that the
custom of partible inheritance has been partly responsible for the
differences in the structure of peasant society in England and on the
Continent, we should be unwise to ignore it as a factor contributing to
the different structure of England's varied local communities. There is
every sign that it at least accentuated the differences already existing
between the communities of highland and lowland England.

Apart from the effect of partible inheritance upon the size of farms
and class structure, more attention deserves to be given to its influence
on the size of populations. Whereas primogeniture often compelled
younger sons to move from their native places, partible inheritance
persuaded them to stay at home by promising them a share in the
family land. A recent study of some fenland villages in Lincolnshire in
the thirteenth century has shown how populations grew at a faster
rate in the villages where partible inheritance was practised. In the
sixteenth century, however, it is more difficult to isolate the effects of
inheritance customs from others operating at the same time. Populations were rising, through natural increase, throughout England and,
indeed, throughout Europe. The consequent shortage of land and the
expansion of industry in town and countryside were also causing much
migration between districts.

Contemporaries, concerned with the great increase of numbers in
some districts, dwelt on both causes—inheritance customs *and* migration—but for different communities they favoured one explanation
more than the other. As we have noted already, partible inheritance was
most commonly adduced as the explanation by commentators familiar
with communities in highland England, whereas in the lowlands they
tended to lay the blame on the presence of abundant commons which
attracted immigrants by giving them a chance to make a living from
their common rights. Extensive pastures and the right to gather
unlimited turves therein was the explanation offered by an observer in
1675 for the great increase of people inhabiting the Isle of Axholme.
The wapentake of Elloe, in south Lincolnshire, sustained a remarkably
rapid increase of population in the period 1563–1723, far in excess of
anything experienced in the rest of Lincolnshire; it too disposed of
unstinted commons. Unstinted commons have been offered by a
recent writer as the explanation for the great congregations of people in

the Northamptonshire forests, and emphatic contemporary testimony supports this conclusion. The surveyor of one estate at Apethorpe, in Rockingham Forest, writing in the 1570's, attributed the preponderance of cottagers entirely to the idleness fostered by the extensive, unstinted pastures.

"In these fields tenants and cottagers have common of pasture for their horses, oxen, kine, and other great beasts without any rate amongst themselves cessed or appointed, which is a great hindrance to the husbands and a maintaining of the idlers and beggary of the cottagers, for the liberty of the common of pasture and the gentleness that is showed in the forest to the bribers and stealers of woods and hedge-breakers without punishment is the only occasion of the resort of so many naughty and idle persons into that town and others adjoining."[1]

Thus, both contemporary observers and later historians distinguish between the causes of abnormally large population increases in highland and lowland England. Nevertheless, the suspicion lingers that both migration *and* inheritance customs were of significance in *both* halves of England, though in different proportions. The highland villages which complained of the effects of partible inheritance also disposed of generous commons. Districts in the lowlands, which still possessed large reserves of land, did not universally observe the rule of primogeniture. In the Lincolnshire wapentake of Elloe gavelkind was practised in the Middle Ages, and there is no reason to believe that it had died out by the sixteenth century. One of the customs found in the Northamptonshire forests at this time was a form of Borough English, by which inherited land passed to the youngest son, and since this custom often meant that other sons had already been provided for, Borough English may have had a similar effect to that of gavelkind. The Weald of Kent observed gavelkind and was also blessed with comparatively plentiful grazings and waste land.

It would not be unreasonable to suggest, as a tentative hypothesis, that the custom of partitioning land among children and the presence of unstinted commons were closely related phenomena in the structure of local communities. Partible inheritance could survive without causing great economic difficulty only so long as the commons and wastes were large and provided a reserve of land on which succeeding generations could draw for their living. But as the commons shrank and the population grew, there came a point when it was no longer economically feasible to allow the subdivision of estates to continue, and either by a once-for-all manorial agreement, or by a slower

[1] Joan Thirsk, *English Peasant Farming*, pp. 140–1; P. A. J. Pettit, *The Economy of the Northamptonshire Royal Forests, 1558–1714*, Oxford D.Phil. thesis, 1959, p. 303: Northants RO, Westmorland, Apethorpe Coll., 4 XVI, 5.

process of persuasion and example, people abandoned the custom of partible inheritance, and stinted their pastures. Because of the abundance of land and the relatively greater tenurial freedom of the peasantry, the trend was slow in the highland zone and had proceeded furthest in the west Midlands only. In lowland England the process had been hastened on individual estates in the Middle Ages by the deliberate policy of ecclesiastical and lay landlords who had kept a vigilant eye on the administration of their property. But even without their deliberate intervention, the trend was inevitably more rapid in this direction because of the greater density of population. By the beginning of the sixteenth century unstinted pastures were hard to find in lowland England, and except on some freak estates so was partible inheritance.

Finally, consideration must be given to the industrial occupations which played so large a part in the livelihood of many agricultural communities. In bestowing minerals, Nature has made its most generous gifts to the highland communities of England, and so compensated them for the disappointments of their farming. Thus, there was hardly a county in the highland half of England without a considerable mining or quarrying industry, carried on for the most part by small family groups or by the partnership of two or three individuals. The working units were small, and except in the coalfields, continued so into the seventeenth century. Most miners were part-time farmers, and while neither occupation by itself yielded them an adequate living, they managed to fit their industrial and agricultural occupations into a satisfactory workable whole.

Highland communities which lacked mineral resources on their doorstep frequently resorted to a domestic handicraft. Clothmaking was the most important of these and was well established in the west country, in certain areas of Wiltshire, Gloucestershire, Somerset, Dorset, and Devon long before the sixteenth century. Further north, a coarse cloth industry had become firmly entrenched by the late fifteenth century around Kendal in Westmorland, in Cumberland, and in Furness. In the course of the next hundred years it attained greater importance than ever before in West Yorkshire in the district around Halifax. Elsewhere, stocking-knitting took hold and grew from a small local trade to an export industry supplying stockings and mittens not only to London but to Holland as well. The main distribution centre and market for the industry was in north-west Yorkshire at Richmond, but there are hints that the industry was growing in other districts too, in the neighbourhood of Doncaster, Rotherham, Northampton, and Norwich, and along the north-east coast of Norfolk.[1]

Lowland England also boasted a number of centres of domestic

[1] PRO E 134, 2 Chas. I, M 38; E 178, 4354.

industry, but they were located for the most part in the pastoral areas where labour was evidently plentiful, and where farming for one reason or another did not afford sufficient monetary rewards or constitute a full-time occupation. In the Weald of Kent, and in the southern half of central Suffolk a large-scale cloth industry had already come to maturity in the fifteenth century and employed many part-time dairy farmers. In pastoral districts cleared from the forest where much timber still survived, wood-turning and other wood-working crafts were another by-employment. In the Isle of Axholme and the fens of Lincolnshire around the Wash a weaving industry developed alongside the growing of hemp and flax: in Axholme people made sack cloth, while in south-east Lincolnshire they wove canvas, harden, and linen. These occupations were in addition to those associated with the curing of the two crops. The growing of hemp was itself regarded as a labour-consuming but profitable occupation for the poor cottagers. It did not grow successfully everywhere, and was best suited to rich alluvial soils, but where hemp crofts were a usual appurtenance to the cottage dwelling, hemp-growing contributed in more than one way to the support of the small holder. Thus the melancholy surveyor of Rockingham Forest, Northamptonshire, bewailing the number of idle cottagers who inhabited it in the 1570's and got their living by keeping stock upon the common grazings, added as an afterthought, and without noticing that it contradicted his main thesis, that in Nassington "the soil is so good and there is such a trade and vent of hemp in that town, an acre of ground well sown with hemp will be worth twenty shillings above all charges."[1]

Rural industries were not altogether unknown in the mixed husbandry areas of lowland England—for example, the broadcloth industry flourished in the Wylye and Nadder valleys of Wiltshire in the sheep-corn region of the county, largely it seems because of their proximity to the old cloth town of Salisbury in which the industry had first been established. In Norfolk cloth-making developed in a similar farming region, next door to Norwich which dominated the industry. But the exceptions were few. Indeed, the economic and social environment was so unfavourable to the maintenance of industries in corn-growing districts that those that did survive deserve closer examination. If an industry was to flourish on a scale sufficiently large to support a specialized market of repute, like Richmond, Yorkshire, for knitted stockings, or to call into existence a group of travelling chapmen and factors like the cloth industry of Halifax, it had to be able to draw on a considerable reserve of labour. This was not so easily found in common-field districts where the system of land distribution, particularly the

[1] Northants. RO, Westmorland, Apethorpe Coll., 4, XVI 5.

scattered strips of arable, were extravagant in the use of labour, and where mixed husbandry made heavy demands on the labour force, requiring attention to the cultivation of the fields virtually throughout the year as well as attention to stock. Given these difficulties alone, it is not surprising that industries did not survive. But these were not the only obstacles: other social factors worked in the same direction. The lowland common-field districts were more highly manorialized, and manorial control had considerable effect in discouraging the immigration of outsiders and squatters on the waste, and the partitioning of land by tenants. The nightmare of many a manorial lord in the sixteenth century was to see his land carved up among too many tenants, or his waste encroached upon and ultimately devoured by landless men seeking a bare subsistence from the commons. Hence his concern to control the size and growth of population on his estate—a policy which sometimes won support from tenants also since it was in their interests too to discourage intruders. These were not ideal conditions for nursing a cottage industry.

Some attempt has here been made to enumerate the economic and social factors which moulded the many different communities of England, and to underline some of the recurring features in their structure in highland and lowland England. These may be summarized thus: the communities most typical of highland England practised pasture farming, produced only enough corn for their own needs, and did so in closes, or in small common fields, many of which were enclosed without commotion during and immediately after the Tudor period. Some of them still clung to the custom of partitioning their land among all or many of their sons, kept their families around them by providing them with holdings, and successfully resisted manorial pressure designed to restrict their freedom to do what they wished with their estates. Many of them mined and quarried while also running their farms and small-holdings, or engaged in a domestic handicraft to supplement their living. The majority of communities in lowland England followed a system of mixed husbandry, cultivated their ploughland in common, submitted to communal regulation of their farming, and to stricter manorial regulation when they disposed of their land. For the most part they were inclined to accept the custom of primogeniture, that is to say, they commonly accepted it as the custom of the manor, though how far evasions in practice, through the devising of land before death or by will, occurred in some districts it is as yet impossible to say. Farming was a full-time occupation, which did not leave much scope for men to engage in a cottage industry.

The highlands had pockets of more fertile land where larger acreages lay under the plough, and usually these were inhabited by communities of the lowland kind. Similarly, the lowland had its pockets of pastoral country and communities which were cast in the highland mould. Everywhere, local circumstances, the personality of the landowner, the accidents of birth, mortality, good and bad fortune among tenants, and the opportunities for marketing surplus produce were liable to lead to local variations upon these two main themes. But at the beginning of the sixteenth century, clear contrasts could still be observed at the extremities of the kingdom. Cornwall and Devon, Cumberland, Westmorland, and Northumberland had many communities dispersed in lonely farmsteads, some still preserving vestiges of the clan spirit, still almost completely isolated from the commercial world. Corn-growing villages in East Anglia and east Kent, on the other hand, were deeply involved in large-scale commercial dealings in food, and conducted their business seemingly without regard for any social obligation whether to clan, family, or manorial lord. Between these two extremes, and particularly on the frontiers between the highland and lowland zones, the contrasts were blurred. The west Midlands, for example, had large tracts of valley land supporting a mixed husbandry in open fields, and dense populations whose understanding of market opportunities was sharpened by the neighbouring presence of growing industrial centres. Market opportunities, indeed, precipitated many changes in agricultural specialization at this period, making farming more profitable, and encouraging individuals to enlarge their enterprise and consolidate and enclose their lands. Thus the expansion of the market started a revolution in methods of farming which erased some of the salient differences in the structure of highland and lowland communities. At the same time, since all communities accepted innovations at a different pace, and adapted them to suit their needs, the individuality of regions was in other ways accentuated.

In these introductory pages, the heaviest emphasis has been laid on the recurring features of social and economic organization. They suggest that some institutions in the life of local communities are intimately linked with, and dependent upon, one another. The more detailed studies that ensue illustrate these points with further examples while emphasizing at the same time many aspects of life in which each community was unique. They are not intended to be read as a continuous narrative, but sampled as the reader's interests dictate.

B. THE NORTHERN PROVINCE: CUMBERLAND, WESTMORLAND, FURNESS, DURHAM, AND NORTHUMBERLAND

The northern province of England affords examples of many typical highland communities, interspersed with a few communities which pursued a mixed husbandry in common fields, and were subject to the stresses and strains of land shortage and commercial ambition, more readily associated at this period with lowland England.

Certain political and economic factors exercised a more or less uniform influence throughout the province in the period 1500–1640, and are worth enumerating first before the differences are considered in greater detail. Much of the district was remote from large industrial and trading centres; much of it was inaccessible to the traveller, and all was generally regarded with repulsion by outsiders. There might be striking differences between the way of life and the farming of the stock farmers and the corn-growers in this province, but to the gentle southerner, and particularly to government officials who waged a losing battle in trying to enforce the law of Westminster, the whole province was a wild savage country, its inhabitants primitive in their passions and morals, and entirely without understanding of the rules of a law-abiding society. Seen through the eyes of the outsider, this was a frontier province, harbouring a characteristic frontier society, and in some ways this verdict was accurate enough. The border country was exposed to the depredations of the Scots both in war and peace, and, at least until 1603 and the Union of the Crowns, the people living nearest to Scotland farmed their land under the constant threat of losing their lives, their cattle, their crops, or their houses in a sudden midnight raid. Attacks across the Solway Firth were especially frequent, since they could be timed with the tides to cover the raiders' retreat and prevent pursuit. On one such errand, a party of sixty Scots raided Holm Cultram on the night of 2 October 1542, and left two burning houses in their wake. In the year after the Armada, the decaying castle of Drumburgh on Solway was still prized as a refuge to which the inhabitants of Bowness manor could flee with their animals whenever the Scots "should happen to make any sudden raid or foray, as when the sea ebbeth they may easily do before other relief can come unto them."[1]

Nor were the Scots the only threat to the life and livelihood of the

[1] F. Grainger and W. G. Collingwood, eds., 'The Register and Records of Holm Cultram', *Cumb. & Westm. Antiq. & Arch. Soc.*, Rec. Ser., VII, 1929, p. 174; Cumberland RO, Survey of Baronies and Lands of Leonard Dacre, attainted, 1589. See also C. M. L. Bouch and G. P. Jones, *The Lake Counties, 1500–1830*, p. 22.

peaceful farmer. The hills were the refuge of outlaws who had nothing to lose but their lives. They wandered to and fro across the Irish Sea, preying upon the countryside of both kingdoms. They got their food by theft and slaughter, and sometimes so intimidated the local people that men were finally driven from their holdings for fear of the out-laws. Others came to terms with the felons and defied the officers of the Crown. The law of Westminster was powerless to safeguard its subjects in parts of this remote region, and law-abiding men had to arrange their own protection. This they did by keeping faith with their own clans and communities and by loyalty also to the most powerful lord of the district. His temper and sympathies, indeed, largely determined the efficiency with which the law was administered locally.[1]

Reports on the situation in James I's reign, when a stern attempt was made to bring the north to heel, illustrate the difficulties of the govern-ment in reducing a region to order against the opposition of, or with only lukewarm assistance from, the influential landowners. Some were sympathetic to the Crown's efforts but threw up their hands in helpless-ness. Speaking of the border region of Liddesdale, Cumberland, in 1618, Sir William Hutton blandly declared that there was not a true man inhabiting it. An influential landowner in Northumberland and north-east Cumberland was Lord Howard, whose bailiff, it was said, on the Sabbath day kept the people of Redesdale in the town streets and churchyard all prayer and sermon time. With the connivance and encouragement of men such as these, the western half of Northumber-land was deemed the haven of "professed Papists, thieves, or atheists," living "without fear of God or regard of any wholesome laws."[2]

Reports such as these seem to be couched in extravagant language, but they become more credible in the light of the statement that there were only twelve English preaching ministers of the church in the whole of Northumberland. It was easy enough to say that a strong man was needed to live in these parts and set an example, but no one "who hath not been bred in those highland countries [will] come from a more civil place to interpose himself in such a business." Here, indeed, we touch the heart of the problem. The largest and most influential landowners were absentees who frequented this "barren wilderness" only when they came to hunt the deer for sport. Much lawlessness, then, was encouraged by their absence. And to this fact also must be attributed much of the alleged poverty of the province. The

[1] SP 14, 97, 60, See also Bouch and Jones, op. cit., p. 91.
[2] SP 14, 97, 60; SP 14, 92, 17; SP 14, 86, 113. See also Penry Williams, 'The Northern Borderland under the Early Stuarts', Historical Essays, 1600–1750, presented to David Ogg, ed. H. E. Bell and R. L. Ollard, 1963, pp. 1–17.

evidence of its farmers' wealth does not support the view that this was a
uniformly poor region, but at subsidy-collecting time there was truth
in the complaint that non-resident landlords took elsewhere much of
the wealth which the region produced.[1]

Desperate situations bred desperate remedies. The law was evidently
best enforced by dramatic scenes of punishment. The earl of Northumberland executed five offenders from Redesdale in Henry VIII's
reign in the presence of many gentlemen of the county, and with this
fearful example before their eyes, many other men from the same
district "submitted themselves in their shirts with halters about their
necks upon their bare knees unto the King's mercy." In January 1618
Sir Henry Widdrington, in a similar mood of zeal to uphold the law of
England, tore the roof from the house of a fugitive, cast out his wife and
children to beg for winter shelter, and so intimidated others that for
the time being another generation of outlaws in Tyndale and Redesdale
likewise made humble submission.[2]

Not surprisingly, outsiders turned away in repugnance from the
harsh landscape, the unfriendly climate, and the rough manners of the
north. But the inhabitants looked upon their countryside with different
eyes. And we who have learned to appreciate the beauty of bracken-
covered hillsides, of rocky, infertile mountain scree, who are not
necessarily repelled by the sense of isolation in lonely valleys, are in a
better position to understand the attachment of the northerner to his
rugged environment. He did not, after all, live on the barren mountain
tops. He chose the more fruitful valleys and plains where he found
shelter for his house, where corn could be grown, where meadows
yielded hay for the winter, where the lower pastures invited enclosure
and improvement with sand and lime, and where, in addition to all
this, he had ample common grazings on the hillsides. The countryside
looked entirely different from that of Midland and southern England
where ploughland often occupied at least half the area of many
parishes, and to strangers it might indeed seem barren and poor. But
this region counted its wealth in different commodities, in its woods,
in its deer parks (though these began to disappear in the sixteenth
century to make room for more cattle), in its birds of moor and fell
(black heathcocks, brown moorcocks, and poots, as tasty as pheasants),
in the fish of its tarns and lakes (the pikes, bass, trout, and eels of Lakes
Windermere and Coniston, and particularly the *charrs*—"like trout,
but with red bellies," which were a delicacy at London banquets), and

[1] SP 14, 92, 17; SP 16, 7, 74 (II). The explanation for the absence of ministers in
Northumberland seems to be that most were from Scotland. See BM Harl. MS
595.

[2] LP IV, part 2, p. 1855; SP, 14, 95 19.

most of all in its cattle (the black and the less common wild white cattle), and in its sheep (small animals, it is true, and yielding a coarse wool, but producing a mutton which some claimed was sweeter than that of the southern sheep). The land did not yield corn bountifully like the south, but it provided a very miscellaneous collection of resources which were used with great economy and efficiency. The court orders of Cartmel Manor in Furness regulated the tenants' use of limestone, freestone, slate, clay, sand, bracken, peat, rushes, juniper berries, and nuts. And, making a virtue of necessity, the inhabitants who used young shoots of holly and ash for feeding their cattle and sheep in winter, argued that the holly cuttings gave the mutton a remarkably fine flavour.[1]

More than this, the conditions of land tenure were in general more attractive than in many other parts of England. Much land was held by a customary tenure which gave tenants the security of freeholders. The 'statesmen' of the north were comparable to the yeomen of the south, but they were more numerous. And when James I attempted to undermine the security of those who held by border tenure, he found himself in conflict with a stalwart and determined class of tenants who were prepared to fight a long lawsuit to preserve their rights.[2]

The principal hazard of all farmers in the northern province was the meagre corn harvest, which placed the whole economy upon a precarious footing. The main crops were barley, or bigg (a poorer and hardier variety of barley), and oats, the two crops varying in relative importance in different districts. In Furness and Cumberland barley seems to have taken first place, and the bread was made of barley flour. In Westmorland oats seem to have been the larger crop, and were not only ground into flour for oat clap bread, the staple food, but malted for the making of beer. March-sown wheat and rye were grown in places scattered all over the province; William Harrison observed both around Kendal, and they appear in lists of farmers' crops in north Lancashire, Furness, and further north, from Elizabeth's reign onwards. In central Durham and throughout lowland Northumberland, however, wheat and rye were widely grown, sometimes even exceeding the acreage of barley and oats, and here the winter varieties were used. For

---

[1] E. Sandford, *A Cursory Relation of all the Antiquities and Families in Cumberland writ about the year 1675*, ed. C. Ferguson, *Cumb. & Westm. Antiq. & Arch. Soc.*, Tract Ser. IV, 1890, pp. 47, 24; Carlisle Public Library, Accounts of Bailiffs, etc., of Gilsland Barony, 1633–4; *The Memoirs of Daniel Fleming*, ed. W. G. Collingwood, *Cumb. & Westm. Antiq. & Arch. Soc.*, Tract Ser., XI, 1928, pp. 83–4; T. H. B. Graham, 'English Park Cattle', *Cumb. & Westm. Antiq. & Arch. Soc.*, NS, XXXIII, 1933, pp. 7 sqq.; Lancs. RO, DD, c a, 7, 2–3; Thos. West, *The Antiquities of Furness*, 1805 ed., p. 40.

[2] Bouch and Jones, *op. cit.*, pp. 65 sqq.; M. Campbell, *The English Yeoman*, p. 148.

fodder, peas, and less commonly beans were grown throughout the province, and seem to have assumed steadily greater importance as time went on. Apart from these, and the grains already mentioned, the only other crops were hemp and flax.[1]

In years of poor harvests this province was liable to suffer serious shortages of corn. Danzig rye was regularly brought in through the port of Newcastle and, in emergency, further supplies came from the corn-growing counties of eastern and southern England. When outside aid was not forthcoming, as in the late 1590's, the whole province was stricken by famine, plague, and cattle sickness. The same sequence of misfortunes followed again in 1622 and 1623, and in 1629.[2]

Men won a hard living in the battle against an ungenerous and fickle climate, but they were not wholly dependent on their agriculture. By-employments in mining, quarrying, and cottage handicraft industries contributed substantially towards maintaining the population. Blue slate and iron were mined in Furness; lead, limestone, blue slate, and copper ore in Westmorland; coal, iron, lead, and building stone in Northumberland; lead, alum, ironstone in West Durham, and coal in the central portion of the county. In other districts a cloth industry provided additional occupations. But it seems to have been confined to the pastoral regions of the province, and is therefore less conspicuous in Northumberland and Durham, where a lowland system of mixed husbandry occupied larger areas, than on the western side of the Pennines. *Cartmels*, coarse woollen cloths, were made in Furness, Westmorland, and Cumberland at the beginning of the seventeenth century, although, judging by their name, they must have originated in Furness. Coloured cloths, and kerseys, together with linen and harden, hung from the tenter bars behind almost every house in Kendal, and fluttered in the wind on the fellsides. Cloth was woven in all the valleys radiating from Kendal, and occupied a large proportion of the population of parishes such as Grasmere where there were eighteen fulling-mills in the 1490's.[3]

[1] Probate Invs., *passim*; William Harrison, *Elizabethan England*, ed. F. J. Furnivall, p. 98.

[2] CSPD 1638–9, p. 349; *ibid.*, 1628–9, p. 450; T. H. B. Graham, *The Barony of Gilsland. Lord William Howard's Survey taken in 1603, Cumb. & Westm. Antiq. & Arch. Soc.*, Extra Ser., XVI, 1934, pp. viii–ix; Henry Barnes, 'Visitations of the Plague in Cumberland and Westmorland', *ibid.* XI, 1892, pp. 178–9; SP 14, 131, 29 & 9; SP 16, 7, 74 (II). See also F. W. Garnett, *Westmorland Agriculture, 1800–1900*, p. 19.

[3] C. Ferguson, ed., 'Account of the City and Diocese of Carlisle by Hugh Todd', *Cumb. & Westm. Antiq. & Arch. Soc.*, Tract Ser., V, 1890, 33; VCH *Lancs.*, VIII, p. 255; M. L. Armitt, 'Fullers and Freeholders of the Parish of Grasmere', *Cumb. & Westm. Antiq. & Arch. Soc.*, NS, VIII, 1908, pp. 137, 155.

At the beginning of the sixteenth century Kendal cloth was being carried to Southampton for despatch to Italy, and to Bristol for transport to Spain. Some falling-off in the prosperity of this industry occurred in the second half of the century (four of the mills in Grasmere were in decay by 1572), but it was a temporary setback only; Kendal merchants in Elizabeth's reign had business connections with God-manchester, Huntingdon, Barnsley, Bradford, Wakefield, Keighley, and London. At the end of the seventeenth century, when Celia Fiennes passed through Kendal, the colourful display of cloth and the activities of its busy traders could still provoke the admiration of the traveller. But by that time the cloth industry was dwindling away, and in the eighteenth century, stocking-knitting took its place as the main textile activity.[1]

Broad generalizations can be made concerning the difficulties of governing this province, the limitations imposed by its geographical situation, and the significance of its industries. At the same time, striking differences in the scale of farming and the commercial opportunities have to be acknowledged between the mountainous fells and narrow valleys penetrating them, which constitute the core of the province, and the plains that lie on either side and reach to the coasts. And these in their turn influenced the structure of the two types of community.

1. *The highlands*

On the fells, the characteristic settlement was the hamlet or single farm, and not the village. The arable land was restricted to a few closes near the farmstead, or, in larger settlements, lay in scattered parcels in one or more fields, which were commonable after harvest. Ample explanation for the perennial corn shortage in the highlands is found in an examination of land use on the typical farm. A fell farm usually consisted of arable and meadow land but not always pasture closes. Since the arable carried a rotation of corn, pulses, and long leys, a holding with five or eight acres of arable might yield no more than two acres of corn crops in the year. The customary acre in the north was half as large again and sometimes three times the size of the statute acre, but even this did not mean a large corn crop. For winter fodder, therefore, men set most store by their common pastures and leys in the arable fields, and by their meadows which frequently equalled or exceeded the acreage of the arable (in the Midlands, the meadow was on average one tenth the size of the arable land). At Watermillock in Cumberland, for example, the standard holding consisted of five customary acres of

[1] Bouch and Jones, *op. cit.*, pp. 134, 137; *The Journeys of Celia Fiennes*, ed. C. Morris, 1947, p. 191.

arable and four acres of meadow. In Grisedale it consisted of four acres of arable, four acres of meadow, and one acre of pasture.[1]

The highland farmer's main business was the breeding of cattle, which were sold as stores into more southerly counties, and the keeping of sheep, which were pastured on the hills and were kept mainly for their wool. Except in the forest districts, no one in the highlands was able to keep pigs in any number, and between a half and three quarters of the farmers had none at all, while the rest had on average one pig per household. One or two horses were kept on all farms since all journeys were made by packhorse. Bees yielded honey, and sometimes an occasional goat grazing the rocky hillsides yielded additional milk. Life was hard for the small farmer; many had stock "to halves," and admitted many debts at their deaths. But the ordinary 'statesman' could make a moderate living with six to nine beasts, two horses, and twenty to forty sheep, while a few richer farmers could compete with any southerner. Henry Swinburne of Crosthwaite parish, Cumberland, dying in 1633, had 37 cattle, 8 horses, 260 sheep; his total fortune in personal goods was valued at £326.[2]

Cattle sickness was a major disaster for fell farmers, but in Cumberland and Northumberland, at least, the risk of infection was reduced by the widespread practice of transhumance. Every summer around Whitsuntide, the herds and flocks from the valleys were led to higher pastures and fresh grazing, and there the cattle herds, and sometimes the whole community, remained until the hay in the valley was ready to be harvested. The inhabitants of Redesdale in Northumberland turned their expedition into a social ceremony in which the whole community took part. The day was chosen by the bailiff, and no one was allowed to remain behind unless he wished to rebuild his house in the village. In 1620 the inhabitants described the ritual in terms which vividly illustrate the danger and uncertainties of life in the north, and portray conditions which the southerner had forgotten many centuries before and could neither recall nor understand. The expedition was planned in the form of a veritable military operation "for that in the time of the late borders, the people were not permitted to go straggling one before another, or remain straggling one after another, in respect of the danger and deadly feuds abroad, and in respect of ill neighbourhood and wronging one another in their husbandry at home."[3]

[1] Cumberland RO, Survey of Greystoke Barony, lands of Leonard Dacre, attainted, 1589.   [2] Cumberland RO, Probate Invs. *passim*.

[3] PRO E 134, 18 Jas. I, E 13; E 134, 18 Jas. I, M 21. See also *A Book of the Survey of the Debatable and Border Lands, 1604*, ed. R. P. Sanderson, 1891, p. 104; J. Hodgson, *A History of Northumberland*, 1828, part III, vol. II, pp. 221, 226.

Detailed descriptions of the custom of transhumance are rare, but the sheilings occupy an important place in the more prosaic records of manorial revenues, for they were extremely remunerative to the landlord. Lord William Howard received in 1633–4 £25 5s. in sheild rents (presumably rents of the huts and small allotments of cultivated land attached to them) and £95 15s. 8d. for the agistment of the cattle. Sheilings seem to be described in a survey of Duston manor—a now lost place in Greystoke barony—where agistment rights were leased in Akeskewe wood together with thirty-three tiny holdings, most of them consisting of half an acre of arable land and two acres of pasture, but without permanent houses of any kind. At Rayboure agistment rights with tiny holdings of land again imply sheilings. Kinniside in Cumberland accommodated tenants of "grasshouses" with six to nine beastgates apiece in summer. In Gilsland barony in Cumberland so-called sheild rents were received in the 1630's for the pasturage of cattle on the North Moor in Askerton. In Furness, the distinction frequently made between cattle "in the country" and those "at home" hints at the practice of transhumance.[1]

Transhumance was one of a number of factors fostering and maintaining a sense of community, and strengthening the still lively clan spirit in the more remote highland parts of the province. The people of Redesdale, for example, claimed their rights of common pasture on the fells at Redeshead not in respect of their tenements in the lowlands, but by virtue of their surnames "for that they are descended of such a surname or race of men to whom such a summering belongeth." And since this isolated community still harked back to its origin in a single family, it is not surprising to find that it practised partible inheritance. Its customary land in the valleys, we are told, was divided among all sons (the eldest having the chief house), while the pastures continued to be enjoyed in common.

The same inheritance rule was observed in other parts of the highlands. It was the formal custom of the manor at Waterhead in Furness on customary land which had not been devised by will. Elsewhere its influence is implied or explicitly admitted in complaints concerning the subdivision of tenements. In 1594 the government attributed the lawlessness on the border to the decay of border service, caused by the division of tenements by landlords, and "by the tenants themselves making partition among their children." In Furness the Crown as landlord displayed anxiety at the division of land which increased the number of poor and indirectly caused serious spoil of the woods. These

[1] Carlisle Public Library, Accounts of Bailiffs, etc., of Gilsland Barony, 1633–4; A159 Egmond Manor Surveys, 1578, Id; Cumberland RO, Survey of Greystoke Barony, lands of Leonard Dacre attainted, 1589.

troubles were attributed explicitly to the practice of gavelkind, and an agreement was finally reached in Elizabeth's reign that no customary holding should be further divided among children unless each divided portion was worth at least 6s. 8d. in ancient yearly rent. Where division did take place, new holdings were all to be provided with proper houses and onsets. At the same time, it was agreed that if customary tenants died without leaving a will, the tenement should pass to the eldest son. Here, as in a number of similar disputes concerning the customs of manors, the suspicion is aroused that while primogeniture was now accepted as the rule in cases of intestacy, a different rule had prevailed before.[1]

Investigation of the effects of partible inheritance in another district of England suggests that it resulted in larger than average populations because the younger children were encouraged by the promise of a piece of land to stay at home, instead of seeking a living elsewhere. The temptations to leave home were in any case weak in communities whose physical isolation and family traditions caged the young almost as effectively as prison walls. Moreover, there was less economic pressure to migrate than in other districts such as the east Midlands. Land was abundant, even though the southerner might sneer at its poor quality. Good cornland was hard to win, but there was plentiful common grazing and much land on the lower hillsides promised to repay enclosure and improvement. Every young man could make a start with a cow and a few sheep, and found in this as much opportunity and freedom as he desired.[2]

The persistence of the custom of partible inheritance coupled with the general rise of population at this period seems to have caused some congestion in the narrow valleys with their meagre resources of arable. Contemporary descriptions of the excessive populations of Redesdale and Tyndale—"There be more inhabitants within either of them than the said countries may sustain to live truly for upon a farm of a noble rent. They do inhabit in some place[s] three or four household so that they cannot upon so small farms without any other crafts live truly but either by stealing in England or Scotland"—must be coupled with the knowledge that in both valleys partible inheritance was the custom: of Tyndale it was said that "they have ever had a custom, if a man have issue ten sons, eight, six, five or four, and sits on a holding but of 6s.

---

[1] PRO E 134, 18 Jas. I, E 13; VCH *Lancs.*, VIII, pp. 377, 299; SP 15, 33, 1; PRO DL 44, 398; Thos. West, *op. cit.*, pp. 226, 228. For further evidence of the dominance of one family name in some townships in the Lake Counties, see Bouch and Jones, *op. cit.*, p. 90.

[2] H. E. Hallam, 'Some Thirteenth Century Censuses', EcHR, 2nd Ser., X, 1958, pp. 340 *sqq.*

rent, every son shall have a piece of his father's holding." The justices of the peace for Westmorland, reporting to the Privy Council in 1622, believed their county to be smaller, more barren, and more densely populated than any other in the kingdom. And looking at the number of tenements in some remote hamlets in the mountains, we can see facts which justified such an opinion. Admittedly, the parishes were vast, and it is impossible to make effective comparisons between the size of population in these mountainous districts and those in the lowlands. But if we take as our measure the average parish of the Midlands and southern England with about 1,000 acres of land, accommodating not more than forty households, the populations of 100, 200, and 300 families in the Westmorland fell parishes, even though their acreages were ten times larger, must surely be regarded as dense. For the habitable places were few. Yet the parish of Grasmere accommodated 186 families in 1563, with another 46 at Ambleside and 40 in Langdale; Orton had 211 families; Ravenstonedale 116; Shap, that large parish of which at least half is still not mapped in detail, had 180 families; Bampton had 140, and Askham 80. In 1589 the manor of Matterdale, resting in a steep-sided valley between Derwentwater and Bassenthwaite, had 52 tenants-at-will.[1]

2. *The lowlands*

The lowlands of this province, lying along the west coast of Westmorland and Cumberland, in the Eden valley, and on the broader coastal plains of Northumberland and Durham, supported a different system of husbandry and a different type of society. Villages were more usual than hamlets. The husbandry was mixed. The common fields were larger and played a more important part in the farming system; the proportion of arable to meadow was sometimes as high as seven acres to one, and this resulted in some places in such a diminution of commons that stints of cattle were imposed. The nominal arable acreage in these lowlands, however, was often deceptive. Some crop rotations lasted 7–10 years and included a long period of leys. Hence the acreage of ploughland recorded in a survey was not a reliable guide to the quantity of arable crops grown in any year. The farmer in lowland Westmorland, for example, who had $1\frac{1}{2}$ acres of wheat, $2\frac{1}{2}$ acres of oats, 2 acres of barley and hemp, and $4\frac{1}{2}$ acres of meadow, was a not untypical lowland farmer on the western side of the Pennines, though

[1] J. Hodgson, *op. cit.*, pp. 233, 237, 243; *Calendar of Border Papers, I, 1560–94,* ed. J. Bain, p. 23; A. L. Rowse, *The England of Elizabeth,* pp. 220–1; SP 14, 131, 25; BM Harl. MS 594; Cumberland RO, Dacre Survey, 1589; Bouch and Jones, *op. cit.,* pp. 91–2.

on the east he was more likely to have between 10 and 20 acres of crops.[1]

The larger areas of ploughland undoubtedly gave greater security from domestic grain shortages, but the bulk of the field crops were used as fodder to maintain the livestock. For animals were the main interest of all lowland farmers. On the west coast the speciality was the production of store cattle and store sheep, although men who had sufficient feeding land supplemented their profits by meat production, finding their markets in the Yorkshire towns such as Rotherham and Wakefield, and occasionally even at Smithfield in London. Herrings and codfish were caught off the coast, and both meat and fish were preserved in the salt, evaporated in saltpans along the Solway Firth. The encroaching sea devoured some of these in the course of Elizabeth's reign, after which Cheshire salt was brought in via Chester and Liverpool. From the ports and havens of Cumberland, regular contact was maintained with the Isle of Man, Scotland, and Ireland. It is probable that by all these routes cattle were imported into Cumberland, and fed for a summer in the lowlands, just as they were imported from Ireland into the counties of the south-west. The trade of the west coast, however, was not sufficient to encourage any great expansion of Cumberland's ports, and in Elizabeth's reign they were still only villages: Workington, the largest, had only thirty householders: others were nothing more than a collection of houses strung along the coast. In short, commercial activity was relatively sluggish on this side of northern England, and the fact was reflected in the scale of farming enterprise.[2]

On the coastal plains of Northumberland and central Durham, a much more concentrated effort at beef and mutton production was discernible by the end of the sixteenth century, stimulated by the more highly developed organization of markets and coastal trade. Here were many graziers with over a hundred cattle apiece, and with sheep flocks which consisted not of a collection of "old sheep,"—the commonest description for a flock in Westmorland and Cumberland—but of a balanced flock of ewes, lambs, and wethers, yielding young sheep for sale to other farms and mutton for sale to the butcher. Some remarkably well-to-do graziers lived here: Sir Cuthbert Collingwood of Eppleton in the parish of Houghton-le-Spring, for example, who in 1596 had three sheep flocks, totalling 958 sheep and 143 cattle, and was engaged

[1] G. Elliott, 'The System of Cultivation and Evidence of Enclosure in the Cumberland Open Fields in the Sixteenth Century', *Cumb. & Westm. Antiq. & Arch. Soc.*, NS, LIX, 1959, p. 92.

[2] W. T. McIntire, 'The Saltpans of the Solway', *Cumb. & Westm. Antiq. & Arch. Soc.*, NS., XLII, 1942, pp. 8–9; E. Sandford, *A Cursory Relation*, op. cit. p. 10; P. H. Fox, 'Cumberland Ports and Shipping', *Cumb. & Westm. Antiq. & Arch. Soc.*, NS, XXI, 1921, pp. 76 *sqq.*

in breeding at Eppleton, fattening on the coast at Dalton and also at Grindon; and Robert Woodrington, esq., who in 1599 had land on the coast at Monkwearmouth, more at Washington further inland, where most of his crops were growing, fattening land at Plessey in Northumberland, and more at Cowpen in the same county where he had a saltpan and was part owner of a coal keel.[1]

Examples like these give the lie to those who labelled the whole of northern England as a backward and primitive region. Moreover, in the eastern half of Durham by the end of the sixteenth century, the demand for food to supply the coalmining districts around Newcastle, and for freighting coastal vessels travelling to Scotland and elsewhere, had driven some farmers even further along the road to intensive agricultural production and careful specialization. Meat production was still the principal object in view, but it was supplemented by dairying, the rearing of oxen for draught, and horse breeding. All this was facilitated by even greater use of the plough. Large arable fields yielded plentiful fodder crops, and although oats were probably the most important single corn crop, a good deal of wheat and often rye were grown.[2]

More intensive farming on the eastern side of the province was accompanied by attempts to rationalize the distribution of land. Common fields and common pastures were everywhere associated with village settlements, and stints were in operation in some villages in east Durham, confirming the impression that land was fairly intensively used and that some pressure on the common pastures was developing. This was not surprising, indeed, since there were few townships without their clusters of newly-built cottages to house a growing population. Efforts were being made to improve fertility by liberal applications of manure: farmers around Newcastle-on-Tyne, for example, used to cart dung from the town to their fields.[3]

By the beginning of the seventeenth century enclosure throughout the eastern lowlands was spreading rapidly. In some places in Northumberland it was facilitated by the fact that much of the common arable land was already occupied on a shifting basis and the reallotment of holdings from time to time was an accepted part of village routine. In a nineteenth-century lawsuit, evidence was brought together by manorial stewards from various parts of Northumberland to show that a farm in Northumberland traditionally signified only a share in the township's land and not a fixed piece of village territory. Reallotment

[1] *Wills and Inventories from the Registry at Durham, part II.* Surtees Soc., xxxvIII, 1860, pp. 267–72; Durham RO, Probate Invs., 1599 bundle.

[2] Durham, The Prior's Kitchen, Probate Invs., *passim.*

[3] PRO E 134, 20 Jas. I, E 18; E 134, 8 Jas. I, T 1.

of village holdings was thus made acceptable to all tenants by a tradition, which had originated probably in practical necessity: none of the land would bear crops or grass for many years in succession without reploughing. When, in the later sixteenth century, some townships chose to divide their land into two halves and allot holdings in one half or the other, the consequent redistribution of land did not seem as drastic to them as to those who judge the north in the light of the customs and practices of the south. Nor was enclosure regarded as a device for robbing one man to enrich another. Like all other rearrangements of land in the township, it was a matter for discussion and common agreement. Most of Northumberland's common fields, in consequence, were enclosed before the age of parliamentary acts.[1]

In Durham, where the scale of farming and the variety of crops bore even closer resemblance to the Midlands and the south, the arguments in favour of enclosure were concerned with the exhaustion of the arable, which, it was argued, would yield better under a rotation that included long leys. In contrast with the east Midlands, however, the complaints against enclosure were not vociferous, partly perhaps because townships arrived at the decision to enclose in the seventeenth century, when agreements were the usual preliminary. On the whole the change was carried out amicably and painlessly.[2]

C. YORKSHIRE AND LINCOLNSHIRE

Yorkshire and Lincolnshire lie for the most part in the lowland half of England, and much of the husbandry and many of the communities in these two counties resembled those of midland and southern England. But a western strip of Yorkshire lies athwart the Pennines, and its valleys supported communities which in many respects were little different from those of the hill country in the northern province. It is necessary therefore, to consider the small territory within Yorkshire which was cast in the highland mould, before considering the greater lowland area of the two counties, and dividing it into various regions.

1. *The highlands of Yorkshire*

The valley settlements of the Pennines south of Otley were deeply involved in the manufacture of cloth at this period, and this industry has received far more attention from the historian than the farming. A recent study of Halifax affords a picture of social and economic develop-

---

[1] H. L. Gray, *English Field Systems*, pp. 206–27; F. W. Dendy, 'The Ancient Farms of Northumberland', *Archaeolog. Aeliana*, 2nd Ser., XVI, 1894, pp. 121–56.

[2] H. L. Gray, *op. cit.*, p. 107; VCH *Durham*, II, pp. 239–40.

ment in one large parish in the district which may fairly be regarded as typical of the neighbourhood. The manor belonged to the Duchy of Lancaster, and embraced 150 towns, villages, and hamlets, extending thirty miles in breadth to the borders of Lancashire. Every township had its common fields and commonable pastures, but as in all other pastoral regions, enclosure by exchange agreements or by consent given in the manorial court was slowly disrupting this orderly pattern.[1]

Copyholders probably accounted for two thirds of the tenants at the beginning of Elizabeth's reign, though the proportion may have fallen a little by 1640 as copyholds were enfranchised in the early Stuart period. Partible inheritance was not the formal custom of the manor, but, in practice, tenants' lands were constantly being divided at death, since families preferred to leave some land, if possible, to all their sons. When the land of one man was subject to different terms of tenure, he often favoured the device of giving the freehold land to one son, the copyhold to another, and the leaseholds to other children.[2]

By the sixteenth century the manufacture of kersey cloth was well established in Halifax parish and was regarded by the inhabitants as essential to their support, the land, they declared, being too barren, cold, and acid to make good farm land, and the number of poor being large. As elsewhere, clothmaking was carried on in conjunction with farming, and about half the people whose wills have survived were engaged in both activities.[3]

Of the agriculture of this manufacturing district in the dales it is difficult to say much for lack of documentary evidence, but it is unlikely that it differed greatly from the system in the more northerly sector of the Yorkshire dales where most holdings consisted of pasture only or of meadow and pasture, and where the main pursuit was cattle rearing and dairying. An acre or so of cornland on which oats were the main crop, and rye a secondary one, provided the principal breadcorn, but a farm without ploughland was by no means unusual. In Middleham lordship, for example, it would have been impossible for everyone to share in the arable for it constituted only about 7 per cent of the total cultivated land, while meadow accounted for 55 per cent, and pasture 37 per cent. In other places in West Yorkshire the proportion of

[1] Martha Ellis, 'A Study in the Manorial History of Halifax Parish in the Sixteenth and early Seventeenth Centuries, part 1', *Yorks. Arch. J.*, CLVIII, 1960, p. 254; T. W. Hanson, 'Ovenden Wood', *Halifax Antiq. Soc.*, 1910, p. 87; J. Lister, 'Some Local Star Chamber Cases', *ibid.* 1927, pp. 199–200; Leeds Public Library, TN, Hx, E; TN, Hx, C4, 1.

[2] Martha Ellis, *op. cit.*, p. 261, and private correspondence with the author.

[3] Leeds Central Library, Archives Dept., TN, Hx, E. Cf. also contemporary remarks on the increase of population and pauperism in Bradford (1589).—PRO DL 44, 440.

arable was higher than this, approaching 30 per cent. But even this allocation of land between different uses was in marked contrast with the proportions found on ordinary lowland manors where between 60 and 80 per cent of the cultivated land was under the plough while about 10 per cent was meadow. As one writer described conditions in the lordships of Middleham and Richmond, the land was "not able to bear corn for the coldness of the soil and the length of the winter there." Thus many substantial graziers possessed large herds and flocks but lacked all implements of husbandry such as ploughs and harrows. William Alderson of Angram in Muker bequeathed to his heirs in 1631 28 head of cattle, including 12 cows, 3 heifers, 7 stirks, 5 calves, and a bull, 2 horses, and 113 sheep, but possessed no cornland.[1]

A holding of 15–20 customary acres was average in the dales, and this included all the cornland (if any), and all the meadow and enclosed pasture. But it left out of account the outmoors or fells, grazed by sheep and cattle in all but the coldest months of winter. These moors were described by one writer as four times as extensive, but one third as valuable as the ingrounds. Large farms with over 100 acres apiece were not unknown, however, and accommodated the large yeomen and gentry. In Wensleydale six such farms occupied 45 per cent of the cultivated land of the manor, although nearly 60 per cent of the holdings, not counting the cottagers' plots, were less than 30 acres and the average (median) was 15–20 acres. In outward appearance, the dale farmstead probably looked much as it does today—a stone building, superseding a former timber one, with garths, closes, and turf house surrounding the house, and barns and hayhouses scattered about the fields. In contemporary surveys, the hayhouses, which are still a characteristic feature of the dales, were indicated in such phrases as a "meadow with a fieldhouse thereupon."[2]

Dale farms were breeding grounds for flocks of sheep and a steadily increasing number of dairy cattle. The cows were milked in the open where they grazed, as they are to this day. The main winter fodder was hay and the land which was most sought after was meadow. In Wensleydale the best meadow was rented at 5s. an acre, the best pasture at 3s. 4d., and the arable at 4s. These were uneconomic rents, however; the surveyor estimated the true value of the meadow at 16s. per acre. The main produce for the market, therefore, was wool, lambs, cheese,

[1] Yorks. Arch. Soc. MS 509; Joan Thirsk, 'The Content and Sources of Agrarian History after 1500', AHR, III, 1955, p. 70; T. S. Willan and E. W. Crossley, eds., *Three Seventeenth-century Yorkshire Surveys*, Yorks. Arch. Soc., Rec. Ser., CIV, 1941, p. xx; Leeds Public Libraries, Archives Dept., Central Library, Leeds, RD, AP, 1A.
[2] Yorks. Arch. Soc. MS 509; DD 121, 31; Willan and Crossley, *op. cit.*, pp. xxiii–iv.

salt butter, and tallow. Pigs were few and seem to have supplied only the household with meat. But most dalesmen had a couple of ponies for carrying their wool and produce down the mountain paths, and bringing back corn from the lowlands. They were called Galloway nags, then as now, and were probably the descendants of the 'Celtic pony'.[1]

The large yeomen and squires in the dales were graziers on an adventurous scale. Charles Dransfield, esq., of Garrestone in Hauxwell, for example, possessed in 1552 258 cattle (201 being dairy animals), 51 horses (he was clearly a horse breeder), and nearly a thousand sheep. But many, and probably the majority, of the dalesmen wrung a fairly hard living from their farming. Lead mining was a by-employment of long standing. And in the course of the sixteenth century stocking-knitting developed into an export industry of some importance. Men as well as women knitted at their doors in the evenings and as they walked with their cattle and sheep out to the pastures. The inhabitants of Dentdale and Garsdale regarded this occupation as vital in rescuing them all from harsh poverty, for their holdings were too small to yield a proper living from the land. Their farms, they declared at an enquiry in 1634, were "so small in quantity that many of them are not above three or four acres apiece, and generally not above eight or nine acres so that they could not maintain their families were it not by their industry in knitting coarse stockings." The diminution of their holdings they attributed to the effects of partible inheritance, and although it is impossible as yet to say how far this custom prevailed throughout the dales at the time, there are hints that it had been fairly common in the not very distant past. Muker in Upper Swaledale was land "of gavel-kind tenure" in the late thirteenth century. The inhabitants of Arkengarthdale were said to have followed the custom of gavelkind until 1571 when it was altered to primogeniture, and since Arkengarthdale falls within the lordship of Richmond, it is possible that the custom was at one time common to the whole lordship.[2]

The effects of a rising population were evident in changes in the use of both houses and land. Extra houses were being built and one-family houses divided into two. Even turf houses, and kitchens, standing apart from the main house, were being turned into separate dwellings. Much improvement of the waste, enclosure of the arable fields, and conversion of arable to meadow was in progress. Many a village was engaged

[1] Cumberland RO and Lancs. RO, Probate Invs., *passim*; Yorks. Arch. Soc., MS 509; Willan and Crossley, *op. cit.*, p. 146; PRO E 178, 2627.

[2] York Probate Registry, Invs., D and C., 1488–1569; PRO E 134, 2 Chas. I, M 38; E 134, 10–11 Chas. I, Hil. 22; E 134, 10 Jas. I, Mich. 26; E. Cooper, *Muker: The Story of a Yorkshire Parish*, 1948, p. 14.

in converting some of its unstinted common into regulated pasture where the quality of the grassland could be improved and better shelter given to young stock by the planting of hedges. And an increasing amount of litigation arose from disputes between townships which had previously intercommoned on each other's pastures without defining their own territory clearly.[1]

All these developments point to more intensive grazing by cattle and sheep. Alarm at the growing shortage of grass was even raised in the wildest and most isolated parishes of the North Riding of Yorkshire, where thousands of cattle traversed the commons on their way over the Pennines from Scotland to the south. In the course of a lawsuit in James I's reign, it was stated that twenty thousand beasts as well as sheep pastured on the commons of Bolton and Bowes on their journey along the road from Carlisle across the Pennines to Middlesbrough.[2]

The Pennine district of Yorkshire, in short, affords an excellent example of a poor pasture-farming country, given over mainly to dairying and cattle rearing, where the increase of employment in domestic handicrafts—clothmaking in the south, stocking-knitting in the north—offered a welcome solution to the problem of occupying a rising population.

2. The lowlands

(a) The vales

The vale lands of Yorkshire and Lincolnshire comprise one of three regions of mixed husbandry in these two counties. They include the vales of York and Cleveland, the vale of central Lindsey, Lincolnshire, situated between the limestone cliff and the wolds, the Trent valley in West Lindsey, and the vale of West Kesteven. For the most part this was a countryside of nucleated villages, common fields, and stinted, shrinking commons. Two or three common fields, still preserving a tidiness in their ground pattern and routine despite enclosure, dominated the landscape and husbandry. As population increased, the fields nibbled at the edges of the pastures until many villages were hard put to it to find sufficient grass for their stock. Grazing shortages were therefore overcome by the use of 'leys' in the common fields or by enclosure. The average husbandman's farm consisted of about 20–30 acres of arable, meadow, and enclosed pasture, and nearly always by this period the commons were carefully regulated. Local variations in

---

[1] Willan and Crossley, op. cit., pp. 39, 51, 56; Inf. on Wensleydale kindly given by Mrs Betty Grant; YAS DD, 121, 31; PRO E 178, 4831; E 134, 17 Jas. I, Hil. I; E 134, 17 Jas. I, Hil. 1; E 134, 2 Jas. I, Mich. 33; E 134, 9 Jas. I, Easter 2. For examples from the more industrialized portion of the W.R., see PRO E 134, 21 Jas. I, Easter 4; Sheffield Central Library, WWM, C 2, 257 (3); PRO E 178, 2747.

[2] PRO E 178, 4831.

the crop rotations and stints were, of course, numerous, and reflected differences in the quality of the land and pressure on the grazings.[1]

The principal crops in Lincolnshire were barley, wheat, and peas, in that order, while in Yorkshire the principal bread corn was rye. A mixed herd of cattle—cows and their followers, fat beasts, and oxen—gave the farmer a finger in several pies, allowing him to breed, rear, and fatten, and keep oxen for drawing the plough. The sheep flock of the ordinary small farmer was large enough to fold the arable: twenty to thirty sheep were normal on a farm of 20–30 acres. Half a dozen pigs supplemented the meat supplies of the house, and sometimes yielded a surplus for sale. It is difficult to judge from the farmers' stock and crops which branch of farming was most lucrative. Contemporaries thought that stock were more profitable than crops, and this verdict was probably correct. In the western half of the vale of York the speciality was cattle rearing and dairying, while farmers in the eastern half bred horses. If any one trend is discernible in the claylands of Lincolnshire, it is the inclination to stock the pastures more intensively than before and by enclosure or by the use of "leys" in the common fields to snatch some ploughland for additional grassland, while at the same time maintaining or even increasing the yield of the corn harvest.[2]

In their farming, therefore, the vales of Yorkshire and Lincolnshire resembled the claylands of the Midlands. And the resemblance went further. Most land in the vales was held within a strong manorial framework. The main centre of settlement was the village, and the lands of the township were frequently coterminous with the lands of the manor. Communal cultivation of the fields was regulated in the manorial court, and in one-manor villages the squire and his steward had undivided authority over the community. The clay vales of Lincolnshire and Yorkshire, like the vales of the east Midlands, perfectly illustrate the pattern of social and economic organization commonly regarded as typical of rural England.

(b) The chalk and limestone uplands

Another type of mixed farming, almost as familiar a part of the English scene as the corn-and-stock system of the vales, was the sheep-barley husbandry of the hills, found in these counties on the wolds of east Yorkshire and on the wolds and limestone heath of Lincolnshire. The sheep pastured on the slopes and summits of the hills and were folded by night on the cornfields. The flocks yielded lambs for sale to lowland graziers, some were fattened on the farm, while wool was dispatched to the clothiers of East Anglia or the West Riding. The chief cash

[1] Joan Thirsk, *English Peasant Farming*, pp. 96–7, 99–101.
[2] *Ibid.*, pp. 96–105; York Probate Registry, Probate Invs., *passim*.

crop was barley, and secondly wheat. Some cattle were reared, and this branch of upland farming expanded in scale in the course of the period, but sheep far outnumbered cattle and claimed the greater share of attention. Indeed, when Henry Best of Elmswell gave advice to his son on the management of his farm, he devoted the first thirty-odd pages of his book to the management and marketing of sheep, and said nothing about the care of the cattle. The worst land in these districts bred rabbits.[1]

The class structure of upland villages was noticeably different from that of the vale townships. They had smaller populations, and the contrast in wealth was sharp between the squire and his relations with their farms of several hundreds of acres, the few yeomen and husbandmen with between 30 and 100 acres, and the wage labourers with less than 10 acres. Nevertheless, the villages of the Lincolnshire wolds contained a smaller proportion of wage labourers than the vales and so were less plagued with the problem of poverty, and the same may well have been true of Yorkshire wold villages. Small populations of course made it easier for the large farmer to enclose and convert arable land into sheepwalk, and to overgraze and even appropriate to himself some of the common pastures. Hence the wold country on both sides of the Humber had more than its share of deserted villages, dating for the most part from the fifteenth century, though some were not depopulated until the sixteenth. Men such as John Thorpe of Appleton, who was said to have taken 460 ewes, 300 wethers, and 360 hogs to pasture at Wharram Percy in 1543, and Henry Best of Elmswell, an astute businessman who could account for every penny, every load of hay, and every quarter of barley, and knew exactly in which markets to get the most profit, clearly wanted the hills to themselves, and disliked accommodating themselves to communal rules of husbandry.

The situation of these upland countries encouraged the large farmer and gave him plenty of alternatives when studying the best markets. He was in easy contact with coastal ports and could dispatch his produce to Scotland, to London, or to the Low Countries if he desired. Hence, the class structure of society in these hill areas and the commercial opportunities readily at hand fostered the growth of a class of large farmers. The hills of Lincolnshire and Yorkshire, like the downlands of southern England, were a fertile field for the development of large-scale farming by the capitalist farmer.[2]

[1] Thirsk, *op. cit.*, pp. 85, 90–1, 88; Alan Harris 'The Agriculture of the East Riding of Yorkshire before the Parliamentary Enclosures', *Yorks. Arch. J.*, CLVII, 1959, pp. 126, 125; C. B. Robinson, ed., *Rural Economy in Yorkshire in 1641*, Surtees Soc., XXXIII, 1857, pp. 1–31.

[2] Thirsk, *op. cit.*, p. 83; M. Beresford, 'The Lost Villages of Yorkshire', *Yorks. Arch. J.*, XXXVIII, 1952, pp. 56–70.

(c) The marshland

The third type of mixed farming in these counties was that practised in the marshlands. These included the ill-drained lowlands south and east of York, the Ouse–Humber marshes, Holderness, and the coastal strip of Lindsey. Here the specialities were cattle and sheep fattening, *and* wheat growing. On a first visit, the traveller in these parts could not but be strongly reminded of the fens. A tithe dispute in 1554 between the rector of Sutton-on-Derwent and a local farmer conjures up the picture before us. Sutton Marsh was not under water, we are told, it was a grazing ground for 200–300 fat cattle, fat sheep, horses, and cows. Commoners who could not make full use of their common rights took in other men's beasts for a fee; the gist of a beast from St Elenmas to Martinmas (18 August–11 November) was 6s. 8d., "now that grass is much dearer than it was." But a grazier could be certain that sheep put in in the spring would be "good mutton" before St Elenmas. In the eighteenth century William Marshall formed a similar impression of Holderness, and labelled it without more ado as fen country. But these first impressions were, in fact, misleading. It is true that the marshland farmer set great store by his cattle and sheep; that the more substantial peasant bred horses; that the cottagers grew hemp; and that fishing and fowling were profitable subsidiary occupations. The similarities were, indeed, striking. But at the same time the differences were profound. Corn-growing for the market was of equal importance with stock fattening, and was carried on in common fields. And most important of all, the class composition of marshland villages was entirely alien to the true fen country.[1]

Both Holderness and the marshland coast of Lindsey consist of boulder clay, silt, and peat carrs. When properly drained, the clay made good cornland. Hence both regions constituted a grazing ground for fat stock *and* a granary. Beans were the main fodder crop, and wheat the main cash crop. The latter was marketed locally—the main corn markets in Yorkshire lay in the East Riding—or was dispatched to the coastal ports of both counties for transport to Durham, Northumberland, and London. In both districts the arable land was almost invariably divided into two common fields, and in some villages, at least, one of these was fallowed every year. This seemingly wasteful practice evidently had some common-sense explanation for it persisted into the age of parliamentary enclosure. Nucleated villages were in both regions

---

[1] J. S. Purvis, ed., *Select Sixteenth Century Causes in Tithe*, Yorks Arch. Soc., Rec. Ser., CXIV, 1947, pp. 60–4; William Marshall, *The Rural Economy of Yorkshire*, I, p. 8. On the drainage history of East Yorkshire see June Sheppard, *The Draining of the Marshlands of East Yorkshire*, London Univ. Ph.D. thesis, 1956.

the most common type of settlement, and, unlike the fenland, which bewailed "the want of gentlemen here to inhabit," afforded a congenial environment for the life of the country gentleman. Leconfield in the East Riding of Yorkshire, for example, boasted "the largest and stateliest house" of the earl of Northumberland in all Yorkshire. It was surrounded by good corn and pasture ground, meadow, and woodland, and possessed three deer parks, a fen stocked with swans, wildfowl, and fish.[1]

The marshland of both counties was a well-populated prosperous county of corn-and-cattle farmers, many of whom were exceedingly rich squires and yeomen. Even the average farm was nearer 40–60 acres than the small-holding of the fenlander. As one writer, describing the Lincolnshire marshes in 1629 expressed it—"it is hard to find a poor man though they sit at great rents, for their cattle are always sound and thriving, and therefore ever merchandable; or if they come to a mischance, yet fit for food."[2]

(d) The forests

Most of the lowland areas of Yorkshire and Lincolnshire illustrate the generalization made earlier that lowland England was a country of mixed husbandry. Two exceptional regions, however, were the lowland forests of Yorkshire and the fens of both counties. They afford the first examples of two types of landscape, which recur in other parts of England, and which exhibited at this period a distinct economy and a personality of their own.

The forests of lowland Yorkshire consisted of Galtres forest in the vale of York, and Pickering forest, which extended across the vale of Pickering to the marshland of the east coast. They were by no means confined to the poorer soils, but royal forest law had placed a brake upon the freedom of the inhabitants to improve their land, and in consequence much of it awaited and invited improvement at this period.[3]

Farmers living within the precincts of the royal forest were chiefly concerned with the production of stock and in the vale of Pickering with dairying. Pasture farming, indeed, had probably been forced upon them by the forest laws, which restricted the felling of trees and the increase of ploughland. The arable usually lay in common fields,

---

[1] Thirsk, *op. cit.*, pp. 57, 75–7, 60–1, 47; Alan Harris, *op. cit.*, pp. 125, 122; PRO E 164, 37, ff. 249–50; East Riding RO, DDCC, Section 143; George Poulson, *History and Antiquities of the Seigniory of Holderness*, 1840, I, p. 271.

[2] H.C., *A Discourse concerning the Draining of Fens and Surrounded Grounds*, 1629, f.B.

[3] PRO DL 42, 124.

but the common pastures were much more extensive than in vale lands outside the forests. The inhabitants therefore enjoyed generous grazing rights and had larger than usual timber allotments for fuel and house repair. Usually, too, they kept more pigs since these were allowed to forage in the woods at certain times of the year. The benefits derived from this privilege are less evident in the documents relating to the Yorkshire forests than, for example, in the New Forest, Hampshire, where pig fattening was a speciality. Nevertheless, pigs were fairly numerous in the eastern half of the vale of York, and the fame of York ham has yet to be traced to its origin.[1]

Forest districts were almost unique in the lowlands in having land to spare, and this fact was of great significance, when populations were increasing everywhere and the neighbouring vales were hard pressed to accommodate their growing numbers: lax administration on the part of the Crown, and its failure to make use of the grazing rights which it reserved for itself in the forests permitted the inhabitants to take by stealth what the law denied them. They drove their cattle into the deer reserves, and freely abused their already generous timber rights. In James I's reign the Crown resolved to disafforest Galtres and Knaresborough forests, belatedly recognizing that it could no longer preserve its ancient privileges against mounting local hostility which even the royal ‖surveyors justified, "the people (especially the poorer sort) increasing in such abundance as they do."[2]

Poverty and the rising number of forest inhabitants were continually emphasized by observers engaged in the detailed arrangements for disafforestation. Lists of tenants were not an accurate guide to the distribution of land for much of it was sub-let to undertenants, and this raised the problem of how compensation should be allotted. The Crown was urged to accept responsibility for compensating both tenants and undertenants, "inclining rather a little more in favour to the undertenants." But this did not settle every problem. The many landless inhabitants had to be considered, and this was no small matter. In Galtres forest, where disafforestation took place in Charles I's reign, the Crown awarded every landless cottager four acres of good land in a convenient place, increasing the allotment in certain villages like Huby and Easingwold to six and seven acres respectively, "in pity and commiseration of the estate of the poorer sort of inhabitants."[3]

[1] PRO E 134, 7 Chas. I, Easter 11; E 134, 5 Jas. I, Easter 12.

[2] PRO DL 42, 124; LR 2, 194, ff. 29, 34, 35. Some of the pastoral areas of west and north-west Yorkshire were royal forests, e.g. Knaresborough forest, Coverdale, Arkengarthdale, and Wharfedale, but the restrictions of forest law do not appear to have caused restiveness among the local population at this period, probably because the land was not worth enclosing either by the inhabitants or the Crown.

[3] PRO LR 2, 194, f. 35v; E 178, 5742.

The class structure of the forest villages has not yet been compared with neighbouring areas in Yorkshire, but there are hints here that the contrasts were similar to those found in other juxtaposed forest and vale lands. A disproportionate number of poor lived in the Yorkshire forests. And, by analogy with other forest districts, where the documentary information is more abundant and has been more thoroughly studied, it is likely that the problem was aggravated by the immigration of outsiders.[1]

(e) The fens

Another region of Yorkshire and Lincolnshire practising a pastoral system of husbandry and possessing a social structure reminiscent of the forests was the fen country. This region included Hatfield Chase in Yorkshire, the Isle of Axholme in north-west Lincolnshire, and a large tract of country surrounding the edge of the Wash, comprising the whole of the division of Holland, the eastern fringe of Kesteven, and the south-eastern fringe of Lindsey. This fen region also extended further east into Norfolk and Suffolk, and in their social organization and economy the fens of East Anglia seem to have differed not at all from the fenland region of Lincolnshire.

Nucleated village settlements were most usual in this country since the risk of flooding discouraged dispersal. Nevertheless, some small settlements grew up in outlying corners of these large fen parishes in the high Middle Ages, following upon drainage improvements which in south Lincolnshire were carried out as a communal enterprise by the fen villages. All the villages had large populations in the sixteenth century, including a great number of poor who, although they had little or no arable land, got their living from their common rights. The commons were spacious and unstinted; they yielded not only hay and grass for animals and geese, but peat for fuel, reeds for thatching, and wildfowl.[2]

As Lord Willoughby wrote in 1597 in protest against a bill for the drainage of the fens, "a poor man will easily get 16s. a week by cutting down of three or four loads of reed for thack and fuel to bake and brew withal, whereof that country hath great want, every load of the same being worth 4s. or 5s. at the least, and likewise 3s. or 4s. a week in fish and fowl serving the next markets...I speak not of hearsay but of mine own knowledge."[3]

Despite the growth of population in the sixteenth and early seventeenth centuries, and despite suggestions that the number of animals grazing the pastures should be regulated, the commons continued

[1] See pp. 95 sqq.   [2] Thirsk, op. cit., pp. 8–10, 27–8.
[3] HMC LXVI, p. 338.

unstinted throughout the period. Yet compared with the rest of Lincolnshire, some of the wapentakes in the fen, particularly those in Holland, had denser populations in the mid-sixteenth century than many on the clays, wolds, or heath. And in the wapentake of Elloe, which had the largest commons, the increase of numbers between 1563 and 1723 (the dates of two ecclesiastical censuses) surpassed all other regions of the county. Two possible causes of growth present themselves: the custom of inheritance and immigration. A recent study of the thirteenth-century records of Holland estates has shown that partible inheritance was practised in some villages in this division of Lincolnshire and that population increased at a greater rate in these communities than in villages where primogeniture was the rule. The later history of the custom has not yet been investigated in Holland, but it is worth noting that in the Norfolk fen, next door, the tenants of customary holdings at Terrington Howards still favoured the rule of gavelkind at the end of the sixteenth century. On the other hand the spacious commons were undoubtedly an attraction to outsiders. One writer, observing the large numbers of poor in the Isle of Axholme in 1675, gave as explanation the commoners' right to cut turves, which "draws multitudes of the poor sort from all the countries adjacent to come and inhabit in the Isle." Both explanations were probably right.[1]

In the sixteenth and early seventeenth centuries, then, the fens supported a large population of small peasants, few of whom were rich but all of whom shared in the varied natural resources of the fenland and enjoyed a reasonable living. The country did not attract gentlemen; it did not provide the environment for splendid living. Instead, the social pyramid sloped gently down to the poorest landless commoner.[2]

Because most fenland townships contained several manors, all communal regulation governing the use of the fens was a matter for village agreement, and could not be wholly decided within the manorial court. Manorial control of farming operations, therefore, was weak, and the sense of community and feelings of communal loyalty were focused upon the village. These had impelled the population to carry through several large-scale drainage schemes in the Middle Ages and it emboldened the inhabitants to wage a fierce struggle against the Crown in the early seventeenth century when the drainage of the fens was planned, and the commoners were threatened with the loss of two thirds of their commons. Everyone was drawn into contributing to a

[1] Thirsk, *op. cit.*, pp. 8–10, 140–1; H. E. Hallam, 'Some Thirteenth-century Censuses', EcHR, 2nd Ser., x, 1958, pp. 340 *sqq.*; Norwich Public Library, NRS 26971, 26972.
[2] Thirsk, *op. cit.*, p. 47.

common purse to pay for the lawsuits that ensued, and some plain language was used to express the fenlander's contempt of government. Who but "a Parliament of Clouts" would have dared to undermine the foundation of their livelihood?[1]

Most of the drainage projects of this period failed in the end, and none produced any fundamental alteration in the economy of the region. This was and remained for another century, at least, a district of pastoral husbandry where the inhabitants' greatest asset was the rich and abundant summer grazing. Cows yielded milk for dairying; cattle were fattened for the butcher; horses were bred on the fens; sheep were fattened on the coastal saltmarshes; geese were kept on the commons; wildfowl haunted the fens; fish were caught in the dykes and rivers. The arable land was meagre; many peasants had none, and even the average holding had no more than 10 acres under the plough on which the chief crops were barley, wheat, and pulses. Hemp and flax were important additional crops grown in a croft beside the house. They employed many women on the curing processes as well as affording an occupation for spinners and weavers.[2] Coleseed began to be planted on the better drained fens and provided cattle cake as well as oil.

Of communal fields and communal cultivation of the fields there is no sign in the fens around the Wash, and no certainty in the evidence from Axholme. The arable in some townships was grouped in large blocks immediately round the village, and holdings were divided into scattered strips, bearing every appearance of a common-field system. But no common grazing was practised on the arable, and this pattern of land distribution could as well have resulted from the division of land through inheritance.[3]

D. EAST ANGLIA: NORFOLK AND SUFFOLK

East Anglia nowadays occupies a somewhat isolated geographical position off the main traffic ways between London and the north. In the sixteenth century, by contrast, its rivers reaching into the heart of East Anglia, its long coastline, and its many ports, placed it in easy communication with the markets of London, north-eastern England,

---

[1] H. E. Hallam, *The New Lands of Elloe*, University of Leicester, Occasional Paper, no. 6, 1954, pp. 23–4; Joan Thirsk, 'The Isle of Axholme before Vermuyden', AHR, I, 1953, p. 28.

[2] Thirsk, *English Peasant Farming*, pp. 29–36, 39–42; Thirsk, 'Axholme', *op. cit.*, pp. 21–2. Cf. the similar situation in the Suffolk fens, inhabited by "a great number of miserable, poor people, which neither plough nor sow for corn." SP 14, 142, 14.

[3] Thirsk, *English Peasant Farming*, p. 14; Thirsk, 'The Common Fields', *Past & Present*, 29, 1964, pp. 3–25.

Scotland, the Netherlands, and the Baltic. Its farming, in consequence, developed early in the service of national and international markets, and specialization was so far advanced that by the early seventeenth century, even in years of good harvest, many districts were far from self-sufficient in corn: the wood-pasture region depended on corn supplies from the sheep-corn region; the coastal hundreds with their large populations of fishermen and boat builders were hungry for all agricultural produce.[1]

The two counties of Norfolk and Suffolk were divided into three farming regions. A mixed sheep-corn husbandry prevailed on the loams and sands which extend in a broad arc from south-west Suffolk round the northern rim of Norfolk and along the eastern coast of Suffolk. The heavier clays, which occupy central Suffolk and an irregularly shaped segment of south-east Norfolk were for the most part given over to grassland. Bearing in mind their formerly forested condition, it is appropriate to call them a 'woodpasture' region. The third region was composed of fenland in west Norfolk and north-west Suffolk, and formed part of a much larger fen area surrounding the shores of the Wash, whose economy has already been described.[2]

The contrast in landscape between the light and heavy lands of East Anglia is vividly portrayed in the words of two contemporary descriptions. Norfolk, we are told, was "compownded and sorted of soyles apt for grayne and sheep, and of soyles apt for woode and pasture." Suffolk consisted "of two several conditions of soil, the one champion which yields for the most part sheep and some corn, the other enclosed for pasture grounds, employed most to grazing and dairy, so as the champion doth not only serve itself with corn but is forced continually to supply the woodland especially in wet cold years."[3]

[1] Basil Cozens-Hardy, 'The Maritime Trade of the Port of Blakeney, Norfolk, 1587–90', *Norfolk Rec. Soc.*, VIII, 1936, p. 19; V. B. Redstone, 'Woodbridge, its History and Antiquity', *Suffolk Inst. Archaeology*, IX, 1897, pp. 348–9; CSPD 1633–4, p. 385. See also Robert Reyce, *Suffolk in the Seventeenth Century*, 1902, p. 13; SP 14, 142, 14, III and VIII.

[2] See pp. 38–40 *supra*. Robert Reyce, writing in the early seventeenth century, qualified this generalization concerning central Suffolk by saying that in the middle parts of this region lay a district with much meadow and pasture but "far more tillage." This statement awaits more detailed examination. If true, such arable parishes would invite comparison with the districts of Hertfordshire, where in the sixteenth century one-time 'woodpasture' was also being transformed into rich cornland. For much help with this and other problems relating to Suffolk, I wish to thank Mr Norman Scarfe.

[3] Norwich Public Library, MS 2641, cited in K. J. Allison 'The Sheep-Corn Husbandy of Norfolk in the Sixteenth and Seventeenth Centuries', AHR, V, 1957, p. 12; SP 14, 128, 65.

1. *The sands and heaths*

The light loams of East Anglia were an open, scantily hedged country of common fields and meadows, and common breckland or heath. The detailed management of the land was different from that practised in the common fields of the Midlands, but the basic principles of the system were the same. The arable fields were divided into strips; ownership of the strips was dispersed; certain common rights—defined in terms of foldcourses for sheep, though not for cattle—existed over the fields, meadows, and commons. Since the light lands were over-hungry for manure and could not be kept fertile by the ordinary Midland rotations, a sufficient arable area was maintained by using the best of the commons as a series of outfields or brecks, manuring each in rotation (usually every seven years), cropping each for two to three years in succession, and then letting each piece fall down to grass till its turn for manuring came round again. Marl was applied in quantity, and the fields of East Anglia are still scored with the pits of an earlier age, but the main fertilizer was the dung of the sheep. The system of sheep folding was different from that used in other sheep country, like the Cotswolds, inasmuch as the right to graze the sheep and the benefit of their manure belonged to the manorial lord or his lessees. This placed irksome restraints on tenants, for the cultivation of their arable had to be ordered in such a way as to leave the land free at the seasons when it was grazed by the lord's flock. By the sixteenth century the foldcourse owners were paying annual compensation or granting alternative land to those tenants who were unable to farm their land because of the lord's rights of foldcourse, while many tenants were paying for the benefit of the tathe or manure which their land received, and for the right to graze some of their sheep in the lord's flock. But these were concessions to equity which modified and complicated the original system.[1]

The lord's near monopoly of the right to graze sheep on the common fields forced his tenants to adopt a different system of husbandry from that of their lord, to keep cattle, which they were allowed to graze with their lord's sheep, and to leave the sheep-keeping to the owners of the foldcourses. Hence, although the region may be dubbed the sheep-corn region, this description has greatest significance and accuracy when applied to the activities of the foldcourse owners—the larger

[1] H. L. Gray, *English Field Systems*, 2nd ed., 1959, pp. 305–54; H. C. Darby and J. Saltmarsh, 'The Infield-Outfield System on a Norfolk Manor', *Economic History*, III, 1935; K. J. Allison, *op. cit., passim.*; PRO E 134, 4 Jas. I, E 26; D. & C. of Norwich, 1649 Parliamentary Survey of Westhall and Easthall, Sedgeforth; H. Prince, 'Pits and Ponds in Norfolk', *Erdkunde*, XVI, 1962, pp. 10 *sqq.*

farmers with anything from one hundred to one thousand sheep. It was they who knew in detail the finances of sheep-keeping—men such as William Stanhawe, gentleman, who in 1637 had rights over eight foldcourses and collected each year a woolclip of 356 stones; and Paul Dewes of Stowlangtoft, who owned a sheepwalk for 600 ewes and 600 wethers, who reckoned on fattening the wethers in three or four years, selling 150 a year fully grown at a profit of £50–60, taking more profit from the woolclip, and most of all from the sale of lambs. For these farmers the sheep were possibly more lucrative than the corn. The smaller farmers, on the other hand, were driven by their restricted common rights to keep cattle, and between two thirds and three quarters of the peasantry had no sheep at all, but concentrated on the dairy—encouraged, no doubt, by the existence of a market built up by the farmers of the wood-pasture region. Other income from stock was derived from the sale of fat pigs, cows fattened off when they were too old for the dairy, and male calves. Along the coast and on the Norfolk Broads the dairying was combined with or replaced by cattle fattening, for here were marshes and fens, undergoing reclamation as opportunity offered. Some graziers even bought in northern steers in order to make full use of the summer grazing and abundant hay crop. The coastal lands mingled the characteristics of the light lands of East Anglia with those of the marshland coast of eastern England. Some land was given over to sheep and corn and subject to a foldcourse, some was marshland grazing where fat cattle were the main prize while fish and fowl yielded additional profits.[1]

Other subsidiary enterprises in the sheep-corn region included hop-growing—Norfolk and Suffolk were among the first English counties to grow hops, hemp-growing—a speciality of Suffolk, poultry-keeping—a speciality of Norfolk, and rabbits, whose skins constituted the fourth largest export from the port of Blakeney Haven in north Norfolk in the late sixteenth century.[2]

Nevertheless, the sheep-corn region was first and foremost an arable area and corn was the main interest of both large and small farmers. It is not difficult, therefore, to see why East Anglia was a forerunner in the use of new agricultural implements and machinery in the eighteenth century. Its farmers in the sixteenth century had by far the most numerous and the widest range of vehicles and arable tools of any

---

[1] Ipswich and East Suffolk RO, Probate inventories, *passim*; Norwich Public Library, MS 1481, Box 1, Fl; BM Harl. MS 98, f. 120; PRO E 178, 2195; E 134, 27 & 28 Eliz., M 15; E 134, 23 Eliz., E 11; Ipswich and E.S. RO, Sl, 10, 9, 4; Robert Reyce, *op. cit.*, p. 38.

[2] H. E. Wilton, 'The Suffolk Hemp Industry', *Suffolk Rev.*, II, 4, 1961; Basil Cozens-Hardy, *op. cit.*, p. 19.

district in England. One example will suffice to illustrate the wealth of a rich farmer's equipment: William Cobb, a gentleman farmer of Gayton, possessed in 1611 four wheelploughs, one pair of iron and five pairs of wooden harrows, three shod carts, ten swathe rakes, six hay rakes, five pitchforks, four three-tined forks, three sickles, three weeding hooks, six scythes, a hook, a hatchet, an axe, two muckforks, a spade, a shovel, and a mattock. These implements served for 321 acres of arable land, of which 215 acres were sown with barley. This was the scale on which the gentry farmed. The ordinary peasant's sown land averaged 20 acres of which something between a quarter and a half was sown with barley. Throughout the region the three main crops in order of importance were barley, rye, and wheat, while oats, peas, bullimong (a mixture of the two), vetches, and buckwheat were grown for fodder. Buckwheat, or brank, was eminently suited to the poorest lands which would not grow oats, and nowhere in England was it grown as freely as in Norfolk. In years of harvest failure the poor were driven to mix buckwheat with barley for their bread, but this was only a desperate expedient. For the most part it was a fodder crop. It could be fed to horses, was excellent for fattening pigs and poultry, and may well have been the crop which dictated the growth of the poultry-keeping business in Norfolk. For already in the Tudor period poultry were kept on a large scale. Anne Arminger, a widow of North Creake, who managed a large farm at the beginning of the seventeenth century, had 50 hens, 2 cocks, 10 geese and ganders, 30 capons, 44 ducks and drakes, and for special feasts 2 turkey cocks and 3 turkey hens. Turkeys were already popular by the 1570's, having been first introduced to England a generation earlier. Here were the forerunners of the turkeys which were to be seen in large flocks walking the road to London in the time of Daniel Defoe.[1]

The light lands of East Anglia, in short, were a corn-growing region, where sheep were the main fertilizing agents as well as being bred and fattened on a large scale by the foldcourse owners. The small farmer often had no sheep, although he had some benefit of cattle, and relied for his manure on his cattle (a herd usually of about half a dozen beasts), and his pigs. Dairying and pig-keeping, however, were not of such importance as beef production. Barley was the main cash crop, and this specialization continued well into the eighteenth century, for in

[1] Norfolk and Norwich RO, Inv. 24, 90; 27, 67; PRO SP 14, 138, 35; SP 16, 187, 12; Daniel Defoe, *A Tour through England and Wales*, Everyman ed., I, p. 59. For a detailed example of cropping, see Coxford farm, 5 miles S.W. Fakenham, in 1620-1, with 162 acres of arable land of which 37 per cent was in barley, 22 per cent wheat and rye, 24 per cent oats, and 16 per cent peas and vetches.—Norfolk and Norwich RO, MS 1505, Box 1, D 2.

Arthur Young's words in 1804 "Norfolk is the greatest barley county in the kingdom."[1]

The class structure of the sheep-corn region was typical of a manorialized society living in nucleated villages, and practising co-operative husbandry. The manorial lords were marked out by wealth and privilege as the leaders of society. Their farms were large and their foldcourse rights dominated the farming routine of the village. At the same time, East Anglia had been conspicuous since Domesday times for its large population of freeholders, who at that time constituted over 40 per cent of the population. They continued to form a larger than average proportion of manorial tenants in the sixteenth and early seventeenth centuries. At Hindringham, in Norfolk, for example, there were three free tenants to every four copyholders in 1649. On two manors in Sedgeforth the number in each group was roughly equal. On some of the manors of the Dean and Chapter of Norwich, situated near Norwich, the freeholders even outnumbered the copyholders.[2]

Leaseholders represented a growing class of people swelling the ranks of the large farmers. Frequently such a man held other land in the parish by free or copyhold tenure, but rented a large portion of demesne on lease, and sometimes the foldcourse rights as well. These leases were often annual, for the land belonging to the foldcourse changed from year to year, and could not be let conveniently for any longer term. Such leases were not, therefore, invariably renewed, and this may well be the origin of the year-to-year leases which were extremely common in the eighteenth century and prompted comment from William Marshall.[3]

Arable regions did not usually give warm hospitality to domestic crafts—there was enough work for everyone in performing all the tillage operations in the fields. But Norfolk may prove to be one of the more notable exceptions inasmuch as it supported a flourishing worsted cloth industry in the fourteenth and fifteenth centuries, which turned over to the making of New Draperies in the sixteenth and seventeenth. The fact that it was basically a town industry, centred on Norwich, which spread into the neighbouring countryside may explain its

[1] Arthur Young, *General View of the Agriculture of Norfolk*, 1804, p. 238.

[2] D. & C. of Norwich, Parliamentary Surveys, 1649; J. Spratt, *Agrarian Conditions in Norfolk and Suffolk, 1600–1650*, London M.A. thesis, 1935, p. 108. See also R. H. Tawney, *The Agrarian Problem of the Sixteenth Century*, Table 1, p. 25, analysing a sample of manors taken from some eleven counties. The highest proportion of freeholders was found in Norfolk and Suffolk.

[3] Norfolk and Norwich RO, NRS 14487, 29, C1; Townshend MS 164; NRS 15152, 30, B6; MS 1509, Box 1, D 2; William Marshall, *The Rural Economy of Norfolk*, 1787, p. 68.

anomalous situation. In this respect it resembled the cloth industry of the sheep-corn region of Wiltshire, linked with the town of Salisbury. Certainly the relationship between the cloth industry and the farming business are matters that call for further research.[1]

It is not difficult, however, to explain the rise of the stocking-knitting industry in the coastal districts of Norfolk in the early Stuart period: it was a fishermen's by-employment. Large populations congregated around the fishing ports, the quaysides were crowded with salthouses and tackle sheds, and the sands were covered with nets drying in the sun. There was plentiful labour for the menfolk in fishing for red and white herring, mackerel, sprats, and spirling off the coast, or in voyaging to Iceland for "the best ling and codfish." But there were slack seasons, and the women, who were probably already skilful knitters of seamen's stockings, afforded a handsome reserve of labour for merchants building up an export industry. The variety of stockings on the market at this period were enough to tempt the money from anyone's purse: coarse white woollen stockings, men's stockings with scalloped tops, men's stockings with large welts and of mingled colours, and children's coloured stockings. For all these there was a ready market in London and Holland by the end of the sixteenth century.[2]

2. *The wood-pasture region*

In contrast with the light sheep-corn lands of East Anglia, the wood-pasture region supported a community with an entirely different class structure in countryside of a quite different appearance. Small hamlets and dispersed farms were generously sprinkled between the villages. Farms were enclosed, and the only observable vestige of co-operative farming in most places lay in the management of commons. The closes were often large, but were divided for practical convenience between several crops. They were shut in by large hedges, and their chequer-board pattern broken at intervals by extensive woodlands. Hedges gave excellent cover to pheasants and partridges, and after the Restoration game-shooting was offered as an attraction to prospective purchasers of estates in the district. The woods were a mixture of oak, ash, and hazel, which was readily sold since timber could be easily

[1] Joan Thirsk, 'Industries in the Countryside', in F. J. Fisher, ed., *Essays in the Economic and Social History of Tudor and Stuart England*, pp. 70 *sqq.*; K. J. Allison, 'The Norfolk Worsted Industry in the Sixteenth and Seventeenth Centuries', *Yorks. Bull. Econ. and Social Res.*, XII, 1960, pp. 73–83.

[2] Ipswich & E.S. RO and Norfolk and Norwich RO, Probate Invs., *passim*; Walter Rye, *Cromer Past and Present*, p. lxi, appendix X; PRO E 134, 2 Chas. I, M 38; E 178, 4354; CSPD 1635, p. 10.

transported by river and coastal vessels. Ash, in particular, was much sought after by the coopers who made herring barrels for the fisheries off the Norfolk and Suffolk coast.[1]

Farms in this region consisted mostly of pasture and meadow, with a very small proportion of arable land. At Ilketshall, on the border between Norfolk and Suffolk, for example, a farm of 88½ acres had 66½ acres of pasture, 7 acres of meadow, and 15 acres of arable. Another of 34 acres had 27½ acres of pasture, 2¼ acres of meadow, and 4¼ acres of ploughland. The region regularly relied on corn supplies from the light lands.[2]

Most farmers were engaged in rearing and dairying, and only the richest farmers combined this with cattle fattening. The dairy house was always numbered among the farm buildings, and it was not unusual to find men with 30 cows and followers, and 30 or 40 milk bowls in the dairy. One of the largest yeomen farmers in eastern England in the early seventeenth century had 87 cattle, 141 cheeses in store, and 93 milk bowls. Pig-keeping was carried on in conjunction with dairying, and provided bacon for London as well as victualling the navy and merchant ships. Two important sidelines were the breeding of horses— the Suffolk Punches, in fact—and poultry-keeping, though this was more popular in Norfolk than in Suffolk. Sheep were of small account. Although sheep grazing was not confined to foldcourse owners, the foldcourse being unknown here, between a half and three quarters of the peasants had none.[3]

Although some large farmers had impressive acreages of arable land (devoted to crops which fed their cattle), the ploughland was meagre compared with the large acreages of the sheep-corn region. The same crops were grown; wheat sometimes received first preference, but in the region as a whole, barley remained the largest crop and these two together with rye occupied between a half and two thirds of the sown land. The smaller crops were oats, peas, and vetches, hops and occasionally hemp. Carrots and turnips were being grown in the 1630's by the more enterprising farmers in the Waveney valley for feeding cows and bullocks, and by this means buttermaking was made possible in the winter months. But grass and hay were the chief support of the cheese producer.[4]

[1] Ipswich and E.S. RO, S1, 2, 7, 15; BM Add. MS 14850.

[2] BM Add. MS 14850.

[3] See probate inventory of Edward Lowe of Shimpling, Sept. 1614—Norfolk and Norwich RO, Inv. 27, 133; Reyce, *op. cit.*, p. 37. See also Frances Davenport, *The Economic Development of a Norfolk Manor, 1086–1565*, p. 36, for medieval evidence of dairying and poultry-keeping in this region.

[4] E. Kerridge, 'Turnip Husbandry in High Suffolk', EcHR, 2nd Ser., VIII, pp. 390–2.

Like other pastoral, dairying regions of the kingdom, this was a thickly populated countryside of family farmers. The manor was a weak institution of little significance in ordering the lives of the inhabitants. The typical manor comprised demesne and only one or two other farms. One manor in Mettingham, for example (the parish had three or four manors in all) consisted of 365½ acres of demesne and only one other farm of 51¾ acres. Sometimes the demesne was not much larger than the farms, and if this was once leased out in parcels, the manor house became a farmhouse or fell into decay. All outward signs of the existence of a manor disappeared, and its only remaining functions were financial and legal: its lord continued to receive rent and other dues, and its court was sometimes necessary to regulate the use of the commons, and to supervise the upkeep of buildings, hedges, and ditches. To the outside observer, coming from the more integrated communities of the common-field regions, this was a community of individualists, who depended hardly at all on their neighbours in their day-to-day farming activities. No manorial lord exercised effective control over the distribution and partition of land, therefore, and partible inheritance was the custom in some places, Borough English in others.[1]

This was also a farming region which had an industry to fall back on. Cloth-making had developed rapidly in the fifteenth century and gave part-time employment to many country folk, particularly those living in the southern half of Suffolk's wood-pasture region, in and around Sudbury, where coloured cloth was made. Large villages and towns had grown up here by the Tudor period, which proclaimed their prosperity in magnificent churches. To the north-east, in the villages around Eye, Debenham, Wickham Market, and Woodbridge, kerseys were manufactured but this industry never assumed the proportions of the coloured cloth industry. In Norfolk the dressing and combing of wool and the weaving of flax were the main industrial occupations. In these areas of the wood-pasture region, therefore, most communities were involved in industry and agriculture. Cloth-making combined well with dairying, for farm work was slack in the winter months, and even in the summer it did not fully engage the whole family.[2]

A remarkable similarity exists between the economy of this region, and that of the dairying-weaving, family farms of Wiltshire and Somerset, and the cattle-feeding, dairying, cloth-making farms of the Weald of Kent. It prompts speculation on the strong influence of

[1] BM Harl. MS 595; Add. MS, 14850; Thirsk, op. cit., p. 77; map of manors where Borough English was the custom, kindly lent by Mr Norman Scarfe.
[2] Thirsk, op. cit., pp. 75–7; R. J. Hammond, The Social and Economic Circumstances of Ket's Rebellion, London M.A. thesis, 1933, p. 12.

landscape and geography upon the affairs of men, for not only did these naturally shape and restrict the system of farming, they seem sometimes to have governed the structure of society as well. East Anglia's wood-pasture region is one of several districts where dairying was associated with small family farmers. Few of them were rich, but the average peasant was better off than his counterpart in the sheep-corn region. Wealth was more evenly distributed, social classes were less sharply differentiated, and the majority of men were not abjectly poor nor the few abnormally rich.

E. FOUR HOME COUNTIES: BUCKINGHAMSHIRE, BEDFORDSHIRE, HERTFORDSHIRE, AND ESSEX

Historians are wont to attach great importance to the influence of London in promoting the growth of a commercialized agriculture in the sixteenth century. Greater knowledge of farming and marketing in different corners of England, however, suggests that all towns exerted a powerful influence within their regions, and that London was only one, though the most influential, among many. Nevertheless, in describing the economy of the Home Counties immediately north of London, there is no reason to minimize the rôle of London. All the main roads and rivers converged upon the capital. Many of the villages had in their midst a good proportion of London citizens as residents and landowners who were constantly travelling to and fro. Local farmers either dealt direct with merchants and drovers frequenting the central London markets, or disposed of their produce in local towns, knowing that these were only transit camps and that the bulk of the food sold there was likewise ultimately destined for London. Romford, Brentwood, Enfield, Cheshunt, Watford, all were half-way houses, halting places and little more, for the great procession of animals, merchants, and packhorse men wending their way to the metropolis.

None of these counties, apart from Essex, has yet received much attention from the agricultural historian. All possess a number of different farming regions. Mixed husbandry was the system in the wide vale of Aylesbury, carried on in conjunction with common fields of the Midland kind. Buckinghamshire had its small, dispersed woodland settlements in the Chilterns, where the system of farming was probably the same as that found in the Oxfordshire Chilterns. Hertfordshire had its common fields and sheep-corn farms on the downs like those of other upland chalk country. Hertfordshire, Middlesex, and Essex had their share of marshes along the banks of rivers, producing fine meadows for cattle fattening. Essex had corn-growing common fields on the western edge of the county in the neighbourhood of the Rodings,

4

a pastoral region of enclosures for stock rearing in the middle of the county, and rich marshlands for fattening cattle and sheep and for dairying along Thames-side. The large amount of enclosed land in these four counties emancipated the farmer from irksome restrictions which might otherwise have checked the development of a commercial agriculture. Thus the magnetic power of London was exerted in full strength, and showed itself in a high degree of specialization. Two of the counties in which this can be demonstrated in detail are Hertfordshire and Essex.[1]

1. *Hertfordshire*

Hertfordshire was blessed with excellent channels of communication with London; the rivers Colne and Lea (greatly improved after 1571) carried corn, the Great North Road and Watling Street carried animals and people. It was almost certainly due to the demands of mealmen, maltmen, and travellers that the southern fringe of Hertfordshire, the parishes stretching from Watford in the west to Cheshunt in the east, paid so much attention to the breeding and feeding of horses, and grew such large crops of oats. Nearly every farmer of any standing in the mid-sixteenth century had mares and colts on his land, and among a variety of arable crops which included wheat, rye, barley, peas, and oats, the last-named crop seems to have occupied the largest acreage. A corn account for Cassiobury manor, in the parish of Watford, confirms the evidence drawn from inventories of corn in the barns of humbler folk. It enumerates the tithe produce from Watford parsonage in the year 1609–10 as follows: 116 qrs 5 bu. of wheat, 38 qrs 1 bu. of rye, 31 qrs 4 bu. of barley, 145 qrs 7 bu. of oats, 39 qrs 1 bu. of peas, and 7 qrs 4 bu. of beans. The demesnes of the manor yielded 55 qrs 3 bu. of wheat, 89 qrs 5 bu. of oats and not more than 10 qrs of rye and peas. The barley harvest on the demesne was not recorded. Some of the oats from these two sources were sold and the rest went to feed horses in the great stable of the house; cart horses, falconers' horses, "Nottingham-shire men's horses," and the horses of some notable people (presumably visitors at the house) such as Baptist Hicks, Sir Edward Noel, Lord Haddington, and Lady Sussex. The rest went to feed poulty, and sows with young pigs, while some was reserved for seed, and some for malting. The main cash crop was wheat which was sold to corn merchants in Watford, Harrow, Bushey, Pinner, and Ruislip. Apart from breeding horses, this district of Hertfordshire also reared and

[1] M. W. Beresford, 'Glebe Terriers and Open-Field Buckinghamshire', *Records of Bucks.*, XVI, 1, 1953–4, p. 6; W. E. Ellis, *The Practical Farmer*, 1732, p. 44; H. L. Gray, *English Field Systems*, pp. 63, 369–402; CSPD 1629–31, pp. 417–18; Herts. RO, MSS. 47311–7.

fattened pigs, chickens, and geese in great number. Barley was used for "cramming capons" and weaning pigs, while peas and beans were fed to hogs and horses. In short, this was a region of mixed farming, where nearly all the arable crops except wheat were used for the production of stock.[1]

On the loams and clays that stretch across central Hertfordshire, pigs were again a speciality and some farmers had a smoking house on the premises for curing bacon. But equal attention was given to the fattening of bullocks for the butcher, and to growing wheat as a cash crop. Few of the bullocks were bred on the farm; most were bought in as stores, and many of them stall-fed. Largish flocks of 50–100 sheep were common, and were needed first of all for their manure, and only secondly for their wool. Grass and hay were small in amount, compared with the large harvest from the arable. Oats, peas, and vetches and some of the barley were fed to stock, while the wheat was sold to the London baker. Two typical crop schedules illustrate the large arable acreage on Hertfordshire farms and the importance of wheat: on a farm with $78\frac{3}{4}$ acres under crops, 33 acres were sown with wheat, 12 acres with barley, and $33\frac{3}{4}$ acres with peas, oats, and vetches. On another with 76 acres, 27 acres were sown with wheat and rye, about 32 acres with oats, peas, and vetches, and 17 acres lay fallow. This then was another region of mixed farming, its system somewhat different in detail from that of southern Hertfordshire, but one in which most of the arable crops, except wheat, were used for stock feeding.[2]

On the chalk hills of north Hertfordshire, another system of mixed husbandry prevailed, namely, the familiar sheep-corn husbandry of wolds and downland. Sheep were folded on the arable, and barley was the main white corn crop, though some farmers also grew a large acreage of wheat. A number of the malting towns of the county were situated in this district—Bishop's Stortford, Hitchin, Baldock, Ashwell, and Royston—and it is probable that some of their barley came from Cambridgeshire as well.[3]

In Domesday times Hertfordshire was a densely wooded county, and some districts in the east were not cleared and settled until the late thirteenth to fifteenth centuries. Some reminder of its former state may be found in the many disputes concerning timber rights which were heard at Westminster in the sixteenth and early seventeenth centuries. Its soils were generally considered to be rather poor and barren, and it would not have been surprising, therefore, to find most of the county still given over to pasture and woodland pursuits, as were many other

[1] Herts. RO, Probate Invs., *passim;* MSS 6604, 6718.
[2] Herts. RO, Probate Invs., *passim.*
[3] SP 16, 182, 40; CSPD 1636–7, pp. 323–4; W. Ellis, *op. cit.*, pp. 27–8.

woodland districts in southern and Midland England. That Hertford-shire had transformed so much of its land into corn-growing country must be attributed to particularly energetic efforts at colonization in the Anglo-Saxon period and the Middle Ages, and also to the advantage derived by the inhabitants from using great quantities of London dung to enhance the fertility of their land. The boats which carried corn and malt down the rivers Colne and Lea to London brought back manure on the return journey, and the value placed upon it is reflected in the remarks of early nineteenth-century writers who believed that Hert-fordshire could not maintain its fertility without London dung.[1]

By the Tudor period, of course, many enclaves of pasture-farming country still survived in arable parishes: in Aldenham, for example, where lived Edward Briscoe, a dairy-farmer who promised in 1592–3 to supply to the Queen's household thirty pounds of sweet butter weekly both in winter and summer; and in the Hundred of Hertford, whose justices of the peace complained in 1622–3 that few people had corn to sell, "which we suppose to be by reason of our enclosure, and waste of commonage for cattle, not employed in tillage." Nevertheless, the greater part of the county had by this time adopted some form of mixed husbandry, and put much of its land under the plough. Yet unlike the long established arable regions, its common fields were not strictly regulated and its enclosures were many. Since all woodland areas under-going clearance passed through a period in which their farming was pas-toral, it is not unreasonable to guess that the enclosure of Hertfordshire had taken place in the pasture-farming period, when, as we have noticed elsewhere, it could be achieved without controversy or commotion.[2]

In specializing in mixed farming and growing so much corn, Hertfordshire provided enough employment to make domestic handi-craft industries unnecessary. It may be for this reason, therefore, that the embryonic cloth industry of the county in the fifteenth century failed to mature in the sixteenth. When the Crown suggested establish-ing a new industry for the making of the New Draperies in James I's reign, it met with a cold response. "The county of Hertford doth consist for the most part of tillage . . . it has better means to set the poor children on work without this new invention than some other counties, viz. by employing the female children in picking of their wheat a great part of the year, and the male children by straining before their ploughs in seedtime and other necessary occasions of husbandry."[3]

[1] CSPD 1595–7, p. 107; W. Ellis, op. cit., pp. 5–8; CSPD 1581–90, p. 230; CSPD 1591–4, p. 499; Arthur Young, General View of the Agriculture of Hertfordshire, 1804, p. 26.

[2] Notes and Extracts from the Sessions Rolls, 1581 to 1698, ed. W. J. Hardy, I, p. 16, SP 14, 140, 41 (I).

[3] PRO SP 14, 144, 24; Joan Thirsk, 'Industries in the Countryside', op. cit., pp. 87–8.

2. Essex

In Essex the various systems of farming were similarly designed to cater for the needs of the London markets. The county had once been as densely wooded as Hertfordshire—the whole of Essex had once been part of the royal forest—and large stretches of woodland still remained on the western fringe in Epping and Hainault forests. Its countryside displayed in even more striking fashion than Hertfordshire the pattern of hamlets, dispersed farms, and enclosures, characteristic of districts colonized from woodland. But although sixteenth- and seventeenth-century writers regarded the whole county as enclosed, it still possessed common fields in the districts of mixed husbandry, though these too were fast disappearing. Again, therefore, we find in Essex the association of common fields with mixed husbandry on the one hand, and enclosures with pasture farming on the other.[1]

The county possessed at least three different regions: the marshland, the wood-pasture, and a champion region of mixed husbandry. The marsh parishes lay along the Thames estuary and extended round the coast to include Dengie Hundred. They resembled the marshlands of Yorkshire and Lincolnshire in their dual interest in corn and stock. Significantly, too, their system of mixed husbandry was associated with common fields, which still lingered along the Thames terraces between London and Thurrock. Dairying was a considerable business on the marshes between Barking and Aveley, and caused the latter to develop a market for butter and cheese, and to attract the regular attention of merchants from Kent. But the farmers who had large dairy herds also fattened beef cattle, including Welsh beasts, on the marshes, and bred horses. On Canvey Island, however, and along the coast between Canvey and Foulness, sheep were more conspicuous, and comprised mainly ewe flocks, whose milk was used to make Essex cheeses. On the stock side, indeed, the Essex farmer's interests were more varied than in the marshlands of Yorkshire and Lincolnshire.[2]

In addition to their grazing pastures, all the Essex marshland parishes had extensive cornlands. In 1619 the farms and demesnes of Aveley, for example, which totalled 2,249½ acres, were made up of 308¼ acres of woodland, 23 acres of reeds, 327½ acres of meadow, 889¾ acres of

[1] Rev. J. L. Fisher, 'The Forest of Essex', *Essex Rev.*, XLVI, 1937, pp. 115 *sqq.*; H. C. Darby, *The Domesday Geography of Eastern England*, p. 238; F. Hull, *Agriculture and Rural Society in Essex, 1560–1640;* London Univ. Ph.D. thesis, 1950, p. 13.

[2] Cf. F. Hull, *op. cit.*, p. 98; Essex RO, D, DTh. Survey of Aveley manor, *c.* 1602; Probate Inv. of William Pownsett of Loxford, 8 March 1553–4; Basil Cracknell, *Canvey Island: The History of a Marshland Community*, Univ. of Leicester, Occ. Paper, 12, 1959, p. 14; Defoe, *op. cit.*, p. 13.

pasture, and 700½ acres of arable. In short 31 per cent of the land was in corn and 54 per cent in pasture and meadow. The importance of corn is also emphasized in the remark of the surveyor, Norden, that Barstable Hundred, between Brentwood, Rayleigh, and the coast, was a granary of oats; in the fact that land in Southchurch manor owed rent partly in herrings, partly in cummin, and partly in wheat; and in the statement that the parishes of Dengie Hundred regularly had a surplus of corn to sell, but being unable to send it by road because of the "foul ways," dispatched it to London by sea. The stock-and-wheat farming of the Essex marshlands, in short, presents a close parallel with the marshlands of Lincolnshire and Yorkshire. The class structure of the region also deserves closer examination.[1]

The rest of the southern half of Essex was an enclosed wood-pasture country criss-crossed by deep winding lanes. Bullocks and sheep grazed on the pastures and pigs were fed in the forest. Important fairs at Brentwood, Romford, and Epping, received drovers from the Midlands, north and west, bringing store animals into the county and removing the fat stock to the slaughterhouse. The farm accounts of the Petre family of Ingatestone Hall illustrate this traffic in the late sixteenth century. They sold steers, wethers, and oxen at Romford, and bought oxen and store wethers at Brentwood. Some of their business at these fairs was done direct with London butchers or their agents, and some with drovers who had travelled a long way to reach Essex. Further income on this estate came from the sale of forest resources: from the bark of trees in the hedgerows for the tanner, and from ash for the cooper for the making of barrels. Over the forest as a whole, these items together with pigs brought substantial profit.[2]

On the lighter and more workable clays in the northern half of Essex more corn was grown than in the wood-pasture region. One specially fertile district lay in the north-western quarter between Bishop's Stortford and Saffron Walden, another lay between Chelmsford and Maldon, while the Rodings were considered to have the best cornland of all. But most of the northern half of Essex was pastoral country, and it was this region which nurtured a cloth industry. It seems at a superficial glance, at least, to afford another excellent example of a community in which a domestic handicraft was dovetailed with a system of pasture farming by family farmers.[3]

The two counties of Hertfordshire and Essex furnish certain material

[1] Essex RO, D, DL, M 14, 2; D, D, Mq, M 12; J. Norden, *The Surveyor's Dialogue*, cited in F. Hull, *op. cit.*, p. 71; PRO SP 16, 182, 67.
[2] Essex RO, D, DP, A 18; D, DP, A 22; D, DH, t, bundle M 49.
[3] N. V. Scarfe, *Land Utilization Survey of Essex*, p. 433; Essex RO, Inv. of Thomas, earl of Sussex, 9 June 1583; SP 16, 186, 62.

for generalization. Both supplied finished produce for London—meat, milk, butter, cheese, malt, and breadcorn—while Hertfordshire sped the traveller on his way with fresh horses and fodder. The opportunities for commercial enterprise were insistent enough to tempt many farmers into credit arrangements with food merchants: this seems to be a fair deduction to draw from the fact that the property of Hertfordshire farmers at death included many more debts and credits than was usual in other parts of England.

Several regions in these two counties resemble others found elsewhere in the kingdom. The farming of the downlands of Hertfordshire resembled that of the wolds of Lincolnshire and Yorkshire. The marshland economy of Essex resembled that of the Lincolnshire marshes. The central district of Hertfordshire and the more workable clay lands of Essex, most of them bordering on Hertfordshire, resembled the mixed husbandry districts of the Midlands, while the heavier clays of Essex bore a marked similarity in their pastoral pursuits, their settlement pattern, and their cloth industry to the Weald of Kent.

F. SOUTH-EASTERN ENGLAND:
KENT AND SUSSEX

The two south-eastern counties of Kent and Sussex were as profoundly influenced in their farming by the proximity of London as the Home Counties to the north. They had in London an almost unlimited market for all agricultural produce, and if London rejected any of their grain on account of its poor quality, both counties had a long coastline and many ports from which the surplus could be carried to other parts of England, and, when export was permitted, abroad. The usefulness of the ports depended to a considerable extent on a good internal river system, and this was denied to the inhabitants of the Weald. But since they were mainly graziers, they did not urgently need a waterway to London. The chief commodity carried by water was grain, while meat was carried on the hoof. Hence the water transport was available where it was most needed, in east Kent and south Sussex, where corn was grown in quantity on the North and South Downs. The Weald, in contrast, was mostly under grass and given over to meat production. Its principal traffic ways were its roads, and it is no wonder, therefore, that they were abominable in winter. They were built on the most unsuitable of materials and they had to carry more animals than men— not only those dispatched by the Wealden farmer to Smithfield but those which travelled through the Weald from the fattening pastures of Romney marsh. When Dr Burton of Cambridge complained in the mid-eighteenth century of the Wealden roads as "more truly the tracks of cattle drivers" he described them more accurately than he knew.[1]

For the most part, the farming of south-eastern England was organized to produce food for the townsman's table. Having a considerable variety of soils, the two counties formed three principal regions, whose activities dovetailed neatly to produce beef, mutton, wheat, barley, hops, and fruit.[2]

1. *The North and South Downs*

The wheat- and barley-growing regions were the North and South Downs, where the hill pastures were used for grazing sheep flocks which were folded at night on the lower arable fields. The system was the same in all hill country where sheepwalks were extensive, and the soil of the cornfields shallow and hungry for manure. Large flocks were the prerequisite of large arable acreages and the manure of the sheep was their most highly valued product. The wool and the lambs, which could be sold to the flockmasters who had fattening pastures in the marsh, were secondary. Through the dung of the sheep some farmers were able to grow as much as 55 or even 86 acres of crops each year.

On the North Downs the largest crop was usually wheat, the second barley or oats, and the third and fourth crops, tares and peas. All were consumed on the farm except the wheat and possibly some of the barley. The wheat was either sent to London, or, if it was deemed inferior in quality (and according to early seventeenth-century witnesses, downland wheat was not the best that Londoners could buy), it was sent coastwise to other parts of England. Durham and Northumberland, for example, suffered an almost perennial shortage of corn, and were eager recipients of the surplus of other counties. On the South Downs and on the coastal plain of Sussex (where the system of management was the same as on the Downs) the chief cash crops were wheat, rye, and barley, different districts showing a marked preference for one or another of these three, while all relied mainly on tares and peas for fodder.[3]

Besides his ewe flock, the downland farmer had a small herd of cows and followers to supply him with milk, cheese, and butter. He fattened what cattle he could on his own land, and sold stores to the farmers of other districts.

[1] E. Melling, ed., *Kentish Sources. Some Roads and Bridges* (1959), p. vii; E. M. Bell-Irving, *Mayfield. The Story of a Wealden Village*, 1903, p. 11.

[2] See T. S. Willan, *The English Coasting Trade*, p. 138, for the statement that Kent supplied more corn to London than any other county.

[3] SP 14, 112, 12; Julian Cornwall, 'Farming in Sussex, 1560–1640', *Sussex Arch. Coll.*, XCII, p. 55.

Downland farms were often large: a yeoman's farm at Findon on the Sussex Downs, for example, had 82 acres under the plough—25 acres of wheat, 34 acres of barley, 2 acres of oats, and 11 acres of tares. A Kentish farm, similarly situated, was that of Nicholas Raignold of Adisham, who in 1601 had 30 acres of wheat, 16 acres of oats, 2 acres of barley, 7 acres of tares and peas. His stock comprised 9 cows and followers, 8 bullocks, 13 pigs, and 94 sheep. Farmers such as these, with large acreages of corn and sheepwalks for nearly a hundred sheep apiece, made a community and a countryside that was markedly different from that of the small-holders and small-holdings of the neighbouring Weald.[1]

2. *The Weald*

The Weald of Kent and Sussex, including both the High Weald and the Low Weald encircling it, was still, even in the sixteenth century, densely wooded. It was this region which caused William Lambard to say of Kent that "wood occupieth the greatest portion [of the county] except it be towards the east." At the beginning of the sixteenth century at least half the large parish of Tonbridge was still waiting to be colonized and transformed from wood and parkland into farmland, even though the town itself was an important market and lay on one of the main roads from London to the coast.[2]

Like other woodland regions of the kingdom the Weald was exceptionally populous. Most parishes housed between two and three hundred families compared with a mere sixty, and frequently less than thirty, on the Downs. The larger size of the Wealden parishes does not invalidate this comparison with the Downs entirely, for the farmland and pasture of the Weald probably occupied only about half the total area.[3]

Land in the low Weald which had been won from the forest was mostly a heavy clay, difficult to drain, and in the High Weald consisted of alternating sand and clay beds. Much of it, in consequence, was heath or coppice (Ashdown Forest alone occupied 14,000 acres), a third of the land was arable, and the rest lay under grass, and was used for the rearing and fattening of cattle. Some men, like John and Nicholas Toke of Godinton, had additional grazing elsewhere, and even sheepwalk on the Downs, in which case their sheep flocks were also large. William Curtis, gentleman, of Tenterden, for example, had 195 sheep in

---

[1] Kent RO, Probate Invs., *passim;* J. Cornwall, *op. cit.*, p. 65.
[2] E. Lodge, *The Account Book of a Kentish Estate, 1616–1704,* 1927, p. xviii; C. W. Chalklin, 'The Rural Economy of a Kentish Wealden Parish, 1650–1750', AHR, x, 1962, p. 30.
[3] BM Harl. MS 594.

Burmarsh besides a flock of eighty sheep and beasts feeding at Tenterden. But the smaller Wealden farmer was more typical, and he specialized in cattle. He had perhaps sixteen animals in his herd and not more than about twice that number of sheep in his flocks. Pigs were also fed, but usually there were not more than half a dozen to be found on each farm, and although the pannage of the beech and oak woods supported many pigs, it seems likely that the bacon and pork satisfied only domestic and local needs.[1]

Dairy houses and cheese chambers were usual on Wealden farms, and again many served little more than household requirements, but some cheese-making, particularly in the Rother valley, was clearly a subsidiary enterprise for the market. The Weald was not nationally renowned for its dairy produce, however, and its dairies in the sixteenth century may have been a legacy from the Middle Ages, destined to be abandoned as the demand for meat in London increased. Nevertheless, cheese production was sufficiently large to persuade the clothiers of the Weald to deal in cheeses as well as in cloth.[2]

The ploughland on the average Wealden farm was small—usually not more than 10 acres—and was devoted to the growing of oats, wheat, and peas. A well-to-do farmer like William Raymes of Staplehurst (1600), with 11 cows and followers, 11 oxen, 4 bullocks and a bull, and 25 sheep, had only 5 acres of oats, 1 acre of peas, and 3 acres of wheat. Oats, peas, and tares supplemented the grass and hay, leaving a meagre ration of corn for the house. On farms with twice this acreage, the proportion of one third domestic corn and two thirds fodder was the general rule.

Since the Weald attracted large numbers of people, and since also the average farm was small, many people relied on by-employments to supplement their income. The woodlands fed the iron industry of Sussex with charcoal and gave a living to many ironworkers, while the inhabitants of the High Weald found supplementary employment in the cloth industry, which made its home in the neighbourhood of Tenterden and Marden in the fourteenth century, and reached the peak of its prosperity in the middle decades of the sixteenth century. The cloth workers were part-time graziers, or dairymen, and part-time spinners and weavers. They managed the two occupations by relying

[1] J. Cornwall, *op. cit.*, pp. 67 *sqq.*, 78; E. Straker, 'Ashdown Forest and its Inclosures', *Sussex Arch. Coll.*, LXXXI, 1940, p. 122; J. R. Daniel-Tyssen, 'The Parliamentary Surveys of the County of Sussex', *ibid.*, XXIII, 1871, pp. 294, 270; E. Lodge, *op. cit.*, pp. xxiii, 5, 14.

[2] Cf. Norden, *The Surveyor's Dialogue*, p. 216, on recent improvements in the Sussex Weald: "In so much as the people lack not, but can to their great benefit yearly afford to others both butter, cheese, and corn;" J. Cornwall, *op. cit.*, p. 76; Kent RO, Probate Invs., *passim*.

on the clothiers, who gave out the wool, collected the finished cloth, and dealt in cheeses also, perhaps even receiving the cheese from the weavers in part exchange for the wool. This seems to be the only reasonable explanation for the activities of clothiers like William Huggett of Pluckley, who in 1618 had 264 lb. of cheese in store at his death.[1]

By the mid-Tudor period by-employments were so usual in the Weald that contemporaries considered them vital to the survival of its large populations. The cloth-making areas, for example, were said to be "so populous that the soil thereof is not able by any increase thereof to maintain and find the one half of the inhabitants except clothing be maintained." This situation was not unique; it was typical of many other pastoral areas, particularly those in the lowlands which had once consisted of dense forest. And the Weald differs not at all in the explanations it offers for this situation. People were attracted to the area by opportunities for more varied employment than those available in the open countryside of the plains. Its common grazings were more extensive than elsewhere; in Lamberhurst, for example, rights of common in 1568 still covered all animals without stint. And as Hartlib remarked in the mid-seventeenth century, "there are fewest poor where there are fewest commons." Manorial control, moreover, was weak in the Weald, and control over immigration was negligible. Customs of inheritance also probably fostered the growth of population, for gavelkind was the common custom, which promised the young people a share of family land, and persuaded them to stay at home rather than seek their fortune elsewhere. However, the importance of this factor is difficult to assess, for we know nothing as yet about the relative strength of gavelkind in the Weald compared with the rest of the county. Theoretically, the custom was common throughout Kent, but judging by the size of farms on the North Downs, for example, it is doubtful whether, by the sixteenth century, it was as frequently observed on the hills and in the marshes as in the Weald.[2]

3. The Marshes

The third farming region of south-eastern England comprised the coastal marshlands of Romney, Walland, Denge, and New Romney marshes in Kent, the Pevensey Levels in Sussex, and the isles of Thanet

[1] J. Boys, *General View of the Agriculture of the County of Kent*, 1813, p. 3 footnote; CSPD 1631–3, p. 64; D. C. Coleman, *The Economy of Kent under the Later Stuarts*, London Univ. Ph.D. thesis, 1951, p. 150; Kent RO, PRC 28, 5; 10, 35.

[2] R. Furley, *A History of the Weald of Kent*, 1874, II, ii, pp. 481–2; Kent RO, U 47, 42, M 12; *Samuel Hartlib, His Legacie*, 1652, p. 42.

and Sheppey and the Thames shore in the north. In Romney the work of reclamation and drainage in the Middle Ages had built up a store of experience concerning the use and maintenance of the marsh pastures. The whole region was a network of drains and dikes, and Kentish men, who had pioneered the system of sewer commissions for the maintenance of these earth works, were past masters of the grazing art. The dikes and ditches divided the marshes into 'several' grounds, on which farmers fattened sheep and, on a smaller scale, cattle. The farming system was somewhat different from that of most marshland country, for farms were almost entirely given over to meadow and pasture, leaving the minimum of arable land for the growing of a few additional fodder crops, mostly peas, beans, tares, and oats, with some domestic corn. By the second half of the seventeenth century, however, parts of the matured marshland were being ploughed up for the first time and marl and sleech were locally available to improve fertility. But until the introduction of corn bounties after the Restoration there was no strong incentive to plough pasture except to procure sufficient bread corn and to supplement the hay ration. A description of 30 acres of marshland in Dymchurch parish in 1669 presents a picture of this countryside which would have stood equally well for most of the region in the sixteenth and early seventeenth centuries. The land was

"divided by good wet ditches into four severals, well fenced with gates, posts, and rails where need is. The same is very well wayed for it is good coming to it and driving of sheep or cattle any time of the winter though the season be very wet...As sound thriving ground for sheep and feeding land for cattle as any in the level of Romney marsh, for when the rot among sheep hath been in Romney marsh, which is very seldom, yet it was never in the said parcel of land known."[1]

Here was an almost wholly green landscape, whose rivers and seashore afforded additional resources to its inhabitants—sea fish, fowl in due season, some land that was "as proper for oyster pits as any land in England," and along parts of the shore beach stone for road-mending, worth at the Restoration 4d. an acre. The subsidiary sources of income were not to be despised, and, indeed, to the poor who lacked land of their own and relied upon common pastures and common perquisites, these were often their main livelihood.

For the larger farmer, fattening mutton and beef was the main business. The grazier's interests are well illustrated in the list of possessions of William Epps of Old Romney, who died in March 1595, and left a flock of 202 sheep (87 ewes, 89 twelve-monthings, 19 wethers, and 7 rams) and a mixed herd of 4 cows, 2 calves, 7 twelve-monthings,

[1] Kent RO, U 214, E 7, 49 and 50; 44; 14.

2 two-year-old heifers, 1 two-year-old bullock, four other bullocks, and 4 oxen. Had he lived to enjoy the summer, he would, no doubt, have bought in more sheep and cattle, and some of them would have appeared in his list of possessions as "northern" or "Welch" steers and heifers. The terms "northern" and "Welch" were applied generally to all store cattle that were brought by the drovers from northern and western England for sale to the graziers of the Home Counties. The steward of the first earl of Dorset bought northern cattle of a drover at Uxbridge fair in 1604. Nicholas Toke of Godinton procured northern beasts at Ashford and Harrietsham, and Cheshire oxen, steers, and heifers at St Bartholomew's fair in London. Welch and northern cattle seem to have been sold at all the fairs in and around London. "Country" cattle were the cattle of one's native county and were bought from local farmers or at the markets. Large marshland graziers had a mixture of both kinds.[1]

The second marshland region of Kent comprised the Isles of Sheppey and Thanet and the whole Thames shore, where the ploughland was more extensive and the system of farming more closely resembled that of the east coast marshlands. The grass and hay, supplemented by peas, tares, and beans, fattened sheep and bullocks for Smithfield. But more land was ploughed along this northern coast of Kent, and some farmers were producing wheat, barley, and even fruit for sale. This region is today regarded as one of the more fertile districts of Kent, and grows much fruit and many market garden crops. It was already differentiated as a marshland region of mixed farming in the sixteenth century.[2]

Both the northern and southern marshes of Kent attracted some of the larger farmers from the hill country and even from the Weald, who wished to feed some of the stock they had reared elsewhere. Like the marshlands of Lincolnshire, therefore, both districts of marsh in Kent and Sussex gave up a certain proportion of their land to outsiders. Farmers on the North Downs between Detling and Canterbury looked northward to the Thames marshes, those living further east and south looked to Romney marsh. Stephen Hulkes of Newnham was among the latter group—a rich farmer, who was six times wealthier than the average downland yeoman. In July 1618 his farm on the Downs gave him 38½ acres of crops (including 17 acres of wheat, the rest consisting of tares, peas, oats, and barley). About the house that summer he had only 3 cows, 12 one-year-old bullocks, a northern heifer, and a nondescript flock of 9 twelve-monthings and 2 lambs. His wealth at the moment of his death lay in Romney marsh where he had an old

[1] Kent RO, A 2, 1, f. 23; E. Lodge, *op. cit.*, pp. 23–4.
[2] VCH *Kent*, III, p. 420.

removable house with lumber, sheepskins, and wool in the loft, worth £93 9s. od., 48 cattle (mostly northern steers and heifers with some country steers as well), and 894 sheep.[1]

By the second half of the seventeenth century south-eastern England, and particularly Kent, was well-known for its hops and fruit. Before this, fruit trees and hop bines were to be seen in scattered places in many parts of the county. But it is difficult to get an accurate measure of their importance. While an orchard was usually part and parcel of the land surrounding the farmhouse, and was as commonplace as the garden, large crops of fruit for the market were unusual. The only districts in which they seem to have been more noticeable than elsewhere were in the Favresham-Sittingbourne area and on the Lower Greensand ridge which divides the Low Weald from the chalk Downs. Here was a comparatively narrow strip of land of mixed sand, loam, and clay of varying fertility. On the map it is amalgamated with the Weald, but more detailed research might justify its separation as a distinct region. Some of it was woodland, and yielded most profit in this condition. Peckham Hurst, for example, was occupied by beech woods where large numbers of pigs found pannage. Some of the sandier soils were fit for nothing but cony warrens, although the conies on Wrotham heath, where a golf course now occupies the land, brought in enough to pay the rent of its farmer-owner. But on the most fertile loams the orchards hint at the appearance of the specialist fruit-grower, whose greatest pride was his trees, even though they did not yet account for much of his annual income.[2]

The development of a comparatively high degree of specialization in south-eastern England was no doubt associated with the fact that much of the land in Kent and Sussex was enclosed. It is probable, indeed, that much of it had never been held in common. The custom of gavelkind in Kent points to the importance of the family as the basic social unit, and despite the superimposition of the manor upon Kentish society in the eleventh century, the underlying structure of independent families and ring-fence farms survived intact in most parts of the county. By the sixteenth century many settlements had already thrown aside the weak manorial superstructure as a useless and inconvenient appendage.

Nor did the custom of gavelkind turn the family farm into a fragmented manorial tenement. Although many farms were partitioned to provide land for the sons of the family, they were not usually broken down into small scattered strips. The effects of partition were continually being cancelled out by amalgamations. And since no system of

[1] Kent RO, PRC 28, 9. See also *infra*, pp. 195 *sqq*.
[2] The clearest evidence emerges in the 1660's. See Kent RO, U 214, E 7, *passim*; U 214, E 7, 58.

common rights ever seems to have developed over the land, however scattered it became, there were never any obstacles to enclosure.[1]

In Midland villages where the manor lands were usually co-extensive with the village lands, and where the arable was cultivated in common fields, the manor drew considerable strength from the fact that it regulated all the vital operations in the farming year. In Kent the manor had little authority in this direction. Sometimes the pastures of a hamlet or township were grazed in common, in which case the manorial courts controlled the stints and maintained order. But regulation of the commons, together with the maintenance of hedges, banks, and roadways, were the only farming tasks which called for co-operative agreement. And they were not by themselves sufficiently important to keep the manorial courts in existence and preserve them as the framework of social and economic life. In any case, the manor in Kent was frequently only a small estate consisting of a demesne and a few freeholds, and when customary tenants were absent the administrative and legal functions of the estate were small indeed. By the sixteenth century, when money values were falling rapidly, many a lord found the freehold rents hardly worth the trouble of collection. The sum owed by a freeholder of Horsmonden in 1645 who had neglected to pay rent to the lord for 22 years was £1 18s. 6d., 110 hens, and 22 cocks.[2] In short, the sums of money which tenants owed to their lord frequently amounted to less than the lord's obligations to his tenants, and in such cases the prudent landowner allowed the manor to die a natural death. The manorial tenants of Hunton who enumerated the customs of the manor in 1598 and complained of the lord's failure to maintain them, listed his duty to provide a bull and a boar, to grant hedgebote and stackbote from the timber on the estate, to maintain hospitality and relieve the poor, and to provide his tenants with a feast every lawday in return for a penny from each of them. The tenants' dues to their lord were not stated, but it is unlikely that they were worth more than £5 a year. Can we blame the landlord who deemed it expedient to let these customs quietly lapse?[3]

The freeholders were a large class in Kentish society. Their farms were held in severalty; co-operation in the day-to-day farming routine was practically non-existent; they had complete freedom to alienate or sell their land; and judging by the thousands of deeds still surviving among Kent archives, the market in land flourished. In such circum-

---

[1] A. R. H. Baker, *The Field Systems of Kent*, London Ph.D. thesis, 1963; 'The Field System of an East Kent parish (Deal)', *Arch. Cant.* LXXVIII, 1963, pp. 96–117; 'Open Fields and Partible Inheritance on a Kent manor', *EcHR*, 2nd Ser., XVII, 1964, pp. 1–23.

[2] Kent RO, U 513, M 9.

[3] Kent RO, U 282, M 13.

stances, it is no surprise to find that large farms were already numerous in the Tudor period on the Downs and in the marsh, as successful yeomen thrust out the small men. To explain the rise of the capitalist farmer in Kent is not difficult: the circumstances of the age were on his side. What is more perplexing is the problem of explaining how the Weald—like many other forest areas in lowland England—remained the refuge of the small men.

G. SOUTH AND WEST ENGLAND: GLOUCESTERSHIRE, WILTSHIRE, DORSET, OXFORDSHIRE, BERKSHIRE, AND HAMPSHIRE

The six counties of Gloucestershire, Wiltshire, Dorset, Oxfordshire, Berkshire, and Hampshire possess many different kinds of country. The large expanse of chalk downland stretching from Dorset, through Wiltshire, Hampshire, and Berkshire, culminating in Oxfordshire in the Chiltern hills, and the limestone hills of the Cotswolds which thread their way through Gloucestershire, north Wiltshire, and Oxfordshire, were given over to a sheep-corn husbandry. Regions of more general mixed farming lay in the vale of Oxford and the eastern half of the vale of the White Horse in Berkshire, in the Kennet valley, Berkshire, and on the marlstone uplands of north Oxfordshire. Vale lands on heavier soils like the vales of Gloucester and Berkeley were in grass and dedicated to dairying. Finally, these six counties contained a remarkable cluster of forests, lying on very diverse soils ranging from the heavy cold clays of Dean and Kingswood forests in Gloucestershire to the heathlands of the New Forest. Some were dairying, some stock-keeping districts, but on the lightest lands these activities were mingled with corn-growing.

1. The Chalk Downs and the Cotswolds

Two recent studies of agrarian organization on the chalk downs and Cotswolds in Wiltshire and Oxfordshire have revealed a pattern similar in outline to that of other upland country in lowland England. Both were districts of nucleated villages, common fields, and spacious downland commons, in which enclosure made little headway until the later eighteenth century. A sheep-corn husbandry, like that followed on the Lincoln cliff, on the chalk wolds of Lincolnshire, and on the downs of south-eastern England, was universal. The relative importance of ploughland and pasture is indicated in the calculation that on the Wiltshire chalklands, sheep down occupied about half the land, while on the other half about three quarters was arable and the rest permanent grass. In the Cotswolds the sheepwalks were only a little less extensive. Hence a thousand and more sheep were not unusual in the village flocks of Wiltshire townships, while on the Hampshire downs nearly as many could be counted in the flocks of individual farmers. The sheep were essential for making the arable fertile, and while the smaller arable crops—oats, peas, and vetches—were used for fodder, it was the barley and wheat which earned for the farmer the largest slice of his income. Sheep fairs at places like Weyhill in Hampshire attracted dealers from far and wide, but to the farmer the sale of lambs and wool was of secondary importance to the production of barley and wheat.[1]

The scale of farming enterprise was grander and more ambitious on the Hampshire downlands than any encountered elsewhere, though an explanation may be difficult to find. Not only were the larger farmers breeding hundreds of sheep for the manuring of their fields, but they were fattening cattle, breeding horses, and keeping pigs as well. The property of Joan Denby of Overton appraised on 2 April 1539, for example, consisted of 12 kine, 4 yearlings, 4 bullocks, 7 horses, 23 hogs, and 660 sheep. Her crops on the ground were 30 acres of wheat and 20 acres of oats and dredgecorn. This picture of farming derived from the 1530's is redrawn again a century later in the inventory of Christopher Archer of Cranborne. His goods were enumerated in October 1639 and included 13 kine, 6 bullocks, 6 weaned calves, 2 bulls, 12 carthorses, 1 store sow, 12 young store hogs, 12 fattening hogs, 600 store ewes, 105 keb ewes, 112 lambs, 26 rams, and about 80 acres of wheat in the ground. As early as Henry VIII's reign, therefore, the downland farmers of Hampshire were engaged in large-scale capitalist farming, which can only have been undertaken with the aid of large numbers of wage labourers.[2]

The structure of society in the chalk country was typical of mixed farming regions in the uplands where settlement was concentrated in villages. The manor continued to be a powerful institution throughout the period. Village society was hierarchical, and since arable farms could be more efficiently run when the units were large, the trend in this period of comparative prosperity was towards the amalgamation of holdings, and a steady increase in the landed resources of the large farmers at the expense of the small family. Farmers did not disappear

[1] E. Kerridge, 'Agriculture, c. 1500–c.1793', VCH Wilts., IV, pp. 43 sqq.; M. Havinden, The Rural Economy of Oxfordshire, 1580–1730, Oxford B.Litt. thesis, 1961, pp. 16, 73, 56 sqq.; Gloucester Public Library and Bristol Archives Office, Probate Invs., passim. I wish to thank Mr Frank Emery for allowing me to use his analysis of Berkshire probate inventories from the Bodleian Library, Oxford.

[2] Hants. RO, Probate Invs. passim, and in particular that of Joan Denby of Overton, 2 April 1539, and Chris. Archer of Cranborne, 12 October 1639 (Pec. Wonston).

overnight, but their number dwindled steadily, for the region had little work to offer outside farming. A small amount of clothmaking was carried on in the Cotswolds and on the downs of Hampshire (Winchester, after all, had been a great cloth centre in the Middle Ages). But the main focus of the cloth industry was now in the vales, which possessed larger and increasing populations of family farmers. Indeed, the decline of the small-holder on the downland was the more noticeable in this period, because of the contrast it presented with the fortunes of small farmers in the dairying regions of Wiltshire, whose numbers steadily multiplied.[1]

2. The vale of Oxford and eastern half of the vale of the White Horse, Berkshire, and the marlstone uplands of north Oxfordshire

The vale of Oxford, lying between the Cotswolds and the Chilterns, and the eastern half of the vale of the White Horse in Berkshire comprised a region of mixed husbandry, similar in its farming system to the Midland plain. It lay on the edge of a large dairying area, since the western half of the Berkshire vale was pastoral, dairying country, and was continuous with the dairying district of Wiltshire, but the frontier between the two zones was noted and mapped by W. Mavor in his *General View of the Agriculture of Berkshire* in 1808.[2] For want of more precise evidence for the sixteenth century, his boundary is adopted in the map of farming regions (p. 4), but the existence of this frontier in the Berkshire vale is clearly indicated in the meagre stores of cheese and butter and the large areas under crop possessed by the farmers in the east in contrast with those living in the western half. In Oxfordshire four sample manors from this region had between 67 and 90 per cent of their cultivated land (excluding commons) under the plough. Much of the corn was grown for the market, for as Robert Loder of Harwell, Berkshire, calculated in the early seventeenth century, wheat and barley malt were the most profitable produce on his type of farm. And he was evidently not alone in this opinion, for barley was by far the largest crop on all farms, and occupied nearly half the sown land each year. Second in importance was wheat, occupying a quarter of the land, while beans, peas, and occasionally vetches occupied the remainder. Oats and rye were rare. The farmers' interest in stock was centred mainly on cattle. Nearly all substantial farmers reared young animals and fattened some, while a few maintained a dairy. Most farmers kept

[1] Kerridge, *op. cit.*, pp. 46, 49, 57, 58, 60; VCH *Hants.*, v, p. 484.

[2] W. Mavor, *General View of the Agriculture of Berkshire*, 1808, p. 23 and map facing title-page.

some sheep, if only for their manure, but they rarely numbered more than twenty. Nevertheless, the stock, including a few pigs and a horse or two, represented a considerable proportion of the value of goods on the farm. This was a region of truly mixed farming.[1]

The marlstone upland of north Oxfordshire was another similar region. Its nucleated villages were composed for the most part of small farms of 20–30 acres apiece, on which the use of leys permitted the growth of livestock farming without enclosure. The red loam soils of this area were eminently suited to corn-growing, but it lacked any rivers to carry its produce to the larger markets. Hence, its arable crops were large, but they were used, as in Leicestershire, to feed cattle which could walk to the towns, while the hill-slopes afforded good grazing for sheep. The chief income of the farmer, in consequence, was derived from wool, mutton, and beef.[2]

3. *The pastoral vales and woodpasture districts*

The regions of open pasture comprised the vales of Gloucester and Berkeley, and a district in south-east Hampshire sandwiched between the downs and the New Forest, both of which specialized in dairying. With them it is convenient to consider two other districts of mixed open and forest pasture: one in Wiltshire lying between the Cotswolds and Salisbury Plain and extending along the western boundary of the county—"sour woodsere land," John Aubrey described it, "very natural for the production of oaks"—and another in Dorset, arc-like in shape, curving westwards around the downlands and heaths of the county. These two districts include the forests of Blackmore, Gillingham, Selwood, Chippenham, Melksham, and Braydon, and for this reason are portrayed on the map of farming regions as woodpasture areas (p. 4). They join up with the woodpasture lands of Somerset and like them were dairying areas.[3] Fragments of common fields and open commons were not difficult to find in these dairying countries, but enclosure by agreement had done much to transform the landscape, and the movement made further headway during the sixteenth and seventeenth centuries. It was accompanied by other improvements and changes in land use. Lime was liberally used as a fertilizer; woodland was cleared, and rough grazing improved and turned into permanent pasture; some of the arable was put under leys.[4]

The result of these changes was to increase the acreage of grassland

[1] M. Havinden, *op. cit.*, pp. 92, 103, 97, 107, 91.
[2] *Ibid.*, pp. 149–65.
[3] J. E. Jackson, ed., *The Topographical Collections of John Aubrey*, 1862, p. 4.
[4] E. Kerridge, *op. cit.*, pp. 43, 55.

which supported the dairy herd. Half the beasts in the Wiltshire dairying districts were milch kine, and sheep were only 50 per cent more numerous than the beasts. Some cattle were fattened for beef, and pigs fed for bacon, but the speciality of the vales lay in the dairy, which produced cheese in the north, and butter in the south. Of less importance was the sale of beef, bacon, mutton, and wool. The arable crops included, in order of importance, wheat, barley, peas, oats, rye, vetches, and beans, but their acreages were small compared with the yield of grass and hay.[1]

The pasture lands of Dorset, consisting in part of former forest—Gillingham forest in the north was not disafforested until 1628—possessed medium to heavy loam soils, which lacked good drainage. Scattered settlement, small farms, much old enclosure, common fields rapidly disappearing as a result of enclosure by agreement, improvement of the soil by marl and lime—these were features which were typical also of the Wiltshire vale lands. And the similarity went further, for while the best pastures were used for feeding cattle, most of Dorset's vale lands were also given over to dairying.[2]

The vales of Gloucester and Berkeley were also districts of heavy, Liassic clay soils which did not submit readily to the plough. Their dairying interest was clearly reflected in the composition of the cattle herds, and in the stores of cheese in the cheese chambers of local farmers. A few animals not needed for the dairy were fattened for the butcher, pigs were kept on a small scale in conjunction with the dairy, and some horses were bred. Sheep were numerous on some farms, particularly those with larger than average acreages of ploughland, but many smaller peasants kept none. The general run of family farmers, moreover, had small acreages of arable yielding only enough crops for their own needs. They included wheat and barley (the main white corn crops), rye, oats, beans, peas, and vetches, while one farmer of Hambrook in Winterbourne, William Bayley, possessed in 1618 two acres of turnips. He was evidently not alone in this parish, for another farmer of Hambrook in 1638 also had a close of turnips. Knowledge of the virtues of the turnip in promoting cheese and butter production was clearly not confined to East Anglia at this time. Both vales also boasted many orchards of apple and pear trees, the fruit of which was exported to Devon, Cornwall, and Wales.[3]

[1] E. Kerridge, op. cit., pp. 44–5.

[2] G. E. Fussell, 'Four Centuries of Farming Systems in Dorset, 1500–1900', Dorset Nat. Hist. & Arch. Soc., LXXIII, 1952, pp. 119, 127–8; L. E. Tavener, Dorset, Land Utilization Survey, part 88, 1940, p. 247; Hants. RO, Probate Invs., passim; H. L. Gray, English Field Systems, p. 32.

[3] Gloucester City Library and Bristol Archives Office, Probate Invs., passim; Gloucester City Library, 16064; PRO E 134, 43 Eliz., E 18.

Hampshire's pastoral region occupied a triangle of land between the New Forest and the downs. When Leland travelled through it, it was enclosed and "reasonably wooded," having passed no doubt through the same process of medieval colonization as other country created out of the forest. Its farmers in the mid-sixteenth century were engaged in rearing and fattening cattle, pigs, and sheep—far more sheep were kept in the Hampshire vales than in the lowlands of Wiltshire and Dorset—and in breeding horses. But by the beginning of the seventeenth century the fattening of beasts was less conspicuous, and many farmers were turning to dairying. This was but one of many pastoral regions which at the turn of the century began to see economic advantages in the production of cheese and butter.[1]

The structure of society in the pastoral dairying regions has not yet been studied for all these counties, but we have a detailed examination of conditions in Wiltshire, which discloses many similarities with the communities of other dairying regions colonized from the forest. It is probably a not unfaithful portrait of all vale lands in these six counties, which were formerly afforested. The strongest impression made upon the traveller in dairying Wiltshire was of a green country of small fields, parcelled between many small farms, and patches of woodland. Enclosure had recently changed the appearance of the countryside, but the population did not fall in consequence. Rather it tended to increase. The explanation has much to do with the weakness or complete absence of manorial control in all districts where common cultivation was fast disappearing. The demesnes of many manors were being sold off, sometimes to tenants, and manorial rights and obligations lapsed. No obstacles then stood in the way of a free market in land, and the number of small-holders increased steadily. Dairying, of course, as we have observed in other regions, was eminently successful when carried on in small family units. And the region could absorb additional population, for it had other work, apart from farming, on which to employ idle hands. It was a country of spinning wheels, and weaving looms, for this was the region in which much of Wiltshire's fine broadcloth was woven.[2]

4. *The forests*

The forest districts not already mentioned in the preceding section include the forests of Dean and Kingswood in Gloucestershire, the forests of Oxfordshire and Buckinghamshire—Wychwood, Shotover, Stowood, and Bernwood, a stretch of once continuous woodland

[1] Hants. RO, Probate Invs., *passim.*
[2] Kerridge, *op. cit.*, pp. 57–60, 63.

extending from the New Forest in the south to Savernake in the north and Windsor to the east, and the Chilterns of Oxfordshire and Buckinghamshire.

The New Forest, here considered in conjunction with the neighbouring district of sands and podsols around Poole in Dorset, is a special case of a forest lying not on heavy clay soils, like so many of the large forests of the kingdom, but on sandy heathland. Its inhabitants pursued a pastoral system of farming, but also grew corn on a larger scale than usual and even marketed some. The economy has resemblances with that of Sherwood Forest, Nottinghamshire. Fertility was maintained by sheep which were folded on the ploughland, and enabled the farmer to keep more land in arable than other forest farmers. The largest corn crop both in Hampshire and Dorset was often wheat, and others included barley, oats, rye, peas, and vetches. Most farmers bred and fattened cattle, but their specialities were pig-keeping and horse-breeding, for both of which pursuits they relied upon the pannage and pasture of the forest, and heath commons. As Fuller later observed of the pig-fattening business, the animals went into the forest lean and returned home fat "without either care or cost to their owners." This region therefore contributed much to the making of Hampshire's fine reputation as a producer of the best bacon in the kingdom. A typical inventory of farm stock and crops for this region was that of Richard Tagg of Brockenhurst, compiled in December 1561. He had 6 kine, 5 calves, 13 heifers and steers, 8 oxen, 6 mares and a colt, 12 pigs and 2 gelts, 14 ewes and tegs, and 2½ acres of wheat in the ground. Later on in the farming year, other farmers made an even braver show with feeding bullocks bought in from elsewhere in the spring, three times as many pigs as Richard Tagg, and often 10–30 acres sown with crops. From a cursory view of the New Forest, it does not appear to have attracted the squatters who plagued the oak forests, but a thorough analysis of the class structure and size of this forest community has yet to be made.[1]

Farming in the Chilterns differed in certain details from that of the sandy forests owing to the fact that the soil was more diversified and London was conveniently at hand, but it may be grouped with them because of its similar economy with its unusual emphasis on corn production. The hills were heavily wooded in parts, and pig-keeping was a speciality in the beech forests, but the chalk subsoil, overlain with gravel,

[1] Hants. RO, Probate Invs., *passim;* G. E. Fussell, 'Four Centuries of Farming Systems in Hampshire, 1500–1900', *Hants. Field Club & Arch. Soc.,* XVII, iii, p. 269. For a later view of the peasants of the New Forest, see C. R. Tubbs, 'The Development of the Smallholding and Cottage Stock-Keeping Economy of the New Forest', *AHR,* XIII, 23 *sqq.*

clay, and flints, provided some good ploughland, while along the Thames lay excellent natural meadows. The countryside was a mixture of scattered farms held in severalty, and smaller holdings, whose land lay partly in common fields, partly in closes, and whose farmhouses were grouped together in nucleated villages. Enclosure made some progress in this period, but most new closes were used as arable, which was kept fertile by small flocks, numbering on average about twenty sheep. Cattle were not of great consequence on the small farm, although some large farmers were dairymen and graziers on a more ambitious scale. So far this description could apply equally well to the clay forests. The difference lay in the fact that corn was a considerable crop for the London market. The principal grain was barley, which occupied one third of the sown land; oats occupied a fifth of the ground; rye was a fairly usual crop and took some acres from wheat; pulses occupied only 12 per cent of the land.[1]

The woodlands of the forest of Dean and Kingswood were likewise pasture-farming districts, but were engaged in cattle-rearing, dairying, and pig-keeping with very little corn-growing. Preliminary indications are that this was the economy of the Oxfordshire and Buckinghamshire forests, but a closer study of these areas is necessary to establish both their farming system and their social organization. From the forests of Dean and Kingswood in Gloucestershire, there issued the common complaint concerning the "great number of unnecessary cabins and cottages built in the forest by strangers, who are people of very lewd lives and conversation, leaving their own and other countries and taking this place for a shelter as a cloak to their villainies." And to employ their populations, there were many supplementary industries— iron smelting in the forest of Dean, coal-mining in Kingswood, glove-making and blanket-making in Wychwood Forest, and lace-making in Bernwood and Stowood.[2]

H. THE SOUTH-WEST: SOMERSET, DEVON, AND CORNWALL

Somerset, Devon, and Cornwall form a group of mainly pastoral counties, with small pockets of fielden, corn-growing country in the valleys and along the coast, a woodpasture region in east and south

---

[1] M. Havinden, op. cit., pp. 26–8, 120 sqq., 174.

[2] PRO SP 16, 44, 45; E 134, 16 Chas. I, M 36; SP 14, 84, 46. It may be significant that one of the customs of inheritance in the Forest of Dean, as in the Northamptonshire forests, was Borough English.—Gloucester City Library, MS RF, 30, 4. See also infra, p. 00. I wish to thank Michael Havinden for much help with the description of Oxfordshire.

Somerset, and a fen district in the Somerset Levels. Cornwall was the least intensively cultivated, and Somerset the most. When Leland travelled through Cornwall in the 1540's, his descriptions made monotonous reading, like a play with only two sets of scenery, each alternating regularly with the other. A patch of enclosed country, possessing wood, grass, and good corn crops, gave way to a landscape of hilly, moorish, barren ground; this was superseded by a patch of corn and grass, which was likewise superseded by another stretch of barren moorland. The county was evidently a series of cultivated oases set in a large expanse of moor, the only continuous stretches of fertile land lying on the coast. Such a landscape expressed as clearly as words the economic circumstances of the agricultural community: the population was too small to feel any compulsion to colonize fresh land or improve the use of the old. There was enough land for all, and most people were content simply to wring subsistence from it.[1]

Somerset, on the other hand, was an exceptionally populous county. Indeed, by 1588 it is believed to have been the third most densely populated county in the kingdom, and this is a credible verdict, for the eastern portion of the county was congested with dairy farmers and clothiers, while the county as a whole offered a varied selection of industrial occupations. Its minerals included calamine, lead, zinc, iron, stone, and coal; cloth-making was an old industry in the east, together with glove-making, which had been carried on since the early fourteenth century, and bone lace-making, which occupied the inhabitants of Yeovil by the early seventeenth century. Judging by the evidence of trade tokens, moreover, stocking-knitting, which was well established by Defoe's day, was already giving employment at Shepton Mallet, Wells, and Glastonbury during the Interregnum, if not earlier.[2]

Somewhere between the two extremes of sparse populations in Cornwall and dense populations in Somerset lay Devon. Dartmoor and Exmoor were bleak and desolate in winter, but were used for grazing cattle and sheep in summer. Most of the northern half of the county, except around Bideford and Barnstaple, was pastoral country, rearing many sheep and cattle, and fattening some in the valleys, for supplying meat to ships' victuallers. Rich corn- and fruit-growing land lay in the vale of Exeter, along the edge of Torbay, and in the South Hams

[1] The verdict of the Crown Surveyors in 1630 was that these three counties had many hundreds and thousands of acres of common land that could be improved.— SP 16, 161, 80.

[2] E. C. K. Gonner, *Common Land and Inclosure*, pp. 134 *sqq.*; H. C. Darby, ed., *Historical Geography of England before A.D. 1800*, pp. 345–6. See also SP 16, 183, 50; CSPD 1547–80, p. 275; VCH *Somerset*, II, pp. 353–4, 409, 427, 426, 358.

district. By-employments in the county were several. Fishing held an important place in the opinion of contemporary writers, and tin and other metals were mined on Dartmoor. The main industrial occupation, however, was cloth-making. Fine kerseys were made all over north Devon, as well as in the vale of Exeter and the Exe valley (Exeter having been one of the original centres of the industry in the early thirteenth century). Coarse cloth was made west of Dartmoor, the principal distributing centre being Tavistock.[1]

Clearly, these three counties presented many contrasts. Some inland districts were remote and sparsely settled, and indeed have remained so to this day. Farmsteads grouped singly, in pairs, or in small hamlets, made up the characteristic pattern of settlement, and many farmers kept in touch with markets and merchants spasmodically or not at all. In contrast, the coastal lowlands, and the valleys with access to the sea, such as the vales of Taunton Deane and Wellington, the Axe valley, and the vale of Exeter, were far from being a commercial backwater even at the beginning of the Tudor period, and by the end they were drawn as securely into the scheme of agricultural specialization and production for the market as the counties surrounding London. Cornwall and Devon had long-standing commercial relations with Wales, France, and Spain. Towns and ports nearer home—Cardiff, Plymouth, and Bristol—grew to rely on the south-west for some of their food supplies. The old link with Ireland was maintained and strengthened, the Irish carrying away some of the harvest of the fields—beans and peas from Somerset's ports on the Bristol Channel, for example—and bringing in return increasing numbers of store cattle for fattening in Somerset, and butter, which they supplied to Cornwall through Padstow.[2]

It was in the valleys and along the coast, where the farming was mixed, that most remnants of strip- and some commonable fields were still to be found. Many more had already undergone peaceful, piecemeal enclosure. In pastoral country some districts, such as the western half of Somerset, showed no vestige of common fields, while others, such as the dairying country of east Somerset, with its many nucleated settlements, and the central Somerset levels, seem to have clung to their strip fields throughout this period. Strips in closes were also very

---

[1] W. G. Hoskins, *Devon*, pp. 62, 93, 96, 124–8; W. T. Blake, 'Hooker's Synopsis Chorographical of Devonshire', *Devon Assoc.*, XLVII, 1915, pp. 343, 345–7; Carew's *Survey of Cornwall*, 1811, p. 16; CSPD 1629–31, p. 363.

[2] *Topographer and Genealogist*, I, p. 224; SP 14, 144, 24; SP 16, 175, 35; E. H. Bates, *The Particular Description of the County of Somerset, 1633*, Somerset Rec. Soc., XV, 1900, pp. 12, 18; SP 14, 130, 81; information kindly supplied by Mrs Veronica Chesher.

common, and suggest that some agreements for cropping and grazing were made between small groups of tenants.[1]

Management of the cornland was not as intensive as in the corn country of lowland England, for much of it throughout the south-west was managed on a rotation that included long leys. And since other pasture was plentiful, the rules of co-operative husbandry were less stringent and were more readily set aside, when need arose, than in regions of mixed husbandry in lowland England. The traditional attitude associated with the highland half of the kingdom, of willing-ness to assist enclosure where it did not injure the rights of others, was universal; it was reflected in the indignant retort of an inhabitant of Ilminster, Somerset, giving evidence in a tithe dispute in 1578. There was no custom in the manor, declared Joan Bonvile, to prevent copyholders from enclosing land in arable fields and converting it to pasture and meadow "at their will and pleasure, without denial of anyone." Another tacit admission that the majority of people looked favourably upon enclosure lay behind the tart remark of the incumbent of Cossington in the central Somerset levels in 1606, that the lord of the manor, "taking then the profits of the said parsonage for the better benefit of his tenants," had allowed the latter to lay their ground together in bigger parcels, and so alter and exchange their land that part of one field was shortly afterwards enclosed. The same lord by agreement with his freeholders had also enclosed and partitioned a beast pasture. Step by step, by one agreement after another, enclosure made headway without commotion throughout the south-west. It is not surprising that contemporaries formed the impression that Devon and Cornwall and, indeed, much of Somerset were for the most part enclosed. In making this generalization, however, they were thinking chiefly of arable land. Common pastures were numerous in all three counties, though these too, of course, were liable to undergo partition and enclosure.[2]

An expanding market for food and a rising population instigated a fresh movement of land colonization and land improvement all over the region. But the changes which astounded and impressed contem-poraries most were those taking place in Devon and Cornwall, hitherto

[1] Cornwall RO, Survey of Landrake Manor, 1578–9; A. L. Rowse, *Tudor Corn-wall*, p. 33; H. L. Gray, *English Field Systems*, pp. 259, 262, 97–101; W. E. Tate, 'Somerset Enclosure Acts and Awards', *Somerset Arch. & Nat. Hist. Soc.*, 1948, p. 21; Exeter City Library, Dynham Survey, 1566; TED I, pp. 60–3; Somerset RO, Glebe Terriers, 195; 66 (3); 26 (2); 28 (1); 341 (1); X WLM, O, 822;

[2] Carew, *op. cit.*, p. 62; G. E. Fussell, 'Cornish Farming, A.D. 1500–1910'; *Amateur Historian*, IV, 1960, p. 339; PRO C 2 Eliz. A 7, 28; Somerset RO, Glebe Terriers, 199 (2); W. J. Blake, *op. cit.*, p. 346; A. L. Rowse, *op. cit.*, p. 37; D. & C., Exeter, MS 676; Exeter City Library, M. B, 8d; 50, 11, 3, 1.

the least intensively cultivated of the three counties. Everyone seemed anxious to improve the yield of his land by enclosure, consolidation, and the use of fertilizers. Sand, seaweed, marl, lime, soap ashes, paring and burning, all helped to increase the harvest. At Clayhidon, in north Devon, and on other estates belonging to Lord Dynham, tenants were freely allowed to cultivate parts of the common, paying 4d. an acre as long as they sowed it. Such efforts brought a personal reward, for farmers were able to improve their diet, smarten their dress, and even find cash to spend at the market. On the economy of the county also, the effects were dramatic. Farms for which it had once been difficult to find a tenant were in great demand, and rents rose ten times over. If we are to believe Carew's reminiscences of the past, the population of Cornwall had hitherto been far from self-sufficient in corn, and had relied on buying grain in other counties. A larger harvest now enabled the county first to meet local demands, and then, as production increased, to export. By the end of Elizabeth's reign Cornwall was victualling all the vessels riding in its harbours as well as exporting corn to France and Spain. By the 1630's its markets were sought out by merchants from Plymouth and Bristol. Indeed, the coastal areas of south-eastern Cornwall were planting orchards and making cider, as well as growing grain, with the Plymouth market deliberately in view.[1]

1. Valley and coast

The regions which responded most readily to the blandishments of the merchants—inevitably perhaps, for they were in closest contact with the main routes of trade—were the fertile coast lands and the vales inland. They enjoyed a high reputation for their grain and fruit, but in most cases their farmers had a finger in many other pies as well. In the vales of Taunton Deane and Wellington, for example, farmers were rearing and feeding cattle and sheep; a few were dairymen; fruit and hops were specialities; and among a selection of field crops, which included barley, beans, oats, and wheat, the latter was the first and largest. No wonder that John Norden in 1607 called the vale of Taunton Deane the Paradise of England.[2]

The coastal lands of Cornwall likewise boasted their fertility in the fact that wheat occupied about half the acreage on the better land each year. Oats and barley were two other important crops and supplied

[1] Hoskins, op. cit., p. 63; W. J. Blake, op. cit., p. 343; Carew, op. cit., pp. 61–2, 183, 115; Exeter City Library, M. B, 8d; Rowse, op. cit., pp. 39, 40; SP 16, 175, 35; CSPD 1629–31, pp. 393–4.

[2] Somerset RO, Probate Invs., passim; J. Norden, The Surveyor's Dialogue, 1607, p. 230.

most domestic needs. Unfortunately few farmers' probate inventories have survived for Devon, but some list the property of lowlanders in the 1640's and portray farmers with large acreages of arable crops. Philip Elston, a rich farmer of Crediton, with goods and chattels worth £665 13s. 4d. in October 1645, had threshed corn worth £94 10s. while his stock, which included 6 kine, 2 calves, 4 oxen, 4 young bullocks, 118 sheep, horses, and pigs, were worth £81. John Weslake of Topsham had 66 acres of corn, worth £196 in May 1646, whereas his stock of 20 cattle, 12 of them being stores, 5 horses, 20 couples of ewes and lambs, 20 lean wethers, and a dozen pigs, were worth £96 10s.[1]

2. *Pastoral Moorland and Marsh*

Pastoral country in the south-west included high, desolate moorland, lashed by wind and rain, and used only for sheep-grazing, steep-sided valleys with lush meadow grass in the bottom for rearing and feeding, and fertile marshland such as that lying along the north coast of Somerset, where cattle fattening was the main preoccupation.[2]

Bodmin Moor, Dartmoor, and Exmoor, and the hills of west Somerset were cattle-rearing, sheep-grazing country where farms were often large but where the minimum of corn (rye, barley, and oats, more often than wheat) was grown to serve domestic needs only. Leland's description of his journey on Exmoor from Exford to Simonsbath portrays one of these more solitary areas from the visitor's point of view: "all by forest, barren, and moorish ground, where is store and breeding of young cattle, but little or no corn or habitation." The natives who knew the situation more intimately, however, believed that the free commoners, such as those living on Dartmoor, were substantial men. They had large farms taken in from the moor, and by ancient custom they were allowed to enclose any part of the moor, paying 1½d an acre for it. In the 1620's they began to make temporary enclosures, preparing it by paring and burning, and growing oats and rye for two or three years, then leaving it to lie common again. Not only did they put their own cattle, horses, and sheep to graze on the moors; they took in other men's beasts as well, employing their poor undertenants—moormen, they were called—to herd and drive the animals. Evidently there were two classes of people on the moor, the richer freeholders and the poor undertenants, who had little land and paid heavily for it, and took on other jobs as well. In addition to shepherding and cattle-herding, tin-mining was a shrinking occupation

[1] Carew, *op. cit.*, p. 16; Cornwall RO, Probate Invs., *passim;* Devon RO, E, C, Inv. files 1, 29.

[2] Carew, *op. cit.*, p. 297.

for them during the sixteenth century. The life was arduous and the reward small. "The tin miner," wrote Hooker, "goeth so near the weather as no man can live more frugally and nearer than he doth."[1]

On the fringes of the moors some well-to-do pasture farmers made more of a better situation by using the moors for summer grazing and wintering their stock in home closes. The poor who were servants to such men enjoyed the use of the commons by putting their sheep in their masters' flocks, and in this way some grew "to be of good ability." The traffic in agisted cattle on Exmoor is described in the course of several lawsuits of the early Stuart period. The prices of agistment were proclaimed every spring in the market towns adjoining the moor, and 42,000 sheep were said to graze there at a cost of 2s. or 2s. 6d. per score. Such large numbers were not regarded as excessive; indeed, they improved the grazing, for the grass was sedgy and coarse, and had to be kept low if the sheep were to thrive. In Charles I's reign the price of agistment was raised to 3s. 4d. a score, and agisters began to withdraw. More followed suit when about 1635 a claim for tithes was made, and the number of sheep grazing on the moor fell to 16,000. The local inhabitants raised about £30 towards the cost of initiating a lawsuit, but the dispute was not finally settled in that decade. Another case was brought in 1657 on the same issue, when agistment rates had risen to 5s. and 6s. 8d. to include the cost of both grazing and tithe.[2]

One example of a substantial farmer, who doubtless benefited from the common grazing on Dartmoor, was Roger Austen of Lifton who left goods worth £460 9s. 2d. in the later 1640's, including 10 kine, 10 calves, 8 young cattle, 8 oxen and 1 bull, a mare, a nag, 2 sucking colts, 6 pigs, 19 old sheep, and 11 lambs. Not only was Austen rearing and feeding cattle, he was breeding horses in a small way as well. This was not unusual in Cornwall and Devon, for many were needed for use in the mines and for the pack-saddle. His sheep flock was small, but this again was characteristic of many farmers in both counties. Single flocks were small, but as Carew put it, "it may sum the total to a jolly rate."[3]

On the coastal marshes, such as those of north Somerset between East Quantoxhead and Clevedon, stock could be fattened in large numbers. Hence the description by the justices of the peace of three hundreds in north Somerset—Winterstoke, Brent, and Bempstone: "the husbandry of these places consisting much in grazing and most proper

[1] Cornwall RO and Somerset RO, Probate Invs., *passim;* W. E. Tate, *op. cit.,* p. 17; PRO E 134, 4 Chas. I, Easter 9; 3 & 4 Chas. I, Hil. 11; W. J. Blake, *op. cit.,* p. 342. [2] PRO E 134, 17 Chas. I, Mich. 21; 1657, Mich. 36.

[3] Devon RO, E.C. Inv. file 12; W. J. Blake, *op. cit.,* p. 345; information kindly supplied by Mrs Veronica Chesher; Carew, *op. cit.,* p. 78.

for it." Hence also the impression formed by Defoe on his journey
from Bridgwater to Bristol that farmers were "wholly imployed in
breeding and feeding of cattle." Indeed, as a generalization about the
whole county of Somerset, this was as accurate a description as any.
The Crown victuallers in Elizabeth's reign regarded Somerset as the
producer of beef and mutton for the larder. The Irish cattle breeders
were importing stores into Somerset in such large numbers in 1621 that
the inhabitants were drawn to utter a loud protest at the drain of money
from the county. Among connoisseurs of bullocks and beef, moreover,
the largest cattle were known to come from Somerset.[1]

3. *The central Somerset Levels*

The central Somerset Levels must be treated separately, for they were
in fact fen country. Contemporary descriptions were couched in much
the same phrases as those used to describe the fens of eastern England.
Thomas Gerard's account of Somerton, written in 1633, speaks of a
prospect over flats and moors which "in winter present but a watery
spectacle, being then for the most part drowned, yet yields it a great
commodity to the fowlers who furnish not only this town but many
other places with such traffic." The Monday market at Somerton was
stocked with cattle, "people hereabouts being much given to feeding
and grazing of cattle." Aller in winter looked like an arm of the sea
rather than land, being surrounded by drowned pastures. The parish
was large, and the inhabitants dwelt in scattered places on the higher
ground, travelling to church in winter by boats. This way of life and
work were all strongly reminiscent of the Lincolnshire fens. The pasture
commons were spacious and unstinted, and the flooding in winter
ensured a rich crop of grass in summer on which cattle were fattened.[2]

Farms may have been somewhat larger on average than those in the
Lincolnshire fens. In Mudgley manor in Wedmore parish, for example,
the average holding in 1558 was 18¼ acres; in Lincolnshire it would
have been somewhere between five and ten acres. But then it is probable that the Somerset Levels were not as densely settled as the fens of
eastern England. At least, the commonest signs of pressure on the land
had not yet appeared.[3]

That not a few farmers relied entirely on the commons for their
grazing pastures is evident in the fact that some holdings consisted of
arable and meadow only. Some land, however, was described as arable

[1] SP 16, 533, 3; Defoe, *op. cit.*, I, p. 270; CSPD 1595–7, pp. 155–6; SP 14, 130, 81;
G. E. Fussell, *op. cit.*
[2] E. H. Bates, *op. cit.*, pp. 231–2, 214, 63, 219; Somerset RO X WLM, O, 822.
[3] *Ibid.*; J. Thirsk, *English Peasant Farming*, p. 42.

and meadow, or arable *and* pasture, hinting at some system of alternate husbandry. On the more fertile ploughland continuous cultivation, such as that practised in the Isle of Axholme in the early seventeenth century, may not have been unknown. It was certainly used at Othery in the eighteenth century.[1]

As for additional sources of food and income: wild fowl and eels furnished the Saturday market at Langport; some farms had withy beds; peat was dug for fuel; fruit and hemp were grown. The main activities, however, were cattle-rearing and feeding, dairying, and horse-breeding—as they were in the fens of eastern England. There were not a great many sheep. The ploughland was more extensive than in Lincolnshire; one probate inventory recording 16½ acres illustrates the variety of the crops and the special importance of wheat: 7½ acres wheat, 3 acres barley, 2 acres beans, 4 acres oats. When the inhabitants of east Somerset declared that some of their grain came from the western half of the county, it is possible that they were referring not only to the vales of Taunton Deane and Wellington but to the Somerset Levels as well.[2]

4. *Wood-pasture in East Somerset*

The eastern third of Somerset—a region stretching in a wide arc from Chard and Ilminster in the south through Yeovil, Shepton Mallet, and Frome to Bath in the north—was the dairying and cloth-making region of the county. It is physically joined to the dairying-weaving district around Mere in Wiltshire, where a similar economy and a similar type of society have been found. The land was divided among many small family farms, constituting a pattern of land distribution already familiar in other dairying districts such as central Suffolk. Cloth-making sustained the members of the family who would not otherwise have been fully employed, and other domestic handicrafts played a lesser rôle. Some glove-making was carried on at Yeovil already in the Tudor period; bone lace-making is also mentioned there in 1620; and stocking-knitting was an established occupation in the home by the middle of the seventeenth century.[3]

This eastern sector of Somerset was the most densely settled part of the county in Domesday times; and dairying, together with the opportunities for work in domestic handicraft industries, did nothing to

[1] Somerset RO, Lease book of Othery manor, 1610; X, WLM, O, 822; F. M. Ward, *Supplement to Collinson's History of Somerset*, 1939, p. 119; J. Thirsk, 'The Isle of Axholme before Vermuyden', AHR, I, 1953, p. 19.

[2] E. H. Bates, *op. cit.*, pp. 132, 232; Somerset RO, Probate Inv. Bath and Wells Cons., Inv. of William Smith of Lillesdon, 7 July 1590; SP 14, 144, 24 (12).

[3] VCH *Somerset*, II, pp. 353-4, 409, 427, 426, 358.

reduce the congestion of population. The region became not only the home of many small farmers and craftsmen in the sixteenth century, but a refuge for the poor. The justices of the peace for the four hundreds of Frome, Batheaston, Wellow, and Kilmersdon, describing the northern part of the region in 1623, depicted an economy and society characteristic of other forest areas in the kingdom.

"The country, a great part of it being forest and woodlands, and the rest very barren for corn, bordering upon the county of Wiltshire, from whence it hath continual supply of corn, and also out of the more western parts of this county, the people of the country (for the most part) being occupied about the trade of cloth-making, spinning, weaving, and tucking. Also we find that by reason of the trade of cloth-making, and the increase of people working about that trade, there have been very many cottages erected within our said division for them to work in, which have no means of living but about that trade."

In 1631, when the justices of Frome again pleaded the poverty of the division, it was the invasion of poor cottagers of which they complained. They congregated in the town of Frome and in the neighbouring forest of Selwood, where squatting rights were easily established.[1]

Much of the settlement in this region consists of small hamlets and scattered farmsteads, but the nucleated centres often had arable land in common fields, and wheat, barley, oats, and peas were grown as well as apples. But corn was small in amount and did not enable the region to be self-sufficient. Farmers set most store by their dairy herds and sheep flocks, and most of their ready cash came from the sale of cheese and wool. In the 1630's Yeovil was one of the great cheese markets of the locality, whence cheese was transported to Wiltshire and Hampshire "in very great quantity." When Defoe travelled this circuit, it inspired him to write one of his most glowing and colourful passages. A low, flat, enclosed country, thickly populated with villages, hamlets, and farms, it hummed with the noise of dairy churns and weaving looms.[2]

I. CHESHIRE AND LANCASHIRE

Lancashire and Cheshire are kindred counties. Both were predominantly pastoral, both possessed broad lowlands of clay loam soils upon marl interspersed with peat mosses, and both were hemmed in on the east by an upland zone of moorland straddling the Pennines.

Most of Cheshire consists of clay, sand, and gravel soils. In the

[1] F. W. Morgan, 'The Domesday Geography of Somerset', *Somerset Arch. & Nat. Hist. Soc.*, LXXXIV, 1938, p. 145; SP 14, 144, 24 (12); SP 16, 185, 40.
[2] Somerset RO, Probate Invs., *passim;* E. H. Bates, *op. cit.*, p. 171; Defoe, *op. cit.*, I, pp. 280–4.

Tudor period it was a grassland county, with no more land under the plough than was necessary to feed the family and the farmers' stock. The same generalization applies to the forest regions of Macclesfield and Delamere, though their farming differed in certain details from that of the open pastoral lowlands.

Lancashire was divided into three distinct farming regions. The lowland plain of south Lancashire and Amounderness consists of Keuper red marl, overlain with boulder clay. The western half of this plain was a pastoral region, possessing a strip of coastal marsh, many river meadows, and large areas of moss inland which had hardly been touched as yet by the hand of the improver, and which yielded turf for fuel and grazing for stock. The region was later to be improved beyond recognition by the destruction of the moss and by marling, and by the beginning of the nineteenth century it was given over to mixed farming. In the Tudor period, however, the greater part of the land was pasture and meadow, and only about two fifths of the cultivated land (38–46 per cent) lay under the plough.[1]

In the eastern half of the Lancashire plain, that is, in the central zone of south Lancashire between the Ribble and the Mersey, and in the central and eastern sectors of the Fylde, the farming was mixed. A higher proportion of the cultivated land was in arable (55–62 per cent) and a greater variety of crops was grown. Nevertheless, when domestic needs were satisfied, the surplus field crops were put to the same use as the grassland of the western sector, for rearing and feeding cattle. Further east still a second pastoral region stretched almost continuously down the side of the county, and consisted for the most part of Millstone Grit moorlands yielding poor acid pastures. This region too could be used for little else but cattle rearing. In short, the whole of Lancashire was first and foremost a producer of stores and fat cattle.

Certain features of agrarian development in this period were common to all regions in both counties. Energetic efforts were being made everywhere to improve land, particularly by marling, by embanking against the sea, and by enclosure. In north Cheshire heath and moss around Halton and Runcorn were being turned into good pasture, and poor pastures in the neighbourhood of Macclesfield Forest were being ploughed and sown with rye and oats. The best illustration of a large-scale work of reclamation is contained in a description of Henbury manor in 1558. The manor house was singularly well equipped, with

---

[1] H. B. Rodgers, 'Land Use in Tudor Lancashire: the Evidence of the Final Concords, 1450–1558', *Inst. British Geographers*, XXI, 1955, pp. 79 *sqq.* For an example of tiny assarts of moss, see Lancs. RO DD Bo, 101 and 102; R. W. Dickson, *General View of the Agriculture of Lancashire*, 1815, p. 18; R. Cunliffe-Shaw, *Kirkham in Amounderness*, p. 278.

several courts of outbuildings, including stables, barns, turfhouses, hayhouses, oxhouses, cowhouses, and dovehouse. The estate also included a deerpark, fishponds, orchard, and hopyard, but not apparently any permanent arable. The rest of the land consisted of woodland and pastures, with names which betrayed their condition: *Little Moorfield*, "not very profitable land;" *Mossfield*, "gorsy and heathy in many places;" other pastures and meadows were "woody," "gorsy and benty," or "full of fern." Their owner was clearly embarked upon an ambitious plan of improvement. Of three pastures of 12 acres apiece, one was full of fern, one was fenny, broomy, and benty, and the third was sown with oats. Of two other pastures, one of 5 acres was "gorsie and bentie," the other of four acres was "this year sown with rye." Altogether five fields, amounting to 28 acres, had been ploughed, and carried crops of oats and rye.[1]

In this survey we catch a glimpse of an estate in the midst of a large programme of improvement. We can also glimpse through this one example the process of reclamation which had already transformed large parts of England. In Domesday times woodland had covered many parts of the kingdom. But the trees had gradually been felled, and the land turned into pasture. The pasture, when neglected, quickly grew a covering of moss, gorse, and bracken. But by ploughing for a few years and then allowing the land to go back to grass again, it could gradually be turned into convertible land and the moss and the bracken kept at bay. It was in this way that much woodland in the west Midland and southern counties had been turned into pasture farms giving enough cornland as well for subsistence. The English landscape owed a great deal to farmers as energetic as the owner of Henbury manor, who had made war upon the wilderness and tamed it.

Both Lancashire and Cheshire afford plentiful examples of common fields and common pastures, but in this age of strenuous land improvement they were quietly disappearing. In Cheshire, where common fields were small and consisted of one or a multitude of fields, more often than three, enclosure had begun as early as the fourteenth century, and was carried through by the method used so successfully throughout highland England, by exchanges of strips and by agreements. By the late eighteenth century only one parliamentary act was necessary for the enclosure of Cheshire's common fields.[2]

[1] Margaret Blundell, ed., *Blundell's Diary and Letter Book, 1702–28*, 1952, pp. 134–5; R. W. Dickson, *op. cit.*, p. 488; G. E. Fussell, 'Four Centuries of Cheshire Farming Systems, 1500–1900', *Hist. Soc. Lancs. & Cheshire*, CVI, 1954, p. 57; Chester RO, Cholmondeley Coll., F 237, E 110, E 125, E 126, E 127; John Rylands Library, Ry. Ch., 2047.

[2] Dorothy Sylvester, 'The Open Fields of Cheshire', *op. cit.*, pp. 4, 12–15, 17, 20, 29–31; D. Sylvester and G. Nulty, *The Historical Atlas of Cheshire*, 1958, p. 28.

In Lancashire also agreements to exchange strips were the usual preliminary to the enclosure of common fields. At the same time, common pastures were being divided between townships, and then divided by consent between individuals. A typical agreement concerning commons was that between the lord of the manor and the thirty-two inhabitants of Lytham in 1608. The lord agreed to allow to his tenants as much land on the waste as they had on their holdings, plus 100 acres more. He then assumed the right to enclose and let the remainder, undertaking, however, to lease as much of this land to his tenants as they could afford to pay for. An even more liberal allotment was that made by Edward Stanley to his tenants at Wray "when he returned from the Scottish field." He allowed them to enclose 3 acres of the common apiece as pasture for 2 kine without paying rent. Generous agreements like these spoke louder than words. Land was relatively abundant, and enclosure in consequence took place in a calm atmosphere.[1]

1. *Pastoral Cheshire*

The Cheshire plain was pasture-farming country with a predilection for cattle rearing and fattening in the north, and for dairying in the south and west where the soils were heaviest. As the justices of Nantwich Hundred declared in 1623, this southern part of the county had much land "converted into pasture and dairies," and it was the dairies which brought Cheshire most fame. The best cheese of all Europe, according to John Speed, was made in Cheshire.[2]

Nowhere in Cheshire was the arable land as plentiful as in regions of mixed farming, but it was somewhat more extensive in the north than in the south, and crops were more varied in consequence. In the north farmers grew barley, oats, wheat, vetches, peas, and beans; in the south, barley and rye were probably the main crops, and oats, hemp, and flax the most commonly mentioned subsidiary ones. The contrasts

---

[1] Augustine Watts, 'Court Rolls of the Manor of Little Crosby', *Hist. Soc. Lancs. & Cheshire*, XLIII, 1891, p. 118; Lancs. RO, DDCL, 1240A; 2160; F. Walker, *Historical Geography of South-West Lancashire before the Industrial Revolution*, Chetham Soc., NS, CIII, 1939, p. 55; Lancs. RO, DDCL, 2162; DD Pt., Bundle 18; H. T. Crofton, 'Moston and White Moss', *Lancs. & Cheshire Antiq. Soc.*, XXV, p. 51; Lancs. RO, DDS Misc. (6), 12; R. D. and T. H. Briercliffe and Ernest Axon, 'The Briercliffes of Briercliffe', *Lancs. & Cheshire Antiq. Soc.*, XXXV, p. 55; Charles E. Higson, 'Quick Moor', *Ibid.*, XXXIX, p. 21; Lancs. RO DDCL, 2162; C. L. W. H. Chippindall, ed., *A Sixteenth Century Survey and Year's Account of the Estatate of Hornby Castle, Lancashire*', Chetham Soc., NS, CII, 1939, p. 37. See also H. L. Gray, *English Field Systems*, pp. 242-9.

[2] Chester RO, Probate Invs., *passim;* SP 14, 140, 78; E. P. Boon, *Cheshire*, Land Utilization Survey, LXV, 1941, p. 185. See also G. E. Fussell, 'Four Centuries of Cheshire Farming Systems, 1500-1900', *Hist. Soc. Lancs. & Cheshire*, CVI, 1954, pp. 57 *sqq.*

of specialization in the two halves of Cheshire can be illustrated by two probate inventories. William Heyward of Audlem, a dairying parish in south Cheshire, died in July 1613 and left 9 kine, 4 calves, 3 stirks, 2 twinter bullocks, 1 steer, 1 bull, 2 nags, 3 pigs, 5 weaning lambs, hens, geese, and turkeys. No crops are mentioned in the inventory of his goods except £5 worth of hay, but his cheeses in the house were valued at £5. Ellen Forshall of Willaston in the Wirral, a rearing-fattening district, left at her death in May 1614 5 kine, 2 calves, 4 oxen, 10 young cattle, 4 horses, 7 swine, 20 sheep, poultry and geese worth 10s., 20 bushels of sown barley worth £8, 5 bushels of peas and oats in the ground worth £2, and £3 worth of winter corn.[1]

2. *The Cheshire forests*

In the forests of Macclesfield and Delamere a somewhat different system of grassland farming was practised. Cattle were reared, but in addition sheep, which were few and far between in the rest of Cheshire, were more numerous, and there are signs, at least in Macclesfield forest, that horse-breeding was carried on. Pannage for pigs was also available. Forest husbandry in Cheshire seems to have been similar to that practised in the other forest regions of the kingdom. And on the western edge of Macclesfield forest employment was diversified by the presence of coal.[2]

3. *Pastoral Lancashire*

One of the pastoral regions of Lancashire lay along the coast and river estuaries, and included the whole of south-west Lancashire between Liverpool and Preston, and two separate districts in the Fylde. Few details of farming in the Fylde are available, but in south-west Lancashire the principal occupation was cattle-rearing and fattening. The ordinary farmer had a herd of about ten beasts, kept some young animals for fattening, but sold most of them as stores. And in the 1630's he began to investigate the business opportunities in dairying. Very few sheep were kept on most farms, no more than one or two horses, and usually a couple of pigs.[3]

---

[1] Chester RO, Probate Invs., 1615 H; 1614 F.

[2] Chester RO, Probate Invs., *passim;* H. Holland, *General View of the Agriculture of Cheshire*, 1808, p. 287. But see also D. Sylvester, 'The Manor and the Cheshire Landscape', *Trans. Lancs. & Cheshire Antiq. Soc.*, LXX, 1960, pp. 3–15, where a manorial organization, unusual in forest areas, is suggested.

[3] Lancs. RO, Probate Invs., *passim;* R. Stewart-Brown, 'Lancashire and *Cheshire Cases in the Court of Star Chamber, part 1, Rec. Soc. Lancs. & Cheshire*, LXXI, 1916, p. 75; E. B. Saxton, ed., 'A Speke Inventory of 1624', *Hist. Soc. Lancs. & Cheshire*, XCVII, 1945, p. 142.

The average farmer was a customary tenant with not more than 5 acres under the plough. His cattle, in consequence, were fed mainly on grass and hay. This was a region in which 48 per cent of the cultivated land was arable, 14 per cent meadow, and 38 per cent pasture. But this calculation, of course, takes no account of the common marshland grazings, which made good feeding land. In the fields the main crops were oats, which were used for bread, and barley, but wheat was more usual here than elsewhere in Lancashire, and rye, peas, beans, and vetches were also occasionally grown.

The second pastoral region lay in east Lancashire, and stretched from Lonsdale in the north through Bowland and Rossendale south to the Manchester district. The eastern half of Rossendale had been developed in the thirteenth and fourteenth centuries by the Lacy family for cattle-rearing, and this was how the land was still being used in the sixteenth century, when the forest had ceased to be a hunting ground, and the pace of land reclamation had quickened. Although little is known about the early colonization of other parts of these grit and limestone moorlands it is almost certain that they too were developed in the first instance as vaccaries.[1]

At the beginning of the seventeenth century the inhabitants held out small hopes of any change in their farming scheme. The vaccary at Accrington was described in 1607 as "cold and barren land, but by manuring, marling, and tilling, they and every vaccary will yield a certain grass called oats, but after such manuring in short time, it will grow to heath, ling, moss, and rushes." A petition from the tenants of the forest added that oats would only grow in dry years "with continual change of every third year's new manurement." The meaning of this last statement is not crystal clear. It may mean that manuring was necessary every third year. Alternatively, it may refer to the practice followed elsewhere in Rossendale of cropping the land for a few years and then allowing it to revert to grass. A survey of Rochdale in 1610 spoke of the difficulty of distinguishing between arable, meadow, and pasture because the land was used for "ploughing, mowing, and pasturage as occasion and necessity doth urge the occupiers thereof."[2]

The stock on the farms of east Lancashire consisted almost entirely of cows and young cattle, which were fed on grass and hay and sold off as stores to other districts, including lowland Lancashire. But by the beginning of the seventeenth century some farmers were turning to

[1] G. E. Tupling, *The Economic History of Rossendale*, Chetham Soc., LXXXVI, 1927, pp. 18–27; Lancs. RO, Probate Invs., *passim*.

[2] Lancs. RO, DD Ta, 216; H. Fishwick, ed., *The Survey of the Manor of Rochdale*, Chetham Soc., NS, LXXI, 1913, p. 10.

dairying—a change of specialization, which as we have seen already, occurred in several other cattle-breeding districts of highland England. Few sheep were seen on these moors; only about half the farmers had any at all, and those that did rarely kept more than thirty or forty. The arable land was small—acreages of 2½–6½ acres are commonly mentioned in probate inventories—and the crop consisted usually of barley and oats alone, although occasionally wheat and peas were sown in tiny quantities.[1]

Hamlets and single farmsteads made up the pattern of settlement, and manorial traditions were weak. So although much land was held by customary tenure, tenants had the privileges of freeholders and were allowed to alienate their land freely after submission in the lord's court. A considerable traffic in land developed in the sixteenth century, in consequence: it was not uncommon for copyholders to alienate or sublet portions of their holdings for long periods of up to sixty years. And the fragmentation of land was carried further by the partitioning of land among sons. Partible inheritance was a common custom in the sixteenth century.[2]

Thus, the farming economy and the structure of society in east Lancashire were similar to those of communities inhabiting the Yorkshire dales. And in Rossendale the resemblance was brought closer in this period, for its inhabitants developed a handicraft industry to supplement their living from farming. In the Yorkshire dales, as we have noticed already, it was the weaving of woollen cloth and stocking-knitting. In Rossendale it was the weaving of flax and wool, and later cotton.[3]

4. Lancashire's mixed farming lowlands

The lowland zone of south central Lancashire, from Preston in the north to Manchester in the south, and the central and eastern portions of the Fylde, were mixed farming regions in which arable land represented between 55 and 62 per cent of the total cultivated area. This fact, which is derived from an examination of feet of fines, suggests a region of mixed husbandry, which is borne out by the study of manorial surveys. At Billington, for example, the substantial freeholders divided their land in 1554 thus: a farm of 140 acres had 60 acres of arable, 40 of pasture, 30 of meadow, and 10 of wood. Another of 68 acres was divided into 20 acres of arable, 20 of pasture, 8 of meadow, and 20 of

[1] Lancs. RO, Probate Invs., passim.

[2] Tupling, op. cit., pp. 75–84; T. Woodcock, 'Haslingden. A Topographical History', Chetham Soc., 3rd Ser. IV, 1952, p. 97.

[3] F. W. Walker, op. cit., pp. 60–1; W. S. Weeks, 'Clitheroe in the Seventeenth Century', Lancs. & Cheshire Antiq. Soc., XLIII, p. 75; VCH Lancs., II, pp. 376–7.

wood. Another of 67 acres had 23 acres of arable, 30 of pasture, 10 of meadow, and 4 of wood. On smaller farms the arable was often in much the same proportion. Tenants-at-will in Billington had no more than 15 acres apiece, but all devoted between a quarter and a half to the plough and the rest was pasture and meadow.[1]

The herd of cattle on the ordinary farm hardly differed from that of the peasant in south-west Lancashire. It consisted usually of cows, calves, and young bullocks—ten was the average number—and the main business lay in selling stores to graziers, although the richer farmers did some fattening, and towards the end of the period some peasants began to turn over to dairying. The region differed from south-west Lancashire in the scale of its other activities. About half the farmers had a sheep flock and sold stores, and the majority bred a few horses, three to four being average. And the arable crops were as varied as in the Midlands. Although oats usually occupied about half the ground and served for bread and malt as well as fodder, the other crops included barley, wheat, beans, peas, vetches, rye, hemp, and flax, ranked roughly in that order of importance.[2]

The size of farms revealed a striking contrast between fielden Lancashire and the fielden country of the Midlands. On most manors a wide gulf yawned between the few large farmers and the multitude of very small men. Billington, already mentioned, affords a good example. The freeholders had large farms of 60 acres and more, whereas none of the customary tenants, although they were five times more numerous, had more than 15 acres apiece. Over half the tenants on the manor of Ulnes Walton in 1614 had between 5 and 20 acres each. Further north, in the Lune valley, the majority of holdings on Hornby manor were no more than 20 acres. And in the lists of property, compiled at death, of peasants inhabiting the regions of mixed husbandry, the usual acreages under crops were less than 8 acres, suggesting yet again that the bulk of holdings were small indeed.[3]

The explanation of this phenomenon calls for much closer investigation than is possible here. But the elements in the situation which seem to be most worthy of investigation are the influence of coalmining upon the economy—it was not often that arable farming was combined with industrial employment as it was in part, at least, of this region—the rights of customary tenants with regard to the subletting and division of holdings, the common custom of inheritance, the rate of

[1] H. B. Rodgers, *op. cit.*, p. 85; Lancs. RO, DD Pt, 22 (Billington Survey 1 and 2 Ph. and M.)

[2] Lancs. RO, Probate Invs., *passim*. See also R. Sharpe France, 'An Inventory of the Goods of John Cuerden of Cuerden, 1601', *Hist. Soc. Lancs. & Cheshire*, XCI, 1939, p. 196.

[3] Lancs. RO, DD Pt, 22 (Billington Survey 1 and 2 Ph. and M.); DDM, 14, 7.

population growth in the sixteenth century through immigration as well as natural increase, and the length of time during which the mixed system of farming had been practised. As the study of other regions has suggested, all these factors were liable to play a part in shaping the pattern of land distribution. And although it may be rash to underline any single aspect more heavily than the rest, we should perhaps stress the subletting and dividing of freeholds and customary holdings, about which there is unusual information. It seems to have been of more significance here than in the fielden country of the Midlands and south. A survey of Penwortham manor in 1570, for example, records much subletting of freeholds to undertenants, while the correspondence concerning an estate in Prescot, in which manorial administration was said to be utterly neglected, illustrates better than any other example yet found how lax manorial control could lead to an excessive subdivision of tenements. The estate at Prescot belonged to King's College, Cambridge, and the earl of Derby was the steward, but the work of administration was in the hands of an underling. He was described in 1583 as an ignoramus, who occupied a copyhold in Prescot, and furthered his own interests by claiming great freedom for his fellows. He cared nothing for the good government of the manor: there were more "lewd tippling houses in Prescot than in all Cambridgeshire;" the town was a refuge of harlots; the tenants took timber at their pleasure, and refused to pay any fines. Neglect, moreover, was evidently an old story: even before Elizabeth's reign the estate had suffered from its steward's inefficiency. In the early part of Henry VIII's reign the Provost of the college had complained to Lord Derby that tenants had been dividing their tenements into several dwellings, selling off land, and building fresh houses on it. In 1592 it was alleged that seventy-six undertenants had taken land in Prescot, "tending much to the impoverishing of the said town besides occasion of divers disorders." And in 1640 the problem of poverty loomed larger still, a great part of the population "living in summer time by digging and winding coals, and in winter time by begging."[1]

So little is known about the amount of subletting in England that it is impossible to say whether this region of Lancashire deserves to be considered as a special case. But by allowing subletting and the subdivision of customary holdings, these townships were following a course that could lead to an uncontrolled rise of population, through

[1] C. W. Sutton, ed., 'A Survey of the Manor of Penwortham, 1570', *Chetham Miscellanies*, NS, III, Chetham Soc., NS, LXXIII, 1915, pp. 7–9; *Selection from Prescot Court Leet and other Records, 1447–1600*, ed., F. A. Bailey, Rec. Soc. Lancs. & Cheshire, LXXXIX, 1937, pp. 283–4, 297–9, 306; F. A. Bailey, 'Early Coalmining in Prescot, Lancashire', *Hist. Soc. Lancs. & Cheshire*, XCIX, 1947, p. 17.

natural increase and immigration. It was a problem with which the pastoral and forest regions were more familiar, and which certainly accounted for the many small farms in those areas. Is it possible that the unusual pattern of land allotment in fielden Lancashire was due to the fact that it had been until recently a pastoral region, and was but newly embarked on a system of mixed farming? Is this a case of a community clinging to customs of land tenure which were only appropriate to another system of farming? South-west Lancashire, after all, was undergoing exactly the same slow transformation of its farming, but was not yet so far advanced upon this road. In the sixteenth century it was still a pasture-farming region, but by the end of the eighteenth century it was a mixed farming area. Since the structure of communities practising pastoral and mixed farming systems was different, it is not difficult to see that a change from one to the other could be accompanied by a prolonged dislocation of the whole structure of society. It is legitimate to interpret the agrarian problem of the east Midlands at this period in this way. And it is not unreasonable to suggest that fielden Lancashire too was in process of adjusting itself, though less painfully, perhaps, to a new agrarian situation.

J. THE EAST MIDLANDS: NOTTINGHAMSHIRE, LEICESTERSHIRE, NORTHAMPTONSHIRE, RUTLAND, AND WARWICKSHIRE

These five counties afford the best examples of the characteristic English landscape, and of the classic common-field system. The villages of Leicestershire, Northamptonshire, and Warwickshire waged the fiercest struggle of all to defend their common fields and slender commons against enclosure in the sixteenth and seventeenth centuries, and were the scene of the Midland Revolt in 1607; many townships in these counties clung to the system of common-field farming until at least the eighteenth century; and Laxton in Nottinghamshire still boasts some of the few surviving common fields in the country.

Much of this region in the Tudor period consisted of fielden country pursuing a mixed husbandry. The whole of the eastern half of Nottinghamshire except the northern carrlands between Hayton and Misterton was of this kind; the whole of Leicestershire excluding Charnwood and Leicester forest; the whole of Rutland excluding the forest in the south-western quarter; half of Northamptonshire excluding the forest and fen areas in the east and north; and the southern half of Warwickshire, south of the Avon, known to contemporaries as the Felden. Nevertheless, other types of countryside which do not accord with the conven-

tional picture of the Midlands occupied at least a third, and possibly
more, of this region. A narrow strip of west Nottinghamshire joins up
with the Peak district of Derbyshire.[1] Northamptonshire and Nottinghamshire both possess small fenny areas in the extreme north of
Northamptonshire, covering most of the soke of Peterborough, and at
the northern end of Nottinghamshire adjoining the Isle of Axholme.[2]
The largest alien region of all, however, consisted of forest country,
and occupied the whole of the northern half of Warwickshire, much
of the western half of Nottinghamshire, parts of west Leicestershire,
the south-western quarter of Rutland, and much of east Northamptonshire. These regions differed sharply from the fielden countryside in
their social structure as well as in their farming.

1. Mixed farming country

The fielden country was managed on much the same farming system
throughout these five counties. Nottinghamshire affords the best
example, for a large part of the eastern half of the county lies on
Keuper Marl soils, which are eminently suited to arable farming. In the
period 1500–1640 its husbandmen usually had a mixed herd of cattle
for breeding and rearing stores; they all bred horses, presumably for
work in the pits of Nottinghamshire and Derbyshire as well as for farm
and town work;[3] they all kept pigs on a considerable scale, to which
were fed some of the large quantities of peas grown in this region;
they also had a good many poultry. Few farmers, however, had more
than thirty sheep and many had none at all. Their arable crops were
varied: wheat, rye, barley, oats, beans, and peas were all grown, but
among the grain crops barley was pre-eminent, as Celia Fiennes observed
in her travels in the later seventeenth century, while peas were often
the largest single crop of all. The probate inventory of William Feilde
of East Markham, clerk, may stand for many farmers throughout the
region. He died in the spring of 1610 and left 5 kine, 7 calves, 8 young
cattle, 7 mares and horses, and 1 foal, 7 pigs, 28 sheep, hens, ducks, and
turkeys, $1\frac{3}{4}$ acres of wheat, $\frac{1}{2}$ rood of rye, $10\frac{1}{4}$ acres of barley, and 19
acres of peas. He had one plough, one great and two small harrows, and
two bound carts. He was fairly well-to-do, for his total goods were
worth £207 16s. 8d.[4]

In the late eighteenth century Robert Lowe, author of the *General*

[1] See *infra*, pp. 102 *sqq.*   [2] See *supra*, pp. 38 *sqq.*

[3] Horse-breeding was still carried on in the eighteenth century.—R. Lowe, *General
View of the Agriculture of Nottinghamshire*, 1794, p. 21.

[4] Cf. also *ibid.*, p. 28; G. E. Fussell, 'Four Centuries of Nottinghamshire Farming',
Notts. Countryside, XVII, 2, 1956, p. 16; York District Probate Registry, Probate
Inventories, D. & C., 1429–1695.

View of Nottinghamshire agriculture, differentiated the parishes lying on either side of the Trent bank from the remainder of east Nottinghamshire. But the differences then and probably also in the sixteenth century did not amount to a different system, but merely showed a slight shift of emphasis: more cattle were fattened in the meadows. In all fielden districts in these counties differences of emphasis were visible, but the system was basically the same.[1]

In Leicestershire and Rutland the chief arable crops were barley and beans, as both counties were "remote from any means of exporting corn." Much of this harvest, together with oats and peas, was fed to stock, which could then walk to market. A mixed herd of 6–9 beasts of all ages, and a flock of about 30 sheep, were usual on the average farm, which comprised some 30 acres of ploughland and 20 of meadow and pasture. The Leicestershire farmer bred horses, like his Nottinghamshire neighbours. He also fattened pigs; hence the lines of William King singing the praises of two of Leicestershire's specialities: "Leicester beans and bacon, food of kings."[2]

Various specialities developed in different parts of these two counties. On the eastern uplands of Leicestershire and in Rutland many farmers kept larger than average flocks of sheep. In the vale of Belvoir they specialized in growing corn for the market, and in the neighbourhood of Market Harborough they fattened beef. But as a generalized summary of the activities of all Leicestershire and Rutland farmers, John Moore's description of Leicestershire in 1653 is accurate enough: "We breed multitudes of hardy men and horses for the service of the Commonwealth if need be; whereby we also send forth abundance of all manner of corn and grain and pease-fed cattle to the city, to victual our shipping at sea and to countries round about us; all fed with the plough in the common fields."[3]

Fielden Warwickshire, in the southern half of that county, also used its large harvest of arable crops (barley, wheat, and peas mainly) to feed stock, breeding and fattening cattle and pigs, and keeping sheep, which were in turn folded on the fields. In the second decade of the seventeenth century some dairying developed, not on the scale on which it was carried on in Arden, but probably with a view to exploiting the same growing markets.[4]

[1] R. Lowe, *op. cit.*, pp. 21 *sqq.*

[2] SP 14, 112, 91; J. Crutchley, *General View of Rutland*, p. 20; CSPD 1619–23, pp. 544–5; W. G. Hoskins, *Essays in Leicestershire History*, pp. 137, 145, 173–7; Leics. Co. RO, Probate Invs., *passim*.

[3] Camden, *Magna Britannia*, IV, p. 589; W. H. Stevenson, 'A Description of Nottinghamshire in the Seventeenth Century', *Trans. Thoroton Soc.*, XI, 1907, p. 120; J. Nichols, *History and Antiquities of the County of Leicester*, IV, i, p. 83.

[4] Worcs. RO, Probate Invs., *passim*.

Except in a few heathy districts in Northamptonshire, where a sheep-corn husbandry was practised, fielden Northamptonshire was managed on the same system. Horse-breeding and pig production were just as considerable. Wheat vied with barley as the chief white corn crop, but peas were the main legume. Larger numbers of sheep were reared and fattened than in the other east Midland counties, however, and this fact caused the justices of the peace to declare in 1620 that wool was Northamptonshire's main cash crop. It is highly doubtful, however, whether anyone could have asserted which was Northamptonshire's principal commodity. Some of the gentry of Northamptonshire at the same period would have said meat. John Morton in the early eighteenth century considered that the county was "of greatest note for grain." In fact, fielden country throughout the kingdom was truly *mixed* farming country; as Norden described Northampton-shire, "it had many and noble sheep pastures, rich feedings for cattle, fertile corn grounds." Except in a small neighbourhood it was difficult to dogmatize about the chief among all the dovetailed branches of farming.[1]

The characteristic community in the fielden country was a nucleated village of not more than about forty families in the mid-sixteenth century, with a squire, who was sometimes resident, several yeomen possessing farms of upwards of 60 acres, more husbandmen with 20–60 acres, while one third of the male population consisted of cottagers and labourers. The latter had little hope of attaining independence by acquiring their own farms; the land in these fielden parishes was already highly cultivated, and there was no waste left. Economic inequality, therefore, was conspicuous: a quarter of the personal wealth of Leicestershire villagers in the early sixteenth century, for example, was vested in the hands of 4 per cent of the population.[2]

The structure of fielden communities in Leicestershire has been made familiar by the writings of Dr Hoskins. In a more detailed study of Wigston Magna, however, he has portrayed a type of village community which was less common in mixed farming regions than in pastoral ones—one which lacked a squire, but included a large number of freeholders. This study illustrates the far-reaching effects upon the class structure and economy of the village, following from the presence of many freeholders and the absence of manorial control, the manorial

[1] SP 14, 113, 21; M. Finch, *The Wealth of Five Northamptonshire Families*, Northants. Rec. Soc., XIX, 1955, *passim;* J. Morton, *The Natural History of Northampton-shire*, pp. 7–15. These conclusions are based on probate inventories of the period 1660–1700, but the accuracy of the generalizations is confirmed in the papers of gentle families, such as those used by Miss Mary Finch.

[2] W. G. Hoskins, *Essays in Leicestershire History*, pp. 126–32, 146.

rights having lapsed when the demesnes were sold to tenants in the later sixteenth and early seventeenth centuries. Immigration caused the population to grow at an exceptional rate. But whereas this led in pastoral regions to the fragmentation of land, here land was consolidated, some large farms developed, but at the cost of an increasing number of landless people. This development, which was exactly contrary to the trend in pastoral areas, where manorial discipline was equally weak and the tenants equally strong, probably reflects the powerful influence of mixed farming in encouraging the growth of the larger farm, as well as the absence of any custom of partible inheritance. But if Wigston was untroubled by small farmers with insufficient land to live on, it was in worse case in possessing a large class that was completely landless. The solution to which its inhabitants came, however, was that familiar already in pastoral regions: in the second half of the seventeenth century they took up framework-knitting.[1]

2. The forests

The forest regions of the east Midlands occupied a substantial proportion of the counties of Nottingham, Rutland, Northampton, and Warwick, as well as part of west Leicestershire, and covered possibly a third of the whole region. It is important, therefore, that in any discussion of the east Midland landscape and of its society, the fielden country should not engross attention.

The essential character of all forest areas was summed up in a brief phrase of Leland referring to Arden Warwickshire: "much enclosed, plentiful of grass, but no great plenty of corn." A summary of the land of Stoneleigh manor in Arden in 1597, giving an example of the way land was distributed between different uses, confirms this verdict. Of the land not in the hands of freeholders, only 37 per cent lay in common fields, 31 per cent was common, 21 per cent woodground, and 9 per cent was held in severalty. This abundance of grazing ground at Stoneleigh was also reflected in the stints of stock. Each yardlander had the right to common 12 beasts, 60 sheep, and 3 horses. In other parts of Arden there were no stints; or, at least, as a custumal of Kingswood tells us, the commoners had the right to common all manner of cattle without stint, but did occasionally, by common consent and "for their own profit," stint themselves.[2]

Although the proportion of arable in Arden townships was small compared with that found in fielden country, it usually lay in common fields, but in a multitude of fields which presented the same disorderly

[1] W. G. Hoskins, The Midland Peasant.
[2] Stratford TSB, Stoneleigh MSS, Survey, 1597; Birmingham Ref. Lib., 379610.

pattern as that characteristic of pastoral regions. And true to type, these arable fields underwent enclosure by agreement without difficulty. In another respect, too, land arrangements in Arden resembled those found in the west Midlands. It was usual for villages to increase their ploughland by occasionally breaking up the common pastures, just as they did in Staffordshire and elsewhere. The parliamentary survey (1649) of Hampton-in-Arden describes the system more precisely. Pasture was broken up for two or three years and then left under grass again for fifteen or twenty years. There were evidently no hard and fast rules.[1]

In the early Tudor period the Arden country was concerned first and foremost with meat production, particularly veal and beef. Some cattle were bred on the farms, but many stores were brought in from outside as well. Remarkable numbers of stores and oxen were in the possession of Arden farmers, a herd of thirty or forty beasts being not unusual. Sheep flocks belonging to the richer farmers were large, but the small peasant kept few sheep in comparison with his herd of cattle: if he had six to eight cattle, he often had less than a dozen sheep. Horses were bred in Arden, as in the other forest districts, and numerous pigs fed on pannage. In the 1590's, however, a gradual shift from beef production to dairying began to take place, and by the 1630's the composition of most farmers' herds had been transformed. This shift in specialization was no passing fancy: by the time Defoe was visiting the district, a regular traffic in cheese was established from Warwickshire along the Trent to Gainsborough and Hull.[2]

Although arable land was more limited in Arden than in fielden Warwickshire, the chief crops were the same: wheat, barley, oats, rye, peas, and vetches, and occasionally flax and hemp. Fruit, particularly apples, began to be mentioned in farmers' lists of property in James I's reign.

In Northamptonshire the forests of Rockingham, Salcey, and Whittlewood lie on a cold, waterlogged clay which is far better suited to grass than crops. Hence, although most townships possessed some common fields, they also had many old enclosures, and their commons were large and usually unstinted. As in Arden, the farming was concerned with the rearing of cattle, sheep, and pigs, and the breeding of horses, and for fodder most reliance was placed on grass and hay.

[1] Warws. RO, Newdegate Coll. C 136, B 1337A; Stratford TSB, Throckmorton MSS, Great Alne, 1550; R. H. Hilton, *The Social Structure of Rural Warwickshire*, Dugdale Soc. Occasional Paper, 9, 1950, pp. 22–5; Birmingham Ref. Lib., 511, 984.
[2] Worcester RO, Probate Invs., *passim;* Warws. RO Newdegate Coll., C 136, B 593; Defoe, *op. cit.,* II, p. 141.

Although little is known about the forest of south-west Rutland, later known as Leighfield forest, it is probable, since it adjoins Rockingham forest, that its husbandry was the same.[1]

Sherwood forest, Nottinghamshire, and Charnwood forest, Leicestershire are singular forest regions for they lie for the most part on sandy, infertile soils, which required different treatment from the heavy clays supporting the other forests of the east Midlands. They could be made serviceable for arable only by the treading and manuring of sheep. One farmer, working this land in Barnby, Sherwood, called it the most barren land in the kingdom, and complained that he was able to grow little more than rye and skegs (*avena stipiformis*) on it. Hence the arable was used for the growing of rye, oats, skegs, and only occasionally barley, and to render it fertile large flocks of sheep were kept. Skegs were grown where nothing else succeeded, and yielded sweet food for horses.[2]

Arable land did not dominate the landscape, however. Much of Sherwood consisted of gorsy heath, cony warrens, and sheepwalks. And because of the absence of any great demand for land, it became the centre of some large parks and stately homes. Nevertheless, some improvement of its commons was under way in the sixteenth century, the procedure being the same as that used in Arden Warwickshire, Staffordshire, and elsewhere: temporary cultivations were sanctioned by the manorial lord; the land was cropped for five or six years usually ending with a crop of skegs, and then left to grass again. In this way some of the waste was slowly but surely improved. In Charnwood the farmer spared himself the arduous task of trying to improve the arable, and accepted the fact that his land was of a "sour, cold, and wild nature," "unfit for corn or sheep pasture but most fit for milch kine and breeding of cattle." Dairying in Charnwood forest is thus an old story.[3]

Large populations of small farmers and an increasing number of immigrants—these were characteristic features of most of the forests in the east Midlands, as they were of the forests in other parts of the kingdom. The region in which the problem of immigrants loomed largest and was most bitterly lamented, however, was the Northamptonshire forests. They lay in a most vulnerable position. The whole county was already considered to be extremely populous, and since the fielden areas had no waste left and were suffering from the worst depopulating enclosures of any in the kingdom, it is not surprising

[1] Northants RO, Probate Invs., *passim*. These relate only to the period after 1660, however.

[2] PRO E 134, 3 Jas. I, Hil. 19; Lowe, *op. cit.*, p. 64.

[3] Lowe, *op. cit.*, p. 9; VCH *Notts.*, I, p. 376; SP 16, 183, 17.

that many folk who were driven thence moved into the neighbouring forests.[1]

Settlements in the Northamptonshire forests usually consisted of nucleated villages, but they were more thinly distributed over the countryside than elsewhere in the county, and their population, judging by the number of householders paying the subsidy in 1524, was larger. This disparity increased in the course of the sixteenth and seventeenth centuries; some villages, indeed, appear to have trebled their size between 1524 and 1670, the rate of growth being greater in the larger open villages than in the smaller ones under the eye of a resident squire.[2]

Complaints about squatters in the forests were voiced on all sides. The wardens of the forest complained of despoilers of the woods who gathered fuel and browse wood and did not hesitate to pull up roots and break down trees in the process. Local property owners bewailed the heavy burden of poor relief, which they carried. In 1623 the lessee of Brigstock Little Park, for example, grumbled about "the continual erecting of new cottages and taking in of new inmates, being at least four score families more in the town of Brigstock in these few years than in any ancient time." Another witness inveighed against freeholders and copyholders who converted stables and barns into dwellings for the poor, and divided houses between two and three families "whereby are raised divers and many unprofitable members of the Commonwealth." Improving landowners resented the "idleness" of their forest tenants, who lived upon their stock of cattle, and wasted their days in sauntering after them. Like the politicians of their day they believed that arable husbandry called for hard work, while pasture farming encouraged loafing.[3]

Restrictions on the building of cottages in the forest were ordered in 1616 and 1620, but they seem to have had little effect. By the time of the Hearth Tax levies the poor who were excused the tax amounted to 44 per cent of the householders in forest townships, whereas the average proportion of paupers in fielden villages was only 35 per cent. How far woodland industries relieved poverty and afforded employment in this period, it is impossible to say. Since Northampton was said to be a centre for stocking-knitting in the early seventeenth century it is more than likely that the knitters were to be found in the Northamptonshire forests. Two other cottage handicraft industries established themselves in the course of the seventeenth century. The weaving of tammies (a

[1] P. A. J. Pettit, *The Economy of the Northamptonshire Royal Forests, 1558–1714*, Oxford D.Phil. thesis, 1959, p. 5.

[2] *Ibid.*, pp. 34–5, 303–7.

[3] *Ibid.*, pp. 269, 308, 370; Northants RO, Westmorland, Apethorpe Coll., 4, XVI, 5.

thin woollen material) and shalloons (a coarse wool stuff) developed into a thriving business in and around Kettering, in the Rockingham forest area, and in Leighfield forest, Rutland, while lace-making (mainly a women's occupation) was carried on in the south-east of Northamptonshire, in Salcey and Whittlewood forests, and in 1698 employed up to a hundred and more workers in some villages. By the eighteenth century other industries were sufficiently important to leave their mark upon the documents: hurdle- and ladder-making, wood-turning, leather-working (with deer skins), and tanning.[1]

In Sherwood Forest, Nottinghamshire, less evidence has so far been found of the immigration of squatters in the sixteenth century. Yet the county as a whole was vexed with the familiar problem of finding a home for those dispossessed by enclosure, and the justices of the peace who explained the dilemma in 1631, without specifying the districts to which the landless population was migrating, may well have had the forest in mind.

"When houses are pulled down the people are forced to seek new habitation in other towns and countries, by means whereof those towns where they get a settling are pestered so as they are hardly able to live one by another, and it is likewise the cause of erecting new cottages upon the waste and other places who are not able to relieve themselves nor any such towns able to sustain them or set them on work which causes rogues and vagabonds to increase."[2]

The class structure of the Sherwood forest townships remains to be investigated, but its economy was one in which a handicraft—stocking-knitting—already played a part. It was, indeed, no accident that the inventor of the stocking frame, which later revolutionized the hosiery industry, William Lee, came from Woodborough and Calverton in Sherwood.

Although no study of Arden Warwickshire has yet been made for the sixteenth century, a valuable account of its social structure in the Middle Ages has already revealed the large population of freeholders and the weakness of manorial control in the thirteenth century. The forest was settled late: colonization had hardly begun before the twelfth century, and when it did it was undertaken by individuals who in return for their pioneering labours received their land as freeholds. Hence by the third quarter of the thirteenth century half the tenants in one sample hundred in Arden—Stoneleigh—were free tenants, compared with 30 per cent in a neighbouring fielden hundred, 27 per cent were villeins or serfs, compared with 46 per cent in the fielden, and 23 per cent were small-holders. The weight of labour services,

---

[1] See *supra*, pp. 12–13; Pettit, *op. cit.*, pp. 309, 310, 345–9; VCH *Northants.*, II, pp. 333, 337; VCH *Rutland*, I, p. 237.   [2] SP 16, 185, 86.

TAH

moreover, rested far more lightly on the villeins in this forest area than on bond tenants dwelling in the fielden country.[1]

Here then we catch a glimpse of the relative freedom of forest folk at an earlier age. Undoubtedly tenurial freedom had an influence upon the distribution of holdings and the rate of population growth in subsequent centuries. Yet another factor that must be considered alongside is the custom of inheritance, for in Arden Warwickshire, and also, it should be added, in the Northamptonshire forests, we come again upon the custom of Borough English.[2]

The history of settlement in Charnwood and Leicester forests seems to have differed from others in the east Midlands for another reason. They were not for long royal forests; both were in private hands during most of the Middle Ages and neither was ever made subject to forest law. It is significant, therefore, that neither of these forests seems to have been plagued with squatters during the Tudor period; no complaints have survived in the records, and such information as we have about the population of the forest villages suggests that none was justified. In other respects the fortunes of Charnwood and Leicester forest diverged. Charnwood remained a well-wooded district until the late seventeenth century, while Leicester forest had suffered such depredations by the beginning of the sixteenth century that a survey of 1523, painting a dismal picture of neglect, precipitated a decision to enclose the northern half of the forest in 1526. Pressure on the remaining commons grew in consequence—the forest was, of course, very near Leicester—and in 1626 when it was recognized that the king's reserves could no longer be satisfactorily guarded, disafforestation of the remainder took place.[3]

Here then are two forest areas in the east Midlands which, because of their singular experience, suggest a possible reason for the common trend of settlement history in the other forests. We know nothing yet about the class structure of the Leicestershire forest villages. The unique element in the situation, so far as we understand it at present, was the fact that the forests were in the hands of lay lords and that neither had at any time suffered the severe restrictions imposed by royal forest law. We have already had cause to suspect that the large reserves of land, particularly the ample commons in areas of royal forest, were due to the obstacles placed in the way of settlement and colonization in the Middle Ages. Did the absence of forest law in the Leicestershire forests permit more settlement in the thirteenth century and thus make the

[1] R. H. Hilton, op. cit., pp. 12, 15–17.

[2] See supra, p. 11; Stratford TSB, Throckmorton MSS, Customs of Sambourne, 1583; Birmingham Ref. Lib. MS 379610.

[3] VCH Leics., II, pp. 265 sqq.; Levi Fox and Percy Russell, Leicester Forest, passim.

forest less attractive in the sixteenth? Or did the owners of the forests in the sixteenth century exert such careful control that they deterred squatters? Or were other factors, not considered here, more relevant?

K. THE WEST MIDLANDS: HEREFORDSHIRE, SHROPSHIRE, STAFFORDSHIRE, WORCESTERSHIRE, AND DERBYSHIRE

In no region of England is the historian so keenly aware of the changes wrought by man in the last three or four hundred years upon the condition of agricultural land as in the west Midlands. Large areas of the counties of Derbyshire, Staffordshire, Shropshire, Worcestershire, and Herefordshire had once been covered by forest: many were still in a semi-cleared state in the sixteenth century, affording spacious commons and waste to their inhabitants and also attracting many landless immigrants. Although efforts were being made to bring new land under the plough and to improve fertility by marling and liming, they brought small returns for many years. In short, much of the present-day fertility of west Midland farms and market gardens was built up slowly between the sixteenth and twentieth centuries under the stimulus of a growing population of industrial workers in towns and villages of the region.[1]

Although the west Midlands probably possessed larger tracts of fielden country than any other region in the highland half of England, pasture and woodland, nevertheless, dominated the landscape. Shropshire was described by a member of the Commons in 1597 as a county consisting wholly of woodland, "bred of oxen, and dairies." Staffordshire was described by the justices of the peace in 1636 as "for the most part barren, one fourth being heath and waste, and another fourth being chases and parks." Derbyshire was said to produce little grain except oats and to be unable to feed more than half the population with hardcorn grown in the county. The surveyors of ecclesiastical land in Worcestershire and Herefordshire in the mid-seventeenth century found themselves using certain descriptive phrases with monotonous regularity, so much of the land being "barren, bushy, or broomy pasture," "bad pasture," "barren meadow," "barren arable on the hillside," or "heathy, barren ground upon rock."[2]

---

[1] Cf. *Land Classification in the West Midland Region, A Publication of the West Midland Group on Post-War Reconstruction and Planning*, 1947, p. 33.

[2] A. F. Pollard and M. Blatcher, 'Hayward Townshend's Journals', *Bull.* IHR, XII, 16; CSPD 1636–7, p. 408; PRO SP 14, 113, 17; *The Parliamentary Survey of the Lands and Possessions of the Dean and Chapter of Worcester, 1649*, Worcs. Hist. Soc., 1924, *passim;* Lambeth Palace Library, MS 911, ff. 11, 19.

At the same time a rising population made it necessary to extend the acreage of arable, meadow, and good pasture, and efforts in this direction were continuously changing the local landscape. Indeed, so much had been done to improve land for corn-growing in Herefordshire that it and the counties adjoining (presumably Worcestershire and Gloucestershire) were described in 1597 as "the barns for the corn." An enquiry into the progress of enclosure in High Peak hundred in Derbyshire in 1631 elicited the reply that enclosure was negligible, the people showing "rather a general desire and daily endeavour to increase tillage." In Staffordshire pressure on the arable was being relieved by ploughing up parts of the commons for two, three, five, or even eight years together, and then allowing these plots to revert to common and ploughing up another part. The decision to plough was a matter of agreement between the inhabitants and the manorial lord, and seems to have been reached amicably, even eagerly, by both parties. Eventually, of course, these temporary cultivations were liable to become permanent, but at this period most were not; they acted as a safety valve ensuring an adequate supply of arable as population rose, and at the same time preparing the land for the more regular routine of cultivation by alternate husbandry. In central Staffordshire it is likely that a substantial increase in the arable acreage resulted from this practice. Nor was it confined to Staffordshire: there are hints of the custom in Derbyshire, as well as in some east Midland and southern counties. In any account of the gradual increase of corn production in the period 1500–1640, the temporary, shifting cultivation of commons must be accorded a place.[1]

Further evidence of the zeal for land improvement is contained in leases insisting on the proper manuring of land before corn was sown, as at Bishops Frome in Herefordshire, in leases providing for the clearance of woodland to make new pasture and meadow, as at Kilpeck in Herefordshire, and in descriptions of common pasture promoted for use as meadow, as at Mayfield on the fringe of the Pennines in north-east Staffordshire. But the most notable enterprise was that of Rowland Vaughan of New Court in the Golden valley, Herefordshire, who in 1610 publicized the virtues of floated water meadows in a book entitled *The Most Approved and Long Experienced Water Workes, containing the Manner of Winter and Summer Drowning of Meadow and Pasture.*

[1] Pollard and Blatcher, *op. cit.*, p. 16; VCH *Derbys.* II, p. 173; Staffs. RO, D 260, Box A (f); Plot, *Natural History of Staffordshire*, 1686, p. 343; PRO E 134, 39 and 40 Eliz., M 21; E 134, 34 Chas. II, Mich. 10; E 134, 10 Chas. I, E 47; G. E. Fussell, 'Four Centuries of Farming Systems in Derbyshire, 1500–1900', *Derbyshire Arch. & Nat. Hist. Soc.*, LXXI, 1951, p. 27. See also E. L. Jones, 'Eighteenth-century Changes in Hampshire Chalkland Farming', AHR, VIII, 1960, p. 13.

Vaughan's technique enabled him to graze his mowing meadows till the 1st of May, and keep 300 kine, 300 young cattle, and 3,000 sheep all winter and summer, thus yielding a plentiful supply of cheese, butter, and meat for the market.[1]

The west Midland counties possessed regions of all three types—forest, open pasture, and fielden—and all yielded examples of commonable fields as well as enclosures. The differences lay in the size of the common fields and the intensity with which they were cultivated. The hamlets in the remote moorlands of the Pennines and the Welsh border frequently possessed only one commonable field, small in size. In the lowland pastoral areas and in the woodland the fields were larger, and often numerous, but the closes also were numerous. Enclosure was a relatively easy matter for the attitude of society was favourable to it. And since people were willing to promote this improvement, they were also willing to accept some eccentric arrangements for maintaining a good supply of common grazing. At Alrewas, Staffordshire, for example, some of the closes of the freeholders were enclosed all the year round, while some were thrown open at Michaelmas. Other townships reached peaceful agreements to enclose on terms that would have raised a riot in the east Midlands. The tenants of Salt and Enson in Staffordshire decided in 1585 to make some of the town fields several throughout the year, "as well winter and summer," and recorded this decision in the manorial court roll. At one fell blow, therefore, they extinguished all common rights and so removed all obstacles to enclosure. Shropshire records are full of agreements between individuals to exchange strips in the common fields as a preliminary to consolidation and enclosure, and of agreements in the manorial court for individuals or groups to enclose parts of the commons. Frequently the agreement was accompanied by a note emphasizing that the closes injured no one.[2]

In the fielden districts of the west Midlands the difficulties attending enclosure were much greater than in the pastoral. But even so the

[1] Nat. Lib. Wales, Kentchurch Court Coll., 320; Pye of the Mynd Coll., 73; *Elizabethan Chancery Proceedings, Series II, 1558–79*, Staffs. Rec. Soc., 1938, p. 143; *Rowland Vaughan, His Booke*, ed. E. B. Wood, 1897, pp. 127, 76, 78.

[2] J. C. Jackson, *A Geographical Study of Open-Field Cultivation in Derbyshire with Special Reference to the Problem of Ridge and Furrow*, Leicester Univ. M.A. thesis, 1959, ch. VIII; PRO E 134, 14 Jas. I, M. 13; William Salt Lib., Stafford, Hand Morgan Coll., Chetwynd MSS, Great Court of Salt and Ingestre Manor 1585; William Salt Lib. D 1788, P 38, B 12; D 1788, P 39, B 8; Aqualate Coll., D 1788, P 58, B 1 Court of Sutton Magna 10 Oct. 1610; Nat. Lib. Wales, Pitchford Hall Coll. (for Shropshire), 2434; 901; for Staffs., see also Staffs RO, D 260, M Box 166; and for Herefordshire, Hereford City Library, LC Deeds 5887. For medieval and later enclosure in Derbyshire, see VCH *Derbys.* II, pp. 170–5.

subject did not arouse as much passion as in the east Midlands. Something of the sweetly reasonable attitude of pastoral and woodland communities towards the problem infected the fielden country too. The principle laid down in the Statute of Merton of 1236, that manorial lords could improve the waste so long as they left enough commons for their free tenants, still commanded assent in the sixteenth century. It persuaded communities to sanction in the manorial court enclosure which did not deprive others of valuable common rights, while accepting without deep rancour a prohibition upon enclosures which did. Many townships reached agreements to enclose. But at the same time many common fields awaited enclosure in the eighteenth century.

1. *Pastoral moorland and lowland*

The pastoral districts differed greatly in situation: some lay in lowland areas such as central Staffordshire where a tenacious soil thwarted the plough; some lay at heights of 800 and even 1,000 feet soaked by heavy rains, like the acid, Millstone Grit moorlands of the Derbyshire Peak and north-east Staffordshire, and the hill country of the Welsh border. All these regions were concerned mainly with the production of cattle and sheep, but they varied in the emphasis they placed on each, and in the amount of arable land they possessed for growing domestic corn and arable fodder crops. On the moorlands around Leek, for example, conditions were graphically described by the clergy who submitted corn acreage returns in 1801: a late cold climate, it was pointed out, was "but ill calculated by nature for the production of grain, excepting oats, and those of an inferior sort, being chiefly black." The daily bread of the inhabitants, in consequence, was oatcake. In the sixteenth and early seventeenth centuries this was a region producing store sheep and cattle: it was not uncommon for farms to carry large flocks of three to six hundred sheep, together with a breeding herd of a dozen cows and followers. The cornfields were small and grew little more than oats. In the Peak district of north-west Derbyshire next door the conditions were much the same, and large breeding flocks were kept for the making of ewes' milk cheese.[1]

The lowland pastoral districts were more specialized cattle-breeding and feeding areas, selling some of their stores to graziers in eastern and southern England, but fattening some themselves to supply to butchers in local markets. One such region was central Staffordshire, a country of strong clay and clay-loam soils, difficult to work. It carried relatively

[1] R. A. Pelham, 'The 1801 Crop Returns for Staffordshire in their Geographical Setting', *Staffs. Rec. Soc.*, 1950 and 1951, p. 237; Probate Invs., *passim;* Fussell, 'Farming in Derbyshire', pp. 3–4; Sheffield Central Library, Beauchief Coll. 684-2.

few sheep; its pigs were not as numerous as in the forests; but its fields displayed goodly herds of breeding and fat cattle. And farmers who did not breed all their own replacements could obtain stores from the moorland districts, and from the Welsh drovers who passed through the county. A complaint about thirty-five oxen and kine, which were driven by Welsh drovers as far as Heywood to rest for the night, and which ate up all the corn in the fields, shows this traffic thronging the roads in the reign of Henry VIII. Later on central Staffordshire was to become a noted dairying region, but the economic attractions of cheese and butter production were slower to manifest themselves here than elsewhere, possibly because of the satisfactory links already established with graziers and butchers. Indeed, this may be inferred from Gervase Markham's statement that cattle bred in Staffordshire and Derbyshire were among the best in England.[1]

In Derbyshire the stock-rearing, cattle-feeding region lay in the central sector of the county. The Dove valley, praised by Norden, and the Derwent valley were the celebrated feeding grounds, but many farms in the region supported large sheep flocks as well as bullocks.[2]

In Herefordshire the graziers and dairymen were most conspicuous in the river valleys, which afforded lush meadows and a good supply of early grass. Rowland Vaughan's achievements in both fattening and dairying in the Golden valley were well publicized, but he was not unique in his interest in dairying. The whole hundred of Ewyas Lacy, in the Black Mountains rising up on the west side of the Golden valley, was described in 1623 as a country consisting more in dairies than tillage.[3]

Another region which began to show an increasing interest in the dairying business by the beginning of the seventeenth century was north Shropshire, between Oswestry and Woore, while the same development is evident in the north-eastern corner of Worcestershire adjoining Arden Warwickshire. The trend is illustrated in the inventories of two farmers of Alvechurch, Worcestershire. Walter Newman, who died in 1596, left among other things 14 kine, 3 calves, 6 young cattle, 9 pigs, and 80 cheeses. John Anger left in August 1598 14 kine, 5 calves, 1 yearling, 1 yoke of oxen, 1 bull, 6 pigs, and 208 cheeses.[4]

[1] Lichfield Joint RO, Probate Invs., *passim;* W. K. Boyd, *Staffordshire Suits in the Court of Star Chamber, temp. Hen. VII & Hen. VIII,* William Salt Arch. Soc., 1907, NS, x, p. 104; G. E. Fussell, *op. cit.,* p. 9.

[2] Lichfield Joint RO, Probate Invs., *passim;* G. E. Fussell, *op. cit.,* p. 9.

[3] SP 14, 140, 25 (II).

[4] This was the region in which dairying was well established by the late eighteenth century. (For the sake of clarity it is depicted on the map of farming regions in England (p. 4) as a wholly dairying region.) See G. E. Fussell, 'Four Centuries of Farming Systems in Shropshire, 1500–1900', *Salop. Archaeolog. Soc.,* LIV, 1951–2, p. 13; Worcs. RO, Probate Invs., Worcester Diocese, 1598, 10 and 62.

All these pastoral areas had a certain amount of arable land. Its quantity and the variety of crops grown depended on geographical situation. In the Pennine foothills oats were almost the only crop and the ploughland was meagre. In central Staffordshire, on the other hand, the arable fields were large and growing larger; and wheat, barley, peas, oats, and rye were grown. In Shropshire, where even in 1801 descriptions of the corn harvest of individual parishes do not suggest anything but low yields, the arable crops included rye, oats, peas, barley, vetches, and wheat, roughly in that order of importance. That rye was the principal crop in Shropshire is confirmed by the observation of Celia Fiennes, who ate rye bread on her travels through the county. It also explains why on occasion land was measured by the amount of rye necessary to sow an acre.[1]

2. *The forests*

Although it is impossible without detailed local studies to estimate the total area of woodland in these five counties, it is likely that in some counties such as Shropshire and possibly Derbyshire it equalled or exceeded the area of open grassland country. Shropshire's forests included Morfe forest, "of large extent," according to Mr Treswell's survey in 1621, together with the forests of Clun, Clee, Hayes, Worthen, Alberbury, and Westbury. In Staffordshire lay the forests of Cannock, Kinver, and Needwood; in Worcestershire Feckenham and Wyre, the latter lying partly in Shropshire also; in Derbyshire lay Duffield forest; in Herefordshire Deerfold, Aconbury, Ewyas, and Haywood.[2]

All these wooded districts were concerned, like the more open pastoral areas and moorlands, with the production of animals, and all afforded their inhabitants generous common rights. Often the grazing of cattle, sheep, and horses was unstinted, while pannage rights permitted the keeping of large numbers of pigs, as, for example, in central Shropshire, where the foundation of Shropshire's pig fattening industry in the nineteenth century was laid, and in Needwood forest in Stafford-

[1] Philip Dodd, 'State of Agriculture in Shropshire, 1775–1825', *Shropshire Arch. & Nat. Hist. Soc.*, LV, 1954, pp. 3–4; Fussell, *op. cit.*, p. 7; Salop RO, 167, 43.

[2] PRO SP 14, 122, 114; *Transcr.* Rev. R. C. Purton, 'A Description of ye Clee', *Shropshire Arch. & Nat. Hist. Soc.*, Ser. 2, VIII, 1896, pp. 195–9; Salop RO, 837, 56; J. Duncumb, *Collections towards the History and Antiquities of the County of Hereford*, I, 1804, p. 205. Only the Staffordshire forests and Feckenham forest, Worcestershire, are included on the map of farming regions (p. 4), since it has not been possible to determine the boundaries of the others.

shire. Horse-breeding supplemented cattle and pig production in some places, such as Cannock Chase, and villages like Penkridge and Brewood acquired some fame as horse fairs.[1]

3. Mixed farming districts

The areas of fielden country in the west Midlands, where the arable land was more extensive and arable crops more important, lay in scattered pockets all over the region. In Derbyshire they lay in the north-east, bordering upon Sherwood forest, and in the south in the Trent valley sandwiched between similar districts in south-east Staffordshire and north-west Leicestershire. Another lay in the south-west corner of Staffordshire, linked with the adjacent district in south-east Shropshire. Yet other regions of mixed husbandry lay in Worcestershire, on the light sandy soils in the north, in the vale of Evesham, and in the Severn valley, both the last two being also fruit-growing districts. The largest corn-growing area of all, however, lay in Herefordshire. This county has been described recently as having "the highest proportion and largest absolute area of first class land of any of the West Midland counties." And this was evidently recognized already in the Tudor period.[2]

Most districts of mixed husbandry depended on the sheepfold for maintaining fertility. And like the fielden country of the east Midlands, the large common fields, intensively cultivated, existed alongside attenuated common pastures, which had to be carefully stinted. At Naunton Beauchamp, Worcestershire, for example, there were two common fields in 1617 managed on a four-course rotation including one year fallow. The cattle were stinted, and for each yardland men were allowed to graze 5 horses, 8 beasts, and 40 sheep. The varied crops of these vale lands are indicated in the probate inventories of individual farmers. One farm at Bretforton, Worcestershire, in July 1598 had 24 acres of wheat and rye, 32 of barley, and 26 of beans, peas, and vetches. Another at Church Honeybourne in March 1592 had 18 acres of wheat, 20 of barley, and 15 of pulse. On John Gilbert's farm at Pershore, the large barley crop, valued at £80 in July 1617, owed much no doubt to the 122 Welsh sheep and 120 other sheep that belonged to the same farm.[3]

[1] Shrewsbury Public Library, MSS. 5384, 2491; Salop RO 167, 43; PRO C 2 Eliz. A 8, 58; G. E. Fussell, 'Shropshire Farming', p. 14; PRO E 134, 41 Eliz., E 7; Staffs. RO, D 590, 435, 1, 2.

[2] *Land Classification in the West Midland Region*, p. 40; Pollard and Blatcher, *op. cit.*, p. 16.

[3] Worcs. RO, Glebe terriers of Naunton Beauchamp; Probate Invs. *passim*.

The different crops varied in importance in different districts. In Derbyshire oats and peas occupied the most ground; in south-east and south-west Staffordshire pride of place was given to barley and rye, in Shropshire to rye and oats. But it is doubtful whether any of the arable crops left much surplus for sale outside the counties or smaller marketing regions in which they were grown. Some counties, like Derbyshire, did not even grow enough to satisfy their own demand for bread-corn and beer. Others, which were less dependent on imported domestic corn, needed all the rest of their arable crops for rearing and fattening their stock. The only county in the west Midlands which may have had a surplus was Herefordshire. Its corn-cattle husbandry drew fulsome praise from contemporaries such as Camden, and his short phrase summing up the county as "fruitful for corn and cattle feeding" is confirmed in the less graceful language of leases and probate inventories. Rents were often paid partly in wheat, oats, and rye, in the Tudor period; and men's crops listed at their death after the Restoration (there are no surviving probate inventories for the earlier period) show that 40–50 acres of arable crops on a farm were not uncommon. A farm on the river Wye at Preston in 1660, for example, had 20 acres of oats, 17 of rye, 5 of wheat, 5 of peas, and 1 acre of barley. In addition many farms grew fruit and hops. The scale of business is indicated in the generous buildings accommodating these varied undertakings on the larger farm. The demesne farm of Buttas Manor in the parishes of King's Pyon and Canon Pyon in 1623 possessed "a large new frame of buildings," including a dairyhouse, kilnhouse, storehouse, six lofts well boarded for malting and other uses, a fair stable with chambers over, of which two were glazed and ceiled, a new tiled barn, and one other large barn, a large beasthouse, a large sheepcot, a swinehouse, and a good pigeon house of stone. The farm included a hopyard with six thousand poles.[1]

Differences in the pattern of settlement between pastoral, woodland, and fielden communities have already been emphasized. The pastoral and woodland communities favoured small hamlets and scattered homesteads, the fielden communities favoured nucleated villages. But every region exhibited some examples of every type.[2]

The density of population calls for more detailed local investigation. Many of the fielden regions were, of course, already fairly densely

[1] J. N. Jackson, 'Some Observations upon the Herefordshire Environment of the Seventeenth and Eighteenth Centuries', *Trans. Woolhope Naturalists' Field Club*, XXXVI, 1958, p. 28; Hereford D. & C. Lib., 3 E; Hereford City Library, LC Deeds 6129 (1).

[2] Cf. Dorothy Sylvester, 'Rural Habitation in Shropshire'. *Report of the Proc. of the International Geog. Congress, Cambridge, 1928*, 1930, p. 364.

settled in Domesday times, and since they were the most attractive agriculturally, medieval pestilences had had no lasting effect in depopulating them. The most thinly settled regions in the sixteenth century were the high moorlands, on the edge of the Pennines for example, and on the Welsh border. But even here the population was rising; commons were being steadily encroached upon and improved; cottages grew like mushrooms on the waste. The standard of living enjoyed by yeoman and husbandman in these less congenial districts was lower than that of his counterpart in fielden country, but at the same time such communities had fewer poor. The parishes of northeast Staffordshire, for example, had a smaller proportion of paupers at the time of the Hearth Tax levy in 1665 than either the forest or fielden areas of the county.[1]

Pastoral districts in the lowlands were more congested than the pastoral highlands and their problems are reflected in new regulations stinting animals on the common grazing, and in the diligent efforts given to the ploughing up of common to make additional cornland. But the region which had to support not only its own increasing numbers but an army of immigrants from elsewhere were the woodlands. Their immediately obvious attraction was their unstinted commons, and the many opportunities they offered for obtaining work in woodland industries, in lead-mining, as in the Derbyshire Peak, in iron-mining, and alabaster digging, as in the Staffordshire forests, and in coalmining, as in Duffield Forest, Derbyshire.[2]

An equally influential factor, as we have seen earlier, was the strength of the freeholders and the corresponding weakness of manorial lords in checking the influx of landless squatters into the forests. The freeholders owed their numerical strength to the methods by which woodland had been colonized in the Middle Ages. Pioneer settlers had received land on attractive terms. In the sixteenth century these freeholders met the housing shortage by building cottages on their land to let for rent. This development can be observed in Deerfold forest, Herefordshire, at the end of Elizabeth's reign when common rights were still unstinted. Not surprisingly, we find inhabitants betraying some alarm by 1640 at the heavy burden of poor they carried. They blamed the poverty of their cottagers on the large-scale felling of timber to meet the demands of the iron-smelting industry, which

[1] See H. C. Darby and I. B. Terrett, eds., *The Domesday Geography of Midland England, passim;* Birmingham Ref. Lib., Norton Coll. 309, 310. The calculation of pauperism is based on the Hearth Tax returns of sample townships. The returns are in W. N. Landor, *Staffordshire Incumbents and Parochial Records, 1530–1680, Staffs. Hist. Coll.,* 1915.

[2] W. Salt Lib., Hand Morgan Coll., Penkridge 1, 11; VCH *Derbys.,* II, p. 178; PRO E 178, 4533; Staffs. RO, D 240, M. Section C, bundle AA1.

deprived the community of many sources of employment. But judging by the experience of other forest areas at this time, we may guess that this was not the only cause of the trouble. When the enclosure of Deerfold forest was being negotiated with the owner, Lord Craven, in 1640 and 1663, the commoners constituted a large, powerful, and vociferous group. "They do absolutely insist," says a resolution of 1663, "on an allotment of 782 acres."[1]

In fielden areas the problem of poverty was due to other causes, to the natural increase of population and to engrossing, which reduced the number of holdings at the moment when an increase was urgently necessary. Complaints from the fielden country in the west Midlands, of course, were less shrill than in the east, for it covered a relatively small area when compared with the woodland and pasture. Hereford-shire, however, is an interesting exception, for it was a considerable corn-growing county. Yet its poor appear to have been unusually numerous. "For so small a circuit as this shire contains," declared the county sheriff in 1637, "there are not in the kingdom a greater number of poor people." And Rowland Vaughan echoed this complaint in his description of the Dore valley, which for lack of employment, he alleged, had the largest number of poor in the realm. Other evidence shows the presence in the county of many rich farmers with substantial houses, enjoying a high standard of living. Here, then, we see the problem of the poor in mixed farming country where corn-growing encouraged consolidation and engrossing by large farmers while allowing the poor commoner only a precarious foothold on the land. It was aggravated in some parts of the county, moreover, by the tenacity with which the inhabitants clung to the customs and institu-tions of their Welsh neighbours, for time had not obliterated all traces of Herefordshire's Welsh associations. Archenfield district around Ross and Llanwarne was a district of mixed husbandry, yet its land was still subject to gavelkind tenure, and this tenure persisted into the nineteenth century. In pastoral districts, as we have noticed elsewhere, the custom was liable to produce economic difficulties. It was worse still in a comparatively highly cultivated arable district, for partible inheri-tance multiplied population while the farming allowed no scope for an increase in the number of holdings.[2]

In the pastoral districts of south-west Herefordshire we have further

[1] Cf. R. H. Hilton, *op. cit.*, p. 12; Hereford City Lib., LC Deeds 5887; 5779A; 5571. For the poor in Duffield forest, see VCH *Derbys.*, I, p. 419. For the large popula-tions in the mining areas of Wirksworth, High Peak, and Scarsdale Hundreds in 1635 (65 per cent of all the men in the county), *see* VCH *Derbys.*, II, p. 184.

[2] CSPD 1636–7, p. 415; Rowland Vaughan, *op. cit.*, p. 30; Hereford City Library, LC Deeds 3144; Nat. Library of Wales, Pye of the Mynd Coll., 223; John Duncumb, *General View of the Agriculture of the County of Hereford*, 1805, p. 24.

cause to suspect the survival of gavelkind—in the hundred of Ewyas Lacy, for example, possibly even in Rowland Vaughan's Golden valley, where unemployment was so pressing a problem as to drive Vaughan to take practical steps to solve it. "For want of employment," he had written, the valley was "the plentifullest place of poor in the kingdom, yielding two or three-hundred fold, the number so increasing (idleness having gotten the upper hand) if trades be not raised, beggary will carry such reputation in my quarter of the country as if it had the whole to halves." The solution, as he shrewdly resolved, lay in finding alternative trades. He set up a commonwealth of traders in the valley, gathering together not only brewers, maltsters, bakers, cooks, etc., but handicraft workers such as hosiers, stocking-knitters, weavers, and glove-makers. Within a short time he had attracted two thousand "mechanicals" into the fold.[1]

As a partial explanation of Herefordshire's many poor, therefore, we must bear in mind that specialization in corn-growing encouraged the growth of larger farming enterprises and tended increasingly to drive out the poor commoners. In these circumstances survival of gavelkind in some parts was anomalous. Gavelkind may have been an irritant in some pastoral areas as well, though this requires further investigation. Refuge for the poor was to be found in the forest and pastoral regions, but these were not as extensive in Herefordshire as in other counties of the west Midlands, nor had they as much to offer. The county lacked secondary employments. It had no mineral industries apart from iron-mining in the forest of Dean, and most of this forest lies in Gloucestershire. It had no domestic handicrafts until glove-making made its appearance some time in the seventeenth century. It is not impertinent to ask whether this industry established itself in direct answer to this pressing social problem.[2]

L. CONCLUSION

The contrast between the communities of mixed and pasture-farming is the main general conclusion to be drawn from this examination of farming regions, and it needs no further emphasis by way of conclusion. Its significance, however, calls for further comment.

It is clear that within these two broad categories, some subdivision of the pasture-farming communities is necessary to distinguish between the open pastoral and the forest communities, for the latter, particularly those inhabiting royal forests, who had been subject until recently to

[1] Vaughan, op. cit., pp. 30, xv–xvi.
[2] J. N. Jackson, op. cit., p. 32.

forest law, possessed unique features. They had rewarding land awaiting colonization; they alone among all the regions of the kingdom offered the greatest opportunities to the land-hungry. And in the more densely populated lowlands, these were the only regions in a position to absorb immigrants.

By examining farming communities at a period when men were unusually zealous to improve their conditions, we are in an exceptionally good position for observing changes under way. It becomes apparent, then, that all three types of community, whether they inhabited forest, open pasture, or mixed farming country, were liable to change their nature. A forest economy could easily give way to a pastoral when once restrictions were lifted on the felling of trees. This in its turn did not necessarily remain a permanent state of affairs. Periodic ploughing of the pasture, as it was practised in the west Midland counties and elsewhere, prepared the land for more permanent cultivation, and in the course of generations such improvements could result in the enlargement of the arable until ploughland and pasture were more evenly balanced and a system of mixed farming evolved.

Indeed, the fact that such changes were in progress has occasionally made it difficult in this narrative to define the frontier between the three types of farming, to differentiate between the forest regions with their spacious commons and lavish timber rights, and the more open pastoral regions with their abundant commons and shrinking woodland, to differentiate between the more fertile pastoral lowlands with a disposition steadily to increase their arable, and the fielden areas which still had pastures awaiting conversion to cornland. In some places, such as the Severn valley, for example, which possessed lush meadows for feeding cattle as well as fertile fields and orchards, only local investigation in detail could establish with certainty in which category this region belongs.

Not all regions, of course, were capable of passing through these three phases of development; some were prevented by physical limitations, some were not impelled to do so owing to the absence of population pressure. But certain districts in the west Midland counties and the south and central lowlands of Lancashire afford excellent examples at this period of communities in process of transforming their land from forest to open pasture, and from open pasture to mixed arable and pasture, while the counties of the east Midlands show that this was not necessarily the end of the process. Economic circumstances could persuade communities to embark on yet another revolution, and turn their land back from mixed to pasture-farming. In counties like Northamptonshire and Leicestershire this change began in the sixteenth century. In other districts it was postponed until the later nineteenth century.

In what circumstances, and at what period, then, did these changes generate tension and cause the worst conflict? This is a question which has hardly been asked as yet. But it is clearly a valid one if we accept the proposition that certain kinds of farming specialization were associated with certain kinds of social organization. Signs of strain would be almost inevitable as the economy of the community underwent fundamental alteration and its long-standing institutions no longer fitted the new framework. Possibly this explains the large populations and onerous poverty of parts of Herefordshire, where specialization in corn-growing was at odds with some of the social institutions appropriate to pasture-farming. The outcry against enclosure in the east Midlands, similarly, must be considered in the light of the fact that its corn-growing economy—so completely in harmony with its highly manorialized society—could not but be disturbed by the change to pasture-farming.

That contemporaries were aware of the distinction between the two types of community and the two kinds of farming is a conclusion difficult to avoid. 'Woodland' and 'champion' were the terms commonly used to contrast them, 'the woodland' describing the forest or pastoral country, the 'champion' describing the countryside of mixed farming in common fields. Suffolk was deemed a county "of two several conditions of soil, the one champion, which yields for the most part sheep and some corn, the other enclosed pasture grounds employed most to grazing and dairy." Norfolk's two regions, and the Arden and Felden regions of Warwickshire were contrasted in similar terms.[1]

Contemporary comment, however, was not confined to contrasting the physical appearance and the farming of the two kinds of country. The contrasting temperament of the peoples inhabiting each also seems to have been familiar to sixteenth-century writers. As Norden explained it: "the people bred amongst woods are naturally more stubborn and uncivil than in the champion countries." John Aubrey described the woodlanders as "the mean people [who] live lawless, nobody to govern them, they care for nobody, having no dependence on anybody." Lord Burghley also alluded to the phenomenon when he declared that the clothworkers, most of whom, after all, were inhabitants of pastoral and woodland country, were "of worse condition to be quietly governed than the husbandmen."[2]

[1] John Leland, *Itinerary in England*, ed. L. Toulmin Smith, II, p. 47; R. J. Hammond, *The Social and Economic Circumstances of Ket's Rebellion*, London Univ. M.A. thesis, 1933, p. 3. See also G. C. Homans, *English Villagers of the Thirteenth Century*, 1942, ch. II.
[2] J. Norden, *The Surveyor's Dialogue*, p. 215; E. Kerridge, 'The Revolts in Wiltshire against Charles I', *Wilts. Arch. & Nat. Hist. Mag.*, LVII, 1958, p. 71; TED, II, p. 45.

This independence of spirit was displayed in the revolts against disafforestation under Charles I in Wiltshire and Gloucestershire, for example, and also in the battles waged by the fenlanders, another pastoral community, when they fought the drainage of their commons. In the light of this evidence it is also worth considering what support these people contributed to other disturbances in the realm which were not connected with enclosure—the Pilgrimage of Grace, for example, which recruited followers from the valleys of Cumberland and Westmorland, and Ket's rebellion, which started in the wood-pasture region of Norfolk. And some attention needs to be given to two comments on the religious inclinations of people living in the forests. Of the forests of Wiltshire, John Aubrey remarked, "It is a sour, woodsere country, and inclines people to contemplation. So that, the Bible, and ease, for it is all now upon dairy grassing and clothing, set there with a-running and reforming." The Weald of Kent was described as "that dark country, which is the receptacle of all schism and rebellion." Was it generally true that pastoral regions were also the most fertile seedbeds for Puritanism and dissent?[1]

[1] D. G. C. Allan, 'The Rising in the West, 1628–31', EcHR, 2nd Ser., v, 1952, pp. 76 *sqq.*; Kerridge, *op. cit.*, p. 10; VCH *Kent*, II, p. 101. I wish to thank Mr C. W. Chalklin for this reference.

CHAPTER II

THE FARMING REGIONS OF WALES

Unless he is qualified as either a hill-farmer or a plainsman, the 'farmer' in Tudor and early Stuart Wales remains an abstraction, for wherever in the Principality he worked the higher valleys and slopes, his strength and patience were very severely and specially tested. The most pervasive control in the agricultural life of Wales is the ecological deterioration caused by increasing height above the sea, and, as a result, the Welsh uplands have a temper of their own. As to their extent, about 58 per cent of the country is higher than 500 feet, though naturally there are broad differences in the lie of the land between one county and another.[1] Anglesey, for instance, scarcely rises above 500 feet anywhere within its shores, whereas Caernarvonshire, just across the Menai Straits, has as much as 5 per cent above 2,000 feet; to the south, land-locked counties like Radnorshire and Breconshire have more than half of their land surfaces higher than 1,000 feet above sea-level.

It is well known that the British uplands suffer from heavy rainfall, cloudy skies, and mists, from scant sunshine and slight evaporation, from boisterous winds, frosts, and blizzards. Neither is it surprising to find that a recent report on technical problems in Welsh farming is couched throughout in terms of upland and lowland: "high land areas," it concludes, "present the greater difficulties."[2] Furthermore, this limiting bleakness sets in very rapidly as one moves upslope and gains height.[3] Even in the coastal lowlands of Wales, spring temperatures rise very slowly to a fairly low summer peak, while, correspondingly, the growing season is sharply reduced on high ground. It is late, slow, and short, so that not only are living conditions worsened for grass, crops, and livestock, but the soils become impoverished and badly drained. In fact, the first lesson learned by a farmer's son, as he looks over the fields, is to know the dry ground from the wet—on the one hand, a few favoured slopes of free-draining, though probably acid, tilth, and on the other, hollows and skirts of cold, rushy, soggy

---

[1] For an account of the physique of the country, see *Wales: a Physical, Historical, and Regional Geography*, ed. E. G. Bowen, 1957, chapters 1–3.

[2] *Report of the Committee on Technical Problems of Welsh Agriculture* (Agricultural Improvement Council for England and Wales), H.M.S.O., 1958, p. 5.

[3] *Hill Climates and Land Usage, with special Reference to the Highland Zone of Britain*, Univ. Coll. of Wales, Aberystwyth, memo. no. 3, 1960, p. 2; see pp. 1–14, 41–8, 56–9, and, in addition, *The Growing Season*, memo. no. 1, 1958.

land. This was, and seems likely to remain, one of the inescapable facts
of Welsh farming life. Today more than one third of Wales is rough
grazing, almost two million acres of moorland, heath, peat, and rocky
waste, a harsh reminder that the hill-farmer has always had to face
unremittingly hard labour and meagre returns. Moreover, during the
phase of rapid agrarian expansion in the sixteenth century, we can
assume that the upland limitations and problems were at least as severe
as they are today. It has been shown that up to about 1550 the climate
was warm and fairly settled, but afterwards it became distinctly colder.
There were very severe winters, such as those of 1564 and 1579, which
were probably followed by cool, late springs. Climatic conditions
seem to have improved in the 1630's, but even then were far less
favourable than those of a century earlier.[1]

Conversely, the coastal and Border lowlands of Wales have enjoyed
for many centuries an array of clear and positive inducements for a
more ambitious kind of farming. Nowadays, rough moorlands give
way there to arable cropping and good grazing on sown grasses, with
open, gently undulating surfaces; fertile, warm soils; and a genial
climate. The more accessible tracts were colonized from the twelfth
century by Anglo-Normans, and many of them were cultivated in
common fields. These manorial Englishries still have an alien appearance, despite their settlement by Welshmen again in the fourteenth
and fifteenth centuries. Village farms cluster around a green, with
names like Reynoldston, Herbrandston, Newton, separated by a broad,
regular pattern of fields—'Longfurlong', 'Limekiln close', 'Sandy-
lands', 'Whitewell mead', bounded by low, straight hedges, some of
which were thrown up and planted in common fields after 1500.

Admittedly, these are the most favoured lowlands, but one cannot
escape the separation of Welsh landscapes into upland and lowland,
two distinct frameworks within which farmers have led their lives
(Fig. 2). Perhaps it is less culpable than Dr Hoskins suggests if we
thoughtfully superimpose upon Wales "the topographical regions"
that, after all, embody the ground conditions in which farming has its
roots.[2] For in Wales the known regions respect by name and location
this distinction between upland or lowland, between *blaenau* or *bro*, a
distinction sometimes seen in the Welshry and Englishry of a single
Marcher lordship. The advantages for a varied regional economy were
vested in the plains, which were marked off from the upland mass of

[1] Gordon Manley, *Climate and the British Scene*, 1952, pp. 238–42; J. N. L. Baker,
'The climate of England in the seventeenth century', *Quart. J. Roy. Meteorological
Soc.*, LVIII, 1932, pp. 421–38.

[2] W. G. Hoskins, 'Regional farming in England: problems and sources', AHR,
II, 1958, p. 9.

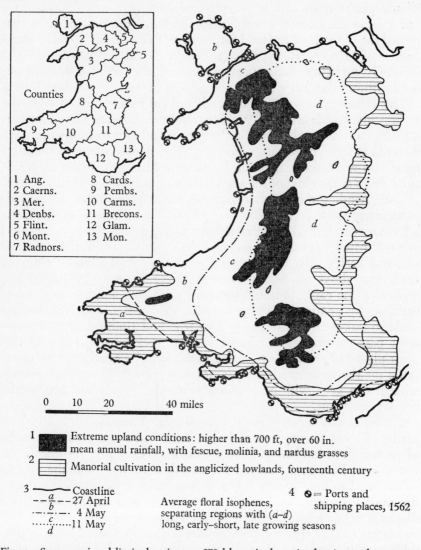

Counties

1 Ang.   8 Cards.
2 Caerns.   9 Pembs.
3 Mer.   10 Carms.
4 Denbs.   11 Brecons.
5 Flint.   12 Glam.
6 Mont.   13 Mon.
7 Radnors.

0   10   20   40 miles

1 ■ Extreme upland conditions: higher than 700 ft, over 60 in.
      mean annual rainfall, with fescue, molinia, and nardus grasses

2 ≡ Manorial cultivation in the anglicized lowlands, fourteenth century

3 ——— Coastline   4 ⊘ = Ports and
  -- a/b -- 27 April   Average floral isophenes,   shipping places, 1562
  -·- b/c -·- 4 May   separating regions with (a–d)
  ····· c/d ····· 11 May long, early–short, late growing seasons

Fig. 2. Some regional limits bearing on Welsh agriculture in the sixteenth century. (1, 3 from *Wales: a Physical, Historical, and Regional Geography*, ed. E. G. Bowen, 1957, figs. 74 and 21 respectively; 2 from Wm Rees, *An Historical Atlas of Wales*, 1951, plate 47; 4 from 'Anglia Wallia' ('A brief declaration of all havens, roads, creeks, and shipping places', 1562), *Arch. Camb.*, 11, 1911, p. 421).

the country rather than from each other. We find this in the vale of Glamorgan, a misnomer in the physical sense (it is a coastal plateau), but in agrarian matters quite comparable with the host of vales that record the old *pays* of lowland England. We also find it in the lowland entities of Llŷn, Anglesey, Gower, Gwent Iscoed and Uwchcoed (i.e. lower Gwent below, and upper Gwent above, the barrier of Wentwood, in Monmouthshire) as well as in the vales of Clwyd, Powys, and Towy.

This cleavage between upland and lowland farming appeared in the earliest first-hand survey of Welsh agriculture. Edward Lhuyd sent his questionnaire through Wales in the 1690's, and four of its queries were directed at soils and agrarian practice.[1] The replies, many of them by men who worked the glebe land, give us at least the outlines of Welsh agriculture at the close of the seventeenth century. They are also useful in understanding the regional contrasts which prevailed in our period, particularly those between mountain and plain. Thus the replies from hill country in central Wales stated that corn ground, where it appeared in small patches among the pastures, was "indifferent fertile" of oats, rye, and barley. On the southern shoulders of Plynlimon, close to 1,000 feet above the sea, these crops were grown "by paring the surface of the earth and burning it, by fallowing and carrying muck upon it, by penting of sheep in folds or hurdles, and by tying of cattle to stakes on it." Between Tregaron and Builth it was "for the most part pasture, mountainous, heathy, rocky, barren; but breeds great plenty of good sheep." One parish kept "a good stock of black cattle for the summer. It affords not hay enough to keep all winter what it can keep with grass in the summer." There was little grain besides small oats.

Conditions became harsher northwards. Trawsfynydd (Mer.), a parish of over twenty square miles, with "oats the grain generally sown, some rye and barley," had 800 cattle, 2,000 lambs, 100 goats, and 100 horses. Peat-bogs "served for excellent turves," and the people were "used to hard labour and a milk diet." Snowdonia could daunt the stoutest traveller on "that solitary, rough, and narrow way from Llanrwst to Llanberis; Llanberis afforded us but cold entertainment, our fare being next to the worst of a soldier's, their best bread being black, thick, tough oatbread...I need not describe Llanberis parish unto you, in which neither miller, nor fuller, and any other tradesman but one

---

[1] F. V. Emery, 'A map of Lhuyd's *Parochial queries, etc., 1696*', *Hon. Soc. Cymmrodorion*, 1959, pp. 41–53. The replies were edited by R. H. Morris and published by the Cambrian Archaeological Association in three parts, 1909–11, as *Parochialia, being summary of answers to 'Parochial queries in order to a Geographical Dictionary, etc., of Wales'*, issued by Edward Lhuyd. Unless stated otherwise, quotations in pp. 116–18 are taken from *Parochialia*.

tailor lives."[1] Transhumance lingered on here and there, for Lhuyd in discussing the meaning of *hafod* wrote that "the word is at present used...to signify a summer hut up in the mountains, made use of only that time of the year for making butter and cheese; as they do at present [1693] not only about Snowdon and Cader Idris, and elsewhere in Wales, but likewise in Switzerland."[2]

The upland margins in southern counties like Cardigan, Carmarthen, and Glamorgan were better off. Grazing dominated, but rye, oats great and small, barley, even some wheat and peas, were grown. Their compost was "generally dung, but some good husbands use lime, a great advantage, and have great herds of cattle and horses, but small." Lime and sea-sand were taken inland. On Teifiside it was "partly mountainous and partly champion," and so "very good for corn, cattle, and pasture." At Llanboidy (Carms.) the plains were "indifferent fertile for corn and hay, the mountains not very barren but yield pasture for sheep and dry cattle," though grass became scarce in scorching summers. The Glamorgan uplands carried plenty of livestock, but were "liable in winter to cold and want of grass." A parish of about four square miles fed 600 sheep, 260 cattle, 80 horses, 60 hogs, and 10 goats. On the coast near Neath, the soil was "subject to wild springs in winter and parchings in summer, having so shallow an upper crust;" yet good husbandry and "the temperate season" furnished crops of oats, barley, wheat, and rye, with dunging and liming—"but most oats in the upper parts," where cattle were smaller.

Agriculture in the fringing lowlands of Wales was more secure and diverse. Castlemartin in south Pembrokeshire was well known for its arable resources, fertile soils, with "only a little rising ground." Where not ploughed for wheat, barley, oats, white and grey peas, beans, with rye on thin soils, the land had a good cover of short grass, "extraordinary feeding for good mutton and lamb." Nearly every farmer had a limestone quarry and lime-kiln. The Gower peninsula in Glamorgan was chiefly corn ground for wheat, barley, rye, white and grey oats, peas, and vetches. One of the most significant replies (1697) reveals that "in divers parts" of Gower "there are much clover grass and seed."[3] Even where the Gower soils were colder and "moorish," with woods and "wet grounds, yet there are many considerable tenements that is

[1] Bodleian Library, MS Ashmole 1816, fo. 229; letter from John Lloyd of Ruthin to Ed. Lhuyd at Oxford, August 1693.

[2] Lhuyd to John Lloyd, 16 June 1693; printed in *Arch. Camb.*, III, 1848, p. 243. For a general discussion of transhumance, see R.U. Sayce, 'The Old Summer Pastures: a Comparative Study', *Montgomeryshire Collections*, LIV, 1956, pp. 117–41; LV, 1957, pp. 37–86.

[3] Bodleian, MS Carte (Collections for Wales) 108, fo. 27. I am grateful to Dr Delwyn Tibbott for this reference.

[*sic*] good ground for corn and hay."¹ The uplands proper, however, were "more apt to feed sheep than large cattle, and great cattle than bear corn; and of grain it bears oats and barley more than any other."²

Farmers in the vale of Glamorgan in the 1690's kept a well-formed, brown breed of cattle, and their sheep gave fat quarters of mutton as well as heavy fleeces. Corn ground was well limed: "lime we use much, and so doth the country in general." Rich meadows in the valleys bore "seven or eight loads of hay upon an acre" in some years. Some of the best land lay in the south-easternmost angle of the vale, "plain and level ground" with red marls "good for corn, pasture, and hay," much of it "peculiarly famous for barley, and good for wheat." One parish of a few hundred acres was heavily stocked with three hundred cattle and a thousand sheep. Thanks to a "low and planey shore" there were several harbours from which farm produce, including livestock, was shipped across the Bristol Channel to the West Country. Again in the Monmouthshire lowlands it was "equally grain and pasture," with hay, and limed crops of wheat, muncorn (wheat and rye), barley, and peas. Bristol bakers were buying corn in Caerwent, at the expense of Warminster market. Near Abergavenny, where the land was more "shelving by hills and mountains," the valleys held meadows, pasture, and arable, with oak- and ash-woods. "It affords all sorts of corn and grain, chiefly wheat, barley, and peas. The land for winter corn is usually limed and dunged. The other grounds are improved by water-courses and the washing of the highways." Here, too, "by sowing clover, greater numbers of cattle are of late bred and fed than was formerly," so widening still further the gulf between lowland and upland.

So much is clear, then, from Lhuyd's investigations in the 1690's. Few authors, on the other hand, gave much attention to Welsh agrarian life in the sixteenth century. Gerald the Welshman had no successor, while for English writers there were the barriers of language and distance. "The Welsh were seen as people slightly more strange than provincials, slightly more familiar than foreigners," and the Welshman was moulded into a stereotyped character.³ Something of this attitude may be detected in the patronizing tone that creeps at times into Leland's and Camden's glimpses of the Welsh scene.⁴ It

¹ Bodleian, MS Carte (Collections for Wales) 108, fo. 27.

² *Ibid.*, fo. 342; letter from Thomas Morgan, of Llangiwg and Cilybebill, 12 December 1697.

³ Penry Williams, 'The Welsh Borderland under Queen Elizabeth', *Welsh Hist. Rev.*, I, 1960, p. 33.

⁴ L. T. Smith (ed.), *The Itinerary in Wales of John Leland, in or about the years 1536–1539*, 1906: William Camden, *Britannia*, revised 1607, translated by Philemon Holland. All quotations from Leland and Camden are taken from these editions.

could not be balanced from within, because in this kind of literature Wales produced little to compare with the English county chorographers, those "able men in each shire" who responded to Lambard's plea (1576) for descriptions of their own regions. Only two or three authors can be mustered in Wales, mainly from the more advanced southern regions, but they all agreed on the apartness of pastoral uplands from the more prosperous coastlands and vales. George Owen described Pembrokeshire, and his classic survey, completed in 1603, compared well with the best in England. He portrayed the "chiefest corn land" in his county, the southern most hundred of Castlemartin, which "yieldeth the best and finest grain and most abundance, a country of itself naturally fit and apt for corn, having lime, sand, weed of the sea, and divers other principal helps to better the soil, where need is; this country yieldeth the best wheat and greatest store."[1] Roose, its nearest rival among the Pembrokeshire hundreds, was "a champion and plain country without much wood or enclosures." Rice Merrick's history of Glamorgan (1578) depicted the regional personalities of its uplands and vale, one relatively barren in corn but with "great breeding of cattle, horses, and sheep;" the other low-lying and fertile, a mild, open, champion country, "apt for tillage, bearing abundance of all kinds of grain."[2]

A different set of values was implied by Robert Vaughan, whose *Survey of Merioneth* was meant to be a revision of Camden's description of the county.[3] The hills and streams of this most mountainous county in Wales were rich in cattle, game, and fish; "the chief wealth of the inhabitants consisteth in cattle and white cottons" (i.e. coarse woollen cloth, see p. 139).[4] The broken relief of Wales, "up hill and down hill, yet enriched with fair valleys, and above all with the benefit of the sea," was appreciated by William Vaughan in *The Golden Fleece* (1626). In his references to the Welsh as "very much impoverished of late" we see perhaps the economic stagnation of the 1620's. Vaughan thought excessive litigation kept men from following "their husbandry diligently;" without it, they could then "fall to enclosures, plant orchards, marl their lands, and not scratch the earth with weak heifers or steers."[5]

[1] George Owen, *Description of Pembrokeshire*, ed. H. Owen and published by the Hon. Soc. of Cymmrodorion, 1892, I, p. 55. See also B. G. Charles, 'The Second Book of George Owen's "Description of Pembrokeshire,"' *National Library of Wales J.*, v, 1948, pp. 265–85.

[2] Merrick's survey was edited by J. A. Corbett and published as *A Booke of Glamorganshires Antiquities*, 1887; these comments are made on pp. 9–12.

[3] E. D. Jones, 'Camden, Vaughan, and Lhwyd, and Merionethshire', *Merioneth Hist. and Rec. Soc.*, II, 1953–6, p. 209.

[4] National Library of Wales Add. MS 472 B, fo. 2.

[5] W. Vaughan, *The Golden Fleece*, 1626, p. 35.

He was also concerned because Wales, even by comparison with one English county like Devonshire, had so few ships, a deficiency emphasized more recently by Professor A. H. Dodd.[1] But it should be remembered that there were other ships to carry Welsh trade, as in 1607, when over one hundred vessels arrived at and sailed from Swansea; only eleven of them were Welsh, the rest coming from the West Country, the Channel Islands, and Brittany.[2] One should not minimize the functions of the fifty or so "shipping places" on the Welsh coast (Fig. 2).

In Wales, as in northern England, cattle and sheep were sold by private bargaining at fairs rather than at the open markets. In view of its size and limitations, Wales compared favourably with England in the abundance of its fairs. It is said that a fair was held somewhere in Wales four days a week, but even this is conservative for the year as a whole.[3] There were about 245 fairs each year *circa* 1602 (some prolonged or recurrent), compared with 494 principal fairs held in all parts of England.[4] Their seasonal incidence reflected the pastoral cycle followed by most Welsh farmers: 75 per cent were in the summer half-year (May–October); 11 per cent in November; and only 14 per cent from December to April (see Fig. 3). More fairs were held in June than in any other month, mainly for lambs and yearling sheep. Wool and cattle fairs began late in July and continued through August and September. The August fairs (e.g. eight of them on the 1st, seven on the 10th) were favoured by farmers from the 'earlier' southern regions. Rhos (Cards.), according to Camden, had "the greatest fair for cattle in all those parts" on the 15th of August; after buying there,

[1] A. H. Dodd, *Studies in Stuart Wales*, 1952, p. 32.

[2] W. Rees, 'Port Books for the Port of Cardiff and its Members for the Years 1606–1610', *South Wales and Monmouth Rec. Soc.*, III, 1954, pp. 69–91. On trade generally, see E. A. Lewis, *The Welsh Port Books (1550–1603)*, Cymmrodorion Record Series, no. 12, 1927; and Figs. 59 ('Elizabethan exports') and 60 ('Milford Haven: creeks and ships, 1566'), in Margaret Davies, *Wales in Maps*, 1951, pp. 66–7.

[3] Dodd, *op. cit.*, p. 31.

[4] George Owen, *The Taylors Cussion*, ed. E. M. Prichard, 1906, I, ff. 74–82, 'Fairs and markets in Wales', by counties; II, ff. 57–61, a longer list arranged by months of the year. Owen explained that the second list "was requested of me by Thomas Adams, a printer in Paul's churchyard, in June 1601" (fo. 61). Both lists were annotated to 1623, and are amended here from other sources (see n. 4, p. 122, *infra*). Richard Grafton, in *A litle treatise, conteyning many proper Tables and rules, very necessary for the use of al men*, 1571, gave a list of 352 principal fairs in England. In the enlarged editions by Thomas Adams (1602, 1608, 1611), the number of fairs had expanded to 494. Grafton in 1571 included a few Welsh fairs (e.g. Ruthin, Denbigh, Holt), but in his 1602 edition Adams printed (pp. 107–15) "All the fairs of Wales .ogether with the Shires wherein they are kept, collected in the year of our Lord 1602. By George Owen, Esquire."

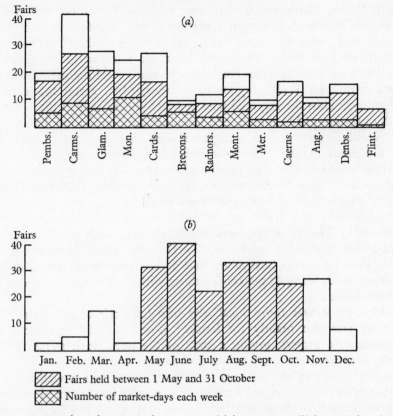

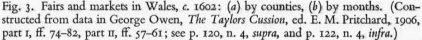

Fig. 3. Fairs and markets in Wales, c. 1602: (a) by counties, (b) by months. (Constructed from data in George Owen, *The Taylors Cussion*, ed. E. M. Pritchard, 1906, part I, ff. 74–82, part II, ff. 57–61; see p. 120, n. 4, *supra*, and p. 122, n. 4, *infra*.)

drovers moved to a fair on the 16th at Rhayader, 14 miles across the high moorland, their cattle following as they journeyed eastwards for England.[1]

Fairs were also uneven in their geographical distribution. Five southern counties (Cardigan, Carmarthen, Pembroke, Glamorgan, Monmouth) had 58 per cent of them. (In Fig. 3(a) the counties are arranged, from left to right, in rough succession from south-west Wales to the north-east.) Their farming was more varied, productive, and accessible to external markets. Carmarthenshire had most fairs (forty-two); Montgomeryshire, smaller by only a hundred square miles, had only twenty. Winter did not proscribe their fairs, as it did in

[1] J. Eurfyl Jones, 'Fairs in Cardiganshire', *Cardiganshire Antiq. Soc.*, VII, 1930, pp. 94–111.

north Wales. Cardiganshire had nine between December and April; Whitland (Carms.), not even a market town, held fairs in February, March, and December, as well as August and September. This national pattern of fairs not only started livestock moving to the English Midlands and metropolitan counties, but also served the movement of stock from one Welsh region to another, often along the ancient ridgeways. Thus the regional fairs at Machynlleth tapped the uplands of Montgomery, Merioneth, and Cardiganshire on the one hand, and the Welsh Border counties, together with Shropshire and Hereford, on the other. There were four summer fairs and another in mid-November. At the May and June fairs in 1632 nearly four thousand sheep and lambs changed hands, and only 345 cattle.[1] In May there was a large sale of yearling sheep, brought from their winter quarters in north Cardiganshire, and taken up by hill-farmers in Montgomery and Merioneth. The June fair was much smaller, with newly-weaned lambs also moving northwards. There were twice as many store cattle then, sold into Shropshire and Brecon; the black breed easily predominated, being 83 per cent of those with their colours recorded in the toll-books.

Although it was more local, the mid-June fair at Newport (N. Pembs.) was also mainly for lambs.[2] Over half of them went to Cardiganshire buyers, giving a start to the northward trend. With cattle, however, this longitudinal exchange went in the reverse direction. Eglwyswrw, also in north Pembrokeshire, had a well-known cattle fair in November, sales rising from almost two hundred head in 1599 to more than three hundred in 1600 and 1602.[3] The buyers were local farmers, but the sellers came from far afield, drovers who handled 46 per cent of sales in 1600 and 60 per cent in 1602. Sixteen of them travelled from north Wales, bringing store cattle from Merioneth to the better pastures of south-western Wales. Leather was sold at this fair (236 hides, 38 sheepskins in 1600), searched and sealed by 'corvisers' from Haverfordwest.

Fairs were increasing at traditional meeting-places and at virgin sites,[4] but at least as remarkable was the new lease of life experienced by the market-towns. More markets were held in the southern coun-

[1] Elwyn Evans, 'Two Machynlleth Toll Books', *Nat. Lib. Wales J.*, VI, 1949–50, p. 78.
[2] E. A. Lewis, 'The toll books of some north Pembrokeshire fairs (1599–1603)', *Bull. BCS*, VII, 1935, p. 284.   [3] *Ibid.*
[4] Owen, in his lists (n. 4, p. 120, *supra*) recorded "a new fair" at Aber (Caerns.) and two new fairs at Raglan (Mon.). Fairs were also held by 1627 at Trefriw and Ysbytty Ifan (Caerns.), one of them probably being "the new fair" mentioned as early as 1569 (Nat. Lib. Wales, MSS Wynn 1522; 61, pp. 75–83). See note 4, p. 123, *infra*.

ties—half of the sixty-four market days each week (1602) were in Monmouth, Carmarthen, Glamorgan, and Pembrokeshire. They were also exceedingly busy. Pembrokeshire had only five days, but the Saturday market at Haverfordwest was reputedly the greatest in Wales for the amount and variety of meats, poultry (including turkeys), game (the pheasant was a recent introduction from Ireland), and fish.[1] Dr Everitt discusses the specialization of Welsh markets on pp. 000–000; from the regional standpoint, mixed farming in the coastlands or Border valleys was very well served by markets. In the vale of Glamorgan few farmers lived more than five miles from a market-town (cf. p. 134).[2] Flintshire had only one market, Caerwys, but it was "furnished with all manner of corn and grain, and with greater store than is brought or carried away by the country people, and that at reasonable prices."[3] As a result, sellers were carrying corn over the border to Chester, Whitchurch, and Ellesmere, or to markets at Wrexham, Ruthin, and Denbigh.

Neither were the remoter stock-rearing counties in northern and central Wales badly off in markets, certainly when their small towns had recovered from the decayed poverty witnessed by Leland. Thus in Merioneth, perhaps the poorest county, by 1592 the burgesses of Dinas Mawddwy were raising money for a charter to hold markets and fairs; Dolgellau, though not a borough, outstripped Bala and Harlech and planned a new Shire Hall. All three towns reintroduced tolls, with books for "the goods and cattle there bought and sold."[4] Similar advances were also made in Radnorshire. Knighton had a market-house "newly built" by 1649, with market and fair tolls worth £20 a year. Presteigne, which had grown, as Camden said, from "a very little village to a fair market town" in our period, came to rival New Radnor, having tolls worth £12 10s. Rhayader, far inland in mountainous country, had a weekly market (which was not listed in 1602), and fairs or "meetings" four times a year (as opposed to three in 1602).[5]

---

[1] J. Phillips, 'Haverfordwest in 1572', *Arch. Camb.* LI, 1896, p. 193; B. G. Charles, 'Haverfordwest Accounts, 1563–1620', *Nat. Lib. Wales J.*, IX, 1955, pp. 157–79.

[2] *A Breviat of Glamorgan, by Rice Lewis*, (1596), transcribed by W. Rees, S. Wales and Mon. Rec. Soc., III, 1954, pp. 92–150, gives distances between each manor and its market.

[3] SP 16, 184, 61 (10 February 1630/1). I am indebted to Dr Joan Thirsk for this reference.

[4] K. Williams-Jones, 'An Inquisition concerning Yearly Fairs in 1606', *Merioneth Hist. and Rec. Soc.*, III, 1958, p. 207; B. G. Charles, 'Court Rolls, etc., of the Borough of Dinas Mawddwy, and Manor of Mawddwy', *ibid.*, I, 1949, p. 48.

[5] John Lloyd, 'Surveys of the Manors of Radnorshire', *Arch. Camb.*, XVII, 1900, pp. 1 *sqq.*, 110 *sqq.*

A. REGIONAL ECONOMIES

The Union of 1536–42 made Wales part and parcel of England, and its legal consequences, which had a close, if indirect, bearing on Welsh agrarian life, must be taken into account when tracing the farming patterns (see *infra*, pp. 00–00)[1]. With the legalization of primogeniture, for example, and the imposition of English forms of manorialism in what had been purely Welsh communities, many farmers (as some of them put it at the time) were soon "brought to a wonderful uncertainty" about tenures.[2] In these conditions of flux, the fittest men not only survived but considerably enlarged their property. From one end of Wales to the other it was a time of estate-building and the laying of family fortunes. Some were on a grand scale, like the Crosswood (or Trawscoed) estate in Cardiganshire, which grew from a dowry of scattered lands brought to Moris Vaughan in 1547. Consolidation, purchase, and marriage gathered in more land, until in 1630 his great-grandson paid £4,300 for 13,000 acres, which a century earlier had belonged to Strata Florida. By 1670 the Crosswood rent roll amounted to £1,200 a year.[3] In other parts of Wales the new estates were smaller. Thus, by the close of the sixteenth century, Llyn in Caernarvonshire had become divided into dozens of properties, fashioned from burgages, bond townships, and free lands. Each had its mansion house, like Cefnamwlch, Boduan, Madryn, and Bodfel, all of which stood near the borough of Nefyn.[4]

How, then, may we proceed to identify the farming regions of Tudor and early Stuart Wales? For this purpose, the most direct and revealing kind of source material are the farmers' own wills and inventories, and we may begin with the digest of livestock and crops

[1] Maps of the territorial framework of Wales before and after Union are given in W. Rees, *An Historical Atlas of Wales from Early to Modern Times*, 1951, especially plates 55–7. See also Professor Rees's *The Union of England and Wales*, 1948.

[2] Quoted by J. Fisher, 'Wales in the time of Queen Elizabeth', *Arch. Camb.*, xv, 1915, p. 237.

[3] J. M. Howells, 'The Crosswood Estate, 1547–1947', *Ceredigion*, I, 1950–1, pp. 70–88.

[4] T. Jones Pierce, 'The Old Borough of Nefyn', *Caernarvonshire Hist. Soc.*, XVIII, 1957, *passim*. G. Dyfnallt Owen's recent book, *Elizabethan Wales. The Social Scene*, 1962, attempts "to illustrate the social and economic environment that conditioned the lives and habits of the different classes of Welsh society" during the latter half of the sixteenth century. It is firmly based on primary sources (especially those at the P.R.O.), and casts much light on the Welsh agrarian scene in chapter 1, 'The Countryside', pp. 18–25 (squires' houses, parks, and home farms), 39–46 (farmhouses and farm buildings), 65–8 (fairs), 75–9 (tenures), 79–90 (farming); and again in chapter 2, 'The Town', especially pp. 91–101. The third chapter, pp. 123–68, is concerned with 'Commerce and Industry'.

in the hands of 340 farmers, as set out in their probate inventories, and given in Table 1. Without these details it would be virtually impossible to appreciate the regional contrasts in Welsh farming, although in Wales inventories were fewer and more sporadic before 1640 than afterwards. As might be expected, the yield of documents from the remoter uplands tends to be restricted in number and terse in content. In addition to the 340 farms included in Table 1, use has been made of another five hundred inventories from Pembrokeshire and Gower, dating from 1580 to 1620.[1]

When the evidence provided by all these farms is arranged geographically, assuming (as Mr Harwood Long puts it) they would then "throw up contrasts in the systems" from county to county, two major farming regions are brought into relief in Wales.[2] First, there were the mixed farming lowlands, fringing the upland massif in seven component parts: Anglesey; Llŷn; the Border lowlands of Flint and Denbighshire, with the vale of Clwyd; the central Borderlands, or middle Marches; lowland Gwent and the vale of Glamorgan; Gower; Pembrokeshire and south-west Wales. These, and the other farming regions, are mapped on Fig. 4. One broad property or characteristic shared by the lowlands, for instance, was that in an average year enough bread- or malting-corn could be grown to satisfy most local needs, while in a good season there would be a surplus for sale. Secondly, there were the pastoral stock-rearing uplands of Wales, much larger in area, and divisible by differences of degree or intensity into southern, central, and northern sectors.

It is also possible to use Table 1 to confirm or amend some of the accepted ideas about Welsh farming in the sixteenth century. A common generalization is that cattle and goats were more numerous than sheep in upland regions.[3] Perhaps the most categorical expression

---

[1] The wills and inventories are kept at the National Library of Wales, Aberystwyth, and I wish to thank the library staff for their kind help in tracing the bundles used here. For the Pembrokeshire and Gower evidence, see B. E. Howells, 'Pembrokeshire Farming circa 1580–1620', Nat. Lib. Wales J., IX, 1955–6, pp. 239–51, 313–33, 413–39; and F. V. Emery, 'West Glamorgan farming circa 1580–1620', ibid., IX, 1955–6, pp. 392–400; IX, 1957–8, pp. 17–32.

[2] W. Harwood Long, 'Regional Farming in Seventeenth-century Yorkshire', AHR, VIII, 1960, p. 104.

[3] This belief may be traced to R. G. White, 'Sheep Farming: a Distinctive Feature of British Agriculture', Report of the Annual Meeting of the British Association for the Advancement of Science, 1932, pp. 229–56. In a discussion of mountain sheep farming, the numbers of different kinds of stock on eight Welsh mountain farms in 1569 are analysed (p. 237); Table 5 is entitled "Eight large farms, 1570." Figures summarized in this table have been quoted repeatedly since 1932, e.g. Margaret Davies, Wales in Maps, 1951, p. 45: "Not until the 18th century did sheep outnumber cattle in Wales."

Table 1. *Welsh Farmers Livestock and Crops*

	Cows and heifers[a]	Store cattle and calves	Horses, mares, and colts	Pigs	Sheep and lambs	Goats	Corn by value	Hay by value	Number of farmers' inventories
		Numbers of							
							£ s. d.	£ s. d.	
A. Mixed farming lowland regions									
1. [Anglesey][b]									
2. [Llŷn][b]									
3. Border lowlands of Flirt and Denbighshire, with the vale of Clwyd	194	185	120	203	1,081	Nil	483 10 6	34 5 2	58
4. The central Borderland	150	156	57	58	582	Nil	56 4 10	17 4	27
5. Lowland Gwent and the vale of Glamorgan	367	253	69	40	918	Nil	146 7 8	4 11 4	21
6. Gower (see below)[c]									
7. Pembrokeshire and south-west Wales[d]	417	320	181	112	2,626	109	244 17 8	18 4	52
Total:	1,128	914	427	413	5,207	109	931 0 8	40 12 2	158
Gower	621	672	319	205	3,390	21	744 9 0	20 15 0	86
B. Stock-rearing upland regions									
1. Southern	606	505	116	41	2,715	26	141 9 0	Nil	36
2. Central	230	277	136	43	1,340	29	43 11 0	2 0 4	38
3. Northern	129	133	38	10	427	Nil	22 0 0	6 8	22
Total (B):	965	915	290	94	4,482	55	207 0 0	2 7 0	96
Total, all regions, including Gower:	2,714	2,511	1,036	712	13,079	185	1,882 9 8	63 14 2	340

a The wide, and sometimes overwhelming, range of particulars about stock and crops is reduced in this Table to eight groups, giving a simplified summary. Cows, dairy cows, and heifers are put together because they would provide the basis for dairy farming, but it is perhaps unwise to go farther than this and separate cattle rigidly into dairy, store, and working animals. Stores were used for ploughing, and heifers (especially in 'dual-purpose' breeds like the Welsh blacks) were kept for breeding and dairying or sold as stores. By 'store cattle' here is meant steers, bullocks, yearlings, bulls, and oxen; where, rarely, "heifers and steers" are cited in the inventories, their number has been divided equally. In all other groups, wherever hogs or teggs or geldings or quantities of oats are not enumerated in the manuscripts, they have been calculated (by comparison with inventories giving numbers) from their monetary values.

b The sample does not have inventories from Anglesey or Llŷn. Fire at the Chapter House of Bangor Cathedral destroyed the Anglesey records, *circa* 1635; and inventories do not become at all numerous there until the 1660's: Hugh Owen, 'A list of Anglesey wills, 1635–1670', *Trans. Ang. Antiq. Soc.*, 1928, pp. 68–81.

c Gower is placed separately because it has a disproportionately high number of inventories dating from 1620 to 1640 (later than the majority), and is given here because it illustrates the scale of mixed farming reached in a favoured region by the end of our period. Of the other inventories, 72 per cent date from 1600 to 1612; some, for instance those from Flint, are as early as 1590, while others (e.g. Caernarvonshire) as late as 1635.

d There are no Pembrokeshire inventories in this sample, but they are used extensively by Mr B. E. Howells in his 'Pembrokeshire farming, *circa* 1580–1620', *National Library of Wales Journal*, IX, 1955–6, pp. 239–51, 313–33, and 413–39. The inventories for region 'A.7' therefore come from Carmarthenshire and Cardiganshire. All the regions are delimited and mapped on Fig. 4.

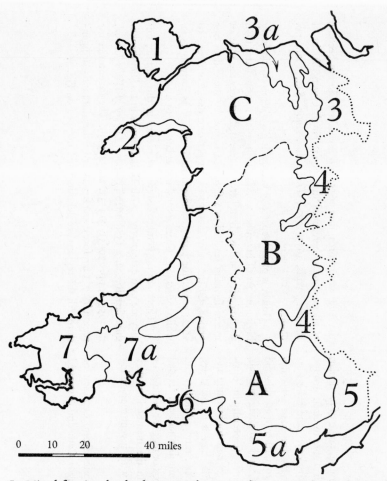

I. Mixed farming lowlands: 1, Anglesey; 2, Llŷn; 3, Border lowlands of
Flint and Denbighshire, with 3a, Vale of Clwyd; 4, Central Borderlands;
5, Lowland Gwent; 5a, Vale of Glamorgan; 6, Gower; 7, Pembrokeshire;
7a, South-west Wales.

II. Pastoral stock-rearing uplands: A, Southern; B, Central; C, Northern

Fig. 4. Farming regions in Wales, 1500–1640. (Based on the probate evidence
summarized in Table 1, p. 126, *supra*.)

of this appears in a report of the Welsh Agricultural Land Sub-commission (1955): "Tudor surveys show conclusively that goats far
outnumbered sheep, while cattle numbers surpassed the totals of goats
and sheep put together."[1] But the inventories of sixty hill-farmers from

[1] *Mid-Wales Investigation Report*, Welsh Agricultural Land Sub-commission,
H.M.S.O., 1955, p. 14. This sentence is accepted by R.U. Sayce, *art. cit.*, p. 123.

north and central Wales tell an entirely different story: sheep and lambs, 1,767; cattle, 769; goats, 29. The ratio of sheep to cattle was 2·3 : 1, with goats of no significance. Those "Tudor surveys" are analysed later (p. 140). Demand for wool and mutton, the making of Welsh cottons, and the over-all rise in driven exports of livestock to England, brought larger and larger flocks of sheep into being. In all the Welsh farms recorded in Table 1, sheep outnumbered cattle by 2·5 : 1.

1. *Mixed farming regions*

Anglesey in 1562 was well inhabited, abundant of corn, cattle, "and all good provision except wood," with "good trade of merchandise and many gentlemen."[1] Favourable conditions for cropping and its maritime position gave the island a varied economy. Cattle, reared for sale in England, were the backbone of its farming. Butter and cheese were shipped from Beaumaris to London, Bristol, Chester, and Liverpool, the barrel-staves coming from Ireland, the salt from Lancashire.[2] Other exports were beef and hides; wool; barrels of herring, cod, and mackerel. Perhaps it may be noted, in passing, that the first systematic work on trade in English, *The Marchant's Mapp of Commerce* (1638), was by a Beaumaris man, Lewis Roberts.[3] Sir Richard Bulkeley (1552–1621) also lived there, "as good an example of the successful business gentleman as could anywhere be found."[4] He bought Crown, Church, and tribal lands; paid interest on money simply to strengthen his bargaining power in the land market; worked several farms, stocked his estate with timber, built and maintained ships in various "maritime affairs."

By the end of our period Anglesey, though far poorer than southern counties like Glamorgan, could show three landowners with over £1,000 per annum, and five with over £500.[5] The mixed farming of one of the lesser gentry can be reconstructed by using the diary of Robert Bulkeley for the period from November 1630 to May 1636.[6] A justice of the peace, with an income from lands which was probably little more than £10 a year, he rented land himself, and was steward to one of the Mostyns. His farm at Llanfachraeth was barely 50 feet above

---

[1] 'Anglia Wallia' ('A brief declaration of all havens, roads, creeks, and shipping places', 1562), *Arch. Camb.*, XI, 1911, pp. 421–32.
[2] W. Ogwen Williams, 'The Anglesey Gentry as Businessmen in Tudor and Stuart Times', *Anglesey Antiq. Soc.*, 1948, pp. 100–14.
[3] R. Lloyd, 'The Mappe of Commerce', *ibid.*, 1954, pp. 88–97.
[4] W. Ogwen Williams, *art. cit.*, p. 112.
[5] Dodd, *op. cit.*, p. 14.
[6] 'The Diary of Bulkeley of Dronwy, Anglesey, 1630-6', transcribed and introduced by Hugh Owen, *Anglesey Antiq. Soc.*, 1937, pp. 26–172.

the sea, facing Holyhead, and very well placed by Welsh standards
He kept a herd of 60 cattle; 15 cows were mainly for breeding, butter
and cheese being made solely for the needs of the house. Store cattle
were the chief product, 20 or 30 heifers and steers, yearlings to three-
year-olds, destined to join the "great multitudes" of cattle which, as
Camden saw, Anglesey "sendeth out." Bulkeley took them to Newborough, a decayed market-place twelve miles off, for the cattle fairs
on the 10th of August and 14th of September. There, for instance, in
1635 he sold eight oxen for £26 16s. His animals were duly listed by
him on the first days of May and November, when the Welsh pastoral
farmer traditionally began and ended his summer season. They also
moved to summer grazings in early May, the cattle from his mowing
land going to the meadows of Cors-y-bol. The lateness of housing
his stock in winter shows how long was the growing season. They were
installed from the 6th to the 22nd of December, usually in mid-month
and by stages, e.g. oxen housed on the 6th; smaller cattle, 12th; cows,
15th. There was no great slaughter; apart from a cow killed for the
house in early December, the herd was unchanged from November to
May. They had plenty of hay, made throughout August and varying
spans of July and September; in 1632 eighteen hands mowed and raked
hay.

Bulkeley built up his flock from 48 sheep and lambs (1631) to 60 in
1635. They were mainly breeding ewes, a dozen or fifteen yearling
wethers being sold to drovers in late April (bringing in £2 15s. in
1634). Shearing and wool are not mentioned in the diary, but the sheep
grazed and fed the fallows. One or two young mares were bought each
year, the nags bred from them fetching £4 or more at Mold fair in
Flintshire. Only a few pigs were kept. Sixteen team oxen supplied the
power for Bulkeley's cultivation. In early October he ploughed and
sowed wheat and rye; ploughing continued until early March, when
four weeks were spent harrowing and sowing oats. Barley ploughing
and planting then lasted well into May. Corn harvest began in late
August (two to three weeks later than in the 1730's), and was spread
over a month or more; in 1633 it was not completed until the 15th of
October. Judging by corn sales, oats was the main crop; it was dried
and winnowed each June (1631–5) to give 51½ qrs of pilcorn, and
6¼ qrs of oatmeal were also sold. (It was said that the Anglesey poor
lived on oat and barley bread, buttermilk, whey, and "such trash.")[1]
More muncorn was sold (5¼ qrs) than wheat or rye, 4½ qrs of malt, but
very little barley.

Most of these sales were made in summer to get good prices, some at
Caernarvon, thus upholding Anglesey's rôle as the "Mother of

[1] Quoted by Dodd, op. cit., p. 16.

Wales" in supplying grain to needier regions. But her reputation was better deserved when Gerald proclaimed it in the twelfth century, for by 1630 the cattle trade was dominant. Bulkeley sold stock worth £33 15s. in 1634; his purchases came to £15 9s. 8d. (twice as much as usual), but even so the balance, less charges, was £18 5s. 4d.—as opposed to £7 4s. 3d. from sales of muncorn, rye, barley, and malt. Yet the arable was tended by dunging for oats and barley in February, and by 'pinfolding', an old and productive method for oats and rye. It meant "securing cattle of all sorts in a well-fenced field at night, and at mid-day during summer and autumn, especially after fallowing"[1] (cf. p. 116). These temporary fences were pulled down after sowing, and so Anglesey was open and bare, "a bleak, forlorn, unfenced country," its growing crops unprotected against trespassing cattle.[2]

Although we have no diaries or inventories to support it, farming in Llŷn approached the mixed economy of Anglesey. Camden noted its fruitful soil, seeing its "larger and more open fields" than those in the rest of Caernarvonshire, "yielding barley most plenteously." We are on more certain ground in the Border lowlands of Flint, where farming on rich loams was as distinctive as the alien flavour of place-names like Aston, Bretton, or Shotton, and family names like Gill, Hubbard, or Messam. Store cattle were rare, save on a few large farms. While most farmers had at least three or four milch cows, dairying was over-shadowed by a kind of sheep-corn husbandry, in which sheep were not very numerous but the crops highly varied. Most farmers had crops worth at least £2 and 20 sheep, rising to £30 and 120 sheep. As to the crops, Thomas Millinton, an Aston husbandman (£57 estate, January 1587), had barley, oats, rye, wheat, peas, vetches, beans, and 'French wheat' or buckwheat, worth £10 1s. 4d. After his four oxen, the most valuable stock were 52 sheep at £7 3s. 4d. Even Edward Weygh, with only £4 8s. had £2 8s. 8d. in those same crops and malt. Camden described the fields as bearing a twenty-fold increase of barley, rye, and wheat at the first breaking-up, then four or five successive crops of oats. The land was certainly well manured (e.g. "sixteen loads of muck, 5s. 4d." in an inventory of 1606). Most men kept half-a-dozen pigs, more than in the other Welsh regions, and many flitches of bacon hung in the roof. Chickens, geese, and ducks were plentiful, even the poorest having two to four shillings' worth of poultry, some probably for Chester market. Linseed, flax, and hemp, with linen and woollen yarn, were often worth ten shillings and more. Hay and straw, generally rare items in the Welsh inventories, were common provisions here and

---

[1] Henry Rowlands, *Idea Agriculturae* (written in 1704, published 1764), reprinted in *Anglesey Antiq. Soc.*, 1936, pp. 54–93.
[2] *Ibid.* p. 62.

worth, say, 10s. with farmers of £20 and less, or £1 with those upwards of £20. As well as ploughs, harrows, and other gear, the wealthier man generally had "an ironbound wain."

The Border lowlands in Denbighshire had an identical kind of farming. Its possibilities were shown in the wealth of Magdalen Puleston (£440 11s. 8d. in October 1606), whose house at Gresford, near Wrexham, had thirteen well-furnished rooms and outbuildings. Corn and malt were worth nearly twice as much as the livestock, with rye by far the biggest crop. With her farmstuff, her clothes (£27 15s.), her virginals, her "piece of unicorn's horn" (£10), she could have bought out all the freeholders in many an upland township. Her farming may be summarized as follows:

Livestock	£	s.	d.	*Crops*	£	s.	d.
13 cows, heifers, and calves, 5 bullocks	33	8	0	Rye	59	5	0
8 horses, mares, and colts	11	19	4	Wheat	29	8	0
109 sheep and lambs	19	12	0	Barley	27	0	0
17 swine of all sorts	4	16	8	Oats	12	11	8
poultry		15	8	Malt	2	10	0
bees		13	4	Vetches	2	8	0
				Peas	1	4	0
Total	71	5	0	Buckwheat	1	1	6
Hay	6	0	0	Hemp	1	0	0
Ploughs, harrows, carts, 'trowls'	7	8	0				
				Total	136	8	2

Apart from her maid's chamber, there was a servants' chamber in the house and another "in the outhouse." These remind us of the greater need for paid labour on such large lowland farms, as opposed to the mainly family-worked units in the stock-farming uplands.

The vale of Clwyd is physically an outlier of the Cheshire plain hemmed in by the Denbighshire hills: it was also an outlier of Border husbandry. A wholesome, fruitful, pleasant region as Camden saw it, the vale had green meadows, yellow cornfields, and "fair houses standing thick." Its farmers kept rather more cattle than those of the Borderlands, and their crops were less varied, barley, wheat, rye, and oats being the mainstays. John Roberts, gentleman, of Dinorben (£56 6s., 1606), farmed with 35 cattle, mainly stores (41 per cent of his estate); 'corn', oats, and malt (34 per cent); 104 sheep and lambs (11 per cent); 5 horses, 4 pigs, poultry (10 per cent).

In the central Borderland—the middle Marches of Montgomery, Radnor, and Breconshire—the anglicized lowlands (using 'anglicized' in a mainly economic sense) were confined to the Severn, Wye, and Usk valleys. The region's mixed husbandry was broadly similar to that in the vale of Clwyd, although more limited, perhaps, and with rather more cattle. At Glasbury-on-Wye, Harry Powell (worth £29) had 23 cattle (58 per cent); 14 acres of wheat and rye, 10 acres of barley and oats (20 per cent); 25 sheep, horses, and pigs (13 per cent). A neighbour, John William John Phillip, held his farmhouse, garden, orchard, a meadow with six 'mens math' of hay, and 21 acres of arable. Eight were sown with oats, five with wheat and rye, one-and-a-half with barley. Arable land really came into its own in the Severn plain, suggested by the team of sixteen working oxen on Edward Herbert's demesne at Montgomery (1594), and other herds including bullocks "which do usually plough with the oxen"; by all the grain stored in barns, and manure in farmyards; and by the wains or other husbandry gear.[1] On the livestock side, this abundance appears in one of the earliest wills (1559), with its bequests of 6 oxen, 34 cattle, 175 sheep, and many breeding horses at grass on the Kerry hills.[2] It also showed through the pattern of mansion houses visited by Lewis Dwnn between 1586 and 1614, many of which were newly built in the black-and-white style of construction. When mapped, they are found to be thickest in the Severn lowlands around Montgomery, along the valley between Newtown and Llanidloes, and again in the Vyrnwy-Banwy valleys.[3]

The economically anglicized tracts of Monmouthshire fall into the coastal plain (lower Gwent) and the middle lowlands (upper Gwent), between Monmouth, Usk, and Abergavenny. Mixed farming was practised in both. Dairy cattle were more numerous in lower Gwent, especially near the low moors or fens fringing the shore from Undy to Goldcliff.[4] These rich reclaimed grazings were still liable to be disastrously flooded by the sea, as in January 1607. Many creeks and harbours were the scene of "great lading of small boats with butter and cheese and other victuals" for Bristol.[5] A typical leaseholder was William Griffith of Llanhenwg Fawr (£20), with 16 cattle (40 per cent of the whole); barley, wheat, and oats (16 per cent); 20 sheep and 8 pigs (10 per cent). As in the English fen country, notably in the Somerset Levels just across the Bristol channel, the spacious common pastures were a vital and necessary part of the system. Inland in upper Gwent farmers relied more on sheep and corn (oats, 'maslin', wheat, barley, and peas); horses, pigs, and poultry were scarce. Here "the husbandry of liming the ground for corn was first practised within the memory

[1] H. L. Squires and E. Rowley Morris, 'Early Montgomeryshire Wills at Somerset House', *Mont. Coll.*, XLII, 1887, pp. 141–248.

[2] *Ibid.* XLIII, 1888, pp. 261–302; XLIV, 1889, pp. 13–58.

[3] E. G. Bowen, *Wales: a Study in Geography and History*, 1941, pp. 74–6 and Fig. 20.

[4] For the agrarian background of the Monmouthshire Levels, see Dorothy Sylvester, 'The Common Fields of the Coastlands of Gwent', AHR, VI, 1958, pp. 9–26.

[5] 'Anglia Wallia', *Arch. Camb.*, XI, 1911, p. 421.

of the fathers or grandfathers of men yet living" (1610).[1] A free tenant with 44 acres (£33 8s.) had 21 cattle (40 per cent); corn in store and 12 acres sown (20 per cent); 11 ewes, 3 hogs, a mare and a colt (10 per cent). In Monmouthshire, and along the Border generally, were found the only extensive orchards in Wales. Out of thirty free-holdings in Skenfrith (1610), twenty-three had orchards.[2] The other categories of land on those thirty farms were arable and pasture, 1,684 acres; wood, 266; meadow, 203; arable, 106; pasture, 44, with 76 acres of common grazing. In the western valleys of the county, however, this was changed to rough hills, thick woods, and occasional pastures, e.g. along the Ebbw to Dyffryn Risca, "as it were a forest ground" (Leland).

Dairy cattle and corn were features of mixed farming in the vale of Glamorgan, some rich farmers having herds of fifty to sixty cows. Even in the *blaenau* or uplands north of the vale, farmers with £70 to £100 followed this pattern, though with larger flocks of sheep: Lewis William Lewis at Merthyr Tydfil had 65 dairy cattle, and 41 stores (53 per cent); 360 sheep (25 per cent), with corn at 8 per cent. The productivity of the vale was a by-word, "a very principal good corn ground" (Leland), which also exported butter, cheese, tallow, and leather.[3] The earl of Pembroke's manors were "the best parts in that country, and all as finable lands as any other, and so every man knoweth;" Boverton and Llantwit Major on the coast had between eight and nine hundred acres of good arable.[4] The Vale gentry counted their regional blessings as proudly as George Owen praised his in Pembrokeshire. Sir Edward Mansel, one of Camden's correspondents, thought that "for corn and good fruits" the Vale was "the Garden of Wales, and for good cattle of all kinds the nursery of the West."[5] From Aberthaw, Newton, Sully, and Cardiff went cargoes of butter, wool, wheat, hides, cattle, and other livestock.[6] Butter shipments to the West Country, Ireland, or France were reckoned to be worth £12,000 a year in Jacobean times, monopolized by Bristol speculators

---

[1] E 134, 13 Jas. I, Mick. 16, quoted by T. I. Jeffreys Jones, *The Enclosure Movement in South Wales in the Tudor and early Stuart periods*, Univ. of Wales M.A. thesis, 1936.

[2] W. Rees, *A Survey of the Duchy of Lancaster lordships in Wales, 1609–1613*, 1953, pp. 92–110.

[3] 'Anglia Wallia', p. 422.

[4] *A Breviat of Glamorgan*, by Rice Lewis (1596), transcribed by W. Rees, S. Wales and Mon. Rec. Soc., III, 1954, pp. 102, 108.

[5] Quoted by D. J. Davies, *The Economic History of South Wales prior to 1800*, 1933, p. 57. Chapter 8 in this book is a good introduction to Tudor and Stuart farming, based chiefly on the printed primary sources.

[6] M. I. Williams, 'Some Aspects of the Economic and Social Life of the Southern Regions of Glamorgan, 1600–1800', *Morgannwg*, III, 1959, pp. 21–40.

before being brought to the open market (1624).[1] The region was said to be plagued by Turkish (Barbary) pirates in 1626, who sold men as slaves at Sallee and captured ships laden with local produce, especially butter: thus "the farmers and dairymen" were unable to pay their rents.[2]

Livestock, corn, and wool from Gower, another coastal region, were similarly marketed in the West Country, at Barnstaple and Ilfracombe.[3] Its mixed farming has been discussed elsewhere, and Gower has a special place in Table 1, its eighty-six farm inventories (1620–40) showing the heights achieved in a favoured region by the close of the period. Cattle rearing, corn (especially oats and wheat), and sheep were the main interests in its varied farming landscape, with plenty of horses, pigs, and poultry, haystacks, 'mexens' or dunghills, straw- and furze-ricks in the yards, carts with iron-bound wheels, and limekilns in the fields or along the lanes. The Gower squires, with their profitable marriages and purchases, were spinning a lucrative web over the region. One of the foremost was Harry Bowen of Llanelen, whose son settled in Cork and established the family described by Miss Elizabeth Bowen in *Bowen's Court*.[4] His personal goods (February 1641) were valued at £248 17s. 6d., with ready money, specialties, and debts worth another £280. Three quarters of his goods were in stock and crops: 95 cattle, 300 sheep, 17 horses, corn, hay, straw and "all other fodder and soil." His relations consistently left property valued at or near £200.

Pembrokeshire has been called the "premier agricultural county" in early Stuart Wales, open to progressive influences from outside.[5] Certainly its farming is better known than most, thanks to George Owen's contemporary picture and Mr B. E. Howells's paper (p. 125, n. 1). It was a mixed farming county, with the emphasis on sheep, corn, and cattle. Even in the best arable districts like Castlemartin (p. 117) most farmers had at least a third of their wealth in livestock. Horses and oxen were used for farm work, pigs were bred for sale to drovers, and there was plenty of poultry, especially geese. Sheep were as important as cattle and their wool was exported rather than made into frieze as formerly. In Castlemartin and the central hundreds on either side of Milford Haven, the crops in order of importance were oats, wheat, barley, peas, beans, and rye. Near the coasts, fields were improved by liming, sanding, marling, and the application of seaweed, as well as by the traditional folding and burning. One should be cautious in accepting Owen's statement that corn was Pembrokeshire's chief

---

[1] Dodd, *op. cit.*, p. 24.
[2] SP 16, 18, 5. I wish to thank Dr Joan Thirsk for this reference.
[3] Emery, *art. cit.*, 1957–8, pp. 25–7.
[4] Elizabeth Bowen, *Bowen's Court*, 1942, pp. 24–35.
[5] Dodd, *op. cit.*, pp. 18, 31.

product, especially as some tillage was being converted to sheep pastures. It is safer to accept his account of cattle-rearing as a growing activity, especially "in the Welsh parts and near the mountains." In those northern hundreds like Cemais and Cilgerran, oats and barley were the main crops, though enclosure of common fields brought more winter corn into the arable routine. Sheep and dual-purpose cattle (cows and heifers rather than beef steers) predominated, and dairying earned profits for the larger farmers. One of Owen's arguments against hiring out cattle was their potential yield in butter and cheese. He gave accounts for three of his dairies near Newport (N. Pembs.), where 274 stones of cheese (worth £36) were made in the summer of 1593, and 146½ gallons of butter (£32).[1] Even so, his largest profits came from wheat, barley, oats, rye, and peas grown there; no fewer than 240 men and women were hired for the corn harvest.

Mixed farming in the rest of south-west Wales produced more sheep, cattle, and horses, but still a good selection of crops. Unlike Gower or the vale of Glamorgan, it was not a compact region physically, and included the vale of Towy, Teifiside, other river and coastal plains, with the low maritime plateaux in Carmarthen and Cardiganshire. Furthermore, the Presceli hills in north Pembrokeshire rise above one thousand feet and imposed the usual upland limitations. All shared a mild climate, long growing season, and easy access to the ports. The vale of Towy had the biggest flocks and herds (its richest farmer even had a herd of nine wild cattle). The value of its sheep may be judged from items like the ton-and-three-quarters of wool stored in a Carmarthen shop (£46 13s. 4d., 1607). In lowland Cardiganshire, sheep, corn, and dairy cattle were main interests; for example Lewis Phillip Lewis of Tremain (£18 4s. 10d., 1607) owned:

	£	s.	d.		£	s.	d.
Four cows	4	0	0	Fifty-two sheep and lambs	5	4	0
Two bullocks	1	6	8	Three ricks of wheat, barley,	5	0	0
One horse	1	10	0	and oats			

Like many of his neighbours, he also had hurdles for folding sheep on the arable, a practice that later made this coastal belt famous for its barley. Most of the foreign trade of Cardigan was with Ireland, importing hoop-staves and boards for the herring fishery, with an occasional boat-load of Irish cattle.[2] The coastal traffic was far more

---

[1] George Owen, *The Taylor's Cussion*, ed. E. M. Prichard, 1906, I, ff. 31–4. He made an error (in his favour) of £10 in totalling the profits of Court Hall for 1593: they should be £182 14s. 8d., not £192 14s. 8d.

[2] E. A. Lewis, 'The Port Books of the Port of Cardigan in Elizabethan and Stuart Times', *Cards. Antiq. Soc.*, VII, 1930, pp. 21–49.

regular, with a steady export of oats, barley, malt, wheat, and rye to the more pastoral regions of north Wales. Bay salt was trans-shipped from the Pembrokeshire ports, which also supplied culm and limestone. One or two cargoes of very varied general merchandise arrived each year from Milford or the West Country.

2. *Pastoral farming*: *stock-rearing regions*

The distinction between mixed farming and upland pastoralism was less sharp in south Wales than elsewhere. Stock-rearing on the southern hills (below the Towy-Wye, Teifi-Severn watersheds) ran on generous lines. This is well illustrated by the richest inventory in the sample, that of Thomas Lloyd of Llangynllo (£495, 1630), a landed proprietor in Cardiganshire. His home, and thirteen farms bequeathed to his eldest son, lay in the low hills of Teifiside. He also owned farms (nineteen of them left to his second son) in parishes lying farther up the Teifi valley, between Lampeter and Tregaron. Since he had stock there, his farming spanned the range of conditions from coastal plateau to moorland pastures. Cattle and sheep accounted for two thirds of his great wealth:

	£
720 sheep and lambs	108
100 milch cows	100
43 oxen and bulls	63
82 cattle of two and three years	54
Corn	45
20 horses, mares, colts	20

Stock and crops in these proportions were usual in the north Carmarthenshire uplands, where even quite modest farms were well stocked: eighteen of them together had 900 sheep, 370 cattle of all kinds, and 60 horses. Some typical farmers were (1600):

Estate	Cows and heifers	Stores	Horses	Pigs	Sheep	Goats	Corn £ s. d.
Hugh Lawrence, Llanllawddog (Carms.)	£26	12	9	3	2	57	–	1 7 0
Jevan Thomas David ap Jevan Goch, Llanddewibrefi (Cards.)	£25	18	12	7	–	50	–	1 0 0
David ap Eynon ap William, Llanllawddog (Carms.)	£11	2	6	2	1	35	3	1 6 8
Rees David Llewellyn, Silian (Cards.)	£10	5	5	3	–	18	–	1 12 0

The term 'dairy' was used for small farms carrying sheep and all sorts of cattle, occupied throughout the year, and used for stock-rearing as much as for butter- or cheese-making. The true *hafod* disappeared as the uplands were used more intensively. Leland saw them at Afon Claerddu, 1,300 feet up on the Cardigan-Carmarthen borders—"two very poor cottages for summer dairies for cattle." The vastness of the open grazings there, stretching fifteen or twenty miles to all points of the compass from Strata Florida, amazed him. It was more than adequate for the demands made on it in his time. He rightly thought the moorland was once wooded, judging from the tree-stumps found (and sometimes deliberately sought) in peat bogs. Deforestation, he thought, was caused by uncontrolled felling; by the close grazing of the much-maligned goat; and by those who regarded woods as dangerous hiding places for lawless men.

Judging by the inventories, stock were half as numerous in the central uplands, with less than a third of the crops grown in the south. The ratio between sheep and cattle was still almost 3:1, many farms having a dozen cattle, thirty sheep, three horses, few pigs, some oats or rye, with proportionately more cattle on the smaller farms. Near Rhayader—according to Camden, "a wilderness, hideous to behold, by reason of the crooked by-ways and craggy mountains"—life was truly pastoral. Meredudd David Lloyd of Llansanffraed Cwmteuddwr (£11 13s. 6d., 1612), a yeoman, had 12 cattle (£8 2s. 6d.); 20 sheep (£1 16s.), and a horse; the rest of his goods were worth 15s. At the other end of the scale was Hafod Cadogan on the eastern slopes of Plynlimon, rented by Edward Herbert of Trefeglwys, "which premises is partly stocked, viz. with twelve kine; 236 sheep, about eighty-six sucking lambs unparted, thirty barren beasts; and twenty mares and horses in the charge of my keeper there." That was in May 1604, and (despite the 352 sheep) he left £40 for the "better stocking" of the farm. There were dairies with milch cattle, butter, and cheese (e.g. at Purk Penprice near Llanidloes, also "a stock of wild cattle upon the mountains" there), and "summer houses, dairy houses, and milking folds" around Machynlleth. Horse-breeding was a feature of Montgomeryshire, where well-to-do farmers had up to two dozen horses and the renowned 'merlins' (or wild mares) from which they were bred.[1]

By virtue of their position, the central uplands attracted to their pastures the "cattle of strangers" from as far afield as the English Midlands. Alongside the streams of thousands of beasts driven from

[1] The Montgomeryshire details in this paragraph, from Hafod Cadogan onwards, are taken from H. L. Squires and E. Rowley Morris, 'Early Montgomeryshire Wills at Somerset House' (see notes 1 and 2, p. 133, *supra*).

Wales each year, we must place this curiosity of some being led into the country from England. Their temporary stay broadened the stock-rearing, at least locally, into fattening as well. In the argument (*c.* 1540) that horse-breeding should be encouraged, Welsh counties like Montgomery were said to have ample pastures and to spare.[1] Each year on the first day of May a thousand or more lean cattle were taken across the border from Hereford, Shropshire, and Staffordshire. They were returned "full fed" in mid-September; payment for grazing was 4d. or 6d. per beast, and even then it was claimed that not a tenth of the pasture was eaten. In this way, the surcharging of the commons with strangers' cattle became a danger for the small farmer (p. 155). At Llanwddyn (Mont.) as many as 292 cattle and ten horses were "wrongfully kept on the waste" in 1591.[2]

The manufacture of Welsh cottons was widespread in the northern uplands, where farmers had most need of a supplementary source of income (p. 157). Indeed, the anonymous author of an Elizabethan tract urged cloth-making as the most promising means of alleviating hardship in regions bordering the high mountains; "their barren soil cannot serve any trade other than summering of cattle," or mining.[3] This was the poorest region and the most pastoral, including what Camden termed "the British Alps, rank with grass." Much of it was open forest land: in Snowdon and its outliers, Leland remarked, "is very little corn, except oats in some places, and a little barley, but scantly rye. If there were, the deer would destroy it." (Red deer ranged freely there until late in the eighteenth century.)[4] In this setting, David ap Griffith of Dolwyddelan (Caerns.) was comfortably off (£39 17s., 1635), owning 28 cattle (£29 5s.), the same number of sheep (£4 10s.), and two horses. Richard ap Hugh Oliver of Pennal (Merioneth, £25 16s.) had 70 sheep (£12 15s. 4d.), six cattle (£7 10s.), two horses (£1 14s.), and corn worth £1 6s. 8d. Besides the lands or annuities given in marriage settlements, numbers of precious livestock also changed hands. A Merioneth dowry (1569) included forty cattle in good condition and "large of bones," with 60 sheep unshorn; at Michaelmas after the marriage another 20 cattle and 20 sheep were

---

[1] *Mont. Coll.*, XXII, 1888, p. 28; cf. Elwyn Evans, 'Arwystli and Cyfeiliog in the Sixteenth Century. An Elizabethan Inquisition', *Mont. Coll.*, LI, 1950, pp. 23–40.

[2] E. A. Lewis, 'Court Leet of the Manor of Llanwddyn (1579–98)', *Mont. Coll.*, XLIV, 1936, pp. 1–31.

[3] Printed by J. Fisher, 'Wales in the Time of Queen Elizabeth', *Arch. Camb.*, XV, 1915, pp. 237–48.

[4] Colin Matheson, 'Notes on Domestic and Wild Animals in Montgomeryshire', *Mont. Coll.*, XLIII, 1934, pp. 75–95. Red deer survived in the wild near Harlech until about 1770, and in the hills south of Bala until 1783.

given.[1] Pastures were cleared and enclosed from the high waste, which even at these extremes was being tamed at its edges. 'Ridding' was the order of the day. 'Stockers or rooters' were paid 2d. a day with food and drink (Merioneth, 1601).[2] "Ditchers for every rood of Great Assize with quicksets" received 6d. The toil involved in such patient extension of the farmed land is seen in a tenant's obligation at Dolwen (Denbs.) "to rid the alders, and to ditch round abouts as need requireth to draw out the water."[3] Conditions were less rigorous, of course, in the lowlands (e.g. the coastal plain of northern Caernarvonshire), and in valley tracts along the lower Conway and upper Dee, where there were some comfortably independent farmers.

It is worth re-examining the evidence which gave rise to the idea that sheep were outnumbered by cattle and goats. This is contained in the estate accounts of Maurice Wynn of Gwydir for 1569–70, when he was high sheriff of Caernarvonshire. It appears that his income from lands in Caernarvonshire, Merioneth, Denbighshire, Anglesey, and Flint in 1569 was £127 13s.[4] This would place him at the summit of the squires, or landed gentlemen on the grand scale of £20 to £40 a year, as distinguished by Mr W. Ogwen Williams.[5] Some of his lands lay in Dolwyddelan, an upland parish of 15,000 acres centred on the river Lledr (tributary to the Conway) and including the massif of Moel Siabod (2,860 feet). It fell into a valley tract or 'Wern', cleared from alder-oak-birch wood and scrub, and the 'Ffridd', rough pastures with open moorland beyond. The bailiff's accounts (written partly in Welsh) covered eight Wynn farms; five were indeed upland, but of the others Gwydir itself was not a mountain farm, lying at 50 feet in the vale of Conway. The total livestock on these eight farms in late June 1570 was 1,049 cattle, 1,032 sheep and lambs, 160 goats, and 16 horses.[6] But these figures must be amended considerably. First, they did not include animals sold, slaughtered, died, lost, given away, or rented from the farms between early July 1569 and midsummer 1570.[7] When these are added, the totals give 1,209 cattle and 1,495 sheep. Secondly, there is a

---

[1] F. Gwynne Jones, 'MSS relating to Merioneth in the Library of U.C.N.W., Bangor', *Mer. Hist. and Rec. Soc.*, III, 1958, p. 184.

[2] T. C. Mendenhall, 'A Merioneth Wage Assessment for 1601', *ibid.*, II, 1953–6, pp. 204–8.

[3] *Calendar of Wynn (of Gwydir) papers, 1515–1690*, Nat. Lib. Wales, 1926, p. 11 (MS Wynn 61, pp. 151–8).

[4] N.L.W., MS Wynn 61 (a book of rentals and accounts, 212 pages long), pp. 55–63.

[5] W. Ogwen Williams, *Calendar of the Caernarvonshire Quarter Sessions Records*, I (1541–58), 1956, pp. lxv *sqq.*

[6] MS Wynn 61, pp. 75–83.

[7] These details are given below the tables of livestock on each farm in June 1570: *ibid.*

list of sheep and lambs rented out by Wynn to nine other farmers (1569-70), which takes the number of sheep to 2,114; in other words, they were almost twice as numerous as cattle.[1] Flocks of sixty or thirty lambs were also sent to farmers at Mawddwy (Mer.) on the same 'bargain' as formerly, "except that they have the whole wool the first year." It was a regular practice; e.g. in 1571 Wynn rented out thirty-six lambs "upon this bargain, that he shall redeliver me again at May in 1572 thirty of the best of the same if they be alive, and if not, thirty made up to me of yearlings of Mawddwy sheep and in their whole wool."

Yet the herds of cattle were surprisingly large. It was estimated that twenty-four Wynn farms "will sustain" 2,820 cattle each year, ranging from 200 to sixty, many of them with 120.[2] The accuracy of this estimate is proven by five Dolwyddelan farms which had 661 cattle (1570): they were estimated as able to carry 620. By custom, farmers could graze on the commons only as many cattle as they kept through the winter: with the intensification of stock-rearing, it was serious when some men "took the cattle of strangers" and summered them on Moel Siabod (p. 155).[3] There was no wholesale slaughter before winter set in; only forty-one cattle were killed during the whole year on those eight Dolwyddelan farms already mentioned. Nearly a hundred, chiefly three-year-old bullocks, were sold to drovers at the fairs; wethers were sold directly off the farms, for in Caernarvonshire (as George Owen observed in his lists of fairs) "they sell no sheep in any fair but at home in their houses." Only Gwydir itself, the home farm, had a team of sixteen plough oxen. There was some dairying; a tenant entering on a four-year lease was given eight cows, and part of his rent was "half the cheese or twenty shillings."[4]

The vagaries of farming here, and its dependence on cattle and sheep, were often used in his defence by Sir John Wynn of Gwydir (1553-1627), "unscrupulous, acquisitive, litigious, and hot-tempered."[5] He excused non-payment for his baronetcy (1613) by the unseasonable weather that burned up grass and corn; according to him, because of reduced cattle sales—their sole means of livelihood—his tenants could not pay their rents, and the Privy Council must wait until his drovers returned from Kent after Michaelmas.[6] Again in 1623 he said he was £3,000 in debt, his rents falling by £400 in the past year: his farms

[1] Ibid., p. 85.   [2] Ibid., pp. 3-9.
[3] W. Ogwen Williams, op. cit., p. 97.
[4] Calendar of Wynn papers, 1926, p. 11.
[5] The Dictionary of Welsh Biography, 1959. Sir John and 'The Wynn Papers' are discussed by J. F. Rees, Studies in Welsh History, 1947, pp. 48-58.
[6] N.L.W., MS. Wynn 627.

were in mountainous country where no corn grew, where neither cattle, wool, sheep, nor butter "have borne any price" for two years,[1] Still, his interests were well served by the more substantial drovers, who carried money to his sons in London as well as driving the herds to Northamptonshire or Kent, while at his death the 'dairy' at Gwydir was stocked with 171 cattle; 66 were sold the previous year, mostly bullocks of two and three years, fetching at least £2 apiece.[2] Although the Welsh drover was known in England as early as the thirteenth century, he became a really familiar figure in Tudor times when the cattle trade greatly increased.[3] This it did because of soaring demand from the English markets; the relative law and order imposed after 1536 (especially in former Marcher territory along the Border); and the settling of many Welshmen in London and provincial towns, where they could mediate between the English graziers and suppliers in Wales. There was always an element of risk in droving. Further, the drovers' roads were cut and their trade strangled by the Civil Wars. Safe conducts were begged for the north Wales herds; by 1642 the price of cattle had "fallen by half in the fairs from two years since," and the position was gravest in the northern rearing regions.[4] "There be many thousand families in the mountainous part of this country [N. Wales] who, sowing little or no corn at all, trust merely to the sale of their cattle, wool, and Welsh cottons for provision of bread."[5] In the south, too, nine hundred cattle were taken from their drovers by parliamentary soldiers at the siege of Gloucester, while after the war, a group of drovers was voted £3,000 in compensation for their losses, proof enough of the scale of the trade.[6] Yet it revived, even securing after the Restoration its old demand for a restriction of imported Irish cattle.

B. SOCIAL STRUCTURE

1. *Size of population*

Several estimates agree that Wales and Monmouthshire had a population of about 275,000 in the early sixteenth century.[7] A more recent calculation (though probably on the low side) will be used here, with

[1] N.L.W., MS. Wynn 1075. [2] *ibid.*, 1522.

[3] H. P. R. Finberg, 'An Early Reference to the Welsh Cattle Trade', AHR, II, 1954, pp. 12–14. For a map of the main drovers' roads in Wales and the Border see Margaret Davies, *Wales in Maps*, 1951, pp. 70–1.

[4] N.L.W., MSS Wynn, 1718, 1834.

[5] Quoted by David Williams, *A History of Modern Wales*, 1950, p. 90.

[6] Dodd, *op. cit.*, p. 23.

[7] They are summarized in *Wales: a Physical, Historical, and Regional Geography*, ed. E. G. Bowen, 1957, pp. 230–1.

the usual reservations, because it suggests detailed figures for all the counties and hundreds, which are very useful for discovering contrasts between the farming regions.[1] It suggests a total population of 251,826 in the middle of the sixteenth century. At one extreme, Carmarthenshire had over 34,000, at the other were Anglesey (9,770) and Merioneth (10,470). The general contrasts were:

1. Southern counties (Cards., Pembs., Carms., Glam., Mon.)   50·6 per cent of the total population
2. Border counties (Flint, Denbs., Mont., Radnors., Brecons.)   35·5 per cent
3. Northern counties (Anglesey, Caerns., Mer.)   13·9 per cent

Although the mixed farming counties were so populous, the most spectacular expansion in numbers during our period was in north Wales. The over-all gain between c. 1550 and 1670 was about 52 per cent, giving a total of 381,000 in that year, but Merioneth increased by 85 per cent, Caernarvonshire by 76 per cent, and Anglesey by 66 per cent. It shows that a more intensive use of the land, capable of supporting more people, reached well into these remoter regions. To take one case: Edyrnion, a hundred on the upper Dee in Merioneth, had a population of 1,545 in 1545–53, increasing by 105 per cent by 1670. An observer had this to say in 1693: "The vale of Edyrnion deserves a better character than Camden gives the country in general. Though I can't deny but most of our neighbourhood has been improved since Camden's days, by liming, ridding, and good husbandry, as much as any country I believe in England or Wales."[2] The counties stood as follows in 1670:

1. Southern   46·5 per cent of the total population
2. Border   37·2 per cent
3. Northern   16·3 per cent

It is more rewarding, however, to convert these figures into population densities per square mile. On a county basis, for what it is worth, Monmouthshire had the highesy density (44 persons p.s.m.) and Merioneth the lowest (15). The newly-formed hundreds are a better

---

[1] Leonard Owen, 'The Population of Wales in the Sixteenth and Seventeenth Centuries', *Trans. Hon. Soc. Cymmrodorion*, 1959, pp. 99–113. I am greatly indebted to Mr Owen for his kindness in giving me the population estimates for Monmouthshire, which do not appear in his paper. The sources on which the estimates are based are the Subsidy Rolls of 1544–6; the Bishops' Census of 1563; and the Hearth Tax returns, 1670. For an analysis at parise level in Gower, see W. R. B. Robinson, 'The First Subsidy Assessment of the Hundreds of Swansea and Llangyfelack, 1543', *The Welsh Hist. Rev.*, II, 1964, pp. 125–45.

[2] Bodleian, MS Ashmole 1816, fo. 232: John Lloyd to Ed. Lhuyd, 19 December 1693.

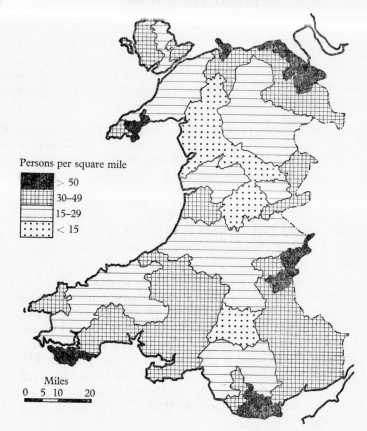

Persons per square mile

> 50
30–49
15–29
< 15

Miles
0   5 10   20

Fig. 5. Density of population in Wales, c. 1550. The densities shown are of 'rural' population in that they exclude the 'urban' population of twenty-five large towns, which are shown in Fig. 6. (Constructed from data given by Leonard Owen, 'The population of Wales in the sixteenth and seventeenth centuries', *Trans. Hon. Soc. Cymmrodorion*, 1959, pp. 99–113; see p. 1, p. 143, *Supra*).

areal framework for mapping, and are used in Fig. 5, although some were curiously delineated and others give incredibly steep population gradients in adjoining hundreds. The highest of all these mainly rural densities were in the richest mixed farming regions. Castlemartin had 53 persons p.s.m., well ahead of the rest of Pembrokeshire, and the vale of Glamorgan also stood at this level, Dinas Powis having 65. In the Borderland, the highest density for any Welsh hundred was 80 persons p.s.m. in Radnorshire itself; next to it, Painscastle had 55. The coastal districts of Flintshire had densities of more than 50; Mold (including the town, with about two hundred people) had 68; Creuddyn, on the coastal plain near Conway, showed 55 and one Llŷn hundred stood out with 68, including Criccieth. A medium density of between 30 and 50 persons per square mile was characteristic of the mixed farming regions as a whole. Such values appear in south-west Wales, Pembrokeshire, and Gower; Monmouthshire, where Caldicot, the most populous district (46), lay along the seaboard; the Border hundreds of Breconshire, Montgomeryshire, and Denbighshire; the vale of Clwyd; Llŷn; and most of Anglesey.

A wide belt of sparse population, from the Brecon Beacons to Snowdonia, marked the transition to upland stock-rearing. Some of its densities were 21 persons p.s.m. in Edyrnion (the highest value in Merioneth); 17 in Cyfeiliog (Mont.); 18 in Eifionydd (Caerns.); and 24 in Isaled, the slightest density in Denbighshire. The relationship between numbers of people, their farming, and the nature of the land may be construed from the lowest densities of all—as in Defynnog (Brecons.), 11 persons per square mile; Ardudwy (Mer.), 12; and Nant Conway (Caerns.), the thinnest in Wales with nine. They were the harshest extremes in a pastoral region of difficulty, "very rare of corn and of good provisions, few gentlemen and no trade of any merchandise" (1562).[1]

The distribution of twenty-five of the main Welsh towns and their estimated population is shown on Fig. 6. They lay in an arc facing outwards to England, from the Menai Straits around the Border to Milford Haven, chiefly in the coastal and Marcher lowlands. The mixed farming regions were more urbanized. Ten southern towns in Pembrokeshire, Carmarthenshire, Glamorgan, and Monmouthshire (seven of them seaports) had 52 per cent of this urban population, with by far the most populous town, Carmarthen (2,150). Carmarthen was a market for corn, wool, fish, and cattle products; its companies of tanners, cordwainers, saddlers, and hammermen were incorporated in 1569; tuckers and weavers, feltmakers, fullers, and shearmen in 1574; and glovers in 1583.[2] About thirty small market towns in all parts of Wales, such as Mold, Newtown, Llandeilo, and Cowbridge, are unfortunately omitted from the estimates. Each had between 200 and 300 people. They would bring the whole urban community to about 28,000, only some 11 per cent of the total population.

Further, the line between town and country was indistinct. Even the largest towns had a rural appearance with closes of crops, hay-stacks, sheephouses, and barns standing among their shops and streets. At Wrexham, the third largest place with 1,515 inhabitants, "the prevailing character of the town was still agricultural" in its malt-kilns,

---

[1] 'Anglia Wallia', *Arch. Camb.*, XI, 1911, p. 430.
[2] C. A. J. Skeel, 'The Welsh Woollen Industry in the Sixteenth and Seventeenth Centuries', *Arch. Camb.*, LXXVII, 1922, pp. 220–57.

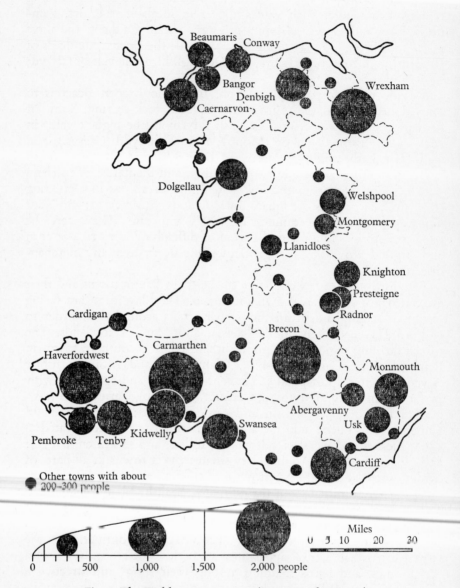

Beaumaris
Conway
Bangor
Denbigh
Caernarvon
Wrexham
Dolgellau
Welshpool
Montgomery
Llanidloes
Knighton
Presteigne
Cardigan
Radnor
Brecon
Carmarthen
Haverfordwest
Monmouth
Abergavenny
Usk
Pembroke   Tenby   Kidwelly   Swansea
Cardiff

Other towns with about
200-300 people

Miles
0   5 10   20   30

0   500   1,000   1,500   2,000 people

Fig. 6. The Welsh towns, c. 1550. (Sources as for Fig. 5.)

tanneries, weaving sheds, dye-houses, and tenter-fields.[1] Swansea, on the southern seaboard, was a growing town of 960 people, and while more and more collieries were opening up nearby, the town was still set in a rural frame. Its tradesmen were weavers, tuckers, tailors, and dyers; tanners, butchers, and shoemakers; bakers and tilers; mercers, haberdashers, and mariners. The richest inventory found so far was that of a mercer, Thomas Hopkin (£753, 1617), followed by a tanner, Rice Davids (£238, 1645). Tanning was one of Swansea's busiest trades; from 1532 all hides brought to market were searched so that "the tanneries have no leather but good."[2] Like other southern towns, it was well placed for all the raw materials used by the tanner: hides and skins from the farms; tannin from oak bark, so abundantly stripped from local timber that some was sent to Ireland; lime, burned from local stone with cheap culm; salt brought in Breton ships from the Biscay ports; and, moreover, it had a wide market for leather in the West Country. When two tanners left £40 to £50 each (1613) their stocks-in-trade accounted for more than half, one of them having seventy hides "in the vats and in the lime."

2. Settlements

There were three main associations of rural settlement in Wales. Single farmsteads, standing apart in a dispersed pattern, were usual in the stock-rearing uplands; very rarely there were small nucleated hamlets; and, thirdly, a blending of single farms, hamlets, and large villages appeared in the mixed farming lowlands. Single farms were the direct outcome of Welsh ways of land-holding, and they multiplied rapidly before and during the sixteenth century, owing to economic inducements and the decay of tribal institutions. The free townships had become minutely subdivided into *gafaelion*, arable blocks held by each clan (twenty or more, perhaps, in a single township).[3] In accordance with the custom of gavelkind, these common fields were shared among male heirs when the head of a clan died, causing further morcellation into *tyddynnod*, new homesteads scattered about or beyond the *gafaelion*.

[1] *A History of Wrexham*, 1957, ed. A. H. Dodd, p. 49; 'Jacobean Wrexham', pp. 45–50. Speed's plans (1610) of some of the Welsh market towns (Carmarthen, Brecon, and Flint), with others of Caernarvon and Pembroke, are given by Margaret Davies, *Wales in Maps*, 1951, 58–65.

[2] W. de Gray Birch, *A History of Neath Abbey*, 1902, p. 259.

[3] T. Jones Pierce, 'The *gafael* in Bangor MS 1939', *Hon. Soc. Cymmrodorion*, 1942, pp. 162–88; Emrys Jones, 'Some Aspects of the Study of Settlement in Britain', *The Advancement of Science*, VIII, 1951, pp. 59–65; G. R. J. Jones, 'The Pattern of Settlement on the Welsh Border', AHR, VIII, 1960, pp. 66–81, and authorities cited there.

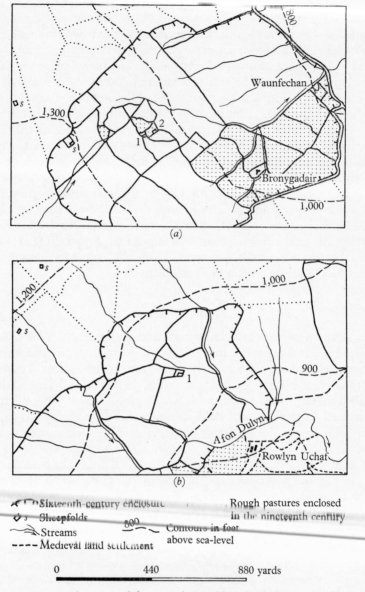

Fig. 7. Single scattered farms in the Welsh uplands (800–1,300 ft)
of eastern Caernarvonshire.

(*a*) Waunfechan and Bronygadair both came into being in the sixteenth century
(Llanbedr-y-Cennin parish). They were cleared and enclosed from upland alderwood,
on very poorly-drained, peaty, drift soils. Their fields varied from a couple of acres
near the farm to great pastures of 10, 20, and (in one case) 40 acres. 1, 2 are no longer

As the average endowment of a medieval clansman was less than ten acres of arable, and the open sharelands of *gafael* arable rarely exceeded a hundred acres, it may be imagined that by 1500 there was little scope for creating economic farms among the old *gafaelion*.

These fragmented lands, however, were being acquired, consolidated, and enclosed, sometimes by burgesses from the alien towns, sometimes by the more prosperous freeholder who was well placed to buy, mortgage, or exchange.[1] Thus, to start with, there might be a reduction in the number of *tyddynnod*. But a growing population and the incentives for asserting or enclosing were bound to bring new single farms into the landscape. To take one example, the medieval *tyddynnod* in a district reaching from the lower Conway to the eastern ramparts of Snowdonia were sited on the best land below 500 feet, where the brown soils were cleared of their oak woodland.[2] Some were to be enclosed (1545) and fenced within ten years, the waste cleared and scoured off, their bounds properly maintained. Then encroachments were made on common pastures, the old winter grazings which may have been cultivated from time to time. Cleared of oak-birch scrub and clumps of alder on poorly-drained drift soils, they offered good hay ground and pasture (Figs. 7 (a) and (b)). Next, the frontiers of land use were pushed into the remoter folds and heads of moorland valleys, as high as 1,400 feet, and traditionally visited in summer by the trans-humant flocks and herds. Their peaty, boggy soils were covered with heather, cotton-grass, rough *nardus* or *molinia* grasses. Nevertheless, new farms were built, four at Cwm Eigiau in 1554, carrying about a hundred cattle in summer; old *hafodau* became permanent rearing or dairy-farms worked in severalty. Diffusion followed these lines in most

---

[1] T. Jones Pierce, 'Some Tendencies in the Agrarian History of Caernarvonshire during the Later Middle Ages', *Caerns. Hist. Soc.*, 1939, pp. 18–36; 'Notes on the History of Rural Caernarvonshire in the Reign of Elizabeth', *ibid.*, 1940, pp. 39–57.

[2] R. Elfyn Hughes, 'Environment and Human Settlement in the Commote of Arllechwedd Isaf', *ibid.*, 1940, pp. 1–25; 'Possible human historical factors determining the distribution of *Eriophorum latifolium* in the north-west Conway valley', pp. 40–5 in *The Changing Flora of Britain*, ed. J. E. Lousley, 1953.

---

occupied as farms. The dotted fields alone appeared (1887) as 'islands' of improved land in a sea of rough grazing, rocks or bog.

(b) Another farm (1), a mile away in the same parish as Waunfechan, also cleared from alder scrub (on similar soils) in the sixteenth century. It is no longer occupied. The larger (10–20 acres) of its irregular enclosures were again subdivided by the many streams. Rowlyn uchaf was a medieval settlement on an outcrop of favourable basic igneous rock; its fields (dotted) were the only improved land (1875). (Based on air photographs used by R. Elfyn Hughes in *The Changing Flora of Britain*, ed. J. E. Lousley, 1953, pp. 40–5.)

upland counties, though many of the farms are identified today solely by the silent remains of 'platform houses.'[1]

Small nucleated hamlets were originally the homes of bondmen. At their most definite, in the *maerdref* (mayor's settlement), they rarely had more than a dozen houses surrounded by a spread of open arable. It is now claimed for them that they not only pre-date the scattered farmsteads in Wales, but were the common origin of settlement patterns in the Welsh *and* English Borderland, dating at least to the Iron Age.[2] Most hamlets, however, had disappeared in Wales by 1500 and very few survived the sixteenth century. Some became free townships with *gafaelion* settlements, particularly where large free clans appeared, as in Gwynedd in the twelfth century. Again, bond townships belonging to the Crown in Caernarvonshire were deserted by 1500, inviting encroachment by those very men establishing themselves on freehold estates. The charter converting bondmen to freeholders in Gwynedd (1507), the Acts of Union, and the anglicization of the Welsh squires, combined to induce men to take up bond lands, often enlarging them by intakes from the waste. Every bond township in Caernarvonshire known from medieval sources was destined to appear in court proceedings over disputed claims.[3] The result in terms of settlement was that bond hamlets (wherever they had survived the aftermath of plagues and rebellion) were replaced by new, compact, single farms. They persisted only where local circumstances offered a means of livelihood in addition to farming (e.g. quarrying), chiefly in the mixed farming lowlands.

Here, in any case, settlement was more diverse. In the Marcher lordships of south Wales, the upland Welshries contained scattered farms and small hamlets, occupied chiefly by freemen, and surrounded by a few hundred acres of open arable with some form of infield-outfield. Besides these, in the lowland Englishries, there were three kinds of farming settlement. A basic pattern of villages was fashioned by Anglo-Norman and Flemish colonists in the early twelfth century, and others (with 'off-shoot' hamlets) were in being by 1300.[4] Their arable common fields were enclosed in varying degrees by Tudor times (p. 153). Secondly, there were single farms standing amidst their quite large, rectilinear fields, often at the margins of parishes and some distance from the villages. Most of them were medieval freeholds,

[1] C. A. Gresham, 'Platform Houses of North-west Wales', *Arch. Camb.*, CIII, 1954, pp. 18–53.

[2] G. R. J. Jones, *art. cit.*, pp. 69 *sqq.*; the argument is taken much further in 'Settlement Patterns in Anglo-Saxon England', *Antiquity*, XXXV, 1961, pp. 221–32.

[3] T. Jones Pierce, *art. cit.*, 1940, p. 57.

[4] B. E. Howells, *art. cit.*, pp. 315–33.

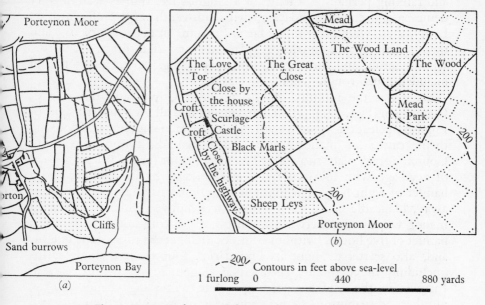

Fig. 8. Farms in the mixed farming lowlands of Wales.

(a) A village farm on the Gower coast in 1551. Griffith Russell leased this 'mansion house', orchard, and 25¾ acres of land. (13¾ were arable, 12 waste, 'rocks and bushes' on the cliffs.) His fields, mostly one or two acres, are shaded on the plan. The nucleus of the farm lay in the former common fields; 10 acres of arable were still unenclosed, 3¾ acres lying in three parcels 'in Horton field'. Russell had to maintain the hedges, ditches and quicksets, as enclosure was in progress. From their disposition it is clear that an attempt had been made to piece together and consolidate the scattered fields, with as much as possible near the farm house, then contiguously from one to another inland, to the common grazings on Porteynon Moor.

(b) A large demesne farm in Gower, c. 1540: Scurlage Castle. Situated two miles inland from (a), it was a capital messuage of 156 acres, comprising 130 acres arable; 20 acres of pasture, furze, and wood; 6 acres meadow. Some of its fields were known (alternatively to those names marked) as "the norther demaines of Scurlage"; they were so large that the whole of Russell's farm at Horton (a) could have been placed within any one of them. The rents of its 20- to 30-acre fields were as high as £1 3s. 4d. or £1 apiece; the farm was leased for £6 8s. 4d. Field names indicate the enclosure of large blocks of common field demesne, one motive being suggested by 'Sheep Leys', which recurs in similar situations in other Gower manors.

The sides of many fields in both (a) and (b) measured exactly a furlong. Dotted lines in (b) represent modern field boundaries. The named fields are now all subdivided into two or three smaller fields. (Reconstructed with data from MSS Penrice 3039 and 6524, National Library of Wales.)

worked in severalty from the start, held in return for military service and ranking perhaps as a tenth of a knight's fee. Others were former demesne land, enclosed and leased in the fourteenth or fifteenth centuries. Lastly, there were other single farms (or sometimes groups of two and three), with smaller and less regular fields, assarted directly from the woods, scrub, and furze as customary holdings; many of them still included much rough ground after 1500.

Such was the mixture of settlement in Gower and the vale of Glamorgan (Figs. 8 (*a*), (*b*)). Their villages had all the outward signs of English nucleation—greens with square-towered churches overlooking them, castles or manor-houses, parish pounds, forges, and mills. Contemporary plans show that Penmark manor (in the vale) consisted of a village with fourteen farms and cottages by the church, and a hamlet of eight houses, without any single farms at all.[1] A few miles away, Llancadle had a village of thirteen houses, while an adjoining manor was divided between a village of ten common-field farms, a hamlet of five houses (without common field) at the edge of the manor, and, also scattered about its boundaries, four or five single farms (including the demesne, enclosed as huge pastures of fifty acres). Farmers in the Marcher lordships were witnessing changes in the numbers, distribution, shapes, and sizes of farming settlements and fields, but less precipitately than on the Crown lands in north Wales.

3. *Size of farms*

Marked inequalities in the size of holdings appeared in the anglicized lowlands before 1500. Demesne and other common-field lands were grouped together and enclosed as compact fields and farms, worked by customary tenants. Some copyholds at Monmouth (1610) were still scattered over three common fields; others were consolidated as farms of 155 or 120 acres; yet others, both customary and freehold, had 200 and 250 acres of arable, built up by marriage, indenture, and lease. On such foundations "the new middle class and the lesser gentry were to rise to wealth and power."[2] At Caldicot, on the coastal fens of

[1] Margaret Davies, 'Field Patterns in the Vale of Glamorgan', *Cardiff Naturalists' Soc.*, LXXXIV, 1955–6, pp. 5–14. For other evidence of English forms in South Wales, see the same writer, 'Common Lands in South-east Monmouthshire', *ibid.*, LXXXV, 1955–6, pp. 5–15; 'The Open Fields of Laugharne', *Geography*, XL, 1955, pp. 169–77; 'Rhosili Open Field and related South Wales Field Patterns', AHR, IV, 1956, pp. 80–96; and Dorothy Sylvester, *art. cit.*, 1958. On common fields in other Welsh regions, see D. Sylvester, 'The Rural Landscape of Eastern Montgomeryshire', *Mont. Coll.*, LIV, 1956, pp. 3–26; R. R. Rawson, 'The Open Field in Flintshire, Devon, and Cornwall', EcHR, 2nd Ser., VI, 1953, pp. 51–5.

[2] W. Rees, *A Survey of the Duchy of Lancaster lordships in Wales, 1609–1613*, pp. xxxi, 1–68.

Monmouthshire, English influence was at its strongest, and nearly all the farms were customary holdings. They rarely exceeded 50 acres, several were between 20 and 50 acres, others merely an acre or two, scattered in fractional parcels over five common fields. Common grazings were vital to them (p. 133).[1] In the lordships of the Three Castles, on the other hand, strung along the Border above Monmouth, Welsh influences were more persistent. Customary farms were rare; the demesnes were large (about 240 acres at Skenfrith), and free-holdings ranged from between 15 and 25 acres to 50, 100, or even 300 acres.[2]

Farm sizes were not as generous in the vale of Glamorgan, but became larger, with growing disparities between the smallest and largest, as consolidation and enclosure went ahead. From surveys of 1622–4 we see copyhold farms at Aberthaw, with common-field remnants, ranging from 19 to 62 acres, 20–30 acres being usual.[3] At Llancadle and Penmark, with more enclosure, there was a wider range, and the typical copyholder had 30–40 acres; as a rule the new fields were four or five acres. Barry no longer had common fields, and its farms were dispersed; seven were between 10 and 26 acres, but four had from 44 to 83 acres. The mixed farms in Gower were mainly customary holdings of 15–22 acres, in varying degrees of consolidation in the common fields.[4] Freeholds were larger, up to sixty acres, but it is hard to be precise because of rapid changes taking place throughout our period. These changes saw copyholders or customary tenants becoming tenants-at-will and leaseholders by deed, not 'by the rod'; their services becoming money payments; and large fines imposed upon alienation or succession. The freeholders were strongly placed, whatever their origins. As socage tenants with token rents, they profited from rising prices, and were eager to enlarge their property. They played a leading part in enclosing the common fields in south Wales, about 90 per cent of which were enclosed by 1640.[5] But their extinction was not uniform: common fields seem to have survived longer in the more westerly parts of the coastal plain, although in Pembrokeshire itself one finds all the many stages of rearrangement. A deciding factor in the stage reached was the size and strength of the freeholding families.

Kittle, one of the Gower manors, illustrates the reduction in

[1] *Ibid.*, pp. 133–72.
[2] *Ibid.*, pp. 69–132.
[3] M. Davies, *art. cit.*, *Cardiff Nat. Soc.*, LXXXIV, 1955–6, p. 8.
[4] Emery, *art. cit.*, 1955–6, pp. 394–5.
[5] This figure is calculated by T. I. Jeffreys Jones in his thesis (see note 1, p. 134, *supra*, p. 401).

customary farms and engrossing of freehold estates by the smaller squires:[1]

	Customary holdings	Customary acreage	Rent £ s. d.	Freeholders	Rent s. d.
1550	11	252	9 16 8	7	9 10½
1650	5	103	3 12 7	7	10 3½
1764	2	103	do	6	do

In 1764 all lands, except three freeholdings, were in the hands of two families. Some idea of the intensification of farming appears from the rise in economic rents and entry fines on two Gower manors belonging to the Mansels:[2]

			£ s. d.	
Oxwich	1540	19 copyholders paying	17 6 2	3 freeholders, 2s. 3d.
	1632	19 copyholders } 7 cottagers	32 14 0	do
		and in fines	300 13 4	
Penrice	1540	21 copyholders paying	18 2 6	4 freeholders, 2s.
	1632	21 copyholders } 7 cottagers	23 10 10	do
		and in fines	312 13 4	

It is difficult to generalize about farm sizes in the less anglicized regions. On low coastal plateaux in south-eastern Carmarthenshire the manorial imprint was slight. Freemen "living in their small farmsteads of a few limited inclosures but enjoying extensive rights of common, made up the main part of the population."[3] Just how small they were, it is hard to say. In Pembrey, where it seems safe to allow two English acres for each acre given in the survey (1609), half the farms were less than 10 acres, many of them between four and six; eleven farms were from 10 to 20 acres in size, five were from 20 to 40, and two farms were large by local standards, 80 and 178 acres.[4] There was scarcely any movement towards larger farms on the scale recorded in Monmouthshire. Stability of this kind, where the farms were about 20 acres at the most, may be presumed for many upland townships where freeholders paid small chief rents. A rental of Crown lands in a Merioneth *commote* (1633) named the Crown lessees and their undertenants in the *tyddy-*

[1] N.L.W., MS Badminton 5533; C. Baker and G. G. Francis (eds.), *Surveys of Gower and Kilvey* (*Arch. Camb.* supplementary volume, 1870,) pp. 78–9, 324–5; Gabriel Powell's survey of the Beaufort estate in Gower, 1764 (MS in the Royal Institution of South Wales, Swansea), ff. 72 *sqq.*

[2] N.L.W., MSS Penrice 2836, 3004; *Surveys of Gower and Kilvey*, pp. 125–40, 235–49.

[3] Rees, *op. cit.*, 1953, pp. xxxiv, 173–303.

[4] *Ibid.*, pp. 200–4.

nnod.[1] Rents ranged from 11s. 8d. to 2d., the most usual being 2s. to 4s. some idea of the acreages represented by these sums may be gained. when 15 acres of arable are known to have been rented for 2s. 6d

In Gwynedd there was greater variation in farm size. Of three neighbouring townships in coastal Caernarvonshire, the largest (4,700 acres) was bond land rented from the Crown in 1531.[2] By 1546 its ambitious lessee had fashioned a series of new enclosed farms, which he rented out, ditching and draining the saltmarshes for grazing. By 1567 there were about twenty of these, and as many again came into being by the close of the century, mostly between 50 and 100 acres in area. The few freeholdings were large; one man owned 137 acres and worked 60 acres in two other farms. Indeed, one of these freeholders became owner *en bloc* of an adjoining free township (540 acres) and carved it into five new holdings: two large and two small farms, with one smallholding, their layout quite erasing the old patterns. By contrast, the third township underwent little change: although free land, its leading family moved away before the tribal holdings could be 'modernized'; these continued as a fragmentation of small farms lying intermingled on the better land. Other townships in Llŷn (which, as a district, lay remote from the early estate-building ventures of the northern burgesses in the county) also retained the old order until late in the sixteenth century. One at the tip of the Llŷn peninsula (now 136 acres) still had common fields with the inter mixed shares of twenty farmers.[3]

Whatever the size of their farms, most Welshmen were acutely dependent on open common grazings. Their reliance naturally became more critical in the uplands, and a main cause of hot disputes was the restriction or enclosure of moorland pastures. Many were poorly defined, like the forest of Snowdon, which the earl of Leicester tried to extend to neighbouring counties, claiming enclosures from it.[4] Crown officials were not always scrupulous about taking in and concealing parcels of waste. Enclosure of Crown commons was particularly widespread in the central uplands of the stock-rearing region. A petition by freeholders in Radnorshire and Montgomeryshire gave their situation in a nutshell (1573): most of those "living near to the said mountains and wastes have but small quantity and but few acres in severalty,

[1] 'A Rental of Crown Lands in the Commote of Estimanner, 1633', *Mer. Hist. and Rec. Soc.*, II, 1953–6, pp. 312–24.

[2] C. A. Gresham, 'The Townships of Gest, Treflys, and Ystumllyn', *Caerns. Hist. Soc.*, XVIII, 1957, pp. 5–33.

[3] T. Jones Pierce, *art. cit.*, 1939, p. 28.

[4] T. I. Jeffreys Jones, *Exchequer proceedings concerning Wales in temp. James I*, Board of Celtic Studies, History and Law series, XV, 1955, pp. xvii, 227. *Ef.* C. Thomas, 'Encroachment on the Common Lands of Merioneth in the Sixteenth Century', *The Northern Universities' Geog. J.*, V, 1964, pp. 33–8.

and the same very barren and fruitless, they cannot without good order being had for the commons and wastes maintain themselves and their families."[1] Disorders took several forms. The forest of Colwyn (Radnors.) was reduced by Crown farmers who built houses on it, enclosed fields for meadow or arable, limited rights of common pasture only to the winter months, and licensed strangers to graze their livestock there. The commoners, faced with less pasture and greater competition for it, protested (1618) that some open lands, far from being common in the manorial sense, were *rhandir* holdings, deliberately left open by co-heirs in gavelkind. Besides common appurtenant for unstinted grazing, they also claimed turbary and—a strong reminder of transhumant traditions—"the free use of summer houses, cottages, and folds for their cattle upon such commons."[2]

This problem recurred in the vast 'manorial districts' in the western uplands of Montgomeryshire.[3] The Crown, its lessees, and the larger freeholders all encroached, enclosed, or over-stocked the commons, an inquisition of 1561 revealing the confusion as landlords tried to impose manorial dues after the Union. There was also stricter control of the woodlands (still quite abundant), which were claimed as common. "Forests or ffreythes" were either open "mountain ground" or "partly replenished with woods and underwoods," but such was the mounting demand for timber that its disposal was newly placed in the hands of six foresters. At Llanwddyn, in the upper fastnesses of Vyrnwy, the leet courts (1579–98) imposed fines for cutting timber in the demesne woods, including oak, birch, hazel, and willow.[4] Again, to safeguard the upland resources, legislation was brought to bear on the omnivorous goat. Tenants at Llanwddyn were forbidden to keep them, under penalty of twenty shillings, while in the Severn lowlands, too, courts fined farmers fourpence for each goat kept "to the damage of their neighbours," or on the commons "to the annoyance of the free tenants."[5] Though smaller in area, the open commons in these mixed farming lowlands were prized by all sections of the community. They offered good grazing, whether on moor, marsh, cliff, or sand

---

[1] Quoted by Elwyn Evans, 'Arwystli and Cyfeiliog in the Sixteenth Century. An Elizabethan Inquisition', *Mont. Coll.*, LI, 1950, p. 26.

[2] Elwyn Evans, 'The Manor of Uwchmynydd, Radnorshire, in 1618', *Nat. Lib. Wales J.*, VI, 1949–50, pp. 385–90.

[3] E. Evans, *art. cit.*, 1950, pp. 23–7

[4] E. A. Lewis, 'Court Leet of the Manor of Llanwddyn (1579–98)', *Mont. Coll.*, XLIV, 1936, p. 31. Timber was also felled in the Teifi valley and taken down-river to Cardigan, 1602: I. J. Sanders, 'Trade and Industry in some Cardiganshire Towns in the Middle Ages', *Ceredigion*, III, 1959, pp. 319–36.

[5] E. A. Lewis, 'Manorial Documents relating to the Manor of Broniarth, 1536–1773', *Mont. Col.*, XLIX, 1946, pp. 225–43.

'burrows'. As such, they invited enclosure when a man wished to enlarge his own lands, or when he wished to place pressure on the smaller farmer by depriving him of pasture.

C. RURAL INDUSTRIES

The making of woollen cloth affected the livelihood of more Welsh farmers than any other rural industry. 'Welsh cottons' were a kind of frieze, warm, hard-wearing, but rough, sold plain, and best used as a lining material. Wool was spun and woven in farmhouses throughout Wales, but by the 1550's a domestic cloth-weaving industry was localized near Carmarthen and, much more strongly, in the uplands of north Wales. The sale of cottons made with wool from their own flocks is known to have benefited the small farmer–clothiers of Montgomery, Merioneth, and Denbighshire, those in Merioneth being the busiest producers. At Bala, the wage for working a yard of best frieze was one penny (by comparison a labourer in summer received twopence a day and his meals); paupers earned fivepence for spinning and carding a pound of wool.[1] Cloth was sold to the drapers of Shrewsbury, who monopolized the trade from 1565. They bought cottons each Monday at Oswestry market, brought by pack-horses, for example, from the valleys around Dolgelley and Mawddwy, paying as much as £2,000 a week by 1620.[2] Shortly afterwards the drapers shifted the cloth market to Shrewsbury, on Fridays. This was hard for the Merioneth clothier, who in any case had an extra journey of twenty miles to Shrewsbury. They were so late getting home on Saturdays that the rector of Dolgelley asked (1648) that the market be put back to Wednesdays.[3] It is a measure of their strength that the drapers compromised and agreed to buy cloth on Thursdays. Flannel was also made in smaller quantities near Wrexham, and the beginnings of a domestic industry of knitting woollen stockings can be traced in the vale of Glamorgan.[4] But the main use of wool in southern counties in our period was for shipment to the West Country.

[1] T. C. Mendenhall, 'A Merioneth Wage Assessment, 1601', *Mer. Hist. and Rec. Soc.*, II, 1953–6, pp. 204–8.

[2] T. C. Mendenhall, *The Shrewsbury Drapers and the Welsh Wool Trade in the Sixteenth and Seventeenth Centuries*, 1953.

[3] D. J. Evans, 'A Note on Dr John Ellis and the Drapers of Shrewsbury', *Mer. Hist. and Rec. Soc.*, II, 1953–6, pp. 69–71; on the later flannel industry, see D. J. Evans, 'The Drapers of Shrewsbury and the Welshpool Flannel Market in the Seventeenth Century', *Mont. Coll.*, LII, 1952, p. 22.

[4] M. I. Williams, 'Some Aspects of the Economic and Social Life of the Southern Regions of Glamorgan, 1600–1800', *Morgannwg*, III, 1959, pp. 30, 32–3; 'A Contribution to the Commercial History of Glamorgan, 1666–1735', *Nat. Lib. Wales J.*, IX, 1955–6, pp. 188–215, 334–53.

The growth of mining and metallurgical industries on a new scale occurred in south Wales. Development was sporadic, achieving a greater intensity only at the seaward margins of the coalfield, between Kidwelly and Neath, and again in Pembrokeshire, where George Owen recorded that "now they sink their pits down right four square about vi or vii foot square, and with a windlass turned by four men they drew up the coals a barrel full at once by a rope."[1] Coal was worked for export wherever the seams outcropped near tidal water. The industry made direct contact with the farming community when men could dig coal from their lands, or when landowners became interested in minerals. Thus there was a growing trade in good 'sea coal' between the Burry estuary in Gower, for instance, and north Devon, carried by shipmasters from Northam and Barnstaple. The producing rôle of Gower farmers shows in one inventory where William ap William of Llanrhidian (1609) had £5 in "coals above the ground already wrought," and "one vein of coals where upon is two pits open." Metal works had a less direct effect on the countryside; they included copper-smelting at Neath, iron furnaces (using nodular ores from the Coal Measures) at Aberdare, Merthyr, Radyr, and elsewhere, with wire-works at Tintern.[2] They all consumed load after load of charcoal, which in turn caused the deforestation of hundreds of acres: timber for 'coaling' was one strong motive for enclosing and clearing the common woodlands. From the forests of Garth Maelwg and Alltgriffith, on the margins of the vale of Glamorgan, "the woods were sold to the iron works" started by Henry VIII at Llantrisant. By the close of the century, together with the forest of Talyfan, they had become "a fair and large sheep leaze."[3] Changes of this sort led to upheaval in Pembrokeshire and in Monmouthshire, where the earl of Pembroke was resisted by his tenants at Usk and Trelech (cf. p. 244). Deforestation also accompanied the lead-mining and smelting in Cardiganshire, started in 1568 north of the Ystwyth, although the growing industry must have benefited some of the farmers both in employment and sale of produce; by 1592 the district yielded 30 per cent of the lead smelted in England and Wales, most of it shipped overseas. Shortly afterwards Myddleton introduced deeper mining by

[1] A. H. John, *The Industrial Development of South Wales*, 1950, p. 3; George Owen, *Description of Pembrokeshire* (1892 ed.), I, p. 89.

[2] David Williams, *A History of Modern Wales*, 1950, pp. 92–3; D. J. Davies, *The Economic History of South Wales prior to 1800*, 1933, chapters 7, 9, and 10; Lionel Williams, 'A sixteenth-century example of regional interdependence and alien participation in the mining industry: the exploitation of Cornish copper and lead ores and copper smelting at Neath', *Morgannwg*, III, 1959, pp. 3–20.

[3] *A Breviat of Glamorgan*, by Rice Lewis (1596), transcr. W. Rees, S. Wales and Mon. Rec. Soc., III, 1954, pp. 104, 108.

shafts, with water-driven engines to pump them dry. He sent silver valued at £50,000 to the Mint, and is supposed to have made £2,000 a month from one lead-mine.[1]

Finally, the well-stocked Welsh rivers were carefully and rewardingly fished—the Teifi and the Conway, for instance; the earl of Pembroke's fishing in the Glamorgan streams was "very profitable by the year," that for the Taff alone being leased for £24.[2] There was a busy herring fishery along the shores of Cardigan Bay, shifting its location after the autumn peak to more northerly waters beyond Anglesey, where it continued until Candlemas.[3] Neither was sea fishing neglected elsewhere, as Glamorgan inventories, with their shares held in small boats and tackle, or the weirs and traps listed in manorial surveys, clearly show.

The farming regions portrayed in this chapter, admittedly and inevitably by a kind of *chiaroscuro*, persisted after 1640, through the eighteenth century (when sheep-farming came into its own on the hills), and at least until the age of railways. Differences between upland and lowland were clear in the 1690's (pp. 116–18). Although we know the northern Welsh counties were gaining ground, we have also seen the steady introduction of new crops and methods in the open lowlands, perpetuating the differences between the more and the less rewarding farming areas. Henry Rowlands in 1704 traced the appearance of three new means of improving the land in Anglesey. Shelly sand from the beaches was first used in the 1640's, many landowners and farmers following suit after 1660. With its help, fields gave heavy crops of barley instead of poor yields of oats. White marl was dug and used in 1652 by the new proprietors who brought their knowledge to the island. Lime was tried in 1666, burned from local stone, and was quickly taken up.[4] The same improvements were introduced in the vale of Clwyd and Flint.[5] By 1700, too, clover was known in Gower probably in the vale of Glamorgan, and in Monmouthshire: "Now they are fallen into the vein of clover, and those which kept no kine before now keep some twelve, some twenty; and they take care that they have two or three pieces of clover under one another, for it holds

[1] W. J. Lewis, 'Some Aspects of Lead Mining in Cardiganshire in the Sixteenth and Seventeenth Centuries', *Ceredigion*, I, 1950–1, pp. 176–90.

[2] *A Breviat of Glamorgan*, p. 108.

[3] 'Anglia Wallia', *Arch. Camb.*, XI, 1911, p. 432.

[4] Henry Rowlands, *Idea Agriculturae*, written in 1704, first published 1764, and printed in *Anglesey Antiq. Soc.*, 1934, pp. 86–107; 1935, pp. 145–81; 1936, pp. 54–93.

[5] Replies to Edward Lhuyd's questionnaire (1696), *Parochialia*, 1909, pp. 46, 60, 137, 142 (see note 1, p. 116, *supra*).

but three years at most."[1] Again, the improvements suggested by Henry Rowlands in his *Idea Agriculturae* (1704) had been speedily adopted on the Bodewryd estate, comprising about 2,500 acres of mixed farming in northern Anglesey. New fields with strong walls or hedges replaced the traditional pinfolds. Barley, rye, wheat, oats, and turnips were grown. The fields were regularly dressed with dung, lime, and sea sand, as well as put down to leys, "for it's no good husbandry to run the land ground out of heart." Clover seed arrived very suddenly at Bodewryd, sent in 1727 from the owner's residence at Ross-on-Wye in Herefordshire—a striking instance of transmission to a Welsh region with the capacity for responding to such revolutionary practices.[2] By contrast, in the hills of northern Cardiganshire, little had changed by 1755. Lewis Morris's vignette shows us farmers growing four or five crops of small oats after 'burn beating' ("too much in use"), milling the oats for bread and feeding the straw to their cattle in winter.[3] Their other crop was rye, for which the land was ploughed three or four times, and strengthened with cow-dung, bracken, and sheep-folding. A simple, light plough was usually drawn by two horses and two oxen. As the farmers had summer pasture without stint on the moorland, they reared "too many sheep...a farm of £10 will have two hundred sheep, which so demolish the quicksets and growing woods that...the whole country is open, almost like a common field." Some of the flocks were "even fifteen or twenty thousand, which is more than Job had." There were still wild cattle and horses "which run out all the winter."

At one stage of his journey through Wales in the 1530's, and in censorious mood, John Leland framed a judgment that "the Welshmen in times past, as they do almost yet, did study more to pasturage than tilling, as favourers of their consuet idleness." Such a remark was manifestly untrue of the lowland farmer, certainly in Elizabethan Wales, and, had he fully realized the rigours of an upland environment, Leland might have avoided such a conventional and shallow comment.

[1] Bodleian, MS Aubrey 2, fo. 152: John Aubrey was informed of this by his friend Henry Milbourne, Recorder of Monmouth.

[2] Leonard Owen, 'The Letters of an Anglesey Parson, 1712–32', *Hon. Soc. Cymmrodorion*, 1961, pp. 72–99; agrarian topics appear mainly in pp. 93 7. I am very grateful to Mr Owen for his further help in correspondence. According to Clark in 1794, clover and rye grass comprised two out of seven years in an "old system" of crop rotation at Ross. (David Thomas, 'Agricultural Changes in the Welsh Borderland', *ibid.*, p. 111.)

[3] BM Add. MS 14927, ff. 24, 27–9, in 'Answers to the Queries of ye Society of Antiquaries of London. By L.M. of the Parish of Llanbadarn vawr in the County of Cardigan, South Wales'. This manuscript is discussed by F. R. Lewis, 'Lewis Morris and the Parish of Llanbadarn Fawr, Cards., in 1755', *Arch. Camb.*, XCIII, 1938, pp. 15–30.

CHAPTER III

FARMING TECHNIQUES

A. INTRODUCTION

All periods of agricultural prosperity in England have given rise to a spate of literature on farming techniques. This was particularly true in the sixteenth and early seventeenth centuries, more especially after about 1560, when methods were more carefully examined and discussed than at any time since the thirteenth century, and the number of books published was greater than ever before. This reappraisal was prompted by the insistent demand for food, which made itself felt in every quarter of the kingdom. For as the population increased, not only were the towns obliged to seek larger supplies of food in the countryside, but every village too found itself supporting a larger number of families. Somehow the land in cultivation had to be made to grow more, the pastures had to be improved to support more stock, and the wasteland put to better use. It is not surprising that contemporary writings on husbandry are full of exhortations to improve the yield of the land and contemporary documents full of examples of how this was done. Men were imbued with the conviction that everything could and should be employed and improved. With economy and ingenuity every living thing, where possible, was pressed into the service of man—wild fruits, wild animals, weeds, wildflowers, insects— all found a use in agriculture or as medicines to promote the health of men and stock. Animals were cured of sicknesses with frogs, the earth of anthills, mugwort, rue, rosemary, savory, bloodwort, seeds of broom, herb robert, alder leaves, and a hundred and one other plants. In years of corn shortage the poor mixed beechmast and chestnuts in their breadflour, and when they were without ale they were urged to distil liquors from the birch tree and gorse flowers, aniseed, fennel seed, and caraway seed.[1]

This life of frugality and careful economy, far from being a painful necessity, was regarded as a positive virtue. Every hedgerow, men argued, could and should be planted with fruit trees. Hemp, they maintained, should be grown on every tiny weed-covered scrap of ground. On wet land, impossible to drain, willows would grow

---

[1] L. Mascall, *The Government of Cattle*, passim; Hugh Platt, *Sundrie New and Artificiall Remedies against Famine*, ff. A4ᵛ, C4ᵛ.

quickly; on the driest carrots would flourish. "I am of the opinion," wrote Norden, "that there is no kind of soil, be it never so wild, boggy, clay, or sandy, but will not yield one kind of beneficial fruit or another." Others evidently shared Norden's opinion. They offered remedies for all types of barren land overrun with heath and ling, sandy land covered with moss, waste moorland, marshes overflowed by the sea, land plagued with moles and anthills, and neglected fields rank with weeds. If men exploited their resources to the full, they argued, they would not need to settle new plantations overseas.[1]

That such comprehensive schemes of improvement were formulated in this period was proof of the favourable economic conditions surrounding the farming business. But every hopeful propagandist of improvement recognized the obstacles in the way of fulfilment. The majority of men, they admitted, were plain countrymen, who lacked resources or ambition or both. They carried on in the way of their forefathers, content with little, and loving leisure above the rewards of toil. "We have, indeed, a kind of plodding and common course of husbandry hereabouts," wrote Norden, "a kind of peevish imitation of the most, who (as wise men note) are the worst husbands." It was impossible to persuade such men to improve their land unless the scheme involved small expense. Hope lay in the ingenious husbandman who was willing to experiment. It was taken for granted that he would be master of his land, that is, that his arable and his pasture would be all, or at least mostly, enclosed.[2]

Even when this condition was satisfied, however, the diligent husbandman might be hindered by other obstacles. Some landlords deterred their tenants by refusing them long leases and by not allowing them compensation for improvements. The floating of land to improve fertility was prejudiced by millers who turned watercourses, and sometimes caused farmland to be flooded. Not all men were willing to co operate in destroying molehills and anthills and keeping their fields clean, and their sins were visited on their neighbours. For even when land was enclosed and freed of the burden of common rights, few men owned ring-fence farms, completely separate from their neighbours. On the contrary their lands lay in scattered bits and pieces, and their neighbour's bad or indifferent farming touched them nearly.[3]

Many were the complaints about bad farming—about those who exhausted their land with a few seasons' crops and abandoned it again,

---

[1] J. Norden, *The Surveyor's Dialogue*, 1607, pp. 204–8; Adam Speed, *Adam out of Eden*, Preface.

[2] Norden, *op. cit.*, p. 226; Gervase Markham, *Farewell to Husbandry*, p. 57.

[3] Gabriel Plattes, *A Discovery of Hidden Treasure*, p. 29; Walter Blith, *The English Improver Improved*, pp. A3–B2, 11.

and those who skimped the ploughings and stirrings. We can see why common-field regulations, and indeed, all village by-laws were necessary to maintain minimum standards of husbandry. Indeed it is tempting to argue that some of the worst examples of bad farming must have come not from the common field but from the enclosed areas which were populated by small family farmers. But we cannot be sure.[1]

On land let by lease some rules of husbandry were enforced by the landlord, but they affected only a small part of the farmer's routine—the rotations he used in his fields, and the frequency with which he manured his crops. Many a landlord tolerated a low standard of farming without complaint. James Bankes of Winstanley, Lancashire, a consider-ate landlord if ever there was one, did not expect his tenants to marl their land, but was content to wait until their leases fell in and they claimed no renewal, to carry out this much-needed improvement himself.[2]

In the cultivation of land, contemporaries regarded the labours of the husbandman as a continuous war upon nature to preserve the land from reverting to scrub and woodland. They believed that most, if not all, land in the kingdom had once consisted of forest, and that by the efforts of man it had been transformed into pasture and cornland. This version of past history meant that the creation of corn land was the supreme end of the farmer's work. The arable farmer was always held superior to the pasture farmer.

B. ARABLE HUSBANDRY

The necessary tools and equipment of the arable husbandman were the plough, the harrow, the clodding beetle, the drag, roller, fork, weed-hook, reaphook, scythe, sickle, pitchfork, rake, flail, sled, and seedlip, the dung cart, and the corn cart or wain, sometimes with iron-bound wheels. Most of the tools were made by hand while the husbandman sat by the fire on winter evenings.

Many different ploughs were at his disposal, varying in shape and detail according to the depth and strength of the soil they were intended to plough, and in part according to local eccentricity and obstinacy which none could logically explain. "The differences," wrote John Mortimer, more sceptical than most, "proceed more from the custom of the country than any usefulness that belongs to them." Despite this diversity, however, it was usual to classify ploughs into four groups:

[1] Blith, *op. cit.*, pp. 9–11.
[2] *The Memoranda Book of James Bankes, 1586–1617*, ed. Joyce Bankes, pp. 7–8.

the double-wheeled; the single-wheeled and foot ploughs; the ploughs without wheel or foot; and the Dutch or plain Dutch ploughs.[1]

The double-wheeled plough was used on flinty or gravelly soil—on the North Downs and in Hertfordshire, for example—where it stood the test of strength. It was drawn by horses or oxen double abreast, and the wheels could be adjusted deep or shallow. The turnwrest or Kentish plough was also double-wheeled, having either two turnwrests, or one which moved from one side to the other when the plough reached the headland. Either way, the turnwrest enabled the ploughman to reverse at the furrow end without turning the plough. Theoretically the idea was good. In practice, it was less successful; the Kentish plough surpassed all others for weight and clumsiness.[2]

The one-wheeled plough was a short, neat implement which, on the lightest soils, such as the brecklands of Norfolk, where the going was easy, could be drawn by one horse. More usually, however, it required a man and two horses. With this complement, the Colchester one-wheeled plough could plough two acres a day, while on the sandy lands of Norfolk and Suffolk with the same man and horse-power, it was possible to plough two or even three acres a day. In the deeper claylands, such as those of Oxfordshire, the foot plough was preferred to the one-wheeled plough. It was drawn by horses in a string, walking in the furrow.[3]

The plain plough without wheel or foot was the common man's plough, the cheapest and simplest of all, usable in most conditions, and indispensable on uneven hilly ground, where the wheeled plough was useless.[4]

Finally, the Dutch plough was used in the fens and marshland where the soil was free from stones. It had a broad sharp share, one-and-a-half feet wide, which could deal with matted weeds and sedge.[5]

The plough was drawn by oxen or horses or both, and the respective merits of each were discussed on a practical basis. Tough land was best left to oxen, whereas on lighter soils horses were faster and nimbler, though more costly to keep. When too old for work, oxen could be sold to the butcher, whereas the horse was profitless, apart from its hide. On the other hand it was unwise to keep oxen if your neighbours kept horses or you would "want their companies in your journey." The same debate in the nineteenth century contained no more original arguments than these.

[1] John Worlidge, *Systema Agriculturae*, p. 228; Norden, *op. cit.*, p. 191; Blith, *op. cit.*, p. 198; John Mortimer, *The Whole Art of Husbandry*, p. 38.

[2] Blith, *op. cit.*, pp. 198–203; Worlidge, *op. cit.*, p. 224.

[3] Blith, *op. cit.*, p. 203; Mortimer, *op. cit.*, p. 39; R. Plot, *The Natural History of Oxfordshire*, p. 247.

[4] Blith, *op. cit.*, p. 215.   [5] *Ibid.*, p. 209; Mortimer, *op. cit.*, p. 39.

The final decision in the sixteenth century rested not so much on the cost of draught animals as on the availability of fodder on the farm. In pastoral areas the grass was abundant, in arable areas oats could be grown. A horse could be tethered on balks in the common fields, oxen could not. Nor was it any good putting oxen to graze on a bare common pasture after a day's work, and expecting them to be fresh for work in the morning. They had to be put to lush grass that was only available in closes. So long as fodder was the decisive factor, then, the mixed farmer with sufficient pasture in severalty and the pasture farmer could keep oxen, although in mountainous districts the latter would have to keep horses as well for transport down the hillsides. The common-field farmer in the lowlands was more likely to use horses. The rich man used both.[1]

Methods of ploughing varied according to the different types of soil. On stiffish clay soils the land was thrown up into high ridges before sowing to lift the seed out of the damp, waterlogged furrows. This method was used in Bedfordshire, in the vale of the White Horse in Berkshire, in Buckinghamshire in the vale of Aylesbury, in the Weald of Kent, the vales of Gloucestershire, and in Durham. On the very heaviest clays, as in Essex, Middlesex, and Hertfordshire, the land was also ridged up but into narrow lands of no more than two or three furrows to prevent the soil from sticking together in a solid mass and to enable weeding to be carried out more easily. On the light soils of the chalk downlands and wolds, on the Isle of Portland, the warm soils of south Devon, and the East Anglian brecklands, the land was ploughed flat without water furrows in order to retain as much moisture as possible. It was in common fields in these areas that, for lack of water furrows, the grass balks were necessary, to define the boundaries of each man's strips.[2]

After the land had been ridged up on heavy soils in the common fields (and, for that matter, in enclosures also) adequate drainage was secured by directing the water from the ends of the furrows into gutters crossing the headlands, by cutting cross-gutters to drain the water to the sides of the fields, and by trenching. Trenching was often carried out at the expense of the whole community, and guttering too might be done on this basis, if it was not the responsibility of the individual.[3]

The work of guttering was carried out by a trenching plough,

---

[1] *The Book of Husbandry by Master Fitzherbert*, ed. W. W. Skeat, English Dialect Society, 1882, p. 15; Mascall, *op. cit.*, pp. 300–1; Markham, *op. cit.*, pp. 153–4.

[2] E. Kerridge, 'Ridge and Furrow and Agrarian History', EcHR, 2nd Ser., IV, i, 1951, pp. 14–20.

[3] E. Kerridge, 'A Reconsideration of Some Former Husbandry Practices', AHR, III, i, 1955, pp. 27–30.

wheeled or unwheeled (Plate II). The smaller type was owned by individuals, the larger, which belonged to the whole township and was maintained at its expense, was drawn by as many as eight or nine oxen, with two or four horses in front, ridden by boys to guide the whole equipage. The town plough, frequently with two coulters, cut drains about one foot deep. Trenching spades and shovels perfected the work of the plough, or if a plough was not to be had, the work could be done more laboriously with the spade alone. Manorial court orders afford ample evidence of the attention that was rightly given to this vital matter of drainage.[1]

Arable land was usually ploughed three times in the fallow year in preparation for wheat, four times by the industrious, twice only on some soils, and in other years only once or twice. In the fallow year a shallow ploughing, casting the ridges down, was given in April when once the crops were sown in the other fields. The second ploughing in about June went deeper than the first and included ridging up the land. The third was performed in July or August when the land was cast down again, if appropriate, or left ridged up if not. The land was then harrowed and sown and harrowed again, and any clods remaining were crumbled with the roller, or by hand with the mattock or clodding beetle, a tool which resembled a carpenter's mallet but with a longer handle. Spring crops were sown after one or two ploughings, and the available dung applied to the barley in April or the beginning of May.[2]

Ley ground, waiting to be ploughed again after several years of grass, was turned over soon after the beginning of the year, and oats were sown as the first crop. Wasteland, such as that on Dartmoor, which was being brought into cultivation for the first time, old pasture overgrown with moss or rushes, and fen and marshland being cultivated for the first time after drainage, was denshired. The turf was pared off with a paring plough in summer, piled into heaps and burned, and the ashes scattered over the land. If oats were not the first crop, then coleseed was recommended, particularly in the fens.[3]

Seed was carefully selected by the best farmers, and the sources of supply changed at regular intervals. In many cases it was bought from far afield, and if possible from a worse soil than that in which it was to be sown. North Staffordshire farmers bought their seed from south Staffordshire, and vice versa; wheat and barley seed for west Suffolk farmers came from Cambridgeshire; the best hempseed was imported

[1] E. Kerridge, *loc. cit.*; G. Atwell, *The Faithfull Surveyour*, p. 88.
[2] E. Maxey, *A New Instruction of Planting and Setting of Corne*, f.B3; Mortimer, *op. cit.*, pp. 44–6; Fitzherbert, *op. cit.*, pp. 24–8, 31–9; W. Ellis, *Chiltern and Vale Farming*, p. 308.
[3] Fitzherbert, *op. cit.*, p. 17; E134, 4 Chas. I, Easter 9; Blith, *op. cit.*, p. 61.

from Holland. Various steeps for seed were used before sowing, and many experiments were carried out to test their virtues, some prompting their inventors to apply for a royal patent granting them sole use of their invention. A much-used method was to steep the seed in brine and then mix it with unslaked lime. This prevented smut and deterred the birds. Another recipe used salt, red lead, and water, and yet another sheep dung steeped in water.[1]

Corn was either sown broadcast and harrowed in, ploughed under furrow, or set with a setting board. Peas, vetches, and beans were sown broadcast and ploughed or harrowed in; beans were sometimes set with a dibbler. At harvest wheat was reaped with a sickle or hook, barley and oats were usually mown with a scythe, peas and beans reaped or sometimes mown. Local practice differed according to custom or the fashion of the moment. Maxey tried to set the fashion of using a setting board for wheat, but the task must have been extremely tedious and he probably had few followers. In parts of Somerset around Martock wheat was shorn very low, the ears cut off, and the stalks used for thatching.[2]

For manure, anything and everything was put to use. At Newcastle-on-Tyne the burgesses cast their ashes and dung on a heap adjoining the castle walls in the middle of the town, which was carted away once a year by country farmers. Some of the muck from Newcastle was also carried away by water to country areas along the coast. Marl was dug from medieval marlpits in Lancashire, Cheshire, Shropshire, Somerset, Middlesex, Sussex, and Surrey. In Shropshire, Denbighshire, Flintshire, and later in Sussex, limestone was carried two to four miles from the hills to be burned in kilns in the fields and then cast on the land. Pebbles from the beaches of Kent, Sussex, and Suffolk were similarly burned and applied to the fields. Around Padstow in Cornwall people led their horses, laden with sacks of seasand, as much as six miles to their farms. In Hertfordshire farmers laid bracken in the lanes in autumn, and in March when it was well trodden down by the feet of horses and men and by the wheels of carts and carriages, it was carried on to the fields. In Sussex and Surrey the cleansing of the many fish-ponds provided more manure. Sludge from the river Colne was transported eight to ten miles to fertilize barren land in Hertfordshire, Buckinghamshire, and Middlesex, and from the river Avon into Hampshire. London's stable dung travelled down the Thames to

[1] Mortimer, *op. cit.*, pp. 50–2; SP 14, 187, 22A; Hugh Platt, *The Garden of Eden*, p. 91; E. Kerridge, 'The Notebook of a Wiltshire Farmer in the Early Seventeenth Century', *Wilts. Arch. & Nat. Hist. Mag.*, CXCVII, 1952, p. 420.

[2] Fitzherbert, *op. cit.*, p. 39; Ellis, *op. cit.*, pp. 221, 230; J. Blagrave, *The Epitomie of the Art of Husbandry*, 1685, pp. 26–7; Plot, *op. cit.*, pp. 255–6.

Chelsea, Fulham, Battersea, and Putney. Malt dust discarded by the maltsters, soap ashes cast out by the soap boilers, brine taken from the Nantwich salt pits, hair from the backs of animals, decaying fish, offal, beasts' entrails and blood, all were laid on the land.[1]

In addition to all this, the dung of cattle, sheep, pigs, horses, and pigeons was employed with the utmost diligence and economy. Pigeon dung was prized most highly, but it was not available everywhere; the counties with the most pigeons were Bedfordshire, Northamptonshire, and Cambridgeshire. For the majority of farmers, the best and strongest dung to be had was sheep's dung, and it was for this reason that sheep-folding on the common fields fertilized them so handsomely. Cattle dung was laid on warm soils, stable dung on cold land, and the better the horses were fed the better the dung. Corned horse dung was therefore richer than hay horse dung. Since barley benefited most from rich manure, the dung was usually laid on the barley at the end of April or beginning of May.[2]

The commonest arable crops were wheat, rye, barley or bigg, oats or haver, beans, and peas, with the addition of buckwheat, vetches, tares, and lentils in certain areas.

Both species of wheat were grown in England and Wales at this period, rivet or cone wheat (*triticum turgidum*) which produces a mealy flour suitable for biscuits, and bread wheat (*triticum vulgare*) which yields a strong flour, suitable for bread-making. The bread wheats, usually, though not always, beardless, seem to have been the most common, although some fifteenth- and sixteenth-century specimens of plant remains from Kent suggest that in this county, at least, rivet wheats may have predominated. Of bread wheats there were many varieties. The most notable were *flaxen wheat*, without awns, with a yellow ear, small straw, and small corn, which made the whitest bread and grew well on indifferent land; *pole-eared wheat*, also without awns and thickset in the ear; *white wheat* with a square ear; *red-stalked wheat*, more resistant to smut, which was said to have been first propagated at Dunstable in the 1620's, spread through Buckingham-shire, and became one of the commonest varieties grown in Oxford-shire fifty years later; and *white-eared red wheat*, introduced about the middle of the seventeenth century, which yielded twenty grains for one, far more than any other variety. When wheat and rye were sown

[1] E 134, 20 Jas. I, E 18; Norden, *op. cit.*, pp. 226–30, 219–22; H. Prince, 'Pits and Ponds in Norfolk', *Erdkunde*, XVI, i, 1962, *passim*; Hugh Platt, *The Jewell House of Art and Nature*, pp. 49, 50, 42, 59.

[2] Worlidge, *op. cit.*, pp. 66–8; John Smith, *England's Improvement Revived*, 1673, p. 174; Blith, *op. cit.*, pp. 147–8; Fitzherbert, *op. cit.*, p. 27; Norwich Public Library, MS 1505, Box I, D 2.

together as maslin, the first three of these varieties were particularly recommended, since they ripened early and were ready with the rye. Rivet wheats, though less common, were growing on the rank clays of Oxfordshire when Plot wrote his *Natural History* of the county in 1676, and were specially resistant to mildew and lodging. A century and a half earlier, Fitzherbert's description of Peak wheat which had a red ear, was full of awns, and would not make bread, almost certainly refers to a variety of rivet wheat.[1]

Almost always wheat was sown in the autumn, and usually in September, but a March or summer wheat, sown in spring, was known in the northern counties, and was remarked by William Harrison when travelling in the neighbourhood of Kendal. The wheat of Heston, Middlesex, was among the most celebrated in England, but wheat was also the principal white grain in some other districts of the lowlands such as central Hertfordshire, the Lincolnshire marshlands and Holderness, the heaths and sands of Hampshire and Dorset, the vales of Taunton Deane and Wellington, and the Kentish downs. Mostly, however, it was second in importance to barley. This meant that barley, even in the lowlands, was the main breadcorn.[2]

Two varieties of rye were grown in the sixteenth century, a winter variety, sown in September, and often eaten down by sheep in the spring, and a spring variety, used in the northern counties, which was sown in March, produced a shorter straw and smaller ear, and made a very brown bread. Rye was a common crop for growing in small quantities, but larger acreages were to be found on gravelly, dry soils, such as the Archenfield district of Herefordshire, in the Wye valley around Clehonger, on the eastern sands of Suffolk, in the vale of York, on the Bunter Sandstones of the Cannock hills in Staffordshire, and in Shropshire. In this last county the spring variety was used and land was often measured according to the amount of rye required to sow it. Rye was also a common crop on the sour soils of the Yorkshire moors and dales, and on Dartmoor, before manuring made the soil fertile for barley. In all these districts, rye was the principal, if not the only, grain used for bread, whereas elsewhere it was more commonly used in a mixture with wheat, for bread made from maslin was thought to keep moist longer than pure wheaten bread.[3]

[1] J. R. B. Arthur, *Plant Remains taken from Medieval Building Material*, n.d. (1963?), *passim*; Fitzherbert, *op. cit.*, p. 40; Plot, *op. cit.*, pp. 151–2; Worlidge, *op. cit.*, p. 36; J. M. Percival, *The Wheat Plant, a Monograph*, pp. 156–7, 241–3, 265–74, 289, 296; Henry Lyte, transl., *A Niewe Herbal*, p. 453.

[2] W. Harrison, *Elizabethan England*, ed. F. J. Furnivall, p. 98; W. Folkingham, *Feudigraphia*, p. 42.

[3] Lyte, *op. cit.*, p. 459; Beale, *Herefordshire Orchards*, p. 36; Salop RO, 167, 43; E 134, 3 & 4 Chas. I, Hil. 11.

Of all the white grains, barley was probably grown in largest quantity, for it served a triple purpose for bread, malt, and stock feed, and since it made fewer demands on the land than wheat, it would grow in the less fertile soils of the common fields. With good reason, then, it was dubbed "the countryman's tillage" (Plate III). The most usual variety of barley was two-rowed barley, of which there were two main kinds in the early sixteenth century, *long-ear*, being a form of *hordeum distichum*, and having a long, narrow ear and smallish corn, and *spratt*, a form of *hordeum zeocriton*, which possessed a larger corn and was considered the best barley. The latter was specially recommended for rank land since it had a stiff, erect straw, a characteristic which has commended it to barley-growers ever since. An early ripening or *rathe-ripe* variety of narrow-eared barley came to prominence in the seventeenth century, which could be sown in May rather than March and returned to the barn in two months or less. It was of the greatest value in wet, backward springs, and was known in Cornwall, and much grown in Oxfordshire. It originated, however, in Patney, Wiltshire, whence the seed was despatched far afield. Another less-celebrated rathe-ripe form of *hordeum distichum* was Scotch barley which was cultivated in Lincolnshire.[1]

Less popular than the two-rowed barleys was *naked* or *wheat* barley, also known as French barley, which resembled wheat in the ease with which the grain came from the ear. It made good bread and malt, and was popular in parts of Staffordshire, such as the Hamstall–Ridware district. The worst barley was six-rowed *bere* or *bigg*, which was spring or sometimes autumn sown and produced a harvest, though a poor one, on the dryest, poorest soils. William Harrison noticed it growing in the neighbourhood of Kendal, and it seems to have been the most common type of barley in Durham, Cumberland, Westmorland, and High Furness.[2]

Although the main uses of barley were for beer—that of Lincolnshire and the Hertfordshire Chilterns was mostly used for this purpose—and also for bread, it was widely used, usually in a boiled mash, for weaning and fattening pigs, and fattening capons, barren cows, oxen that were past work, and sheep that were short of grass in winter. A large amount of barley was used in this way in counties such as Hertfordshire and Leicestershire, particularly in the latter where barley was the main corn crop and lack of river transport prevented its being marketed far afield.[3]

[1] Worlidge, *op. cit.*, pp. 36–7; Fitzherbert, *op. cit.*, pp. 22–3; H. Hunter, *The Barley Crop*, 1952, pp. 5, 31–2; Plot, *op. cit.*, pp. 152–3; Lyte, *op. cit.*, pp. 460–1; Mortimer, *op. cit.*, p. 100.

[2] Mortimer, *op. cit.*, p. 100; Lyte, *op. cit.*, p. 460; *Elizabethan England*, p. 98.

[3] Worlidge, *op. cit.*, p. 51.

On the very poorest and wettest soils the only cereal that would succeed was oats. Hence it was the main crop of the Derbyshire Peak, the Staffordshire moorlands, the Yorkshire dales, south Lancashire, and parts of Wales, and came second only to bigg in all other parts of the northern counties. It was the largest crop on Dartmoor and in north Devon, and a common one elsewhere in Devon and Cornwall. It was also extensively grown in some pastoral areas in lowland England such as the Weald of Kent and Sussex.[1]

In mountainous counties where wheat-growing was rarely possible and barley was needed for beer, oats were used to make bread and sometimes for malting as well. But their main purpose was to make oatmeal concoctions, such as pottage, hasty pudding, gruel, washbrew, and gertbrew, which provided starch in the diet in more varied forms than oat bread and oat cake. Further south, oats were grown to feed cattle, pigs, horses, and poultry. The large acreages in Hertfordshire, for example, were intended for its many stables which provisioned horses on their way to and from London. In Somerset they were put to yet another use by clothiers who used them to thicken their mingled cloths.[2]

The varieties grown were white, black, and red oats. Red oats were best for oatmeal and were grown in Staffordshire and the north. Black (Tartarian) oats, found in Westmorland, for example, were sown early in spring, at the end of February or beginning of March, but made inferior oatmeal. White oats were sown in April and yielded the heaviest grain, good for both bread and pottage (Plate III).[3]

Of peas there were several sorts; white, green, grey, and black, and the local varieties of each were innumerable. *Hotspurs* were ripe soonest, *sugar peas* were the sweetest, the *White Hastings* were large and ready among the earliest, grey *Runcival* peas were the fullest, *Red Shanks* were best for freshly broken land, *Vale grey* for strong land, *Hampshire kids* for newly chalked land, and the *Cotswold* pea for gravelly land. Since beans required a strong soil if they were to do well, peas were the usual alternative for lighter land, though various mixtures were also sown. In Durham oats and peas were cropped together, and in other places beans and peas. Their principal use was for feeding horses, sheep, pigeons, and fattening pigs.[4]

[1] Mortimer, *op. cit.*, p. 105; E 134, 3 & 4 Chas. I, Hil. 11; W. J. Blake, 'Hooker's Synopsis Chorographical of Devonshire', *Devon Assoc..*, XLVII, p. 345.

[2] Markham, *Farewell to Husbandry*, p. 133; CSPD 1629-31, p. 406. For the difference between the oatbread of north-west England and the oatcake of north-east England, Scotland, and Wales, see F. Atkinson, 'Oatbread of Northern England', *Gwerin*, III, 1960-2, pp. 44 *sqq.*

[3] Mortimer, *op. cit.*, pp. 103-5; Worlidge, *op. cit.*, p. 37; Fitzherbert, *op. cit.*, p. 23.

[4] Lyte, *op. cit.*, pp. 474-5; Worlidge, *op. cit.*, p. 149; Plot, *op. cit.*, p. 153.

Among beans, the domestic variety was grown in gardens only, and the great field bean—usually white, but sometimes red or brown and flat in shape—made only a rare appearance. Much the most common were the small horse beans, which were sown in February, and when harvested in the north country and the Midlands, at least, were usually made into small ricks. But they were widely grown on all stiff clay soils, and of all pulses were probably grown in largest quantity. They were used to fatten pigs—a speciality of Leicestershire and Hertfordshire, for example—to feed pigeons, horses, sheep, and in lean years to make meal for bread.[1]

Lentils were highly praised by agricultural writers as the best of all pulses for feeding calves and pigeons, but if the evidence of farmers' inventories is to be trusted they were not a common crop, though they were found in south Lancashire and Oxfordshire.[2]

Winter and summer varieties of vetch were grown, but it was a crop of southern England and in the north seems to have been entirely neglected. In Oxfordshire the *Gore* and *Pebble* vetch were sown on sour land, the rathe-ripe or early-ripening variety on cold, moist ground. On the North Downs in Kent, a considerable acreage was grazed by cattle, and afterwards ploughed in. But when vetches were to be mown, they were often planted with a cereal, oats in particular, to act as a support.[3]

Lupines were recommended in at least one contemporary textbook of husbandry as a good crop in the arable rotation for sheep feed, but the exhortation to grow it seems to have been in vain. No reference to a growing crop of lupines has been found in documents, and it is probable, as some writers, indeed, imply, that it was a plant better known to gardeners and herbalists than to farmers.[4]

Buckwheat or French wheat was grown on barren, sandy land which would not grow much else, and was supremely good for fattening poultry and pigs, while in years of dearth it was used by the poor, mixed with barley, to make "a very hearty and well-relished bread." If it did not instigate, it certainly promoted the growth of the poultry business in Norfolk and Suffolk, for the largest acreages of buckwheat in the whole kingdom seem to have been grown on the sands and brecks, where hundreds of turkeys, geese, chickens, and ducks were fattened for the table. It was also grown on the Bagshot

[1] Lyte, *op. cit.*, pp. 472–3; Markham, *Farewell to Husbandry*, pp. 135–6; Mortimer, *op. cit.*, p. 107.

[2] Worlidge, *op. cit.*, p. 38; Mortimer, *op. cit.*, pp. 107–8; M. Havinden, 'Agricultural Progress in Open-Field Oxfordshire', AHR, ix, 1961, p. 82.

[3] Worlidge, *op. cit.*, p. 38; S. Hartlib, *His Legacie*, p. 49.

[4] Markham, *Farewell to Husbandry*, p. 43; Hartlib, *op. cit.*, p. 49; H. Lyte, *op. cit.*, pp. 480–1; Worlidge, *op. cit.*, p. 38.

heaths in Surrey, on the downlands of Hampshire, and in Essex (Plate IV).[1]

It is evident from this enumeration of the many varieties of common arable crops, both cereals and legumes, that considerable attention was paid to the quality of each variety, and that there were always men on the look-out for new strains that would yield better, prove more resistant to disease, or easier to harvest. In addition, some new, and some not so new, crops were being developed in special localities. Information about them was passed on to literate farmers by enthusiastic writers who thought it possible to extend to other places the cultivation of these less usual plants. One of these was coleseed or rape, a plant that was already indigenous on the seashores of this country. The full circumstances of its introduction as a field crop are not yet known, but Barnaby Googe, a Lincolnshire squire, who saw it growing in the Principality of Cleves, publicized it in print in *The Four Bookes of Husbandry* in 1577, commending it as a green manure, as sheep fodder, and as a source of oil. Since strenuous efforts were being made during the same decade to promote the manufacture of oil in England and so to reduce the imports of expensive foreign oils, it is unlikely that the usefulness of coleseed passed unnoticed, particularly since it was more productive of oil than either linseed or hempseed. Not until the 1590's, however, is there proof of coleseed being grown on a large scale, and by then it was being exported from eastern England, a fact which suggests that the volume of production was considerable.[2]

Most early references to coleseed relate to the fens and marshes of eastern England, where the soil was admirably suited to it. In 1593 it was being exported from Boston; in September 1599 a farmer of Terrington St Clements, Norfolk, was in possession of ten coombs of rapeseed; in 1611 and 1631 it was being exported from Maldon, and in 1631 from Colchester; in 1632 it was one of the crops sown on four thousand acres of Sutton Marsh, Lincolnshire, and was frequently mentioned as a crop in other Lincolnshire fens newly drained by the Dutch. The chronological order of these documentary references makes it impossible to continue to attribute the introduction of coleseed to the Dutch drainers who came to England with Vermuyden in the early seventeenth century. However, it is more than likely that the crop was introduced from the Netherlands, for it had been extensively grown there ever since the Middle Ages, and, since it seems to have been first deliberately cultivated in the field in Elizabeth's reign, and since all seed was always recommended to be brought from

[1] Worlidge, *op. cit.*, p. 37; CSPD 1629–31, p. 545; SP 16, 187, 12.

[2] G. E. Fussell, 'History of Cole (Brassica Sp.)', *Nature*, CLXXVI, no. 4471, p. 48; H. W. Brace, *History of Seedcrushing in Great Britain*, pp. 15–17.

Holland, it seems reasonable to guess that it was introduced by the refugees who settled in East Anglia and recognized the suitability of the crop in their new environment. Its value as oil seems to have been regarded as its first asset, but when the oil was pressed out, the residue was made into cakes for fodder and for fuel. Towards the end of the seventeenth century the value of the stubble as winter food for sheep was more widely publicized, and at the same time the acreage was greatly increased.[1]

Other crops urged upon the enterprising farmer were plants used for dyes. Weld, otherwise known as *dyer's weed*, which produced a yellow dye, was one of these. It needed a warm, dry soil, but since it did not produce a crop until the second year, it was recommended to be sown with barley or oats in the first year. Large claims were made for its profitability—that it would repay the farmer four times the charge of the land and its cultivation. However, the only known centre for the crop seems to have been the chalklands of Kent, particularly around Canterbury and Wye, where the seed was marketed.[2]

Greater success was had with woad owing to the additional propaganda of the government. Although woad grew wild in various parts of England, and had also been deliberately cultivated on some monastic estates in the Middle Ages, the necessity for growing it was not urged until the second half of the sixteenth century. The rising demands of the wool-textile industry induced farmers to plant more of it and thus enable the clothiers to dispense with imports from France. It had long been regarded as an exhausting crop. Now the opinion gained ground that it was, nevertheless, a very profitable one. A report of woad growing in Surrey in 1585 described the profit from two acres after all charges as five guineas, or, as another report put it, six times the profit of corn. The commercial attractions of the crop may also be inferred from a proclamation of 1587, a famine year, limiting the amount of woad that might be grown on individual farms and in parishes as a whole, and forbidding its cultivation near royal palaces, cities, market towns, and thoroughfares. Woad-growing had become so popular a business that it prompted the fear that land would be exhausted on a large scale, and the poor deprived of means to sustain them. The panic of 1587 was quickly allayed, however, and in 1589 a more liberal policy was announced allowing anyone to grow woad who wished.[3]

Because of the intensive cultivation necessary to grow woad, it is probable that the land benefited in the long run from this crop. As a

[1] H. W. Brace, *loc. cit.*; Fussell, *op. cit.*, pp. 48–9; Thirsk, *English Peasant Farming*, 180, 79; Blith, *op. cit.*, p. 249; Worlidge, *op. cit.*, p. 52; Mortimer, *op. cit.*, pp. 120–1. p. 133; SP 14,   [2] Blith, *op. cit.*, pp. 222–4.
[3] J. B. Hurry, *The Woad Plant and its Dye*, 1930, pp. 59–64.

reporter from Surrey expressed it in 1585, "we have seen good wheat and barley after woad, which we take not to be because of the woad but the rather by so much marling, stirring, and soiling of the ground in far more better sort than they do for corn." Every one agreed, however, that after woad it was no good trying to grow grass for many years.[1]

One of the principal and earliest areas in which woad was grown in the Middle Ages was Somerset, but by the later sixteenth century there were woad farms in Hampshire, Bedfordshire, at Lathbury in Buckinghamshire, and at Alphamstone in Essex. By the mid-seventeenth century, it was also being grown in Worcestershire, south Warwickshire, Oxfordshire, Gloucestershire, Northamptonshire, Leicestershire, and parts of Rutland. It had to be cultivated in a deep, well-drained soil, and it was for this reason that many sites lay on alluvial land near rivers.[2]

Yet another dye plant was madder for red colouring. It was grown at Barn Elms, Barnes, in Charles I's reign, and at Deptford in the 1650's, but it was a crop that took three years to come to perfection, and was not likely to commend itself to many. It was more popular with gardeners who grew it for the apothecary.[3]

Saffron was used as a dye as well as a condiment, medicine, and perfume, and was a speciality in the neighbourhood of Saffron Walden, Essex, in Suffolk, around Walsingham in Norfolk, and in Cambridge-shire. It was planted at midsummer and was ready to yield a crop the following autumn. It was said to prepare the ground for splendid harvests of barley.[4]

Various plants for culinary use were grown as field crops in special localities. Caraway was grown in Oxfordshire at Clanfield. Mustard seed was grown in the Norfolk fens and around Tewkesbury, onions in the Lincolnshire fens, and liquorice at Worksop in Nottinghamshire, at Pontefract, Yorkshire, and at Godalming, Surrey. Carrots were grown in east Suffolk, at Orford, Ipswich, and along the coast; at Framlingham inland; at Bury St Edmunds in west Suffolk; at Norwich and other places in Norfolk; and at Colchester, Essex. At Fulham, near London, where market-gardening was becoming the principal occupation, carrots were grown together with parsnips, turnips, and other vegetables in common fields, parts of which were ploughed, parts dug with the spade, and all kept fertile by an occasional change from vegetable to wheat-growing. Although most of this crop was destined for the table, some carrots were used to feed poultry, and probably in Suffolk, at least, to feed cows and fatten bullocks thus leading men on

[1] Guildford Muniment Room, Loseley MS 1966, 3 and 1.
[2] Hurry, op. cit., pp. 65–70, 11.   [3] Blith, op. cit., p. 235.
[4] Folkingham, op. cit., pp. 31, 42; Blith, op. cit., p. 244.

to the idea of using turnips in the same way. The use of carrots for cattle is strongly suggested by an inventory of Robert Beversham of Sudbury, yeoman, who in January 1638 had eighteen cows, forty bullocks, 38 acres of rye, and five acres of carrots.[1]

More original than any of the plants mentioned already was tobacco, first cultivated in England about 1571. Experiments were made with both *nicotiana tabacum* and *nicotiana rustica* or yellow henbane, but by the early seventeenth century the latter had supplanted the former. Repeated attempts were made by the Crown in the reigns of James I and Charles I to suppress the cultivation of tobacco in England and Wales in order to ensure a market at home for the Virginian crop, but they had not the slightest effect. The acreage of land growing tobacco increased by leaps and bounds. In the early seventeenth century it was grown in yards and gardens in London and Westminster, in the Home Counties, the Channel Islands, in Lincolnshire and Yorkshire, Worcestershire, Warwickshire, and Wiltshire, and above all in Gloucestershire, where the districts around Winchcombe, Cheltenham, and Tewkesbury became the most important centres of tobacco-growing in the kingdom. The history of this crop illustrates better than any other, perhaps, how adventurous English farmers from all districts could be when once they had been persuaded of the success of a new farm enterprise.[2]

Another newly introduced plant of this period was hops, said to have been introduced into England at the time of the Reformation. They were first grown in Suffolk, Kent, Surrey, and Essex, and later moved westward into Hampshire and Herefordshire, where John Beale, a proud native of the latter county, claimed in 1657 that with the hops around Bromyard "we make haste to be the chief hopmasters in England." Despite high labour costs the financial rewards of hop-growing were attractive to large farmers who had suitable, well-drained soil: twenty acres of hop bines, growing at Earls Colne in Essex in 1631, were valued at £400.[3]

Among crops grown for the making and processing of various kinds of cloth and for the making of domestic goods such as baskets, some were common to most parts of England and Wales, some were confined to special areas. Among the latter were teasels, used in the

[1] Plot, *op. cit.*, p. 155; Folkingham, *op. cit.*, p. 42; Blith, *op. cit.*, pp. 246–8; Worlidge, *op. cit.*, p. 147; Norden, *op. cit.*, p. 207; P. McGrath, *The Marketing of Food, Fodder, and Livestock in the London Area in the Seventeenth Century*, London M.A. thesis, 1948, p. 197; Hugh Platte, *The Jewell House of Art and Nature*, p. 13.

[2] C. M. MacInnes, *The Early English Tobacco Trade*, pp. 76–93. For the villages growing tobacco in Glos., Worcs., and Wilts., see *Acts of the Privy Council*, Jan.–Aug. 1627, p. 409.

[3] Robert Reyce, *Suffolk in the Seventeenth Century*, p. 31; Norden, *op. cit.*, p. 206; John Beale, *Herefordshire Orchards*, p. 47.

finishing of cloth, which were grown in the Cheddar area of Somerset, and were considered excellent as a preparation for wheat, because their strong roots opened out the soil. Osiers were a speciality of the fens of eastern England and the Somerset Levels, and were used for making baskets. The more common crops were hemp and flax. They were grown in small tofts and crofts by the peasantry, who, after the harvest, found further employment in dressing them for the weaver. At the same time, some districts grew these crops on a larger scale, and here too the harvest, coming after other harvests, gave much-needed work to the poor. Hemp requires a rich, alluvial soil, and was particularly suited to fenland. It occupied a large acreage in the fens of south-east Lincolnshire, Norfolk, and the Isle of Axholme, and along the rivers in east Suffolk, Sussex, Dorset, and Somerset. Good flax land lay in Essex, along the rivers of Kent, particularly around Maidstone on the Medway (where the best thread in all England was spun), in Warwickshire, Worcestershire, the forests of Northamptonshire, and, finally, in Gloucestershire, where at Winchcombe in James I's reign an agriculturist who had formerly bought flax from the Eastland company to be dressed by the poor, planted 40 acres and claimed to employ eight hundred people in cultivating and dressing it. Both crops had many uses besides being woven into cloth. Linseed oil from flax was used in paint and soap, and the chaff and the stalks for fuel. Hemp made exceedingly strong ropes that were used as horse halters and for shipping purposes. The seed was good for feeding poultry.[1]

It is clear from the variety of crops grown in the kingdom, from the fact that some of the unusual ones such as teasels and saffron were fitted into the crop rotation of modest peasant farmers, while even market-gardening was carried on in common fields, that the cropping schedule of every locality, sometimes also of every field in one township, was subject to the greatest variety. On newly reclaimed land, and on all poor soils in the northern counties, the rotation often consisted of two, three, or four years of arable crops, followed by seven or eight years of leys. In Cumberland, for example, the rotation was oats, barley (usually bigg), oats, and then grass for seven to ten years. In the more fertile vale lands of the kingdom, including the lowlands of Durham, a more intensive rotation of two year's crops and one of fallow was the rule. Sometimes it consisted of winter corn, spring corn or pulses, and a fallow, as in the vale of Aylesbury, or wheat or barley one year, oats or pulses in the second, and a fallow in the third, as in the vale of York. In the marshlands of Lincolnshire and east Yorkshire a two-course rotation was customary, which meant that one field lay

[1] VCH *Somerset*, II, p. 542; Thirsk, *op. cit.*, p. 30; Norden, *op. cit.*, p. 207; Blith, *op. cit.*, pp. 254–5; Worlidge, *op. cit.*, pp. 40, 52; SP 14, 180, 79.

fallow while the other was divided into furlongs, some growing spring, some winter crops. On the brecklands of Norfolk a four-course rotation was followed, consisting of barley, rye, then barley or another spring crop, then fallow. In the fens of Lincolnshire some land alternated between arable and pasture, some supported crops year after year without a fallow. And in many parts of England farmers in common fields sometimes grew tares on parts of the common fields that would otherwise have lain fallow.[1]

It is impossible to discover all the various rotations that suited each locality and, indeed, each season. But one innovation affecting the rotations in mixed farming areas in the lowlands deserves special notice. It was the introduction of years of leys on arable land which had previously been subject to a regular course of grain, legumes, and one year's fallow. It is possible that the practice was suggested by rotations used in the north where leys of seven to ten years were not unusual. What is certain is that the use of leys in old arable fields revived a lot of ploughland which badly needed a rest under grass. The logic behind the system was described by Fitzherbert in his *Book of Husbandry* for the benefit of those who had enclosed lands. "And if any of his three closes that he hath for his corn be worn or wear bare, then he may break and plough up his close that he had for his leys, or the close that he had for his common pasture, or both, and sow them with corn and let the other lie for a time and so shall he have always rest ground, the which will bear much corn with little dung." The first reference so far found to leys in common fields relates to Wymeswold in Leicestershire in the early fifteenth century. In documents of the sixteenth and seventeenth centuries there are numerous examples of leys among the common fields and village agreements have been adduced to show how the system worked. It was necessary for the owners of the strips to agree to put them under grass, and when the ley was established it could be grazed by them all. How long the leys were left before they were ploughed up is a more difficult question to answer. It has been suggested on the evidence of leys in Cambridgeshire that some became permanent pasture, though termed 'leys'. But other references to leys newly ploughed or to "broken up leys" suggest that they were genuinely temporary, though they might last ten years or more.[2]

---

[1] See *supra*, p. 175; Ellis, *op. cit.*, p. 197; Thirsk, *op. cit.*, pp. 61, 23, 100; E 134, 4 Jas. I, E 26; Havinden, *op. cit.*, pp. 78–9; E. Kerridge, 'The Notebook of a Wiltshire Farmer in the early Seventeenth Century', *Wilts. Arch. & Nat. Hist. Mag.*, CXCVII, 1952, p. 419.

[2] TED, III, p. 23; W. G. Hoskins, *Essays in Leicestershire History*, pp. 139–43; Thirsk, *op. cit.*, pp. 100–1; M. Havinden, *op. cit.*, p. 75; Margaret Spufford, 'Rural Cambridgeshire, 1520–1680', Leicester M.A. thesis, 1962, p. 19, and correspondence with the writer.

Common-field farming might be an irksome system to the farmer in districts of mixed husbandry who wished to turn the bulk of his land to pasture, and to the individualist, like Henry Best, who hated to think that the fruits of his labour would be appropriated for the benefit of others, that his hay, for example, which he had to contribute along with other villagers to feed the village flock in the coldest days of winter, would be used to feed other men's animals. But by the standards of the plain countryman the system was efficient and flexible enough to suit his needs. The regular fallow every second or third year was essential to keep down weeds and restore the land if manure was not abundant, and was still used in the eighteenth century on lands that had long been enclosed. Changes of agricultural routine could be, and were, accepted after discussion in the manorial court. New crops and unusual rotations were introduced into common fields as well as closes. And for some farming systems such as the sheep-corn farming of the downlands, where sheep-folding by a communal flock was the foundation on which the success of the arable crops depended, the co-operation of the community was essential. Thus people were willing to tolerate the inconveniences of common fields—the risks of having other men's stock trampling their crops on intermingled strips, having their animals stolen overnight from the common pastures, or having the wool stolen from the sheeps' backs just before they were shorn. They tolerated these risks because there were others attending enclosure. Mildew in wheat, for example, was a serious disease in closes because the hedges prevented the sun and wind from drying the grain.[1]

The result of this attachment to a traditional system was not always third-rate farming. The two most famous corn-growing areas in the kingdom, where the greatest pains were taken in the preparation of the arable, were the vale of Taunton Deane—the *Paradise of England*, in Norden's words—which was mostly enclosed at this period; and the brecklands of Norfolk and Suffolk, which lay for the most part in common fields, and where farmers possessed the largest array of arable implements anywhere.[2]

C. GRASSLAND AND STOCK

Meadows, whether enclosed, or commonable after harvest as in common-field townships, were of two kinds. Dry upland meadows consisted of the best pasture shut up for hay. Low meadows lay along

[1] Henry Best, *Rural Economy in Yorkshire, 1641*, Surtees Soc., XXXIII, 1857, pp. 74, 94, 118; Ellis, *op. cit.*, p. 4; E. Kerridge, 'The Sheepfold in Wiltshire and the Floating of the Watermeadows', EcHR, 2nd Ser., VI, 3, 1954, pp. 283-4; Hartlib, *op. cit.*, p. 17; Markham, *The Inrichment of the Weald of Kent*, p. 6.
[2] Norden, *op. cit.*, p. 230.

river banks and in the fens and were overflowed in winter, thus making "the grass grow cheerful." Natural water meadows were far superior to dry meadows, and along the banks of the Dove, the Severn at Welshpool, in the vale of Taunton Deane, and at Crediton, were the best meadows in the kingdom. They lay under water during the winter, and in spring were drained off when the old sewers and water drains were cleaned out or renewed. Upland meadows had to be manured at least once every three years if they were to survive continual mowing. Chalk and lime, coaldust, ashes, chimney soot, and marl were applied, and in south-west England water, washed from the streets and ditches, was led into the meadows. Good grasses recommended for hay and grazing were clover, white melilot or sweet clover, milfoil or yarrow, septfoil or tormentil, cinquefoil, and ribgrass. Bare patches, advised Norden, should be resown with clover and grass honeysuckle or other seeds from the best hay. But if more drastic remedial treatment was needed, the meadow was ploughed in spring, left all summer, ploughed again in autumn, and sown the following spring with peas or vetches. This was followed by wheat, and in the third year by vetches or hayseed, after which the meadow was ready to be grazed once more. The fourth year it was ready to be mown again. That the value of clover in the meadow was already recognized is evident in the advice of Norden and Folkingham quoted above. Moreover, cloverseed was being imported into Norfolk in 1620. But whether the idea of the clover ley had yet been introduced is not certain. It was well-tried on the Continent, and since Norfolk was the centre of so many innovations in farming that seem to have been brought over by the Flemish immigrants, it is possible that the clover ley was also introduced by them. But it was not until the 1650's that its merits were advertised in print and that clover seed was being bought by farmers in quantity outside East Anglia.[1]

The great innovation in the management of meadows in the late sixteenth and early seventeenth centuries, which in western England solved the problem of finding fodder early in the year for increasing numbers of stock, was the deliberate flooding of upland meadows—a technique that was undoubtedly suggested by the natural action of the rivers in overflowing low meadows.

The first known experiment was made by Rowland Vaughan of New Court in the Golden valley in Herefordshire, who publicized his method and proclaimed his success in a book published in 1610,

---

[1] Norden, op. cit., pp. 193–202; Folkingham, op. cit., p. 25; G. E. Fussell, 'Adventures with Clover', Agriculture, LXII, 7, 1955, pp. 342–5; E. C. Lodge, The Account Book of a Kentish Estate, 1616–1704, p. 237. Honeysuckle was a common term for all the clovers.

entitled *The Most Approved and Long Experienced Waterworks*. In it, he implied that he had been engaged in this work for some years, possibly since the later 1590's.

To float a meadow, it was necessary first to construct a hatch to dam up the river. When this was opened, the water flowed through a specially dug main duct, and thence into a series of lesser ducts, spaced at intervals of 30–40 feet, all of which were floored and walled with timber. Between each duct a drain was dug to take the water off the meadow when necessary, and to lead it into a main drain and back to the river. The water was allowed through the hatch in November and covered the meadow to a depth of one inch. Not only was it charged with chalk and other deposits, so enhancing the fertility of the meadow, it also acted as a blanket, protecting the grass from frost. Thus the water was kept on the meadow until the danger of severe frosts had passed, and only if scum began to appear on the surface of the water was it necessary to drain it off temporarily and allow the grass to breathe. By about the middle of March the grass was five to six inches high, and the water was then drained off, and the meadow allowed to dry for a few days. It was then ready to be grazed by sheep. The farmer thus had rich grass at his disposal at least a month and sometimes nearly two months before most other farmers. In consequence, he could over-winter more stock, knowing that the lean month of April was catered for. He could also advance lambing time and so gain a considerable financial advantage when he came to sell early lamb to the butcher.[1]

At the end of April, when the grass had been eaten low, the meadows were floated again for a few days, and then put up for hay. The harvest in June was generally four times as heavy as from ordinary meadows. If necessary a second or even a third crop of hay could be had in one year by repeating the same procedure. Alternatively, and more usually, the farmer grazed the meadow with dairy cattle until about October, when the drains and ducts had to be cleaned out and the waters let in again for the winter.

The floating of meadows demanded skill and experience, and by the mid-seventeenth century it was customary to entrust the work to a professional 'floater'. The initial cost of construction was high, but it was not always necessary for one individual to bear a heavy burden of expense. Although Rowland Vaughan, working alone, spent £2,000 on his meadows, the work was carried out on some common meadows

[1] This and the following paragraphs are based on E. Kerridge, 'The Floating of the Wiltshire Watermeadows', *Wilts. Arch. & Nat. Hist. Mag.*, CXCIX, 1953, pp. 105 *sqq.*; id., 'The Sheepfold in Wiltshire and the Floating of the Watermeadows', EcHR, 2nd Ser., VI, 3, 1954, pp. 282 *sqq.*; *Rowland Vaughan, His Booke*, ed. E. B. Wood, 1897; Hugh Platt, *The Jewell House of Art and Nature*, p. 46.

in Wiltshire by agreement with, and at a cost that was shared between, the whole community.

Although Rowland Vaughan publicized his pioneer efforts through his book, the written word did not persuade many of his fellow farmers. His example was much more effective. His methods were adopted before the middle of the seventeenth century in several places on the chalk lands of Salisbury plain, notably on the estates of the earls of Pembroke, who had family connections with the Vaughans, and had presumably seen and applauded the result of his efforts in Hereford-shire. Indeed, Vaughan wrote a dedicatory letter to William, earl of Pembroke. As with some later farming innovations, the new technique seems to have spread first through personal recommendation and example. Experiments in Wiltshire were probably being made around 1616. On the authority of Aubrey, we know for certain that floated meadows were started at Wylye and Chalke about 1635 and in other Wiltshire villages in the 1640's. After the period with which we are concerned, the use of floated watermeadows spread into other down-land areas in Berkshire, Dorset, and Hampshire, even into the Midlands and eastern England. It led to a sharp increase in the number of cattle and sheep that could be maintained both in winter and summer.

Pasture for the grazing of stock was plentiful in some areas through-out the year except when snow fell. In others it was adequate in summer and meagre throughout the winter, though many farmers had a close or two near the house where they could graze some of their animals when the commons were bare. All except the minority, whose pasture as well as arable land was enclosed, depended on the commons for feeding their animals during the summer and autumn. The risks of infection among stock grazing together in large numbers were reduced by strict by-laws, which imposed penalties on anyone who allowed a sick animal on to the common.

The value of rights of common pasture varied greatly between mixed farming and pastoral regions. In the less fertile pastoral areas—in the Pennines, and on the fells of the northern counties—common pasture rights were unlimited, and it was not unusual for a holding to be without pasture closes, and to have all its cultivated land in use as arable and meadow. Near the Scottish border, in Tyndale and Redes-dale, so spacious and neglected were the more distant pastures that the inhabitants of the valleys still practised transhumance in the early seventeenth century. In less remote nucleated settlements in the north some improvement of these vast commons was carried out by enclosing a portion where stock could have shelter and graze without the attention of a cattleherd or shepherd. And wherever pasture was plentiful, it was customary for the commoners by agreement to take in some of the common when necessary, plough it for a while and then put it back to common again. There are abundant references to this practice in Staffordshire where the ploughing usually lasted about five years, and greatly benefited the subsequent pasture. In the northern counties this taking in of common was the usual way of replacing one worn-out common field by a fresh one.[1]

The quality of the grazing on most commons was as nature made it and the stock ate and fertilized it. The practice of folding deprived the commons of much needed manure, but on the other hand some bene-fited more than ever before from the increasing number of animals put out by the commoners. The larger the flocks and herds, the more effectively they kept down the bracken and coarse, sedgy grass. As one of the graziers of Dartmoor explained it, "Pasture is just as good when there are many sheep [as when there are few] because the lower the sedge and grass is eaten in spring, the sweeter the pasture all the year after and the sheep prove the better." The argument suggests that perhaps some of our hillsides which have been surrendered to bracken may have been more profitable to our forebears when there were more cattle, wild horses, and sheep in these lonely places to keep the bracken at bay.[2]

Common pastures were also unstinted in the forest areas of the lowlands, even in comparatively populous districts such as east Northamptonshire and the Weald of Kent, and in all fen areas in eastern England where some of the wet commons were being drained and made more profitable in the early decades of the seventeenth century. So abundant was the grazing in the fens of Lincolnshire, indeed, that the commoners were allotted each year a portion of the fen to be shut up for hay. And in years of special abundance when there was still grass to spare, the bailiff of the manor agisted strangers' cattle for the summer at a few pence per head. But on all commons, however spacious, restrictions on unlimited grazing were imposed indirectly, since no one was supposed to keep more stock in summer than he could support on his home farm in winter. The rule was intended to stop the greedy opportunist from taking more than his share of the common, and judging by the prosecutions for infringement, it was sometimes strictly enforced.[3]

Grazing was a comparatively scarce commodity in some pastoral areas of the west Midlands and in all mixed farming districts every-

[1] E 134, 8 Jas. I, Easter 15; 34 Chas. II, Mich. 10; *Star Chamber Proceedings, Henry VIII & Edward VI*, Wm. Salt Archaeolog. Soc., 1912, p. 169; *Chanc. Proc. temp. Eliz.*, ibid., 1926, pp. 91–2.

[2] G. Plattes, *A Discovery of Hidden Treasure*, p. 30; E 134, 17 Chas. I, Mich. 21.

[3] E 134, 17–18 Eliz., M 6.

where. The number of animals which each tenant was allowed to graze on the common was related to the size of his holding, and the seasons at which stock could be grazed were agreed in the manorial courts. These measures did not prevent over-grazing, however, for large increases in stock numbers were taking place everywhere in this period. In some cases, the commoners met the difficulty by introducing stints for the first time, or reducing old ones.

The majority of townships in England and Wales, as we have seen, had a fixed allotment of common land, which could be improved but not enlarged. Some coastal townships, however, were in the exceptionally fortunate position of being able to count on a gradual increase in their land resources through the action of the sea along the shore. Some stretches of the coastline, of course, were being eroded at the same time, for example, in Holderness, Yorkshire, along the Lincolnshire coast at Mumby Chapel, at Benington along the Wash, at Penychen in Caernarvon, Rhuddlan in Denbigh, and Overton in Lancashire. But the losses here were small in comparison with the gains elsewhere. Large-scale marshland reclamation was being carried out, as opportunity offered, during the reigns of Elizabeth, James I, and Charles I. On the Suffolk coast reclamation of saltmarsh was carried on at a number of places, including Hemley, Bawdsey, Lowestoft, and Walberswick. Along the southern edge of the Wash extensive reclamations became possible in the early seventeenth century, because, the inhabitants said, of a change in the course of the channel which occurred during a storm in or about 1592 and once thereafter. The coastline started to silt up rapidly and hundreds of acres of marsh were built up between the old seabank and the sea. As the men of Whaplode graphically described it, creeks of the sea on which the wives of fishermen had once stood to call their husbands home to dinner had now become dry land. In Romney Marsh, Kent, at Lydd and Broomhill, the existence of some hundreds of acres of saltmarsh outside the seawall attracted the notice of the queen, who was lord of the manor, and became the subject of litigation to establish the queen's rights to draw rent from them. Thereafter the Crown conducted regular enquiries into the extent of reclaimed marsh along the whole coast of England and Wales, and discovered further small acreages on the banks of the Severn, and along the Devon, Hampshire, and Welsh coasts.[1]

Saltmarsh was a valuable asset to the inhabitants of coastal areas since it added fresh acres of grazing to their existing resources and made good pasture for horses and sheep. Although the marsh was damp,

[1] E 178, 5922; 3382; 2195; 2917; 1078; 6016; 5629; 3409; E 134, 27 & 28 Eliz., M 15; 23 Eliz., E 11; PRO DL 44, 67; Ipswich & E. Suffolk RO, Blois Coll., 50, 22, 3-1; Thirsk, *op. cit.*, pp. 15-19, 62-6.

sheep were unaffected by foot rot because of the salt. As soon as the spring tides drained off the marsh, it was left for a few days until the rain had washed out some of the salt. It was then ready for grazing until the next spring tide. The use of these unprotected saltmarshes was not without risk. An unexpectedly strong tide might drown the marsh before the animals had been driven to higher pastures, but the danger was reduced in some places by the presence of shepherds who kept watch in huts on the marsh. As silting proceeded, the saltmarshes were raised above the level of the tides, and lost their saltiness. Samphire and cotton lavender began to grow and the marsh was soon covered with coarse sedgy grass. Gradually its quality improved and it became dry pasture and meadow. Later still it became possible to plough it: at Holbeach, for example, four hundred acres of wheat, oats, barley, and rye were growing on the marshes in 1640.[1]

Sheep and horses were not the only occupants of the saltmarshes. Saltcotes were dotted along the coast from the shores of Lincolnshire to Essex. The salt evaporated here could not have been more conveniently situated to serve the needs of the graziers who thronged the marshes. They could have their meat slaughtered nearby and immediately salted down for ships' victuallers. The industry, which had been carried on in some places since the Iron Age, did not surve throughout this period, however. It came to an end in Lincolnshire at the beginning of the seventeenth century, possibly, as one contemporary alleged, because of the large imports of salt from Scotland at the accession of James I, possibly, as a recent writer has suggested, because of the dearth of turves as fuel for boiling the salt, caused by the gradual flooding of the turbaries during the later Middle Ages. Thereafter salt came to Lincolnshire by sea or by road, along the Salt Way which led from the saltmines at Droitwich in Worcestershire and entered the county near Saltby.[2]

Since common rights were granted to all men possessing a house and some arable land, and in some places, where pasture was plentiful, to all inhabitants whether they had land or not, there were few men who did not have an animal of some kind, usually a cow, sometimes a couple of sheep, and sometimes a horse, since the owner of a horse could always get a living as a carter. A cow was the most usual possession of the small man, whatever else he lacked, so that he could have milk, cheese, and butter even if he was too poor to buy meat. Among large farmers, for whom cattle breeding or fattening was a business, it was not unusual to find between forty and eighty animals in the yards and the fields.

[1] Thirsk, *op. cit.*, pp. 17, 133.
[2] H. E. Hallam, 'Saltmaking in the Lincolnshire Fenland during the Middle Ages', *Lincs. Archit. & Arch. Soc.*, NS VIII, 1960.

In the cattle-breeding areas of the north and west, whence stores were sold into the lowlands, and where it was important to give the calves a good start, they were left to run with the cows all the year. In the dairying areas they were weaned at between two and eight weeks and the milk sent to the dairyhouse throughout the summer and autumn for making into butter and cheese. In Hertfordshire, Essex, and other counties round London, calves were fattened for the butcher as there was a good market for veal in London. Otherwise, it was years before beef was ready for the butcher, and by that time many a bullock had come a long way from its birthplace. From the cattle-breeding areas of the north, west, and south-west stores were sent to the fattening areas of the Midlands, the Home Counties, and East Anglia. In the mixed farming areas cattle that were not bred on the farm were bought in between August and October and fattened for sale in winter or spring. In pastoral areas in the lowlands and on some enclosed farms elsewhere some cattle were overwintered, and more were bought in in spring to be ready for the butcher between July and September. Barren cows and oxen were used for draught until they were about ten years old and then fattened on hay, vetches, peas, boiled barley, or beans, and sold to the butcher.[1]

Contemporary writers on husbandry distinguished three principal breeds of cattle which they considered gave England its high reputation. First were the long-horned cattle, which were the main breed in Yorkshire, Derbyshire, Lancashire, and Staffordshire—black-haired, with large white horns tipped with black, square stately bodies, and short legs. They were especially good for tallow, hide, and horn, but also made good milkers and were strong in labour. Second came the Lincolnshire cattle of the fens and marshes, pied, but more white than anything else, with small crooked horns, tall, large bodies, and large but lean thighs. They were the strongest of all cattle for work and made good meat. The third type were the red Somerset and Gloucestershire cattle, with tall, large bodies, and small horns. They made excellent milkers.[2]

In addition to these, there were many other local breeds which did not enjoy the same celebrity. Woodland Suffolk, for example, had its polled dun-coloured cow, which produced the milk for Suffolk cheeses. Anglesey and Wales had a breed of black cattle that were considered excellent for fattening on barren or poor land, and were distinct from the red and brown cattle of the more fertile lands in south and central Wales. North Devon fostered a breed of red cattle, excellent for draught, and Sussex and Kent a dark red animal, also esteemed for draught and for beef. Cheshire cattle were large, big-boned long-

---

[1] Mortimer, op. cit., pp. 168, 171; Mascall, op. cit., pp. 52–8, 61.
[2] Markham, Cheap and Good Husbandry, pp. 85–6; Folkingham, op. cit., p. 9.

horns, which yielded milk for cheese or good beef for those who wanted it.[1]

Despite the existence of these local breeds the fields in every shire were liable to hold a motley collection of cattle, for the trade in live-stock reached into every corner of the kingdom. There were red cattle in Durham, Cumberland, and Furness, as well as the black and brown longhorns. There are signs that imported Frisian cattle were already in Cumberland and Furness in the 1590's, if that is the correct interpreta-tion of references to *Frisent* and *Fristneck* cattle. The wild white cattle were to be found in Cumberland, at Gilsland and probably elsewhere. Irish cattle were imported in great numbers into Somerset and other counties in the west country. Indeed, it was alleged, in the House of Commons in 1621, that 100,000 Irish cattle came into the kingdom each year. In the lowland areas where fattening was the business, it was still more difficult to distinguish the most favoured breed, since cattle were brought in from Wales and the north. There were Welsh and northern steers in the Weald of Kent and in Essex, black and brown cattle in Hertfordshire.[2]

If cattle, and particularly cows, were considered the most desirable farm animals, sheep undoubtedly came next. "Sheep in mine opinion," wrote Fitzherbert, "is the most profitablest cattle that a man can have," and this belief was reflected in the care lavished on them. In southern England, at least, they were regarded as tender animals, prone to disease, and unable to endure the cold. Hence houses were recommended for them in winter, and were certainly used in Gloucestershire and Herefordshire. In arable areas having common fields and meadows, lambing took place between the beginning of January and the end of March so that the lambs would be strong enough before May to be moved out of the meadows, then being closed for hay, and to follow the ewes over the rough stubble and water furrows of the common fields. Pasture sheep dropped their lambs in April when the grass was ready for them, and were weaned at 16–18 weeks, or at 12 weeks if the ewes were to be milked for cheese, as in the Derbyshire Peak. Meat from suckled lambs was considered vastly preferable, however, to that of grass lambs.[3]

Sheep were normally shorn about mid-June and culled at Michael-mas, when a great movement of sheep took place from breeding to feeding grounds and from feeding grounds to the butcher. The regular slaughter of stock at Michaelmas is a myth: it occurred in

[1] R. Trow-Smith, *A History of British Livestock Husbandry to 1700*, pp. 197, 210; Mortimer, *op. cit.*, p. 166.

[2] Notestein, Relf, and Simpson, *Commons Debates, 1621*, III, p. 214; V, p. 492.

[3] Fitzherbert, *op. cit.*, p. 42; Mascall, *op. cit.*, pp. 202, 229; Beale, *op. cit.*, p. 54; Markham, *Cheap and Good Husbandry*, pp. 105, 108, 113.

occasional years when the hay crop had been exceptionally poor, but otherwise the only slaughter that took place was of fat animals. In the winter sheep were fed on grass, hay, or straw, chaff, peas in the straw, or mashes of barley, beans, and acorns. In the worst of the winter ash and elm leaves and holly were used for fodder. In the spring the sheep were driven into the fields to graze the tares, where grown, or the green shoots of rye and wheat. Ewes before lambing were put on the best pasture available, or fed on threshed oats or peas and oats in the straw. Before taking the ram they were brought into good condition with oat or barley stubble. Wethers were finished for the butcher at four or five years either on grass during the summer or on peas during the winter, to be ready for sale between December and May. Lamb was in the shops at any time from Christmas onwards, for the sheep of Dorset, Hampshire, and Wiltshire lambed about November, and many ewes in lamb were bought up by Middlesex graziers for early sale at Christmas. Otherwise lambs fattened for the butcher were not ready until July.[1]

The soundest precept offered to the purchaser of sheep was that he should buy from land of poorer quality than his own, so that his flock would thrive when moved to better grazing. The best cure for sick sheep and the best way to increase the milk from ewes was a change of pasture. The principal diseases were liver fluke and rot, the latter avoided by moving the sheep regularly to fresh pastures, the former cured quickly (without much loss to the farmer) by despatching the animal to the butcher.[2]

In all areas of mixed farming, the folding of sheep on the arable was a pillar of the farming system, and the breeds of sheep used for this purpose were specially conditioned to it. In common-field areas the sheep were put into a common village flock, since a small flock was useless, hurdled at night, and the pens moved from one part of the field to another daily. On enclosed farms the farmer needed a large flock or the system did not work. A thousand sheep would fold an acre of common-field land in a night, and folding was arranged so that each field should be dunged in time for sowing. Folding was only possible on land that was fairly dry, otherwise the sheep were liable to rot. In Wiltshire on the warm chalk soils of the downs folding continued all the year round. But in other places it was carried on during the summer months only, between about May and September.[3] Contemporaries believed that environment and feed were the principal

[1] A.S., *The Husbandman's Instructor*, p. 53; Trow-Smith, *op. cit.*, pp. 242–4; Mascall, *op. cit.*, pp. 303–4, 306; Mortimer, *op. cit.*, p. 180.   [2] Beale, *op. cit.*, p. 54.

[3] E. Kerridge, 'The Sheepfold in Wiltshire', *loc. cit.*, pp. 284–5; Mortimer, *op. cit.*, p. 180; Mascall, *op. cit.*, p. 230; Henry Best, *op. cit.*, p. 14.

factors which shaped the breeds, and that all sheep were liable to change their characteristics when moved from one place to another. Strangely, they attached no importance to the effects of selective breeding, though their textbooks insisted on this matter, and the results of selection, haphazard though it may often have been, cannot have been negligible. Thus while modern geneticists give much more weight to the effects of selection than to environment, contemporaries considered the influence of the latter paramount and so did not attempt to enumerate all the many local breeds and define their relationships. All we can do, therefore, is to note the principal types, knowing that minor deviations occurred in every locality.[1]

All the mountain breeds were small, horned animals, some white, some black-faced, usually wild and restless, and producing a sometimes hairy but often fine wool, and excellent mutton. Many reared on the mountains were sold at two or three years or thereabouts into the lowlands, sometimes far distant, where they were fattened for the butcher. Wales had a breed of mountain sheep, horned, small-bodied, usually dark in colour, either black, grey, or brown; Cornwall had a sheep similar to the Welsh, called the South-West Horned. In the hilly areas of the north Midlands and beyond, the principal breed was the black-faced heath sheep, otherwise known as the Lintons, big-boned with large spirally twisted horns, and carrying rough, shaggy, hairy wool. From this breed are descended the modern Scottish Blackface, the Rough Fell, the Swaledale, and the Dalesbred breeds. In the Lake District the Herdwick—a white-faced horned breed—was more favoured. They were the very smallest of the hill sheep, and extremely agile at climbing rough mountain sides. Their wool was grey in colour and coarse in texture, and was already used for making carpets. The sweet taste of their mutton was said to be enhanced by the holly and ash leaves fed to them in winter. Numerous local breeds, descended from these two types of black-faced and white-faced horned mountain sheep, were to be found in the forests and on the moors of the Midlands and the south-west. Dartmoor had one type, Exmoor another, the Mendip forest another, Cannock another, Delamere another, Charnwood another. Their faces and legs were sometimes white, but generally black, grey, or dun-coloured, and usually they had horns. But all yielded fine wool and fine-flavoured mutton.[2]

[1] Markham, *Cheap and Good Husbandry*, p. 103; A.S., *op. cit.*, p. 48. The following account has benefited greatly from discussions with Dr Michael Ryder and his article, 'The History of Sheep Breeds in Britain', AHR, XII, 1964.
[2] David Low, *On the Domesticated Animals of the British Islands*, 1845, pp. 64–8, 80–4; Mortimer, *op. cit.*, p. 177; Markham, *op. cit.*, p. 104; Sydney Moorhouse, 'Herdwick Sheep of the Lake Country', *Wool Knowledge*, III, 12, 1956, pp. 14–19.

The finest wool of all, however, came from the short-woolled sheep of the lowlands, all reared on sweet, but short, not to say scanty, herbage. The best producers of fine wool were the Ryelands, which came from Herefordshire, particularly around Leominster, Shropshire, and Worcestershire, though they were also to be found in various forest districts in the neighbourhood, such as the Forest of Dean, and even in Wales. They were small white-faced animals, with a short delicate fleece, weighing between one and two pounds. These were the animals which were housed at night in the belief that this preserved the fineness of their fleeces.[1]

Dorset had another breed of white-faced short-wool sheep which was unique in that the ewes received the ram early in the season and produced lambs in October which were ready for the butcher by Christmas. Hence some ewes in lamb were sold to Middlesex graziers for the supply of the gourmet's table in London. This long breeding season is still exploited in the modern Dorset Horn breed. The Dorset sheep had white legs and faces, small horns in both sexes, long limbs, low shoulders, and a fleece of medium-fine wool. They were hardy and suited to folding. But the best breeds for this last purpose were the Old Wiltshires of Wiltshire and Hampshire, the Southdown—the "hillish breed" kept by Toke of Godinton, Kent, in the early seventeenth century—and the Norfolk sheep. The Wiltshires were the largest of the white-faced short wools, with clumsy heads, arched faces, horns in male and female, long, straight back, and long, large-boned legs. Their mutton was tolerable but they were slow to fatten, and usually it was not for the butcher that they were kept. Their great virtue was their ability to be driven long distances up hill and down dale from the downland pastures to the fold on the arable fields, and to make good on scanty herbage. Their fleeces were fine and weighed about two pounds. Equally suited to the fold were the black-faced short wool Southdowns and Norfolks. The Southdown was a small animal, with light fore-quarters, narrow chest, long neck, and the long limbs characteristic of most fold sheep. Its home was the Sussex downs. The Norfolk had a long body and legs, was a sturdy walker, and a producer of sweet mutton as well as wool. It was a popular breed on the brecklands of Norfolk and Suffolk and in Cambridgeshire.[2]

Long-wooled sheep were the sheep of the rank marshes and fens and of the fertile vales inland. The Lincolnshire marsh and fen sheep was a Lustre Long-wool, like the Midland sheep, and the largest of all, with

---

[1] Mortimer, *op. cit.*, p. 177; Markham, *op. cit.*, p. 103; Beale, *op. cit.*, p. 54; Low, *op. cit.*, pp. 155–7.

[2] Low, *op. cit.*, pp. 120–4, 162–3, 187, 114–16; E. Kerridge, 'The Sheepfold in Wiltshire', EcHR, 2nd Ser., VI, 1954, p. 283; Folkingham, *op. cit.*, p. 9.

long legs, a long naked belly, admirably adapted to survive on lush but damp grazing. It fattened slowly but butchers liked it nevertheless for its large proportion of fat. It had a heavy fleece of long, coarse wool. The Romney Marsh sheep—a Demi-lustre Longwool—was bred in a similar environment. It is a more primitive breed than the Midland Longwool, with which it too has affinities, but on the fat grazings and under the harsh climate of the marsh it had developed in flesh, wool, and hardiness. As a meat animal it was as slow to mature as the Lincolnshire, but again it yielded a large quantity of fat and offal. Its principal asset, however, was its fleece, which although shorter than the Lustre Longwool commonly weighed three to five pounds.

The sheep of the inland vales were again Lustre Longwools—the large Teeswater on Teesside and the Midland Longwool sheep, found in Warwickshire, east Worcestershire, Leicestershire, Buckinghamshire, Northamptonshire, and most of Nottinghamshire except Sherwood Forest. The Midland was a large-boned lank-bodied animal with a coarse head, and produced a medium-fine fleece weighing two to three pounds. When kept in enclosed pastures, as opposed to common fields, all these qualities of size and weight were further exaggerated.[1]

The two main types of horse used in agriculture were the packhorse for cross-country transport and the cart-horse for labour in the fields. In addition, farmers had to satisfy a considerable demand for saddle and coach-horses. These were usually of cart-horse stock mixed with other, mainly foreign breeds, for horses were imported from abroad more often than any other farm animals. Thus Gervase Markham recommended that for the saddle an English mare be bred with a Turk or Irish Hobbie, for coach and cart with a Flanders or Friesland horse, and for heavy transport with a German horse. And in suggesting this mixing of breeds, he claimed to have had practical experience of the results.[2]

Horses were reared in considerable numbers in all the forests of England. Some were wild, like the ponies of the New Forest, some were farm-bred. The wild horses were usually of pony size, though better grazing sometimes produced a larger animal. Others were of mixed blood and included horses for the hunt, and towards the end of the period, for the racecourse. Their importance among horse fanciers may be judged by the fact that many horse fairs were held in towns within or adjoining the forests: for example, at Woodstock, Rothwell, Northampton, and Brewood. The common packhorse, which carried cloth from the Yorkshire dales to the towns and ports, coal from the

[1] Markham, *op. cit.*, pp. 103–4; Low, *op. cit.*, pp. 171, 176; A.S., *op. cit.*, p. 49; E. Topsell, *The History of Fourfooted Beasts*, p. 484; Mortimer, *op. cit.*, p. 177.
[2] Gervase Markham, *Cavalarice or the English Horseman*, 1625, p. 18.

coalpits, and peat and fuel from the moors of Cornwall and Devon, was probably descended from the same stock of forest ponies. He was a small, sure-footed animal, also used for riding.

The vales of England bred larger horses which were used for draught. They were not speedy but had great strength. Some were mixed with foreign blood to produce saddle horses and lighter carriage horses, but their quality of endurance was best revealed in work on the farm. There were many local breeds known to contemporaries, of which we have no record. But there are incidental references to coach-horses which came from Rothwell fair, near Kettering; plough and cart-horses from Durham; horses from Cleveland, Yorkshire, the Cleveland bays, in other words, excellent for ploughing lighter soils; and the chestnut-coloured Suffolk Punch from wood-pasture Suffolk, which, with its thickset body and short legs, was an ideal horse for work on heavy soils, and would pull a heavily laden wagon till it dropped. The Lincolnshire fens bred horses for the coalpits of Nottinghamshire, the leadmines of Derbyshire, and for Yorkshire breeders who mated fenland mares with their local types.[1]

As we have seen, horse-breeding was mainly the speciality in pastoral areas, where it was usual to have a team of mares and work them gently till near foaling. Hence the preoccupation with horse-breeding in the Lincolnshire and Norfolk fens, the Somerset Levels, the Essex marshes, the Yorkshire dales, Cannock Chase, the forests of Pickering, Macclesfield, Northamptonshire, and Arden, and the New Forest. In mixed farming areas, with more arable land at their disposal, horses and geldings were a better proposition. These were the choice in south Hertfordshire and Cambridgeshire, counties which were traversed by main roads into London, and had to meet a large demand for coach-horses. Hertfordshire horses were bought in as colts from Leicestershire, at two or three years, and sold at six years.[2]

Pig-keeping was regarded as one of the peasant's standbys. It was a common saying that "he that hath sheep, swine, and bees, sleep he, wake he, may thrive." Many a peasant, therefore, kept a pig or two as "the husbandman's best scavenger, the housewife's most wholesome sink." And in due course he had meat that hung in the roof and kept better than all other flesh. It would be an exaggeration, however, to think that all peasants kept pigs. Many a family did not have enough kitchen waste to keep even one pig: in Northumberland, Durham, Cumberland, and Westmorland, therefore, the majority of peasants had none at all. Thus, although pig-keeping enabled the small peasant

---

[1] David Low, op. cit., pp. 521, 524, 602, 619; infra, pp.   ; Robert Reyce, Suffolk in the Seventeenth Century, pp. 42–3; Thirsk, op. cit., pp. 176, 32.

[2] Worlidge, op. cit., p. 160; Mortimer, op. cit., p. 149.

to enjoy meat at the lowest cost, to produce pigs for the market was mainly a business for the larger farmer, or for the specialized husbandman who happened to have suitable feed that cost him little. Thus, dairymen kept pigs in large numbers to consume the whey from the dairy. In the forests they were fattened in droves on acorns, beechmast, crab apples, medlars, and hazelnuts, and in Herefordshire, when nuts were short, on elm leaves. In mixed farming areas, however, particularly in the Midlands, they were fattened, not on kitchen waste or on the common harvest of the woods, but on grain and pulses, specially grown for their benefit. In Germany at this period this would have been regarded as a most uneconomic and extravagant method of farming.[1]

The best pig was considered to be one that had a long, deep-sided, deep-bellied body, with thick thighs, short legs, and a thick neck. They might be pink, sandy, or white, but very few were black. They were fattened in various ways according to the facilities available. In forest areas they were turned into the woods for fattening in six to eight weeks, and were then brought home, and finished off in sties, feeding for ten to fourteen days on old dried peas, split beans, or tares. In Elizabeth's reign a dispute developed between two men who arranged to send 240 pigs from Buckinghamshire and Oxfordshire to be fed in the woods of Sussex and Hampshire, and to receive them back "well and sufficiently fed for bacon." It was this kind of forest pig-keeping that made Hampshire hogs "allowed by all for the best bacon." This business maintained many a peasant in the Chilterns and the Shropshire and Herefordshire forests. In Suffolk's wood-pasture region the pigs were reared with the dairy, and then fed on the mast and acorns of the woods. Acorns were claimed to make the hardest, firmest flesh which salted down the best.[2]

In the neighbourhood of towns such as London and York pork and bacon were much in demand, and for that reason pigs were kept in great numbers in Hertfordshire and in the vale of York. One of the feeding methods was to put them in sties and feed them on the dregs and offal of tallow, mixed with a warm wash, till the pigs fattened up, when their flesh was hardened off with peas. This procedure produced bacon speedily, though, as may be imagined, it lacked much flavour. For lard or brawn swine were fed with barley mash, followed by raw malt and dried peas, washed down with sweet whey or the dregs of ale barrels.[3]

[1] Blagrave, *op. cit.*, p. 73; Mascall, *op. cit.*, p. 257; Speed, *Adam out of Eden*, p. 86; Markham, *Cheap and Good Husbandry*, p. 121.

[2] G. Markham, *op. cit.*, pp. 122, 128; PRO Req. 2, 270, 39; VCH *Hants.*, v, p. 496; Reyce, *op. cit.*, p. 37; A.S., *The Husbandman's Instructor*, p. 74.

[3] Markham, *op. cit.*, pp. 129–30.

The largest pigs, and the very best meat of all, came from Midland counties, such as Leicestershire and Northamptonshire, where peas and beans were grown in quantity, mainly for the purpose of feeding pigs. At nine months or a year old, they were shut up in sties and fattened in four to five weeks, or turned out, as in Leicestershire, to feed from the peas ricks in the fields.[1]

Another source of food for the modest husbandman was poultry. All but the poorest had a few hens, chickens, and sometimes ducks, while those who enjoyed generous common rights kept geese as well. Hence the fenlanders of eastern England and the foresters of Dartmoor kept geese in large numbers and earned something from the sale of feathers and grease as well as meat. At the same time a poultry-keeping industry was already in existence in Norfolk and to a less extent in Suffolk. Not only were chickens fattened for the market but ducks, geese, and turkeys, too. Turkeys were not introduced into Europe from Mexico until the second decade of the sixteenth century but by the end of Elizabeth's reign there were already considerable numbers in Norfolk.

Buckwheat was one of the foods most used in East Anglia for fattening poultry. But in the 1590's, carrots and turnips also were used for this purpose which may have suggested their use for cattle too. Various other grains served their turn when available. Turkeys were fed on sodden barley and oats, and sometimes on bruised acorns; chickens were crammed with wheat meal and milk for fourteen days; capons were crammed with corn and peas at the barn door, or penned and fed with barley malt. Geese were fed on grass or other pastures; the young were fattened with ground malt and milk, old and stubble geese with new malt. Outside East Anglia poultry-keeping as a speciality was the eccentric choice of individuals, but it is worth mentioning William Dockray of Matterdale, Cumberland, whose labours suggest that the market for poultry was not restricted to London. In 1639 Dockray possessed 160 head of poultry, worth £42.[2]

Finally, among the activities of the peasant, from which the poor were not debarred by the cost of equipment, was bee-keeping. Since honey was the main sweetening agent in the kitchen, there were beehives everywhere. In the forests they were made of hazel wood, in champion country of long rye straw, and in the west country of wheat straw. If they were more in evidence in some districts than others, it was on the moorlands where heather honey was produced.[3]

[1] Mortimer, *op. cit.*, p. 184; Markham, *op. cit.*, pp. 128–9; A.S., *op. cit.*, pp. 73–4.
[2] H. Platt, *The Jewell House of Art and Nature*, p. 13; Markham, *op. cit.*, p. 139; Worlidge, *op. cit.*, p. 165.
[3] Markham, *op. cit.*, p. 169.

Goats were kept only in mountainous areas, in High Furness, for example, Northumberland, and Wales, where "cattle of better profit can hardly be maintained." Besides giving milk to their owners, their skin was useful for clothing, their hair excellent for ropes, since it did not rot in water, and their flesh when young as tasty as venison.[1]

Deer which had been kept in parks in the Middle Ages were gradually thrust out in the second half of the sixteenth century by deliberate action on the part of lay landowners, and by neglect on the part of the Crown in administering royal chases. Almost everywhere, even in Cumberland, where it might be thought that land was not always put to the most profitable use, deer gave way to more profitable cattle.[2]

Rabbits were not regarded as pests but as a valuable source of additional income for those who were willing to go to the expense of making a warren. For besides providing meat at six weeks, the rabbit had a skin that made a useful fur. For those whose crops were liable to be eaten by rabbits they were a nuisance but not an incurable one. Rabbits could be contained in the warren if good banks were erected and maintained around the perimeter. Most warrens were situated on heathy, sandy, or other waste land that was of little use for other purposes. There were warrens on the Yorkshire and Lincolnshire wolds, on the moors of Barnsley, in Sherwood Forest, on the Northamptonshire heaths, on the Norfolk brecklands, on the eastern sands of Suffolk, and on the heath at Wrotham, Kent, where one warren owner paid his rent with the profit of his rabbits.[3]

D. FRUIT AND MARKET-GARDENING

Finally, two branches of farming which assumed a new importance in this period and which have since become the principal, and sometimes the only activity, of some farmers, were fruit-growing and market-gardening. Great emphasis was placed on fruit-growing as a profitable enterprise with an assured market in the sixteenth century. In most of the fruit-growing counties—Kent, Hertfordshire, Worcestershire, Gloucestershire, Herefordshire, Somerset, and Devon, fruit trees grew in every hedgerow, and farmers elsewhere were urged to plant them likewise. But in these counties orchards too were rapidly increasing in number.[4]

[1] Markham, *op. cit.*, p. 116; A.S., *op. cit.*, p. 91; Worlidge, *op. cit.*, p. 162.

[2] Norden, *op. cit.*, pp. 114–15.

[3] Speed, *Adam out of Eden*, p. 3.

[4] This and the following three paragraphs are based on Alicia Amherst, *A History of Gardening in England*, 1895, pp. 93–8, 143–55; Norden, *op. cit.*, pp. 208–9; S. Hartlib, *op. cit.*, p. 20; John Beale, *op. cit.*, pp. 3, 10, 32. I wish to thank Miss W. Dullforce for help with the bibliography of this subject.

Fruit-growing seems to have benefited greatly from royal encouragement, for it was to royal gardens that attention was always directed by contemporaries whenever they discussed the history of fruit-growing in their own lifetime. Henry VIII's gardener, Richard Harris, is said to have been among the first to import French grafts of cherry, pear, and apple, and among apples "especially pippins, before which time there were no pippins in England." The anonymous writer of this account (1609) added that Harris's orchard at Teynham, Kent, was "the chief mother of all other orchards for those kinds of fruit in Kent and divers other places." The apricot, too, was a novelty of the first half of the sixteenth century, probably introduced by Henry VIII's gardener, Wolf, about 1524, while among the first gooseberries to be planted in gardens were those growing in Henry VIII's garden in 1516.

By Charles I's reign the varieties of apples were too numerous for the compilers of botanical descriptions to list them all. Of pears there were at least sixty-five varieties, of cherries thirty-five, of plums sixty-one, and of apricots six, including one brought back from "the Argier voyage" against pirates in 1620 by John Tradescant, a great fruit-grower who "laboured to obtain all the rarest fruits he can hear of." The fruits of warmer summers than those enjoyed in England were still patiently coaxed and coddled. Lord Burghley planted vines at Hatfield about 1607, and having an orange tree already, ordered a lemon tree from abroad. The peach was grown but not with much success, its fruit being soft and fleshy and "hoary without." James I tried hard to encourage the planting of mulberry trees and issued a circular letter to Lords Lieutenant of the counties in 1609 announcing that he would be sending one thousand mulberry trees to each county town the following March, and requiring the inhabitants to plant them.

The fruits that reached the market in largest quantity were cherries, apples, and pears, and the connoisseur knew the best varieties from each part of the country. Hertfordshire and Kentish apples and Hertfordshire pears were sold in London as fruit. Perry was best made from west country and Kentish pears. Pippins, that is to say dessert apples, and cherries were a speciality in Kent around Faversham and Sittingbourne. Cherries grew plentifully at Ketteringham, Norfolk. Worcestershire grew pears and cherries better than Herefordshire. Herefordshire grew excellent cooking apples but for lack of river transport had difficulty in selling its cider.

Market gardening developed rapidly in the late sixteenth century—mainly in the 1590's—with the encouragement and active participation of alien immigrants from the Low Countries. The areas around London which specialized in this activity can be gauged from the addresses of members of the Gardeners' Company, which received its first charter in 1605, and quickly grew in importance. Some of the centres of market gardening were Westminster, Lambeth, Battersea, Fulham, Putney, and Brentford, and, in the opposite direction along the Thames, Whitechapel, Stepney, Hackney, and Greenwich. These were all districts with easy access to the river, which enabled market produce and the dung that was essential in large quantities for this kind of intensive cultivation, to be transported by water. More distant from London were market garden centres in Surrey, Essex, and Kent, particularly at Colchester and Sandwich. The Sandwich carrot, indeed, was as famous as the Fulham parsnip and the Hackney turnip.[1]

E. CONCLUSION

We have enumerated the various branches of farming in which both plain countrymen and ingenious husbandmen were engaged in the sixteenth and early seventeenth centuries. The individual's choice of a suitable combination of these activities was to a large extent determined for him by the condition of his land—its soil and topography, and the climate of the district—and by the routine that was necessary to maintain each branch of farming. Some activities could be undertaken together by a peasant family with little land and large pasture commons, which were out of the question for the man with a virgate of land and small pasture rights. The main specialities, however, can be summarized thus: pastoral areas were engaged either in cattle or sheep breeding, fattening, dairying, pig-keeping, or horse breeding, or, more usually, doing something of each. The main stock-breeding areas lay in the moorland and mountainous parts of the highland zone, most stock fattening was done in the vales, dairying was carried on in both, pig-keeping and horse breeding were the specialities of the forests, but pig-keeping was also an adjunct to the dairy. Always the arable land in these regions was no more than adequate to satisfy domestic and farm needs for grain, and the large-scale market production of arable crops was impossible. The mixed farming areas usually contained far more ploughland than pasture, except perhaps in parts of the Midland counties such as Leicestershire and Northamptonshire, where enclosure in some areas had wrought drastic changes in the proportions of each. Mixed farming regions specialized in growing grain and fodder crops. Cereals were marketed, if water transport by river or sea was available, and if not, were used to feed and fatten stock for the butcher. Some mixed farming areas, in consequence, had the same objectives as the

[1] P. McGrath, 'The Marketing of Food, Fodder, and Livestock in the London Area in the Seventeenth Century', London M.A. thesis, 1948, pp. 193–206; Norden, *op. cit.*, pp. 229–30; Folkingham, *op. cit.*, p. 42.

pastoral vales, though their methods were different. Less usual crops such as saffron, teasels, and vegetables for the table, which were grown in specialized areas, were not necessarily products of enclosed farms, but were incorporated in arable rotations in common fields. Hemp and flax, of course, were grown everywhere in crofts and closes beside the house, though some pastoral districts, such as the fens, specialized in them.

Although much specialization was an ancient tradition, it was not a fixed and unchanging one. Slight modifications, and some more drastic ones, can be observed in the course of this century and a half. Some breeding areas, such as Arden in Warwickshire, for example, turned to dairying; fruit growing spread from the Canterbury area of Kent to other districts on the edge of the Weald; dairying in the Weald disappeared for good and cattle fattening became the principal activity. Moreover, as one region prospered by means of its speciality, it influenced its neighbours. Cheese production in the wood-pasture region of Norfolk, for example, spread into the sheep-corn region, and the dairying of the Arden in Warwickshire infected the Felden.

The land's capacity, the custom of the country, capital resources, and the influence of market prices were paramount influences governing the choice of speciality by individual farmers. But no mean consideration was the cost of labour. We catch fragments of the discussion on this matter in the advice given by James Bankes of Winstanley to his son. He was lord of the manor and an employer of labour on his demesne. Writing in 1600 he recommended corn growing "for in breeding of cattle is great loss." "Make tillage of your best land that is good and therein your gain will be greatest for corn is ready money and cometh once a year." By 1610 experience had caused him to revise his ideas. His labourers had caused him much anxiety and trouble, and he had decided that a system of pasture farming which required the least labour paid best.

"Make no more tillage to get corn than to serve your house, for I have been hindered by keeping of servants in getting of corn that I have rather desired to die than to live for they care not whether end goeth forward so that they have meat, drink, and wages. Small fear of God is in servants, and thou shalt find my counsel just and most true."

This problem of the labourer's inefficiency and its influence upon the farming programme of the larger farmer is also referred to in a letter by a Yorkshire steward to his master in the 1620's. "Nothing is more unprofitable than a farm in tillage in the hands of servants where the master's eye is not daily upon them."[1]

[1] Joyce Bankes, *op. cit.*, pp. 23, 28; Sheffield RO, Strafford Letters, WWM, 20(a), 17

In the course of the sixteenth century, most noticeably after about 1560 when our records become abundant, farm production made rapid strides. It is impossible to say how far yields per acre were raised during this period since there were wide differences in the rate of seeding and in the yields from different kinds of soil, and documentary evidence between different periods never affords comparisons of like with like. But we can confidently speak of other reasons for the increase in agricultural production: namely, the use of more intensive rotations, accompanied by heavier manuring; the use of improved varieties of grain; and, probably most important of all, the impressive increase in the total acreage of land under the plough as a result of the reclamation of waste and the conversion of pasture. This increased acreage, it should be noted, was regarded by contemporaries as the main explanation for the improved supply of corn. It led an unknown writer to the Commissioners for Pardons to write in 1621 that "there is no want of cornland at this time, but want of pastures and cattle, for much woodlands and barren grounds are become fruitful corn lands instead of pasture." Heavier manuring of the arable, of course, was made possible by keeping larger numbers of animals, which resulted in a great increase in the supply of meat and wool and other animal products. Heavier rates of stocking were made possible by the improvement of pastures and meadows by fertilizers, by the improved supply of spring grazing, through the watering of meadows in the west country, the growing of tares elsewhere, and by the increased supply of summer grazing through the use of leys and the reclamation of coastal marshland and fen. Thus improvements in arable and pastoral husbandry went hand in hand, each helping the other, and both serving to promote the specialization and interdependence of regions.

CHAPTER IV

ENCLOSING AND ENGROSSING

A. INTRODUCTION

Enclosing and engrossing were two of the most controversial topics in sixteenth-century England. They provoked animated discussion in the alehouses, inspired outspoken sermons from the pulpit, and stirred passions and community loyalties in the fields as men ploughed their strips side by side in the common fields and muttered imprecations against the selfish and the rich. They incited many minor local riots and one larger disturbance which spread across three Midland counties. Popular indignation prodded the government into action, and commissions of enquiry, proclamations, and statutes form a continuous series from the beginning of Henry VII's reign to the end of Elizabeth's and beyond.

A movement which was so widespread, in which so many people of all classes participated, and yet which aroused such loud popular outcry, poses problems for the historian. He cannot make sense of the seeming contradictions without recognizing first that the word 'enclosure' was a very loose general term for a number of different dealings concerning land and changes in land use, and, secondly, that the economic advantages and social consequences of enclosing and engrossing differed profoundly from one region to another. To those who observed or experienced some of the more ruthless enclosures of land in the Midland counties, all enclosers were agents of Satan and all enclosures inflicted grievous harm on the community. Such hardened opponents of change would hardly have recognized as part of the same movement the amicable enclosures taking place at the same time in some of the northern and west Midland counties.

To arrive at a fair definition of enclosing and engrossing, it is first necessary to strip the subject of all reference to the controversies which surrounded it in the Tudor period. To enclose land was to extinguish common rights over it, thus putting an end to all common grazing. To effect this, it was usual for the encloser to hedge or fence the land. Thus in contemporary controversy anger was directed mainly at the hedges and fences—the outward and visible signs of enclosure. To make it economically worth while, enclosure was often preceded by the amalgamation of several strips by exchange or purchase. If the enclosed land lay in the common arable fields or in the meadows, the encloser now had complete freedom to do what he pleases with this land throughout the year, instead of having to surrender the stubble or aftermath after harvest to the use of the whole township. On the pasture commons, enclosure by an individual signified the appropriation to one person of land which had previously been at the disposal of the whole community throughout the year. All enclosures, then, whether they concerned land in the common fields, in the meadows, or in the common pastures, deprived the community of common rights. The seriousness of the loss depended entirely on whether the needs of the villagers' stock were adequately met by the common grazing which remained. Engrossing signified the amalgamation of two or more farms into one. The superfluous farmhouse was either left to fall into decay, or, with a small piece of land attached to it, was down-graded to accommodate a cottager. Engrossing and enclosing were frequently referred to in the same breath as twin evils in the countryside. But they did not inevitably accompany one another. Many an encloser was innocent of the charge of engrossing. Many an engrosser of land was free of all temptation to enclose. The two sins ranked together because, by different means, they both caused depopulation.

To analyse the significance of enclosing and engrossing first of all in the electric atmosphere of sixteenth-century popular agitation is to see two commonplace changes in the use and distribution of land at one special moment in history when tempers were high and perspective was distorted. Enclosing and engrossing were as ancient as farming itself. They could and did occur without riot or revolution, and, in less inflammable situations, were regarded as part of a sensible and reasonable plan of agarian improvement.

Much enclosure had already taken place without trial or tribulation in the early Middle Ages. Enclosure from the waste had been as commonplace a part of the farming round as ploughing. And as long as the commons remained plentiful, such enterprise went unchallenged. Individuals who wished to enlarge their holdings cleared an acre or two, on the vacant land adjoining their farms, if possible, or at a convenient distance. Others made a small clearing in the forest, and started a pioneer operation which was not completed for several generations. Their labours might end in the creation of a family farm, or even in a small hamlet. Settlements like this of medieval origin are scattered all over England, and lie usually on the fringes of parishes. Sometimes a group of farmers, or even whole villages, enclosed some common land by agreement and by co-operative labour. In this way, much land in the fen was diked, drained, enclosed, and then partitioned among the tenants of the fen villages. The community thus added to its land resources as population grew.

The growth of population, indeed, had been the sharpest goad behind the enclosure of pasture and waste in the Middle Ages and continued so until the nineteenth century when the movement virtually reached completion. At the beginning of settlement all townships had had extensive wastes for which they had no immediate use. As population increased, this land formed a reserve upon which the community could draw to support its growing numbers. So long as the reserves remained plentiful, no one counted the loss of a few acres enclosed here and there to provide a better living for one member of the community, while manorial lords welcomed all improvements which increased their income from rent. Indeed, as late as the sixteenth century in thinly populated districts—for example in many parts of Lancashire, Yorkshire, and the more northern counties, neighbouring villages intercommoned on the waste lying between their townships without observing any frontiers.

Serious disagreements between villages did not arise for centuries, often not until the Tudor age, when the diminishing waste and the growth of population taught people to look at first anxiously, and then angrily, at the slightest new encroachment on their commons. They learned at last, by bitter practical experience, that the commons were not unlimited, and that their diminution beyond a certain point could pose grave economic problems. The changing situation in the sixteenth century is best described by a tenant of Holme on Spalding Moor, Yorkshire, giving evidence in 1620 in a dispute about common rights. A cottage built on the common some sixty years before had enjoyed common rights "by sufferance or negligence of the freeholders," for at that time "the freeholders made little reckoning of common for so small goods [i.e. so few stock] as was then put upon the said common by the said tenants." The situation changed radically in the next two generations. The population as a whole increased, and this cottage, originally a small hut 15 feet by 12 feet, containing two small rooms, was altered to accommodate another and more affluent farmer who added a parlour, a chamber over the parlour, a milkhouse, a stable, and at the end of the building a new hall house, kitchen, barn, and beast-house. He had a great many stock and claimed the right to graze them all on the commons.[1] Since this kind of incident recurred many times in townships all over England, it is not difficult to see how in the end the enclosure of the waste became a highly controversial issue. The same episode serves to illustrate a further point, namely, that the crisis of land shortage was liable to occur at different times in different districts, for not all townships grew in population at the same pace, nor did they start with the same amount of land. Hence in Shropshire or

[1] E 134, 18 Jas. I, Hil. 15.

Lancashire in the sixteenth and early seventeenth centuries enclosure was usually an amicable and peaceable proceeding, which reflected the fact that land was still an abundant commodity. The indignation which enclosure aroused at the same period in the east Midlands, on the other hand, leaves no doubt that in this region the shortage of common grazings had reached a critical point.

The enclosure of strips in the common fields and meadows raised much the same issues as the enclosure of commons, for it further reduced the area of common grazing land. But again the significance of the problem differed from district to district and period to period. In some parts of England and Wales common arable fields were neither extensive nor of great economic importance. In the Pennine Hills, for example, arable fields were usually small and were separated from each other by large areas of pasture; moreover, the farmer's livelihood depended more on the exploitation of his pastures than on his corn harvest. In certain counties much common-field land was enclosed before 1500. Sixteenth-century writers regarded the counties of Suffolk, Essex, Hertfordshire, Kent, Devon, Somerset, Cornwall, Shropshire, Worcestershire, and Herefordshire as completely, or largely, enclosed. And although no one nowadays would agree that any of these counties was completely without common fields, and many still had large areas of common pasture, the historian accepts the substantial truth of these generalizations. Somehow in the Middle Ages these counties had put an end to most of their common fields and common rights without commotion.[1]

In districts of England which possessed large areas of old enclosed land, or a local system of husbandry which was not yet endangered by shortage of land, the enclosure controversy had little meaning and stirred few passions. But in others the zeal to enclose caused the maximum social disturbances and distress. What elements in the local situation signalled danger for the intending encloser in the Tudor period, and where were they most commonly found? The most inflammable situations seem to have arisen in lowland villages possessing attenuated common pastures, large areas of common field, and an increasing population which leaned heavily on its common grazing land for the feeding of its animals. In such villages no one could enclose without risk of hurting others. Even when the individual

[1] W. Cunningham, *The Growth of English Industry and Commerce in Modern Times*, 1921 ed., II, pp. 898–9; E. F. Gay, 'Inclosures in England in the Sixteenth Century', *Qtrly. J. Econ.*, XVII, 1903, p. 593; *A Discourse of the Common Weal of this Realm of England*, ed. E. Lamond, 1954, p. 49; John Nichols, *History and Antiquities of the County of Leicester*, IV, i, 1807, p. 99; A. H. Johnson, *The Disappearance of the Small Landowner*, 1909, p. 39.

encloser surrendered a proportion of his share in the common grazings
to compensate for the close he had made in the arable fields, the
remaining commoners might derive less benefit from their commons
than before, because the enclosure divided the land into scattered bits
and pieces, and forced men to keep moving their stock from one small
piece of grazing to another, thus damaging the grass, and often rendering it almost worthless. Moreover, every argument against enclosure
carried extra weight because the enclosure of the common fields *and* the
waste was often under way at the same time. When the process took
place on both fronts in a single township, the farming routine of the
community was liable to be severely disrupted by the sudden reduction
in its total resources of common pasture.[1]

Why was the demand for grassland so insistent in the sixteenth
century? The answer lies in the economic trends of the period, in the
rise of population, and the prosperity of farming. After the Black
Death, labour had been short and land plentiful. This situation did not
endure. After a little more than a century of stagnation, population
began to grow again. The increase cannot be measured by any exact
counting of heads, but it was apparent from 1470 onwards in the
rising price of land.[2] By the beginning of the seventeenth century it
was sufficiently obvious to contemporaries to call for public comment.
No doubt, the rate of increase differed from region to region, and no
full understanding of economic and social changes in the countryside
at this period will be attained until this subject is examined in greater
detail. But here it is sufficient to note that it was a national phenomenon.
The population of Leicestershire, for example, increased by 58 per cent
between 1563 and 1603, that of 74 parishes in Hertfordshire by the
same amount.[3] In other parts of England, the increase has not yet been
studied in the same detail but it manifested itself to contemporaries in
other ways. They noticed first of all the number of new houses built
in their townships, and then the increasing numbers of stock which were
put out to graze on the commons. In the Isle of Axholme, the inhabitants of Epworth manor observed one hundred extra cottages built
between about 1590 and 1630. At Misterton, in the same district, thirty
new cottages were erected in forty years. Equally good examples could
be drawn from other English counties. The consequence everywhere
was a substantial increase in the numbers of cattle, sheep, horses, pigs,

[1] PRO C 78, 1581, 5.
[2] M. M. Postan, 'Some Economic Evidence of Declining Population in the later
Middle Ages', EcHR, 2nd Ser., II, 1950; E. Kerridge, 'The Movement of Rent,
1540–1640', EcHR, 2nd Ser., VI, 1953.
[3] VCH *Leics.*, III, p. 140; L. Munby, *Hertfordshire Population Statistics, 1563–1801*,
1964, p. 21.

and geese seeking herbage on the commons. Many of the predominantly pastoral counties could absorb this increase without practical inconvenience. Others could not. They became involved in innumerable lawsuits concerning common rights, or they solved the problem with less expense by reducing the number of stock which each tenant was entitled to put on the commons. In some townships stints were already in operation, and these were reduced to give every commoner a fair share and at the same time preserve the common from ruin by over-grazing. In other places, stints were introduced for the first time in the Tudor period. In others, for example in the fenland of Lincolnshire, stints were discussed but never operated.[1]

Apart from the difficulty of finding pasture for a rising population, most villages were subject to additional stress and strain because large farmers wished to increase the scale of their undertakings. Rising prices for agricultural produce throughout the sixteenth century stimulated enterprise among all farmers who produced a surplus for the market. Its effects can be observed in indirect ways—in the growing number and size of markets, and in increasing specialization by the farmers themselves. It can be illustrated more directly in complaints from villages all over the country against John Brown and Henry Smith who overcharged the commons with their herds and flocks, brought in strangers' cattle to graze on the summer pastures, or kept more stock on the commons in summer than they could support in winter on their home grounds. The complaints were all of one kind, recording the resentment of the many at the selfish ambitions of the few. And they echoed from Solway Firth to the East Anglian fens, from the Essex marshes to Land's End.

The demand for pasture reflected agricultural prosperity and the pressure of a rising population. It demonstrated too the basic imporance of livestock in all farming systems. The land could not be made to yield more until more manure was put into it. All over England farmers were making the most of their local resources with this end in view. Marl, chalk, seasand, alluvial silt, seawrack, night soil from the towns—all were spread upon the land where available. But the distance and costs of transport were considerable, and none was as efficient in increasing yields and maintaining humus as dung. To get more manure it was necessary to keep more animals. Hence in all farming regions, both those which concentrated on crops and those specializing in animal production, more intensive farming could only be achieved by carrying more livestock. Hence the universal pressure on grazing.

Public hostility to engrossing was prompted by the same economic

[1] Joan Thirsk, 'The Isle of Axholme before Vermuyden', AHR, I, 1953, p. 24; *Tudor Enclosures*, Hist. Ass. pamphlet, General Series, 41, 1959, p. 6.

stresses and strains as enclosure. Modern agricultural economists recommend engrossing, or, as we would term it today, the amalgamation of farms, as a means to more efficient business. The adverse social consequences weigh lightly in the scale of modern values. But in the sixteenth century, when most country people expected to get their living by farming, and when the idea of an ordered society in which no man took advantage of his neighbours was regarded as the only philosophy by which communal farming could work, the social drawbacks of engrossing carried greater weight than the economic advantages. Hence the outcry against it was vociferous, and claimed as much attention from the government as enclosure. Though Tudor landlords might prefer to let their land to one man rather than to many, they were constantly thwarted by the more powerful social argument that engrossing constituted the loss of a holding which could have supported a deserving family. As the vicar of Quinton in Gloucestershire observed bitterly to the President of Magdalen College, Oxford, in the early part of Henry VII's reign, "To let your lordship to one man, to prefer him, and he to keep under your tenants, and have all the vayle and they the burden, will there none tenants come to the town."[1]

Hunger for land and particularly for pasture impelled both those who enclosed and those who resisted. The two opposing attitudes towards enclosure mirrored two different ways of farming—the individualist and the communal systems. We have seen the simpler and more immediate reason for the opposition to enclosure—that it deprived the community of common rights. Others, more involved, however, weighed strongly in the formation of public opinion. They concerned first and foremost the adverse social consequences which followed when land was put to a new use, especially when old arable was put under pasture.

The regulations governing the common fields had never been so rigidly enforced as to preserve a permanent equilibrium between the arable and pasture of a township. But so long as a community pursued its traditional course of husbandry, some such balance tended to be preserved naturally. This did not mean that the same land remained under the plough or in grass century after century, without any change of use. The drawbacks to any such permanent routine were obvious when yields were reckoned up after harvest. It was usual for individuals and whole communities to alter the use of land as occasion required. By village agreement arable strips were converted into common pasture and a piece of common taken in to make a new

[1] W. Denton, *England in the Fifteenth Century*, 1888, p. 318. See also Warws. RO L2, 86.

arable field. In Northumberland villages, the redistribution of land was frequent and radical, and is probably to be attributed to the fact that good pasture did not last long in this wet climate and, unless ploughed out at frequent intervals, became overgrown with moss. In many pastoral districts where the commons were still plentiful, it was customary for whole communities to agree upon a change of land use from time to time. Alternatively, a man was permitted by custom to enclose and cultivate a piece of land from the common at any time, so long as the community was compensated by an equivalent piece of formerly enclosed land. In these ways a rough balance was always maintained between plough and pasture. And so long as the traditional system of husbandry was observed, the balance was not too rudely shaken even though the commons continued to undergo piecemeal enclosure.

The rapid spread of enclosure in the fifteenth and sixteenth centuries, however, was accompanied by some radical changes in the traditional husbandry of the different regions. Enclosure liberated men from restrictions and communal regulations. They used this liberty to alter their system of husbandry. In some places the old equilibrium of plough and pasture abruptly disappeared. In the fifteenth century the conversion of arable to pasture was so usual after enclosure in parts of England that in the sixteenth it was popularly regarded as the inevitable consequence. And since it was generally admitted that land in grass employed fewer hands than land under corn, the drastic fall in the arable acreage threatened to create serious unemployment among wage workers. Of the justice of popular complaints on this score there is no doubt. Unemployment and depopulation were writ large across the face of the landscape. Already by the accession of Henry Tudor hundreds of deserted or decaying villages gave a miserable daily reminder to all neighbours and travellers that this was the meaning of enclosure.

To contemporaries, in brief, enclosure signified first the loss to the community of common rights, and, when arable land was converted to pasture, depopulation. Engrossing likewise caused depopulation. Herein lay the logic behind all contemporary allegations that enclosure impoverished and depopulated the countryside. What, then, were its advantages to the encloser? By extinguishing common rights it freed men from subjection to the rules of communal husbandry. From the landlord's point of view this meant that the land was worth more and the rent could be increased. An acre enclosed, declared John Norden, was worth one and a half in common. Writing in 1641 Henry Best thought enclosed land was worth thrice the value of common land. Its benefits to the farmer depended entirely on the way the land was employed after enclosure. This in turn depended on the farming system of the locality and the policy of the individual farmer. The advantages of enclosure were as varied as the farming types.[1]

The least contentious enclosures were those which effected no change in land use or else resulted in the conversion of pasture to arable. These were common enough in the mainly pastoral districts where grass was a more successful crop than corn and where grazing was still relatively plentiful. Pasture from the commons was sometimes enclosed and kept in grass, because its feeding capacity could be improved by controlled grazing and more systematic manuring, and because the hedges of a close provided better shelter for stock than that afforded on a wind-swept open common. Sometimes pasture was enclosed and put under the plough because the inadequacy of the arable land caused a shortage of fodder or domestic corn and made the farmer undesirably dependent upon purchased foodstuffs. The fenland peasant, for example, whose arable land on average amounted to no more than eight acres, and who enjoyed unstinted grazing rights on the common, was more likely to turn pasture into cornland than the reverse. Hence the meagre crop of enclosure cases found in the Lincolnshire fenland by the commissioners of 1607.[2]

Sometimes the conversion of pasture to arable after enclosure was accompanied by the conversion of an equivalent amount of arable to pasture. Many such rearrangements were described in detail in the lawcourts after the enclosure commissioners had reported on one half of the operation, the conversion of arable to pasture, and neglected to mention the other. Here the enclosure and change of land use preserved the same balance of corn and grassland as before, but improved the yield of both by introducing a convertible husbandry. The wisdom of this practice had long been recognized. It had prompted many redistributions of land in the Middle Ages when common was put under the plough and cornland reverted to common. But now men were beginning to see the benefits of a change in land use accompanied by enclosure, and undertook both operations together. They justified it by describing the progressive exhaustion of their arable. Their observations led Miss Harriet Bradley, some forty years ago, to argue the universal exhaustion of the soil in England by the end of the Middle Ages. It was a greatly exaggerated hypothesis, quickly discredited when others were able to demonstrate from monastic estate records of the same period an impressive series of rising corn yields. The two opposing arguments can only be reconciled by admitting the truth of

[1] J. Norden, *The Surveyor's Dialogue*, p. 97; Henry Best, *Rural Economy, in Yorkshire, 1641*, Surtees Soc., XXXIII, 1957, pp. 129–31.

[2] E 134, 2 Jas. I, Mich. 33; Thirsk, *Tudor Enclosures*, pp. 14–15.

both. There *were* estates on which crop yields increased. Equally, there were farmers, more particularly perhaps those farming on a small scale, who noticed diminishing yields and recognized its cause, namely that the fields had been too long cropped without respite and needed a rest under grass.[1]

The solution to the difficulty did not inevitably lie with enclosure. The radical redistribution of land by common agreement but without enclosure was one alternative and had long been customary in Northumberland. Another was to let some arable strips in the common fields lie in ley. The ley strips were fenced off in order to permit stock to graze them when the adjoining arable land was in corn. Alternatively, the stock grazing on the leys were tethered. This compromise, which stopped short of enclosure, worked well enough. It could be carried out by a number of tenants agreeing together to leave a whole furlong in ley, or it could be undertaken by individuals converting a few of their own strips. The only disadvantage lay in the necessity for fencing or tethering cattle. The tenants of Fulbeck in Lincolnshire found themselves tethering 300 draught cattle and milch kine in the township on leys, headlands, and small pieces of ground in the cornfields and suffering constant damage to their corn when the animals broke loose. The inhabitants were driven in the end to accept the final remedy—to agree upon the consolidation of strips and enclosure.[2]

The most contentious enclosures of all, however, which vexed the government, and caused the greatest hardship, and the loudest popular outcry, were those which led to the permanent conversion of arable to pasture. To understand the economic motives for this movement it is necessary to refer briefly to agrarian changes in the century before 1500. The disastrous mortality in the plagues of the mid-fourteenth century had radically altered the relationship of land and labour. Land became plentiful and labour short. Men acquired holdings easily and large demesne farmers found it difficult to hire sufficient labourers to work their land efficiently. Some ceased to farm and leased their land to tenants, but others solved the problem of dear and scarce labour and untenanted holdings by turning their land over to sheepwalk and cattle pasture. Their labour costs fell, and the land was kept in use.

The demand for wool to supply the expanding wool trade and cloth industry justified the keeping of increasing numbers of sheep. Less is known about the parallel increase in the keeping of cattle at this time, but it is probable that with the spread of pasture farming it was as

[1] E 178, 3749; E 134, 23 Eliz. H6; TED I, pp. 61–2; Harriet Bradley, *The Enclosures in England—an Economic Reconstruction*, 1918; R. Lennard, 'The Alleged Exhaustion of the Soil in Medieval England', Econ. J., cxxxv, 1922.

[2] C 2, Jas. I, F 135.

marked in some regions as was sheep-keeping in others. Dairying developed in the wood-pasture region of Suffolk, for example, in the fifteenth century. When the vaccaries of Rossendale ceased to be managed by the great lords and were leased to smaller tenants from the fourteenth century onwards, there is nothing to suggest that they did not continue in use as cattle rather than sheep farms. The full story of regional specialization in the Middle Ages has yet to be told, but when complete, it is unlikely that the sheep will be allowed to dominate the historical scene as they have done in the past. Flocks were certainly conspicuous in the landscape, particularly on the hills throughout southern England, where a sheep-corn husbandry prevailed, but in other grassland regions, where better water supplies were available, it is likely that some of the beef and dairy cattle, which were well in evidence by the sixteenth century, were already in occupation of the pastures.[1]

For the present the place of sheep and cattle in the agrarian changes of the late Middle Ages cannot be assessed, but there is no doubt of the increasing popularity of pasture farming in areas where formerly a mixed corn and cattle husbandry had prevailed. Economically it had every advantage for the large farmer. But by the end of the fifteenth century, when population had begun to rise again, more attention was given to the awkward social problems it created. As common field arable was turned over to grass, the fall in the demand for labour caused unemployment; the profits of pasture farming tempted the larger farmers to overstock the common pastures with their animals and then to engage in illegal and ruthless measures for getting control of more land, and driving out the commoners. In one way and another the small farmer and the hired man were being edged off the land. In the worst cases small hamlets were completely abandoned and larger villages seriously depopulated. At the accession of Henry VII the increase in pasture farming had already cost the country a heavy price in human suffering.[2]

And yet the movement continued for a time into the Tudor period. Population rose, and the prices of farm produce and rents followed suit. Now the cloth industry was expanding, and the demand for wool rose to new and hitherto undreamed of proportions. Indeed, in areas marginal to corn, it is probable that the profit from wool in the early part of the sixteenth century was higher than for any other produce of

[1] A. H. Denney, *The Sibton Abbey Estates. Select Documents*, Suffolk Rec. Soc., II, 1960, pp. 26–7; G. H. Tupling, *The Economic History of Rossendale*, Chetham Soc., NS LXXXVI, 1927, p. 39; R. H. Hilton, 'A Study in the Pre-History of English Enclosure in the Fifteenth Century', *Studi in Onore di Armando Sapori*, pp. 680–2.
[2] *The Anglica Historia of Polydore Vergil*, ed. D. Hay, Camden Soc., LXXXIV, 1950, p. 277; Maurice Beresford, *The Lost Villages of England*, passim.

the farm. Not that this is anywhere explicitly stated in contemporary records, but in 1539 Fitzherbert held the view that "of all stock the rearing of sheep is most profitable," while the superior profits of sheep *and* cattle production over other farm enterprises are to be inferred from Sir Thomas Smith's suggested remedy for enclosure in 1549—to permit corn export and prohibit wool in order "to make the profit of the plough to be as good, rate for rate, as the profit of the graziers and sheepmasters." In the end, of course, this aim was achieved in the second half of the century through the impersonal intervention of economic forces.[1]

The decline of the cloth trade after 1551 dealt the wool producer a serious blow and farmers' interests shifted somewhat from wool to meat and cheese production. While some grassland regions concentrated on meat, others in west and north-west England showed signs (from about 1590 onwards) of shifting their interests from meat to cheese and butter production. Furness farmers engaged in cheese-making and invested less capital in cattle fattening; the small farmers of the Warwickshire Arden began to keep fewer bullocks and feeding oxen, and to fill their yards with cows and heifers—a trend which became more and more noticeable under the early Stuarts.[2]

Meanwhile the demand for farm produce of all kinds was growing in the towns. London began to sprawl further along Thames side; the cloth-producing areas of the west country and west Yorkshire became more populous; the metal-working centres around Birmingham and the coalmining towns of Durham called for more and more workers. All these industrial centres depended increasingly on all kinds of produce—not merely meat and cheese but grain as well—brought to the market by local farmers. And local farmers responded. Two excellent examples of regions catering particularly for the needs of the town lie ready to hand in eastern Durham, sending meat, cheese, and grain to the coalminers around Newcastle, and central Hertfordshire supplying pork, bacon, beef, and wheat to London. Neither, it should be noticed, displayed an overweening desire to convert all its ploughland to pasture.

The 1590's mark a turning point in the agricultural history of this period. They include a run of bad harvests which caused grain shortages, plague, and near famine. Thereafter, profit margins no longer favoured grass at the expense of grain. The enclosure movement did not cease, but the conversion of arable to pasture did not hold out the attractive possibilities of two generations earlier.

[1] R. H. Tawney, *The Agrarian Problem in the Sixteenth Century*, pp. 195 sqq.; *A Discourse of the Commonweal of this Realm of England*, p. 53.

[2] See *supra*, p. 94.

The generalizations offered here concerning the economic incentives in farming during the period 1500–1640 must not be allowed to dominate this account of the enclosure movement. Indeed, they are dangerously misleading unless handled in their proper context. Farming is not a highly flexible business which can twist and change direction at every trick and turn of the price curve. The land and its buildings impose severe limitations on most farmers. Moreover, within the framework of what is practicable, the successful farm business is a union of several interlocking enterprises. Complex problems arise for the man who makes a change in any one of them. Even if he can reorganize and rearrange them satisfactorily, he may find the short-term benefits cancelled out by the long-term disadvantages. Understandably, then, the ordinary farmer is rarely a revolutionary, and often his knowledge of his land and his experience of the vagaries of the market will make him a hardened conservative in agricultural matters. When we speak of changes in the relative profits of wool, meat, dairy produce, and grain, therefore, we describe economic forces which left thousands of farmers unmoved. They could not or would not respond. The downland farmers who at one time found themselves able to take advantage of rising wool prices and to keep more sheep were not able at another time to change over to preparing beef for the butcher. Those who reared cattle in Lancashire and the west Midlands could turn to dairying if they chose, but the farmers on the light lands of Norfolk and Suffolk were chained to a sheep-corn husbandry with no room to manœuvre. The farmers on the lower slopes of the Pennines could alter within limits the proportion of sheep to cattle as prices lured them, but the farmer on the damp waterlogged clays of the Weald of Kent could never do any good with sheep and was bound to rest his fortune on other stock. As circumstances changed through this century and a half, the trend towards increasing specialization affected every corner of the kingdom, but it led the farmers of the different regions in various directions. Every region possessing common fields or common pastures had some experience of enclosure. But it was not equally advantageous to the individual everywhere nor equally injurious to the community. And when enclosures were accompanied by the conversion of cornland to grass, not every farmer was prompted by the desire to accommodate a larger sheep-flock.[1]

[1] See also pp. 00.

B. PUBLIC OPINION, POPULAR COMMOTION, AND LEGISLATION

Throughout the sixteenth century Tudor governmental enquiries and legislation reflected concern at the progress of enclosing, the conversion of arable to pasture, and engrossing. But policy vacillated between mild and rigorous measures, from acts which were vaguely phrased and could not be enforced to strenuous county-by-county enquiries, followed by prosecutions in the courts and heavy money fines. In addition to these direct attacks on the problem, a number of statutes were passed which struck a glancing blow at enclosure and engrossing by attacking sheepmasters and those who leased cottages without sufficient land to support their occupants. Under James I and Charles I, however, the government lost much of its zeal for the cause. Indeed, after 1607, when the last large-scale enclosure enquiry took place, it abandoned all opposition to the principle of enclosure, but continued to keep up the appearance of opposing it in practice. Commissions were issued from time to time for the discovery of offenders, but their crimes were pardoned on payment of a money fine. The punishment of enclosers had degenerated into a revenue-raising device and little else.[1]

Some of the reasons for this change of attitude can be inferred from the preceding pages: as economic circumstances altered, so did the pace, purpose, and social consequences of enclosing and engrossing. It is now necessary to consider the legislation against the movement, in order to see more clearly the gradual growth of understanding in Parliament of its multifarious causes, and to set alongside all this the evidence of public opinion in so far as it can be gauged in political and other literature, and was revealed in popular disturbances.

The first acts to deal with the problems of depopulation at the beginning of Henry VII's reign did not appear like bolts from the blue. Some public complaint against the effects of enclosure had already reached the ears of Parliament, though just how vociferous the outcry had been it is impossible to say. But since, in the words of John Hales writing in 1549, "the chief destruction of towns and decay of houses was before the beginning of the reign of King Henry VII," it is certain that before the Tudor age began tempers in the countryside already ran high, and that the country gentry who sat as members of Parliament at Westminster were well aware of local grievances. But as yet people had no easy means of gaining wide publicity for their distress through the printed word, and the surviving evidence of popular

[1] M. Beresford and J. K. St Joseph, *Medieval England. An Aerial Survey*, p. 120.

complaint is extremely meagre. Two petitions to Parliament in 1414 from the Crown tenants of Darlton and Ragnall in Nottinghamshire against enclosure, and from the inhabitants of Chesterton, tenants of the prior and canons of Barnwell in Cambridgeshire, against engrossing, together with a petition by John Rous to the Parliament at Coventry in 1459, are the only protests known to have been presented formally to Parliament. But at the opening of Parliament in 1484 a reference by the lord chancellor to enclosures and depopulation implied that the government considered these matters urgent enough to call for action.[1]

The first act, passed in 1488, concerned the Isle of Wight. It was an attack on engrossers who took many farms into their hands and turned them all into grazing grounds for cattle and sheep. The government expressed dismay at the depopulation which followed, and the consequent threat to the defence of the kingdom, and enacted penalties for anyone who engrossed holdings whose total value exceeded ten marks a year. This was followed by a general statute in 1489 "agaynst pullyng doun of tounes" prompted by the same considerations as the act of 1488. Its provisions, however, were framed differently, and were preceded by a more verbose preamble. Deploring the decay of villages and the conversion of arable to pasture, the act enumerated all the evil consequences thereof: the growth of unemployment, the decay of tillage, the destruction of churches, and the weakening of England's defences against her enemies. Finally, it provided that all houses with twenty acres of land should be preserved with all necessary buildings and land for the maintenance of tillage. Until the decayed buildings were rebuilt, offenders had to surrender half the profits of the holding to the lord of the fee. It was a vaguely worded act and a little muddled. Despite the preamble which deplored the conversion of arable to pasture (without, be it noted, mentioning enclosing), the act was in fact directed against engrossing. It is true that both these things *and* enclosure were inextricably mixed in contemporary discussion and blended together into one massive agrarian problem. But this does not excuse a muddled act. The legislature seems to have been no more clear-headed on the subject than the public.[2]

No further acts against engrossing and the conversion of arable to pasture were deemed necessary for almost another generation. In 1515 the issue flared up again, at the same time as London officials were anxiously investigating the export of corn. The immediate cause,

[1] *A Discourse of the Commonweal of this Realm of England*, p.lxiii; E. F. Gay, *Zur Geschichte der Einhegungen in England*, Inaugural Dissertation zur Erlangung der Doktorwürde, Friedrich-Wilhelms-Universität zu Berlin, 1912, pp. 23–5. I wish to thank Professor Herbert Heaton for the loan of this thesis.

[2] Beresford, *The Lost Villages of England*, pp. 103–4; TED I, pp. 4–6.

therefore, may well have been fear of corn shortage in the capital. An undated bill against engrossing, and a proclamation against the conversion of arable to pasture, were drafted at about the same time. The bill inveighed against the engrossers of farms, and named in particular the merchant adventurers, clothmakers, goldsmiths, butchers, tanners, and other artificers who held sometimes ten to sixteen farms apiece, and were totally unable to maintain tillage in all of them. It deplored the consequent scarcity of victuals, and the depopulation of townships, which had once possessed twenty or thirty dwellings, and now were populated only by a neatherd, a shepherd, or a warrener. In short, it attacked merchants who engrossed farms, engaged in pasture farming, and kept cattle, sheep, and rabbits, at the expense of tillage. Having delivered this thrust at townsmen-turned-farmers, it suggested that no one should be allowed to occupy more than one farm. It was a sweeping, and also an illogical proposal. It would not by itself have arrested the spread of pasture farming, while to prohibit engrossing throughout the whole of England was an unworkable scheme and economically undesirable. Not surprisingly, then, this draft bill was discarded. The act of 1515 followed much more closely the lines of the draft proclamation, also drawn up in 1514, which dealt with the conversion of arable to pasture. The proclamation alluded to complaints from justices of the peace and commissioners of shires concerning the continued scarcity of grain owing to the conversion of arable to pasture, and the engrossing of farms. It laid special stress on the "infinite number of the king's subjects, [who] for lack of occupation, have fallen and daily do fall into idleness and consequently into theft and robberies." It then proposed that all land in tillage in 1485 should revert to tillage. Like the bill on engrossing, this proclamation was phrased in sweeping general terms with little regard for the practical difficulties of enforcing its provisions throughout the kingdom.[1] The act which finally emerged in 1515, and was made perpetual in 1516, showed more understanding of regional diversity, and seems to have been modified under pressure from members of Parliament who knew something of the variety of local conditions. For "advoidyng pullyng downe of townes" the act declared that all villages and habitations which on the first day of the present Parliament were for "the more part" occupied in tillage were to continue so; all buildings which were decayed were to be rebuilt within a year; and all land turned to pasture since 1 February 1515 was to be restored to arable "after the maner and usage of the countrey where the seid lond lyeth." The penalty for disobedience was again the forfeiture of half the profits from the holding to the lord of the

[1] N. S. B. Gras, *The Evolution of the English Corn Market*, p. 223; LP I, ii, pp. 1493, 1494.

fee so long as the offence continued. The act, in brief, attempted to arrest the decay of farm buildings (through engrossing), and the conversion of arable to pasture. It legislated for the districts where a substantial proportion of land was under the plough, and omitted the predominantly pastoral areas from the reckoning.[1]

Two years later Wolsey appointed a commission of enquiry into depopulation—a more effective instrument for measuring the scale of the problem than any used hitherto. It reflected the importance attached to the subject by the government, and, presumably, the complete failure of the earlier legislation. The commissioners were ordered to conduct investigations in all but the four northern counties of England, to report on villages and houses pulled down since 1488, the amount of land then in tillage and now in pasture, and the amount of parkland enclosed for the preservation of wild animals. In 1518, when the commission was still conducting enquiries, the first offenders began to appear in Chancery, and in a decree of the court issued that year it was ordered that all who pleaded for pardon should, within forty days, pull down all enclosures made since 1485, unless they could prove that their enclosures were beneficial to the commonwealth. Failure to obey the court's decrees laid the offender open to a penalty of £100. Prosecutions, consequent upon the information gathered in 1517 and 1518, continued for the next twenty years, but always they were initiated by the Crown. Although the immediate overlords of enclosing tenants had equal rights with the Crown to start proceedings, they utterly failed to do so. Herein lay the chief obstacle in the way of enforcing the early anti-enclosure legislation. The interests of landlords were identical with those of enclosing tenants. Their land was far more valuable enclosed than open. The Crown could not hope to find many allies among landlords.[2]

Prosecutions by the Crown in the court of Chancery and in the court of King's Bench continued for the next two decades. At the same time the acts of 1489 and 1515 remained on the statute book, and public attention was drawn to them from time to time by proclamation. In May 1528, for example, the lord chancellor asked for information to be passed to him secretly of all persons who kept more than one farm and made enclosures. In February 1529, again by proclamation, all enclosed grounds were ordered to be laid open and the hedges or palings removed before the following Easter. For nearly two decades the hunt for engrossers, enclosers, and converters was carried on with

---

[1] Statutes of the Realm, III (1509–47), p. 176.
[2] I. S. Leadam, The Domesday of Inclosures, 1517–18, I, pp. 1–11; E. F. Gay, 'Inquisitions of Depopulation in 1517 and the Domesday of Inclosures', RHS NS XIV, 1900, p. 235; Beresford, The Lost Villages of England, pp. 106–10.

the imperfect weapons forged in 1489 and 1515–1517. Then in 1533 the government turned to attack the problem from another angle.[1]

In a new act (25 Hen. VIII, c. 13) with a freshly-worded preamble it fastened responsibility for the spread of enclosure on the "great profit that cometh of sheep" and declared (a little wildly, perhaps) that some individuals had five, six, ten, twenty, even twenty-four thousand sheep apiece. Henceforth no person was to keep more than two thousand sheep, reckoned by the long hundred, i.e. 2,400 animals, on pain of forfeiting 3s. 4d. for every sheep above that number. The act then enumerated various important exceptions to the new ruling. "Spiritual persons" and lay lords occupying their own demesnes could keep as many sheep as they liked. So could those who needed them for household consumption. Lambs under one year did not count as sheep according to this definition, so that the breeder of sheep was less hampered in his business than those who specialized in wool and meat production. Finally, the act legislated against engrossing. No one after Christmas was to take up more than two farms or tenements, and those who had two holdings must dwell in the parishes in which they lay or forfeit 3s. 4d. for every week in which their offence continued. The act was a puppet, wearing a bold face but stuffed with straw. Indeed, it has every appearance of having been put forward by the government in strong terms, and modified subsequently under pressure from the large landlords sitting in Parliament. The explanatory clauses of the final act enabled them to escape from its restrictions almost scotfree, leaving the smaller farmers to submit. In one respect, however, the act proclaimed stern intentions. Responsibility for the discovery of offenders was placed for the first time on private informers as well as on the Crown, and the former were encouraged to produce information about enclosing and engrossing by the promise of an equal share with the Crown in the money penalties imposed on offenders. Informers had now taken the place of landlords in implementing the law, and were to share with the Crown the fines imposed on offenders. Common informers were used by Tudor and early Stuart governments on many other occasions for enforcing the law. Indeed, they have been called the "chief instrument for the enforcement of economic legislation" between 1550 and 1624, and though their performance was uneven, and their motives and methods always questionable, their poking and prying doubtless had a deterrent effect.[2]

[1] J. L. Lindsay, *Bibliotheca Lindesiana. Bibliography of Tudor and Stuart Proclamations*, nos. 111, 115.

[2] *Statutes of the Realm*, III, p. 451; M. Beresford, 'The Common Informer, the Penal Statutes, and Economic Regulation', EcHR, NS x, 1957, pp. 221 *sqq.;* see also *infra*, p. .

If the sheep population was increasing as fast as the government feared, this was due to the remarkable expansion of the cloth industry in Henry VIII's reign. Export figures suggest a steady upward movement from the beginning of the reign, and it is reasonable to suppose that the demand for wool had prompted more and more farmers to concentrate on this branch of farming. At the same time, pamphlets were beginning to appear emphasizing the rôle of sheep in the depopulation of villages, and these helped further to tilt the argument against sheep rather than against the evils of pasture farming in general.[1]

Meanwhile the earlier acts of 1489 and 1515 continued in operation though the machinery for enforcing them had proved ineffective. To remedy this weakness another act was passed in 1536 (27 Hen. VIII, c. 22). It did not introduce any new crimes, but its preamble observed that while the king had taken steps to enforce the earlier acts on Crown land, manorial lords had entirely neglected their duty of enforcing the law on their own estates. The new statute provided that if a landlord did not prosecute a tenant who let a house of husbandry fall into decay or converted arable to pasture, then the king was entitled to take the profits due to the immediate overlord so long as the offence continued. In other words, the new act allowed the Crown to take the initiative in prosecuting all enclosers, whether Crown tenants or not. Two further clauses took account of varied regional conditions. They conceded the existence of local husbandry practices in a vague phrase which stated that when pasture was converted to arable again, it should be done "according to the nature of the soil and course of husbandry used in the country where any such lands do lie." Secondly, the act applied only in the counties of Hertfordshire, Cambridgeshire, Lincolnshire, Nottinghamshire, Leicestershire, Warwickshire, Rutland, Northamptonshire, Bedfordshire, Buckinghamshire, Oxfordshire, Berkshire, Worcestershire, and the Isle of Wight. This choice of counties may not seem entirely logical, but it was doubtless arrived at, as was the list of counties in the later tillage statute of 1597, after much debate in Parliament and after many interventions by local members. Its merits were that it grouped together, in one large region, thirteen contiguous counties, all of which possessed a considerable amount of arable land or common field or both; and it concentrated on the portion of central England from which most complaints emanated, as well as including others on the fringe of this area.[2]

It is worth speculating, however, whether the act of 1536 would not have contained different provisions if it had been deferred for a few

---

[1] F. J. Fisher, 'Commercial Trends and Policy in Sixteenth-century England', EcHR, x, 1940, pp. 96–7.

[2] *Statutes of the Realm*, III, p. 553.

months. For in the late summer of 1536 disturbances broke out in the North Riding of Yorkshire, Cumberland, and Westmorland which were not unconnected with enclosure. They could easily have been used to justify the inclusion of these counties in the act of 1536.

The main strength of the rebellion in 1536, as its name—the Pilgrimage of Grace—implies, was drawn from discontent at religious innovations, in particular the dissolution of the monasteries, and it recruited its most enthusiastic supporters in the north and in Lincolnshire. But social and economic issues were inextricably intertwined with religious dispute in the north-west, for the monasteries and their farms often constituted the social centre of community life as well as its economic framework. When Furness Abbey was dissolved, the people of the district described how hitherto they had supplied various provisions to the monastery and received in return "almost as much as they supplied," namely sixty barrels of single beer or ale, thirty dozen loaves of coarse wheat bread, iron for their ploughs, and other farm tools, and timber to repair their houses. Moreover, everyone having a plough was allowed to send two people to dinner in the refectory one day a week from Martinmas to Pentecost, all tenants were allowed to send their children to school in the monastery, and to dinner or supper in the refectory each day; and if any child was "apt for learning," he was elected a monk, or given a post in the monastery in preference to all others. Finally, the monks paid all the charges for repairing the banks of the Isle of Walney. At the dissolution, the abrupt end of this mutual aid in Furness and elsewhere dealt a severe blow to those relatively poor communities in the highland parts of England who derived little benefit from the life-bringing arteries of national commerce. If their new landlord proved to be a non-resident country squire, or an absentee merchant, who expected his land to bear him financial profit before all else, he was a miserable substitute for the monastic brotherhood.[1]

The principal agrarian grievances voiced in 1536, therefore, arose from changes in lordship and landownership following the dissolution of the monasteries. Enclosure was only one, and seemingly a lesser cause of complaint, than quarrels about the rights and duties of customary tenants. Customary tenure was the most common tenure in the four northern counties, and because it laid onerous obligations on tenants—they were obliged to render border service, when necessary, to protect their land from the incursions of the Scots, and this was

[1] LP XII, i, p. 405; Thomas West, *The Antiquities of Furness*, 1805, p. 195. This and the following paragraphs are based on M. H. and Ruth Dodds, *The Pilgrimage of Grace, 1536–7 and the Exeter Conspiracy, 1538*, 1915, and R. H. Tawney, *The Agrarian Problem in the Sixteenth Century*, pp. 318 *sqq.*, and the authorities therein cited.

more than a nominal duty—their rights were more guaranteed than those customary in the south. The rebels who assembled at Doncaster in 1536 had evidently come fresh from wrangles with their landlords on the meaning of "tenant right," and their chief claim, therefore, was that lands in Westmorland, Cumberland, Kendal, Dent, Sedbergh, Furness, and abbey lands in Mashamshire, Kirkbyshire, and Nidderdale should be held by "tenant right," and that the customary payments for entry fines should be two years' rent. Enclosure was mentioned only once in a plea that the statutes against it should be enforced—a difficult task in this region where local government officials were too few to make much impression—and that intakes of land made since 4 Henry VII (except those made in mountains, forests, and parks) should be laid open. This seems to be a reference to the enclosure of commons, which became much more frequent in this part of the country later in the century without arousing any loud outcry. It seems probable, therefore, that it loomed large at this time because the traditional life of the community was under attack from many different directions, and this grievance was magnified in the light of all the rest. New interpretations of tenant right, rent increases, enclosure, and the knowledge that justice was expensively bought, made the inhabitants of these remote highland valleys feel themselves beleaguered and defenceless against their new landlords.

The northern rebels who joined the Pilgrimage of Grace gathered under the leadership of certain men of Richmondshire, a district in the north Yorkshire dales inhabited by many small pasture farmers, whose poverty was later alleviated by the growth of a secondary occupation—the knitting of stockings—to supplement their meagre farm earnings. Their leaders were called the four captains of Penrith: Faith, Poverty, Pity, and Charity, and judging by the confessions later elicited from two of the rebels, their support was drawn almost entirely from north western England, the highland districts of north-west Yorkshire, Westmorland, and Cumberland, where people were poorer and, owing to the meagre quantity of their arable land, lived in more congested conditions than in the north-east. Not surprisingly, these northern insurgents who set agrarian grievances alongside the religious in their campaign did not co-operate easily with the leaders of the religious insurrection. Indeed, how could it have been otherwise, since the background of their experience was entirely different from that of the rebels in the lowlands of East Yorkshire and Lincolnshire?[1]

The whole outbreak was ruthlessly put down in the early months of 1537 and the executions that followed terrorized the rebellious into subjection. A more powerful and authoritative King's Council in the

[1] LP XII, i, pp. 300–4; see also pp.   – .

North was set up to administer the five northern counties, and to hear and deal with agrarian grievances. The rebellion of 1536 did not necessitate any new agrarian legislation, but more conscientious efforts were made in the north at least to enforce existing acts.

The problem simmered for more than a decade until a new government under a Protector who lent a fresh and sympathetic ear to complaints from the peasantry unwittingly fomented unrest until it issued forth in another political crisis. But by that time economic conditions had undergone a profound change since 1536. The country was now living through a period of sharp inflation. Three debasements of the coinage in 1542, 1547, and 1549, accompanied by harvest failures in 1545, 1549, 1550, and 1551, caused a sharp rise in prices, particularly of food. The price index of articles consumed in the ordinary labourer's household, which stood at 100 in 1508, had risen to 231 by 1547, and rose again to 285 in 1551.[1]

The price revolution, which had made a slow start in the first three decades of the century, had now gathered such speed in the forties that it was racking the foundations of the economy. The sins of the government were at once laid at the door of the pasture farmer, and particularly the sheepmaster. He was charged with the responsibility for everything, for the poverty of the poor, the high price of food, and even the high price of wool. He was the canker that poisoned the economy at its roots, forcing it into complete servitude to the foreign cloth market. The remedy for this imbalance seemed to Somerset's advisers to lie in curbing the activities of the sheepmaster, and this, as Sir Thomas Smith, an influential figure in government circles, defined it, lay in making "the profit of the plough to be as good, rate for rate, as the profit of the graziers and sheepmasters." In March 1549, persuaded by these arguments and the propaganda of the Commonwealth men, Parliament sanctioned a novel tax on sheep and cloth. Although its overt objective was to raise money, its promoters were evidently well aware of its wider repercussions on agriculture.[2]

The idea of a tax on the cattle grazier or sheepmaster had been in the air since the beginning of Edward VI's reign. An estimate had been made about October 1547 (the document is undated, so this date is conjectural) by an unknown writer of the probable sum of money which would accrue from a tax on sheep and fat cattle. It involved elaborate calculations concerning the amount of wool, woolfells, and

[1] See infra, p.   ; Y. S. Brenner, 'The Inflations of Prices in Early Sixteenth-Century England', EcHR, NS XIV, 1961, pp. 231–2; E. H. Phelps-Brown and Sheila V. Hopkins, 'Seven Centuries of the Prices of Consumables compared with Builders' Wage Rates', Economica, NS XXIII, p. 312.

[2] Discourse of the Commonweal, p. 53.

cloth exported in the reign of Edward III and in 1546, and the number of sheep which must have accounted for this output. It arrived at an estimate of nearly seven million sheep in the mid-fourteenth century and nearly $8\frac{1}{2}$ million in the mid-sixteenth—a calculation, incidentally, which suggests a rather modest increase in sheep numbers, hardly supporting the wild allegations of contemporaries that sheep-keeping had displaced all other kinds of husbandry. The memorandum then went on to make a number of alternative proposals, one for a tax on sheep, wool, cloth, fat cattle, and leather, and another on sheep alone. When John Hales presented his *Causes of Dearth*, probably in a speech to Parliament in the summer of the following year, he engaged in similar estimates of sheep numbers, which betrayed the influence on his thought of the earlier draft proposal. On this occasion, however, the tax on sheep and cloth was proffered as a substitute for revenue that would be lost by the suggested abolition of purveyance. Parliament accepted it : purveyance was abolished for three years, and in an act of March 1549 a "relief" on sheep and cloth was imposed in its place. It entailed a nation-wide, parish-by-parish census of sheep, which was scheduled to take place in June of that year. But the incidence of the tax was modified according to the amount which taxpayers paid at the same time on personal goods. This clause seems to have been an amendment insisted on by Parliament, since it did not appear in Hales's original proposal, and it had the effect of easing the burden on the rich while leaving it on the poor. The act, therefore, defeated its author's intentions before it even reached the statute book.[1]

Parliament rose in the middle of March, and the commissioners began their enquiries that summer. But general discontent in the countryside, coupled with political manœuvring at Westminister, wrought the downfall of Protector Somerset that autumn, and he was succeeded by the more cautious Northumberland. When Parliament met again in November 1549, it repealed the tax on sheep. The preamble of the act (3 & 4 Edward VI, c. 23) explained that the tax had fallen harshly on the poor commoners—a result that might have been foreseen—and that the money had been cumbrous to collect—a readily credible statement. So the tax by which Hales had hoped to redress the balance between tillage and pasture was abandoned before it had time to show effect.[2]

The vigorous opposition to the sheep tax of 1549 and its speedy repeal early the following year cannot be fully understood, however, without due reference to more serious agrarian disturbances that

[1] TED I, pp. 178 *sqq.*; *Discourse of the Commonweal*, pp. xlii *sqq.*; M. Beresford, 'The Poll Tax and Census of Sheep, 1549', AHR, I, 1953, pp. 9–15; II, 1954, pp. 15–29.
[2] *Statutes of the Realm*, IV, p. 122.

occurred in the same year. Before the tax on sheep was introduced, Somerset's government had dealt another blow at enclosure by initiating in 1548 an enclosure enquiry on the same lines as that of 1517. A principal instigator, and one of the commissioners appointed to undertake local enquiries, was again John Hales. Before this, a proclamation had been issued on 1 June 1548, inveighing against engrossing, enclosing, and the conversion of arable to pasture, declaring that rots and murrains were the punishment, sent by God, for "this uncharitable conduct," and ordering the laws of Henry VII and VIII to be put into execution. The enclosure commissioners in the same month were given precise instructions to enquire into the towns, villages, and hamlets decayed and laid down to pasture by enclosure since 1488, to discover the number of ploughs put down, the houses fallen into decay, the number of parks created or enlarged, the names of the persons responsible, the names of those who kept over 2,400 sheep, those who had robbed their tenants of their commons, and those who occupied more than two farms. The commissioners were despatched first of all to the Midland counties and later to other areas as well.[1]

Sponsored by a government which promised to show special sympathy for the poor, the commission raised hopes for the redress of grievances which could not but be frustrated by promises of legal prosecutions that might take years to produce results. Riotous attacks on enclosures broke out all over the country, and the commissioners who had been bidden to work for "a charitable and quiet reformation by the order only of the law" encountered a peasantry with staves and bludgeons in their hands ready to effect quicker remedies. Three anxious proclamations in 1549, in May, mid-June, and mid-July, betrayed an ugly situation. By exhortation and the threat of dire penalties, they tried to repress seditious and disobedient persons, and to put an end to riotous assemblies. All three proclamations dealt particularly with enclosure disturbances and associated the outbreaks of violence with the enclosure commissioners' enquiries.[2]

The uproar was widespread in southern England. It had started in Hertfordshire before the enclosure commission set to work, and spread to Buckinghamshire, Wiltshire, Sussex, Hampshire, Kent, Gloucestershire, Suffolk, Warwickshire, Essex, Leicestershire, Worcestershire, and Rutland. For the most part the outbreaks were disorganized and uncoordinated, but eventually the uproar crystallized in two more formidable risings centred upon widely separated districts—the south-west, and Norfolk. And although neither of these outbreaks was expressly concerned with enclosure, nor the two districts much plagued by the

[1] Lindsay, *op. cit.*, no. 333; TED I, pp. 39–44; S. T. Bindoff, *Tudor England*, p. 134.
[2] Lindsay, *op. cit.*, nos. 353, 356, 362.

movement, their leaders recruited many aggrieved men with personal experience of agrarian abuses, including enclosure and engrossing, whose enthusiasm for their cause sprang from a seedbed of many discontents. Sir William Paget, for example, expressing some personal knowledge of the circumstances behind the rising in the west country, dwelt not only upon religious indignation, provoked by Cranmer's new prayer book, but also upon high prices and enclosures. This view of the causes of discontent is confirmed by the character of the disturbances in many scattered places throughout southern England.[1]

In Norfolk, where the disturbances of 1549 took the form of an open rebellion, led by Robert Ket, agrarian discontent was outspoken. The rebels came mostly from the populous district of north and east Norfolk, where pressure on the land within a community of small farmers had bred tension enough to kindle a riot at the smallest provocation. But enclosure was not the outstanding grievance; it was not even mentioned directly in Ket's programme, and the only reference to enclosure was ambiguous, and seemed to concern closes reserved for saffron-growing. But underlying the particular list of abuses concerning selfish lords who overgrazed the commons with their animals, kept dovecotes, allowed their pigeons to damage their tenants' crops, and kept rabbits in unprotected cony warrens, was general exasperation at the shortage of land and the greedy exploitation of the commons by the few. Local discontents mirrored the economy and the social structure of the region as they had done in 1536 in north-western England. But all were rooted in the shifting sands of a changing economy, a growing population, and expanding agricultural enterprise.[2]

Ket's rebellion failed miserably, the Western rebellion was crushed, and Somerset was overthrown. The government learnt its lesson and was not disposed to embark again on legislation which would act as a clarion call to a restive peasantry. The sheep tax had gone. The enclosure enquiry of 1548 was prematurely brought to an end, and the only surviving information collected by it relates to Warwickshire and Cambridgeshire. But despite the general verdict that Northumberland was the friend of the large landowner, his period of government saw the passing of two agrarian statutes in 1550 and 1552 to help the homeless cottager find accommodation in the countryside, and to maintain tillage. Though hardly forceful enough, they at least made a show of defending the poor against the powerful. The first act of 1550 "concerning the ymprovement of comons and waste groundes," was in fact concerned with protecting small cottagers who sought to build a

---

[1] E. F. Gay, 'The Midland Revolt and the Inquisitions of Depopulation of 1607', RHS, XVIII, 1904, p. 200; Strype, *Ecclesiastical Memorials*, 1822, II, ii, p. 432.

[2] S. T. Bindoff, *Ket's Rebellion, 1549*, pp. 7–10, 17–18.

house and take a small plot of land on the wastes. It reaffirmed the principles set out in the Statutes of Merton and Westminster in 1235 and 1285 that lords might improve their commons so long as they left enough for their free tenants, but reminded them that houses built on the waste with not more than three acres of land "dothe noe hurt and yet is muche commoditie to the owner thereof and to others." Only when more than three acres of land were annexed to the cottages was an offence committed, and the land ordered to be laid open to common again. In short, the act recognized that housing had to be found for increasing numbers of people, that squatting on the commons was the only solution to the housing shortage in many places, and that some distinction had to be made between such encroachments and enclosures by farmers who sought to carve out more substantial farms.[1]

The second statute, in 1552 (5 & 6 Edward VI, c. 5), reverted to the familiar problem of maintaining and increasing tillage. It harked back to the beginning of Henry VIII's reign and ordered that all land which had been in tillage for four years at any time since 1509 should be put back to tillage. The act thus instituted an enquiry into the use of land over the previous forty-two years. Another clause excluded land that had lain in pasture for forty years, and all land on marshes, heaths, common downs, fens, and moor, which had not been ploughed for forty years, as well as pasture kept only for the maintenance of houses and hospitality. It also exempted from penalty all those who, having converted arable to pasture, converted an equivalent amount of land in the same township from pasture to arable. Commissioners were to be appointed to discover the lands which offended against the new regulations, cases were to be heard in the court of Exchequer, and a penalty of 5s. was imposed on every acre discovered which was not put back into tillage. The act was to endure for ten years at least and after that to the end of the next Parliament.[2]

Under Mary Parliament reiterated and elucidated the meaning of the old statutes of husbandry. It provided for the appointment of commissioners to see that the statutes were observed, while allowing some latitude in the enforcement of the acts in areas where it was considered unnecessary to insist on the strict letter of the law. It also attacked another problem, which had been voiced much earlier in the century, though it is not easy to measure its importance beyond the clauses of the statute. In 1556 it was ordained that all men who kept more than 120 sheep should keep one cow per sixty sheep and rear one calf for every 120 sheep. The preamble justifying the act tells us that "of late yeres" people had turned their land over to the feeding of sheep, oxen, steers, heifers, etc., and in concentrating on meat produc-

[1] *Statutes of the Realm*, IV, pp. 102–3.   [2] *Ibid.*, pp. 134–5.

tion had neglected rearing, and so caused a shortage of store cattle. This complaint had already been made by Thomas More in his *Utopia* (1516). The decline of cattle breeding, he had argued, was due to the fact that rich men preferred to engage in the more profitable pursuit of keeping sheep or fattening bullocks. The argument was repeated by John Hales in his *Causes of Dearth* (1548): the universal dearth of victuals, he said, resulted from the failure to breed and rear cattle and poultry. By 1555 Hales had ceased to have any influence on government policies, but this proposition, following so closely the reasoning in *Utopia*, probably expressed a widespread popular notion about the causes of high food prices.[1]

Judging by the records we possess of the animals kept by the larger farmers in the sixteenth century, there were few men keeping large numbers of sheep who did not also keep a sizeable herd of cows and rear calves. Nor did the act, having attacked the producers of mutton as well as beef, suggest how to compel those who fattened sheep to give attention to rearing them. It was certainly true that some regions tended to concentrate more and more on fattening—this was the trend in the Weald of Kent, for example—but then these districts were served by farmers from north and west where rearing was the principal business. Towards the end of the sixteenth century the tendency grew for the rearing regions to engage in a certain amount of fattening as well. The farmers in the four northern counties, for example, seem to have taken more interest in fattening, probably in response to a larger demand for meat from the local cloth-and coal-producing towns. This may well have reduced the number of store cattle available for sale to the farmers of the Home Counties, who concentrated on fattening because of their favourable geographical position in relation to London. By the beginning of the seventeenth century, moreover, there were other signs that the home production of store cattle was inadequate. The gap was being met by imports from Ireland, a solution which prompted bitter complaint from some of the breeders in Somerset.[2]

It would not, therefore, have been surprising to see the act of 1556 in the 1590's or at the beginning of James I's reign. But it is difficult to show that fifty years earlier it dealt with an urgent problem. Rather it would seem likely that increasing specialization on meat production in certain districts around London had forced itself upon the notice of contemporary writers and politicians, and persuaded them that this was the trend all over England. Had this been true, it would certainly have been arguable that legislation was needed to encourage cattle

---

[1] *Statutes of the Realm*, IV, pp. 274–5; *The Utopia of Sir Thomas More*, ed. H. B. Cotterill, 1937, p. 30; *Discourse of the Commonweal*, p. xlii.

[2] See also p. 187; CSPD 1619–23, p. 291.

breeding again. In fact, it was not, and there is nothing to suggest that at this date the breeding regions failed to supply all the needs of the fattening areas.

It is noteworthy that the attack on sheepmasters, which had prompted punitive legislation in 1533, had now died away. The one and only statute which had singled out the wool producers rather than the pasture farmers as a whole was a period piece, belonging to a decade when cloth exports were reaching their peak. By 1550 the Crown had turned its attention elsewhere—to the graziers who produced meat and bought in their store animals from elsewhere. And in the nineties, when bad harvests and high food prices yielded signs of considerable rural distress and occasioned a fresh burst of legislation, it was again meat producers who were cast in the rôle of villains of the piece, while the sheepmasters were allowed to retreat into the shadow. The change of emphasis between 1533 and 1555 seems to reflect a change of opinion concerning the mainspring of the enclosure movement. The profit from sheep had been regarded as the main motive until the middle of the century. Now it was the profit from fat cattle.

Enclosure cases presented in the court of Exchequer from 1517 onwards dwindled to a mere trickle after 1556. This slackening off in the zeal of informers explains the provisions of a new act for maintaining tillage, passed early in Elizabeth's reign (1563). It repealed all agrarian statutes passed under Edward and Mary on the grounds that they were imperfect, in some cases too mild, and did not produce results, and it ordained that the acts of Henry VII and VIII should continue in force, that from 1564 all land tilled for four successive years at any time since 20 Henry VIII (1528–9) should continue in tillage, that all arable converted to pasture between 7 and 20 Henry VIII should be restored to tillage, and that no further conversions from arable to pasture should be carried out anywhere. The act heralded a new enclosure enquiry, which began in 1565. For some reason, not yet clearly understood, however, this commission came to a premature end, and the only surviving returns consist of fragments relating to Leicestershire and Buckinghamshire.[1]

Before the dearth of the nineties again focused anxious attention on enclosure, one other agrarian statute was passed in 1589, dealing with the problem of landless cottagers. It forbade the building of cottages with less than four acres of land. This may have been inspired by the

---

[1] Beresford, *The Lost Villages of England*, p. 115; E. F. Gay, 'Inclosures in England in the Sixteenth Century', p. 577. Gay suggests elsewhere that the enquiry of 1566 ended abruptly because Parliament did not renew the act of 1563. The Crown had to rest content with a proclamation in 1568.—E. F. Gay, *Zur Geschichte der Einhegungen in England*, p. 45.

Crown's own experience of the problem as landowner. As population increased in certain areas, holdings and tenements were being divided in order to provide accommodation for everyone, sheds and barns were being turned into dwellings, and cottages were being built by freeholders on small sites as a speculation. Often they lacked any land, and became a desperate refuge for paupers who had little hope of supporting themselves and who made heavy demands on the charity of the rest of the community. The new legislation, therefore, was designed to preserve the principle that all countrymen should have some land for their essential support.[1]

The act of 1563 for maintaining tillage had contained nothing novel, and the enquiry of 1565 had proved abortive. We must conclude from this and the fact that the rebellion of 1569 did not let loose an avalanche of agrarian complaints that enclosing and engrossing had lost some of their sting. Not that the movement came to a halt in the second half of the sixteenth century—it did not. But it may well have slowed down. This seems to have occurred between 1530 and 1580 in Leicestershire, for example, one of the counties most plagued by enclosures in the Tudor period. Moreover, the idea that enclosure had some merit was gaining ground, as reasonable methods of carrying it through became more common and the peasantry shared in its benefits. Finally in the Parliament of 1593 the Commons decided "because of the great plenty and cheapness of grain," and "partly because of the imperfection and obscurities of the law" that the statutes against the conversion of arable to pasture should be discontinued. It proved to be an ill-chosen moment at which to loosen the reins. The autumn of 1594 brought a disastrous harvest failure, and this was but the first of a series of four. The subsistence farmer was quickly reduced to abject helpless misery; he could not feed his family, let alone pay his rent. The middling farmers could support themselves but had nothing to sell at the market; they too fell in arrears with their rent. Only the large farmer who still had a considerable surplus to sell did well out of the famine.[2]

In 1597 Parliament took fright and decided to revive the statutes against enclosing and engrossing. In doing so, it expressed the conviction that enclosing had greatly increased since 1593, and this statement has been confirmed by detailed investigation in one Midland county—Leicestershire—showing a great burst of activity between 1591 and

[1] *Statutes of the Realm*, IV, pp. 804–5; PRO DL 44, 398.
[2] L. A. Parker, *Enclosure in Leicestershire, 1485–1607*, London Ph.D. thesis, 1948, p. 189; TED I, pp. 84–5; C 2 Eliz., P 7, 34; P 1, 5; D 8, 31; H 11, 46; Thirsk, 'Industries in the Countryside', pp. 82–3; CSPD 1595–7, p. 348. The influence of the harvests on this legislation is analysed in W. G. Hoskins, 'Harvest Fluctuations and English Economic History, 1480–1619', AHR, XII, 1964, pp. 28–46.

1597. The loosening of the reins had evidently accelerated the movement in the Midlands towards the conversion of arable to pasture and convertible leys.[1]

E. F. Gay once remarked of the anti-enclosure legislation of the sixteenth century that most of it coincided with periods of dearth. Legislation became necessary because the government feared the social tension bred by these changes within a community of hard-pressed anxious peasants. Nothing illustrates this better than the legislation of 1597. From all parts of the country the Privy Council received news of meagre corn supplies and plague. Enclosing and engrossing, the old bones of contention, seemed doubly offensive to the peasantry, and were doubly dangerous to the government, as a threat to social peace. Fear and reality were brought face to face in disturbances in Oxfordshire "to overthrow enclosures, and to help the poor commonalty that were to famish for want of corn."[2]

The two statutes of 1597 emerged as a result of the initiative taken by the Commons. The first act against the decaying of towns (39 Eliz. c. 1) tackled engrossing by ordaining that all houses of husbandry (i.e. all houses having twenty acres or more of land) which had been allowed to fall into decay within the last seven years should be rebuilt and forty acres of land (or if so much land was not available, twenty acres) laid to them. Half the houses decayed for *more than* seven years were to be rebuilt with the same allotment of land. The second act "for the maintenance of husbandrie and tillage" (39 Eliz. c. 2), having stated in the preamble that the repeal of the old statutes in 1593 had caused more depopulations by turning tillage into pasture than at "anie time for the like number of yeares heretofore," ordered that lands converted since 1588 into sheep pastures or used for the fattening or grazing of cattle, and having been tilled for twelve years before conversion, should be restored to arable before May 1599. Certain exceptions followed, however, which show that by now members of the Commons were well drilled in the routine of pointing out the unpractical and unrealistic aspects of the tillage statutes. The act did not apply to lands converted to pasture in order to regain heart by being grazed—official recognition, at last, for the virtues of ley farming. The act did not apply to common graziers or butchers who needed only grazing grounds for the temporary keep of fat beasts and sheep. Nor did it apply to commons and wastes which were unsuited to corn. Finally, the statute was ordered to

[1] Parker, *op. cit.*, pp. 93, 189.
[2] E. F. Gay, 'The Midland Revolt and the Inquisitions of Depopulation of 1607', RHS, xviii, 1904, p. 213 note; Henry Barnes, 'Visitations of the Plague in Cumberland and Westmorland', *Cumb. & Westm. Antiq. & Archaeolog. Soc.*, xi, 1892, pp. 178–9; SP 14, 28, 64.

be kept in certain counties only. The original bill, having been designed to apply throughout the kingdom, was amended in committee to omit Devon, Cornwall, Shropshire, Staffordshire, Cheshire, Lancashire, Cumberland, Westmorland, and all counties in eastern England lying east of a line drawn through Hampshire, Berkshire, Buckinghamshire, Bedfordshire, and Cambridgeshire. The reasoning behind the geography of this act is not readily obvious. But it seems to have been decided upon after vigorous discussion in committee, as a result of intervention by members of Parliament with local knowledge of farming in their own counties. One member, for example, remarked in debate that Shropshire was wholly given over to woodland, oxen, and dairies—in other words, it was a pastoral county. To include it in the act would breed a greater scarcity than the scarcity of corn. This then explains the omission of Shropshire from the act, while Herefordshire, one of the counties described as "the barns for the corn" in this part of the country, was included. Sir John Neale has expressed the view that some counties suffered inclusion in the act simply for want of an M.P. to speak for them. But all in all the counties selected for investigation seem to have been wisely chosen. They were counties with common fields and considerable arable land, while many, though not all, the omitted counties lacked common fields or were mainly engaged in grassland farming. The final singular exception in this statute related to land "lying within two miles of Watling Street leading from Dunstable to Westchester so that the same ground be not above five miles from the parish church of Dunstable nore within two miles thereof." This clause smacks especially of strong intervention by a member of the Commons with local interests, and may have been designed to ensure that the drovers of cattle had sufficient pasturage at this halting place on their road to London. But it will require a local historian to settle this problem with certainty.[1]

Surviving records of the Commons debate on these two statutes in 1597 suggest that the anti-enclosure bill met much opposition while that against engrossing did not. It was, indeed, difficult to defend engrossing against those who argued the paramount importance of defending the realm and the necessity for keeping the country well populated with husbandmen and yeomen. Economic rationalism—the strongest argument in favour of engrossing—could not compete against the patriotic appeal for military security at home. But enclosure had become a highly controversial subject, because greater knowledge had shown it to be a many-sided issue. Nothing illustrates better the

[1] J. E. Neale, *Elizabeth I and her Parliaments, 1584–1601*, pp. 337–45; *Statutes of the Realm*, IV, pp. 891–6; A. F. Pollard and Marjorie Blatcher, 'Hayward Townshend's Journals', *Bull. IHR*, XII, 1935, p. 16.

increasing awareness of its complex nature than the tone of the speeches in debate, and the content of some of the rejected clauses of the Act against the Decaying of Towns. At one stage a clause was proposed to allow any tenant to enclose land belonging to his farm if he had the consent of his lord. Another amendment suggested allowing anyone to enclose as much land as he desired, so long as it was for the maintenance of his household. In the midst of these debates, a bill "for the most commodious usage of land dispersed in the common fields" was presented. This also must have been intended to assist consolidation of holdings, if not enclosure. The discussions leading up to the legislation of 1597 were throughout hampered by uncertainties about the wisdom of anti-enclosure legislation. For the immediate cause of the proposed acts was the shortage of grain, and who could be certain that this was really due to the decay of tillage? In the opinion of one speaker in debate, the true cause was the weather. If pasture were converted to arable, it would raise the rents of pasture, cause cattle and sheep to be scarce, wool to fall short of demand, grain to be overabundant, and its price to fall unduly low. Here, indeed, was displayed a much fuller understanding of the complementary nature of arable and pastoral husbandry than in any of the statutes passed earlier in the Tudor period.[1]

The two statutes of 1597 served their turn while high prices lasted. But in 1601 they fell under criticism again, for the previous harvest had been good, and grain prices had fallen. The Commons began to consider the possibility of repealing them. Policy was now vacillating and uncertain. The conviction that enclosure was wrong and the tillage laws were right, which had governed opinion at Westminster for so long, had gone. The statutes seemed necessary when grain prices were high, but when they fell, some politicians, at least, saw the folly of compelling men to convert pasture to arable to grow more grain and so force the price of corn even lower. "In the time of dearth, when we made this statute [for the maintenance of tillage]," said Mr Johnson in the Commons in 1601, "it was not considered that the hand of God was upon us; and now corn is cheap. If too cheap, the husbandman is undone, whom we must provide for, for he is the staple man of the kingdom. And so, after many arguments, he concluded the statute to be repealed." Sir Walter Raleigh also argued in favour of repeal, desiring to leave every man free, "which is the desire of a true Englishman." Cecil, on the other hand, was against repeal because he believed that in years of abundance the surplus corn could be

[1] Neale, *op. cit.*, pp. 342–3; M. Beresford, 'Habitation versus Improvement. The Debate on Enclosure by Agreement', *Essays in the Economic and Social History of Tudor and Stuart England*, ed. F. J. Fisher, pp. 52–3.

readily exported, and national defence demanded a good supply of ploughmen.[1]

Cecil's speech shows that the government opposed repeal of the tillage statutes, and on this occasion its view prevailed. But the tenor of the debates of 1597 and 1601 suggests that the weight of opinion in the House was gradually shifting towards a *laissez-faire* attitude, leaving "every man free" as Raleigh phrased it. Probably the tillage laws would have been discarded altogether in the next ten years had the harvests been plentiful. But events took another turn. Suddenly in 1607, with little warning, an angry peasantry in three counties rose in revolt against enclosure, and in a matter of days the Midlands were ablaze with tumult and rumours of worse to come.

A full explanation of the outbreak of 1607 must wait upon a local historian who can examine in detail the enclosure history of all those villages in Northamptonshire, Leicestershire, and Warwickshire which were the ringleaders of the revolt. All five villages lay within a small tract of country—none more than twenty miles from any other—between Rugby, Kettering, and Market Harborough, a district now given over almost entirely to grazing and dairying, where the enclosure movement had made rapid strides in the Tudor period. No national legislation touching enclosure can be blamed for encouraging the insurgents, nor had Westminster recently intervened with economic aid or promises of aid to raise hopes of a remedy for agrarian distress. The long-term irritant was almost certainly the prolonged agricultural distress, which had begun with a bad harvest in 1594, and had continued with a whole series of misfortunes, mounting grain shortage, high prices, and sickness among men and stock. A contemporary reporter described the purpose of the revolt in 1607 as the desire "for reformation of those late inclosures which made them of the porest sorte reddy to pyne for want." In the light of other information about this decade, it seems that enclosures were the scapegoat for other more immediate ills. We have noticed already how in depression falling profits drove the larger farmer to economize in the employment of labour. This immediately aggravated the plight of the poor by increasing unemployment just at the time when food was in short supply and expensive. Even those who had some land of their own reaped such a meagre harvest in bad years that they had nothing to sell, and were driven, if they had money enough, to buy domestic supplies at the market. Everything conspired against the labourer and small farmer in bad times, and it was almost certainly in a situation like this, of mounting

[1] Bland, Brown, and Tawney, *English Economic History. Select Documents*, pp. 274–5. It seems to have been a conventional assumption that "shepherds be but ill archers."— TED III, p. 55.

economic difficulty offering little hope of a speedy remedy, that the Midland revolt broke out.[1]

The disturbance started with a riot in Northamptonshire on the last day of May. Already in 1604 complaints had been heard in this county against "the depopulation and daily excessive conversion of tillage into pasture." Parts of Northamptonshire, like Leicestershire, had fallen readily into the grasp of the enclosing farmer, for its soils were nowhere specially fertile for corn whereas it grew good grass, and was eminently suited to cattle and sheep grazing. Thus although bad harvests between 1594 and 1597 had raised the price of grain and so encouraged the large corn-grower, the difficulties of distributing corn in these east Midland counties, and the hazards of growing it, were too great to divert the farmer from his course. The extent of the enclosure movement can be roughly measured by the reports submitted to the enclosure commission later in 1607. The acreage of Northamptonshire reported enclosed since 1578 was far higher than in any other Midland county investigated by the commission. Over 27,000 acres were reported, affecting 118 townships.[2]

As for the immediate cause of the revolt, it is evident that grain shortage had raised prices in the Midlands by the spring of 1607, though they were not as high as they were to be on the eve of the harvest of 1608; Arthur Standish who referred in *The Commons Complaint* (1611) to mutinies "only for the dearth of corn in Warwickshire, Northamptonshire, and other places" can only have been referring to the troubles of 1607. Since this was a district which could export little grain for lack of good water transport, and so presumably did not normally produce much more than it consumed, it was easy enough for a bad year to precipitate a serious crisis. Certainly, on the eve of the harvest of 1608 the shortage of grain was unmistakable in the Midland counties. William Combe wrote to Lord Salisbury from Warwickshire foreseeing trouble because of the dearth of corn, and because of the activities of maltsters in the bigger towns engrossing barley under the very eyes of the justices of the peace.[3]

Hunger and threatening starvation drove the peasants to vent their wrath on the most obvious offenders, the enclosing farmers. The first rising in Northamptonshire was followed by others at Hillmorton in Warwickshire, Cotesbach in Leicestershire, and Rushton, Pytchley, and Haselbeech in Northamptonshire. Parts of Bedfordshire were affected, and in Derbyshire people were restive. The local circumstances of the

[1] Gay, 'The Midland Revolt', p. 215.
[2] *Ibid.*, pp. 212, 240.
[3] *Ibid.*, p. 213, note 3; J. D. Gould, 'Mr Beresford and the Lost Villages: a Comment', AHR, III, 1955, p. 112; PRO SP 14, 113, 90; SP 14, 34, 4.

outbreaks have not yet been examined in detail except in the case of Cotesbach, but this one example is enough to illustrate the bitterness of local quarrels about enclosure which had frayed tempers to breaking-point.[1]

Cotesbach lies in the southern tip of Leicestershire on the borders of Northamptonshire and Warwickshire. The bulk of the land in the parish belonged to the Devereuxs of Chartley (Staffs.) until 1591 when the estate was sold to pay off heavy debts. By 1626 it had passed through the hands of six different owners. Except for the enclosure of the demesne—some 200 acres, or one-fifth of the lordship—which took place at the beginning of the sixteenth century, the organization of farming at Cotesbach had undergone no fundamental alteration for a hundred years. Then suddenly, between 1603 and 1612, everything was changed. The lordship was enclosed and the income of the lord was doubled. The revolution was brought about by John Quarles, a London merchant, who bought the estate in 1596 and promptly had it wrested from him by the Crown to pay off the debts of the previous owner. He did not recover possession until about 1601–2, when he resolved to recoup his losses. His tenants' leases had expired, and he offered them new agreements at a rent of £5 per yardland, which they refused. He therefore resolved to enclose the lordship. He bought out one of the four freeholders, came to agreements with the second freeholder, and with the rector, owner of the glebe, and ignored the fourth, who, in any case, had only two acres of freehold land. The leaseholders were given another opportunity to renew their leases, but again refused. In 1603 Quarles procured a royal licence to enclose, and the courts turned down a petition of the tenants against it. After enclosure, the tenants had no option but to accept new leases or leave the village. Some remained but took up less land than before, since the new rents were appreciably higher; some rented cottages only and refused all land, contenting themselves with grazing rights at 6d. per cow on the lord's closes; others declined the new terms altogether and left the village. The tenants had suffered a complete defeat and their numbers had been reduced by about a half. No wonder that seething discontent boiled over in revolt in 1607. Cotesbach became the rallying point in Leicestershire where "there assembled of men, women, and children to the number of full five thousand" to cast down the hedges. But the revolt did not spread. Indeed, both here and in Northamptonshire and Warwickshire, the term *revolt* exaggerated the scale of the disturbances. A gallows was erected in Leicester as a warning to miscreants on 6 June, and the borough began to train the militia. It, expecting worse violence. The gallows were torn down by an angry

[1] Gay, 'The Midland Revolt', pp. 215 *sqq*.

crowd on the 8th, but no worse commotion occurred, and by 14 June the trouble was over.[1]

Brief though the disturbances were—they lasted little more than a month—they caused enough alarm in government circles to prompt the appointment of a new enclosure commission in August 1607. Its work was limited to seven Midland counties: Northamptonshire, Warwickshire, Leicestershire, and Bedfordshire, which had set the stage for the summer disturbances, together with Huntingdonshire, Buckinghamshire, and Lincolnshire. Oxfordshire, which had shown itself to be a much-enclosed county in 1517, was unaccountably ignored, and so was Derbyshire, where the alarm had been sounded in 1607, though all fears in that quarter had proved groundless.

This first and last enquiry of James I's reign harked back thirty years and called for a return of the townships depopulated since 1578, the land enclosed and converted to cattle and sheep pasture, the land severed and engrossed, the farmhouses vacant or turned into cottages, the farm buildings decayed, the tenants evicted, the highways blocked up or diverted, and the churches decayed. The results of the enquiry filled in some of the background to the Midland revolt by showing that the acreage of the county reported to be affected by enclosure was far higher in Northamptonshire than in any other county, while Lincolnshire, Leicestershire, and Bedfordshire each reported over 10,000 acres of enclosure and over sixty villages affected. The enquiry of 1607 was followed up by numerous prosecutions and fines in Star Chamber, but much resentment lingered in the Midlands owing to the universal belief that nothing was being done to bring offenders to book. From Northamptonshire, for example, came a report to Salisbury in August 1608 of fresh enclosures and a burning sense of grievance among the people "that no reformation doth follow." Nothing further occurred, however, to fan these embers into flame.[2]

Viewed in the light of changing public opinion towards enclosure, the Midland revolt was something of an anachronism. At Westminster, where the problem was discussed in its national setting, passions were no longer deeply engaged. Politicians forgot that in certain districts, particularly in Leicestershire and Northamptonshire, people had had to swallow a highly concentrated pill, and were still brooding over their long and bitter memories. The appointment of the enclosure com-

[1] L. A. Parker, 'The Agrarian Revolution at Cotesbach, 1501–1612', *Studies in Leicestershire Agrarian History*, Leics. Arch. Soc., XXIV, 1948, pp. 41 *sqq.*

[2] E. F. Gay, 'Inclosures in England in the Sixteenth Century', *Qtrly J. Econ.* XVII, 1903, p. 581; John Gould, 'The Inquisition of Depopulation of 1607 in Lincolnshire', EHR, LXVII, 1952, pp. 392–5; L. A. Parker, 'The Depopulation Returns for Leicestershire in 1607', *Leics. Arch. Soc.*, XXIII, 1947, p. 4; SP 14, 48, 4; SP 14, 35, 52.

mission of 1607 showed that the government was not disposed to overlook the causes of the Midlander's discontent. But neither was it to be driven into panic legislation. Nothing could be better reasoned or more reasonable than the memorandum of July 1607—*A Consideration of the cause in question before the lords touching depopulation*—apparently prepared for the benefit of the Privy Council immediately after the revolt, and arguing the *pros* and *cons* of enclosure. It claimed, quite rightly, that enclosure did not inevitably cause depopulation, and cited Somerset as an example of an enclosed, wealthy, *and* populous county. It pointed out that open fens and forest commons were often the nurseries of beggars, while enclosed land in counties like Essex, Devon, and Somerset afforded fuel for the poor, and work in hedging and ditching. It reached the heart of the matter by concluding that depopulation was the evil to be rooted out, and not enclosure, and that depopulation was as readily caused by engrossing as converting. "By redressing the fault of depopulation and leaving enclosing and converting arbitrable as in other shires, the poor man shall be satisfied in his end, habitation, and the gentleman not hindered in his desire, improvement."[1]

The *pros* of enclosure were beginning to outweigh the *cons*, and, not surprisingly, the 1607 commission turned out to be the last large-scale enquiry. In 1618 the government decided that "tillage is become much more frequent and usual, corn is at reasonable rates," and appointed a commission of judges and others to grant exemptions from the tillage statutes in order that "the rigor of the statutes may be mitigated according to these present times and occasions." It was admitted that legislation had forced men to put land in tillage which was unsuitable for crops, and that the work of informers in exposing the crimes of those who converted arable to pasture had been more of a nuisance to the king's subjects than a benefit to the commonwealth—"some great offenders were spared by connivance of the informer, and others that were innocent were vexed without end." Finally, in 1624, when Parliament agreed that the nation's corn supply was no longer in danger, the tillage statute of 1563 was repealed, while those of 1597 died for want of enforcement. In the words of Chief Justice Coke, they had been "so like labyrinths, with such intricate windings or turnings as little or no fruit proceeded from them." It was at about this time that John Shotbolt, in his *Verie necessary considerations for the Weale publique*, put forward a plan for a general permission to enclose land by exchange, believing that the public might now be willing to accept "so good a business . . . for so general enriching to

[1] W. Cunningham, *The Growth of English Industry and Commerce in Modern Times*, II, pp. 898–9.

all sorts." The idea of enclosure had, indeed, "hardened and become more durable."[1]

The last attempt by the Crown to flog a dead horse into life was made in the 1630's, when bad harvests caused alarm and the Privy Council instituted another investigation into enclosure. This last enquiry began in 1630 and has been termed a display of "paternalism and pick-pocketry," for it brought benefits to the Crown in the shape of fines, and appeared to appease the victims of enclosure. But it did nothing to sweeten relations between Charles I and his subjects, for, in fact, the commission condoned as much enclosure as it condemned. In any case, public opinion had undergone a considerable change: in 1644, when Archbishop Laud was tried for high treason, the charges against him included the allegation that "he did a little too much countenance the commission for depopulations." A century before, such a charge, far from causing the bishop to be arraigned before Parliament, would have endeared him to it.[2]

By 1640, then, a strenuous attack on enclosers was no longer the sure way to court popularity. Depopulation was still universally condemned, but people no longer assumed that enclosure was always and alone responsible. They saw more clearly the tangled complexity of the problem, and, moreover, they now knew by experience the shortcomings of penal legislation against enclosure which was enforced regardless of individual circumstances. Private informers, who had been made responsible for the first time in 1538 for bringing offenders against the tillage statutes to book, had done as much as anything to antagonize the public. Indeed, the commission of 1618 to compound with enclosers justified itself on these grounds. More than this, people had groped their own way towards a solution of their difficulties. Increasingly efficient methods were being employed for carrying out enclosure, without depopulation, by agreement. Private agreements between individuals for the exchange of land as a preliminary to enclosure show the principle at work in its simplest form in the Tudor period. Private agreements on a larger scale, between lords and their tenants, were not uncommon in the later sixteenth century. Finally, to save the parties to these agreements from the fear of later litigation, the habit developed of getting them enrolled in one of the

[1] Beresford, 'Habitation versus Improvement', pp. 49–50, 55 note, 54; Commons Debates, 1621, ed. Notestein, Relf, and Simpson, VII, p. 512; E. Gay, 'Inquisitions of Depopulation in 1517 and the Domesday of Inclosures', RHS, NS, XIV, 1900, pp. 236, 240; The Anglica Historia of Polydore Vergil, ed. Denys Hay, Camden Soc., LXXIV, 1950, p. 277.

[2] See, for example, SP 16: 531, 82; 187, 7; 184, 7; 181, 6; 185, 86; 176, 11; E. M. Leonard, 'The Inclosure of Common Fields in the Seventeenth Century', RHS, NS, XIX, 1905, pp. 127 sqq.; CSPD 1631–3, p. 490; Beresford, 'Habitation versus Improvement', p. 50.

courts at Westminster. Tenants of the Crown had enjoyed this privilege in the sixteenth century when seeking permission to improve land. When their landlord investigated the situation and agreed, he gave his endorsement by having the agreement enrolled in the court of Exchequer. At some time in the early seventeenth century private lords began to follow this example, and secured the enrolment of their agreements in the court of Chancery. The parties claimed, truthfully or otherwise, that the agreement was being challenged by a few wanton troublemakers. They brought a lawsuit into the court, the result of which was a decree approving the enclosure, which was duly registered on the Chancery rolls. The date of the first of such Chancery decrees cannot yet be ascertained owing to the deficient indexes to this large class of records. But in the 1630's enrolled agreements were not unusual, and after 1633 the court of the Palatinate of Durham also began to sanction and record enclosure agreements.[1]

C. PAMPHLET LITERATURE

The pamphlet literature of this century and a half of enclosure controversy reflects the changing moods of the public in much the same way as do the statutes and parliamentary debates. The subject remained controversial, but the indignation which charged the pens of writers at the beginning of the period was much diluted with tolerance and sweet reasonableness at the end. The matter could still provoke fierce debate in the 1650's within the Midland shires. It prompted a petition from Leicestershire to the Council of State in November 1655, and a bill in Parliament to regulate enclosure in 1656. But three years earlier, when John Moore, minister of Knaptoft, Leicestershire, rose up like a ghost from the past to launch a bitter attack on enclosures in *The Crying Sin of England of not caring for the Poor*, he found an equally redoubtable adversary in Joseph Lee, rector of Catthorpe, who from his own personal experience could compile an impressive list of Leicestershire villages which had been enclosed in the previous fifty years without depopulation and without the decay of tillage.[2]

Viewed as a whole, the pamphlet literature mirrors as many different aspects of depopulation as anyone seeking local differentiation could wish for. Even Thomas More, whose impassioned and dramatic passage in *Utopia* is the best remembered of all the diatribes against depopulation, in fact castigates a regional phenomenon only, the increase of sheep in those areas which were already dedicated to sheep-keeping and which grew the finest wool. It is true that his remarks

[1] Beresford, *op. cit.*, pp. 49, 53 *sqq.*; L. A. Parker, 'Enclosure in Leicestershire', pp. 190–1; TED I, p. 61; Leonard, *op. cit.*, p. 109.   [2] VCH *Leics.*, II, pp. 218–19.

begin with a general comment on the sheep which cause depopulation, and this has resulted in their being generally remembered as an indiscriminate and vigorous onslaught upon enclosure for sheep everywhere. "Your sheep, that were wont to be so meek and tame and so small eaters, now, as I hear say, be become so great devourers and so wild, that they eat up and swallow down the very men themselves. They consume, destroy, and devour whole fields, houses, and cities." But in fact More particularizes in the very next sentence. The passage continues, "For look, in what parts of the realm doth grow the finest and therefore dearest wool, there noblemen and gentlemen, yea and certain abbots, holy men, no doubt, not contenting themselves with the yearly revenues and profits that were wont to grow to their forefathers and predecessors of their lands, nor being content that they live in rest and pleasure, nothing profiting, yea much noying the weal public, leave no ground for tillage." More, in short, was as precise a reporter on the evils of his day as were the members of the House of Commons defending the local interests of their constituencies against the tillage statutes.[1]

The dominant theme of the pamphlet literature of 1500–1640 was depopulation and its varied causes. But different writers singled out different abuses for special attention. Altogether, they were five in number: first, enclosure of the common pastures and fields, and the subsequent conversion of arable to pasture, which deprived the poorer people of common grazing and reduced employment in arable farming; secondly, sheep-keeping on a large scale—the crime of the rich and ambitious farmers—because it too reduced employment as well as causing beef, dairy produce, and corn to be scarce and dear; thirdly, cattle-keeping, which, when more exactly defined, meant fattening, again because it employed few hands and caused a scarcity of young cattle and dairy products; fourthly, engrossing of farms, because it drove small men off the land—another crime usually attributed to the rich and powerful farmers and landlords, and sometimes coupled with the crime of rackrenting; fifthly, the making of parks and chases for deer, which again reduced the amount of land in tillage. This last recreation of the landed gentleman was a fashion in vogue in the first half of the sixteenth century, but it received less attention in the literature than other agrarian changes because it passed out of favour in the second half of the century when many of the parks were turned to more profitable use for cattle grazing.[2]

---

[1] *The Utopia of Sir Thomas More*, ed. H. B. Cotterill, 1937, p. 28.
[2] See the list of contemporary pamphlets and sermons on enclosure in Conyers Read, *Bibliography of British History. Tudor Period*, 1933, p. 169, and Godfrey Davies, *Bibliography of British History. Stuart Period*, 1928, pp. 203–4; E. Kerridge, 'The Revolts in Wiltshire against Charles I', *Wilts. Arch. & Nat. Hist. Mag.*, LVII, 1958–9, p. 64.

D. THE LOCAL HISTORY OF ENCLOSING
AND ENGROSSING

Through the eys of pamphleteers and politicians, we have observed a large-scale enclosure movement in the period 1500–1640, concentrated mostly in the Midland counties, and provoking great controversy there because it served as the prelude to the conversion of much arable to pasture, and the increase of stock farming at the expense of corn. Regional differences can now be elaborated, using the more detailed evidence of the contemporary enquiry commissions, and other miscellaneous documentary material now available to the historian.

The evidence of the enclosure commissions is, of course, woefully imperfect. The 1517–19 enquiry was directed at only twenty-three counties, and the surviving documents even from these twenty-three are incomplete. All that remains of the report of 1548 concerns two counties only, Warwickshire and Cambridgeshire, and from the commission of 1566 there survive only fragments for Leicestershire and Buckinghamshire. In 1607 seven Midland counties were surveyed, and reports are at hand for all of them. But though they are packed with information, they reveal only too clearly the difficulties of the commissioners' task, and the imperfections of the final result. The returns were collected hundred by hundred from empanelled juries who can never have hoped to collect information of all enclosures in the area. Moreover, the reports submitted were usually inaccurate in minor ways, and sometimes complete distortions of the truth.[1]

Taking the information submitted to the enclosure commissioners, the lawsuits that followed, together with other evidence from local records, however, certain general observations seem to be justified. Enclosing and engrossing were taking place all over England, but unemployment and depopulation which accompanied these changes were mainly Midland problems. Clement Armstrong's *Treatise concerning the Staple* (c. 1519–33) spoke of enclosure "in the middle parts of the body of this realm." And we have traced already in the statutes and enquiries the government's growing recognition that the worst distress was indeed concentrated there. Whether engrossing was a Midland rather than a national matter is less certain. It was liable to occur wherever land was in short supply and farming seemed a profitable business. Many enclosed counties, therefore, must have been as much plagued by engrossers as the common-field areas. However, the government clung to the view that the two things were inseparable,

[1] Gay, 'Inquisitions of Depopulation in 1517', p. 238; E. Kerridge, 'The Returns of the Inquisitions of Depopulation', EHR, LXX, 1955.

and never considered asking for reports of engrossing from counties that were already enclosed.[1]

In counties with common fields there was plentiful evidence of both enclosing and engrossing. But the two problems were not evenly distributed everywhere. Enclosure and conversion to pasture, for example, were unusual in the Lincolnshire marshlands. As various inhabitants pointed out when accused of this crime in 1607–8, they had little arable land, the district comprising "almost all pasture and feeding ground, employed for the feeding and grazing of sheep and cattle." On the other hand, because of the excellent feeding qualities of the land, engrossing was a common grievance. Indeed, the occupation of marshland by farmers from other districts was a continual annoyance to the inhabitants until the eighteenth century, when the upland farmer finally found a way of fattening his sheep on his own land.[2]

The surviving returns of the enclosure commissions of 1517–19 are so incomplete that no conclusions about the extent of enclosing and engrossing can be built upon them. The more impressive figures— showing over 4,000 acres of land enclosed and over fifty farmhouses decayed or reduced to cottages—relate to ten counties:

Table 2. *Findings of the 1517–19 Enclosure Commission in ten counties*

County	Acreage affected by enclosure	No. of villages from which returns are available	Houses of husbandry		No. of[a] persons displaced
			Decayed	Made cottages	
Nottinghamshire	4,470	80	71	—	188
Warwickshire	9,694	70	189	18	1,018
Leicestershire	5,780½	49	136	12	542
Northamptonshire	14,081½	112	345	9	1,405
Oxfordshire	11,831	107	176	10	720
Buckinghamshire	9,921	70	160	12	887
Bedfordshire	4,137	36	89	—	309
Berkshire	6,392	86	116	—	588
Lincolnshire	4,866½	63	70	—	158
Norfolk	9,334	122	70	—	—

[a] I. S. Leadam, *The Domesday of Inclosures*, 1897, I, pp. 38, 40.

For 1548 and 1565 the returns are so fragmentary as to be valueless; they have survived by chance and merely record what would in any case have been assumed, that enclosing and engrossing were still in

[1] TED III, p. 100.
[2] PRO St Ch. 8, 17, 23; Thirsk, *English Peasant Farming*, pp. 154–6, 177.

progress. In 1607, when the returns were confined to seven Midland counties, the following acres were reported.

Table 3. *Findings of the 1607 Enclosure Commission*

County	Acreage enclosed and converted to pasture	No. of villages from which returns are available	Houses of husbandry		No. of[a] persons displaced
			Decayed	Made cottages	
Warwickshire	5,373	28	62	26	33
Leicestershire	12,290½	70	151	21	120
Northamptonshire	27,335½	118	201	157	1,444
Buckinghamshire	7,077½	56	29	51	86
Bedfordshire	10,004	69	47	75	259
Huntingdonshire	7,677½	52	59	87	290
Lincolnshire	13,420	?	⌐1,290⌐		?

[a] Gay, 'Inclosure in England in the Sixteenth Century', p. 581; Gould, 'The Inquisition of Depopulation of 1607 in Lincolnshire', p. 395.

None of these figures bears close examination. In the first place, no county investigation was thorough and complete. In the second place, each county was made up of two or more regions, each with a different farming routine and a different social structure, and they were not all equally susceptible to enclosing and engrossing. No fair statistical comparison between the counties, therefore, is possible. In the third place, the allegations which were made against enclosers to the commissioners were often found later to be based on flimsy evidence, to distort the true facts, or even to be downright falsehoods. The courts investigating these cases afterwards rejected many as unfounded, and listened sympathetically to the extenuating circumstances surrounding others. All that the enclosure enquiries do is to point an accusing finger at certain counties in the Midlands which had suffered more, or at least complained more, than the rest. Those which attracted notice consistently throughout the period were Leicestershire, Lincolnshire, Warwickshire, Northamptonshire, Bedfordshire, and Buckinghamshire. In the agrarian history of these counties, then, we may expect to find the explanation for the controversial nature of enclosing and engrossing in the period 1500–1640. Other counties await the closer attention of the local historian. Oxfordshire, Berkshire, Norfolk, and Nottinghamshire kept Wolsey's clerks busy in 1517–19, and were included in the tillage statutes of 1597, but were passed over in 1607. Huntingdonshire did not attract attention in 1517–19 or in 1597, but justified the visit of the enclosure commissioners in 1607 by producing evidence of considerable engrossing and over 7,500 acres enclosed. Its sudden appearance on the stage in the final act of the drama is not easily explained, but it was probably due to the intervention of a local member of Parliament who could argue from experience the necessity for governmental interest in this usually neglected county. Some hint of what was afoot may be found in statements made in Charles I's reign that many citizens of London owned land in the county and leased it to tenants, while the county as a whole was complaining of its poverty and inability to contribute to a levy. Since the county was proving an attractive field of investment to the London business man, its experiences of enclosing, and, more noticeably, of engrossing may well derive from this fact.[1]

Before considering the special circumstances of the Midland counties, some brief observations on enclosure in other parts of England and Wales must be made. Wales was not singled out for special mention in legislation until 1597, when the tillage statute of that year included Pembrokeshire at the suggestion of the House of Lords. Before this the government at Westminster had not considered that Wales had any serious enclosure problem, although the Council of Wales, being obliged to enforce the laws of England, had been instructed from time to time to investigate the decay of tillage and the enclosure of commons, and had heard appeals from injured parties against enclosure. However, the loss of most of the records of the Council of Wales makes it impossible to say how large the problem loomed in its deliberations. That enclosure was under way throughout Wales there is no doubt. The country had plentiful open commons and wastes, and much arable land which was divided into scattered strips, some of it subject to common rights, and which required consolidation. And since Welsh farmers were subject to the same economic stimuli as English farmers, they too responded by specializing more than hitherto, cultivating their land more intensively, keeping more stock and threatening to overcharge the commons, using temporary leys, clearing fresh land from the waste, and enclosing their common pastures and arable fields. But Wales was for the most part a pastoral country depending on its sheep and cattle for a living, and like the pastoral districts of England, it possessed the secret of enclosing land amicably. Since common rights over the arable were not greatly valued, and sometimes did not exist at all, many fields were enclosed without opposition of any kind. Enclosure of the commons was more liable to provoke disturbance, and did so in Monmouthshire and Carmarthenshire, where protests were accompanied by some colourful incidents: at Ffinnant, Breconshire, in 1560

[1] Kerridge, 'The Returns of the Inquisitions of Depopulation', *passim;* SP 16, 8, 44 and 86.

the hedges were overthrown and their planters tied to the tails of horses; at Dreuthen, Monmouthshire, in 1619 the tenants gathered to watch the enclosures, saying "Work if you will, for it shall not stand very long." Nevertheless, even the enclosure of commons did not inevitably enrage or injure the community. Many commons were so large that the allotments after partition satisfied everyone, while in the most thinly settled mountain districts enclosure often resulted from customary usage rather than deliberate agreement; people used different portions of the mountain as their sheepwalk until at length they claimed them as their own. Viewed as a whole, enclosure made more progress in this period in the eastern half of Wales than in the west, particularly in north Monmouthshire and the more accessible parts of Radnorshire and Breconshire, which were more influenced by English develop- ments and the English market than west Wales. But nowhere did the movement cause wild commotion. The pastoral husbandry of the country, like that of highland England, could accommodate enclosure without disrupting social peace and destroying the poor.[1]

The government's lack of concern for the four northern counties of England at the time of the 1517–19 enclosure commission can be explained as a tradition of much economic legislation and one which persisted to some extent throughout the century. It was not intended to imply that enclosure was unknown in this area. But it would have been as futile to attempt an enclosure survey in 1517 as it was to collect a subsidy. The gentry, on whom the Crown relied to do the donkey work, were too few and too remote from central control, and the government, therefore, had to admit its inability to administer this distant territory efficiently. Later on, these four counties were included in some of the tillage statutes, since after 1536 the Crown had a re- constituted council sitting in the North which could deal with enclo- sure information and put the statutes in execution. But even then little concern was shown for the northern counties in this matter, and this attitude was in part justified by the knowledge that they were not corn-growing counties, and were not likely to be much distressed by the "decay of tillage." They were not, however, immune from the effects of depopulation, and in 1597, when some exemptions to the tillage statutes were being considered, the dean of Durham pleaded for the inclusion of Northumberland, Cumberland, and Westmorland. "The decays are not, as supposed, by the enemy, but private men have

[1] Beresford, 'Habitation versus Improvement', p. 48; T. I. J. Jones, *The Enclosure Movement in South Wales in the Tudor and early Stuart Periods*, Univ. of Wales M.A. thesis, 1936, *passim;* David Williams, *A History of Modern Wales*, pp. 83–4; John Rhys and D. Brynmor-Jones, *The Welsh People*, p. 432. I owe this paragraph to Mr Frank Emery

dispeopled whole villages." In the end, Northumberland alone was included in the provisions of the act but was omitted in 1601 when the statute was re-enacted.[1]

Much work could profitably be done on the enclosure history of these northern counties, for the chronology, and the means by which enclosure was carried through, are still not yet fully understood. Westmorland and Cumberland seem at first glance to have suffered more depopulation from Scottish raids than from enclosing and engrossing, for except on the coastal plains, their common fields were small, and their unstinted commons extensive. And wherever enclosure occurred, it tended to take place silently and painlessly. Northumberland and Durham did not escape some depopulation, however, particularly during the last years of Elizabeth. But engrossing seems to have been a more common cause of the demise of villages than enclosing, and the problem was localized—in the eastern plain and in the wider valleys inland, which possessed large common fields, grew corn in some quantity, and were accessible to good markets and ports. By the end of Elizabeth's reign enclosure agreements were fairly common. Farmers in the more mountainous western parts of these counties, however, were more interested in pasture-farming than in corn-growing, and since, in the words of a reporter writing on rural conditions on the border, "the people that inhabit there are very poor and rude, having much more ground than they can manage, not having stock to store a third part thereof," there was no purpose in engaging in depopulating enclosure. Even the acquisitive instincts of their landlords were held firmly in check by the physical difficulties of getting their goods to market. We should not, therefore, expect to find many of Philip Stubbs's "caterpillars and locusts that massacre the poor and eat up the whole realm" in this part of the kingdom.[2]

· Other counties of the north, west, and south-west, for example, Lancashire and Yorkshire, Cornwall and Devon, Cheshire, Shropshire, and Derbyshire, were omitted from the later enclosure commissions because they too were largely grass-growing counties, and the government was concerned with those which lay "for the more part" in tillage. Some of these counties had fertile districts of mixed farming, but they were small enclaves in predominantly pastoral regions and could safely be ignored in the spacious generalizations of the politicians.

[1] CSPD 1595–7, p. 542; Beresford, 'Habitation versus Improvement', p. 48.
[2] Beresford, *The Lost Villages of England*, pp. 172–7, 372–3; H. L. Gray, *English Field Systems*, pp. 207, 105–7; G. Elliott, 'The System of Cultivation and Evidence of Enclosure in the Cumberland Open Fields in the Sixteenth Century', *Cumb. & Westm. Antiq. & Arch. Soc.*, NS LIX, 1959, pp. 85, 89; *Phillip Stubbes's Anatomy of Abuses in England in Shakespere's Youth*, ed. F. J. Furnivall, 1877–9, part i, p. 117; SP Jas. I, IX, 97.

Some of these counties, also, were, or were reputed to be, largely enclosed. And although the modern historian can produce evidence of enclosure in the sixteenth century from all of them, it was either small in scale, or if extensive, was of an amicable kind. In pastoral districts the path for both the enclosing landlord and the enclosing peasant seems to have been smoothed by the common assumption that enclosure was a reasonable and not an anti-social improvement of land, and that so long as others were not injured thereby, an enclosure would normally be approved by the community, often in the manorial court. Rossendale in Lancashire yields perhaps the best evidence of the enclosure of small pieces of waste, a process which was deemed thoroughly commonplace, and passed unchallenged since land was plentiful. Shropshire yields good evidence of the enclosure of strips in the common fields. Agreements, by deed, to exchange strips and consolidate them, are plentiful in the local records of this county and were the avowed prelude to enclosure. In Wiltshire too, most enclosures were carried out by agreement, not by force. Why agreements were so much more numerous in the pastoral counties than in the mixed farming areas is a subject which deserves closer investigation than it can receive here. But we may see some part of the explanation in the fact that grazing rights over the arable were not so jealously guarded in a pastoral county, nor was land so scarce. The documents relating to an enclosure at Ilminster in Somerset convey to us something of the surprise of the inhabitants that any one should object to the enclosure of strips in the common fields. In reply to the charge that arable land had been converted to pasture, Joan Bonvile replied that there was no custom in the manor of Ilminster preventing the enclosure of arable land and its conversion to pasture. She had known the copyhold tenants for half a century to convert arable to meadow or pasture "at their will and pleasure without denial of anyone." Some such basic attitude, which was entirely foreign to the eastern Midlands, seems to have been usual in the pastoral counties, and to account for the generally peaceable progress of enclosure.[1]

The counties of southern and eastern England were exempt from the plague of enclosure for other reasons. Kent, Sussex, and Essex were by this time commonly deemed enclosed counties. East Anglia was regarded as enclosed, though in fact only the wood-pasture region was

[1] J. Lister, 'Some Local Star Chamber Cases', *Halifax Antiq. Soc.*, XXIV, 1927, p. 199; G. H. Tupling, *The Economic History of Rossendale*, Chetham Soc., NS LXXXVI, 1927, pp. 47 *sqq.*; Nat. Lib. Wales, Pitchford Hall Coll., nos. 2434, 2029, etc.; C 2 Eliz., A 7, 28; VCH *Wilts.*, IV, p. 47; Woburn Abbey Muniments, Court Roll of the earl of Bedford's manor of Werrington, 21 September 1557. I owe this reference to the kindness of Professor H. P. R. Finberg.

enclosed and much of the light lands and brecks lay open. Only about 9,000 acres of newly enclosed land were reported from Norfolk in 1517–19, and in 1549 Ket's complaints suggest that engrossing and encroachments by large farmers were a greater irritant than enclosure. To this extent official unconcern for the problem of enclosure in these districts was justified.[1]

The government, therefore, appraised the situation as accurately as it could when it sought in the Midlands for the heart of the matter. But even then, in designating whole counties for investigation, it was making only a rough and ready generalization. Even within the Midland shires certain regions of fen and forest were almost untouched by the controversies about depopulation. Most of the deserted villages in Warwickshire listed by Rous at the end of the fifteenth century, as well as those where enclosure was reported to the Tudor commissioners, were situated in the common-field districts of south Warwickshire, and not in the forest area of Arden in the north. The fenland and forest districts of Northamptonshire, the Chiltern forest areas of Oxfordshire, and the fens of Lincolnshire were likewise oases of peaceful farming, standing apart from the turmoil of the common-field areas in the same counties. Even Midland England then was not all of a piece.[2]

But since the government administered affairs by counties, and not by farming regions, it was not far wrong in directing its whole attention to the Midland shires. What, then, can we add by way of explanation?

In the first place, the Midland counties were among the most densely populated of the common-field counties. The poll tax returns towards the end of the fourteenth century suggest that Leicestershire, Rutland, Northamptonshire, Bedfordshire, East Anglia, and the fens of Lincolnshire were the most populous districts of England, and this may be taken as a guide to the situation at the beginning of the sixteenth century. In many townships the farming community had used up all the waste land on which it had formerly relied for accommodating an increasing population. Few Leicestershire townships except those lying in Charnwood Forest had any waste by the sixteenth century, and many others had only small amounts of regulated common pasture. Grazing thereon had to be carefully controlled, in consequence, and the overcharging of the commons was jealously watched. Young men wishing

---

[1] M. R. Postgate, 'The Field Systems of Breckland', AHR, x, 1962, pp. 85–6; K. J. Allison, 'The Sheep-Corn Husbandry of Norfolk in the Sixteenth and Seventeenth Centuries', AHR, v, 1957, pp. 13, 22–3; 'The Lost Villages of Norfolk', *Norfolk Archaeology*, XXXI, 1955, pp. 134 *sqq.*

[2] M. Beresford, 'The Deserted Villages of Warwickshire', *Birmingham Arch. Soc.*, LXVI, 1950, p. 80; *The Lost Villages of England*, pp. 234–7, 379.

to make a living in their native places were hard put to it to find land to farm, and as village populations grew—the population of Leicestershire increased by almost a half between 1563 and 1603—stints of stock on the common pastures had to be reduced, to ensure that all had their fair share. The whole community tended to feel oppressed by the irksome restraints imposed by its straitened land resources. Enclosing or engrossing in such circumstances only made matters worse. And yet, from the point of view of the individual, such measures were one of the few means left of increasing efficiency and so making the best use of a restricted supply of land. Deprived of the chance to change things by enclosure, they were trapped. For price changes whipped up ambition and offered to farmers a golden chance to make more money if their husbandry could be made more flexible, at the same time goading the landlord with the certain knowledge that by enclosure he could raise the rents on his estate.[1]

Large populations and land shortage explain why it was difficult to enclose and engross land in the Midlands without injuring the community and arousing hostility. Further trouble arose after enclosure because so much land was put down to pasture. The advantages of pasture farming have already been described in general terms. Good prices were paid for meat, wool, sheep skins, leather, and tallow, and the labour costs of pasture farming were lower than for crop-growing. But over and above this, local circumstances pulled in the same direction. The Midland counties had difficulty in exporting grain for lack of a convenient river system. Two contemporary comments underline the seriousness of this handicap. In defence of enclosure, a writer of a memorandum to the Privy Council in 1607 argued that the Midland shires should be allowed to develop naturally into pasture counties, because of their poor transport facilities, "the charge far exceeding the full worth of the corn they sell." In 1620 the same point was underlined yet again when the Leicestershire justices argued the absence of any need for a local storehouse for corn, "the county being remote from any means of exporting grain."[2]

Yet another more technical reason for the conversion of arable to pasture must be emphasized. Large areas of the Midlands are covered with a heavy clay soil. Even today it is difficult to grow crops on this land. The conversion of arable to permanent pasture was a change of

---

[1] H. C. Darby, *An Historical Geography of England before A.D. 1800*, 1936, p. 232; W. G. Hoskins, 'The Leicestershire Farmer in the Seventeenth Century', *Agric. History*, XXV, 1951, p. 10; SP 16, 402, 12 and 13; PRO C 78, 526, 8; C 78, 67, 21; Leicester City RO, Clayton MSS, 35' 29, 292; 383; 447; 57; John Rylands Library, Ry. Ch. 2659.

[2] W. Cunningham, *The Growth of English Industry and Commerce*, II, pp. 898–9; CSPD 1619–23, p. 124, quoted in J. Gould, 'Mr Beresford and the Lost Villages', p. 112.

use which subsequent generations of farmers have applauded and endorsed. East and south Leicestershire, for example, which underwent much enclosure in the Tudor period, have remained for the most part in permanent grass to this day. In short, while the prices of pastoral products rose in the Tudor period, and the Midland movement was much influenced by this fact, we must not ignore the sound technical reasons also which justified it.

Another system of cultivation favoured on the lighter clay soils of the same region was that known as convertible husbandry, whereby the arable land was put under grass for a number of years in order to "regain heart" and old pastures were ploughed up. The conversion of arable to pasture frequently proved to be one stage of a programme for introducing ley farming. It gave rise to the usual complaints on the grounds that the plough had been permanently put down, but often what looked like another permanent pasture was in fact a temporary ley. Here again the modern farmer can help us to see the issue in better perspective, for he understands the issues involved. In the last thirty years the principles of ley farming have been scientifically analysed and diligently publicized. The system is now widely understood and practised by English farmers.

The spread of permanent pastures and of convertible leys in the Midlands, therefore, had a technical justification as well as an economic one. And since the ordinary peasant undoubtedly understood the practical problems of agriculture better than the economics, it would be unwise to assume that he attached more weight to the financial than to the technical arguments in favour of growing grass. It is worth noting, for example, how often technical arguments were used in the law-courts to defend enclosure. Moreover, this was an age of practical farming manuals, and although the majority of peasants could not read, they could certainly talk. Indeed, the social life of the village community in common-field England probably gave more time and opportunity for talk and the exchange of ideas than that enjoyed by the modern farmer. The advantages of temporary leys and permanent pasture may well have been as much argued in the alehouses as Elizabeth's religious settlement.[1]

While the increase of pasture was the commonest consequence of enclosure in the Midlands, the farming system carried on in the new closes differed from region to region. In general it may be said to have accentuated the existing specialization of the district. On the Lincolnshire wolds and the limestone edge, and in the eastern uplands of Leicestershire, enclosures were used to extend the area of sheepwalk and to increase the quantity of sheep feed in winter. But while sheep

[1] E.g. SP 16, 183, 25.

were profitable in themselves, they were also essential for manuring the thin soils of the uplands and increasing the yield of corn. For the upland farmer, therefore, the sheep flock was only one pillar of his system; his arable, and particularly his barley or wheat crop, were an equally important part of his farming business, even though the profits were not as spectacular, as those from his sheep. The same system ruled farming in parts of Oxfordshire and Buckinghamshire, and explains why the writer of *The Decays of England only by the great multitude of shepe* (1550–3) drew particular attention to these two counties as well as Northamptonshire. The generalization would have been more precise had it been made of farming regions, and not counties. On the Cotswold hills of Oxfordshire a sheep-corn husbandry similar to that of the chalk and limestone hills of Lincolnshire was the general rule. Even without enclosure, therefore, the incentive to keep more sheep was so strong, that we may accept without undue scepticism the charge that enclosure here had led to an increase of sheep numbers.[1]

Northamptonshire had other reasons for its addiction to sheep. In the Middle Ages more than half the county lay within the royal forests of Rockingham, Salcey, and Whittlewood, and this had undoubtedly acted as a brake upon the improvement of the land for cultivation by the plough. Much of this forest land, therefore, lay under grass in the sixteenth century as it had done in the Middle Ages. The special attractions of pasture farming in the period did not procure as complete a revolution as has sometimes been suggested. Moreover, as a modern account of Northamptonshire farming tells us, "no part of the county is remarkable for the exceptional productivity or fertility of its arable land." Even in 1939 "the most outstanding feature of Northamptonshire farming" was the amount of land laid to grass; the county carried more sheep per hundred acres of grass crops and rough grazings than any other lowland county of England. Since the present-day farmer with all the resources of science at his command cannot find a better use for his land than in sheep-keeping, we cannot altogether condemn the gentry and husbandmen who were perspicacious enough to see this four hundred years ago. The Ishams of Lamport, who purposefully reorganized their estates between 1560 and 1584 in order to expand their wool dealing business to include wool production, the Spencers of Althorp, and the Treshams of Rushton, who concentrated on fattening mutton for the butcher, were all making good use, and perhaps the best use, of their land. Despite the predominance of sheep, however, the county had other goods to sell. Many farmers were producing beef for the market, and many bred horses for sale at the

[1] Thirsk, *English Peasant Farming*, pp. 84–6, 88–9; TED III, p. 52; M. A. Havinden, 'Agricultural Progress in Open-Field Oxfordshire', AHR IX, 1961, p. 81.

horse fairs at Rothwell and Fotheringhay. Nevertheless, all these activities only served to emphasize the county's predilection for pasture-farming.

In explaining the outcry against enclosure in Northamptonshire, however, what was just as significant as the increase of grazing was the fact that Northamptonshire was generally acknowledged to be a densely populated county, and was becoming more so as its forest areas with their ample commons continued to attract immigrants throughout the period. Enclosure and conversion to pasture stood condemned, therefore, mainly for its harmful social consequences. It satisfied the ambitions of the larger farmers, but only at the expense of the small men and the many poor.[1]

In Warwickshire enclosure and the conversion of arable to pasture in the fifteenth century had had disastrous effects in depopulating common-field villages in the southern half of the county. Many large farmers and landlords had turned from mixed farming to sheep-keeping on a large scale, and the worst depopulations had certainly occurred before the reign of Henry VII. But the movement to evict men for the benefit of sheep lost much of its force in the next four reigns, even though some eighteen more villages were depopulated between 1485 and 1558. By the end of the sixteenth century, the Warwickshire Felden was still a country of mixed farming, growing large corn crops as well as keeping stock. True, it boasted some large sheep-flocks, but the production of store cattle was also a considerable business, and by the early seventeenth century, dairying also. The northern half of the county, the Arden or forest region, on the other hand, suffered little from the pangs of enclosing, converting, and depopulation, for its economic and social organization was quite different from that of the Felden country. It had many similarities with the wood-pasture region of Suffolk and the dairying districts of Wiltshire, and it too specialized in the same kind of farming. Indeed, the fact that the Arden had organized the markets and the means of transport for the sale of dairy produce probably explains the trend towards dairying in the Felden in the early Stuart period.[2]

In south, and parts of east, Leicestershire, where the heavy clay soils favoured the spread of permanent pastures, new closes were most frequently used for cattle fattening. Here was land which later enjoyed a high reputation for its feeding quality. Already by the late sixteenth

---

[1] *Land Utilization Survey: Northamptonshire and the Soke of Peterborough*, parts 58, 59, pp. 349, 355, 361; Mary Finch, *Five Northamptonshire Families*, Northants. Rec. Soc., xx, 1956, *passim*; P. A. J. Pettitt, *The Economy of the Northamptonshire Royal Forests, 1558–1714*, Oxford Univ. Ph.D. thesis, 1959, pp. 35–6, 269, 303, 306–7.

[2] Beresford, 'The Deserted Villages of Warwickshire', pp. 80, 85.

century south Leicestershire as well as parts of Northamptonshire had become acknowledged suppliers of beef to the butchers of the Midland towns and London. In west Leicestershire on the poor soils in and around Charnwood forest the traditional pasture-farming of the region tended to develop a special emphasis on breeding and dairying, and this trend was accelerated in some places by enclosure. But enclosure was not nearly so common in west Leicestershire as in the eastern half of the county, and the breeding of cattle with butter and cheese making were common on open as well as on enclosed lands. The technical arguments in favour of this specialization were stated in an enclosure report in 1631. Pleading the case in extenuation of an enclosure at Market Bosworth, the justices of the peace explained that some part of the land "is of indifferent quality for corn, the rest unfit for corn or sheep pasture, but most fit for milch kine and breeding of cattle, being of a sour, cold, and wild nature." At Nailstone they described the land as "all, or the greatest part, of a light wild nature, full of springs of a spongey nature, wet and cold, not fit for continual tillage. And yet in the best use of husbandry must in eight or ten years be ploughed to destroy the broom, gorse, and heath it is subject to bear." At Donington on the Heath (Castle Donington) the land was deemed of the same quality as at Nailstone, "but worse, greatest part thereof rocky, stony, cold and moorish, only fit for breeding cattle [if] without the help of lime." So, they concluded, "in our opinion, there is no likelihood of depopulation or decay of tillage."[1]

These more detailed explanations in defence of enclosure indicate the complexity of local circumstances surrounding the spread of the movement. Over and over again, farmers argued that their newly converted land was better suited to pasture than to arable. And if they did not plead this excuse, then they extolled the virtues of ley farming. John Bluett of Harlaxton, in Lincolnshire, for example, defended his conversion of 200–300 acres of arable as a means of building up fertility. For the time being, he explained, he was using the land as meadow, eating part of it every fourth year and mowing it in the other three years, grazing part for two years and mowing for two years, and mowing and grazing the rest every other year. Arable which he had converted already had been the means "to make good corn ground of that which before was very barren and bare and lay waste by reason there was not sufficient grass ground to maintain stock to manure it before this was converted. For," he continued, "we find that one land well manured is better than two that want heart."[2]

Apart from the technical reasons for enclosing and converting arable to pasture, practical convenience moved many a landlord and farmer

[1] SP 16, 183, 17.   [2] PRO St Ch. 8, 17, 23.

to enclose or to engross after a change of occupier had taken place. These cases illustrate another set of circumstances justifying changes in land arrangement. William Walcote, esquire, defended the conversion of sixty acres of arable to pasture at Walcot in Kesteven on the ground that he needed the additional pasture to maintain his household because his mother had an estate for life in half his land. Thomas Manisby had a farm of 100 acres in Cadeby and another farm in Binbrook, Lincolnshire, and was using the two in conjunction, altering the use of the land in each in order to achieve a proper balance of husbandry over the whole. Sir Edmund Bussey, having land in Heydour, Oseby, Aisby, and Culverthorpe, Lincolnshire, claimed that when he entered into possession the manor house was in ruin and the land inadequate to keep his household. A considerable reorganization of houses and land was necessary until everything was arranged to his liking. From the details which he gave, it would have required a Solomon sitting in judgement to determine whether the new pattern of occupation was less socially desirable than the old. Sir Thomas Cony claimed that his manor and demesne in North Stoke, again in the same county, had been let to a tenant who had divided the house and land among several undertenants, and that all he did on taking possession again was to restore the *status quo*, moving the three tenants elsewhere "to their better contentment."[1]

The justices who sat in Star Chamber and listened in 1608 to these and many more circumstantial explanations in defence of enclosing and engrossing must have ended that year of hearings chastened and wiser men. For in all the lawsuits arising from the enclosure enquiry in these seven Midland counties they heard many reasonable arguments in favour of enclosure, which bore eloquent witness to the desire of optimistic and hopeful farmers to make changes in order to improve their land and their yields.

The lawsuits of 1608 emphasized the rational advantages of the enclosure movement. But it was, of course, in the interests of every defendant to present a sweetly reasonable case. We must not be too gullible. The stories of evicted peasants departing their villages in tears and lamentation showed the other side of the medal. And the two differing accounts of one and the same episode were not necessarily deliberate or gross distortions by one or other party, but merely the forceful expression of two strongly held and different points of view. A course of action which seems reasonable to a man who has bought an estate and sets about organizing it to his liking will appear ruthless and inexcusable to his tenants whose forefathers have long occupied farms on the estate. The dispute at Cotesbach, which ended in a riot,

[1] PRO St Ch. 8, 17, 23; 8, 10, 4.

admirably illustrates the irreconcilable attitudes of two opposing sides, while each party justified itself to its own satisfaction.[1]

At the same time, it must be acknowledged that the reasonable tone of the arguments heard in the court of Star Chamber by 1608 agrees with many of the expressions of public opinion on the subject at the same period. The changing attitude towards enclosure was already evident by the end of Elizabeth's reign. Its explanation lay partly in the strength of the technical arguments in favour of enclosure, and secondly in the gradual change of procedure by which it was carried out. For the peasantry had learned the advantages of enclosure from the gentry. The evidence of enclosure in Leicestershire, for example, suggests that in the early years of the sixteenth century it was mainly the work of the nobility, gentry, and religious houses. Something like 70 per cent of the reported enclosures in the period 1485–1550 were carried out by the nobility and squirearchy alone. But in the second half of the sixteenth century the peasantry of this Midland county began to take the initiative, and between 1551 and 1607 were responsible for 19 per cent of the land reported enclosed. Moreover, the method of enclosing land changed. Since the very word 'enclosure' had become an incitement to violence, landlords were forced to proceed more cautiously. And statutes, government proclamations, and public opinion generally were not without their deterrent effect. Amicable agreements became more common. William Brocas of Theddingworth, Leicestershire, for example, came to an agreement with his freeholders in 1582, giving "gratuities and leases of good value" in addition to land in compensation. At least six and possibly a dozen enclosure agreements in Leicestershire date from the second half of the Tudor period. And what was happening in Leicestershire was happening also in other Midland counties.[2]

In the course of the next fifty years, the machinery for carrying out enclosure agreements was improved, and gave such satisfaction that the parliamentary enclosure commissioners a hundred years later were disposed to copy it in some detail. An agreement to enclose was accompanied by the appointment of (usually) five referees and two surveyors, chosen by all parties, who were responsible for allotting the new holdings. They were obliged to pay due regard to the "quantity, quality, and convenience of every man's land;" cottagers with common rights were granted land in compensation; the poor were provided for, frequently by a piece of open common. The final agreement was made binding on all parties by being enrolled in the court of Chancery after a fictitious suit had been brought to test it.

[1] See *supra*, pp. 234 *sqq.*
[2] L. A. Parker, 'Enclosure in Leicestershire', pp. 83, 149, 114.

Friendly agreements which dealt fairly with tenants' claims took the sting out of the enclosure movement. And in 1656, when the last bill to regulate enclosure was introduced into the House of Commons by Major-General Edward Whalley, the governor of five of the Midland counties, it was rejected. Thus ended all attempts by the government to arrest the progress of enclosure, and for a time, until the movement entered upon another energetic phase in the mid-eighteenth century, it ceased to be an urgent subject of public debate.

By 1640 few strong arguments could be advanced in favour of common fields and pastures. And not surprisingly, the strongest of them all was one which no contemporary ever mentioned, for it was one which only the observer from a later age could appreciate. Common fields and pastures kept alive a vigorous co-operative spirit in the community; enclosures starved it. In champion country people had to work together amicably, to agree upon crop rotations, stints of common pasture, the upkeep and improvement of their grazings and meadows, the clearing of ditches, the fencing of fields. They toiled side by side in the fields, and they walked together from field to village, from farm to heath, morning, afternoon, and evening. They all depended on common resources for their fuel, for bedding, and fodder for their stock, and by pooling so many of thene cessities of livelihood they were disciplined from early youth to submit to the rules and the customs of their community. After enclosure, when every man could fence his own piece of territory and warn his neighbours off, the discipline of sharing things fairly with one's neighbours was relaxed, and every household became an island unto itself. This was the great revolution in men's lives, greater than all the economic changes following enclosure. Yet few people living in this world bequeathed to us by the enclosing and improving farmer are capable of gauging the full significance of a way of life that is now lost.

CHAPTER V

LANDLORDS IN ENGLAND

A. THE CROWN

1. *The golden age of the crown estate, 1461–1509*

The nature of early Tudor kingship is now recognized to have been not a 'new monarchy' but fundamentally medieval. The strength of the government lay in feudal power and in the possession in the king's hands, as Sir John Fortescue pointed out, of as much land as possible. Edward IV made a famous statement on the royal finances to his Commons in 1467: "I purpose to live upon my own, and not to charge my subjects but in great and urgent causes, concerning more the weal of themselves, and also the defence of them and of this my realm, rather than my own pleasure."[1] The phrase, 'to live of his own', meant strictly that the king should live on what was lawfully his, or in other words that he should live within his income. It was found expedient, by sovereigns who sought independence of action and by parliaments which were loath to grant taxes alike, to interpret this as meaning that, apart from the revenues from the customs, the king should ordinarily live on the rents from his Crown lands and on the income from his rights, especially escheat and wardship, as a feudal suzerain.[2]

There was no considerable landed estate in the country which did not include land held directly from the Crown, and the extent of the Crown land was greatly increased in the reign of Henry VII. Besides his own estates as earl of Richmond, Henry confirmed the addition to the Crown lands of those of the duchy of York and the earldom of March by his politic marriage to Elizabeth of York. Parliament assured him of the ancient inheritances of the Crown, including the duchy of Lancaster, as well as restoring all lands alienated from the Crown during the Wars of the Roses, by acts of resumption passed within two years of the victory at Bosworth, and a further act of 1495 gave him the authority to resume certain alienations made by Edward III and Richard II and all lands which Henry VI had possessed on the 2nd of October 1455.[3] Not all these resumptions were effected, but the

[1] *Rotuli Parliamentorum*, 1783, V, p. 572, quoted by B. P. Wolffe, 'The Management of English Royal Estates under the Yorkist Kings', EHR, LXXI, 1950, p. 1.

[2] On the phrase, 'to live of his own', see B. P. Wolffe, 'Acts of Resumption in the Lancastrian Parliaments 1399–1456', EHR, LXXIII, 1958, p. 584.

[3] *Rotuli Parliamentorum*, VI, pp. 270, 336, 403, 459.

legislation provided the Crown with an additional formidable hold over the nobility. Moreover, parliamentary attainders, of which there were 122 in the period 1485 to 1503 alone, led to further and often large accretions to the Crown lands; for example, the lands of Sir William Stanley, the lord chamberlain who so dramatically fell from power in 1495, added more than a thousand pounds a year to the royal income.[1] Precisely what the extent of the Crown lands were at this time, we do not know, but we do know that Chief Justice Fortescue estimated that one-fifth of England was in the hands of the Crown at one time or another in the course of the reign of Edward IV and that the duchy of Lancaster, admittedly the largest single entity of the royal demesne, included not only the county palatine but also estates in Wales, London, Calais, and thirty-three English counties. It has been estimated that, whereas the income from the Crown lands in the last year of Edward IV was £6,471, Henry VII received some £13,633 in the first year of his reign.[2]

The degree to which the Crown benefited from its advantageous position clearly depended upon the efficiency of the administration of this vast collection of lands scattered through the length and breadth of the kingdom. Royal finances were normally controlled in the later Middle Ages by the Exchequer, a department of state with an established 'course' or process of passing accounts. The Exchequer was divided into the Lower Exchequer or Exchequer of Receipt, for the receipt and disbursement of revenue, and the Upper Exchequer or Exchequer of Account, for the auditing and recording of accounts. By the later fifteenth century the Exchequer had experienced personnel with a reputation for probity but suffered from a number of defects which made it a less flexible organization than the situation demanded. It had come to deal not so much in cash as in instruments of credit, the famous 'tallies'. Its processes were slow—audits commonly took two years—and its system of accounting was designed rather to provide a record of the responsibilities of individual officers than to reveal the overall position of the royal income. The estate management of the Crown lands was cumbersome and its divisions dictated by political rather than by geographical factors. The larger palatine estates were administered separately, each with its own staff of officials; large estates which accrued to the Crown demesne were arbitrarily grouped together; and many particular properties were administered directly or leased to tenants. In the face of these rigidities, Henry VII, like his Yorkist predecessors, found it convenient to develop the Chamber as a

[1] W. C. Richardson, *Tudor Chamber Administration, 1485–1547*, 1952, p. 12.

[2] F. C. Dietz, *English Government Finance, 1485–1558*, 1921, p. 21. The figures given by Dietz are less than reliable and must be used with caution.

financial department and not to attempt any major reform of the Exchequer. For the creation of a new system of royal estate management to provide the king with an income independent of the Exchequer and of an organization capable of assigning money to different departments of state independently of Exchequer control began not, as was at one time supposed, in 1485 but in 1461.[1] As Professor Richardson has written: "the 'newness' of the Tudor rule lay not in any novelty of the governmental system, but in the thoroughness with which it was administered."[2]

The organization of the Chamber was not designed to replace the Exchequer in its fundamental functions as a treasury for the receipt of such revenues as the customs and as a court of record, but to supplement the Exchequer where it failed to meet the vital Crown requirements of the provision of ready cash and of that close and personal supervision of the localities without which there could be no adequate augmentation of the Crown revenues at a time of rapid change. The new system which the Crown adopted for its estate administration was essentially that which had been developed on the larger lay estates. The Crown lands came to be grouped into territorial divisions, each with professionally trained officers as surveyors, receivers, and auditors, men such as were beginning to appear on the larger noble estates in the middle of the fifteenth century. These men, often trained in the law, were eminently qualified to make a survey of the lands, to compile a *valor*, to search out feudal rights, and to advise on the problems of estate management at a time when demesne farming was declining and when money rents were showing "a universal, though uneven, tendency to fall."[3] The duties of the royal officers were well expressed in a signet office docket book of 1484: "to ride, survey, receive and remember on every behalf that might be most for the king's profit and thereof yearly to make report."[4] Many of these men were drawn from the service of the nobility, like John Touke, in the royal service after 1478, who had been auditor to the duke of Clarence and to Margaret, Lady Hungerford. Many of them, again, were drawn from the personnel of the Household or Exchequer, like Richard Harper, the first receiver-general of the duchy of Lancaster in Henry VII's time, who had been in the Exchequer of Receipt.[5] Such men were equally at home in central and local appointments and indeed the lesser administrative posts of the Crown estate provided a useful training for men who later progressed to high offices of state.

[1] Wolffe, EHR, LXXI, 1956, pp. 1–27.
[2] Richardson, *op. cit.*, p. 1.
[3] *Ministers' Accounts of the Warwickshire Estates of the Duke of Clarence, 1479–80*, ed. R. H. Hilton, Dugdale Soc., 1952, p. xx.   [4] Wolffe, *op. cit.*, p. 9.
[5] *Ibid.*, p. 4; R. Somerville, *History of the Duchy of Lancaster*, I, 1953, p. 263.

It was a system which depended for its success upon no elaboration of process but upon constant, informal, personal control from above and upon simple checks and balances. The treasurer of the Chamber received and paid on direct commands from the king and only rarely by warrants under the signet, the chancellor of the duchy of Lancaster learnt the king's mind upon details of administration by conversation and not by any more formal direction, and the responsibility for the tightening of the entire revenue administration fell upon a small group of personal servants of the king. Chief of these in Henry VII's reign was Sir Reginald Bray, who had been receiver-general and steward to Sir Henry Stafford, the second husband of Henry's mother, Lady Margaret Beaufort, and who remained in Lady Margaret's service after he had become *de facto* chief financial minister. It was Bray who became chancellor of the duchy of Lancaster upon Henry's accession, who revitalized the administration of that institution which had enjoyed a separate organization ever since it came under the royal control by the accession of Henry IV. Arrears were the perennial thorn in the flesh of all land administrators in the period; under Bray, letters were sent under the duchy seal every year in February and March, after the audit, to tenants or lessees, demanding the payment of arrears. As in the reign of Edward IV, many special commissions of enquiry were appointed to investigate neglect or decay—the derelict state of the demesne lands at Willingdon in 1491, or the defects of the town wall of Leicester and the occupation of Crown land without payment of rent in 1497, or the inefficiency of the duchy officers at Tutbury in 1498. Sometimes commissioners were appointed with wide powers, as were those who were charged with the improvement of all the royal lands in Gloucestershire in 1466 and as were Andrew Dymock and John Cutte who were sent on a progress of the duchy lands in the north in 1497. These latter have left us a record of their recommendations for improvements in administration and of their success in adding £120 annually to the revenue, by new or increased rents or by the restoration of rents which had decayed or been withheld. The sale of wardships was often dealt with by the king in person, or by Bray on his behalf, and, from the first year of the reign, receivers-general were appointed for the lands of royal wards and for the investigation of concealments in groups of counties at a time. So energetic was the pursuit of the Crown's feudal rights that the Chancery issued a writ for the holding of an *inquisition post mortem* wherever there was the least chance of finding that the land was held *in capite*.[1]

---

[1] *Ibid.*, pp. 265–6, 267; *Cal. Pat. Rolls, 1461–7*, p. 553; H. E. Bell, *An Introduction to the History and Records of the Court of Wards & Liveries*, 1953, pp. 3–5. For a biographical sketch of Bray, see Richardson, *op. cit.*, pp. 451–8.

The success of these policies was such that the period from 1461 to 1509 has been termed "the golden age of the Crown estate."[1] After the assignments for the maintenance of the Wardrobe and Household have been deducted, the net annual yield of the Crown lands was approximately £2,500 in the early years of Henry VII. It rose from £3,765 to £24,145 between 1491 and 1504. The extent to which the Chamber was responsible for this remarkable increase may be judged from the surviving accounts. By the end of the reign the Chamber was receiving five times the Exchequer's income from the landed revenues, and where the total receipts of the Exchequer, apart from subsidies, benevolences, and loans, varied between £32,000 a year in 1485 and £48,000 in 1509, the Chamber's receipts multiplied ten times at least.[2] Yet the estates increased in size more than in yield, for they were encumbered with such charges as pensions and annuities and burdened with arrears which defied collection, and they were utilized to reward the services of government officials of every description. The surplus which Henry VII accumulated was not appreciable until 1497 and most of the wealth which he left at his death was not fluid; his income from ordinary revenues had not sufficed to save him from borrowing, from benevolences, or from occasional resort to parliamentary grants.

Even before Henry VII's death, a degree of more formal organization of the Crown revenues was necessary. Immediately after the death of Bray in 1503, the office of master of the wards was established to oversee, manage, and at any rate initiate the sales of wardships, though even now the income from sales and from fines for liveries continued to be collected by less formal methods. In August 1508 Sir Edward Belknap was appointed 'surveyor of the king's prerogative', with the task of supervising the exploitation of the king's rights independently of Exchequer control. Meanwhile, Richard Empson and Edmund Dudley, the king's servants, were pursuing through the 'king's council learned in the law', again outside Exchequer control, that active collection of fines on penal statutes which earned them such notoriety.[3]

2. *The decline of the Chamber system, 1509–1554*

The death of Henry VII, "the most uniformly successful of English kings,"[4] and pressure from vested interests in the Exchequer threatened the continuance of the 'Chamber system'. The office of surveyor of

[1] R. B. Pugh, *The Crown Estate*, 1960, p. 9.

[2] Dietz, *op. cit.*, pp. 28–30, 80–4.

[3] Bell, *op. cit.*, pp. 6–7; Richardson, *op. cit.*, pp. 153–6, 198–214; G. R. Elton, *The Tudor Revolution in Government*, 1953, pp. 29–30.

[4] S. T. Bindoff, *Tudor England*, 1950, p. 66.

the prerogative quickly fell into abeyance and the learned council met only spasmodically from this time. The use of the Chamber as the leading revenue department, however, was too well established to be abandoned as yet; instead, it was gradually placed upon a more formal, and therefore more bureaucratic, basis. First by letters patent from 1511, then by statutes renewed and frequently revised from parliament to parliament between 1515 and 1535, when the offices were made permanent, two general surveyors of the Crown lands were appointed, one at least of whom was always a baron of the Exchequer, and these offices came to constitute "the first distinct organ of government permanently concerned with the profitable management of Crown lands."[1] The Chamber auditing system begun by Henry VII was perfected and the management of all the lands, woods, and revenues, other than those of the duchy of Lancaster, was centralized and made more efficient, while legal and judicial business continued to be the concern of the Exchequer. The restoration of some lands to their former owners by act of parliament at the start of the reign, grants to royal favourites, and increased assignments for the Household, meant that the treasurer of the Chamber was receiving £24,719 less from the annual land revenues within his province in 1515 than in 1508 and that the total income from revenues in the survey of the general surveyors and of the duchy of Lancaster was only £16,367. By 1531, however, the importance of the office of the surveyors had exceeded that of the Exchequer, for it was yielding more than £40,000 annually against £30,000 to £40,000, and the net revenue of the duchy of Lancaster was averaging £13,000.[2]

A radical change in Crown land administration was to take place between 1536 and 1554, which was to establish a pattern of organization which survived with only minor modifications until the middle of the eighteenth century. The occasion of this change was the vast extension of the lands in the possession of the Crown. The attainders which followed the Pilgrimage of Grace, Lady Jane Grey's abortive attempt for the succession to the throne, and Wyatt's rebellion, added markedly to the steady accretion of attainted lands which had taken place since the accession of the Tudors and before. From 1531 to 1545, too, the royal honorial units were consolidated by the judicious purchase or exchange of lands. Most important of all, of course, the dissolution of the monasteries made the king incomparably the largest landowner in the country; by 1539 over eight hundred religious institutions, many of them richly endowed, had passed to the Crown.

[1] Elton, *op. cit.*, pp. 45–51, 167; *The Tudor Constitution*, ed. G. R. Elton, 1960, pp. 134–6; Pugh, *op. cit.*, p. 9.
[2] Dietz, *op. cit.*, pp. 89–90; Richardson, *op. cit.*, p. 278.

From 1536 Thomas Cromwell initiated a policy which, whether deliberately conceived (as Dr G. R. Elton has argued convincingly) or not, was effectively to reduce the importance of the Chamber and ultimately to re-establish the position of the Exchequer in the administration of the land revenues. The very act which made their office permanent restricted the general surveyors to the supervision of the Crown lands which were already within their purview; they were reduced to the fixity of a court by an act of 1542 which, though passed after Cromwell's fall from power, was the logical conclusion of his reforms. Another act of 1536 had established the court of Augmentations to administer not only the lands of the dissolved monasteries but also all lands purchased by the king—a responsibility which until this time had belonged to the general surveyors. The court of Augmentations modelled its procedure on that of the duchy of Lancaster and had identical fees and allowances, but subsequently broke new ground by abandoning the honorial structure of the lands, so largely preserved by the general surveyors, and adopting a new system by which all its lands, regardless of their previous tenure, were included in the accounts for the county in which they were situated. In 1540 two further courts were given statutory basis—the court of First Fruits and Tenths, and the court of Wards and Liveries.[1]

By 1542, then, six departments of state had been created, each with its own curial establishment and each with specific responsibilities for the collection of the royal revenues. The fall of Cromwell removed the unifying factor which was needed to promote efficiency and to prevent corruption, but the reforms which were subsequently introduced to simplify the administration and which resulted in the final elimination of the Chamber from control of the Crown lands were the work of experts who had been trained under Cromwell, and especially of Sir William Paulet. A patent of January 1547, adopting the recommendation of a commission of enquiry into the state of the revenue, amalgamated the court of Survey with the court of Augmentations to form the second court of Augmentations. It was the dissolution of this second court of Augmentations, again as the result of a commission of enquiry, which in 1554 established the control of all the land revenues, except those from wardships and the duchy of Lancaster, in the Exchequer.[2]

These experiments and measures of reorganization occurred when an unprecedented expansion of the Crown lands was taking place, largely as the outcome of the dissolution of the monasteries, and it was

[1] Elton, *Tudor Constitution*, pp. 139–42; Elton, *Tudor Revolution*, pp. 177 *sqq.*, 203–19; W. C. Richardson, *History of the Court of Augmentations, 1536–1554*, 1961, pp. 38–9; *Statutes of the Realm*, III, pp. 798 *sqq.*; 802 *sqq.*; 860 *sqq.*
[2] *Ibid.*, IV, pp. 208–9; LP, XXI, ii, no. 770 (1).

the court of Augmentations which proved the most important of the Crown's treasuries in the period. The average annual net receipts of the court between 1536 and 1547 were £120,000; in the peak year, 1543–4, it collected over £253,292. None of the other departments approached Augmentations in importance—the court of First Fruits never collected more than £78,000 a year, the court of Survey seldom more than £38,000, while the duchy of Lancaster was yielding for the king's use at the most £11,000 and the court of Wards produced a mere £4,466 in 1542. Precise figures for the profits of the Dissolution properties are difficult to calculate, but the average annual income of the Augmentations from the rents of the former monastic lands was over £36,000 in the first decade, and it has been estimated that the sale of Crown estates between the time of the first important commissions for sale of December 1539 and March 1540 and the dissolution of the court in 1554 exceeded one million pounds.[1] Cromwell's wish to reserve the monastic properties as a means of enabling the Crown to live of its own, a policy which might have had far-reaching effects upon the development of English constitutional history, was doomed to frustration by the incessant demands of the government to meet its increasing expenses and, in particular, those of a series of costly wars—the fighting with Scotland and France in the early 1540's cost nearly £2,200,000 in itself.[2] It is difficult to believe that large-scale land sales could have produced the best possible capital gains; moreover, the rents which were reserved to the Crown upon lands conveyed in fee farm were fixed and, therefore, liable to be rendered less valuable by inflation. Yet it is clear from the studies which have been undertaken of alienations in particular counties that the monastic lands were not given away at bargain prices as used to be thought; grants were usually made at twenty years' purchase at this time and subsequent increases in the rates were adopted to allow for the rise in annual values as the century progressed. Equally, it is clear that not all the monastic lands were disposed of by 1547; Dr Youings has estimated that only three fifths of the monastic property in Devon had been sold or given in reward for services by the time of Henry VIII's death, for example, and a few vestiges of monastic land, indeed, are in Crown hands today, like Burwell manor in Cambridgeshire.[3] The amalgamation of the court of

[1] Richardson, *Tudor Chamber Administration*, pp. 322–3, 368; Somerville, *op. cit.*, p. 304; Bell, *op. cit.*, p. 47; J. Hurstfield, 'The Profits of Fiscal Feudalism', EcHR, 2nd Ser., VIII, 1955, p. 55; Richardson, *Court of Augmentations*, pp. 24, 77, 235.

[2] Dietz, *op. cit.*, p. 147.

[3] H. J. Habakkuk, 'The Market for Monastic Property, 1539–1603', EcHR, 2nd Ser., X, 1958, especially pp. 363–70; J. A. Youings, *Devon Monastic Lands*, Devon and Cornwall Rec. Soc., NS I, 1955, *passim*, and 'The Terms of the Disposal of the Devon Monastic Lands, 1536–1558', EHR, LXIX, 1954, pp. 18–38.

Survey and the first court of Augmentations is not, therefore, to be interpreted as "a measure of the speed of alienation." Although lands worth about £8,250 a year and £3,500 respectively were alienated in 1545 and 1546, the receipts in Augmentations were £59,255 in 1545–6 and £48,303 in 1546–7, sufficiently useful sums in any context. Moreover, the court of Augmentations left one legacy which was to be of lasting benefit to the administrators of the Crown estate—surveys of all lands and property assigned to it, usually the work of its local officials but upon occasion compiled by its central staff sent out upon special commissions. These surveys were neither as well organized nor as uniform as those made for Parliament in the next century, though some were nearly as complete, and with the acquisition of the records of the court of Survey in 1547 the court of Augmentations had full descriptions of the vast majority of Crown lands.[1]

There is no doubt, however, that the opportunities for peculation, for graft, and for the oppression of the weak by officers of the courts of revenue were many, or that the succession of a boy king in 1547 increased those opportunities. Much of the property which accrued to the Crown by the dissolution of the chantries under Edward VI, which had been planned in the reign of his father, was disposed of before 1553 and lands of an annual value of £27,000 were given away, more in fact than were sold in the reign. The wasteful overstaffing of offices in the various departments was a source of considerable expense to the Crown, just as the excessive fees charged by court officials were to the public. The court of Augmentations, for instance, was paying its principal officers, according to one contemporary estimate, £7,085 a year in 1551 as against £4,749 in 1536, and to salaries must be added expense accounts. The absence of a strong minister led to laxity in administration which seems to have gone virtually unchecked in Edward VI's reign until the report of the commission of investigations in 1552, which in effect documents the charges made against the revenue courts some years earlier by Henry Brinkelow, when he declared that "for their own advantage they make many times the king to rob his subjects, and they rob the king again." The act of 1552–3 for improving the revenues required all receivers to be bonded, and noted that they had been keeping in their own hands revenues which they had collected on behalf of the Crown.[2] The two outstanding examples of this practice

[1] Pugh, op. cit., p. 10; Elton, Tudor Revolution, p. 225; Richardson, Court of Augmentations, pp. 300–3.

[2] Dietz, op. cit., p. 180; 'The Certificate of Thomas Lord Darcy', BM Add. MS 30198, ff. 40–52; Richardson, Chamber Administration, pp. 425–32; H. Brinkelow, Complaynt of Roderyck Mors, ed. J. M. Cowper, Early Eng. Text Soc., Extra Ser., XXII, 1874, p. 24; Statutes of the Realm, IV, pp. 161–4.

were provided by Richard Whalley, receiver of the Crown revenues in Yorkshire from 1546 to 1552, who confessed to a series of misdemeanours which involved an embezzlement of over £2,000, part of of it accomplished by the disguising of revenues received as 'arrearages', and Sir John Beaumont, receiver-general in the court of Wards, who concealed in his arrearages various sums which totalled over £21,000.[1]

3. *The weaknesses of Crown land administration, 1554–1603*

The value of the attainted lands which came to the Crown under Mary was in great part off-set by her surrender of the first-fruits and tenths, by her restorations to the church of spiritualities received at the dissolution of the monasteries, and by the re-establishment of half a dozen monasteries. The gross value of the lands and properties surrendered or given away by Mary was given in a contemporary document as £49,000; of this, Elizabeth quickly recovered by resumptions £24,429, and, with the approval of Parliament, exchanged the spiritualities for most of the temporalities of the bishops. This measure was to prove a valuable addition to the Crown revenue. The lands lately the bishop of Ely's, for instance, yielded £638 in 1559–60 against an income from the rest of the Crown lands in Norfolk and Suffolk of £3,049, while in 1573 the lands of the bishops of Winchester and of Bath and Wells contributed £625 and £113 respectively to a total income from the Crown estate in Somerset of £4,920. Accretions by attainder, escheat, and inheritance continued to occur from time to time, of course; the confiscations which followed the Rising in the North of 1569 were the largest of the reign and added lands of an annual value of £2,502. Major sales, on the other hand, were carefully restricted in Elizabeth's time to periods of extreme national crisis— to meet the debts of the Scottish campaign of 1560, to pay for the defences against the Spanish Armada of 1588, and to finance the Irish expeditions at the turn of the century; the capital realization of Crown lands on these three occasions amounted to £263,000, £126,000, and £213,000.[2] Elizabeth had, in the words of her able lord treasurer, Burghley, "as great care to preserve the revenues of the Crown as a mother could have for her children;" she had energetic and competent ministers; and this was an age of rising rents. Yet the Crown estates in the last year of her long reign produced only £88,767, merely £22,319 above the yield in 1558. Where the duchy of Lancaster estates had

[1] Richardson, *Court of Augmentations*, pp. 232–3; J. Hurstfield, 'Corruption and Reform under Edward VI and Mary', EHR, LXVIII, 1953, pp. 24–7.

[2] F. C. Dietz, *English Public Finance, 1558–1641*, 1932, pp. 19, 64, 87, 294–5; BM Lansdowne MS. 4, ff. 182 *sqq.*; SP 12: 1, 64; 12, 50; 228, 3, 30; 274, 146.

provided Henry VII with £8,040 in 1508–9, the revenues received from the ancient duchy lands in 1579–80 were £8,038. The net revenue of the court of Wards was £7,638 in the first year of Edward VI, including £1,117 from the sale of wardships; by 1559 the income had risen to £20,290, with sales contributing £5,003; but there followed, under the mastership of Burghley himself, a period of static or even declining income—the net revenue from the court in 1607 was no more than £17,810.[1]

Corruption and moderation have been put forward as the two most likely explanations of this failure to secure a substantial improvement in the royal revenues in Elizabeth's time, and both certainly existed. The sheer size of the administrative problem presented by the Crown estate, coupled with the strength of the resistance in the period to the feudal exactions of the Crown, are likely to prove the more important factors when further research has been undertaken. Professor Hurstfield has drawn attention to the increasing use of socage tenure 'as of the manor of East Greenwich' in grants for sales from the reign of Edward VI onwards, which was one significant expression of the resistance to feudal charges, and the administrative history of the court of Wards in Elizabeth's reign provides a striking illustration of the problems which the Crown faced in its relationship with its tenants.[2]

As Professor Plucknett has pointed out, the Crown had had increasing difficulty in keeping track of its tenants-in-chief from the time of Edward I at least. Under Burghley's mastership, the court of Wards made consistent but not altogether successful efforts to discover tenants-in-chief. Commissioners were appointed in 1556–7 to compile a list of lands held by knight service in the county palatine from the Exchequer records at Chester, feodaries—the officers responsible for maintaining this information—were provided with notes from the court's own records in 1570 and were required to keep their own books in 1600, but the task was, in Plucknett's words, "wellnigh hopeless." For all who held the smallest item of land, or even a reversion, by knight service in chief were affected. Even though from early in Elizabeth's reign the Crown began to reward informers, not all tenants were as unfortunate as John Sheparde who suffered the full exactions of wardship in Mary's reign because out of lands of an annual value of £18 2s., two shillings' worth was held *in capite*. It was only in the second half of Burghley's mastership that the Crown appreciated

[1] Dietz, *op. cit.*, p. 296; Somerville, *op. cit.*, p. 305; Bell, *op. cit.*, pp. 47, 48, 57; Hurstfield, EcHR, 2nd Ser., VIII, p. 55; SP 12: 255, 84; 282, 75.

[2] J. Hurstfield, 'Lord Burghley as Master of the Court of Wards, 1561–98', *Trans. RHS*, 4th Ser., XXXI, 1949, pp. 95–114; and 'The Greenwich Tenures of the Reign of Edward VI', *Law Qtrly. Rev.*, LXV, 1949, pp. 72–81.

that the feodaries' surveys could not only act as records of lands held but also provide a more realistic valuation of the lands than the *inquisitions post mortem* and so make a positive contribution to the increase in revenue which was so necessary.[1]

What the Crown lost by its inability to make a maximum profit out of its possessions, the lessee and the grantee gained. "The significance of the feudal revenues in the Tudor period," Professor Hurstfield has stated, "lies not in their direct yield to the state but as a method of payment, albeit indirectly and capriciously, to ministers and civil servants," and a contemporary recorded that Elizabeth had granted more leases in reversion "to her servants and captains and such like in her time than has been granted since the Conquest."[2] There was no general increase in duchy of Lancaster rents in leases granted under its seal from early in the reign of Henry VIII to the end of the sixteenth century, and even the fines were increased only moderately. In Elizabeth's time twice the annual rent was normally exacted for a lease lasting thirty-one years, and thrice for a twenty-one years' lease. There is every reason to believe that what was true of the duchy estates was generally true of all Crown lands.[3] Three examples will serve to show how the grantee could benefit. When Writtle in Essex escheated to the Crown in 1521 by the attainder of the duke of Buckingham, it had an income which was valued at £140 a year. By 1547 the rents had fallen to £109, about a quarter of the customary tenements were in abeyance, and the lord's profits of courts were being plundered. Sir William Petre, secretary of state, had receipts of £200 a year from the manor within two years of his being granted it at a valuation of £76 13s. 4d. in 1554, and this was achieved by recoveries alone without rent increases or fines.[4] Two patents under Chancery and duchy of Lancaster seals in 1575 empowered Sir Henry Lee to search out bondmen and agree with them on terms for their manumission on any of the Crown lands, including those alienated since Elizabeth's accession. Just how much Lee profited is not known, but the duchy records contain numerous mentions of such manumissions between 1575 and 1599, and many bondmen were well-to-do men who were able to pay anything from twenty to sixty pounds.[5] In 1587, again, the third

[1] T. F. T. Plucknett, *The Legislation of Edward I*, 1949, p. 105; Bell, *op. cit.*, pp. 50–7.

[2] Hurstfield, EcHR, 2nd Ser., VIII, p. 59; BM Lansdowne MS. 105, no. 31, f. 141.

[3] Somerville, *op. cit.*, p. 306; Habakkuk, *op. cit.*, pp. 370–2; E. Kerridge, 'The Movement of Rent, 1540–1640', EcHR, 2nd Ser., VI, 1953, pp. 30–3.

[4] W. R. Emerson, *The Economic Development of the Estates of the Petre Family in Essex in the Sixteenth and Seventeenth Centuries*, Oxford D.Phil. Thesis, 1951, pp. 101–2.

[5] S. Peyton, 'An Elizabethan Inquisition concerning Bondmen', *Beds. Hist. Rec. Soc.*, IX, 1925, p. 62; E. K. Chambers, *Sir Henry Lee*, 1936, pp. 45–6; TED, I, p. 71.

earl of Huntingdon, lord president of the council in the North, successfully petitioned for the exchange of a compact holding of land in fee
simple, the manors of Bradbury and Hilton in Durham, worth £400 a
year, for 101 scattered parcels of Crown lands of a nominally equivalent
value which he could resell, through agents, in smaller lots. Huntingdon
had no difficulty in disposing of the lands and had completed the resales by July 1591; again, no total is available for the profit made, but
he recovered the value of Bradbury and Hilton when he sold the
manor of Framfield for £8,400.[1] These grants did not represent total
loss to the Crown, for its servants were rewarded and they were often
of items from which a private individual could more readily profit than
an institution, because of more energetic management and of local
knowledge, but they do illustrate the weaknesses of Crown land
administration.

4. *The failure of efforts at reform in the reign of James I*

Elizabeth, it has been calculated, sold Crown lands in her reign of an
annual value of £24,808 at a cash yield of £813,332, but many of her
sales were advowsons or small quillets of land, so that the real reduction
in income must have been much smaller than is indicated by the
nominal rental value of the properties. James I did not even attempt
seriously to keep the landed inheritance of the Crown intact. He quickly
embarked upon a lavish distribution of grants to favourites and had
sold Crown lands for £426,151 by 1609; the net receipts of the general
receivers of Crown lands fell in the first five years of his reign by
£13,000 compared with the last five years of Elizabeth's.[2] The interest
of the period for the historian, however, lies in the information left in
the state papers on the problems of the Crown estate, revealed by the
unprecedented series of commissions for selling, leasing, or farming the
king's possessions which were appointed at the rate of one or two a
year for the first part of James's reign. Many of these problems clearly
were not peculiar to James and much of the history of Crown land
administration in the later sixteenth and early seventeenth centuries is
illuminated by the reports of these commissions. In the face of a
demanding sovereign and of the refusal of intransigent parliaments to
give the king an adequate income from other sources, James's treasurers
in these early years, Dorset and Salisbury, achieved more than Burghley
had done in improving the management of the lands which remained,
but the years from 1603 to 1613 may be said to constitute the moment

[1] M. Claire Cross, 'An Exchange of Lands with the Crown, 1587-8', *Bull.* IHR,
xxxiv, 1961, pp. 178-83.
[2] Dietz, *op. cit.*, pp. 114, 125; SP 14: 44, 61; 47, 61, 99-102; 48, 35; 52, 6.

of truth for the Crown lands when the formidable nature of the obstacles to any dramatic increase in their yield was revealed.

At the beginning of the reign a proposal was made for the enfranchisement of the royal copyhold and customary lands. In return for the remission of their labour services and other incidents, customary tenants were to pay in two instalments a cash equivalent of one hundred years' purchase of their rents, which were to be reserved to the Crown with such heriots, reliefs, and suits of court as the commissioners should think expedient. But enfranchisement, as the king was to be told by his commissioners, was "rather to be wished than hopeful suddenly to be effected." The enfranchisement was not likely to be general, "for as it is not to be expected that it will be desired in all manors, so it is also improbable that all the tenants in any one manor will agree in that desire"—many would be either unwilling or unable to be purchasers. The days of payment would have to be set at least at two six-monthly intervals after the date of composition, to allow for the preparation of the assurance and because "many a tenant, not expecting he should have been a purchaser, must sell part to pay for the rest." Nor would the price be as high as the king wished, for there were many precedents of cheaper compositions. The whole undertaking would demand a great many commissioners who would be hard to find and the fees of the bailiffs would have to be increased to ensure efficiency of collection, for "the copyhold doth and must pay his rent, or else he forfeits his estate; but a fee farmer not often payeth till he be, or be afraid to be, distrained." Even when the Crown reduced its demands, copyhold tenants did not prove keen for enfranchisement, as is witnessed by the "careless" response of the tenants of Spaldwick manor in Huntingdonshire to Salisbury's offer of enfranchisement at seven years' purchase in 1611. They were afraid that they would lose their rights of common, that their freedom would not be secure, and that they would be subjected to such fresh burdens as jury service, while they suspected that the reliefs alone might amount to as much as their fines had done.[1]

Other attempts were made to convert uncertain fines into certain on the Crown lands. Some of these were more successful; the instructions sent in the summer of 1609 to all stewards of Crown manors where there were customary tenants led to a number of compositions which raised "good sums of money" and broke "the ice for the stream to run more currently after," it was reported in February 1610. The directions for these conversions make it clear that the Crown's attitude in the matter of fines had compared favourably with that of private landlords. Heriotable estates had previously been subject to a fine of one and a half year's rent at an improved value, and unheriotable to a

[1] SP 14: 59, 44; 71, 91.

fine of two years' rent; these rates were now reduced to one year's rent. "For every 20s. the king had formerly, he shall have £10 for ever, and £10 fine, in some places £20. And so if his copyholds yielded him £1,000, they shall yield him £10,000 besides the present fine." Even where the rack-rent was ten or twenty times the copyhold rent, the terms were reasonable, and there was little opposition evidently to these proposals, except where the copyhold tenants believed that their fines had been certain, as at Pontefract in Yorkshire where the officers found the people "the most headstrong...in that country."[1]

Leases which had been granted on Crown lands were either compounded for or renewed at improved rents; a note made in 1609 shows that rents on demises of the king's lands had been increased by nearly a quarter within the reign, and the Crown was constantly being advised to convert its copyhold tenements to leases. "By this means," Sir Lawrence Tanfield, the chief justice, told George Calvert in December 1609, "the abuses of stewards will be prevented, his Majesty's charge of many stewards and bailiffs eased, and his yearly revenue much increased, for if the lands be let at half the improved value, every 20s. rent of assize would yield twenty marks per annum." Several commissions were issued to enquire into 'concealed lands' and individuals also undertook, in the best Elizabethan manner, to search out such estates on condition of being granted the whole or part of the lands discovered. Six commissions were issued in five years from 1605 for compositions for assarts, wastes, and purprestures, and by the end of 1609 £26,013 had been received from this source.[2] But the fundamental need then, as it had surely been very much earlier, was for a thorough survey of all the Crown lands. A report which appears to have been prepared for Salisbury early in 1608 lists some fifteen advantages which would accrue to the Crown from such a survey and marks the following six points as of especial importance—the true understanding of the quality, quantity, rent, and value of the lands; the general controlment of the accounts of all officers, the discovery and maintenance of all manner of tenures, "which now are so generally omitted as scarce there is the remembrance of them, except of known tenures *in capite*;" the prevention of suits arising from uncertainties; the hindrance to the erection of cottages on the waste; and the avoiding of confusion in the custom of manors. "By the untruth and uncertainty thereof," the report remarks about the last point, "infinite loss doth daily grow unto his Majesty." With that one could not quarrel, but when the report goes on to suggest that it is "as much disadvantage to the tenants," one is rather

[1] SP 14: 37, 107; 43, 113.
[2] SP 14: 38, 25; 50, 30. See also CSPD 1603–10, pp. 163, 196, 331, 335, 379, 432.

dubious. It was a cogently argued report, however, and Salisbury proceeded to act upon it.[1]

Another suggestion which was made at this time was that income could be raised from an improved administration of the Crown forests and woods, set as they were in the rigour of tradition with a large staff of permanent officials paid both in cash and kind. A surveyor-ship of Crown woods, outside the ancient forest organization, had been established as early as 1521, and the office had been enlarged and become better organized in response to the acquisition of the woodlands of the monastic estates. But the office never became important in the way that other accounting offices did, and it is clear from the fragmentary and scattered records of woodsales in the 1540's and 1550's that woods never yielded any considerable income. In 1546, for example, only two counties showed a profit of more than £100 each, while twenty counties produced less than £300 between them; in 1558–9 the total receipts were only £2,845 or an average of £89 a county. So desultory was the exploitation of the Crown woods and forests under Elizabeth that in 1598 John Manwood was able to declare that the forest laws "are gone clean out of knowledge"—doubtless an overstatement of the case, but a clear indication of the trend of events. By the early seventeenth century there appears to have been a growing shortage of timber for building and wood for fuel. Whereas in the sixteenth century timber prices had lagged behind agricultural prices, now they rose more rapidly. In much of the east Midlands and of the eastern counties of England the shortage of fuel was so great that men were burning dried dung and furze for lack of it. Yet, though most Crown woods were specially surveyed between 1604 and 1612, and a conscious effort made to produce coppices for quick sales and ready returns of profit, no great success was had. For want of buyers, no more than sixteen of the forty or fifty thousand acres of coppice surveyed had been let by August 1612. Some 9,301 acres of the portion which was let produced an income of only £3,157. The shortages of which contemporaries complained and of which historians have made so much were probably highly localized, as Mr Hammersley has suggested. Although the iron works and shipbuilding took so much wood and timber in Kent and Sussex, for example, there was no general shortage in those counties. Even labourers were almost invariably burning wood there till 1640, few areas show more timber building of this period at the present time, and these counties remain among the best wooded in the country. Administration costs of scattered woods in local fees and the expenses of sales were at all times heavy, and for the Crown inevi-tably so. The woodward of Yorkshire who was left in 1545 with only

[1] SP 14: 37, 102.

£56 in ready money, after his costs of £10 were allowed, had many successors in the course of the next century; local commissioners reported in 1617 that the profit to the Crown of the wood in the forest of Dean, with its advantageous access to lines of communication, was only £21 a year before 1610, and the total income from all royal woods in a good year probably did not exceed £10,000 in the early seventeenth century, of which perhaps as much as a quarter was taken by the costs of administration. It was even more true of Crown woods than of Crown lands that they "had their value for men who did not legally own them." Fraudulent officials like the keeper of Needwood forest who sold over eight hundred loads of wood in a single year in 1540 before being discovered, and those who lawfully possessed rights of common in the forests and Crown woods, profited more than the monarchy. It is no wonder that from 1607 till after the death of Charles I revenue commission after revenue commission advocated the sale of forest land, with its consequent reduction in staffing costs, rather than the exploitation of the Crown's resources of timber for building and wood for fuel, of which there was no general shortage except in the immediate vicinity of London and for which there was consequently no ready market.[1]

While Salisbury lived, he made every effort to preserve the Crown estate and to improve the royal income from it. By entails of July 1604 and May 1609, the most valuable of the Crown lands were assured against alienation; the entail of 1609 provided for the assurance of manors and lands in the Exchequer and duchy of Lancaster of the value of £50,089 and of £16,782 worth of fee farms and rents reserved. The surveys of 1608 were never completed, though those which were carried out showed clearly enough that by raising ancient rents to their true level the Crown could have increased its income, as Sir Julius Caesar, the chancellor of the Exchequer, calculated at the time, in the proportion of five to two. In the North and East Ridings of Yorkshire the surveyor reported improved valuations of £11,449 against ancient rents of £3,291; in Cumberland, Westmorland, and the West Riding, Crown tenants were found to be paying £2,206 for lands worth £9,294; and in the west country lands worth £7,500 were producing as little as £506. Under alert administration, fees and expenses on the Crown lands were reduced from £18,448 in 1606 to £9,329 in 1619. The size of the Crown debts in the 1600's and the extravagance of the Court rendered some sales unavoidable; hence the need for the second entail of 1609. But Dorset and Salisbury were able to restrict them very

[1] Richardson, *Chamber Administration*, pp. 261–74, and *Augmentations*, pp. 302–15; G. Hammersley, 'The Crown Woods and their Exploitation in the Sixteenth and Seventeenth Centuries', *Bull.* IHR, xxx, 1957, pp. 136–61.

largely to items which were relatively uneconomic from the Crown's point of view, to parsonages and tithes scattered in small parcels throughout the land and to mills removed from any large Crown holding.[1]

In 1610 a strenuous effort was made to exchange the king's feudal rights for an annual allowance from Parliament which would permit him to put his finances upon a sound basis—the 'Great Contract'. It was defeated by disagreement over the manner of levying the allowance and by Sir Julius Caesar's belief, which may well have been shared by Salisbury, that the sum of £200,000 which was offered was an insufficient recompense for the surrender of royal incomes of £115,000 —£44,000 from the court of Wards, £50,000 from the royal prerogative of purveyance, and £21,000 from assarts, defective titles, and information upon penal statutes.[2] Had abatements in expenditure taken place, had the policy of improving Crown rents systematically continued, and had sales of Crown land been halted, Caesar's argument would have been justified. In fact, the failure of the negotiations for the Great Contract and the death of Salisbury were the prelude to a disastrous period in which precisely the reverse occurred. The expenses of administration and the assignments for Household purposes from the Crown lands were alike increased, the improvement in Crown rents was not pursued, and sales on a large scale were resumed. In 1619 James I was receiving only £72,664 net from the Crown lands, excluding the revenues of the duchy of Cornwall, which were assigned to the prince of Wales, and those of the duchy of Lancaster, which did not normally exceed the £11,000 to £13,000 a year which they had yielded at the start of Elizabeth's reign. Lands of the value of £216,310 were conveyed to the city of London in 1625 in satisfaction of loans and by 1635 some £642,742 had been raised in ten years from Crown land sales. The average yield of the Crown lands, including the duchy of Cornwall, was only £86,000 between 1630 and 1635. Assignments had reduced the net income to the Crown from lands accountable in the Exchequer to as little as £22,980 in 1619; after 1628, it fell to less than £10,000.[3] In short, the Crown lands had ceased to be an important part of the royal income, where a century before the Crown had been the principal landowner in the country and might have been rendered independent of parliamentary sources of supply.

[1] Dietz, op. cit., pp. 106, 116–18, 298, 299; BM Lansdowne MS. 169, fols. 83, 85, 87, 91.

[2] BM Lansdowne MS 151, ff. 23 sqq., 126 sqq.

[3] Dietz, op. cit., pp. 223, 271, 296, 297, 300, 301; BM Harleian MS 3,796, ff. 35–6; BM Add. MS 11598.

TAH

5. *The exploitation of wardships under the early Stuarts*

The consequence was that the Crown extracted from the court of Wards what it could no longer hope to obtain from the Crown lands. Assignments from the revenues of the court of Wards multiplied in the 1620's and 1630's especially. In 1624 pensions were granted from its income to the duke of Buckingham, Sir Thomas Edmondes, and Sir Edward Villiers of £1,000, £750, and £500 respectively. In 1625 the dowager duchess of Lennox was given an annuity for three lives of £2,100, besides a cash payment of £3,350 that same year, and another of £1,000 in 1628. As much as £27,051 might be spent on pensions and gifts in a single year. A series of instructions to the masters of the court in the 1610's and 1620's produced a dramatic increase in the court's yield. This could not have taken place without the preparatory work of Burghley and Salisbury in the encouragement of private informers of concealments, in the production of the feodaries' surveys and other checks on the validity of the *inquisitions post mortem*, and in the raising of the rates for sales of wardships from the one or one and a half times the yearly value of the lands which had been customary in Elizabeth's time to three times the yearly value which prevailed by 1610. Where between 1617 and 1622 the net revenues of the court averaged just under £30,000 a year, in the last four normal working years of the court between 1638 and 1641 inclusive they were little short of £69,500. When these figures are examined more closely and an analysis made of the way in which the increase came about, a fascinating and significant fact emerges—namely, that the various elements of the increase are directly related to the sort of difficulties of administration and collection which beset the Crown in its land revenues. The largest increase was achieved in the simplest transaction, sales of wardships; here a thirty-one fold increase occurred between 1540 and 1640. Where the average sales in 1547–9 were £1,271 a year, in 1639–41 they were £39,819. The next largest increase was achieved from the relatively straightforward leasing of wards' properties, though, as with lands, profits were reduced by the allowances demanded by the collecting officials, in this case the feodaries, and by the problem of arrearages, which was partly solved by granting them as rewards under James and Charles. Here the increase over the century was seven-fold; 'issues', as the profits of leasing were termed, rose from an average of £5,420 in 1547–9 to £36,968 in 1639–41. By contrast, fines for liveries never attained a steady level and yielded surprisingly little more in 1639–41 than in 1547–9—£3,798 a year against £2,363.[1] Feodaries'

[1] HMC Cowper, I, p. 291; Bell, *op. cit.*, pp. 46–7, 51, 54, 57–62, Table A opposite p. 192; SP 14: 61.

surveys of liveries of full age tended to return lower values than those of liveries within age, and abuses arose from the over-continuances of liveries and from the high fees charged by the court's officers of those who sued livery. The subject could hope to share with the Crown in the spoils of a sale or lease of a wardship, but in a suit for livery the subject stood to lose and there were opportunities for the officers of the court to benefit themselves rather than the Crown.

The financial consequences of the exploitation of wardships were satisfactory enough under the early Stuarts, but the political price which was paid was too high. The court of Wards was increasingly unpopular; as early as Burghley's death in 1598 propositions had been made for its abolition, and the ruthless exactions of the court under Charles I helped to undermine the Crown's standing in the country. Feudalism was felt to be an anachronism and it would have been better if the Crown had accepted the Great Contract, for "bearing in mind how many of the Parliament party held lands in chief of the Crown, it is not unfair to include the court as an important subsidiary cause of the Civil War."[1]

Some at least of the sins which have been attributed in the past to the policies of sales and grants carried out in the reigns of Henry VIII and Edward VI must now be seen as the evils of administrative problems connected with the Crown lands which proved too great for the Crown to remedy sufficiently. It was not so much sales which rendered the Crown revenues from land so inadequate by 1603 as the failure of the Crown to secure its feudal dues and generally to adapt the administration of its lands to the changed circumstances brought about by a new demand for land and by a price revolution. No matter what aspect of revenue from land, whether direct or indirect, one examines closely, the same recurring themes arise—a conservatism of management, a rigidity of procedure, a baffling complexity of circumstance varying from one area to another, and a veritable army of officials to be paid. If Cromwell's policy of keeping the acquisitions from the dissolution of the monasteries as an endowment had been pursued, it seems likely that the Crown would never have extracted a proper return from its lands within the sixteenth century by reason of these overwhelming administrative difficulties. If, on the other hand, the composition for the feudal dues had been accepted by James I, if the improvements envisaged by Salisbury had been carried through on a Crown estate rationally consolidated into compact areas and shorn of uneconomic isolated holdings, then the Crown lands might have

[1] Bell, *op. cit.*, p. 149.

become, as Caesar called them in 1610, "the surest and best livelihood of the Crown,"[1] and the possibility of an English Civil War would have been decidedly reduced.

B. NOBLEMEN, GENTLEMEN, AND YEOMEN

1. *The historian's sources*

The basic difficulty which besets any discussion of lay landownership in the Tudor and early Stuart periods is the absence of any considerable body of systematic and objective evidence. This is true even of such prosaic records as accounts. The accounts of the largest of landowners were not designed to yield a balance of income and expenditure. Proceeds from entry fines and from the sales of lands and woods were commonly included with rents, for the good reason that clear distinctions between capital and income, and between recurring and non-recurring income, did not exist in the contemporary mind. The system of accountancy which was used in both estate and household accounts, 'charge and discharge', differed in no material respect from the methods employed in medieval times and was, as the earl of Northumberland's auditor reminded his master in 1606, "more material for matter of records, posterities, and royalties than for any present profit."[2] The 'charge' of an account, for instance, would include for years in succession 'arrearages' which had not been collected, merely to provide a record of them. On a large estate a number of receivers would be employed at any one time, just as in a large household perhaps as many as ten officers might account in any audit-period. Since there was never any sharp or rigid distinction between the responsibilities of either estate or household officers, and any one type of receipt or expense might be entered under three or four different heads, neither income nor expenditure may be calculated with any degree of accuracy without the examination of a long series of accounts. Recurring items, like 'rents resolute' on the leases of particular properties and formal fees accruing to the landlord for a position of state or to the estate officer for his duties, may fairly readily be traced from *valors* or accounts. Yields from estates which came in kind instead of cash, and perquisites of office and 'casualties' of all descriptions which were incidental or spasmodic (but nonetheless substantial), on the other hand, are likely to be concealed from the historian's view. Household accounts of all kinds, whether preliminary, diurnal records, or formal declarations made at the annual audit, which may be very useful in assessing a

---

[1] Dietz, *op. cit.*, p. 138.
[2] Syon House MS at Alnwick Castle, Q. I. 31.

landlord's pattern of expenditure, have proved especially ephemeral records; few families still possess, as the Percies do, virtually complete records of their ancestors' domestic expenses for the century before the Restoration.

The estate papers of many families, especially the lesser landowners, have been lost altogether, and, indeed, in some instances the accounts were never set down formally. Thomas Buttes of Riborough, Norfolk, for example, who had a part interest in a group of small manors on the borders of Essex and Suffolk, took the deliveries of cash from his bailiffs in person and kept such records as he needed in his notebook.[1] Among the manuscripts of larger landowners, some have been steadily dispersed over the centuries and others have lain for years, ill-sorted and little used, in repositories to which access has been difficult. One must look for the Cliffords' Westmorland estate documents at Appleby, for their Craven records at Leeds, for their Bolton Priory and Londesborough muniments at Chatsworth, and for other cognate papers at Althorp. The bulk of the Talbot estate papers for the sixteenth and early seventeenth centuries were taken from the duke of Norfolk's Arundel Castle collection and from his Sheffield estate office to the Sheffield City Library only as recently as 1959; other manuscripts likely to supplement our knowledge of the Talbot estates are still to be found scattered between the collections at the College of Arms, the British Museum, Lambeth Palace Library, Chatsworth, Longleat, and Leeds.

The records of land transactions and of the borrowing of 'ready money' are equally dispersed and incomplete, and demand equally cautious interpretation. The patent rolls, feet of fines, and close rolls, which together form a record of conveyances of land, are collectively incomplete and separately very inadequate. The variety of form of obligation for debt in the period is confusing and makes it exceedingly difficult to trace any man's borrowings completely. Bonds and bills obligatory, which were used extensively for small loans and current debts in the later sixteenth and early seventeenth centuries, were unrecorded in any court of law and consequently rarely survive. Recognizances and statutes, which were recorded obligations, were sometimes entered into for legal and not financial reasons, and present particular difficulties of interpretation. Many transactions, again, were done in the names of servants and not directly by the landowner.

Documents arising at death are no more satisfactory; in any case many have disappeared. Wills, which Gervase Holles held to be "the noblest sort of records,"[2] were proved in a great variety of courts in

---

[1] Alan Simpson, *The Wealth of the Gentry, 1540–1640*, 1961, p. 9.
[2] Gervase Holles, *Memorials of the Holles Family*, ed. A. C. Wood, Camden Soc., 3rd Ser., LV, 1937, p. 20.

the period—prerogative courts, archdeacons' courts, peculiar courts, manorial courts, and local courts like London's court of Hustings—and even now are dispersed among a great variety of repositories, public and private, national and local. The inventories of all the deceased's "goods, chattels, wares, merchandizes, as well moveable as not moveable" which were required by the statute of 21 Henry VIII c. 5 were appraised by friends, neighbours, or dependants and related only to personal estate; they did not, for instance, include lands in entail, but they did include leases, though often the mention of deeds was laconic. The court of Wards was constantly seeking to avoid frauds in the *inquisitions post mortem* required when lands were held *in capite*, but never approached success and this type of record notoriously undervalued lands, besides presenting the difficulty of being made separately for holdings in each county. The feodaries' surveys, which frequently set down the true or 'improved' value of the properties, have not survived in all instances and did not become generally reliable in their valuations until towards the end of Burghley's long mastership of the court of Wards. Taxation records are no more reliable or better preserved. At first sight, the papers of the Committee for Compounding, established to deal with the royalist delinquents in the Civil War, offer extensive and reliable data on the estates of one section of the landed class in the late 1640's, for the committee was not likely to be biased in favour of the landowners and any significant concealment was subject to heavy penalties. But many prominent royalists were not allowed to compound and the papers are incomplete. Again, from 1523 peers were assessed as a class for their subsidies by special commissioners, where the rest of the nation was assessed regionally. Quite apart from the fact that not all the assessments have survived, their evidence of peers' incomes, though reasonably accurate for the reign of Henry VIII, is for most of the reign of Elizabeth very unsatisfactory. Sir Walter Raleigh commented in 1601 on subsidy assessments in general: "our estates, that be thirty or forty pound in the Queen's books, are not the hundred part of our wealth."[1]

It is little wonder that, in the face of these and similar obstacles, historians have turned to the literary evidence of the age in attempts to gain an understanding of the general trends in landowning. These sources are, if anything, more misleading still, for they are essentially

[1] H. E. Bell, *An Introduction to the History and Records of the Court of Wards*, 1953, pp. 53–5; W. G. Hoskins, 'The Estates of the Caroline Gentry', in W. G. Hoskins and H. P. R. Finberg, *Devonshire Studies*, 1952, pp. 334–6; E. L. Klotz and G. Davies, 'The Wealth of Royalist Peers and Baronets during the Puritan Revolution', EHR, LVIII, 1943, p. 217; H. Miller, 'Subsidy Assessments of the Peerage in the Sixteenth Century', *Bull.* IHR, XXVIII, 1955, pp. 16, 23, 30–1.

subjective accounts. The lack of objectivity in Philip Stubbs's *Anatomy of the Abuses in England*, A.D. *1583* is obvious enough in such a passage as this:

"...when a gentleman or other has a farm or a lease to let, first he causes a surveyor to make strict enquiry what may be made of it, and how much it is worth by year, which being found out and signified to the owner, he racks it, strains it, and as it were sets it on the tenterhooks, stretching every vein and joint thereof, as no poor man can live of it... though he pay never so great an annual rent, yet must he pay at his entrance a fine, or (as they call it) an income of ten pound, twenty pound, forty pound, threescore pound, a hundred pound, whereas in truth the purchase thereof is hardly worth so much...The devil himself, I think, will not be so strait-laced nor yet so niggardly to his servants, as they are to their poor tenants."[1]

But both Professors Tawney and Trevor-Roper, as Professor Hexter has pointed out, have quoted Sir Edward Montague's claim of penury in Northamptonshire in the time of James I—"most of the ancientest gentlemen's houses in the county are either divided, diminished, or decayed" and "there has been within these three or four years many good lordships sold within the county, and not a gentleman of the county has bought any, but strangers, and they no inhabitants"— without apparently realizing that this was but one of the many examples of special pleading to be found in the official correspondence of the age. For Sir Edward had a considerable estate in the county and was writing to the lord lieutenant in 1614, when the government was pressing the landed proprietors throughout the country for a benevolence.[2] When Thomas Wilson made his famous estimates of the incomes of the various social classes in his *The State of England Anno Domini 1600*, he was able to claim unusually good sources for his material:

"I have seen divers books which have been collected by secretaries and counsellors of estate which did exactly show the several revenues of every nobleman, knights and gentlemen through the realm, and curiously collected by an uncle of mine which not long since was principal secretary to the Queen."[3]

Wilson was the nephew of Dr Thomas Wilson, secretary of state 1577 to 1581. A statistical approach, however, was basically alien to the

[1] *Phillip Stubbes' Anatomy of the Abuses in England*, A.D. *1583*, ed. F. J. Furnivall, 1882, part II, p. 29.
[2] J. H. Hexter, 'Storm over the Gentry', *Encounter*, X, 1958, p. 23.
[3] 'The State of England Anno Domini 1600 by Thomas Wilson', ed. F. J. Fisher, *Camden Soc. Miscellany*, XVI, 1936, p. 21.

thinking of the era, even at governmental level, and Wilson's estimates must be used with as much caution as Stubbs's polemics.

It is true, then, of lay landownership, as Professor Simpson has written, that "our present state of knowledge is one of mitigated ignorance."[1] It is also true, as Klotz and Davies commented of the parliamentary compositions made by royalists between 1643 and 1660, that "in historical studies the absence of full data is no reason why what survives should not be used."[2] The dust has settled sufficiently on the controversy over the 'rise of the gentry', and the interest which that controversy aroused has stimulated the production of such a number of detailed studies of the fortunes of individual landowners and of the state of landowning in particular areas at this time, for it to be possible to essay an analysis of the principal factors affecting lay landownership in Tudor and early Stuart times.

2. The peerage: A declining class?

Professor Tawney attempted to draw a clear distinction between the trends in the fortunes of the peerage and in those of the gentry in this period.[3] He argued that the peerage differed from the gentry both quantitatively and qualitatively in that, first, the proportion of land held by the peers was tending to decline where the landholding of the gentry was tending to increase and, secondly, the peers were failing as a class to extract adequate incomes from their estates. A conservatism of management kept peers' incomes down, Tawney held, at a time when prices were rising and the expenditure associated with their status, such as hospitality and the building of great houses, was notably increasing. The evidence upon which he based his thesis—a combination of literary references and statistical analysis based upon the counting of manors held by various types of landowner at particular dates—has been subjected to several reappraisals. While it now seems clear that the total amount of land held by the peers did not rise in proportion to their increased numbers when new creations doubled the size of the class in the early seventeenth century, the consensus of recent opinion has placed less emphasis than did Tawney upon the division between the old and the new families among the peers, and between the peerage and the gentry, and more emphasis upon the factors which affected all landowners alike.

For the peerage did not constitute a sharply defined class clearly

[1] Simpson, op. cit., p. 21.

[2] Klotz and Davies, op. cit., p. 217.

[3] R. H. Tawney, 'The Rise of the Gentry', EcHR, XI, 1941, pp. 1–38, and 'The Rise of the Gentry: a Postscript', EcHR, 2nd Ser., VII, 1954, pp. 91–7.

separable from the gentry under the Tudors and early Stuarts. The English peerage is not, in the strictest sense, a nobility; an English peer's position, though admittedly normally hereditary, is personal and is not shared with the cadets of his family. The composition of the English peerage in 1640 was radically different from its composition in 1485 and, with a few exceptions, the new creations came from the gentry families. One half of the medieval noble families of England had been extinguished in the male line by the end of Henry VIII's reign, partly by attainders which removed in Pollard's phrase, "the tallest heads," but natural failure of new as well as old families was numerically the more important cause.[1] Elizabeth was sparing in her creations, but so was Charles I after 1629 and the Elizabethan peerage was scarcely less new than the Stuart; of the sixty-two peers in 1560, thirty-seven held titles which had been conferred since 1509. James I raised forty-six commoners to the peerage and Charles I as many as twenty-six in the first four years of his reign, but the majority of the newly ennobled came from the same sort of families as had been given titles under Henry VIII. It is, therefore, wrong to think of the early Stuart peerage as different in kind from the Tudor peerage.

Mr Lawrence Stone has analysed the evidence of land transfers in twelve and a half counties recorded by the Victoria County Histories for the period 1558–1642. The area covered happens to be predominantly the Home Counties and therefore normally (with the exception of the old-enclosed county of Kent) most subject to the pressure of the London land market; properties which remained in continuous ownership throughout the period may in some instances have been omitted; and some transfers from the Crown, which tend to be recorded as gifts, may in point of fact have been purchases. Allowing for all these factors, each of which would weight the figures against the peerage, Mr Stone's analysis supports other calculations, such as those made by Professor Tawney, which lead to the conclusion that the landholding of peers was tending to decline at this time. Between 1558 and 1602, the net sales of manors by peers created before 1602 amounted to 28 per cent of the manors owned, inherited, and granted in the area within the reign of Elizabeth. Between 1603 and 1642, the net sales by the Elizabethan peerage amounted to 16 per cent of those owned, inherited, and granted within the reigns of James I and Charles I. Though the peerage had doubled in numbers, the class as a whole held slightly fewer manors in the area in 1642 than it had in 1558. Nor is there much evidence to support the hypothesis that many of these sales may

[1] A. F. Pollard, *The Reign of Henry VII from Contemporary Sources*, 3 vols., 1913–4, III, p. 319; H. Miller, 'The Early Tudor Peerage', (thesis summary), *Bull*. IHR, XXIV, 1951, pp. 88–91.

have been the result of a deliberate policy to consolidate estates in compact, easily-managed holdings.[1]

Some individual case-studies of the fortunes of peers in the period have been made which rest upon a sufficient corpus of documentary material to remove the conclusions drawn from the realm of speculation or debate. The third earl of Cumberland could be said to epitomize the decadent peer of the Elizabethan age who drew his income from inherited lands and spent it on the conspicuous waste which has been held to be characteristic of the class. He was the heir to one of the richest land inheritances of the reign. The Cliffords had acquired their considerable northern estates, centred round their principal houses at Appleby, Brougham, Brough, and Pendragon in Westmorland, Skipton in Craven, and Londesborough in the East Riding of Yorkshire, partly by exchange and purchase, but chiefly by Crown grants and by a series of well-chosen marriages with heiresses. Henry the tenth Lord Clifford, the 'Shepherd Lord', had been restored in blood and lands by Henry VII after the family troubles in the Wars of the Roses, and by careful management had grown rich in "money, chattles, and goods, and great stocks of ground."[2] His son was created earl of Cumberland in 1525. Both the first and second earls had periods of extravagant living at Court, but followed them by periods of prudence and prosperity from royal favour. Two particularly valuable acquisitions made in Henry VIII's reign were the Percy fee in Craven, which the first earl's second wife brought to the family, and the grant of Bolton and other monastic properties in 1542. The third earl's net income from land was returned to the Crown (and therefore probably underestimated) as £1,821 a year; the death of a childless uncle in 1578 added further to his estate.

At first, Cumberland continued the policy of his father and grandfather of selling minor and widely dispersed parts of the estate and consolidating the lands in compact groups. From the early 1580's, however, he attended Court regularly and lived extravagantly, with the result that he began to sell land for quick returns and by 1585 was in debt for £5,000. His famous privateering ventures seem to have been motivated in the first instance by this indebtedness, but the profits of some of his early voyages did no more than pay the debts of others and a more general lack of success with voyages after 1594 meant that his debts rose to over £20,000. He was obliged to look to his lands to

---

[1] L. Stone, 'The Elizabethan Aristocracy—a Restatement', EcHR, 2nd Ser., IV, 1952, pp. 309–11. For the wealth of the gentry in Kent, see Alan Everitt, *Kent and its Gentry 1640–60*, London Ph.D. thesis, 1957, pp. 494–8.

[2] 'A Summary of the Lives of the Cliffords' by Lady Anne Clifford, in *Clifford Letters of the Sixteenth Century*, ed. A. G. Dickens, Surtees Soc., CLXXII, 1962, p. 135.

overcome his financial embarrassment, first mortgaging some to his tenants but subsequently embarking upon more desperate measures. Individual manors, capital messuages, demesnes, and woods, especially on his Craven estates, were exploited by a variety of methods—outright sales, fee farm grants, long leases with nominal or full rents reserved— and the income of his successors imperilled. He died in 1605 in debt for £80,000. Even so, his heirs might have survived successfully, for the third earl left, as well as debts and lands impoverished of their full rents, the legacy of a cloth licence which for a quarter of a century after 1601 made a substantial contribution to the family income, and the Clifford estates were producing as much as £4,500 a year in 1646. However, a disputed inheritance, the weak estate policy of the fourth earl, an inability to compete for office under Charles I because of the reduced income, and a failure in the male line, added to the depredations of the third earl, ultimately made recovery impossible, and a great estate disintegrated.[1]

The older peerage families did not as a class show any lack of energetic management of their lands. The sixth earl of Shrewsbury, the guardian to Mary, Queen of Scots, for instance, pursued an active, if not very profitable, exploitation of the mineral resources of his vast midland estates, working coalmines, establishing smelting works, founding ironworks, promoting the nascent steel industry, and making glass, as well as engaging in shipping ventures, farming many of his demesnes, and taking an active interest in the collection of his general estate revenues. During the widowhood of his equally business-like second wife, 'Bess of Hardwick', his son enjoyed a net revenue from land of £5,396 in 1592, which by a particularly ruthless approach he was able to improve in the course of the next few years.[2]

The story of the Percies' estate management in the Tudor and early Stuart periods is as fully documented as that of any family and shows the ability of a large medieval collection of lands, scattered from Sussex in the south to Northumberland in the north, to survive economic, political, and personal adversities. The heads of the family in the first four decades of the sixteenth century, the 'Magnificent' fifth earl and the 'Unthrifty' sixth earl, were not improving landlords, but there is no evidence of lax estate administration. The rise in the receipts from rents and farms on the Percy lands between 1471 and 1537 was slight over the estates as a whole. Yet individual properties

[1] R. T. Spence, *The Cliffords, earls of Cumberland, 1579–1646*, London Ph.D. thesis, 1959, *passim*.

[2] L. Stone, 'The Nobility in Business, 1540–1640', in *The Entrepreneur*, 1957, pp. 14–16; 'A Breviary of the Rents of the Earl of Shrewsbury, 1592', Sheffield Corn Exchange MSS of the duke of Norfolk, A.P./C, now in Sheffield City Library.

showed marked increases, and the appointment of commissioners to travel the estates from 1474, to supervise their management and grant leases, is a clear indication of an active policy. The fifth earl paid attention to entry fines and extended to the estates in Northumberland and Yorkshire the custom of Cumberland, which stressed their significance, but the rates were no more than one or one and a half year's rents, so that there was no dramatic addition to the family revenues. The net annual value of rents and farms on the Percy estates was approximately £3,600 in the early 1520's, to which should be added perhaps £300 as the average receipt from entry fines. Contrary to popular tradition, the sixth earl inherited in 1527 an estate which was free of serious encumbrance. For psychological reasons, and not from any necessity, he elected in the course of the next decade to alienate his inheritance, first large portions of lands to favourites and then the remainder to the Crown, which received it the more willingly because it was hostile to the power of great feudal nobles, especially in the north.[1]

The effect of this drastic, eccentric step was, in the event, mitigated by the attainder of the sixth earl's heir for his part in the Pilgrimage of Grace, since the family titles and most of the lands were restored after an interval of twenty years. The seventh earl was himself executed for rebellion in 1572, but the letters patent of 1557 had provided for a remainder to his brother. The lands were consequently unimpaired by this attainder and, more than that, the entail of the vast majority of the Percy estates by the 1557 restoration successfully prevented their dispersal in the later 1580's. At that time, the *abandon* of the young ninth earl incurred heavy debts which, as he has himself attested, might have been met by ill-considered land-sales, had it not been for the entail. As it was, heavy wood-sales, the raising of some fines on the renewal of leases for twenty-one years at low rents, a failure to pay some debts promptly, and the raising of a little borrowed money sufficed. In the mid-1590's the earl turned to a remarkably sound administration of his estates which so improved the income from them in the course of the next fifty years that, aided by the fact that his mother was co-heiress of the last Lord Latimer and by his own marriage to a widow, he became one of the wealthiest landowners in England. The adoption of scientific surveying of his estates, the judicious purchase of lands and leases to consolidate his inherited holdings in some eight counties of England and Wales, the granting of leases on carefully calculated principles, large-scale enclosure on his northern lands, and, above all, unremitting personal supervision based on serious study, all these measures allowed

[1] J. M. W. Bean, *The Estates of the Percy Family 1416–1537*, 1958, pp. 43–68, 135–57.

the ninth earl to leave his son a vastly improved estate. This was achieved without his holding for any length of time any significant office of state, and despite a period of personal disgrace which involved his imprisonment for sixteen years, as well as payment to the Crown of some eleven thousand pounds. It was not achieved without heavy borrowing, but heavy borrowing, we have come to understand, may be an indication of economic health rather than of impending bankruptcy.[1] It certainly was a case of economic health with the ninth earl of Northumberland, for his debts never exceeded twice his landed income and for every period when his borrowing increased markedly it is possible to find an extraordinary expense—a military expedition, house-building, the payment of his fine in Star Chamber, exceptional purchases of land, or the provision of a dowry for a daughter. The earl told Salisbury in 1612 that "my wife, children and myself must starve," as a result of his fine, but whereas in 1582 the net annual income from Percy lands had been £3,602, it was as much as £12,978 by 1636, after the second renewal of the leases which he had misguidedly granted in the early 1590's had taken effect. A policy of modernization and reorganization under an alert landowner had overcome political adversity, the peculations of officers, the resistance of tenants to feudal claims and to rationalized rents, reductions in the income from large parts of the estates in years of bad harvest such as the early 1620's, and increases in household expenditure in years when the earl was sowing wild oats or indulging the taste of his class for glorifying its residences.[2]

3. *The profits of office, profession, and trade*

If we can no longer accept unreservedly Professor Tawney's thesis that the gentry rose at the expense of the peerage between 1540 and 1640, or that the Jacobean peerage differed markedly in its estate management from the Elizabethan, there is no gainsaying the rise within the landed class of certain families, or that many of these families, especially in the early Stuart period, owed their improved status to the profits of office, profession, or trade rather than to the yields of their lands. Professor Trevor-Roper found that only one of seventy Elizabethan and Jacobean great houses was founded on a largely landed fortune; all

[1] H. R. Trevor-Roper, 'The Elizabethan Aristocracy: an Anatomy Anatomized', EcHR, 2nd Ser., III, 1951, p. 297.

[2] G. R. Batho, 'The Finances of an Elizabethan Nobleman', EcHR, 2nd Ser., IX, 1957, pp. 433–50, and *The Household Papers of Henry Percy, ninth Earl of Northumberland*, Camden Soc., 3rd Ser., XCIII, 1962, pp. xlvii–lvi; M. E. James, *Estate Accounts of the Earls of Northumberland 1562–1637*, Surtees Soc., CLXIII, 1955, pp. xxxv–lv; E. B. DeFonblanque, *Annals of the House of Percy*, 2 vols., 1887, II, p. 314.

the rest were built with fortunes derived mostly from important offices of state, professional careers, or success in business. Again, the evidence of *inquisitions post mortem*, of building, of the subsidy assessments of 1546, 1560, 1572, and 1626, and of contributions to the Armada loans has been analysed for seventy-eight gentry families in Elizabethan Sussex. Among the twenty-five families which on this evidence appear to have been flourishing, four were supported chiefly by land, but the majority had heads who were ironmasters, managers of forges and furnaces, merchants, or lawyers.[1]

Sir William Petre, one of the commissioners for the surrender of monasteries, a master in chancery, and principal secretary of state from 1544 to 1557, is an interesting example of a man who rose to wealth in the middle of the sixteenth century largely on the profits, direct and indirect, of his profession and of office. He came of a family which ranked between the yeomanry and gentry. He had, therefore, no considerable inheritance. His first wife was the youngest daughter of an Essex squire, his second a widow whose father was a London alderman and merchant; this second marriage in 1542 brought him lands which were worth £284 a year at the time. He made no extensive gains from the dissolution of the monasteries, for he paid in cash to the Crown or to lay vendors market prices totalling £2,946 for the church lands of an annual value of £180 which he bought, and his single gift from the Crown was the manor of South Brent, Devon. His salaries and fees, even when swollen for two years by a pension from King Philip, never exceeded £871 a year, and there is no evidence of his receiving any substantial gifts or bribes. Yet he was able to spend some £22,000 on land purchases between 1537 and 1571 without incurring debt, and at the end of his life he owned over twenty thousand acres in his native west country and nearly as much again in the county of his adoption, Essex. What Petre did, he did slowly and methodically, not by any dramatic strokes of fortune. Office had furnished him with a satisfactory, if relatively small, income, and he had used the knowledge of the property market which office had given him to invest that income to advantage in acquiring, almost manor by manor, two compact estates. His estate policy was conservative; his sole important innovation was the introduction on his Essex estates of rents in kind to be paid by leaseholders above their money rents, thus facilitating the provisioning of his London and Ingatestone households. A lawyer, he kept administrative costs to the minimum and used the "court roll, the custumal, and the estreat roll rather than the rack-rent" to improve

[1] H. R. Trevor-Roper, *The Gentry 1540–1640*, 1953, pp. 16, 17; J. E. Mousley, 'The Fortunes of Some Gentry Families of Elizabethan Sussex', EcHR, 2nd Ser., XI, 1959, pp. 476–7, 481.

his income. He granted no beneficial leases and made no attempt to obtain from his tenants rents which represented the market values of his properties but in 1570 he was receiving a net income from his estates of £2,274.[1]

There are remarkable parallels to Petre's career in that of Sir Nicholas Bacon, solicitor to the court of Augmentations from 1536, attorney in the court of Wards from 1545, and lord keeper to Queen Elizabeth from 1558. Like Petre, he came of a yeoman family. He married the daughter of a mercer first and the sister-in-law of Burghley second. He invested heavily in former monastic lands, mostly in Suffolk, but also in London, Norfolk, Hertfordshire, and Dorset, and bought at market prices. His salaries and fees were larger than Petre's naturally, as were the expenses of his position, but even as lord keeper they amounted to only £960 a year, besides an annuity from the Queen of £100. He acquired twenty-one wardships but seems to have made no appreciable profit from them and some may have been taken out of friendship to the families involved. Yet he was able to invest about £500 a year in land in the two decades after his appointment to the court of Augmentations, and about £1,150 a year during his lord keepership, without incurring debt. His estate policy, like Petre's, was conservative; its main features were thorough surveys of his estates, the consolidation of his properties by purchase as the occasion offered, the provision of a stock of sheep or cattle where appropriate, an interest in rents in kind, and a restrained pressure for higher entry fines and for improved yields from woods. In these ways his income from land rose from under £1,000 in 1559 to nearly £2,500 in 1575—and the increase was due more to purchase than to improvement.[2]

The survival of the receiver-general's accounts for Robert Cecil, first earl of Salisbury, between 1608 and 1612 has enabled Mr Stone to calculate with some degree of precision the profits from office of a great Jacobean statesman. It is clear that these were of great proportions, even if one singles out only the three main sources of profit from his offices. The fees of his most important office, the lord treasurership, were no more than £400 a year, but the sales of offices in his gift and other more dubious receipts added perhaps as much as £4,000 a year to his income. The fees of the mastership of the court of Wards were of the order of £480 a year, but private sales of wardships yielded about £2,100 a year more. The farm of the silk customs, for which he

[1] F. G. Emmison, *Tudor Secretary*, 1961, especially pp. 185-6, 271-6; W. R. Emerson, *The Economic Development of the Estates of the Petre Family in Essex in the Sixteenth and Seventeenth Centuries*, Oxford D.Phil. thesis, 1951, pp. 53, 98, 108-9, 149, 160.

[2] Simpson, *op. cit.*, pp. 28-89.

secured leases from Elizabeth in 1601 and from James in 1604 and 1610, were sublet to farmers, producing £1,333 a year in the later 1600's and as much as £7,000 after 1610. His father had settled on Salisbury his estate at Theobalds and most of his lands in Hertfordshire and the Home Counties, properties which produced an annual income of £1,700. From his political rewards and from his successful ventures in privateering and in the acquisition of a monopoly for the manufacture of starch, he was able in the course of fourteen years from his father's death to acquire one of the largest estates in England; his average receipts from land in the last four years of his life were about £7,000 a year. Salisbury's expenses were high—the maintenance of his large household cost an average of £8,500 a year at this time and he was spending as much as £13,500 a year on building—and by July 1611 his debts were no less than £53,000, but these were shortly reduced by land-sales and his successors inherited estates which have formed the nucleus of a great family's fortune.[1]

Salisbury profited from office, sometimes by means which were less than scrupulous, but he served the country well and retained some principles of conduct. Sir Arthur Ingram, by contrast, founded a landed family in the early Stuart period by ruthless exploitation of opportunities which came his way through the patronage of a succession of James I's ministers, and his outlook has been compared by his biographer with that of the dustman in Shaw's *Pygmalion*. He inherited his father's London business as a tallowchandler, but he would never have made a fortune with the limited capital placed at his disposal by that business. In Salisbury's time he established a position for himself in the customs service. He was a controller of the port of London from 1603 to 1613 at a salary of £200 a year, he was collector of the new impositions paid by alien merchants from 1608 on a commission and expenses basis, and he assisted Salisbury with his negotiations for the leasing and subletting of the silk farm in 1604, for which he was rewarded with annuities of £217 out of the Exchequer. His major profits, however, came from the holding of large cash balances for considerable periods from his customs positions, and from his activities as a middleman who brought together the courtiers who had grants and the businessmen who had the capital which was needed to exploit them. He organized syndicate after syndicate, to dispose of the cargo of captured ships, to sell Crown lands, to develop a monopoly of starch-making, and to establish the alum industry in England. After Salisbury's death he found new patrons, first in the Howard family whose right to license taverns and wine shops he helped to exploit,

[1] L. Stone, 'The Fruits of Office', in *Essays in the Economic and Social History of Tudor and Stuart England*, ed. F. J. Fisher, 1961, pp. 89–116.

then in Lionel Cranfield, earl of Middlesex, under whom he formed a syndicate to raise the rates over the renewal of the great customs farm in 1621, and finally, until they had a bitter quarrel, in Thomas Wentworth, earl of Strafford, for whom he secured the farm of recusancy fines in the north of England. Exactly what his profits were, it is impossible to assess in most instances. But they were sufficient for him to be able to purchase the secretaryship of the council of the North in 1613 and for him to found a landed family. At first he bought lands from the Crown or from private individuals which he improved and then sold again. After 1622 he deliberately consolidated his estates in Yorkshire. He already had one large house in the city of York and another at Sheriff Hutton in the forest of Galtres, ten miles away, as well as some lands in the county. In 1622 he acquired the estate of Temple Newsam, outside Leeds, for £12,000 and exchanged large estates in Warwickshire with Cranfield for even larger in Yorkshire. With other acquisitions, these purchases and exchanges meant that in the 1630's Ingram had a landed income of eight or nine thousand pounds. The parvenu had arrived among the landed class.[1]

The importance of office-holding and of political influence in raising some families in the social hierarchy must not, however, be exaggerated. While large incomes were enjoyed by the fortunate few, the majority of household and central government posts were poorly paid and did not permit of large gains apart from the official fees, even in Stuart times. Of 240 office-holders in the period 1625–42 whose finances have been examined, only forty acquired landed property worth more than £1,000 a year or increased their landed income by that amount. If the rise of some families can be directly related to office-holding, as was the case with the Egertons, earls of Bridgwater, and with the Fanshawes and the Osbornes of the upper Exchequer, the rise of other families is to be attributed at least as much to the good management of lands acquired as to the fruits of office, as was the case with the Brownlows of Belton and the Henleys of Hampshire and Somerset. Among both big men and small, office could involve debts which spelt disaster to their families. Sir Thomas Shirley, treasurer at war to the earl of Leicester's expedition to the Netherlands, left debts which the sale of old family property did not suffice to meet and ruined his family. George Goring, receiver-general in the court of Wards, died in debt to the Crown for nearly twenty thousand pounds and much of the family income was appropriated to the Crown throughout his son's lifetime. Sir Christopher Hatton, receiver of tenths and first fruits and lord chancellor to Queen Elizabeth, left debts to the Crown of approximately £42,000; his heirs were obliged to dispose of his personal

[1] A. F. Upton, *Sir Arthur Ingram*, 1961, especially pp. 1–22, 43–52, 148–71, 192.

property and to convey to the Crown his hereditary manor of Holdenby.[1]

Strafford provides a fascinating instance of the perils of office. He had a personal fortune; his grandfather had married the heiress of the Gascoignes, his father left him a landed income of £4,000 a year, and he married the daughter of the earl of Clare, one of the newly-risen gentry. He held high office which brought him opportunities for corresponding gain. He was president of the council of the North from 1629; he was able to use large cash balances in his hands from the collection of the knighthood fines in 1630–1 and from his receivership of recusants' rents in the north from 1629; he enjoyed the lease of the alum farm from 1638 with a probable income of £2,500 a year; and he was lord deputy of Ireland from 1632 until his fall from power, a position which brought him incidentally the farm of the Irish customs. Both in England and in Ireland he was able to invest heavily in lands. By 1639, apart from his salaries and the farm of Irish tobacco which he had acquired for himself in 1637, his income amounted to £22,800 a year. He was also heavily in debt. Had political trouble not intervened, he would have been able to eliminate his debt easily, but as it was he died owing £107,000. His son sold nearly half of the English lands and the family might have been ruined for ever if they had not retained the Irish lands which, though worthless in the 1640's and 1650's, came to be the salvation of the family fortunes.[2]

4. The gentry and the enduring qualities of land

That land could be a successful basis for the rise of a family in the sixteenth century is proved by the remarkable story of the Spencers of Althorp. Sir John Spencer the first came from a family of Warwickshire graziers. At first he rented his pastures, but from 1506 he was sufficiently affluent to buy carefully selected sheepwalks in compact groups on the borders of Warwickshire and Northamptonshire, which he stocked with animals largely of his own breeding. His successors added to both lands and flock. From at least the 1570's to the late 1620's the Spencers had a flock of 14,000 head or so; moreover, they dealt direct with the powerful London market and so were assured of ready sales. Their prosperity allowed them to make advantageous

[1] G. E. Aylmer, *The King's Servants*, 1961, pp. 264, 314, 331–3; E. Hopkins, *The Bridgewater Estates in North Shropshire in the first half of the Seventeenth Century*, London M.A. thesis, 1956, pp. 1–10, 221–2; Mousley, *op. cit.*, p. 478; E. St J. Brooks, *Sir Christopher Hatton*, 1946, pp. 360–1.

[2] J. P. Cooper, 'The Fortune of Thomas Wentworth, Earl of Strafford', EcHR, 2nd Ser., XI, 1958, pp. 227–48.

marriages from the first. Sir John's son, Sir William, allied the family with one of the oldest and wealthiest Northamptonshire gentry families, the Knightleys; Sir John the second married the daughter of the city of London merchant, Sir Thomas Kitson; Sir John the third, the heiress of the prosperous lawyer, Sir Robert Catlin; William, the second Baron Spencer, the eldest daughter of the earl of Southampton. Though they came to match with some of the great families in the land, the Spencers did not adopt aristocratic expenses. They built no large house in this period, they lived simply but well, and they refused the earldom which was offered them in 1618 for £10,000. By the early seventeenth century they came to have an annual income of between £6,500 and £8,000, of which perhaps £4,000 was derived from their flock and the rest from their investments in lands which they were leasing out.[1]

The Spencers have been held to be a great exception, and it must be said that they enjoyed great advantages in the siting of their lands, in the size of their transactions, and in the consistent efficiency of their management over several generations. Sheep-farming did not constitute a short cut to wealth in the period, but it is clear that it was usually profitable in the long run for any landowner who had some capital available to counteract the temporary depressions in returns which disease and variations of demand were liable to bring in the conditions of the age. The labour costs were particularly light and profits rose, at first steeply and then slightly. It has been calculated for East Anglia that the owner of a thousand sheep (in long hundreds) could confidently expect a profit of forty pounds a year by the late 1540's, perhaps twice as much as he would have received in the 1520's. This figure must be trebled for the late 1580's; by the 1630's it would have been of the order of £140.[2]

There is no reason to believe that it was only sheep-farmers who prospered among those landowners of the period whose income was derived primarily from land. All landowners from the 1540's on had relatively fixed expenses and increasing selling prices. Wages, especially of unskilled labour, rose less than prices from the second decade of the sixteenth century; this remained true despite the gradual, though irregular, rise of wages which occurred from the 1620's on. Food prices rose almost continuously, and in some decades dramatically, from 1500 to 1640. By 1550 they were at least double the level in 1500, by 1590 they were almost quadrupled, the 'great dearth' of 1594-7

---

[1] M. E. Finch, *The Wealth of Five Northamptonshire Families 1540–1640*, Northants. Rec. Soc., XIX, 1956, pp. 38–65.

[2] J. H. Round, *Studies in Peerage and Family History*, 1901, p. 281; Trevor-Roper, *op. cit.*, p. 16; Simpson, *op. cit.*, p. 194.

brought a sharp increase which was not quite maintained in the 1600's, but by 1640 food prices were almost six times what they had been in 1500. Nor is it true that rents lagged behind prices and as a consequence impoverished the landlords of Tudor and early Stuart England. In general terms, rents rose considerably, especially on new takings, before and especially around the middle of the sixteenth century; in the sixties, seventies, and eighties rents tended not to rise appreciably in most areas, though on the Bures estate in East Anglia they doubled in the period; from 1590 to the early 1620's rents rose considerably, while the bad harvests of the 1620's led to a general decline. A building labourer's daily wage rate in 1650 was less than twice what it had been a century before; food prices were more than double; rents were on many holdings at least twice what they had been in 1550.[1]

There were, of course, variations between areas and between different tenures. The rent of some meadowland in Derbyshire rose fourfold between 1543 and 1584, that of some arable even more. In East Anglia the rent of arable land rose six times between 1590 and 1650, but the rent of pasture and meadow rose only two or three times. The rent yield of some manors in Wiltshire increased as much as ten times between 1510 and 1650. The prosperity of the Kentish gentry was legendary, because of the proximity of their lands to the London food market; as Lambarde commented in the early 1570's, this was "not so much by the quantity of their possessions, or by the fertility of their soil, as by the benefit of the situation of the country itself." The poverty of Northumberland was readily exaggerated by its inhabitants when the occasion served, but it was nonetheless real. Dean James of Durham held in 1597 that five hundred ploughs had decayed in the previous half century within the bishopric and "want and waste have crept into Northumberland, Westmorland, and Cumberland." The ninth earl of Northumberland, again, wrote to his receiver in 1623, "I am made the more sensible of the general poverty of those parts by the poor reckonings which I in my particular have received of those demesnes which rest in my hands, and the ill proof of the stock upon them."[2]

In Northumberland, as in the other counties in the far north, such as Cumberland and Westmorland, tenants could offer an especially strong resistance to the attempts of the landlord in this period to raise

[1] Y. S. Brenner, 'The Inflation of Prices in Early Sixteenth Century England', EcHR, 2nd Ser., XIV, 1961, pp. 227, 231, 237, and 'The Inflation of Prices in England, 1551–1650', EcHR, 2nd Ser., XV, 1962, pp. 266–8, 270–3, 279–84; E. Kerridge, 'The Movement of Rent, 1540–1640', EcHR, 2nd Ser., VI, 1953, pp. 16–34; Simpson, op. cit., pp. 197–202.

[2] Kerridge, op. cit., p. 17; P. Laslett, 'The Gentry of Kent in 1640', Camb. Hist. J., IX, 1948, p. 153; SP 12: 362, 10 and 11; Syon House MS at Alnwick Castle, P. I. 3 n.

his income. For many held their lands by a customary tenant-right which varied from manor to manor but which was, in effect, "tantamount to freehold." The security which was given to customary tenants by the growth of copyhold tenure throughout the country was such that Coke declared in the reign of James I that, provided the copyholder had performed the duties and services required of him, "then let the lord frown, the copyholder cares not, knowing himself safe." Few landowners anywhere, indeed, could escape the presence on their manors of a bewildering complexity of tenures. John Rowe had been the steward of the manors of Lord Abergavenny in Sussex for a quarter of a century when in 1622 he was asked to compile a survey of them. Yet he wrote of one manor: "Its customs I find so variable as that I cannot certainly resolve myself thereof, much less satisfy others." Of another manor he reported: "I find their estates to be entangled with the like difficulties, fitter for the reverend judges of this kingdom upon mature deliberation than for mine insufficiency to determine."[1]

New families like the Spencers benefited by being able to select their lands with these and other landlord difficulties in mind, but old families with scattered properties like the Percies could off-set stable or declining incomes from some lands by increased yields from others. Even in the far north, the landlord wishing to improve his rent from lands which were largely in the hands of copyholders could treat with them for the substitution of leases for copyholds, as did Sir Thomas Chaloner at St Bees in 1560; or he could deny the customary nature of the tenure, as Anthony Knipe denied in 1561 that Myles Briggs of Crosthwaite held by tenant-right; or he could claim high entry fines, as Sir Thomas Wharton did from his Cumberland tenants in 1537; or, what amounted to the same thing, he could exact entry fines with great frequency, as the Percies did in Cumberland between 1527 and 1537. Where entry fines were uncertain, and many either were or could be made to appear so by a steward who knew his business, they could be raised to the limits which tenants would pay; many tenants in the period would have echoed the statement of the Methwold jury in 1606: "For our fines, they were certain; but now, by what means we know not, our custom is so broken that they are arbitrable." In any case, few landlords had manors which were composed solely of copyholds, and leases yielded markedly increased profits in many areas not merely after the 1580's, when the process became general, but also before. The manor of Ilketshall Hall, part of the Mettingham College estate which Sir Nicholas Bacon bought of Henry Denny in

[1] C. M. L. Bouch and G. P. Jones, *A Short Economic and Social History of the Lake Counties 1500–1830*, 1961, p. 65; Sir Edward Coke, *The Compleat Copyholder*, 1719, p. 31; W. H. Godfrey, ed., *The Book of John Rowe*, Suss. Rec. Soc., XXXIV, 1928, p. 93.

1562, was leased for £10 a year in the 1530's; Denny granted a lease for 21 years at £13 6s. 8d. in 1561, but when this expired in 1581, Bacon was able to lease it for £60, and by 1646 it was being leased at £160. The leasehold income of the whole estate showed an increase of nine hundred per cent between 1530 and 1656. William Harrison commented in 1587: "whereas in my time, although peradventure four pounds of old rent be improved to forty, fifty, or a hundred pounds, yet will the farmer think his gains very small toward the end of his term, if he have not six or seven years' rent lying by him, therewith to purchase a new lease," and he went on to speak of entry fines being doubled, trebled, and even increased seven times. On the other hand, even on manors where entry fines were uncertain, it was by no means always the case that tenants were squeezed; on many holdings rents remained virtually unchanged between 1500 and 1640.[1]

Sir Thomas Cornwallis, treasurer of Calais and comptroller of the household to Queen Mary, held no office under Elizabeth and acquired little land after his retirement from a mere five years at Court. His papers, therefore, give some indication of how far land could provide a satisfactory income when other sources were lacking. His patrimony had amounted to perhaps £300 a year, to which he added by his marriage and from the fruits of his office. Just what his profits were from office we do not know, but contemporary gossip held that he built his house at Brome in Suffolk from the proceeds of his treasurership and his household accounts show that his income of approximately £2,500 was more than halved when he left office. Twelve years after his father's death in 1544 he had a landed income of £650–700; in 1558 he received grants of leases of two manors from the Crown, Walsham in Suffolk which he sold to Sir Nicholas Bacon, and Wilton in Cleveland, Yorkshire, for which he paid a yearly rent of £50 but which yielded a net income of £180 a year without casualties. After the accession of Elizabeth, Cornwallis added little to his lands, apart from the purchase of a thousand pounds' worth of land in Brome and Oakley, the centre of his main estate, between 1565 and 1570, and the purchase of a town house in Norwich in 1571 for £400. His net income averaged £1,200 between 1575 and 1595. Some rents did not expand at all; these were from manors with little leasehold income. Entry fines and wood-sales on some of the larger of the manors, however, could inflate the income in certain years appreciably; thus Wilton, which normally produced £240 a year, yielded over £850 in 1573–5 and £1,500 in 1593–4, when entry fines were levied, and contributed £245 in wood-sales in 1595. Fines were rarely charged in

[1] Bouch and Jones, op. cit., p. 72; Bean, op. cit., p. 66; Simpson, op. cit., pp. 80, 202–8; TED, III, p. 71.

East Anglia on leasehold, but rents were raised as elsewhere; the income from the manor of Tivetshall was trebled between 1565 and 1579 and that from the manor of Basildon in Essex doubled between 1558 and 1595 in this way. Cornwallis's retirement from Court meant that he could reduce his living expenses from about £1,800 a year to a thousand a year, but, without selling any land, he built two houses afterwards, he lived as a county gentleman, and he was buried in an impressive tomb. A recusant, he was commanded by the queen to reside in London in 1587–9, but his estate income shows no signs of the economic decline which Miss Mousley has suggested for the catholic gentry of Sussex. His land did not make him a rich man, certainly; with the expenditure of no more than £1,500 capital, however, it was yielding an income in 1595 which was about 80 per cent better than that of 1560.[1]

The Yorkshire gentry, it is generally agreed, were relatively poor and the vast majority of them were entirely dependent upon their lands. They enjoyed none of the advantages of easy marketing which the proximity to London gave the Kentish gentry, and more than half of them had an annual income in 1642 of less than £250. The average Yorkshire knight probably disposed of less wealth than a Buckinghamshire or Worcestershire squire, and a yeoman in Norfolk or Kent was sometimes as well off as a lesser gentleman in Yorkshire. Yet there is every indication that as a class the Yorkshire gentry were prospering in the early Stuart period. They built in that time over eighty manor houses. The gentry who owed their position to office, business, or the law, like the Ingrams at Temple Newsam and the Wandesfords at Kirklington Hall, built the larger houses and carried out the bigger improvements to existing houses, but older gentry were also building and reconstructing, like the Kayes at Denby Grange and at Woodsome. The Yorkshire gentry were indulging in hunting and hawking on some scale. William Vavasour of Hazlewood declared on the eve of the Civil War that within eight miles of his family seat there were no fewer than thirty-two parks and two chases of deer, and a number of families obtained grants of free warren on their property to allow them to keep rabbits, hares, and game. In 1611 seven Yorkshire gentlemen bought baronetcies, and several purchased peerages from the early Stuarts, as Sir Thomas Fairfax of Denton bought the Scottish barony of Cameron in 1628. It was becoming increasingly common for the gentry to educate their sons expensively, to send one or more to the university or to one of the inns of court, and for the upper gentry families like the Wentworths to send their eldest sons on foreign tours. Nor was it only the wealthiest families who had a surplus in this

[1] Simpson, *op. cit.*, pp. 142–69; Mousley, *op. cit.*, pp. 478–9.

period. Sir Marmaduke Langdale of North Dalton had a patrimony which was one-eighth of Thomas Wentworth's—he was receiving a mere £500 a year on his succession to his estates in 1617. A good marriage and particularly shrewd estate management sufficed to allow him to expend over twelve thousand pounds in land purchases between 1627 and 1635. Steady acquisition over a long period was naturally more common among the country gentry. The Kayes afford a Yorkshire parallel to the Furses of Devon whose story has been told by Dr Hoskins; John Kaye (1578–1641) improved his estate by careful husbandry and, like his father and grandfather before him, added to the family property, buying land of the value of £279 a year in his time. Even a recusant family could prosper in the period, as the Gascoignes of Barnbow demonstrated. The head of the family was a convicted recusant throughout the period 1603–42 and the family was paying sixty pounds a year rent for its properties in consequence. By prudent management, including enclosure, mining ventures, and improved rents, and by purchases with the profits of land management, they raised their income from about a thousand a year in 1603 to about £1,700 a year in 1642, and in 1635 John Gascoigne was able to afford to be the first Englishman to purchase a baronetcy of Nova Scotia.[1]

What Sir John Oglander of the Isle of Wight wrote with his own blood in 1632 may have been true for the lesser country gentleman— "by only following the plough he may keep his word and be upright, but will never increase his fortune." But many families did succeed in living comfortably off quite small estates. Westcote records of the Brembridges of Devon, for example, that they had lived on an estate of seventy-five acres "with such a temperate moderation in every succession, that greedy desire of riches hath neither much increased, nor prodigality decreased it." Good estate management could bring rewards to noble and gentry families as well as to yeoman families like the Loders, as the advices to heirs which were so fashionable in the early seventeenth century were concerned to stress. "Understand your estate generally better than any one of your officers," the ninth earl of Northumberland exhorted his son; "before your lordship can direct your estate," John Guevara told Robert Bertie, Lord Willoughby of Eresby, soon after his father's death, "you ought necessarily understand what it is: for more have been undone by blindfold expense than by youthful courses." Sir Thomas Tresham suffered penalties for recusancy of nearly eight thousand pounds, had to provide for a large family of three sons and six daughters, and indulged in expensive hospitality,

[1] J. T. Cliffe, *The Yorkshire Gentry on the Eve of the Civil War*, London Ph.D. thesis, 1960, pp. 86, 90, 92, 96, 98, 99; W. T. Jordan, *Philanthropy in England 1480–1660*, 1959, pp. 332–4; Hoskins, *op. cit.*, pp. 356–65.

extensive litigation, and some building. But the application of business methods to his estates and his employment of an outstanding surveyor, George Levens, allowed him to survive all, to leave debts of under £11,500 which amounted to no more than four years' income. Without his handicaps, and if he had not been succeeded by irresponsible sons, he would by sheer acumen have developed the family fortunes beyond fear of damage.[1]

Disaster was obviously more common among the smaller gentry families than among the larger landowners. The smaller landowners had none of the resources of the larger, either to overcome temporary financial embarrassments or to apply professional expertise to estate management. The estate officials on the smaller manors were, Smyth of Nibley, steward to the Lords Berkeley, tells us, often ill-educated, and Clay testifies in 1619 to the losses sustained by the smaller landowners by trying to administer their own estates. Many a family like the Elands of Carlinghow, who had been landowners in Batley for three hundred years, were forced to sell their estates and sank unheralded into oblivion. Above the level of landowning where contemporaries might have been left in doubt whether to call the head of the family yeoman or gentleman, however, it required an exceptional combination of circumstances to destroy a landed family. The earls of Oxford had been declining for some time when in Elizabeth's reign Edward de Vere, the seventeenth earl, was reduced by quite extraordinary extravagance to "the mentality of a failed gambler" and to living on a royal pension. The main line of the Markhams of Nottinghamshire, whose ancestry can be traced to pre-Conquest times and who had served the Crown from the twelfth century onwards, was severely impoverished in the early seventeenth century. But Robert Markham, the heir to Sir John, had been left a reduced inheritance, for the greater part of Sir John's lands were willed away to the sons of a second marriage, and his manor house at Cotham had been virtually stripped of furniture and heirlooms. Robert's resources were drained by service at Court and by his having to provide for eight children; his heir, Sir Robert, not only had eight children himself but was also, according to Thoroton, "a great unthrift and destroyer of this eminent family."[2]

[1] *A Royalist's Notebook*, ed. F. Bamford, 1936, p. 75; T. Westcote, *A View of Devonshire in 1630*, 1845, p. 119; *Advice to his Son by Henry Percy, ninth Earl of Northumberland*, ed. G. B. Harrison, 1930, p. 75; Lincs. AO, 2 Ancaster MSS 14/17; Finch, *op. cit.*, pp. 72–92.

[2] J. Smyth of Nibley, *The Lives of the Berkeleys*, ed. Sir J. Maclean, 3 vols., 1883–6, II, p. 416; T. Clay, *A Chorological Discourse of the Well Ordering of an Honorable Estate*, 1619, pp. 52–5; Cliffe, *op. cit.*, p. 21; A. L. Rowse, *The England of Elizabeth*, 1950, p. 257; F. N. L. Poynter, *A Bibliography of Gervase Markham*, Oxford Bibliog. Soc., 1962, pp. 5–8.

One common cause of decline among landed families was beyond their control—the vagaries of the demographic factor. No fewer than 102 of 859 gentry families in Yorkshire, for example, died out in the male line between 1603 and 1642. The Onleys of Pulborough in Sussex were a family which suffered particularly in this regard. Owen Onley died in October 1590 leaving an only son, William, a minor; William was later found to be a lunatic and the Onley inheritance passed to a married sister. Large families could imperil the maintenance of a landed estate as an entity and the continuance of the family as landowners, especially if there were no supplies of ready cash to meet such contingencies, and among the smaller families who were dependant upon land there rarely was any ready cash. Provision for younger sons had often enough to be made by carving estates out of the main inheritance, so reducing it seriously, and the size of marriage portions for daughters, which were always a major expense for a family, was tending to increase in the early seventeenth century. The Spencers of Althorp did not materially alter their provision for younger sons between the early sixteenth century and the middle of the seventeenth century, but they provided marriage portions for their daughters which were ten times as large in 1642 as they had been two generations earlier, and thirty times as large as in 1532. Where large families occurred in two successive generations it was often ruinous. Sir John Mallory of Studley in Yorkshire, for example, had to provide for his nineteen children; his father had had seventeen children and his grandfather nine.[1]

The personality of the landowner was even more material in making or marring a family's fortunes. The industry and care with which John Isham of Lamport and his blind son Thomas husbanded the resources of their estates were as important factors in founding that landed family as John's wealth acquired as a merchant. Sir Richard Gargrave of Nostell Priory inherited an estate which was so large that he could ride over his own land from Wakefield to Doncaster, but his penchant for gambling was such that he had lost most of it within twenty years and he was found dead in 1649 with his head resting on the saddle of one of the packhorses with which he had been travelling in his poverty. Ignorance could waste an inheritance; Dr Nathaniel Johnston has recorded of Sir Francis Foljambe of Aldwark, who succeeded to property worth £3,000 a year but left only £1,000 a year at his death, that he was "a man of no estate or fortune, and of small understanding by reason of his education to manage so great an estate."

---

[1] Cliffe, op. cit., p. 20; Mousley, op. cit., p. 478; Finch, op. cit., pp. 59–60; *Memorials of the Abbey of St Mary of Fountains*, ed. J. R. Walbran and J. Raine, Surtees Soc., LXVII, 1878, pp. 325–6.

Extravagance combined with ignorance was even more catastrophic; witness the career of Henry, Lord Berkeley, which is recorded for us by his steward, John Smyth of Nibley. He knew nothing of business, was married above his station to the sister of the duke of Norfolk, and lived, until wiser counsels prevailed, far above his income. He was also unfortunate, for litigation about the will of the marquis of Berkeley, who had died in 1492, continued for more than a century, and his son inherited the youthful extravagance of his father. In sixty years Lord Henry had sold lands worth £41,400.[1]

The need to balance income and expenditure was imperative for landowners in the period. "Except you do this," Sir Nicholas Bacon warned his son-in-law, Sir Henry Woodhouse, in the 1570's, "surely that will follow that will bring great disquietness and grief to yourself and your friends." It was sound advice which John Guevara had to offer Lord Willoughby a generation later: "the surest course, for any man that will live, and better his estate, is by casting it up truly, and dividing it into three parts: whereof the one is to be bestowed in maintaining himself and family, in household charges; the second may be dispended in apparel, and extraordinary expenses; the third ought to be laid up, or disposed, for the good of posterity." There were no long-term credit facilities in the sixteenth and early seventeenth centuries and interest rates were high—the statute of 13 Elizabeth c. 8 fixed interest at 10 per cent and scriveners' charges were commonly another pound per cent. If the landowner was unable to repay a loan on the appointed day, he forfeited his bond or, worse, his mortgage, his personal credit was impaired, and he would find it difficult to renew his short-term loans, usually for six months only at a time, or to secure new loans. Land-sales would then be probably his only recourse.[2]

By the 1630's, the situation had altered considerably. Usury charges were reduced, the statute of 21 James I c. 17 fixing them at 8 per cent, and scriveners were now charging only five shillings per cent. The development of the equity of redemption, even more significantly, converted the mortgage into a long-term security and freed the land-owner from fear of forfeiture, provided that he could meet the interest charges. Indebtedness could now be a method not merely of providing ready cash for a particularly large expenditure, but of gaining a long respite in which a family's fortunes which had been seriously impaired could be restored by careful management over a long period. Land-sales could thus be avoided and family estates retained intact. Christopher

---

[1] Finch, op. cit., pp. 6–28; J. Hunter, South Yorkshire, 2 vols., 1828–31, II, pp. 213–14; N. Johnston, 'History of the Family of Foljambe', Collectanea Topographica et Genealogia, II, 1835, pp. 79–81; Rowse, op. cit., pp. 257–8.

[2] Simpson, op. cit., p. 15; Lincs. AO, 2 Ancaster MSS 14/17.

Wandesford, for example, has explained in his *Book of Instructions* how he paid off his father's debts: "by the credit of my friends and my own good and careful performance (I mean keeping time) with my creditors, I supplied my occasions with money at the usual rates; which I was forced to do continually, rather than by the sale of some part of my lands, by mortgages or some more disadvantageous bargains, to weaken my estate and lessen my revenue." Where Sir Thomas Tresham in the 1590's and 1600's had been forced to sell land and to undertake drastic schemes of improvement which affected his relationships with his tenants adversely, the Fitzwilliams half a century later were able to survive debts which consumed two-thirds of their annual income in interest alone. It was these changes in credit facilities which allowed many of the Caroline gentry to survive their high degree of indebtedness which has been observed in many areas, and which was brought about by such factors as the extravagance or incompetence of one generation, the religious penalties of a recusant head of family in the 1600's and 1610's, the economic difficulties of a decade like the 1620's, or the political adversity of a royalist in the 1640's.[1]

Where a family chanced to suffer a multiplicity of misfortunes, however, even a fair-sized estate could not readily prevent a decline, as the story of the Temples of Stowe demonstrates. Peter Temple founded the family in the middle of the sixteenth century by a combination of successful sheep-farming on leased lands and good management of purchased properties. The active policy of his son John, who had the reputation of being "a frugal and provident gentleman," assured the Temples' position among the county gentry of Buckinghamshire. John's purchase of lands in Burton Dassett in Warwickshire, to consolidate an important family holding there, for some £9,000 in 1593 and his expenditure of a further £3,200 to buy leases which had been granted by the previous owner meant, however, that he left the estates heavily encumbered with debt at a time when it was not easy to obtain long-term credit. He also left eleven children for whom provision had to be made. His eldest son, Sir Thomas, moreover, had fifteen children. Despite careful management, the reduction of interest charges after 1624, and the sale of some lands, Sir Thomas was unable to remove the burden of debt from the family. For the family debts were increased in his time not only by provision for cadets of the family but also by the agricultural depression of the 1620's, by prolonged litigation between him, his brothers, and eldest son, and between his sons, and by the extravagance of his heir, Sir Peter. By 1653 Sir

[1] Finch, *op. cit.*, pp. 167–9; T. Comber, ed., *Christopher Wandesford's Book of Instructions*, 2 vols., 1777–8, I, p. 92; on indebtedness of the Caroline gentry see e.g. Hoskins, *op. cit.*, p. 353.

Peter was reduced to agreeing to a settlement by which trustees were to administer his estates for a term of years on behalf of his 105 creditors to whom some £24,000 was owed. Sir Peter's death that year resulted in a more favourable settlement which ultimately enabled his heir to straighten out the family finances, but it is clear that the debts of John Temple, the incidence of large families, and the unthrifty personality of Sir Peter had imperilled for more than fifty years the stability of what was otherwise a prospering landed family.[1]

5. The yeomanry and the opportunities for the capable

Thomas Fuller called the yeomanry "an estate of people almost peculiar to England, living in the temperate zone between greatness and want." But there was no sharp division between the lesser gentry and the richer yeomen. The position of men of both classes was determined, as Tawney has written of the lesser gentry, "not by legal distinctions, but by common estimation." Sir Edward Coke, following a century-old precedent, defined a yeoman in the early seventeenth century as "a freeholder that may dispend forty shillings per annum." In fact, the definition was virtually meaningless, for many a yeoman in Tudor and early Stuart times, like Latimer's father, had no land of his own, but was a copyholder or leaseholder. In innumerable wills and legal documents of the age a man is described in one place as a yeoman and in another as a gentleman, or a man describes himself as a gentleman but is described by others as a yeoman. For it was not gentility of birth nor degree of wealth which distinguished the classes. Many of the younger sons of the lesser gentry became yeomen; many gentry were newly risen from the yeomanry or, with the aid of business or professional profits, from humbler origins still. Few gentry could have traced back their ancestry for three centuries, as some yeomen families like the Reddaways of Devon could. Many yeomen, again, were far richer than some gentry, like Thomas Bradgate of Peatling Parva in Leicestershire, who was not merely the richest yeoman in the county in 1524 but had the second highest tax assessment there in any class. The principal characteristic of the yeoman was his contentment with a simple way of life, even when he could afford more comfort; he was, in Fuller's phrase, "a gentleman in ore," and he could live without the expenses of a gentleman. Even in the prosperous south-east, yeomen houses remained until late in the sixteenth century distinguished from lesser men's by the number of rooms rather than by the quality of their

[1] E. F. Gay, 'The Rise of an English Country Family', *Huntington Lib. Qtrly.*, I, 1938, pp. 367–90, and 'The Temples of Stowe and Their Debts', *ibid.*, II, 1939, pp. 399–438.

furnishings, and the long house persisted in parts of the north until very much later.[1]

Although some yeomen combined agricultural and industrial activities, as did the yeomen clothiers of the Huddersfield district of Yorkshire and the Northumberland men who made some profit from the salt and coal on their lands, yeomen relied for their income primarily upon the land. As direct producers, they were among the first to benefit from the rise in prices of the age and were always assured of food and clothing, but they shared most of the perils as well as the opportunities of other landowners in the period. They were subject to the same natural misfortunes—a failure of heirs or the succession of a reckless spendthrift could ruin yeomen as well as gentry families. They were subject to the same fluctuations in prices—the sudden falls in the price of wheat in years such as 1582-4, 1591-2, 1603-4, and 1619-20 affected them as it affected others. They were subject to the same variation of conditions between different districts. In arable areas yeomen farmed anything from twenty-five to two hundred acres, and a Kentish yeoman with only twenty-five acres, like Alexander Paramore in the 1570's, could be sufficiently well off to make friendly loans to his neighbours; in pastoral areas no man could have made a good living from so small a farm, and the wealthy yeoman might have as many as five or six hundred acres. The chances to amass wealth were far greater within reach of London than in the more remote areas of the country, and the average wealth of a Norfolk yeoman, which has been calculated at £443 in the period 1480-1660, was perhaps four times as much as that of a Somerset yeoman.[2]

It was an age when, in the words of Gras, there was "opportunity for the capable, loss for the incapable." From the 1540's there was taking place what Hoskins has termed "the largest transference of land ownership since Domesday." Many yeomen became owners of the lands which their fathers and grandfathers had farmed before them as tenants, and rose into the gentry as a result of successful landownership. If contemporary opinion may be accepted, the land market was especially active about the turn of the century. Thomas Wilson wrote in 1600: "I find great alterations almost every year, so mutable are worldly things and worldly men's affairs," and John Norden, who surveyed so many noble estates and made topographical studies of so

[1] M. Campbell, *The English Yeoman under Elizabeth and the Early Stuarts*, 1942, pp. 23-4, 62; R. H. Tawney, 'The Rise of the Gentry', EcHR, XI, 1941, pp. 2-3; Jordan, *op. cit.*, p. 324; W. G. Hoskins, *Devon*, 1954, pp. 88-9, and *Essays in Leicestershire History*, 1950, pp. 153-4; M. W. Barley, *The English Farmhouse and Cottage*, 1961, pp. 41-3, 52-4, 121.

[2] Campbell, *op. cit.*, pp. 102, 162-4; Barley, *op. cit.*, pp. 41-3; Jordan, *op. cit.*, p. 334.

many counties, wrote in 1610: "lands pass from one to another more in these latter days than ever before." Yeomen as well as gentry were building up estates, in the north as well as in the favoured south. Adam Cooke, a yeoman of Kendale, for example, owned at his death in 1624 seven messuages and tenements in Killington and eighty-six acres of land, including thirty-six of arable. The extent to which yeomen were benefiting as a class from this transference of land may be illustrated from two counties, though it could be seen almost every-where in England. The 1634 visitation of Lincolnshire contains the names of seventy-eight families who were not listed in 1562; two dozen of these families came from other counties, but of the remaining forty-four, half were risen yeomen. One hundred and fifty eight of the 679 gentry families in Yorkshire in 1642 were 'new' in the sense that they had entered the county or the class since the accession of Elizabeth. The families who were new to the county were mostly those of business or professional men who were settling in the country, or men who had married heiresses and had come to reside on their newly acquired estates. But of the fifty-seven Yorkshire families who were granted arms between 1603 and 1642, more than half were wealthy yeomen.[1]

Yeomen were not perhaps "worldly men" in some respects, but there was nothing unworldly about the attitude of many to the exploita-tion of their lands. The survival of his accounts has made Robert Loder of Berkshire immortal. He was not content with subsistence farming, but grew for commercial marketing the wheat and barley which he knew would sell readily at London and at the market towns within reach of his estate. He improved his land in the manner advo-cated by the plethora of books on good husbandry which appeared in Elizabethan and early Stuart times and bought lime, for example, every year to fertilize his ground. As the editor of his accounts has written of him: "He wanted as large a financial return for his expenditure of capital, managerial work, and manual work as he could get, and did his utmost to maintain it." It is hard to believe that Loder's approach was not typical of hundreds more, for whenever an individual farmer's records have survived, their predominant themes are experimentation and diversity of farming. At the other end of the scale, the decline of villeinage to the point of extinction by the early seventeenth century meant that others were rising from the husbandry to be yeomen and the distinctions between husbandmen and yeomen were being blurred. Hoskins has remarked of the division between the two groups in

[1] N. S. B. Gras, *The Economic and Social History of an English Village*, 1930, p. 99; W. G. Hoskins, *Essays in Leics. Hist.*, p. 155; Wilson, ed. F. J. Fisher, *op. cit.*, p. 22; J. Norden, *The Surveyor's Dialogue*, 1610, p. 10; Bouch and Jones, *op. cit.*, p. 94; Campbell, *op. cit.*, pp. 37–8; Cliffe, *op. cit.*, pp. 27 *sqq.*

Leicestershire, and it was evidently the case generally, that "in the main it seems to have been, by the sixteenth century, a matter of personal wealth and of a man's scale of activities and living."[1]

The interest of the landlord and of the tenant was often consistent. Thomas, Lord Brudenell of Deene, demonstrated this when he succeeded in doubling the yield of his estate in Northamptonshire between 1606 and 1642 by the creation of new demesne enclosures and by the adoption of improvements on his lands not in demesne which were designed to advance his more substantial tenants as well as to increase his own profits. "Be very kind and loving unto your tenants," James Bankes of Winstanley in Lancashire exhorted his children, "so shall you prosper." Robert Furse of Morshead, a yeoman, had much the same advice to offer his children on their dealings with their tenants in 1593: "Burden them not with more fines, rents, or services more than they be well able to pay you, displace not an honest, friendly tenant for a trifle or small sum of money." Constant enquiry into the customs of manors and into the evidences of tenants' titles was, however, one of the outstanding features of Elizabethan and early Stuart times, as literally thousands of surviving documents testify. "In these days there go more words to a bargain of ten-pound land a year than in former times were used in the grant of an earldom," Norden commented in *The Surveyor's Dialogue* in 1607. The rise in rents which occurred in the 1590's was coupled with the adoption of more scientific surveying of their estates by many landlords and was more marked than any previous general rise in rent level, but it was in most areas only one of many attempts by landlords to safeguard themselves against the inflation of prices of the age. The yeoman who failed to protect his title was lost, entry fines as well as rents rose markedly in the period, and the length of leases, which were increasingly substituted for other tenures, was generally reduced, especially in the south-eastern counties, where the pressure on land was greatest. Competition for land among yeomen was so marked by the early seventeenth century that Robert Churton was able to declare that tenants "by reason of this greediness and spleen one against another [are] more their own enemies than is either the surveyor or the landlord." John Taylor wrote of the smallholder in 1630:

> ". . .if a gentleman have land to let,
> He'll have it, at what price so 'ere 'tis set,
> And bids and overbids, and will give more
> Than any man could make of it before."

[1] G. E. Fussell, ed., *Robert Loder's Farm Accounts, 1610–1620*, Camden Soc., 3rd Ser., LIII, 1936, pp. xxiii–vi; Campbell, *op. cit.*, pp. 16, 178; Hoskins, *op. cit.*, p. 151.

Taylor's poetic licence must not deceive us; the landlord could not have raised rents or fines beyond the levels which tenants were both able and willing to pay, so that this movement was probably no more than a redistribution of profits from land. Some yeomen were landlords themselves and more were living like landlords by the early seventeenth century. As Hooker remarked of the Devonshire yeoman about 1599: "his fine being once paid he liveth as merrily as does his landlord and giveth himself for the most part to such virtue, conditions, and qualities as doth the gentleman."[1]

For there is every reason to believe that yeomen were advancing as a class both absolutely and relatively more than any other landed group of the time. Robert Reyce thought that the Suffolk yeomen were the one group who were doing well in 1618: "Continual underliving, saving, and the immunities from the costly charges of these unfaithful times, do make them so to grow with wealth of this world that whilst many of the better sort, as having passed their uttermost period, do suffer an utter declination, these only do arise, and do lay such strong, sure, and deep foundations, that from thence in time are derived many noble and worthy families." Where in the early sixteenth century the yeoman were in many counties no more than "an emerging class," according to one modern estimate based on records from areas covering one third of England, their average wealth doubled between the time of Elizabeth and the Civil War. The yeoman way of life with its emphasis on frugality buttressed the majority of families against the sudden demands for resources which a bad harvest or a rise in rents could make, and many rose slowly but surely over the period, perhaps like John Lyon, the founder of Harrow School, having no desire to be termed anything other than yeomen. An examination of more than three thousand deeds describing the land transactions of yeomen between 1570 and 1640 showed that 59 per cent were for purchases amounting to less than a hundred pounds, and 78 per cent were for purchases involving less than two hundred pounds. What Robert Furse recorded in 1593 of his ancestors, who a century before had been farming tenements of no more than ninety acres in Devon, must have been true of most yeomen families—they "always kept themselves within their own bounds that by these means we are come to much more possessions, credit and reputation than ever any of them had."[2]

[1] Finch, op. cit., pp. 154–63; The Memoranda Book of James Bankes 1586–1617, ed. Joyce Bankes, 1935, p. 6; H. J. Carpenter, 'Furse of Morshead', Devon Assoc., XXVI, 1894, p. 172; Campbell, op. cit., pp. 58, 77–83, 106; cf. Simpson, op. cit., p. 202.

[2] Campbell, op. cit., pp. 53, 62, 78; Jordan, op. cit., p. 334; Hoskins, op. cit., p. 159; Rowse, op. cit., p. 233.

Professor Campbell has written of the Elizabethan yeomen that "their profits came by small rather than by large gains. And in their struggle for those gains, their own wit, industry, and initiative counted for much." So it was of all who owned land in the Tudor and early Stuart period. Some by recklessness, extravagance, over-large families, or a failure to adapt themselves to economic changes fell into "an utter declination." Some rose by royal favour, commercial success, or profits made in profession or office. Some by good marriages and good management were able to increase their landholdings. But most, like the Furses, progressed "by little and little" and constituted what Professor Simpson has called "the perdurable gentry." These were the families who in succeeding generations by their industry and initiative countered adverse circumstances and benefited from advantageous situations to remain stable within their class but in possession of their land, the soundest long-term investment of the age and the surest means of support for their descendants. Only a failure in the male line could remove these families, such were the enduring qualities of land.[1]

C. THE CHURCH[2]

1. *The Monasteries*

(a) *Introduction*

There can have been few parishes in England in 1500 the products of whose fields and pastures were not contributing in some way towards the maintenance of one or more of over eight hundred religious communities. The nature of the contribution varied, from fixed rent-charges through the whole range of rents, customary, 'at will', and leasehold, both in cash and in kind; tithes, great and small; profits of manor courts; labour services and other customary obligations; to the crops and stock produced on land kept in hand by the monks and nuns themselves. It is impossible, therefore, to define the extent of the monastic landed estate in terms of acreage. The counting of manors and other types of property is equally inappropriate and offers only a very rough indication of the economic value of the monastic lands.

[1] Campbell, *op. cit.*, p. 220; Simpson, *op. cit.*, p. 216.

[2] Professor Dom David Knowles and Professor H. J. Habakkuk were kind enough to read an early draft of this section and to make some valuable suggestions. I am most grateful to them and also to the following who have allowed me to draw upon their unpublished dissertations: J. Kennedy (*The Dissolution of the Monasteries in Hampshire and the Isle of Wight*, London M.A., 1953); G. W. O. Woodward (*The Benedictines and Cistercians in Yorkshire in the Sixteenth Century*, Trin. Coll. Dublin, Ph.D., 1955); S. M. Thorpe (Mrs Jack) (*The Monastic Lands in Leicestershire on and after the Dissolution*, Oxford B.Litt., 1961); and R. J. Mason (*The Income, Administration, and Disposal of the Monastic Lands in Lancashire*, London M.A., 1962).

More realistic in this respect, and by far the most ambitious reckoning attempted by a modern scholar, is Professor Savine's calculation, based on the *Valor Ecclesiasticus*, that the gross annual value of the monastic lands of England in 1535 was in the region of £160,000.[1] The addition of several large estates, such as that of St Augustine's Abbey, Bristol, and the lands of the colleges and some of the hospitals, all of which, for various reasons, Savine excluded, together with some allowance for under-valuation of demesne, would bring the total much nearer £200,000. It is impossible to say exactly what relation this bore to the total landed wealth of the kingdom, but it was probably between one fifth and one quarter of the whole.[2]

To the majority of early Tudor countrymen the monastery was first and foremost a landlord, a powerful possessor of wealth. Monastic tenants would no doubt have regaled the stranger with talk of crippling rents, low prices, neglected repairs, and inescapable tithes. At the abbot's table the tale would have been a different one, of miserably low rents, quite unrelated to the profit being enjoyed by his tenant farmers, of the high cost of foodstuffs and of the other bare necessities of the convent, and of the profitless task of improving such parts of the estate as could from time to time be taken in hand. But all this in 1500 was mere neighbourly chaffing, the rubbing along together of members of the farming community, their relations little affected as yet by the busy world of politics. A whole generation of monks was to pass before rumours of the disendowment of the Church began to be spread abroad, and a third of a century before Henry VIII and Thomas Cromwell embarked upon the wholesale confiscation of monastic resources. Meanwhile the life of the countryside was relatively undisturbed, save by the challenge of an increasingly buoyant national economy.

(b) The monastic estate

Inextricably entwined as were the landed resources of the monks with those of their lay and ecclesiastical neighbours, the monastic lands nevertheless comprised a clearly identifiable estate. Continuity of ownership, and the care with which, as corporate bodies, the monasteries cherished their title deeds, went a long way to ensure this. Equally important was the persistence of the manor as a tenurial unit. Even for agrarian historians, impatient to get to grips with fields and pastures, this is important. Well over half of the monastic landed estate took the form of manors. In Devon in 1535 one hundred and

[1] A. Savine, *English Monasteries on the Eve of the Dissolution*, Oxford Studies in Social and Legal History, ed. P. Vinogradoff, I, 1909, pp. 76–100.

[2] This proportion has no statistical basis: it represents the consensus of the more reliable contemporary and modern impressions.

thirty monastic 'manors', using the term in its contemporary connotation, accounted for over 60 per cent of the total monastic landed resources in the county.[1] Disintegrating forces had long been at work. Not only had there been the retreat from demesne farming and the commutation of labour services, but also, on the estates of some of the larger houses, the fragmentation of manorial issues among monastic obedientiaries. But the administrative framework had held firm. The manors retained their identity, buttressed by the regular holding of their courts, and by an administrative system which, however it might change at the centre, in the countryside rested firmly on the duties and perquisites of an army of lay bailiffs.

Monastic manors were for the most part indistinguishable from their lay neighbours, comprising the lord's demesne, often described as the 'chief messuage' of the manor, the lands of the tenants, woods, commons, mills, fisheries, and the manor court. Like them, too, they varied enormously in size, in geography, and in tenurial composition. Most of the large, territorially compact, manors had a long history of uninterrupted administrative cohesion going back beyond the time when they had first been given "to God and the church of St...and to the abbot and monks there serving God." Such were the manors of Abbots Ripton, Upwood, Houghton, Holywell, and Warboys, to name only a few of the twenty-five in Huntingdonshire alone which had belonged to Ramsey Abbey since the tenth century. Each manor had its own peculiar combination of old demesne and free and customary holdings, overlaid to varying degrees by leasehold tenancies. To select at random, the manor of Alvington in Gloucestershire belonged to the priory of Llantony. In 1535 the priory was drawing 40s. in freehold rents, £24 16s. 9d. from customary tenements, 40s. for the 'farm' of the chief messuage, and 110s. 4d. from the rest of the demesne, all of which had been let. The mill was at farm for 46s. 8d. and court profits amounted to 13s. 7d. in an average year, making a gross revenue of £37 7s. 4d. The customary holdings characteristically provided the greater part, about two thirds, of the rent income, but it is more than likely that the lands of the customary tenants accounted for an even greater proportion of the total area of the priory estate in Alvington.[2]

Other 'manors', so-called, were more artificial creations, being

[1] This figure is based on the gross annual value, as set down in the *Valor Ecclesiasticus*, ed. J. Caley and Jos. Hunter, 1810–34, of all the monastic lands in the county, irrespective of the location of the monastery to which they belonged, allowing for regular deductions such as manorial bailiffs' fees and clerical stipends, but not for the fees of the higher administrative officers nor for charitable disbursements. For a discussion of the value of the *Valor*, see *infra*, pp. 324–5.

[2] J. A. Raftis, *The Estates of Ramsey Abbey*, 1957, pp. 20–1; *Valor Eccles.*, IV, pp. 271–5; II, p. 426.

composed of scattered tenements, accumulated piecemeal over the years by gift and purchase, and grouped together for convenience of administration. The 'manor' of Pilton in north Devon comprised most of the resources of the small priory there, and was made up of dozens of farms, parts of farms, and semi-urban tenements, scattered around at least eight local parishes. Rather more compact was the 'manor' of Canonbury, a collection of tenements belonging to St Augustine's Abbey, Bristol, mostly lying within the bounds of the large lay lordship of Berkeley and gathered piecemeal over the years. It included a portion of demesne, and the abbot held a court. Syon Abbey in Middlesex derived part of its income, a mere 68s., from a dozen freehold rents in the Devon parish of Washfield. Here was no demesne and the abbess did not hold a court, but she did claim the sole right of granting licences to fish that part of the river Exe which runs through the parish, and also profits arising from waifs, strays, felons' and fugitives' goods.[1]

Rather more organic in their composition than the agglomerations of odd rents were the numerous monastic estates which had originated with the gift of a parish church, with its glebe and its tithes and other parochial revenues, and which had been augmented over the years by gifts and purchases of nearby property. Such estates, which were of course at this time owned only by the Church, were to be found in all parts of the country. Their characteristic feature was that the income from tithes usually greatly exceeded that from land rents or demesne farming. In such cases while the monastery was far from being the principal landowner in the parish, as owner of the tithes it was deeply involved in local farming operations. No form of income could be closer to the actual yield of the soil. Out of every ten stooks of corn, every ten new lambs, every ten gallons of milk, every ten loads of hay, or apples, nine were a man's own. The tenth belonged to the Church, and, in a very large number of cases, this meant a monastic house, near at hand or at a distance.[2]

Equally characteristic of monastic estates up and down the country were the great tracts of land known as 'granges' and associated particularly with houses of the Cistercian order. Little attention has been paid to these outside Yorkshire, but hundreds of them can be identified up and down the country. Granges normally consisted of enclosed demesne land, arable or pasture, sometimes running into

[1] E 318, 946, 180, 945; A. Sabin, *Some Manorial Accounts of Saint Augustine's Abbey, Bristol*, Bristol Rec. Soc., XXII, 1960, pp. 147–54; PRO SC 11, 164.

[2] R. H Hilton, *The Economic Development of Some Leicestershire Estates*, 1947, pp. 36–7, and VCH *Leics.*, II, p. 171; J. S. Purvis, *Select Sixteenth Century Causes in Tithe*, Yorks. Arch. Soc., Rec. Ser., CXIV, 1949, *passim*.

hundreds of acres, and unencumbered by ancient customary tenures. Many of them lay adjacent to or within a few miles of the house to which they belonged. Sibton Abbey, a small Suffolk house, possessed at least half a dozen of these enclosed farms, containing nearly three thousand acres in all, the two largest, South Grange and North Grange, in the parish of Sibton itself, comprising 963 and 818 acres respectively. Fountains Abbey possessed at least a score of granges, some of them a considerable distance from the abbey. As one would expect these granges were particularly numerous in the old enclosed south-western counties, where they were known as 'bartons'. Hartland Abbey in Devon, for instance, situated in the parish of Stoke St Nectan, possessed not only the large manor of Stoke but also Stoke Barton. This large home farm, still identifiable today, consisted of over five hundred acres of land divided into about twenty-five 'closes', some of which, for instance Southdown Close, Langland Close, and Putshole Close, extended to over fifty acres each.[1] On these great farms the monks had enjoyed exclusive occupation at a very early date. Their character is best appreciated when one compares them with the demesne of many Midland monasteries, scattered abroad, or only partially consolidated, among the strips of open fields. Newnham Priory in Bedford, for example, according to a rental of 1506-7, possessed over three hundred acres of demesne, three and a half acres in Conduit Field, seventy-two acres in Middle Field, one hundred and thirty acres in Bury Field, and 114 acres in East Field. A further seventy-two acres purchased by the priory as recently as 1502-3 also lay in strips, subject probably to a rigid customary routine. The demesne of De La Pré Abbey, North-amptonshire, when surveyed by the royal commissioners in June 1539, was found to consist of forty-six acres of meadow, only eight of which were "severell all the yere," sixty-six acres of pasture, partly enclosed and partly open, and over one hundred and seventy acres of arable land, nearly all of which lay in the East Field and West Field of Hardingstone. At Canons Ashby in the same county the demesne pasture, 153 acres, lay in closes, but the whole of the demesne arable, 341 acres, lay in the open fields. The nuns at Catesby had over two hundred and fifty acres of enclosed pasture and shared a further 535 acres with their tenants. Of their one hundred and sixty acres of arable land, all but seven acres lay open.[2]

[1] T. A. M. Bishop, 'Monastic Granges in Yorkshire', EHR, LI, 1936; A. H. Denney, *The Sibton Abbey Estates. Select Documents*, Suffolk Rec. Soc., II, 1960, p. 148; *Valor Eccles.*, v, p. 253; E 315, 215, f. 4. For the derivation of the word 'barton', see H. P. R. Finberg, *Tavistock Abbey*, 1951, p. 49.

[2] B. Crook and W. N. Henman, *Rentals of Bedford Priory*, Beds. Rec. Soc., 1947, pp. 15–103; E 315, 399, ff. 118, 126, 120.

In spite of much judicious purchasing and exchange of lands, few monasteries possessed compact estates. A good deal of the dispersal was, or had once been, convenient for intermanorial husbandry, but in many cases possession of remote properties can have been convenient only for peripatetic abbots. A map plotting every part of the monastic estate would show some eight hundred overlapping networks, some reaching out across several counties. The nuns of Canonsleigh in Devon owned property in East Anglia. Studley Priory, Warwickshire, had to send for part of its revenues to Devon. Neighbouring estates, on the other hand, belonged to different houses. Sherborne Abbey, Dorset, owned the Devon manor of Littleham-and-Exmouth, while the adjoining manors of East Budleigh and Otterton belonged to Syon Abbey, Middlesex. So great was the dispersal, however, that of few localities anywhere in the kingdom can it be said that the interests of monastic landlords predominated over those of the laity.

(c) Monastic estate management

(i) *The early decades of the sixteenth century.* The pattern of late medieval estate management, monastic, episcopal, capitular, as well as lay, is familiar enough in its broad outlines. With whatever sizeable estate one is concerned, at some point, usually during the century 1350–1450, large-scale demesne farming operations ceased, land hitherto in hand was let, piecemeal or *en bloc*, to peasant farmers, labour services due from customary holdings were commuted, and the landlord became a *rentier*.[1] By 1500 the economic conditions which had been largely responsible for these almost universal developments were fast disappearing. The energetic landowner sought wherever possible to take land in hand, either to farm himself or to create new tenancies for shorter terms and with a higher cash yield. Monastic records for the reign of Henry VII are few, and fewer still have been intensively studied, so all conclusions about monastic reactions to the new possibilities must be very tentative. No religious house has yet been found pursuing a really aggressive policy of resumption. Canterbury Cathedral Priory probably enjoyed the rule of one of the most enlightened superiors of his age in Thomas Goldston II (1495–1517). But all the demesnes of the priory except one had been let out as early as 1411 and in the middle of the fifteenth century leases had been regularly made for terms of up to ninety years. From about 1470 the terms of new and renewed leases became much shorter but there was

---

[1] R. A. L. Smith, *Canterbury Cathedral Priory*, 1943, pp. 192–4, 200; E. M. Halcrow, 'The decline of demesne farming on the estates of Durham Cathedral Priory', EcHR, 2nd Ser., VII, 1955, pp. 345–56; R. H. Hilton, *The Economic Development of some Leicestershire Estates*, pp. 88–94.

no apparent revival of interest in active farming. In the west country, by contrast, the retreat from demesne had not gone quite so far by 1500. Lacock Abbey in Wiltshire had leased out very few of its manorial demesnes by 1476. Thereafter the process continued, slowly but steadily, with no noticeable change of policy in the early Tudor period. Some time before 1517 the great East Farm at Chittern was leased, with the abbey flock of fifteen hundred sheep. There followed a lull until 1527–33 when extensive leasing took place, and by 1535 all the demesnes were let except those in Lacock itself. At Tavistock Abbey as late as 1497 the demesnes of four manors were still in hand. One of these, at Werrington, was let for the first time in 1500, and another, at Morwell, in 1501. This time-lag was not due to sheer west-country inertia, for more than once during the preceding century the abbey had embarked on a policy of converting arable land to pasture on its large demesne farm at Hurdwick, arriving by the early Tudor period at a situation in which a stable balance between arable and pastoral farming had been achieved. The leases of Werrington and Morwell were made only for the comparatively short terms of forty and twenty years respectively. This was prudent but hardly energetic estate management.[1]

Signs are not lacking however that some monasteries in other parts of the country, not long after the turn of the century, were reclaiming part of their arrented demesnes. For example, accounts relating to the estates of Oseney Abbey, Oxford, for a number of years between 1507 and 1520, show that each year more land formerly leased was taken in hand. On the manor of Weston, in 1509–10, demesne lately farmed by John Cocks for £6 was reserved for the abbot's husbandry. This represented an estate of at least sixty acres and probably much more. At Turkdean, pasture for one hundred and sixty sheep, summer and winter, was let for 40s., but only for as long as it was not required by the abbot. At Hampton Gay, pasture for two hundred and forty sheep which the abbey had previously leased for 20s. was kept in hand this year. All this meant, of course, forgoing rents. At Walton this amounted to 40s. previously paid for cattle and sheep pasture, and the abbot put it on record that the herbage of a meadow called Kingsmead, now in hand, used to be sold for £13 13s. 4d., suggesting that even he was not sure how long this new policy was going to last. In 1520–1 the abbey thought better of it and sold the herbage, for only £5 18s.

It will be noticed that it was mostly pasture land that Oseney took in hand. The steward's accounts show that in 1507–8 twenty sacks of wool were sold to "Mr Audelet" of Abingdon, part at £6 13s. 4d. a sack and the rest at £7 6s. 8d., a total of £142 13s. 4d. Nearly half this

[1] Smith, op. cit., pp. 192–200; VCH Wilts., III, pp. 312–3; Finberg, op. cit., pp. 256–7, 253, 258.

wool, however, had been purchased by the abbey, possibly from tenants. Two years later total sales fell to £91 15s. 8d. The price and the abbey production remained about the same but less had been bought. In 1520–1 only nine sacks were sold, but John Busby of Burford paid £9 2s. per sack. Here, unfortunately, the accounts end, but they are enough to suggest that the monks at Oseney were not altogether lacking in enterprise. In 1530 and 1532, according to a list among the state papers, wool for export to Calais was coming not only from Oseney but also from Bruern Abbey in the same county, from Cirencester, Gloucester, Winchcombe, Hailes, Pershore, Evesham, Llantony, and Bordesley further west, and from Canons Ashby in Northamptonshire. Not all of this was necessarily from the abbeys' own flocks: some will have been collected from tenants, either by purchase or in rent or tithe.[1] There are indications, however, that pastoral farming was being carried out on a considerable scale by a number of monasteries during the first two decades of the sixteenth century. On the estates of Norwich Cathedral Priory expansion was impressive, from one flock of about one thousand sheep in 1475 to eight flocks numbering nearly eight thousand five hundred sheep in 1515. In 1521 the abbess of Wilton paid to one Richard Thurston over £180's worth of wool, presumably from the abbey's own flocks, for vestments, and even at Tavistock the marketing of wool, although it was never on a large scale, never actually ceased during the early sixteenth century. During the first two decades of the century it varied between two hundred and fifty and four hundred fleeces and between fifty and one hundred lambs' fleeces a year. But at Tavistock conversion to pastoral farming was never carried to extremes, and receipts from the sales of corn, largely oats, usually equalled those from pastoral farming.[2]

Sibton Abbey in Suffolk, having leased out most of its demesne, retained half of North Grange, and established there, in or before 1507, a new dairy farm. Katherine Dowe was in charge, with four other women as her assistants, and the abbey kitchener travelled to Norwich and Stourbridge to purchase additions to the stock. There were sixty-six cows in 1507, rising to one hundred and forty by 1513. The main product was cheese, over half a wey per cow, as well as considerable quantities of butter, milk, and also cream. In their spare time the dairy-maids wove woollen and linen cloth and looked after pigs, geese,

[1] H. E. Salter, *Cartulary of Oseney Abbey*, vi, Oxford Hist. Soc., CL, 1936, pp. 208 *sqq.*; LP *Addenda*, I, pt. i, pp. 244, 320.
[2] K. J. Allison, 'Flock Management in the Sixteenth and Seventeenth Centuries', EcHR, 2nd Ser., XI, 1958, p. 100; VCH *Wilts.*, III, p. 237; Finberg, *op. cit.*, pp. 150, 145, 148–9, 157.

chickens, and ducks. In the accounts an attempt was made to show a profit, which rose from £29 in 1507 to £45 in 1513. In fact, the 'sales' were to the abbey guest house and the abbot's stables, but since trouble was taken to enter up market prices it suggests at least an attempt to discover whether the project could pay its way.[1] The interest in careful purchasing is noteworthy at a time when most of the smaller houses were less particular about the way in which they augmented their stock. There is, for instance, evidence from many houses of stock being accepted in payment for corrodies. These involved contracts between laymen and the monasteries whereby the latter undertook to provide the former with board and lodging for their lives. In 1518 John and Agnes Hudson surrendered to Esholt Priory, Yorkshire, thirteen cattle, three calves, forty sheep, six wethers, thirty-four lambs, and 20s. in cash, in return for their maintenance. This must have been a considerable addition to the stock of the small priory. John died shortly afterwards, but Agnes was still alive, aged 80, in 1536, enjoying the nuns' hospitality.[2]

One would very much like to know whether the produce of the Sibton dairy was at any time sent to market. The Tavistock Abbey accounts, which are more complete, show a modest but regular sale of from thirty to fifty stones of cheese and from a dozen to fifteen stones of butter each year, right down to the eve of the abbey's dissolution.[3] But the home farm, part arable, part pastoral, was a normal adjunct to the life of any religious community, and it was a far cry from marketing small surpluses to embarking on a deliberate policy of large-scale farming for the market. Only where there is a record of intensive sheep-farming can one safely assume that the monks had their eyes on the expanding market. An increased demesne production of crops and meat and dairy products may only point to an enlarged conventual household, and we know that the number of monks and nuns, and with them their household servants, reached a high level in the 1520's.[4] Moreover, too much must not be expected of the monasteries in an age when their lay neighbours were only just beginning to take the initiative. Demesne farming on any appreciable scale raised problems of the recruitment of lay labour and the developing of entrepreneurial talent within the community, as well as those of resuming fields and pastures. In fact, had the internal life of the monastic communities been of a higher standard during these years, the monks might have been commended for continuing to turn their backs on the outside world. There was also the administrative factor. The widespread

[1] Denney, *op. cit.*, pp. 37–9, 141–4.   [2] Woodward, *op. cit.*, pp. 78–9.
[3] Finberg, *op. cit.*, pp. 135–44.
[4] D. Knowles, *The Religious Orders in England*, III, 1959, pp. 256–7.

attachment to the obedientary system was hardly conducive to agrarian enterprise. Each official was allocated certain sources of revenue, or, in the case of those responsible for catering, of produce. If his sources were inadequate, he merely asked that they be augmented. Within his restricted sphere there was little room for enterprise. Only the abbot would be likely to show any initiative. Hence it was in those abbeys where a centralized financial system persisted, as at Oseney, that interest in marketing possibilities was more likely to emerge.

In 1529 a statute was passed curtailing monastic commercial activities, especially in the larger houses. The monks were in future to confine themselves to supplying the needs of their own households and of their guests. There must have been some excuse for parliamentary action, but the object of the legislation was probably merely to irritate.[1] It seems unlikely that laymen were either genuinely afraid of monastic competition or concerned about monks wasting time on worldly pursuits. There was, in fact, no apparent outcry by the victims, nothing comparable with the cries of woe which went up from abbots who, very soon after, were prohibited from leaving the precincts of their houses. By 1529, in fact, as far as most houses were concerned, the legislation was out of date. The evidence so far available points to the years 1505–25 as the period of monastic agrarian enterprise. Thereafter, with a few exceptions, the general picture is one of steady retreat.[2]

More important on a long-term view than commercial ventures was the energy being expended by the monks in improving their land, either by drainage or by reclaiming it from the marsh. The work of the priors of Canterbury in reclaiming Appledore marsh is already well known. Recently some details have come to light of the progress made by St Augustine's Abbey, Bristol, in extending its lands at Almondsbury in Gloucestershire by draining the marshy banks of the river Severn. Initial operations were complete by 1500, but in the following decades the new pastures demanded constant expert attention. Until the 1520's special *appruatores* were appointed for this work. The new lands fetched high rents but most of the increased income went on maintenance. Similar evidence may yet emerge from other parts of the country. Very probably, however, it will be found that most houses which were interested at all in improving their land preferred to let their tenants do it for them. At Haseley in Warwick-

---

[1] *Statutes of the Realm*, III, pp. 292–6. The statute of 1533–4 (*ibid.*, pp. 453–4) which prohibited individuals from keeping more than 2,400 sheep, exempted from its provisions not only all flocks kept for household purposes but also those of "spiritual persons," a clear contradiction of the act of 1529.

[2] Relying largely on the *Valor Ecclesiasticus*, Professor Knowles (*op. cit.*, p. 250) does not admit of any revival of monastic high farming in the early sixteenth century.

shire, for instance, in 1523, the prior of Wroxall leased a messuage, three crofts, and a grove to Richard Shakespeare and Richard Wood-ham for twenty-five years, on condition that they eradicated all briars, brambles, thorns, and underwood, and prepared the ground for arable or pasture farming, leaving it well-enclosed and fenced at the end of the term. The term was not a long one, but long enough to encourage the tenants to take trouble over effecting improvements and offering to the abbey the prospect of cashing in on the improved value at a not-too-distant date.[1]

Finally there must be included under the general heading of improve-ments some mention of enclosure. It is now generally agreed that the greater part of the most ruthless enclosure, involving the depopulation of whole villages, took place before 1485. And certainly all that is known of monastic activity in this direction bears this out, and under-lines the point already made that the monks were not incapable of energetic action. A good deal of enclosure was no doubt effected quite peaceably by arrangement with tenants and neighbours. But there is also sufficient evidence of the kind of enclosure which led to depopulation of the countryside to justify Sir Thomas More's "yea and certain abbotts, holy men no doubt..." In Leicestershire, the county for which we have the most comprehensive information, the monastic houses appear to have played a part at least commensurate with their share of the county's landed wealth. Leicester Abbey itself, having first acquired the manor of Ingarsby in 1352, added gradually to its lands there and carried through the complete enclosure of some 1,152 acres in 1469. In 1500–1 the process was repeated at Baggrave, north of Ingarsby, where 216 acres of arable land were converted to pasture and a year later this new 'grange' was extended by the acquisition of adjoining lands by exchange. Leicester's example was followed by Launde Priory, which, partly by exchanges and partly by purchase, managed to extend its control over the village fields of Whatborough, which it then proceeded to enclose and depopulate. Other notorious enclosers were Garendon Abbey, Langley Priory, Croxton, and Kirby Bellars. Generally speaking, in their engrossing of tenements, their encroach-ment on commons, and their conversion of much land to pasture, there is little to distinguish the monasteries from their lay neighbours, except that they had done it all before, and that the monastic enclosures of the late fifteenth and early sixteenth centuries simply added to the granges and bartons with which the monks had long been familiar. There were, incidentally, the odd occasions when the monks, in this

<hr/>

[1] Smith, *op. cit.*, pp. 203–4; Sabin, *op. cit.*, pp. 133 *sqq.*; W. B. Bickley, *Bailiffs' Accounts of Monastic and other Estates in the County of Warwick*, Dugdale Soc., 1923, p. 20.

matter of enclosure, were on the side of the angels. In or about 1509 Thomas Walshe, prior of Bradenstoke, Wiltshire, accused one of his tenants, John Anne, lessee of the priory's manor of North Aston for a term of thirty-three years commencing in 1485, of enclosing some 142 acres out of a total arable of three hundred acres, resulting, he alleged, in the decay of twelve houses and seven ploughs.[1]

Contemporary opinion of the monks as *rentiers* was somewhat divided. In the late 1520's they were the objects of much popular denunciation, especially as raisers of rents:

> Wheare a farme for xx *li.* was sett
> Under xxx they wolde not it lett,
> Raysynge it vp on so hye a some
> That many a good husholder
> Constrayned to geve his farme over
> To extreme beggary did come.[2]

Charges of extortionate practices were regularly brought against them in the court of Star Chamber. For example, the abbot of Fountains was accused of refusing to accept rent from one of his leasehold tenants in order to effect his eviction.[3] But the evidence from their accounts, indentures of leases, etc., is quite overwhelming. The early Tudor monks were not increasing their regular rents to any appreciable extent. Irrespective of their relation to the real value of the land, the "old and accustomed" rents were normally reserved at the renewal of tenancies, including leaseholds. Occasionally rent increases were made in renewing leases of demesne land. For instance, the rent of Staunton Grange was twice raised by Garendon Abbey, Leicestershire, between 1500 and its dissolution, first from £4 13s. 4d. to £8, and then, in 1529, to £12. The same abbey raised its rents from three other granges during the same period by over 50 per cent. Far more often, however, even rents for demesne land remained unchanged over a long period. In 1489 St Augustine's Abbey, Bristol, leased the chief messuage of its manor of Roborough, comprising buildings, land, and woods, to William Harris and John Squire, and John's wife, Joan, for sixty years determinable on their lives, at a rent of 60s. Nearly forty years later, in 1527, the property was leased to John and Margaret Backewell and their son John for their lives at the same rent.[4]

[1] I. S. Leadam, *The Domesday of Inclosures, 1517–18, passim;* W. G. Hoskins, 'The Deserted Villages of Leicestershire', *Essays in Leicestershire History*, 1950, pp. 75, 80, 105; VCH *Wilts.*, III, pp. 285–6.

[2] TED, III, pp. 20–1.

[3] J. Lister, *Yorkshire Star Chamber Proceedings*, iv, Yorks. Arch. Soc., Rec. Ser., LXX, 1927, pp. 1–3.

[4] Thorpe, *op. cit.*, p. 47; Sabin, *op. cit.*, pp. 31–2, 194.

The increased value of land at this period, whether customary or leasehold, was reflected, if at all, not in rents but in entry fines. Information on this score for the very early decades of the sixteenth century is, however, very scrappy. The amount of the fine, and we can take it for granted that a fine was always paid at the commencement or renewal of a tenancy, was rarely recorded in rentals or in the indentures of leases. Tenants often claimed in the course of court actions that they had paid heavy fines. For example, John Clerke of Loddiswell, Devon, pleaded in Chancery that on the 1st of June 1523 he had paid to the prior of Studley, Warwickshire, £9 for the reversion of forty acres of land in Loddiswell, to himself, his wife, and their son, for their lives. But he had not been able to get his lease put into writing. If this was the same land which he subsequently held by a lease dated 1530 at a rent of 10s., then indeed he had paid considerably more than the fine of two years' rent which contemporaries apparently regarded as reasonable. Court rolls provide some details of fines for copyholdings. At the manor court of the abbess of Syon at Yarcombe, Devon, held in September 1527, fines totalling more than £40 were recorded. These were payable in instalments over a number of years, an indication that they were regarded as additions to the regular manorial income. Christopher and John Hellier agreed to pay £13 6s. 8d. for the reversion, for their lives, of two furlongs of land then in the tenure of their father, Thomas Hellier. The next entry concerns Alice Hellier, who was to pay £8 for a lease of half a virgate. By contrast John Gardiner paid only 40s. for the reversion of four closes of barton land, to hold for the lives of himself and his two sons after the death of the present tenant. The relatively low fine can probably be accounted for by the barton land being let at a more economic rent.[1] A great deal more information from many parts of the country is needed before any firm conclusion can be reached about the extent to which entry fines were being levied to offset low rents in the early decades of the sixteenth century. But the information so far available goes some way to counter the other contemporary belief, current after the Dissolution, that the monks were easy-going landlords. Professor Knowles, in dealing with the overall monastic budget, has drawn attention to the apparent ease with which abbots who wished to rebuild or to embellish conventual buildings were able to lay their hands on large sums of ready cash.[2] It would be interesting, if the necessary accounts and court rolls were available, to collate monastic building activity, of which there was a great deal in the early Tudor period, with the renewal of tenancies. It was the same type of masterful, energetic, abbot who embarked on

[1] C 1, 623, 23 and E 318, 1390, m. 5; Devon RO, 346M/M2.
[2] Knowles, op. cit., pp. 22, 252–3, 259.

ambitious building schemes who would discover ways and means of applying pressure on his tenants.

Reference to court rolls raises the question of the difference between customary and leasehold tenure. In theory the lease was a form of grant entered into by two freely contracting parties, their agreement involving no customary obligations and recorded in indentures sealed by both parties. This remained the legal theory, but when the contents of some of the monastic indentures are examined it is very difficult to see how their conditions differed in practice from those of copyhold grants. Of the dozens of surviving indentures of leases made by the abbots of Buckland in Devon during the fifteenth and early sixteenth century, nearly all bind the lessee to pay suit of court twice a year, and mill-suit, and also to perform harvest work, and carry out repairs to weirs, fisheries, mills, etc. They were also all bound to pay 2d. a year "geld", and heriots. Similar conditions have been found in conventual leases from many other west country houses, and also in Warwickshire. Dr Hilton found them in Gloucester Abbey leases for lives in the late thirteenth century and concluded that they resulted from conversions from old customary tenures. There was a case on the lands of Tilty Abbey, Essex, of an expressly double tenure. On Easter Saturday 1487 at a court at Tilty, in the abbot's presence, John Pampheton of Great Easton, husbandman, was granted some land by copy of court roll and for a rent of 40s., the term being unspecified; and at the same time, at John's request and without impairing his copyhold, he was given a lease of the property at the same rent, on condition that he paid suit at Tilty, kept his fences in repair, etc., and John had the right to alienate or sell or assign the property at death, provided that the lands were not divided.[1] In their conversion from customary to leasehold tenure the monks and their tenants clearly had a foot in what lawyers regarded as two completely different worlds.

Monastic policy with regard to the length of terms of leases varied to such an extent during this period that it is impracticable to write of "long" and "short" terms. Terms of forty years were "long", apparently, in Leicestershire and Huntingdonshire.[2] But monasteries in other parts of the country were regularly granting tenancies for terms as long as ninety years during the greater part of the fifteenth century and right down to the Dissolution. Buckland Abbey in Devon granted

[1] Plymouth RO, Roborough MSS., 126–52, 180–6, 206, 214–17, 247–59; Finberg, *op. cit.*, pp. 249–51; Bickley, *op. cit.*, *passim;* R. H. Hilton, 'Gloucester Abbey Leases of the Late Thirteenth Century', *Univ. Birmingham Hist. J.*, III, ii, 1952, pp. 9–14; W. C. Wallen, 'Tilty Abbey', *Essex Arch. Soc.*, New Ser., IX, 1904–5, pp. 118–22.

[2] R. H. Hilton, VCH *Leics.*, II, p. 195; Raftis, *op. cit.*, p. 291, n. 19.

leases for sixty, seventy, and even ninety years, from the 1430's. In 1486 the abbot leased to Richard Talbot, his son Philip, and Philip's wife, Joan, a farm at Gnatham in Walkhampton for seventy years at a rent of 66s. 8d. The farm was still held by Joan, widow of Philip Talbot, at the same rent, in 1538, when a reversionary lease was granted to John and Agnes Servington on the same terms. At Dunkeswell Abbey, at the other side of the county, during the same period, leases for lives, those of two, three, and four members of a family, were the rule. But up at Hartland, in north Devon, when John Heard, tenant of a farm called South Chaladon, tried to persuade the abbot to add his son's life to those of his own and his wife's, the abbot said he would not do it, even for £20, for none of his tenants had terms of more than two lives.[1]

Leases for lives were frequently surrendered before the lessees had died, so that, for a consideration, a new life or lives might be added. Many of the longer leases for terms of years were also surrendered long before they expired, usually at the death of the lessee. A reversionary interest had usually already been created. For example, in 1531 the prior of Bridlington leased to Isabel Tunstall, widow, the rectory of Fraystrop for sixty years. In 1536 he granted a lease of the property in reversion to Brian Tunstall, also for sixty years, to date from Isabel's death.[2] It is possible that no term of years was regarded as secure, and, indeed, although the law decided in favour of the tenant for years in 1499, the lease for years remained a chattel interest only, unlike a lease for life, which was a form of real property.[3] Hence, it would appear that Buckland Abbey, in spite of the length of its terms, was being less generous than Dunkeswell, and that the changeover at Tavistock Abbey in 1517, from leases for forty years to leases for lives,[4] marked a victory for the tenants. A number of the long monastic leases for term of years were, in fact, expressly determinable on lives. This type of lease is usually thought to have made its appearance in the later sixteenth century, but examples are to be found over a century earlier among monastic leases. The lease by St. Augustine's Abbey, Bristol, in 1489, of its demesne at Roborough, even has the phrase so familiar later on, "si tam diu vixerint seu unus eorum vixerit," but at this period there was more often the rather clumsy provision that if all the named lives expired within the specified term of years, the tenement

[1] Plymouth RO, Roborough MSS, *passim* and 252, 261; Exeter City RO, DD. 22593–22734; E 321 12, 98.

[2] J. S. Purvis, *A Selection of Monastic Records and Dissolution Papers*, Yorks. Arch. Soc., Rec. Ser., LXXX, 1931, pp. 7–10.

[3] W. S. Holdsworth, *Historical Introduction to the Land Law*, 1927, pp. 71–3.

[4] Finberg, *op. cit.*, p. 250.

would revert to the grantor.[1] It was a type of lease which, carrying a life interest, had obvious attractions for the tenant. In 1530 Robert Howe, who already held a number of properties at Cullompton on leases from the abbot of Buckland for terms of seventy and eighty years, took yet another piece of land from the monastery, this time for eighty years determinable on five lives. All the life-tenants had to be living already, of course, but this sounds like a very good bargain on Howe's side and suggests a weakening on the part of the abbey.[2] The whole subject needs further study, but it seems likely that when later Tudor lay landlords, seeking to convert their copyholdings, turned to the lease for years determinable on lives, they were following an example already set on west-country monastic estates.[3]

Reference has already been made to the payment of monastic rents in kind. There is no sign of any tendency towards their commutation in the early sixteenth century: rather were they on the increase. They were, of course, a splendid cushion against inflation, every bit as effective as demesne farming, as well as being useful to abbots who liked to spend part of the year at their outlying manor houses. In 1504-5 the garnerer of Christ Church Priory, Canterbury, gathered in nearly seven hundred quarters of corn from food-farms, leaving less than one hundred quarters to be purchased that year. In 1521-2 the under-cellarer of Worcester Priory took delivery of over three hundred quarters of grain from leasehold and customary tenants. A lease made by Coventry Priory in 1533 provided that the rent, eight quarters of corn and twenty of barley, was to be drawn from the best grain grown by the tenant, or was to be bought at Coventry market.[4] That rents in kind were to the monks' advantage is confirmed by the fact that indentures of leases usually provided for future commutation, at the lessor's option. It was a particularly convenient arrangement when demesne hitherto in hand was being leased, perpetuating the arrangement whereby the demesnes provided the main source of supply for the abbey household. It was also convenient that when the monks ceased to cultivate any part of their estate for themselves, demesne stock and implements should be handed over to the lessee as part of the contract, to be returned in kind at the termination of the lease. Bath Abbey leased its grange at Launcedon, part of the manor of Weston, with a stock of eighteen oxen, ten cows, five yearlings, five

[1] *Supra*, p. 417, n. 4; Bickley, *op. cit.*, pp. 59–61.
[2] Exeter RO, DD. 22505.
[3] W. G. Hoskins, *Devon*, 1954, p. 91; R. B. Pugh, *Antrobus Deeds before 1625*, Wilts. Arch. & Nat. Hist. Soc., Records Branch, III, 1947, p. xl; I. P. Collis, 'Leases for Term of Years determinable with lives', *J. Soc. Archivists*, I, 1957, pp. 168–71.
[4] Smith, *op. cit.*, p. 201; J. M. Wilson, *Account of Worcester Priory, 1521-2*, Worcs. Hist. Soc., 1907, p. 6; Bickley, *op. cit.*, p. 59.

calves, and other stock appertaining to husbandry, for an annual rent of fifty-two quarters of wheat, seventy quarters of barley, five quarters of oats, six loads of hay, four loads of straw, and the feeding of two fat oxen from St Martin's Day to Holy Cross. For a further rent of £20 2s. 6d. the farmer also leased the abbey flock of 440 wethers and 540 ewes. The actual amount of produce rent was usually fixed in the indentures, but when, in 1500, Tavistock Abbey leased its demesne and stock at Werrington to its bailiff, for forty years at a rent of £3 and thirty-two quarters of wheat and all the cheese produced on the manor, there was also a proviso that if the price of wheat varied the rent should be adjusted accordingly. In 1529 a new agreement was made whereby the rent was raised to £8 and the wheat reduced to twenty quarters.[1] Not all 'stock and land' leases were accompanied by rents in kind, nor, of course, do rents in kind necessarily imply the initial provision of stock. But where both were present it seems fairly clear that here was a very convenient arrangement with the advantages equally balanced between both parties.

Another regular source of provisions for the monastic households was tithe. In fact, in the case of some houses whose resources included a good deal of 'spiritual' income, collection of all of it in kind would have embarrassed the abbey kitchens. In any case, transport from distant parishes was expensive. The most common practice seems to have been to sell the tithes from year to year, to local dealers. Leasing, too, was commonly resorted to, but usually for short terms, perhaps from five years to five years, rarely more than ten or twelve, and occasionally for one life. St Augustine's Abbey, Bristol, made new contracts each year, falling back on leases only in the later 1520's.[2]

By and large the early Tudor monks did not lease out their manors in their entirety and in fact this period probably saw the reversal of earlier tendencies in this direction. The usual pattern was to retain the seigneurial rights, including the manor court, in hand, let out the demesne or chief messuage to a farmer, and retain a bailiff to collect the rents and deal with repairs. Bailiff and farmer were very often one and the same. Thereby the monks retained full control over the granting of tenancies and collected the fines. In a number of cases they also retained the manorial sheepwalks long after they had let out the demesne arable land, or at least made an arrangement with the farmer

---

[1] PRO SC 6, Henry VIII, 3144, m. 17 and E 321, 6, 97; Finberg, *op. cit.*, p. 99. Savine (*op. cit.*, pp. 164–5) associates food-rents, even from demesne, with "a certain lack of progress to be observed in the monastic economy," and is followed by Dr Finberg (*op. cit.*, p. 241). Their advantages were rediscovered, however, by many lay landowners during the period of inflation later in the sixteenth century.

[2] Sabin, *op. cit.*, *passim*.

for the continued pasturing of the abbey flocks. Sometimes the farmer undertook to manage the stock as part of his 'rent', and in that case he accounted for sales of wool, etc., in his manorial account. Winchcombe Abbey leased its arable demesne at Sherborne in Gloucestershire as early as 1464, but must have reserved the pasture, for in 1485 nearly three thousand of its sheep were collected there for washing and shearing. As late as 1535 the demesnes of the abbey manor of Frampton were still in hand in their entirety, and at Snowshill, Hawling, and Charlton Abbots pastures were still in hand although the rest of the demesnes had been leased.[1]

Finally, even when the last of the pasture had been let, there were the woods, which were always reserved by the monastic landlords. A typical provision was that made in a lease by Wroxall Priory, Warwickshire, on the 1st of April 1529, whereby three acres of land were let for thirty-two years. The farmers were expressly forbidden to fell any timber growing on the premises but they were permitted to "lop and crop the same, according to the custom of the manor there, for repairs to the fence and hedge."[2] Monastic estates were well provided with timber, continuity of ownership having resulted in greater conservation than elsewhere. Wood sales brought in welcome supplies of ready cash and were always negotiated under the direct supervision of the abbots themselves. Bailiffs disposed only of fallen timber and underwood.

It is, of course, a well-known fact that laymen were employed in great numbers by the monasteries as stewards, auditors, receivers, and manorial bailiffs. But it would be a great mistake to assume that the monks thereby relieved themselves of worldly cares. Not even unpleasant tasks were delegated to laymen. It was the monk treasurer of Garendon Priory in Leicestershire who informed the tenants at Dishley that they were no longer to enjoy common rights there on land which the priory had enclosed. At Merevale Abbey, too, a house which was still deeply involved in sheepfarming in the early sixteenth century, the movement of flocks from one grange to another was organized by the monk treasurer. In 1535 the abbot of Glastonbury, in a letter to Thomas Cromwell, explained that leases made "at a courte and letten by copie of the courte roll" were always arranged "by on(e) of the religion and ceculer men appoynted to hym." Incidentally he adds, in defence against the very common charge that leases were being made without the consent of the whole convent, "if they schuld made no leese but by assent of the more parte of the covent, it

[1] R. H. Hilton, 'Winchcombe Abbey and the Manor of Sherborne', *Gloucestershire Studies*, ed. H. P. R. Finberg, 1957, pp. 110 *sqq.; Valor Eccles.*, II, pp. 456-7.

[2] Bickley, *op. cit.*, p. 18.

schuld be verie tedyous bothe to them and to ther tenauntes."[1] In fact, lay officers were for the most part either servants, responsible to the monks and accountable to them for their day-to-day duties, or sine-curists, being men of some influence in lay society who were retained by the monks for what the monks called their 'counsel'. It seems unlikely that either group dictated monastic agricultural policy.

The regular fees to be earned as manorial bailiffs will have augmented many a peasant farmer's income, but it was as lessees of the abbey lands that laymen, during the early sixteenth century, were making their greatest inroads into monastic landed wealth. Until we know more about the capital outlay required by way of entrance fines the question of the actual extent of their advantage must remain un-answered. It is, however, among the ranks of those farmers who were both bailiffs and lessees of the monks that we should look for the ancestors of some of the more prosperous yeomen farmers of later Tudor England.

(ii) *The last decade: 1529–39.* The late 1520's saw the end of normal economic relationships between the monks and their tenants. Between about 1527 and 1534 external pressures, especially from government circles, increased steadily, and after 1535 the floodgates were wide open. Monastic lands, acquired over many centuries, sometimes mismanaged but never before wholly despoiled, were exploited with the full legal connivance of their owners, with little thought for the future, and with a great deal of overt encouragement by the Crown and its representa-tives, at times apparently indecently anxious to allow others to anticipate its own depredations. The actual story of the Dissolution need not be retold here: it has already been related with admirable clarity else-where.[2] One point only needs to be emphasized in this context, namely that the process of confiscation was a protracted one, beginning, for all practical purposes, in the summer of 1536, but not completed until well into 1540, with the dissolution of the colleges and chantries still to follow later. What must concern us is the effect of this situation, when some houses had already fallen and others were still fully operational, on the relations of the monks with their tenants, and, more particularly, on the extent of their own farming operations.

Descriptions of the state of the monastic lands on the eve of the Dissolution so often rely entirely on the *Valor Ecclesiasticus* of 1535. This was, of course, a remarkable survey, and it is quite indispensable to the historian of monastic lands. No other record can rival its com-prehensiveness, and its compilation made the subsequent confiscation

---

[1] Thorpe, *op. cit.*, pp. 31–3; T. Wright, *Three Chapters of Letters relating to the Suppression of the Monasteries*, Camden Soc., 1843, p. 64.

[2] Knowles, *op. cit.*, chaps. xxii–xxix.

of the monastic lands by the Crown administratively possible. But for all its considerable reliability it is only a survey of current regular gross income. As has so often been demonstrated, its valuations of demesne still in hand were, to say the least, conservative.[1] But this was as much due to underestimation of the extent of the demesne as to actual undervaluation. In dealing with Studley Priory, Oxfordshire, the commissioners put it on record that demesne pasture in hand had been valued at 1s. per acre and arable at 4d.[2] This was low but resulted in figures which were almost certainly nearer the real value of the land than the bare rents which represented the customary holdings. On the other hand, the commissioners must have exaggerated the actual net income from arrented land for no allowances were made for expenditure on repairs, or for rents in arrears, both of which figure prominently in most current bailiffs' accounts. Setting the one deficiency against the other, it seems probable that the gross values of the *Valor* were not far off the mark. Its most serious limitation as a record of what passed to the Crown is that it takes no account, naturally enough, of the tenurial developments of the years 1536–9. These, however, can be very largely reconstructed from post-Dissolution records, notably the surveys made at the moment of surrender, together with the enrolments of confirmations of conventual grants.[3]

The smaller houses which were dissolved in the summer of 1536 had never farmed on any scale and their preparations to avert the crisis had been negligible. Most of them had a small domestic home farm to provide for their daily needs and in most cases this was in working order right up to the last. At the dissolution of Thremhall Priory in Essex the commissioners found there a dairy stock of six milking cows, two bullocks, and a dozen pigs. In the stable were eight cart-horses, a cart, a dung-cart, and a plough with coulter and share. In store were six bushels of wheat and a load of hay, and in standing corn, thirty-six acres of barley and fourteen of wheat. There were also thirteen sheep. Here was a small mixed farm comparable with those of the more substantial yeomen farmers of the district. At Prittlewell Priory in the same county arable fields were not mentioned but the stock was much larger than at Thremhall. There were seventeen horses in all, various cattle, including a bull, 139 sheep, and seventy-six lambs. In store were one pack and seventy-one pounds of wool, on which the commis-

---

[1] Savine, *op. cit.*, pp. 73–4, followed by Knowles, *op. cit.*, pp. 245, 312. See also A. Evans, 'Battle Abbey at the Dissolution', *Huntingdon Lib. Quart.*, IV, July 1941, pp. 393–442 and Nov. 1942, i, pp. 53–105.

[2] *Valor Eccles.*, II, p. 186.

[3] For further details of post-Dissolution sources see J. A. Youings, *Devon Monastic Lands: Particulars for Grants, 1536–58*, Devon and Cornwall Rec. Soc., New Ser., I, 1955, pp. xxxiv–xxxvii.

sioners placed a value of £4 3s. 4d. Stock and dairy farming predominated on the rest of the smaller Essex houses for which inventories
have survived. Plough and cart-horses were valued by the commissioners at prices varying between 6s. and 12s., sows at 1s. or 1s. 6d.,
and sheep about the same. In fact the variety in prices suggests that the
king's officers took a great deal of trouble, and took careful note of the
quality of the stock and of prevailing local market prices. Local men
were no doubt only too ready to proffer advice, but town and country
were not so far divorced in Tudor England that civil servants like
Richard Pollard and Sir Thomas Moyle would not be perfectly
capable, if time allowed, of distinguishing between good and poor
stock. At Sawtry in Huntingdonshire in May 1536 the commissioners
proceeded from the abbey church and domestic quarters to a forge,
where they listed a vice, hammers, tongs, and bellows, and then to the
"cart-ware," which included three shod carts, shares and coulters,
seven pairs of cart gear, eight pairs of plough-traces, a dung-cart,
roller and harrows, spades and dung-forks. Here, among the so-called
'paper surveys' of 1536, is much material for the historian of farming
gear, and a great deal of information on current local prices.[1] The
same surveys also provided in some cases lists of agricultural labourers.
At Cockersand Abbey, Lancashire, in May 1536, the commissioners
enumerated sixteen hands, including two women "winnowers of
corn." Wages ranged from 33s. 4d. for the wright down to 8s. 2d. for
the women. An odd "tasker" and a plough-driver received only
food and clothing. This seems a more than adequate labour force for a
farm whose stock amounted only to eighteen pigs, fifty-eight milking
cows, thirty heifers, forty-two bullocks, twenty-four oxen, and a
miscellaneous collection of horses. Only forty-seven acres of land was
under crop. The abbey was, in fact, reprieved until 1539. However,
according to figures given by Professor Knowles relating to seventy
of the houses dissolved in 1536, the average number of agricultural
labourers, male and female, on these smaller establishments, was
twenty.[2]

Though no one in 1536, not even the king and Cromwell, knew if,
and certainly not exactly when, the larger houses and those which had
bought exemption would ultimately surrender or be forcibly dissolved,
the acquisitive instincts of all parties, court, country, and the monasteries
themselves, except a few quite exceptional communities, now came

[1] R. C. Fowler, 'Inventories of Essex Monasteries in 1536', Essex Arch. Soc., New
Ser., x, 1909, pp. 345, 390, and passim; E 315, 402, ff. 45v–48; Knowles, op. cit.,
p. 313.
[2] W. Farrer, Chartulary of Cockersand Abbey, iii, pt. 3, Chetham Soc., New Ser.,
LXIV, 1909, pp. 1154 sqq.; Knowles, op. cit., p. 262.

into full play. Outright conveyance of monastic lands, either by gift or sale, although suspected by the Crown, was not widely detected, if indeed it took place. In any case there was little need. The process of capitalization was effected so much more easily by the granting of long leases in return for heavy fines, or, when the prospect for the monks became really black, merely in the hope of lay favour. Conventual leases from all parts of the country point to 1538 as the peak year.[1] Buckfast Abbey in Devon may not be typical, but its operations illustrate very well what was happening. Few leases for long terms were granted by the house in the early 1530's, but from 1536 Abbot Gabriel Donne became very busy with the abbey seal. Out of thirty leases made in 1538 for which details survive, thirteen were for terms of ninety-nine years, and all but three were for three or more lives or for sixty years and over. What is more important is the much fuller information now available about entry fines. For one tenement paying an annual rent of 20s. a lessee paid £40 for a lease for one life. On the other hand, for a lease for four lives at a rent of £5 4s. another tenant paid only £5 13s. 4d. For leases each of ninety-nine years' duration at rents of 19s. 3½d. and 24s. 4d. two others paid £2 and £20 respectively. The abbess of Wilton, who in 1530 and 1531 had been content with fines of one or two years' rent, was exacting five or six times the annual rents for the renewal of copyholdings for life in 1534 and 1535. In 1537 and 1538 she obtained ten, and even fifteen, times the rent. For instance, on the 29th of April 1538 Richard Ellis paid her £7 13s. 4d. for a lease of a messuage on the manor of Fugglestone in Wiltshire. This comprised nineteen acres in the open fields, two small closes, and common pasture for six cattle and fifty sheep. The rent was low, only 11s. 11d. and a cock and a hen.[2] There is absolutely no pattern and no means of discovering how these terms were made. Personal and political considerations as well as purely economic ones no doubt played a part. But there can be no doubt that many houses, or more likely their abbots, were able during the last few years to put by very considerable sums of ready money which the Crown was never able to touch. It is perhaps ironic that the Crown later paid out large sums in settlement of monastic debts.[3]

The royal agents frequently reported to Cromwell that leases had been made "unthrifftelye," i.e. at reduced rents. But only one clear

[1] PRO SC 6, Henry VIII (Ministers' Accounts of Monastic Lands), *passim.*

[2] *ibid.*, 597 and Exeter City RO, DD. 22786, 22867, 22809, 22810, 22808, 22843; C. R. Straton, *Surveys of the Lands of William, first earl of Pembroke*, Roxburghe Club, 1909, I, pp. 57 and *passim.*

[3] Professor Knowles' conclusion (*op. cit.*, pp. 253–5) that the monastic houses were not, generally speaking, heavily in debt, does not alter the fact that large numbers of monastic creditors obtained repayment from the court of Augmentations.

instance has been found of an old rent being lowered by the monks and balanced by a large fine. This was at Holme Cultram in Cumberland, where in 1537 for a fine of £13 13s. 4d., the abbot leased some land to Steven Skelton for twenty-one years at a rent of 10s. instead of at the old rent of 20s. Over the full term, had he remained to enjoy the rent, the abbot would have made £3 3s. 4d. on the deal. As it was, he had a substantial part of the total in hand.[1] If such practices were indeed more widespread, the Crown was well and truly forestalled.

After 1535 a much larger proportion of the conventual leases, especially those of demesne hitherto in hand, was taken up by knights and gentlemen. In 1538 Sir Philip Champernon obtained from the abbot of Buckfast a lease for sixty years of the chief messuage of the manor of Englebourne, to date from the death of the tenant in occupation, Robert Screech, a local farmer, who with his son had leased the property in 1528. The same thing was happening in the Midlands, too, especially on the coveted granges. Edward Villiers succeeded the Pickering family who had farmed Cortlingstock, Nottinghamshire, since the late fifteenth century. Of the Leicestershire houses, only Croxton, for reasons unknown, resisted offers from gentlemen as long as possible, even inserting in indentures a prohibition against sub-letting to gentlemen or even to gentlemen's servants. Finally, it gave in and leased its demesne at Waltham to Sir John Uvedale, one of its stewards.[2] Many of the lessees of the later 1530's were friends, potential supporters, and relations of the monks. For example, in 1536 Sir Thomas Dennis, very prominent among the Devon gentry and steward of Newenham Abbey (among others), obtained from the abbot a ninety-nine year lease of some abbey land. The last abbess of Lacock in Wiltshire, Joan Temmse, made sure of keeping a good deal of the abbey resources in her own family. In 1529 her brother Thomas, who was also her auditor and steward of her courts, took her manor of Sherwell for eighty years; in 1533 another brother, Christopher, steward of her household, took Hatherop for sixty years; and at the same time her brother-in-law, Robert Bath, clothier, leased Bishopstrow for ninety-nine years. Christopher also leased a tenement in Lacock with pastures and part of the tithes. This was in 1537, and the following year Thomas bought the abbey flock at Chittern for £150.[3] But there was also a market for leases among the gentry, for they are to be found paying reasonable, if not heavy, fines. Examples have been found in all parts of the country. In 1538 William Westby, esquire, paid the

[1] E 315, 399, fo. 26v.
[2] Exeter City RO, DD. 22838, 22823; Thorpe, op. cit., pp. 20–7.
[3] Exeter City RO, DD. 6800; VCH Wilts., III, pp. 313–4. See also A. L. Rowse, Tudor Cornwall, 1941, pp. 178–80.

abbot of Cockersand, Lancashire, a fine of £10 for a ninety-nine year lease of some lands in Medlar in Amounderness, at the accustomed rent of £4. Sir Robert Hesketh paid twenty marks to the same prior for a similar lease of lands in Tarleton, Lancashire, at the old rent of £4 19s. 8½d. William Standish paid a fine of £50 on the 30th of August 1537 for a lease of the Ulverscroft Priory grange of Chorley, and in 1536 Simon Catesby, a Nottinghamshire gentleman, paid Lenton Priory £40 for a forty-five year lease of Wigston rectory, the rent being £22 7s. 4d.[1]

But the gentry had by no means entirely ousted the yeomen farmers from the best of the abbey lands by 1538-9. Many thousands of yeomen were securely entrenched with long leases, all over the country. In Leicestershire they held more than half of the monastic leaseholdings.[2] Many manorial bailiffs now obtained, or renewed, leases of the demesne which they already administered. In 1535 John Collins, bailiff of the St Augustine's Abbey manor of Leigh, obtained from the abbot a lease for three lives of the manor house and demesne, at a rent of £10. Two years later he added a lease for sixty years of the sheephouse, Sheephouse Close, and common pasture for five hundred sheep, at a rent of £1; and finally, in 1538, the office of bailiff was assured to him for life, by indenture, with a fee of £1 6s. 8d. Collins was one of thousands of manorial bailiffs, mostly small local farmers, who, following the lead given by the gentlemen who held the higher monastic administrative offices, had their contracts put in writing in the 1530's.[3]

It would be a mistake to conclude that during the last year or so before the Dissolution conventual seals were being used carelessly. Very few of the leases and other grants were ever called in question. Occasionally the omission of a clause of distress or failure to reserve woods came to light in the course of subsequent litigation. But such cases were rare: the monks knew their business in this respect. Most of the legendary roguery took place after the Dissolution, usually through the convent seals getting into the wrong hands.

Enough has perhaps been said to indicate that even during the last year or so before the Dissolution the monks were still able to strike a hard bargain, and that they were not nearly so pliable as Thomas Cromwell and his circle would have liked them to be. It would be unwise, in fact, to assume that in every case the Dissolution was casting

[1] Farrer, op. cit., pp. 1189-1200; E 303, 292; W. G. Hoskins, The Midland Peasant, 1957, p. 131. [2] Thorpe, op. cit., p. 28.
[3] Sabin, op. cit., p. 16; PRO, SC 6 (Ministers' Accounts) passim. Dr R. H. Hilton (VCH Leics., II, p. 195) places greater emphasis on the advantageous position gained by the gentry. See also A. G. Dickens, Register of Butleigh Priory, Suffolk, 1951, passim.

its shadow before. A great many of the leases of the 1530's, even those made almost on the eve of surrender, merely represent the culmination of a long process of retreat from demesne farming and not a frantic attempt to prepare for the end. One house, at least, prepared for any eventuality. St Werburgh's Abbey, Chester, on the 10th of October 1538 leased the parsonage of Sutton in Wirral to William Goodman and Hugh Aldersey, "uppon condycon yf the seyd monastery be nott dissoluyd that then the seyd William and Hugh to redelyver the seyd indenture."[1]

The royal officials who were engaged in effecting the 'surrender' of the monasteries adopted an air of great concern about these last-minute leases of demesne hitherto in hand. In 1538 John Freeman reported from Lincolnshire that all the houses remaining in the county were "in readiness to surrender," which, he went on, "doth appear by their acts, for they are in a customed sort of spoil and bribery...for they leave neither demesnes unlet nor honest stuff in their houses, but also minisheth the greater part of their stock and store."[2] What Cromwell's informants did not mention, even if they were aware of the fact, was that the leasing of demesne on distant manors had been almost complete by 1535. In Hampshire, according to the *Valor Ecclesiasticus*, less than one fifth of the monastic manors had at that time any demesne in hand.[3] By 1538–9 the withdrawal had gone a good deal further, and portions of nearby demesne had been leased. But in nearly every, case as the commissioners' own surveys show, the core of the estate, the adjacent home farm, was being worked by the monks right up to the end. Selby Abbey in Yorkshire was one of the last to be dissolved and had plenty of time to prepare for suppression. In March 1540 its demesnes were listed. Within the precincts were the usual gardens and orchards and beyond them some 190 acres of arable, which the commissioners valued at rates varying from 6d. an acre for the coarser ground to 1s. 0d. an acre for meadow. All of this was still in hand, as also were a further two hundred acres, mostly woodland, known as Stayner Grange. But Haysteads meadow in Wystowe Inges, extending to five acres and formerly kept for the abbey mill horses, had been let in August 1538 to Robert Good for 10s. a year. The fishery of the Ouse, previously reserved by the monks for their own use, had been let very recently to Richard Kirk for 13s. 4d., and four corn mills to Robert Beverley of Selby for 40s. Thorpe Grange had been let as recently as January 1539.[4] Clearly the final retreat had

[1] E 315, 397, f. 42.   [2] LP XIII, ii, p. 207.
[3] Kennedy, *op. cit.*, p. 57. See also Savine, *op. cit.*, pp. 153–4.
[4] J. T. Fowler, *Coucher Book of Selby Abbey*, Yorks Arch. Soc., Rec. Ser., 1893, pp. 349 *sqq.*

begun, but in very few cases had there been sufficient time for it to be complete.

For the county of Leicester it has been calculated that 20–25 per cent of the total monastic land (in terms of the gross values set down in the *Valor Ecclesiasticus*) was still in hand at the Dissolution. Broken down, this proportion ranged from 9 per cent at Kirby Bellars, of which five sixths was arable land, to 51 per cent at the small priory of Bradley, which was still pasturing considerable flocks on its 130 acres of pasture.[1] These figures illustrate something which is probably true for the whole country, namely that the houses which had retained the greater proportion of land in hand were those most interested in pastoral farming. This is particularly true of the granges. Pastoral farming, of course, involved greater acreages, so that the actual amount of land still in hand in some counties was quite considerable. In Devon, where the monastic economy had been less weighted on the side of pastoral farming, the proportion of demesne still in hand at the Dissolution, whether in terms of value or acreage, was much less than in Leicester-shire. In Hampshire there was great variety between the houses, but here also, pasture predominated on the land acquired by the Crown with vacant possession.[2]

Few communities, or at least their superiors, can have lacked warning of impending dispersal, and even if tenants had not actually been installed, it was hardly to be expected that the commissioners would find farming operations in full swing. In many there will have been divided counsels. The Carthusian brothers at Axholme, in Lincolnshire, for example, less anxious than their prior to prepare for the end, complained bitterly of his negligence. Not only, they asserted in 1538, had he been selling off their goods and stock and let part of the demesne to his kinsmen, but, worst of all, he had dismissed their labourers, so that,

"...our husbandry is not lokyd upon, our lond is not tylde, muke is not led, our corne lyth in the barn, sum is threshte, and sum is husbondyd, and mych is yit to threshe, and taketh hurt with vermyn... and shortly hay tyme shall cum, and when it shuld be sped, other thynges shalbe to do."[3]

Many indeed were the reports reaching London of the wholesale selling-off of stock by the abbots and priors, and these are very difficult to check. The most that can be said is that, here again, the com-missioners' own reports belie some of the hair-raising tales which they were sending to Cromwell. At Fountains Abbey, in 1539, for instance, they listed a 'store' of over two thousand horned cattle, over one thousand

[1] Thorpe, *op. cit.*, pp. 38–9, 291, 296.
[2] Kennedy, *op. cit.*, pp. 47–9, 54. [3] Wright, *op. cit.*, pp. 175–6.

sheep, eighty-six horses, and nearly as many pigs. There cannot have been much excess marketing of stock here. There is, moreover, evidence of the purchase of stock by some houses not long before the Dissolution. Oxen were being purchased for the farm at Hurdwick by the bailiff of Tavistock Abbey in 1538, and at Glastonbury, during 1538-9, at a time when most of the other Somerset houses had already fallen, money was being laid out on the restocking of Shapwick moor.[1]

The retreat from active farming had undoubtedly accelerated considerably in the 1530's, and especially during the years 1538-9, but there was still a good deal of land left to be handed over to the Crown with full possession, and in good shape, land fit for the immediate occupation of the king himself or of one of the more fortunate of his subjects. Richard Pollard, having sent the abbot to his tragic fate on the tor just outside the town, wrote from Glastonbury in November 1539:

"The house is greate, goodly, and so pryncely as we have not sene the lyke, with iiii parkes adjoynynge, the furthermoste of them but iiii myles distaunte from the house; a great mere, which ys v miles cumpas...well replenished with greate pykis, bremes, perche, and roche; iiii faire manour placis, belonginge to the late abbott...beynge goodly mansions."[2]

(d) The Crown takes over

The statute of 1539, unlike that of 1536 which actually authorized dissolution, was merely intended to set aside all doubts about the legality of the royal title to monastic lands, especially, no doubt, the misgivings of those who had already purchased portions or were contemplating doing so.[3] There was assured to the king the "very actual and real seisin and possession" of the property of all dissolved monasteries, whether suppressed by the act of 1536, voluntarily surrendered or to be surrendered in the future, or whose superiors had been attainted. The king was to be regarded as absolute owner of the property, "in as large and ample manner and form" as the monasteries. Henry and Cromwell could, presumably, have gone one stage further, either in 1536 or 1539, and obtained a statutory declaration that all contracts entered into by the monks were null and void. This they did not do. It was most important that the interests of laymen should not be disturbed. The statute only invalidated leases made within a year of surrender, and then only of lands not usually let to farm, or leases in reversion or not reserving the old rent, or leases of growing wood, and even these provisions the Crown chose very

[1] Dugdale, *Monasticon*, v, p. 291; Finberg, *op. cit.*, p. 135; Dom Aelred Watkin, 'Glastonbury, 1538-9', *Downside Review*, LXVII, 1949, p. 448.

[2] Wright, *op. cit.*, p. 258.   [3] *Statutes of the Realm*, III, pp. 375-8, 733-9.

largely to ignore. Many hundreds of long leases which could statutorily have been called in were allowed to run their full term. For example, only a few months before the dissolution of Kenilworth Priory, Warwickshire, the priory manor of Salford Priors had been let for ninety-nine years. The manor was still in Crown hands in 1547, its conventual lease still running. The same priory had, as long ago as 1521, leased its wool tithes at Bidford for forty-six years to commence on 20 April 1540. This lease also was still operating in 1547.[1] Only very occasionally was the term of a long lease reduced or a rent 'restored', i.e. raised, by the Crown to what was regarded as the customary figure. Moreover, there is no substance in the records of the court of Augmentations for the suggestion often made that the tenants of the former monastic lands were in a state of "anxious suspense," eager to exchange their titles for new ones and only too willing to pay a heavy fine to the Crown to ensure security.[2]

The ease, the speed, and the comparative lack of local disturbance with which the great confiscation was carried through was largely due to the establishment, at the very commencement of the operation in 1536, of the court of Augmentations, with its central and local officers. The same local, i.e. regional, officers who carried out the dissolution of the smaller houses in 1536, remained to administer the property, and, as the larger houses fell, in their case to bodies of special commissioners, to deal with their property too. Apart from the estates which were handed over to the duchy of Lancaster, only the lands of the attainted abbots were dealt with separately, by the General Surveyors of Crown lands. Once the Augmentations men arrived the 'take-over' was swift and remarkably simple. The *rentier* character of so much of the monastic estate facilitated this. The monastic bailiffs and farmers accounted to the Augmentations receivers instead of to monastic treasurers. Where they had formerly been accountable to more than one monastic obedientiary this must have been a welcome relief, or at any rate a simplification. For the great mass of monastic tenantry the changeover can have made very little difference.[3]

[1] Bickley, *op. cit.*, pp. 34–6. These conclusions are confirmed by a recent study of Lancashire monastic lands (Mason, *op. cit.*, pp. 137–9). It must be stressed that the Augmentations officers had no statutory authority to 'meddle' with leases made, on whatever terms, more than a year before the dissolution of the house concerned.

[2] Savine, *op. cit.*, p. 54. The confirmations of conventual leases are in E 315, 90–105. The act of 1540 requiring the observance of all covenants in conventual leases (32 Henry VIII, c. 34), applied to both landlords and tenants.

[3] *Statutes of the Realm*, III, pp. 574, 734. For the parallel administration of the court of Augmentations, the General Surveyors, and the duchy of Lancaster, in the county of Lancashire, see Mason, *op. cit.*, *passim*. The workings of the court of Augmentations in the county of Devon are dealt with in Youings, *op. cit.*, pp. viii–xiv.

At the earliest opportunity, however, the administration of the new Crown estate was rationalized. No longer were there monastic households to feed. All resources in kind were converted into ready cash or into a regular cash income. Stock, live and dead, stores of all kinds, and standing corn were sold. Many people, including the monks, no doubt made the most of any period of confusion, or of delay in the arrival of the king's officers, to spirit away stock, goods, and even parts of the fabric. But great quantities were sold by the royal officers. The prices which are recorded seem reasonable and there are few reports of difficulty in finding purchasers. At Netley Abbey, Hants., in 1536, Michael Lister and William Sharland paid over £100 for all the cattle and other stock. At Wintney, Richard Paulet, receiver of the court of Augmentations, bought half the grain crop himself.[1] Sales of stock invariably realized far more than sales of standing crops or grain. It seems likely, as Savine suggests, that such a wholesale dispersal must have depressed local prices for a time, although it is reported that in 1537 people came from all parts of the south to buy the Furness Abbey cattle.[2] In a very large number of cases, stock, and even household equipment, was sold to those who took over the demesnes. Lord Scrope bought a good deal of the stock in hand of Easby Priory, Yorkshire, and also obtained possession of the site and demesnes. John Herbert did the same at Ellerton Priory. In some cases part of the stock and grain was distributed among the departing monks. At the surrender of Roche Abbey, Yorkshire, in 1538, the abbot, in addition to a pension of £33 6s. 8d., was sent on his way with £30 in cash and a quarter of the abbey stock, including sixty oxen, 120 sheep, and forty swine.[3] Rents in kind were an embarrassment to the Crown and were speedily commuted. For example, in 1539 the leasehold rent due to Bath Abbey from Weston in Somerset was converted into £24 8s. by pricing the wheat at 5s. 4d. per quarter, barley at 2s. 8d., and oats at 1s. 4d. The cartloads of hay were valued at 1s. each, and those of straw at 4d., and the feeding of the oxen at 4s. a head.[4] Cash equivalents had sometimes already been provided for in the indentures of leases. In a number of cases the rent in kind, instead of being commuted, was farmed out by the Crown to a third party. For example, in December 1542 Sir George Throckmorton of Coughton, Warwickshire, took from

[1] Kennedy, op. cit., p. 149.

[2] Savine, op. cit., p. 196; LP XII, ii, p. 88. Savine bases his conclusions on the valuations of stock set down in the commissioners' surveys. The actual sale prices are to be found in some of the accounts of the Receivers of the court of Augmentations (PRO SC 6, Henry VIII, Monastic Lands).

[3] J. M. Clay, Yorkshire Monasteries: Suppression Papers, Yorks. Arch. Soc., Rec. Ser., XLVIII, 1912, pp. 99, 105; Woodward, op. cit., p. 362.

[4] PRO SC 6, Henry VIII, 3144, m. 17.

the Crown for twenty-one years a lease of thirty-seven quarters of wheat, eighty-two quarters of barley, besides a small quantity of rye, payable by various tenants of the lands late of Worcester Cathedral Priory. He paid a total rent of £24 4s. 10d. One of these rents in kind was payable by John and Thomas Charlett and John Harborne, lessees of the former abbey's tithes at Cleeve, who, unfortunately for Throckmorton, "off theyr malycyous froward synyster myndes and intentes," did not pay up promptly, and Robert Throckmorton and William Sheldon, assigns of Sir George, complained to the court of Augmentations.[1] As prices rose many of these lessees of grain rents must have made handsome profits.

Most important of all, such monastic property as came into the king's hands with vacant possession was very promptly rented on a temporary basis. Richard Pollard wrote from Glastonbury, "Cattell we intende to sell for redy money, and to let owte the pastures and demeynes now from Mighelmas for the quarterly, untill the kingis pleasure therin be further knowyne to thentente his grace shall lease (lose) no rent, for thabbott had muche pasture grounde in his hande."[2] In 1536 the rent of vacant demesne was usually fixed by reference to the *Valor Ecclesiasticus*, or by some hasty estimation, and was for the most part below its market value. Robert Southwell reported from Yorkshire in 1537 that monastic demesnes were being sublet by Crown lessees at a profit. Sir Thomas Wharton had the demesnes of Healaugh Park Priory for £23 and was subletting at £26 13s. 4d. Leases were being sold even more profitably. According to Southwell, that of Rosedale Priory had changed hands for £200 although the rent due to the Crown was only £7. He knew, he said, of local men who would give a great deal for these 'farms', and he begged Cromwell to hold his hand until the property could be surveyed "by eye and measure, and not by credit, as the commissioners for the suppression did."[3] But to have leased these lands on the open market would have put an almost impossible strain on the newly-established administrative machinery. Moreover, the possibility must not be ruled out that the government was deliberately enabling numbers of laymen to share in the proceeds of the Dissolution. In 1538-9, however, demesne in hand was more carefully surveyed. At De la Pré Abbey, Northamptonshire, meadow subject to common grazing for part of the year was valued at 3s. per acre, meadow lying 'several' all the year at 3s. 4d. Pasture was valued at 1s. 6d. per acre, and arable land in the open fields at 6d. At St Andrew's Priory in the same county, arable land described as

---

[1] E 321, 16, 73.
[2] Wright, *op. cit.*, p. 258.
[3] LP XII, i, p. 255; ii, pp. 88, 206.

lying in furlongs was valued at 8d. per acre, and meadow at 5s. At Pipewell Abbey commonable meadow was set at 2s. 4d. and open field arable at 8d., and at Welbeck closes of pasture were valued at 8d., closes of arable at 4d., and of meadow at 1s. 4d.[1] These initial lettings of demesne were most important, for the rents fixed then were usually adhered to in subsequent more formal leases, and also formed the basis of later valuations for outright grants. Formal leases followed at a later date, sometimes within months, and in a few cases only after some years had passed. As laid down in the statute of 1536, Crown leases were normally for twenty-one years. Woods were always carefully reserved.[2]

As a landlord the Crown was always conservative. Rents remained fixed, although land values more than doubled between 1540 and 1590. In the 1530's and 1540's fines for leases were low, rarely more than one year's rent. In the 1550's some attempt was made to take account of the rise in the value of land, in the 1560's fines for new leases reached four and five times the annual rent. If this came anywhere near to closing the gap early in Elizabeth's reign, it failed to keep up with subsequent inflation, so that by the end of the century, according to Professor Habakkuk's calculations, "fines were probably only some five years' purchase of the excess of annual value over annual rent."[3] Winchcombe manor in Gloucestershire had been in Crown hands during the greater part of the sixteenth century. In the early seventeenth century it was sold to the Whitmores, one of whom went down to inspect the property in 1612 and tried to hold a court. He reported as follows:

"...and for herriots wee might have had naked children, and for distresses for rent, patched petticoats, the Common pasture for all the quicke Cattle, and when we spake of fines and raysinge of rentes, we had a Chain of Scoulds, raysinge their voyces to 'God save the Kinge and the lawes; and they and their ancestours had lived there And they would live there,' and without the danger of hotte spittes and scaldinge water and fiery tongues, there is no gaineinge of possession."

---

[1] E 315, 399, fo. 118; fos. 131–8; fo. 148; fos. 216–7. For a longer Crown lease in Mary's reign, see M. E. Finch, *The Wealth of Five Northamptonshire Families, 1540–1640*, Northants Rec. Soc., 1956, p. 70.

[2] Attention is often drawn to the fact that the revenues recorded in the early post-Dissolution ministers' accounts considerably exceed those set down in the *Valor Ecclesiasticus*, implying that the Crown was effecting 'improvements' in its income. But in most cases detailed examination of the figures will show that the increases are due to the inclusion in the Crown accounts, or the more realistic valuation of, demesne which had been in hand in 1535.

[3] E 323, 1–8, *passim;* H. J. Habakkuk, 'The Market for Monastic Property, 1539–1603', EcHR, 2nd Ser., x, 1958, pp. 370–72.

He went on to report that in the end the poorer tenants, who could not afford to pay fines, agreed to their rents being raised.[1]

The court of Augmentations, besides administering the former monastic lands, was charged, through its chancellor, with "minister(ing) equal justice to rich and poor to the best of (his) cunning, wit and power," and was soon very busy dealing with a multitude of complaints. Many were of the kind regularly being dealt with by the king's other courts, cases of disputed tenure, claims to leases for which no written evidence could be shown, and so on. Many, however, arose from the peculiarities of the lands concerned. Liability to pay tithe was a frequent subject of litigation. Quite apart from the reputed freedom from tithe of certain monastic land, a good deal of it had not paid tithe before the Dissolution simply because the monasteries concerned were themselves owners of the tithe. The Dissolution inevitably altered the situation when tithes and demesnes were leased or sold separately. The lessee of the site and demesnes of Tywardreath Priory, Cornwall, when charged with non-payment of tithe by the lessee of the parsonage, cited the statute of 1539 which assured the lands to the king exactly as they had been enjoyed by the monks.[2] Many disputes arose over boundaries between adjacent manors now in separate occupation. A great many people were no doubt hoping to take advantage of the confusion brought about by the change in ownership to lay false claims. The settlement of the ensuing disputes led to many former abbots and monks being called on for their testimony. On the whole the proceedings of the court make dull reading for the historian of agriculture. Only occasionally did a refreshing whiff of country air blow through the courts at Westminister, as when one of the tenants of the manor of Lenthall Stark, late of Wigmore Abbey, Herefordshire, told the court about five parcels of meadow, part of the lord's demesne, called Lady Plocks, where, immediately after midsummer and the gathering of the first "math" and crop, until Candlemas, the tenants had been accustomed to enjoy with their beasts "the later math, crop, vesture, edgrowe, or depasturacon." One is reminded, too, of the benevolent abbots of the legends when one reads the plea of the parishioners of Longney in Gloucestershire. The prior of Great Malvern, the court was told, owner of fifty messuages in their village, had always contributed half the cost of repairing their sea defences, giving them two "crybbes" and certain "throughes" and gates. Since the Dissolution no help had been forthcoming and they had had to sell

---

[1] D. Royce, *Landboc sive Registrum Monasterii de Winchelcumba*, II, 1903, p. lxx. The conservatism of Crown management is amply demonstrated in Lancashire by Mr Mason (*op. cit.*, pp. 157–63, 224–6).

[2] E 321, 9, 69. See also Savine, *op. cit.*, pp. 108 *sqq.*

TAH

jewels from their church to raise the necessary money.[1] But by and large the proceedings of the court of Augmentations, together with those of the courts of Star Chamber and Requests, which also dealt with cases concerning monastic lands, do not give one the impression that the Dissolution had inflicted great hardships on the peasants. In fact, the plaintiffs were very often the new landlords, endeavouring to establish their right to enjoy their grants. With only the depositions extant it is usually very difficult, at this distance, to judge which of the parties was at fault. But we can sympathize with Isabel Best who, in 1544 bought, at second-hand, a tenement in Hawksworth, Yorkshire, late of Esholt Priory. She complained that Thomas Wood of Hawksworth, "having neither right nor title" to the property, refused to give her possession. In this case, reference to the particulars prepared for the initial sale by the Crown establishes that he was a tenant-at-will.[2]

(e) The disposal of monastic lands

(i) *The break-up of the monastic estates.* Whatever the king and Cromwell may or may not have intended, outright alienation of the monastic lands began almost at once and rapidly rose to a peak in the early 1540's. The first grant according to the date of the letters patent was that on the 1st of April 1536, to Sir Henry Parker, of the site of Latton Priory, Essex, with property belonging to the priory in Essex, Hampshire, and Middlesex.[3] Over the country as a whole well over half of the total monastic estate had been alienated by the Crown before the end of Henry VIII's reign. Large portions of the remainder were disposed of during the reign of Edward VI, and a smaller amount during that of Mary. By 1558 about three quarters had left Crown ownership. Elizabeth continued the distribution, along with other church lands, but a not inconsiderable estate still remained to be drawn on by her early Stuart successors. These are conclusions based on the only national estimates available, those of Professor Dietz, modified by the more detailed figures now available for several counties.[4] If the figures for the counties so far

---

[1] E 321, 9, 2; 11, 49.

[2] E 321, 20, 71, and E 318, 755.   [3] LP x, p. 325, g. 6.

[4] F. C. Dietz, *English Government Finance, 1485–1558*, 1920, p. 149. Here Dietz speaks of two-thirds of the monastic lands having been "alienated" by 1547. One can only assume that he is including grants by exchange, gift, and sale. In a later work (*English Public Finance, 1558–1641*, 1932, p. 291) he puts the proportion of the monastic lands "sold" during the same period at seven-eighths. The county of Lancashire, where, owing to the large proportion of the former monastic lands which had been annexed to the duchy of Lancaster, less than half the total had been alienated by the Crown by 1558 (Mason, *op. cit.*, p. 146), may be regarded as an extreme case, probably unparalleled elsewhere.

studied are representative, Professor Dietz's figures are rather high. The discrepancy is probably to be explained by the fact that at county level it is possible to be more precise on details, to allow, for instance, for the restoration of part of the land to the Crown by sale, exchange, or escheat. The figures for the counties agree remarkably well for the separate reigns, but they differ a little when compared over the years. Whereas in Leicestershire the peak came early, some 36 per cent of all the monastic land in the county having been alienated by 1542, in Hampshire the climax came in 1544–6.[1]

On whatever terms the grant was to be made, the initiative was taken by the prospective grantee in deciding what particular estates he wanted. Even from 1539 onwards, when the lands were put on the open market, although the total amount which the commissioners were empowered to sell was limited, the officers of the Crown did not attempt to sell specific properties. From time to time attempts were made to dispose of certain types of property. In the case of odd tenements of small value which were expensive to administer, this was done by making tenurial or financial concessions.[2] A certain brake was always applied to the disposal of properties which, usually on account of their size or because they were near other royal estates, it was not advisable for the Crown to part with. But, broadly speaking, all the monastic land was potentially on the market.

Given the initiative to this extent, it was obvious that prospective grantees would pounce first on the most desirable properties. The sites of monastic houses figure very largely in early grants. These included the remains of extensive buildings, gardens, fishponds, orchards, and in fact the makings of desirable country residences, whether for letting or occupation. A good deal of the fabric, especially of the conventual churches, had been dismantled and sold by the royal commissioners. The greater part, however, especially of the domestic quarters and agricultural buildings such as barns, was left intact. Equally sought-after were the monastic home-farms and the bartons or granges which so often lay conveniently adjacent to the conventual buildings. But most grantees had to be satisfied with the monastic manors. These were sought not so much on account of their size, though available capital must often have been a limiting factor, as of their location, and the opportunity this offered of adding to an already existing estate, or, especially where monastic manors lay adjacent, of accumulating a new one.

[1] Thorpe, *op. cit.*, pp. 119–21, 191; Kennedy, *op. cit.*, p. 167; J. A. Youings, 'The Terms of the Disposal of the Devon Monastic Lands, 1536–58', EHRi xix, 1954, pp. 34, 37.

[2] Youings, *ibid.*, pp. 31–3; J. Hurstfield, 'The Greenwich Tenures of the reign of Edward VI', *Law Quart. Rev.*, lxv, 1949, pp. 72–81.

The size of grants varied greatly, from the enormous grants, mostly confined to the very early years and to the reign of Edward VI, to men like John Lord Russell, Thomas earl of Rutland and others, through hundreds of grants of land worth £20 or thereabouts, to numbers of grants of small properties or groups of tenements worth less than £5 in all.[1] While subsequent grants and also resales did on occasion re-unite parts of the total monastic estate, the general effect of disposal was to split the whole into thousands of portions, most of it to be loosely joined to lay estates of infinite variety as regards both size and geographical distribution.

Some of the early grants, especially those made on favourable terms to the king's closest associates, included the site, demesnes, and practically the whole of the former monastic estate appertaining thereto. Thus, in July 1537, Sir Edward Grey, lord Powis, was granted the site and demesnes of Buildwas Abbey, Shropshire, ten of the abbey's granges in Shropshire, Staffordshire, and Derbyshire, and three of its rectories.[2] But for the most part, and especially when sale of the property was in full swing after 1539, purchasers were more selective and the estates of individual houses went into the melting pot. The *rentier* character of most of the monastic lands meant that the break-up of the estate did not materially affect the agricultural management of constituent parts or leave them in novel isolation. Indeed the dispersal of the property among lay owners made for more compactness in the geographical pattern of landownership. For whereas monasteries had been largely dependent on benefactors, the new lay owners had more freedom to select their acquisitions. In the long run this must have led to improvements in local agrarian efficiency.

Monastic manors, however, were invariably disposed of intact. Such fragmentation as did take place was confined to the more loosely knit and territorially scattered 'manors' of more recent origin. But, whether of ancient or recent origin, the monastic manor came, in lay hands, to assume more than an administrative significance, the manor being the key unit of landholding in the feudal tenurial structure which the Tudor monarchy was energetically striving to perpetuate. In this respect, as far as most of the monastic tenants were concerned, the effect of the transference of ownership was of little consequence. The great majority of them, free, customary, and leasehold, merely became tenants of the king, instead of tenants of the monasteries. Most of the free tenants held by 'socage' tenure which was free from feudal incidents. A handful of landowners in each county, however, who had held part of their land by military tenure of the monasteries, became, as a result of the Dissolution, military tenants of the Crown, and later of

[1] LP, CPR, and E 318, *passim*.   [2] LP XII, ii, p. 166, g. 13.

other landowners, with all the accompanying disadvantages.[1] Far more important, however, when the monastic lands were alienated in fee by the Crown to its subjects, care was taken to secure, and potentially to expand, the Crown's feudal interests. It was laid down, in the statute of 1536 which established the court of Augmentations, that on all convey-ances of monastic property in fee there should be reserved tenures by knight service in chief of the Crown, and, with minor concessions later on, this provision was carried out. As a result, the amount of land which was of interest to the Office (from 1540, the Court) of Wards was considerably increased. The combined outcome, therefore, of the Dissolution and the disposal of monastic lands was to perpetuate the existing tenurial structure of the countryside, the only difference being that almost the whole of the former monastic estate was now held either by, or immediately of, the Crown itself.[2]

Finally, as the result of the Dissolution and of the subsequent aliena-tion of the monastic property by the Crown, in thousands of parishes throughout the kingdom, some or all of the tithes, which had often been leased by laymen, now came, for the first time, into the outright ownership of laymen.

(ii) *The terms of Crown disposal.* In December 1539 Sir Richard Rich, chancellor of the court of Augmentations, and Thomas Crom-well, were empowered by letters patent to sell the former monastic and other Crown lands to the total annual value of £6,000, at twenty years' purchase. Urban property could be sold at a lower rate.[3] A good deal of the monastic property had already been alienated by the Crown during the three preceding years, some as free gifts, some by exchange for other land, some at fee-farm rents, and some by sale. It can be shown that the standard rate of twenty years' purchase had already been adopted, though there is no record of its having been officially authorized.[4] The procedure for obtaining a grant had also

[1] The abbess of Wilton had a considerable number of tenants by knight service, and, as the surveyor of the earl of Pembroke, who acquired most of the Wilton Abbey lands, wrote of them in 1567–8, ". . . and so Homage, Fealtie, and Escuage draweth unto them Warde, Maryage, and Reliefe" (Straton, *op. cit.*, 1, pp. 3–6, and *passim*).

[2] J. Hurstfield, *The Queen's Wards*, 1958, Part 1, 'The Revival of Royal Wardship', pp. 3–29. [3] LP XIV, ii, p. 301, g. 36.

[4] For example, in March 1537 there was granted to Sir Edmund Bedingfield and his wife, Grace, the site and estates of Redlingfield Priory, Suffolk. No purchase price appears in the letters patent (LP XII, i, p. 353, g. 39), but the annual value of the property is given as £31 4s. 5d. and an annual rent of 63s. 6d., i.e. one tenth, is mentioned. The accounts of the Treasurer of the court of Augmentations, however, record the payment by Sir Edmund of £400, part of £561 19s. due for the purchase of Redlingfield (E 323, 1, 1, m. 5). This works out at almost exactly twenty years' purchase of the net annual value. See also TED, 1, p. 18. Dietz states, quite unaccoun-tably, that sales commenced in March 1539 (*English Government Finance*, p. 148).

already been established. The suitor had first to seek out the appropriate auditor of the court of Augmentations and obtain a certificate of the current annual value of the property he wished to acquire. This valuation was then placed before the appropriate royal officials, either the chancellor of the court of Augmentations if any royal bounty or any exchange of land was involved, or, in the case of a straightforward sale, the commissioners. In either case a 'rate' was appended. From the net annual value as certified by the auditors was deducted the statutory reserved rent of one tenth, and any allowance by way of royal gift, or for lands surrendered to the king in exchange. Additions were made for woods. Finally the balance was made payable, either as a perpetual fixed 'fee-farm' rent or as a capital sum calculated at a number of years' purchase. For example, in 1545 William Sneyd desired to purchase the manor of Keele in Staffordshire, lately belonging to the Order of St John of Jerusalem. The auditor certified that the current annual value was confined to the rent of £18 reserved on a lease of the manor in 1528 for forty years to Sir Henry Dewes. The commissioners noted this, deducted the normal reserved rent of one tenth, i.e. 36s., and rated the balance at twenty years' purchase. To this they added £10 for the woods and required the total, £334, to be paid in hand.[1]

The auditors' basic valuations were obviously very important. Except where, as at Keele, manors had been farmed out as a whole, individual totals were given for free and customary rents. Leasehold rents were usually given in detail and the date and term cited if the information was to hand. Like the *Valor* of 1535, from which, in fact the auditors would seem often to have copied, the particulars for grants contain accurate summaries of strictly current regular annual income. It is likely that the figures given for an average year's casual revenue, court profits, fines, etc., were low. On the other hand, as in the *Valor*, no allowances were made for arrears of rent, 'decayed' or vacant holdings, or for expenditure on repairs. Full allowance was made for inescapable charges such as outgoing rents, bailiffs' fees granted for life, and stipends, synodals, etc., payable out of 'spiritual' revenues. Very rarely, however, were grantees burdened with the 'fees', annuities and other general expenses with which the monks had charged their revenues. Responsibility for these, together with the pensions granted to the monks, was usually retained by the Crown. Only in the case of some of the 'gifts' of land were these burdens passed on, thereby limiting considerably the grantees' immediate enjoyment of the royal bounty. Woods were separately valued, at a capital sum based on acreage or on the number of growing trees. In Devon the normal value put on timber by the Surveyor of Woods was 6d. per acre per year's

[1] E 318, 1021.

growth, i.e. ten acres of eight years' growth were set at 40s. Odd trees were priced at from 4d. to 1s., according to age, and a further sum was added in respect of the natural increase and the herbage, usually 4d. or 6d. per acre, *per annum*. By comparison the treatment of such conventual and farm buildings as had survived the stripping of their lead was casual, and these rarely figured in the valuation. In most cases, however, they were already occupied by the farmers or their assigns, whereas woods had always been carefully reserved by the owners.[1]

Using the gross figures of the *Valor* of 1535 as a rough guide, together with the details in the particulars for grants, it is possible to ascertain, very approximately, how much monastic land was actually given away by the Crown, how much went by exchange, etc., and how much was sold. Calculations of this kind have so far been made only on a county basis, and they are complicated by the grants which included land from more than one county. However, for Devon, it has been calculated that during the period 1536–58, rather less than 25 per cent of the total monastic landed wealth in the county was given away by the Crown. For Leicestershire the proportion seems to have been considerably less, under 15 per cent of the whole.[2] Calculation of the proportion alienated in exchange for other lands is even more difficult. For Leicestershire a figure of $7\frac{1}{2}$ per cent of the whole monastic estate has been suggested.[3] Apart from the small amount which was accounted for by the reservation of a fee-farm rent, the rest was sold, and in this category one can safely include by far the greater part of the former monastic lands throughout the country. Savine calculated that nearly three quarters of the grants made by Henry VIII were by sale, and recent local studies have amply confirmed what H. A. L. Fisher wrote as long ago as 1906, that the greater part of the monastic lands throughout the kingdom was sold at or above the "good market price" of twenty years' purchase.[4]

During the very early years, when there was rather more likelihood, and certainly greater hope, of royal generosity, there was something of a scramble for grants. Everyone in Court circles, and many who were hardly known at Court, hoped for a share of the confiscated lands on favourable terms, and few hesitated to press their suit in what they hoped was the right quarter, usually with Thomas Cromwell. Some even offered to pay whatever the king might regard as a fair

[1] The form of the particulars for grants is more fully described in Youings, *Devon Monastic Lands, loc. cit.*, pp. xiv–xx.

[2] Youings, EHR, LXIX, 1954, p. 30; Thorpe, *op. cit.*, p. 133.

[3] Thorpe, *ibid.*, where the figures are given as proportions of the total monastic estate alienated before 1558. They have been corrected by reference to the estimate (*ibid.*) of a total alienation of the Leicestershire property by 1558 of 75 per cent.

[4] H. A. L. Fisher, *Political History of England, 1485–1547*, 1906, pp. 482, 499.

price. After 1539, when sales began in earnest, supply and demand, at the Crown's price, seem to have been about equally balanced. There is no reflection in the terms of the grants either of competition for individual properties, or of any greater demand for estates in the home counties as opposed to those in the more distant parts of the kingdom. Whatever the location, the commissioners calculated the price in accordance with current routine instructions. In fact the Crown seems to have found little difficulty at any time in disposing of as much of the monastic property as it wished to sell, and those of its subjects who possessed the necessary capital had little difficulty in acquiring the lands they wanted.

During the 1540's, when the volume of sales was at its height, the standard rate of twenty years' purchase was adhered to with great regularity, and this was the case whatever the length of time which remained before the grantee might, by the falling-in of leases, enjoy the advantages of full possession of his property. Thus, in 1544, John Maynard bought a number of properties scattered over several counties. These included a mill and some land in Chaddesley, Worcestershire, leased to a tenant by Bordesley Abbey in 1479 for eighty years, and a farm in Sherrington, Buckinghamshire, let in 1534 by the Northamptonshire abbey of De La Pré for ninety-nine years. Of the former, and of several similar properties, the auditor noted, "I think ther wold be good fynes given for the same if they were nowe to be letten," but the commissioners rated all together at twenty years' purchase.[1] The commissioners alone were responsible for arranging the terms of sale, and they were busy ministers of the Crown. It would have been impossible for them to have gauged the value of each piece of property on the open market: there had to be a simple formula. The practice of rating the property at twenty years' purchase of the net annual value worked very well in the early years, and, bearing in mind existing leases, it probably ensured a reasonable bargain to both sides until about the end of Henry VIII's reign. Occasionally, even in these early years, when the auditors indicated that a property was considerably under-rented, the rate was slightly increased. By the mid and later 1540's the rise in prices was making nonsense of most existing rents, and twenty years' purchase of current annual values was clearly realizing much less than the real value of the land. Gradually, therefore, the rate of sale of all but fixed or 'improved' rents was increased, first to twenty-five and thirty years' purchase, and, by the 1590's, to as much as forty times the current annual value.[2] This was the rough-and-ready

[1] E 318, 755.
[2] Habakkuk, op. cit., pp. 372–6. The whole of this paragraph owes a great deal to Professor Habakkuk's article.

method adopted of obtaining something approaching twenty years' purchase of the real value of the land, which nobody doubted was a fair price, and it was not, as has sometimes been suggested, a response to a greater demand for monastic land, although the fact that it apparently did not depress sales suggests that the demand was always a resilient one. The rise in the rating from the 1550's probably never quite caught up with the general rise in land values during the following century. Whether this was due to administrative inertia or to deliberate Crown policy, it probably helped to sustain interest in the purchase of monastic lands. Far more important in this respect, however, was the appearance in the land market during the half century following the Dissolution of a steady stream of men on the look-out for land with which either to form the nucleus of a new estate or to augment a patrimony. Such men were not easily persuaded to pay greatly inflated prices, but neither were they speculators, needing to buy cheaply. Location was more important to them and they were quite prepared to suffer a low yield for a generation or more.

(iii) *Profits*. What was monastic land worth to the grantee, were he a recipient of royal bounty or one of the majority who had paid ready money for his estate? By and large such a question must form part of a general inquiry into land values and profits during the century between the Dissolution and the Civil War.[1] There were, however, certain features which characterized, even if they were not peculiar to, monastic estates. It is quite obvious from what we have seen of the activities of the monks during the decade preceding the Dissolution that the majority of monastic tenants enjoyed considerable security of tenure. Moreover, as we have seen, the Crown did nothing to undermine or lessen this security. The amount of revenue which the Crown, and after the Crown, the lay grantees, could hope to enjoy, immediately and in many cases for decades, was limited almost entirely to the regular current rents being paid in the 1530's. This is easily illustrated from estate accounts and surveys of former monastic lands in private hands up and down the country. A survey made in 1590 of the manor of Brilley in Herefordshire, once belonging to Abbey Cwmhir, shows tenant after tenant still in possession of lands granted to their predecessors for ninety-nine years in the early years of the century. Richard ap Thomas paid 4s. a year for thirty-five acres leased to his forebears by the abbot for ninety-nine years on the 28th January 1495; David ap Richard, 7s. for forty-three acres on a ninety-nine year lease made in 1527.[2] The disadvantage to the landlord of such long terms lay not so much in the persistence of old and accustomed rents as in the length of time that must elaspe before he could levy fines for the renewal of

[1] See pp.   .   [2] Hereford RO, LC Deeds, 6581.

tenancies. In so far as the monks had gathered in large sums on the eve of the Dissolution, by that much were the lay owners precluded from repeating the process for some considerable time.

Tenancies-at-will, of course, offered the greatest scope to the new owners. But, on the whole, the proportion of monastic land held on such terms was small. Few abbots had been able to resist the offers made by their tenants for some security of tenure, on the eve of their departure if not before. A few tenancies fell in, in the normal course of events, within a short time, but the number of reversions granted shortly before the Dissolution kept these at a minimum. Life tenancies offered to landlords at least a sporting chance of profitable resumption. Many of the customary holdings of Wilton Abbey, most of which were for one life only, fell in in the 1540's, but, whether debarred by the custom of the manors, or by a glut of available holdings, or by inclination, the new owner, the earl of Pembroke, exacted entry fines which were appreciably lower than those which the abbess had levied a decade earlier.[1] Of the leases for years with which the monastic lands were encumbered, the comparatively short Crown leases for twenty-one years probably offered the earliest hope of surrender. When John lord Russell acquired the site and demesnes of Woburn Abbey in 1547, at a partial fee-farm rent, any immediate profit or possession was barred by two Crown leases held by Sir Francis Bryan and Sir John Williams or their assigns and not due to expire until 1565–6.[2] But this, by current standards, was but a short interval. Customary tenures were, in the long run, less profitable to the landowner, and some of the latter found ways of persuading their customary tenants to exchange copies for indentures of leases. At Tavistock, in the 1540's, Russell had done this with some success. Even so, the increase in his income was probably far from commensurate with the real value of his estate. On his large manor of Werrington, for example, valued at £125 for the grant of 1539, conversion from copyhold to leasehold tenure had little effect on rents. By the death of Francis Russell, fourth earl of Bedford, in 1585, regular annual income had risen to only £128. Fines levied at the granting of tenancies during the preceding two decades amounted to approximately £3,000, but, spread over the years, this barely doubled the annual income.[3] Sir Nicholas Bacon built up an estate in East Anglia and the neighbouring counties during the period 1540–79, much of it former monastic property. By 1646 some of this was producing an annual rent income ten, and even fourteen, times that of

[1] Straton, *op. cit.*, pp. 7–11 and *passim*.
[2] G. Scott Thomson, 'Woburn Abbey and the Dissolution of the Monasteries', RHS, 4th Ser., XVI, pp. 129 *sqq.*
[3] Finberg, *op. cit.*, p. 271, and PRO SP 1, Elizabeth, case 9, no. 2.

a century earlier. To a certain extent Bacon was fortunate, and also showed himself to be a shrewd judge of property, in that his purchases were not encumbered with unduly long leases. But he, or rather his descendants, had to wait until at least the turn of the century before their income rose appreciably. At Redgrave in Suffolk, where Bacon wanted immediate possession, he had to buy out existing interests. At Rickinghall, too, he had to buy out Crown leases which still had seventeen years to run. In 1558 Sir Robert Molyneux, having purchased the manor of Altcar in Lancashire from the Crown for £1000, then paid 500 marks to the tenant in occupation for the remaining sixty years of a conventual lease of 1537.[1] Thus, in order to obtain immediate possession, both Bacon and Molyneux had had to find two lots of capital.

There were, no doubt, many landowners who resorted to oppressive and illegal means of evicting tenants and of increasing rents. But the history of landlord-tenant relations cannot fairly be reconstructed from the records of law-suits, especially from those cases for which we have only the plaintiffs' depositions and not the decrees of the courts concerned. Moreover, it has yet to be proved that the grantees of monastic lands were more successful than the Crown in upsetting conventual grants, or even any more intent on doing so.[2] Not all Tudor landowners valued financial gain more than a well-chosen complex of properties and a good name. Sir John Gostwick was a typical servant of Henry VIII's new regime. He was also busy in the 1540's augmenting his estate. His purchases of monastic lands were made with great deliberation, beginning with properties late of Warden Abbey near his home at Willington in Bedfordshire. Later he added to his estate, mostly in the same county, but with outlying portions in Northamptonshire and Staffordshire. For all of this he paid the full standard price. But he seems to have had no desire for quick returns, even if these were possible. He advised his son neither to levy large fines nor to raise his rents unless this could be justified by the fact that his tenants were subletting at a considerable profit.[3]

[1] A. Simpson, *The Wealth of the Gentry, 1540–1660*, 1961, pp. 66–84, 202–9, 214; Mason, *op. cit.*, p. 215. See also J. H. Hexter, *Reappraisals in History*, 1961, pp. 132–3.

[2] It is possible (I owe the suggestion to Professor Habakkuk) that those who, in the latter part of the century, purchased at more than twenty years' purchase property still encumbered by long leases, did so in the hope that they would be able to upset conventual grants. Further study of the judicial records of the courts of Augmentations and Exchequer and of private estate records is needed before we can be sure how far such hopes were either experienced or fulfilled. Meanwhile, this at least is certain: at no time was there any discernible relation between the number of years' purchase and the unexpired terms of existing leases.

[3] A. G. Dickens, 'Estate and Household Management in Bedfordshire', c. 1540, *Beds. Hist. Rec. Soc.*, XXXVI, 1956, pp. 44–5, and H. P. R. Finberg, 'The Gostwicks of Willington', *ibid.*, pp. 57–75.

For the majority of laymen, whether gentlemen or yeomen farmers, quicker profits were to be made by leasing than by buying monastic lands. A jury in 1549 found that Simon Catesby's rectory of Wigston was worth £60 a year more to him than the £22 7s. 4d. which he was paying to the king. The fine of £40 which he had paid to Lenton Priory in 1536 had been money well spent, and his lease still had over thirty years to run. In 1531–2 the earl of Cumberland obtained from the abbot of Furness a lease for eighty years of Winterburn Grange. The rent was £40. In 1537 the property was valued by the king's officers at £51 6s. 8d., but the earl had no difficulty in obtaining confirmation of his lease and his assigns were still paying the same rent to the duchy of Lancaster in the early part of Elizabeth's reign.[1] Finally, when Sir Thomas Dennis died in 1561 he was still enjoying the lease of sixty acres of marsh and moorland which his old employer, the abbot of Newenham, had granted to him in 1536. His son and heir later assigned the remainder of the term to his brother, who sold the residue of thirty-five years to a Henry Parson in 1600 for £220. Not until 1631 did Parson surrender the lease to the owner, Sir William Petre, who had brought the property, along with a great deal more, from the Howards in 1605.[2] It seems possible that it was the gentlemen lease-holders, most of them well versed in the law, who led the way in showing that the long lease for term of years could be made to run its full term.

Without any doubt the laymen who were in the best position of all to profit from monastic lands were those who were able to buy land of which they themselves were already conventual or Crown lessees. This applied particularly to those who bought monastic sites, with home farms which had been kept in hand to the very end by the monks, provided they were able to complete the purchase before the Crown granted a lease to a third party. The site of Marrick Priory, Yorkshire, was first leased by the Crown and then sold to John Uvedale. That of Nun Appleton fell in similar fashion to Robert Darkenall.[3] Both were active and energetic royal servants, alert to the speed with which their fellow Crown officers installed tenants into vacant properties. Others were not quick enough. Arthur Plantagenet, Lord Lisle, was at a disadvantage in that he carried on his negotiations from Calais through his agent, John Hussey. He actually began his bid for Frithelstock Priory in north Devon before the house was dissolved on the 27th of August 1536. The royal commissioners installed a local farmer, John Winslade, as temporary tenant. On the 6th of September Hussey informed Lisle that the site and barton had been let by the Crown to

[1] W. G. Hoskins, *The Midland Peasant*, 1957, p. 131; Mason, *op. cit.*, p. 138
[2] Exeter City RO, DD. 6800.　　　[3] Clay, *op. cit.*, pp. 134–5, 140–1.

George Carew, and that unless Lisle could compound with Carew he would have to be content with the bare rent for twenty-one years. As Lisle later remarked in a letter to Ralph Sadler, he did not expect to live that long. Meanwhile, Carew sold his interest to John Winslade. Hussey advised Lisle to content himself with the reversion of the property, for the woods would be worth at least £100. The grant, in part a gift from the Crown and part at fee-farm, was completed on the 4th of September 1537.[1] Here and there one comes across individuals who purchased manors, direct or at second hand, whose demesne they already held by conventual lease. For example, the Horners, Thomas and John, who bought the manor of Mells and Leigh in Somerset from the Crown in 1543, already enjoyed possession of a farm called Melcombe which Thomas had leased from the abbot of Glastonbury at a rent of £6 6s. 8d. But this formed only a small part of the total property, for which, at a net valuation of £56 3s. 2½d., they paid twenty-four years' purchase. Unless Horner had Melcombe at a very low rent, this was not a very good bargain, for the greater part consisted of customary holdings, not easily 'improved'.[2]

Woods, which were extensive on monastic lands in many parts of the country, having been carefully reserved in leases, offered to the new owners some of the best opportunities of immediate profit. For instance, when Sir Philip Champernon bought the manor of Maristow, near Plymouth, in 1544, he obtained seventy-three acres of woodland, of which nineteen had already been felled, and eight appertained to the chief messuage for repairs, etc., leaving forty-six acres of timber varying from six to sixty years' growth. At 6d. per acre per year's growth, and £12 10s. for the "spring of the wood," Champernon paid the Crown £41 19s. Five years later his son Arthur sold the wood and underwood, but not the land, to four local farmers for £109.[3]

A great deal of the monastic land was resold by the original grantees, some of it changing hands many times, but the market was not so brisk, nor the speculation so rife, as many writers have suggested. In the county of Leicestershire out of about 64 per cent of the total monastic property, i.e. excluding the land still in Crown hands, which can be accounted for in 1558, nearly 40 per cent of the total was still in the hands of the original grantees or their heirs. These comprised only thirty-two out of the 105 original private grantees, excepting corporate bodies, but they were, on the whole, the recipients of the best estates. In Hampshire, in 1558, out of a total of 124 monastic manors, sixteen were still in Crown hands, seventy-seven in the

[1] Youings, *Devon Monastic Lands*, pp. 1–2; LP XI, pp. 111, 168, 513; LP *Addenda*, I, pt. I, pp. 391–2; LP XII, ii, p. 281.
[2] E 318, 619.   [3] E 318, 257; Plymouth RO, Roborough Mss., 197.

possession of the original grantees, and only thirty-five had changed hands. Of the 130 manors in Devon which accounted for 60 per cent of the monastic property, seventeen were still in Crown hands in 1558, eighty-two were held by the original grantees or their descendants, twenty-two had changed hands once more, six twice more, two three times more, and one, the manor of Sherford, five times more, including two restorations to the Crown. Not all these changes of ownership were clear sales. Releases of parts of property between partners to a grant have been ignored, but some of the early 'resales' may have been simply releases by agents to their principals.[1]

Attention has often been drawn to the small band of grantees who would seem, from the patent rolls, to have hunted in pairs all over the country, buying up an extraordinary collection of scattered, and, on the whole, smaller, properties, most of which they disposed of at once. Richard Andrews, a native of Hailes, Gloucestershire, and Leonard Chamberlain of Woodstock, Oxford; the same Andrews in partnership with one Nicholas Temple; John Bellow of Grimsby and John Broxholme of London; Richard Brokylsbye of Glentworth, Lincolnshire, and John Dyon; and others, they are all familiar names to those who pursue monastic lands in any county. Apart from their activities in the monastic land market they were quite unknown in contemporary society. However, as Professor Habakkuk has pointed out, they were not necessarily speculators, buying to sell at a profit. Their purchases were too diverse and deliberate for that. They were agents, engaged in negotiating grants for clients all over the country, many of whom were unfamiliar with the procedure for acquiring monastic lands from the Crown.[2] This interpretation of their activities is strengthened by the fact that, where prices are recorded they were apparently disposing of the property for the same money as they gave for it. They were most active in the middle 1540's when, over the country as a whole, the disposal of monastic property was at its peak.

For something nearer pure speculation one has to look for purchases of accumulations of small properties confined to one or more localities. George Rolle and George Haydon certainly made a relatively large profit by buying most of the scattered north Devon properties of Pilton Priory in 1544 at twenty years' purchase and selling them to the occupiers or to other local men. To John Downe of Pilton, husbandman, they sold three messuages for £80, which was more than twice what they had paid for them. A farm called Lilly in the parish of Goodleigh, which they had bought for £18, they sold within six weeks to

[1] Thorpe, *op. cit.*, pp. 195–6; Kennedy, *op. cit.*, p. 202; Youings, *Devon Monastic Lands*, p. xxiii.
[2] Habakkuk, *op. cit.*, pp. 377–80.

William Downe of Pilton, for £28.[1] Both Rolle and Haydon were lawyers, sprung from minor local freeholding families, and their descendants, by the early seventeenth century, were among the greatest landowners in the county. But the scale of their dealings in monastic lands was not such as to bring them great wealth. It was just one of many ways in which modest fortunes were founded. They had their counterparts in other counties, but perhaps not many.

It is by no means easy to find out at what price monastic lands were resold. Only very occasionally was the 'consideration' recorded, either in the actual conveyances or in their enrolments in the various courts of record. It is never mentioned in the royal licences to alienate land held by military tenure. Profits made after the lapse of a decade or more are relatively insignificant: it was to be expected that the value of land would appreciate in an age of fairly rapid inflation. Thus it is hardly surprising that the earl of Bedford sold his Devon manor of Burrington in 1577 for £700, a profit of 100 per cent on what it would have cost him at the standard rate in 1539.[2] Evidence of considerable short-term gains on large manorial properties does emerge here and there, but careful enquiry usually reveals that this had been made possible by some peculiarity in the terms of sale by the Crown, such as a valuation based on the nominal or low rent reserved on a life grant, as opposed to a lease, to a favourite subject. The officers of the court of Augmentations, especially in the early years, could usually be relied upon to 'work to rule' in such cases and the shrewd purchaser was able to buy the reversion to the property very cheaply. For example, in 1549 the earl of Warwick bought the site, demesne, and manor of Polsloe, near Exeter, by exchange and fee-farm rent, the whole being valued at just under £30 a year. Two days later he sold the property to Sir Richard Sackville, who sold it less than a year later to Sir Arthur Champernon for £1,048, a capital appreciation, assuming the standard rate of twenty years' purchase had been charged to Warwick, of 75 per cent. Either Warwick or Sackville had made a handsome profit, but at the expense of the Crown, not of Champernon, for the real value of the estate was about £70. It had been granted in 1541, for their lives, to Sir George Carew and Mary, his wife, at the low rent set in Warwick's particulars. Sir George had died in 1545 and his widow had married Sir Arthur Champernon.[3] He, presumably, was very happy to pay just under

[1] Youings, *Devon Monastic Lands*, pp. 44, 71. These were not all urban properties as suggested by Professor Habakkuk (*op. cit.*, p. 377, n. 2).

[2] Woburn Abbey, G 1, 54, for details of which I am indebted to Miss Gladys Scott Thomson.

[3] Youings, *op. cit.*, p. 102. See also G. W. O. Woodward, *EHR*, LXXIX, 1964, pp. 778–83.

fifteen years' purchase for the freehold rather than merely to occupy the estate in the right of his wife's life interest.

Generally speaking, however, the evidence, though limited, suggests that short-term capital gains were very rare in the monastic land market. Moreover, not even the use of agents will account for the number of people, courtiers, lawyers, and country gentry, who were content to buy at second hand. Had there been a larger profit on resales, more purchasers would surely have bought direct from the Crown, and this, in its turn, might have led to competitive offers. In fact, however, it is open to doubt whether contemporaries thought of land as a source of quick returns, least of all monastic lands, whose value could not rapidly be improved. At any rate, the comparative absence of short-term gains on resales confirms the impression that the Crown, having decided, rightly or wrongly, to alienate the monastic lands, normally obtained a fair capital return.

In the final analysis it will probably be found that the balance of economic advantage from the Dissolution lay neither with the Crown nor with any particular section of society, aristocratic, old or new gentry, or peasant. In the short run it undoubtedly lay with the tenants, whether peasants or gentlemen, and in the long run with the owners of the freehold. It was the latter, however, who were the real successors of the religious communities, and it is they who must now be considered.

(iii) *The grantees*. The task of discovering who were the new owners was begun over fifty years ago by Professor Savine, who established from the patent rolls the names of all the original grantees during the reign of Henry VIII. His method of classifying them, partly by class, and partly by occupation, has not been generally acceptable, but it is still the only attempt to achieve results on a national scale. In very round figures Savine's analysis indicates that, of that portion of the monastic land which was alienated by the Crown before 1547, 14 per cent went to peers, 18 per cent to courtiers and royal officials, and 21 per cent to country gentry.[1]

The main drawback of Savine's table is that it deals only with original Crown grantees, and in printing it H. A. L. Fisher drew attention to the need to consider the effect of subsequent resales. Over thirty years later this point was taken up by Professor Tawney, and he himself gave a lead by considering the history of some two hundred and fifty former monastic manors in Gloucestershire, Northamptonshire, and Warwickshire. He found that initially rather more than one sixth was acquired by seventeen peers. Crown officials and business men also had a share but the greater part went immediately to members of already well-established local landowning families.

[1] Fisher, *op. cit.*, p. 499.

Pursuing his manors through almost to the eve of the Civil War, Professor Tawney found that, as time went on, more and more came into the possession of local gentry, but their names included those of Thynne, Spencer, and Cecil. In fact, in these particular counties the long-term effect of the Dissolution was "not so much (to) endow an existing nobility, as (to) lay the foundation of a new nobility to arise in the next century."[1]

Some progress has been made in recent years in pursuing the ownership of former monastic lands on a strictly county basis, but the study has in no case been carried systematically beyond the end of Mary's reign. In three widely separated counties, Leicestershire, Hampshire and the Isle of Wight, and Devonshire, results so far obtained suggest certain local peculiarities, but the general pattern is remarkably uniform, and, on the whole, Professor Tawney's conclusions have been considerably reinforced. In each of the three counties large initial grants were made to men very close to the king, and, in each case, the lands were retained almost intact by their descendants for several generations. In Leicestershire the earls of Rutland acquired and retained lands worth, on the eve of the Dissolution, some £300 a year, and by 1558 about 30 per cent of the total monastic estate in the county had gone to peers of the realm. This included over half the demesne and land held 'at will', and it had been granted mostly as royal gifts or in exchange for other lands. In Hampshire, by 1558, the Wriothesleys, earls of Southampton, owned just over 20 per cent of the former monastic manors in the county, about half of which they had paid for in cash. The Lords Sandys and Paulet had acquired a further 18 per cent between them, so that nearly 40 per cent of the monastic estate in the county, in terms of manors, if not in value, had gone to three owners. In Devon one very large estate was carved out of monastic lands, that of the Russells, later earls of Bedford, worth in 1535 over £800 a year. This comprised about 12 per cent of the monastic land in the county. Altogether, by 1558 just over 27 per cent of the Devon monastic lands were held in large portions by seven owners, including, besides the earl of Bedford, the dean and canons of Windsor.[2]

The next largest share in Devon, nearly 20 per cent, went in parcels of land worth between £50 and £100 a year, mostly to men bearing the names of established local families but who were also themselves well known in London political and administrative circles. Such men

[1] R. H. Tawney, 'The Rise of the Gentry', EcHR, XI, 1941, pp. 23–8.
[2] Thorpe, *op. cit.*, pp. 184–7 (figures relate to original grants only); Kennedy, *op. cit.*, pp. 190, 195 (figures relate to lands alienated by 1558 and have been adjusted to indicate proportion of total monastic estate); Youings, *Devon Monastic Lands*, pp. xxv–xxvi (do.).

almost without exception had paid in full for their monastic property. By comparison the share of the lands acquired by purely local interests was rather less. Some sixty persons in this category in Devon had, by 1558, purchased a bare 15 per cent of the whole.[1] In none of the counties so far investigated do yeomen figure appreciably. Occasionally they bought small farms or parts of farms already in their own occupation, but rarely did they buy manors or lordships. Such men stood to gain far more by using what capital they had either to buy leases or to improve land they already held on long monastic leases.

With the notable exception of the rising aristocracy such as the earls of Bedford and Southampton, very few new or appreciably enlarged estates were built up by 1558 entirely or even principally of monastic lands. In Devon it is possible to identify only nine of these. In Leicestershire some fourteen had appeared by 1558, but of these only five lasted very much longer.[2] There is no particular significance in the fact that so few men put all their capital into monastic lands. Sir Arthur Champernon showed quite exceptional caution among his contemporaries when, in 1550, he had inserted in the deed of bargain and sale to him of the Polsloe Priory estate near Exeter, a covenant whereby the vendor, Sir Richard Sackville, was to repay the purchase money should the property ever be seized by the Crown.[3] The attitude of most men of his time amounted to a firm resolution that capital expended on the purchase of monastic lands would not lightly be surrendered. Politics hardly entered into it, and, it must be remembered, even Mary Tudor sold portions of the monastic estate. As always, men bought, when they were able to afford to, with discrimination, building up in the process either a compact or a dispersed estate, whichever suited their purpose. They kept an eye on the land market as a whole, and monastic lands were not by any means all that were available, nor were they necessarily the best bargains. John Arscott, of the Middle Temple and surveyor of woods beyond Trent for the court of Augmentations, the younger son of an old-established family of minor gentry in north-west Devon, was in a very fair position to purchase when and what he wanted directly from the Crown. But in fact he confined his monastic acquisitions to the two manors of Bradford, late of Launceston Priory, and Hatherleigh, late of Tavistock Abbey, which he bought in 1552 at second-hand, though within a matter of days after the original grant, from Lord Clinton and Saye. Both manors lay near his old home, but when he retired it was to the non-monastic manor of Tetcott, also on the Cornish border, which he bought, also in 1552, from Sir John Neville. Richard Duke, another

---

[1] Youings, *ibid.*   [2] Youings, *ibid.*, p. xxvii; Thorpe, *op. cit.*, pp. 286–7.
[3] Exeter RO, DD. 41941.

Devon lawyer and clerk of the court of Augmentations, was earlier in the field. He was, in fact, the first purchaser of monastic land in Devon. He made a number of further purchases, building up a compact estate in the vicinity of his small patrimony in east Devon where his descendants flourished for at least two centuries.[1] Men like Arscott and Duke, most of them younger sons of already established landowning families, were building up new patterns of landownership all over the country during the century following the Dissolution. Only in so far as the capital with which they acquired their new estates had been accumulated in the service of the Crown did they owe their landed wealth to the dissolution of the monasteries.

2. *The Secular Clergy*

The administration of the non-monastic ecclesiastical estates, from those of the archbishops to those of the parish clergy, has attracted very little attention from agricultural historians of the period 1500–1640. There is insufficient scholarly work available upon which to base a long account of the subject. In part this is due to the scanty nature of the ecclesiastical estate records of the period and, until quite recently, these have not all been easily accessible. But no one has yet analysed that part of the *Valor Ecclesiasticus* of 1535 which deals with non-monastic lands, so that it is not yet known what was the extent of the Church's landed resources at a time when complete disendowment was being seriously envisaged.[2]

During the century 1540–1640 episcopal and capitular estates were extensively plundered, both by the Crown, and by the laity aided and abetted by the Crown. But although examples abound, neither the rate nor the short and long-term effects of the process are yet at all clear. It appears, on the evidence so far available, that the Church's regular income was depleted more by the granting of long leases at old rents than by the outright alienation of large properties, although the latter was certainly taking place.[3] The only large estate so far thoroughly investigated is that of the bishop of Bath and Wells. The results

[1] CPR Edward VI, IV, pp. 224, 231; PRO, CP 40, 1151, m. 6d.; LP xv, p. 105, XVIII, i, p. 539, XXI, i, p. 250; PRO C 142, 163, 13. For further examples of families who built up considerable estates during the period 1540–1640, partly but not exclusively from former monastic lands, see M. E. Finch, *op. cit.*, pp. 50–1 (Sir Robert Catlin), p. 69 (Thomas Tresham), p. 141 (the Brudenells), and p. 176 (the Spencers).

[2] LP VII, pp. 551–2 for Chapuys' well-known despatch; L. Stone, 'The Political Programme of Thomas Cromwell', *Bull. IHR*, XXIV, 1951, pp. 1–18.

[3] C. Hill, *The Economic Problems of the Church*, 1956, *passim* and especially chap. ii, 'The Plunder of the Church'; F. R. H. du Boulay, 'Archbishop Cranmer and the Canterbury Temporalities', EHR, LXVII, 1962, pp. 19–36.

suggest that the most disastrous inroads were made before the accession of Queen Elizabeth, who has traditionally been held to blame for the impoverishment of the secular clergy. Between 1539 and 1559 the gross annual revenue of the see fell by 55 per cent, from over £2,000 to under £1,000, largely as the result of the surrender of lands to Henry VIII and the Protector Somerset. In 1560 the first Elizabethan bishop, Berkeley, complained to the queen about the improvident leases granted by bishop Bourne, his Marian predecessor. Like the departing monks, Bourne had obliged not only neighbouring gentry but also his own family, some of whom were still in possession of the house and demesnes at Wiveliscombe in 1623. In spite of the statutory prohibitions of 1559 and 1571, Berkeley was able to raise large sums by way of fines for long leases. However, both he and Bourne exerted pressure on their smaller tenants, and Berkeley succeeded in stabilizing the revenues of his see. Although these never reached pre-Reformation levels, they did rise to over £1,300 by the turn of the century.[1]

Rather more attention has been given to the parochial clergy of the period. For the most part theirs was an ever-increasing struggle to extract the tithes upon which they very largely depended. But most of them kept a few animals and tilled their glebe acres.[2]

Conflicting solutions for the economic problems of the Church— Puritan disendowment *versus* Laudian resumption and conservation— these certainly loomed large in the public controversies of the early Stuart period. But we are still far from knowing how great those problems really were. It is even possible that the archbishop himself had little cause for concern over his own revenues.[3] To the agricultural historian the more important question is whether the dead hand of the Church over so considerable a part of the landed wealth of the country had a stifling effect on agricultural experiment. Certainly the day had long since gone when bishops had produced crops and stock for the market. At the same time there is no reason why some of those long leases should not have acted as a spur to improvement by others.

---

[1] P. Hembry, *The Bishops of Bath and Wells, 1535–1647: a Social and Economic Study*, unpublished London Ph.D. thesis, 1956, *passim*, and especially pp. 97, 111, 126–48, 181, 164, 184, 191–8, 200–1, 286–9, 304.

[2] Hill, *op. cit.*, chaps. v and vi; A. Tindall Hart, *The Country Clergy in Elizabethan and Stuart Times, 1558–1660*, 1958, pp. 28, 51; W. G. Hoskins, 'The Leicestershire Country Parson in the Sixteenth Century', in *Essays in Leicestershire History*, 1950, pp. 1–23.

[3] Du Boulay, *op. cit.*, p. 36.

CHAPTER VI

LANDLORDS IN WALES

A. THE NOBILITY AND GENTRY[1]

Although there are many familiar features in the agrarian history
of the period under review which are common to both sides of the
border, there is every reason why Wales should in some measure be
the subject of separate treatment in this volume. It is true that on a
purely physical level there are very few elements in the Welsh settlement pattern which are not found elsewhere in the highland zone of
Britain. Wales, moreover, had experienced most of the tensions which
had been at work in England during the later Middle Ages—tensions
which had exposed traditional methods of landholding to much the
same kind of influence which concurrently was beginning to reshape
the manor in England. On the other hand, a fundamental distinction
emerges from the fact that manorial institutions never took natural
root in Wales outside certain Normanized parts of the March which
were situated in the coastal lowlands and eastward-facing valleys of the
south—areas which account for only a fraction of the total land surface
of the country, and with which for the time being we have no concern.
As for the rest of Wales, including some districts lying to the east of the
present Anglo-Welsh border, landownership in 1500 rested on a basis
of intrinsically native institutions. Those institutions were admittedly
already passing through a process of internal modification at that date,
but the essential framework of the so-called 'tribal system' had survived
virtually intact.

In the chaos which followed the failure of the Glyndŵr rising at the
opening of the fifteenth century, alienation of small clan holdings,
though not unknown before the outbreak of the rebellion, began for
the first time to be a critical factor in the fate of the older hereditary
tenures; and in the course of the century the process continued at so
phenomenal a pace that by 1500 several freehold estates of considerable
size had appeared, as well as a great many nuclei of smaller estates on
which the economic and social power of an emergent squirearchy

[1] This section was received from the late Professor Jones Pierce a few days before
his untimely death. The text was complete but it lacked footnotes. The editor is
deeply indebted to Mr Beverley Smith, Mr Glanville Jones, Dr Colin Thomas, and
Mr Ogwen Williams for supplying, from their own knowledge, the majority of the
footnotes.

would rest in the ensuing century. Notable though these inroads into
the crumbling organization of the clan were, the essential features of
the medieval landscape were nevertheless clearly visible at the beginning of the sixteenth century; and small peasant proprietors whose
rights in the soil derived from clan status were still the most prominent
element in Welsh rural society. Moreover, the fact that a new type of
proprietor, having as often as not no personal association with the
clan in occupation, was replacing some of the hereditary owners, had
not disrupted the unity of clan territories as a whole since knowledge
of the precise nature of a constituent holding and its appurtenances,
whether alienated or not, continued to be necessary both for safeguard-
ing the fiscal interests of the Crown or marcher lord, and for ensuring
the landed title of old and new owners alike. For it must be realized
that even under these conditions of mixed proprietorship, all title to
rights appurtenant to arable holdings—particularly to those relating to
common pasture—were regarded as being derived from a common
juridical source and therefore continued to be linked to the clan
territory in its entirety. This is reflected in the fact that the increasing
tempo observed in transfers of land during the fifteenth century was
not much facilitated by the intrusion of English legal practice, except
perhaps along the borderlands, where, despite the survival of the clanland and many of the native customs associated with it, English methods
of conveyancing would appear to have entirely replaced the sanctions
of native custom. But over the greater part of Wales, and in particular
within the area of the two principalities of north and west Wales, the
majority of ordinary Welshmen in 1500, and, as will be seen, for a
considerable time afterwards, thought in terms of their own legal
concepts where landownership, including the processes of alienation,
was concerned. Such changes as had appeared in 'tribal' society by
1500, and indeed all the developments which will occur during the
next century or so, must therefore be viewed against a continuing
institutional background of early medieval origin, with stress on
four major surviving factors, namely (1) a long-established settlement
pattern; (2) a widespread peasant proprietorship, (3) a network of rights
anchored to ancient clanlands; (4) a body of innate tenurial law and
custom. Each of these factors will be treated in turn.

1. *The settlement pattern*

The mould in which settlement had been shaped in Wales during the
central period of the Middle Ages was the township (*tref*) which func-
tioned both as a sphere of influence for a number of interrelated kindreds
and as a unit of fiscal and agrarian administration. In places like

Anglesey and the promontories of Llŷn and Pembroke, and indeed all along the narrow coastal lowlands and the broader estuarine valleys of the north and west, townships normally occupied a relatively small superficial area, although even in these low-lying territories there were townships of considerable size, some virtually co-extensive with entire commotes (the commote being the local government division later identified with the English hundred), and others broken up into two or more members including pastoral detachments in the hills. The townships of the interior, on the other hand, were in general very extensive, and included a large acreage of mountain land which merged valleywards with lower-lying pastures (*ffridd*) and the scattered homesteads (*tyddyn*) which were characteristic of the settlement pattern in these upland districts. It was in these narrow valleys of the interior, where the balance of activity was heavily slanted on the pastoral side, that the isolated homestead, traditionally associated with the 'celtic' countryside, dominated the landscape. Under suitable physical conditions, however, stretches of arable and meadow, shared among several proprietors, occurred—a feature which on a more extensive scale was normal in lowland settlement where there was greater stress on field husbandry. Here on the periphery of the mountain zone, the unit of settlement was the hamlet (*rhandir*) which basically consisted of open field made up of irregular-shaped parcels of varying size and engirdled with a cluster of homesteads set in small enclosures. Modifications of landscape in the lowlands, and to some extent in parts of the uplands, during the fifteenth century were produced by alienation and concentration of holdings in these open sharelands—a term which conveys the literal meaning of *rhandir* rather better than the word hamlet. This was a continuing process which was accelerated in the course of the sixteenth century, when further modifications appeared through complete or partial hedging in the open fields, and, though purely in a secondary sense, through enclosure of common appurtenant to arable holdings. The most prominent factor, however, in reshaping the rural scene in the uplands was undoubtedly the practice of assimilating portions of waste to the land already appropriated round an isolated homestead, a practice which, as will be seen,[1] assumed no small proportions as the sixteenth century advanced, and which in fact was then considerably extended by large, independent intakes from the waste on the part of the more powerful landowners who had emerged from, and had profited by, the breakdown of the medieval social system.

[1] See *infra*, pp. 377 *sqq.*

2. *Peasant proprietors*

Control of the soil in the average free township (a minority class of bond township will be examined in a separate context), at the beginning of the sixteenth century was shared among a mixture of small, medium, and, in varying degrees, fairly substantial proprietors—the small proprietor still predominating and the larger proprietor representing both resident and non-resident interests. While the records reflect a greater concentration of ownership than had existed a century earlier, small survivors of an older social system continued to be very numerous. Outside one or two areas where escheat for example had facilitated the premature creation of rather larger estates in land, free townships had remained almost to the end of the fourteenth century in the hands of exclusive groups of resident kindred, among whom there would appear to have been few glaring disparities of wealth or social status. It has been calculated that the average lowland holding of arable land in the fourteenth century consisted of some six to ten acres which were usually dispersed in scattered parcels over the fields of several hamlets; and that this was also the average size of enclosures associated with homesteads in areas where the detached farmstead predominated. Even if the exercise were feasible, however, no useful purpose could be served by attempting to strike an average in the circumstances which had supervened by the beginning of the sixteenth century, because in broad general terms, although the position varied widely from district to district and township to township, the gulf between smaller and larger proprietors is one of the more striking features of the agrarian situation in Wales at this time—the large proprietor, as well as many of the medium-sized owners, having evidently benefited meanwhile from the morcellation of the average fourteenth-century holding.

What would appear on a superficial acquaintance with the agrarian problem in Wales at the close of the Middle Ages to have been a relatively sudden internal collapse of the medieval system of tenure— itself the product of a movement going back no further than the twelfth century—occurred largely as a logical consequence of the operation within a system which, in at least a juridical sense, had become fully extended before 1350, of the traditional practice of partible succession—known in the vernacular as *cyfran*, and better known to English readers as *gavelkind*. This fragmentation of holdings, which in some parts had clearly begun on the eve of the Glyndŵr rising, and which was reaching its climax during the period of the early Tudors, was naturally felt more acutely in lowland vills with their more tightly-woven agrarian structure, and in so far as the interior was affected, in those areas where joint appropriation of land had led to the creation of sharelands. Commentators writing at the close of the period covered by this volume were very much aware of this as a major factor in producing the agrarian changes of the preceding two centuries. George Owen, writing of conditions in south-west Wales, observed that "the use of gavelkind among most of these Welshmen to part all of the father's patrimony" had led in process of time to the whole country being "brought into small pieces of ground and inter-mingled up and down one with another, so as in every five or six acres you shall have ten or twelve owners."[1] Sir John Wynn, commenting on a similar situation in the north, refers to descendants of certain well-known tribal stocks who had been brought "by the division and subdivision of gavelkind (the destruction of Wales)...to the estate of mean freeholders, and so having forgotten their descents and pedigree have become as if they never had been."[2] Both writers were of course concerned in retrospect with the results of a process to which Welsh rural society had been sharply exposed between say 1425 and 1535, but which in some degree was halted by the Union legislation of 1536–42. It is therefore of interest to observe that the writer of a fifteenth-century legal tract can assume quite incidentally in dealing with an entirely different matter that an inheritance of land could descend "in small shares among forty or sixty co-inheritors."[3] The witness of contemporary record, moreover, bears out the observations of the writers who have been quoted, since the average size of holdings subject to alienation or falling in by way of escheat during the period in question is shown to have been much lower than the fourteenth-century average. Apart from the fact that an aggregate of one or two acres is far more common than in the preceding century, a significant feature of the late fifteenth-century accounts is the appearance within these aggregates of items which fall below one acre. So striking indeed is this feature in contrast with earlier conditions that one tends to conclude that extreme morcellation had been formerly avoided by assarting from individual assets in waste; and that this procedure was becoming increasingly difficult for many proprietors in lowland vills because of the contraction of their stakes in the waste, and in some cases perhaps because of growing physical limitation on expansion.

George Owen realized that it was this proliferation of uneconomic units which, more than any other single factor, had encouraged those developments, still proceeding at the time when he was writing,

[1] George Owen, *The Description of Pembrokeshire*, ed. H. Owen, I, 1892, p. 61.
[2] Sir John Wynn, *The History of the Gwydir Family*, 1927, p. 14.
[3] *Ancient Laws and Institutes of Wales*, ed. A. Owen, II, 1841, pp. 430–3.

whereby fragmented holdings had been "brought together by purchase and exchange."[1] These were of course conditions which had appeared in the type of country with which Owen was familiar in west Wales, where shareland farming had long been customary and where dwindling resources placed a limit on the extension of holdings. But in hill country, where the possibilities of expansion were far less restricted, the effects of partible inheritance could not have been felt in quite the same way. Under mainly pastoral conditions of living, holdings in mountain districts could remain undivided for several generations on a quasi-patriarchal basis, a method of circumventing the acuter consequences of gavelkind not uncommon in the lowlands. Since the evidence points to the fact that there was not much hiving-off of families into new settlement during the later Middle Ages, and since the population of inland regions does not appear to have been much, if at all, thinner than along the coastlands, increasing needs must have been met by appropriations from joint common or *cytir* in the immediate neighbourhood of farmsteads, thus foreshadowing in the years before 1500 those massive invasions of the waste which went on steadily as the sixteenth century advanced.[2] At the same time, at the beginning of the century estates had also emerged in the Welsh heartland, although they were growing at a slower pace, in response to the same influences as were at work elsewhere in Wales, including the factor of partible inheritance. While at least one of these upland estates can be shown to have had its origin in a single farmstead enlarged by absorption of surrounding waste (there are many others which have all the appearances of having been launched in this way), most of them began as concentrations of small holdings in valley sharelands, and were subsequently extended by the acquisition of more isolated hill farms—a salutary warning against drawing too rigid a distinction between highland and lowland.

Owen, however, seems to have been under the impression that the consolidation of holdings to which he refers was a process which began only with the statutory abolition of gavelkind some threescore years before his time. But we have already indicated, and the point will be illustrated in rather greater detail at a later stage, that within the limitations already stated, the growth of the modern freehold estate was already reasonably advanced when the parliamentary provisions which finally brought Wales within the complete orbit of English administration between 1536 and 1542 gave a new *legal* direction to the business of estate building without impinging, at least directly and in the short-term, on the continuity in organic growth of these estates.

[1] George Owen, *op. cit.*, p. 61.
[2] See *infra*, pp. 377 *sqq.*

Whatever the impact of 1536 and the years which immediately followed on Welsh society (and this too is a matter which will have to be considered in due course), this is a date which in the study of the rise of modern freeholds in Wales can no more be regarded as crucial than the year 1500, since the sixteenth and early seventeenth centuries merely witnessed the continued operation of agencies which had their effective origin in the crises which followed the political cataclysm of the early fifteenth century. The problem here is to discover in broad terms (detailed calculations are not at the moment practicable) the extent to which the structural growth of these estates from 1500 onwards altered the overall pattern of small peasant proprietorship which, in spite of the preludial changes which have been noted, was still, when our period opens, the most prominent surviving phenomenon of an older agrarian order.

3. *The ancient clanlands*

The student of English agrarian history will not be altogether unfamiliar with some of the features which have been hitherto unfolded. But at this point the picture becomes complicated by the intrusion of those other factors mentioned at the outset which centre round the survival of certain institutions traditionally associated with the former working of the kindred system. The fact is that the influences which had brought about the slow erosion and, with the Edwardian conquest, the collapse of most aspects of kindred organization, did not begin seriously to impinge on the function of kindred in relation to the native law on 'land and soil' until the fifteenth century. It is true that here and there an association of kindred had lost control of some individual holdings which had passed to the lord by way of escheat, holdings which thereby ceased to be held by Welsh tenure, but rarely had this happened on a scale large enough to effect serious breaches in the unity of clan territories. Of much greater significance is the fact that commutation, where not already completed, became more or less universal at the time of the Edwardian settlement, thus making the discharge of communal dues and services, which had been one of the more important collective functions of kindred, no longer necessary.[1] With cash rents henceforth anchored to recognizable units of land, and with the personal bonds of kindred in consequence loosened and undermined, the substitution of alienees for hereditary proprietors was

[1] T. Jones Pierce, 'The Growth of Commutation in Gwynedd during the Thirteenth Century', *Bull. BCS*, x, 1941, pp. 309–30; Idem, 'Some Tendencies in the Agrarian History of Caernarvonshire in the later Middle Ages', *Trans. Caernarvonshire Hist. Soc.*, 1939, pp. 18–36.

facilitated when in due course other factors, such as the onset of morcellation, gave rise to the kind of situation earlier described as existing during the initial decades of the sixteenth century. But the steady dissolution of established groupings of agnatic kindred which that situation reveals had not resulted in much corresponding loss in local knowledge of where and how alienated as well as surviving hereditary holdings fitted into an aggregate of rights once enjoyed by an undisrupted kindred. In other words, the growing divorce which had been taking place between personal and tenurial elements in the structure of kindred—or in vernacular terms between the *gwelygordd* (clan) and its territorial basis in *gwely* or *gafael* (clanland)—did not, until the repercussions of the Act of Union began to be felt, eliminate the need to know how the clanland was related *inter alia* to shareland and farmstead, so vital did this knowledge continue to be if proprietary interests, whether official, innate, or acquired, were to be safeguarded.

Originating far back in the twelfth century in a primary settlement set in a township over which a single occupying family normally had sole control, the nuclei of the multipartite and often sprawling clanlands (*gwelyau*) which are described in some Tudor and Stuart rentals,[1] arose out of the partition of a primary settlement among a first generation of co-heirs whose names became permanently associated with these clanlands throughout all subsequent stages of growth and subdivision. The peculiar shape which the clanland eventually assumed grew out of the need for simultaneous appropriations from the waste as families with heritable interests, derived from the original stocks, increased in number and spilled over into secondary sharelands, thus producing an intermingling of clanland offshoots and a pattern of landholding in which every quillet and plot could be identified as a member of one of the clanlands represented in a township's fields. It should be added, however, that in the hillier parts of the interior the differences already observed in the matter of settlement are also reflected in the institutional overlay. Whereas in townships where the *gwely* type of clanland flourished (usually in lower-lying districts) unappropriated waste continued to be undivided, larger upland townships were parcelled out into separate pastoral divisions known as

---

[1] T. Jones Pierce, 'An Anglesey Crown Rental of the Sixteenth Century', *Bull. BCS*, x, 1940, pp. 156–76; Idem, 'Medieval Settlement in Anglesey', *Trans. Anglesey Antiq. Soc.*, 1951, pp. 1–33; Idem, 'Agrarian Aspects of the Tribal System in Wales', *Géographie et Histoire Agraires, Annales de L'Est*, Mémoire no. 21, Nancy, 1959, pp. 329–37; G. R. J. Jones, 'Medieval Rural Settlements in North Wales', *Trans. Inst. British Geographers*, XIX, 1953, pp. 51–72; Idem, 'The Distribution of Medieval Settlement in Anglesey', *Trans. Anglesey Antiq. Soc.*, 1955, pp. 27–96; Idem, 'Medieval Open Fields and Associated Settlement Patterns in North-west Wales', *Géographie et Histoire, op. cit.*, 1959, pp. 313–26.

gafaels in each of which a particular stock (*gwelygordd*) had exercised exclusive rights. Nevertheless, sharelands developed the same features here as elsewhere, except that the number of stocks participating in the formation of sharelands had normally been larger in *gafael* than in *gwely* settlement, a factor which tended to impose somewhat greater complexity on the ultimate form of sharelands falling within the former category. Otherwise the similarities were so close that an expert English observer when recording his impressions of shareland conditions in the fourteenth century failed to understand why there should have been a distinction of nomenclature at all.[1]

Now the actual outlines of some of these medieval clanlands continue as late as the time of Elizabeth and James I[2] to figure in official rentals where internal arrangements are described in such expansive detail that problematical factors in the purely medieval evidence can often be resolved in the light of data which they contain. These rare documents, moreover, are invaluable as standards whereby one can interpret very similar detail in other contemporary rentals from which known *gwely* and *gafael* affiliations are nominally omitted.[3] The primary purpose, of course, which all these rentals served, apart from the few extant examples compiled for private use, was to pinpoint sites on which ancient quit-rents were leviable; and certainly by the end of our period this was virtually the only practical value which can be ascribed to them. But the kind of information which such rentals preserve, whether actually recorded or verbally transmitted, had more than merely fiscal implications for those who paid chief-rents, until, during the half century or so which followed the union with England, circumstances on the periphery of ancient holdings became, both from the legal and physical angles, progressively more confused. After all, the very fact that a holding formed part of a clanland imposed certain restrictions on the individual freedom of proprietors, if for no other reason than the need for mutual protection of rights appurtenant to arable holdings, and for the preservation of the intrinsically hereditary nature of clanland or *gwely* tenure—both matters which now call for brief consideration.

[1] *Survey of the Honour of Denbigh, 1334*, ed. P. Vinogradoff and F. Morgan, 1914, p. 211. See also T. Jones Pierce, 'Pastoral and Agricultural Settlements in Early Wales', *Geographiska Annaler*, XLIII, 1961, pp. 182–9.

[2] T. Jones Pierce, *Bull. BCS*, x, *loc. cit.*; *The Lordship of Oswestry, 1393–1607*, ed. W. J. Slack, 1951, pp. 38–141. See also PRO SC 12, 21, 13; E 178, 7213.

[3] PRO LR 2, 205; LR 2, 236; SC 12, 23, 42; SC 12, 24, 1. See G. R. J. Jones, 'The Llanynys Quillets', *Denbighshire Hist. Soc. Trans.*, XIII, 1964, pp. 133–58.

4. Tenurial law and custom

Although at higher levels English administrative procedure had tended from the start to regard Welsh proprietors (*priodorion*) as *liberi tenentes*, in practice the underlying realities of the native system of tenure were observed in accordance with official policy, thus ensuring the survival into the sixteenth century of traditional tenurial concepts and of the technicalities of language in which these were expressed—a survival which was made all the easier by the fact that the business of administration at commote level was continuously in the hands of local officials drawn from the ranks of native proprietors themselves. The weightiest claim which a hereditary proprietor (*priodawr*, pl. *priodorion*, a term which would appear to have been still current in the sixteenth century) had in the general assets of the community was to a share in the pasture, wood, and waste which the community controlled, and which constituted what was known as *cytir* or joint-land. Limited to the *gafael*, rather than to the township as a whole, in districts where that class of clanland flourished, a *priodawr's* share in *cytir* formed an integral part of his patrimony (*treftadaeth*), the extent of which share was determined by the past operation of partible succession (*cyfran*), and calculated in comparable acreages of land already appropriated (*tir priod*), such as homesteads (*tyddynod*) and scattered arable holdings (*tir gwasgar*). Concentration of holdings therefore involved a corresponding accumulation of hereditary rights in *cytir*, or for that matter in other appurtenances such as shares in collective mills, which were sometimes bought in infinitesimal fractions over a period of several generations. By 1536 large engrossers on the fringes of hill country are known to have acquired considerable tracts of unenclosed wood and pasture in which their claims had to be assessed in relation to those arable units of clanland to which such claims were tied, and to a variety of similar interests likewise based on *gwely* tenure.

The chances of disengagement for acquired interests were still further restricted by another cardinal feature of native custom which enshrined hereditary proprietorship in a kind of fiction of indestructibility. A measure of flexibility had, however, been attained quite early by permitting, in exceptional circumstances, and with the combined consent of the lord and coheirs, the substitution of a guardian (*gwarcheidwad*) who, in return for an agreed consideration (*pridwerth*), would have possession of the whole or part of a patrimony for a defined period without prejudice to the innate title of the hereditary proprietor. The most advantageous of the permissible arrangements, and the most far-reaching in its long-term consequences, allowed for a kind of lease or mortgage (*prid*) covering in the first instance a four-year term, which could be renewed for additional quadrennial periods in the event of the *prid* continuing to be unredeemed. Although resort to this principle was unusual before 1400, in the exigencies of the period which followed *prid* provided the one loophole through which large-scale, permanent alienation of land could be brought about without trespassing unduly on native custom. This trend seems to have been facilitated by the rule (possibly evolved late in the day by the action of native jurists themselves) which gave absolute title to the mortgagor (*pridwr*) if *prid* was unredeemed after sixteen years, a contingency which it is on record was sometimes followed by the execution of a deed of quitclaim on the English model.[1] Records are extant which show how several small estates in the fifteenth century were built up along these lines; and in the case of the largest landowner in north Wales at the end of the century, his estate is said to have consisted entirely of either hereditary land or *terre pridate*. Though the growth of the vast majority of small estates in Wales is undocumented, particularly during the earliest phases, the models we have and the numerous cross-sections which emerge from collections of early deeds suffice to show, in the light of our knowledge of native custom, how the revolutionary extension of a principle which was originally intended to alleviate the rigours of native tenure proved, while still continuing for a long time ahead to impede the process of complete extrication, the most effective bridge in easing the transition from medieval to modern conditions of tenure over a large part of Wales.

In the long run, the more substantial estate builders naturally preferred to allow *prid* lands, on ceasing of the time bar, to pass into estates in fee simple rather than revert, as would have been the case if they had adhered to native custom, to the condition of a new hereditary tenure. With clefts already in being through the withdrawal of escheat holdings, this imposed new pressures on the overall cohesion of the traditional system of tenure; and with the voluntary rejection of gavelkind and the open adoption of English methods of conveyancing, including entail, by certain landowners, among whom there were some who lived in more remote western districts, the resultant picture during the first half of the sixteenth century was in some ways strikingly different from what it had been a century earlier. But the average countryman still turned in a familiar *milieu*, seeking to have his interests protected by Welsh law which, as interpretations recorded in current law-books make clear, had been trying to keep pace with the agrarian trends of the age. On the eve of the Union, litigants in west Wales persisted in submitting claims in the Welsh manner to the judgement

[1] T. Jones Pierce, 'The Law of Wales—The Last Phase', *Trans. Hon. Soc. Cymmrodorion*, 1963, pp. 17–19; Idem, *Trans. Caern. Hist. Soc.*, 1939, pp. 31–3.

of native suitors in established commote courts, or as elsewhere, were resorting to quasi-judicial arbitration by local landowners, versed in the intricacies of Welsh tenures, who, in this twilight phase of the older jurisprudence, must have been called upon to unravel many a knotty problem arising from the interlocking claims which had been fostered by the transitional nature of the times.[1] With forward-looking agencies thus working relentlessly against the grain of a conservatively oriented agrarian structure, the legislation of 1536–42, at least in so far as it was directed towards the assimilation of Welsh tenures, must have been received with profound relief by those aggressive elements in Welsh society who were bent on increasing and consolidating their stake in the soil.

In addition to introducing new and streamlining existing judicial machinery, the cumulative force of the legal provisions incorporated in the statutes of 1536 and 1542[2] was to give English legal processes, including the exclusive use of the English language, an all-embracing warrant throughout the recently completed Welsh shire system. In relation to most sectors of legal practice this decisive step amounted to virtual recognition of a *fait accompli*, as, indeed, it also was to some extent in its bearing on dealings in real property, a fact which the statute of 1542 seems to imply in certain references to current procedures in the principality courts of north Wales. The proscription of what the redactors of the statutes regarded as "sinister customs and usages" could only have been seriously motivated therefore by a desire to eradicate methods of landholding which were still tied to ancient clanlands, and to bring Welsh tenure (*terra Wallensica* or *tir Cymraeg*) into line with those holdings of English land (*terra Anglicana* or *tir Saesneg*) with which, although they were as a rule a minority element, the average Welsh township was by this time inlaid. This is borne out by the fact that specific statements about such "usages" mention only tenurial customs which, after having been the subject of some hesitation and uncertainty when the statute of 1536 was enacted, were dealt with, in concise but no uncertain terms, in *three key clauses* towards the end of the later statute of 1542.[3] All real property due to descend by inheritance after 24 June 1541, it was enacted, was to be held by English tenure according to the common law of England, and was to devolve henceforth without division among male heirs "according to the custom of gavelkind." All impediments on freedom to part with land, moreover, were swept away by the clauses which provided that after the same 24th June transfers of property in fee-simple, fee-

[1] T. Jones Pierce, *Trans*. Hon. Soc. Cymmrodorion, 1963, pp. 2–4, 20–6.
[2] I. Bowen, *The Statutes of Wales*, 1908, pp. 75–93, 101–33.
[3] *Ibid*., pp. 122–3.

tail, or for terms of life or years could proceed without restriction; and that mortgages not executed in compliance with the common and statute law of England would no longer be legally valid, "Welsh law and custom heretofore used in the said country or Dominion of Wales to the contrary thereof notwithstanding."

It will no doubt have been observed that the provision governing future modes of inheritance allowed an ample margin of time for lands held under Welsh tenure to become gradually merged into an integrated system; and if events had followed a logical course, the desired adjustments could have been completed in a generation or so. But in actual fact the transition was prolonged far beyond the preconceived span, although it has to be admitted that we are here confronted with one of the most tantalizingly blurred phases in Welsh social history, for the simple reason that from the time of the Union onwards, matters calling for the attention of courts and lawyers were interpreted in terms of an alien law and recorded in a foreign tongue, so that record evidence rarely more than hints at continued conflict between law and custom, as a rule concealing the reactions of that creature of ingrained habit, the inarticulate smaller man. There are however clear indications that Welsh custom persisted until well into the seventeenth century in colouring the attitudes of the humbler freeholder—the kind of man who managed to avoid involvement in litigation, or if the law did catch up with him, succumbed to the threats or blandishments of his betters who had become expert at manipulating the new legal position in their own interests; and who did not scruple about encouraging false witness, securing custody of title deeds, or extracting a full measure of advantage from the inability of their victims to prove an interest in customary freehold in the language of the newer jurisprudence. Among other social customs, such as *cynnwys* (this had allowed natural sons to share inheritances, and although banned by an Edwardian ordinance as far back as 1284, the prohibition had been consistently evaded by direct personal conveyance),[1] the usages surrounding partible inheritance and native forms of mortgage lingered on in the folk life of parts of Wales into the nineteenth century; and until at least the second half of the seventeenth century, it would appear that such matters were the subject of extracurial arbitration in unofficial assemblies which are described in a contemporary diary as *dadlau*,[2] the term used in medieval law books for the old moots in which legal issues had been determined.

[1] *The Extent of Chirkland, 1391–93*, ed. G. P. Jones, 1933, pp. 61–2.
[2] T. Jones Pierce, *op. cit.*, p. 19.

5. Social change

Meanwhile, released finally from the limitations of the old order, families who had already risen above their neighbours, together with others who had similar aspirations, pressed forward, in fierce competition with each other, in the business of extending existing estates or fashioning new ones, a process which would have accelerated at a far quicker rate after 1542 if the cash resources of the average Welsh landowner of this class had not been so restricted. The opportunities afforded before 1536 for acquiring modest emoluments and exercising a degree of local pressure through the enjoyment of office at commote level (and sometimes through service in quite humble capacities at court or in great English households)—opportunities which had given certain families an initial advantage in the contest which lay ahead— were after that date vastly increased for the enterprising with the admission of Welshmen into the full civic and social privilege of the Englishman. When the fruits of office fell short of expectation or were unattainable, entry on a professional career in the Church or in legal practice could prove a profitable additional source of income—forms of livelihood into which, with trade, younger sons were now freely launched; and there were also the possibilities afforded by expanding English markets which as time went on were increasingly exploited from the resources of those unshared 'dairy farms' which were now appearing in hill country, not to mention the splendid openings for illicit commerce available in coastal regions. When it could be asserted, not without some degree of truth, that in 1536 there were very few landowners above Brecknock with lands worth ten pounds a year,[1] and again about a century later, that it was then easier to find fifty gentlemen of a hundred pounds per annum in Wales than five of five hundred pounds,[2] it will be appreciated how great was the need for seeking out all avenues for supplementing income. Considering the handicaps from which most Welshmen suffered before the Union, some of the results were indeed astounding. A notably impressive feature of the period is the swiftness with which so many families of sparse means, with no other backing than an intense pride of lineage, rose to positions of no mean eminence in Church and State both at home and across the border, ploughing back their financial gains into estates which soon brought them power and influence in their shires, rivalling that of established families who had started off with rather more fortunate inheritances from the tribal past.

But viewed in terms of English social stratification, the average

---

[1] PRO SP 1, 102, f. 199, calendared in LP, x, p. 182.
[2] A. H. Dodd, *Studies in Stuart Wales*, 1952, p. 2.

member of the so-called 'squire' class attained a position which was little more than that of a reasonably substantial, home-keeping yeoman —an ascription which is found substituted for "gentleman" in certain items included in the same run of family deeds, so unsure were English notaries of how to equate Welsh social attitudes with English usage. Living mainly on the produce of a consolidated demesne situated on the site, and bearing the name, of a former *rhandir* or *tyddyn* (or possibly still farming partially consolidated tenements in different parts of a township), and with an undertenant or two holding leases on land acquired in marginal areas, the squireen was distinguished from lesser neighbours by the subtlest of social nuances. Conscious of distant ties of kinship with smaller surviving freeholders, and even with some of the emergent tenantry (more solidly based families, such as the Wynns of Gwydir or the Vaughans of Nannau, continued to be very much aware of blood relationships with humbler folk),[1] they rarely, until well into the seventeenth century, copied the growing fashion among the more substantial squires of adopting territorial or personal surnames in place of the traditional triple patronymic. The common social denominator among all gradations of the squirearchy was their tenacity in continuing to endow personal pedigree with a social significance which in concrete terms it no longer possessed since the protection of tenurial interests was fast ceasing to depend on expert interpretation of genealogical affiliations. The sense of belonging to a "gentle" (*bonheddig*) society which was so widely diffused among the agnatic clan groupings of medieval Wales, together with the egalitarianism which such a feeling engendered, endured at lower levels of rural society[2] until, with the approach of the Restoration, the ranks of the dispossessed having become increasingly enlarged with freeholders diminishing in number and middling families shedding their numerous offspring into a growing mass of unlineaged peasantry (*gwerin didras*), social cleavages gradually broadened, and under the stress of subsequent agrarian and cultural pressures there emerged the peculiar sociological pattern which characterized rural Wales in Victorian times.

While cultural pressures from without were naturally intensified after 1536, at no level of society did anglicization before 1640 prove to be more than superficial in its effects, manifesting itself mainly in material standards and modes of living, and, among the upper crust, in close identification with English methods of administration which in

[1] John Wynn, *op. cit.*, pp. 35–6; Univ. College North Wales, Bangor, Nannau MS 1178.
[2] W. Ogwen Williams, *Calendar of the Caernarvonshire Quarter Sessions Records*, I, pp. lxviii–lxix.

itself called for increasing acquaintance with the English language. But even the wealthiest and most sophisticated of the squire class, who had every reason to welcome the legal provisions of the Union legislation, had no hesitation in clinging to ancient customs when such customs, *cymortha* and *arddel*[1] for example, continued to serve their interests. On one issue in particular the largest landowner, when it suited him, could appeal on the same footing as the smallest freeholder to former custom, and that was when it was thought desirable to defend his real or reputed claims to *cytir*. Welsh tenures in the class of township which we have been considering, having been reduced in law to the common category of free socage, the township itself had in turn to be fitted into the manorial framework of English real property law. The official tendency after the Edwardian conquest in the principalities of north and west Wales, and in the newly created marcher lordships of the north-east, to identify the commote for fiscal purposes with the manor, on the lines of the manorialized hundreds of northern England, took on a definite and permanent shape after the Union.[2] Thus over a large part of Wales, except for townships which as former bond vills were regarded as manors in themselves or as church lands were members of dispersed ecclesiastical manors, the tacitly assumed interests of the Crown as manorial lord came at once into conflict with traditional attitudes on ownership and control of the waste. In older established manors of the March, moreover, where Welsh tenure had persisted until late in the day, the same issue of principle led to much tension between lord and freeholder at a time when all over Wales, in Crown and private manor alike, more and more holdings were being carved out of the waste, and when it was becoming increasingly difficult to distinguish even in terms of Welsh custom between legitimate appropriation and illegal encroachment, or indeed to determine, in view of the stress on the force of custom in English manorial theory, the exact position of Welsh manorial lords under the legislation of 1536–42. This is one of the major problems surrounding the development of landownership in our period, and will call for rather closer attention at a later stage.

6. *Types of freehold estate*

Up to this point we have been concerned in general terms with the broad background, and with the principles which alone can explain the character of the early freehold estate in Wales. The growth and structure of these estates now calls for slightly more detailed considera-

[1] For *commorth* see G. Dyfnallt Owen, *Elizabethan Wales, the Social Scene*, 1962, pp. 26–8.

[2] W. Ogwen Williams, *op. cit.*, pp. li–lii, lxv.

tion, and for convenience of exposition they can be divided into four categories:

(a) the estate of adventitious origin created by foreign settlers in Wales;

(b) the privileged estate established by members of a native official class;

(c) the clanland estate of hereditary origin;

(d) the clanland estate of non-hereditary origin.

(a) Estates of adventitious origin

Estates of adventitious origin were those established outside areas of Norman settlement by non-Welsh families, which, allowing for some inevitable cross-fertilization in an indeterminate borderland, were almost wholly confined to the hinterlands of English urban foundations in north Wales. The earliest large concentration of this kind, which appeared among clanlands near Conway between 1420 and 1453,[1] was inherited by the Bulkeleys who, with a modest cluster of seven burgages of their own in Beaumaris, were at this time poised for a similar drive into the clanlands of Anglesey.[2] By 1630 the estimated annual value of the Anglesey estate alone had reached the phenomenally high figure of £4,000. Compared with the Salusburys, who were next in importance among landowners of English origin, and who emerged with a rent-roll of some £1,400, having started off, in 1334, with thirty acres of escheat land outside Denbigh,[3] the Bulkeleys, it will be seen, are the outstanding example of a class of landowner, bearing English surnames, who in this period launched out, with varying degrees of success, as estate builders from bases in burgage and escheat holdings. Most of them in time retired from the fray, either sinking into the ranks of the small freeholder, or becoming grafted on to native stocks; and certainly not many succeeded in attaining genuine county status, still less in acquiring the means to enable cadet branches to secure estates of their own, which was a conspicuous feature in the annals of the more notable families. Furthermore, in the course of the sixteenth century these descendants of former garrison elements in the population of north Wales became less and less distinguishable

---

[1] T. Jones Pierce, 'The Gafael in Bangor MS 1939', *Trans. Hon. Soc. Cymmrodorion*, 1942, pp. 158 *sqq.*

[2] D. C. Jones, 'The Bulkeleys of Beaumaris, 1440–1547', *Trans. Anglesey Antiq. Soc.*, 1961, pp. 1–17; C. M. Evans, *The Borough of Beaumaris and the Commote of Dindaethwy, 1200–1600*, unpublished M.A. thesis, University of Wales, 1949, pp. 147 *sqq.* and pp. 328–34.

[3] Vinogradoff and Morgan, *op. cit.*, pp. 63, 66, 69; W. J. Smith, *Calendar of Salusbury Correspondence*, 1954, pp. 1–17.

from the rest of society, so closely were they identifying themselves with Welsh speech and culture. They were, nevertheless, a minority force in comparison with those native operators who were equally diligent in playing havoc with clanlands on the purlieus of urban settlement. Among Welsh estate builders there was also a resistive instinct at work which was seemingly opposed to settler penetration much beyond urban hinterlands, so thinly distributed were English pickings in the hills and valleys situated at no great distance from the towns themselves. Indeed, west of Caernarvon almost every trace of English settlement had disappeared by the end of the sixteenth century from boroughs facing the Cardigan Bay; and the phenomenon of mixed racial participation in the dissolution of medieval agrarian institutions in Wales ceases to have much relevance until it appears in rather different guise in and around the lowland manors of south Wales.

(b) Privileged estates

Estates in the second category, namely those derived from official status antedating the Edwardian conquest, were far less numerous, although it is in this class that the true prototypes of the modern estate, one in north Wales and the other in the south, occur. In both cases the bases of attack on circumjacent clanlands were certain bond vills (constituents of a widely scattered feudal complex granted to a highly favoured official of the thirteenth-century princes) which had devolved on the founders of the Penrhyn and Dinefwr estates under the rule of partible inheritance. A striking feature in the rise of Penrhyn is the scale on which the clanlands of neighbouring free townships had been penetrated from these quasi-manorial units even *before* 1400. By 1500 the estate (including incidentally almost the entire inheritance of the Tudor branch of the house of Ednyfed) had expanded so rapidly along both banks of the Menai Straits that successive members of the Griffith family (among the first families in Wales to adopt the English fashion in surnames) succeeded in attaining high office in principality administration, not altogether unaided by a calculating choice of brides from distinguished settler stock. When the estate in its original form began to disintegrate towards the middle of the sixteenth century, it must have been worth at a rough estimate at least £400 a year. Although not so firmly delineated, the Dinefwr estate arose from a nucleus of Ednyfed manors in Carmarthenshire and Cardiganshire, to which much Welsh freehold (*uchelwrdir*) had been added quite early in the fourteenth century. When under Sir Rhys ap Thomas, the leading supporter of Henry VII in south Wales, this estate was amalgamated through maternal inheritance with lands recently accumulated by himself and his immediate forbears, the annual value of the entire estate at the time of Sir Rhys's death in 1525 has been estimated at about £600, a figure which belies the exaggerated notions about his wealth which arose from the power and influence which had been his in south-west Wales. Though for personal reasons both estates suffered premature contraction before mid-century, their history illustrates the advantages which could accrue from an early application of entail, in contrast with lands in the upper valley of the Dee, also based on old Welsh barony (*tir pennaeth*) lands which by the sixteenth century had become so highly morcellated from the operation of gavelkind that descendants of princes had been reduced to 'yeoman' status, or which at best had become indistinguishable from the estates of the mass of Welsh squires,[1] the vast majority of which can be placed in one or other of our final categories.

(c) The clanland estate of hereditary origin

Estates in the third category had evolved along lines already indicated from hereditary nuclei in clanlands in which the owners' ancestors had in unbroken succession enjoyed an interest since the central period of the Middle Ages. A considerable proportion of the squirearchy living in the northern coastal shires (including at least half the leading landowners of Anglesey)[2] could trace their original title back in this way, and that in regions where English settlement had left so deep an impress; and the proportion could be shown to have been even higher south of Snowdonia and throughout central Wales.

(d) The clanland estate of non-hereditary origin

Barely distinguishable from these estates of hereditary origin were those in the equally numerous category of estate built up from a base in clan holdings which had been alienated to an interloper, not infrequently a scion of an ancient clan, bent on matching parental enterprise or urged by a desire to avoid the consequences of gavelkind. Although, irrespective of type, the growth of only a select number can at present be traced in reasonable detail, the general indications are that in every shire literally dozens of these estates had rapidly crystallized during the fifteen and early sixteenth centuries, thereafter increasing at a slower, though on the whole a progressively steady, pace. Certainly there were very few districts where, by 1536, at least one complex of small estates,

[1] A. D. Carr, *The Barons of Edeyrnion, 1282–1485*, unpublished M.A. thesis, University of Wales, 1963, pp. 226–8.

[2] Emyr Gwynne Jones, 'Some Notes on the Principal County Families of Anglesey in the Sixteenth and Seventeenth Centuries', *Trans. Anglesey Antiq. Soc.*, 1939, pp. 61–75, and 1940, pp. 46–61.

united by close family and heraldic ties, had not appeared as the result of a break-away by junior branches from a parent estate of hereditary origin, thus renewing in a different setting the impulsions which had given shape to the clanland several centuries earlier. As the sixteenth century advanced, this outward drive led to the spread of some of these family alliances over a wider field, when younger sons acquired whole estates at a single bid through marriage, purchase, or investment in Crown lands, a tendency which gave a sharper edge to a form of bastard 'tribalism' which preceding developments had encouraged, and which was not without a strong impact on the local politics of the Welsh shires in the post-Union period.[1]

7. The growth of estates and enclosure

On the evidence at present available it is impossible to suggest an overall range of rentals in areas of Welsh tenure much before 1580. With the exception already noted, the largest estate to have emerged before that date (an estate which was unique in that it already had ramifications in four counties) was Gwydir; and yet between 1569 and 1571 Gwydir rents produced less than £150 a year. It will therefore be seen that, allowing for a measure of increase meanwhile in the size of estates, a decidedly upward trend in rents between 1580 and 1640 is revealed in the fact that the norm in this period for reasonably substantial estates, such as Nannau or Mathafarn, Cochwillan or Bryn-kinallt, which were much smaller than Gwydir, was about £300 to £400. Rentals above £1,000 (those exceeding £2,000 are rare) are as a rule found to have been inflated, as in the case of Trawsgoed or Gelli Aur, by the profits of leasehold or monastic land, or as with Llewenni and Clenennau, by early coalescence of estates through intermarriage, thus bringing the freehold content nearer to the £500 bracket which, as we have already observed, was regarded as a rather exceptional thing in Wales. There remained the profusion of potty 'gentlemen', including the proverbial 'mountain squire', with estates under £100, who merged almost imperceptibly with the legion of smaller freeholders who had survived into the seventeenth century.

Records in which chief-rents are listed show much local variation during these forty years in the number of small owner-occupiers, a variation which was no doubt dictated by differences in the pressures exerted by the land-hungry; and when comparison is possible, a decline, though by no means dramatic, can be detected in the number of tenants responsible for chief-rents. At one extreme we have Anglesey

[1] For an account of the growth of a typical estate within this category, see Professor Jones Pierce's introduction to *Clenennau Letters and Papers*, 1947.

and some of the lower-lying sectors of south-west Wales where the number of minor freeholders had dwindled considerably in comparison with large areas of central Wales and even parts of the borderland. An analysis of a substantial cross-section, covering forty-nine townships in Merionethshire, has shown that there were only eleven townships in which more than half the land had ceased to be held by owner-occupiers, and in only one of these had the proportion of owner-occupied land fallen to as low as a quarter; there were three vills in which there were no tenanted farms at all, and fourteen in which the proportion of tenant farmers was never higher than 25 per cent.[1] In a rather similar sample embracing an entire commote in Montgomeryshire, which can well be regarded as typical of this region, 50 per cent of landowners possessed less than thirty acres; whereas, with the exception of the leading squire who had over two thousand acres, there were only four landowners in the 500–1000 acres class.[2] Indeed, in districts as far apart as Llŷn and Oswestry, there were entire townships which had scarcely felt the hand of the large exploiter, and so still retained a landscape which preserved much of its medieval character. There was therefore still plenty of room for upcoming families to expand their properties when near home opportunities became circumscribed because of the initiative of competitors or the resistance of smaller men. Thus the Vaughans of Nannau, whose ancestors had been *priodorion* of a single *tyddyn* in Nannau, had by 1600 acquired only a third of the holdings in that vill, the rest of the estate lying characteristically scattered over a dozen other townships within a ten-mile radius of the mansion house, and intermingled with offshoots of sundry other estates of various shapes and sizes.[3]

One of the most striking changes in landscape, however, was produced by the enlargement of holdings to which quit-rents were tied through permanent enclosure of portions of adjoining waste, and further afield by taking into severalty larger blocks of upland pasture. The extent to which this erosion of common had proceeded is vividly illustrated in Leicester's dealings with the freeholders of five counties in north Wales where between 1561 and 1588 he controlled the greater part of the Crown's manorial interests. When Leicester's agents raised the equivocal issue of the commons, they were met with such explosive and tenacious opposition that one is left with a firm impression that by

---

[1] This analysis, based on PRO LR 2, 236, is made by Colin Thomas in Ph.D. thesis, University of Wales, 1965 *The Evolution of Rural Settlement and Land Tenure in Merioneth*.

[2] Elwyn Evans, *Arwystli and Cyfeiliog in the Sixteenth Century*, unpublished M.A. thesis, University of Wales, 1939, p. 133.

[3] Colin Thomas, *op. cit.*

1560 encroachment had become widespread, and that the legal questions involved had become matters of crucial importance to every
grade of freeholder. This impression is confirmed when, an uneasy
accommodation having been eventually reached whereby freeholders
undertook to pay *new* in addition to established rents, fresh surveys
were prepared—surveys in which these new rents appear so consistently
alongside the old as to indicate that the habit of encroachment had
become well-nigh universal.[1] An inventory of encroachments covering
four commotes in which Leicester's agents were active, gives some idea
of the extent to which intakes along the edges of ancient freehold had
taken place, as well as the degree to which the hill commons had been
invaded. Of 631 recorded plots, as many as 322 (51 per cent) were
below ten acres; 257 (30·8 per cent) were under sixty acres; 16 (2·5 per
cent) varied between sixty and one hundred acres; and 36 (5·7 per cent)
exceeded one hundred acres. But it is of the utmost significance that the
landowners represented in the last bracket claimed between them to
control 5,080 acres, or 40·2 per cent of the total area surveyed, namely
12,729 acres, in contrast with 1,405 acres possessed by smallholders
in the lowest bracket. Almost without exception, the really large
encroachments of several hundred acres consisted of high pasture and
sheepwalk which had been enclosed, usually within convenient distance
of demesne and mansion house, by local figures of county standing. On
the other hand, the mass of small and medium encroachers (the
inventory[2] which is by no means exhaustive contains about five hundred
names) had advanced in the main into moorland fringes (*ffriddoedd*)
from established bases in *tyddyn* and *rhandir*, reproducing in this new
phase of colonization the irregular field pattern of medieval settlement.

Now this remarkably microscopic view of a considerable cross-
section of the Welsh countryside mirrors tendencies which, through
the medium of much patchy and uneven documentation, can be
discerned at work in every Welsh shire, as well as in those cymricized
regions along the border which had been incorporated into English
shires at the time of the Union.[3] That pressures on the waste would
appear to have been heavier in smaller, lower-lying, coastal townships
(where minor freeholders were tending to be squeezed out by actual
physical restrictions on their capacity to enlarge their stakes in the soil)
is suggested by endeavours to improve marshy ground, a process which
is seen to stem as a rule from the individual enterprise of smaller men
bent on wresting a few additional acres from the poorer margins of

[1] Colin Thomas, *op. cit.*
[2] Colin Thomas, 'Encroachment onto the Common Lands in Meirioneth in the
Sixteenth Century', *Northern Universities' Geogr. J.*, v, 1964, pp. 33–8.
[3] W. J. Slack, *op. cit.*

attenuated *cytiroedd*.[1] But even in the larger townships on the edges of the mountain zone and along the valley basins of the interior, where there were fewer quantitative limitations on expansion (after all two fifths of the entire land surface of the country still consisted of moor and mountain at the end of the eighteenth century), large sectors of mountain land were being withdrawn from communal use and the rims of our moorlands were being increasingly absorbed into private ownership, thus blurring the contours of the medieval landscape, bringing a new threat, despite some small temporary gains, to the traditional livelihood of the smallholder, and confining future settlement to barren squatter holdings high up in the hills.[2] Moreover, when shacks for temporary use under customs of seasonal transhumance (*hafodtai* and *lluestai*) are sometimes found converted into permanent settlements, one can also detect the beginnings of that breach between lowland and upland farmstead which in time produced the modern social dichotomy between valley and mountain communities. Finally, slight though the evidence is, there is no reason to suppose that dubious invasions of the commons unsanctioned by communal custom had assumed serious proportions until the sixteenth century was reasonably well advanced, nor that encroachments had amounted to much more than cautious movement into waste in the immediate vicinity of existing holdings. Actual enclosure of upland pasture on the scale indicated could not have been set in motion until time-worn procedures for controlling the waste began falling to pieces, and this did not occur until near mid-century when separable interests became so discordant as to encourage irresponsible elements to overstock the commons to the hurt and detriment of fellow proprietors, who then, from motives of sheer self-preservation, proceeded to seize and enclose pasture on a scale commensurable with personal status or influence.[3] As for lowland enclosure, although much cultivated land still lay open, particularly in areas where estate building had been slight, even in central Wales there were men at the beginning of the seventeenth century, who, while recalling a time when fences and enclosures were little known except for "a dead hedge round an acre of wheat," could assert that unenclosed arable was an unusual phenomenon in their day, that enclosure was still proceeding consequent upon partition among co-heirs of legitimately heritable waste, and that land which was once "waste and wilderness" had been brought into "present fertility" through the diligence and foresight of freeholders.[4]

[1] *Ibid.*, p. 71.   [2] This statement is based upon the work of Colin Thomas.
[3] T. I. Jeffreys-Jones, *The Enclosure Movement in South Wales in the Tudor and Early Stuart Periods*, unpublished M.A. thesis, University of Wales, 1936, pp. 395–7.
[4] Elwyn Evans, *op. cit.*

It will be seen that England and Wales faced different problems in relation to 'enclosure', although in Wales there are aspects of the movement which without doubt did set the stage for the peasant discontents of a later age. In Wales enclosure was accompanied by an actual extension of tillage which was encouraged among the more enlightened by the abandonment of old predatory techniques in favour of improved agricultural methods; and displacements of population resulting from lowland consolidation and enclosure were to all appearances cushioned by local need for labour and migration to England. Exploitation of pasture, stimulated, it is true, by the need to meet the requirements of steadily increasing numbers of livestock reared for commercial purposes, went on almost fortuitously and in piecemeal fashion within the familiar context of the native pastoral tradition. The tensions which enclosure of waste did engender in Wales arose from the competitive scramble which followed a rather sudden collapse of the physical and legal controls which had governed the management of the commons for centuries past. Hence the frequent difficulty in determining, in face of local reticence or resentment, and after generations of official neglect, the exact boundaries between the various intercommoning divisions of a commote; or within townships themselves the infinitely more troublesome question of distinguishing between enclosure which on the one hand represented improper invasion of the waste and quasi-legitimate intake sanctioned by ancient custom on the other.[1] Disorders, even the rather more serious outbreaks of violence caused by 'enclosure', were wholly sporadic and impetuous protests motivated by particular local circumstances, and, as one would expect from the nature of Welsh society at that time, free of any flavour of class struggle; and if there was a common factor in all these commotions, it is usually found to have been discord between rival groups of freeholders. On the other hand, unless manorial lords or their assignees happened also to be members of the local squirearchy, or unless, as for example in the Leicester affair, there were freeholders who were prepared to side with the enemy, the outsider who ventured to oppose the claim of freeholders to control their own common lands with foreign notions of what was due to the lord of the manor met with a united front. To the very end of our period it was insistently asserted in face of repeated threats from manorial lords that the wastes were not "commons" but *cyd-tir* (joint land) the ownership of which was vested in *cyd-tirogion* (co-parceners) who, as tenants of adjoining freeholds, were entitled to enclose and improve them without licence and at their will and pleasure. Chief rents, it was claimed, were paid for waste and severed land "as well for the one as for the other";

[1] T. I. Jeffreys Jones, *op. cit.*, p. 394.

and as late as 1637 objections were being raised to the claim that certain unenclosed wastes in central Wales were commonable on the ground that the land in question was in fact made up of "distinct and several holdings" owned by "co-parceners in gavelkind."[1] These successors of the medieval *bonheddig* were, however, engaged in a rearguard action against official insistence on treating the term *cytir* as no more than the Welsh equivalent of *common*, and on regarding the claim for which it stood as no more than an "ancient dream." Nevertheless, the confusion surrounding this "vain conceit" remained for several centuries ahead to benight manorial theory and to bewilder those who were concerned with what emerged as the problem of Crown lands.[2]

B. THE CHURCH

1. *Introduction: before the Reformation*

The Welsh Church before the Reformation was not wealthy.[3] Three of the four Welsh bishoprics—Bangor (£131), Llandaff (£144), and St Asaph (£187)—had a total net annual value, according to the *Valor Ecclesiasticus*, of not much more than the poorest English bishopric, Rochester (£411). The remaining one, St David's (£457), came below every other English bishopric but Rochester. Gross temporal income (i.e. income from landed estates and their perquisites) of the dioceses ranged from £311 19s. 3d. (63 per cent) in St David's through £131 14s. 1d. (76 per cent) for Llandaff and £85 13s. 7d. (56 per cent) for Bangor, to £25 10s. 0d. (12 per cent) for St Asaph. Gross spiritual income (i.e. income from tithes and other comparable offerings) showed corresponding disparities: £179 18s. 11½d. (37 per cent) for St David's, £38 (24 per cent) for Llandaff, £65 9s. 5½d. (44 per cent) for Bangor, and £177 1s. 6d. (88 per cent) for St Asaph. Both temporalities and spiritualities were leased out on a considerable scale, in many instances to the same families who were active in leasing monastic possessions. The endowments of the cathedral clergy, all of whom belonged to chapters of secular clergy in Wales, were correspondingly as modest as those of the bishops. Some of the best, for example the archdeaconry of St Asaph or the archdeaconry of St David's, were worth only £74 and £56 respectively, while most of the Welsh prebends were far less valuable than many of the richer

[1] Elwyn Evans, *op. cit.*

[2] Professor Jones Pierce approached the problem of the Crown lands in his paper 'Notes on the History of Caernarvonshire in the Reign of Elizabeth', *Trans. Caernarvonshire Hist. Soc.*, 1940, pp. 35–57.

[3] Details in Glanmor Williams, *The Welsh Church from Conquest to Reformation*, 1962, chs. VIII and X.

rectories and vicarages in England. Apart from the cathedrals there were only six collegiate churches, namely, Holyhead, Clynnog, Ruthin, Llanddewibrefi, Abergwili, and the College of B.V.M. at St David's, in the whole of Wales, and they were worth on the average between £40 and £50 a year. Among the parochial clergy poverty was widespread: an analysis of the livings listed in *Valor Ecclesiasticus* shows that only 6 per cent of them were valued at more than £20 a year, 23·5 per cent at between £10 and £20, 46 per cent at between £5 and £10, and the rest at less than £5. Examination of the sources of incumbents' income in a typical rural deanery like that of Abergavenny reveals that on the average glebe accounted for 16 per cent, the tithes of corn and hay for 39 per cent, and the tithes of natural increase (i.e. livestock) for about 30 per cent, while the remainder was made up from miscellaneous minor sources. In addition to the beneficed clergy there were about as many unbeneficed stipendiary clergy whose average income was about £4 a year. Chantries, guilds, and fraternities were comparatively rare in Wales. They were nearly all slenderly endowed, usually with tenements and small acreages of land in and around the towns, and with stocks of sheep and cattle or small sums of cash in the rural parishes.[1]

There were in all some forty-seven religious houses in Wales before the dissolution, i.e. about one to every twenty parishes, as compared with one to every ten parishes in England. Not one was rated at more than £200 a year, and the clear annual value of their total endowments, as listed in the *Valor Ecclesiasticus* at £3,178, was worth less than that of the single great house of Westminster (£3,470). They varied considerably in the sources of their income, though all of them, except the seven houses of canons, depended chiefly on their landed estates, and the thirteen Cistercian houses, especially, were by Welsh standards landowners on a big scale. Monastic lands were in the hands of tenants except for a small fraction kept in hand to meet the needs of the now very small numbers of monks—there were probably no more than 250 men and women in religious orders in the whole of Wales—and their household servants. There is no conclusive evidence that Welsh monastic landlords were trying to draw back land into their own hands for direct exploitation early in the sixteenth century as some English houses are known to have been doing.[2] Among their tenants conditions of tenure varied widely, but, broadly speaking, the usual four classes of tenants were recognized: freeholders, copyholders, tenants-at-will, and leaseholders. There had been a growing tendency for leaseholds to

---

[1] *Ibid.*, pp. 284–6 and Appendix A (for beneficed clergy); pp. 287–8 (unbeneficed clergy); and pp. 288–95 (chantries etc.).

[2] See *supra*, p. 312.

displace other tenancies in the fifteenth and sixteenth centuries. But the custom was far from prevalent even on the eve of the dissolution, and most surviving Welsh leases show that there had been a rush to secure them in 1535 and 1536. Unlike many of the earlier sixteenth-century leases, which were usually entered into for a term of lives, many of these late leases were for long terms, ranging from forty to one hundred years, and may have represented an attempt by landlords and tenants to reap the maximum benefit in the form of high entry fines and security respectively in the brief space at their disposal. Late as many of these leases were, they were almost without exception confirmed when the Crown took over, and evidence from the early seventeenth century shows that some of the pre-dissolution leases were still valid.[1]

2. *The dissolution of the monasteries*

Welsh houses, like those of England, were surveyed by commissioners appointed by the Crown in 1535 and their possessions recorded in the *Valor Ecclesiasticus*. None was valued at more than £200 and all should have been dissolved under the terms of the first act for the dissolution of the religious houses. In fact, three—Whitland, Strata Florida, and Neath—were reprieved for a short time on payment of fines to the Crown; and others, like Ewenni or Malpas, which were daughter priories of the large English monasteries of Gloucester and Montacute, survived until the dissolution of the mother house. The Welsh friaries, all of which were meagrely furnished and held only the scantiest possessions in land, much of it leased to local laymen, disappeared in 1538. The commandery of the Knights of St John at Slebech, Pembrokeshire, and the possessions of the order in north Wales survived until 1540. Finally, the chantries and similar endowments were appropriated in 1549, after an abortive proposal of 1545. The chantry certificates place the total value of the assets of Welsh chantries at just over £950. Even allowing for the very considerable degree of concealment and embezzlement which took place at the time of the dissolution, it is clear that chantry property was not very extensive in Wales and much of it was already being diverted for secular purposes even before 1549.[2]

The broad pattern of the subsequent disposal of these confiscated properties was, as might be expected, much the same for Wales as for England. In the years immediately after the dissolution the intention of the government seems patently to have been to retain most of its

---

[1] *Exchequer Proceedings concerning Wales in Tempore James I*, ed. T. I. Jeffreys Jones, Cardiff, 1955, pp. 29, 35, 92, 109, 119, 226, 292, 309.

[2] Details in Williams, *Conquest to Reformation*, pp. 288–95.

newly won assets in its own hands. The process of leasing began in
1537 and rapidly gained momentum in 1538–9 when the bulk of the
leases were concluded, though others continued to be made in smaller
numbers during the remaining years of Henry VIII's reign. The
possessions thus leased consisted for the most part of vacant sites,
demesne lands, and rectories not already farmed out by the monks.
Rents were based on the assessments made in 1535 and the term
of years was always twenty-one. The majority of these early leases
were entered into by members of the royal household or men in close
touch with it. Some had no connection with Wales at all, but many of
them were drawn from local Welsh families, like Morgan Wolfe, the
king's goldsmith but a Monmouthshire man by origin, who took
out leases of properties formerly belonging to Chepstow and Abergavenny priories. Three of those concerned with monastic visitations
would appear to have taken advantage of inside information and
contacts to acquire leases—John Price (Brecon Priory), Edward Carne
(Ewenni Priory), and John Vaughan (Grace Dieu, Pembroke, and
Whitland).

Whatever its original intentions may have been, the Crown found
itself obliged, from about 1539 onwards, to begin selling its interests in
the former monastic lands. The first official statement of the terms,
i.e. twenty years' purchase, comes in December 1539, and the first sales
in Wales are recorded in 1540, the earliest being the sale of the priory
of Cardigan together with three of its rectories to William Cavendish,
auditor of the court of Augmentations, on 26 February.[1] This was
followed by a number of other sales in the same year; then followed a
relatively quiet period until the crisis of the years 1544–6, when heavy
war expenditure forced Henry to make many more sales. At first the
Crown was anxious to dispose only of small, isolated tenements and
sought to attach the lucrative but burdensome military tenure to them.
Under the pressure of necessity, however, smaller properties were
offered in free socage or burgage, and large blocks of the more valuable
granges were disposed of. Similar financial embarrassments forced
Edward VI and Mary to sell further parcels of monastic land, and it is
clear that by Elizabeth's reign a large part of it had been alienated.
Close examination of the disposal of former monastic lands in the
diocese of Llandaff, which broadly speaking covered the two counties
of Glamorgan and Monmouth, and contained within its borders much
the heaviest concentration of monastic possessions in Wales, shows that
by the end of Henry VIII's reign about 50–60 per cent had been disposed
of. A further 20–30 per cent followed during the next two reigns, so
that by Elizabeth's accession less than a quarter remained in the queen's

[1] LP, xv, 282 (108).

hands. This compares broadly with comparable estimates made for some English counties, and the picture for the rest of Wales seems not to differ significantly.

Only a very small amount of this property found its way back to the Church or to educational foundations. The new dioceses of Gloucester and Bristol founded by Henry VIII benefited to some slight extent by being allowed to take over some of the former interests in south Wales of the abbeys of Tewkesbury, Gloucester, and St Augustine's, Bristol; and grammar schools were founded at Brecon, Carmarthen, and Abergavenny with buildings and/or endowments partly from the former priory of Abergavenny, friaries at Brecon and Carmarthen, and the collegiate church of Abergwili.[1] Nor was a very large amount of given away or disposed of monastic land on highly favourable terms. The only really significant gift of it in Wales was that made to the earl of Worcester as early as March 1537 when the site and the possessions of Tintern Abbey in south Wales were bestowed upon him.[2] The rest was bought for hard cash, for rarely less than the market rate of twenty years' purchase, and in some instances for considerably more, as for example when Sir Edward Carne, a trusted royal servant, non the less in 1543 paid twenty-three years' purchase for lands in Conwilston and twenty-seven years' purchase for the site of the Austin Friars' house in Newport.[3]

At first sight it might seem that many Welsh properties were bought by large-scale speculators. But closer inspection usually reveals that even men like Henry Audley or Sir Thomas Heneage were for the most part agents who were subsequently given licences to alienate land to local buyers. In fact, the biggest buyers of Welsh monastic land were local gentry who made application direct to the court of Augmentations on their own account. In some instances, they were men already leasing the site and some of the demesne of former monasteries, some of whose larger estates they now wished to purchase—Sir John Williams at Cwm-hir, John Scudamore at Dore, John Price at Brecon, Rice Mansel at Margam, John Bradshaw at St Dogmael's, Edward Carne at Ewenni, and Nicholas Arnold at Llanthony, are the most notable examples. The only individuals who could thus benefit were those who had ready cash or who could raise it quickly. Quite often they were men who had done well out of service to the Crown, or in trade, or at the law, or by all or a number of these means. To acquire their new estates they were often able to raise impressive sums; Rice Mansel, for instance, put up no less than £2,600 in all for the estates

---

[1] LP, XVI, 503 (30), 1226 (5); XVII, 1154 (60), 556 (25); XVIII, i, 226.
[2] LP, XII, i, 795 (16).
[3] E 318, 243.

of Margam Abbey between 1540 and 1556.[1] In general it is probable that many of these purchasers, though not without an eye to business, were more concerned with prestige than profits. There is very little evidence that they were unduly oppressive or inequitable in their treatment of under-tenants; at all events there are very few of the protracted lawsuits that might have been expected to ensue in so litigious an age if they had been. Often, indeed, the boot was on the other foot, with new monastic proprietors or lessees complaining of being unable to get former monastic tenants to fulfil obligations.[2] Nor can they be said to have constituted a 'new' gentry. Certainly the purchase of extensive monastic holdings might help to establish a new family in a county, as it did the Barlows of Slebech, the Bradshaws of St Dogmael's, or the Steadmans of Strata Florida. But in general, the families that benefited most, the Herberts, the Somersets, the Devereux, the Carnes, the Gunters, or the Morgans of Monmouthshire, were already well established and rising clans. Their stake in monastic property did not create, but helped to emphasize, the differences between them and less successful families. It has often been suggested that their acquisitions from this source, especially when paid for at the market price, helped to ensure the permanence of the English Reformation, yet it is noteworthy that in Wales, at least, some of the families who did best out of the dissolution were also among the most tenacious upholders of the Roman religion, the Somerset earls of Worcester being among the foremost recusants in the whole realm.

By Elizabeth's reign almost all the surviving Crown leases of former monastic possessions relate to rectories and tithe.[3] Examined decade by decade over the whole reign they reveal some interesting trends. During the years 1558–70 profits anticipated from such leases seem to have been sufficient for the Crown to try to offset the effects of inflation by exacting high entry fines, averaging about four years' rent and rising to as high as six years'. Between 1570 and 1580 entry fines were still fairly high, averaging about three years' rent. During the whole period down to 1580 the term of a lease was invariably twenty-one years. In the decade between 1580 and 1590 the market hardened against the Crown; entry fines were down to an average of about two years, and leases for three lives began to appear, though those for twenty-one years were still more common. By the time of the agri-

---

[1] *Penrice and Margam Manuscripts*, ed. W. de G. Birch, 1893–1904; cf. G. Williams, 'Sir Rhys Mansel of Penrice and Margam', *Morgannwg*, VI, 1962.

[2] *Records of the Court of Augmentations relating to Wales and Monmouthshire*, Cardiff, ed. E. A. Lewis and J. C. Davies, 1954, *passim*; *Exchequer Proceedings (Equity) concerning Wales*, ed. E. G. Jones, Cardiff, 1939, *passim*.

[3] *Records...Augmentations*, part II.

cultural crises of the 1590's leases for three lives began to predominate and entry fines were down to an average of about one year. The lessees continued to be local gentry in the main, though it was comparatively rare for a family to maintain an unbroken lien on the lease of any rectory. Where urban tenements, notably parcels of the former chantries, were still being leased, complaints of their decayed and ruinous state were not infrequent.

3. Lay pressure on the secular clergy, 1536–58

The transfer of such enormous assets from monastic to lay owners threatened to put the possessions of the secular clergy in almost equal danger. It had been proved that the patrimony of the Church could be despoiled with impunity and advantage; a large part of the property of the secular clergy was already farmed out to a laity which regarded them as being hardly less grossly over-endowed than the monks had been; and the nature of Protestant doctrine, particularly Puritan versions of it, rendered it sharply critical of the worldly wealth of the clergy.[1] As the pace of economic and doctrinal change began simultaneously to quicken the secular clergy came under increasingly heavy pressure. They were perhaps at their most defenceless during the reign of Edward VI, when they could hope for no protection by the government. In three of the Welsh dioceses we have clear evidence of attempts by the laity to extend their control over the possessions of the bishops and chapters. At Llandaff, Bishop Kitchen (1545–66) has a bad reputation for having granted away to the Mathew family of Radyr his marcher rights over the lordship of Llandaff and for selling and leasing land to the prejudice of his successors. While we can only guess what pressures on the part of the local gentry Kitchen had to contend with, we are left in no doubt of the part of the dominant Salusbury family in the diocese of St Asaph. Here the efforts of the vigorous Marian bishop, Thomas Goldwell (1555–9), make it plain that this family, which for a generation or two had been the outstanding family in the diocese, had exercised its influence to such an extent as almost to turn the endowments of the deanery and archdeaconry of St Asaph, not to mention the chapter seal, into its own private property. At St David's during the same period no small part of the violent contentions between Bishop Ferrar (1548–55) and clergy and laymen of his diocese, which ended in his being imprisoned at the order of the Privy Council, arose out of Ferrar's attempts to undo some of the unduly favourable leases and concessions made by his predecessor, William Barlow (1536–48). They brought him into conflict with some of the most powerful

[1] Christopher Hill, *The Economic Problems of the Church*, 1956.

families in the south-west, above all the Devereux. In all these episodes
the possessions of the cathedrals and the higher clergy were as much the
subject of the laity's attention as those of the bishops. In many instances
the laity's task was made easier by weakness or even collusion on the
part of friends, relatives, or dependants among the cathedral clergy.
At Llandaff, where leading canons had in 1538–9 been implicated in the
spoliation of the treasures of their own cathedral, the chapter was found
by a commission of enquiry to have made favourable leases to friends,
and the archdeacon confessed to having removed the chapter seal
contrary to the bishop's will. Similar accusations were brought against
some of the canons at St David's, and there, too, there were unedifying
squabbles over custody of the chapter seal, while at St Asaph Bishop
Goldwell later accused Sir John Salusbury of having entered into
"very corrupt and simoniacal pacts and agreements" with the former
dean and of appending the chapter seal to forged leases.[1]

Mary's reign brought some relief to the bishops. There were even
attempts at St Asaph and Llandaff to make good some of the earlier
spoliation. But Mary's appeal for the restitution of monastic land
brought no better response in Wales than it did elsewhere. Her policy
of depriving many of the parish clergy for heresy and removing them
for marriage gave rise to a series of disputes over the validity of leases
of tithe and glebe agreed upon by the deprived clergy. About seventy
to eighty Chancery suits of this period for England and Wales give
some indication of the ways in which a clergyman about to be deprived
had leased his benefice in such a way that a "great part of the profits of
the same might come to the relief of himself, his wife, and children."[2]
Such juggling with leases was not to be wondered at. Chancery suits
for the period before the Reformation record many disputes concerning
the leasing of tithe and glebe and embody numerous allegations of
forgery, tampering with seals, ante-dating, and the like. The rapid
changes of religious policy, repeated attacks on ecclesiastical property,
and the inflationary spiral, all taught men to anticipate disaster and to
think only of their own interest in their freehold. Many of the economic
problems of the clergy of Elizabethan and Stuart times and the solutions
they were obliged to find to them are in embryo much older than is
often supposed.

[1] Lawrence Thomas, The Reformation in the Old Diocese of Llandaff, 1930, pp. 75–82;
An Inventory of the Early Chancery Proceedings concerning Wales, ed. E. A. Lewis, 1937,
pp. 130–2, 274; Glanmor Williams, 'The Protestant Experiment in the Diocese of
St David's', Bull. BCS, xv, 1953, pp. 212–24; xvi, 1954, pp. 38–48.
[2] Lewis, Early Chancery Procs., passim; cf. Early Chancery Proceedings, List of, x, 1936.

4. *Economic Tensions, 1558–1640*

The reigns of Elizabeth and the first two Stuarts were a period of sustained tension between the economic interests of the clergy and laity, in which religious conviction reinforced the latter's ambitions to curtail the privileges and property rights of the former. The events of the century had immeasurably weakened the clergy's position and given the laity reason to anticipate that continued pressure would bring them further gains. Elizabeth's own attitude towards the clergy was ambivalent: while she was determined for political reasons to preserve the authority of the hierarchy, she missed no opportunity to milch the bishoprics of every possible source of revenue.[1] Her lay subjects were not loth to follow her example, and from all four Welsh dioceses there are protests by the bishops against the rapacious pressures of greedy laymen, typified by Sir John Wynn of Gwydir, whom the best of the Welsh bishops, William Morgan, described as "a sacrilegious robber of my church, a perfidious spoiler of my diocese." One of the favourite devices of such laymen was the commission of concealment, i.e. a royal commission to enquire into ecclesiastical possessions such as those of former monasteries or collegiate churches which allegedly ought to have passed into the hands of the Crown but which were said to be illicitly detained. The instigators of such a commission generally hoped to derive some reward for their efforts in the form of a lease of the concealed lands brought to light by them. The bishops of St David's suffered particularly badly from such commissions when they were deprived of their interests in the former collegiate church of Llanddewibrefi and came near to losing their rights in the other college of Abergwili. The fortunate Queen's farmer who was allowed to rent these possessions for £40 a year was reputed by 1600 to be making a profit of close on £400 on his bargain. It is true that the Stuart kings were more disposed to defend the interests of their bishops than Elizabeth had been, but even so the bishops of early Stuart Wales were as doleful in their complaints of the impoverishment of their sees by lay rapacity as their Elizabethan predecessors had been—and with reason.[2]

The surviving chapter records for the dioceses of Llandaff and St

---

[1] Gordon Donaldson, *The Scottish Reformation*, 1960, p. 172, n. 2, for refs.

[2] D. R. Thomas, *The History of the Diocese of St Asaph*, 1908, I, 101; A. G. Edwards, *Landmarks in the History of the Welsh Church*, 1913, pp. 104 *sqq*; E. J. Newell, *Llandaff*, 1902, pp. 145–51; Glanmor Williams, 'Richard Davies, Bishop of St David's, 1561–81', *Hon. Soc. Cymmrodorion*, 1948, pp. 147–69; CPSD, *passim;* Thos. Richards, *A History of the Puritan Movement in Wales, 1639–53*, 1920, ch. 1; Glanmor Williams, 'The Collegiate Church of Llanddewibrefi', *Ceredigion* (IV, 1963.).

David's[1] show the eagerness of laymen to enter into leases of episcopal and capitular property, in both glebe and tithe. Most of the lessees were local gentry, though there was also a sprinkling of lawyers and merchants, particularly among those who appear to be related to the lessors. Leases of Llandaff capitular possessions were dominated to a large extent by the families of Herbert and Morgan, but those of St David's, with its much wider geographical spread, show a greater variation. The records themselves, of course, reveal little of the pressures exerted or the inducements offered to obtain such leases, though it may be significant that the registrar of St David's recorded in 1563 that he had no record of any lease before 1559, "such hath been the alteration and misorder in these later days of our predecessors," and it is certainly noticeable that before the act of 1571 preventing leases for longer than three lives or twenty-one years, a number of St David's leases had been entered into for terms ranging from thirty to seventy years. But we know from other sources what kind of pressures bishops and chapters were in general subjected to and there are indications from Welsh bishops' comments that things were not different in Wales. Bishop Richard Davies of St David's (1561–81) attacked the "insatiable cormorants" in his own diocese, "greedy for Church spoils and contemptuously intolerant of the Church's rulers." His successor, Marmaduke Middleton (1581–93), complained how all the best prebends in his diocese were leased out for long terms, and there were comparable complaints from the dioceses of Llandaff, Bangor, and St Asaph.[2] Middleton also bemoaned that the endowments of a large number of the rectories and vicarages within his diocese were leased out, and averred that the incumbents of livings worth £10 and even £30 were glad to take £6 13s. 4d., or even less, "and yet bound in bonds that they cannot avoid it without their undoing." Parsonages impropriate to the bishop and chapter, "the chiefest part of the revenues of the see," were all leased out so that "almost none" would return for fifty years to come. Middleton is not the best of witnesses and his sweeping statements cannot safely be taken at their face value. Yet there is corroborative evidence from his own chapter's records and those of Llandaff and other sources that such endowments were regularly leased.

On the subject of lay impropriations Welsh bishops were outspokenly critical. Many of these livings were "the very best things in all the whole diocese," but were regarded by the impropriators solely as a source of profit to themselves. Where there was an endowed vicarage

[1] National Library of Wales, LlCh 4; SDCh, B, 1–4.
[2] SP 12, 65, i; B. M. Lansdowne MS 120; Thomas, *St Asaph*, I, pp. 98–100; cf. *infra*, p. 394, n.1

they squeezed the incumbents hard trying to cut down on their income and making no allowance in lieu of former oblations and other "superstitious offerings" which had formerly accrued to them. The parish of Llanbadarn Fawr in Jacobean times affords an outstanding example of their methods. In this enormous parish of 180 square miles, with its 2,400 communicants, the farmer's issues were alleged to be worth over £1,000 a year while his rent was £120. He paid £20 to the vicar and had also allowed £40 or £50 in tithes to make up for the loss of former oblations, but had withdrawn this concession, with the result that the vicar took him to the Exchequer Court.[1] Where there was no vicarage endowed and no vicarial tithes, but only a stipendiary curate, the farmer could do even better. Here it was usual for his rent to remain at its customary level when a lease was renewed, and in so far as the Crown reaped a profit at all it did so by means of entry fines. Meantime the customary stipend, often small in pre-Reformation times, was grossly inadequate for a married clergy in an inflationary age, and was maintained unchanged from decade to decade, while the impropriator stood to gain handsomely from rising prices. Richard Davies's report on his diocese in 1570 speaks of many churches of this kind. In a return for St David's diocese in 1583, out of seventy-nine curates' stipends listed, eleven only were worth £10 or more and thirty-three were worth £5 or less—it was hardly a matter of surprise that seven of the curates should be fugitives from their cures. A similar report on Llandaff in 1603 listed seven curacies out of thirty-one as worth more than £5 a year, and four were without anyone to serve them at all. The parishioners of Churchstoke, situated in one of the most fertile spots in north Wales, yielding a yearly revenue of £160 for a rent of £6 or £7, so it was claimed, in a bill of complaint alleged that the farmers had for years paid their stipendiary curates less than twenty nobles a year. The result was that the ministers were "unlearned, poor, bare and needy fellows," forced to leave their wives and children to the mercy of the parish, "such a mischief and inconvenience... happening in the parts of Wales so often," that their lordships of the Exchequer should attend thereto. The chancel of the church there, like that of many others in the possession of impropriators, was in a ruinous condition on account of their unwillingness to spend money in fulfilling their obligations as rectors to maintain the chancel in good repair.[2]

[1] SP 12, 66, 26, i; D. R. Thomas, *The Life and Work of Bishop Davies and William Salesbury, etc.*, 1902, pp. 37–44; Jeffreys Jones, *Exchequer Procs. James I*, pp. 103, 119, 224.

[2] SP 12, 65, i; BM Harleian MS 595; J. Jones, *op. cit.*, pp. 123, 293, 333; W. H. House, 'Contest for a Radnorshire Rectory in the Seventeenth Century', *Hist. Soc. Church Wales*, VII, 1957; G. Gruffydd, 'Bishop Godwin's Injunctions for...Llandaff, 1603', *ibid.*, IV, 1954.

Nor was the process of impropriation and annexation everywhere at an end even as late as the first decade of the seventeenth century, judging by the comment of Bishop Parry of St Asaph, who in 1611 wrote to Salisbury that the miserable state of his diocese, lacking a learned resident ministry, might be made all the worse by the many efforts being made and bribes being offered to procure annexations.

Along with the leasing of the endowments of benefices went the eager acquisition of rights of advowson. A record from the diocese of St Asaph for the years 1536–8 shows that the practice of granting away rights of next presentation to livings within the bishop's gift was prevalent at least as early as Henry VIII's reign, and later records from Llandaff and St David's showed that it remained usual throughout our period.[1] Bishops rarely parted with these rights except for a consideration, and laymen's motives for acquiring them were usually self-interested: either they wished to place relatives or clients in employment, or they intended to extract a favourable lease or some other simoniacal agreement from the incumbent they presented. The more creditable motives of raising the standards of the ministry associated with the acquisition of advowsons by Feoffees for Impropriations, though they made some impact upon Wales and the border English counties, were not given much encouragement in a country so little touched by Puritan influences as Wales was.[2]

5. The reaction of the clergy

In face of all this pressure from laymen, clerics were not, of course, entirely defenceless or invariably the losers. If only they could maintain their sources of income intact they stood to benefit as much as anyone else from the rise in prices. It was thought reasonable in 1583 to estimate the benefices of St David's diocese as being then worth three times what they had been valued at in 1535 for the *Valor Ecclesiasticus*, though the incumbents not surprisingly maintained that they were hardly worth double the earlier estimate, especially since so many of them were leased out anyway. At St Asaph four years later, livings were reckoned to be worth five or six times what the *Valor* rated them, but this estimate comes in too partisan an account to be wholly reliable. Scattered fragments of information from the early seventeenth century certainly point to a striking increase in the value of the tithe-yield from Welsh parishes, and this may be reflected in the much larger number of graduates and preachers who were being ordained in

[1] NLW, SA, M, 21; Cf. p. 390, n. 1 *supra*.
[2] Howse, *loc. cit.*; C. Hill, 'Puritans and "the Dark Corners of the Land",' RHS, 5th Ser., XIII, 1963, pp. 91–3.

Welsh dioceses by Stuart times as compared with the pre-Reformation era or even the early Elizabethan period, when Welsh livings were said to be too poor for the most part to attract men with such training.[1] Nevertheless, it is doubtful whether the resident clergy in Wales gained more than a small fraction of this increased prosperity. Most of the cathedral dignitaries and the best rectories were held by non-resident absentees and their endowments were normally leased out, or were impropriate, to laymen. Even where this was not so, the lesser tithes of natural increase, where the largest increments were likely to accrue, were notoriously the most difficult to collect.

Almost inevitably, therefore, the consequence of frequent and bitter exchanges between the clergy and laity was that the former tended to become as shameless in their methods as their adversaries. The example was set at the top and spread down from the head to members. Even the best of the bishops did not entirely escape the taint, while the administration of many rapidly degenerated into avarice and corruption. Most of them were men of middle-class origin and hardly any, apart from Rudd of St David's (1594–1615), had private income of any consequence. Obliged to maintain state and hospitality appropriate to their station on their miserably inadequate incomes, they were querulous and persistent in their expostulations, though only Carleton of Llandaff (1618–19) had the unabashed frankness to admit that he accepted his unwelcome "promotion" there because "the favours of princes are not to be rejected."[2] *Commendams* and pluralism, common in Wales since the fifteenth century, were normal among all the higher clergy, and even Laud as bishop of St David's proved no exception. Some took to systematically acquiring some of the better rectories in their gift, the most notorious offender being Hughes of St Asaph. (1573–1600) Allegations of simony and greed were made, probably with justice, against a number of them. It comes as no surprise that Marmaduke Middleton, deprived of his see in 1593, should be accused of simony and many other extortions and corrupt practices, but some of the best bishops have their reputations hardly less tarnished in this respect, among them Lewis Bayly, author of *The Practice of Piety* and bishop of Bangor (1616–31) and Richard Davies of St David's (1561–81). The unusually well documented activities of Davies and his precentor Thomas Huet, show that even men who had a conscientious regard for their office were obliged to provide for themselves and their families by unashamed nepotism in granting rights of next presentation

---

[1] Williams, *Conquest to Reformation*, pp. 327–31; Idem, 'The Episcopal Registers of St David's, 1554–65', *Bull. BCS*, XIV, pp. 45–54, 125–38; NLW, SD, BR, 3; Richards, *Puritan Movement*.

[2] CPSD, 1611–18, p. 500.

to livings, leasing of prebends, and conferring livings.[1] The temptation of *sauve qui peut* was made the stronger by short episcopates
and frequent changes. Pressed by poverty, high taxation, and rising
living-costs, they took what they could in the way of high entry
fines and other short-term gains. They cut down on overheads
like residence, repairs, and hospitality; palaces, parsonages, chancels,
the cathedrals themselves, were allowed to fall into disrepair and even
ruin.[2]

So that when in Charles I's reign, under Laud's direction, a determined drive was made to safeguard what remained of the Church's
property and to recover from profane hands as much as possible, it was
directed nearly as much against some of the practices of the clergy as
against those of the laity. Bishops were required not to be absentee
landlords nor to prejudice their successors' rights or possessions before
being translated. These were eminently salutary regulations as far as
Welsh dioceses were concerned, where short-term bishops were all
too usual, though neither of Laud's appointments to his old diocese of
St David's, Field (1627–35) and Manwaring (1636–53), did much to
comply with his wishes. On the other hand there are a few small
signs of the changing times to be discerned in the contemporary
ecclesiastical records. The chapter of Llandaff in 1626, considering the
"great decay" of the church, piously resolved not to renew the lease
of the rectory of Eglwysilan but to "convert the entire profits and
annual rent (being not minished by taking any fine) to the best use and
most valuable advantage" of the church of Llandaff. Encouraged
perhaps by a concession in its favour from Charles I over a lease, in
1629 it refused rent from so great a figure as the earl of Worcester on
the grounds that it was not certain just how much of its possessions the
sum was being tendered for; and in 1634 it carefully entered into its
records royal letters forbidding the negotiation of leases for a term of
lives by the whole chapter or individual members of it. The bishop
of St David's had already laid down as early as 1629 that the chapter
was not to lease for a term of lives or to agree upon any leases in his
absence.[3] Laud in 1637 settled on the bishop the perpetual annexation
of two rectories *in commendam*. In the still poorer dioceses of north
Wales he was also active, settling commendams on the bishop of St
Asaph and providing him with a new palace. In Bangor, where

[1] St Ch. 5, G15, 23, 580, 25; H. R. Trevor-Roper, *Archbishop Laud, 1573–1645*,
1962 ed., p. 188; Williams, *Hon. Soc. Cymmrodorion*, 1948, pp. 163–4.
[2] Gruffydd, *Hist. Soc. Ch. Wales*, IV, pp. 18–19; W. T. Morgan 'Two Cases
concerning Dilapidations to Episcopal Property etc.', *National Library Wales J.*,
VII, 1951, pp. 149–54.
[3] NLW, LlCh, 4, pp. 106, 111, 126–8; SDCh, B, 4, p. 30.

"everything was let for lives, down to the very mill that grinds his corn," by his predecessors, the bishop was required to make a survey of all the lands of his see; and, moreover, in 1637 the archdeacon of Anglesey was promoted to be bishop of the diocese as a reward for having recovered for the see concealed lands to the value of £1,000.[1] But this was a quite exceptional piece of good fortune for the Church. Much of its property was gone beyond recall and more still was to be lost in the vast upheaval that was soon to shake it and the whole realm to their foundations.

[1] Trevor-Roper, *Laud*, p. 189; Hill, *Economic Problems*, pp. 312, 315.

CHAPTER VII

FARM LABOURERS

A. THE LABOURING POPULATION

"...I think it fit to begin with the poorer sort, from whom all other sorts of estates do take their beginning. And therefore of our poor thus much:...as well the poor as the rich proceed from the Lord...the rich cannot stand without the poor...and the humble thoughts which smoke from a poor man's cottage are as sweet a sacrifice unto the Lord as the costly perfumes of the prince's palace."[1]

In these words Robert Reyce opened his description of the social order in Suffolk, in the early years of the seventeenth century; and his homily may serve to remind us of a field of study still largely unexplored by English historians.

The reason for the comparative neglect of the Tudor and Stuart farmworker is not far to seek. No one has written his signature more plainly across the countryside; but no one has left more scanty records of his achievements. No diaries, no letters, no account books; few lawsuits, a handful of wills and inventories, an inchoate mass of manorial surveys, subsidy assessments, royal commissions, and parish registers: these, with the observations of a few contemporaries, are almost all we have to go on.

Yet the history of the Tudor farmworker is surprisingly full of interest and variety. The work of labourers in the cornlands of Hertfordshire was quite unlike that of shepherds on the Yorkshire Wolds, hopmen in the Weald of Kent, neatherds on the Cumberland mountains, or warreners in the cony country of Wiltshire. The lives of farmhands who lived with their master in the farmhouse bore little resemblance to those of labourers who lived with their wives and children in cottages in the village street. The economic standing of a skilled farmworker with a holding of his own and unstinted pasture rights on the common waste was altogether different from that of a disinherited day-labourer with no property but his wages, and a mere hovel of sticks and dirt to live in. If all the relevant material could be studied, the Tudor farmworker's story would, indeed, furnish sufficient information for a book. In the space of a single chapter only the bare outlines of the subject can be traced.

[1] Robert Reyce, *Suffolk in the XVIIth Century: the Breviary of Suffolk by Robert Reyce, 1618...*, ed. Lord Francis Hervey, 1902, pp. 56, 57.

The first problem confronting the student of Tudor farmworkers is that of definition. For the bulk of the labouring population the question does not arise; but in the topmost rank of the working community there was sometimes no sharp distinction between the better-off labourer working his own holding and supplementing his income with seasonal wage-work, and the poor husbandman whose holding was insufficient to support his family and who turned to occasional wage-work to augment his resources. All that can be said is that the employment of the former tended to be regular, and of the latter spasmodic. This distinction is sometimes difficult to observe in practice; but the difficulty affects only a marginal section of the working community, though it should be borne in mind in interpreting the figures given below.

For an estimate of the size of the labouring population, in proportion to that of the country as a whole, we must turn to the subsidy assessments of 1524, the Hearth Tax Returns of the 1660's, two occupational censuses of the early seventeenth century, and a sample of manorial surveys.[1] In the subsidy of 1524 people were assessed on lands, goods, or wages, and in rural parishes most of those in the latter category can probably be regarded as farm servants. In forty-four parishes scattered throughout Devonshire the average proportion so assessed was 36 per cent, though in some places it rose as high as two thirds. In Lincolnshire it was about one third, ranging from 28 per cent on the sparsely populated wolds to 35 per cent in the marshland, and 41 per cent in the middle marsh. In Leicestershire, by contrast, only about 20–22 per cent of the rural population were assessed on wages, though here there was even wider diversity between different parishes, and in some places the proportion was as high as 90 per cent.

In the Hearth Tax Returns poor people were usually returned as "not chargeable," and most people so described were probably labourers. In Kent, the proportion so accounted was one third: ranging from 16 per cent on the thinly settled sheep pastures of Aloesbridge hundred in Romney Marsh, to 44 per cent in the populous countryside

---

[1] W. G. Hoskins and H. P. R. Finberg, *Devonshire Studies*, 1952, pp. 419–20; W. G. Hoskins, *Essays in Leicestershire History*, 1950, pp. 129–30; Joan Thirsk, *English Peasant Farming*, 1957, pp. 41, 74, 83, 98, 149; A. J. and R. H. Tawney, 'An Occupational Census of the Seventeenth Century', EcHR, v, 1934–5, pp. 39 and n., 46 *sqq.*; information on Kentish Surveys (1562–1639) and Hearth Tax Returns kindly given by Dr Felix Hull; PRO LR, 2, 230, ff. 42–3, 223–34; SP 14, 44, 28; SP 14, 47, 75; Bradford Corporation, Cunliffe-Lister MSS (2), Bdle 29; Lancs. RO, DDM. 14. 7, DD Pt. 39, DD F. 112, DD He. 61.5; Carlisle, Dean and Chapter Records, Hugh Todd's Account of Rentals (1490); Cumb. RO, Surveys of Dacre Lands (1589); Yorks. Arch. Soc., MS Collns., DD.121.31; *Yorks. Arch. Jnl*, xxxi, 1934, pp. 245, 246; Yorks. Arch. Soc., *Rec. Ser.*, CIV, p. xxiii. Most of the surveys relate to 1570–1640; three to 1651 (Yorkshire); one to 1490 (Cumberland). cf. also VHC *Wilts.*, IV, 1959, p. 57

round Maidstone, Ashford, and the Wealden cloth villages, and 51 per cent in the rich cornlands of Downhamford hundred, between Sandwich and Canterbury.

Between the 1524 subsidy and the Hearth Tax Returns, two county 'censuses' were compiled, one for Gloucestershire in 1608, and another for part of Northamptonshire in 1638. In the latter, the proportion of agricultural labourers in the ten hundreds of the eastern division of the county was probably about 31 per cent.[1] In Gloucestershire, where an exceptionally large number of people were employed in the cloth industry, farmworkers formed only one fifth of the population, although labouring people as a whole comprised nearly 30 per cent of the total. From this latter census it is also clear that the actual number of farmworkers in Gloucestershire, between the ages of 20 and 60, was about 3,500, out of a total male agricultural population of about 8,000.[2]

The evidence of manorial surveys is more difficult to interpret. It is probably safe to assume, however, that most rural tenants with holdings of less than five acres occasionally, at least, augmented their income by working as wage-labourers. (The Act of 1589, it will be recalled, stipulated that no cottage should be erected with less than four acres of land attached.) On the fifty-one manors in the sample here analysed, nearly thirty-seven per cent of tenants occupied smallholdings of this kind. As between different farming regions, the proportions varied from only 19 per cent on the fell-side manors of the north to 34 per cent in mainly arable clayland areas, 35 per cent in marshland manors, and almost 70 per cent in the fens. (In this last area, however, commons were unusually extensive and the arable exceptionally fertile, and smallholdings do not necessarily represent labourers' tenements.)

Taken together, these various sources suggest that in the Tudor and early Stuart period the labouring population probably formed about one quarter or one third of the entire population of the countryside. The figure was lowest in moorland areas, a little higher on wolds and downs, and a good deal higher in fertile corn-growing districts. In unenclosed heath- and forest-lands, it was probably higher still, especially at the end of the period. The foregoing evidence does not

[1] Tawney, op. cit., p. 39 and n. . I have reckoned half the "servants" of unspecified occupation together with all the "labourers" as agricultural employees; but the interpretation of these categories is doubtful.

[2] Tawney, op. cit., pp. 46 sqq. I have reckoned two thirds of the 430 knights, esquires, and gentry in the census as engaged in agricultural pursuits. I have also counted half the 750 servants and half the 283 servants of unspecified employment as probably engaged in farm-work. These proportions may be either too high or too low; but on any estimate they can hardly affect the relevant percentages by more than two or three either way.

cover such areas; but contemporaries like Hartlib and Norden expressed this opinion, and their statements are supported, as we shall see, by other evidence from manorial surveys and Exchequer Commissions.[1]

The size of the labouring population did not remain constant, however. Between the opening and closing decades of the period, it almost certainly expanded, both absolutely and relatively, till by the end of the seventeenth century labourers, cottagers, and paupers were said to comprise as much as 47 per cent of the entire population.[2] The consequences of this expansion of the working population were far-reaching. As the number of labourers increased, the pressure on land also increased, and smallholdings were either divided up amongst children, and subdivided again till they shrank to mere curtilages, or else bequeathed to the elder son alone, so that the younger children were left propertyless. As the period proceeded, therefore, a growing army of landless, or almost landless, labourers appeared, dependent on wages alone for their livelihood, often forced to wander from place to place till they found employment, or else to hire themselves out at the autumnal labour fairs held in many market towns. At the same time, largely because the development of commercial farming and the progress of regional specialization in agriculture greatly intensified the *demand* for seasonal or occasional labour, a new population of migrant labourers gradually came into being, principally recruited from among the ranks of these disinherited peasants. In all probability the labouring population had always been more mobile than we realize: droving and transhumance were, after all, long-standing practices in pastoral areas, from Wales and Northumberland to Romney Marsh and the Weald; the enclosure movement and the dissolution of the monasteries, moreover, had set many labourers adrift from their moorings; and the expansion of urban areas, especially London, attracted an increasing influx of labourers from rural parishes all over the kingdom.[3] But the appearance of an army of migrant wage-

[1] Cf. *Samuel Hartlib, his Legacie*, 1652, p. 42. of Hartlib's remarks, however, on the fewness of commons in Kent need qualification in view of the extensive wood-lands in the county, where according to Cobbett in the nineteenth century a similar economy prevailed. For Norden's opinion, see *Harrison's Description of England in Shakespere's Youth*, ed. F. J. Furnivall, Part IV, New Shakespere Soc., 6th Ser., VIII, 1881, p. 180 [Quoted hereafter as Harrison, *op. cit.*].

[2] D. C. Coleman, 'Labour in the English Economy of the Seventeenth Century', EcHR, 2nd Ser., VIII, 1955-6, p. 283 ; Cf .C. W. Chalking, *Seventeenth Century Kent*, 1965, p. 247.

[3] Cf. E 134, 7 Car. I, M 15; E 134, 3 Car. I, M 35; Gloucester City Lib., MS 16064, f. 14; R. U. Sayce, 'The Old Summer Pastures', Pt. II, *Mont. Coll.*, LV, i, 1958, p. 71; SP 14, 138, 11. For the mobility of the rural population in Leicestershire, see W. G. Hoskins, *Essays in Leicestershire History*, 1950, pp. 131-2.

earners in the Tudor countryside was essentially a different phenomenon, and it was directly attributable to the demands of commercial
farming and the growth of the labouring population.

We must not exaggerate either the novelty or the extent of these
new developments, however. Judged by modern standards, the working population of Tudor and early Stuart England was still relatively
small. England still remained an overwhelmingly peasant community:
a land of small family farms where outside labour was only occasionally
employed at peak periods. On the holdings of yeomen and husbandmen in Gloucestershire, for instance, masters outnumbered men by at
least two to one: only one husbandman in ten employed any servants
at all, and scarcely one in 350 more than two. In Kent and other
counties, even substantial landed families, like the Tokes of Godinton
Place, sometimes employed nephews and cousins of neighbouring
branches of the family, when in need of farm servants or stewards.[1]
Despite the development of capitalist farming and the virtual extinction
of serfdom,[2] the structure of farming society yet remained intensely
patriarchal, even on sizeable estates. In many counties, from Cumberland to Cornwall and Kent, it continued to be so till long after the
Civil War and the Revolution of 1688.

B. HOLDINGS AND COMMON-RIGHTS

In most parts of England the labourer's landed property, like that of
other country people, was of two kinds: his individual holding, and
his common rights in the village fields, meadows, and wastes. Individual
cottage-holdings, according to the Act of 1589, were supposed to
consist of not less than four acres of land, and many examples of tenements of this size and larger existed. William Hobson, for example, a
labourer of Wheldrake in the vale of York in James I's reign, inherited
a farm of six acres from his father, consisting of a house, barn, homestead, and garth of one acre, together with arable strips amounting to

---

[1] Tawney, op. cit., pp. 52, 53; E. C. Lodge, ed., The Account Book of a Kentish
Estate, 1616–1704, British Academy, Records of Social and Economic History, VI,
1927, passim. Professor and Mrs Tawney's figures relate only to known employers;
on any showing, however, it is not likely that more than one husbandman in six
employed a servant.

[2] For bondmen and manumission under the Tudors see A. Savine, 'Bondmen
under the Tudors', RHS, NS, XVII, 1903, pp. 235–89. Savine's opinion is that even in
the early sixteenth century bondmen formed little more than 1 per cent of the population, although he shows that Tudor villeinage was "not in all cases a harmless fiction
..." (pp. 248, 263). His evidence relates almost entirely to the first half of our period.
Exchequer Special Commissions and Depositions show that bondmen not infrequently
bequeathed property worth £30 or £40.

four acres in the east and north fields of the village, and a further acre of arable land in the Flatt. His neighbour Richard Penrose rented a similar tenement, with five and a half acres of arable in the four common fields of the village, a quarter of an acre of meadowland, and a house, a barn, a homestead, and a small garth. Two generations earlier, Robert Plommer of Nassington, in Northamptonshire, was renting a cottage with a garden and an acre of land belonging to it, together with twenty selions of arable and an acre of meadowland in the village fields. Robert Sharpe, his neighbour, lived in a cottage with a garden and a close of one acre, "lying between the king's lands" there, with nearly four acres of meadowland belonging to it.[1]

In general, however, labourers with as much as four or five acres of land were exceptionally fortunate. A study of holdings of five acres and less listed in manorial surveys of the period suggests that the lot of most village labourers was very different. Out of about 650 small-holdings on forty-three manors scattered over thirteen counties, only 7 per cent covered four or more acres; a further 26 per cent, each consisting of a cottage and garden with toft, croft, close, or orchard attached, comprised under one acre; and 41 per cent consisted of little more than a cottage and garden.[2] Even assuming that all the four-acre holdings belonged to labourers (some may have been worked by husbandmen), and taking account of holdings of over five acres, it seems probable that the tenements of at least two labourers out of three consisted of little more than a garden, with possibly a small close or two attached. As the period advanced, moreover, the proportion of labourers with very small tenements almost certainly increased. There can be little doubt that, between 1500 and 1640, the labourer's share of the cultivable area of the country as a whole was declining.

As between different counties, the size of labourers' holdings varied widely. In the marcher counties, cottagers often seem to have been relatively fortunate, barely half of them renting less than one acre of land, and one in five more than two acres. In east Northamptonshire the relevant proportions were 56 and 17 per cent, and in Yorkshire and Lancashire 61 and 24 per cent. In the southern parts of Sussex, however, three labourers in four cultivated holdings of less than one acre; and in some of the densely populated manors of East Anglia nearly four out of five. Only a tiny minority of labourers on these eastern manors—some 3 per cent—farmed the statutory holding of four acres or more.

---

[1] PRO LR, 2, 230, ff. 279, 281; Northants. RO, Westmorland Apethorpe Colln., 4, XVI, 5 (1551).

[2] See Table 4 and note thereto for names of manors. In interpreting the evidence of surveys, however, it must be remembered that they tell us nothing about the sub-letting of holdings.

On the manor of Hartest, near the Suffolk wool town of Lavenham, there were, in 1608, no fewer than "40 small and poor copyholders, the best of them not having above two acres, the most of them being cottingers, and 35 other poor households that have no habitation of their own, nor cow nor calf..." It was in such areas, as Dr Thirsk has pointed out elsewhere, that labourers were forced to turn to by-employments like spinning and weaving to eke out a living.[1]

Table 4. *The size of labourers' holdings (percentages)*[a]

	Cottage with garden or croft, etc., only	Under 1 acre	1–1¾ acres	2–2¾ acres	3–3¾ acres	4 and 5 acres
Cumberland	60	12	10	5	8	6
Yorks. and Lancs.	31	30	14	7	8	9
West Midlands	16	33	28	8	6	8
Sussex and Hants.	20	57	8	6	5	5
Eastern Counties	73	5	10	7	2	3
Northants.	4	52	26	0	4	13
All areas	41	26	13	6	7	7
Fell parishes	47	18	13	3	7	11
Forest parishes	10	34	30	2	10	15
Plain parishes (Sussex)	22	50	8	8	8	5
Plain parishes (Cumb.)	60	12	10	5	8	6
Before 1560	11	31	28	7	11	11
1600–10	35	36	13	6	5	5
After 1620	40	23	14	8	7	8

[a] The first section of the table covers 651 labourers' holdings in forty-three manors; the second 356 holdings in twenty four manors, the third 447 holdings in twenty-eight manors. For the Surveys used, see pp. 397, n. 1, 401, n. 1, 402, n. 1, 404, n. 1. The manors covered are: North Bersted, Falmer, Preston, Stanmer, St Leonards, and Tarring (Sussex); West Linton, Bowness, Drumburgh, Cardurnock, Glasson, Easton, Rockcliffe, Orton, and Wetheral (Cumb.); Hoff and Drybeck (Westm.); Castleton and Butter-Aikton, worth (Lancs.); Elloughton, Wheldrake, Sheriff Hutton, Temple Newsam, Wensleydale, Pickering, Grassington, Ellingtons, Healey, Howsham, and Swine (Yorks.); Church Aston and Longford (Salop); Hallow (Worcs.); Hartest (Suffolk); Great Wigborough and Salcott Wigborough (Essex); Prior's Barton (Hants.); The Lea in Mitcheldean and Gotherington (Glos.); Nassington and Apethorpe (Northants.); Great Abington (Cambs.).

[1] SP 14, 40, 21; Joan Thirsk, 'Industries in the Countryside', in *Essays in the Economic and Social History of Tudor and Stuart England*, ed. F. J. Fisher, 1961, pp. 75–7.

Quite as diverse was the average size of holdings in different agricultural regions.[1] In both the coastal plain of Cumberland and the coastal plain of Sussex nearly three quarters of the labouring population rented less than one acre of land apiece, and only one fifth more than two acres; scarcely one labourer in twenty worked the statutory acreage. In such districts, especially in the north and Midlands, it was not uncommon for two or more labouring families to share a single cottage, dividing the croft or garden between them.[2] In some of the fell-side villages of Yorkshire and Lancashire, labourers were a little more fortunate, though there too nearly two thirds held under one acre; while in valleys like Garsdale a rising population, coupled with gavelkind tenure, compelled peasants to turn to by-employments, such as stocking-knitting, to supplement the resources of their dwindling holdings. In woodland areas, by contrast, or on manors where wasteland was still abundant, many labourers were relatively well off. In the vale of York with its extensive royal forests, and in the vale of Pickering with its neighbouring marshes and moorlands, about half the working population rented at least one acre of land. On a group of woodland manors in Sussex, Northamptonshire, Staffordshire, and the marcher counties, the proportion was well over half, and one labourer in four worked at least three acres. In Kinver Forest one cottage holding amounted to no less than eleven acres and another to thirty; whilst at the enclosure of Deerfold Forest in Herefordshire all cottagers were allotted at least four acres of land, "that so they may be able to maintain their families and not continue a great charge and burden to the several townships."[3]

Important though the labourer's individual smallholding was, the vital factor in his fortunes was his rights of common.[4] Pre-eminent among these privileges were his grazing rights on common pastures, which in moorland and woodland districts were often extensive. On the forest manor of Feckenham in Worcestershire all the inhabitants, including labourers, enjoyed common at all times of the year, for all kinds of beasts without number, whether sheep, swine, geese, or cattle. At Alberbury in Shropshire, in Elizabeth's reign, the tenants had common pasture in the village woodlands for all cattle without stint, and for 100 hogs without rate of pannage. In Northamptonshire the

[1] For a map of agricultural regions, see p. 4.
[2] Cumb. RO, Surveys of Dacre lands, 1589. For examples of shared holdings a in Midland county: cf. Northants. RO, Westmorland Apethorpe Colln., 4, XVI, 5.
[3] E 134, 10–11 Car. I, H 22 (for Garsdale); E 178, 4959 (for Kinver forest); Hereford City Library, L.C. Deeds, Bdle 5571 (1611).
[4] Cf. Chalklin, op. cite., p. 22,

fifty-two cottagers of Nassington were allowed to pasture three cattle
and ten sheep each on the common lands of the village, and were able
"to live in such idleness upon their stock of cattle [that] they will bend
themselves to no kind of labour; for there is few of the 52 cottagers
but has as much cattle in the Forest [of Rockingham] over and above
the rate aforsesaid as any husband [man] in the town..." In thickly
populated vales and plains, however, the labourer's pasture rights were
often being restricted, challenged, or extinguished in this period. At
Broughton near Stokesley, in the vale of Cleveland, where at one time
each of the poorer inhabitants had been suffered to pasture ten or twenty
cattle, sheep, or horses on the common, their privileges were threatened
by enclosure in Charles I's reign. At Sutton on Derwent, near York,
the "gressmen" or cottagers, who comprised nearly two thirds of the
village farmers, were in the mid-sixteenth century allowed to put
only one beast each on the common between Lammas and Martinmas;
while at Kirkby Moorside, where in 1560 every inhabitant had kept at
least one or two kine, the poor cottagers seem to have lost their common
rights altogether by 1570.[1]

Rights of pasture were not the only communal benefits enjoyed by
labourers. They also claimed privileges in the shrubs, woods, under-
growth, stone-quarries, and gravel-pits of the common: for building
and repairing their houses, for making gates, fences, and hurdles, and
for fuel for cooking and heating. In some parishes, like Kennington in
east Kent, commoners were allowed to take loam and sand for making
bricks for their cottages, and turves "for amending their highways..."
In some, like Cartmel in Furness, they were permitted to lop and crop
underwood for the browse of their cattle in wintertime. At Burnley
and Ightenhill in Lancashire they might dig what coal they pleased
from the pits on the common, for use in their cottages. In parts of
Holmesdale and the Weald of Kent labourers possessed an almost unlimited supply of top and lop in the woods and copses, and of fallen
wood after winter storms. On the peat moors of the Pennines, the
Cheviots, and Devonshire, on the moorlands of the Lancashire plain, on
the sandy heaths of Surrey and Hampshire, cottagers often took what
turf, bracken, and furze they pleased. On Cattell Moor, near Wetherby
in Yorkshire, the "poorest sort" of inhabitants, "through the whole
year, as they had occasion to use them, have usually gotten all such
elding or fuel (*viz.*, whins and brake)...as they did usually burn...
within their houses," carrying them home "on their back..." Where-
ever woodland or commonland was short, however, as in much of

[1] Worcs. RO, 705, 78 (1590 or 1591); C 2, Eliz., A 8, 58; Northants. RO, Westmorland Apethorpe Colln., 4, XVI, 5 (1551); E 134, 9 and 10 Car. I, H 37; Yorks.
Arch. Soc., *Rec. Ser.*, CXIV, 1947, p. 64; E 164, 37, f. 386.

Leicestershire and the East Riding, common rights of this kind were closely restricted and the labourer's lot in winter weather was hard.[1]

Labourers also shared in the wild bird- and animal-life of the common. In the parishes of the Isle of Axholme poor people possessed rights of fishing and fowling. In Hatfield Chase they were said to have almost lived off the abundance of rabbits breeding on the commons. Until the enclosure of the royal forests, they frequently poached the king's deer, sometimes maiming a young kid so that its dam was forced to feed it where it lay, till it became "as fat as brawn", and then returning "in a dark night" to cut its throat and carry it home.[2] In many parishes poor people also appropriated hares, fish, wood-pigeons, and birds' eggs; together with beech-mast from the copses, for their pigs; crab-apples and cobnuts from the hedgerows; brambles, whortles, and juniper berries from the heaths; and mint, thyme, balm, tansy, and other wild herbs from any little patch of waste. Almost every living thing in the parish, however insignificant, could be turned to some good use by the frugal peasant-labourer or his wife.

All these customary rights of rural labourers were more or less carefully regulated by village by-laws and manorial customs. At Cartmel, for example, villagers were not permitted to cut rushes on Windermoor before 26 September; those with meadow on the common were ordered to mow the same on 1 or 2 July; and no one was allowed to gather nuts before Nutday, 1 September, or shear his bracken for thatching, bedding, or burning before Brackenday, 2 October.[3] Judged by modern standards of individual freedom, restrictions of this kind may seem petty and repressive; but in a society where resources were strictly limited and the sense of community intense, they were both natural and necessary. The labourer's rights of common formed part of a carefully integrated economy, whose balance could rarely be altered without serious consequences for the commoners themselves. When we read of old William Hall, of Amble in Northumberland, solemnly striking the village boundary stone with his staff in the presence of his two sons, or of Mistress Clarke compelling her grandson to sit on it with "his bare buttock" that he might "remember the same so long as he should live," we sense something of the importance of communal privileges in the

[1] E 178, 3960 (1615); A. P. Brydson, *Some Records of two Lakeland Townships*, 1908, p. 162; PRO DL, 43, 4, 12; E 134, 20–21 Eliz., M 10; *Lancs. and Ches. Rec. Soc.*, XXXII, p. 139; SP 14, 58, 7; E 134, 41 and 42 Eliz., M 22; William Burton, *The Description of Leicestershire*, [1622], p. 2.

[2] *Yorks. Arch. Jnl.*, XXXVII, 1951, p. 386; BM, Lansdowne MS 897, ff. 50–1; cf. SP 14, 31, 74.

[3] Lancs. RO, DDCa.7.3 (mainly late seventeenth- and early eighteenth-century customs).

aspirations of the village.[1] Poor though they seem, those rights alone added a few simple graces to an otherwise bare existence, and bred in the labourer a sense of hope and independence. For the cottager with ample common rights, there was profound truth in Sir Henry Wotton's dictum:

> How happy is he born and taught
> That serveth not another's will.

C. ENCLOSURE AND ENCROACHMENT

Such an economy was peculiarly vulnerable, however, to the new economic forces of the period, and it is no accident that the fiercest opposition to the Tudor enclosure movement stemmed from poor commoners. In using the word 'enclosure' it is important to differentiate between two distinct phenomena: first, large-scale enclosure of common fields and commons, usually undertaken by wealthy tenants or proprietors without the poor commoners' consent, and often involving depopulation; secondly, small-scale enclosures of common-land, consisting of a few roods of land only, usually undertaken by poor commoners themselves, and involving no depopulation. In contemporary usage 'enclosure' often covered both kinds of activity. Here it is confined, in the interests of clarity, to the former, while the latter is designated 'encroachment'. For the labouring community, enclosure and encroachment had diametrically opposite, though often complementary, consequences.

The effect of enclosure upon the lives of poor commoners was notorious. At its worst, where arable land was forcibly converted to pasture, enclosure led to the eviction of whole villages, and compelled their inhabitants either to seek employment elsewhere or to join the swelling army of perhaps 20,000 vagrants already roaming the Tudor countryside.[2] Where depopulation did not occur, the effects of enclosure might still be revolutionary. As the complaints of labourers themselves in countless lawsuits indicate, it could hardly fail to undermine the way of life to which they and their forebears had, for generations, been accustomed. When two hundred poor inhabitants of Oakley, Brill, and Boarstall in Buckinghamshire were threatened in 1611 with the enclosure of their common, they complained that they would "be utterly undone and have small or no means to relieve

[1] E 134, 13 Jas. I, M 4.
[2] This is probably a conservative figure. Gregory King estimated the number of vagrants at 30,000 in the late seventeenth century.—Andrew Browning, ed., *English Historical Documents, 1660–1714,* 1953, p. 517.

themselves." At Preston in Holderness the parishioners asserted in 1601 that, if their pasture was turned over to new usages, it would lead "to the utter undoing of the poorer sort, for that they shall thereby be enforced to leave off their tillage for want of pasture for their draught oxen." As a result of the enclosure of commonland at Easingwold in James I's reign, "the poor sort" of villagers were "utterly overthrown in the best means of their livelihood," for they "had no other means or relief at all whereupon to live..." When the Lord President of the Council of the North visited the area, "a great multitude...of people assembled...to make complaint," and an inhabitant of the neighbouring village of Crayke "cried to the said Lord President and commissioners to take pity of the poor inhabitants thereabouts..." Wherever enclosure took place, similar stories abounded: in Warwickshire, in Monmouthshire, on Sedgemoor, in the Isle of Axholme, in the Lincolnshire fenland, in the West Riding of Yorkshire, in County Durham.[1]

The realization that their whole way of life was at stake was a prominent factor in the peasant risings of the period. It is important not to overestimate the labourer's part in these rebellions. Magnates like the Northumbrian Percys and knightly families like the Yorkshire Constables were also behind them. Quarrelsome local gentry, like the Nortons of County Durham, were only too eager to array themselves "in warlike manner, with weapons as well invasive as defensive," and "in most riotous and disordered manner" break into their neighbours' cony-warrens. Rebel leaders were sometimes drawn, not from the ranks of countrymen at all, but from those of tanners "of good estate," carpenters "placed in very good service," or artisans and tradesmen of towns like Louth. Both the Gillingham Forest riots and those of the forest of Dean, in Charles I's reign, seem to have been led by a certain Henry Hoskins, a substantial yeoman whose Dorset followers included nearly fifty urban tradesmen and weavers, but only twenty-five countrymen, of whom no more than two were labourers.[2]

Nevertheless, much of the initiative behind these risings indubitably

[1] SP 14, 54, 15; C 2, Eliz., C 16, 55; SP 14, 116, 133; E 178, 4852; CSPD, 1640–1, p. 371; CSPD 1625–49, p. 617; CSPD 1636–7, p. 257; Yorks. Arch. Jnl., xxxvii, 1951 p. 386; Joan Thirsk, English Peasant Farming, 1957, p. 111; PRO DL, 44, 440; E 134, 16 Jas. I, E 25.

[2] LP xii, i, pp. 166–7, 82; Req. 2, 106, 55; D. G. C. Allan, 'The Rising in the West, 1628–1631', EcHR, 2nd Ser., v, 1952, pp. 78, 80; SP 14, 28, 64; LP xii, i, pp. 173–5; E 159, 472. Trin. 8 Car., rot. 38. Hoskins received the maximum fine of £200, and was evidently a substantial farmer. I am indebted to Dr T. G. Barnes for references to the Gillingham Forest riots. For further information on labourers' risings, see D. G. C. Allan, Agrarian Discontent under the early Stuarts and during the last Decade of Elizabeth, London M.Sc. (Econ.) thesis, 1950.

came from labouring peasants. In the Northern Rebellion of 1536 poor commoners gathered in hundreds to throw down enclosures and defend their tenurial privileges in Cumberland and Westmorland. In the Midland risings of James I's reign, multitudes of "the meaner sort of our people" assembled and armed themselves in Northamptonshire, "sometimes in the night and sometimes in the day," alleging sundry villages had been depopulated and "divers families undone." Nor were these riotous activities confined to the menfolk: women, and even children, joined in them with equal vigour, arming themselves with stones and bedposts, and breaking down newly erected enclosures.[1]

Although rarely successful, such risings at least drew the attention of the government and the church to the labourers' problems. The policy of the Crown was necessarily ambivalent; but both Tudors and Stuarts were firmly set against depopulation, and often tempered their natural severity against rebels with compassion "towards the simplicity of such offenders." The attitude of ecclesiastics, though in the fifteenth century they had themselves often enclosed, was also animated by a tradition of opposition to depopulation, stretching from Latimer and Grindal to Abbott and Laud. The outlook of the gentry was more divided. Many were themselves responsible for enclosure, and, as the poor of Cockfield in Durham complained, did not "spare to enclose us up even to our own doors..." Others, however, like the Scotts of Scots' Hall in Kent, endeavoured to protect their poorer tenants, and when "certain rich men who had great stock of cattle" transgressed their common rights, commanded "the said greedy-minded tenants" to "desist from their said oppression..." In many cases, there is reason to think, it was primarily new or minor gentry and self-assertive tenants who were the real culprits, while the indigenous or greater gentry endeavoured to restrain them in the interests of the poor.[2]

Nevertheless, from almost every point of view, enclosure increased the dependence of labourers on their landlords. Where they were compensated with land in severalty, their allotment was usually too small to support their livestock. Where they were compensated in kind, like the poor of Conisborough who received an allowance of milk in lieu of their cattle-rake on Firsby Moor, they had to walk to the farmhouse each Sunday, vessel in hand, to collect it.[3] Where they lost

---

[1] Cf. LP XII, i, pp. 182, 234, 304 et passim; SP 14, 73, pp. 139, 140, 147; SP 14, 35, 52; LP VIII, p. 393; SP 16, 116, 37. See also E 134, 13 Jas. I, E 18 and M 17, though it is not clear whether these cases refer to labourers or other peasants.

[2] Cf. R. H. Tawney, *The Agrarian Problem in the Sixteenth Century*, 1912, pp. 371 sqq., 420–1; SP 14, 73, pp. 139–47; SP 14, 142, 23; *Cumb. and Westm. Antiq. and Archaeolog. Soc.*, NS, XLIII, 1943, p. 178; E 134, 26 Eliz., E 11; C 2, Jas. I, G 5, 70; E 134, 10 Car. I, E 47.

[3] E 134, 21 Jas. I, M 14.

their rights altogether, they became mere wage-earners, tied to the wayward favour of a possibly temperamental employer. Wherever the labourer of the enclosed village turned, he was forcibly reminded of his loss of independence. The sole purpose of his existence was to serve "another's will."

Meanwhile *encroachment* was producing a very different effect on the labouring community. Largely under the impulse of peasant-workers themselves, and as a consequence of their steady nibbling at the remaining areas of uncultivated commonland, a new wave of settlement was taking place in this period. Driven partly by the depopulation of old-established villages, partly by the rapid rise of population and morcellation of their ancestral tenements, and in part by the attraction of new industries like mining and smelting, many labourers were drifting away from the old centres of rural population in this period, and resettling themselves, wherever land remained unappropriated, in royal forests, on sandy heaths, and beside wooded spaces.[1] While some villages were enclosed and depopulated in the fertile arable plains, new settlements began to appear round small commons, greens, and forstals; old hamlets received an influx of fresh blood, and extended their boundaries further into the waste. Not all the new encroachments were originated by new settlers; many consisted of small parcels of land added to already ancient holdings. But although contemporaries may have exaggerated the phenomenon, the existence of a new wave of settlement by squatters in search of living-space is undeniable.

In Kingswood Forest in Gloucestershire, for instance, John Norden found in 1615 "very many cottages raised upon the forests, maintained under the toleration of the statute for erecting houses near mineral places: but in this forest are far more erected than the necessity of the coalmines requireth..." In the moorland forest of Wensleydale, about 1610, one contemporary averred that, within his own memory, the number of forest inhabitants had increased, while another stated that

[1] The increasing population of these areas was also connected with the prevalence of gavelkind inheritance (e.g., in Kent and in the Pennine dales) and possibly borough-English customs, leading to excessive subdivision of tenements (cf. SP 14, 45, 94; E 134, 10–11 Car. I, H 22; Thomas Robinson, *The Common Law of Kent, with an Appendix concerning Borough English*, 1822, pp. 9, 17, 42 *sqq.*, 391 *sqq.*; Joan Thirsk, 'Industries in the Countryside', p. 77). For the influence of industries like mining and smelting on the populations of forest areas and wastes, cf. E 134, 22 & 23 Eliz., M 17 (Benwell, Northumberland); SP 14, 84, 46 (Kingswood Forest, Glos.); E 134, 16 Car. I, M 36 (Forest of Dean); E 178, 4533 (Cannock Chase). Quite apart from private forests and unappropriated wastes, there were probably at least one hundred royal forests and chases at this time: SP 14, 32, 26, lists over eighty in thirty-two English and five Welsh counties.

many of the new settlers were poor people and lived "very hardly."
In Galtres Forest, a few years later, the "poorest sort" of people were
said to be especially numerous, and in Easingwold manor alone there
were 150 poor commoners. In Feckenham Forest in Worcestershire,
in 1573, five hundred inhabitants brought a suit before the court of
Requests and asserted that the population of the Forest was then "above
five thousand people." In the Forest of Dean "many townships,
parishes, and hamlets adjoining unto and depending on the forest"

Table 5. *Distribution of population in rural Kent: analysis of
the Compton census, 1676*[a]

(Acres per head of population)

	East Kent	Mid Kent	West Kent	All Kent
Weald	14·5	6·2	9·6	7·7
Chartland	7·4	6·9	7·2	7·2
Upper downland	10·8	9·4	12·1	10·7
Lower downland	7·1	5·7	8·1	6·1
Northern marshland	15·7	25·1	16·2	18·3
Romney Marsh	44·2	—	—	44·2
All agarian regions	9·8[b]	7·3	9·9	9·1[c]

[a] The census is edited by C. W. Chalklin, in *A Seventeenth Century Miscellany*,
Kent Arch. Soc., Records Publication Committee, XVII, 1960, pp. 153–74. Urban
parishes and parishes covering more than one agrarian region have been omitted
from the calculations. The census appears to list inhabitants over sixteen only, and in
estimating the total population I have followed Mr Chalklin's suggestion of an
average of forty children to sixty adults (pp. 155, 157). The table covers nearly two
thirds of the area of the county and about half the total population. It is not possible
to calculate any valid figures for the Isle of Thanet and the Forest of Blean, owing
to *lacunae* in the material and to subsequent boundary changes.
[b] Excluding Romney Marsh.
[c] Including Romney Marsh (excluding Romney Marsh, the figure is 8·8).

were said, about 1640, to be "full of poor people, and that such poor
people have much increased and multiplied..." In Nottinghamshire
many new cottages were erected on wasteland and some settlements
were so "pestered" with squatters that "they are hardly able to live
one by another..." In Rossendale Forest, in Lancashire, the same
process seems to have been at work, and "the whole system of landholding was in a state of continuous dissolution" as a consequence.
In Kent, the forest parishes of the Chartlands and the Weald were
among the most thickly settled in the county, and the parishioners were
often forced to take to by-employments, such as clothing and iron-

working, to make a living. According to James I's surveyors, the inhabitants of forests were everywhere "increasing in such abundance" that they would soon thrust one another out of their possessions by violence, from mere "want of habitations." Wherever a Jacobean traveller like Norden crossed "great and spacious wastes, mountains, and heaths" he observed "many such cottages [of poor people] set up..."[1]

The character of these new and expanding forest communities is plain enough. They usually consisted, on one hand, of a small core of substantial peasant labourers, with sizeable holdings of their own, decidedly better off than common-field labourers, and probably identifiable with the indigenous settlers of the original community. On the other hand, they often included a much larger body of new squatters and "beggarly people," who had little legal right to the land they appropriated, but "adventured upon" the erection of their cottages—as two Kentish squatters remarked—"for that they were destitute of houses, and had seen other cottages upon the same waste, built by other poor men."[2] Not infrequently these hovels existed for two or three generations before they were tracked down by manorial surveyors, and their owners forced to pay rent.

By and large, the new forest communities were squatters' settlements, and were formed of scattered hamlets rather than nucleated villages. They often consisted solely of husbandmen and labourers, without either squire or parson to diversify their social structure, or to keep them in order. According to the Londoner John Norden, their inhabitants were "given to little or no kind of labour, living very hardly with oaten bread, sour whey, and goats' milk, dwelling far from any church or chapel, and are as ignorant of God or of any civil course of life as the very savages amongst the infidels..."[3] For "the people bred amongst woods," he remarked, "are naturally more stubborn and uncivil than in the champion countries." As each generation came and went, they became more and more inbred, more and

---

[1] SP 14, 84, 46; E 134, 7 Jas. I, E 34; SP 14, 116, 133; Req. 2, 66, 84; E 134, 16 Car. I, M 36; SP 16, 185, 86; G. H. Tupling, *The Economic History of Rossendale*, Chetham. Soc., LXXXVI, 1927, pp. 95, 97; Joan Thirsk, 'Industries in the Countryside', p. 79; PRO LR, 2, 194, f. 35; Harrison, *op. cit.*, p. 180; cf. SP 16, 44, 45; SP 14, 144, 24; G. E. Fussell, *The English Rural Labourer*, 1949, pp. 3–4; Hoskins and Finberg, *op. cit.*, p. 327. So late as 1656 Cromwell sent to suppress "near 400 cabins of beggarly people" in the Forest of Dean.—Allan, *loc. cit.*, p. 84. For the distribution of the population in Kent, see Table 5.

[2] E 178, 3960; Allan, *op. cit.*, p. 84. They may have trusted to the widespread belief that a cottage erected on the waste overnight constituted a lawful piece of property: cf. Hoskins and Finberg, *op. cit.*, p. 327; Fussell, *op. cit.*, p. 10.

[3] Quoted in Harrison, *loc. cit.*

more tenacious of their real or supposed customs and common-rights, and gradually more alienated from the common-field villages whence their inhabitants originally migrated.[1] Their greens and inns became the resorts of cattle-drovers and wayfaring badgers; their woods and dingles the haunts of vagabonds, gipsies, and bandits; their cottages the meeting places of millenarian sects. For the government and for local justices, their expanding population raised many a problem in preserving peace and providing work.[2] By the inhabitants of established villages their disorderly habits were regarded with fear and aversion, and their encroachment on the waste with jealousy. In the Forest of Dean they were described as people of very lewd lives and conversations, leaving their own "countries" and "taking this place for a shelter as a cloak to their villainies."[3] But for many a poor labourer forest hamlets afforded not only a footing, but a certain freedom denied to the farmworker of the village, whose life was lived under the shadow of the manor-house. For these workers the sixteenth century was an age not only of depopulation, but of settlement on heaths and wastes: and on these wastes, as we shall see, there was still opportunity for many an enterprising labourer to make a comfortable living.

D. COTTAGE HUSBANDRY AND PEASANT WEALTH

For a picture of the husbandry of rural workers, it is necessary to turn to the inventories of goods drawn up for probate purposes after their death. Only the uppermost layers of the labouring population possessed sufficient property to leave inventories; but those who were too poor to do so probably possessed little farm property worth valuing, so that the pattern of cottage husbandry presented in the inventories is in fact substantially complete.[4] In the following account, the terms 'cottager' and 'cottage farmer', which in contemporary usage were applied to labourers and husbandmen indiscriminately, are used of labourers only. Like the term 'peasant labourers', they refer to those workers whose livelihood was based partly on their holdings and who were wealthy

[1] John Nordon, *Surveyor's Dialogue*, p. 215. Of the Knaresborough Forest commoners, it was said in James I's reign: "they observe their customs curiously" and "are the most headstrong people in that country..."—SP 14, 37, 107.

[2] The policy of disafforestation and attempts to 'suppress' new cottages and forbid the entertainment of "inmates and undersetters" helped to foment the labourers' revolts of the early seventeenth century.—SP 14, 120, 35; cf. SP 14, 37, 102; SP 14, 124, 137; Helmingham Hall MSS, D.L's' and J.P's' Committee Book, *passim;* and see Allan, *op. cit.*, pp. 77 *sqq.*

[3] SP 16, 44, 45 (?1626), and cf. E 178, 3960; E 134, 18 Jas. I, H 15; SP 16, 143, 41.

[4] A small but increasing proportion of labourers who left inventories possessed no farmstock.

enough to leave inventories. For this study, the inventories have been grouped in six broad regions: northern lowlands, northern highlands, eastern England, the west country, the woodland areas of the Midlands, and the fielden areas of the Midlands.[1] For all except the last area and the west country, the inventories have been subdivided into two periods, those between 1560 and 1600, and those between 1610 and 1640.[2]

In all regions, the basis of the labourer's farming was livestock.[3] Only a small proportion of cottage farmers possessed no stock what-

Table 6. *Peasant Labourers' cattle*[a]

| Region | Period | Percentage of peasant labourers possessing | | Number of cattle per 100 labourers |
		Cows, calves and heifers	Other cattle	
Northern lowlands	1560–1600	74	26	227
	1610–1640	88	12	161
Northern highlands	1560–1600	84	16	197
	1610–1640	87	13	163
Eastern England	1560–1600	82	18	122
	1610–1640	79	11	153
Midland forest areas	1560–1600	92	8	142
	1610–1640[b]	93	7	237
Midland fielden areas	1590–1640	91	9	153
West of England	1590–1640	90	10	82

[a] Based on probate inventories. For the term 'peasant labourers' see p. 412.
[b] Including a few inventories of the 1660's for Northants.

[1] For a map of these regions, see p. 4.
[2] For the west country and Midland fielden areas there are insufficient labourers' inventories before 1600 for separate analysis. In selecting the inventories I have in general included: (a) all those described as belonging to labourers, (b) all those which belonged to country people whose social status is not described and were valued at under £5 before 1570, under £10 during the 1590's, and under £15 during 1610–40. I have not always followed this rule blindly in the north-west, where money-values were lower and labourers fewer, and where farmers with inventories of these values were sometimes obviously not labourers. Some inventories of small value evidently belonged to retired yeomen or others living with their family, and these also have been excluded. Most of the Northants. inventories unavoidably relate to the 1660's, since few before 1640 have survived. Any rules of selection are bound to contain an arbitrary element; but the fact that in Hertfordshire (where social status is usually described) Stuart labourers not infrequently left property worth more than £15 suggests that these limits are, if anything, set rather too low than too high. But I do not think they are likely to be very wide of the mark either way.
[3] See Table 7.

ever: about one in twenty before 1600 and one in seven or eight thereafter. In all parts of the country the staple item in the worker's stock-farming was cattle.[1] In the north of England about 75 per cent of cottage farmers possessed cattle, in eastern England about 70 per cent, in the Midlands 60 per cent, and in the west of England 55 per cent. The great majority owned no more than one or two beasts each, and the number of labourers with more than five never exceeded 6 per cent except in the woodland areas of the Midlands, where in the seventeenth century it rose to 16 per cent. For every hundred peasant labourers, there were something like 80 cattle in the west country, 140 in the eastern counties, 150 in Midland fielden areas, 180 in the northern highlands, and 190 or more in the lowland areas of the northern counties and the woodland areas of central England.

The great bulk of this livestock consisted of milch kine, heifers, and calves: nowhere less than two thirds, and generally more than four fifths. Only a few labourers, chiefly in the north, interested themselves in breeding or fattening livestock for the expanding Tudor meat-market; still fewer either possessed or needed draught beasts. The primary agricultural concern of the labourer was to provide milk, cheese, and butter for his own family, while he or his wife disposed of surplus produce at the butter-cross in the neighbouring market town. Sometimes an exceptionally pushing or resourceful labourer, with a well fitted out-dairy, manufactured cheese or butter specifically for the or local market. Richard Gurleye of Knebworth in Hertfordshire, for instance, died possessed of as many as twenty cheeses in his store-rooms, and Robert Wood of Nuneaton left more than seventy. But people like Wood and Gurleye comprised only a fraction of the working population: except in a few favoured districts, the husbandry of Tudor cottagers reflected only to a limited degree the agricultural specialities or the commercial opportunities of their region.

Next in importance to the labourer's cattle were his sheep. In eastern England the proportion of peasant labourers who possessed sheep was only 19 per cent; in the west the figure rose to 45 per cent, in the Pennines to 48 per cent, and in the Midlands to 55 per cent. Most labourers' flocks, if such they can be called, were exceedingly small, often of less than three sheep, and rarely of more than nine. Everywhere, however, there were a few labourers, generally shepherds with little or no other stock of their own, who possessed twenty or more sheep. It was a well-recognized custom for shepherds to be allowed a few lambs from their master's flock each year, to be run on their employer's sheep-pastures.[2] In this way many a poor shepherd in

[1] See Table 6.
[2] See, for example, BM Harleian MS 98, f. 31v.

Table 7. *peasant Labourers' livestock*[a]

		No stock	Cattle				Sheep			Horses				Pigs				Poultry
Region	Period		0	½-2	3-5	6+	0	1-8	9+	0	½-1	1½-2	3+	0	1	2-3	4+	
Northern lowlands	1560-1600	7	13	53	27	6	77	16	6	57	27	10	6	67	23	0	10	30
	1610-40	6	32	37	27	4	72	10	18	61	29	0	0	80	14	6	0	39
Northern highlands	1560-1600	3	13	53	33	0	47	27	13	63	33	3	0	93	0	3	3	47
	1610-40	13	29	39	23	3	56	13	8	59	39	3	0	85	15	0	0	30
Eastern England	1560-1600	0	22	67	11	0	78	11	11	100	0	0	0	45	22	22	11	56
	1610-40	21	39	45	10	6	84	11	5	76	21	0	3	58	21	17	4	29
Midland forest areas	1560-1600	9	38	33	29	0	54	24	21	63	17	12	8	54	17	25	4	42
	1610-40	16	47	11	26	16	37	31	32	79	11	0	10	63	16	11	10	16
Midland fielden areas	1590-1640[c]	13	32	44	18	0	44	25	25	88	6	6	0	50	32	12	0	12
West of England	1590-1640	15	45	40	15	0	55	30	10	70	25	5	0	70	20	10	0	35

a Based on probate inventories; for the basis of selection of inventories, see p. 413, n. 2. For the term 'peasant labourers' see p. 412.

b Small discrepancies in percentage totals are due to the fact that some inventories do not specify the *number* of livestock owned by the labourer. The references to 'half beasts', and 'half-horses' arise from the custom, in some areas, of sharing stock. There are too few inventories for Midland fielden areas and the west of England for separate analysis of the period before 1600.

c Including a few inventories of the 1660's for Northants.

the Midlands, and a few in the north and south, built up a stock of twenty or thirty sheep; while, very occasionally, a labourer like Henry Joyce of Winwick in Northamptonshire possessed nearly one hundred, or, like John Power of Longstock in Hampshire, as many as eight score. By such means a few Tudor and Stuart labourers were still able to work their way up in the social scale, step by step, till they reached the ranks of the yeomanry.

Pigs were not so ubiquitous an adjunct of the labourer's cottage in the sixteenth century as they became in the nineteenth; in the west of England and the Pennines they were still a rarity. Until labourers began to grow potatoes, they were rarely in a position to rear and fatten swine. In Midland and eastern England, however, about 40 or 50 per cent of peasant-workers kept swine, and bacon flitches hung from many a cottage chimney and roof-tree. In the forest areas of the Midlands a few labourers had as many as six pigs, no doubt fattened on mast in nearby woodlands, or on the waste products of dairies.

Horses were kept by only a minority of the peasant-labouring population, in most areas by less than one third. They were relatively numerous in the north of England where 40 per cent of cottage farmers kept horses, and least common in the eastern counties (12 per cent). Most labourers had little need for plough-animals of their own, or else, when they required them, either borrowed those of a neighbouring farmer for a day or two, or employed the common draught-team bequeathed to the parish by a former vicar or landowner. (Charitable bequests of this kind were not uncommon, and suggest that more labourers might have grown crops if they had possessed draught animals.)[1] In the woodland areas of the Midlands, it is true, near horse-markets like Stratford on Avon and manufacturing districts like Birmingham, a few well-off labourers seem to have been breeding horses: there was a growing demand for packhorses in these areas, and labourers' inventories often mention mares-with-colts or -with-fillies. The typical labourer's horse, however, served much the same purpose as the peasant's donkey in modern Ireland: it was employed, as inventories and lawsuits suggest, in carrying turf and bracken in packs, panniers, and 'nets', slung across its back; in carting hay, corn, and wood; and in conveying the labourer's wife and neighbours to the nearest market town.[2]

Hens or geese were kept by about one third of the labouring population. The proportion was rather higher in East Anglia, Cornwall, the

[1] See R. H. Tawney, *The Agrarian Problem in the Sixteenth Century*, 1912, p. 109; E 134, 8 Eliz., E 2; and cf. Req. 2, 29, 62 (26 Elizabeth) for a bequest of heifers and calves.

[2] Cf. C 3, 185, 47 (n.d., c. 1560–70).

East Riding, and Furness; rather lower in the lowland areas of Cumberland and Lancashire, in Hertfordshire and Somerset, and in the fielden areas of the Midlands. Only a few cottagers kept ducks or turkeys, and scarcely any owned bees; most labourers must have eaten all their food unsweetened, for few can have afforded the luxury of sugar.

Between the earlier and later parts of the period, so far as the evidence of probate inventories reveals, a number of significant changes seem to have occurred in the pattern of labouring stock-farming as a whole. On one hand, the number of *really poor* labourers—i.e. without *any* livestock of their own—rose from 5 per cent (of those who left inventories) to 13 per cent; the proportion with no cattle increased from 13 to over 30 per cent in the north, from 22 to 39 per cent in the east, and from 38 to 47 per cent in the Midlands; the numbers of small stockmen, with only one or two beasts, dropped from 53 to 38 per cent in the north, from 67 to 45 per cent in the east, and from 33 to 11 per cent in the Midlands; the percentage of labourers without any pigs or poultry increased, and in most areas the numbers with only one or two pigs, or three or four sheep, or a single horse, declined.[1] Over against this picture of declining fortunes, it seems that in most districts the *better-off* labourers, with herds of four or more cattle, were able to maintain their position: while in the Midland forest areas their numbers actually increased from 4 per cent to nearly 40 per cent. In the northern lowland areas, moreover, an increasing number of labourers began to keep poultry, and the number with sizeable sheep flocks rose threefold. In the dales and fells of the north a clear increase occurred in the proportion of labourers who kept horses and pigs; in the eastern counties a number of labourers began to keep horses and a few seem to have begun breeding them; in Midland forest parishes, the proportion of better-off pig farmers rose from 4 per cent to 10 per cent, and the average sheep flock rose from eight to twelve.

What do these facts and figures suggest? They seem to show that, as the period advanced, two distinct developments were taking place in the pattern of labourers' stock-farming. In the first place, as the population rose and land-hunger increased, most peasant labourers were keeping fewer cattle, and turning their attention instead to other kinds of livestock requiring less extensive grazings. Secondly, while the *better-off* labourers were able to increase their stock, the agrarian fortunes of the *poorer* peasant workers were declining, and the number of

---

[1] It may be thought that these changes were due to a growing habit among poorer labourers of leaving inventories; but I see no evidence for such a habit. In fact, the lower ranks in the sample were not usually poorer in *total* wealth than before but in *agricultural* wealth; instead of investing in stock, they were turning to by-employments to augment their income, and were also investing more in domestic goods.

labourers with *no* stock increased. In other words, the smaller labouring
stockman was gradually being squeezed out in favour of the larger: the
larger man was working his way up into the ranks of the husbandmen,
and the small peasant was becoming a mere wage-worker.[1] In both
these developments we can trace the influence of deep-seated economic
forces: in each case the determining factor was the diminishing supply
of land.

Arable husbandry played a far smaller part in cottage farming than
stock-husbandry. Few workers possessed either sufficient land or
sufficient capital to grow corn or other crops on even the smallest
scale. The great majority of labourers purchased their grain requirements in the local market town week by week, or from the travelling
badgers and mealmen who frequented the country districts of Tudor
England. Of those labourers whose inventories were drawn up in the
corn-growing season, less than one third left any sown land, and in the
Midlands only one seventh. Very occasionally, a labourer in the vale
of York kept as much as seven acres of land under the plough; but
elsewhere the figure did not rise above three acres. In the country as a
whole, the sown area (excluding inventories listing, no crops) averaged
little more than one acre, declining from seven roods before 1600 to
four thereafter; the average was slightly higher in the north of England,
where the pressure on land was less acute, rather lower in the Midlands
and the east, and very low in the west country. Barley, the poor man's
usual breadcorn, seems to have been the most frequent crop, followed
by peas, wheat, and oats. The labourer was usually accustomed to vary
his sowing, however, and he often planted a little of each kind of grain,
with perhaps a small quantity of rye and beans as well, and in some
districts, such as Hertfordshire, the Pennines, and the East Riding, a
small garth or croft of hemp, or occasionally flax. Quite probably,
if later custom is any guide, the worker's corn was sometimes literally
planted, grain by grain with a dibber, with a correspondingly good yield,
no doubt, at harvest-time.[2]

In marketing their produce, labourers rarely went beyond their
local town. Corn was usually sold soon after harvest in order to pay

[1] It may be argued that these conclusions are influenced by the basis of selection of
inventories (see p. 413, n. 2), and that the apparent decline of poor stockmen's fortunes
is because the £15 datum for the 1630's is set too low. But this would not explain the
rising fortunes of the better-off. I believe the interpretation in the text is correct,
more particularly since it tallies with other lines of argument, such as the shrinkage
in size of most labourers' holdings, the restriction of common-rights, and the fact
that stockless labourers were usually most numerous in 'advanced' agricultural
areas like the eastern counties.

[2] This was a nineteenth-century custom in Surrey.—George Bourne, *Memoirs
of a Surrey Labourer*, 1911, p. 150.

rent, and butter and eggs were disposed of weekly at the nearest market-cross. A few labourers, it is true, especially in forest districts, seem to have definitely oriented their production towards the private market, and to have ventured on individual contracts with butchers, drovers, and cheese-factors. In Hertfordshire an important barley county, a number of labourers engaged in malt dealings. In Kent, Thomas Strowde and Joseph Mayowe of Marden "dealt together in the working and sale of...wood:" purchasing timber from local gentry, hiring other workmen to help them hew and cleave it, and reselling it in the form of boards, laths, pales, faggots, roundwood, and "checker-timber" to the wheelwrights, carpenters, and spoon-makers of the area. But in fact such men were exceptional. As a rule, labourers lacked either the education to keep accounts, or the experience and 'credit' necessary to deal as private traders; they were frequently defrauded by more knowledgeable people as a consequence. The partnership of Mayowe and Strowde came to an untimely end because Mayowe kept no note of his dealings, "being a mere layman and illiterate." A note on the inventory of a Hertfordshire labourer records that £20 was owing to him "upon bonds and bills, which is all lost by ill debtors." A "man of power and credit" in Dorsetshire was able to extort a composition far short of his just debt from a local labourer who had sold him forty-one sheep, and eventually, "by taking advantage of his poverty and want, and...unableness to follow suits," compelled the labourer "to leave his own country of Dorsetshire, and live in service in Devonshire..." In fact, as William Harrison indicated, marketing was one of the labourer's most serious problems: for the worker was either forced to dispose of his produce in an un-favourable market in order to raise ready money for his rent, or else to risk his whole farmstock in a single private contract, with the possibility of ruining his family in the upshot.[1] The changing market conditions of the period were undoubtedly responsible, in part, for the gradual decline in the fortunes of the smaller labourer peasant.

We must now re-examine the probate inventories with a view to reconstructing the pattern of wealth as a whole among peasant labourers. The subject is most easily approached by posing four separate questions. First, what was the proportion of cottage farmers to the farming community at large? Analysis of about 3,600 inventories, between 1540 and 1640, scattered over seventeen counties, suggests that labourers' inventories comprised about 8 per cent of the total. The number of

[1] Req. 2, 28, 5; Req. 2, 30, 30; Herts. RO, inventory of Robert Pearman of Ardeley, Herts., 1619; C 2, Jas. I, H 18, 64; Harrison, op. cit., Part I, New Shakespere Soc., 6th Ser., I, 1877, pp. 296–7.

cottage farmers naturally varied widely between different regions.
It was more than twice as high in the lowland zone (9 per cent) as it was
in the highland zone (4 per cent). As between different agricultural
regions, it was exceptionally high in the woodland parishes of the
lowland zone, where it varied from 7 per cent in the 1560's to 18 per
cent in the 1590's, falling away again to 12 per cent in the 1630's. It
was lowest in the fielden parishes of both zones, where it rarely exceeded
6 per cent and sometimes dropped to *nil:* not so much because labourers
were few in such areas as because most of them were too poor to leave
inventories.

Secondly, what was the proportion of cottage farmers to the
labouring population as a whole? If, as has been said, labourers' inventories comprised about 8 per cent of the total number, and if, as we
saw earlier, labourers comprised about one third of the whole population, it seems that perhaps one labourer in four was sufficiently well-off
to leave an inventory. Allowing for the fact that about one tenth of
those workers who left an inventory possessed no farm stock, and
assuming that those who left no inventories were too poor to bequeath
any stock worth speaking of, we shall not be far wrong in thinking
that cottage farmers, as distinct from rural craft-workers and labourers
dependent solely on wages, comprised something like one quarter of
the farmworking population as a whole: a figure which roughly
tallies with the number of labourers who possessed holdings of two or
more acres.[1] There can be little doubt that the proportion of cottage
farmers varied widely in different parts of the country; but no valid
figures can be arrived at until we know more accurately the proportion
of labourers in each county. It is safe to say, however, that they formed
a higher percentage of the farmworking population in the woodland
areas of Hertfordshire, Somerset, and the Midlands than in East Anglia,
the north, and, in all probability, other parts of the west country.

Thirdly, what was the pattern of personal wealth, amongst labourers,
in each region and period? It is not possible to calculate any very
reliable averages, owing to the basis of selection necessarily adopted for
this study;[2] but the overall pattern is clear enough nevertheless.[3]
In the Pennine fells and the lowland areas of the far north, cottage
farmers were relatively few and never well-off, but not often totally
indigent, and the labouring community was relatively equalitarian in
its social structure. In the fielden parishes of the Midlands, the vale of
York, and East Anglia, labourers were usually poor (most of them
far too poor to leave inventories), though a very small sprinkling left
property worth £30, £40, and even £50. In the forest parishes of the
Midlands, few peasant labourers in the earlier part of the period were

[1] Cf. Table 4.   [2] See p. 413, no. 2.   [3] See Table 8.

either very poor or very rich, and most left property worth £5–£10; after 1610, however, a substantial proportion of the working population left goods valued at more than £30, and the general level of labouring wealth was higher than in any other region. In the woodland parishes of Hertfordshire wealthy peasant labourers were also numerous, and few cottagers were very poor, though none left as much as £40. In Somerset, where the inventories also relate mainly to woodland parishes, there were no very wealthy labourers, although in the early seventeenth century many left a comfortable cottage estate of £7–£12. Thus in the north of England cottage farmers were relatively few and, though never well-off, rarely destitute; in the Midland fielden areas they were more numerous, but mostly very poor; in the forest areas they were very numerous, but not infrequently quite well-to-do.

Table 8. *The pattern of peasant labourers' wealth*[a]

	Percentage of wealth invested in domestic goods		Average value of domestic goods	
	1560–1600	1610–40	1560–1600	1610–40
			£ s. d.	£ s. d.
Northern lowlands	18	29	10 0	1 9 4
Northern fells	34	—	1 6 8	—
Midland fielden areas[b]	35	46	2 16 6	3 12 8
Midland forest areas[b]	44	39	2 9 6	4 10 0
Hertfordshire	59	69	4 3 9	7 9 10
Eastern counties	—	48	—	3 18 4
Somerset	—	65	—	5 17 0
All England	40	50	2 5 3	4 9 6

[a] Based on probate inventories; for the basis of selection of inventories (in some degree affecting the reliability of the 'Average Value of Domestic Goods'), see p. 413, n. 2.

[b] Including a few inventories of the 1660's for Northants.

Lastly, what was the proportion of personal wealth invested by labourers in farm goods and household goods respectively, in each region and period? In the country as a whole, the domestic proportion rose from 40 per cent to 50 per cent as between the Tudor and Stuart periods, and the agricultural percentage dropped in the same ratio. (The tendency to invest a higher proportion of wealth in domestic goods seems to have characterized all levels of society in this period.) In the north-country lowlands, household property comprised only 18 per cent of total wealth before 1600, and 29 per cent thereafter;

while in the dales and fells it was approximately 34 per cent before
1600. In the fielden areas of the Midlands the proportions were 35
per cent and 46 per cent for the two periods; in the woodland areas of
central England, 44 and 39 per cent; and in Hertfordshire 59 and 69
per cent. For the eastern counties and Somerset no reliable figures can
be computed for the period before 1600, but for the Stuart period the
East Anglian proportion closely approached the Midland fielden figure,
and the Somerset percentage that of Hertfordshire. The average value
of household goods during the latter part of the period thus ranged
from under 30s. in the northern lowlands to £3 13s. in the fielden
areas of central England, £3 18s. in East Anglia, £4 10s. in Midland
forest parishes, £5 17s. in Somerset, and £7 10s. in Hertfordshire.[1]
In other words, it was relatively low in the fielden areas of England
and comparatively high in the woodland districts.

In explanation of this varying pattern of wealth in different regions
of England, no single factor of universal application can be adduced.
Each part of the country was affected by influences largely peculiar to
itself, and before stating any general conclusions, it is necessary to
depict the broad economic characteristics of each region.

In the north, in both field and fell parishes, cottage inventories were
relatively few because of the general poverty of the region, and because
there was comparatively little demand for agricultural labour. The
typical agrarian unit in the north, especially on the fells, was the small
family farm, on which outside help was rarely required. Among farmworkers themselves, the sharing of holdings, livestock, crops, and
implements—as is shown by references in inventories to 'half-tene-
ments,' 'half-beasts,' and 'half plough teams'—suggests that labourers
also cultivated their holdings on a family basis. The comparatively
equalitarian structure of the labouring community in the north was
largely due, no doubt, to the relative poverty of the small farmer in the
area and his general lack of interest in the market.

The poverty of the labouring population in the fielden areas of
East Anglia, the Midlands, and the southern parts of the vale of York
arose from different causes. In all three areas, though in varying degrees,
the *demand* for labour was relatively intense (especially in the arable
areas of Norfolk), but cottage-holdings were often small, and commonland, except near wolds, fens, or forests, was scarce. The working
population was therefore numerous, but labourers' inventories were
relatively few and their value small. Many workers had evidently
won what little wealth they possessed only by taking up by-employments, such as thatching, spinning, and hemp-weaving. Their domestic

[1] The scale of valuation evidently tended to be higher in the south, but not to this
degree.

goods, though two or three times as valuable as in the far north, were generally modest. Only where a man of exceptional energy or good fortune built up a healthy herd of cattle and took advantage of the unrivalled commercial facilities of a county like Norfolk, or, like Henry Joyce of Winwick, bred a large sheep flock on the pastures of Northamptonshire, was the labourer likely to prosper. In such cases a man might justly style himself 'husbandman' in his will, although his neighbours still remembered his lowly origins and described him as 'labourer' in his inventory.

In the woodland areas of the Midland and Hertfordshire the picture was quite different. Here peasant labourers formed an exceptionally large section of the population; and although the local demand for labour was mainly seasonal and many of the workers were intensely poor squatters, many others possessed valuable holdings and common rights and were remarkably well-to-do. Some, like Robert Pearman of Ardeley, farmed as much as nine acres of arable land. Others, like Robert Wood of Nuneaton, rented stretches of pastureland and made a living by cheese-making. Others again, like Thomas Hall of Fillongley, built up sizeable sheep flocks. Many also engaged in by-employments, such as wood-turning, carpentry, forestry, and charcoal-burning; a few became carriers for Black Country manufacturers; a few were gardeners, gamekeepers, and petty maltsters in Hertfordshire. Nearby, there were many busy market towns in Hertfordshire, many sheep- and cattle-fairs in the Midlands, a rising industrial region round Birmingham, and the largest commercial city of the kingdom in London. There can be little doubt that a significant minority of labourers, especially in Hertfordshire and Warwickshire, exploited these commercial opportunities, for their inventories mention debts owing to them, in all probability for goods sold by private contract. The two regions differed significantly in only one respect. In the Midlands, well over half the typical labourer's wealth was sunk in his farming stock, whereas in Hertfordshire almost two thirds consisted of household property. It is tempting to attribute the difference to the influence of metropolitan wealth and the higher standard of living generally credited to south-eastern counties; but the explanation would be misleading, since purely domestic wealth was insignificant in value in other eastern counties, such as Suffolk, and relatively high in some counties remote from London, such as Somerset. More probably, with more ample commons at their disposal, Midland forest labourers were able to add to their stock more readily than their cousins in Hertfordshire, who depended increasingly on by-employments and work in neighbouring arable areas for their livelihood.

Until many more local studies of the economic structure of rural communities have been undertaken, the conclusions suggested by this study can only be tentative. Nevertheless, the broad economic pattern seems clear. Over the country as a whole, the wealth of peasant labourers appears in general to have reached a peak in the latter part of Elizabeth's reign, and to have tended to decline during the first half of the seventeenth century. Although well-off peasant labourers became more numerous, the proportion of labourers' inventories declined, the middle ranks of the labouring community became poorer, while the lower ranks ceased to possess any stock of their own, and sank to the level of a landless proletariat. In other words, the labouring class was becoming increasingly differentiated within itself.

Perhaps the most striking conclusion emerging from the inventories is the difference in the condition of labourers between forest and fielden areas. In the latter the decline in the wealth of peasant labourers was much more striking than in the former. By Charles I's reign a very few fielden cottagers of exceptional force of character were still able to make fortunes of £50 or even £150, and so work their way up into the ranks of the husbandmen; but the vast majority were slowly sinking in the social scale, and in many villages the poor stock-man virtually ceased to exist. In the woodland parishes of Hertfordshire and Somerset, by contrast, the decline in labouring wealth was slight, and in the forest areas of Warwickshire and Northamptonshire the worker's fortunes actually seem to have improved; the number of labourers dependent solely on wages probably increased, but well-off labourers certainly became wealthier and more numerous. Beneath these distinctions it is not difficult to trace that gradual disinheritance and increasing dependence of the fielden labourer, due to a rising population and enclosure, which has already been remarked, and the consequent resettlement of poor peasants in unappropriated wastes and forests. As in the early nineteenth century, a rich land was apt to breed poor Cobbett found labourers, whilst a poor or wooded countryside often promised them prosperity.[1]

Both probate inventories and other sources suggest that labouring society was less rigid in its structure than might have been supposed. It is abundantly evident that the fortunes of peasant workers and their families fluctuated from one generation to the next almost as much as those of other people. A labourer like Henry Feltnes of Mereworth in Kent was descended from a yeoman grandfather farming sixty acres of his own land at Speldhurst; whilst a labourer like Christopher Tomlinson of Wilton near Pickering in the North Riding was able to amass a fortune of £40, purchase a second farmhold at Great Driffield, and bequeath it as a jointure to his widow. Indeed, it was not unknown for

[1] Cf. William Cobbett, *Rural Rides*, Everyman edn., 1957, I, pp. 247–8, 256.

labourers who were still technically 'bondmen in blood' to bequeath property worth £30 or £40.[1] Where labourers still owned small-holdings, prudent marriage alliances often helped to make their fortunes; where they held extensive common rights, they sometimes built up substantial flocks or herds from quite modest beginnings; where neither condition obtained, they might still augment their resources by turning to spinning, weaving, wood-turning, charcoal-burning, or some other by-employment. It was the conjunction of all three circumstances in woodland areas—large holdings, generous commons, numerous by-employments—that enabled enterprising labourers to better their lot at a time when the labouring community, as a whole, was being gradually disinherited and impoverished.

E. BY-EMPLOYMENTS

Of the labourer's other sources of income, by-employments were therefore of considerable importance. Of those labourers wealthy enough to leave an inventory, nearly two thirds took up some kind of by-industry: the figure varying from under one half in the northern lowlands to nearly four fifths in the woodland parishes of Somerset, Hertfordshire, and the Midlands.[2] Most of these industries were connected either with forest and woodland crafts, or with the spinning and weaving of flax, hemp, or wool. There were, of course, countless other local industries, such as glove-making in Dorset, lace-making in Buckinghamshire, and rush-mat-making in Cornwall; but only the principal employments can be mentioned in this brief survey.[3]

Woollen industries probably occupied the spare hours of at least one quarter of the cottage-farming population in England as a whole, and nearly half of that in the Midlands: generally in spinning and carding wool or in knitting stockings, only occasionally in weaving cloth. In parts of Suffolk, where poor people were exceptionally numerous, labourers' wives often used to "go spinning up and down the way"

[1] Req. 2, 206, 12; York Probate Registry, will and inventory of Christopher Tomlinson, 1610; cf. Req. 2, 226, 30 for an account of an Elizabethan yeoman of Huntingdon sinking to the level of a wage-labourer; E 178, 7064; cf. Savine, op. cit., pp. 277–9.   [2] See Table 9.

[3] The following paragraphs are based largely on probate inventories, in addition to the sources cited below. For Cornish mat-making, see Richard Carew, The Survey of Cornwall, 1602, p. 18. I have omitted extractive industries, because in some counties inventories and Exchequer special commissions and depositions suggest that some mining and quarrying was undertaken by labourers not engaged in agriculture. In Devon, Hooker seems to suggest such a division between farm-labourers and tin-miners (Devonshire Association, XLVII, 1915, p. 342). In south Wales, however, probate inventories show that mining and farming were closely connected. Cf. also Joan Thirsk, 'Industries in the Countryside', p. 73.

with a distaff in their hands. In populous Pennine valleys like Garsdale and Dentdale, and in parts of Wales, both men and women knitted stockings as they walked from house to house and village to village. In the two townships of Sowerby and Warley, near Halifax, a great part of the 400 copyholders were said, about the year 1600, to live by "spinning, weaving, dighting cloth, or work pertaining to clothing..." In the poor heathy areas of west Surrey at least 1,100 "poor workfolk" depended for their livelihood, in Charles I's reign, on the clothiers of Wonersh and Godalming, "besides a great number in the county [of Hampshire] adjoining." In Hertfordshire, too, despite the assertion of certain inhabitants that tillage offered a "better means to set the poor children on work," many of the better-off labourers spun and carded wool, no doubt for the clothiers of Hatfield and the neighbouring parts of Essex and Suffolk.[1] Wherever travellers went, in scores of parishes in Tudor England—in Dorset, Somerset, Gloucestershire, Warwickshire, Northamptonshire, East Anglia, the Pennines, or the Weald of Kent— they would have heard spinning-wheels turning, or seen the distaff twirling, in countless farm labourers' cottages.

Spinning and weaving of hemp and flax were not so widely undertaken, although together (so far as inventories indicate) they occupied the spare hours of nearly one third of the labouring population. Hemp spinning was particularly widespread in the far north and in east Yorkshire: generally, no doubt, for the coarse sheets and pillow-cases used by the poorer classes, sometimes for sacks, ropes, and fishing nets. Elsewhere, except in the Northamptonshire forests, Lincolnshire, East Anglia, and Somerset, comparatively little hemp seems to have been grown or woven by Tudor farm labourers, although in the eighteenth century it was widely cultivated by labourers in the Welsh Marches and elsewhere.[2] Flax-spinning was undertaken by labourers in most parts of the country, except the eastern counties; it was especially common in the lowland parishes of the north and in the woodland areas of Hertfordshire and the Midlands.

[1] Cf. HMC, *Reports*, XIII, ii, p. 266 (*temp* Restoration); Reyce, *op. cit.*, p. 57; E 134, 10–11 Car. I, H 22, Leeds, TN, Hx, E, f. 6; SP 16, 177, 56 and 56, i, SP 14, 96, 39; C 2, Jas. I, M 12, 41 (which relates how a Hatfield, Herts., clothier in 1616, employed fifty poor children and many other poor townsfolk). Until Gilbert White's time the women of Selborne "availed themselves greatly by spinning wool for making of *barragons*...chiefly manufactured at Alton..."—*The Natural History of Selborne*, Everyman edn., 1945, p. 17.

[2] Cf. Henry Best, *Rural Economy in Yorkshire in 1641, being the Farming and Account Books of Henry Best of Elmeswell in the East Riding*, Surtees Soc., XXXIII, 1857, p. 106; *Yorks. Arch. Jnl.*, XXXVII, 1951, p. 386, referring to a stock of £400 worth of hemp to be set aside to employ the poor of Axholme in making sackcloth, in compensation for loss of fishing and fowling rights due to enclosure in Charles I's reign; Joseph Plymley, *General View of the Agriculture of Shropshire*, 1803, pp. 177–8.

Forest industries were more localized. In the wooded districts of central England one peasant labourer in three, and in Hertfordshire two in three engaged in some kind of woodcraft. Many labourers in woodland parishes possessed tools for felling, hewing, cleaving, sawing, adzing, and carting timber. They must often have spent their spare days, and probably much of the wintertime, in making spiles, pales, poles, gates, posts, rails, and laths for fencing and walling. In Gillingham Forest in Dorset some labourers made parts for weavers' looms; on the borders of Hampshire and Surrey they carved wooden bottles; around Wymondham in Norfolk wooden taps and handles; near the South Downs in Sussex shepherds' crooks; in the Weald of Kent 'checkerwork' objects and wooden spoons; in Staffordshire wooden trenchers and 'treenware'; and in the Forest of Arden they made brooms and besoms.[1] Sometimes farm labourers were also small village carpenters; sometimes coopers or turners; sometimes wheelwrights, cartwrights, or ploughwrights. Some of these crafts, it is true, such as the wheelwright's, called for lengthy training, and were more generally undertaken by townsmen; others, however, like those of the wooden spoon- and bottle-makers, seem to have been the traditional arts of a small dynasty of local labouring families. All over the country, woodland wares must have been exported in considerable quantities in this period to the neighbouring fielden districts, and in both Hertfordshire and the Midlands labourers acted as packmen or carriers of their neighbours' products. Forest areas were the natural workshops of an agrarian civilization largely dependent on wooden tools and implements for its work: the number and variety of local crafts, often highly specialized and recondite, was legion.

Other by-employments, such as potting, tiling, nailing, coaling, and iron-smelting, which required plentiful supplies of fuel, were also centred in woodland districts. In Cannock Chase and the Weald of Sussex and Surrey some labourers burnt charcoal for the forges and furnaces of local ironmasters. In Gloucestershire many hamlets "adjoining unto and depending on" the Forest of Dean were "full of poor people" employed in the ironworks. On Dartmoor the 'venville men' cut and burned turf-coal, and were said in 1610 to have carried not less than a hundred thousand horse-loads "out of the forest every year to the parishes about the said forest," both for domestic use and for "the blacksmiths thereabout, [who] use no other coal to work withal." On the borders of Staffordshire and Warwick-

---

[1] Req. 2, 30, 30; E 159, 472, Trin. 8 Car., rot. 38 (for a Gillingham Forest slay-maker). Wymondham was a noted market for small woodware objects. Was 'checkerwork' possibly an early form of the well-known 'Tunbridge-ware'? 'Treenware' was wooden or 'tree' ware—usually domestic utensils.

Table 9. *Labourers' by-employments: percentage of labourers engaged in different rural industries*[a]

	Spinning or weaving			Woodland crafts	Other by-employments	All by-employments
	Wool	Hemp	Flax			
Northern Lowlands	17	20	20	0	10	46
Northern Fells	25	19	9	0	22	59
East Riding	8	35	14	8	22	68
Midland Fielden areas	38	0	13	13	13	56
Midland Forest areas	41	9	18	36	27	77
Hertfordshire	41	4	26	59	22	78
Eastern counties	11	11	0	32	26	58
Somerset	33	0	11	22	22	78
All areas	23	15	14	17	19	60

[a] Based on labourers' probate inventories. Many labourers, especially in Hertfordshire and Midland forest areas, engaged in more than one by-employment, so that the percentages in the final column do not equal the sum of those in the previous columns. The low percentages for the eastern counties are probably due to the fact that a larger proportion of labourers who engaged in spinning and weaving were too poor to leave inventories.

shire, and occasionally in Yorkshire and Lancashire, labourers took up nail-making and other smiths' work; around Newcastle-under-Lyme they engaged in both nailing and potting. In the neighbourhood of Bernwood Forest, in Buckinghamshire, villagers apparently dug tile-earth and potters' earth, and in James I's reign scores of "poor women and little children" were employed "for the greater part of the whole year" in making woad, without which employment they would have been forced to "starve or wander begging..." "Amongst those who inhabit[ed] in the cottages on the outwood" of Wakefield in Yorkshire, there was, in 1709, "a manufactory of earthenware pots of all sorts;" the inhabitants paid the lord of the manor 4d. per 1000 for their right to make bricks.[1] All over England there were hundreds of local 'manufactories', of which little or no trace remains today, save perhaps in an occasional place-name like Kilnwood or Collier Street in the woodland parishes of counties like Kent.

The factors underlying the location of these rural by-employments

[1] E 178, 2098; C 2, Jas. I, N 1, 5; SP 14, 58, 7; SP 14, 54, 15; Yorks. Arch. Soc., *Rec. Ser.*, CI, 1939, p. 184.

have been discussed elsewhere by Dr Thirsk; the foregoing evidence fully bears out her thesis. For the most part, country industries were established in areas at one time well-wooded, now largely given over to dairying or pasture farming. As a result of the custom of partible inheritance and possibly also of Borough English, both characteristic of these areas, and the migration of labourers from common-field villages, the population of woodland districts rose rapidly during the sixteenth century, and by the mid-seventeenth century regions like the Weald of Kent were among the most thickly settled in the country.[1] Yet it was precisely in these districts, with their pastoral economy, that the local demand for agricultural labour was relatively slight, or at best spasmodic.[2] During the slack months, therefore, labourers naturally took up those employments for which woods and forests furnished at once the fuel supplies and the raw materials.

The importance of by-employments in raising the labourer's standard of living has already been emphasized. Wherever peasant industries were combined with agriculture, farmworkers tended to be relatively wealthy. In Hertfordshire, where labourers often engaged in two or three employments at once, they were better-off than in almost any other county. In Gloucestershire, too, where "many families… were almost equally interested in farming and manufacturing," labourers were sometimes comfortably off.[3] It was in regions where rural industries were divorced from agriculture, as apparently in some of the mining villages of Derbyshire and wool villages of Suffolk, or where they were absent altogether, as in Herefordshire, that labourers were very poor.[4] The income which a working family derived from any particular by-employment may have been small; but it was often sufficient to pay the rent of their cottage-holding, and it enabled them to lay aside a small surplus against times of dearth or unemployment. It was an evil day for farmworkers when rural industries left the countryside and returned to the towns.

[1] Joan Thirsk, 'Industries in the Countryside', pp. 70 sqq.; cf. E 134, 10–11 Car. I, H 22 (for the connection between gavelkind, a rising population, and by-employments in Garsdale). See also Table 5.

[2] For the "persistent chronic unemployment" of agricultural workers in Stuart England, cf. D. C. Coleman, 'Labour in the English Economy of the Seventeenth Century', EcHR, 2nd Ser., VIII, 1955–6, pp. 283–8.

[3] A. J. and R. H. Tawney, 'An Occupational Census of the Seventeenth Century', EcHR, V, 1934–5, p. 42; Gloucestershire probate inventories.

[4] In a sample of over sixty Herefordshire inventories, none related to labourers. It was the absence of local industry that led Rowland Vaughan to found a "commonwealth" of tradesmen living on the products of his estate, which by 1604 had been joined by 2000 "mechanicals."—N. Jackson, 'Some Observations on the Herefordshire Environment in the 17th and 18th Centuries', Woolhope Naturalists' Field Club, XXXVI, i, 1958, pp. 32, 36. See also p. 425, n. 3.

F. WORK, WAGES, AND EMPLOYERS

By-employments, nevertheless, benefited only a section, possibly only a minority, of the labouring population as a whole. The mainstay of all but a few labourers, apart from the income from their holdings, was their work as wage-labourers on a farm. Contemporaries and historians have sometimes seemed to describe farmwork in terms implying unrelieved hardship and monotony. Sir Thomas More, for instance, remarked in *Utopia* that "almost everywhere the life of workmen and artificers" involved "continual work, like labouring and toiling beasts," from "early morning to late in the evening..."[1] There is a good deal of truth in such statements; but a glance at a few estate account books and diaries may serve to modify More's somewhat over-pessimistic picture, and illustrate the great variety of farming tasks undertaken by Tudor and Stuart farmworkers.

Amongst the labourers employed by Nicholas Toke of Godinton, a landowner of East Kent in Charles I's reign, were gardeners, bailiffs, lookers, haywards, thatchers, carpenters, masons, shepherds, plough-men, ploughboys, and mole-catchers. The squire's cherry orchards at Great Chart were tended by "Old James," his hop-gardens by one of his head-labourers, Tom Finn, and his sheep in Romney Marsh by Barnaby Punyer. His wage-accounts include payments for washing and shearing sheep in marsh and upland; for ploughing, harrowing, and sowing the arable lands at Great Chart; for mowing, reaping, binding, and carrying hay and corn; for felling timber, digging stone and gravel, setting quicks, mending hedges, scouring drills and ditches, and for work "about the ponds." In Berkshire, at a slightly earlier period, the account book of Robert Loder of Harwell, yeoman, records the wages paid to William Weston, his carter, John Austen his harrower, Dick [?Cottes] his shepherd, John Andrews his plough-boy, and Joan Colle and Alice Keates his two maids. Many sums were paid out each year for thatching, hedging, reaping, mowing, cocking, threshing, winnowing, and 'ruddering'; for pilling hemp, gathering walnuts, picking cherries, pulling hops, carrying fruit and pigeons to market, and managing the watermeadows. In the north of England, on the estates of the Shuttleworths near Burnley and Bolton, the steward or bailiff records payments to Roger Harper for mowing rushes, to Nicholas Pendleburie for clipping sheep, to "wife Turner and her folks" for clipping and washing, to Robert Houlden for scouring watercourses, to "divers women of Bolton" for turf-gathering, to fourteen persons at Hoole for dressing hemp, to John Hackings for

[1] *The Utopia of Sir Thomas More*, ed. J. H. Lupton, 1895, p. 141; cf. pp. 301 *sq.*

walling on Broadheale Moor, to a man for watching and warding cattle at Burnley Fair, to three women for weeding in the garden, and to "Mr James Andertone's man"—for bringing a porpoise.[1]

This variety in the labourer's work was neither eclectic nor haphazard, however: it was closely related to the rhythmic pattern of the seasons. On John Clopton's farm at Great Wratting in Suffolk the month of March was largely spent in ploughing; April was taken up with "fallowing" and grafting crab-stocks; August with reaping and "pitching cart;" September and October with picking apples, making cider, and sowing wheat and rye; and the winter months with pruning apple trees, cleaving logs, ploughing and sowing the arable lands, and threshing and dressing 'bullimong'. On Nicholas Toke's estates, the winter months were spent in ploughing and sowing the fields, dunging the meadows, felling timber and bushes, topping and clearing oats, scouring the river, and "drilling in the new hop-garden;" the months of March and April in lambing, hedging, "diking," "sharping and carrying" hop-poles, and setting and poling hops. May and June were spent in mole-catching, mowing hay, washing and shearing sheep, and carrying and spreading marl; July and August in burning lime, weeding barley, dressing and hoeing the hop-gardens, mowing bracken, making hay, and thatching the barn at Yardhurst; September in reaping tares and wheat, cutting and binding 'podware', stacking and stripping hop-poles, and "driving and spreading marl;" and October and November in ploughing, felling, diking, 'clodding,' clearing the ponds, dressing the hop-grounds, and cutting timber.[2]

Some further insight into the variety of the labourer's work may be gained from a study of his work-tools. For men who were boarded in the house, the farmer himself usually seems to have supplied the necessary implements; but outworkers and day-labourers were often expected to bring their own gear with them—sometimes their own horse and cart too—when they came to work on the farm each morning. In a sample of some 300 labourers' probate inventories, more than sixty different kinds of work-tools and farm-gear are mentioned: ploughs, harrows, spades, rakes, shovels, skoppets, and dung-forks for preparing and manuring the ground; scythes, sickles, pitch-forks, pease-hooks, flails, sieves, and riddles for harvesting, threshing, and sifting grain; carts, 'courts', cars, barrows, wains, and drays for carrying

[1] Lodge, op. cit., pp. xxxii–ix et passim; G. E. Fussell, ed., Robert Loder's Farm Accounts, 1610–1620, Camden Soc., 3rd Ser., LIII, 1936, passim; John Harland, ed., The House and Farm Accounts of the Shuttleworths of Gawthorpe Hall..., Parts I and II, Chetham Soc., XXXV, 1856, and XLI, 1856, passim.

[2] Essex RO, B 7, B.38.1502, John Clopton's Diary, entries relating to 1649–50; Lodge, op. cit., passim.

corn, hay, dung, furze, and turf; mattocks, bills, axes, hatchets, saws, augers, adzes, drags, chains, wedges, and a dozen other implements for grubbing, hedging, felling, cutting, carting, and preparing wood. Not to mention the ladders and apple baskets for use in the orchard; the crooks and shears and bells for the sheep; the "doggchyne" for the labourer's sheep dog; the small metal or wooden bottles for his own drink; and the bridles, saddles, nets, packs, and panniers for his horse or mare. A well-furnished labourer, like Richard Perkins of Acton Beauchamp in Herefordshire, might possess a rake, a shovel, two trowels, a bill-hook, three sheaf-picks, a hair sieve, a wire sieve, four ladders, a hand-barrow, two hurdles, a manger, and various coils of rope; together with an axe, a hatchet, two augers, a handsaw, a hammer, a pair of puncheons, a crowbar, and a "little pewter bottle." Altogether, Perkin's gear was worth nearly £1, although the whole of his worldly wealth did not amount to £5. All his tools were carefully listed by the neighbours who drew up his inventory; for they had doubtless been purchased at some expense from the wheelwright or blacksmith of the next market town, or perhaps from some travelling iron-merchant from the Black Country.[1] They were the symbols of his calling, as well as the tools of his trade.

The work of labourers on the farm was not only characterized by variety, however, but by an increasing tendency for certain men to specialize in particular crafts. Many of the tasks so far mentioned, and much of the work allotted in particular to women and children, such as stone-gathering, weeding, rush-cutting, treading hay, and picking apples, required little skill.[2] On small yeoman-farms, moreover, only one or two labourers were employed, and there was little scope or necessity for division of labour. But there were numerous farm-tasks, such as ploughing, shepherding, and dairywork, that were highly technical arts requiring careful training, and were undertaken by certain expert men and women only. Skills of this kind did not, of course, originate in this period; but with the progress of commercial farming and regional specialization in husbandry, agricultural tasks themselves became more highly specialized, and on large farms the number of specialist labourers was sometimes remarkable. On the sheep-farms of the earl of Winchilsea at Watton in Holderness, for example, the number of shearers alone ran to forty or fifty. On monastic demesnes, quite minor houses like Cockersand or Conishead employed forty or

---

[1] Judging from inventories, however, only one labourer in three possessed any farm—or work—gear; but it should be remembered that inventories do not always list gear in detail, and many workers needed only the tools of their particular craft.

[2] Harland, *op. cit., passim.*

fifty hinds and labourers, and a small nunnery like St Sexburga's in Sheppey maintained a carter, a carpenter, a thatcher, a horsekeeper, a maltster, two cowherds, and three shepherds; the average number of agricultural labourers or 'hinds' on the estates of seventy small houses dissolved in 1536 was nineteen. On the home-farms of Nicholas Toke in Kent there were carters, shepherds, haywards, ploughmen, gardeners, thatchers, carpenters, hopmen, and overseers of the orchards. And on the co-operative peasant farms of common-field villages it was not unusual for the community to employ its own shepherd, cowherd, swineherd, moorman, hayward, and "fen-clerk."[1]

The development of these specialist labouring skills exerted a profound influence on the structure of the labouring community as a whole. Without doubt it helped to accentuate that distinction between forest and fielden settlements which has already been remarked. In many fielden parishes, with their emphasis on arable husbandry, the supply of work was relatively abundant and farms were large enough to employ a sizeable labour force; the structure of society was intensely patriarchal, manorial organization was rigid, and the working population was relatively static. On the farms of Nicholas Toke, for instance, a number of ancient village families, like the Gillams and Punyers, were employed from one generation to the next almost *en masse:* sons, sisters, daughters, and brothers evidently worked side by side; as their children grew up, they were taken to work each morning by their fathers, and gradually trained up, over the years, to follow in their footsteps as ploughmen or shepherds.[2] In parishes like these, labourers could afford to stick to the particular farm-crafts in which they had been trained; certain arts became traditional in certain families, and a kind of rigid pattern or hierarchy of skills came into being. Many tasks on the farm acquired their own peculiar customs and *mystique;* the farmer was careful to enquire into a new employee's "true knowledge in his art;"[3] and few labourers, for their part, would have consented to divagate

[1] Best, *op. cit.*, pp. 96–7 (Best confuses the earl with his cousin, Lord Finch; Finch was the family name); LP XII, i, p. 1; R. H. Tawney, *The Agrarian Problem in the Sixteenth Century*, 1912, p. 21n.; David Knowles, *The Religious Orders in England*, III, 1959, p. 262; Lodge, *op. cit., passim;* Lancs. RO, DDCa 7.3. (relates to Cartmel in 1703); E 134, 5 Jas. I, E 12; *Yorks Arch. Jnl.*, XXXV, 1943, pp. 298, 300; E 134, 9 Jas. I, E 4; E 134, 17–18 Eliz., M 6.

[2] Lodge, *op. cit.*, pp. xxxiii, xxxvii, xxxix, *et passim;* cf. Lancs. RO, DDM 1.1 (Heskin rental, 1572), ff. 12, 15, 19. Richard Jefferies described these same patriarchal influences in agricultural society, in the nineteenth century, in *The Toilers of the Field*, 1892, pp. 49–54.

[3] Cf. BM Harleian MS 98, f. 25, in which Paul D'Ewes of Stowlangtoft, Suffolk, engages Ambrose Clarke of Bury, gardener. For a modern account of the customs and *mystique* of the horseman's art, see G. Ewart Evans, *The Horse in the Furrow*, 1960, especially chapters I–VI.

from their particular calling and take up that of another man. In these areas, as Richard Jefferies remarked of labourers in the nineteenth century, "work for the cottager must be work to please him; and to please him it must be the regular sort to which he is accustomed, which he did beside his father as a boy, which *his* father did, and *his* father before him; the same old plough or grub-axe, the same milking, the same identical mowing, if possible in the same field. He does not care for any new-fangled jobs. He does not recognize them, they have no *locus standi*—they are not established."[1]

In forest areas, by contrast, labourers were compelled to be more versatile and more adventurous. The influence of kinship and the tendency for certain crafts to become traditional in certain families may have been little less apparent; but the supply of work was less plentiful, and the labourer was often forced to look for employment elsewhere. In this way a sizeable population of migrant workers came into being, occupying the winter months at home, in woodland crafts or other by-employments, and, as seed-time or harvest came round, seeking work on the arable farms of fielden villages. In Kent the high wages paid by corn-farmers "invite[d] many stout workmen hither from the neighbouring country to get in their harvest: so that you shall find, especially on Sundays, the roads full of troops of workmen with their scythes and sickles, going to the adjacent town to refresh themselves with good liquor and victuals." In Yorkshire, when reaping began, Henry Best of Elmswell used to send to Malton to hire "moor-folks" from the Cleveland Hills, and set up boards and bedsteads in his folks' chamber, his kiln, and any other "convenient house," for their accommodation. In Pembrokeshire George Owen gathered a labour force of as many as 240 people to get in his corn harvest.[2] If we may judge from contemporary account books and from later evidence, the same practice obtained in the arable districts of Norfolk, Suffolk, and Sussex, and in other areas where a seasonal demand for additional labour existed, whether for haymaking, harvesting, hop-picking, or any other kind of farmwork.[3]

[1] Richard Jefferies, *Field and Hedgerow*, 1904, p. 198

[2] HMC, *Reports*, XIII, ii, p. 280 ('An account of some remarkable things in a journey between London and Dover', n.d., but from internal evidence *c.* 1664); Best, *op. cit.*, p. 48, and cf. pp. 110, 115; G. Owen, *The Taylors Cussion*, ed. E. M. Pritchard, 1906, I, ff. 31–34.

[3] Cf. Harland, *op. cit.*, *passim;* Bradford Corporation, Cunliffe Lister MSS (2), Bdle I (2); William Marshall, *The Rural Economy of Norfolk*, 1787, I, pp. 184 *sqq.* Since the population increased perhaps 50–75 per cent in this period, and at the same time corn exports rose rapidly, areas like Cambridgeshire, Hertfordshire, Thanet, Holderness, Norfolk, and the Thames basin became major granaries for England and parts of Europe, and required a large population of seasonal labourers.

It is of course important not to exaggerate the differences between the two kinds of community. Many labourers neither remained rooted in one village for life nor became truly migratory, but hired themselves out from year to year at the autumnal hiring-fairs, where they stood in rows in the market-place, with ribbons in their caps to indicate their craft, waiting for some farmer to engage them.[1] Neither is it possible to mention here the special characteristics of the working population in fen and fell areas, where wage-labour, however, was generally less in evidence.[2] The foregoing account stresses only the distinctive tendencies in the two principal types of labouring community, and indicates the dominant trends of the future. Quite certainly those trends helped to foster a relatively free and mobile society in heath and wood parishes, and a relatively static and subservient one in the parishes of the fielden plains.

Labourers' wages are discussed elsewhere in this volume by Dr Bowden, and only a brief commentary is called for here. The figures Dr Bowden has worked out show that, on a group of college estates in the south and east Midlands, farm wages increased in money terms three-fold between 1500 and 1640, rising on the average from 4d. *per diem* to 1s. *per diem*, without allowance for meat and drink. The cost of living, however, rose sixfold in this period, and the labourer's real wages therefore dropped by 50 per cent. In the north of England wage-rates were rather lower than on these estates, and in the west and south somewhat higher; but in all areas the general trend was similar.[3]

[1] Cf. Richard Blome, *Britannia*, 1673, p. 70. For examples of hiring agreements between masters and men, see BM Harleian MS 98, ff. 25, 30, 31 v., 32; Hereford City Library, LC Deeds 3731.

[2] Some marshland areas (as in Kent) were very thinly populated in any case (see Table 5); moorland areas were sometimes characterized by the same features as forest regions, however. See also p. 438, n. 4.

[3] I am indebted to the Price History Committee of the Economic History Society for permission to utilize the material on which these statements are based. Cf. also J. E. Thorold Rogers, *A History of Agriculture and Prices in England*, IV, 1882, chapters XVII and XXVII; V, 1887, chapters XXIII and XXVIII. The above rates for agricultural labourers resembled those paid to building labourers: cf. E. H. Phelps Brown and Sheila V. Hopkins, 'Seven Centuries of Building Wages', *Economica*, NS, XXII, 1955, pp. 195–205. For other information on wages, see J. E. Thorold Rogers, *Six Centuries of Work and Wages*, 1903, pp. 388 *sqq.*; N. C. P. Tyack, *Migration from East Anglia to New England before 1660*, London Ph.D. thesis, 1951, Part II, pp. 153–68; E. M. Leonard, 'The Relief of the Poor by the State Regulation of Wages', EHR, XIII, 1898, pp. 91–93; Sir William Beveridge, 'Wages in the Winchester Manors', EcHR, VII, 1936–7, pp. 22–43 (between 1208 and 1453). For information on wage-assessment, the reader is referred, *inter alia*, to articles in EHR, IX, XII, XIII, XV, XLI, LVII; in EcHR, I; and to HMC, *Reports*, XII, iv, pp. 460–62, and *Report on the Records of The City of Exeter*, 1916, pp. 50–1.

The consequences of this decline in the wage-labourer's economic
position are obvious; they became ever more serious, moreover, as the
working population multiplied, and the number of labourers dependent
solely on wages for their livelihood increased.

Nevertheless, these figures do not tell the whole truth about rural
wages. They refer only to basic rates for regular tasks like hedging and
ditching. Specialized tasks and seasonal work were more highly paid,
and most labourers received a number of perquisites, gifts, and allowances in addition. On large farms, like those of Nicholas Toke, there
was in fact a great deal of variation in the actual economic fortunes of
farm employees. Most of Toke's permanent labourers seem to have
lived in the manor-house or one of the farmsteads, and their annual
wages ranged from 20s. to 30s. for a newly engaged lad, to £2 10s.–£3
for women workers, £3–£7 10s. for most of the men, £8 for Pack
the bailiff, £10 for Masters the gardener, and £15 (probably including
meat) for one of the lookers in Romney Marsh.[1] For day labourers,
with no allowance for meat and drink, the usual rate was 1s. a day;
but in the mid-seventeenth century 1s. 1d. was paid for haymaking,
1s. 2d. for ploughing, 1s. 3d. for work about the ponds, 1s. 4d. for
lading water, 1s. 2d.–1s. 6d. for felling timber, 1s. 6d. for reaping,
1s. 9d. for hedge-mending, and 2s.–2s. 6d. for thatching.[2] For men
employed upon piecework it is difficult to arrive at reliable comparisons; but occasionally they earned higher wages than workers engaged
by the year. For ploughing, piece-rates varied from under 1s. an acre
for a boy to 1s. 4d. for working fallow and barley land, and as much as
5s. 6d. an acre, presumably for work on specially intractable soils.
For harrowing, pieceworkers received 1s. 4d. an acre; for hay-making
1s. 8d.; for reaping fodder 4s.–5s.; and for reaping wheat 3s. 4d.–5s. 6d.
Hedging and ditching were paid at 2d.–9d. a rod; "making quickset"
at 1s. the rod; shearing sheep at 1s.–1s. 4d. the score, and washing sheep
at 2d. or 3d. the score.[3] Such rates may seem to suggest that Nicholas
Toke's estates were run on unusually generous lines, and they lend
colour to Thomas Baskerville's remark that Kentish labourers received
"the best wages…of any in England." But in fact, though well above
the levels fixed by the local justices and the wage-rates actually paid in
the Midlands and Lancashire, Toke's payments were not unique. In
Baskerville's own county of Berkshire one of Robert Loder's men

[1] These figures relate to the mid-seventeenth century; Master's wages may also
cover purchases for the garden, and the looker's an allowance for food.

[2] Some of these rates were probably paid to men working specially long hours, or
using their own carts or horses. In Yorkshire Henry Best's field-workers started work
by 7 o'clock, or 6 o'clock when carrying corn from the wolds, and worked till half an
hour after sunset.—Best, *op. cit.*, p. 52.

[3] Lodge, *op. cit.*, pp. xxxii–vii.

received in 1617 the "exceeding great wages" of £13 9s. 4d.: a sum which Nicholas Toke certainly never paid to any of his resident labourers in Kent.[1]

On most farms, labourers' wages were also supplemented by various allowances and perquisites. At Holme on Spalding Moor, in the vale of York, Marmaduke Dolman allowed his herdsman the milk of three kine, in addition to his annual stipend. In Suffolk, Paul D'Ewes agreed to give one of his workers five combs of rye and five of barley annually, together with a house and farmhold. In Berkshire, Robert Loder allowed his shepherd several bushels of malt or "four sheep's wintering," and his carter a load of bushes or "a hog's keeping all the year." In Kent, during the Civil War, Nicholas Toke paid his labourers' monthly tax-assessments for them. In Norfolk, the Southwells and Townshends sometimes allowed their shepherds and sheep-reeves a number of lambs and fleeces, a provision of corn, and a rent-free cottage and land. In most districts there were also customary allowances of clothing: harvest gloves for the men, boys, and girls on the estates of Nicholas Toke; a new shirt for the men and a new smock for the maids, each year with their wages, on Robert Caton's farm at Cark in Cartmel; a pair of shoes for his boy, and shoes and knitting wool for his maid, on Robert Loder's near Abingdon.[2]

Where labourers lived in the farmhouse or were boarded out in other workers' cottages, the value of their food and drink also has to be taken into account. Robert Loder estimated the annual cost of meat and drink for each of his three men and two maids at £9 16s. 6d. in 1614, and £11 18s. 6d. in 1616. Nicholas Toke allowed one of his sheep-lookers in Romney Marsh £10 a year for his board and £36 a year for the diet of two men and two boys.[3] Such men were clearly well-fed, often, it appears, at their master's own table, and probably a good deal more generously than in their own cottages. At haysel and

[1] Ibid., pp. xxxiii–iv, xxxvi; HMC, Reports, XIII, ii, p. 280 (relating to c. 1664); Harland, op. cit., passim; Price History Committee's wage-material, transcripts of Stowe estate records; Fussell, Loder's Farm Accounts, p. 137. According to Baskerville, writing about 1664, Kentish labourers received 4s.–5s. an acre for reaping wheat plus 2s. a day for meat and drink; but he probably exaggerated.

[2] E 134, 6 Car. I, M 29; BM Harleian MS 98, f. 30, and cf. ff. 31v, 32 (1628, 1629); Fussell, Loder's Farm Accounts, pp. 23, 49, 107, 123, 137; Lodge, op. cit., pp. xxxiii, xxxvi, 137; K. J. Allison, 'Flock Management in the Sixteenth and Seventeenth Centuries', EcHR, 2nd Ser., XI, 1958, p. 110; cf. also Best, op. cit., pp. 96–7; Yorks. Arch. Jnl., XXXVI, 1944, p. 446; Lancs. RO, inventory of Robert Caton and his wife, of Cark in Cartmel, Lancs. (1590); cf. Essex RO, D.Dk.M.135, Foulness bailiff's account (1424).

[3] Fussell, Loder's Farm Accounts, pp. 108, 122; Lodge, op. cit., p. xxxvii. There was no farmhouse on Toke's marsh estate, and his men probably lodged in one of the 'removable houses' of the kind mentioned in Kentish inventories at this time.

harvest time they and the outworkers were granted an additional allowance for beer, which on Toke's farms sometimes amounted to as much as 1s. a day. And when all the harvest had been gathered in, they were invited by the farmer to a great feast of boiled beef and bacon, puddings and apple-pies, and hot cakes and ale.[1]

Nevertheless, we must not make the fortunes of the wage-worker appear too rosy. The labourer with a good master, or with adequate seasonal work and suitable by-employments for the winter months, was relatively well-off. But the chronic problem of the labouring community as a whole was an inadequate supply of work.[2] For many thousands of rural workers every slack period or harvest failure brought unemployment and hunger. Neither the Privy Council nor the local justices were unsympathetic to their necessities; and somehow or other, by charity, or poor relief, or poaching, they and their children managed to procure the means of subsistence. But behind the laconic sentences of conciliar enquiries and justices' reports there must have been countless unrecorded tales of human suffering and tragedy.

Relationships between masters and men are largely a matter of personality. In all ages there are good and bad employers, in the sixteenth century no less than our own day. When a Stuart farmer complained that his "men can work if they list, and so they can loiter," or a Tudor labourer left behind him a list of unpaid wages due from a succession of employers, it may prove little about working conditions in general or the characteristic attitudes of masters and men.[3] Our present concern is not with these personal considerations, but with the economic and social conditions underlying them.

On most farm, the social conditions in which Tudor farm-labourers worked were still intensely 'feudal' or patriarchal. In the north of England the abiding strength of feudalism is well known. Although the characteristic Pennine farm was a small family holding worked with little outside assistance, the territorial dominion of the monastic houses and of magnates like the Percys and the bishops of Durham was a social force of immense power in the lives of the poor.[4] In the south

---

[1] Lodge, op. cit., p. xxxv; Best, op. cit., p. 93; cf. Carew, op. cit., p. 68. Even a close-fisted yeoman like Robert Loder spent £2 16s. "extraordinary" on "our feast" in 1614.—Fussell, Loder's Farm Accounts, pp. 68, 107. According to Baskerville, Kentish labourers were sometimes allowed 2s. per diem for meat and drink at harvest time, though probably he exaggerated.—HMC, XIII, ii, p. 280.

[2] Cf. p. 429, n. 2.

[3] Fussell, op. cit., p. 59; Worcester Diocesan Registry, inventories of William Nurthall of Halesowen (1544–5), John Hyende of Blockley (1560).

[4] According to a Jacobean puritan, Northumbrian people were "merely led by the example of their masters, which is for the most part papistry or atheism..."—SP 14,

of England, feudalism, though different in quality, was in many ways little less firmly entrenched. It is only necessary to glance at the probate inventory of a Kentish squire or a Hertfordshire corn-farmer, with its detailed description of the manor- or farm-house, to sense the auto-cratic influence of south-country landowners in the lives of their rural labourers. William Smyth's Caroline farmhouse at Three Houses in Hertfordshire, for instance, comprised a hall, kitchen, chambers, garrets, buttery, and men's chambers within doors; and a mealhouse, henhouse, hayhouse, brewhouse, beer-cellar, stables, and barns round the yard: it was a microcosm, in fact, of each aspect of rural and labouring life. The Rudstones' Elizabethan manor-house at Boughton Monchelsea in Kent consisted of a great hall, dining-room, parlour, court-room, gallery, nursery, buttery, kitchens, chambers, and garrets looking southwards over the Weald; and adjoining them, grouped round the courtyards, a milkhouse, stilling-house, wheat-loft, brewhouse, fish-house, boulting-house, bakehouse, workhouse-cham-ber, barns, and stables.[1] Quite clearly, farms of this kind resembled, in Norden's phrase, virtually independent "commonwealths"; their rulers wielded very considerable power in the local community, and the life of the labourer was entirely bound up in their agricultural and social routine.[2] It is no accident that the political theory of patriarchal-ism received its most extreme enunciation, not in the north of England, but in Kent, in the writings of Sir Robert Filmer of East Sutton—the next village to Boughton Monchelsea.

Of the labourer's working conditions on these farms something has already been said. It was from these conditions that a distinctive ideal of conduct, governing the relationships between masters and men, took its rise. From Henry VIII's reign to that of Charles I it is possible to trace the development of a definite social code by which high-minded employers believed they should regulate their conduct towards employees: a code that governed not only the social and spiritual welfare of their own labourers, but that of all the poor in their neigh-bourhood generally. When their labourers were ill, farming squires like Nicholas Toke and John Clopton assisted them in their expenses

92, 17; cf. LP, XII, i, pp. 82, 166, 167, 234. For evidence of the fewness of wage-labourers in Georgian Westmorland see A. Pringle, *General View of the Agriculture of the County of Westmorland*, [1813], p. 333, and cf. p. 301; according to J. Bailey and G. Culley, *General View of the Agriculture of the county of Northumberland*, 1813, p. 164, there were few servants kept in Northumbrian farmhouses.

[1] MSS of Michael Winch, Esq., at Boughton Monchelsea Place: inventory of Belknap Rudstone. I am indebted to Mr Winch for a transcript of this document.

[2] "And is not every manor a little commonwealth, whereof the tenants are the members, the land the body, and the Lord the Head?"—Quoted in R. H. Tawney, *The Agrarian Problem in the Sixteenth Century*, 1912, p. 350n.

and paid other workers or women to nurse them; when their wives
were in childbed, they sent their own wives to attend their labour;
when disputes with other villagers arose, they endeavoured to mediate
between them; when their rights in the local commonland were
challenged, they took up their cause in the court of the manor, or
filed a bill in their behalf in Chancery or Requests.[1] In 1529, when Sir
Thomas More heard of the "loss of our barns and our neighbours'
also," he instructed his wife to "take all the household to church and
thank God, both for what He has given and for what He has taken from
us," and "to make some good ensearch what my poor neighbours
have lost and bid them take no thought therefor; for if I should not
leave myself a spoon," he added, "there shall no poor neighbour of
mine bear no loss by any chance happened in my house." At the end
of the period Sir George Sondes of Lees Court in Kent considered that
it was "the master's part" not only to find work for the labourers of
his own parish and to relieve and feed the poor at his table, but also
to see them "perform the outward duties of God's service, as prayer
and going to church, and to show them the way by his own godly
example:" calling upon his servants to do the same, and attending
family prayers in his own house "once, if not twice every day." For a
period of some thirty years Sondes spent "at least a thousand pounds a
year" on his labourers and workmen, and relieved upwards of twenty
poor people weekly: providing each week a bullock of about fifty
stone, a quarter of wheat, and a quarter of malt for his household.[2]
There is no reason to suppose that these philanthropic customs were
universally adopted; but even where they did not obtain, they were
sometimes held up as an ideal.

On many farms, however, the semi-feudal conditions underlying
ideals of this kind were beginning to give way to a specifically commercial nexus between masters and men. On large arable farms
especially, where many labourers were employed in production for the
market, and where it was imperative for farmers to keep an eye fixed
firmly on prices and profits, the frictions between masters and men
were often acute. In the vale of York, the earl of Strafford's steward
remarked to his patron in the 1620's that "nothing is more unprofitable
than a farm in tillage in the hands of servants, where the master's
eye is not daily upon them." (It would be interesting to know the
opinion of his labourers.) In the corn-growing area of Berkshire
Robert Loder was continually complaining of his "unruly servants,"

[1] Cf. Lodge, op. cit., passim; Essex RO, B, 7 B.38.1502, John Clopton's Diary,
passim; Req. 2, 223, 40; C 2 Jas. I, G 5, 70.
[2] LP, IV, p. 2651, and cf. II, p. cclxxvi, citing More's Utopia; Harleian Miscellany,
X, pp. 49, 51.

and nicely calculating the less and more of their wages and expenses: for "all workmen almost (it is to be doubted) will play legerdemain with their masters and favour themselves..." In the arable plain of Lancashire, James Bankes, a London goldsmith-turned-corn-farmer, at the age of seventy counselled his son to "make no more tillage to get corn than to serve your house, for I have been hindered by keeping servants in getting of corn that I have rather desired to die than to live, for they care not whether end goeth forward so that they have meat, drink, and wages; small fear of God is in servants, and thou shalt find my counsel just and most true." As Richard Jefferies pointed out in the nineteenth century, short terms of service and frequent changes of employment (which were little less characteristic of many arable districts of Stuart England) necessarily deepened the social gulf between masters and men.[1]

Partly as a result of this manifest animosity between labourers and employers, a new attitude to the working community as a whole was emerging in this period. As labourers increased in numbers and came more and more to depend on wages alone for their livelihood, some farmers came to think of them as mere employees, to be taken on or dismissed at pleasure, as commercial prudence alone dictated. They ceased to think of their labourers as their own "folk" and neighbours, and began to regard their responsibility towards them as something of a problem, and even a nuisance. In Suffolk, Robert Reyce remarked severely on "the corrupt and forward judgement of many in these days, who esteem the multitude of our poor here to be a matter of heavy burden, and a sore discommodity;" he felt himself bound to remind his countrymen that "as well the poor as the rich proceed from the Lord, and that the rich cannot stand without the poor..."[2] In Norfolk, poor people seem to have felt very bitterly "how little favour" the local gentry "bear to us poor men," and threatened to "go to their [sc. the gentry's] houses and get harness and victuals and kill those who will not join us, even their children in the cradles; for it were a good turn if there were as many gentlemen in Norfolk as there be white bulls."[3]

Once again, it is important not to exaggerate either the novelty or the extent of these changing attitudes. In point of fact, people like Loder were often more generous than their critical or plaintive comments suggest. But the change itself can hardly be gainsaid. And it is

[1] Fussell, *Loder's Farm Accounts*, p. 25, and cf. pp. 36, 59, 68, 71, 90, 108, 118; Sheffield Central Library, Strafford Letters, no. 17; J. H. M. Bankes, 'James Bankes and the Manor of Winstanley, 1596–1617', *Hist. Soc. of Lancs. and Ches.*, XCIV, 1943, p. 75; Richard Jefferies, *The Gamekeeper at Home*, 1948 edn., p. 32.

[2] Reyce, *op. cit.*, p. 56.

[3] LP, xv, p. 354, quoting depositions of four local men against John Walter of Griston. The phrases occur in a projected speech to rioters in 1540.

not without significance that it was most marked in the economically advanced eastern counties, and in those arable and fielden districts where cottage holdings were smallest and labourers were perforce most dependent on their masters' favour. By many of their contemporaries in the seventeenth century farmworkers were ceasing to be thought of as respected members of a distinct social order, with peculiar rights and privileges of their own; they were coming to be regarded, instead, as a class of pariahs, and spoken of collectively, and a little condescendingly, as "the poor." It would not be many years before they were described as the "rude forefathers of the hamlet."

G. DOMESTIC LIFE

The farmworker's cottage has often been described as a one-room hovel of sticks and dirt, and for the majority of landless labourers the description is probably not far off the mark. A glance at a few probate inventories, however, will show that not all farmworkers were so ill-housed as we might expect. Out of about three hundred inventories, approximately one quarter afford some description of the layout of labourers' cottages. It would not be safe to assume that the rest were too poor to be worth describing, since rooms were mentioned only to facilitate the description of goods; but the number of cottages whose rooms *were* described probably provides a rough, if exaggerated, indication of the proportion of relatively well-housed labourers in each region. In the Welsh Marches and the north-west the proportion of cottages with more than one room was almost *nil;* in the East Riding it was nearly one third, in the east Midlands nearly two thirds, and in Hertfordshire more than nine tenths. In forest parishes the proportion was nearly twice as high as in fielden parishes, although the number of small, two-roomed cottages was greater, and three- and four-roomed houses were rather less numerous. Houses with five or more rooms were naturally rare in any region, although a few, probably former yeomen's houses, had six, seven, and even eight rooms. As the period progressed, the standard of housing definitely improved, and by 1640 four labourers in five (of those who left inventories) lived in cottages with at least three rooms.[1]

Of the cottages described in the inventories, nearly all contained a hall or 'house' as their principal living-room, with at least one chamber, either at the end of, or more usually above, the hall, though the exact position is not always specified. Many also had a parlour, generally indistinguishable in function from the chamber. In Hertfordshire the space above the hall was often boarded off into lofts for sleeping

[1] See Table 10.

quarters and storage; the term 'loft' was rarely used in labourers' inventories in other areas, but some of the 'chambers' in the Midlands would probably have been called mere lofts in Hertfordshire. Cooking was generally done in the labourer's hall or 'house', for even in 1640 few cottages had separate kitchens. Opening off one end of the hall, there was usually a buttery, and a number of the larger cottages also boasted a milkhouse, dairy, or cheese-chamber. In the yard often stood some kind of outhouse, usually a barn, occasionally a stable, wood-house, or some other kind of 'hovel', although in more than half the inventories describing the cottage building no kind of outhouse is mentioned.[1]

Table 10. *Labourers' houses—1*

	Percentage[a] of labourers' houses with				
	2 rooms	3 rooms	4 rooms	5 rooms	6 or more rooms
1560–1600	44	28	11	17	0
1610–20	22	22	34	11	11
1630–40	21	41	23	9	6
Fielden parishes	17	43	25	8	8
Forest parishes:					
Midlands	33	39	17	0	11
Herts.	36	16	28	20	0
All regions	27	32	24	10	7

ᵃ Based on all labourers' inventories in which rooms are specified (about eighty in a sample of 300). These probably cover only one sixteenth of the labouring population as a whole; most of the remainder probably inhabited one-room houses, but it is not always safe to assume so, since rooms were listed only to facilitate the description of goods. A few inventories relating to the 1660's for Northants. are included.

Quite clearly not every Tudor and Stuart labourer was condemned to live in a miserable one-roomed cabin. But probate inventories, it must be remembered, represent only the upper levels of the labouring population. How did farmworkers fare who were too poor to leave an inventory? For a description of their houses we are indebted to a few scrappy remarks by contemporary travellers and topographers. In Cornwall, according to Richard Carew, the older cottages were built with "walls of earth, low thatched roofs, few partitions, no planchings [*sc.* floor-boards] or glass windows, and scarcely any chimneys other

1 See Table 11.

Table 11. *Labourers' houses—2*

	Hall or house	Chambers			Parlours		Kitchen	Buttery	Lofts		Milkhouse, dairy, or cheese-room	Other rooms[b]	Out-houses[c]	
		1	2	3	1	2			1	2			1	2
Fielden parishes	92	67	13	9	38	9	25	33	0	0	17	17	25	4
Forest parishes:														
Midlands	94	75	22	0	61	0	22	28	0	0	11	17	33	6
Herts.	100	84	24	0	4	0	12	32	20	16	16	12	40	0
All regions	96	63	20	3	32	3	20	32	8	6	15	15	33	3

Percentage[a] of labourers' houses with

[a] See note to Table 10.
[b] Entry, backhouse, firehouse, little house, 'other room', or shop.
[c] Barn (fourteen instances), stable, woodhouse, hovel (five instances), outhouse, kiln.

than a hole in the wall to let out the smoke..."[1] In Suffolk, according to Robert Reyce, the mean person or cottager "thinks he doth very well if he can compass in his manner of building to raise his frame low, cover it with thatch, and to fill his wide panels (after they are well splinted and bound) with clay or culm enough well tempered, over which it may be some of more ability, both for warmth, continuance, and comeliness, do bestow a cast of hair, lime, and sand made into mortar and laid thereon, rough or smooth as the owner pleaseth." Elsewhere the poorer worker's cottage was probably little better. Sometimes, as in Cumberland and Northumberland, it was built of stone and clay; sometimes, as in Devon and Leicestershire, of cob or earth; occasionally, as on the North Downs, of flints and clunch; most often, however, of wattle and daub over a wooden frame, thatched with straw, reeds, or bracken. The common belief that a cottage erected on the waste overnight entitled its builder to undisputed possession, and the fact that few, if any, labourers' cottages of the period are known to survive, provides the most eloquent evidence of their flimsy construction.[2]

In heath and forest areas, poor cottages like these were being erected in great numbers in this period.[3] For labourers turned adrift from other districts, woodlands afforded both living-room and building materials. And not infrequently, statutes notwithstanding, the judges at assizes ordered local landlords to allow such poor men to retain "quiet possession" of their hovels merely "in regard of [their] misery."[4] In all probability, however, the story of two Kentish labourers who built themselves cottages on Longbridge Leaze, in the valley of the Stour, in James I's reign, was typical of many others. Because "they had erected

[1] Richard Carew, *Survey of Cornwall*, 1602, p. 66. Carew is actually referring to husbandmen's cottages in "times not past the remembrance of some living;" but by his own day those of husbandmen had generally improved, and probably the above description is more applicable to those of labourers of his time. He does not mention labourers' houses as such. See also G. E. Fussell, *The English Rural Labourer*, 1949, pp. 6–12 for further information regarding cottages; much of Mr Fussell's evidence, however, relates to husbandmen's or yeomen's, not labourers', houses.

[2] Reyce, *op. cit.*, p. 51; Bailey and Culley, *op. cit.*, p. 27 (published 1813, but referring to the older Northumbrian cottages); CSPD 1629–31, p. 562; *Cumb. & Westmorland Antiq. & Arch. Soc.*, NS, LIII, 1953, pp. 150, 151. In Cumberland, labourers' clay houses were said to take three or four hours to build; they were "rude earth and timber shanties that would not readily burn." For further information on labourers' houses see M. W. Barley, *The English Farmhouse and Cottage*, 1961, *passim*.

[3] Cf. PRO LR, 2, 194, f. 35. Many cases regarding "spoils of woods" in the Exchequer Special Commissions and Depositions also bear witness to cottage encroachment in woodland areas at this time; cf. also SP 14, 124, 137.

[4] Cf. T. G. Barnes, *Somerset Assize Orders, 1629–1640*, Som. Rec. Soc., LXV, 1959, p. 25.

the said cottages without any authority or lawful licence given them,"
and only "for that they were destitute of houses and had seen other
cottages upon the same waste built by other poor men," the two men
were fined by the parishioners of Willesborough in the court leet,
forced to pay "recompense" for repair of the parish church, and ordered
by three justices of the peace, themselves goaded into activity by the
Exchequer, to pull down their hovels "according to his Majesty's
commission." The two outcasts then wandered abroad, no doubt, till
they found some other corner of land where they might squat down
unmolested and unobserved.[1]

The furniture in labourers' cottages was often listed in great detail
in probate inventories. It varied much in kind and value in different
parts of the country. James Caddie of Cleator, in Cumberland, who
died in the winter of 1597, left furniture valued at no more than 4s.,
although his cattle and sheep were worth nearly £4. John Cuthbertson
of Wormington, who died in 1635, was rather better off, and left three
chests, two chairs, two stands and coolers, three pots, three pans, an
iron pot, a grate, a pair of tongs, and the "old bedclothes which the
children lie on, at small value." In general, however, there were very
few labourers in Cumberland, Westmorland, or north Lancashire
whose domestic goods were worth more than £2. There was evidently
very little money to spare in the north for anything but farmstock and
the barest domestic necessities.

In the East Riding of Yorkshire a number of labourers lived in
almost equally poverty-stricken circumstances. A labourer of Reedness,
William Waterhouse, whose property was worth £6 5s. when he died
in 1632, possessed only a cupboard, a little table, a chair, a single pot,
one pan, and one "reckon." But a number of labourers' houses in this
region were surprisingly well-furnished. William Heptinstall of
Carleton, dying in 1611 worth £18, left in his dining parlour a livery
table, a cupboard, two chairs, a little stool, two forms, two glass
windows, various painted cloths, nineteen pewter dishes, two salts,
four saucers, five porringers, two candlesticks, six cushions, and a
carpet. His three lodging chambers were well supplied with beds,
linen, and chests (together with crooks, pitchforks, and swine-grease);
and in his kitchen, buttery, and 'firehouse' stood an impressive array

[1] E 178, 3960. The record of the case is very stained and partly illegible, but I
believe the above account represents the gist of it, though possibly these two men
were not actually fined. The Leaze was crown property. Village by-laws (cf., e.g.,
E 134, 18, James I, H 15, regarding Holme on Spalding Moor, Yorks.) often specified
that only cottages of "ancient toft and croft" should have common rights, and new
houses should have "no common at all." This jealousy over common rights naturally
tended to divide local communities between the old and new settlers.

of pots, pans, bowls, chafing-dishes, skimmers, grid-irons, barrels, stands, liquor-tubs, flasks, flaskets, copper ladles, brewing vessels, and an iron range.

In Suffolk and Norfolk few labourers were so well off as William Heptinstall. On the whole, their domestic goods were rather meagre. A number of agricultural craftsmen, however, such as thatchers and daubers, lived in comparative comfort, and few labourers who were rich enough to leave inventories lived so hardly as in Cumberland.

In the Midlands, the counties to the north and west were markedly poorer than those to the south-east. In Derbyshire, Staffordshire, Shropshire, and Worcestershire, only one labourer in twelve left domestic goods worth more than £4; in Warwickshire and North-amptonshire, by contrast, one labourer in two. In forest parishes cottages were sometimes well-furnished, and the household property of a relatively wealthy peasant labourer, Robert Wood of Nuneaton, was valued in 1617 at nearly £11. Robert Wood lived in a seven-roomed farmhouse with kitchen, milkhouse, two chambers, two parlours, and a wainscoted hall. He had evidently made his money by weaving and cheese-making. When he died in the summer of 1617 he possessed nearly eighty cheeses stored in two chambers over 'the entry', and his milkhouse contained cheese-vats, milk-benches, butterpots, barrels, puncheons (or casks), and various brazen vessels. In his kitchen stood a cheese-press, a churn, a wash-tub, three pails, two looms, two spinning-wheels, and a number of meal-sieves, boulting-tubs, and brass and iron pots. In the chamber and parlours were beds and bedding, napkins, sheets, and a hand-towel; in his own bedroom a valuable joined bedstead and feather bed; and in the hall a set of pewter dishes, salts, cups, and candlesticks. Clearly Robert Wood was tiptoeing his way up into the ranks of the husbandmen; but he was still regarded by his neighbours as a farm-labourer when they came to compile his inventory.

In the west of England, as in the Midlands, the remoter counties were much the poorest. In Cornwall the labouring population was relatively small, and the household goods of farmworkers were generally meagre. John Tregellest of Cubert, for instance, who died in 1637, left only a table-board, a form, a coffer, three dishes, and an old coverlet and bedstead worth in all only 14s. 9d., or less than one third the value of his solitary cow, four sheep, one lamb, and labouring tools. In the wooded parishes of Somerset and Gloucester, on the other hand, though labourers were rarely as well off as in the east Midlands, two out of three left domestic goods worth over £4. The household gear of Philip Wilkins of Chillington was valued at nearly £5 when he died in the autumn of 1634. Like Robert Wood of Nuneaton, though in a smaller way, he had made his money by making cheese and butter, no doubt for sale in the neighbouring dairy markets of Yeovil and Ilminster. His goods included a cheese-rack, a cheese-stean (a stone weight or vessel), a cheese-stock, a butter-barrel, a skimmer, and various buckets, pails, and barrels; his furnishings comprised a press, two forms, two coffers, two dustbeds, a little bedstead with coverlet, blankets, feather-bolsters, and pillow; together with the usual array of pothooks, platters, porringers, brazen crocks, kettles, a cup, a salt, and a candlestick.

In Hertfordshire, peasant-labourers' cottages were particularly comfortable. Their furnishings were usually worth at least £7 in the early seventeenth century, and occasionally more than £25. Even a labourer with no farm stock, and only his wages and work as a wood-man to support him, like Thomas Carter of Pirton, sometimes left household property valued at nearly £10. One of the wealthiest Hertfordshire labourers was William Layfield of Shenley, who died in the spring of 1612 leaving property worth no less than £38 11s. 2d. Layfield's income, apart from his wages, came partly from dairying and bee-keeping, partly from a small piece of arable land recently sown with wheat, and partly from work in the neighbouring woods and from spinning flax and wool. In his hall stood a cupboard, table, form, bench, joined stool, wicker-chair, two little chairs, three cushions, and a collection of pewter spoons, brass pots and kettles, tin dripping pans, and posnets. In the chimney-space hung his wife's cob-iron, frying-pan, bellows, tongs, spit, grid-iron, and trivet. In the milkhouse and buttery were bowls, tubs, firkins, cheese-moots, powdering-troughs, boulting-hutches, and a butter-churn; in his own chamber there were beds, chests, boxes, a clothes-press, and a bedstead worth no less than £5; together with eight pairs of sheets, four table-cloths, a dozen table-napkins, two cupboard-cloths, and four towels. The comfort of William Layfield's home evidently owed much to the diligence of his wife: for not only would she have been responsible for the butter- and cheese-making, but for spinning flax and hemp for her prized store of sheets, towels, cloths, and napkins. There can have been few idle moments for the busy fingers of Mistress Layfield.

For the domestic goods of labourers too poor to leave inventories, we are dependent on a few comments of topographers. According to Carew, the bedding of poor people in Cornwall consisted of nothing but straw and a blanket, and the rest of their substance "a mazer and a pan or two." The Elizabethan Harrison, referring to earlier generations, remarks that if servants "had any sheet above them, it was well, for seldom had they any under their bodies to keep them from the pricking straws that ran oft through the canvas [of the pallet] and rased their hardened hides." John Taylor, the water-poet, describes a poor weaver's cottage at Hastings as offering

> ...no lodging but the floor,
> No stool to sit, no lock upon the door,
> No straw to make us litter in the night,
> Nor any candlesticks to hold the light.

According to Bishop Hall, the "thatched spars" of a poor man's cote were

> ...furred with sluttish soot
> A whole inch thick, shining like blackmoor's brows
> Through smoke that through the headless barrel blows.
> At his bed's feet feeden his stalled team,
> His swine beneath, his pullen o'er the beam.

None of these descriptions, however, comes from the pen of labourers themselves; *they*, no doubt, would have distinguished many varying degrees of poverty and cleanliness in the cottages of their fellow workers, such as the casual glances of poets and gentlemen failed to observe.[1]

Labourers living in the farmhouse were often relatively well-off. Until Charles I's reign, they usually fed at their master's table, and were lodged in simply furnished folks' or servants' chambers, or else on boarded bedsteads put up in barns and outhouses at harvest time.[2] Their life was often hard, but not necessarily any more so than that of a hop-picker in a modern Kentish hutment. John Doggett's folks' chamber at Albury in Hertfordshire, for instance, contained two bedsteads, with flock beds, bolsters, and blankets; Thomas Granwine's at Sandridge, four beds, together with bedding, valued at £6; John Gybbe's at Rickmansworth two beds and a coffer. On some farms seasonal workers, instead of being boarded in the house, were lodged in the cottages of local widows and labourers, their diet being paid for by the farmer who employed them.[3]

Probate inventories also sometimes afford us a brief description of the labourers' clothing. Generally speaking, it was worth about 7 per cent of his total wealth: rather more in poor districts like the north-west (12 per cent), rather less in prosperous areas like the south Midlands (5 per cent). In Cumberland, in the early seventeenth century, the

[1] Carew, *loc. cit.*; Fussell, *op. cit.*, pp. 9, 11, 8; Harrison, *op. cit.*, Part I, p. 240. Carew actually refers to husbandmen of previous generations; but by his own day husbandmen were better-housed and his remarks would probably be more applicable to labourers.

[2] Best, *op. cit.*, p. 48.

[3] Harland, *op. cit.*, *passim*.

labourer's apparel was worth on the average about 10s.; in the north and west Midlands about 8s.; in East Anglia 13s. 4d.; and in Warwickshire, Hertfordshire, and Somerset, usually about £1, sometimes as much as £2.[1] Only very occasionally do inventories describe the labourer's clothing in any detail. The apparel of George Sprott of Abbey Holme in Cumberland is said to have included a leather doublet and a pair of blue breeches; that of John Hyende of Blockley in Gloucestershire a new coat, a new shirt, a shift, a jerkin, and an old ragged coat; that of John Fessher of Portbury in Somerset, two coats, two jackets, a doublet, three pairs of hose, and a cap, in all worth £1. On working days, labourers often wore cloths made of sack-cloth, canvas, or skins; their holiday wear might consist of a suit of woollen cloth, containing six yards of material and lasting them perhaps two years. At the end of each year of service, their master might provide them with a new smock or shirt, and a pair of shoes and stockings, and at harvest time with a pair of gloves.[2]

The labourer's food, like his furniture and clothing, varied much from region to region. The staple articles of his diet were bread, pies, and puddings. Judging by probate inventories and the reports of local justices, the poor man's breadflour was usually made from barley, occasionally, however, from oats, wheat, and rye.[3] During times of dearth, and at all times amongst the very poor, mixed grain was often used: either oats, peas, beans, and acorns, or else beans, peas, oats, tares, and lentils, and no doubt other mixtures. In the East Riding, according to Henry Best, "poor folks put usually a peck of peas to a bushel of rye, and some again two pecks of peas to a frundell [sc. two pecks] of massledine [sc. wheat and rye], and say that these make hearty bread." In Norfolk, during the dearth of 1623, "the poorer sort" were forced to mix buckwheat with their barley-flour, although, according to the justices, they had not formerly been "acquainted with [it], and therefore shew much loathness to use [it]."[4]

During the greater part of the period, as already remarked, very few cottagers grew their own breadcorn. The great majority depended for

---

[1] To some extent, however, these figures are affected by local differences in the value of money.

[2] SP 16, 537, 17; Fussell, *Loder's Farm Accounts*, pp. 70, 107, 123; Lancs. RO, inventory of Robert Caton and his wife, of Cark in Cartmel, Lancs. (1590).

[3] Sir William Ashley, in *The Bread of our Forefathers*, 1928, seems to me greatly to over-emphasize the importance of rye as the standard breadcorn at this time: justices' reports, *inter alia*, frequently indicate that barley was the staple grain among the poorer classes. See also, *supra*, p.   .

[4] Harrison, *op. cit.*, Part I, p. 153; Fussell, *English Rural Labourer*, p. 30; Best, *op. cit.*, p. 104; SP 14, 138, 35.

their supplies on small weekly amounts bought in local market towns, or on occasional purchases from some itinerant "badger of the Forest."[1] In Somerset, for instance, nearly seven thousand labourers and artizans obtained their weekly corn and meal from the two small markets of Bruton and Wincanton. In Derbyshire, many poor workmen and miners attended the great corn mart in the county-town, to which barley was brought by way of the Trent from as far afield as East Anglia and even Danzig. At Bury St Edmunds, in James I's reign, "four millers at the least weekly...brought every day in the week three or four horseloads of meal of rye and barley, to the great relief and comfort of the poorest sort of people, who being very many in number, can buy meal of them by the penny and twopence, and such small sums...and employ part to bread, part to make a pudding for the relief of them and their children."[2] In consequence of this increasing dependence on local markets, periods of dearth struck the labouring population with growing severity. When prices rose, they were not able to compete with brewers and maltsters for the available supplies of barley, and, as the reports of justices to the Privy Council, indicate, they were often reduced to extreme misery.[3]

Next to bread, the principal items in the labourer's diet were cheese, lard, milk, and occasionally butter. Judging from probate inventories, cheese was frequently to be found in labourers' store-rooms, and it was certainly more widely eaten than inventories themselves suggest. Even the tin-miners of Devon, the poorest of the poor, reckoned some kind of hard cheese in their diet. Together with butter and lard, "skimmed cheese" (as Baxter called it) probably formed the only fat and protein elements in the poorer farmworkers' meals.[4]

Of the various kinds of butchers' meat eaten by farmworkers, the most usual was swine-flesh. Though few labourers kept pigs of their own, many had flitches of bacon hanging in their roof or chimney, presumably cured by their wives and purchased from neighbouring smallholders when they slaughtered their own animals. Beef was eaten by labourers who fed at their master's table, but in the inventories of out-labourers it is rarely mentioned.[5] The cottager's own cattle were primarily milch-beasts, or if, on occasion, fatting animals, they were usually destined for the market. A whole beef would have lasted a labourer's household several months, and would probably have

[1] Worcester Diocesan Registry, inventory of Chrystyan Darby, 1545 (of Old Swinford, Worcs.).

[2] SP 16, 187, 51; SP 14, 137, 33.i, and cf. 33 and SP 14, 138, 18.

[3] Cf. Harrison, *op. cit.*, Part I, pp. 297–300; and see 'The Marketing of Agricultural Produce', pp. , *supra*.

[4] Fussell, *English Rural Labourer*, p. 28; *Devonshire Association*, XLVII, 1915, p. 342.

[5] Harland, *op. cit.*, II, p. 244 *et passim*.

required an expenditure on salting and storing beyond his means. Mutton is not referred to in any of the three-hundred labourers' inventories analysed for this study: judging by references to wool in store, the farmworker's sheep were valued rather for their wool-clip than for their capabilities as mutton-producers, though their carcases may have been sold to local butchers.

Except in areas where wildfowl or deer were plentiful, other kinds of meat were rarely eaten by labourers. Occasionally, a cottager may have slaughtered one of his hens or ducks, and possibly, at feast times, a goose. But the labourer's own fowls were invariably too few to have formed a regular part in his diet, and it is improbable that he purchased much in the open market. He or his wife were more likely to be found among the sellers than the buyers at the poultry-cross of the neighbouring town. In the vicinity of parks and deer-forests, however, labourers not infrequently varied their fare with a haunch of venison. There was certainly a good deal of illicit deer-hunting in forests like Galtres in Yorkshire and in royal parks like Knole, Postern, Leigh, and South Frith in Kent. In Hatfield Chase, on the borders of Yorkshire and Lincolnshire, the poor were said at one time to have "almost lived" off the abundance of deer and rabbits, before the Chase was enclosed in Charles I's reign.[1]

The rest of the labourer's food came mostly from his own garden or from the wild places of the parish. Roots like radishes, carrots, and parsnips, green vegetables such as cabbage and lettuce, and probably herbs like mint, sage, balm, and parsley were commonly grown in cottage gardens; their value was too slight to be worth mentioning in inventories, but occasionally a labourer kept a load of roots in his loft, worth 3s. or 4s. In some cottage gardens there were also a few apple trees (the crop is occasionally mentioned in inventories); and by the end of the seventeenth century turnips and potatoes were being grown by the poor. For the rest, the labourer gathered brambles and herbs in the hedgerows; juniper berries on Lakeland fells and Surrey downs; sloes and bilberries on southern heaths and chartlands; chestnuts and cobs in Kentish woods and hazel copses; and wild nuts of various kinds, when the annual Nutday came round, on north-country manors like Cartmel.[2] In a land with a population of only four or five millions, and at a time when many heaths and moors were still partially uninhabited, wild life of all kinds was more abundant than it is today, and rural labourers profited accordingly.

The labourer's drink, like his food, differed much according to his

---

[1] BM, Lansdowne MS 897, f. 51; LP, XIII, ii, pp. 542–3, and cf. XIII, i, p. 106.
[2] Harrison, op. cit., Part I, p. 259; Lancs. RO, DDCa.7.3; cf. Fussell, *English Rural Labourer*, p. 33.

neighbourhood and his own resources. Some labourers had plentiful supplies of milk from their kine, a few from sheep. Some evidently brewed their own ale and beer. In East Anglia and the south and west of England, they drank cider; in the Welsh Marches, meed and metheglin. According to Norden, poor heath-dwellers drank "sour whey and goats' milk;" according to Richard Baxter "skimmed milk and whey-curds." Few farm-workers were so poor as the Devon tin-miner, whose drink was "commonly the dew of heaven, which he taketh either from his shovel or spade, or in the hollow of his hand." In the hayfields and at harvest time, at any rate, there was no lack of beer and ale for even the poorest day-labourers.[1]

Fuel supplies varied greatly from county to county and according to the extent of the village waste. In mining areas like Kingswood forest and the forest of Dean, or in parts of Derbyshire, Lancashire and Northumberland, labourers not infrequently burnt coal. In woodland parishes and in royal forests and chases, rights of fuelboot and top and lop were sometimes valuable; in parts of Kent labourers took fallen branches and brushwood whenever they pleased. In northern fell parishes, on the barren heathlands of Surrey and Hampshire, and on west country moorlands, they dug turf or peat. Elsewhere, if wood and coal were lacking, furze, bracken, thorn-bushes, and elder-scrub were widely utilized. Over much of England, however, particularly in the Midland champion areas and on chalk downlands, the labourer's fuel problem was often acute. The long winter months can have brought little joy to labourers on the Yorkshire Wolds or in the wood-less parishes of Leicestershire, where people burned straw and cow-dung, or in those Wiltshire villages where groups of cottagers were forced to cook their daily meals by the meagre heat of a single common fire.[2]

Taken as a whole, the proportion of wealth invested in domestic property by the wealthier labourers markedly increased as the Tudor and Stuart period proceeded. As already remarked in England as a whole this proportion expanded from 40 per cent before 1600 to 50 per cent thereafter: rising in the northern lowlands from 18 to 29 per cent, in the common-field villages of the Midlands from 35 to 46 per cent, and in the woodland parishes of Hertfordshire from 59 to 69 per cent. The average value of the labourer's domestic property, in the

[1] *ibid.*, pp. 28, 31–35 (but much of Mr Fussell's evidence relates to yeomen or husbandmen, not labourers); Thomas Westcote, *A View of Devonshire in MDCXXX*, 1845, p. 53. Harrison, *op. cit.*, Part III, p. 180. HMC, *Reports*, XIII, ii, p. 280; Lodge, *op. cit.*, p. xxxv.

[2] Much information on village fuel supplies may be gleaned from village by-laws, and from disputes in Exchequer Special Commissions and Depositions in PRO; cf. also SP 14, 58, 7; Burton, *loc. cit.*

reigns of James I and Charles I, ranged from about £1 10s. in the northern lowlands to £3 10s. in Midland field parishes, £4 in East Anglia, £4 10s. in Midland forest parishes, £6 in Somerset, and £7 10s. in Hertfordshire.[1] To some extent, these varying levels reflect local differences in the value of money; but they also indicate real differences in home comfort. One telling indication of the rising standard of living amongst the better-off labourers may be mentioned. The furniture of early Tudor cottages was evidently rough carpentry work, of small value, quite possibly constructed by the labourer himself: whereas by Charles I's reign many a cottager possessed at least one article of *joined* furniture, properly constructed by a trained craftsman, carefully described by the neighbours who drew up his inventory, and lending a new touch of modest luxury to his home.

Amongst the poorer labourers, however—that anonymous majority who were too indigent to leave any wills or inventories—there can have been few luxuries. We know little enough about them, and the comments of contemporaries were often vague and undiscriminating. But all the evidence suggests that their economic fortunes were declining; that their cottages were cramped and poverty-stricken; and that their lives were rich in nothing but hungry children.

H. THE CHANGING PATTERN OF LABOURING LIFE

Until the end of the sixteenth century, the labouring community was still an essentially peasant society. With infinite local variation in detail, and in spite of the growing number of very small holdings, it was still characterized by a certain unity of outlook, and that unity was based, in the main, on distinctively peasant preconceptions. Hitherto, it has been primarily the economic aspects of that community that have engaged us; it now remains to penetrate, if possible, into the mind of the peasant-labourer himself, and to envisage, as far as may be, his aspirations and ideals. The evidence is necessarily slight, since cottagers rarely recorded their own thoughts and can only be observed through the eyes of outsiders; but, such as it is, it may enable us to visualize the labourer as a human being, instead of an economic abstraction, and to sense the difference in his outlook from that of the rural wage-worker of today. We may do so most simply by posing a series of questions: what was the characteristic attitude of peasant-labourers to their land, their stock, their families, their work, their pastimes, and their religion?

Land is the basis of all peasant societies, and the traditional attachment of the labouring peasant to his own farmhold and common

[1] See Table 8.

rights can be sensed in many Tudor and Stuart lawsuits. At Pontefract in 1611, for instance, the poorer tenants kept certain proposed land-dealings in which they were involved "very secret" from the other party concerned, lest "their offers should be refused, and so in the end be turned to their prejudice."[1] At Leeds in Kent, when it was rumoured in 1608 that the tenants' leases would not be renewed, it "went so near...the heart" of one "poor and simple man, as he lived but few days after, leaving behind him a poor wife lying bedrid, and 3 small children, having no other dwelling, nor means but the alms of the parish to live on." Of the lengths to which poor commoners were prepared to go in defence of their common-rights, mention has already been made; so late as the nineteenth century, the tenants of Southowram, near Halifax, refused to give their landlord permission to enclose a few yards of waste land near his lodge at Stonyroyd.[2]

The attachment of labourers to their farm property is equally evident. It comes to light in many probate inventories of the period, with their carefully listed details of each cottager's stock and crops. It also appears in a number of Chancery disputes relating to the property of Tudor and Stuart farm labourers, of which one concerning Richard Veredy, a labourer of Sedgeley in Staffordshire, in Elizabeth's reign, may be taken as typical. Veredy, "a very poor man and having a wife and seven children, all at his own only cost and charges," possessed one single "horse of his own, being worth to be sold fifty shillings, and did use to let out the said horse to hire by the day to divers persons...as well for his own relief as for the necessity of his neighbours, which was a good stay of his living and the greatest part of his substance." One day, a certain Mistress Annes Gestone, "naming herself to be a surgeon and coming and going divers times to the said town of Sedgeley," requested to hire the horse for a period of four days. Riding it away into Worcestershire, with its saddle, bridle, and pillow, she the resold it to John and Joan Moole, and pocketed the proceeds. Thereupon, Richard Veredy "made great move and labour to seek out the said Annes," and followed her as far as Droitwich, where he found John and Joan Moole and offered them the full price they had paid Annes Gestone for the horse, in order to regain his one animal.[3]

The regard of peasant labourers for their families, and the strength of family ties in labouring households, comes to light in the scrupulous

---

[1] SP 14, 65, 75 (relating to 1611). The other parties were Sir Henry Savile, jr., Sir Henry Slingsby, and Thomas Blande, on behalf of the king.

[2] SP 14, 37, 35; J. Lister, 'Some Local Star Chamber Cases', *Halifax Antiq. Soc.*, 1927, pp. 199–200.

[3] C 3, 185, 47; for other cases relating to poor people and their animals, cf. C 3, 20, 83 and Req. 2, 242, 30.

care with which they endeavoured to provide for them in their wills. Of many examples which might be adduced, four must suffice. John Perry of Brinklow, in Warwickshire, who died in 1634, left his property to his son, with the request that he should provide his widow with "all needful, sufficient, and convenient meat and drinks, apparel and lodging, landresses and all other necessaries decent and meet for a woman of her age, state, and condition." John Goosy of Old, in Northampton-shire, dying in 1613, left "the cottage-house where I now dwell in, with...the timber and hovels in the yard," and "all the outhouses and floors to that cottage belonging" to his second son Thomas; half his cattle and goods to his daughter Avice, together with "a little house called the stable, to be in, if she need, so long as she lives unmarried;" £10 in money to his third son Edward, to be paid within six months by his brother Thomas; but nothing to his eldest son Robert, because he had already received the lease of "a quartern land in Naseby, and a great brass pot." Robert Pearman of Ardeley in Hertfordshire, dying in 1619, left all his property to his wife, so long as she remained a widow, but if she remarried, it was to be equally divided between his two sons: Robert was to have the east end of the house, the north half of the barn, the "little garden-place fenced in with faggots behind it," and two acres of the family holding in the common fields: Edward was to have the west end of the house, the little garden attached, the south half of the barn, and the other half of the family holding; while the orchard and well were to be held in common between them. Finally, Thomas Smith, a poor widower of Great Amwell, who died in 1567, left "one cow and one bullock, and my daughter Joan" to his brother-in-law in Cheshunt; "one cow and one bullock, and my son John" to his cousin in Hertford; and "the residue of my goods and movables, and the residue of my children," to his neighbour John Rolfe, whom he entreated to look after all his children, and receive all his property, if his kinsmen refused the care of them.[1] Quite clearly labourers like these regulated their conduct towards dependants by the recognized social customs of their order, and went to considerable lengths to keep their children out of the workhouse, even to the extent of 'bequeathing' them along with their goods and cattle. Neither is it without significance that they were careful to provide, more or less equally, for *all* their dependants: for the tyranny of primogeniture did not usually hold sway in the cottages of the labouring peasantry.

[1] Smith's will is quoted in C. M. Matthews, 'Annals of the Poor: taken from the Records of a Hertfordshire Village', *History Today*, v, 1955, p. 701; the rest are in the relevant county record offices. Smith is not stated to be a labourer, but the conditions of his will suggest he was either a labourer or possibly a husbandman.

The attitude of labourers to their work has already been referred to. In the sixteenth century, quite as much as in the twentieth, farmworkers were "masters of many complicated and exquisite crafts—land-drainage, shepherding, forestry, hedge-laying, thatching, plowing—and the repository of much knowledge, part-traditional and part acquired by experience and acute observation, of the vagaries of nature."[1] They did not think of themselves as *labourers* merely, but rather as ploughmen, horsemen, hopmen, shepherds, hedgers, cowmen, reapers, shearers, thatchers, foresters, haymakers, or experts in any of the other score or more of skilled crafts on the farm. The detailed lists of their work-tools in probate inventories—the bills, scythes, shovels, skoppets, dung-picks, spittles, and trowels; the axes, hatchets, handsaws, augers, mattocks, chisels, and other implements—suggest something of that "unsuspected fame amongst their own people" which many a skilled labourer of the period enjoyed in his own community.[2]

The pleasures and pastimes of farm-labourers were closely interwoven with their work. Many of the old country songs seem to have been connected with agricultural tasks, such as ploughing, milking, and churning. Labourers, no doubt, played a major part in the Plough Monday plays of the period. Wandering pipers were sometimes paid a few pence by Yorkshire farmers to play through the long spring days to the sheep-clippers on the Wolds.[3] Cornish labourers, according to a Georgian topographer, used to sing to their plough-oxen "in a sort of chaunt, of very agreeable modulation, which, floating through the air from different distances, produces a striking effect both on the ear and imagination..."[4] The great feast of the year, the harvest-home, celebrated the successful completion of the year's work, when the farmer invited "all the work folks and their wives that helped them that harvest" to a supper of boiled beef, apple pies and cream, and hot cakes and ale.[5] Although not diectly connected with farm-work, sports such as wrestling, hurling, and vaulting, at which "the meaner sort who labour hard all the week" were encouraged by the Stuarts "to refresh their spirits," also served to "inseme their bodies with hardenes and strength," and to fit them for the heavy labour of the fields.[6] Even a purely political occasion, like the restoration of Charles

---

[1] Quoted from F. Brett Young, *Portrait of a Village*, 1937, by F. A. Walbank in *The English Scene*, 1947 edn., p. 67, and referring to a modern Midland village.

[2] The words quoted in the text are from George Bourne, *The Bettesworth Book*, 1920, p. 7. 'Spittles' are small spades or spuds.

[3] Best, *op. cit.*, p. 97; cf. *Montgomeryshire Collections*, LV, Part I, 1958, p. 80.

[4] Quoted in W. H. Hudson, *A Shepherd's Life*, Everyman edn., 1949, p. 100.

[5] Best, *op. cit.*, p. 108.

[6] *Devonshire Association*, XLVII, 1915, p. 342; S. R. Gardiner, *The Constitutional Documents of the Puritan Revolution, 1625–1660*, 1906 edn., pp. 99, 101.

II, coinciding as it did with traditional Maytime games, was welcomed in Kent with "a kind of rural triumph, expressed by the country swains in a morris dance, with the old music of tabor and pipe,... with all agility and cheerfulness imaginable..."[1] Unlike the leisure pastimes of today, the recreations of Tudor and Stuart labourers were not merely a means of escape: they formed a kind of inherited art or ritual, centring round their daily occupations, and based upon the ordinary sights and sounds of the village.

No less closely bound up with the work of Tudor and Stuart labourers was their religion. In the frequent recitation of the Psalms in church, for instance, the sights and sounds of the village fields where they worked were continually re-echoed. "I will take no bullock out of thine house," they might have heard, "nor he-goat out of thy folds. For all the beasts of the forest are mind, and so are the cattle upon a thousand hills." Or, again: "Thou crownest the year with thy good-ness, and thy clouds drop fatness... The folds shall be full of sheep; the valleys also shall stand so thick with corn, that they shall laugh and sing." Or, yet again: "So we, that are thy people, the sheep of thy pasture, shall give thee thanks for ever, and will alway be shewing forth thy praise from generation to generation." For the peasant-labourers of Stuart England, the vivid imagery of the Bible must have come with an immediacy it has largely lost for the urban worker of today. Was not King David himself once a shepherd boy, and Ruth a poor gleaner in the fields of Boaz? It may be that farmworkers did not regularly attend their parish church, but, when they did, the pastoral poetry of the Bible came native with all the warmth of familiarity.

The survival of many distinctly peasant attitudes and aspirations amongst the labourers of Tudor England was of course not fortuitous. The aspirations remained, because the social institutions and traditions essential to their existence also remained, largely intact. The abiding force of local loyalty, of manorial custom, and of feudal authority, was still sufficient, in a changing world, to maintain the vitality of many peasant preconceptions.

The force of local loyalty, if gradually (and perhaps temporarily) being undermined by the increasing mobility of the labouring popula-tion, was still immensely powerful. For the great majority of labourers, the local community was still the natural sphere of life and thought, and a place, despite its jealousies, "where much affection and pity of neighbours doth reign." The past events of their lives they still reckoned, not by the regnal or dominical year, but by some local "commotion

[1] Alan Everitt, *Kent and its Gentry, 1640–1660: a Political Study*, London Ph.D. thesis, 1957, p. 469, quoting contemporary tracts.

in the time of the reign of the late King Edward VI."[1] The narrowness of their environment was often such that, when a handful of Suffolk labourers were sent across the county border into Essex, during the Civil War, to a military rendezvous at Saffron Walden, they soon found themselves in a "strange country" and "benighted." Even the administration of the new Elizabethan poor law, which might have been expected to create a sense of class solidarity, only served to root the typical labourer more deeply in his own community. When local jealousy between towns and villages could force the justices of two counties to spend weary hours in determining whether a single "poor impotent person" should be cared for by Dunster or Tiverton, it was not surprising if the sense of class loyalty among farmworkers remained rudimentary. The inhabitants of the two places were quite as likely to fight with one another as with their employers and landlords.[2]

Closely bound up with the strength of local loyalty was the continuing force of manorial custom. The custom of the Tudor village was no vague body of tradition, but a rigorous, detailed, and precise *corpus* of local law. It regulated the lives of all the people on the manor; it sometimes governed the usage of the remotest corner of the parish, even to the empty mountain tops of Lakeland fells. Customs of inheritance, rules of cultivation, stints for sheep and cattle, maintenance of paths and hedges, rights of fuelboot, houseboot, and hayboot, precautions against fire: these and countless other matters affecting the welfare of labourers came within the purview of the manorial court. According to the Court Book of Billington in Lancashire, for instance, no one was to dig turves on the Moor before 12 May; no one was to "play at the ball" or any other unlawful game, such as quoiting and pitching, in Chapel Garth; the nests of crows or magpies on local farmhouses were to be pulled down, and their young destroyed; and every tenant paying a rent of 10d. annually was to plant, near his house, at least one apple- or crab-tree, one birch, six alders, and four quick-staves yearly. At Burton Agnes in the East Riding, a Book of Pains and Orders for 1632 laid down that no man should allow his servant to keep above four shorn sheep and lambs; that no one should keep any geese from 3 May till average-time (viz. till after harvest); that no kine, oxen, or other horned beasts should be tethered in west field or middle field; and no one should cut or cart away more whins (viz. furze) than he could carry upon his back. At King's Langley in

---

[1] LP, XII, i, p. 234; Cecil Torr, *Small Talk at Wreyland*, 1926, pp. 43–4 (quoting document of 1602 referring to the Cornish Rising of 1549; the words cited are from the deposition of a yeoman, but would have been no less typical of a labourer).

[2] Alan Everitt, *Suffolk and the Great Rebellion, 1640–1660*, Suffolk Records Society, III, 1961; p. 94; Barnes, *op. cit.*, pp. 6, 11, 50, and cf. p. 24.

Hertfordshire, no inhabitant was allowed to leave any timber, dung, or wood on the king's highway; no one was to receive any "foreigner" into his house without first giving security; no one was to put any cattle in the lanes or highways, except in charge of a keeper no one was to pick any cherries or other fruit growing on the lord's waste in Chipperfield; and every villager with lands adjoining the river was to cut down the water-weeds adjoining his property, once a year.[1]

That such orders were duly enforced, with more or less strictness, is clear from any number of court-rolls of the period. At Whitmore in Staffordshire, Thomas Stevenson was fined in the manor-court for putting horses and mares into his neighbour's field in the night-time, and Richard Blackeshawe for chasing the sheep of other tenants "with his doggys." At Wentworth Woodhouse in Yorkshire, Robert Lowden was presented for not sending his servants to the common work, Francis Burton for tethering his horses in the sown fields, Gilbert Crowden for driving six oxen through the hardcorn field, Thomas Swift for plowing a common balk in the Barron Field going towards Lanehead, and seventeen persons for not having their swine duly ringed. At Little Crosby, in Lancashire, Ellen Davie was fined 3d. for tethering horses in the Town Field, Elizabeth Rice 4d. for "carting down a butt of meadow and treading corn," Margaret Brough 6d. for putting more cattle than her stint into the Town Field, and Margaret Rice, worst offender of all, 3s. 4d. for reviling the jury in open court.[2]

Judged by modern notions of individual freedom, such repressive customs may appear pettifogging; but for the peasant labourer they were rather a protection against overmighty neighbours than a restriction. Their readiness to defend them is shown by the records of many a Tudor lawsuit; and even today the empty court-room of an Elizabethan manorhouse like Boughton Monchelsea Place, with its bare wooden benches ranged round the whitewashed walls, still conveys some impression of the stark, yet not entirely unwelcome, authority of manorial custom in the peasant labourer's life.

The protection of the manor-court would have been of little avail, however, without the feudal authority of the gentry to uphold it. So much has been written, not without reason, about rack-renting and enclosing landlords, that it is easy to forget that, unless vital economic

---

[1] Lancs. RO, DD Pt, Box 22, Billington (1559–66); C. V. Collier, 'Burton Agnes Courts, Miscellanea II', Yorks. Arch. Soc., Rec. Ser., LXXIV, 1929, pp. 87, 93; 94, 95; Herts. RO, 20737, m. 1 and dorse.

[2] William Salt Library, Stafford, D 1743, M 130 and M 123 (1569 and 1597); Sheffield Central Library, Wentworth Woodhouse Muniments, C 7, 80, 99, 122, 85 (1626, 1629, 1653, 1666, 1641); Lancs. RO, DD BL.48.35 (1667).

interest were at stake, rural squires were as anxious to preserve the customary order as their tenants and labourers. Only a fraction of the 800 or so gentry of counties like Suffolk, Kent, and Somerset, probably only a small proportion of the 300 or so of counties like Leicestershire and Wiltshire, were in any way concerned with enclosure. As the Civil War was to show, the great majority of the gentry and peasantry, in their almost morbid anxiety to preserve the traditional fabric of local society generally stood side by side.

The kind of feudal protection, in the widest sense, afforded by a well-disposed squire to the labourers of his neighbourhood might be illustrated from many examples. Three instances, all drawn from the county of Kent, must suffice. At Sellindge, in the east of the county, when the local parishioners' title to certain lands was disputed by one Alexander Lewknor about 1586, Squire Ralph Heyman undertook, and paid half the charges of, a lawsuit to re-establish their rights, and the whole charge of a second suit two years later, when two labourers' leases of these lands were challenged by a wealthy local yeoman. In the next parish of Brabourne, about 1574, when "certain rich men who had great stock of cattle did go about to break the...custom [of the common]," Sir Thomas Scott, "being then lord of the said manor of Brabourne...caused the court-rolls of the said manor to be produced and read unto divers...of the said tenants," and, in the interests of the poorer inhabitants, commanded "the said greedy-minded tenants" to "desist from their said oppression and surcharge of the said common..." At Barham, in Charles I's reign, when Goodwife Gilnot was "accused to be a witch," and was likely to lose her good name and her livelihood, Squire Henry Oxinden wrote to his brother-in-law, a justice of the peace, requesting "that you will not lightly believe such false and malicious reports as you hear, or may hear, alleged against this woman, whom I believe to be religiously disposed. Certain I am," he added, "she hath undergone a great deal of labour to bring up her charge of children, and hath taken no small care to have them instructed up in the fear of God, and therefore it is the more pity to have her labour under so great a scandal. And for so much as the neighbours healp [sic] themselves together, and the poor woman's cry, though it reach to heaven, is scarce heard here upon earth, I thought I was bound in conscience to speak in her behalf..." Quite clearly, men like Heyman, Oxinden, and Scott, all of them representatives of ancient Kentish families, took their responsibilities to their local community seriously.[1] The economic gulf between them and their farmworkers was already wide; but they were still as interested in farming as their

[1] Req. 2, 223, 40; C 2, Jas. I, G 5, 70; Dorothy Gardiner, ed., *The Oxinden Letters, 1607–1642*, 1933, p. 222.

own labourers; they still spoke or understood the local Kentish dialect; and they still believed in old notions of social duty and 'hospitality'.

During the seventeenth century, however, the unity of peasant labouring society, and the protection afforded to the labourer by the customary order of society, were beginning to break down. That unity had no doubt never been complete, and its basis was not finally destroyed till the eighteenth or nineteenth century. But it was probably in the latter half of our own period, with the growth of population, the decline in real wages, and the progress of commercial farming, that some of the most distinctive changes in labouring society took their rise. By the time the Civil War broke out, the labouring community was manifestly split by a twofold cleavage within its own ranks.

In part this cleavage was an economic one. As the labouring population increased, the pressure on land became continually more acute, an ever-growing army of landless labourers came into being, and the distinction between rich and poor labourers became more pronounced. A minority of farmworkers, still possessed of sizeable holdings or valuable common rights, were enabled to profit by the new commercial openings of the age and work their way up into the ranks of the husbandmen; while the middle and lower ranks of cottagers were slowly losing their landed rights and sinking to the level of mere wage-workers. The former were able to add new rooms to their cottages, invest an increasing proportion of their income in domestic comforts, purchase a few pieces of good joined furniture, and leave a modest competence to their sons and widows. The latter inhabited flimsy cots and hovels, fed "very hardly with oaten bread, sour whey, and goats' milk," lived very close to the poverty line, and in time of dearth sank far beneath it.[1]

The cleavage in labouring society was not only economic, however. It also consisted in a growing distinction between working communities in forest and in fielden areas. In the nucleated villages characteristic of the latter, forms of society were often deeply rooted, social classes were relatively stable and distinct, manorial customs fairly rigid, political habits comparatively orderly, and the labourer's outlook deeply imbued with the prevalent preconceptions of church and manor-house. In these fielden areas, labourers often tended to remain rooted in the same district from one generation to the next: working on the same farm, specializing in the same crafts, passing on the same customary skills to their children, and more or less freely accepting their dependence on squire and parson. Few of them were really well-off,

[1] Harrison, *op. cit.*, Part III, p. 180; and see 'The Marketing of Agricultural Produce', pp.   , *supra*.

their holdings were usually small, and their common rights often negligible; but the very poor were less numerous than in remote woodland settlements, and manorial charity was probably more abundant.

In the isolated hamlets characteristic of forest settlements, by contrast, the roots of society were often relatively shallow, the population was largely composed of a single social class, the customs of the manor were sometimes vague or difficult to enforce, the instincts of the poor were anything but law-abiding, and the authority of church and manor-house seemed remote. In these areas, labouring society frequently consisted, on one hand, of a core of indigenous peasants with sizeable holdings and a relatively high standard of living; and, on the other, of an ever-growing number of very poor squatters and wanderers, often evicted from lately enclosed fielden villages, "given to little or no kind of labour...dwelling far from any church or chapel, and...as ignorant of God or of any civil course of life as the very savages amongst the infidels..."[1] In consequence of their semi-vagrant origins, many forest labourers were less rooted in their own community than their fielden cousins; more willing to migrate at certain seasons in search of employment elsewhere; more independent and eager to take up the cudgels in their own defence; and more prone to pick up new ways and new ideas. It was primarily in heath and forest areas, visited as they were by travelling badgers and tinkers, that the vagrant religion of the Independents found a footing in rural communities;[2] it was principally thence, there is reason to think, that the godly (or not so godly) troops of the Parliamentarian armies were recruited during the Civil War. It was also in heaths and forests that the millenarian leaders of the Interregnum, the Methodist preachers of the eighteenth century, and strange messianic sects like that of John Nichols Tom in East Kent, found many of their most devoted adherents.[3]

Essentially, the difference between fielden and forest societies was that of a relatively static and a relatively mobile way of life. Of the

[1] Harrison, op. cit., Part III, p. 180; cf. SP 16, 176, 55 for an account of Irish vagrants in Somerset in 1630, and Carew, op. cit., p. 67, for poor Irish people flocking into Cornwall.

[2] During the sixteenth century the Familists spread their doctrines in Cambridgeshire by going round as travelling basket makers, musicians, etc. (Ronald Knox, Enthusiasm, 1950, p. 171). During the Interregnum, Gerrard Winstanley, the well-known Independent and Digger, wished to take in "all the commons and waste ground in England" for the poor (W. Schenk, The Concern for Social Justice in the Puritan Revolution, 1948, p. 102).

[3] P. G. Rogers, Battle in Bossenden Wood, 1961, pp. 201 sqq. Tom's supporters came from the Forest of Blean; after the collapse of his movement (in a battle in 1838 in which twelve lives were lost), a church was built at Dunkirk specifically to 'civilize' the area.

latent jealousy between them, the last embers continued to smoulder on until the closing years of the nineteenth century. In Oxfordshire, at the end of Queen Victoria's reign, the hamlet people of 'Lark Rise', though then bereft of all their common rights, still maintained an attitude of independence and mild animosity towards the parent village of 'Fordlow', with its parish church, its Tory parson, and its decrepit little manor-house; while the labourers of the village itself, still sunning themselves in the fading rays of parish gentility, retorted by calling the hamlet children, "That gypsy lot from Lark Rise."[1]

Hand in hand with the break up in the unity of labouring society itself, went a decline in the protection afforded to the labourer by the customary social order. There was of course no sudden or universal change in that order; traditional ideas of social duty still lingered on for generations after the end of the period. But in some districts, at least, a definite decline in the sense of responsibility to dependants and a widening psychological gulf between gentry and peasantry was coming into evidence. In newly-enclosed parishes, and in the eastern counties with their relatively advanced economy and acute land-hunger, these developments seem to have been particularly pronounced. In Norfolk, some poor people apparently felt "that the gentlemen had all the farms and cattle in the country in their hands, and poor men could have no living..." In Suffolk, a sharp linguistic division between gentry and peasantry was already emerging, and the "honest country toiling villager" would "many times let slip some strange different-sounding terms, no ways intelligible to any of civil education..." In Essex, the abominable Lord Rich actually wished "none else to be put to school, but only gentlemen's children," since the poor were fitted for nothing but to be unlettered ploughmen and artificers: a sentiment which Archbishop Cranmer, to his credit indignantly repudiated.[2]

With the Civil War, these social cleavages were suddenly deepened. The reins of traditional authority were inevitably relaxed, the bonds of society weakened, and the gentry driven into harsh repressive measures to restore order. The strict enforcement of military discipline, more-over, and the herding together of social classes in cramped quarters with the King or with Fairfax, unavoidably accentuated those status symbols by which rich and poor were distinguished. With rival

[1] Flora Thompson, *Lark Rise to Candleford*, 1957 edn., pp. 188 *et passim*. 'Lark Rise' was Juniper Hill in north Oxfordshire, and 'Fordlow' the village of Cottisford.
[2] SP 14, 28, 64; LP, XII, i, p. 482; Reyce, *op. cit.*, p. 55; R. H. Tawney, *The Agrarian Problem in the Sixteenth Century*, 1912, p. 135. Cranmer retorted that "the poor man's son by painstaking will be learned, when the gentleman's son will not take the pains to get it..." Rich was an Essex landowner; the "other gentlemen" with him are not named by Professor Tawney.

armies plundering the countryside, and with thousands of estates under sequestration, many labourers could not tell to whom their rents, and their loyalty, were due.[1] With many squires taking up arms for Charles I or Parliament, and leaving their home locality for years on end, the direct interest of many landlords in farming ceased, and absenteeism became, first a military necessity, then a social habit. As a consequence, an attitude of supercilious contempt for social inferiors developed, amongst both cavaliers and puritans, which must have filled old-fashioned squires like Sir George Sondes with shame and dismay. In a word, the Civil War and the Interregnum dealt a death-blow to the old-age conception of society as a heirarchy of interdependent orders, and went far to replace it by the notion of society as a series of independent and necessarily antagonistic classes.

From the Civil War onwards, the preconceptions of labouring society thus became increasingly alienated from those of the country at large. In all the cant of contemporary demagogues about "the people," Hodge was the one individual whose aspirations were never considered: it was scarcely proper that he should have any. Even the well-meant lucubrations of his few champions, like William Walwyn, displayed no real understanding of his problems: the wish of that London silk-merchant "that there was neither pale, hedge, nor ditch in the whole nation" must have struck village labourers, of all people, as strangely absurd.[2] But for another two centuries, Hodge's feelings necessarily remained unspoken and unknown; for his was a way of life whose secret springs became more and more unintelligible to polite society. Yet nowadays, in the mid-twentieth century, as we watch the autumnal sunshine cast lengthening shadows across the meadows of a Pennine valley, or the deserted cattle-pastures of a Wealden farm, it is but just to remember how much we still owe to the labours of the Tudor and Stuart farmworker. For the fact that "things are not so ill with you and me as they might have been, is half owing to the number who lived faithfully a hidden life, and rest in unvisited tombs."[3]

[1] Cf. Alan Everitt, *The County Committee of Kent in the Civil War*, University of Leicester, Dept. of English Local History, Occasional Papers, no. 9, 1957, pp. 41-2; HMC, *Reports*, VII, p. 553.

[2] Schenk, *op. cit.*, p. 50. Winstanley's well-known Digger experiment at St George's Hill in Surrey, where he attempted to found an ideal labouring community, was bitterly opposed by local people, who smashed his followers' tools, tore down their houses, and pulled up their corn and vegetables.—*ibid.*, p. 102.

[3] The quotation is from the concluding sentence of George Eliot's *Middlemarch*.

CHAPTER VIII

THE MARKETING OF AGRICULTURAL PRODUCE

By the year 1500 England had moved a very long way from the era of fully self-supporting rural communities. In all probability such arcadian conditions had never existed. A number of fairs and markets can be traced back to the Anglo-Saxon period, and by the time of Domesday there was a sprinkling of market towns in all parts of the country. In the sixteenth century, it is true, there were probably still many villages whose food was grown entirely within the confines of the parish. Even a prosperous gentleman, like Richard Cheston of St Lawrence in Suffolk, farmed his land "as well for the provision of [his] house and family, as also to sell in divers fairs and markets..."[1] Quite possibly the bulk of agricultural produce still never reached the market. Nevertheless, the development of regional specialization in agricultural products, and the existence of a score of market towns in many English counties, indicate some sort of marketing on a considerable scale well before 1500. The theme of this chapter is the extent, the organization, and the impact of this activity between 1500 and 1640.

By the sixteenth century the organization of marketing can be separated into two more or less distinct parts. The ancient or customary centres of trade were the market towns, with their more or less rigorous regulation and vigilant, ordered system summed up in the contemporary phrase 'the open market'. At the same time, much 'private bargaining' was carried on between individual traders, beyond the scrutiny of official eyes, either central or local. The distinction between the two was not always clearly defined, and many men, at all times, engaged in both spheres. Nevertheless, the open and private markets were essentially distinct in the minds of contemporaries, and as the period progressed the latent jealousy between them became increasingly pronounced. The often antiquated facilities of the market town proved incapable of accommodating the expansion of marketing; its regulations were not sufficiently adaptable to the scale of the new transactions; and the new wine of private bargaining was continually breaking through the old bottles of regulated dealing.

[1] C 2 James I, C 26, 36.

A. THE MARKET TOWN

1. *The number and origin of market towns*

Despite the expansion of private bargaining in the sixteenth century, the market town was still, and was destined to remain, the normal place of sale and purchase for the great majority of country people. Scattered up and down the countryside, at intervals of every few miles, there were about 760 market towns in Tudor and Stuart England and 50 in Wales, each with its official weekly market day or days and its fairs held once or twice a year. Although the population of the country was then less than one tenth that of today, there were far more market towns than now. The intense localism of society and the absence of mechanical transport demanded their proliferation.

Some of these markets had been founded well before the Conquest, like Gloucester, Winchcombe, and Bristol in Gloucestershire. Other early foundations, like Sevenoaks in Kent, originated spontaneously at casual or traditional meeting places, and never received an official charter.[1] But the great majority of markets came into existence in the period which Dr Finberg has described as "the golden age of borough-making in England," the two hundred years or so following the Norman Conquest. Of the thirty-four Tudor and Stuart market towns of Gloucestershire, all but five had been founded before the Black Death, and more than half before the reign of Edward I; they had existed for upwards of 250 years before our period began.[2] In Lancashire the peak of development came rather later, but there too more than half the thirty markets extant under the Tudors and early Stuarts had been flourishing for two centuries before 1500. Many new towns were entirely fresh creations on hitherto unoccupied sites; not infrequently, as at Newmarket, Northleach, and Market Harborough, the new territory was carved out of the corner of an existing parish or group of parishes, whose boundaries often became a source of contention in the sixteenth century.[3]

Despite this proliferation of markets, there were far fewer market towns and villages in the sixteenth century than three centuries earlier—probably less than one third as many. The population of the country may by that date have returned to or surpassed its former peak; but

[1] H. W. Knocker, 'Sevenoaks: the Manor, Church, and Market', *Arch. Cant.*, XXXVII, 1926, pp. 51–68.

[2] See H. P. R. Finberg, *Gloucestershire Studies*, 1957, pp. 64 *sqq.*; G. H. Tupling, 'The Origin of Markets and Fairs in Medieval Lancashire', *Lancs. and Ches. Antiq. Soc.*, XLIX, 1933, pp. 75–94.

[3] G. H. Tupling, 'An Alphabetical List of the Markets and Fairs of Lancashire recorded before the year 1701', *Lancs. and Ches. Antiq. Soc.*, LI, 1936, pp. 88–110.

Fig. 9 (a). Markets in northern England, c. 1500–1640.

Cumberland: 1. Alston; 2. Blennerhasset; 3. Bootle; 4. Brampton; 5. Carlisle; 6. Cockermouth; 7. Egremont; 8. Holme Cultram; 9. Ireby; 10. Keswick; 11. Kirkoswald; 12. Penrith; 13. Ravenglass; 14. Whitehaven; 15. Wigton; 16. Workington.

Durham: 1. Barnard Castle; 2. Bishop Auckland; 3. Darlington; 4. Durham; 5. Hartlepool; 6. Staindrop; 7. Sunderland.

Lancashire: 1. Ashton-under Lyne; 2. Blackburn; 3. Bolton; 4. Burnley; 5. Bury; 6. Cartmel; 7. Chorley; 8. Clitheroe; 9. Colne; 10. Dalton-in-Furness; 11. Garstang; 12. Haslingden; 13. Hawkshead; 14. Hornby; 15. Kirkham; 16. Lancaster; 17. Leigh; 18. Liverpool; 19. Manchester; 20. Ormskirk; 21. Padiham; 22. Poulton-le-Fylde; 23. Prescot; 24. Preston; 25. Rochdale; 26. Salford; 27. Ulverston; 28. Walton-le-Dale; 29. Warrington; 30. Whalley; 31. Wigan.

Northumberland: 1. Alnwick; 2. Bellingham; 3. Berwick; 4. Haltwistle; 5. Hexham; 6. Morpeth; 7. Newcastle-upon-Tyne; 8. Wooler.

Westmorland: 1. Ambleside; 2. Appleby; 3. Brough; 4. Burton-in-Kendal; 5. Kendal; 6. Kirkby Lonsdale; 7. Kirkby Stephen; 8. Orton.

Yorkshire: 1. Aldborough (near Boroughbridge); 2. Askrigg; 3. Barnsley; 4. Bawtry; 5. Bedale; 6. Beverley; 7. Boroughbridge; 8. Bradford; 9. Bridlington; 10. Doncaster; 11. Driffield; 12. Guisborough; 13. Halifax; 14. Harewood; 15. Hedon; 16. Helmsley; 17. Hovingham; 18. Howden; 19. Hull; 20. Kettlewell; 21. Kilham; 22. Kirkby Moorside; 23. Knaresborough; 24. Leeds; 25. Malton; 26. Market Weighton; 27. Masham; 28. Middleham; 29. Northallerton; 30. Otley; 31. Pickering; 32. Pocklington; 33. Pontefract; 34. Richmond; 35. Ripley; 36. Ripon; 37. Rotherham; 38. Scarborough; 39. Seamer; 40. Sedbergh; 41. Selby; 42. Settle; 43. Sheffield; 44. Sherburn-in-Elmet; 45. Skipton; 46. Snaith; 47. Stokesley; 48. Tadcaster; 49. Thirsk; 50. Wakefield; 51. Wetherby; 52. Whitby; 53. Yarm; 54. York.

In addition to the markets indicated on the map, the following are listed in John Adams, *Index Villarum*, 1690 edn, *passim*. They are omitted from the map because no clear evidence has been found of their existence between 1500 and 1640. *Cumb.*: Longtown; *Durham*: Stanhope, Stockton, Wolsingham; *Lancs.*: Broughton; *Northumb.*: Elsdon, Learmouth, Rothbury; *Yorks.*: Aberford, Cawood, Easingwold, Gisburn, Hornsea, Huddersfield, Hunmanby, North Frodingham, Patrington, Thorne, Tickhill. In all probability local research would reveal that some of the markets Adams lists (for example, St Austell, Stockton, Dedham, Huddersfield) existed between 1500 and 1640; that others were unofficial or ephemeral in character; and that some, especially in the North and in Wales, were not created until after 1640.

scores and hundreds of markets had perished in the generations following the Black Death, and were never revived. In Norfolk, where at one time there had been 130, there were now only thirty-one. In Gloucestershire, where there had formerly been at least fifty-three, there were now no more than thirty-four. In Lancashire, where charters were granted for no fewer than eighty-five markets and fairs while a further fifty arose by prescription, there were in 1640 not more than thirty market towns in the county.[1] In Kent and Devonshire and most other counties there had been a similar decline in numbers. The truth was that many towns had been founded on a wave of enthusiasm like that of the Railway Age, and were left high and dry when it subsided; for neither kings nor abbots could annul the facts of geography and economics. Perhaps the history of England's vanished market towns would be as interesting a study as its lost villages. The old market cross which today stands forlorn among the trees of Stapleford

---

[1] See map, p.   , and cf. Finberg, *op. cit.*, pp. 86–8; Tupling, 'Origin of Markets and Fairs', pp. 92–93. The Lancashire figures relate to grants up to the end of James I's reign. For the figure of 130 for Norfolk I am indebted to Dr W. G. Hoskins. Mrs J. R. Green, in *Town Life in the Fifteenth Century*, 1894, II, p. 26, states that almost 5,000 markets and fairs were established by grant between 1200 and 1482; R. B. Westerfield, in *Middlemen in English Business...*, 1915, p. 334, gives a figure of over 2,800 between 1199 and 1483. Both figures appear to be exaggerations. The *Royal Commission on Market Rights and Tolls*, 1889, I, pp. 108–31, lists 2,713 between 1199 and 1483; but some of these were to places overseas, some were for the translation of the market to a new site, many were re-grants to places already possessed of market rights, and many were for fairs only.

Fig. 9(b). Markets in western England and Wales, c. 1500–1640.

ENGLAND

Cheshire: 1. Altrincham; 2. Chester; 3. Congleton; 4. Frodsham; 5. Knutsford; 6. Macclesfield; 7. Malpas; 8. Middlewich; 9. Nantwich; 10. Northwich; 11. Sandbach; 12. Stockport; 13. Tarvin.

Cornwall: 1. Bodmin; 2. Boscastle; 3. Camelford; 4. East Looe; 5. Falmouth; 6. Fowey; 7. Grampound; 8. Helston; 9. Launceston; 10. Liskeard; 11. Lostwithiel;

12. Marazion; 13. Millbrook; 14. Padstow; 15. Penryn; 16. Penzance; 17. St Columb Major; 18. St Germans; 19. St Ives; 20. St Stephen's by Launceston; 21. Saltash; 22. Stratton; 23. Tregoney; 24. Truro; 25. West Looe.

Devonshire: 1. Ashburton; 2. Axminster; 3. Bampton; 4. Barnstaple; 5. Bere Alston; 6. Bideford; 7. Bovey Tracey; 8. Bow; 9. Bradninch; 10. Chagford; 11. Chudleigh; 12. Chulmleigh; 13. Colyton; 14. Combe Martin; 15. Crediton; 16. Cullompton; 17. Dartmouth; 18. Dodbrooke; 19. Exeter; 20. Great Torrington; 21. Hartland; 22. Hatherleigh; 23. Holsworthy; 24. Honiton; 25. Ilfracombe; 26. Kingsbridge; 27. Lifton; 28. Membury; 29. Modbury; 30. Moretonhampstead; 31. Newton Abbot; 32. North Bovey; 33. North Molton; 34. North Tawton; 35. Okehampton; 36. Ottery St Mary; 37. Plymouth; 38. Plympton St Mary; 39. Sidmouth; 40. South Brent; 41. South Molton; 42. South Tawton; 43. Tavistock; 44. Tiverton; 45. Totnes.

Dorset: 1. Abbotsbury; 2. Beaminster; 3. Bere Regis; 4. Blandford; 5. Bridport; 6. Cerne Abbas; 7. Corfe Castle; 8. Cranborne; 9. Dorchester; 10. Evershot; 11. Frampton; 12. Lyme Regis; 13. Milton Abbas; 14. Poole; 15. Puddletown; 16. Shaftesbury; 17. Sherborne; 18. Sturminster Newton; 19. Wareham; 20. Weymouth; 21. Wimborne Minster.

Gloucestershire: 1. Berkeley; 2. Bisley; 3. Blockley; 4. Bristol; 5. Cheltenham; 6. Chipping Campden; 7. Chipping Sodbury; 8. Cirencester; 9. Coleford; 10. Dursley; 11. Fairford; 12. Falfield; 13. Frampton-on-Severn; 14. Gloucester; 15. Great Witcombe; 16. Horton; 17. Lechlade; 18. Leonard Stanley; 19. Marshfield; 20. Mitcheldean; 21. Minchinhampton; 22. Moreton-in-Marsh; 23. Newent; 24. Newnham; 25. Northleach; 26. Painswick; 27. Stow-on-the-Wold; 28. Stroud; 29. Tetbury; 30. Tewkesbury; 31. Thornbury; 32. Wickwar; 33. Winchcombe; 34. Wotton-under-Edge.

Herefordshire: 1. Bromyard; 2. Hereford; 3. Kington; 4. Ledbury; 5. Leominster; 6. Pembridge; 7. Ross-on-Wye; 8. Weobley; 9. Wigmore.

Monmouthshire: 1. Abergavenny; 2. Caerleon; 3. Chepstow; 4. Grosmont; 5. Monmouth; 6. Newport; 7. Raglan; 8. Usk.

Shropshire: 1. Bishop's Castle; 2. Bridgnorth; 3. Church Stretton; 4. Cleobury Mortimer; 5. Clun; 6. Ellesmere; 7. Ludlow; 8. Market Drayton; 9. Much Wenlock; 10. Newport; 11. Oswestry; 12. Prees; 13. Shipton; 14. Shrewsbury; 15. Tong; 16. Wellington; 17. Wem; 18. Whitchurch.

Somerset: 1. Axbridge; 2. Bath; 3. Bishop's Lydeard; 4. Bridgwater; 5. Bruton; 6. Chard; 7. Crewkerne; 8. Dulverton; 9. Dunster; 10. Frome; 11. Glastonbury; 12. Huntspill; 13. Ilchester; 14. Ilminster; 15. Keynsham; 16. Langport; 17. Martock; 18. Milverton; 19. Minehead; 20. North Curry; 21. North Petherton; 22. Norton St Philip; 23. Pensford; 24. Porlock; 25. Queen Camel; 26. St Michael Church; 27. Shepton Mallet; 28. Somerton; 29. South Petherton; 30. Stogumber; 31. Taunton; 32. Watchet; 33. Wellington; 34. Wells; 35. Weston Zoyland; 36. Wincanton; 37. Wiveliscombe; 38. Wrington; 39. Yeovil.

Staffordshire: 1. Abbots Bromley; 2. Betley; 3. Brewood; 4. Burton-upon-Trent; 5. Cannock; 6. Cheadle; 7. Eccleshall; 8. Leek; 9. Lichfield; 10. Newcastle-under-Lyme; 11. Penkridge; 12. Rugeley; 13. Stafford; 14. Stone; 15. Tamworth; 16. Tutbury; 17. Uttoxeter; 18. Walsall; 19. Wolverhampton.

Wiltshire: 1. Aldbourne; 2. Amesbury; 3. Bradford-on-Avon; 4. Calne; 5. Castle Combe; 6. Chippenham; 7. Cricklade; 8. Devizes; 9. Downton; 10. Highworth; 11. Hindon; 12. Maiden Bradley; 13. Malmesbury; 14. Market Lavington; 15. Marlborough; 16. Mere; 17. Salisbury; 18. Swindon; 19. Trowbridge; 20. Warminster; 21. Westbury; 22. Wilton; 23. Wootton Bassett.

Worcestershire: 1. Bewdley; 2. Bromsgrove; 3. Droitwich; 4. Dudley; 5. Evesham; 6. Kidderminster; 7. Pershore; 8. Stourbridge; 9. Tenbury; 10. Upton-on-Severn; 11. Worcester.

WALES

Anglesey: 1. Beaumaris; 2. Newborough.
Breconshire: 1. Brecon; 2. Builth; 3. Crickhowell; 4. Hay.
Caernarvonshire: 1. Bangor; 2. Caernarvon; 3. Conway; 4. Nefyn; 5. Pwllheli.
Cardiganshire: 1. Aberystwyth; 2. Cardigan; 3. Lampeter; 4. Tregaron.
Carmarthenshire: 1. Carmarthen; 2. Kidwelly; 3. Llandilo; 4. Llandovery; 5. Llanelly; 6. Llangadog.
Denbighshire: 1. Denbigh; 2. Ruthin; 3. Wrexham.
Flintshire: 1. Caerwys; 2. Flint.
Glamorgan: 1. Bridgend; 2. Cardiff; 3. Cowbridge; 4. Llantrisant; 5. Neath; 6. Swansea.
Merioneth: 1. Bala; 2. Dolgelley; 3. Harlech.
Montgomeryshire: 1. Llanfyllin; 2. Llanidloes; 3. Montgomery; 4. Machynlleth; 5. Newtown; 6. Welshpool.
Pembrokeshire: 1. Haverfordwest; 2. Newport; 3. Pembroke; 4. Tenby.
Radnorshire: 1. Knighton; 2. New Radnor; 4. Presteigne; 4. Rhayader.

In addition to the markets indicated on the map, the following are listed in John Adams, *Index Villarum*, 1690 edn, *passim*. They are omitted from the map because no clear evidence has been found of their existence between 1500 and 1640. In ENGLAND—*Cornwall*: Callington, Redruth, St Austell, Wadebridge; *Devon*: Sheepwash, Topsham; *Dorset*: Stalbridge; *Salop*: Hodnet, Shifnal; *Som.*: Castle Cary, Chewton Mendip, Stowey. In WALES—*Caerns.*: Criccieth; *Carms.*: Laugharne, Newcastle; *Denbs.*: Llangollen, Llanrwst; *Flint.*: St Asaph; *Glam.*: Caerphilly, Llantwitfarde, Penrice; *Mer.*: Dinas Mawddwy; *Pembs.*: Cilgerran, Fishguard, Narberth, Nevern, St David's, Wiston.

Park in Leicestershire, where the village too has now all but disappeared, bears silent testimony to the forgotten aspirations of scores of villages and their manorial lords in medieval England.

In the sixteenth and seventeenth centuries there were still many markets which hovered on the verge of extinction. That at Thornbury in Gloucestershire maintained only the slenderest thread of life. The market at Waltham-on-the-Wolds in Leicestershire was described about 1670 as "very inconsiderable and in a manner disused," while that of Billesdon was "very mean." That at Tutbury in Staffordshire was "very inconsiderable, if one at all;" at Brewood "almost discontinued;" at Great Eccleston in Lancashire "so inconsiderable that it is not worth the taking notice of;" at Holme Cultram in Cumberland "very mean;" at Ewell in Surrey "so inconsiderable that it does not deserve the name." The market at Heacham in Norfolk was extinguished by a great fire in Charles I's reign; that of St Mary Cray in

Fig. 9(c). Markets in eastern England, c. 1500–1640.

Bedfordshire: 1. Ampthill; 2. Bedford; 3. Biggleswade; 4. Dunstable; 5. Leighton Buzzard; 6. Luton; 7. Potton; 8. Shefford; 9. Toddington; 10. Woburn.

Berkshire: 1. Abingdon; 2. East Ilsley; 3. Faringdon; 4. Hungerford; 5. Lambourn; 6. Maidenhead; 7. Newbury; 8. Reading; 9. Wallingford; 10. Wantage; 11. Windsor; 12. Wokingham.

Buckinghamshire: 1. Amersham; 2. Aylesbury; 3. Beaconsfield; 4. Buckingham; 5. Colnbrook; 6. High Wycombe; 7. Ivinghoe; 8. Little Brickhill; 9. Marlow; 10. Newport Pagnell; 11. Olney; 12. Princes Risborough; 13. Stony Stratford; 14. Wendover; 15. Winslow.

Cambridgeshire: 1. Cambridge; 2. Caxton; 3. Ely; 4. Linton; 5. Littleport; 6. March; 7. Reach; 8. Wisbech.

Derbyshire: 1. Alfreton; 2. Ashbourne; 3. Bakewell; 4. Bolsover; 5. Chapel-en-le-Frith; 6. Chesterfield; 7. Derby; 8. Dronfield; 9. Tideswell; 10. Wirksworth.

Essex: 1. Aveley; 2. Barking; 3. Billericay; 4. Braintree; 5. Brentwood; 6. Burnham-on-Crouch; 7. Castle Hedingham; 8. Chelmsford; 9. Chipping Ongar; 10. Coggeshall; 11. Colchester; 12. Epping; 13. Great Dunmow; 14. Halstead; 15. Harlow; 16. Harwich; 17. Hatfield Broadoak; 18. Horndon-on-the-Hill; 19. Maldon; 20. Manningtree; 21. Newport; 22. Rayleigh; 23. Romford; 24. Saffron Walden; 25. Thaxted; 26. Waltham Abbey; 27. Witham.

Hampshire: 1. Alresford; 2. Alton; 3. Andover; 4. Basingstoke; 5. Christchurch; 6. Fareham; 7. Havant; 8. Kingsclere; 9. Lymington; 10. Newport; 11. Odiham; 12. Petersfield; 13. Portsmouth; 14. Ringwood; 15. Romsey; 16. Sandown; 17. Southampton; 18. Stockbridge; 19. Whitchurch; 20. Winchester; 21. Yarmouth.

Hertfordshire: 1. Baldock; 2. Barkway; 3. Berkhamsted; 4. Bishop's Stortford; 5. Buntingford; 6. Hatfield; 7. Hemel Hempstead; 8. Hertford; 9. High Barnet; 10. Hitchin; 11. Hoddesdon; 12. Rickmansworth; 13. Royston; 14. St Albans; 15. Sawbridgeworth; 16. Standon; 17. Stevenage; 18. Tring; 19. Ware; 20. Watford.

Huntingdonshire: 1. Earith; 2. Godmanchester; 3. Huntingdon; 4. Kimbolton; 5. Ramsey; 6. St Ives; 7. St Neots; 8. Yaxley.

Kent: 1. Appledore; 2. Ashford; 3. Bromley; 4. Canterbury; 5. Cranbrook; 6. Dartford; 7. Dover; 8. Elham; 9. Faversham; 10. Folkestone; 11. Goudhurst; 12. Gravesend; 13. Hythe; 14. Lenham; 15. Lydd; 16. Maidstone; 17. Milton Regis; 18. New Romney; 19. Northfleet; 20. Orpington; 21. Rochester; 22. St Mary Cray; 23. Sandwich; 24. Sevenoaks; 25. Sittingbourne; 26. Smarden; 27. Tenterden; 28. Tonbridge; 29. Westerham; 30. West Malling; 31. Woolwich; 32. Wrotham; 33. Wye.

Leicestershire: 1. Ashby-de-la-Zouch; 2. Billesdon; 3. Castle Donington; 4. Hallaton; 5. Hinckley; 6. Leicester; 7. Loughborough; 8. Lutterworth; 9. Market Bosworth; 10. Market Harborough; 11. Melton Mowbray; 12. Mount Sorrel; 13. Waltham-on-the-Wolds.

Lincolnshire: 1. Alford; 2. Barton-upon-Humber; 3. Beckingham; 4. Binbrook; 5. Bolingbroke; 6. Boston; 7. Bourne; 8. Brigg; 9. Burgh-le-Marsh; 10. Burton-upon-Stather; 11. Caistor; 12. Crowland; 13. Dalderby; 14. Donington; 15. Folkingham; 16. Gainsborough; 17. Grantham; 18. Great Limber; 19. Grimsby; 20. Holbeach; 21. Horncastle; 22. Ketsby; 23. Kirton-in-Holland; 24. Kirton-in-Lindsey; 25. Lincoln; 26. Louth; 27. Market Deeping; 28. Market Rasen; 29. Market Stainton; 30. Saltfleet; 31. Sleaford; 32. Spalding; 33. Spilsby; 34. Stallingborough; 35. Stamford; 36. Tattershall; 37. Wainfleet.

Middlesex: 1. Brentford; 2. Edgware; 3. London; 4. Staines; 5. Uxbridge; 6. Westminster.

Norfolk: 1. Attleborough; 2. Aylsham; 3. Burnham Market; 4. Castleacre; 5. Cawston; 6. Cley; 7. Cromer; 8. Diss; 9. Downham Market; 10. East Dereham; 11. East Harling; 12. Fakenham; 13. Harleston; 14. Heacham; 15. Hickling; 16. Hingham; 17. Holt; 18. King's Lynn; 19. Loddon; 20 New Buckenham; 21. North Walsham; 22. Norwich; 23. Reepham; 24. Snettisham; 25. Swaffham; 26. Thetford; 27. Walsingham; 28. Watton; 29. Worstead; 30. Wymondham; 31. Yarmouth.

Northamptonshire: 1. Aynho; 2. Brackley; 3. Daventry; 4. Higham Ferrers; 5. Kettering; 6. King's Cliffe; 7. Northampton; 8. Oundle; 9. Peterborough; 10. Rockingham; 11. Rothwell; 12. Thrapston; 13. Towcester; 14. Weldon; 15. Wellingborough.

Nottinghamshire: 1. Bingham; 2. Blyth; 3. Mansfield; 4. Newark; 5. Nottingham; 6. Retford; 7. Southwell; 8. Tuxford; 9. Worksop.

Oxfordshire: 1. Bampton; 2. Banbury; 3. Bicester; 4. Burford; 5. Chipping Norton; 6. Deddington; 7. Henley-on-Thames; 8. Hook Norton; 9. Oxford; 10. Thame; 11. Watlington; 12. Witney; 13. Woodstock.

Rutland: 1. Oakham; 2. Uppingham.

Suffolk: 1. Aldeburgh; 2. Beccles; 3. Bildeston; 4. Blythburgh; 5. Botesdale; 6. Brandon; 7. Bungay; 8. Bury St Edmunds; 9. Clare; 10. Debenham; 11. Dunwich; 12. Eye; 13. Framlingham; 14. Hadleigh; 15. Halesworth; 16. Haverhill; 17. Ipswich; 18. Ixworth; 19. Lavenham; 20. Lowestoft; 21. Mendlesham; 22. Mildenhall; 23. Nayland; 24. Needham Market; 25. Newmarket; 26. Orford; 27. Saxmundham; 28. Southwold; 29. Stowmarket; 30. Sudbury; 31. Wickham Market; 32. Woodbridge; 33. Woolpit.

Surrey: 1. Chertsey; 2. Croydon; 3. Dorking; 4. Farnham; 5. Godalming; 6. Guildford; 7. Haslemere; 8. Kingston-upon-Thames; 9. Reigate; 10. Southwark.

Sussex: 1. Arundel; 2. Battle; 3. Brighton; 4. Chichester; 5. Cuckfield; 6. Ditchling; 7. Eastbourne; 8. East Grinstead; 9. Hailsham; 10. Hastings; 11. Horsham; 12. Lewes; 13. Midhurst; 14. Petworth; 15. Rye; 16. Shoreham; 17. Steyning; 18. Storrington; 19. West Tarring; 20. Winchelsea; 21. Worthing.

Warwickshire: 1. Alcester; 2. Atherstone; 3. Bidford-on-Avon; 4. Birmingham; 5. Coleshill; 6. Coventry; 7. Henley-in-Arden; 8. Kenilworth; 9. Kineton; 10. Nuneaton; 11. Rugby; 12. Shipston-on-Stour; 13. Solihull; 14. Southam; 15. Stratford-upon-Avon; 16. Sutton Coldfield; 17. Warwick.

In addition to the markets indicated on the map, the following are listed in John Adams, *Index Villarum*, 1690 edn, *passim*. They are omitted from the map because no clear evidence has been found of their existence between 1500 and 1640. *Bucks.*: Chesham; *Cambs.*: Soham; *Derbys.*: Winster; *Essex*: Dedham, Great Bardfield, Grays Thurrock, Rochford; *Hants.*: Bishop's Waltham, Brading, Fordingbridge, Overton; *Middx.*: Enfield; *Norfolk*: Castle Rising, Foulsham, Litcham, Methwold; *Surrey*: Ewell; *Warws.*: Polesworth.

Kent lingered on, though "very inconsiderable," till the great storm of 1703, when its ancient market house was blown down, and its history came to an end.[1]

On the whole, however, the process of elimination was not characteristic of the sixteenth century. Most markets were expanding again, many were obtaining new rights and franchises,[2] and some were being refounded. Almost every county, moreover, could boast a few fresh creations: Ketsby in Lincolnshire in 1524, for instance; Sedbergh in Yorkshire and Little Brickhill in Buckinghamshire in 1526;

[1] Richard Blome, *Britannia*, 1673, *passim;* Edward Hasted, *History of Kent*, 2nd edn., 1, p. 260; cf. CSPD 1639–40, p. 252, regarding Attleborough (Norfolk).

[2] Leicester and Grantham, for instance, obtained the right to hold wool markets.— CSPD 1598–1601, p. 197; 1603–10, p. 115.

Chertsey in Surrey in 1599; Aynho in Northamptonshire in 1622; Earith in Huntingdonshire about 1623; Stevenage in Hertfordshire in 1624; and Puddletown in Dorset in 1626.[1] Generally speaking, these new grants were made to small places not destined to develop a truly urban status; but there were a number of important exceptions, particularly in the north of England. Several of the principal towns of modern Lancashire were emerging in this period and setting up markets of their own: Blackburn, Colne, Haslingden, Leigh, Padiham, and Whalley among them.[2]

Many of the new markets and extended franchises of the sixteenth century owed their origin to the spontaneous action of local people. Frequently they flourished for many years before any formal grant was sought by the lord of the manor or by the town tradesmen.[3] In all probability there were many unofficial markets of which we know nothing; for their life was often brief and fugitive, and it is only when disputes concerning their status arose that we hear of them. A case in point is that of the new wool market set up at Marshfield in Gloucestershire in Queen Elizabeth's reign. According to the citizens of Bath, the inhabitants of Marshfield and the surrounding countryside had hitherto purchased their wool in *their* market; but early in Elizabeth's reign,

"perceiving your Majesty's said city of Bath to be infected and greatly visited with the plague, in such sort as the inhabitants of the country bordering upon...Bath did stay their repair to the said city upon the market days aforesaid for the buying or uttering yarn and other merchandises...the same inhabitants...of Marshfield very uncharitably, withal meaning in the time of the said infection the utter subversion, ruin, and decay of...Bath, did cause, upon proclamation to be made as well in...Somerset as also in...Gloucester[shire], that all your Majesty's subjects...might have their access to...Marshfield for the uttering and buying of yarn, woollen cloth, and other merchandise...And so by the uncharitable...devices of the said inhabitants of the town of Marshfield...the country people...do make their whole repair...to the town of Marshfield..."

The little Gloucestershire town could claim ancient market rights, but not, it was objected, the further privilege of a wool market.[4]

Another, and more auspicious, venture of local enterprise was the revival of the market at Westerham in Kent in James I's reign. Here the

[1] E 134, 9 Car. I, E 30; SP 14, 141, f. 352; CSPD 1598–1601, p. 155; 1625–6, p. 367; W. Le Hardy, *County of Buckingham: Calender to the Sessions Records, Records, 1933*, I, p. 344; LP IV, pp. 81, 898, 902.
[2] Tupling, 'Alphabetical List of the Markets and Fairs', pp. 89, 93, 96, 99, 103, 109.
[3] Tupling, 'Origin of Markets and Fairs', pp. 89, 92.   [4] Req. 2, 213, 15.

old market granted about 1337 to the then lord of the manor, the abbot of Westminster, had long since fallen into desuetude. So, too, had the markets granted to other villages in Holmesdale—Kemsing, Shoreham, Seal, and Otford. Only Sevenoaks, at the junction of the roads traversing the valley, had survived the vicissitudes of the late fourteenth and fifteenth centuries. The village of Westerham itself, however, still survived as a small trading centre, with its mercers', grocers', and bakers' shops, and its inns and alehouses. There was no other market, north and south, between East Grinstead and Bromley, a distance of thirty miles, nor, east and west, between Sevenoaks and Reigate, a distance of twenty. Towards the end of 1620, therefore, a group of local tradesmen joined together in an attempt to restore the market "as it had been of ancient time." Richard Dawling, a local grocer, "went about to persuade divers other inhabitants of the said town of Westerham" to contribute to the expense of procuring a new grant, and Raphe Twigg, George Fuller, and nine others entered into a bond of £100 in support of his venture. After considerable delay a patent was obtained in the name of Sir Thomas Gresham, the new lord of the manor, who leased the market with its "tollage, stallage, and pickage," rent-free, to Dawling and Twigg. As Gresham himself was unwilling to incur expense in providing market facilities, he also leased to Dawling and Twigg a plot of land in front of the George and Dragon to erect shambles. The plot covered barely 300 square yards and the term of the lease was for 21 years only; the rent was only 12d., but the shambles were to revert to the lord at the end of the period. Well aware "that the erecting of a market house and shambles would be a furtherance and increase of the [market], and would be very profitable for the general good," the two tradesmen erected thirteen shops or shambles on the site, and a stone "market house with a lanthorne and a market bell." The royal patent was publicly proclaimed, and the market formally declared open. Altogether Dawling and Twigg spent something like £300 in providing the new market—a very considerable sum for two village tradesmen of the reign of James I. Within fifty years Westerham developed into a centre of the Kentish cattle trade; and despite their complaints that other inhabitants refused to share the expenses and that they themselves were "great losers" by it, both Dawlings and Fullers (as their monuments in the church indicate) played a conspicuous part in the prosperity of the town during the succeeding century.[1] The history of Westerham's re-foundation can be taken as typical of that of many rising market villages in the later sixteenth and early seventeenth centuries.

[1] C 2 James I, F 9, 33. Similar disputes occurred in connection with the new market grant at Bovey Tracy in Devon: Req. 2, 45, 93.

2. *The size and functions of market towns*

Quite as various as the origins of market towns were their size and functions. Many markets were held in obscure villages unknown beyond their own borders, or inhabited, like Kirkby Moorside, only by poor people and cottagers.[1] Such places as Elham, buried in its downland valley, or Smarden in the Weald of Kent, or Billesdon in Leicestershire, or Bow and Bradninch in Devon, could scarcely be accounted urban even by Tudor standards. With a population of perhaps three or four hundred, their influence was confined to a few square miles of neighbouring countryside. Within that area, each played a vital rôle in the lives of several thousand husbandmen and labourers.

More characteristic of Tudor England were the numerous market towns with a population of perhaps six hundred or one thousand, or occasionally two thousand, inhabitants. There were few counties without half-a-dozen such centres: Ashford Cranbrook, Dartford, Faversham, Sevenoaks, Tonbridge, Tenterden, and Sandwich in Kent, for example. Or Abingdon, Newbury, Wallingford, Windsor, and Reading in Berkshire. Or Burton, Stafford, Lichfield, Newcastle, Tamworth, and Wolverhampton in Staffordshire.[2]

At the other end of the scale were the shire towns.[3] In each of the five large counties of the south-east of England there were two rival shire towns: Winchester and Southampton in Hampshire, Chichester and Lewes in Sussex, Canterbury and Maidstone in Kent, Colchester and Chelmsford in Essex, and Bury St Edmunds and Ipswich in Suffolk. With a population usually of several thousand inhabitants, and with a long tradition of independence behind them, such towns influenced both the economy and the ways of thought of a wide tract of country-side. Bury St Edmunds, we are told, was accounted the place "of most credit" in Suffolk, "a fine neat town, and much inhabited by the gentry, who resort thither from all parts of the country." Ipswich, with twice or thrice the population, was "the most remarkable [town] towards the sea...a very fair and spacious town, well peopled and well traded too; adorned with fourteen churches for the service of God and many a fair and goodly edifice for private use." Maidstone, already the social capital of West Kent, was described a century later by Defoe,

[1] E 164, 37, f. 386.
[2] For towns in Sussex, Bucks., and Rutland, see Julian Cornwall, 'English Country Towns in the Fifteen Twenties', EcHR, xv, i, 1962, pp. 54–69.
[3] The phrases 'shire town' or 'county town' came into use by Henry VIII's reign (cf. LP VIII, p. 241, referring to Dorchester in 1535), but were unusual before the end of the century.

as "a very agreeable place to live in, where a man of letters, and of manners, will always find suitable society...so that here is what is not often found, namely a town of very great business and trade and yet full of gentry, of mirth, and of good company."[1]

Towns like Maidstone, Ipswich, and Bury were not only centres for the distribution and sale of agricultural produce, but also for its consumption. The feeding of the populace in towns like Canterbury and Preston involved, in little, the same economic and administrative problems as that of London. In recalling the overwhelming preponderance of the metropolis in this period as a factor in agricultural marketing, the parallel growth of these provincial towns must not be overlooked. It was less meteoric, but it was none the less significant. The population of Norwich in Henry VIII's reign has been estimated at about twelve thousand persons; of Bristol, about ten thousand; of Salisbury, Exeter, and York about eight thousand each; and of Coventry 6,600. Taken together, the inhabitants of these six places were equal in number to those of London.[2] By the time of the Hearth Tax, London had far outstripped them; but, judged by the number of their hearths, there were then sixty provincial towns with an average of six or seven thousand inhabitants each, and a total population still exceeding that of London and Westminister.[3]

The factors underlying the growth of towns from purely local markets to provincial centres were many and varied. The necessity of adequate roads and an extensive and varied hinterland are obvious. Quite as important was the presence of a sizeable river. Few major towns were situated away from navigable streams, and the growth of towns like Leicester was indubitably limited by their absence. Another important factor was the topographical suitability of the site. The expansion of Manchester, far excelling "the towns lying round about it, both for the beautiful shew it bears and the resort unto it of the neighbouring people," was evidently facilitated by the convenience of its market place, so "remarkable...in those parts" for its size.[4] Many a market town like Brentford in Middlesex or Shaftesbury in

---

[1] Peter Heylyn, *A Help to English History...*, 1709 (first published in 1641), p. 504; Daniel Defoe, *A Tour through England and Wales*, Everyman, 1959, I, p. 115.

[2] W. G. Hoskins, 'English Provincial Towns in the early Sixteenth Century', RHS, 5th Ser., VI, 1956, p. 5.

[3] Based on C. A. F. Meekings, *Dorset Hearth Tax Assessments*, Dorset Nat. Hist. and Arch. Soc., 1951, pp. 108–10.

[4] William Burton, *The Description of Leicestershire*, [1622], p. 160; Heylyn, *op. cit.*, pp. 375, 389. According to Tupling, however, the Manchester market-place was severely congested.—'Lancashire Markets in the Sixteenth and Seventeenth Centuries', *Lancs. and Ches. Antiq. Soc.*, LVIII, 1947, pp. 15–16. The Soar was not navigable to Leicester in this period.

Dorset was restricted by its "narrowness and straytness" and "by reason of the continual thoroughfare...of travellers through the same, whereby the said street became altogether unfit and inconvenient for the purpose..." At Brentford the townsmen eventually removed the market place to a new site in "the orchard and backside of...the Crown" inn.[1] But generally the opposition of tradesmen with burgage tenements in the old market place precluded removal; at Shaftesbury, although the market was so cramped that wealthy corn farmers threatened to carry their grain elsewhere, the site was not altered.[2]

3. *The topography and facilities of market towns*

The topographical layout of market towns in the sixteenth century was thus of considerable importance. Though no two towns were identical, there were certain distinctive shapes or types of market place. The simplest form, characteristic of small country towns, consisted of a single, long, wide street, expanding in the middle and narrowing at either end, such as may be seen today at Yarm, Thame, or West Malling. Little less common were the triangular shape, often formed at the meeting place of three roads, at Sevenoaks or Ormskirk; the plain rectangle, as at Grantham and Preston; and the cross-shape, as at Warrington and Maidstone. In larger towns there were many deviations from these basic patterns. In some places, like Canterbury and Northampton, the expansion of the market obliterated the original layout or necessitated the dispersal of trade through various streets devoted to the sale of particular commodities. Quite modest towns, like Banbury and Newark, had their "horse fair", "beast market hill," or "cornhill;" such names are still met with in places as small as Ottery St Mary. At Exeter there was a Butcher Row, Shambles, Fish Market, Corn Market, Cloth Market, and Wool and Yarn Market;[3] at Northampton a Horsemarket, Cattle Market, Marehold, Hay Market, Cornhill, Sheep Street, Woodhill, and Malthill. At Warrington the market stalls and standings extended along the four arms of the cross-roads in the centre of the town, with the Butter Market to the east, the Horse Market to the north, and the Forum or Corn Market in the north-west angle of the cross-roads. At Liverpool the general market was held round the White Cross, extending along the High Street into

[1] C 2, Eliz., H 22, 34.
[2] E 134, 5 James I, H 22.
[3] E 134, 42 and 43 Eliz., M 3; E 134, 3 James I, E 20; W. G. Hoskins, *Industry, Trade, and People in Exeter, 1688–1800*, 1935, pp. 23, 25; cf. M. W. Beresford, *History on the Ground*, 1957, chapter VI, for Toddington and Higham Ferrers. The name 'cornhill' arose from the need to choose the driest and cleanest site for the sale of grain; livestock were generally penned in the lower-lying parts of the market.

Castle Street and along Dale Street. In the High Street was the Corn Market, the Lancashire dealers standing on one side and those of Cheshire on the other; nearby were the Shambles; while the fish boards stood nest to the Town Hall, and the fruit and vegetable stalls near the High Cross. Until 1567 the Liverpool Cattle Market was also held in this part of the town; but about 1570, owing to the "greater repair of people than in times past," it was removed first to the Castle fields and then to Chapel Street: for like many other towns Liverpool was rapidly outgrowing its original site.[1]

Situated alongside the market place of every country town were its public and official buildings. Practically every town had its market cross. In the smallest places, like West Malling, it was the solitary symbol of market status. With the expansion of markets in the sixteenth century, crosses were often multiplied till in towns like Yeovil and Shaftesbury there were four or five of them: one for the sale of fish, another for cheese, a third for poultry, and others for hemp and butter. The building or rebuilding of these structures was a common act of civic piety in the two centuries preceding 1640. At Shaftesbury the butter cross was built about 1570, by Edmund Bower the mayor, "for all those who sold butter, cheese, eggs, poultry, or the like to stand or sit dry in during the market."[2] At Canterbury the old Poultry Cross was built by John Coppin of Whitstable and William Bigg of Canterbury in 1446, and the new Cross by John Somner, brother of the antiquary, "at the expense of upwards of £400," two centuries later. In the same town there was also a 'Bull Stake' erected for the baiting and chasing of bulls, "used by an ancient order and custom of the city by the city butchers before their killing, not for pleasure, but to make them proper meat and fit to be eaten."[3]

The principal official building was the market house, variously styled market hall, booth hall, toll booth, town house, town hall, guildhall, or courthouse. It was generally built in the open market place, often with a row of shops to one end; and it gave rise to a common topographical feature of modern town centres namely a row of buildings on an island site, with a narrow lane to one side and a wide

---

[1] J. C. Cox, ed., *The Records of the Borough of Northampton*, 1898, II, p. 186 (most of these Northampton street-names still survive); Tupling, 'Lancashire Markets in the Sixteenth and Seventeenth Centuries', pp. 12–14; cf. pp. 15–16, 19. For a valuable account of the markets of York, see H. Richardson, *Medieval Fairs and Markets of York*, St Anthony's Hall Publications, No. 20, 1961, pp. 21 *sqq.*

[2] E 134, 5 James I, H 22; E 134, 9 James I, M 31.

[3] Hasted, *op. cit.*, XI, p. 115n. The new 'cross' comprised a "handsome market place, with several rooms over it for public use, part of which was used as a repository for corn, against a time of dearth..." The Crediton market accounts refer to a "bull collar."—Devon RO, 252 B, APF, Bdle 75, No. 13. The custom seems to have been usual.

street on the other. The precise functions of the market house varied from place to place. Some were little more than covered crosses, or open shelters supported on rows of pillars, as at Oakham; many included a hall or court room built above, with a weigh house, toll chamber, and gaol or cell below.[1]

In all parts of the country many market houses were rebuilt under the Tudors and Stuarts. The market house at Rothwell and the pillared guildhall of Much Wenlock both date from 1577. The guildhall at Sandwich is also Elizabethan. At Liverpool the Common Hall was the gift of John Crosse, a London vicar, who in 1515 bequeathed to his native town his "new [house] called our Lady house to keep their courts and such business as they shall think most expedient."[2] At Barking the Town House was rebuilt early in Queen Elizabeth's reign, the structure itself being erected by the Crown, while the inhabitants spent £100 in levelling the site and putting up sixteen shops "and certain sheds" for the benefit of the market. At Clare, in Suffolk, the timber, tiles, and workmanship for the new market house were supplied by Roger Barrow, a local grocer, while the townsmen agreed to raise a fund amongst themselves to repay him.[3] At Newtown, in Montgomeryshire, the town hall was built by Thomas Turner, under a lease of the market tolls from the corporation; it comprised "a courthouse where the bailiffs keep their courts and the judges keep their great assizes" for the county, with "two or three fair chambers in the lower end thereof," "two strong rooms to keep prisoners," and an open chamber beneath "for market folks to sell their grain of corn, meal, malt, and such like…" At Shaftesbury three market halls appear to have been built in this period: the Old Guildhall, where the mayor's court was held every Saturday afternoon; the new "market house or guildhall near adjoining unto St Peter's Church there, wherein the said balances and weights do stand;" and "a fair building made with timber and covered with lead over the said cornmarket, and a bell to ring when the said market shall begin…"[4]

The statutory obligation to provide a 'common beam', with its accompanying weights and measures, was one of the principal reasons for erecting market halls. Goods sold in the open market were usually

[1] In large towns the legal and municipal functions were carried on in a separate building.

[2] Tupling, 'Lancashire Markets in the Sixteenth and Seventeenth Centuries,' p. 4. Crosse's house served till 1675, when a new building was erected at the High Cross.

[3] E 178, 843; C 2, Eliz., B 5, 58. The Clare market house was put up in 1592 to shelter market folk "from the rain, which might and did fall to the great loss and spoil" of their corn.

[4] E 134, 12 James I, E 16; E 134, 12 James I, T 2; E 134, 5 James I, H 22; E 134, 18 James I, E 1.

supposed to be weighed by the common balances, and, as trade increased, the right to levy toll at the beam often became a valuable source of revenue. At Crediton "cries [were] usually made in the said market to call such as had anything which ought to be weighed at the said common beam, to bring it away to the beam. And if any were found to weigh any commodities away from the common beam... such commodities were threatened or declared to be forfeited, half to the king, and half to the lord of the market." In the great summer wool market at Doncaster the mayor appointed yearly four sufficient men, with weights and scales, to levy toll of $\frac{1}{2}$d. per stone from the wool sellers, allowing large merchants to compound at 6d. per pack of 15 or 16 stone, "in regard they were good customers to the said market."[1]

In practice there were many loopholes in these urban regulations. At Doncaster in Charles I's reign the freemen of Lincoln claimed to be toll-free by virtue of their charter, and many merchants refused to pay the dues demanded, alleging "deceit and cozenage" on the part of local officials. In other towns private beams were set up. At Crediton one Shilston let out one of his rooms with a beam to a woolman from Chudleigh; another Chudleigh woolman set up a beam in Clement Piddesley's house; and Mistress Katherine Berry had a beam "openly set up in her hall." Altogether not a "half part" of the wool sold in Crediton market was lawfully weighed; the town was so full of a "great multitude of weavers" that every market day great quantities of wool and yarn were carried "away out of the market and weigh[ed] ...at their own or other private houses."[2] In the neighbouring wool market of Ashburton, two rival beams were set up, and a heated dispute arose between two local climants to the profits, Thomas Prideaux and William Abarrow. For "divers market days together" Thomas Prideaux "did walk up and down the said market...with a sword by his side, and did threaten the said William Abarrow...that his father...would spend a thousand pounds but that he would have and keep the profits...and...did also unhang the weights set up by the said William Abarrow to weigh wool and yarn, and did also threaten the market people there coming to sell their wares, that if they did not weigh their wool and yarn at our weights they should pay for it," and "did also overthrow the stalls and standings of others and terrify them much..."[3]

In addition to crosses and halls, market towns also possessed shops and shambles. The two terms were not sharply distinguished, but the

---

[1] E 134, 9 James I, M 31; E 134, 4 Car. I, E 36; E 134, 17 Car. I, M 8.

[2] E 134, 4 Car. I, E 36. Private beams were legitimate in shops. The Crediton weigh-house had been enlarged in 1615, but was evidently still too small.

[3] E 178, 5236.

latter were generally small premises erected for the sale of fish and flesh by the town and let out to townsmen or foreigners on market days only. Frequently, as at Crediton, the shambles stood in the centre of the market place adjoining the market house; the borough court, as at Tavistock, was sometimes called the "Shammel-Moot".[1] In some places shambles still survive, and at Sevenoaks butchers' shops are still gathered near them.

Shops were more permanent structures than shambles, generally burgage tenements, built with pentices before them, with signposts set up in their pavement, and opened for sale to the public each day.[2] Some places, like Westerham, had their row of mercers' and grocers' shops many years before they acquired the grant of a market; there were also shops in villages like Leeds, in Kent, where no market grant seems to have been sought. In thriving towns, like Blandford and Chichester, competition for shop sites was keen, and many new shops were built in this period. At Shaftesbury in James I's reign "shops and houses," had recently been erected, it seems, called "Chapman's Standings." At Crediton there was a street of new shops, some let out at rents of 40s. and 56s. a year.[3] Such buildings were sometimes of considerable size. The two shops of Edward Baylie, a butcher at Frome Selwood in Somerset, consisted of "17 felde of building;" the three of Robert Acourt, another butcher, of "25 felds;" that of Anthony Treheren, a smith, was smaller, comprising only "6 felds." Like other shops in the town, they were of "timber and stone building, and...covered with stone tile..."[4] Sometimes shop tenants were expected to undertake their own "glazing [of windows], making of partitions, setting up of shelves, lining the walls with boards, [and] hanging up of a cupboard" for their "more convenient occupying of the said rooms and premises ..." Ranged as they were round the market place, and often rented by the same family for several generations, such buildings provided an element of continuity in the market town which would otherwise have been lacking.[5]

[1] E 134, 4 Car. I, E 36; Tavistock deed of 1315 cited in W. G. Hoskins and H. P. R. Finberg, *Devonshire Studies*, 1952, p. 181.
[2] 'Signposts' are referred to at Brackley, Crediton, etc.—Northants RO, Elles-mere MSS, 2345/77; E 134, 4 Car. I, E 36. A sign-rent was often payable to the lord or corporation, in addition to shop rent.
[3] C 2, James I, F 9, 33; Req. 2, 114, 17; Req. 2, 55, 64; E 134, 18 James I, E 1; E 134, 4 Car. I, E 36. Many village 'shops' were workshops rather than trading centres.
[4] E 178, 1934. The width of a 'feld' is not stated, but an inn of "21 feld" is des-cribed as a "house of great room."
[5] C 2, James I, P 25, 4. Treheren's shop at Frome was held by a succession of smiths who drew their custom from the market folk, "for that the same was the nearest smith house" to the market place. A shop at West Malling was held by at least three generations of the Tresse family.—E 134, 15 Car. I, E 13.

The wooden pentices formerly attached to shop fronts have disappeared from the modern country town. Their position is still visible in the pavement of a number of market places, and the cloth 'tilts' or awnings occasionally employed were a direct ancestor of the modern shop blind. In the sixteenth century, when business was still carried on in open premises, the wooden pentice was a necessity of trade. It extended several feet into the street, as far as the 'eavesdropping'; the work of shoemakers or tailors was carried on beneath it, under the public eye, the master sitting in the centre of a trestle table, with his apprentices at either end.[1] The right to erect 'standings' with 'balks' or counters beneath the pentice and to let them out to country folk on market days was sometimes a valuable privilege of burgage tenure. In most towns burgage tenants also claimed the right to erect stalls or sheep pens in front of their shops, as far as the channel in the centre of the street. At Ashburton, those who held "ancient burgages near the places where the said market is kept" claimed this right in virtue of their responsibility for "reparations of the pavements afore their several houses..." At Shaftesbury, freeholders who were responsible to repair the "pavements and pitchings right before their houses and lands unto the channel" claimed the right "to take the profits of the pickage and standings set before their said houses and lands on fair and market days..." At West Malling, where one side of the High Street lay in the bishop of Rochester's liberty and the other in the manor or lordship of Malling, stalls were erected by shopkeepers on either side of the "posts or dowls" set up in the centre of the street to mark the manorial boundary.[2] In corporate towns, the erection of stalls and pens was usually the responsibility of municipal authorities. At King's Lynn, the profit of the market reaped by the corporation must have been considerable, for the butchers alone rented thirty stalls in the Tuesday market from the corporation.[3]

No summary can do justice to the infinite variety of market towns. Each had its own customs and peculiarities, familiar to those who frequented it, a source of curiosity and wonder to strangers. One instance of an unusual market was the annual "great mart" held at Howden in Yorkshire. Each year the old manor house of the bishop

[1] E 134, 4 and 5 Car. I, H 1.

[2] E 178, 5236; E 134, 18 James I, E 1; E 134, 12 Car. I, E 26; E 134, 15 Car. I, E 13. For this right the Malling shopkeepers paid a rent called "street gable." The erection of market stalls back to back in the middle of the street, as at Malling, probably explains the broad high streets of many country towns. In some towns, as at Rayleigh, stalls descended from father to son and were bought and sold like other forms of real property.—Req. 2, 303, 74.

[3] E 134, 24 Car. I, M 7. According to E 178, 6104 one fourth of the profits were claimed by private individuals.

of Durham was let out as warehouses to merchants from London and the West Riding; stalls were erected in the courtyard and against the kitchen walls; the stables were converted into shops; and goods were transported by ferry boats from the river Ouse to the Briggate.[1]

4. Regulation of market towns by local authorities

Everywhere marketing was subject to more or less strict regulation. Each town had its own company of market officers, varying in number from the four or five of Newtown or Ashton-under-Lyne to the forty or fifty of Manchester or King's Lynn. Sometimes they were elected annually by the borough or manorial court; sometimes appointed for a term of years; not infrequently the office descended *de facto* from husband to widow or father to son. Virtually every town had its toll-gatherers, sweepers, and bellmen, and many appointed a couple of 'market lookers' for the general inspection of the market. Aleconners and bread-testers enforced regulations and statutes governing the price and quality of bread and beer; leather searchers carried a hammer with a die or seal in its head and stamped skins and hides; 'aulnagers' performed similar functions for various types of cloth; and 'appraisers' were appointed to settle the value of goods in event of dispute. In large market towns there might be half-a-dozen of these officials. In Manchester there were six or seven corn-lookers, four fish-and-flesh-lookers, and ten whitemeat-lookers; in Liverpool there was a host of paid employees, ranging from the stewards of the Common Hall and the keeper of the Common Warehouse to the setters of booths and fleshboards.[2]

Under the auspices of these officers the market was closely controlled in the interests of the consumer or the lord of the market. Market days were usually fixed in the original charter; but market hours were settled by the town, and as a rule no one was allowed to sell his corn till the country folk had arrived from distant villages and the toll-gatherer had made his round of the cornsellers, dipping his toll-dish into the mouth of each man's sack. The provision and testing of measures, balances, and weights; the control and licensing of badgers, broggers, corn-carriers, maltsters, engrossers, forestallers, and other traders; the fixing of prices of bread, malt, meal, and corn; the preven-

[1] Durham, Prior's Kitchen, Ch. Com. 23, 384.
[2] The above account is based principally on Tupling, 'Lancashire Markets in the Sixteenth and Seventeenth Centuries', pp. 20–25, supplemented by information in Exchequer Special Commissions and Depositions relating to Newtown, Gainsborough, St Ives, St Neots, and Reading.

tion of cozenage and civil disturbance: these and other activities were among the responsibilities of market authorities.[1]

Their most onerous task was the levying of tolls and the entering of receipts and expenditure therefrom in toll-books kept in the market hall or tollbooth. The fiscal value and utility of these dues varied greatly. No tolls were payable in the corn markets of Shaftesbury, Huntingdon, or St Ives. At Hertford in 1536–7 they amounted to no more than 18s. 8d. At Gainsborough no official corn toll was levied, but the bellman took "some small quantity of corn to his own use... and in consideration thereof he kept clean the streets," for which he was also given "twenty shillings in the year...and some old coat" by the lord of the market. At Romford the corn toll amounted to one pint in every four bushels, or 6d. a cartload, and the beast toll to 2d. a head; the butchers paid 6d. for every stall, or 12d. if "twice filled," and other tradesmen 3d., 2d., 1d., "or what could be gotten of them." At Newark the tolls appear to have been sufficiently valuable to farm out to five or six different people: the passage toll and "week toll" to Richard Stacye; the beast-market toll and swine drift to Nicholas Hopton; the horsemarket toll to an inhabitant of Balderton; the corn toll to the man who "dresseth...the market place;" and the toll for "pickage and stallage" to the earl of Rutland and Mr Anthony Foster. Generally, dues levied on townsmen were lower than those paid by strangers, perhaps half or less. Quite frequently local people refused to pay toll. An angry scene occurred at Denbigh in 1537, when the Welsh countrymen came in arms on market day and proclaimed at the cross "that Welshmen were as free as Englishmen and that they should pay no stallage there."[2]

The proceeds from tolls, when not farmed out to private people, were generally devoted to some charitable or civic purpose. At Crediton they were employed in paying the rent of the market, mending the standings of butchers and shoemakers, cleansing the town wells, providing a ladder and fire-buckets, improving the pavements and causeways, enlarging the weighing house, repairing the almshouses and market clock, relieving the sick, and purchasing corn for the poor, "a shroud for poor Rose," and bread, wine, beer, and cheese, spent "at the passing of this account."[3] This annual auditing of the toll-

[1] For a detailed account of market regulation in one county cf. G. H. Tupling, 'Lancashire Markets in the Sixteenth and Seventeenth Centuries', *Lancs. and Ches. Antiq. Soc.*, LVIII, 1947, pp. 26–34, LIX, pp. 1–33.

[2] E 134, 9 James I, M 19; Herts. RO, Hatfield Deposit, Bailiff's Account of Hertford Vill; E 134, 24 Car. I, E 9; E 134, 42 and 43 Eliz., M 3; LP, XII, i, p. 543. At King's Lynn, about 1648, tolls were apparently worth at least £130 p.a.

[3] Devon RO, 252 B, APF, Bdle 75, No. 13. Cf. Req. 2, 77, 77, E 134, 18 James I, E1, Devon RO, 257 M/T.5, lease of 30 Jan. 1629, and C2, James I, G2, 19, for Dulverton, Shaftesbury, Tiverton, and Burton upon Trent.

gatherers' accounts was often a local ceremony of some importance. At Dover it was heralded by blowing the borough horn through the streets of the town; at Stow-on-the-Wold the town bailiffs came to the courthouse "attired in their gowns, and round Leominster caps, with other velvet night caps under them, and their sergeants...before them with maces and sergeant's staves..."[1]

Some glimpse of market regulation may be gleaned from the Courts' Books of the borough of Ipswich. By regulations passed in the reigns of Elizabeth and James I, no one in Ipswich was permitted to have a stall upon the Cornhill "but only such as shall be free of this town, and every of them shall pay for his standing there 4d. for every market day, to be paid to the chamberlains..." None of the "butchers of this town or country" were to sell "in any other place but in the butchers' stalls of this town," on pain of forfeiting their licence for one year. No one was to bring any wheeled vehicles into the market except "carts and tumbrils unshod." No one was allowed to open his shop doors or windows upon the [Sabbath day, and the carriers of the town who had caused "great offence [to] Almighty God" and brought "infamy and slander" on the town by travelling on Sunday were ordered to discontinue their profanity. Elaborate regulations were passed regarding the selling of tallow, hides, and cloth, the licensing of foreigners who wished to rent stalls in the market, the charges of carriers and wagoners, and the purchase of corn for the poor.[2] Similar restrictions could be traced in the records of many another town: of Manchester, Leicester, Whitchurch, Beverley, Royston, or Northampton, for instance.[3] When we come to study private marketing, however, we shall find that this kind of restriction was not altogether unnecessary.

5. *The community of the market town*

The market town was not simply a centre of trade; it was the focus of the rural life around it. Its square and taverns provided the meeting place for yeomen and husbandmen not only to buy and sell, but to hear the news, listen to sermons, criticize the government, or organize insurrection.[4] Its carpenters, wheelwrights, ploughwrights, and other

[1] LP IV, p. 3113; E 134, 7 James I, E 18.
[2] Ipswich and East Suffolk RO, Ipswich General Courts' Books, 1582–1608 and 1609–43 *passim;* HMC, *Reports,* IX, i, pp. 254, 256; cf. E 134, 43 Eliz., H 18.
[3] At Royston in 1633 more than 100 traders were fined at the manor court "for overcharging."—Herts. RO, No. 66,344, Royston Manor Court Book. For Northampton cf. J. C. Cox, *op. cit.,* II, pp. 278, 280–4, 290, 293 *et psssim;* for Whitchurch, Salop RO, Bridgewater Collection, No. 212.
[4] Henry VIII's activities were frankly discussed in Fakenham market place in 1534,

craftsmen existed principally to minister to the needs of its dependent villages. Its society was closely intertwined with that of the countryside and its prejudices and convictions governed those of the farmers who bought and sold in its streets. Its conservatism was upheld and strengthened by the hard core of aldermanic families who by the end of the period had come to dominate the society of most country towns. At Ipswich, Daundys, Sparrows, and Bloyses governed the borough from the early sixteenth century till the end of the seventeenth. In Northampton a number of shops remained in the same ownership for seventy or eighty years, and families like the Maynards, Mackerneses, Scrivens, and Lyons dominated the town for upwards of a century. At Petworth there was a succession of Libards as millers, Barnards as chandlers, Lucases as locksmiths, Bowyers as shoemakers, and Haslens as barber-surgeons. In Leicester three freemen out of four followed in their father's footsteps; and even in the smallest towns, like Westerham and West Malling, family businesses sometimes descended from father to son for three or four generations.[1] Many town churches still contain memorials to half-a-dozen local trading dynasties of this kind, whose history would repay detailed investigation. Although the drift of wealth back into the countryside precluded the development of rigid burghal hierarchies like those of continental cities, the web of urban society was remarkably close-knit and enduring.

The wealth of urban tradesmen varied much with the size and situation of the town.[2] In the small market towns of East Anglia, like Diss and Bungay, the tradesman's property was often worth no more than £30 or £40. In the middle-sized towns of Hertfordshire, such as St Albans, many merchants possessed goods worth £80 or £90, and some more than £600. In Northampton, a town of three or four thousand people in this period, the richest mercers and innkeepers left over £1,000. In Newcastle, one of the principal ports of the country, a number of grazing butchers possessed personal property valued at

where "honest men...marvelled much what the king meant by polling and pilling the realm...more than he did in times past, and thought he intended to make a great hand by money, and then to avoid the realm and let the people shift as they could."—LP VIII, p. 46. Public sermons were preached on market days in many places, such as Cranbrook, for "the amendment of men's manners..."—Cf. *Thomas Wotton's Letter-Book, 1574–1586*, ed. G. Eland, 1960, pp. 24–5.

[1] Nathaniel Bacon, *Annalls of Ipswiche*, 1884, *passim;* Northants. RO, Northampton wills and probate inventories; G. H. Kenyon, 'Petworth Town and Trades, 1610–1760: Part I', *Sussex Arch. Colls.*, XCVI, 1958, pp. 64–6; W. G. Hoskins, 'An Elizabethan Provincial Town: Leicester', in *Studies in Social History: a tribute to G. M. Trevelyan*, ed. J. H. Plumb, 1955, p. 60; cf. D. Charman, 'Wealth and Trade in Leicester in the early Sixteenth Century', *Leics. Arch. Soc.*, XXV, 1949, pp. 69 *sqq.*

[2] The following paragraph is based on tradesmen's probate inventories for thirty-three towns situated mainly in Hertfordshire, East Anglia, and the north.

over £2,000, and merchant-venturers more than £3,000. Since most towns still retained their open fields and commons, much of this wealth was invested in agricultural goods. In many places, such as Leicester, leading tradesmen were often graziers or farmers; and in large ports like Ipswich and Newcastle, agrarian wealth still accounted for half the property of a number of burgesses. In few towns was there as yet a complete divorce between the trading community and the land, although by the end of the seventeenth century that breach was becoming much clearer in a county town such as Northampton.

In urban communities as much as in the countryside, everything was still carefully made by craftsmen. Essentially it was still a hand-made world, and the trading classes often enjoyed a substantial measure of comfort. Thomas Webster, a tanner of St Albans who died in 1612, left domestic goods worth £175 out of a total estate of £600. His house contained no fewer than seventeen rooms. The hall and parlour were furnished with carpets, cushions, and chairs. In the kitchen hung a fine array of dripping pans, frying pans, pothooks, spits, and bellows; in the offices and outhouses stood the powdering troughs, boulting hutches, churns, hogsheads, stills, and other paraphernalia of a large farming-tradesman. His pewterware was valued at £5 and his silver at £2. His wife's store of linen, perhaps spun on the spinning wheel in the parlour, comprised 20 pillowberes, 30 pairs of sheets, 15 table-cloths, and 42 napkins; it was worth nearly £20. Both the house and goods of Thomas Webster bear witness to the solid prosperity of an urban tradesman, and to a kind of wealth not easily spent or quickly come by, but the fruit of a lifetime of patient toil. For the society of the Stuart market town was no mushroom growth; it was embedded in traditional ways of life of exceptional strength and obstinacy. Those ways of life have now vanished, but they surviced every wind of fortune, with only minor changes, until the time of George Eliot's *Middlemarch*.

B. THE OPEN MARKET

1. *Products and specialities of market towns*

There can be little doubt that in the sixteenth century most towns still served a purely local area and specialized in marketing no particular type of commodity. Nevertheless, a tendency for the more important towns to market certain kinds of product had inevitably gone handin hand with regional specialization in agriculture. By the end of the period, or a little after, the broad pattern of specialization becomes clear. About two English towns in five and one Welsh town in four tended to specialize in the marketing of either corn, cattle, horses, sheep, cheese and butter, poultry and fish, wool, yarn, cloth, or some other product. For the country as a whole, the available sources are not sufficiently detailed to admit of very precise differentiation; local studies would doubtless reveal more minute specialization, in some towns, in marketing different types of grain and cattle.[1] Neither was their a sharp distinction between all corn markets and all cattle markets; nor were their specialities mutually exclusive. To some extent specialization varied with the time of year, and many markets specialized in the sale of more than one kind of product. An important city, such as Exeter, might be equally noted as a trading centre for cattle, corn, and wool. The town of Bedford, situated near diverse agrarian regions, was both the chief cattle market and the chief corn market of its area, the former held on the south side of the river on Tuesday, the latter on the north side on Saturday.[2] Only a general outline of the subject, however, can be given here. In this outline six different regions of the country are distinguished, each with its peculiar features: north, south, east, west, Midlands, and Wales.

The pattern of specialization emerges most distinctly in the east of England.[3] In this area seventy-seven out of a total of nearly 200 market towns showed a tendency to specialize in one or more products. Four were primarily devoted to the sale of cheese and butter, nine to poultry, ten to fish, five to swine, five to sheep, ten to cattle, thirteen to malt, and as many as forty-five to corn. The cattle markets were mainly situated on the Midland fringe of the area in Bedfordshire, or near the fenland pastures of East Anglia; the fowl and fish markets near the fens, or in other wildfowl areas, or on the sea-coast. The principal corn markets were almost uniformly sited near navigable rivers. Here, as elsewhere, there were many purely local corn markets, but few English towns were likely to develop into major grain entrepôts,

[1] Best's farming book, for instance, shows that Bridlington was noted for oats, Malton for wheat and maslin, Pocklington for barley.—Henry Best, *Rural Economy in Yorkshire in 1641...*, Surtees Society, XXXIII, 1857, pp. 100-1.

[2] Richard Blome, *Britannia*, 1673, p. 44. The following generalized account is based on numerous cases in Exchequer Special Commissions and Depositions, and many references in State Papers Domestic and local histories. I have also relied heavily on Leland, and on Richard Blome, though I have checked the latter's information, whenever possible, from other sources, and I believe his facts to represent, broadly speaking, developments apparent by 1640. For a list of the specialities of market towns see Appendix, Table I. There is urgent need for local monographs on market specialization; they would probably reveal many specialities I have not discovered and modify or amplify the conclusions of the following paragraphs.

[3] The area so designated here includes Middlesex, Suffolk, Norfolk, Hertfordshire, Buckinghamshire, Cambridgeshire, Bedfordshire, Oxfordshire, Huntingdonshire, Lincolnshire, most of Nottinghamshire, part of west Essex, and a few Thamesside markets in Surrey and Berks.

unless they were situated on the sea-coast or near a navigable stream.[1] And no other region of England was so plenteously served by waterways as the eastern counties. Nottinghamshire and Lincolnshire were watered by the Witham, Trent, and Foss Dyke; Norfolk, Cambridge, Bedford, Huntingdon, and West Suffolk by the Wensum, Welland, Nene, Cam, and Great and Little Ouse; Hertfordshire by the river Lea; and Buckinghamshire, Middlesex, and Essex by the Thames. Of the many great corn markets of the area, Gainsborough was sited on the river Trent, Peterborough on the Nene, Bedford, St Neots, and King's Lynn on the Ouse; and Oxford, Abingdon, Wallingford, Reading, Kingston, and Brentford on the Thames.

The Midland counties provide a marked contrast with the east.[2] Here the predominant speciality was not corn and malt, but livestock. Out of about eighty markets where specialization is descernible, of a total of over 160 in the area, twenty-nine concentrated on cattle, fourteen on sheep, at least six on horses, and seven on swine. A further five towns held markets for leather products, including Northampton for shoes, Burford for saddles, and Congleton for "purses and points." Among the numerous cattle markets of the Midlands were Kington in Herefordshire; Banbury, Bicester, and Thame in Oxfordshire; Shrewsbury, Oswestry, Whitchurch, Ludlow, Bridgnorth, Wem, and Newport in Shropshire; Newcastle, Leek, Uttoxeter, Wolverhampton, and Tamworth in Staffordshire; and Coventry, Birmingham, and Southam in Warwickshire. A number of these towns also held large sheep markets; while others were held at Hereford, Leominster, Loughborough, Market Harborough, Daventry, Kettering, and Stow-on-the-Wold. Among the principal horsemarkets of the area were Banbury, Daventry, Hinckley, Northampton, and Market Harborough; among the chief cloth markets Shrewsbury and Oswestry.[3]

[1] In Kent, for instance, the chief corn-towns were Faversham, Maidstone, and Sandwich; in Sussex corn for the royal household was furnished at Chichester, Arundel, Shoreham, and Newhaven. Allegra Woodworth, 'Purveyance for the Royal Household in the Reign of Queen Elizabeth', American Philosophical Society, NS, XXXV, 1946, p. 44. Leicestershire, by contrast, could not develop as a corn county, for it was "far remote from any means of exportation of corn..."—SP 14, 112, 91. For river navigation see T. S. Willan, River Navigation in England, 1600–1750, 1936, especially pp. 125 sqq. and 136–8; cf. also R. B. Westerfield, Middlemen in English Business, 1915, pp. 150, 169–70.

[2] 'The Midlands' here comprises Warwickshire, Worcestershire, Northamptonshire, Rutland, Leicestershire, Staffordshire, Shropshire, Derbyshire, Cheshire, Herefordshire, Monmouthshire, part of Nottinghamshire, Gloucestershire (north of the Stroud Water), and Oxfordshire (except Oxford and Henley).

[3] For Shrewsbury and Oswestry, see T. C. Mendenhall, The Shrewsbury Drapers and the Welsh Wool Trade..., 1953.

In the west of England the pattern was again different. Here there were about fifty-five specialized markets, or rather more, out of a total of some 170.[1] Of these, twenty-four were devoted primarily to the sale of cattle; five to cheese and butter (including Yeovil, Chipping Sodbury, and Wincanton); and three to leather or gloves (including Ilminster and Grampound). The principal specialities of west country markets, however, were wool, yarn, and cloth. According to Hooker, virtually every town in Devon was a market for kerseys, wool, or yarn.[2] One such town was Crediton, where there dwelt "a great multitude of weavers" who every market day dealt "very much in buying and selling of wool." Another was Norton St Philip, where for three weeks before SS Philip and James's day "the great house or inn called the George" was converted into an emporium for the use of Somerset clothmen, and all the "tables and household stuff" were "displaced...out of the hall, kitchen, two parlours, cellars and chambers" to receive their woollen and linen packs and fardels. Among the many other wool markets of the area were Launceston in Cornwall, Ashburton in Devon, and Shaftesbury in Dorset.[3]

In both the west of England and the Midlands there was also a goodly number of grain markets: seventeen in the former area and twenty in the latter. Most of these corn marts were of merely local importance, but a few were remarkably lively centres. The two markets of Bruton and Wincanton in east Somerset supplied corn to nearly seven thousand people in the surrounding clothing villages; most of it, apparently, imported from other districts. The corn market at Derby served a similar function for the miners and quarrymen of Derbyshire, and was furnished with corn principally by way of the river Trent.[4] At Shaftesbury as many as twenty cartloads of corn were brought in for sale, each market day, by farmers from Dorset and Wiltshire, "besides divers other horseloads;" while it is clear that only the restrictions of the site prevented further expansion.[5]

[1] 'The West' here comprises Dorset, Devon, Cornwall, Somerset, Whiltshire, and Gloucestershire south of the Stroud Water.

[2] W. J. Blake, 'Hooker's Synopsis Chorographical of Devonshire', *Devonshire Assoc.*, XLVII, 1915, p. 346. The transcript has "voirne", but no doubt "yarn" is intended. Hooker probably exaggerated, but local searches would doubtless reveal many wool and cloth markets in the West.

[3] E 134, 4 Car. I, E 36; E 134, 37-8 Eliz., M 15; E 178, 5236; E 134, 20 James I, E 10; E 134, 5 James I, H 22. For the great Exeter serge market, at a rather later date, cf. W. G. Hoskins, *Industry, Trade, and People in Exeter, 1688-1800*, 1935, pp. 41-3.

[4] SP 16, 187, 51; cf. SP 14, 113, 17 and 90.

[5] The corn market was constricted by the cattle market, likewise expanding: one large corn farmer from Bridmore (Wilts.), who had sold in Shaftesbury for forty years, threatened to "bring no more corn into the said market" unless "such straitening of the corn market place be reformed..."—E 134, 18 James I, E 1.

In the north of England over half the 124 market towns and villages of the area showed a tendency towards specialization, a higher proportion than in any other region.[1] Of the twenty-six corn markets of the area, eleven were situated near the drier arable areas of the north-east, many of them close to navigable rivers; a further five were found in the manufacturing dales of the West Riding and distributed corn imported from Hull and York; while the remainder were probably of local importance only, among them being Penrith, Ulverston, Wooler, and Keswick.[2] More truly characteristic of the area were its seventeen major cattle markets, with which many north-country cattle fairs must also be reckoned. Equally significant were the nine or more markets devoted to wool or yarn, and the nine to cloth. The rising cloth marts of south Lancashire and the West Riding were by 1640 of considerable importance, and the great wool market at Doncaster was undoubtedly one of the largest in the kingdom, attended by purchasers from all parts of Yorkshire and the Midlands.[3]

Of the sixty market towns in Wales only nineteen are known to have specialized to any marked degree. Most Welsh towns were exceptionally small. In the mid-sixteenth century only Carmarthen had over two thousand inhabitants, and only five other towns more than one thousand, most of them situated either near the border or by the sea-coast.[4] Of the nineteen, twelve were devoted primarily to the sale of corn. Presteigne was the market town for the Maelienydd district of Radnorshire (the north-east corner of the county); Denbigh, where "the confluence to the market on Tuesday [was] exceeding great," for the vale of Clwyd. Brecon, Builth, and Tenby were other corn markets of some consequence.[5] All these towns were situated in the drier areas near the border or the southern sea-board. Five Welsh markets also specialized in the disposal of livestock, to which must be added numerous annual fairs; for in Wales, as in the north of England, cattle and sheep were more usually sold by private contract or at fairs than in the weekly markets.

[1] The region comprises Lancashire, Yorkshire, Durham, Westmorland, Cumberland, and Northumberland.

[2] Very large quantities of grain were dispensed from Hull and York. The two towns were jealous rivals in this trade: Hull was said to have purchased 30,000 quarters of corn in 1622 (?) from "strangers" and to have resold it to "country chapmen... not suffering the marchants of York to buy any part thereof..." SP 14, 138, 120.

[3] E 134, 17 Car. I, M 8; E 134, 18 Car. I, E 9.

[4] L .Owen, 'The population of Wales in the Sixteenth and Seventeenth Centuries', *Hon. Soc. Cymmrodorion*, 1959, pp. 107–12. For this reference and other information regarding Wales I am indeibted to Mr Frank Emery.

[5] *The Itinerary in Wales of John Leland...1536–1539*, ed. Lucy Toulmin Smith, 1906, pp. 10, 41, 97. For further information on Welsh markets, see Chapter   , *supra*.

In the south of England only one market town in four tended to specialize.[1] There were a few grain markets in Surrey and Berkshire, such as Dorking and Newbury, and in the rich cornlands of north-east Kent. There was also a handful of important sheep and cattle markets in Hampshire, Sussex, Kent, and the Berkshire Downs; together with three or four markets for poultry and wildfowl in Essex, Surrey, and Sussex. In an area accessible to the metropolis and supposedly progressive, the comparative absence of specialization may seem surprising. In part it may be due to a less specialized economy; in part, perhaps (though this is doubtful) to a tendency to deal privately rather than in the open market; and in part to certain *lacunae* in the sources. It was also affected by the absence of navigable rivers, the notorious state of the roads, the presence of extensive forests and heathlands, and a plethora of exceptionally tiny market towns, such as Smarden, Elham, Ditchling, Tarring, Havant, and Kingsclere. The situation in southern England as a whole, however, is a salutary reminder that, even within the orbit of the metropolis, commercial penetration of agriculture was limited to pockets or *caches* of farmland in a countryside still largely given over to peasant husbandry. As Mr Kenyon found at Petworth and Mr Chaltlin at Tonbridge, the market town of the south were surprisingly self-centred and self-sufficient places.[2] It is difficult to avoid the conclusion that, away from the sea-coast, many of them were still largely asleep.

In summary, it appears that out of a total of some 800 market towns in England and Wales, rather more than three hundred tended to specialize in the marketing of some particular product. Of these eight hundred, 134 were devoted principally to corn, twenty-six to malt, and six or more to fruit; ninety-two to cattle, thirty-two to sheep, thirteen to horses, and fourteen to swine; thirty or more to fish, seventeen to wildfowl and poultry, and twelve to cheese and butter. There were probably well over thirty wool and yarn markets, and twenty-seven or more cloth markets; eleven markets for leather or leather products, eight for linen, and at least four for hemp.[3] Scattered about the country were a number of highly specialized markets, such

---

[1] The region comprises Kent, Sussex, Hampshire, most of Essex, and Berkshire and Surrey excluding Thames-side markets. Judged by its marketing specialities, Essex seems to group more naturally with these counties than those of the East, though its economy was somewhat enigmatic.

[2] Cf. Kenyon, *op. cit.*, pp. 45, 94; C. W. Chalklin, 'A Seventeenth-century Market Town: Tonbridge', *Arch. Cant.*, LXXVI, 1961, p. 160. Mr Chalklin shows the intense poverty of most inland towns in Kent at this time, and suggests similar conditions obtained in Surrey and Hampshire.

[3] For further information on wool markets, see P. J. Bowden, *The Wool Trade in Tudor and Stuart England*, 1962, pp. 57 *sqq.*

as Bewdley for caps, Malton for farming implements, Langport for pecked eels, Evesham for stockings, and Wymondham in Norfolk for wooden spoons, taps, and handles. Of the corn markets, two out of five were situated in the east; of those for cattle, one third in the Midlands, a quarter in the west, and a fifth in the north country. The markets for sheep and horses were also mainly situated in the Midlands; those for swine in East Anglia and the Midlands; for butter and cheese in East Anglia and the west; for poultry in the east and the south; and for wool and cloth in the west, the north, and East Anglia.

How far this pattern of specialization in Caroline England obtained before, say, 1575, it is impossible to say with precision. The information given by Leland, though in general confirmatory, is patchy and incomplete. Short of a series of local monographs, there is no means of arriving at a generalized picture. But it is probable that it was clearly marked by the fourth quarter of the sixteenth century, and that some of its principal features were emerging by the 1530's. Certainly many of the corn markets of East Anglia had appeared on the map at least by Henry VIII's reign, and in all probability many of the cattle markets of the Midlands.

2. Market areas

The eight hundred or so market towns of England and Wales in the sixteenth and seventeenth centuries were distributed by no means evenly over the landscape. In Yorkshire there were at least fifty-four markets, in Devonshire forty-five, in Somerset thirty-nine, in Lincolnshire thirty-seven, in Gloucestershire thirty-four and in Kent thirty-three.[1] In Northumberland, on the other hand, there were only eight markets, and in several of the small Welsh counties no more than three or four. The regions served by market towns thus varied greatly in different parts of the country. The average market area in Wales extended to 100,000 acres, or 156 square miles; in England it averaged 45,000 acres, or 70 square miles, ranging from 20,000 acres for each of the twenty markets in Hertfordshire to the 161,000 acres of the eight markets in Northumberland.

On the whole, towns clustered most thickly in the south-western counties, in Hertfordshire and the neighbouring Midland areas, and in Suffolk and Kent. In these shires there was, generally speaking, at least one market town to every 35,000 acres of countryside. Next came Lancashire and the remaining Midland and East Anglian counties; followed by a group of shires containing extensive tracts of moorland, forest, heath or fen—Cambridge, Nottingham, Hampshire, Surrey, and the Welsh Marches—where the average market area exceeded

[1] See Appendix, Table 12, and map p.   .

Average market area

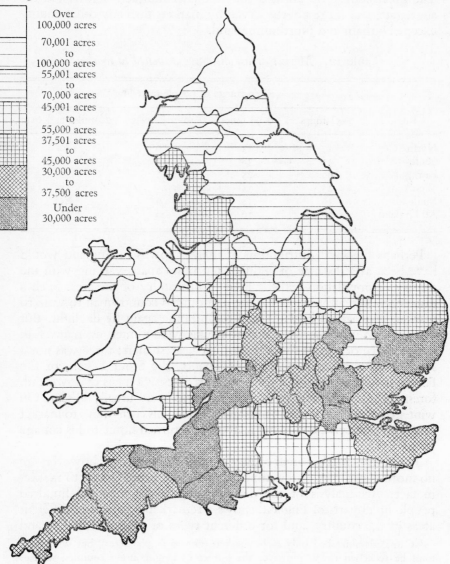

Fig. 10. Market areas in England and Wales, c. 1500–1680.

45,000 acres.[1] At the foot of the scale stood the six remaining Pennine counties, with one market, or less, to every 63,000 acres of countryside. The great county of York, despite its large number of towns in the aggregate, was more poorly served by markets than any other county except Durham and Northumberland.

Table 12. *Market areas: distances travelled to market*

Region	Percentage of people travelling			
	1–5½ miles	6–9½ miles	10–19½ miles	20 miles and over
North	17	13	20	50
South	31	38	31	0
East	60	25	13	2
West	25	35	25	15
Midlands	36	14	29	21
All England	39	26	20	15

Perhaps the ideal distribution of market towns in England would have been at a distance of eight or ten miles apart, varying with the density of population and the kind of husbandry of the area. Such a distance would afford time for the unmounted countryman to walk to market, transact his business, and reach home again by daylight. But even in a county like Kent, where towns were numerous, many folk lived twelve or fifteen miles from their nearest mart; three was not a single market town in the Isle of Thanet, the Stour Levels, or the Forest of Blean. Few shires were without extensive tracts of downland, forest, heath, or moor, from which towns were usually absent. On winter days many a yeoman must have driven his corn-wains to market long before sunrise, and many a labourer returned home to his cottage by starlight.

The *average* market areas of English and Welsh towns, however, are no more than a part of the story. How far did people travel to market in fact? An analysis of the distances travelled by several hundred people in all parts of England shows a remarkable variety in different areas of the country, and for different types of product.[2] In England

[1] Cambridgeshire had only eight markets (one to 69,000 acres), but with these must be reckoned towns just over the border of neighbouring counties, such as Royston and Newmarket.

[2] The following account is based principally on information in Exchequer Special Commissions and Depositions, State Papers Domestic, farming diaries, and private estate account books, printed and manuscript; it relates almost entirely to the period after 1560. For Wales the available sources are too scanty to bear much weight; the situation there probably resembled most closely that of the north.

and Wales as a whole the average distance travelled was seven miles, varying from under one mile to over one hundred.

The market area tended to be least extensive for corn markets. Much corn, it is true, was conveyed great distances by sea and river. In the north of England (for the most part an importing area) many thousands of quarters were sold annually at York and Hull to the chapmen of Yorkshire and Lincolnshire, and transported by way of the Aire, Don, Trent, and other rivers to the markets of the north Midlands and the woollen towns of the Pennines.[1] But elsewhere few people, always excepting merchants and badgers, travelled so far. In East Anglia not many buyers or sellers of corn went more than ten miles to their market, and most no more than five. At Spilsby in Lincolnshire corn was brought from the surrounding villages of Scremby (three miles to the north-east), Hundleby (one mile to the west), Toynton (two miles to the south), and Orby (six miles to the east); only two out of the twelve villages served by Spilsby lay more than six miles away. Even at High Wycombe, one of the principal corn markets of Buckinghamshire, most cornsellers travelled no more than seven miles to market.

At livestock markets the position was different. Cattle and sheep were more easily transportable than corn; and though most sales were still local, the average cattle-market area extended to a radius of eleven miles, while to the great sheep marts of the Midlands and the north people occasionally travelled forty, fifty, and even seventy miles. At Rotherham market, late in Queen Elizabeth's reign, one purchaser came from Carleton in Lincolnshire, forty miles to the south-east, and one seller from Ellerburn in the vale of Pickering, seventy miles to the north-east. At Newcastle-under-Lyme sheep were brought from Macclesfield and from Wales; and in Somerset they were conveyed across the Bristol Channel from Wales and sold at Minehead, Chard, and Taunton.

The market areas of wool, yarn, and cloth towns were sometimes very large. Their radius generally exceeded twenty miles and not infrequently forty. One of the greatest of these wool markets was Doncaster, to which buyers in Charles I's reign came from Gainsborough (21 miles away), Lincoln (40 miles), Warsop (25 miles), Pleasley (26 miles), Blankney (50 miles), and many other places in Yorkshire, Lincolnshire, Nottinghamshire, Derbyshire, Leicestershire, and Warwickshire.[2]

Regarded regionally, market areas were equally diverse. Villagers in the Midlands, the west of England, and especially the north often

---

[1] SP 14, 138, 120; cf. SP 14, 113, 17.
[2] E 134, 17 Car. I, M 8; E 134, 18 Car. I, E 9. See also Bowden, *op. cit.*, pp. 57–72.

travelled further afield in their weekly trading activities than in the east and south. In the sample here analysed more than half the north-countrymen attended markets upwards of twenty miles from their homes; half the inhabitants of the Midlands and two fifths of those in the west country travelled more than ten miles. In eastern England, by contrast, nearly two thirds of the population lived within six miles of their habitual market, and in the south of England the propor-tion was larger still. In part these differences are explained by the comparative fewness of north-country towns, separated as they often were by extensive moorlands; in part, perhaps, by the unavoidable vagaries of the sample. But only in part: they also reflect regional differences in agrarian specialization and in economic outlook. The broad market areas of the north arose from the region's concentration on cattle and wool; those of the Midlands from an emphasis on cattle and sheep; the comparatively narrow areas of East Anglia from its numerous corn markets; and the yet narrower ones of the south from its plethora of small towns and a certain lack of commercial push on the part of its inhabitants.

It must not be supposed, however, that market areas were sharply defined or mutually exclusive. Everywhere large towns trespassed on the territory of their neighbours, and nowhere was it unusual for villagers to frequent two or three different markets. When towns began to specialize in selling particular types of product, such tres-passing was inevitable. In east Devon the people of Broadhembury regularly marketed in Honiton, Ottery St Mary, and Exeter, and an inhabitant of Broadclyst in Exeter, Honiton, Ottery, and Cullompton. In Berkshire the townsmen of Hungerford sold their grain in the important corn market of Newbury; in Buckinghamshire those of Amersham and Wendover at High Wycombe; and in Oxfordshire those of Watlington at Reading. At Crediton the wool mart attracted buyers and sellers from the market towns of Chudleigh, Bow, and Exeter itself; at Doncaster from towns all over the Midlands and the North. In Lancashire the rising county town of Preston succeeded in stealing a good deal of the trade of Kirkham, Chorley, Walton-le-Dale, and Garstang.[1] In almost every county the same process is discernible. For economic *concentration* is one of the salient themes of inland trade in this period: everywhere agricultural traffic tended to be drawn away from the smaller markets, ports, and fairs, and centred in the larger provincial centres like Maidstone, Canterbury, Reading, Newcastle, or King's Lynn.

From the standpoint of many a commercially minded farmer,

[1] H. B. Rodgers, 'The Market Area of Preston in the Sixteenth and Seventeent h Centuries', *Geographical Studies*, III, i, 1956, pp. 49–55.

there was thus often not one market to be considered in disposing of his produce, but several. There might be little in the way of published treatises or trade directories to guide him in his selection; but a keen yeoman, such as Henry Best of Elsmwell, in Yorkshire, would be thoroughly versed in the marketing ways of his own county. Best knew well that the north-country shipmasters bought their corn at Bridlington and sold it at Newcastle; that a fine Tuesday would bring the Lincolnshire mealmen to the Wednesday market at Beverley (they crossed the Humber the previous night); that in summer time Malton was a better barley market than Beverley; that if you would catch the "moorfolk" from the Cleveland Hills, you must get there early; and that if the king was at Malton (as he was in 1641) the market was like to be "very quick." In all parts of the country, and among all classes of people (except the peerage and the poor) the same lively observant interest in agricultural markets was apparent. In Suffolk Sir Nathanial Barnardiston, the richest man in the county, might be seen every week in the market place of Haverhill or Clare. In Kent, families like the Oxindens and Twysdens were fully aware that Canterbury was a rising hop market, that Maidstone was the best fruit mart, and Ashford a flourishing centre of the cattle trade. In Lincoln-shire, John Hatcher of Careby was in the habit of selling his weathers at Stamford and his cows and oxen at Newark, while he bought his steers at Spilsby, his fish at Boston, his wine at Bourne, and his luxuries in London.[1] In Lancashire, the Shuttleworths of Gawthorpe Hall sold their beans and wheat at Preston and Ormskirk, their meal at Padiham, their horses at Wigan, their heifers at Blackburn, their sheep at Has-lingden, and their geldings in London.[2]

Nevertheless, for most people, the economic horizon was still bounded by the local market town. The great majority of agrarian debts and credits recorded in farmers' probate inventories relate to purely local transactions. Those of Richard Green of Little Wyreley in Staffordshire did not extend beyond Walsall, six miles to the south, and West Bromwich, five miles beyond; nor those of Richard Coveney of Elmsted in East Kent beyond the neighbouring villages of Monks' Horton, Wootton, and Boughton Aluph, or the market towns of Sandwich and Wye.[3] In Tudor and Stuart England a certain temerity was required to venture into unfamiliar territories, and the poorer

[1] Best, op. cit., pp. 100–1; Essex RO, B, 7.13, 38.1502, Clopton Diary, passim; Lincs. AO, Holywell MS, 97, 22, passim.

[2] John Harland, ed., The House and Farm Accounts of the Shuttleworths of Gawthorpe Hall..., Chetham Soc., xxxv, 1856 passim. The Shuttleworths also bought cattle at Chorley, Bolton, Bury, Blackburn, Wigan, Newburgh, Colne, and Preston.

[3] Kent AO, PRC 10, 35.

peasant did not often possess it. If he was wise, he restricted himself to the regulated safety of his local market: the records of the Courts of Chancery and Requests contain numerous cases recording the sad fate attending temerarious village labourers who sought to break away from traditional practices.

3. *Expansion and disputation*

The Tudor market town was clearly neither a moribund nor a stagnant place. From about 1570 onwards its trade began to expand rapidly, and the expansion did not go unremarked by contemporaries. Market tolls suddenly became an important source of revenue; the half-forgotten customs of urban freemen began to take on a new significance; burgage rights were stretched or challenged by tradesmen, corporations, and manorial lords; and a spate of lawsuits flooded the Tudor courts. Of these disputes, perhaps the most interesting may be found in the records of Special Commissions and Depositions in the Court of Exchequer, of which about one hundred have been examined for the present study. With much variation in detail, nearly all run to a similar pattern. The market at Great Newton, we learn, has greatly expanded in the last twenty years, after having been "little worth" so long as any one can remember. Not infrequently the tolls have fallen into desuetude and the market charter has been lost or mislaid. Someone has suddenly realized the potential value of the tolls, staked a claim to them, and acquired a new grant from the crown. After a while the corporation challenges his rights, or a sturdy group of townsmen or country folk refuse to pay toll and are prosecuted. In their defence these people usually assert that no one has ever paid tolls before; or that at any rate their village is exempt; or that Mr Smith the complainant is "a great rich man" and a notorious oppressor of the poor. Not infrequently the defendants themselves turn out to be wealthy local tradesmen, or unscrupulous manorial lords, or graziers who have erected half-a-dozen stalls without licence on the king's highway, and are determined to reap their profit.[1] Two or three examples will suffice to illustrate this general theme.

During the early years of Queen Elizabeth's reign the town of St Neots, on the river Ouse, began to emerge as a corn market of some importance, serving the barley farmers of the neighbouring parts of Bedfordshire, Cambridge, and Huntingdon. Its capabilities were readily apprehended by Robert Payne, the local squire, "a gentleman

[1] Many of these disputes turned on a question of town boundaries. They were thus common in towns of late creation, like Stow-on-the-Wold, where the urban area had been carved out of other parishes and was small in extent.

of great wealth" who "might pleasure and displeasure many inhabiting in the said town...and in the country." He railed in the Cornhill, paved it at considerable expense, caused it "weekly to be swept and kept clean for the safeguard of the sacks of corn"—and proceeded to levy toll of one quart of corn for every quarter sold, or twopence for each cartload. There was apparently little legal justification for his action, but the benefit could not be gainsaid, and people conceded it for quietness' sake and because they "would not contend with the said Robert Payne..." But there was a more sinister side to Payne's action. He had leased his rights, such as they were, to one Thomas Newman, whose brother Hugh had obtained a commission as purveyor to the Queen's household. Those who denied toll to Thomas Newman were quietly mulcted, an hour or so later, by his brother Hugh. Unfortunately for Payne and the Newmans, there were a few redoubtable (or possibly perverse) farmers who refused to be coerced. Men like Thomas Archdeacon of Paxton, who had frequented the market for fifty or sixty years, asserted that toll had never been paid in *their* time; and Robert Payne's son and heir Edward was therefore obliged to go to law to establish whatever claim he may have had.[1]

At Doncaster in Yorkshire the position was more complicated. In this case the aggrieved parties were the mayor and corporation. By Charles I's reign the Doncaster wool market had become one of the largest in the country, sometimes as many as eighty packs, or about six thousand fleeces, being sold each Saturday during the summer months. The traffic was so considerable that it was impossible for the four men appointed by the corporation to weigh all the wool sold in the market: it became the custom for some buyers to accept the weight of fleeces on the seller's own word. For those weighed at the corporation's beam, a toll of $\frac{1}{2}$d. per stone was levied on the seller. Or was it in fact a toll—or a mere gratuity? That was the great question. The corporation affirmed that it was a toll, the defendants a voluntary gratuity. Most probably, as in other towns, the dues had originated as small, amicable gratuities when the market was in its infancy, and had become more strictly enforced as the market expanded and the corporation perceived their fiscal potentialities. But in this instance there were two complicating factors. In the first place the official wool-weighers were accused of "cozenage;" they engaged, on the quiet, in a considerable trade in wool on their own account, and it was alleged that they used their official position to blackmail a number of factors and farmers who habitually sold their wool in the market. In the second place, a number of the wool-sellers who came from the city of Lincoln claimed to be toll-free in all markets and seaports

[1] E 134, 3 James I, E 20.

throughout the country. They had recently won their claim to be free in the city of London, and now incited a number of their colleagues to refuse to pay toll in the market at Doncaster too. The corporation, as a consequence, was damnified, and brought the whole question of the Doncaster tolls before the Chancellor of the Exchequer.[1]

The third dispute relates to the market for butter, cheese, and sheep at Yeovil, and to the right to the profits of the town beams and the stalls and standings in the market place. Until the closing years of Queen Elizabeth, Yeovil had boasted only one town beam, used principally for the weighing of wool, and lent or leased to one Master Hobbes, the portreeve's bailiff. The informality of the arrangement is shown by the fact that after Hobbes's death his widow was permitted to remove the beam to her own house, and make what profit she could of it, "in regard of her poor estate." With the expansion of Yeovil's trade, however, the profits of the market became a valuable piece of property, and everyone was anxious to lay claim to them. A second beam for the weighing of cheese and butter was set up about 1595, and the right to the profits of the old one was disputed. According to one deponent, the wool beam had been set up by Sir John (or was it Sir Ralph?) Horsey, the lord of the market; according to another by Mr Penny of East Coker, the farmer of the parsonage; according to a third, by the portreeve of the borough. Meanwhile, as everyone was busy disputing, the inhabitants of the neighbouring manor of Hendford (alias Newland), whose boundary actually traversed the middle of the market place, quietly took it into their heads to assume that their tenements were ancient burgages, and claimed the right to the profit of stalls and pens which they had recently erected in front of their doors. Before long a number of valuable standings had been set up in Hendford manor; and by the middle of James I's reign there were at least two lawsuits in progress—between Jonathan Penny and the inhabitants of Hendford, and between the corporation and Jonathan Penny—over their respective rights to tolls, beams, stalls, pens, and burgage rights in general. Sir Ralph Horsey, it seems, more wise than his hot-headed rivals, had made his peace with the corporation in private.[2]

Finally, the case of Builth in Breconshire may be cited. By the seventeenth century Builth was becoming an important centre of the Welsh cattle and sheep trade, visited by drovers from the counties of Radnor, Brecon, and Carmarthen on their way to fairs and markets across the border. The tolls levied at the bridge over the Wye—3d. for every beast and 1s. for every score of sheep, in addition to a 'drift'

---

[1] E 134, 17 Car. I, M 8; E 134, 18 Car. I, E 9.
[2] E 134, 9 James I, M 31; E 134, 13 James I, E 19. The deponents' evidence is contradictory, but I believe the above account to be substantially correct.

or 'passage' toll—were a lucrative source of revenue. They were acquired, either by purchase or grant from the Crown, by Sir Edmond Sawyer, whose right was disputed by the local squire and justice of the peace, John Williams of the Park. Mr Williams was a colourful, if illogical, personality. He maintained, in the first place, that the tolls were due to himself or his tenants; in the second place, that no tolls were due to anyone.[1] He forbade the townsmen to pay any dues to Sir Edmond Sawyer—no doubt a highly popular act—and, accompanied by a group of his followers, strode into the market on 5 July 1631 to enforce his command. Seeing Sir Edmond Sawyer's octogenarian bailiff, William Thomas, exacting toll "under the market house," he at once demanded by what authority he did so. Thomas rashly replied by putting his hat on his head and defying the squire to his face. Thereupon Mr Williams struck the hat off again with his own hand and did "throw the same to the ground" while his attendants "took hold on the said William Thomas and hauled him and pushed him into the Cage, by means whereof the said William Thomas fell to the ground..." The Cage, as one inhabitant remarked, was "a very loathsome place;" through the bars the market folk could "see the said William Thomas sitting upon the stocks..." When Mr Williams returned later in the day, however, with the town constable, the wretched bailiff pleaded to be left there, where at least his life was safe from the incensed squire and the crowd. But Mr Williams willed the constable "to haul or pull out the said William Thomas out of the Cage in quarters or in pieces if he would not come forth by fair means." Next morning, Mr Williams despatched Thomas, by his own *mittimus*, to the county gaol. And shortly afterwards Sir Edmond Sawyer cited Mr Williams before the chancellor of the exchequer.[2]

These disputes were not merely parochial feuds. They bear witness to the expansion of the agrarian economy and to certain fundamental changes in English rural life. Their geographical distribution is of considerable interest. Two cases in five relate to the eastern counties, with their many corn markets; nearly one quarter to the south-western counties, with their wool and cloth markets; a further seventh to the Midland counties; and only one quarter to the whole of the south of England, the northern counties, and Wales.[3] Barley, malt, wheat, wool, cloth: these were the great culprits. Or in other words, it was in those areas where the influence of 'man's manufacture' was most powerful, by way of the clothing and brewing industries, that the new tensions became most acute.

[2] E 134, 7 Car. I, M 19; E 134, 7 Car. I, E 19.
[3] In the two latter areas, however, market disputes may have been dealt with by the Councils of the North and Marches.

The widespread attack upon market tolls also bears witness to an impatience of old restraints which was highly characteristic of the period. At Wells in Somerset, where tolls were levied by the bishop, a group of tradesmen went so far as to assert that "there ought not any toll at all, by the laws or customs of this realm, to be taken of any corn or grain sold in any market, but the buyers and sellers there ought to be free. And if any such outrageous toll...be taken in the said market by the owner...the king's Majesty shall seize the said market into his hand as forfeited...And this by the Statute of Westminster the first, the thirtieth chapter."[1] Even in the closely regulated community of the market town, the force of individual enterprise was breaking down the barriers of social custom.

C. THE DEVELOPMENT OF PRIVATE MARKETING:
(A) SPECIAL MARKETS

Outside the 'open market' striking changes were also taking place in the sphere of 'private marketing', or individual dealings between traders, farmers, and manufacturers. Since the local market town proved incapable of accommodating much of the increasing trade in agricultural products, the resourceful Englishman turned to more private methods of business. He did not invent the new methods: they were at least as old as the medieval wool trade. Nor did he invent the expression: the economic historian is obliged to coin it for him. The 'open market' was an honoured phrase on the lips of every peasant and politician; the newer phenomenon of a 'private market' was at once nameless and suspect, as unpopular in the country at large as the decline in 'housekeeping' and the lamented privacy of the Caroline court.[2]

The distinction between private marketing and the open market was rarely a sharp one. The penumbra separating them was broad and vague. Many traders naturally engaged in both spheres, as opportunity offered. Bargains between individual farmers and tradesmen took place wherever they happened to meet one another, and as often as

[1] C 3, 262, 7. Tenants of Duchy manors (cf. E 134, 3 James I, H 19) and inhabitants of London, Lincoln, and other towns could invoke genuine claims to be toll-free in English markets. The significant fact is that frequently such rights had fallen into desuetude (though not, of course, in London) till their revival under the impulse of Elizabethen expansion.

[2] Cf. W. Harrison, *Description of England*, New Shakespere Soc., Ser. VI, No. 1, ed. F. J. Furnivall, 1877, pp. 297–302. In 'private marketing' I do not include small transactions between neighbours and the like (usually in cash or by barter) which rarely came into dispute and of which few records survive; what proportion of agricultural marketing they covered it is impossible to say.

not they met in the inns surrounding the market place of the country town. But the new stimulus to private bargaining originated in the expansion, during the Tudor period, of three special or particular markets: the London market, the export market, and the provisioning of the royal household and armed forces. These three special markets were not sharply differentiated: the first and last overlap at many points, and traders frequently engaged in all three in turn. They are distinguished here partly for the sake of simplicity in presentation.

1. *The Metropolitan market*

The development of the London food market has been treated at length by Professor Fisher and Mr McGrath, and there is no need here for more than a brief résumé. The capital's most striking period of expansion occurred during the latter half of the period. The rapid increase in its demands was perhaps most noticeable in its imports of corn. Except during years of dearth metropolitan grain requirements were satisfied almost entirely by English supplies; and between 1500 and 1638 its annual coastwise imports expanded from 17,380 quarters to 95,714 quarters. There was a threefold increase in wheat imports, a ninefold increase in oats, and a sixteenfold in malt.[1]

The principal areas for the supply of wheat lay in Essex and Norfolk, and along the northern fringes of Kent, in that highly fertile tract of undulating countryside between the downland and the sea, where a prosperous yeoman, like Arthur Seath of Rodmersham, might devote more than half his capital and over 100 acres of his farm to the production of wheat.[2] Most of the Kentish wheat was dispatched from Faversham and Milton Regis, and the principal wheat-farming area did not extend for more than a few miles to the south and west of these two narrow creeks; it was bounded by the flinty downland southward and the sterile Forest of Blean to the east. Owing, probably, to the vagaries of the local climate, Kentish wheat seems to have varied greatly in quality from season to season, and London's imports from the country fluctuated violently. In some years exports to the capital amounted to three quarters of the total (i.e., *via* the coasting trade); but in 1625 they fell to less than one third, and in other years went a-begging

[1] F. J. Fisher, 'The Development of the London Food Market, 1540–1640', EcHR, v, 1935, pp. 47, 49; see also N. S. B. Gras, *The Evolution of the English Corn Market...*, 1926, pp. 105–9 and Appendix D; T. S. Willan, *The English Coasting Trade, 1600–1750*, chapters VI, VIII, and IX; Bowden, *op. cit., passim;* P. V. McGrath, *The Marketing of Food, Fodder, and Livestock in the London Area in the Seventeenth Century...*, London M.A. Thesis, 1948. Mr McGrath's study will be found to amplify the following account at many points. Cf. also Table 8, p. 00.
[2] Kent AO, PRC 10, 35.

altogether, or were sent instead to the less exacting markets of Tyneside and the Midlands.[1]

In prosperous years a large proportion of London's malt and barley imports also came from Kent: principally from the farmlands to the east of the Forest of Blean, from the countryside between Sandwich and Canterbury, and from the Isle of Thanet. In 1638 over 19,000 quarters of malt were exported from Kent to London; while a further 17,000 quarters and more were sent from Norfolk, shipped from Blakeney and Hunstanton or down the Ouse and its tributaries and *via* King's Lynn. Oats came principally from the county of Essex, whose supplies were augmented on occasion by considerable shipments from Kent or Norfolk.[2]

In addition to the coasting trade, there was an extensive inland corn traffic to London; in all probability, indeed, its volume greatly exceeded that of the coastal trade. Much of it came from Oxfordshire, Berkshire, and Buckinghamshire, shipped from the many grain towns strung out along the Thames: Oxford, Abingdon, Reading, Kingston, and above all Henley. Out of 121 shipments received in London and recorded in the Bridgehouse *Corn Book* for 1568–73, as much as one third came from Henley. Between October 1573 and March 1574 that town sent over three times the amount of grain dispatched by the whole county of Kent: 8,050 quarters out of a total of 18,897 quarters received in London from England as a whole.[3] Malt and meal were dispatched in large amounts from the numerous market towns of Middlesex, Hertfordshire, Bedfordshire, Cambridgeshire, Surrey, and Buckinghamshire. Prominent among these towns were Royston, Enfield, Croydon, Luton, Dunstable, High Wycombe, and Ware. Malt was sent either by cart and packhorse, or by the navigable waters of the river Lea, or by the Ouse and Cam and the coasters of King's Lynn.[4]

---

[1] Kent AO, PRC inventories; Fisher, *op. cit.*, pp. 50, 56. In 1619 a group of east Kent farmers complained that much of their corn was returned to them after failing to find purchasers in London.—SP 14, 112, 12 and 12 (i).

[2] C 2, James I, O 3, 20; C 2, James I, L 8, 47; Fisher, *op. cit.*, pp. 49, 50; Req. 2 67, 45; LP xiv, i, p. 171; N. J. Williams, *The Maritime Trade of East Anglian Ports, 1550–1590*, Oxford D. Phil. thesis, 1952, p. 179; C 2, James I, C 23, 72. In certain years there were also large grain imports (especially wheat) from Sussex, the southwest, and the north-east; by the 1630's Devon and Cornwall were more frequently importers, however, though occasionally substantial amounts were still sent to London.—W. G. Hoskins, *Industry, Trade, and People in Exeter, 1688–1800*, 1935, pp. 95–6. C 2, James I, H 36, 17.

[3] Gras, *op. cit.*, pp. 105, 106; Fisher, *op. cit.*, p. 50; E 134, 21 James I, T 12; C 2, James I, H 31, 4. Mr McGrath suggests that the corn trade by road and river was probably six times as large as the coasting trade.—*op. cit.*, p. 119.

[4] C 2, James I, G 9, 16; C 2, James I, T 13, 34; Req. 2, 63, 99; SP 16, 177, 50; SP 16, 183, 37; Fisher, *op. cit.*, p. 60; Gras, *op. cit.*, p. 109 and n.

The extent of the metropolitan corn trade was largely determined by the availability of water transport, and its kaleidoscopic pattern varied much from year to year with local circumstances of weather and harvest.

The metropolitan livestock trade drew from a larger area than the traffic in grain. Livestock of most kinds made their way in droves or flocks from many parts of England and arrived on foot. Lean cattle from Wales and the north country were bought and sold by country drovers in the cattle centres of the Midlands, like Shrewsbury, Coventry, Market Harborough, Northampton, and St Ives. They were then fattened alongside the lean 'country' or local cattle of East Anglia and the south, in the marshlands of Lincolnshire, Norfolk, Essex, and Kent. Many instances of this traffic could be cited. A group of London butchers bought steers, runts, heifers, and other beasts at Northampton, Hanging Houghton, Boston, and Sleaford. Three graziers of Hertfordshire and Middlesex purchased steers at Coventry to store their grounds at Rickmansworth, Cowley, and Harmondsworth. A Warwickshire drover bought heifers at Ashbourne, Coventry, and Newcastle-under-Lyme, and drove them into Essex. Two citizens of Chester purchased cattle by the score in Wales, and at Shrewsbury, Whitchurch, and Newport, selling them again "at several fairs in Essex and other places in the up-countries."[1] Oxen and fatware were driven towards London from Siddington in Gloucestershire, Northallerton in Yorkshire, and Stockton-on-Tees. Bullocks, sheep, and lambs were bought from inhabitants of Marsh Chapel, Sleaford, and North Kyme in Lincolnshire, Clyro in Radnorshire, and winwick in Northamptonshire. There were "very many several droves of hogs" sent towards London from Suffolk; and poultry and fowl were dispatched from Hertfordshire, Bedfordshire, Northamptonshire, Suffolk, Essex, and Surrey. A warrener of Hertfordshire sold the whole of his annual stock of conies to a single London poulterer. Another London poulterer purchased thousands of black and grey rabbits from his factor in Reading, and from warrens in Aldbourne Chase in "the coney country of Wiltshire."[2]

[1] *The Account Book of a Kentish Estate, 1616–1704*, ed. E. C. Lodge, British Academy Records of Social and Economic History, VI, 1927, *passim;* Fisher, *op. cit.*, p. 51; E 134, ? James I, Misc. Deps., No. 1; C 2, James I, N 3, 54; Req. 2, 297, 5; Req. 2, 240, 58; E 134, 20–21 Eliz., M 14; E 134, 11 Car. I, E 20.

[2] C 3, 108, 61; Durham, Prior's Kitchen, Ch. Com. Ref. 190, 187; J. S. Purvis, 'A Note on XVI-Century Farming in Yorkshire', *Yorks. Arch. Jnl.*, XXXVI, 1944, p. 449; C 2, James I, R 2, 59; Req. 2, 297, 5; C 3, 78, 43; E 134, 9 Car. I, M 24; Robert Reyce, *Suffolk in the XVIIth Century: the Breviary of Suffolk by Robert Reyce, 1618...*, ed. Lord Francis Hervey, 1902, p. 37; Req. 2, 266, 37; Req. 2, 38, 3; E 134, 22 James I, M 21; E 134, 22 James I, M 37. See also Joan Thirsk, *English Peasant Farming*, 1957, pp. 152, 177.

The sources of London's dairy produce were less diverse. According to Norden milk was supplied by the dairy farmers of Middlesex, whose wives twice or trice a week conveyed butter, eggs, milk, cheese, and bacon to the London markets, much in the manner of butter-wives in provincial towns. Metropolitan demands for cheese and butter were met chiefly by exports from the eastern counties by way of the coasting trade. The bulk of the city's requirements came from Essex and the 'wood-pasture' region of central Suffolk, shipped from Ipswich and Woodbridge and the villages fringing the winding estuaries of the two counties. Robert Reyce speaks of as many as nine hundred loads of butter and cheese being dispatched from a single Suffolk harbour in one year, and three times as much from other havens in the county. There was also a large and rapidly expanding trade in butter from the north-east coast, an area which in 1638 seems to have shipped larger quantities to London than Suffolk itself.[1]

Market garden produce was supplied principally from the immediate hinterland of the capital. Largely as a result of Dutch and Flemish influence the art of 'gardening for profit' spread rapidly in the latter half of the period; its success was crowned in 1605 by the incorporation of the London gardeners' company. Much of the new cultivation was fitted into the old network of open-field land in the suburbs bordering the river Thames, particularly in Chelsea, Fulham, and Kensington. By the mid-seventeenth century a labour force of some 1,500 persons was employed. An aldermanic report of 1635 speaks of 24,000 loads of roots—no doubt carrots, parsnips, and turnips—being sold annually in London and Westminster.[2]

The fruiterers of London drew their supplies from more distant areas. Until Queen Elizabeth's reign probably the bulk of the city's fruit came from the Low Countries and France, purchased by London factors from the merchant fruiterers of Rouen and other towns.[3] The culture of Kentish cherries and apples, however, was already ousting the foreign trade. It had prospered exceedingly since its establishment at Teynham Newgardens in Henry VIII's time. By the end of the sixteenth century it had spread into the neighbouring parishes of Borden, Hartlip, Rainham, and Newington-on-the-Street: a small, compact area, hemmed in by the Downs behind, open to convenient creeks alongside Swale and Medway to the north, and still a principal fruit-growing district of the county. In this area a number of London

[1] Fisher, *op. cit.*, pp. 48, 55; SP 18, 135, 40; Req. 2, 393, 28; Williams, *op. cit.*, pp. 188–90; LP viii, pp. 413, 430, ix, pp. 23, 35, 208; Reyce, *op. cit.*, p. 42.
[2] Fisher, *op. cit.*, pp. 52–5.
[3] *Ibid.*, pp. 52–3; Req. 2, 64, 112.

fruiterers leased their own orchards. Others came down into Kent towards "cherryty time, which was the season for cherries," or purchased in springtime the prospective crop of "cherries, pears, pippins, apples, wardens, and medlars," sometimes for several years in advance.[1]

London's supplies of hops also came partly from Kent. Hops had been grown in the county since before 1500, though probably not on a commercial scale until the end of the sixteenth century. By Charles I's reign the county possessed a rudimentary hop-exchange, situated in Canterbury and visited by factors from London and other counties, who sometimes purchased hops in quantities of a couple of tons at a time.[2] Probably more extensive at this time than the Kentish hop trade was that of Suffolk, Essex, and possibly Surrey. According to Robert Reyce, writing in James I's reign, many Suffolk farmers had become "hop-masters" and "in short time proved wealthy thereby, many leaving their wonted trade" and devoting themselves wholly to the "new-found mystery of planting, setting, drying, and trimming..." Much of this Suffolk trade was not destined for London, but for the west country and Stourbridge Fair, where bargains of twelve tons, or £640 worth at a time, were not unknown.[3] Of the Suffolk trade to the metropolis, much, like that from Kent and Surrey, was waterborne, by way of the east coast estuaries or the river Ouse and North Sea.

The organization of the London market and the methods of supplying it bore little resemblance to those of the small provincial towns described in a previous section. Transactions involving several tons of goods at a time and sums of several hundred pounds sterling necessitated an altogether different kind of organization from that of the modest and carefully regulated open market of country towns. When we read of a Hertfordshire knight sending 2,000 quarters of malt to London in four years; of a Smithfield cooper buying 80,000 boards from a Sussex yeoman; of a Cheshire drover sending 600 cattle a year to be fattened in Essex; and of 1,700 or 1,800 veals being sold in Cheapside every Saturday, we glimpse something of that system of restless and far-reaching enterprise which the expansion of the London market, after 1570, did so much to create.[4]

[1] Req. 2, 61, 39; Req. 2, 97, 55; Req. 2, 220, 15; Req. 2, 34, 38; Req. 2, 35, 92. It is still a common practice in Kent to auction fruit before the crop is picked.

[2] Fisher, op. cit., pp. 52–3; ex inf. Dr Felix Hull; C 2, James I, H 13, 24.

[3] Reyce, op. cit., p. 31; Req. 2, 239, 57; SP 16, 6, 77. Hops from Surrey and Kent were also shipped by sea and river to Stourbridge Fair.

[4] C 2, James I, G 9, 16; Req. 2, 226, 52; E 134, 11 Car. I, E 20; SP 16, 167, 28. Further figures of cattle sold are given in McGrath, op. cit., pp. 167–8. 1,700 veals would be equivalent to the farming stock of perhaps 100 yeomen.

Quite apart from the fact that dozens of new London market places were formed in this period, while the older ones became "unmeasurably pestered with the unimaginable increase and multiplicity of market folks," a whole community of factors and drovers came into being to serve the London market—travelling up from the country, or traversing the provinces in search of cattle, corn, and fruit.[1] Four yeomen and brewers of Essex, for instance, formed a partnership for the sale of East Anglian hops to metropolitan brewers. A butcher of St Botolph's, Aldgate, travelled into the Midlands to purchase thirty steers and bullocks from a gentleman of Hanging Houghton in Northamptonshire. A London wool-winder journeyed into the counties of Gloucester and Northampton, and made "diligent search by his travayle" for "fourscore tods of Cotswold wools." Two metropolitan hop factors "came down unto the city of Canterbury...to buy hops, and made inquiry there what hops were there to be sold..." A butcher of Whitecross Street entered into partnership with a gentleman of Boston for the purchase of Lincolnshire cattle.[2] Two London fishmongers established regional factors in Suffolk for the purchase of East Anglian butter and cheese. A group of Thanet barley farmers "send up and transport" their annual crop "to the city of London, and do there sell the same...by such factors and agents as...are always resident in London," at a fee of 2d. in the pound for their "help or broking." As for the "new company...called hop merchants," Robert Reyce records that, each year, "prying into the last year's store then remaining, diligently hearkening from beyond the sea what likelihood there was from those parts, and carefully looking into every garden and hop yard here at home, in what towardness they stood, comparing the former years' experience with the time present, [they] at length with themselves resolved and concluded of a price, who travelling into the country where these hops were, they offered to the owners at their own doors, either for those remaining or for new at the next gathering to come."[3]

Yet for all its busyness the new organization of the metropolitan market was neither unregulated nor haphazard. Its individualism was

[1] Fisher, op. cit., pp. 57–8; cf. Blome, op. cit., p. 155. By James I's reign the growth of the meal-trade alone necessitated the extension of Newgate and Leadenhall markets and the creation of fresh markets at Queenhithe and Billingsgate. A detailed account of London's new markets is given in McGrath, op. cit., Part III. It was for the carrying trade to London that books like John Taylor's Carriers' Cosmography were published (1637).

[2] Req. 2, 239, 57; C 2, James I, N 3, 54; Req. 2, 206, 7; C 2, James I, H 13, 24; Req. 2, 61, 55.

[3] Req. 2, 393, 28; C 2, James I, O 3, 29; Reyce, op. cit., pp. 31–2. The organization of London's middlemen is analysed in detail in McGrath, op. cit., chapters XI–XVIII.

still tempered by custom, both old and new. The factor's "books of reckonings" were still often written in roman numerals; his system of accounting was still medieval; his rabbits and poultry were reckoned by wooden tallies, scored and notched and split down the centre.[1]

Neither was the 'new company' of travelling merchants which arose to satisfy the expanding demands entirely governed by impersonal competition. One must not read into Tudor 'partnerships' and 'syndicates' the conditions of the twentieth century. They were still held together principally by ties of personal friendship and family connection. The supplies of cattle received by one London butcher were arranged in conjunction with his own father and were often dispatched from the parental pastures in Lincolnshire. The Suffolk cheese factor appointed by two London fishmongers was their own brother-in-law, Thomas Hoorth of South Elmham. A droving partnership engaged in purchasing cattle for the London market in Warwickshire and Staffordshire comprised a father, a son, a friend, and a brother. The wool sales of a Barnet glover and woolman were arranged, during his absence in Norfolk, by his wife, who herself travelled to Harborough Fair to meet him with news of her bargaining.[2] A group of Thanet farmers who sent malt to the capital in James I's reign were not only themselves related, but operated through London factors who were their own nephews and cousins. Nearly all the farming gentry of East Kent who served the London market with wheat and barley, and who signed the petition of 1619 for relief from grain dues, were close kinsmen or neighbours of one another, such as the Philpots, Knowlers, Dennes, and Paramores.[3] The purchase of Kentish fruit by London fruiterers, and their ownership of orchards in the countryside about Teynham, often arose from their intermarriage with the daughters of Kentish farmers and from the fact that they were themselves sons or cousins of Kentish yeomen.[4] There is, after all, nothing surprising in these close personal connections. Most Londoners were still countrymen by birth, and their native county was still their proper home.[5]

It is in the light of these considerations that the question of London's

[1] Req. 2, 266, 37.

[2] Req. 2, 61, 55; Req. 2, 393, 28; E 134, 20–21 Eliz., M 14; Req. 2, 49, 37.

[3] C 2, James I, O 3, 29; SP 14, 112, 12 (i).

[4] Among such Kentish families were the Osbournes, Roothes, Farrells, Harrises, and Palmers. They were clearly a close little group, the same names occurring in various disputes.—cf. Req. 2, 34, 38; Req. 2, 61, 39; Req. 2, 97, 55; Req. 2, 220, 15.

[5] Various Chancery cases in which Welshmen in London dealt in the cattle of their homeland suggest that the cattle trade may have been stimulated by the immigration of Welsh people into England following the accession of the Tudors, though such cases do not necessarily relate to cattle for London: see, for example, C 3, 4, 85; C 3, 243, 37; C 3, 78, 43; C 3, 101, 84; C 3, 111, 90; C 3, 116, 51.

commercial penetration of the countryside must be regarded. How far did that penetration extend? How was it determined? How was it limited? How far did Defoe's assertion of a "general dependence of the whole country upon the city of London...for the consumption of its produce" hold good in the sixteenth century?[1] The answer of Professor Fisher is that the situation a century earlier "differed from that described by [Defoe] in degree rather than in kind." There was, he says, a "steady permeation of the countryside by London retailers purchasing for resale in their shops." He describes vividly how the "corn-growers of Cambridgeshire...the dairy farmers of Suffolk, the graziers of the south Midlands, all looked to the London market as the hub of their economic universe." "The city's tentacles," he affirms, spread "over the provinces until by the middle of the seventeenth century they reached to Berwick, Cornwall, and Wales." Yet Professro Fisher is the first to point out that it is "impossible to measure and easy to exaggerate the novelty, rapidity, and efficacy of these various responses to the growing London market."[2]

A few tentative facts relating to London's population during the period will serve to reinforce his warning. For the year 1534, the population of London has been estimated at 60,000—no more than that of modern Worcester. In 1582 it was probably about 120,000— the size of modern Norwich. In 1605 it was somewhere about 250,000: or still less than half the size of present-day Dublin, in a country twice as large and one-and-a-half times as populous as modern Eire.[3] The expansion of London was an astonishing phenomenon, and it frightened many contemporaries. But it is doubtful if at any time between 1500 and 1640 its numbers reached 7 per cent of the whole population of England and Wales. Even at the end of the period its population was probably more than equalled by that of the two counties of Kent and Suffolk. The proportion of the agricultural output of England consumed by Londoners can never have been more than a small fraction of the whole.

The growth of the capital and its effect upon agriculture must in fact, be viewed in the larger context of the expansion of the English

[1] Daniel Defoe, *A Tour through England and Wales*, Everyman, 1959, I, p. 3.

[2] Fisher, *op. cit.*, pp. 51, 61, 57, 50, 64. Dr Williams has shown that London influence in Norfolk was greatly exaggerated by Professor Gras: Williams, *op. cit.*, pp. 176–7. Cf. also Willan, *Coasting Trade*, especially chapter VI.

[3] N. G. Brett-James, *The Growth of Stuart London*, 1935, pp. 496–500; Gras, *op. cit.*, p. 75. The Bills of Mortality suggest a figure for 1631 of only 173,000; Gras suggests for 1634 339,824. Gras's figure is probably too high, and so too is Brett-James's 250,000 for 1605. It is undeniable, however, that London's population was subject to sudden fluctuations, and it seems likely that there was a temporary decline between 1605 and 1630.

economy as a whole. Relatively, London expanded more quickly than other parts of the kingdom; absolutely its growth was much smaller than that of the rest of the country. Its increase of some 200,000 persons between the reigns of Henry VII and Charles I was probably paralleled by an increase of quite one-and-a-half millions, or between 50 and 75 per cent, in that of the whole country. The needs of these one-and-a-half million souls, not to mention the increasing demands from abroad, required satisfaction as much as those of London; and it would be a grave error to suppose that they were met from local resources alone. Even in purely rural areas certain food supplies often came from a distance. The reports of country justices in the reigns of James I and Charles I show that counties like Derby and Warwick were always grain-importers, and that the labouring population almost everywhere depended on the market for its supplies of corn.[1]

Such considerations do not imply that metropolitan influence was unimportant. But its importance consisted, not in dispersal through England as a whole, but in its regional selectivity and local intensity. As Professor Fisher points out, one *can* find evidence of London factors operating in Cumberland, Cornwall, and Wales; but, it must be admitted, not very often. Large numbers of Welsh cattle undoubtedly were driven across the English border; but Chancery and Exchequer disputes, and the Shrewsbury and Leominster toll books, show that many of them were sold to farmers and tradesmen in the Midlands, and suggest that only a fraction infiltrated, by devious stages, to the south. In the north of England, the stimulus of London's demand certainly had a remarkable effect upon the exports of cheese and butter from Stockton-on-Tees; but the region so affected comprised only a restricted area in Yorkshire and County Durham. In the south of the country, the orchards of Teynham and Hartlip owed their prosperity, and conceivably their establishment, to the expansion of the capital; but, though many contemporaries commented upon them, they were in fact untypical of the Kentish economy as a whole. The wealth and enterprise of the barley farmers of Thanet, the hop merchants of Canterbury, and the wheat farmers around Faversham was evidently based upon the needs of London brewers and bakers. Yet even in Kent the wooded tracts of Holmesdale, and the higher parts of the Weald and Downland, or some two thirds of the county, seem to have remained largely unaffected by these requirements. It must always be remembered, moreover, that outside the immediate vicinity of London, few save yeomen and gentlemen were in a position to take advantage of the expansion of metropolitan demand; while for every commerci-

[1] Gras, *op. cit.*, p. 75.

ally-managed farm there were perhaps a hundred peasant holdings still cultivated in the traditional manner.[1]

The territories in which London's influence was intense thus resembled islands or pockets of countryside, surrounded by areas in which its effect was of little importance. Within these former territories, as for instance in East Suffolk or Romney Marsh, metropolitan demand, if it rarely originated, invariably stimulated and exploited an initial tendency to specialize in certain types of product. Beyond them, London's penetration was limited by the availability of water transport and the adequacy of local roads. In all parts of England the old ways survived alongside the new. In Kent itself, which impressed Stuart travellers by the efficiency of its farming, the wild red deer still roamed at will in the forests of Holmesdale, within twenty-five miles of St Paul's.

2. *Purveyance and victualling*

The purveyance of corn, cattle, and provisions for the royal court was a source of much concern to both farmers and ministers of state in the Tudor period. The iniquities of the system do not concern us; they have been examined by Miss Woodworth, upon whose researches much of the following account is based.[2] Our concern is with the influence purveyance exerted upon private marketing; and this influence made itself felt in the following way. During the sixteenth century purchasing for the royal court was still undertaken primarily in provincial market towns, but part of the royal requirements was met by contract with individual farmers, and during the latter half of the period this proportion rapidly increased. As a result of the composition agreements arranged between court and county by Lord Burghley, the shires were induced, in return for freedom from the activities of royal purveyors, to undertake for themselves the supply of corn and livestock to the queen. The responsibility for the organization of purveyance thus devolved upon the justices of the peace, and they, very frequently, farmed it out to metropolitan or provincial factors.[3]

The proportion of the agricultural output of England and Wales taken by the royal court can never have been more than fractional; but it was by no means insignificant. Every year the household of Henry VIII consumed something like 1,500 cattle, 8,000 sheep, 3,000

[1] Dr Thirsk came to the same conclusions in analysing the impact of metropolitan demand in Lincolnshire (*English Peasant Farming*, 1957, p. 91).

[2] Allegra Woodworth, 'Purveyance for the Royal Household in the reign of Queen Elizabeth', *American Philosophical Society*, NS xxxv, 1946, pp. 3 *sqq.*

[3] By 1603 nearly all counties had compounded for the bulk of the supplies due from them.—Woodworth, *op. cit.*, p. 42.

quarters of wheat, and 3,500 quarters of oats. For a single banquet in 1526, held "in the gallery within the tiltyard" of Greenwich Palace, the king's cooks required 120 calves' tongues, nine dozen geese, eight dozen rabbits, 36 dozen chickens, and 3,875 eggs; not to mention the cranes, herons, peacocks, pheasants, fish, sheep, fruit, and "six great branches of rosemary." Altogether the annual expenditure of the king's household exceeded £20,000, in addition to the expenses of those of Prince Edward, the duke of Richmond, the two princesses, and a succession of consorts.[1] The equivalent sum allocated to the household of Queen Elizabeth amounted to £40,000, and in a single year the court consumed 4,330 cattle, 8,200 sheep, and over 4,000 quarters of wheat. In the reign of James I the annual requirements of the royal entourage rocketed to unprecedented heights: in 1618 they amounted to some 13,000 sheep and lambs, 2,000 cattle, and 19,000 dozen hens and chickens.[2] It is not surprising that four years later the single little county of Middlesex was eager to compound for its responsibilities in supplying the court at a figure exceeding £1,750 per annum.[3]

The regions supplying these products were less sharply distinguished than those that furnished London. The purveyors' purchases were often arbitrary and haphazard, and the composition quotas raised by the justices were levied on county sub-divisions in proportions we can now rarely discover. Nevertheless, the same broad patterns of regional specialization are discernible as in the metropolitan market. The remoter counties of the north and west were comparatively lightly burdened; the responsibility rested most heavily upon the southern counties, the nearer parts of the Midlands, and the east. Of the 4,000 or so quarters of wheat supplied by composition at the end of Queen Elizabeth's reign, more than three quarters came from the same three regions that already supplied much grain to London: the eastern counties sent 1,000 quarters, Hertfordshire, Middlesex, and the counties of the upper Thames 1,500 quarters, and Kent and Sussex 750 quarters. In a proposed composition agreement of 1590 for the delivery of 6,400 quarters of oats, the proportions to be delivered from these areas were respectively 2,900, 1,400, and 1,000 quarters each. Apart from corn sent from Wiltshire there was virtually no grain delivered to the court under composition agreement from the west of England or the Midlands. There were, however, considerable numbers of livestock

[1] LP IV, pp. 1383, 967–8; cf. pp. 710, 927–8 for Princess Mary's and the Duke of Richmond's households.

[2] Woodworth, op. cit., pp. 17, 54–5, 62; R. H. Tawney, Business and Politics under James I..., 1958, pp. 153–4, citing Cranfield MSS, No. 4801 (1618).

[3] HMC, Reports, VII, p. 592. The king demanded £1,849 3s. 4d., Middlesex offered £1,755 4s. 2d.

dispatched from these regions: 1,050 sheep and lambs from Dorset, 900 from Northamptonshire, 1,000 from Leicestershire, and 900 from Buckinghamshire, supplemented by 1,500 from Essex and 600 from Romney Marsh. Of oxen and veals, Somerset and Buckinghamshire supplied 100 each, a group of four Midland counties forty each, and Essex 320. Of hens and chickens, Hampshire furnished 100 dozen, Hertfordshire 150 dozen, Leicestershire 190 dozen, and Essex 230 dozen.[1]

The demands of the smaller courts of the royal consorts and princesses were of course less extensive. On occasion, however, these establishments drew supplies from a wide area. When the household of Princess Mary was in residence at Waltham in Henry VIII's reign, oxen were bought at half a dozen fairs and markets in Essex, and in Northamptonshire, Derbyshire, Nottinghamshire, Bedfordshire, Berkshire, Wiltshire, and Sussex.[2]

The details of the organization of purveyance need not concern us. More significant for the present purpose is the *scale* and *elaboration* of the system. The annual supply of 600,000 gallons of beer to Queen Elizabeth's household entailed operations quite beyond the scope of the local market town. It was entrusted to fifty-eight or sixty official brewers, who must have placed very considerable orders for malt and hops with private provincial factors.[3] Even modest transactions like the annual purchase of two hundred sheep and twenty fat oxen in the Parts of Holland might bring regular orders of £350 at a time to men like William Porey of Sutton, "a great grazier and a great dealer for cattle in the county of Lincoln." Similarly, the supply of delicacies to the private London shops run by Queen Elizabeth's purveyors entailed a network of commercial contacts with the specialized farms of different areas and demanded a rare professional expertise.[4]

Perhaps the most interesting feature of the organization of purveyance is its gradual transfer from royal to private hands. The antiquated methods of the unreformed household were too inflexible to meet the expanding requirements of the court; the Board of Green Cloth was riddled with wastage and abuse. A thorough overhaul of the traditional method of supply was called for; but it was not forthcoming. Instead, Burghley and his successors entered into composition agreements with the counties, and the organization was taken over by local justices. The hard thinking and thankless labour essential to reform

---

[1] Req. 2, 125, 4; Req. 2, 111, 42; cf. E 134, 16 Car. I, T 2; Woodworth, *op. cit.*, pp. 39, 54–5, 74, 77–80; HMC, *Reports*, VII, p. 592.

[2] LP III, p. 1408.

[3] Woodworth, *op. cit.*, pp. 57–8. They also purchased in local markets.

[4] E 134, 16 Car. I, T 2.

were done, not where they should have been done, in the Poultry and Acatry at Westminster, but in the court-rooms of country magistrates and the dusty corn-chambers of provincial merchants.[1] What the court saved itself in time and trouble it lost in administrative experience. The significance of these developments became increasingly apparent with the passage of time and the gradual progress of the country towards civil war.[2]

The victualling of the army and navy of Tudor England runs to much the same pattern as that of purveyance for the household, of which at the beginning of the sixteenth century it was one particular branch. Although the influence of victualling upon the development of private marketing was necessarily more intermittent than that of purveyance—and indeed precisely because it was intermittent—it was in some ways more striking. The scale of operations involved was certainly larger. The monthly requirements of grain, hops, and wood officially allocated (though not necessarily delivered) to the garrison of 20,000 men at Calais in 1524 amounted to 2,500 quarters of wheat, over £1,500 worth of bread, 5,600 quarters of beercorn, 28 thousand-weight of hops, 42 hundred-weight of 'talwood', and 200,000 billets. For the carriage of these goods 1,000 carts were required every eight days. The needs of the garrison of 20,000 men at Berwick in the same year were equally large; and for the king's army of 40,000 men raised for the invasion of France in 1544 the cost of purchasing grain in fourteen counties of the south and east of England was estimated at over £15,500 a month. No doubt these quantities were rarely supplied in full. But it is clear that they entailed operations on a very large scale; and except in years of acute dearth, when supplies were occasionally purchased in the Low Countries, they were met entirely from English resources.[3]

From the *corpus* of material relating to victualling in the *Letters and Papers of Henry VIII*, it is possible to compile tentative figures indicat-

[1] Records of the justices' meetings for Suffolk may be found in their Committee Books preserved among Lord Tollemache's manuscripts at Helmingham Hall. I am indebted to Lord Tollemache for permitting me to consult them.

[2] For the later history of purveyance see G. E. Aylmer, 'The Last Years of Purveyance, 1610–1660', EcHR 2nd Ser., x, 1957, pp. 81–93. Under James I and Charles I, a third method of purveyance became common, by which J.P.'s etc., levied the composition money and paid it in direct to the officers of the Household, who undertook the buying from local factors, farmers, and traders on an ordinary business basis. To some extent this reversed the trends apparent under Elizabeth I, described above; but Dr Aylmer's conclusion is that the varying methods of purveyance "reveal the faltering, though sometimes elaborate, administrative techniques of the age..."—p. 93.

[3] LP IV, p. 428, XIX, i, pp. 145–9, XXI, i, p. 23.

ing the regions from which these supplies were purchased. Though too much weight should not be placed upon the figures mentioned below, there is no reason to suspect the reliability of the sample. They relate to several hundred transactions, involving purchases of some 50,000 quarters of corn and 18,000 head of stock.[1]

The principal area for the supply of grain to the English army and navy was once again East Anglia. More than half the total corn required for Berwick and nearly two thirds of that for France was purchased in Norfolk. Of the different types of grain sent to France, 9 per cent of the oats, 29 per cent of the peas and beans, 65 per cent of the wheat, and 66 per cent of the malt and barley was dispatched from the same county. The corresponding figures for legumes, wheat, and barley sent from Norfolk to Berwick were 22, 26, and 63 per cent. Except for wheat, peas, and beans dispatched to Berwick, Norfolk sent more grain, of every type, than any of the other twenty-two counties involved. It was followed by Suffolk, with 12 per cent of the total; the East Riding of Yorkshire, with 7 per cent (exported mainly to Berwick); and Essex, with 6 per cent. There were also substantial quantities of corn dispatched from Bedfordshire, Hertfordshire, the Thames-side granaries of Oxfordshire and Berkshire, and from certain parts of Hampshire, Sussex, and Kent. The figures for Norfolk, therefore, probably tend to exaggerate its apparent monopoly of the trade, since some of that grain sent from Lynn was no doubt brought down the Ouse and Nene from Cambridgeshire and Huntingdonshire, and perhaps further afield. But there can be no doubt that the Ouse basin as a whole was the leading wheat and barley region, with Suffolk, Holderness, and the south-east of England some way behind, and the upper Thames district bringing up the rear. The striking predominance of Norfolk is one of a number of indications that the agricultural economy of East Anglia came of age a generation or so earlier than that of other areas. And once again the principal factor was the presence of water transport. Victualling traffic in all parts of the country was carried by river and sea. From Southampton, Sandwich, London, Ipswich, Lynn, Hull, or Newcastle. Some, probably much, of the Hertfordshire malt was transported by road through Ware and Highgate;[2] but the only riverless county from which any great quantity of grain was sent to victual the Henrician forces was Wiltshire.

The areas from which livestock were supplied were equally distinct.

---

[1] Other transactions, recorded only in monetary terms (including a total of £26,257 worth of grain) have necessarily been excluded from the figures. These latter transactions broadly confirm the following account, though giving less prominence to Norfolk.

[2] LP IV, i, p. 23.

As with the corn of Holderness and the sotthern seaboard, proximity to Berwick or Calais played a part in the marketing development of these areas. The principal livestock county for the supply of Calais and Boulogne was Kent, especially the level tracts of Romney Marsh, with its Wealden hinterland to the north. About four times as many cattle (principally oxen) and seven times as many sheep and lambs were supplied from this region as from the rest of the country. Many of the 10,000 or so animals known to have been purchased there may, it is true, have been driven from other parts of England; but the predominance of Kentish cattle in the Calais traffic can hardly be questioned. For the supply of Berwick the information is too scanty to formulate reliable figures. Originally much of the stock required seems to have been furnished locally; much continued to be obtained by border raiding. But for both border garrisons and troopships, as well as for the forces raised to suppress the Northern Rebellion in 1536, large numbers of cattle seem to have been obtained in the countryside around Peterborough, Kettering, Rothwell, Oakham, Spalding, and Huntingdon. This district, together with the Newark area to the north-west, was to remain an important cattle region throughout the period.

For the supply of horses for the Henrician armies there is unfortunately little information. For the northern armies the majority were requisitioned in the border counties, though numbers were also purchased in Northamptonshire and probably in Suffolk. Supplies of cheese and butter came mainly from Suffolk and Essex, dispatched from Harwich in quantities of up to 100 weys and £1,000 worth at a time. The butter trade of Whitby and Stockton does not seem to have developed until the end of the period; by then it provided a useful basis for the supply of Charles I's forces during the Bishops' Wars.[1]

The importance of victualling as a factor in the agricultural development of these various regions was probably considerable. That it originated their several specializations is improbable. But in the large quantities of corn sent to Berwick and Newcastle for the victualling of Henry VIII's armies it is difficult not to trace an important source of the later grain trade from East Anglia to the north, which by 1600 had reached impressive proportions.[2] Similarly, the traditional devotion of Romney Marsh to stock-raising cannot have remained unaffected

---

[1] CSPD 1639–40, p. 563.

[2] Originally grain supplies for the Border were requisitioned locally. But the northern counties were too poor to support the burden during the frequent dearth years, and the government was forced to look further afield—first to Holderness, then to Lincolnshire, finally to Lynn—to supply both its own garrisons and the local population.

by Henry VIII's demands for thousands of cattle and sheep for the English garrisons in France. In all probability the victualling of military forces in the later years of Elizabeth and during the Civil War exerted a similar influence upon English husbandry. Undoubtedly the naval victualling of the Interregnum period affected the economy of Suffolk.[1] The study of these latter topics is too extensive a field to be undertaken here; but the effect of military victualling upon agricultural development as a whole would repay detailed investigation.

A study of the organization of victualling reveals many points of similarity to that of purveyance. Its gradual transfer from royal purveyors to private factors and merchants was quite as striking. In Henry VIII's reign it was still undertaken mainly by the Board of Green Cloth. From the outset, however, a certain amount was entrusted to "the adventure of the merchants," and little by little the purveyors' share declined while mercantile purchasing increased.[2] Where purveyors began by requisitioning goods in local markets in person, they continued by contracting with provincial factors to assist them, and ended by committing the organization to the capable hands of metropolitan and provincial merchants. Under the Tudors, for example, the supply of cheese and butter for Berwick was organized by a medley of royal purveyors visiting the eastern counties; in 1640 the supply required for Charles I's armies in the north was entrusted to a group of five London cheesemongers.[3] The political significance of this development became apparent when, during the Civil War, such merchants found Parliament a more reliable paymaster than the king.

Little less important was the new commercial experience which victualling afforded to provincial factors. The necessity of supplying large numbers of men encouraged them to think in terms, not of hundreds, but of thousands of quarters of corn, and not of scores, but hundreds of sheep and cattle. The grant of 'protections' to the tradesmen of country towns who travelled in the retinue of Henrician generals and governors opened the eyes of many an obscure merchant to the possibilities of European commerce. A victualler of Canterbury, an innholder of Guildford, a wheelwright of Long Melford, a vintner of King's Lynn, a horse-seller of Hythe, a clothier of Halifax, a grocer

---

[1] For the reign of Elizabeth, cf. Brian Pearce, 'Elizabethan Food Policy and the Armed Forces', EcHR XII, 1942, pp. 39–46. Dr N. J. Williams mentions that in 1588–9 16,000 quarters of corn, and in 1589–90 21,000 quarters, were shipped from Lynn when the English army was in the Netherlands: *op. cit.*, p. 89. For victualling in the Interregnum period there is much information in the Navy and Admiralty Records in the State Papers.

[2] Cf. LP, 1st edn., 1509–14, p. 768, and XX, i, p. 252. Many commissions to purveyors for victualling forces going abroad are calendared in LP, 2nd edn., I.

[3] Cf. Req. 2, 55, 50; CSPD 1639–40, p. 563.

of Cranbrook, a draper of Coventry, a butcher of Bury St Edmunds: these and scores of other men from market towns all over the country obtained their first glimpse of the great world as private victuallers to Lord Berners, Sir Robert Wingfield, or Sir Thomas Clifford.[1]

Nor were mercantile men the sole beneficiaries. If royal purveyors and private victuallers are known to have made personal fortunes in supplying the troops, the gentry from whose ancestral acres they purchased their corn and cattle also benefited. The names of many a well-known family of the seventeenth and eighteenth centuries figure prominently in the victualling records in the *Letters and Papers*. Stanhopes in the North; Faunts and Hastingses in the Midlands; Auchers and Lovelaces in Kent; Rouses, Wentworths, Moundefords, Calthorpes, Jernynghams, Pastons, and Wodehouses in East Anglia: these and other families owed not a little of their riches to the hunger of Tudor troops.

Yet it is important not to exaggerate the novelty or extent of these new influences. As in the metropolitan market, family connection continued to play as large a part in the victualling of the forces as individual competition.[2] The traffic in barley, wheat, and malt from Norfolk to Calais was no casual or haphazard venture. It was controlled by a knot of relatives and neighbours; by men like Anthony Rous, his kinsman George Rous, his friend Robert Bonde, his neighbour John Marshall, and a handful of other neighbouring gentry and yeomen. When Edward Fogge, a gentleman "of great wealth and very well-friended in the country" of Kent, travelled to France as lieutenant to Sir Maurice Dennis, it was his own countryman, Marcks Questonbury of Canterbury, who attended him as victualler to his officers and troops.[3] The pattern can be taken as typical of the system as a whole.

Neither must it be supposed that the stimulus of victualling and the new market which it opened up were universally welcomed. A few people were enthusiastic, many were opposed, perhaps most were unaffected. The government experienced much local antagonism in obtaining supplies. Its wholesale purchasing caused frequent local dearth and disrupted the commercial life of market towns like Dover and Hythe.[4] Like the feeding of London, the feeding of troops benefited certain sections of the community only and affected small pockets of countryside in a landscape still largely untamed by commercial farming.

[1] LP IV, *passim*.
[2] The office of purveyor frequently descended in the same family for several generations.—Woodworth, *op. cit.*, p. 30.
[3] Cf. LP XX, i, pp. 28, 64, *et passim;* Req. 2, 257, 4.
[4] See, for example, LP V, p. 685, VIII, p. 201, XX, i, p. 553, XII, i, p. 21.

3. The export market

The development of the export market went hand in hand with that of victualling: the two were to some extent complementary. English farmers who in wartime increased their production or extended their acreage to meet the requirements of Tudor armies found themselves saddled, when peace was restored, with a considerable surplus. In all probability their wartime experience suggested the expedient of exploiting European markets, and their surplus was switched from the English soldier to the French or Flemish artisan. Agrarian export did not commence with the Tudor era; but its revival after the decline of the preceding century was certainly stimulated by the victualling of Henrician forces abroad.

Apart from the export of wool in the early decades of the sixteenth century, the most important agricultural export was corn, particularly barley and wheat. The export trade in grain was an ancient one, and during the fourteenth century had achieved notable proportions. Between 1300 and 1399 the average annual grain exports of each English port amounted to some 866 quarters, and in one year more than 6,600 quarters were dispatched from the single harbour of Sandwich.[1] During the following century the average (i.e. annual *median*) figure for each port fell sharply to 410 quarters. With the first half of our period it rose again to 446 quarters, and in the latter half to almost double the fourteenth-century figure: 1,501 quarters per port, and some 20,000 quarters for the whole country. In all probability the peak was reached between 1570 and 1600 and was followed by a temporary decline under the first two Stuarts, with a second revival after 1660.[2]

How far do these figures present an accurate picture of the exportation of English grain? They are useful chiefly as an indication of the changing pattern of trade as a whole, but they require a good deal of care in interpretation. In the first place, mere averages conceal large fluctuations in the annual volume of traffic from the same port. A typical example is the 'port' of Sandwich, that is the complex of harbours and creeks of East Kent. During the sixteenth century Sandwich exported, on the average, 342 quarters of grain a year; but its

[1] The following paragraphs are based mainly upon an analysis of the export figures listed in Gras, *op. cit.*, Appendix C. The reader should be warned, however, that for some periods Gras's information is very sparse, and overmuch weight should not be placed on the averages mentioned in the text. Information in Williams, *op. cit.*, and in numerous cases in Requests, Chancery, and the Exchequer has also been taken into account.

[2] But the early Stuart figures in Gras's Appendix relate mainly to 1600–15 and are too few to bear much weight.

trade varied from 40 quarters in 1559–60 to 2,112 quarters in 1572–3. At Lynn exports rose from 180 quarters in 1509 to a peak of over 20,000 quarters in 1588–9, with troughs of 450 quarters in 1553–4 and 280 quarters in 1590. Or take the instance of Southampton, with recorded exports of 70 quarters in 1491–2, 4,856 quarters in 1516–17, 10 quarters in 1519–20, and 1,985 in 1538–9. In all its aspects the grain trade was a risky business, but nowhere more so than in the export market.

Secondly, the *total* expansion of exports during the sixteenth century was greater than the *average* figures suggest. During the fifteenth century the number of years in which less than 500 quarters was exported from the whole country was large—more than three in five—while in only one year in six was more than 1,500 quarters sent abroad. Between 1500 and 1569, on the other hand, annual exports exceeded 1,500 quarters in every fourth year, and between 1570 and 1640 in nearly every other year. In the absence of figures covering the whole century it is impossible to estimate total Tudor grain exports: but it is safe to say that in the last half of the sixteenth century they were several times higher, probably quite six or eight times, than in the first half of the fifteenth. The expansion of grain exports during the reign of Elizabeth was not an entirely novel phenomenon, but it was a striking achievement.

Finally, since the figures are based upon customs accounts and port-books, they reveal nothing of the unlawful traffic in grain which escaped the easy eyes of Tudor officials. It has been suggested that at least half the traffic between England and France was illicit, and that in some years as much as 20,000 quarters of Norfolk's wheat and barley exports evaded the customs officers at King's Lynn.[1]

Despite these reservations, which must be given full weight, a clear pattern emerges in the corn export trade between 1500 and 1640. The most important trading area was again East Anglia. Probably about one third of grain exports during the fourteenth century was dispatched from east coast ports. Between 1500 and 1570 the proportion rose to about 50 per cent, and between 1570 and 1640 to 75 per cent. The volume of corn sent from northern ports, considerable in the fourteenth century, dwindled almost to nothing in the fifteenth, but rose again nearly fourfold between 1500 and 1640; its proportion of the whole trade expanded from some 6 per cent in the first half of the period to 8 or 9 per cent in the second. The south-coast traffic also increased absolutely, but its relative proportion remained stationary at 11 or 12 per cent of the English grain trade as a whole. In the west of England corn exports declined, from an average of 416 quarters to only 242

[1] Williams, *op. cit.*, pp. 82, 131.

quarters per port, and from 36 per cent to probably less than 8 per cent of the whole trade. The years 1500–1640 thus seem to have witnessed a striking expansion of grain exports from the eastern counties, a smaller increase in those from the north, relative stagnation in the south, and virtual extinction in the west of England.

In all areas trade tended to become concentrated in fewer ports. Virtually the whole grain surplus of northern England, from the corn-lands of Holderness and north Lincolnshire, was exported from Hull; that of the west of England, primarily from Bristol and Bridgwater; that of the south, from Sandwich and, on occasion, Chichester. Nowhere was the concentration clearer than in East Anglia, where more than 80 per cent of the trade was handled by King's Lynn and Yarmouth. It is probably safe to say that during the latter half of the period at least 60 per cent of the country's grain exports were sent from these two latter ports. Of this 60 per cent, probably more than half consisted of malt and barley, a further quarter of rye, and about one eighth of wheat.[1] The bulk of the East Anglian corn was probably harvested in Norfolk itself, though much barley and malt was also brought down the Ouse and Cam from Bedfordshire, Cambridge-shire, and Huntingdonshire.

The principal destination of English grain, at least from eastern counties, was the Netherlands: Antwerp and the other great cities of the Scheldt, Amsterdam and those of Holland. One Amsterdam merchant purchased 360 quarters of wheat, malt, and barley through the agency of an innholder in Boston.[2] Thomas Mascall of Maidstone and Martin Cann of London had "great dealings together by the space of six or seven years" in purchasing grain in Essex, Norfolk, and Kent, and dispatching it to their factors in Flanders. A couple of Ipswich merchant-adventurers sent regular supplies of malt—50 and 140 quarters at a time—in the *Katherine*, *John*, and *Thomas* of Ipswich to the "macklers and brokers" of Bruges. They obtained it through their partner Thomas Dennett, the Ipswich innkeeper in whose house it was made; they loaded it "by stealth" at Holbrooke, and (all too typically) "transported the same into the parts beyond the seas without warrant, licence, or docket."[3]

The Low Countries were not the sole destination of grain exports. The same Thomas Mascall and Martin Cann, and a number of other merchants of Sussex and Kent, and sometimes of Norfolk and Suffolk,

[1] Williams, *op. cit.*, p. 179 (figures for 1575–6 and 1586–7).

[2] *Ibid.*, pp. 80, 82, 89; Req. 2, 38, 41; cf. Req. 2, 94, 3, Req. 2, 109, 60, E 134, 19–20 Eliz., M 12.

[3] Req. 2, 60, 3; E 178, 2164; Req. 2, 112, 24; cf. Req. 2, 95, 16, Req. 2, 96, 21.

also traded to Rouen and other cities of northern and western France. From Devon and Cornwall, considerable cargoes of wheat and other grain were dispatched to Brittany and Bordeaux. [1]During the earlier and later years of the century corn was sent from Bristol, Bridgwater, and Bideford to Spain, the extent of the trade waxing and waning with the state of Henry VIII's matrimonial enthusiasms and the exigencies of Elizabethan foreign policy.[2] A certain amount of corn was also shipped down the Severn from Tewkesbury and Worcester, and exported to European markets from Gloucester. In the later years of the century grain was sent to Spain and the Atlantic islands from the eastern counties as well. In 1582–3 fourteen vessels left Blakeney laden with 2,000 quarters of corn for Spain; the same year a shipment of 231 quarters of wheat left Hull for "Vego in the isles of Byon;" and in Charles I's reign there seems to have been some traffic in wheat, beans, and peas from Newhaven and London to the Canaries.[3]

The grain trade with Ireland was probably a largely west country affair. Between Bristol and Youghal in County Cork the connection was close and frequent. Beans, malt, and wheat figured most prominently in these west country exports. By Queen Elizabeth's reign a further connection with Ireland was established by the ports of Ipswich, Weymouth, and Dover: a merchant of Ipswich and London established factors in both Dublin and Galway for the disposal of regular shipments of English malt there. From Northumberland, and occasionally East Anglia, grain and malt were exported to Scotland. During the Henrician wars "immense quantities" of corn were said to be passing across the border daily, no doubt to feed hungry armies on the other side.[4]

Compared with the trade in grain and malt, that of other agricultural products was small.[5] The export of livestock was probably insignificant, apart from a certain surreptitious traffic from Dover and Romney Marsh. England was already a large importer of cattle from other parts of the British Isles, notably Scotland and Wales. No doubt

[1] Req. 2, 60, 3; Req. 2, 95, 16; LP v, pp. 414–5, x, p. 145; HMC, *Reports*, xi, vii, p. 166; E 178, 656; E 134, 28 Eliz., H 8.

[2] E 134, 26 Eliz., H 1; E 134, 25–26 Eliz., M 16. There are many references in LP (e.g. ii, pp. 339, 806, 916, iii, pp. 892, 1287) to export of corn to Spain. Licences were often granted to members of Katherine of Aragon's household or at the emporer's specific request.

[3] E 134, 14–15 Eliz., M 9; cf. LP xviii, i, p. 202; Williams, *op. cit.*, p. 145; E 134, 26–27 Eliz., M 19; CSPD 1639–40, p. 152.

[4] Req. 2, 290, 35; LP iii, p. 1324; cf. LP ii, pp. 486, 536, 1269, iii, p. 1285, v, pp. 79–80, viii, p. 304.

[5] The overseas wool-trade in the early sixteenth century is of course an exception. It has been considered too large and specialized a subject to treat in the present context. The reader should refer to Bowden, *op. cit.*, chapter VI *et passim*.

the greater part of the 40,000 beasts said, in the early seventeenth century, to be transported annually from Ireland found their ultimate destination in English markets; and certainly large numbers of Irish cattle were exported to the fattening grounds and market towns of Somerset.[1]

By Charles I's reign, small numbers of English horses seem to have been exported. Between October 1631 and September 1632 nearly five hundred geldings, horses, and mares were shipped across the Channel from Dover to Calais, no doubt bred on the Kentish downland, where many of the wealthier farmers possessed considerable numbers of horses (on the average more than three times as many as in the Weald).[2] It would be interesting to know whether horse-breeding on the Yorkshire Wolds and the export of horses from Ipswich for Tudor forces in France led to similar exportation by this date. The breeding of blood horses was already a highly technical art, and few but gentry possessed sufficient leisure or education to indulge in it. It was an enthusiastic pursuit of families like the Oxindens of Deane and Great Maydeken in East Kent, and the Barnardistons of Kedington, near Newmarket, in Suffolk.[3]

More important was the export of butter and cheese. The trade was centred primarily in Suffolk, in South Wales, and, by the end of the period, in the Whitby and Stockton area. The bulk of Suffolk's cheese output was taken by London; but much was also "stolen from havens commodious for that purpose for foreign markets;" for their was generally a ready sale for Suffolk cheese at Calais and other Channel ports—English, Flemish, and French. Of Welsh butter, some was transported to Ireland and much to Bordeaux and La Rochelle. It was manufactured principally in Glamorgan and dispatched from Cardiff, Barry, and Aberthaw. Not infrequently Welsh vessels travelled via west-country ports and loaded further supplies at Barnstaple or Minehead. During Charles I's reign the Welsh trade was officially organized through a trading company, operating under a royal patent in the hands of Lord Goring and Sir Henry Hungate, with a joint stock of £5,000 for the export of 3,000 barrels of butter per annum. Much of the traffic was actually conducted by metropolitan and provincial merchants, who purchased their licences from the noble

[1] Cf. Req. 2, 285, 32; LP xviii, i, p. 492; SP 16, 14, 36. In 1665 nearly 100,000 Irish sheep, of English breed, were imported, so that the export of foundation stock to Ireland at some time "must have been very considerable."—R. Trow-Smith, *A History of British Livestock Husbandry to 1700*, 1957, p. 230.

[2] E 134, 8 Car. I, M 20. Kentish probate inventories suggest an average of two horses on each farm in the Weald, and six on the Downs.

[3] Essex RO, B/7. 13, 38.1502, Clopton Diary, *passim;* Dorothy Gardiner, ed., *The Oxinden Letters 1607–1642*, 1933, *passim.*

promoters: for the "Welsh butter business" was a typical Stuart racket for the benefit of penurious gentry.[1]

Leather and skins were exported in some volume from various parts of England. In Queen Elizabeth's reign, coney skins in quantities of 26,000 at a time were purchased in London by a merchant of Ipswich for export to Danzig. No doubt they were a by-product of the metropolitan trade in coneys from Wiltshire, Berkshire, and other counties.[2] There was also a substantial trade in leather and skins to Scotland. In James I's reign "a great number of sheepskins and pelts [were] every year conveyed and sold forth of this realm [of England] and carried by land carriage into the realm of Scotland..." A Cumbrian gentleman, Thomas Blennerhassett, had seen "horses loaden with sheepskins going over the Sands" of Solway. The markets of Wigton and Carlisle were regularly visited by merchants from Edinburgh and Dumfries, who conveyed their purchases by packhorse across the fells. No doubt wherever the farming emphasis was laid on livestock and the sea-coast was near, a more or less illicit trade in hides and leather developed.[3] There are numerous cases touching upon the subject in the Exchequer Special Commissions and Depositions.

Finally, a few special exports from the southern counties may be mentioned. Wood was sometimes exported in considerable quantities from Kent and Sussex to France, especially during time of war. It was evidently conveyed principally to the Parts of Calais, and consisted largely of billet wood. In Henry VIII's reign one Sussex wood merchant obtained licences to export up to eight million billets in four years. From Kent small quantities of hops were at times exported, and considerable quantities of beer. In Henry VIII's reign many hundreds of tuns of Kentish beer were sent to slake the thirst of Frenchmen and Flemings. The trade continued at least until the time of the Spanish Armada.[4]

A full account of the organization of the export market would require a volume to itself. Only its salient characteristics can be mentioned here. As a whole it broadened yet further those new horizons which private marketing, in all its forms, began to open up

[1] Reyce, op. cit., p. 41; LP xxi, i, p. 727; Williams, op. cit., p. 129; SP 16, 18, 5; E 134, 23–24 Car. I, H 1; E 178, 3445; E 178, 4143; E 134, 23–24 Car. I, H 1.

[2] Cf. Req. 2, 121, 3. In this case, however, the Londoner neglected to fulfil his contract.

[3] Cf. E 134, 11 James I, T 2. At Carlisle the customer was known to turn an indulgent eye in return for an occasional gratuity.

[4] LP iv, passim, xi, p. 179; E 178, 1134. The Kentish hop trade seems to have existed before 1524, when Sir Edward Guldeford, a Kentishman, obtained a licence to export hops and madder.—LP iv, p. 125.

to provincial people. London drew its supplies, by and large, from the shires of lowland England, or in north-country phrase "the up-countries." Victualling took the English factor or tradesman as far afield as Berwick and Boulogne. But in the export market the country merchant sometimes travelled with his barley to Flushing, his oats to Brittany, his malt to Galway, his butter to La Rochelle, and his wheat to St Sebastian and the Canaries. It was only a small company to whom these new vistas were being opened; but within it many an export merchant was a truly cosmopolitan figure.

Yet, as in other spheres, the new methods and techniques, however apparently advanced, still operated through a network of family connection and personal friendship. Grants of Henrician export licences were rarely made to merchants direct, but to courtiers and knights of the body, servants of Katherine of Aragon, or personal favourites of the king. These men either granted their rights away to their own friends and dependants, bartered them to merchants of their native county, or sold them for hard cash to metropolitan tradesmen. The local merchant, after purchasing his licence, set on foot a similar process in his own town, forming a working partnership from among his relatives and neighbours. How closely this community of seafaring traders was bound together by kinship and acquaintance is demonstrated in the records of many a legal dispute in the courts of Exchequer and Requests. One London merchant, anxious to procure "a ship's loading of wheat" for Spain, desired his neighbour's brother in Norfolk to "help him to [it]." A Glamorgan merchant, wishing to dispose of a load of butter at La Rochelle, asked his brother, who was travelling as a passenger in the ship, to undertake the business for him. A Norfolk merchant, William Castell of King's Lynn, formed a partnership with his sons George and Robert and with their brother-in-law Mr Myllecent Smythe, because of the "great...charity and acquaintance between them."[1]

The underworld of crime and violence which existed in English ports owed much of its vitality to the *esprit de corps* of this seafaring community. Unlawful exportation was closely intertwined with local feuds and family rivalry. Port books and customs accounts convey an impression of orderly marketing which is belied by the flotsam and jetsom cast up in commercial lawsuits. It will be sufficient to cite here a single example. In March 1579 the *Peter* of Looe was standing half laden with wheat, the goods of John Trevyll, merchant, in West Looe harbour. Hearing that the cargo was destined for Spain, apparently without licence, the queen's officer entered the ship, chalked on the mast "the sign of the broad arrow for the Queen's Majesty," and

[1] Req. 2, 65, 79; E 178, 4143; Req. 2, 109, 60.

ordered his servants to remain in the vessel overnight. At midnight Trevyll and his men re-entered the ship, claiming authority from a "justice of the peace to send [the officer] and his company to the gaol," threatening to "carry them into the holly house of Spayne, and that [the officer] should never come into England again to stay or arrest him any more corn..." The searcher's assistants were then "expulsed" from the ship with the assistance of such "horrible weapons" as "sherehokes, bills, bows and arrows, and callivers." One unhappy individual "was taken out of his cabbye asleep and his mouth stopped, and carried between men, [and] was cast out into the sea, where he was like to have been drowned, but that God provided a remedy for him by swimming." The *Peter* of Looe then sailed away to Spain "by stealth," passing by Plymouth, where further corn was laden, and by Saltash Passage, where the searcher was quietly bribed off with eight bushels of wheat. The significance of the case lies in the fact that such occurrences were not merely acts of haphazard violence; they were also calculated incidents in the course of local rivalries and long-standing feuds between families like the Devonian Courtenays, Bullers, Glanvilles, and Keckwickes.[1]

If much of the process of exporting farm produce, from the grant of a licence to the bribery of searchers, seems but a series of abuses, it must be remembered that the kind of impersonal society essential to administrative efficiency had scarcely begun to exist. The abuse was merely symptomatic of a malady inherent in Tudor and Stuart society. It arose from the rapid development of a national, and indeed international, system of commerce within an intensely personal and localized form of society.

D. THE DEVELOPMENT OF PRIVATE MARKETING:
(B) IN THE PROVINCES

Despite the importance of the aspects of private marketing so far considered, they accounted for only a minor part of agricultural dealing outside the market town. Their effect upon the development of private trading was far-reaching; but the bulk of private trade was undertaken with provincial consumption in mind. A few figures relating to the population of the country will bear this out. Between 1500 and 1640 the population of England probably expanded by something like 75 per cent, from under three millions to over four-and-a-half millions. Of this increase, perhaps 200,000 was added to London and one-and-a·

[1] E 134, 23 Eliz., E 14; for a similar case involving the same group cf. E 134 28-9 Eliz., M 18.

half million to the countryside.[1] There must, therefore, have been an expansion of quite two thirds in the consumption of agricultural produce in the provinces. Much of this expansion was met locally; but for various reasons much could not be. In the first place, the increase in population was unevenly distributed. On moorland, down, or wold it was slight; in areas of new enclosure population sometimes declined. But in towns like Norwich, Ipswich, and Exeter; in the clothing areas of the west country, the north, and East Anglia; and in manufacturing districts like Tyneside and the borders of Staffordshire and Warwickshire, the increase of population was relatively rapid. As these latter areas expanded, they were compelled to import supplies from more productive or less densely populated districts. In the second place, not all parts of the country were equally capable of increasing their production to meet the expansion in demand. In some parts little or no 'waste' remained, and the area of cultivation could not be extended; in some, poor soils or an unfavourable climate precluded more intensive farming; in some, social custom or local prejudice retarded it. Elsewhere, however—as in the cornlands of East Anglia, the sheep pastures of Northamptonshire, or the grazing lands of Somerset and the fens—conditions were ripe for an extension of traditional specializations and an increase of production. The former areas thus tended to become dependent on the latter for their supplies.

Much of the increase in agricultural trade resulting from this regional interdependence took place in the 'open' market and there were many Tudor towns which attracted traders from distant places. The primary *raison d'etre* of the Tudor market town, however, was still the disposal of a *local* surplus. For trade on a regional or national scale either annual fairs or private transactions in inns and farmhouses provided a more usual method of dealing. To these two forms of private trading we must now direct attention, bearing in mind at the same time that the distinction between the 'private' and 'open' markets was not always so sharp in practice as a generalized account may seem to suggest.

I. *Trading at fairs*

The fair was a very ancient feature of English life. According to Cornelius Walford there are "very distinct traces of fairs of Roman origin at Helston (Cornwall), at Barnwell (by Cambridge), at Newcastle upon Tyne, and at several places along the line of the Roman wall in Northumberland." Some fairs seem to have developed from heathen festivals or from customary tribal meetings. Several of the

[1] Gras, *op. cit.*, p. 75, and see note , p. , above.

great downland sheep fairs of the South, like Tan Hill and Yarnbury Castle in Wiltshire, were held on prehistoric sites, or near the junction of Roman roads or ancient trackways, as at Weyhill in Hampshire. A number of fairs came into existence during the Anglo-Saxon period, generally by prescription and as a result, it has been conjectured, of the meeting of litigants and others at county courts held about Eastertide and Michaelmas. But the golden age for the establishment of fairs, as of markets, was the period between the Norman Conquest and the Black Death, with a further spurt of activity, in some counties, in the later fifteenth and sixteenth centuries. In Somerset alone more than 90 fairs were founded between 1066 and 1500. Of these later fairs the majority were established by charter, though sometimes charters merely confirmed prescriptive rights while turning the potential profits of the fair into a source of revenue. In general, fairs were held in summer or autumn, often on the patronal festival of the parish church; in Kent, for instance, two fairs out of three were held between June and October.[1]

In origin fairs were thus frequently associated with the regulated 'open market'. But although the grant of market rights to a town or village almost always included the right to hold fairs—generally once or twice a year, occasionally four or five times—many fairs were not held under the aegis of a market town. In Somerset in the early eighteenth century there were no fewer than 180 fairs held each year, of which the majority were in existence in 1600; yet there were no more than 39 market towns in the county. In Kent there were thirty-three market towns; whereas Lambarde, writing about 1570, lists over sixty annual fairs, and a good number of others certainly escaped his notice. Numerous obscure villages like Bethersden and Mereworth in the Weald, or Challock and Stelling on the Downs, or Kemsing and Brasted in Holmesdale held annual fairs—but no weekly markets.[2] The same situation obtained in Cornwall and no doubt in most other counties.

[1] Cornelius Walford, *Fairs, Past and Present: a chapter in History of Commerce*, 1883, pp. 13, 14; *Royal Commission on Market Rights and Tolls*, 1889, I, pp. 1, 7; N. F. Hulbert, 'A Survey of the Somerset Fairs', *Som. Arch. and Nat. Hist. Soc.*, LXXXII, 1937, pp. 86, 155-6; William Lambarde, *A Perambulation of Kent*, 1826, pp. 53-5. For a valuable account of the fairs of York, see H. Richardson, *op. cit.*, pp. 3-21. Quite half the south Somerset fairs were founded by the church, and two fifths were held on the patronal festivals of parish churches. Forty-seven of the sixty-nine fairs in Suffolk were held between May and September.—Ipswich and East Suffolk RO, MS copy of Reyce's *Breviary*.

[2] Hulbert, *op. cit.*, p. 86; Lambarde, *loc. cit.* Richard Grafton, in *A Little Treatise containing many proper Tables and Rules...*, 1572, lists 352 "principal fairs" in England; the 1602 edition lists 494.

Only a small part of the business transacted at fairs, moreover, was regulated in the same strict sense as in markets. Sales were supposed to be recorded, and in some towns, like Leominster and Shrewsbury, careful toll books were compiled. But in many places much traffic slipped through unrecorded.[1] Perhaps no more than a tithe of the many thousands of sheep sold annually at Stow-on-the-Wold passed through the official channels of tollbooth and turnstile.[2] A handful of urban officials could not hope to keep track of the whole traffic; still less a village constable or manorial steward. It was, indeed, largely as a result of this relative freedom that fairs were able to respond more readily to the stimulus of expanding demand than market towns.

The staple commodity of the majority of fairs was cattle. There was no region of England and Wales without its chain of cattle fairs: Maidstone, Lenham, and Ashford in Kent; Somerton, Bath, and Frome in Somerset; Preston and Burnley in Lancashire; Northallerton, Wakefield, and Rotherham in Yorkshire; Coventry, Northampton, and Market Harborough in the Midlands; Rhos Fair, Eglwyswrw, and Knighton in Wales; and a series of fairs in the counties north and east of London—Aldreth, Epping, Waltham, Uxbridge, and many others in the country stretching away into Lincolnshire. Total cattle sales at these major fairs, though allowance must be made for the vagaries of Tudor arithmetic, sometimes ran into thousands. Single purchases of fifty northern cattle at a time were made by one minor Kentish gentleman at Maidstone Fair. Droves of eleven score or more were driven by two partners from Cheshire and Shropshire to Epping, Blackmore, and Could Fairs in Essex. Thousands of Welsh cattle are said to have been sold at Knighton Fair, "a very great trade" coming thither over Builth bridge and passing into England. And up to 20,000 beasts gathered yearly, it was said, on Bowes Moor in Yorkshire in James I's reign.[3] There were, in addition, scores of minor cattle fairs scattered up and down the country, like Appledore, Bethersden, Cranbrook, Hawkhurst, Smarden, and Tenterden in the Weald of Kent. At many of these latter fairs, probably no more than a few hundred cattle were sold, and these in the main were bought by local farmers and tradesmen. At Leominster, in 1556, the toll book of the horse and beast fair

[1] Some Welsh fairs may be an exception. Surviving toll books for two Machynlleth fairs in 1632 record sales of 3,800 sheep.—Elwyn Evans, 'Two Machynlleth Toll-Books', *Nat. Lib. Wales Jnl.*, VI, 1949–50, p. 79. See also E. A. Lewis, 'The Toll-Books of some North Pembrokeshire Fairs (1599–1603)', *Bull. BCS*, VII, 1934, pp. 284–318. For further information on Welsh fairs see chapter   .

[2] E 134, 6 James I, E 36. The Stow tolls for the two fairs in 1612 were worth £60 6s. 4d.; in the 1660's, £70 10s. on an average each year. Thereafter their value declined to £49 p.a. in the 1690's—Glos. RO, D.621/M.18.

[3] Lodge, *op. cit.*, p. 47; E 134, 11 Car. I, E 20; E 134, 7 Car. I, M 15; E 178, 4831.

records sales of only ninety-eight cattle, though, as has been mentioned, many may have been sold without being recorded.[1]

Next in importance to cattle fairs were those for sheep. These were not so numerous, but they were often more exclusively devoted to the one type of animal. The principal sheep fairs were situated either near marshland pastures, like Romford in Essex, Aldreth in Cambridgeshire, and Cowlinge in Suffolk; or on southern downlands, like Yarnbury Castle in Wiltshire, East Ilsley in Berkshire, and Alresford in Hampshire; or on the fells and wolds of the North, like Kilham in the East Riding and Bowes in the Yorkshire Dales; or near the moors and mountains of Wales, like Machynlleth in Montgomeryshire. On these windswept sites, often far out in the country, it was not unusual for several thousand sheep to be sold at a time. Three thousand eight hundred sheep are recorded in the toll books of two Machynlleth fairs in 1632; fifteen or sixteen thousand are said to have been sold at Stow-on-the-Wold in James I's reign; and 30,000 or so in a single part of Weyhill Fair in 1683.[2]

Horse fairs were also numerous, but were more modest in scale. They rarely accounted for the sale of more than a few hundred animals at a time. There were probably few counties without two or three horse fairs for the supply of local draught animals. For riding and blood-horses, as well as cart-horses, the principal fairs were grouped in a few select regions. One district, on the borders of Cambridgeshire, Suffolk, and Essex, included Newmarket, Woolpit, Bardfield, Barnwell, Cowlinge, Newport Pond, Reach, and Earith; another, stretching from the edge of Oxfordshire through Warwick to Northampton and Leicester, included Abingdon, Woodstock, Banbury, Stratford, Towcester, Rothwell, Northampton, Fotheringhay, Melton Mowbray, and Market Harborough. There were also two or three smaller groups of horse fairs in Herefordshire, Shropshire, East Yorkshire, and East Kent, including Leominster, Brewood, Shrewsbury, Howden, Bethersden, and Challock.[3]

No other commodity sold at fairs approached cattle, sheep, or horses in importance, with the possible exception of the wool and hops sold at Stourbridge. According to the charter of 1589, Stourbridge Fair "far surpassed the greatest and most celebrated fairs of all England;

[1] Leominster Corp. Records, Toll Book, 1556. I am indebted to Mr Philip Styles for lending me his transcript of this manuscript.

[2] Evans, op. cit., pp. 78–9; E 134, 6 James I, E 36; VCH Hants., IV, p. 398.

[3] Horse fairs were more strictly regulated than others; horses were costly animals and dealers were well versed in the arts of deception. The toll-books of Brewood Fair show that toll-gatherers were appointed to guard all four entrances to the fair. Names, places, and occupations of sellers and buyers were noted in the toll books and all animals minutely described.—Staffs. RO, D. 590/435, Nos. 1, 2.

whence great benefits had resulted to the merchants of the whole kingdom, who...sold their wares and merchandises to purchasers coming from all parts of the realm..." With its elaborate layout of streets and squares, its booths for jewellers, perfumers, silkmen, haberdashers, drapers, upholsterers, cabinet-makers, potters, pewterers, braziers, gunsmiths, and ironmongers, Stourbridge Fair provided for sixteenth-century provincials much of what a departmental store in the West End of London does today. With its inns and theatres, its fortune-tellers, its harlots, and "Lord of the Taps," it had developed to a fantastic degree the gay, licentious side of fairs which often led to their proscription in Victorian England.[1] But the fame of Stourbridge Fair has probably exaggerated its importance as an agricultural mart. As a cattle and sheep fair it was probably not of great significance, and as an emporium for horses it was rapidly declining—by Defoe's time it was extinct. Its purely agricultural importance was largely limited to the two products, wool and hops. If Defoe's description of the wool and cloth fair, held in the great central square called the Duddery, can be applied to the previous century, it was certainly immense. There is little readily accessible evidence of its scale in the sixteenth century, but cloth was brought from as far off as Stow-on-the-Wold and Bristol; the trade in wool was probably not so considerable.[2] For hops, Stourbridge was probably the only major fair in this period, though certain quantities were also sold at fairs in Hampshire, Kent, and Surrey.[3] The local trade from Essex and Suffolk, perhaps the first two counties to grow hops on a commercial scale, was augmented by supplies from Maidstone, Canterbury, and Farnham, transported by way of the Medway, Stour, and Wey, and thence by sea and river to the edge of the fairground itself. In an age when beer was the staple drink of the community and was necessarily brewed for longer periods than now, great quantities of hops were required by all sections of the community. Stourbridge became the mart not only for the east Midlands, but for much of the west country and the north, where soil and climate did not favour extensive local production.

The remaining products dealt in at fairs require only brief comment. A few fairs in Hampshire, Dorset, Somerset, East Anglia, and the Midlands specialized in the disposal of cheese: among them Frome,

[1] Walford, op. cit., pp. 78, 106, 108, 109, 123; cf. Williams, op. cit., p. 64; VCH Cambs., III, pp. 92–5. The Lord of the Taps was the aletaster.

[2] Defoe, op. cit., I, pp. 81–2, 85; Walford, op. cit., p. 91; Bowden, op. cit., p. 65 and n. 'Dud' is a dialect word for cloth.

[3] Req. 2, 239, 57; Essex RO, B, 7.13, 38.1502, Clopton Diary, passim; Lincs. AO, Holywell MS. 97, 22, passim; VCH Cambs., III, p. 94. According to Marshall, the hop fair at Weyhill had "formerly" lasted a week or more: The Rural Economy of the Southern Counties, 1798, II, pp. 76–7.

Andover, Magdalen Hill, Leicester, and St Faith's near Norwich. Some fairs, like Retford and Romford, dealt in swine; some like Norton St Philip in Somerset in linen or woollen cloth; a few, like, Shaftesbury, in leather, shoes, or gloves; one or two, like Glossop, in geese or poultry. Fish and wildfowl fairs were mainly sited near the coast, like Rye and Hastings, or in marsh and fenland, like Langport, Ely, Stourbridge, and St Ives in Huntingdonshire. In most regions of England two or three of the principal fairs also carried on a vital trade in agricultural implements and household utensils. Of these fairs, the most important was Stourbridge, to which ironware was brought from the west Midlands, cutlery from Sheffield, pewterware from London, glass from Nottingham, together with grindstones, pack-saddles, hurdles, cartspokes, nails, shovels, baskets, kettles, skeps, pails, jacks, frying-pans—and featherbeds.[1]

For an estimate of the extent of areas served by fairs, a sample of approximately four hundred recorded sales and purchases has been analysed.[2] From these it is clear that at most fairs there were three or four more or less distinct areas from which buyers and sellers were drawn: the first, within a radius of ten miles of the fair, corresponded to the normal area of the weekly market; the second, between 10 and 30 miles off, might be termed the 'local fair area'; the third, between 30 and 75 miles, the 'regional fair area'; and lastly, the 'national fair area', over 75 miles distant. In England and Wales as a whole, about one third of both sellers and buyers lived within the local market area; a further 20 per cent lived more than thirty miles away; and 11 per cent of buyers and 23 per cent of sellers more than 75 miles distant.

More detailed analysis reveals striking differences in the relative distances travelled in different parts of the country. In the south of England, 66 per cent of purchasers lived within 10 miles of the fairs they attended, and none came from more than 30 miles away; 55 per cent of sellers, however, travelled over 75 miles. In the eastern counties, 48 per cent of buyers travelled more than 30 miles to fairs, and 44 per cent of sellers. In the Midlands, 49 per cent of buyers travelled over 30 miles, and 19 per cent more than 75 miles; only a small percentage of buyers or sellers were natives of the local market area, living within 10 miles of the fairground. In the Welsh Marches, 75 per cent of sellers lived within 30 miles of the fair, and 40 per cent of buyers came from beyond it. For the north and west of England there is insufficient evidence to form reliable percentages; but it seems probable that in the former area an exceptionally large number of buyers lived over 75 miles off, whereas in the west the situation resembled that of southern

[1] Walford, *op. cit.*, pp. 89, 94–6, 104; cf. Defoe, *op. cit.*, p. 84.
[2] See Table 13, p. 538.

England; in Somerset, at least, sellers came from a great distance, often from Ireland, and sold primarily to purchasers from the local clothing towns, or from Bristol. Too much weight should not be placed on the foregoing figures (particularly those of sellers in the north and south), since they are necessarily based on haphazard examples. But they are not without significance. What do they imply?

Table 13. *Fair areas*

Distance Travelled (miles)	Percentage of sellers (S) and buyers (B) travelling									
	To northern fairs		To southern fairs		To eastern fairs		To Midland fairs		To all fairs	
	S	B	S	B	S	B	S	B	S	B
Under 10	37	28	36	66	22	26	11	14	33	38
10–29	27	28	9	34	34	26	29	38	24	30
30–74	18	22	0	0	15	35	42	30	19	20
75 and above	18	22	55	0	29	13	18	19	23	11

They show that in the south of England purchasers rarely travelled far to attend fairs, at any rate for cattle, just as they rarely travelled far to their local market.[1] Nicholas Toke of Godinton in the Weald of Kent seems to have relied on his stock being *brought* to him by drovers and cattle sellers, often from a considerable distance. Of the eighty-six fairs at which Toke or his son or servants bought or sold livestock between 1616 and 1704, only nine were in other counties; these were Bartholomew Fair in London, which they attended six times, and Northampton, Brentwood, and Bush Fair in Essex, each visited once. The bulk of Toke's marketing, so far as fairs were concerned, was done at Ashford, at which he bought or sold cattle or sheep on twenty-one occasions, at Maidstone (fifteen times), and at Charing (twelve times). All the other thirteen fairs which he or his servants attended, in downland, Weald, or Marsh, lay within 20 miles of his manor-house: principally Appledore, Harrietsham, Bethersden, Chilham, and Wye.[2]

In the eastern counties both buyers and sellers frequented fairs at a considerable distance. The purchases of the Barnardistons of Kedington took them to fairs all over Suffolk and Cambridgeshire, and to

---

[1] See p. , *supra.*

[2] Lodge, *op. cit., passim.* At Magdalen Hill horse fair (Hants.) in the 1620's, however, many buyers came from Somerset and some buyers and sellers from Wiltshire, Sussex, Dorset, Middlesex, Surrey, and Hertfordshire.—Winchester, Dean and Chapter Library, Reference II, D 3.

Bedfordshire, Norfolk, Essex, Lincoln, and London. During the Civil War horses for the earl of Manchester's East Anglian armies were bought in fairs as far apart as Cambridge, Bedford, Huntingdon, Stamford, and Northampton. Between 1633 and 1636 John Hatcher, squire of Careby in Lincolnshire, travelled 20 miles to buy a gelding at Melton Mowbray, 30 miles to buy oxen, steers, and cows at Newark, 31 miles to buy horses at Rothwell, over 50 miles to purchase ewes, hops, onions, sackcloth, and utensils at Stourbridge, and 90 miles to buy cattle at Waltham Fair in Essex. A number of these fairs, including Stourbridge and Waltham, Hatcher attended fairly frequently.[1]

In the Midland counties, with their large volume of through traffic from north and west towards Stourbridge and the south, the situation was again different. Possibly in the thickly populated and more self-supporting open-field villages of counties like Leicestershire both the local demand and the surplus available for other areas was smaller: possibly what was exported was the surplus of large estates whose owners naturally looked to markets further afield than those of the locality. At any rate, cattle, horses, and sheep were driven or ridden exceptionally great distances in the Midlands, and purchasers came from towns and villages all over the country. Men of Hertfordshire and Middlesex bought oxen, kine, and steers 75 miles away at Coventry. A drover of Meriden in Warwickshire bought cattle 45 miles away at Ashbourne in Derbyshire, reselling them at Bromwich. Seven persons of North Kilworth in Leicestershire bought horses worth nearly £60 at Stratford-on-Avon in Warwickshire. A drover of York sold twenty cattle at Chesterfield Fair to a gentleman from London.[2] A gentleman of Kent bought a horse and a butcher of Surrey bought cattle at Northampton Fair. A "poor serving man" from Denbighshire sold three oxen and three kine in Leicester. A man from Farnley, near Leeds, sold his "great grey gelding" at Rothwell Fair in Northamptonshire. The great cattle and horse fair at Market Harborough attracted buyers and sellers from as far off as Hertfordshire, Lincolnshire, London, York, and Northallerton.[3] In short, the

---

[1] Alan Everitt, *Suffolk and the Great Rebellion*, Suffolk Records Society, III, 1961, p. 18; SP 28, 139, John Weaver's Account Book; Lincs. AO, Holywell MS. 97, 22, *passim*. Waltham may, however, refer to Waltham-on-the-Wolds (Leics.) or Waltham near Grimsby. For a more detailed account of Hatcher's marketing activities see Joan Thirsk, *English Peasant Farming*, 1957, pp. 175–6.

[2] Req. 2, 240, 58; E 134, 20, 21 Eliz., M 14; VCH *Warwicks.*, III, p. 236; C 2, James I, G 1, 72.

[3] Lodge, *op. cit.*, p. 391 (relates to 1681); E 134 ? James I, Misc. Deps., No. 1; C 3, 150, 72; Bradford (Farnley) Cunliffe-Lister MSS (Ser. 2.), Bdle 15; Herts. RO, R.6582; Lincs. AO, Holywell MS. 97, 22; C 2, James I, G 1, 72; J. S. Purvis, 'A note on XVI-Century Farming in Yorkshire', *Yorks. Arch. Jnl.*, XXXVI, 1944, p. 449.

cattle and horse fairs of the Midlands not only served local needs, but acted as major agricultural entrepôts between the north and south of England, and between the east and west.

In Wales, the Marches, and the north of England there was also a large through trade for distant consumers. At the great cattle fairs of the Borders, like Knighton in Radnorshire, or of West Wales, like Rhos in Cardiganshire, or of the north country, like Bowes in Yorkshire, farmers and drovers from all parts of Wales, Cumberland, or Galloway gathered to dispose of their lean stock to people from the Midlands, Essex, Lancashire, and the south.[1] At Brough Hill Fair in Westmorland, purchasers came from 45 miles away in County Durham and 50 miles off in Lancashire. At Northallerton, in Yorkshire, "the throngest beast fair on St Bartholomew's day that I ever saw," as Camden observed, they came from more than 200 miles off in Middlesex. At Shrewsbury, Whitchurch, and various fairs in Wales cattle to the value of £1,000 at a time were purchased by drovers from Chester and Malpas, and subsequently resold in Essex.[2] At the horse fairs of Herefordshire and Shropshire buyers and sellers came from Cheshire, Berkshire, Lancashire, Glamorgan, Carmarthen, Cardigan, the Cotswolds, and Surrey. At the great beast fairs of Rotherham and Wakefield cattle sellers came from as far off as Middleton St George in County Durham. In the third quarter of Queen Elizabeth's reign people of Sheffield and its neighbourhood were buying cattle at Ashbourne Fair in Derbyshire, at Retford Fair in Nottinghamshire, at Bedale Fair in the North Riding, and at Middleham Fair, eighty miles off in Wensleydale.[3]

Quite clearly in all regions a general drift of cattle was taking place from the north and west of the country towards the south and east.[4]

[1] Cf. E 178, 4831; E 134, 11 Car. I, E 20; E 134, 7 Car. I, M 15; E 134, 40 Eliz., E 20.

[2] Durham, Prior's Kitchen, G 4, Instaurer's Accounts (relating to 1458); William Camden, *Britannia*, ed. Gibson, 1773, II, p. 116; E 134, 11 Car. I, E 20.

[3] See Table 14. Leominster Borough Records, Toll Book, 1556; Shrewsbury Borough Records, No. 2650: Durham, Prior's Kitchen, Probate Inventory of Marmaduke Audray of Middleton St George, 1611, Sheffield City Library, Misc. MS MD.192.

[4] The volume of this movement cannot be estimated. Mr Trow-Smith speaks, vaguely, of "the Tokes in Kent and thousands of other graziers elsewhere" buying Cheshire cattle for fattening; and of "an overwhelming preponderance of Scots [as compared with Welsh] stock in the southern graziers' fields and yards by the middle of the seventeenth century." He cites a figure of 18,574 cattle passing through Carlisle in 1663. He also mentions that 61,000 head of cattle were sent from Ireland annually in the early 1660's, and that 88,400 beeves were brought to London (at the end of the seventeenth century) each year. Against these figures must be set Gregory King's estimate of 4,500,000 cattle in England and Wales as a whole in 1696. (Trow-Smith, *op. cit.*, pp. 211, 213, 229, 233.) Large though the Scots, Irish, and Welsh cattle trade was, its *relative* importance has perhaps been exaggerated. Despite the impression given by Mr Trow-Smith, most of the Tokes' store cattle, and those of other Kentish farmers, were bred and bought locally.

Table 14. *Purchasers at Leominster fair (1556) and Shrewsbury fair (1608)*[a]

| | Number of purchasers | | |
| | Leominster | | |
Purchaser's place of residence	Cattle	Horses	Shrewsbury—Horses
Herefordshire	18	18	2
Shropshire	5	15	40
West Midlands[b]	58	5	25
Wales	—	2	5
Gloucestershire	6	5	1
Cheshire	—	3	3
Lancashire	—	1	—
Berkshire	—	—	1
Surrey	—	—	3
London	—	—	1
Total	87	49	81

[a] For sources see p. 3, n. 540.
[b] Mainly Birmingham-Stourbridge-Bromsgrove area; a few from Tenbury, Worcester, Warwick, etc.

In part this movement was dictated by conditions of soil and climate, since on the whole the north and west were naturally more suited to breeding, and the east and south to fattening and corn-growing. It was also to a considerable extent explained by the attraction of the London market. It would be a mistake, however, to exaggerate metropolitan influence. In all parts of England and Wales a most important cross-country traffic existed, in both cattle and sheep. In the Midlands much of the trade in Welsh and northern cattle was destined for local towns and manufacturing districts. Of the beasts sold at Leo-minster Fair in 1556, two thirds were bought by purchasers from the fringes of the Black Country: cattle of Herefordshire were sold to men of Stourbridge and Kingswinford, of Radnorshire to men of Hales-owen, of Pembrokeshire to purchasers from Clent, and of Llanyre, Builth, and Machynlleth to those of Birmingham; the remainder were either sold to local butchers or farmers, or were sent north into Shrop-shire or south into Gloucestershire.[1] In Wales, too, a substantial

[1] Leominster Borough Records, Toll Book, 1556. The trade in Welsh cattle through Herefordshire and Gloucestershire went back at least to the mid-thirteenth century.—H. P. R. Finberg, 'An Early Reference to the Welsh Cattle Trade', AHR, II, 1954, pp. 12–13. For the Welsh trade as a whole see Caroline Skeel, 'The Cattle Trade between Wales and England...', RHS, 4th Ser., IX, 1926, pp. 135–58.

internal trade existed between north and south, for local fattening and consumption: considerable numbers of cattle were driven from Caernarvonshire, Merioneth, and Montgomeryshire to the cattle fair at Eglwyswrw in Pembrokeshire. In the north of England, probably many of the 20,000 cattle which were said to have passed annually over Bowes Moor (no doubt from Cumberland, Galloway, and Dumfriesshire) travelled no further than the populous clothing dales of west Yorkshire.[1] Of the thousands of cattle exported annually from Ireland to the harbours of north-west Somerset, many were either driven across the county into Dorset, or sold to local dealers, fattened on the Bridgwater levels, and marketed at Bristol or in the fairs of west country clothing towns. In the Weald of Kent, the bulk of Nicholas Toke's 'northern' and 'western' cattle were marketed locally: of 223 cattle disposed of between 1616 and 1620, eighty-one were sold to tradesmen in Ashford, thirty to people in Canterbury, fifty-two to other local men, and only sixty to Londoners.[2]

Everywhere the broad streams of the south-easterly drift were thus fretted with local cross-currents. The metropolitan cattle trade of Kent was no more than a part, and of Wales and the North Country probably only a marginal part, of the produce of those regions as a whole. The journey towards London was not often taken at one leap or by a single drover. Frequently, statutes notwithstanding, Welsh and northern cattle were driven from one fair or farm to another, and sold two or three times over *en route*. At each stage, only a certain proportion, perhaps only a minority, continued east or southward: the rest were bought by provincial tradesmen and dispersed locally, or were resold in some other town or village. There is nothing surprising in this conclusion when it is remembered that, irrespective of metropolitan expansion, the Midland and eastern counties were generally more populous than Welsh and northern shires, and that the population of provincial towns as a whole greatly exceeded that of the metropolis itself. As we shall see, the general drift towards south and east was reciprocated by a notable trade in corn in the opposite direction.

[1] E 178, 4831. The Bowes cattle are said, rather vaguely, to "pass into the south parts;" but people in the south of the county certainly purchased cattle in north Yorkshire fairs.—Sheffield City Library, Misc. MS. MD. 192. For an account of Scottish droving, principally in subsequent centuries, see A. R. B. Haldane, *The Drove Roads of Scotland*, 1952.

[2] Lodge, *op. cit.*, pp. 484–9. Most of Toke's beasts were in fact 'country' or local cattle, no doubt bred in the Weald. I am doubtful whether the cattle Toke describes as 'northern' and 'western' can always be regarded as driven from the far West or north. In contemporary Kentish usage, 'western' often meant simply west Kent, and Toke's 'northern' cattle may sometimes have come from no further off than the Midlands.

The value of the fair to the agrarian economy in the sixteenth century consisted in the ease with which, in contrast with the market town, it could be expanded and adapted to meet new requirements. The two forms of marketing were not always in rivalry, however; they were complementary. What the local market was to the husbandman each week, the regional fair was each year. The farming calendar was regulated by the days when the fair fell due, and fairs themselves by the pattern of seasons. In the west country, as Mr Minchinton has shown, economic life in the eighteenth century revolved round two pivots, the local fairs and markets and the great September fair at Bristol.[1] In East Anglia and the Midlands it centred on a galaxy of local cattle fairs, and a few regional fairs like Stourbridge, Norwich, and Market Harborough. The frequent proscription of these fairs during Charles I's reign, through fear of plague, resulted in widespread consternation and certainly contributed to the king's unpopularity in the eastern counties. Nowadays the word 'trade' has come to refer primarily to traffic by sea; in the sixteenth and early seventeenth centuries it signified, for perhaps four people out of five, the market town and the local fair.

2. *Free trading between individuals*

None of the forms of private trading so far considered was entirely free from official regulation. Fairs, purveyance, victualling, the export trade, and the metropolitan market were all subject, if only spasmodically, to the official sanction of company, corporation, or privy council. The present section turns to that type of bargaining which was most nearly 'free', or emancipated from official control: to dealing between individual traders, farmers, and manufacturers in private. All the indications are that such trading was rapidly increasing during the latter half of the period.

Most types of agricultural commodity were from time to time

[1] W. Minchinton, 'Bristol—Metropolis of the West in the Eighteenth Century', RHS, 5th Ser., IV, 1954, p. 80. Mr Minchinton's remarks apply with little less force to the previous century. The statements of Westerfield (*op. cit.*, p. 339) that by the sixteenth-century fairs were "superannuated" and falling into decrepitude, and that the age of fairs was succeeded by the age of markets (in turn to be superseded by the era of retail shops), are most misleading. Fairs and markets (and retail shops) may both have been in decline in the fifteenth century, but both expanded together, and from the same causes, in the sixteenth and seventeenth centuries. They can never have been larger or more numerously attended than between 1600 and 1750, although it is probable that a few fairs, like Stourbridge, did not attract so large an *international* clientèle as in the earlier Middle Ages. If anything, fairs expanded in this period more rapidly than markets.

bought and sold in this way, but not all to the same extent. Out of some 800 private transactions recorded in cases brought before Chancery and Requests, 9 per cent refer to wood, 13 per cent to cattle, 13 per cent to sheep, 14 per cent to wool, and 38 per cent to corn.[1] Of the wood transactions, 63 per cent relate to counties in the south of England; of the wool cases, 54 per cent to the Midlands and 27 per cent to the eastern counties;[2] of sheep disputes, 32 per cent to the east, 31 per cent to the Midlands, and 19 per cent to the west. Of cattle dealings, 30 per cent relate to the north, 24 per cent to the east, and 24

Table 15. *Private transactions: regions and product*[a]

(S = sellers, B = buyers)

| | Number of transactions | | | | | | | | | | | | |
| | North | | South | | East | | West | | Midlands | | Wales | | All regions | |
	S	B	S	B	S	B	S	B	S	B	S	B	S	B
Corn	2	7	27	25	107	85	16	13	9	13	1	3	162	146
Cattle	19	13	8	10	10	15	4	2	12	13	—	—	53	53
Horses	—	—	—	—	4	3	3	3	2	3	—	—	9	9
Sheep	4	5	4	6	13	21	10	10	20	13	—	—	51	55
Wool	—	3	1	2	18	13	5	10	39	22	—	—	63	50
Wood	1	1	27	18	4	9	2	2	4	4	—	—	38	34
Misc.[b]	4	5	1	1	18	16	3	6	13	25	1	1	40	54
All goods	30	34	68	62	174	162	43	46	99	93	2	4	416	401

[a] Based on records of disputes in the Courts of Chancery and Requests.

[b] Comprises the following commodities: leather (1 case), woad (9), hops (12), saffron (1), poultry and eggs (3), reeds (1), hay (3), butter and cheese (3), fruit (1), stockings (1), linen (16).

[1] These cases may be found in Req. 2, C 1, C 2, and C 3. The vast majority relate to the latter half of the period. For more detailed analysis, see Table 7, p. 415. Although not all cases are stated to have taken place outside the open market, the presumption is in favour of their private character for several reasons: very few took place in market towns; many took place in inns and farmhouses; many, if not most, plead absence of witnesses to the bargain; many refer to dealings on too large a scale to have taken place in the market-place; most relate to goods to be delivered at a date subsequent to the bargain, frequently in several instalments; all relate to credit, not cash, transactions, for which legal bonds were drawn up (usually bipartite) by a lawyer or scrivener. A few wool cases may refer to transactions in the open market, since market dealings in wool were often on a large scale; but only a small fraction of the sample can refer to such transactions.

[2] A further 8 per cent probably relate to the Midlands, but their provenance is not clearly specified.

per cent to the Midlands; and of corn 62 per cent to the east and 17 per cent to the south. Put in another way, in the north of England 50 per cent of these cases related to cattle dealings; in the south 40 per cent to corn and 35 per cent to wood; in the east 57 per cent to corn and 19 per cent to sheep and wool; in the Midlands 49 per cent to sheep and wool; and in the west 39 per cent to sheep and wool.

What do these figures indicate? First, they show that the principal goods privately dealt in were on one hand corn and on the other sheep and wool: what the fair was to commerce in cattle and horses, individual trading was to that in corn and wool. Secondly, they show that in the eastern counties and the Midlands individual trading was far more widespread than elsewhere. Altogether more than two fifths of these transactions relate to dealings in the east, nearly one quarter to the Midlands, and only one third to the south of England, the west, the north, and Wales.[1] The three principal commodities privately dealt in—sheep, wool, corn—will repay more detailed examination.

There is nothing surprising in the fact that nearly three quarters of the sheep and wool transactions referred to East Anglia and the Midlands. As Dr Allison has shown, gentry like the Townshends and Southwells in Norfolk ran very large sheep-flocks on their fold courses; and perhaps nowhere were sheep more numerous than in the Cotswolds and on the newly enclosed pastures of Northamptonshire, Warwickshire, and Leicestershire. The Spencers, most famous of all sheep-farmers, possessed flocks of 10,000 sheep and lambs in the Midland counties. Sir Richard Knightley of Fawsley may have possessed flocks of 5,000 sheep in Northamptonshire; William Willington some 15,000 in Warwickshire; and William Fermor flocks of between 18,000 and 27,000 in the Cotswolds.[2]

Of these sheep transactions, many relate to dealings between local butchers, gentry, and yeomen. In the thirty-ninth year of Elizabeth, for instance, a minor gentleman of Fletton in Huntingdonshire bought twenty wether sheep for £10 from a yeoman of Benefield in Northamptonshire. In 1559 a miller of Luton sold forty sheep to one Mr Tucke, a local squire. In Warwickshire a butcher of Rugby bought ten sheep from one Lord, of Brownsover, "in the said Lord's yard,

[1] The four latter areas cover about 23 million acres, the two former about 19 million.

[2] K. J. Allison, 'Flock Management in the Sixteenth and Seventeenth Centuries', EcHR, XI, 1958, pp. 102 *sqq.*; Bowden, *op. cit.*, p. 7; Maurice Beresford, *The Lost Villages of England*, 1954, pp. 193–4. Professor Beresford's figures are based, however, on the number of sacks of wool, and since, in Fermor's case, these are said to be of his own "growing and *gathering,*" it is not possible to say how much Fermor grew himself, and how much he obtained from other people.

feeding as they had been there fed all the winter before."[1] In general, however, small-scale sheep transactions were more characteristic of the south-west of England; in East Anglia and the Midlands both sheep and wool transactions sometimes involved very considerable purchases. A yeoman-factor of Gransden in Cambridgeshire sold 340 sheep for his master, a parson, to a gentleman of Guilden Morden. A farmer of Easton-upon-Welland in Leicestershire sold 700 wethers to a factor of Stamford in Lincolnshire. A flock of 1,218 sheep at West Barsham in Norfolk was sold in 1599 for £406 to a Norfolkman. And as many as 2,060 sheep changed hands, at a price of £2,820, between Dame Elizbeth Hatton and William Knight of Holdenby in Northamptonshire.[2]

Wool dealings were rarely on so large a scale as sheep, but sometimes involved bargains of several hundred pounds. At Shrewsbury in 1584 two hundred tods of wool were sold for £305 to a clothier from Shepton Mallet. About 1596 Sir Edward Mountague sold 400 tods to a glover of Northampton. In 1571 James Cottesford obtained a licence to purchase 500 tods annually during a period of twelve years, of which he sold 200 tods a year to three Northampton merchants. And in 1619 Thomas Hills of Sharnbrook in Bedfordshire sold 5,090 fleeces for £790 to a Huntingdonshire yeoman and his partner, of whom the former had brought wool from Hills at various times to the value of at least £4,000.[3]

The regional concentration of individual trading in corn was equally remarkable. Nearly four fifths of grain disputes related to transactions in the east and south of England. The evidence of the port books and customs accounts relating to the coasting trade will reinforce this conclusion.[4] Of the average of 534 grain shipments sent annually from fourteen principal ports between 1500 and 1640, two fifths were dispatched to London and three fifths to provincial towns. In the provinces, in the period before 1570, some 52 per cent of these shipments were sent from ports in the eastern counties and 28 per cent from those in the south; after 1570, 80 per cent were dispatched from the east and 8 per cent from the south. By 1640 East Anglia had become the principal granary of many thousands of provincial people, particularly in the north of England and the Midlands. The expansion of King's Lynn was very remarkable. Its average exports to other provincial towns increased by more than 100 per cent between the

[1] Req. 2, 130, 49; C 3, 137, 73; E 134, 20 James I, H 4. For further information on the marketing of sheep for meat, see Bowden, *op. cit.*, pp. 8–12.

[2] C 2, James I, H 1, 28; C 3, 38, 22; Req. 2, 32, 73; C 2, Eliz., K 2, 54.

[3] Req. 2, 113, 13; Req. 2, 45, 100; Req. 2, 243, 53; C 2, James I, C 2, 46. See also Bowden, *op. cit.*, pp. 57 *sqq.* Dr Bowden also shews the importance of the coasting trade in the marketing of wool: *ibid.*, and p. 74.

[4] See Table   , p.   ; and cf. Willan, *Coasting Trade*, chapters VI, VIII–X.

Table 16. Coasting trade in grain: average annual shipments from principal ports[a]

From	To northern ports		To southern ports		To eastern ports		To London		To western ports		To Welsh ports		To unspecified ports		Total	
	1500–1569	1570–1640	1500–1569	1570–1640	1500–1569	1570–1640	1500–1569	1570–1640	1500–1569	1570–1640	1500–1569	1570–1640	1500–1569	1570–1640	1500–1569	1570–1640
Northern ports	8·7	11·5	—	—	0·1	0·5	4·1	14·0	—	—	—	—	3·5	—	16·3	26·0
Southern ports	—	12·5	49·3	11·0	4·0	1·0	150·4	164·5	1·4	—	—	—	32·4	1·5	237·7	190·5
Eastern ports	78·7	136·0	11·5	13·4	9·9	34·9	58·7	55·4	—	0·3	—	—	57·0	34·9	215·7	274·9
London	—	1·8	3·0	1·3	1·0	6·7	—	—	1·5	—	—	—	1·5	15·7	7·0	23·7
Western ports	0·5	1·8	1·2	1·0	0·1	—	0·2	0·6	11·0	7·1	26·7	12·8	11·7	1·2	51·4	24·4
Total	87·9	161·8	65·0	26·7	15·1	43·1	213·4	234·5	13·9	7·4	26·7	12·8	106·1	53·3	528·1	539·5

[a] Based upon Gras, op. cit., Appendix D. Gras gives no figures for Ipswich and Southampton after 1570, and only one year's figures for Boston, Chichester, and Yarmouth. The figures above are calculated to the nearest decimal point. 'Southern ports' includes those from Kent to Hampshire; 'northern' those from Yorkshire northwards.

two halves of the period, and by 1600 accounted for no less than two thirds of the whole trade.[1]

Of the different types of corn sold by private bargain, the coasting trade figures printed by Gras tell us nothing.[2] For the inland trade it is possible to be more specific. The cases in Chancery and Requests suggest that 51 per cent of grain transactions related to barley, 31 per cent to malt, 13 per cent to wheat, and only 5 per cent to other crops—oats, rye, maslin, meal, and legumes. More than four fifths of the trade was thus destinesd for the brewing industry or the poor.[3] Most of these transactions involved small quantities of 10 or 20 quarters at a time, but large contracts were not unusual. In 1590 Lyonell Bostocke of Abingdon bought 200 quarters of barley from William Harman of Langley in Buckinghamshire, at a price of £70. In 1587 Henry Glanfield of Langford in Bedfordshire, yeoman, paid £300 for the barley growing in the fields of a farmer at Winteringham and St Neots in Huntingdonshire. In the 1590's Michael Potter of Fen Stanton in Huntingdonshire, waterman, supplied 500 quarters of malt to the brewers of Peterborough, at a price of £750, for the supply of the Queen of Scots' household at Fotheringhay. And in 1568 Thomas Fenner of Harting in Sussex bargained with Thomas Mascall of Chart Sutton in Kent for 1,000 quarters of malt, to be delivered at Yarmouth, Burnham, or Wells in Norfolk.[4]

The bulk of the traffic in barley and malt was centred in four small counties: Hertford, Bedford, Cambridge, and Huntingdon, together with the Soke of Peterborough and part of west Norfolk and Suffolk: the same counties, it will be recalled, that supplied so much malt and barley to London and the Low Countries. Climate, soil, and navigable rivers combined to render them an ideal malting area, and the wealth of many of their brewers, maltsters, watermen, and barley farmers was remarkable.[5] A series of thirty-five probate inventories relating to

[1] This shows once again the tendency to economic *concentration* during this period (cf. p   ); by 1640 Hull, Lynn, Yarmouth, Sandwich, and Bristol were the only corn ports of much consequence in the coasting trade. For a detailed account of the East Anglian coasting trade in corn see Williams, *op. cit.*, pp. 175–87. There was also an extensive coasting trade in butter and cheese, principally from Suffolk and Essex to London: *ibid.*, pp. 188–92.

[2] Gras's figures (*op. cit.*, Appendix D) do not particularize the types of grain; but Professor Willan gives information for certain selected years, principally after 1640 (*Coasting Trade*, chapters VI, VIII–X).

[3] Many contemporary references in J.P.s' reports to the Privy Council show that barley was the commonest bread-corn of the poor.

[4] C 2, Eliz., G 6, 45; Req. 2, 255, 65; Req. 2, 104, 75.

[5] A waterman of Peterborough, dying in 1694, left an estate of over £245, including nine boats (£25), four horses (£9), credits of over £70, and furniture in his fourteen-roomed house worth £70. He was also an innkeeper, with over £40 worth of ale and beer in his cellar. Northants. RO, inventory of John Yates, June 1694.

Hertfordshire corn farmers shows that over half their wealth was sunk in corn production, a further quarter in household goods and farming implements, and about one fifth in livestock. A yeoman of Tring on the borders of Hertfordshire and Buckinghamshire, dying in 1610, left an estate worth over £217, and bequeathed portions of £100 each to his two daughters; in his barns there were 60 quarters of barley worth £48. A maltster of Hexton near Hitchin, on the border of Bedfordshire, dying in 1565, left over £90: nearly half his wealth consisted of 95 quarters of malt; more than 33 acres of his strips in the open fields were sown with barley; and he ran three shops, one in St Albans, one in Ashford, and one in Potton in Bedfordshire. In 1614 James Puddevatt of Hemel Hempstead died leaving an estate of nearly £309, including 100 quarters of malt in his malthouse. His premises contained a hall, parlour, kitchen, four chambers, a cellar, buttery, millhouse, malthouse, and malt kiln. His rooms were elaborately furnished with joined furniture, covered stools, carpets, cushions, and painted cloths; his linen, silver, pewter, and brassware were worth over £20; and in his hall there were two bibles, a Testament, and a prayer-book.[1] In brewing and malting towns all over the country it would be possible to find men like James Puddevatt: in Leicester, Sleaford, Abingdon, Maidstone, Reading, Wellingborough, Burton, Bury St Edmunds, or Derby, for instance.[2] But nowhere, were they more numerous than in the towns and villages of Hertfordshire, Bedfordshire, Huntingdonshire, Cambridgeshire, and Norfolk.[3]

In private trading the market area varied greatly between different districts and different products. In general, private traders travelled further in their dealing than those of the market town. In every dozen transactions, three took place between buyers and sellers in wholly different regions of England, four between buyers and sellers in different but adjacent counties, and only five between men within the same county. In the Midlands, north, and east of England relatively few private transactions took place locally, that is between men in the same

---

[1] Herts. RO, inventories relating to Thomas Grace the elder (also his will), Tomas Golsmythe, and James Puddevatt.

[2] For Sleaford, cf. E 134, 12 Car. I, E 26; for Reading and Abingdon, Westerfield, *op. cit.*, p. 180; for Leicester, Eric Kerridge, 'Social and Economic History of Leicester', VCH *Leics.*, IV, pp. 95–6; for Wellingborough, at an earlier period, F. M. Page, *Wellingborough Manorial Accounts, A.D. 1258–1323*, Northants. Rec. Soc., VIII, 1936, p. xxxi. Urban maltsters also bought extensively in the open market.

[3] In the same counties (especially Hertfordshire and Norfolk) there were also many prosperous mealmen and corn-badgers. A mealman of Bushey left personal estate of £51 in 1635; a carrier of Redbourne £114 1s.—Hertfordshire RO, inventories of Ralph Weedon and Amphabell Marshall.

county; in the south nearly two thirds were local; and in the west nearly half. In the east and the Midlands, approximately two thirds of all dealings took place between men in different counties; and in the north private traders travelled particularly far afield in selling and buying agricultural goods.[1]

Table 17. *Private transactions: places of origin of buyers and sellers*[a]

(Figures in percentages)

	Buyer and seller living in same county	Buyer and seller living in different county but same region	Buyer and seller living in different regions
Region			
North	37	19	44
South	62	21	17
East	36	45	19
West	46	35	19
Midlands	32	36	32
All England	42	35	23
Product			
Corn	46	40	13
Cattle	41	30	29
Sheep	46	37	18
Wool	34	28	38
Wood	67	33	—
Miscellaneous	26	32	42
All products	42	35	23

[a] Based principally on records of disputes in the Courts of Chancery, Requests, and Exchequer. The samples for dealings in horses and for Welsh transactions are too few to afford reliable percentages.

Trade in wood, timber, and charcoal most often took place locally. Charcoal was fragile; wood was generally sold standing and was too bulky to carry far save in exceptional circumstances. Wealden timber was frequently sold to the government for shipbuilding, or ready sawn and mortised to Londoners to erect houses; most usually, however, it was bought by local ironmasters and tradesmen.[2] When

[1] See Table   , p.   .
[2] See, for example, Req. 2, 63, 49; Req. 2, 30, 30; C 2, James I, N 1, 5; C 3, 182, 54; and, for charcoal, C 2, Eliz. D 8, 31; Req. 2, 43, 15.

Lady Elizabeth Isley sold her woods in East and West Farleigh on the Medway in 1555, they were bought by "sundry persons dwelling thereabouts." When a Kentish thatcher and his partner purchased timber from the Wealden estates of the Bathursts and Osbornes, they resold it in the form of poles, laths, posts, rails, 'roundwood', squared timber, 'checker timber', and oak bark to carpenters, wheelwrights, tanners, spoonmakers, and others in the vicinity. The mast of woodland, by contrast, was sometimes bought by distant purchasers. In 1591 a south Midland swineherd acquired the mast of woods in Sussex, Surrey, and Hampshire, and drove 240 swine belonging to farmers of Oxfordshire and Buckinghamshire to be fattened there for seven weeks, after which they were to be returned to their owners "well and sufficiently fed for bacon."[1]

Fruit was generally sold in the open market, except in Kent and the lower Severn valley, where the private market was extensive. Of the "great store of apples, pears, and such like fruit" growing "near and about the said river of Severn," much was exported in small vessels from Newnham, Gloucester, Tewkesbury, and Berkeley into Devon, Cornwall, and south and west Wales.[2] The hop trade of Suffolk, Essex, and Kent attracted dealers from London, the Midlands, the north, and the west country, although it usually took place at fairs rather than in inns and farmhouses.

Cattle and sheep were easily driven on foot and most private livestock transactions took place between dealers living in different counties or regions. In the neighbourhood of Coventry, two oxen were sold which had been driven from Stowe in Buckinghamshire; £130 worth of cattle were bought by a group of three dealers from Hertfordshire; and twenty steers and heifers were bought by a drover who also purchased cattle in Warwickshire and Staffordshire and resold them in Oxfordshire. When Oliver Bainbridge, a large sheep and cattle farmer of Kirkby Lonsdale in Westmorland, died in 1560, debts of nearly £60 were owing to him from people in Sleaford, Barnsley, Bradford, Huntingdon, and Godmanchester, evidently for sheep and cattle delivered to them. In James I's reign a gentleman of Shipdham near East Dereham in Norfolk regularly purchased sheep from farmers of Chapel-en-le-Frith in Derbyshire, and sometimes dealt with factors in Manchester as well.[3]

---

[1] Req. 2, 48, 4; Req. 2, 30, 30; Req. 2, 270, 39.

[2] E 134, 43, Eliz. E 18.

[3] C 3, 73, 93; Req. 2, 240, 58; E 134, 21 James I, T 5; Lancs. RO, Westmorland inventory of Oliver Bainbridge, 1560; C 2, James I, M 7, 46. Distances travelled in connection with cattle sales were of course affected by the Statutes forbidding resale within certain specified limits.

Most wool dealings also took place between traders and farmers living in different counties or regions. A clothier of Otley in Yorkshire bought wool from a squire of Normanby in Lincolnshire; another, of Benenden in Kent, from a gentleman of Milton near Cambridge; a third, of Sudbury, from a yeoman and clergyman of Gedney in Lincolnshire; a fourth, of Wiltshire, from a yeoman of Aston Magna in the Cotswolds; and others, of Norton St Philip and Slaughterford in the west country from a glover of Northampton.[1]

In the corn trade, private dealing was usually local; but the river traffic of East Anglia and the coasting trade formed an important exception to this generalization. Apart from grain sent to London, some 45 per cent of the coastal trade passed from one region of England to another before 1570, and 58 per cent thereafter; the rest passed from one port to another within the same region. On the average, King's Lynn alone sent 107 shipments annually to Northumberland and twenty-one to Hull; Yarmouth sent fifteen shipments to Northumberland, Sandwich thirteen, and Hull nine. The south of England was on the whole self-supporting in corn and imported little for its own needs, though a few shipments found their way from Norfolk to Kent, perhaps for re-export. The west country also was at first an exporter of corn; but by 1640 it was usually an importing area, save in exceptionally prosperous years. Its annual coasting exports dropped from fifty-one shipments to twenty-four, mainly dispatched from Bristol, which was itself supplied from Gloucester, Tewkesbury, and Bridgwater. South Wales was partly supplied from these ports and from Bristol while on occasion shipments of malt reached the area from as far off as Dover and King's Lynn.[2]

3. The organization of private marketing in the provinces

The organization of private marketing resembled neither the corporate system of the market town nor the individualism of modern commerce. It operated more or less freely, except during periods of dearth or political disturbance. Those who engaged in it were remarkably enterprising and were not usually swayed by considerations of sentiment. But private marketing was not without its own strict body of custom, and its bonds were still personal and local. It was, in a word, a

[1] Req. 2, 291, 40; Req. 2, 61, 93; Req. 2, 206, 29; Req. 2, 45, 100.
[2] See Table . E 134, 14–15 Car. I, H 19; Req. 2, 290, 77. South Wales itself also exported to Bristol, from the corn-growing areas of Glamorganshire; cf. also Willan, loc. cit.

system of enterprise operating within a network of personal connections.[1]

Those who engaged in private marketing were rarely peasants or labourers. Occasionally, quite humble men bought and sold outside the market town;[2] but in general traders who claim to be "very poor men" turn out, on closer acquaintance, to be substantial merchants or farmers. By and large, it was gentlemen, yeomen, brewers, maltsters, millers, and the like, with an occasional knight and squire, who engaged in private trading. Sir John Packington of Aylesbury, for instance, buys forty sheep from a certain John Saunders; a gentleman yeoman, and innholder of Hertfordshire bargain for grain with a corn-seller of Stevenage; the squire of Boughton Monchelsea in Kent purchases bullocks from his neighbour Nicholas Crumpe of Linton, yeoman; and Charles Dudley of Long Sutton in Somerset pays £12 for "a very fair and comely gelding" to a gentleman from the village of Higham.[3] The majority of East Anglian malt dealings took place between men like John Birde of Wickingham, yeoman, and John Blackheade of Norwich, maltster; or William Shelstone of Marston Moretaine, gentleman, and his neighbour Thomas Impie, yeoman; or Thomas Marshe, a hard-headed maltster of Cambridgeshire, and two wealthy farmers of Whittlesford and Wentworth. Quite frequently private dealing enabled such men to amass substantial fortunes. A "great rich" brewer of Hitchin seems to have engrossed into his hands a substantial part of the trade of his native town. The wealth of not a few East Anglian gentry was founded on intensive corn husbandry; and one Norfolk barley merchant was said, though no doubt with exaggeration, to have made £10,000 in the space of a few years.[4]

Sometimes private dealers traded alone; but frequently they operated together, in partnership with one or two other men of their

---

[1] Only a generalized outline of the subject can be given here. For the functions of different middlemen engaged in the brewing, livestock, corn, wool, and other trades, the reader should refer to Bowden, *op. cit.*, pp. 77–106, and Westerfield, *Middlemen in English Business*, especially pp. 134–74, 187–208, 255–323. Westerfield, utilizing mainly late seventeenth- and eighteenth-century sources, and analysing the subject abstractly, seems to suggest a sharper distinction between the various types of middlemen than usually obtained between 1500 and 1640. Badgers, broggers, carriers, kidders, factors, jobbers, etc., had not yet all developed into separate commercial species. Westerfield's account of the livestock and dairy trades relates principally to the London market, and should not be regarded as presenting an entirely faithful picture of the organization of these trades in provincial centres. His telescoping of the evidence from different periods is also apt to mislead.

[2] C 3, 24, 76; Req. 2, 115, 44.

[3] Req. 2, 74, 36; C 2, James I, N 3, 49; Req. 2, 106, 40; C 2, James I, D 11, 68.

[4] Req. 2, 27, 50; Req. 2, 32, 121; Req. 2, 109, 10; Req. 2, 65, 62; C 2, James I, G 13, 50.

acquaintance. Two Cornish butchers in 1609 thus dealt together as partners, the one to buy wares for the common profit of both. In the Weald of Kent, Joseph Mayowe of Marden and his neighbour Thomas Strowde "dealt together in the working and sale of...wood," which they bought from neighbouring squires. In the Midlands in the 1590's articles of partnership were drawn up between Thomas Forren of St John's Hospital, near Lutterworth, and William Knight of Holdenby, in Northamptonshire, for the joint purchase of sheep.[1] In Huntingdon-shire in James I's reign, two men agreed to "join together in partner-ship and put equal stocks together, and therewith buy cattell and sell the same again for their benefit and advantage," the profits and charges to be divided "upon every return...according to the propor-tion of such stock or sums of money as either of them should disburse." In Bedfordshire Henry Glanfield of Langford and his partner John Creake of Biggleswade dealt together in the purchase of growing barley, the one undertaking to see it "inned," and the other threshed and ordered "in frugal manner" and sold to their greatest advantage. In Staffordshire William Cutts, Francis Burton, and William Tarte of Wolverhampton agreed, about Easter 1618, to become "chapmen, partners, copartners, or parting fellows of divers wares," especially of certain great quantities of hops to the value of £2,000, "by factor-ship and exchange:" they each supplied one third of the necessary stock, sharing equally in the profits, and agreeing to account truly to one another "presently after the sale..."[2] Many of these partnerships were ephemeral arrangements; but it was not unusual to find men dealing together for many years, and occasionally their agreements took on a more formal status. The stocking-dealers of Yorkshire seem to have organized a kind of company, with its headquarters at Rich-mond: they traversed the dales of the North Riding, collected stockings at the houses of knitters and spinsters, brought them to their depôt, and dispatched them in packs of forty to one hundred dozen at a time to London, to other parts of the country, and overseas.[3]

Most dealers or middlemen of any substance, whether in corn, cattle, sheep, wool, or hops, had their own more or less modest staff. Some of the larger merchants, both in London and the provinces, established private factors in various provincial towns. William Holidaye of London had "a factor of his, one Robert Mico, lying at Plymouth...who did use to deal in buying and selling of many

[1] C 2, James I, I 8, 25; Req. 2, 30, 30; C 2, Eliz., K 2, 54.
[2] Req. 2, 300, 33; C 2, Eliz., G 6, 45; C 2, James I, C 24, 4.
[3] E 134, 2 Car. I, M 38; E 178, 4354. For an account of wool-broggers and other middlemen in Norfolk see K. J. Allison, 'Flock Management in the Sixteenth and Seventeenth Centuries', EcHR XI, 1958, pp. 107–8.

commodities there," both for his master and, as opportunity offered, for his master's friends. Others desirous of establishing contacts in distant counties, like Stephen Muryell of Shipdham in Norfolk, depended on the independent corn and sheep factors who had established themselves in large centres like Manchester. Others again, like John Northropp of Ramsey, originally an independent maltster, became "factors or agents" to large brewers like Thomas Joynes of Wisbech, undertaking "the buying of all such malt as he...should have occasion for" at a "salary" of 8d. per quarter.[1] Probably the majority of these 'factors', however, were simple employees, often living in their master's house and travelling to different parts of the country as occasion demanded. They were assisted by, and were sometimes scarcely distinct from, their master's clerks and men-servants. They or his clerks undertook the writing of his order books, notes, and letters, and compiled the account books audited at his quarterly or annual 'days of reckoning.'

In addition to private merchants and their factors and servants, a small but powerful élite of professional men emerged in the sixteenth century. Every provincial town of any size had its corps of notaries, lawyers, and scriveners; boroughs of the size of Northampton or Maidstone might have half-a-dozen such men, often styling themselves 'gentlemen', and descended from minor landed families, such as the Godfreys of Hodiford in Kent.[2] Few of them made great fortunes; but the drawing of bipartite bonds or bills, by which private transactions were ratified, provided them with an increasing source of income. As agricultural techniques became more recondite, moreover, many a country town gathered a handful of men whose expertise in buying and selling certain kinds of goods became much sought after. Humphrey Hunt of Crick in Northamptonshire was considered a man of "great skill in buying of sheep" in those parts. At Coventry there were several "men of skill" and "understanding" in buying and selling horses, and in the event of dispute their word was often decisive. At Basingstoke in 1588, when John Goringe, dyer, was offered a parcel of forty hundred-weight of woad by a yeoman of Bishopstoke, he sent a sample of two bags and had it 'assayed' or tested by a "man of judgement in such cases."[3] In sheep transactions the "skill and diligence" of a specialist sheep factor or a trusted shepherd was often called in to settle the

---

[1] Req. 2, 209, 10; C 2, James I, M 7, 46; C 2, James I, N 3, 56.

[2] Lambarde Godfrey, a lawyer in Maidstone, was eldest son of Thomas Godfrey of Hodiford, grandson of William Lambarde, and half-brother of Sir Edmund Berry Godfrey: typically, he became Kentish solicitor-general for sequestrations in the Civil War.

[3] Req. 2, 76, 44; C 3, 141, 98; Req. 2, 210, 35.

terms of the bargain, with the reward of a small gratuity for his advice.

Of those who were engaged in private marketing, none held a more powerful position than maltsters and brewers. The secret of their influence was two-fold. As manufacturers, they were concerned to obtain regular supplies of grain at fixed and certain prices. Their problem was the insecurity arising from unpredictable harvests. They therefore resorted to bargaining for regular deliveries of corn several months in advance of requirements; not infrequently they purchased the prospective crop of selected fields many weeks before they were reaped. Richard Ford and Michael Webb of Henley-on-Thames were "usually men that deal upon such advantageous bargains for great quantities of corn, while it is upon the ground, to be paid [*sc.* delivered] some short time after harvest..." After carefully viewing the corn-lands of Thomas White of Idston, Ford and Webb earmarked the crop of two enclosed fields where the barley was "discerned to be better than that which [White] had elsewhere, in the common fields..."[1] By this method of advance bargaining the farmer was assured of a ready market, though in the event of harvest failure he was placed at the mercy of the maltster with whom he had bargained.

As local capitalists, moreover, brewers and maltsters often became the moneylenders of the rural community, and sometimes obtained a powerful hold over feckless tradesmen or husbandmen. The instance of John Cooper, the rich brewer of Hitchin, has already been cited. The methods of Henry Oliver of Fen Ditton in Cambridgeshire in dealing with Walter Reynolds of Longstanton were equally typical. About Stourbridge Fair time in 1607, finding himself in "great want of money," Reynolds applied to Oliver for a loan and obtained £14 3s. 4d. for which he was to supply Oliver with twenty quarters of barley. In the following September, being once more "utterly destitute of money," Reynolds sought a further loan and parted with sixty quarters of barley, for which he received £41. One year later, still "in great want and need" and absolutely "driven to a strait...for that he had a great sum...to pay," Reynolds again had recourse to the moneylending maltster. This time, though "moved with the pitiful complaints and lamentations of the distressed estate" of his suppliant, Henry Oliver demanded a further sixty quarters of barley—in return for only £36. Needless to say, when the day of reckoning came round, Reynolds was unable to fulfil his obligations, and was prosecuted by

---

[1] C2, James I, W 7, 41. Barley was frequently delivered in agreed quantities at regular intervals over a period of some months, instead of in a single amount. For further details on the malting trade, cf. Westerfield, *op. cit.*, pp. 172–4. In 1721 an Abingdon maltster died worth, by report, £60,000 (*Northampton Mercury*, 6 Feb. 1720/21).

his benefactor (who had "over-many such debtors") and summoned to appear in the Court of Chancery.[1]

The whole structure of private marketing rested upon a basis of *credit*.[2] Some idea of the increase of credit dealing in this period may be gathered from the debts and credits listed in farmers' probate inventories. These do not always relate to marketing activities; but in counties where their nature is usually specified, especially in corn-growing areas, credits rapidly increased during the latter half of the period.[3] In general, they reached a peak during James I's reign, remaining stationary or tending to decline again, probably temporarily, during that of Charles I. In Shropshire the proportion of credit dealing to total personal wealth rose from 6 per cent in the 1590's to 24 per cent in the 1610's, and declined again to 19 per cent in Charles I's reign. In Derbyshire it increased from 4 per cent in the 1590's to 10 per cent in the 1610's and 17 per cent in the 1630's. In Hertfordshire, with its many large corn farms, it rose from 13 per cent in the 1590's to no less than 53 per cent in James I's reign; falling away again to 33 per cent under Charles I, perhaps as a result of a temporary decline in the population of London.[4] All the evidence, then, bears witness to the great extent of private marketing during the latter half of the period, and to the large part played in it by credit.

Yet despite the use of apparently sophisticated methods, private marketing under the Tudors and Stuarts bore little likeness to the impersonal commerce of more recent times. In the social conditions of the sixteenth century commerce could not be impersonal. In the absence of banks a man's 'credit' could only be what he was personally reputed to be worth in his local community. Individual enterprise necessarily operated through a network of neighbours, friends, and relatives. Sons, fathers, brothers, cousins, wives, uncles, mothers, brothers-in-law: all were drawn into the circle. When, about the year 1566, Lawrence Pake of Dagenham wished to arrange a bargain of cattle, he approached his wife's brother John Wright of South Weald, purchased seven kine from him, and received in addition three

---

[1] C 2, James I, O 3, 8.

[2] For detailed accounts of credit dealings in the wool trade, see Bowden, *op. cit.*, pp. 95–106, and 'The Home Market in Wool, 1500–1700', *Yorks. Bull. Econ. and Soc. Research*, VIII, 1956, pp. 130–48.

[3] In Kent, credits were much higher on the cornlands bordering the Downs than in the pastoral areas of the Weald: the average figure in the former area being £287 and in the latter £99, or respectively 43 per cent and 28 per cent of total wealth, between 1600 and 1640. In Devon, primarily a pastoral county, the corresponding figures were £90 and 27 per cent for 1630–40.

[4] For the probable decline in London's population at this time see note 110, p.   .

or four more "in token and shew of the good will [Wright] then bare unto his said sister" and brother-in-law. When Thomas Fetherstone of Canterbury, maltster, wished to purchase barley from John Videon of Patrixbourne, he "drew from [him]...many good bargains of corn, by which he was a great gainer," merely by calling him "cousin" and other such "glozing terms," and using "manifold and great protestations of love" towards him. When Maud Tesdale of Glympton in Oxfordshire sold corn to Priscilla Tesdale of Abingdon, she gave her advantageous terms because she was her niece and was left "a very poor widow" with "many small children unprovided for, the said Maud...commiserating her necessity...".[1]

Quite as powerful as the influence of kinship was that of personal friendship. In purchasing 103 ewe sheep in 1589, Thomas Taverner of Kettleston in Norfolk "altogether depended upon the friendly speeches and faithful promise" of his acquaintance Thomas Thursebye of Ashwicken, esquire. At the request of the merchant father of two of his pupils, Thomas Rateclif of Woodbridge, clerk, travelled "into divers places in Norfolk for to buy wheat" for him, and "did offer unto a friend of his...a certain sum of money to help him to the bargain..." When the tenants of Sir Thomas Barrington in Essex wished to dispose of their surplus wool, Sir Thomas's steward wrote to his brother-in-law in London and his friend Mr Adames, either "to deal with some chapmen to come down hither out of Kent or some other places, [or] at least to give me speedy notice what rate wool yields with you, that so I may give intimation to some friends that perhaps will adventure to come themselves..." In Northamptonshire, a sheep bargain between William Allen of Benefield and Thomas Greenehall of Fletton in Huntingdonshire was struck solely because two of Allen's neighbours "did much labour and entreat him" to deal, and "commended [Greenehall]...to be a very honest man and a good paymaster... whereas otherwise [Allen] had never dealt with the said Greenehall." At Bristol, when a shipload of rotten malt arrived in 1639, Henry Floyd and his friends summoned a meeting of the city brewers "and used means with some of the company to buy the said malt," because it was brought by one of their regular suppliers and they wished "to do him a courtesy to help him in distress...".[2]

In consequence of this network of kinship and acquaintance, the packmen, carriers, woolmen, and factors who engaged in the private agricultural market were not simply unrelated individuals. By the end of Queen Elizabeth's reign, they had developed into a distinct and

[1] Req. 2, 53, 14; Req. 2, 63, 70; C 2, James I, S 17, 37.
[2] Req. 2, 27, 35; Req. 2, 114, 28; BM, Egerton MS 2648, f. 80; Req. 2, 130, 49; E 134, 15 Car. I, T 1.

self-conscious community on their own: a kind of society of wayfarers, partially separate from the settled society of manor house, village, and market town. It must not be supposed that this society was altogether new; its origins went back to the medieval wool merchant, and perhaps beyond. But it was at the end of Elizabeth's reign, so far as the agricultural market is concerned, that it became a recognizable *community*, with its own characteristic customs, traditions, and ideals.

Much of the dealing in which travelling merchants engaged took place in farmhouses. Some took place in barns, and some in warehouses and corn-chambers. Perhaps the most characteristic meeting-place of the wayfaring community, however, was the provincial inn. The Elizabethan and Stuart inn has no exact counterpart in the modern world. It was the hotel, the bank, the warehouse, the exchange, the scrivener's office, and the market-place of many a private trader. Few English towns or market villages were without their handful of inns. At Romford in Essex, there were the Blue Boar, the Swan, and the White Horse. Round the market-place at Shaftesbury in Dorset were the Raven, the Lamb, the George, the Bush, the New Inn, the Lion, and the Star. According to a census taken in 1577, there were over 1,600 inns in twenty-five English counties: seventy-two in Buckinghamshire, seventy-seven each in Essex and Surrey, eighty in Devon, 119 in Suffolk, 152 in Hertfordshire, and 239 in Yorkshire. By the end of the period there were many more. In Wiltshire, in 1686, nearly 200 towns and villages boasted at least one inn. The city of Salisbury afforded accommodation for some 548 travellers and 865 horses. Of the many inns in Northampton, the Bull contained thirty-six rooms and the George no fewer than forty.[1]

In thoroughfare towns, like Dunstable, Nuneaton, St Albans, or Basingstoke, such hostelries were especially numerous. Of the thirty or more inns at St Albans, about the year 1630, William Mosley's contained twenty-one rooms, including a hall, three parlours, and nine chambers, each with its own name: the Swan, the Star, the Bear, the Falcon, the Elephant, and so on. Most of these chambers were

---

[1] For Romford and Shaftesbury, cf. E 134, 24 Car. I, E 9, E 134, 18 James I, E 1; for Wiltshire, N. J. Williams, *Tradesmen in Early-Stuart Wiltshire*, Wilts. Arch. and Nat. Hist. Soc., Records Branch, xv, 1960, pp. xiv–xv. For information on the 1577 census of inns (based on SP 12, 96; SP 12, 116–19; SP 12, 122; SP 12, 141), I am indebted to Professor M. W. Beresford; the missing counties were mainly in the Midlands. An 'inn' was technically distinct from an 'ale-house', which in theory did not offer accommodation. There were over 14,000 alehouses listed in the census. For further details of the census, see Westerfield, *op. cit.*, pp. 177–8. Westerfield oversimplifies in stating that the proportion of inns and taverns to alehouses was higher in counties near London. The proportion was equally high in the west country, and in Kent it was very low.

remarkable only for the number of their beds; but a few were adorned with pictures, hangings, joined furniture, gilded andirons, and cushions and coverings of Norwich work and black and yellow needlework. In the neighbouring village of Redbourne, on Watling Street, John Tappin's inn consisted of thirteen rooms. Its furnishings included carpets, rugs, curtains, pictures, leather chairs, turkey-work cushions, joined stools, a glass cupboard, at least nineteen beds, quantities of pots, pans, trenchers, and spoons, more than £10 worth of silver, and sheets and table napkins by the score. Men like John Tappin and William Mosley were clearly in the habit of entertaining a considerable company of 'commercial travellers'.[1]

By James I's reign many such inns were acquiring a reputation as marts for particular kinds of product, and were visited year after year by the same clientèle. The George at Milton Regis in Kent was a barley-mart, where merchants, maltmen, and yeomen from Faversham, Ospringe, Margate, Borden, Sittingbourne, and other places sold their goods. Master Child's inn at Reading was an important wool mart, where Midland woolmen disposed of their packs to the clothiers of Berkshire. The Bear Inn at Exeter was one of the principal centres of business in the town, "where thousands of pounds changed hands every Friday."[2] A number of inns at St Ives in Huntingdonshire received "sheep into their yards and backsides," some of them "to a very great number," where they were bought and sold and "conveyed away out at a back gate" to avoid paying tolls.[3] Many country inns offered special facilities to drovers, sometimes having forty or fifty acres of pasture ground nearby. At Wakefield in Yorkshire John Jacksons's "host House" was apparently a mart for wool and woad, attended by clothiers from Halifax, dyers from Wakefield, and yeomen from the Dales. At Norton St Philip in Somerset the "great house or inn called the George" was an important west country wool mart: every year, for three weeks before SS. Philip and James's day, the "tables and household stuff" were "displaced...out of the hall, kitchen, two parlours, cellars, and chambers to place the [wool and linen merchants'] packs in," and its "great store of rooms" for "lodging and entertainment" were filled with travellers and guests.[4]

---

[1] Herts. RO, inventories of Tappin (1635) and Mosley (1631–2).

[2] E 134, 9–10 Car. I, H 14; Req. 2, 30, 56; W. G. Hoskins, *Industry, Trade, and People in Exeter, 1688–1800*, 1935, p. 25. In this and other instances much of the business was done on market days, but outside the control of the authorities of the 'open market'. At Salisbury and Devizes, too, the principal inns were centres of commercial life.

[3] E 134, 11–12 Car. I, H 10. It is not clear, however, whether all these yards belonged to innkeepers; some appear to have been those of local tradesmen.

[4] Req. 2, 227, 16; E 134, 37–8 Eliz., M 15. At Exeter the Cloth Fair was held in the New Inn.—W. G. Hoskins, *Two Thousand Years in Exeter*, 1960, p. 128.

The Tudor and Stuart innkeeper was thus in a powerful position to influence the course of private trading. Many a publican provided cellars or outbuildings for the storage of his clients' goods. Some converted their halls or parlours into private auction rooms. A few engaged in private dealings on their own account. Every week, it was said, John Byde, an innkeeper of Keynsham near Bath, bought corn at Warminster in Wiltshire and resold it to the citizens of Bristol. In Huntingdonshire Michael Potter of Fen Stanton, in addition to running an inn, brewing beer, and renting a reed-ground, also "used the trade of buying and selling divers things," in particular malt, with which he supplied brewers in the neighbouring counties. In Northamptonshire, at the end of the seventeenth century, an innkeeper of Peterborough ran a prosperous business as a waterman, with nine boats on the river Nene; his personal property was valued at nearly £250.[1]

Most innkeepers, however, confined their activities to 'finding chapmen' for customers and arranging bargains between their patrons. The methods by which they did so are of some interest. Frequently the landlord would open negotiations between two of his customers himself, as they were sitting at supper in the hall of the inn. Agreement between the two prospective dealers was rarely reached without a lengthy series of "speeches" and "communications," and the company sat far into the night before the transaction was concluded. Sometimes an unscrupulous innkeeper would allow some hapless yeoman (well plied with ale) to be "cozened of his money" by the "glozing terms... smooth words, and fair speeches" of the other party concerned; though no doubt most landlords, for the sake of their own reputation, endeavoured to encourage fair dealing. When the bargain was agreed, the local scrivener (sometimes himself one of the guests) was called upon to draw up the bonds, and the deed was read out to the assembled company. Finally, perhaps at a later date, the bill was sealed by the two parties concerned, with solemn oaths and vows, and prayers for "the blessing of God."[2] Occasionally neither party fully comprehended its repetitive and antique expressions; not infrequently one of the signatories later confessed himself unable to read it, or, like John Watson of Dalby in Leicestershire, cast his bonds or acquittances "into the fire and burned [them]" because "he did not know what to do with [them]."[3]

[1] E 134, 21 James I, M 29; Req. 2, 255, 65; Northants. RO, inventory of John Yates, 1694.

[2] Details of transactions in inns may be found in many cases in Chancery and Requests. Examples of 'simple' bonds or covenants occur in BM, Harleian MS 98, ff. 35, 41, 44.

[3] Req. 2, 291, 24. Watson's residence is not altogether clear from the document, but was probably Dalby.

By 1640 the community of wayfaring merchants covered the whole of the country. Its members were often familiar with the towns and villages of half a dozen different counties. Two linenmen of Lancashire disposed of their wares to customers in Oxfordshire, Warwickshire, Berkshire, Cheshire, Staffordshire, and Buckinghamshire. A gentleman factor of Nottinghamshire set out to purchase peas from farmers in Huntingdonshire, which he was to deliver at Peterborough in North- amptonshire to a yeoman from the Black Monks near Lincoln. [1] A yeoman-factor of Bythorne in Huntingdonshire bought over five thousand fleeces from a farmer of Sharnbrook in Bedfordshire, became bound in a bill of £790 with a man from Wimbledon in Surrey, and travelled "far northward" and then "likewise into Gloucestershire, and so westward" in order to "procure a chapman." [2] One week a draper of Bury St Edmunds attended Stourbridge Fair to buy wool; another he was in Warwickshire collecting debts from his customers; and from there he proceeded to Ipswich on further business, before returning to his home. Many adventures and dangers from time to time beset such merchants. One man had his corn barges frozen in the river Ouse; another saw his vessels stranded in a Cambridgeshire river through drought; a third was attacked by bandits in a forest in Staffordshire; a fourth was drowned in a flooded river in Warwickshire; and many were robbed of their money, or lost their lives at sea. [3] But nothing deterred them. In northern cities like York, in Cotswold markets like Cirencester, in Wealden wool-villages like Brenchley, and sometimes in foreign towns like Bruges, they were equally at home.

It is not surprising if the wayfaring community developed an ethos of its own dissimilar to that of the settled society of town and village. Its spirit of speculation and adventure ran counter to the stable tradi- tions of the English peasantry. The privacy of its dealings rendered it suspect in the eyes of peasant and government alike. And yet it was principally the private trader who wrestled with the new commercial problems of the age. Without his enterprise, the task of feeding and clothing an extra one and-a-half million people would not have been solved. He was rarely a popular figure; but he was indubitably an indispensable one. What his own feelings were in the face of his unpopularity can rarely be discovered. But it is not fanciful to trace a connection between the rapid spread of private trading in the early seventeenth century and the rapid rise of Independency. For Inde- pendency was not a rural and static religion, like anglicanism, nor

[1] Lancs. RO, inventories of Wm. Bannester of Croston (1595) and Henry Bannester of Heskin in Eccleston (1595); Req. 2, 86, 17.
[2] C 2, James I, C 2, 46. His travelling expenses for visiting the North and West amounted to £11 10s.   [3] Cf. Req. 2, 266, 35; Req. 2, 240, 58; C 3, 251, 59.

rigid and urban, like presbyterianism, but mobile, virile, and impatient of human institutions, like the wayfaring community itself. And it is in the works of Independents like John Bunyan, or in the sermons of the Cornishman Hugh Peter, that we sometimes catch a glimpse of the aspirations of that community. "Oh, the blessed change we see," said Peter, in a sermon preached shortly after the Civil War, "that can travel now from Edinburgh to the Land's End in Cornwall, who not long since were blocked up at our doors. To see the highways occupied again; to hear the carter whistling to his toiling team; to see the weekly carrier attend his constant mart; to see the hills rejoicing, the valleys laughing."[1]

E. THE MARKETING PROBLEM IN THE SIXTEENTH CENTURY

The increase in private bargaining during the latter half of the period did not go unnoticed by contemporaries. It led to a torrent of lawsuits in the courts of Chancery, Requests, Star Chamber, and Exchequer.[2] These disputes cannot be dismissed merely as evidence of litigiousness; they also bear witness to a fundamental problem of the Tudor and Stuart economy. They illustrate the fact that the new methods of private bargaining were gradually breaking down the protective barriers of the customary marketing system. The distribution of these lawsuits is therefore of considerable interest. Out of a sample of some 350 in the Court of Requests, 57 per cent relate to the eastern counties, 18 per cent to the south of England, 11 per cent to the Midlands, 9 per cent to the west country, and 5 per cent to Wales and the north.[3] The high proportion of disputes arising from dealings in the eastern counties is in part explained by the presence of London (accounting for 18 per cent of the transactions) and by the populousness of the region. The Midland proportion, when similar cases in Chancery are taken into account, is probably an under-estimate. In Wales and the north many disputes were brought before the Council of the Marches and the Council of the North.[4] But by and large there can be no doubt

---

[1] Quoted from *God's Doing, Man's Duty*, p. 24, in C. V. Wedgwood, *The King's War, 1641–1647*, 1958, p. 551.

[2] Cf. p.   , n.   . These disputes also need to be viewed in a larger context. They were not confined to agricultural dealings: of those in Chancery, the majority relate to mercantile and manufacturing activities.

[3] The high percentage for the south is affected by a large number of timber disputes, apart from which it would be 13 per cent.

[4] Rachel Reid, *The King's Council in the North*, p. 305, says that actions for debt, upon obligations with penalties and upon leases, were numerous; the court was popular with traders.

that traders in the eastern counties figured most prominently in these disputes, followed, a long way behind, by those of the Midlands, the south, the west, the north, and Wales.

Analysed by type of product, 35 per cent of these lawsuits relate to dealings in barley, malt, or hops; 24 per cent to dealing in sheep, wool, and woad; 11 per cent to cattle; 6 per cent to wood, mast, and charcoal; and barely one quarter to all other types of product—wheat, oats, rye, legumes, fruit, flax, hemp, hay, horses, swine, poultry, fish, cheese, butter, and leather. Something like 60 per cent of all disputes, then, were attributable to the demands of the brewing or clothing industries.[1]

The causes of the expansion in priva tetrading underlying these disputes have already been touched on. The rapid rise in the population and its increasing concentration in urban or industrial centres like London, Norwich, Tyneside, and the west country clothing towns, upset the balance of communities hitherto largely self-supporting, and compelled them to depend upon market supplies. The same concentration, together with the expanding scale of marketing transactions, the declining area of cultivable 'waste', and the increase of regional specialization prevented their being met by local resources. At the same time, the price rise of the sixteenth century seems to have led to an increase in agricultural productivity, while the shortage of ready money in the early seventeenth century, so often complained of at the time, stimulated credit dealings. In the upshot some years showed a large surplus of certain commodities in the more productive areas, which only the private trader could dispose of.[2]

The increase in private trade and credit dealing would not have led to social unrest, however, had not other factors been at work. The truth was that current economic practice gave comparatively little guidance in either the operation or the regulation of private trading. Many fresh questions were raised by agricultural marketing to which traditional experience gave little or no answer. Some of these problems

---

[1] A few wool cases may have related to open market, not private, dealings: but cf. p.   , n.   . Some sheep purchases were by butchers, not clothiers, but generally local butchers bought in fairs or market towns. Sixty per cent is probably a conservative estimate of disputes attributable to brewing and clothing. Virtually all barley dealings recorded in these cases were for brewing: bread-corn for the poor was generally purchased in the open market, though also hawked from door to door by mealmen, etc.

[2] Probably the Dissolution and the composition agreements for victualling the royal household also transferred a certain amount of agricultural trade from institutional hands to those of private individuals. For a discussion of the effects of a shortage of corn in the first half of the seventeenth century, see Barry Supple, *Commercial Crisis and Change in England, 1600–1642*, 1959, pp. 176 *sqq.*

arose from the shortcomings of the 'economic mechanism' itself; some from a conflict between the social assumptions of the market town and wayfaring community; and some from the unpredictable forces of warfare, dearth, and civil confusion.

1. Problems of the Economic mechanism

One of the problems to which the expansion of the Tudor economy gave rise, and to which the experience of the open market gave little answer, was the increase in the *scale* of marketing operations. One man buys over £500 worth of malt; another exports over £300 worth of beer; another buys six thousand coney skins; another over two thousand sheep; another the whole crop of several Kentish orchards; another over four hundred tods of wool; and others again, several hundred pounds worth of hops, over five thousand sheep-skins, the annual produce of a Hertfordshire rabbit warren, and chicken by hundreds and thousands in Bedfordshire and Berkshire. Even in the realm of private marketing such bargains were unusual; but they were not unknown, and the experience of the open market offered little or no guidance in their organization. It is not surprising if many such transactions went awry, or that a factor with a large parcel of sheep accidentally left on his hands, after the default of a customer, should fine himself "full of care and travail" in trying to dispose of them.[1]

Closely connected with the increasing scale of transactions was the inadequacy of Tudor business methods in implementing them. For although by 1640 an elaborate code of custom had come to govern private bargaining, it was inadequate to contain its wayward tendencies. It was cumbersome, inflexible, and inexact. The system of accounting employed by private dealers was still primitive; much business, especially in poultry dealings, was still reckoned by fragile wooden tallies, notched and split down the centre, easily broken or mislaid. The method of binding parties by bonds obligatory, generally bipartite, was hard to enforce.[2] One party might lose his part of the bond; or perhaps his witnesses could not be discovered; or else the phraseology of the legal instrument confused him; or the scrivener who drew it up had misunderstood his agricultural expressions. The penalty for non-

[1] Large-scale agricultural dealings were not, of course, an entirely new phenomenon. The sheep flocks of monastic houses like Canterbury Cathedral and Fountains Abbey, not to mention the export trade in corn, had in an earlier period involved business dealings of a very large order. On any view, however, Elizabethan expansion drew into the field of private marketing many hundreds of new traders with little or no commercial training. They had to buy their experience, and they ofen paid dear.
[2] For an account of wool dealings by means of bonds seeBowden, *op. cit.*, pp. 143–8.

delivery of goods at the due time, usually amounting to double the value of the bargain, was often unenforceable. Quite trivial transactions were ratified with all the verbiage of the law; perhaps only for a farmer to discover, too late, that his lawyer, "being trusted to make a sufficient bond, hath devised such a bauble as tended rather to cozen him of the whole" of his money.[1] Little less perilous were the agreements by which business partnerships were drawn up, and many disputes arose through some flaw in the original deed. The life of an agricultural partnership was too often poor, nasty, brutish, and remarkably short.[2] The remedy for such evils was a reformation of business methods. The homilies of ecclesiastics were not without effect; but they rarely curbed the appetites of unscrupulous traders, and they offered no guidance in cases of genuine misfortune. The arts of commercial co-operation were difficult, and the hazards of agricultural trade considerable. A more carefully thought out system of regulation was called for; but it was not forthcoming.

At the root of the problem was the inadequacy of the Tudor educational system. Many marketing disputes arose through the illiteracy of one or other of the parties concerned. A timber merchant of Marden in the Weald of Kent, sued by his former partner, confessed that he never kept "any note or other writing" of his dealings "being a mere layman and illiterate...." The pathetic bill exhibited by the widow of a woolman in Buckinghamshire was said (only too accurately) to contain "neither any manner of form, sense, reason, or matter whereby to charge the defendant, either by law, equity, or conscience, but only a great heap of senseless words and terms without any manner of order."[3] An acquittance drawn up by Stephen Grene, a factor of Ipswich, was scarcely more intelligible: "Be it knowen to all men," it ran, "that I Steveyen Greyne doveth kovenleyege me seyevlef to rest yen me haynd the sovem of xviii povend feleyemes moveney, to me George Sparke at the sayem pelayes of ey pch thell hes retoveren to bereyges ageyne...."[4] It was the possibility of exploiting similar ignorance that tempted Nicholas Tayler, of Ticehurst in Sussex, to effect his "covenous practice and fraudulent device" against John Awoode of Wadhurst. Perceiving Awoode to be "weak and easy to be deceived," Tayler induced him, for the sum of £20, to agree to deliver four corns of wheat "upon the Sunday next following," eight wheat

---

[1] Req. 2, 109, 60.

[2] Cf. Req. 2, 131, 47; Req. 2, 240, 58; Req. 2, 30, 30; Req. 2, 61, 55; C 2, James I, L 14, 35.

[3] Req. 2, 30, 30; Req. 2, 30, 56.

[4] Req. 2, 112, 24. The meaning is: "...doth acknowledge myself to rest in my hand the sum of 18 pound Flemish money, to me George Sparke at the same place of Ipswich till his return to Bruges again...."

grains the next Sunday, sixteen the next, and so on, doubling the amount week by week, for the space of a year. The unfortunate Awoode apparently thought he had struck a good bargain, till the end of the year revealed his terrifying catastrophe: his debt was over four thousand billion grains of corn.[1] Perhaps such cases shed some light on the foundation of so many grammar schools in this period. For the small transactions of the open market, little education was necessary; but with the growth of private dealing some grounding in writing and accounting was imperative.

Equally inadequate was the essentially *personal* conception of credit upon which private trading was based. There were no banks, and a man's 'credit' could only be what he was taken to be worth in his local community. The very word 'credit' was synonymous with a man's 'estate,' 'worth,' or 'standing' in local society; but when factors and drovers were travelling all over the country, such a conception became nugatory. It was only through the highly personal links of the wayfaring community that it retained any meaning. The problem was really twofold. First, there was a strong temptation for those with much address or little acumen to engage in dealings beyond their means or worth. All went well till some customer defaulted or the harvest failed; then disaster ensued, perhaps involving a score of other victims, unaware of their client's shaky status when they dealt with him.[2] Secondly, there was the temptation to inflict injury on the credit of one's opponent. The dread of 'losing reputation' was not simply a fear of losing caste. It might mean the end of one's business and the impoverishment of one's family. When a wool dealer of Warwick caused his former partner John Lee, glover, "to be arrested in Cirencester in the county of Gloucester in the open market there, where [Lee's] most credit was, by writ of *capias ad satisfaciend*'," that partner found himself greatly damnified and "almost utterly undone."[3] The reputation of Humphrie Grigg of Beaudesert in Warwickshire, as a result of the "unlawful and unconscionable proceedings" of Robert Wheeler of Tanworth in Arden, was "called into question and his estate descanted upon, so far as that whereas before such time...his word and credit was current and would pass in the country with and amongst his neighbours...now they make it very scrupulous to take [his] word or promise, yea scarcely his bond for a matter of five pounds:" so that he is "prejudiced and damnified exceedingly not only in his reputation and credit but also in his private estate;" his creditors calling on him "for their money faster than [he] can provide... threatening [him] with arrests and suits, so as [he] dare not stay at home in his own house or in the country, but is enforced to fly and obscure

<hr>

[1] Req. 2, 49, 46.   [2] Cf. Req. 2, 255, 65.   [3] C 2, James I, L 14, 35.

himself from his own house, wife, and family, to his exceeding great loss…" Little wonder if Robert Reyce of Suffolk, describing the kind of trader who "in short time climbeth to much credit and wealth," could remark that "such is the world, which is nothing but a shop of all change, that too often it falleth out for these riches thus hastily gotten, which can abide no enduring continuance, [that] they receive in exchange first decay, which when willingness in suretyship hath laid open too manifestly, then poverty too, too quickly remedyless seizes them."[1]

2. *The problem of conflicting ideals*

The shortcomings of Tudor marketing arrangements were further accentuated by the conflicting aspirations of the market town and private trader. As already remarked, many traders engaged in both spheres of activity, and it would be misleading to draw too sharp a distinction between them. Nevertheless, a certain essential antipathy between the open market and the private trader was manifest in the eyes of contemporaries, and the historian cannot altogether ignore it. At the risk of over-simplifying a complex situation, a brief analysis of these differences must be attempted.

Much of the animosity is traceable to the mutual jealousy of town and countryside. For although in 1640 at least four English people in five were still engaged in agriculture, there were by that date many towns sufficiently urban to develop an ethos of their own that was alien to that of surrounding parishes. In counties like Hertfordshire, the fear of metropolitan penetration and of London's claim on local food supplies was often intense.[2] In East Anglia, the mercantile interests of a port like King's Lynn were by no means identical with those of surrounding villagers. The economic loyalties of Ipswich during the Interregnum conflicted increasingly with those of countryfolk in west Suffolk. And when a wealthy maltster of Canterbury sued John Videon of Patrixbourne, in the Mayor's Court at the Town Hall, "the jury, being all townsmen that live by their trades and their books of reckonings" and "neighbours and friends" of the maltster, "seemed little to weigh the evidence" on behalf of the village yeoman.[3]

Yet the antagonism between the open and private marketing communities was not simply a question of townsman *versus* countryman. The essential conflict arose from their incompatible views of society and social duty. This fact comes to light in the comments of peasants, gentry, and urban tradesmen on what they regarded as the excessive *acquisitiveness* of the wayfaring merchant and his kind. A cattle-dealer

[1] C 2, James I, G 9, 36; Reyce, *op. cit.*, p. 57.
[2] Cf. Fisher, *op. cit.*, p. 62.   [3] Req. 2, 63, 70.

serving the London market, for instance, was accused of "not respecting any conscionable course of dealing, but altogether his own private gain..." A merchant in the habit of transporting barley from Ipswich to Ireland was said to be a man of a "greedy and covetous humour... [who], being willing to take all extremities, is contented to colour his unconscionable desire to gain with a supposition of great loss." A wealthy drover of Braborne in Kent was said to have "raised to himself and gotten great wealth and ability" by converting the whole village common "to the benefit of himself" and to the "almost utter undoing of many" of the poorer parishioners.[1] A merchant of Bermondsey who purchased timber in Kent and sought to advance himself "from the base condition of a fellmonger unto the worshipful title of a squyer" was reminded that he "hath not yet the thankful heart inclined to speak truth and less care to remember that the same God" who had endued him "with such circumspection...hateth and utterly abhorreth the rich man that is a liar."[2] A corn merchant of Burnham Deepdale in Norfolk was said to be "a man of very covetous mind and desire, and hunting exceedingly after gain and bargains, and engrossing of corn...who is and long time hath been both hasty and greedy to buy up and engross into his hands great sums and quantities of corn as well when it was dear as when it was and is cheap...and doth usually transport the same beyond the seas, one ship after another, with as much haste and speed as he can load them...thirsting and greatly desiring to enrich himself thereby;" by reason whereof "many poor people...endure want and fare much the worse..." No doubt such picturesque stories need to be taken with a good deal of salt, and there is no reason to suppose that they always represent the complainant's personal convictions. But whatever the objective facts, a difference of ideals was clearly in dispute. It is to be feared that Reyce's frequent lamentations over "the continual desire of merchants in traversing all the countries and kingdoms of this inferior world for gain" were not entirely without foundation.[3]

A similar conflict comes to light in the attitude of contemporaries to the claims of *social responsibility* in agricultural bargaining. In the open market the idea of the 'just price' was still a governing consideration. To us that notion may seem antiquated and even chimerical. But it must be remembered that in the eyes of most contemporaries bargains were not simply commercial transactions; they formed part of the

[1] C 2, James I, W 14, 59; Req. 2, 290, 35; C 2, James I, G 5, 70.

[2] Req. 2, 63, 49. The fellmonger (who had described himself as 'esquire' in the bill) retorted that his opponent had fallen "from the degree of an esquire to the base condition of a cozener to cozen this complainant of his money."

[3] C 2, James I, G 13, 50; Reyce, *op. cit.*, p. 33, cf. pp. 29, 40.

network of human intercourse which held society together. Every agricultural transaction both could and should be 'equitable'. For since every man occupied an appointed place or degree in the body politic, every man had a claim on that body to provide him with the means of livelihood. Transactions or contracts that militated against his right to subsistence, however arrived at, were unjust and invalid. For most people the ultimate appeal in disputed dealings was to social, in contrast with economic, duty. A maltster of Marlborough, for instance, was accused of "little respecting the necessity of the commonwealth...or yet the utter undoing of...Thomas Packer [of Pewsey and] his wife, children, and family, but wholly seeking his own gain and the extremest ad[vantage]" of his bargain. The "rigorous dealing" of John Pechye of Huntingdonshire was said to have led to the "utter undoing and impoverishment of [the] wives and children" of William Joyce the elder and younger, who were "like to be utterly bereaved of their liberty, and spoiled of their goods, chattels, and maintenance," unless John Pechye "either for fear of almighty God or upon remorse of his own conscience" should yield to the claims of social justice. The "most foul and wicked" dealings of Thomas Wynde of Norfolk, gentleman, were likely, it was said, to lead "to the utter undoing of [Roger Sedgwick of St Ives and] his wife, family, and children for ever," "clean contrary both to all right equity and good conscience" and "to the ill and perilous example of others..." As for those of Robert Wheeler of Tanworth in Warwickshire, they were so "unlawful and unconscionable," so utterly "vile" and "base," that his very "neighbours...did in course of common humanity reprove the said Wheeler for his said...dealing, telling him that he might be ashamed thereof."[1]

For many a wayfaring merchant, by contrast, the notion of social duty as the ultimate criterion was of little practical importance. Few, perhaps, were so "past shame and void of all feeling of Christianity" as Robert Wheeler, who made answer to his neighbours' reproofs "that if all that he had done in that behalf were to do again, he would do it." Occasionally, a merchant who put his client's penal bonds in suit and been accused of his "utter impoverishing and undoing" was made to feel some compunction, and admit that "he never meant nor intended" such a lamentable consequence. But for many private traders there could be no conceivable reason why debts justly incurred should not be fulfilled, or why people guilty of breaking their bonds, albeit the penalty was double the principal, should not be prosecuted with all the rigour of the law. Two Ipswich merchants, questioned for prosecuting a corn farmer of Hunstanton, replied by asserting their right to put the bond in suit "as it is lawful for them to do." A maltster

[1] Req. 2, 29, 38; Req. 2, 135, 61; Req. 2, 122, 32; C 2, James I, G 9, 36.

of Over in Cambridgeshire, accused by a customer of "covetous and hard dealing," replied that "if the complainant hath endangered his credit and weakened his estate and ability with his undiscreet bargains, yet he, this defendant, hopeth that he shall not be barred...from that benefit that the laws of this realm do afford for the obtaining his said debt due by virtue of the said obligations..."[1] A corn merchant of St Catherine's Hill in Surrey, whose purchase of barley from John Egell of Hampshire could not be fulfilled "by reason of the great dearth of corn that happened the last year," replied that John Egell "never performed any part of his said promise, and now as it seemeth having had intelligence of the defendant's just suits commenced against him at the common law, seeketh unduly the protection of this honourable court to detain from the said defendant his said true and just debts, contrary both to law and conscience." Or take the ingenuous (and highly ungrammatical) amazement of a maltster of Fulmer in Cambridgeshire, when accused by one of his suppliers of exacting 'forbearance' of 100 per cent "without any Christian respect of your Highness's subject his poor estate and charge of children." "What conscience or equity," says the maltster, "can any require in so plain a bargain, to wit that layeth forth his money beforehand for any goods, chattels, or merchandise to be delivered, should not when the time cometh be truly delivered, let the price or value fall forth either great or less? And...for answer to the frivolous declaration that [the complainant is] fallen in loss of cattell and charge with wife and children, thereto the said defendant saith that if it were true it is not material to the bargain...And as to the allegation that there should a gain rise to the defendant after the rate of one hundreth pounds [per cent]...the said defendant sayeth that it is a very rude and frivolous allegation..."[2] Once again, such tales need to be treated with caution, and do not necessarily represent personal convictions. But the conflict of social ideals can hardly be questioned.

Finally, the animosity against private traders comes to light in the attitude of contemporaries to 'secrecy of dealing'. For most people the publicity of the market place afforded at least a measure of protection to both customer and tradesmen. The fact that transactions became the common talk of the town discouraged, if it did not prevent, wholesale cozenage. But the privy dealings of the wayfaring community were rarely amenable to social sanctions of this kind. When so much bargaining was undertaken in alehouses, inns, and farm-kitchens all manner of abuses might occur. The case of one Richard Snellinge of London may be taken as typical. Employed by a poulterer of Grace-

[1] Req. 2, 28, 5; Req. 2, 67, 45; Req. 2, 28, 10.
[2] Req. 2, 88, 17; Req. 2, 86, 43.

church Street, "in journeying and riding to country markets to buy and provide poultry wares," Snellinge was despatched by his master with two horses "worth twenty nobles apiece" to Potton in Bedfordshire. Meeting there in "riotous manner with two country chapmen" from whom he apparently bought poultry, he "went to the Sign of the George in Potton and there continued drinking until they were all drunk, and being drunk...slept in the stable of the said inn until seven o'clock at night. And then...with too much haste [he] came with the said horses towards London, the one being loaden with two hundredweight and the other with two hundred-and-a-half weight, and...drave them" forty-five miles without once baiting them, so that one horse died, the other was thereafter useless, and "the market was past, through such his...drunken neglect...And thus from time to time in most riotous and expensive manner [Snellinge] negligently performed [his master's] businesses..."[1]

More serious than particular instances of abuse was the privacy regarded by contemporaries as essentially characteristic of individual trading. When the cloth merchants of Suffolk visited London in Queen Elizabeth's reign, they customarily travelled together to the same inn, the George in Lombard Street, dined together at the same table, purchased together from the same dealers, and supported one another in their own dealings and lawsuits. When the wool dealers or clothmen of the Weald of Kent had goods to sell, it was their ancient and "usual custom" to take the responsibility for marketing them in turn, each dealer travelling to his appointed market in his allotted week, and trading for the whole community at home.[2] When a Midland factor bought corn or livestock in advance and promised to send his drover or servant at a later date to receive it, he sometimes agreed upon a "secret sign or token" with the seller, usually some peculiar form of handshake, by which the latter might recognize his servant. (Was there, one wonders, some link with the handshake peculiar to societies like the freemasons?) And if any merchant dealt dishonestly or transgressed the customs of the community, it was sometimes extremely difficult for him to escape from its clutches. When Steven Grene, an Ipswich merchant in the habit of exporting grain to Bruges, went bankrupt and fled from his native town in the 1560's, leaving many debts behind him, he was pursued with remorseless importunity by his various creditors: first to Salisbury, then to Shrewsbury, then into Lincolnshire, then to the Rose and Crown at Smithfield, and finally

---

[1] Req. 2, 308, 1. The distance mentioned in the manuscript is 37 miles, but Potton is 45 statute miles from London. For other typical stories of abuses in inn bargaining see Req. 2, 396, 56; Req. 2, 51, 22; Req. 2, 291, 40; Req. 2, 227, 16.

[2] See, for example, Req. 2, 62, 34; C 2, James I, D 3, 44.

to Hill Morton in Warwickshire. In each place he lived a few perilous months or years, changing his name to Leafe, or Greneleafe, or Buckell, attempting to start business anew; until one morning some "Ipswich man in travelling" happened to "meet with him," or some "cunning man to help diseases in men and beasts" casually noticed him passing down the street, and gave information to his creditors.[1]

For the wayfaring trader, it must be acknowledged that the contemporary fear of 'private dealing' was unnecessarily morbid. For every unscrupulous merchant there must have been many who were straightforward, and it was obviously not in their interest to spread social discord. Neither need one suppose that equity, still less common-sense, was usually on the side of their opponents. Private dealing could not be carried on apart from the proper enforcement of bargains freely entered into, and without private trade the marketing problem could not have been solved. Yet it is impossible not to regard the system of private marketing and the community of wayfaring merchants as transforming elements in the Tudor and Stuart economy. The rapid ascendancy of that community in the second half of the period cannot be gainsaid, and was certainly not unconnected with the rise of the revolutionary party during the Great Rebellion. So early as 1640 it was averred that the Scottish Covenanters were making use of travelling merchants "to convey intelligence and gain a party all over England, by insinuating fears and jealousies into the minds of people, of the frightful design of the Court and bishops to introduce popery and arbitrary government..."[2] The abolition or suspension, by the Long Parliament, of the Conciliar Courts in which the new methods of bargaining were frustrated can hardly be without significance. And it does not seem fanciful, as we have observed, to trace a parallel between the vagrant life of the wayfaring community and the vagrant religion of the Independents.

3. The problem of insecurity

These economic and social problems would not have become so serious, however, apart from the frequent occurrence of natural and civil calamity. The rural economy of Tudor England was more subject

---

[1] Req. 2, 112, 24. The evidence is contradictory, but the above account seems substantially correct. Grene was also accused of deserting his wife and living with his maid.

[2] John Nalson, *An impartial Collection of the great Affairs of State...*, 1682, I, p. 285. The Familists in Elizabeth's reign spread their doctrines by "going round the country as travelling basket makers," etc.—Ronald Knox, *Enthusiasm*, 1950, p. 171. Private letters were often carried by packmen and travelling merchants (cf. G .Eland, ed., *Thomas Wotton's Letter-Book, 1574–1586*, 1960, p. 12).

to sudden catastrophes of this kind than our own, and there was certainly less to cushion their effect upon society. One such danger was the threat of warfare. Events like the Spanish Armada caused widespread consternation amongst English villagers. As one Sherborne sheep dealer complained, that "intended and practised invasion of foreign enemies...put your Highness's subjects in so sudden a maze as your said subject could neither sell such things as he had, nor by any means borrow any money to make satisfaction according to his goodwill therein."[1]

A more frequent source of trouble was the lawlessness of the countryside, by means of which many bargains were upset and bonds lost or destroyed. When the Suffolk factor of two London fishmongers called at a farm in South Elmham to purchase cheese and butter, he and his assistants were robbed of £40 in money and "were by the [farmer's] said wife and [his] sons and daughters...being many in number and of great force, or by most of them, grievously battered and beaten in so much as...[they] were driven and enforced to fly away for avoiding of greater danger..."[2] When John Walter, a clothier of Belbroughton in Worcestershire, was travelling with two packhorses through Stourton Wood, near Kinver, "in God's peace and the Queen's, suddenly there issued out of the same wood" a company of bandits who "caught the packhorses and the packs" and "took violently [his]...cloak; whereat he being greatly amazed (for that it was a suspicious place and the said parties being appointed with dangerous weapons wherewith they did very desperately[?] assault [him]...) he stood greatly in fear that they would presently have taken...[his] life..." Fortunately, one Thomas Longman of Kinver happened to "come travelling that way, whom when your said orator saw, he was somewhat comforted." But John Walter never regained his packs, nor a bond of £100 in which he was bound to a yeoman of Northampton, by means of which he was brought to the verge of bankruptcy; for those "said riotous persons...most of them are vagrant and wandering, and cannot easy be found..."[3] Around Diss and Harleston in Norfolk, the countryside was dominated by a man "of such conversation and condition as he will not be obedient to any law," but confederates himself "with divers others of like conversation...such as have rescued divers persons that have been

[1] Req. 2, 50, 7. The document is undated, but from internal evidence appears to relate to this period.

[2] Req. 2, 393, 28.

[3] C 3, 221, 46. The bandits made use of the fact that Stourton Wood was in the Liberty of Kinver; they cited Walter before the court of the Liberty, of which their master was high beadle.

arrested by virtue of the Queen's Majesty's lawful process, and have maimed divers bailiffs, and cut off with swords some of their fingers, some have been also overrun with horses, some otherwise hurt, so as divers times within the markets of Harleston, Diss, and other places... the greater or more part of the market folks have been commoted together with weapons very dangerously;...the company of which disordered persons doth so daily increase...as...it is like to be a very dangerous thing within the country."[1]

The most serious problem of the Tudor and Stuart economy, however, was dearth. The failure of the harvest struck a community still largely agrarian with a force we can hardly imagine. The fluctuations in crop yields were a problem which affected everyone, yet none could solve. In prosperous years a large grain surplus was exported from counties like Cambridge to London, the Netherlands, and the north; but in poor seasons Cambridgeshire people went short and those of cities and manufacturing regions might starve. In 1579–80 London's coastwise cereal imports were only 17,380 quarters; in 1585–6 they rose to 48,401 quarters; two years later they dropped to the level of 1579–80, and in 1615 soared to nearly 70,000 quarters.[2] For the different 'exporting' counties the figures also varied greatly, and the number of annual corn-shipments from ports like King's Lynn followed a most erratic curve. No doubt these vagaries were attributable to a number of factors; but fluctuation in harvest yields was unquestionably the principal cause. Successive periods of shortage and dearth in the first half of the seventeenth century—in 1608, 1621–3, 1630–7, and 1645–51—contributed much to the political malaise of the era. As Professor Tawney remarked, the depression of the early 1620's was a political as well as economic disaster of very considerable magnitude.[3]

The effect of these periods of dearth was twofold. For the maltster and cornmonger they spelt delayed deliveries and broken agreements. To counteract such troubles traders resorted to bargaining in advance, enforcing their transactions by bonds with a penalty generally of double the contract price. For the dealer this ensured regular supplies, with the advantage of an 'unearned increment' if the harvest was poor and the price of grain in the open market rose; for the farmer it offered the advantages of a guaranteed market. The danger of the system lay in the determination of the dealer to exact the full penalty in the event of non-delivery. Every poor harvest was followed, in consequence, by a spate of legal disputes in which farmers pleaded their inability to

[1] C 2, Eliz., L 8, 53.
[2] Cf. SP 14, 130, 9; Fisher, *op. cit.*, table p. 47, and cf. p. 49.
[3] R. H. Tawney, *Business and Politics under James I...*, 1958, p. 185.

fulfil their bargains and the inequity of maltsters and cornmongers in attempting to profit from natural calamity. In the spring of 1596, for instance, Thomas Packer of Pewsey, having borrowed £12 from a Marlborough maltster, for which he entered bond of £24 and promised delivery of 12 quarters of barley, was unable to complete delivery because, "by the will and pleasure of Almighty God and the unseasonable weather and scarcity of the year, the grain of barley did forthwith" grow to 6s. or 7s. a bushel. The maltster, however, refused to receive his money again, even with interest, and the farmer was threatened with the "utter undoing" of himself, his wife, and his children. Or take the case of a Hampshire farmer who in the same year sold 20 quarters of barley to a Surrey factor. "By reason of the great dearth of corn...," he says, and because his "crop and increase of corn greatly in the same year failed, as it hath also done in this present year to the great sorrow and heart's grief of your said subject,...[he], his wife, and vi small poor children are utterly impoverished, and so thereby made altogether unable to make delivery." Yet his customer has put the bonds in suit, refuses the mediation of his "good friends," and covets the whole gain "of the penalty of the aforesaid obligation."[1]

Equally serious was the effect of harvest failure upon the poor. As probate inventories and other sources show, only a small proportion of the poor grew their own corn; the majority purchased their small weekly requirements either in the open market or from badgers and corn factors. Since the usual breadcorn of the poor was barley, a grain shortage thus led to sharp conflict between the brewing industry and the poor, and to serious danger of social disturbance.[2] The effect of dearth upon the poor comes to light in a case filed in the Court of Requests by one Robert Taylor, a wealthy clothier of Bisley in Gloucestershire, in 1598. In the preceding year, "much suspecting.. the great scarcity and want of corn which was like to be and ensue in divers parts of this...realm," Taylor had entered "into communication and speeches with Richard Lewys of the city of London, merchant, for the bringing in of rye into this...realm, from Danske or other the eastern parts," to the value of £1,000, to be delivered at Bristol. He also agreed with one John Knapp of Ipswich, merchant, for a further £1,000 worth, to be delivered along with Lewys's bargain. Returning into Gloucestershire, Taylor made it known "unto divers of the wor-

---

[1] Req. 2, 29, 38; Req. 2, 88, 17.

[2] Sir William Ashley, in *The Bead of our Forefathers*, 1928, overemphasizes the importance of rye as the standard breadcorn at this time: justices' reports, *inter alia*, indicate that barley was the staple grain among the poorer classes, though rye and mixed grain were also utilized.—Cf., for example, CSPD 1629–31, p. 539. See also *supra*, p.   .

shipful and the better sort of men who he thought to be most careful for the relieving of the poorer sort of people inhabiting within the same, as also to divers men of great account of other countries thereunto adjoining, who your subject thought were likewise well affected to their poor neighbours; and did offer unto them that, at the delivery of the same corn, they should receive the same at such prices as he might conveniently afford it, and did bargain with them what quantity of corn they should have from him." Accordingly, "the whole country of Gloucester, as other countries thereabouts, wholly depending upon the receipt thereof, did leave themselves altogethers unprovided otherways..." After a series of delays due to storms at sea, for which Taylor was "greatly threatened" for breach of "his former promises ...and especially for that a number were likely to be starved," the grain ships were reported to be approaching Bristol. Thereupon Taylor "sent into the countries where he had promised to deliver the same corn that the country people might repair to Bristol aforesaid for the fetching away thereof; and thereupon great multitudes of people did resort thither, where they remained divers days...looking for the same corn..." But when the sacks were opened, the corn was "so hot and so insufficient" as to be virtually useless. The reactions of the starving Gloucestershire populace are not recorded; but Robert Taylor was like "to be utterly spoiled and undone" as a result of that "hot, naughty, and ill-conditioned" rye.[1]

The fact that many districts had by 1640 ceased to be self-supporting in grain rendered these conditions doubly dangerous. When people were coming to depend increasingly upon travelling merchants to supply their requirements, the consequences of harvest failure could no longer remain local. Because Smith could not fulfil his bargain to Jones, Jones could not fulfil his to Black and White, nor White his own to Robinson, Johnson, Jackson, Wilson, and Thompson. The ripples of distress spread all over the pool. There is no occasion to believe all the stories of "weeping wives" and "fatherless infants;" but it is indisputable that many families might be brought to the verge of ruin by breach of a single contract, and thousands of townsmen and countryfolk by the failure of the harvest.

4. *The regulation of marketing by the state*

Such is the background against which government attempts to control the marketing of agricultural produce must be reviewed. For the regulation of certain special markets the reader is referred to Dr Bowden's account of the wool market and to Professor Gras's and

[1] Req. 2, 130, 38.

Dr McGrath's studies of the export and London markets.[1] This study concentrates on the regulation of provincial marketing, particularly in corn; for it was in this sphere that control was most vigilant.

In regulating the open market, the government's principal concern was to safeguard the interests of the consumer, and especially the poor.[2] As trade increased, the tendency to protect the consumer increased, and there was a distinct attempt under Queen Elizabeth and especially the first two Stuarts to revive the powers of the clerk of the market.[3] These powers had never died out; but until James I's reign the clerk's primary concern was with the control of measures and prices within the verge of court, for the presence of the royal retinue often caused acute local shortage.[4] Thereafter, as a result of the revival of his office, the duties of the clerk or his deputies became all but universal and, if proclamations were heeded, more or less all-pervasive. By the proclamation of February 1619 the clerk was required to ensure that all duties allotted to him by statute and otherwise were properly carried out both in the verge and elsewhere. He was to enquire into the abuse of weights and measures; ensure that provisinos sold were of good quality; punish forestallers, engrossers, and regrators, "who by their inordinate desire of gain do enhance the prices of all things vendible to the decay and overthrow of all open markets;" keep his sessions at least once a year in every county and as many towns as possible; and appoint deputies only from among those "of sufficiency and ability to perform the place," and not from the ranks of inn-keepers or tradesmen. Notice of the clerk's sessions was to be given by the high constables; at least one justice of the peace in the circuit was to attend him; a jury of twelve men was to be impanelled at each centre; the constables of each parish were to give evidence before them; and the proclamation was to be read, before All Saints, in every market town and "hanged up and fastened in a table in every market place by an officer, where it may continue to be seen and read by any that will." Special attention was to be devoted to the regulation of weights and measures at inns, "that so the traveller or passenger may not be

[1] Bowden, *Wool Trade*, chapters IV–VII; McGrath, *op. cit.*, chapters III, IV, IX; Gras, *op. cit.*, pp. 77–89, 130–55, 221–50. The reader is also referred to Williams, *Tradesmen in Early-Stuart Wiltshire*, pp. vii–xxii; and D. G. Barnes, *A History of the English Corn Laws from 1660 to 1846*, 1930, chapter I.

[2] Cf. SP 14, 73, pp. 29–31.

[3] Many other matters were involved in the extension of these powers, in particular new methods of compounding for purveyance for the household: cf. Aylmer, *op. cit.*, pp. 82 *sqq.*, and see note , p. , *supra*. See also N. J. Williams, 'Sessions of the Clerk of the Market of the Household in Middlesex', Lond. and Middx. Archaeol. Soc., XIX, 1957, p. 82.

[4] Cf. SP 14, 73, pp. 11, 76; SP 14, 187, 25.

deceived of his due measure;" to the punishment of dilatory or dis
honest officials, "because we are informed that the greatest deceits-
and abuses are committed in cities, boroughs, and towns corporate, by
the chief officers there;" and to the protection of "the buyers, the
poorer sort especially," because "we are informed that [they]...are
much pinched by sleights and deceits used in measuring..."[1]

This proclamation was to remain in being for five years in the first
instance. It was enforced with remarkable vigour, and it aroused much
unpopularity amongst provincial tradesmen. Protests against the
clerks' unwelcome activities abounded; justices or traders of various
counties lodged interminable complaints against them; occasionally
town authorities offered some inducement to mitigate the severity of
their inspection; and the stream of opposition contributed not a little
to the political unrest of the period.[2] Local governing bodies resented
what they regarded, quite unhistorically, as interference with their
peculiar privileges; and one of the earliest acts of the Long Parliament
was to restrict the clerk of the market's activities to the verge of court.[3]
It may well be that the clerks had abused their powers; but the numerous disputes relating to market towns in the Court of Exchequer show
that essentially the Stuart policy was neither unnecessary nor obscur-
antist. The poorer consumer needed the protection of the state, and
by the legislation of the Long Parliament he largely lost it. As a consequence of the opposition of farmers and tradesmen, local confusion in
weights and measures continued unchecked until the nineteenth century
and contributed both to the proliferation of marketing disputes and to
the enrichment of country lawyers.[4]

In the regulation of private trading, regard for the interests of the
poorer consumer does not seem, at first sight, to have been so evident.
Closer examination, however, shows that government policy differed
sharply in years of plenty and years of dearth. During years of plenty,
little restraint was imposed in the domestic sphere upon the activities
of private traders. Even before the act of 1552, which legalized a certain
measure of private dealing, an extensive private trade in corn and
victuals was allowed *de facto*. After 1552, any badger, lader, kidder, or

---

[1] SP 14, 187, 64.

[2] Cf. the complaints of the Essex, J.P's in 1622: SP 14, 130, 13. See also Williams,
Tradesmen in Early-Stuart Wiltshire, p. ix.

[3] G. H. Tupling, 'Lancashire Markets in the Sixteenth and Seventeenth Centuries',
Lancs. and Ches. Antiq. Soc., LVIII, 1947, pp. 31–4.

[4] In estimating the corn available in the dearth of 1623, the Derbyshire J.P.'s
found "nothing of so great hindrance to this service as the variety of bushels and other
lesser measures, no one market within the said county using the like measures one to
another."—SP 14, 145, 16. The clerk of the market was supposed to relate all measures
to the London standard.

carrier licensed by three justices of the peace in his district might buy grain, cattle, fish, butter, or cheese where he wished, and resell it in the open market or transport it coastwise under cocket, provided that he did not forestall the market and that the price of corn was not above a certain level.[1] Eleven years later, this act was confirmed and modified by further legislation, and the licensing system tightened. Drovers, badgers, corn-carriers and the like were to be licensed only in the general quarter sessions; they had to be married householders, of at least thirty years of age, and resident in the county for at least three years. The clerk of the peace was to keep a register of licensees as a check on their numbers and residence; the licences were of two types, either for sale and purchase in any public or private place or only in the open market; they were valid for one year at a time only.[2] Despite the superficial impression of a restrictive policy, however, the wayfaring merchant from this time onwards enjoyed a very broad liberty, and the act of 1563 no doubt exerted a considerable influence upon that expansion of private trading which was so marked a feature of the latter part of the period. If the proclamation of July 1618 may be trusted, this liberty was perhaps too generous: for it complained that rogues and wandering persons "carrying about trifles in the habit of pedlars or petty chapmen, so misbehave themselves as indeed they are no other but sturdy beggars, thieves, and absolute dissolutes, and many of them being of no religion, or infected with popery, carry abroad... superstitious trumperies." Evidently the licensing system, operated as it was by local gentry, was not always an efficient method of control.[3]

For a detailed description of the regulation of thee xport and import markets during years of plenty, the reader should refer to Professor Gras's account of the corn trade.[4] So far as the elaborate statutory policy is concerned his conclusion is that it was "almost negligible as far as it concerns the trade in corn." The level of prices at which the acts came into force rarely obtained, and the acts themselves were frequently overridden by the crown. More successful was "The

[1] These prices were: wheat 6s. 8d., rye and maslin 5s., peas and beans 4s., barley and malt 3s. 4d., oats 2s. They were raised at subsequent dates, and in the act of 1627 fixed at: wheat 32s., rye 20s., peas, beans, barley, malt 16s.

[2] Gras, op. cit., pp. 152–4.

[3] SP 14, 187, 56. The fact that offices were to be set up in London and two provincial towns to license "well disposed" chapmen suggests that many travelling merchants were in practice exempt from the earlier acts. For the regulation of local tradesmen and the enforcement of Lenten fasting, see Williams, Tradesmen in Early-Stuart Wiltshire, pp. xi–xv.

[4] Gras, op. cit., pp. 138–43, 221–32. Cattle and sheep do not seem to have been exported to any great extent. The minor export trade in horses from Kent to France was spasmodically regulated by the Privy Council. Of the Suffolk cheese trade, much, like that of corn, slipped through without paying customs.

Commission for the Restraint of Grain," which "ushered in a remarkable attempt to restrain the corn trade."[1] But this also in effect applied principally during years of dearth, with which the following paragraphs deal. Here it is sufficient to say that, although in plentiful periods the corn trade was not always left entirely uncontrolled, restraint was not of primary practical consequence. A large and more or less lawful export in grain in fact existed throughout the period; and, despite the activities of informers, much unlawful export also slipped through the ports without paying custom. According to Dr Williams, this illicit trade may have amounted to 20,000 quarters a year from East Anglia alone.[2]

In years of shortage or expected dearth, the tendency of the government to let well alone was sharply reversed. It was then that the rival claims of private traders and the poor became most acute, and the government was compelled to intervene. How those rival claims were to be reconciled was an exceedingly difficult problem. The solution adopted by the Tudor State was comprised in the celebrated 'Book of Orders', issued by the privy council to justices of the peace. First issued in 1587, and again in each subsequent year of dearth, the thirty-three clauses of the 'Book of Orders' called upon the local magistrates to enquire into the corn supplies in every farmer's, factor's, maltster's, and baker's hands in each county division; to restrict and regulate malting, brewing, and corn selling; to force the owners of grain to supply the markets with corn at low prices for the benefit of poor artificers and labourers; to prevent or limit private dealings and the licensing of badgers and the like; to attend the markets in person and see that the poor were favourably treated; to suppress unnecessary taverns and the expenditure of corn in manufacture; to stay all export abroad, save under special licence, and to limit transportation at home.

What was the purpose of this elaborate and troublesome regulation? According to Professor Gras, the 'Book of Orders' "marks indeed the apogee of paternalism in the history of the corn trade." "The middleman," he says, "whose special business it is to balance supply and demand...was to a considerable extent eliminated from the situation." "With the customers lax, and the justices unmanageable, there was little hope for the successful working of the complicated plan." The whole system, in fact, was a lamentable instance of that "experimenting in governance which the Tudors were pushing into

---

[1] Gras, op. cit., pp. 229–30, 234.

[2] Williams, Maritime Trade of East Anglian Ports, 1550–1590, Oxford D.Phil. Thesis, 1952, p. 82; cf. Req. 2, 65, 79; E 178, 656; E 134, 25–26 Eliz., M 16; E 134, 14–15 Eliz., M 9; E 134, 23 Eliz., E 14; E 134, 28–29 Eliz., M 18; E 134, 26 Eliz., H 1.

almost every field of national life."[1] But was the Tudor and Stuart system so unreasonable as Professor Gras suggests?

The essential fact to bear in mind in interpreting the 'Book of Orders' is that Tudor and Stuart governments were continually haunted by the spectre of popular upheaval. As Dr Hoskins has shown, at least two thirds of the urban population lived close to the poverty line; the failure of the harvest immediately plunged them beneath it, and there was no adequate local force to restrain an outbreak of civil strife in either town or countryside.[2] The justices who administered the regulations were quite as well aware of the potential danger as the Privy Council; and they devoted a great deal of time and energy to the implementation of the scheme.

A few extracts from their reports to the council may be illuminating.[3] From Warwickshire in 1608, one of the justices informed the Lord Treasurer that dearth and engrossing of corn "make the people arrogantly and seditiously to speak of the not reforming of conversion of arable land into pasture by enclosing..." In Norfolk in 1623 the magistrates wrote of "this time of so extraordinary a want both of corn and of work wherein to employ [the poor]...which oftentimes breeds in those of their condition a dangerous desperacy." In Buckinghamshire, "by reason the trades of clothing and bonelace-making are much decayed and do daily fail, the poor are greatly hindered and impoverished and grown into such multitudes that we know no means to set them on work;...and the inconvenience growing thereby is so great that it enforceth many to steal or starve..." In Lincolnshire in the same year the "country was never in that want it now is;" many thousands of people had been forced to sell all they possessed, even to their own bedstraw; dog flesh became "a dainty dish...and the other day one stole a sheep, who for mere hunger tore a leg out and did eat it raw." In Suffolk, in the winter of 1630–1, two justices averred that, "To see their bread thus taken from them and sent to strangers has

[1] Gras, op. cit. pp. 230, 241–2.

[2] W. G. Hoskins, 'English Provincial Towns in the early Sixteenth Century', RHS, 5th Ser., VI, 1956, pp. 17–18; cf. also Brian Pearce, 'The Elizabethan Food Policy and the Armed Forces', EcHR XII, 1942, pp. 39–46, and Westerfield, op. cit., pp. 148–9. Professor Gras seems to lay overmuch stress in this connection (e.g., op. cit., p. 242) on the problem of feeding the London populace. Immense though that was, it was but part of the larger task of feeding the labouring population of the whole country. The difficulty was essentially similar in both London and the provinces: namely, the feeding of an increasing population dependent on the market instead of on local resources. In Somerset nearly 7,000 labourers and artificers relied for their supplies of corn on Burton and Wincanton markets, and in Derbyshire thousands of miners and quarrymen were equally dependent.—SP 16, 187, 51; SP 14, 113, 17.

[3] I do not find, as Gras suggests, that justices on the whole opposed the scheme. Essentially they were in close sympathy with its intention, as their reports indicate.

turned the impatience of the poor into licentious fury and desperation...
they must needs starve if this corn, which, only, they were able to buy,
be taken from them..." In Kent, the poor people fell "upon such as
carry corn by cart or horse in the highways, especially if they conceive
them going to Faversham," from whence corn was exported to
London. The corporation of Maidstone baked its own loaves and sold
them at twopence apiece to the poor; and at Wye some desperate
villagers dropped a 'libel' in the minister's porch:

> "The corn is so dear,
>   I doubt many will starve this year;
>   If you see not to this,
>   Some of you will speed amiss...
>   Note: the poor there is more
>   Than goes from door to door...
>   You that are set in place,
>   See that your profession you do not disgrace."[1]

Quite clearly these conditions provided a golden opportunity for
unscrupulous traders to exploit. They could either force up the price
at home till only the rich could buy, or else send their corn to wealthy
customers overseas. There is evidence that many private dealers did
not let either opportunity slip, and that the middleman's "personal
interest" was not necessarily, as Professor Gras remarks, "very much
in common with that of the community..."[2] Despite the vigilance of
privy council and local magistrates, a great deal of corn continued to
be exported to foreign customers, who, unlike the poor at home, could
afford the high prices the merchant demanded. Still more was sold to
provincial maltsters, brewers, and innkeepers, who had bargained for
supplies some time before harvest and insisted on exacting their full
orders. A great deal of the conciliar regulation was thus directed to
diverting corn supplies away from the insatiable demands of the
brewing industry and towards the open market town and rural
miller who supplied the poor.

A few further extracts from justices' reports will show that the
regulation of the private trader's activities was not unnecessary. During
the dearth of 1622-3, the Suffolk magistrates complained that the corn
sellers of "Norfolk and other places from whence we were wont to
provide ourselves, understanding our wants, have highly enhanced

---

[1] SP 14, 34, 4; SP 14, 138, 35; SP 14, 142, 44; SP 14, 143, 34; SP 16, 187, 12;
SP 16, 175, 81; SP 16, 186, 74.

[2] Gras, *op. cit.*, p. 241. For a contemporary opinion of the maleficent influence of
middlemen, see William Harrison, *Description of England*, ed. F. J. Furnivall, New
Shakespere Soc., Ser. VI, I, 1877, pp. 297–302.

their prices..." In Norfolk itself the justices said that such was "the exceeding inclination of some to their private ends and profits as, to effect the same, they both neglect the accomplishment of what they know his Majesty...so much affecteth" in favour of the poor, and disobey the orders of the justices prohibiting export. In Leicestershire there were "some, and they for the most part of greatest wealth and therefore least subject to control, who neither regard our order made October p[ast?]...nor the [Books of] Orders themselves...[and] will not be persuaded to forbear their old way of devouring peas with sheep and swine." At Norwich, after the suppression of malting by the mayor, the "brewing maltsters, having means...to raise the price of barley at their pleasure, find out cautelous devices to frustrate the order of suppression; for though they themselves desist...yet most of their malting houses are still employed by others whom we cannot eftsoon suppress but by Order in Sessions..."[1] The same kind of story was repeated in almost every corner of the country: in Oxford-shire, Lincolnshire, Wiltshire, Somerset, Nottingham, Warwick, and Essex, for example. There was, it is to be feared, some reason for the assertion of the privy council that high prices and the calamities of the poor proceeded principally "from the innholders, victuallers, and chandlers...who [receive] from brewers into their houses a greater quantity of beer than necessarily is requisite, in that they have and continue at all times provision beforehand for six months or more, whereas if they had store only but for one month it would save as much corn as would serve for the expense of five months."[2]

There was also, however, much to be said on the side of the private trader round whom the contention centred. It is not difficult to imagine a maltster's feelings upon learning that "all the maltsters and alehousekeepers" in a certain county were to be "suppressed." Many maltsters, moreover, were men "of mean ability...chiefly employed by gentlemen and others who send their barleys to them to be malted," and many were said to be "very useful to the county and [to] pay good rents..."[3] Many, too, were forced to break their own bonds as a result of the restraint of trade, and were themselves prosecuted by their customers, and brought into financial distress. Some, like the Lincolnshire victuallers in 1620, complained "much of their own poverty, caused by a late commission whereby they are all generally

---

[1] SP 14, 142, 14. viii; SP 14, 138, 35; SP 14, 140, 81. i; SP 16, 531, 94.
[2] SP 14, 138, 118. The complaints were not peculiar to London: cf. Westerfield, *op. cit.*, pp. 179–80.
[3] SP 16, 342, 93. Many widows and trustees of orphans, too, "who like not to put their money to usury," made a living by purchasing small quantities of barley and malting it.

drawn to compound for their recognizances…and think they shall be drawn to pay a yearly fee for their quiet…" Few can have welcomed the visits of bailiffs and constables to inspect their supplies of barley; while the inquisitorial methods of common informers were a very real grievance. The farmers of east Kent complained in 1620 that the 'portsmen' to whom they sold their surplus wheat were so persecuted by informers for transporting wheat, even within the kingdom and when the statutes allowed, that they had "altogether left off to deal therein at all…" In Lincolnshire, in the same year, there were "so many men…daily vexed with informers, which never so much abounded amongst us, as most men know not how to direct the course of their lives to keep themselves free from their annoyances."[1] But perhaps the most serious problem for men of business was an apparent tendency for conciliar restraint to increase as the periods of dearth became more frequent. The evidence is not quite conclusive, and in some spheres (notably the coasting trade and the export market) control seemed to have declined. But on the whole, regulation was possibly more effective and more far-reaching, as it was certainly from the consumer's viewpoint more necessary, under Charles I than under Queen Elizabeth.[2]

In the short run, the Tudor and Stuart policy of restraint during years of dearth was not unsuccessful. In practice it was neither so inelastic nor so impolitic as Professor Gras suggests; a good deal of transportation to the areas of most acute dearth was encouraged. The scheme as a whole was in fact a form of rationing on behalf of the poor, which perhaps alone prevented their starvation and forestalled rebellion. "By this means," said four Kentish justices concerning the regulation of 1623, "the corn and grain which before was concealed was now discovered, the prices somewhat abated, and much more plenty

---

[1] SP 14, 113, 26; SP 14, 112, 12. i. For the activities of informers see Williams, *Tradesmen in Early-Stuart Wiltshire*, pp. xv–xxi. Various syndicates of informers flourished, specializing in particular offences and regions, and headed by London merchants who maintained agents in the counties. By the Act of 1624 "for the ease of the subject concerning the informations upon penal statutes," these activities were virtually brought to an end. In 1615 the number of Exchequer informations was 867, ten years later only 27.

[2] I gain the impression that there was less 'slack' in this regulation under Charles I than under James I or Elizabeth; the justices were more vigilantly directed. On the other hand, control of the coasting trade deteriorated in the second half of the period. The population of the country increased perhaps 75 per cent between 1500 and 1640, but the average annual figure of coastwise corn shipments *as recorded in the port books and customs accounts* increased only from 528 to 539. Shipments to London, despite a perhaps fourfold increase in population, rose only from 213 to 234; those to provincial ports slightly declined from 315 to 305. Probably, therefore, a growing proportion passed unrecorded by port officials.

appeared in the market, to the great benefit of the poor, and content of all good and charitable people, and those parts of all good and charitable people, and those parts established in good order and tranquility." In Leicestershire, as a result of the restraint, the justices conceived that "there will be, though not an universal and absolute reformation on the sudden, yet so even and peaceable an order holden as shall not minister either to the merchant (whose guide is their lucre) or to the poor (whose steersman is necessity) any just cause of grievance or complaint." And in Hertfordshire, the sheriff declared, the "good and charitable examples and persuasions" of the justices and gentry had "so far prevailed with all men of ability that every parish where need requireth hath provided sufficient quantities of corn…almost at half the price which it is sold for in the markets…whereby we hope no complaint of the poor shall hereafter add any disturbance unto his Majesty's most gracious, pitiful, and charitable mind for the reliefing of his poor subjects' wants."[1]

In the long run, however, it is doubtful if the policy of regulation did not do as much harm as good. The Tudor and Stuart economy was, in fact, in many respects ill-fitted to deal with either surplus or shortage; while in a period when agricultural trade was rapidly ceasing to be primarily local and becoming so largely national and international, restraint in some respects only aggravated the difficulty. It often tended to raise rather than stabilize prices. It upset the system of regular deliveries demanded by industrial concerns. It toppled over the already rickety structure of credit. The truth was that the early Stuart policy was out of touch with a number of fundamental changes in the English rural economy. It failed to recognize that an increasing proportion of agricultural output was produced with distant markets, and not the local village or town, in view. It did not realize that the men whose acquisitive propensities it set out to restrain in the interests of the poor were no longer a number of isolated individuals, but a distinct and self-conscious community whose enterprise, however unwelcome, was essential to the well-being of the country at large. By alienating that community, the Stuarts made some of their most implacable enemies. For while Charles I and his ministers should have been endeavouring to find a new place for it in a changing world, and working out new policies and wiser administrative methods to deflect its activities into useful channels, that community was busy working out its own salvation, carving out its own place in the economy, devising its own methods of organization, and acquiring that administrative skill and commercial wealth by which it assisted Parliament in the Stuarts' ultimate overthrow.

[1] SP 14, 138, 18; SP 14, 140, 81. i and 41.

frowned at and repressed by Stuart governments, such men provided some of the firmest supporters of the revolutionary party during the Great Rebellion.

APPENDIX

THE SPECIALITIES OF MARKET-TOWNS IN THE SIXTEENTH AND SEVENTEENTH CENTURIES

NOTE: The following tentative list makes no claim to be an exhaustive catalogue. Local monographs would undoubtedly amplify, and probably correct, it at many points. It does not include the specialities of fairs. It is based principally on Exchequer Special Commissions and Depositions; on references in State Papers, local histories, and Leland; and on Blome, whose *Britannia*, though not published till 1673, presents, I believe, a substantially accurate picture of developments already apparent in 1640. For a definition of the regions employed, see footnotes to pages.

CORN MARKETS

North: Appleby, Barnsley, Bawtry, Berwick, Beverley, Bridlington, Carlisle, Cartmel, Cockermouth, Halifax, Hull, Keswick, Leeds, Malton, Penrith, Pickering, Pocklington, Poulton le Fylde, Seamer (Yorks.), Sheffield, Stockton-on-Tees, Ulverston, Wakefield, Wigan, Wooler, York.

South: Basingstoke, Canterbury, Croydon, Dartford, Dorking, Farnham, Faversham, Guildford, Horsham, Lewes, Newbury, Reigate, Sandwich, Wokingham.

East: Abingdon, Baldock, Barking, Bedford, Biggleswade, Boston, Bourne, Brentford, Brigg, Bungay, Bury St Edmunds, Diss, Gainsborough, Grantham, Harleston, Henley-on-Thames, High Wycombe, Hitchin, Horncastle, Ipswich, King's Lynn, Kingston-on-Thames, Luton, Market Rasen, North Walsham, Olney, Oxford, Polton, Reading, Retford, Royston, Saffron Walden, St Neots, Shefford (Beds.), Sleaford, Stamford, Stony Stratford, Swaffham, Thetford, Uxbridge, Wallingford, Ware, Watford, Winslow, Yarmouth.

West: Bruton, Crediton, Hindon, Honiton, Lavington (Wilts.), Marlborough, Pensford (Som.), Salisbury, Shaftesbury, Sherborne, Tavistock, Totnes, Warminister, Wells, Westbury (Wilts.), Wincanton, Yeovil.

Midlands: Bewdley, Birmingham, Bishop's Castle, Burton-on-Trent, Cheltenham, Chepstow, Chesterfield, Cirencester, Derby, Evesham, Hinckley, Lichfield, Loughborough, Lutterworth, Shipston-on-S̶t̶ Stratford-on-Avon, Stopford (Ches.), Stretton (Salop.), Welling̶ Wenlock.

Wales: Aberystwyth, Brecon, Builth, Caernar̶ Denbigh, Haverfordwest, Lampeter, P̶ Ruthin, Tenby.

MALT MARKETS

North: Barnsley, Halifax.

South: Dartford, Dorking.

East: Abingdon, Baldock, Berkhamsted, Bury St Edmunds, Grantham, Henley-on-Thames, Hitchin, Mansfield, Oxford, Reading, Royston, Stamford, Wallingford.

West: Bruton, Devizes, Keynsham, Lavington (Wilts.), Marlborough.

Midlands: Bewdley, Birmingham, Burton-on-Trent, Derby.

FRUIT AND HOP MARKETS

South: Canterbury, Maidstone.

East: Buckingham.

Midlands: Gloucester, Leominster, Tewkesbury.

Wales: Knighton.

CATTLE MARKETS

North: Burnley, Clitheroe, Colne, Dalton in Furness, Darlington, Doncaster, Howden, Kendal, Malton, Morpeth, Northallerton, Penrith, Pontefract, Richmond, Ripon, Rochdale, Rotherham.

South: Alton, Ashford (Kent), Chichester, Lenham, Maidstone, Rye.

East: Attleborough, Bedford, Biggleswade, Gainsborough, Glamford Bridge (Lincs.), King's Lynn, Leighton Buzzard, Newark, Polton, St Ives.

West: Barnstaple, Blandford, Bradford-on-Avon, Bridgwater, Chard, Crewkerne, Devizes, Dodbrook (Devon), Dunster, Highworth (Wilts.), Hindon, Lavington (Wilts.), Modbury (Devon), Plymouth, Salisbury, Shaftesbury, Sherborne, Somerton, Swindon, Taunton, Torrington, Totnes, Wimborne Minster, Yeovil.

Midlands: Abergavenny, Banbury, Bicester, Birmingham, Bridgnorth, Bromsgrove, Bromyard, Coventry, Hereford, Kidderminster, Kington, Ledbury, Leek, Leominster, Ludlow, Newcastle-under-Lyne, Newport (Salop.), Newport (Mon.), Oswestry, Shrewsbury, Southam (Warwicks.), Tamworth, Thame, Uppingham, Uttoxeter, Wem, Whitchurch (Salop.), Wolverhampton, Worcester.

Wales: Brecon, Builth, Haverfordwest, Knighton, Llandovery, Swansea, Welshpool

HORSE MARKETS

North: Appleby, Malton, Northallerton, Ormskirk.

East: Louth.

West: Devizes.

Midlands: Banbury, Daventry, Drayton (Salop.), Hinckley, Market Harborough, Newcastle-under-Lyme, Northampton.

SHEEP MARKETS

North: Cartmel, Ormskirk, Ulverston.

South: Alfriston, East Ilsley (Berks.)

East: Attleburgh, Grantham, Horncastle, St Ives, Sleaford.

West: Blandford, Crewkerne, Sherborne.

Midlands: Banbury, Bicester, Daventry, Hereford, Kettering, Kington, Leek, Leominster, Loughborough, Market Harborough, Newcastle-under-Lyme, Stow-on-the-Wold, Tamworth, Uttoxeter.

Wales: Builth, Cardiff, Cowbridge, Lampeter, Llandovery.

SWINE MARKETS

East: Barnet, Horncastle, Louth, Mansfield, Norwich, Romford.

Midlands: Chepstow, Hereford, Hinckley, Kettering, Melton Mowbray, Stourbridge, Uttoxeter.

Wales: Cardiff.

CHEESE AND BUTTER MARKETS

North: Whitby.

East: Ipswich, Southwold, Woburn (Beds.), Woodbridge.

West: Chipping Sodbury, Marlborough, Tetbury, Wincanton, Yeovil.

Midlands: Uttoxeter.

Wales: Aberystwyth.

POULTRY AND WILDFOWL MARKETS

North: Dalton, Whitby.

South: Chichester, Dorking, Horsham, Maldon.

East: Boston, Bury St Edmunds, Luton, Mildenhall, Newmarket, Potton, Ramsey (Hunts.), Shefford (Beds.).

West: Glastonbury, Langport.

Wales: Cardigan, Carmarthen, Haverfordwest, Pembroke, Tenby.

WOOL AND YARN MARKETS

North: Carlisle, Chorley, Clitheroe, Doncaster, Garstang, Halifax, Kendal, Ripon, Wakefield.

South: Newbury.

East: Diss, East Dereham, Norwich, Reading.

West: Ashburton, Bath, Cirencester, Crediton, Exeter, Launceston, Liskeard, Marshfield, Moreton Hampstead, Norton St Philip, Okehampton, Shaftesbury.

Midlands: Brackley, Leominster, Oswestry, Shrewsbury.

Wales: Aberystwyth, Carmarthen, Llanfyllin.

CLOTH MARKETS

North: Bolton, Cockermouth, Kendal, Kirkby Lonsdale, Leeds, Manchester, Preston, Rochdale, Wakefield.

South: Canterbury, Newbury.

East: Norwich, Reading.

West: Bath, Bruton, Crediton, Exeter, Frome Selwood, Ilminster, Shepton Mallet, Taunton.

Midlands: Kington, Oswestry, Shrewsbury.

Wales: Dolgelly, Knighton, Welshpool.

LINEN AND HEMP MARKETS

North: Manchester, Preston, Warrington.
East: Diss, Donington (Lincs.), East Harling, Woodbridge.
West: Bridport, Yeovil.
Midlands: Kington.

MARKETS FOR LEATHER AND LEATHER PRODUCTS

North: Doncaster.
East: Norwich.
West: Grampound, Ilminster, Shaftesbury.
Midlands: Bewdley, Burford, Congleton, Hereford, Northampton, Walsall.

CHAPTER IX

AGRICULTURAL PRICES,
FARM PROFITS, AND RENTS[1]

A. THE LONG-TERM MOVEMENT OF
AGRICULTURAL PRICES

1. *Introduction*

Though much obscurity still exists about the origins, extent, and even the nature of agrarian changes in the Tudor and early Stuart periods, certain broad generalizations may be made. Under the stimulus of growing population, rising agricultural prices, and mounting land values, the demand for land became more intense and its use more efficient. The area under cultivation was extended. Large estates were built up at the expense of small-holdings, and subsistence farming lost ground to commercialized agriculture. Changes in the balance of land distribution were accompanied by an increase in the number of agricultural wage-earners and a decline in their standard of living. There was a growing inequality of income among the different classes of rural society.

These features, indicative of growing population pressure and land hunger, are familiar to all students of thirteenth-century agrarian history. During the greater part of the fourteenth and fifteenth centuries, however, conditions were far otherwise. Severe and recurrent outbreaks of plague, of which the Black Death of 1348–9 is the most notable instance, resulted in extremely high mortality and a marked reduction of population. Beginning in the early decades of the fourteenth century and continuing until the third quarter of the fifteenth, agriculture, together with other sectors of the economy, experienced a prolonged recession; agricultural prices and rents fell, and the area of cultivated land contracted. The task of land reclamation, actively pursued in the thirteenth century, petered out, and on marginal lands

[1] I wish to thank the University of Sheffield for financial assistance from the Knoop Research Fund, which helped make possible the examination of a wide range of source material for this study. I am grateful to a number of colleagues and friends for constructive criticism and advice, but especially should like to mention Dr Joan Thirsk, Mr R. Wilkinson, Prof. A. J. Brown, and Mr A. J. Odber. Any errors remain my own. The diagrams were kindly prepared by Miss M. Lawson, and the typing of the manuscript was undertaken by Mrs M. L. Smith and Mrs B. Jobling.

colonized during the earlier period of expanding demand and high prices, whole settlements were abandoned. Tenants were hard to find in the fifteenth century, and farms were at a discount. Unfavourable land, whether it was infertile or burdened with a heavy rent or an irksome customary service, reverted to nature. On large estates it became increasingly common for the lords to retire wholly or in part from direct farming and to lease their demesnes to tenants on easy terms. On peasants' customary holdings rents were reduced, and labour services, once rigorously exacted, were now commuted. This was "an age of recession, arrested economic development, and declining national income."[1] But if there were losses in the national product, there were gains in social distribution. The latter change resulted partly from the increase in the average size of peasant holdings and their multiplication at the expense of commercialized agriculture. The ease with which a tenancy could be obtained resulted in a general 'upgrading' of the village community, and this, together with the decline in the population as a whole, greatly reduced the size of the wage-labour force. While agricultural prices declined, money wages increased. Between 1300 and 1480, on the estates of the bishop of Winchester, the purchasing power of wages in terms of wheat more than doubled.[2] It is not surprising that Thorold Rogers should refer to the fifteenth century as "the golden age of the English labourer."[3] Not until the nineteenth century was the wage-earner's standard of living again so high.

2. The long-term trend of prices

The question of the antecedent conditions, out of which the agrarian changes of the Tudor period arose, is obviously an important one for our study; just how important becomes apparent when the pressure exorted by the market is considered. The century and a half before 1650 was marked by a long, large rise in the general level of prices. This rise was greater for agricultural commodities than for other products. If the period 1450–99 is taken as base (= 100),[4] the average price of agricultural goods had increased to 644 by the decade 1640–9. This compares with prices indices of 524 for timber and 306 for industrial

[1] M. M. Postan, 'The Fifteenth Century', EcHR, IX, 1939, p. 161.

[2] Ibid., pp. 161–7; M. M. Postan, 'Some Economic Evidence of Declining Population in the later Middle Ages', EcHR, 2nd Ser., II, 1950, pp. 221–46; 'The Chronology of Labour Services', RHS, 4th Ser., XX, 1937, pp. 169–93; J. Saltmarsh, 'Plague and Economic Decline in England', Camb. Hist. Journ., VII, 1941, pp. 23–41.

[3] J. E. T. Rogers, Six Centuries of Work and Wages, London, 1886, p. 326.

[4] All subsequent price indices mentioned in the text refer to this base, unless otherwise specified.

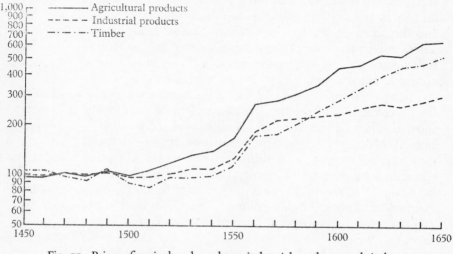

Fig. 11. Prices of agricultural products, industrial products, and timber.
1450–99 = 100.

products.[1] The position is graphically represented in Fig. 11. The secular movement of prices was similar throughout Europe.[2]

There had been periods of rising prices in earlier ages, but the inflation of the sixteenth and early seventeenth centuries was of hitherto unprecedented proportions. Until recent decades, explanations of this

[1] Statistical Appendix, Table XIII.

[2] See Statistical Appendix, Tables VII and XIV; G. Wiebe, *Zur Geschichte der Preisrevolution des XVI. und XVII. Jahrhunderts*, Leipzig, 1895; M. J. Elsas, *Umriss einer Geschichte der Preise und Löhne in Deutschland vom ausgehenden Mittelalter bis zum Beginn des Neunzehnten Jahrhunderts*, I, II, Leiden, 1936–49; A. F. Pribram, *Materialien zur Geschichte der Preise und Löhne in Osterreich*, I, Vienna, 1938; F. Simiand, *Recherches Anciennes et Nouvelles sur le Mouvement Général des Prix du 16e au 19e Siècle*, Paris, 1932; E. J. Hamilton, *Money, Prices, and Wages in Valencia, Aragon, and Navarre, 1351–1500*, Harvard, 1936; *American Treasure and the Price Revolution in Spain, 1501–1650*, Harvard, 1934; G. Parenti; *Prime ricerche sulla rivoluzione dei prezzi in Firenze*, Florence, 1939; J. Pelc, *Ceny w Krakowie w latach, 1369–1600, Badania z dziejóu spolecznychr i gospodarczych*, Livow, 1935; C Verlinden, *et al.*, 'Mouvements des prix et des salaires en Belgique au xviē siècle', *Annales E.S.C.*, 1955, pp. 173–98; C. M. Cipolla, 'La prétendue "révolution des prix," Réflexions sur l'expérience italienne', *Annales E.S.C.*, 1955, pp. 513–16; H. G. Koenigsberger, 'Property and the Price Revolution (Hainault, 1474–1573)', EcHR, 2nd Ser., IX, 1956, pp. 1–15; D. I. Hammarström, 'The Price Revolution of the Sixteenth Century: Some Swedish Evidence', *Scand. Econ. Hist. Rev.*, V, 1957, pp. 118–58; E. H. Phelps Brown and S. V. Hopkins, 'Wage-rates and Prices: Evidence for Population Pressure in the Sixteenth Century', *Economica*, NS XXIV, 1957, pp. 289–306; 'Builders' Wage-rates, Prices and Population: Some Further Evidence', *Economica*, NS XXVI, 1959, pp. 18–38.

sustained fall in the value of money emphasized the effect of monetary influences, and in particular laid stress on the debasements of the coinage and the influx of precious metals into Europe from Spanish America. These monetary factors may have been partly responsible for the inflationary process, but by themselves they do not appear to provide a complete explanation.

The upward movement of prices was far greater than can be allowed for by reductions in the fineness and weight of the coinage, as Wiebe showed when he translated all his money-of-account values into silver prices.[1] Moreover, on close examination, the relationships between currency debasement and rising prices appears less positive than is sometimes suggested.[2] The general level of agricultural prices showed no tendency to rise in the years immediately following 1465, when the quantity of silver in English coins of a given nominal value was cut by 20 per cent. Prices moved upward in the decade following 1526, when the metal weight of coins was reduced by 8 per cent, but the increase was not steep and by then a rising trend had already set in. During the period of the great debasements between 1542 and 1551, the metal content of coins was progressively reduced, eventually by 75 per cent for silver and by 25 per cent for gold.[3] But the rise in prices at this time was not uninterrupted—the price of wheat, for instance, was lower in 1547 than it had been for more than twenty years—and not until the end of the 1540's did the general price level move sharply upwards. Even then, continental prices followed a broadly similar curve, and this suggests other, probably real, economic factors at work.[4] The recoinage of 1560–2[5] had no noticeable effect on the level of prices, and the upward trend continued until the middle years of the seventeenth century.

How far the price inflation was a direct consequence of the influx of silver and gold into Europe from Spanish America is an open question. The upward movement of prices began in the early years of the sixteenth century, before the import of bullion into Spain had assumed very substantial proportions.[6] In several continental countries the price rise commenced even earlier, in the closing decades of the fifteenth century.

---

[1] Wiebe, *op. cit.*, pp. 354–62, 374–7.

[2] See, for example, Y. S. Brenner, 'The Inflation of Prices in Early Sixteenth-century England', EcHR, 2nd Ser., xiv, 1961, pp. 227–8.

[3] Sir John Craig, *The Mint. A History of the London Mint from* A.D. *287 to 1948*, Cambridge, 1953, pp. 94, 109, 111.

[4] See Statistical Appendix.

[5] For details, see Craig, *op. cit.*, A. E. Feaveryear, *The Pound Sterling. A History of English Money*, Oxford, 1933, pp. 71–8.

[6] E. H. Hamilton, 'American Treasure and Andalusian Prices, 1503–1660', *Journ. Econ. & Bus. Hist.*, i, 1928–9, p. 6.

There may, of course, have been some relationship between these earlier price movements and the fact that silver production in Central Europe entered upon a phase of secular expansion in the second half of the fifteenth century, to reach a peak in the decade 1526–35.[1] But even at its peak, Europe's output of coinage metal was only small compared with American production later in the century; and the theoretical substitution of European for American silver still leaves certain apparent contradictions unresolved.

In England, output of silver was insignificant, while the activities of privateers and bullion smugglers in bringing treasure into the realm have probably been exaggerated. This being so, the major part of any additions to the country's monetary stocks must have come by way of a favourable external balance of trade. Statistics of overseas commerce during this period are incomplete, but a favourable balance may have been achieved in the first half of the sixteenth century, when England's export trade underwent a marked expansion.[2] In the second half of the century, however, when the price rise was at its height, the export trade ceased to grow, and England's overall external balance was probably either slightly adverse or in rough equilibrium.[3] Moreover, the level of export-good prices rose less than that of domestic products. Finally, it is only during the second quarter of the seventeenth century that there is any definite evidence of large quantities of silver from Spain actually reaching England. Most of the silver was, however, re-exported, and, in any case, by this time the inflationary movement of prices was coming to an end.[4]

A factor which undoubtedly exercised a powerful stimulating influence on prices in the sixteenth and early seventeenth centuries was population growth. Precise population statistics for this period are not available, and such estimates as there are contain a very large element of guesswork. According to Sir John Cldpham, the population of England and Wales increased, after the setbacks of the earlier period, to perhaps 2,500,000 or 3,000,000 in the year 1500, and to 5,800,000 in 1700.[5]

[1] J. U. Nef, 'Silver production in Central Europe', *Journ. Pol. Econ.*, XLIX, 1941, pp. 584–6; 'Mining and Metallurgy in Medieval Civilisation', *The Cambridge Economic History of Europe*, ed. M. Postan and E. E. Rich, II, Cambridge, 1952, pp. 469–70.

[2] F. J. Fisher, 'Commercial Trends and Policy in Sixteenth-century England', EcHR, X, 1939–40, pp. 95–7.

[3] L. Stone, 'Elizabethan Overseas Trade', EcHR, 2nd Ser., II, 1949, pp. 36, 54.

[4] Y. S. Brenner, 'The Inflation of Prices in England, 1551–1650', EcHR, 2nd Ser., XV, 1962, pp. 277–8.

[5] Sir John Clapham, *A Concise Economic History of Britain from the Earliest Times to 1750*, Cambridge, 1949, pp. 77–8, 186. For other estimates of population in this period see J. C. Russell, *British Medieval Population*, Albuquerque, 1948, *passim;* D. V. Glass, 'Gregory King's Estimates of the Population of England and Wales, 1695', *Population Studies*, III, 1950, p. 338.

On the basis of these estimates, a growth of population of 75–100 per cent between the mid-fifteenth and mid-seventeenth century seems likely. Although the actual extent of demographic change is unknown, the evidence of mounting land hunger, increasing poverty, and diverging relative price movements, in sum, leaves no doubt that the rise in population must have been substantial. The subject of land hunger will be discussed later. For evidence of declining living standards we must look first at changes in the wage-earner's position.

Wage-earning is not a pursuit that is normally engaged in for its own sake, and in a peasant economy it is followed only by men with little or no land of their own. At the beginning of the Tudor period, many— perhaps the majority—of agricultural wage-earners were sons or brothers waiting to take over the family holding. At this time, lifelong agricultural wage-earners, who had no such prospect ahead of them, were probably outnumbered by the land-holders. But as the sixteenth century progressed the position changed, with an increasing proportion of the population becoming dependent upon wages or poor relief for the major part of their livelihood. In 1641 the opinion was expressed that "the fourth part of the inhabitants of most of the parishes of England are miserable poor people, and (harvest time excepted) without any subsistence," while towards the end of the seventeenth century it was estimated that labourers, cottagers, and paupers constituted as much as 47 per cent of the total population.[1]

This growth in the size of the labour force need not have resulted in a decline in the wage-earner's standard of living had there been a compensating increase in the amount of employment available; but there was not. Employment in agriculture, which was much the most important economic activity, may well have fallen, despite an increase in the area under cultivation. Enclosures, especially for pasture farming, engrossing, evictions of small cultivators, and the creation of large estates, meant fewer agricultural holdings and probably less work for labourers. Manufacturing industry could not have employed more than one fifth of the working population, even in 1650, and its expansion was quite inadequate to absorb the surplus labour made available by population growth and agrarian change. Government measures served to aggravate the situation. The free movement of labour, which would have facilitated economic expansion and the absorption of unemployed workers, was impeded by Poor Law enactments and the Statute of Artificers (1563)[2] as well as by the restrictions of the gild system. One

[1] Clapham, op. cit., pp. 212–13; Considerations Touching Trade, with the Advance of the King's Revenue, 1641, p. 15; Gregory King, Natural and Political Observations, 1696, reprinted in G. Chalmers, An Estimate of the Comparative Strength of Great Britain, 1820, pp. 424–5.   [2] Statutes of the Realm, 5 Eliz. I, c. 4.

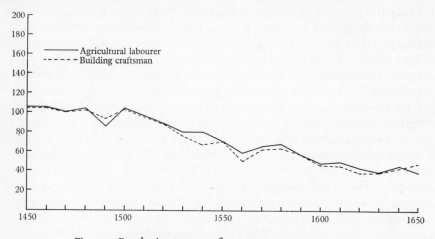

Fig. 12. Purchasing power of wage rates. 1450–99 = 100.

clause of the afore-mentioned Statute sought to preserve the wage-earners' standard of life by putting the power of assessing wage-rates into the hand of the employer class! However, in practice, the machinery of assessment seems to have exercised little long-term influence over actual wage levels, one way or the other; the wage-earner's position had been deteriorating before this measure was passed, and it was to become even worse in the future. There was some improvement in the workers' position in the decade or so following the 1563 Act; but this was not a purely English phenomenon, and was associated with the return of better harvests after the famine years of the 1550's and the probable temporary slowing down of population growth.[1]

Some idea of the extent of the fall in the wage-earner's standard of living is provided by Fig. 12, which indicates changes in the purchasing power of the daily wage-rates of agricultural labourers and building craftsmen in southern England in the period under review. In both cases money wages increased: from 4d. to 1s. 0d. a day for agricultural labourers, and from 6d. to 1s. 5d. for building craftsmen.[2] These increases, though substantial, did not offset the much greater advance in the general level of prices. In real terms, therefore, these workers became much poorer. Beginning in the early years of the sixteenth

[1] Real wages in, for example, Antwerp and Valencia temporarily improved after 1560. See C. Verlinden *et al.*, *Annales E.S.C.*, 1955, pp. 191–8; E. H. Phelps Brown and S. V. Hopkins, 'Builders' Wage-rates, Prices and Population: Some Further Evidence', *Economica*, NS XXVI, 1959, pp. 35–6.

[2] See Tables XV and XVI; E. H. Phelps Brown and S. V. Hopkins, 'Seven Centuries of Building Wages', *Economica*, NS XXII, 1955, p. 205.

century the purchasing power of the daily wage-rate declined, though not continuously. There was a sharp fall in the middle years of the century, when prices rapidly increased, and this was followed by a partial recovery. The improvement in the worker's position, however, was not maintained. At the lowest point, in the second decade of the seventeenth century, the purchasing power of the agricultural labourer's daily wage-rate was only 44 per cent of its level in the second half of the fifteenth century, and the building craftsman's wage-rate was only 39 per cent of the comparable level. Possibly workers in other industries fared somewhat better, for agriculture and the building trades are occupations where rates of pay tend by tradition to be relatively inelastic.[1] The number of wage-earners in other industries, however, was probably only a small proportion of the total working population.

It should be further borne in mind that, for several reasons, Fig. 12 represents only an approximation of changes in the standard of living of agricultural labourers and building craftsmen. In the first place, because of the lack of statistical data, any 'cost of living' index for this period must be based largely on the prices of primary products, such as grain. The prices of the processed products and the manufactured goods actually bought by wage-earners would have risen less than those of the relevant primary commodities, since they would have been influenced to a greater extent by comparatively rigid labour costs.[2] Furthermore, changes in daily wage-rates do not provide an exact measure of changes in the wage-earner's income over a period of time; the number of days in which employment is found must also be taken into account. It has been argued that the Reformation resulted in an increase of one-fifth in the number of working days in the year.[3] Such may have been the case; but, against this, it seems probable that employment became more irregular as the general level of unemployment among the working population increased. Again, the daily wage may not have been the wage-earner's only source of livelihood. Many agricultural labourers (if not building craftsmen) possessed an acre or two of land and enjoyed traditional rights to graze livestock on the common, while in some parts of the country the pursuit of a by-occupation in the home was encouraged by the predominantly rural form of industrial organization. For numbers of wage-earners these supplementary sources of income may well have spelt the difference between existence and starvation.

[1] T. S. Ashton, *An Economic History of England: the Eighteenth Century*, London, 1955, pp. 224–6.
[2] The possibility of reductions in manufacturing costs due to improvements in production methods will be discussed later, see p.   .
[3] E. H. Phelps Brown and S. V. Hopkins, 'Wage-rates and Prices: Evidence for Population Pressure in the Sixteenth Century', *Economica*, NS XXIV, p. 293.

The significance of all these various factors, however, cannot be accurately determined. On balance, it seems probable that the deterioration in the average wage-earner's position was not as drastic as Fig. 12 suggests. Nevertheless, the decline in living standards must still have been very considerable.

3. *The long-term movement of relative prices*

If, as seems probable, a growing surplus of labour arising from population pressure was mainly responsible for increasing poverty among the labouring classes, we should expect to find confirmatory evidence of this in the relative long-term price movements of different commodities.

In the first place, we should expect a rise in the relative price of foodstuffs, reflecting increased pressure on the country's limited natural resources, especially land. Since most other European countries were experiencing similar demographic changes, and since imports were, in any case, restricted by relatively high costs of transport, the major part of any increase in food supplies must have come from home production. There were three principal ways in which domestic farm output could have been increased: by extensions to the agricultural area; by the application of improved technical methods; and by changes involving the better utilization of land, i.e. by specialization upon those products which gave the highest physical returns. Apart from enclosures, improved methods of agricultural production were little in evidence before the mid-sixteenth century, while, with the notable exception of wool production, limitations of transport and marketing organization still imposed severe restrictions on the use of land. This being so, the ex ra food required by a growing population must have been obtained mainly by bringing more land into cultivation. In the late fifteenth century good agricultural land was probably still lying idle in many parts of the country, and its cultivation need not have led to any significant increase in the price of food. But as the demand for agricultural produce continued to rise, less fertile soils and more remote areas would be taken in hand, necessitating heavier outlays and transport over greater distances. Marginal costs of production, particularly for arable crops, would increase.

If the supply of agricultural products was inelastic, so also was the demand. There was no substitute for bread in the diet of the mass of the people. With falling real wages and increasing unemployment, it can be assumed that a relatively larger proportion of consumer demand was directed towards the necessities of life, such as bread. Moreover, in an effort to keep down their expenditure on food, there would be a tendency for consumers to buy less of the more expensive foods and more of the cheaper ones—for example, to buy less wheaten bread, and more rye and barley bread. If we compare the movement of grain prices between the mid-fifteenth and mid-seventeenth centuries we do, in fact, find that whereas the price of wheat increased sevenfold, that of the cheaper grains increased eightfold.[1] Other arable crops—hay, straw, peas, and beans—went up less in price. The demand for these other crops would have been influenced as much by the needs of the animal as of the human population, and the actual increase in price to between six and seven times the 1450–9 level was approximately the same as for livestock.

This line of argument can be developed further. One measure of a country's standard of living is the amount of dairy produce, eggs, and meat consumed per head of the population. At the stage above bare subsistence, expenditure on these products tends to rise proportionately more than income. But in Tudor and Stuart England many families were living at the very margin of subsistence, and though milk, butter, cheese, eggs, and meat may not have been classed as luxuries, they probably did not figure very prominently in the landless labourer's diet, and may well have become less important as his real income declined. When, in addition to this consideration, we allow for a more responsive supply than in the case of arable crops, it is not surprising that edible animal products should have risen less than fivefold in price between the mid-fifteenth and mid-seventeenth centuries. To the very poor man clothing is much less vital than food, and the comparatively small rise in the price of cloth in the latter part of our period suggests that this was an item on which substantial economies in expenditure were made. The price of wool reflected the demand for cloth, and although wool prices rose more than cloth prices during the two hundred years under consideration, the increase over the period was only fourfold. There was a somewhat greater rise in the price of hides and skins, possibly because a higher proportion of leather goods than of cloth was sold to the middle and upper classes.

Another feature which calls for comment is the considerable divergence between the movement of livestock prices, on the one hand, and animal produce prices, on the other, as illustrated in Table 18.

It will be noted that the animal products listed above do not include meat; and it might conceivably be argued that if meat were also brought into the reckoning, the disparity between stock and produce prices would largely disappear. However, the weight of evidence is against this supposition. In the first place, pigs and rabbits, which—to a greater extent than other farm animals—would be purchased mainly

[1] For these and subsequent prices mentioned, see Statistical Appendix.

for their flesh, rose much less in price than other livestock, the comparable indices being 575 (pigs) and 463 (rabbits). Secondly, beef and mutton prices little more than doubled between the mid-sixteenth and mid-seventeenth centuries, the increase being of the same order of magnitude as for other edible animal products. At Cambridge, for example, the price of beef increased from an average of 1s. 5¼d. per stone in the decade 1550–9 to 3s. 3½d. in 1640–9.[1]

Table 18. *Prices of livestock and animal products in 1640–49 as percentages of prices in 1450–1499*

Cows and heifers	823	Dairy products	439
Cattle	713	Hides	577
Poultry	698	Eggs	500
Sheep	681	Wool	396

One possible explanation of the divergence between the prices of livestock and animal products is that improvements in management and feed were resulting in larger and healthier stock, with corresponding increases in the yield of meat, wool, and other produce. The increased supplies would thus tend to exercise a restraining effect on the rise in the prices of these commodities. How far this actually happened is unknown. There is certainly evidence that, compared with nearby common-field areas, enclosed lands in the Midlands produced larger sheep with heavier fleeces, and it is not unreasonable to suppose that, under similar circumstances, the size and yield of other livestock may also have improved. Unfortunately, information about the weights of livestock before the nineteenth century is extremely sparse, and there are insufficient data to enable any clear trend to be established. Such evidence as there is, however, suggests that Gregory King's estimates made at the end of the seventeenth century—which put the average weight of a bullock at 370 lb. and of a sheep at 28 lb.—were too low. Oxen purchased for the household of the bishop of Winchester in 1567–8 averaged 484 lb. in weight, while the figure for wether sheep was 44 lb. The average weight of runts (i.e. undersized bullocks) killed for domestic consumption on the Kentish estate of Sir Roger Twysden in 1641–2 was 370 lb. (allowing 8 lb. to the stone, in accordance with

[1] For meat prices see J. E. T. Rogers, *A History of Agriculture and Prices in England*, III, Oxford, 1882, pp. 119–202, 692–6; *ibid.*, VI, Oxford, 1887, pp. 241–306, 671; W. Beveridge *et al.*, *Prices and Wages in England from the Twelfth to the Nineteenth Century*, I, London, 1939, pp. 83, 144–5, 236.

common contemporary practice) or 647 lb. (allowing 14 lb. to the stone). It is not clear from Twysden's accounts whether these figures include the weight of hides (average, 12·1 lb.), tallow (11·7 lb.), and suet (8·7 lb.).[1] However, in view of what has already been said concerning changes in the pattern of consumer expenditure in times of falling real wages, the main feature of Table 18 that calls for explanation is probably not so much the comparatively small increase in the price of animal products, as the much greater increase in the price of stock. On the demand side, one factor which must have exercised some influence on the prices of cattle, horses, and sheep, was the area of arable cultivation. Not only were oxen and horses (price index number, 675) used for draught purposes, but, before the age of artificial fertilizers, animal manure was essential if the fertility of the arable land was to be maintained. The common-field system of agriculture and, at a more refined level, the growing practice of ley farming demonstrated this interdependence of livestock and tillage. It may, therefore, be assumed that the extension of arable cultivation, unless undertaken at the expense of pasture farming, was accompanied by an increase in the demand for stock. This was one reason why in many common-field villages it became increasingly necessary to stint rights of common as the sixteenth century progressed: the extension of the arable area often meant less waste on which to support more livestock.

Moreover, the overcrowding of the common land was associated with another feature of the period, which also probably exercised a stimulating effect on livestock prices. Attention has already been drawn to the growth in the number of cottagers and labourers with little or no land of their own, but with the traditional right to graze livestock on the common. The land available to such peasants, together with their lack of capital resources, imposed very strict limits on the nature of their farming activities, if, indeed, they were able to farm at all. The urgent need to obtain regular returns in the form of produce directed the attention of many cottagers to the keeping of one or two cows and a few hens, whose milk, cheese, butter, and eggs could be consumed at home, or perhaps sold at the local market. Other stock were also sometimes kept but in general were of subsidiary importance. The disappearance from the agrarian scene of the poor man and his cow was later to be lamented by a generation of economic historians. The very marked rise in the price of dairy animals noted in Table 18 suggests that these partnerships of man and beast were still very much

[1] P. J. Bowden, *The Wool Trade in Tudor and Stuart England*, London, 1962, pp. 26–7; Phyllis Deane and W. A. Cole, *British Economic Growth, 1688–1959*, Cambridge, 1962, pp. 69–70; Surrey RO, Loseley MS 927, 4; BM Add. MS 34162, fo. 5. See also BM Add. MS 37419, fo. 11[v]; Bury and W. Suff. RO, Tem. 1, 7, fo. 6.

in evidence in the sixteenth and early seventeenth centuries, and indeed, were probably becoming increasingly numerous.

So far, our analysis of relative price movements has been concerned with the period 1450–1650 as a whole. The analysis may now be taken further by breaking down the period into three parts, as in Table 19.

Table 19. *Percentage change in price*

+	Agricultural commodities	Timber	Industrial products	Agricultural wage-rates
1450/9—1490/9	+3	−14	−2	—
1490/9—1540/9	+71	+26	+31	+17
1540/9—1590/9	+167	+151	+87	+86
1590/9—1640/9	+43	+81	+29	+39

From the above figures it can be seen that the level of agricultural prices tended to rise throughout the period, with the most rapid rate of advance occurring in the second half of the sixteenth century.

The rise was by no means even or uninterrupted. In the 1490's agricultural prices fell on average 7 per cent compared with the level reached in the previous decade; in the 1550's they jumped 60 per cent. A comparable increase of 26 per cent in the 1590's was followed by a slowing down in the inflationary process. The high point was reached in the fifth decade of the seventeenth century, but by then the prices of some agricultural products (e.g. barley, wool, fells, eggs, and poultry) had already ceased to rise. In the second half of the seventeenth century the general trend of agricultural prices was downward.

If we are looking for a real, as opposed to a monetary, explanation of this slowing down in the upward movement of prices in the early Stuart period, there seems good reason to believe that the forces of both demand and of supply were working in this direction. On the demand side, the probability is that the rate of population growth was greatly slowed down after 1620. In a society where many went hungry, even in prosperous times, and where medical knowledge was practically non-existent, famine or plague could double the mortality rate almost overnight. Neither was ever far away, but both scourges visited the 1620's and 1630's with particular severity. Whether the population actually decreased at this time is not known; in some parts of Europe apparently it did.[1] When we recall the rise in real wages after 1620 and

[1] See, for example, E. J. Hamilton, 'The Decline of Spain', EcHR, VIII, 1938, p. 171; M. J. Elsas, 'Price Data from Munich, 1500–1700', *Econ. Hist.*, III, 1935, p. 77.

the comparatively small increase in the price of grain in the first half of the seventeenth century (33 per cent, as against 43 per cent for all agricultural commodities), a similar occurrence in England does not seem wholly improbable.

On the supply side, various factors were making for an increased output of agricultural commodities and a reduction in prices. Improved farming techniques, described in detail elsewhere in this volume, such as the enclosure of common-field land, the use of lime and marl, the floating of water meadows, and the practice of 'convertible husbandry', all tended to increase the yield from arable and pasture. It would be wrong to infer that these improved methods of agriculture (apart from enclosure) had more than a limited application in the early Stuart period, but certainly they were becoming more widely adopted. Other factors were also working in the same direction. Though some contemporaries were inclined to believe that the concentration of agricultural holdings in fewer hands resulted in the engrossing of produce and rising agricultural prices, the probability is that the trend in favour of the larger farming unit made for more efficient production and lower costs.[1] The market for many commodities in the early Stuart period was still largely local; but the rise of classes of professional middlemen and carriers, together with developments in coastwise transportation, were gradually facilitating the growth of regional economic specialization, with resulting increased farming efficiency. The overall effect of all these influences cannot be precisely measured. One modern authority estimates that the average British wheat yield per acre may have risen from $8\frac{1}{2}$ to 11 bushels in the period 1450–1650; but this is very much guesswork. Also not entirely reliable is the statement made in 1610 that "one sheepe beareth as muche woolle as twoe or three did" formerly.[2] However, the evidence points the same way, and there seems some justification for supposing that towards the end of our period, if not before, improved farming techniques were having some effect in raising yields, at least on the lands of the more progressive farmers.

The increase in the country's agricultural output in the two centuries before 1650, however, probably owed less to improvements in productivity than to extensions in the cultivated area. The breaking in of new land was a piecemeal process, and at first was achieved mainly by intakes from the forest and waste. Later, as the area of easily accessible land diminished, attention was increasingly turned in marshy regions to reclamation by means of drainage. The sixteenth century

[1] TED III, pp. 52, 319; Bowden, op. cit., pp. 2–3.
[2] M. K. Bennett, 'British Wheat Yield Per Acre for Seven Centuries', Econ. Hist., III, 1935, pp. 23–6; B. M. Landsowne MS 152, fo. 229.

saw, for instance, the embankment of the Greenwich, Plumstead, and Wapping marshes, and the stock these newly-created grazings supported helped to supply the needs of the growing London market. In the middle decades of the seventeenth century some thousands of acres of fertile land were drained in the Fenlands in the biggest and most expensive reclamation scheme yet attempted. The resulting addition to the country's output of agricultural produce must have been considerable, and came at a time when other factors were also tending to check the rise in agricultural prices.[1]

The process of land reclamation, which continued throughout the Tudor and early Stuart periods, exercised an important influence on the price of timber. This is understandable, when it is recalled that to bring land under the plough often involved the clearance of woodland areas. The revival of economic activity in the second half of the fifteenth century is suggested, not only by the slight rise in the general level of agricultural prices, but also by the significant fall in the price of timber (see Table 19). It is evident that, at this phase of agricultural expansion, the clearing of woodland was outstripping the demand for wood. In the sixteenth century timber prices, though increasing, still tended to lag behind agricultural prices, but the position was changing. As remoter areas were cleared for cultivation, timber had to be moved greater distances at high and steeply-rising costs of transport. Moreover, the growth of population and industry meant a greater demand for wood as fuel or raw material. More timber was needed, for example, for ordinary domestic use, house-building, ship-building, and the manufacture of iron. By the early decades of the seventeenth century, therefore, as a result of all these various influences, wood prices were rising more rapidly than agricultural prices, thus giving emphasis to contemporary complaints about a growing shortage of timber.

If the gap between timber prices and agricultural prices was narrowing during the early Stuart period, it was not until the middle years of the seventeenth century that industrial prices also began to catch up. During the preceding century and a half the purchasing power of industrial goods over agricultural products had progressively declined. By 1630–9 it needed 226 units of industrial goods to buy the same volume of agricultural commodities that 100 industrial units would have bought in the late fifteenth century.[2]

This lag of industrial prices behind other prices is probably to be explained largely in terms of changes in the pattern of consumer expenditure over the period. As real wages fell, so the proportion of

[1] H. C. Darby, *The Draining of the Fens*, Cambridge, 1940, *passim;* N. Harvey, 'Farm and Estate under Elizabeth the First', *Agriculture*, LX, 1953, pp. 108–11.

[2] Statistical Appendix, Table XIII.

income spent on industrial goods declined, while the proportion spent on foodstuffs and other essential items increased. Since agricultural prices kept ahead of most other prices, the class with the largest proportionate increase in income must have been those agricultural producers who farmed primarily for the market. The growing purchasing power of this section of the community would have helped to stimulate the demand for industrial goods, but only to a limited extent. In the first place, farmers with large marketable surpluses were very much a minority group. The great majority of agricultural producers were subsistence farmers with little to spare for the market; indeed, in times of harvest failure many small cultivators were turned into buyers of grain. Secondly, as a group, the large and middling farmers who engaged in commercialized agriculture seem also to have possessed a comparatively high propensity to save. Many yeomen and gentlemen, as well as the occasional lord, practised thrift, not only to accumulate capital for the future enlargement of their estates, but also simply in order to hoard. It is unlikely, therefore, that the growth in the income of these agricultural producers was accompanied by a corresponding increase in the demand for industrial products.

On the supply side, the probability is that industrial costs of production rose less than agricultural costs. Professor J. U. Nef has claimed that technological changes in the period 1540–1640 amounted to a minor 'industrial revolution'. How far industrial costs of production were lowered in real terms is a matter for debate, but the extent of the application of new industrial techniques has probably been exaggerated by Nef. Certainly, the main manufacturing activity—the production of cloth—was scarcely affected by cost-reducing innovations. Moreover, agricultural and industrial prices were diverging before 1540, i.e. before the technological advances described by Nef could have exercised any effect on costs. Even after 1540, it is doubtful whether technical progress in most spheres of industry greatly exceeded that in agriculture. The growing shortage of fuel, which Nef singles out as supplying the mainspring of industrial advance in the period 1540–1640, did not, in fact, become a major problem, to judge by timber prices, before the early decades of the seventeenth century. To say all this, however, is not to deny that, even with static techniques, there were probably factors on the supply side which tended towards a relative cheapening of industrial products. The greater elasticity of supply of industrial goods, as compared with agricultural commodities, meant that the output of the former could be increased more quickly and at smaller marginal cost. Industrial prices were probably influenced to a greater extent than agricultural prices by comparatively sticky labour costs. Evidence concerning industrial wage movements in the Tudor and

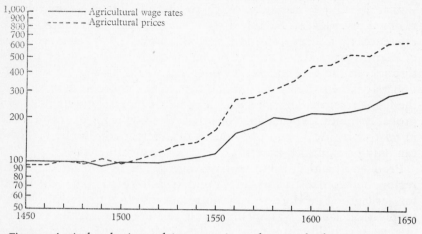

Fig. 13. Agricultural prices and wage rates in southern England. 1450–99 = 100.

early Stuart periods is scanty, but available data suggest that the wages of industrial workers followed a broadly similar trend to the wages of agricultural labourers and building craftsmen. If this was so, then the alleged widening profit-margin, between industrial prices and labour costs, which Professor Earl Hamilton saw as the main causative factor in the development of early capitalism, disappears. As can be seen from Table 19 (p. 605), industrial prices and (agricultural) wage-rates moved very closely together during the late sixteenth century, and in the first half of the seventeenth century—when population may have temporarily stopped growing and the rate of technological advance may have increased—wages began to move ahead of prices. In so far as there was a 'profit inflation' in the Tudor and early Stuart periods, clearly, as Figure 13 indicates, it must have been in agriculture and not in industry.[1]

4. Regional prices

So far, our discussion has been in terms of the secular movement of prices in the national economy as a whole. The market, however, was very imperfect, and while the long-term trend of agricultural prices was

[1] J. U. Nef, *The Rise of the British Coal Industry*, London, 1932; 'The Progress of Technology and the Growth of Large-Scale Industry in Great Britain, 1540–1640', EcHR v, 1934, pp. 3–24; 'A Comparison of Industrial Growth in France and England, 1540–1640', EcHR, VII, 1937, pp. 155–85; E. J. Hamilton, *American Treasure and the Price Revolution in Spain;* D. C. Coleman, 'Industrial Growth and Industrial Revolutions', *Economica*, NS, XXIII, 1956, p. 14; D. Felix, 'Profit Inflation and Industrial Growth', *Quart. Journ. Econ.*, LXX, 1956, pp. 441–6.

similar in all regions, there were significant differences in relative regional price-levels. Thorold Rogers, in discussing this subject (with reference to a later historical period), argued that regional price differences were the outcome of an unequal distribution of money throughout the country, the Thames valley area having a disproportionately large share of the nation's monetary resources, and therefore the highest prices. This, however, can be no more than a partial, and probably minor, explanation, for it fails to account for the divergence in relative regional price movements of different commodities. These can only be explained in terms of real economic differences.[1]

Production and distribution costs varied, not only from region to region, but from district to district within each region; and the demand for agricultural produce was by no means evenly distributed. On the supply side, labour was an important element in the costs of commercial agriculture, especially for the arable farmer.[2] Assuming that there were no significant differences in the productivity of labour, as between regions, a comparison of agricultural wage-rates in different parts of the country may be expected to provide an indication of relative regional labour costs. Wage data for this period are, unfortuately, piecemeal, but there is sufficient evidence to suggest that London, the south-eastern and south-western parts of the country, were high wage-cost areas, that northern and central England were low wage-cost, and that the southern and eastern regions occupied an intermediate position. It is perhaps not without significance that the high wage-cost areas were also high-price areas for arable produce. The relatively high level of wages in the vicinity of London may be attributed to a growing demand for labour engendered by general economic expansion, while in south-western England the developing textile industry was effectively competing with agriculture for workers. To account for the low level of wages in the northern region it should be recalled that this, like parts of the west Midlands, was primarily a pastoral region, and that pasture farming requires less labour than arable production. Elsewhere in central England, where common-field farming was the rule, population growth unsupported by compensating industrial development was creating an unemployment problem of formidable proportions, and one would expect this to be reflected in a relatively low level of agricultural wages.

The costs of agricultural production, however, are affected more by climate and by the nature and fertility of land than by the price of labour. Where soil is rich and well-drained wheat is comparatively cheap to produce; on thin sandy soils rye is a better economic proposi-

[1] Rogers, *Agriculture and Prices*, v, p. 241.
[2] For further on this, see p.   .

tion. Barley does well on light, calcareous ground; while oats, being a hardy crop, will grow almost anywhere. Tudor and Stuart farmers were well aware of these differences. They were also aware that wet soils are better suited to pasture than arable, and that on coarse grassland cattle are preferable to sheep. Where market conditions were favourable this knowledge was reflected in the regional farming pattern. Thus, on the drier, lighter soils of eastern and southern England, barley and sheep predominated; further inland, the claylands grew much wheat, as well as wool; the wet uplands of northern and western England, on the other hand, specialized more on cattle breeding and forage crops. Types of farming, however, varied, not merely from region to region, but from locality to locality. Thus, in the early seventeenth century a sheep-corn husbandry was practised on the chalklands of Sussex, while on the heavier land of the Weald arable farming was subordinate to cattle grazing. Such examples could be multiplied.[1]

Had there been in Tudor and Stuart England a cheap and efficient means of transport, there seems little doubt that the pattern of farming everywhere would have conformed closely to the potentialities of the soil, given the relative level of prices. In some areas, as we have seen, it did, but in others, high costs of transport imposed severe limitations on the nature of agricultural production. Most roads were extremely difficult to negotiate with goods, and many were impassable in winter. The transport of heavy products, therefore, even over comparatively short distances, was normally by water, whenever possible. When, in 1631, the J.P.'s for Essex stated that the inhabitants of the hundred of Dengie "by reason of foulness of ways, have not vented their corn at any country markets, but have always sent it to the City of London by sea and there sold it," they were describing a situation which would have surprised nobody.[2]

The availability of water communications, inadequate though they may seem by present day standards, was an immense advantage to the farmer in the disposal of his produce, and in spite of the ever-present dangers of famine, permitted a degree of economic specialization in some part of the country which was impossible in areas less well-endowed with transport possibilities. While central England had perforce to produce its own grain, it was thought unnecessary in 1620 for the coal-mining and lead-mining districts of Nottinghamshire and Derbyshire to be self-supporting in this respect, since the port of Hull

---

[1] J. C. K. Cornwall, *The Agrarian History of Sussex, 1560–1640*, University of London M.A. thesis, 1953, p. 146. For further on this subject, see chapter I *supra*.

[2] SP 16, 182, 67.

and the river Trent had always been found capable of meeting any deficiency in local corn production. London, which is estimated to have increased threefold or fourfold in size during the course of the sixteenth century, and which by the year 1600 probably contained something like 300,000 people, was a monument to the efficacy of water transport; so too, on a smaller scale, were Bristol and the other major provincial ports. Indeed, there were few important urban areas in predominantly pastoral districts which were not within comparatively easy reach of river transport or coastal shipping.[1]

The significance of water-carriage can be more readily understood when the relative costs of the different methods of transportation are examined. In the late fifteenth and early sixteenth centuries, when the average price of barley was approximately 3s. per quarter, and the normal cost of transporting grain by land carriage was 1d. per ton mile (at 5 quarters to the ton), a journey of 180 miles by road would have meant a doubling of the price of this commodity. At 2d. per ton mile, a rate occasionally charged, a journey of 90 miles would have achieved the same effect. By comparison, the conveyance of a load of barley from Wroxham to Yarmouth by the river Bure, at a slightly earlier period, was undertaken at a freight charge of ¼d. per ton mile—i.e. at between one-quarter and one-eighth of the above-specified rates for land carriage. Wheat, being more than twice the price of barley, was cheaper to transport in relation to its value, and so could be carried longer distances. As a cash crop it had obvious advantages over barley in those parts of the Midlands poorly served by inland waterways. On the other hand, soil and climatic considerations apart, it is hardly surprising that East Anglia, with its excellent water communications, should have been a leading centre for the production of barley. Similarly, the comparatively cheap and perishable nature of dairy produce was reflected in the siting of the principal dairy farming districts along the eastern seaboard and near major groupings of population. In relation to the value of the product, timber was the most expensive agricultural commodity to transport, and since a formidable number of horses, oxen, carriages, and men were normally involved in the passage of any significant quantity overland, water carriage was essential if the destination were more than a few miles away. In an estimate made in the early seventeenth century of the cost of conveying a large consignment of sawn timber from Conisbrough Parks, in the West Riding, to London, we find 5s. per ton allowed for carriage overland to Doncaster, only five miles distant, as against 6s. per ton for the very much

[1] SP 14, 112, 12 (i); SP 14, 112, 91; SP 14, 113, 17: SP 14, 113, 22; SP 14, 142, 14 (vii, viii); SP 16, 175, 35 (i); G. N. Clark, *The Wealth of England, from 1496 to 1760*, Oxford, 1947, pp. 5, 43, 93.

longer journey, in miles, by sea from Hull to London.[1] Accessibility by water, in fact, gave the capital a comparative advantage over many other parts of the country in respect of the price of timber.

Of all agricultural products, wool was the cheapest to transport, by virtue of its high value in relation to weight, and, as in the case of livestock (which were generally driven on the hoof to fattening pastures or to market), wool destined for home use was normally conveyed overland. The wool dealer and his packhorse were a familiar part of the rural and industrial scenes. The corn badger paid much more dearly for transporting his produce in this way. In relation to value, and at the level of prices ruling in the late fifteenth century, wheat was twenty to thirty times more expensive to transport by land carriage than the equivalent weight of good-quality wool, and barley fifty to seventy times more expensive. It should therefore occasion no surprise to recall that the trade in fine wool was the first to be developed on an extensive scale; nor is it difficult to explain the attraction of wool growing (and, to some extent, cattle feeding) for large numbers of capitalistic farmers in the Midlands cut off by transport deficiencies from profitable extra-regional markets in grain.

Efforts to improve the country's transport system were concentrated primarily on the ports, harbours, and inland waterways, whose effective working was especially vital to the economical carriage of corn. A series of statutes was passed, especially in the reign of Henry VIII, with the object of facilitating the removal of obstructions from rivers and clearing them of silt. The first pound-locks in England were built on the canal at Exeter in about 1564; Dover pier was financed, and Trinity House chartered. Such improvements became essential with the growth of London and other urban areas, and particular attention was paid to the removal of obstacles from the Thames, where pound-locks were also constructed. In 1541, as in the fourteenth century, Henley appears to have been the furthest point to which the Thames was ordinarily navigable. But in the early seventeenth century it became possible for barges to navigate as far as Oxford and even beyond.[2]

Such developments as these were bound to have an effect on regional price levels. The growing influence of London demand on the Thames valley area is suggested by Table 20, which indicates the prices of wheat in selected markets in the various regions.[3]

[1] Rogers, *Agriculture and Prices*, IV, pp. 694–710; V, pp. 755–77; Worcester RO, 705, 24, 355 (89).

[2] Clark, *op. cit.*, pp. 45, 95–6; Rogers, *op. cit.*, V, pp. 757–60; T. S. Willan, *River Navigation in England, 1600–1750*, Manchester, 1636, *passim*.

[3] For the sources of these and other prices mentioned in the text, see the 'Note on Sources and Methods' in the Statistical Appendix.

Table 20. *Decennial average prices of wheat (s. per quarter)*

Market	1450–9	1640–9	Percentage increase 1450/9—1640/9
London	6·88	49·91	725
Exeter	6·44	44·95	698
Winchester	5·24	38·75	740
Cambridge	4·70	36·76	783
Oxford	4·63	42·53	919
Canterbury	6·79	—	—
Durham	5·85	—	—
Windsor	—	47·04	—
Nottingham	—	46·59	—
Shrewsbury	—	43·84	—
English general average	5·70	43·85	770

The figures shown in the table make it quite clear that the market for wheat was very local in the mid-fifteenth century, and there seems no doubt that prices were greatly influenced by the availability of supplies grown in the immediately surrounding districts. At this time, much of the fertile Thames valley region was apparently little affected by metropolitan demand, since prices in the London area were very nearly 50 per cent higher than in Oxford, a town less than sixty miles distant. It seems probable that any deficiency in the balance of production and consumption in the vicinity of the capital was met mainly from the south-eastern sector of the country rather than from further inland. This view is supported, not only by the relatively high price of grain in Canterbury in the fifteenth century, but also by the heavy dependence of London on wheat imports from Kent later in the period. Among the other towns indicated in Table 20, relative price-levels were much as one would expect. In Exeter and Durham, both situated in regions relying mainly on spring-sown cereals and pastoral activities, wheat was dear; in Cambridge and Winchester it was cheap.

Two hundred years later the pattern of regional price differences was in many respects the same as in the mid-fifteenth century, but some significant changes had taken place in the intervening period. The most remarkable of these was a narrowing of regional price-differentials, this being a development which one would expect to occur as the market became wider and better organized. Prices in different regions often diverged widely in years of scarcity, but the general tendency was for them to converge more closely together. The latter was particularly the case with prices in London and the Thames valley area; by 1640–9, a margin of only 17 per cent separated Oxford prices from those in the capital. At Windsor, the difference was 6 per cent. However, since the districts through which the upper reaches of the Thames flowed had developed greater pastoral interests in the early Tudor period it would probably be unwise to attribute a ninefold increase in the price of wheat since 1450–9 solely to the growing influence of the London food market. In eastern and southern England (as illustrated by the data relating to Cambridge and Winchester), the growth of London had apparently exercised a much less stimulating effect on prices, and it was in these two regions, and no longer in the Thames valley area, that the cheapest wheat was to be obtained in the mid-seventeenth century.

The scattered nature of the data makes it impossible to attempt a regional analysis of the prices of other grains in the same detail as for wheat; nevertheless, the general picture which emerges is clear enough. Owing to the limitations of the transport system, the prices of inferior cereals varied much more widely from locality to locality than the prices of wheat, since the markets for these cheaper grains were more narrowly restricted. The broad pattern of regional prices, however, was much the same for rye and barley as for wheat, with each grain tending to become more expensive as one moved north, west, and south-east from the low-cost producing areas of eastern and southern England. Barley was a speciality in the eastern districts, being much in demand by the maltsters and brewers of East Anglia and London, though the capital appears to have relied more upon Kentish sources for the supply of this commodity. The production of barley was the principal aim of the sheep-corn husbandry of Norfolk, and it was a major crop in all the main farming regions of Lincolnshire. In the early 1620's the average price of barley in Oxford, at 17s. 7d. per quarter, was 11 per cent higher than in Lincoln. By way of comparison, barley sold at Theydon Garnon, in Essex, was 29 per cent dearer. At Laughton, in the pastoral Weald of Sussex, where oats competed strongly with barley for spring-sown land, barley prices in the 1630's were about on a level with those in Oxford.[1]

The chief strength of the pastoral areas lay in their fodder crops, and both barley and rye prices were often higher in the northern and south-western parts of the country than in the London region. The production of oats was strongly favoured in northern districts, where soils were generally poor and where oatcake and porridge provided the major sustenance of the human population. Thus, the average price of

[1] F. J. Fisher, 'The Development of the London Food Market, 1540–1640', EcHR, v, 1935, pp. 47–51; Joan Thirsk, *English Peasant Farming: the Agrarian History of Lincolnshire From Tudor to Recent Times*, London, 1957, p. 103; BM Add. MS 33147.

oats at Worksop in the 1590's, at 9s. 3d. per quarter, was approximately 13 per cent less than that in Cambridge. In western England a greater emphasis was placed on the production of peas and beans than of oats, and this was reflected in a corresponding price advantage in respect of these commodities. The eastern and south-eastern districts, on the other hand, with their fens and marshes, had generally less need to grow crops for fodder purposes, since hay was in many places plentiful and cheap, though extremely costly to transport any distance. Thus we find that, throughout the Tudor and early Stuart periods, the price of hay at Cambridge was constantly some 40 per cent lower than that at Eton. In general, it was in the central and southern parts of England that hay, oats, and pulses commanded the highest prices. This fact should occasion little surprise, for it fits in well with our knowledge of the growing pressure on common grazing land in these areas and underlines their concentration upon the major bread and drink cereals.

Differences in the cost of feed, not unexpectedly, exercised a strong influence on the price of livestock and animal produce. Pigs, for example, were generally cheapest in woodland and dairy-farming districts, where they could be fed on acorns, beechmast, and the waste-products of dairying, and dearest in unwooded areas devoted largely to tillage. Again, all kinds of poultry, and especially geese, were exceedingly cheap in the north of England, where extensive commons often existed, while they were dearest in London, the south-east, and south. In these latter regions the prices of dairy produce, cattle, horses, and sheep were also generally higher than those elsewhere; but in the absence of comparative data relating to the quality of produce and the size, age, and condition of stock, any attempt at detailed regional price analysis would be unwise.

Local differences in the price of stock arose partly from differences in the value of their produce, and this was especially so in the case of sheep and wool. The quality of wool and weight of fleece varied enormously in different parts of the country, depending largely upon the nature of pasturage and climate. In the south and east midlands, where the quality of wool was generally good and the fleece weight often considerable, sheep fetched high prices and wool growing was a major occupation of many capitalist farmers. In the northern and south-western districts, on the other hand, sheep were comparatively inexpensive, since they produced a fleece of coarse quality and inconsiderable weight. This fact doubtless helps to explain the greater emphasis on cattle rearing and dairy farming in these areas, once the market had become sufficiently well organized.

[1] Bowden, *op. cit.*, pp. 25–37.

B. FLUCTUATIONS AND TRENDS IN THE AGRARIAN ECONOMY

1. *Introduction*

The upward movement of agricultural prices which has been described in the earlier part of this study did not proceed without interruption and prices varied widely from season to season, year to year, and decade to decade. These fluctuations had to be endured as one of the penalties of a backward economic system and of the narrowly confined physical world in which Europeans lived. Agricultural prices always tend to fluctuate more markedly than other prices because in the short-run the supply of agricultural produce is mainly dependent upon variable weather conditions. But in respect of the weather, as well as in various other respects, modern economic systems are provided with a number of built-in stabilizing influences which have the effect of offsetting the worse consequences of scarcity and glut. The wide dispersal of primary producing countries over the globe ensures that climate and crop yields will be favourable in some parts of the world, if not in others, while the operation of an efficient marketing mechanism permits the storage and cheap distribution of stocks, for domestic and foreign consumption, as and when required.

These conditions, which tend towards the stabilization of prices, were largely absent in England and the rest of western Europe in the sixteenth and seventeenth centuries. The agricultural potentialities of the New World had yet to be developed, so there was little hope of outside relief in times of harvest failure. Meanwhile, extreme climatic condition sin the Old World tended to affect all countries ingreater or lesser degree.[1] This is clearly brought out in Fig. 14, which compares wheat prices in England between the mid-fifteenth and mid-seventeenth centuries with the average of wheat prices in Germany, France, and the Netherlands during the same period. Bearing in mind the comparatively wide geographica larea covered by the latter countries, the coincidence, both as regards short-term fluctuations and long-term trends, is striking. The broad similarity of climatic conditions throughout western Europe, together with limitations of the transportation system, largely explain why, even in famine years, the amount of grain imported into England was only a negligible proportion of domestic output and why exports were never very large. The year ending December 1638 was one of extreme food shortage. During this period London, which accounted for the bulk of the country's external

[1] For further on this, see G. Utterström, 'Climatic Fluctuations and Population Problems in Early Modern History', *Scand. Econ. Hist. Rev.*, III, 1955, pp. 3–47.

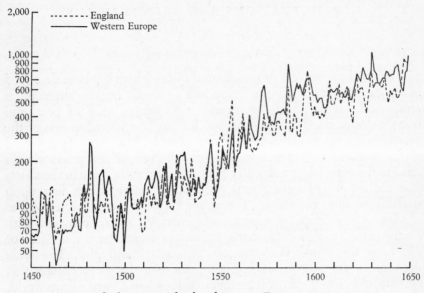

Fig. 14. Price of wheat in England and western Europe. 1450–99 = 100.

trade, imported from abroad a record quantity of 160,545 quarters of different types of grain.[1] If we allow an average crop yield of two quarters per acre, this quantity of produce could have been grown on 125 sq. miles, or about 1 per cent of the nation's arable area. Doubtless, the greater climatic differences of the Baltic countries, as compared with those of western Europe, partly explain why Danzig should have been looked upon as a principal source of supply in times of need.

Adequate storage facilities, which would have helped to mitigate the worst effects of harvest failure, were largely lacking. The corn trade was mainly in the hands of small dealers—an indication of the limited extent of the market. These lacked the necessary capital for the provision of warehousing, and in the face of government intervention when food was scarce must have been hard put to it at times to carry on their business. Larger merchants who dealt in grain did so mainly on an occasional and speculative basis, and were said to lack "the pollices to kepe Corne and wheate for the space of Vj or vij yeres good if nede require."[2]

Among the growers of corn, small producers had little to spare for market, and many were forced by necessity to sell their surplus as soon

[1] PRO E 190, 41, 145. Information kindly supplied by Mrs A. M. Millard.
[2] Fisher, EcHR, v, 1935, p. 59; TED III, pp. 329–30; Gervase Markham, *Markham's Farewell to Husbandry*, London, 1638, p. 110 *seq.*; John Worlidge, *Systema Agriculturae*, 1675, pp. 52, 53.

as crops had been harvested, irrespective of the current market price. The larger farmers were generally in a better position, when prices were low, to wait for a favourable market. That some adopted this course is shown by the practice of Robert Loder, who in 1619, a year of bumper harvest, stored part of his wheat crop in a rick, selling it three years later at twice the original value. Self-interest thus helped to stabilize prices, but only to a limited extent. Not all large corn-growers followed Loder's example, and some, especially in inland areas, made a constant practice of selling their grain in small quantities every week or few days to local buyers. This could suggest an inability to store large quantities of grain for any appreciable length of time; but on the other hand, these small sales may have been forced on growers by the limited nature of the accessible market, or have been preferred because a higher unit price was obtainable than on larger transactions. Local and conciliar regulation also aimed at keeping markets regularly supplied in times of scarcity. Government proposals made in 1619 for the provision of public granaries received no support from J.P.'s in several corn-growing counties, on the ground of the expense involved in providing the necessary buildings. One suspects that this was not the real reason, but that the J.P.'s were looking to their own profit, as Loder had done. Subsequently, the public storage of grain figured prominently in the government's programme to combat the effects of a series of disastrous harvests.[1]

Storage facilities for the other main marketable commodity—wool— were better organized than for grain, since the wool trade was well developed and had long attracted men with substantial amounts of capital. Many large growers also stored wool when prices were low, in order to await a seller's market; but the small sheep farmers, like the arable husbandmen, were often in urgent need of cash and seldom lost much time in the disposal of their produce.[2]

2. Seasonal fluctuations

Even in a highly developed economy, some seasonal movement in the prices of agricultural commodities can be expected, since the supply of some types of produce varies considerably with the seasons, while other

[1] G. E. Fussell (ed.), *Robert Loder's Farm Accounts, 1610–1620*, Camden Soc., 3rd Ser., LIII, 1936, pp. 158–9, 161, 174, 177; BM Add. MS 34682; BM Add. MS 37419 Beds. RO, D.D.T.W. i, i; Herts. RO, 6604 and 6718; Kent RO, U 269, A 418, 5, ff. 11–16; SP 14, 112, 91; SP 14, 113, 26; SP 14, 113, 90; SP 14, 128, 65; SP 14,1 44, 24; SP 14, 144, 32; SP 16, 117, 61; SP 16, 185, 6; SP 16, 186, 16; SP 16, 186, 62.

[2] Bowden, *op. cit.*, pp. 77–80, 86–7, 91–2; A. Simpson, *The Wealth of the Gentry, 1540–1660: East Anglian Studies*, Cambridge, 1961, pp. 188–93.

crops, such as corn, hay, and wool, are gathered only once a year.
Adequate statistical material for an analysis of seasonal movements in
the price of grain in the Tudor period is unfortunately lacking, but
when the relevant data relating to the early Stuart period are analysed,
an unfamiliar picture meets the eye. Normally, we should expect grain
prices to be lowest in the months immediately following the harvest,
since at this time supplies would be at their most plentiful. Subsequently,
as stocks dwindled, we should expect prices to rise, reaching a peak in
the late summer months before the next harvest, though the actual
extent of the price rise would obviously be influenced in some degree
by forecasts, which could be made with reasonable accuracy as early as
April, about forthcoming crop yields. This seasonal pattern had clearly
established itself by the late eighteenth century and may also have been
normal in the earlier part of the period covered by our study. It does
not, however, appear to have been the experience in the early Stuart
period, as Table 21, relating to the price of wheat in Exeter, suggests.[1]

Table 21. *Price of wheat in Exeter (1626–1640)*

Average quarterly price as percentage of average annual price

Oct.–Dec.	Jan.–March	April–June	July–Sept.
98·9	100·1	102·7	98·7

The most striking feature of this table is the fall in the price of wheat
in the late summer months, when the presumption is that growing
scarcity should have forced prices to rise. The only feasible explanation
of this must be that growing scarcity was more than offset by declining
demand. Either people ate less bread of any kind at this time of the
year or they turned from the consumption of wheaten bread to the
consumption of bread made from inferior cereals. Price data for other
grains, had they been available, would have enabled the probability
of these two hypotheses to have been tested. Irrespective of which is the
more likely explanation, however, the evidence presented above
points to a society where many experienced extreme poverty, living
desparately from one meagre harvest to the next. Wheat prices fell in
the late summer months because, by then, any capital accumulated
from the sale of produce the previous year had largely disappeared, and
starvation stared many starkly in the face. This viewpoint is supported

[1] T. S. Ashton, *Economic Fluctuations in England, 1700–1800*, Oxford, 1959, p. 11.
Exeter wheat prices have been obtained from the Beveridge collection of price
material at the Institute of Historical Research, London.

by the fact that the steepest fall in prices in the late summer months occurred at the end of years of severe harvest failure, as was the case in 1630 and 1637, when August wheat prices in Exeter were only 77 per cent and 81 per cent respectively of those obtaining the previous June. The whole weight of evidence, in fact, of this and other sections of this study indicates that the third, fourth, and fifth decades of the seventeenth century witnessed extreme hardship in England, and were probably among the most terrible years through which the country has ever passed. It is probably no coincidence that the first real beginnings in the colonization of America date from this period.

If seasonal fluctuations in the level of consumer income and capital played an important part in determining the price of grain, the same was probably less true of livestock, since large farmers, whose receipts were usually spread throughout the year, figured more prominently as purchasers. However, many small men must have found it necessary to sell stock before the arrival of harvest time in order to raise capital for food and other necessary expenses, and this would obviously have tended to exert a depressing influence on prices. Figures relating to sales of livestock at Shrewsbury, as given in Table 22, appear to lend support to this supposition.[1]

Table 22. *Average prices of livestock at Shrewsbury, 1600–12 (s. each)*

	May	June	August	September
Horses	63·13	45·71	48·71	49·69
Mares	53·05	52·66	46·33	46·36
Oxen	74·50	74·75	70·51	64·76
Cows	49·14	45·46	44·78	44·20
Heifers	39·56	46·09	40·53	35·85

Probably the most decisive factor in the seasonal movement of stock prices, however, was the availability of feed. In the spring and early summer months the growth of natural pasture encouraged the purchase of stock, which could be fed cheaply on grass, but with the approach of autumn and winter it became increasingly necessary to rely upon hay and other fodder crops, which were not only expensive but sometimes almost impossible to obtain. Hay might double in price between one crop and the next, though a rise of about one-third was more usual. Unwanted stock, which could not be supported, were therefore usually sold off before winter set in. The difficulties which were

[1] Figures from the Beveridge collection of price material.

encountered even by large farmers in respect of feed are clearly brought
out by two mid-sixteenth-century entries in the account books of the
depopulated manor of Misterton, in Leicestershire, belonging to the
Poulteney family, but at this time under the wardship of Sir William
Paget. The first entry, relating to the sale of 66 lambs in July and August
1553, reads: "Recept for culling lambes not fatt this yere for wante
grasse to the ewes and yet sold for haueing their dames depryving
them," £3 11s. 8d.; and the second entry, in a list of cattle sales the
following year: "Item, of Wallener the bocher for an other Runte
despayring in the cold weder and sold partelye for lakke of haye,"
£1 7s. 8d.[1] Such sales as these naturally tended to affect the price of
animal products. Cheap livestock in the autumn meant cheap meat. By
the early spring the number of animals being sent to market had
dwindled, and meat, especially beef, was at its dearest. Cows could be
made to yield milk in winter, but only at a disproportionate cost and in
comparatively small quantities. Dairy produce was therefore usually
much dearer, sometimes by as much as 50 per cent, in winter and early
spring than in summer. Thus at Wormleighton, in Warwickshire, in
1621-2, the price of butter in April was $5\frac{1}{4}$d. per lb.; in June it was
$3\frac{3}{4}$d. Since a considerable part of the value of the sheep consisted of its
fleece, the curve of sheep prices normally reached a peak just before
shearing time—usually between the beginning and middle of June—
and thereafter fell to a low point towards the end of the year. The price
of wethers in May was commonly twice that in November. The movement of sheep-skin prices followed a broadly similar curve, since the
value of the pelt depended primarily on the amount of wool covering
the animal when it is slaughtered or otherwise died. Thus, an entry
made in 1583 in the farming accounts of the Clopton family of Kentwell, in Suffolk, notes a price of 2s. 6d. for the fells of sheep killed
between Shrovetide and shearing time, as against 7d. for those killed
between clipping time and Michaelmas. Wool, itself, tended to increase
in price with the coming of autumn and was generally at its most
expensive in the late spring. Detailed information about the seasonal
movement of wool prices is, unfortunately, not available, but this must
have been considerable since many wealthy growers held back their
clips from the market until late in the wool-growing year.[2]

[1] Beveridge, op. cit., pp. 21-2; W. G. Hoskins, Essays in Leicestershire History,
Liverpool, 1950, pp. 88-9; William Salt Library, D 1734, 22, fo. 4; D 1734, 38, fo. 6.
[2] Rogers, Agriculture and Prices, IV, p. 308; V, pp. 337, 358-60; Bowden, op. cit.,
pp. 3-4, 13, 14, 87; Beveridge, op. cit., pp. 238-9; BM Harl. MS 127, fo. 36; Val
Cheke, The Story of Cheese-Making in Britain, London, 1959, p. 84.

3. *Annual fluctuations*

The prime cause of annual fluctuations in agricultural prices was the weather. In the short run, this largely determined the supply of agricultural produce. Moreover, changes arising from supply conditions affected the level and distribution of agricultural income, and in a predominantly agrarian economy this was bound to influence significantly the demand, not only for agricultural commodities, but for things in general.

The weather, however did not affect all branches of farming equally, since different crops and kinds of livestock react differently to climatic conditions. Moreover, as the climate must have varied somewhat from one locality to another, and as sowing and reaping times also differed, an unfavourable spell of weather would have affected some districts more adversely than others. However, the possibilities of bumper harvests in some areas coinciding with crop failures elsewhere were extremely remote.

In England, drought is normally advantageous to the wheat harvest and, unless prolonged, is seldom a cause of failure among the other cereal crops. This, as Professor Ashton has pointed out, is due to the predominance of heavy, moisture-retaining clayland over lighter, sandy soils. The majority of serious crop failures in Tudor and early Stuart times do not appear to have been the result of excessive drought, but one of the most disastrous harvests to be experienced—that of 1637—was apparently due to this cause. The main danger to cereal farming was heavy and prolonged rainfall in summer, accompanied by an almost total absence of sunshine. Under such conditions crops failed to ripen, yields were poor, and prices rose to famine heights. An excessively cold winter and frosty spring were also harmful to the wheat harvest. The weather in winter scarcely affected barley, oats, and pulses, which were spring-sown cereals, but a cold spring could add to the difficulties of sowing, since the ground would be hard, while a late frost might do damage to the crops.[1]

The climatic conditions which ensured a bumper cereal harvest were, in general, less suitable for a plentiful crop of hay. This explains why grain prices and hay prices in Tudor and early Stuart England frequently diverged, with the noticeable exception of the decade which marked the Civil Wars. Since the growth of grass depended primarily on moisture and warmth, a plentiful supply of hay required a mild, wet spring followed by a spell of dry, sunny weather in the early summer months. Late frosts, low rainfall, or prolonged drought were generally

[1] Ashton, *Economic Fluctuations*, p. 15; Yorks. Arch. Soc. Lib., MS 311; SP 14, 123, 62; SP 14, 187, 20; SP 14, 187, 90; SP 16, 90, 35; SP 16, 167, 28; SP 16, 168, 126.

harmful, tending to reduce the supply of good-quality hay and leading to a rise in price.

While farmers in the sixteenth and seventeenth centuries were by no means entirely dependent upon hay for the winter keep of their livestock, since peas, beans, tares, straw, oats, and, occasionally, other grains were used for fodder purposes, hay played a much more vital rôle in the animal husbandry of these earlier centuries than it does today. In the period with which we are concerned, the large-scale use of roots, artificial grasses, oilcake, and the other aids of the modern breeder or grazier were still in the future. A failure of the hay crop meant that the ability of many farmers to carry their stock through the winter months was seriously impaired, and large numbers of animals were slaughtered or sold. This tended to create a short-run buyers' market in respect of livestock, meat, hides, and tallow, followed inevitably by a shortage of these commodities, as well as of dairy produce and young stock. This sequence of events was outlined by the Lord Mayor of London to the Privy Council in a letter dated 26 May 1630, wherein the causes of "the excessive prices of victuals" were set out. The Privy Council was informed that in 1629 "spring fell out so unseasonable that grass grew very short...so much smaller store of hay, straw, and stover for feeding cattle...the last winter...causing a great slaughter in the end of last summer and the winter following and discouraged the Butchers from making their provision of fat cattle and the country people here about London from storing themselves with Cowes as formerly they have done...Of late years have been brought to Cheapside market upon a Saturday 1700 or 1800 veals and this spring not above 200 or 300..." In 1629–30, in fact, the prices of both calves and dairy produce were higher than in any previous year. The state of the hay crop was of special concern to the cattle-farming industry, for other kinds of livestock were probably less dependent than cattle upon hay. Horses were fed mainly on oats, while the practice of feeding pulses to sheep appears to have become increasingly common throughout the period. Pigs and poultry grubbed around for much of their keep, and the acorns favoured by the former were at their most plentiful following the kind of hot summer weather so detrimental to hay.[1]

Apart from influencing the price of livestock and animal produce through the supply of feed, the climate had an important direct bearing on the mortality of stock. Extreme cold in winter, whereby animals may perish from lack of food or shelter, has always been a major hazard in the English livestock industry, and in the sixteenth and

[1] Rogers, Agriculture and Prices, IV, pp. 295–6; V, p. 305; Ashton, Economic Fluctuations, pp. 15–16; W. Salt Lib., D 1734, 22, ff. 4, 22, 24ᵛ; D 1734, 38, fo. 6; SP 14, 113, 89; SP 16, 167, 28.

seventeenth centuries it was a problem which caused farmers much concern. High mortality among stock, however, was probably due less to the effects of cold than to outbreaks of animal diseases, such as the liver fluke in sheep and lung worm in cattle. Though runs of very dry summers were conducive to the spread of disease, the main danger was excessive rain, from which sheep, in particular, were liable to suffer. In such periods one would expect the initial tendency to be for livestock prices to fall, since the reaction of owners of infected animals would be to sell them as quickly as possible, while buyers would be wary. Subsequently, shortages of stock and animal produce would tend to develop and prices to rise. The "great rottes and murryns, bothe of sheepe and bullockes" referred to by Hales in his *Defence* of 1549, suggests that this year experienced abnormal climatic conditions: an impression which gains support from a consideration of the relevant price data relating to stock and corn. Similarly "sore winters" and "immoderate rains" were partly responsible for "great decay and dearth of cattle and sheep" in the early and late 1620's. The loss of stock at such times was often considerable. In 1627–8 disease eliminated one third of the flock of twelve or thirteen hundred sheep kept by Sir Ralph Delaval at Seaton Delaval in Northumberland; while in the stormy weather of 1570, Sir Henry Lee of Quarrendon, in Buckinghamshire, was alleged—probably with great exaggeration—to have lost three thousand sheep besides other horned cattle.[1]

Apart from its effect on the *supply* of agricultural commodities, the climate also indirectly influenced *demand* since, in a peasant economy, purchasing power was largely determined by the size of the harvest. A crop failure, however, did not affect all classes equally, and it was followed by a shift in the distribution of income from other people to large arable farmers, whose propensity to consume was low. Since the demand for bread was inelastic (i.e. only a little less was consumed when the price increased substantially), large grain-growers who produced for the market could expect to enjoy increased receipts in times of general harvest failure. But for most agriculturalists, as well as for the industrial sections of society, a bad harvest meant high bread prices, with less to spend on other things, and a general decline in the standard of living. For the many small subsistence farmers, who normally sold a little surplus produce in the market in order to raise money for rent and other necessary expenses, a crop failure was disastrous. These now found the mselves buying grain at famine prices, using up any small

[1] Bowden, *op. cit.*, pp. 15–16; W. Salt Lib., D 1734, 22, fo. 4^v; E. Lamond (ed.), *A Discourse of the Common Weal of this Realm of England*, Cambridge, 1929, pp 149–50; SP 14, 131, 29; SP 16, 90, 35; SP 16, 167, 28; *Dictionary of National Biography*, ed. S. Lee, XXXII, London, 1892, p. 356.

reserves of capital and falling into arrears with their rent. Preparations for the coming year's harvest might also be threatened by inability to purchase seed-corn and other essential supplies. For the large and growing class of agricultural labourers, a bad harvest meant not only a higher price of subsistence, but less opportunities for work and reductions in already pitifully small incomes. A crop flattened by heavy rain may not have required less labour than usual to reap it, but fewer workers would have been needed to move, stack, thresh, and winnow the grain. Moreover, these reductions in demand for labour may have been preceded by many months of unfavourable weather conditions in which opportunities for work in the fields were restricted. With meagre earnings and dear food, survival for agricultural wage-earners and other depressed sections of society could only have been accomplished by a lowering in the standard of diet and a reduction of expenditure on the minor luxuries, and even bare essentials, of working-class life. One would thus expect to find a contraction in demand for such goods as clothing and footwear, with consequent unemployment in these industries. The consumption of ale, beer, dairy produce, and meat would also be affected, though, in the case of meat, it appears that beef and, to a lesser extent, mutton were supplied mainly to a middle and upper-class market, while bacon and pork were more commonly eaten by the poor. These contractions in demand would in turn be transmitted back to the primary producers, and, above all, to the growers of wool. However, if the hay crop had been good, and if the farming enterprise were of a mixed character, as was often the case, any fall in receipts from the sale of livestock and animal produce might be carried without too great difficulty.[1]

The arguments outlined above can be developed further by reference to our price data. The movement of grain prices in the period under review is illustrated by Fig. 15. This graph has several interesting features, one of which is the wide fluctuation in prices from year to year, this being a consequence of the inelasticity in demand and supply conditions which distinguishes arable agriculture from most other economic activities. The short-term movements in the price of each of the main cereals—wheat, barley, oats, and rye—were broadly similar, since each grain was, in some degree, a substitute for the others, while any extremes of climate in spring or summer affected the yield of all. The degree of price fluctuation, however, varied from one grain to another, being greatest in respect of the inferior cereals. This tendency seems to have become more pronounced in the latter part of our period, when the standard of life of the mass of the people was at its lowest level.

[1] Ashton, *Economic Fluctuations*, pp. 42–4; W. Salt Lib., D 1734, 22; fo. 24ᵛ; D 1734, 38 fo. 28ᵛ. See also *infra*, pp.   .

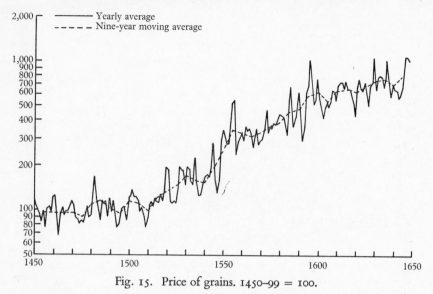

Fig. 15. Price of grains. 1450–99 = 100.

Thus, while wheat harvested in 1637 was only 16 per cent dearer than in the previous year, the prices of rye, barley, and oats were increased by 59 per cent, 50 per cent, and 22 per cent respectively. The climatic conditions of 1636–7 were probably less unfavourable to wheat than to the other cereals. In 1595–6 barley seems to have been the crop least adversely affected by the weather, since the price of barley, like the price of wheat, increased by only approximately one-third. By comparison, oats doubled in price, while rye advanced by more than 50 per cent. At Worksop seed rye was more expensive than wheat. During the same period peas and beans, which, because of their comparative cheapness, were consumed in the form of bread by many people in years of famine, increased in price by 78 per cent and 68 per cent respectively. Barley was primarily a drink cereal, although it was also a principal breadcorn of the poor, and in times of great scarcity was used mainly for this purpose. In this connection it is instructive to note that the price of hops fell sharply in years of harvest failure. This suggests a contraction in the output of the brewing industry, due mainly one supposes, to the income-effect of dearer bread on consumers, and the inability of brewers and maltsters to obtain supplies of scarce grain, rather than to the efforts of the government to curb the activities of the alehouses and their suppliers.[1]

[1] SP 14, 112, 91; SP 14, 132, 52; SP 14, 142, 14 (ii); SP 16, 177, 43; SP 16, 182, 40; SP 16, 186, 62; SP 16, 186, 98; G. E. Fussell, *The English Rural Labourer. His Home, Furniture, Clothing and Food from Tudor to Victorian Times*, London, 1949, pp. 31–3. For hop prices, see Beveridge, *op. cit.*, pp. 145–5 and 193–4.

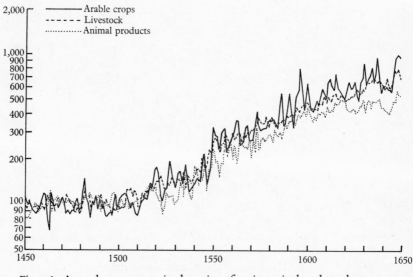

Fig. 16. Annual movements in the price of main agricultural products.
1450–99 = 100.

The relationship between the price of arable crops (including hay) and other agricultural commodities is illustrated in Fig. 16. It should be borne in mind that our price data, especially those relating to livestock and animal produce have certain basic weaknesses (discussed in the Statistical Appendix) which make it unwise to push year-to-year comparisons very far. Nevertheless, the evidence presented in Fig. 6 does appear to lend support to the thesis outlined earlier, especially in respect of the latter part of the period, for which data are more plentiful.

Compared with the wide fluctuations which characterized the short-term movement in arable crop prices, those for livestock and animal produce were much less volatile. Both tended to fall after a crop failure and to rise after a good harvest, but this tendency was much stronger in the case of produce than of stock. Probably part of the explanation of the smaller degree of sensitivity of livestock prices to harvest conditions is the fact that the poorer classes who suffered most severely in times of scarcity were, in general, more important as consumers of produce than as buyers of stock, though many cottagers kept one or two hens, pigs, or a cow. Beef production and sheep husbandry, on the other hand, were mainly the business of substantial and well-to-do farmers for whom a contraction in demand for animal products might mean smaller profits but not an immediate contraction in the scale of enterprise. Moreover, owing to the heavy dependence of arable farming on animal manure, livestock were often not easily dispensed with, and large cereal growers who made windfall gains from the failure of crops might decide to invest some of their profits in adding to their flocks and herds. The demand for livestock, as we have seen, was also greatly influenced by the state of the hay crop, and this was more likely to be good than bad when the harvest was poor.

Among livestock farmers, the adverse effects of a harvest failure were felt with particular severity by the wool growers, since clothing was the principal consumer good on which income might be saved in times of food scarcity. The production of cloth was the main industrial activity in many parts of the country, and its export, together with that of raw wool in the earlier part of our period, accounted for between 75 and 90 per cent of England's total export trade. Any large contraction in demand was therefore likely to create unemployment for many hundreds of industrial workers and adversely affect the balance of payments position. A comparison of statistics relating to cloth exports, wool prices, and English and continental grain prices leaves little doubt that good harvests, at home and abroad, were fundamental to the industry's prosperity, leading to a buoyant demand for wool. Such harvests occurred towards the end of the 1540's, and gave a final great boost to a broadcloth industry already producing at its longer-term equilibrium level; they occurred again at the very beginning of the seventeenth century to inject some life into a trade by then almost stagnant. On the other hand, bad harvests in years such as the early 1550's, mid- 1580's, late 1590's, and early 1620's had the effect of contracting home and export demand for cloth, resulting in a substantial fall in the price of wool.[1]

In much the same manner, though not to the same extent, the prices of dairy produce and meat (e.g. rabbits) tended to rise after a good harvest and fall after a bad one. On the other hand, egg prices usually increased after a crop failure, this suggesting either that necessity had forced cottagers and other small poultry keepers to part with their birds, thus creating a shortage of eggs, or that there was a rising demand for eggs because these were found to be a cheap substitute for dear bread. Since the general tendency was for the prices of capons, hens, geese, and ducks to decline after a bad harvest, the supply of poultry was apparently more plentiful at such times, in relation to demand, than was the supply of eggs. Pigs generally seem to have maintained their price in years of crop failure, this suggesting, perhaps, that there was a switch on the part of some consumers from beef and mutton to the inferior meat, though there are insufficient data for testing the accuracy of this hypothesis.

[1] Bowden, *op. cit.*, pp. xv–xviii.

The general economic effect of changes in the size of the harvest can be further illustrated with specific reference to the years around 1550 and 1620, when comparative prosperity was changed within a short span of time to deep depression. The 1540's have long been thought of as a period of rising prices, for which the debasements of the coinage have been held mainly responsible. The point has generally been missed that, although wheat prices at the very end of the decade were more than double those in 1540, and other prices also much enhanced, the crops harvested in 1546, 1547, and 1548 were exceptionally bountiful and grain prices in those years were very low. This fact did not escape the attention of contemporaries, who were at a loss to explain the apparent paradox of "dearth of victuals" in the midst of abundance. The main blame was laid at the door of land-hungry sheep masters and beef farmers, though covetous engrossers and rack-renting landlords were also roundly condemned.[1]

It is possible that part of the price rise was due to the usurpation of common land for grazing sheep and oxen, since the presumption is that this would tend to result in a shortage of other stock; the high incidence of animal diseases, alleged by contemporaries in the late 1540's, could also have temporarily reduced the supply of livestock and victuals. We must also admit the possibility that the depreciations of the coinage helped to stimulate the price rise in its final stages. But when all this has been said, it still seems reasonable to suppose that the purchasing power engendered by the abundant harvests of 1546–8 not only acted as a stimulus to the economy during these years but also helped to carry it along on a crest of buoyant demand for a period afterwards. Moderately good harvests on the continent in 1549 and 1550, together with the need of foreign armies for clothing, served to sustain the demand for English cloth, and the economy remained active, in spite of a jump in the price of home-produced grain. By 1550, however, the prices of some commodities had already begun to fall, and cloth exports in this year were no higher than in the mid-1540's, in spite of the devaluation of sterling. In the following year, a combination of exchange appreciation and poor crop yields led to a marked contraction of trade and a general collapse of prices.

Cloth exports from London, which had amounted to almost 132,800 pieces in 1550, fell to less than 112,800 pieces in 1551 and 85,000 in 1552. Wool prices, which had more than doubled between 1546 and 1550, fell sharply. At Misterton, in Leicestershire, wool sold for 12s. 6d. per stone in 1550–1 fetched only 6s. 8d. per stone a year later; while an entry made in the manorial accounts in 1552 recorded that "shepe

[1] Lamond, op. cit., pp. lvix–lxv, 15, 17, 38, 48, 52–3, 104, 122, 149–51, 162–3, 167, 185–7; TEDi ii, pp. 7–8, 40, 51–4, 57, 59, 61, 316, 319–21, 337–8.

fells kept from Februare bycase the price then was small" were sold in July for "lesse price." The wheat harvests of 1552 and 1553 appear to have been somewhat better than those in the two preceding years, but the prices of spring-sown cereals remained high, this suggesting not only less favourable yields as compared with wheat, but also a change in the pattern of consumer expenditure in favour of the inferior grains. The depression continued, and at Misterton receipts from the sale of wool averaged only £93 per annum in the three years 1552–4, as compared with £171 in 1550–1. The depth of the slump was reached in 1553, with livestock and animal produce prices well below the levels of 1550. Thereafter, recovery was uncertain and irregular.[1]

The depression of the early 1620's had much in common with that just described. As with the slump of the mid-sixteenth century, several excellent harvests were followed by a number of crop failures. This combination, of a run of exceptionally good harvests followed by a series of crop failures, by impoverishing first one section of the community and then other sections, appears to have provided the optimum conditions for the onset of trade depression. The harvests of 1618 and 1619 were very good, while that of 1620 was even better. A "marvellous yield," noted Loder in his account books in 1620, scarcely able to believe in crops which gave a return of 14·55 quarters of wheat and 8·43 quarters of barley for each quarter of seed sown—figures which represented increases of 36 per cent and 27 per cent respectively over the average yields obtained in the years 1612–17. To Loder, and other substantial arable farmers, the price, as against the yield, of grain gave less cause for rejoicing. For wheat sold in 1620 Loder received only 17s. 7¼d. per quarter, compared with an average price of 32s. 0½d. in the period 1612–17; for barley he received 14s. 4d. per quarter, as against an average price of about 22s. 5d. in the earlier years. While the low price of wheat was enabling many poor people to enjoy wheaten bread for possibly the first time in their lives, the J.P.'s of Norfolk were reporting to the Privy Council in November 1619, "that divers farmers, whose farms consisted upon tilth and corn, are utterly disabled and enforced to leave the same and the owners to leese their farms." From Lincolnshire, in March 1620, the J.P.'s argued that it was "better to endure with patience the present inconvenience" than to adopt the Privy Council's proposal for public granaries. The complaints of abundance continued, Sir Symonds d'Ewes noting in his diary in 1621 that as a result of the excessive cheapness of wheat the price of some

---

[1] L. Stone, 'State Control in Sixteenth-Century England', EcHR, XVII, 1947, pp. 106, 119; F. J. Fisher, 'Commercial Trends and Policy in Sixteenth-Century England', EcHR, X, 1940, pp. 96, 103–4; W. Salt Lib., D 1734, 4 and 5 Edward VI (not numbered); D 1734, 24, ff. 3, 4ᵛ; D 1734, 22, fo. 4ᵛ; D 1734, 38, fo. 5ᵛ.

lands had been reduced from twenty years' purchase to sixteen or seventeen.[1]

Meanwhile, a number of factors had combined to undermine the prosperity of the livestock industry. The hay crops of 1619 and 1620 were disappointing, while the difficulties experienced by mixed farmers with substantial arable interests also encouraged the disposal of stock on easy terms. Abroad, English cloth exporters were meeting with increased foreign competition and trade protection. Bad harvests in 1621 and 1622 underlined the cloth industry's weak position, which was reflected in a rising level of unemployment at home and a steep fall in the price of wool. In 1622—a year which saw a trebling of rye prices in parts of Germany—cloth exports from London amounted to 75,600 pieces: a decline of some 26,700 pieces on the 1618 figure. During the same period the price of Lincolnshire wool sold by Sir George Heneage of Hainton fell from 14s. to 10s. per stone.[2]

Reports received by the government from the northern counties between 1621 and 1623, spoke of great distress among livestock farmers occasioned by recent crop failures and by the "abatement of the wonted prices of cattle sheep and wool." Many small tenants, it was stated, had been unable to pay their rents, and had left "their farms untimely to their landlords"—a position reminiscent of that reported from the bishopric of Durham after the disastrous harvest failure of 1597. From Cambridgeshire, in May 1622, the J.P.'s informed the government that many small husbandmen had been forced to sell crops not yet harvested in order to provide for themselves in the meantime. The following year witnessed no perceptible improvement, and the terrible hardship which many endured was vividly described by Sir William Pelham of Brocklesby, Lincs., in a letter to his brother-in-law, Sir Edward Conway, in 1623. He wrote: "There are many thousands in these parts who have sold all they have even to their bed-straw, and cannot get work to earn any money. Dog's flesh is a dainty dish, and found upon search in many houses, also such horse flesh as hath lain long in a deke for hounds, and the other day one stole a sheep, who for mere hunger tore a leg out, and yet the great time of scarcity not yet come." During the course of the next thirty years, suffering and extreme hunger were to become all too familiar.[3]

[1] *Robert Loder's Farm Accounts, passim;* T. Tooke, *A History of Prices and of the State of the Currency from 1793 to 1837,* London, I, 1838, pp. 23–4; SP 14, 111, 11; SP 14, 113, 26.

[2] Bowden, *op. cit.,* pp. 187–90; M. J. Elsas, 'Price Data from Munich, 1500–1700', *Econ. Hist.,* III, 1935, p. 65; F. J. Fisher, 'London's Export Trade in the Early Seventeenth Century', EcHR, 2nd Ser., III, 1950, p. 153; Lincs. AO, HEN. 3/2.

[3] CSPD, 1621–23, p. 305; SP 14, 113, 21; SP 14, 130, 107; SP 14, 130, 9; SP 14, 131, 9; SP 14, 131, 25; SP 14, 131, 29; SP 14, 140, 10; SP 14, 144, 24 (xii); Joan Thirsk, 'Industries in the Countryside', *Essays in the Economic and Social History of*

Recurrent outbreaks of plague added to the distress caused by famine and trade depression. As Creighton noted many years ago, it is possible to search through the annals of Tudor and early Stuart times, and find scarecely a year when pestilence was not reported from one or another part of the country. The striking coincidence of serious plague outbreaks with harvest failures, however, leaves no doubt that these two events were closely related. Whether this was because the rat hosts of the fleas (*Xenopsylla cheopis*) which carried the plague migrated to towns and granaries in search of food in times of crop failure and were imported with shipments of foreign grain, or whether it was because these fleas multiplied most rapidly in climatic conditions conducive to bad harvests, need not concern us here. Whatever the explanation, the mortality rate in plague years was often extremely high. In London, where many of the severest outbreaks occurred, a record number of 41,313 people were registered in the mortality bills as having died of the plague in 1625. Total recorded mortality in London for this year amounted to 63,001 persons, so if we allow for a population of some 200,000, the death rate in the capital in 1625 approximated to 300 per 1,000 inhabitants. In 1563, another year of severe plague epidemic, the death-rate in London was possibly 200 per 1,000. Outbreaks of this order not only adversely affected the economy by sweeping away large numbers of consumers and producers, but also led directly to stoppages of trade. Few buyers visited markets and risked infection when the plague was rampant, as at least one seller of oxen found after a fruitless visit to Smithfield market in the 1590's. The plague of 1625 stopped all organized trade in the city of London for a season, and subsequent outbreaks of the pestilence in some of the provincial towns, such as Plymouth, also brought commerce to a halt. From Essex, in September 1625, the Deputy Lieutenants informed the Privy Council: "Scarce any man has half an ordinary crop of corn, clothiers have no vent of their wares, graziers and marketmen have no sale on account of the infection in London, hopmasters cannot sell at Stourbridge fair or London, Michaelmas rents and an assessment of the subsidy are becoming due, and extraordinary taxes for the relief of the sick poor." It is not surprising that, at such times, attempts at arbitrary taxation should have met with opposition.[1]

Tudor and Stuart England, ed. F. J. Fisher, Cambridge, 1961, pp. 82–3; J. W. F. Hill, *Tudor and Stuart Lincoln*, Cambridge, 1956, p. 142.

[1] C. Creighton, *A History of Epidemics in Britain from* A.D. *664 to the Extinction of Plague*, Cambridge, 1891, pp. 202, 229 *sqq*, 304, 470, 507–12; L. F. Hirst, *The Conquest of Plague. A Study of the Evolution of Epidemiology*, Oxford, 1953, pp. 213, 260 *sqq.*, 303 *sqq.*; E. Hobsbawn, 'The General Crisis of the European Economy in the Seventeenth Century', *Past and Present*, v 1954, pp. 35; PRO E 133, 1224, 37–8 Eliz. I; SP 16, 29, 46; SP 16, 6, 77.

4. Cycles and trends

Though agricultural prices, and especially grain prices, were subject to violent fluctuations from one year to another, some regularity in the longer-term movement of prices can be discerned (see Figs. 14–16). More than forty years ago, Lord Beveridge commented on the periodicity which he had discovered in the movement of European wheat prices in the early modern period, stating that "this would establish climatic variations as one cause, not as the whole or perhaps even the main cause, of cyclical fluctuations of industry." Our own investigations lend support to this view. Whatever we may think of Jevons's sunspot theory, it does appear that good harvests and bad harvests tended to cluster together, and that at fairly regular intervals—e.g. 1551, 1562, 1573, 1586, 1597, 1608—exceptionally bad harvests occurred as a result of a deterioration in weather conditions. To some extent also, one bad harvest helped to generate others, hunger resulting in the consumption of corn intended for the next year's seed. Conversely, with good harvests.[1]

Moreover, apart from recurrent trade cyclical fluctuations, it is possible to denote alternate periods of ten or more years when the predominant tendency was for the price of grain to rise in relation to other agricultural prices or for other agricultural prices to rise in relation to the price of grain. These different phases or cycles are set out in Tables 23 and 24 and provide a key to the main trends in the agrarian economy during our period. The outstanding feature of those years, when grain prices surged upwards, was relative economic stagnation or decline; whereas in the alternate periods when corn was cheap, the economy was buoyant and growth comparatively rapid.

Doubtless, part of the explanation of these different phases can be traced to deliberate shifts in the balance of agricultural production in favour of one or another branch of farming activity. When grain prices were relatively low consumers would have surplus purchasing power to spend on other things and these would tend to rise in price, while producers would be encouraged to move out of corn into the

[1] W. H. Beveridge, 'British Exports and the Barometer', *Econ. Journ.* XXX, 1920, pp. 13–25, 209–13; 'Weather and Harvest Cycles', *Econ. Journ.*, XXXI, 1921, pp. 429–52; W. S. Jevons, *The Solar Period and the Price of Corn*, 1875; *The Periodicity of Commercial Crises and its Physical Explanation*, 1878; *Commercial Crises and Sun-spots*, 1879—all reprinted in *Investigations in Currency and Finance*, 2nd edn, London, 1909. See also H. S. Jevons, *The Causes of Unemployment, The Sun's Heat and Trade Activity*, London, 1910; 'Trade Fluctuations and Solar Activity', *Contemporary Review*, August, 1909; H. L. Moore, *Economic Cycles: their Law and Cause*, New York, 1914; *Generating Economic Cycles*, New York, 1923; W. G. Hoskins, 'Harvest Fluctuations and English Economic History, 1480–1619', AHR XII, 1964, pp. 31–3.

Table 23. *Percentage change in average annual price and volume*

Percentage change in average annual price — Harvest years

Commodity	1450–61/1462–86	1462–86/1487–1503	1487–1503/1504–18	1504–18/1519–36	1519–36/1537–48	1537–48/1549–73	1549–73/1574–84	1574–84/1585–1600	1585–1600/1601–20	1601–20/1621–49
Grain	−2	+6	+2	+49	+2	+104	+15	+49	+3	+26
Wool	+29	−11	+12	+9	+19	+45	+21	+14	+25	+9
Wethers	+27	−2	+23	+17	+27	+73	+23	+8	+21	+30
Lambs	+15	−8	+17	+41	+22	+55	+28	+20	+9	+17

Percentage change in average annual volume — Calendar years

Commodity	1450–62/1462–82		1510–19/1520–37	1520–37/1538–47	1538–47/1550–73	1550–73/1574–85	1574–85/1586–1600	1586–1600/1601–20	1601–20/1622–40
Total exports of wool and cloth[a]	+15	—	—	—	−8	+6	+0·4[c]	+7[d]	−15[e]
Exports of short-cloths from London[b]	—	—	−7	+20	—	—	—	—	—

[a] Based on figures given in M. Postan, 'The Trade of Medieval Europe', *The Cambridge Economic History of Europe*, ed. M. Postan and E. E. Rich, Cambridge, 1952, ii, p. 193; L. Stone, 'State Control in Sixteenth-Century England', EcHR, xvii, 1947, p. 119.

[b] Based on figures given in F. J. Fisher, 'Commercial Trends and Policy in Sixteenth-century England', EcHR, x, 1940, p. 96; 'London's Export Trade in the Early Seventeenth Century', EcHR, 2nd ser., iii, 1950, p. 153. These figures exclude exports of raw wool and worsted fabrics and exports of woollen cloth from the provincial ports. In the period 1549–73 exports of raw wool almost completely dwindled away, while exports of worsted cloth were also of relatively small importance. Subsequently, especially after the beginning of the seventeenth century, there was a marked expansion in the export of worsted fabrics. Throughout the period the overwhelming bulk of cloth exports were shipped from London.

[c] Statistics of cloth exports in the famine years of 1595–7 are not available. Had they been included, the figure in the table would probably indicate a substantial decline.

[d] Owing to the probable decline in the preceding period (*vide* [c] above) and to the fact that statistics of shipments by alien merchants are not available for every year, this figure almost certainly underestimates the growth in cloth exports.

[e] This figure probably underestimates the decline in cloth shipments (*vide* [d] above).

production of these other, more profitable, commodities. Eventually, this movement would lead to a shortage of grain and a rise in its relative price, as a result of which producers would again find it profitable to devote more attention to cereals. This argument, of course, assumes that farmers possessed the necessary flexibility to switch from one crop to another in response to relative price movements. Most large farmers had room for manœuvre, within limits. But there must also have been many producers who were greatly restricted in their activities by limitations of marketing, capital, or soil.

The main explanation of these price cycles, however, seems to lie less with the decisions of planned farming enterprise than with the impersonal intervention of the weather, which affected not only crops, but also, indirectly, population. Periods of predominantly good weather and predominantly bad weather appear to have alternated with considerable regularity. Moreover, one finds that records of contemporary complaints about severe weather conditions relate primarily to phases when grain prices were relatively high and when outbreaks of disease (with the notable exception of the London plague of 1603) were most severe. The main explanation would seem to be that in a good weather cycle the low price of subsistence and the reduced incidence of disease encouraged population to grow comparatively rapidly. In the ensueing phase of worsened climatic conditions population was found to have outgrown the means of subsistence. The Malthusian checks of famine and pestilence thus served to restrict further growth for a period, and in some cases, as with the 'Sweating Sickness' of 1551 (from which 50,000 people were estimated to have died in England), the dreadful famine of 1556, and the virulent plague of 1563, probably exacted such a toll that population took some years to recover.[1] The pressure on grain supplies would eventually be eased as a result of improved weather conditions, aided by a possible reduction of population, and a switch to grain on the part of some producers affected by a relative fall in the prices of other commodities.

Since the income-elasticity of demand for clothing was high, the sheep-farming industry was particularly sensitive to changes in harvest conditions, and its fortunes fluctuated inversely with the level of grain prices at home and abroad. A long run of good harvests meant a rising demand for clothing and the need for more wool. Under such conditions, cloth exports increased, wool prices rose, and the sheep-farming industry expanded. It seems quite clear from Table 23 that the urge towards increased wool production was very strongly felt in the years 1462–86, when the average annual price of wool was almost one third

[1] Barbara Winchester, *Tudor Family Portrait*, London, 1955, p. 272; Creighton, *op. cit.*, pp. 304, 470, 477; Hoskins, AHR XII, 1964, p. 36.

higher than in the previous period. On the evidence of prices alone it seems possible to pinpoint these years as marking the most destructive phase in the sheep enclosure-movement. But other evidence is not lacking. The author of the *Discourse of the Common Weal*, an acute Midland observer, stated that the great decay of husbandry was before the reign of King Henry VII (i.e. before 1485), while the impressive array of case-histories, investigated by Professor M. W. Beresford in his work on depopulated villages, lends irrefutable support to this view.[1]

The evidence of relatively high grain prices and relatively low wool prices during the next sixteen years or so, suggests that this spectacular phase in the development of the sheep-farming industry was succeeded by a period of contracting demand. In the early years of the sixteenth century, however, demand revived and wool growers enjoyed a further period of rising prosperity. In the years 1450–62, before the boom in sheep farming had commenced, annual exports of raw wool and cloth (allowing $4\frac{1}{3}$ cloths to one sack of wool) had averaged 15,690 sacks of wool or its equivalent. By the decade 1511–20 this figure had risen to 30,440 sacks. Following two exceptionally good harvests on the continent, a peak export was reached in 1519–20 of 35,890 sacks: a level that was not to be attained again until the boom years of the 1540's. The rise in the price of wool which accompanied this growth in export demand (and also, it may be assumed, home demand) encouraged the resumption and expansion of demesne agriculture by monastic and lay landowners alike. The flocks of Norwich Cathedral Priory, which had averaged some 2,700 sheep in the 1470's, increased to a peak of more than 8,600 sheep in 1517 (a year of exceptionally high wool prices and the appointment of the first royal commission on Depopulation) and thereafter declined. In 1520–1 Sir William Fermour of East Barsham, Norfolk, possessed some 17,000 sheep, distributed among twenty-five flocks; but, by this time, the boom was already receding, and a sharp contraction followed. While grain prices continued on an upward trend, wool prices in the years 1520–35 were, on average, 4 per cent lower than those in 1511–20. During the same period the volume of wool and cloth exports fell by 13 per cent to an annual average of 26,560 sacks, the growth of cloth exports being more than offset by a decline in the shipment of wool.[2]

By 1537 another cycle of good harvests had set in, providing the

[1] Lamond, *op. cit.*, p. lxiii; M. W. Beresford, *The Lost Villages of England*, London, 1954, pp. 142, 148; 'The Lost Villages of Medieval England', *Geog. Journ.*, CXVII, 1951, pp. 145–6.

[2] K. J. Allison, *The Wool Supply and the Worsted Cloth Industry in Norfolk in the Sixteenth and Seventeenth Centuries*, University of Leeds Ph.D. thesis, 1955, p. xli; Simpson, *op. cit.*, pp. 182–3.

necessary purchasing power and incentive for a resurgence of sheep-farming activition. Both date and motive are clearly stated by the Husbandman in the *Discourse:* "manie of vs saw, xij yere ago [i.e. 1537], that oure proffittes was but small by the plowes; and therefore divers of my neighboures that had, in times past, some two, some thre, some fowre plowes of their owne, have laid downe some of them [parte, and som of theym] all theire teames, and turned ether part or all theire arable grounde into pasture, and therby have wexed verie Rich men." The year 1548 marked the last of a series of exceptional harvests and the appointment of the second royal commission on Depopulation. Even before the crash of 1550–1 some producers had ceased to expand their sheep-farming activities, and with the sharp decline of cloth exports and wool prices in the early 1550's the business of raising sheep lost much of its former attraction.[1]

Exports of cloth and raw wool in the third quarter of the sixteenth century were at a distinctly lower level than in the boom years of the late 1540's. Assuming that there was a proportionate contraction in the home market for cloth, the total demand for English wool in the third quarter of the century was only between two thirds and three quarters of demand in the years immediately preceding 1550. Supply had now to adjust itself to a lower level of demand, and it was not until the late 1570's that wool prices showed any definite tendency to rise. Many large landowners who had been drawn into wool production during the earlier period of rising demand now decided to reduce the size of their flocks or to give up sheep farming altogether. In Northamptonshire the Fitzwilliams were leasing out whole manors in 1549, and by 1576, at the latest, even the home farm at Milton had ceased to support sheep. Subsequently, a comparatively small number were kept on the family's newly acquired estate at Dogsthorpe, a hamlet of Peterborough. Similarly, the Brudenells of Deene, Northants., began to abandon wool production after 1551, at first on their Leicestershire pastures and then elsewhere. In East Anglia Sir Nicholas Bacon, the rising lawyer, had six flocks totalling about four thousand sheep in 1556. By 1561 the foldcourses on which these sheep ran had all been leased, and the same practice was followed with subsequent acquisitions of land. Indications of a substantial fall in the size of the total sheep population during the third quarter of the sixteen century are suggested, not only by the aforementioned facts, but also by a consideration of certain other price movements. We find, for example, that sheepskins, which are a by-product of wool production, doubled in price between 1550–9

[1] Lamond, *op. cit.*, p. 56; W. Salt Lib., D 1734, 2–4 Edward VI (not numbered); D 1734, 56; K. J. Allison, 'Flock Management in the Sixteenth and Seventeenth Centuries', EcHR, 2nd Ser., XI, 1958, p. 100.

and 1560–9, and continued to rise at a less rapid rate thereafter. If this suggests a reduced supply of pelts as compared with the earlier period, the tendency of pea and bean prices to fall in the decades before 1580 suggests a reduced demand for feed.[1]

The price of grain, which had almost doubled between 1540–9 and 1550–9, fell slightly in the subsequent decade, owing partly, it would seem, to fewer years of severe harvest failure, and partly to an expansion in the area devoted to corn production. The increase in the acreage under grain was achieved in several ways. More land was taken in from the unproductive waste; many acres of pasture were probably converted to tillage; more intensive rotations may have been used, giving more years of grain crops and fewer fallows; and arable land was reallocated with less emphasis on fodder crops such as peas and beans. We should also expect the relatively greater rise in the prices of inferior cereals to encourage grain growers to give more attention to these crops and less to wheat. Some of these tendencies were clearly at work in Leicestershire during this period. Comparing the distribution of arable land in the county in 1558 with that in the early years of the sixteenth century, Dr Hoskins found a substantial decline in the proportion of land devoted to pulses and wheat, and a marked increase in that given over to rye and oats.[2]

By the early 1570's the demand and supply of grain were tending towards equilibrium, and with the return of better harvests the economy again entered upon a phase of comparatively rapid growth. A partial recovery was made in cloth exports, but probably more important in providing an impetus to the revival of sheep farming in the Midlands and East Anglia was the growth in the production of the new draperies, these being worsted fabrics made wholly or in part from long-staple wool. The growing raw material requirements of this new manufacture was clearly the main reason why the Clopton family of Kentwell, in Suffolk, extended their sheep-farming interests in the 1570's and early 1580's, making periodic purchases of long-wool Northamptonshire and Norfolk sheep. References to dairy cattle and beef animals also figure prominently in this family's account books during much of the period, but such references cease after 1582. Another landowner to be attracted by the profits from wool at this time was Sir Thomas Tresham of Rushton, Northants., who turned sheep farmer in the 1570's and by January 1581 had a total flock of 3,600 head.[3]

This boom in the economy, however, was of comparatively short

---

[1] Finch, op. cit., pp. 114, 117, 122, 147; Northants. RO, F. (M) Misc. vol. 52.
[2] Hoskins, op. cit., p. 169.
[3] Bowden, op. cit., pp. 64–5, 130; BM Harl. MS 127, ff. 17–33; Finch, op. cit., pp. 73–5.

duration. A series of severe crop failures and plague epidemics in the last fifteen years of the sixteenth century depressed trade and cast an air of gloom over the country. Cloth exports stagnated, and while some sheep farmers maintained their flocks, others, like John Isham of Lamport, Northants., cut back their production of wool.[1]

Economic revival came at the turn of the century with the beginning of an exceptional cycle of good harvests, which continued until 1620. In England the long-term rise in the price of grain was halted, while in western Europe wheat prices in the period 1601–20 were, on average, 14 per cent lower than in the years 1585–1600. This stimulus generated a rate of economic growth which was probably as great, if not greater, than in any other comparable period of our study. As in the case of other periods of bouyant demand, growth was greatest in the wool-textile industry. There was a marked expansion in the output and export of woollen cloth, and a much more spectacular development in the production of worsted fabrics. Since the new draperies were well suited to the Spanish and Mediterranean markets, the ending of the Anglo-Spanish war in 1604 provided the worsted industry with an additional stimulus to growth. By 1620 the volume of worsted exports was possibly treble that at the beginning of the seventeenth century.[2]

This expansion of the wool-textile industry brought with it a rising demand for wool, and sheep farmers were not slow in responding. Contemporary complaints made in the early years of the seventeenth century about the conversion of arable land to pasture give emphasis to this point. Some large landowners who had abandoned direct farming for the market in former years of trade depression were now lured back by the expectation of high profits from the sale of wool. The Fitzwilliams of Northamptonshire, for example, resumed their pastures in or before 1605, and their sheep-farming activities were no longer confined to Milton or Dogsthorpe but embraced surrounding manors which the family owned. Other landowners extended the scale of existing sheep-farming enterprises, adding to their flocks and utilizing additional pastures whenever possible. Among these was Sir Thomas Temple of Stowe, who had more than 6,600 sheep (excluding lambs) grazing on lands in Buckinghamshire, Warwickshire, and Leicestershire in 1605. Temple's receipts from the sale of wool in this year exceeded £1,260, as compared with receipts which were never in excess of £800 in the 1590's.[3]

The events leading up to the economic collapse of the early 1620's have already been described. Coming after a period of unusual abund-

[1] Finch, op. cit., pp. 19, 74; Simpson, op. cit., p. 190; Northants. RO, F (M) Misc. vol. 52.   [2] Fisher, EcHR, 2nd Ser., III, 1950, pp. 153, 155.
[3] Finch, op. cit., pp. 115, 117, 128; Henry E. Huntington Library, ST 48.

ance and prosperity, the contrast in conditions was striking. Bad
harvests, plague outbreaks, poverty, and unemployment were among
the dominant characteristics of this and the two subsequent decades.
The woollen-cloth industry was as depressed in the 1640's as it had been
twenty years earlier. Efforts to export cloth to western Europe, also
struggling in the throes of economic malaise, were made even more
difficult by a deterioration in the quality of English wool, which had
been very gradually changing its character since the days of the early
Tudors. An increasing proportion of longer and coarser wool was
being produced. This wool was eminently suitable for use by the worsted
industry, whose exports (mainly to southern Europe and the East)
continued on an upward trend throughout the period, thus providing
the most encouraging feature in an otherwise very gloomy picture.
The demands of the worsted manufacturers for more raw material,
however, failed to make the business of wool production as profitable
as it had been in the early decades of the century—even in the Midlands,
where the bulk of the country's long-staple wool was produced. The
English wool-grower's position, already undermined by the chronic
depression in the domestic cloth industry, was further aggravated by
increased imports of the raw material from Ireland and Spain. The
price of wool remained low; and many landowners let their sheep
pastures or turned their attention to other forms of farming enterprise.
In 1622, a year which saw the lowest wool prices for more than three
decades, the Ishams of Lamport were leasing out grazing land, while
still apparently retaining a direct interest in sheep. In 1623 and 1624
Sir Thomas Temple of Stowe disposed of his flocks and established a
system of leaseholds on his pastures. A few years later the Fitzwilliams
of Milton followed his example. In 1628 Sir George Heneage of Hainton, in Lincolnshire, sold the bulk of his sheep for £400 and let out
some of his best grazing land. In November 1630 Lionel Cranfield,
first earl of Middlesex, had more than 6,780 sheep and lambs, besides
cattle, grazing on his recently acquired estates in the west Midlands.
Within four years his flocks had been reduced by more than half and
some of his pastures let out on lease. Even the Spencers of Althorp,
the outstanding flock masters of the age, lost their appetite for sheep
farming in the conditions of the second quarter of the seventeenth
century. By 1639 the family flocks in Warwickshire and Northamptonshire had been reduced to about one third their former size of 10,000
sheep plus lambs, and in the next few years direct farming was abandoned altogether.[1]

[1] Bowden, *op. cit.*, pp. 6–7, 25–7, 43–5, 214–17; Finch, *op. cit.*, pp. 31, 46, 48,
130, 166; E. F. Gay, 'The Temples of Stowe and their Debts', *Huntington Lib. Quart.*,
II, 1938–9, p. 430; Lincs. AO, HEN. 3/2; Kent AO, U 269, A 421; U 269, A 423.

How far the pastures let out by landowners like Spencer in periods of reduced profitability continued to support sheep, and how far they were used for cattle grazing or tillage, cannot be determined. Doubtless much depended on the nature of the land, the accessibility of markets, and the covenants of leases. What does seem to emerge fairly clearly from our study, however, is that for many large Midland landowners, decisions about commercial agriculture and the scale of demesne farming hinged primarily upon the demand for wool. This appears to have been almost as true of the early seventeenth century as it does of the late fifteenth, in spite of a long-term tendency for sheep prices to rise in comparison with wool prices, this suggesting a growing appreciation of the sheep as a supplier of meat, dung, and pelt, as against wool.

It may be safely assumed that sheep's dung increased in value in periods of rising grain prices, and in areas where the lightness of the arable land necessitated heavy application of manure, as in the sheep-corn regions of Norfolk and Wiltshire. Here sheep numbers might be maintained, and even increased, in spite of a contraction in the demand for wool. Thus, Sir Richard Southwell of Wood Rising, in Norfolk, possessed an average of approximately 16,850 sheep in 1561–2, as compared with 14,170 in 1544–5.[1]

It seems reasonable to suppose that the *per capita* consumption of mutton and lamb, like that of clothing, tended to decline in periods when poor harvests predominated. Since, however, mutton did not figure prominently in the diet of the lower classes, the income-effect of high bread prices was presumably smaller than in the case of cloth, and overall demand more inelastic. This being so, wool growers whose pastures were eminently suitable for the grazing of sheep, or who for other reasons decided to stay in the industry, had an incentive to concentrate more of their attention upon the production of meat— possibly lamb, but, more especially, prime mutton. The latter entailed an increase in the proportion of wether sheep in the flock, and one would expect this to be reflected in a tendency for the price of wethers to rise more than the prices of other types of sheep and that of wool. A greater emphasis on mutton production appears to have been the main reason why the number of wethers kept by Sir George Heneage, in Lincolnshire, increased, while the proportion of ewes among his sheep declined from 53 per cent in 1618–20 to 23 per cent in 1633–5.[2]

Whether sheep farmers were willing, or even able, to devote their attention to the production of mutton depended, among other things, on the scale of their enterprise and their accessibility to consumers, especially in the larger urban centres. In the Tudor and early Stuart

[1] Allison, *thesis*, pp. xlv–l.
[2] Fussell, *The English Rural Labourer*, pp. 26–9; Lincs. AO, HEN. 3/2.

periods the market for meat was probably never uppermost in the minds of the smallest farmers. The fattening and sale of stock required time, capital, and a knowledge of marketing techniques, and in all these small men were deficient. But even among large producers there is little evidence to support the view sometimes put forward that the mutton market was the primary reason for sheep-farming activities in early Tudor times. The complete absence of price data for beef before the mid-sixteenth century and for mutton before the early seventeenth, together with the fact that many large households and institutions purchased livestock for the kitchen, and not carcasses—a practice which Eton College, for example, continued until the seventeenth century— suggests that the market for meat was very poorly organized before Elizabeth's reign. In the 1540's and 1550's large Norfolk sheep farmers, like Sir Roger Townshend of East Rainham, Coke of Holkham, and Sir Henry Bedingfield of Oxborough, were selling prime sheep, presumably for use as mutton, but many of their sales were of poor quality stock. At this time, and possibly for more than a century afterwards, the market for meat was supplied with many old, weak, and inferior animals, which were sold either because of a shortage of feed or to make way for stock of higher quality. In the years 1548–51 between one half and two thirds of the sheep pastured at Misterton, in Leicestershire, were ewes. Wethers, as well as oxen, were fattened, but the majority of these were eventually despatched, along with other provisions, to the Paget household at Drayton, in Middlesex. Receipts from the sale of sheep between 1550 and 1554 at no time approached receipts from the sale of wool, and many of the animals which were marketed were noted in the estate account books as being "refuse," "barren," "sick," or "giddy." In only one of these years (1553–4) was the sale made of a substantial number of fat wethers. A basically similar situation was to be found in many other parts of the country at an even later period. On estates in, for example, Lancashire and York-shire (in the 1570's), Buckinghamshire, and Warwickshire (in the 1600's), Lincolnshire, Worcestershire, and Gloucestershire (in the 1630's), a number of substantial and great flock masters, at least, were relying much more upon wool than upon mutton for their income. Similarly, although west country store beasts were coming into Kent as early as the 1530's, indications from later in the century suggest that, with the exception of prime beef produced for the household, many large arable farmers fattened their cattle only at the end of a useful working life.[1]

[1] Simpson, *op. cit.*, p. 192; Rogers, *Agriculture and Prices*, v, pp. 406–7; Allison, EcHR, 2nd Ser., XI, 1958, pp. 108–9; Bowden, *op. cit.*, pp. 4, 8–10; W. Salt Lib., D 1734/22, 24, 38, 56, 2–4 Edward VI (not numbered), 4–5 Edward VI (not numbered);

It is not until the latter half of the sixteenth century that evidence begins to accumulate of the growth of a market-orientated livestock fattening industry of any significance. The main impulse to this development came from the growth of the London food market, and it was in districts adjoining the capital—above all, in the Wealden and marshy coastal regions of the south-east—that specialization on fattening was most pronounced. Already, by the late 1550's, Sir William Petre of Ingatestone, Essex, was placing the emphasis of his demesne farming activities on stock-fattening, mainly of cattle but also other livestock, and was selling considerable numbers of animals to butchers from London and elsewhere. Before the end of the century metropolitan demand was making itself felt much further afield, encouraging an enterprising handful of market-conscious farmers to give more attention to the production of meat. In the summer of 1565, for example sales made by the Northamptonshire Spencers included 706 fat wethers sold to the butchers of London. In the year ending October 1577 a total of 3,071 lambs and 2,765 sheep (including 1,800 wethers) were sold, partly to local butchers, but mainly, it would seem to London men. The lambs were almost certainly home-bred, but it is clear from the family estate accounts that some of the sheep were purchased during the year in order to be fattened for the butcher. At a slightly later date Sir Thomas Tresham of Rushton, was also selling substantial numbers of sheep: some at Northampton, others in London. In 1581 a Buckinghamshire dealer owed him £400 for fat sheep which had subsequently been resold at Smithfield. At the end of the sixteenth century Sir John Dormer of Rousham, who had extensive pastures in Oxfordshire and Buckinghamshire, was buying large numbers of sheep and cattle for grazing and ultimate despatch to markets in London and its vicinity. In the year 1600, he received at least £797 from the sale of sheep and £1,690 from the sale of cattle. Further expansion of the business brought in gross receipts of almost £8,750 from the sale of cattle, sheep, hides, and fells in the seven-month period 25 March—30 October 1616. Many hundreds of wethers were purchased by Dormer in Wiltshire and elsewhere, while oxen and bullocks were bought mainly at Coventry, Tamworth, Burton, and other places in the west and north Midlands. The pastoral regions of northern and western England were thus caught up in the growth of metropolitan demand, since it was in these districts that many of the livestock destined to satisfy the

Finch, *op. cit.*, p. 18; W. F. Rea, 'The Rental and Accounts of Sir Richard Shireburn, 1571–77', *Lancs. & Ches. Hist. Soc.*, CX, 1959, p. 50; Henry E. Huntington Library, ST. 48; E. F. Gay, *op. cit.*, pp. 421–2; Kent AO, U 269, A 423; Lincs. AO, H 97, 22/1, 2; R. Trow-Smith, *A History of British Livestock Husbandry to 1700*, London, 1957, pp. 188–9.

appetites of Londonders, were bred. The early seventeenth-century account-books of the Toke family, who occupied lands in the Kentish Weald and Romney Marsh, are full of references to "northern" and "country" steers and other beasts. In the years 1618 and 1619 Nicholas Toke estimated that, on average, sheep accounted for 58 per cent of the family's farming assets. A further 20 per cent was attributed to other livestock (mainly oxen and steers "a fattinge") and 11 per cent to wool. Hay, arable crops, and other produce accounted for the remaining 11 per cent. In subsequent valuations made by Toke in the years 1624–30 sheep accounted for an average of only 16 per cent of the gross value of stock and produce, while other livestock were credited with 34 per cent. There was a sharp increase in the relative importance of arable crops and other commodities, these now constituting approximately half the total assets of the enterprise. Considerable quantities of wheat and barley were being grown in the 1620's, but the main expansion was in the output of fodder crops, notably oats, beans, peas, and tares. The fattening of livestock remained a major part of the undertaking, but in the latter part of the decade Toke developed an interest in dairy farming, producing quantities of butter and cheese for sale, while pig-keeping and hop production also claimed more of his attention. These various changes in the farming pattern were doubtless partly due to the fact that at some time between 1619 and 1624, Toke gave up valuable marshland grazings at Cheynecourte, though whether voluntarily or not is uncertain. But it also seems reasonable to suppose that, in part, these changes represented adjustments in response to the pull of market forces, and, in particular, to the reduced profitability of sheep.[1]

Cattle grazing and dairying were not, of course, carried on only as a poor second choice to sheep farming. In some pastoral regions physical conditions were much more suitable for cattle than for sheep; and given accessibility to markets, farmers in such regions were probably little influenced by the ebb and flow in the demand for wool and mutton. In other, more marginal, areas the balance between different pastoral activities was doubtless largely determined, at least as far as market-conscious farmers were concerned, by the relative movements in the prices of the main animal products. We should, however, expect there to be a tendency for these prices to move together, since any large swings in consumer demand would be likely to affect all

[1] W. R. Emerson, *The Economic Development of the Estates of the Petre Family in Essex in the Sixteenth and Seventeenth Centuries*, University of Oxford D.Phil. thesis, 1951, pp. 330–1; Finch, *op. cit.*, pp. 42, 75; Lord Dormer's Papers, 1600–30 (in the possession of T. Cottrell-Dormer, Esq., of Rousham Hall, Oxfordshire); W. Salt. Lib., D 1734, 110, 111, 123; Eleanor C. Lodge, (ed.), *The Account Book of a Kentish Estate, 1616–1704*, Oxford, 1927, *passim;* BM Add. MS 34162; 34163; 34166.

animal products in greater or lesser degree. A comparison of Table 23 and Table 24 lends support to this view. The inverse price relationship with grain, already noted in the case of wool, will be seen to apply also to dairy produce and beef. But since the income-elasticity of demand for wool was greater than for the other products, its price increased relatively more in periods when good harvests predominated and less in periods when crops were poor.

On turning more specifically to Table 24, a comparison of oxen and hide prices, on the one hand, with those of kine, calves, and dairy produce, on the other, lends weight to contemporary assertions that the early Tudor enclosure movement was partly motivated by a desire to keep more bullocks and oxen, as well as more sheep. Though the first great spate of depopulating enclosures in the period 1462–86 was apparently directed solely at the production of wool, the resurgence of pasture farming in the years 1504–18 and 1537–48 appears from the evidence of prices, as well as from the statements of contemporaries, to have embraced beef and draught animals as well as sheep. In both of these latter periods the price of oxen substantially increased, while the price of hides (a by-product of cattle farming) changed comparatively little. The relatively greater rise in the price of hides than of oxen in the years 1519–36, when harvests were poor, suggests that sheep farming may not have been the only pastoral industry to contract at this time. Similarly, in the depressed conditions of the second quarter of the seventeenth century, a decline in the numbers of oxen and bullocks can be noted in the account-books of more than one substantial grazier. At the same time, a growth in the import of Irish cattle added to the English stock-breeder's difficulties. The Petres of Ingatestone, who had let out some of their cattle-fattening pastures in 1551, abandoned demesne farming completely for a period after 1638, and they were not the only large graziers to do so. How far the production of hides was a mere by-product of cattle farming, incidental to the business of providing meat for the table or stamina for the plough, is a moot question. The manufacture of leather goods—footwear, gloves, belts, saddles, bellows, and the like—was a major industrial activity, second only to that of cloth; and although the industry was most highly localized in the London area, where it was based upon abundant supplies of hides resulting from the traffic in meat, there were also important centres in cattle rearing and grazing districts, such as south Yorkshire, the east and west Midlands, the Weald, and the forest of Dean. Accounts relating to the provisioning of the army in 1513 attribute one third of the value of oxen purchased to their hides and tallow. On the other hand, the average price received for ox-hides sold by Eton College in the years 1566–1600 was one eighth of that

Table 24. *Percentage change in average annual price*

Commodity	Harvest years									
	1450–61/ 1462–86	1462–86/ 1487–1503	1487–1503/ 1504–18	1504–18/ 1519–36	1519–36/ 1537–48	1537–48/ 1549–73	1549–73/ 1574–84	1574–84/ 1585–1600	1585–1600/ 1601–20	1601–20/ 1621–49
Dairy produce	+11	+2	−10	+10	+23	+75	+9	+28	+14	+11
Beef	—	—	—	—	—	—	+7	+26	+22	+17
Hides	−8	+33	+12	+35	+3	+47	+22	+18	+14	+20
Calves	+19	−21	+57	+1	+12	+76	+41	+12	+19	+27
Dairy cattle	+24	−22	−2	+64	+13	+80	+42	+25	+17	+22
Oxen	−8	−8	+28	+25	+22	+59	+21	+20	+16	+16

paid for live oxen purchased for slaughter. It seems unlikely that the value of tallow could account completely for the difference between this and the 1513 figure, and the most likely explanation is that, by the end of the sixteenth century, beef-producing animals were being valued relatively more for their meat and relatively less for their hides than they had been at the beginning of the Tudor period, in spite of an expansion in the long-term demand for leather goods in the intervening years. Table 24 suggests that it was in the closing decades of the sixteenth century that this growing emphasis on meat made itself most strongly felt. From then onwards, the prices of oxen, beef, and hides did not widely diverge as they had done hitherto, but moved much more closely together. This development is significant. It suggests an improvement in the organization of the market, which doubtless owed much to the increasing activity of middlemen, common carriers and drovers, and to the establishment of direct contact with producers by some of the big retailers from the larger towns, especially London.[1]

The operation of similar tendencies is discernible in the movement of the prices of kine, calves, and dairy produce. Table 24 suggests that, whatever the reason for keeping cows in the early Tudor period, it had no strong connection with the market for milk, butter, and cheese. The relationship between the prices of dairy cattle and calves, on the other hand, was much closer, even if, at times, it was a negative relationship. The large rise in the price of calves in the period 1504–18 seems to have been clearly due to a decline in the number of dairy cattle in the face of increased competition for pasture from sheep and bullocks. In the subsequent years, 1519–36, the demand for kine greatly increased, and so presumably did the supply, since there was a sharp fall in the relative price of calves. The greatly increased demand for dairy cattle during these years is interesting. We must reject the hypothesis that this was mainly due to large farmers switching from other, temporarily less profitable, forms of livestock husbandry to the commercial production of milk, butter, and cheese. Not only were the necessary price incentives to do this lacking, but prevailing market conditions were generally unfavourable for the wholesale disposal of produce of this type. Some large farmers may indeed have kept more kine and reared calves, in place of sheep and oxen; but, if so, it was

[1] H. B. Cotterill (ed.), *The Utopia of Sir Thomas More*, 1937, p. 30; Lamond, *op. cit.*, pp. xlii, lxiii–lxv, 52–3, 149; Kent AO, U 269, A 421/1, 3, 4, 5; BM Add. MS 33147; Thirsk, *English Peasant Farming*, pp. 151, 192; *House of Commons Journals*, I, pp. 527, 615, 625; CSPD, 1621–23, pp. 393, 498; E. Lipson, *The Economic History of England*, III, London, 1947, pp. 198–200; Emerson, *thesis*, pp. 328–9; L. A. Clarkson, 'The Organisation of the English Leather Industry in the late Sixteenth and Seventeenth Centuries', EcHR, 2nd Ser., XIII, 1960, p. 245; LP, I, 1118; F. J. Fisher, EcHR, V, 1935, pp. 46–64.

undoubtedly the market for stock, and not dairy produce, which attracted them. There were also large institutions, such as Sion Monastery in Middlesex, Tavistock Abbey in Devon, and Sibton Abbey in Suffolk, which possessed considerable numbers of cows, but these were kept mainly, if not entirely, for the provisioning of the household. It was, however, among small farmers and cottagers that the main market for dairy cattle existed. It therefore seems probable that the fundamental reasons for the marked rise in the price of dairy cattle in the years 1519–36 were an increase in dairying activity in districts where small peasants predominated and a substantial growth in the number of poor farmers and near-landless cottagers, who produced milk, butter, and cheese from grazing on the common.[1]

It was not, it may be suggested, until towards the end of the sixteenth century that dairy farming ceased to be an almost exclusive province of the poorer sections of rural society, and began to be organized on wider commercial lines. With the improved marketing outlets which we have already noted in connection with the meat trade, substantial farmers in districts physically best suited to dairy farming but hitherto tied to the production of beef, mutton, or wool, now found it possible to turn their attention to the output of butter and cheese. In this, they may also have been influenced by the fact that dairy production brings in quicker returns than meat fattening: a not unimportant consideration in such uncertain years as the 1590's or 1630's. Nevertheless, the small man continued as a major support of the industry throughout the period.

C. EXPENDITURE AND INCOME

1. *Introduction*

The profitability of any farming enterprise depended not only upon the prices received for produce and stock, but also upon the costs of production and distribution incurred by the farmer. Our information about costs is, unfortunately, piecemeal, and for it we are dependent upon two main types of record: manorial accounts compiled by officials in the employ of large landowners; and the personally written farm accounts of substantial yeoman and gentry who played a direct part in commercial agriculture. Both types of record have drawbacks which seriously impair their usefulness for any assessment of profitability. Normally no clear distinction is drawn in contemporary accounts between capital and income; no allowance is made for the depreciation of capital assets; farming and non-farming expenditures are occasionally lumped together; little or no attempt is made to

[1] H. P. R. Finberg, *Tavistock Abbey*, Cambridge, 1951, pp. 135–44.

allocate overheads to different parts of the enterprise—indeed, overheads and other items of expenditure are often completely disregarded;
while the value of home-consumed produce is also frequently omitted.
Moreover, as Mr Batho points out elsewhere in this volume, manorial
accounts were essentially statements of the receipts and expenses of the
accountants (the bailiffs, sheep-reeves, and receivers) and not of the
estate. They were primarily concerned with the liability of the collectors
of revenue and not with the determination of profit. Bad debts were
not written off, but were carried forward year after year, merely for
the record.[1]

A much greater concern with the question of profit is revealed by the
surviving account-books of early seventeenth-century yeomen and
gentlemen farmers such as Nicholas Toke and Sir Roger Twysden of
Kent, Robert Loder of Berkshire, John Hatcher of Lincolnshire, and
Henry Best of the East Riding. These men, and others like them, took a
direct interest in the running of their estates, noting down particulars
of transactions, prices, costs, yields, and other matters relating to the
business of farming. The accounts which they left to posterity tell us
much; but unfortunately, these records suffer in varying degrees from
the defects already mentioned, and are insufficiently detailed or
comprehensive for profits to be accurately assessed. This did not
prevent some farmers from making the attempt; but the science of
accountancy was in its early stages, and the figures which were arrived
at should be viewed with great caution. They are probably of more
significance as indications of the businesslike approach of the compilers
than as accurate statements of their affairs. Our knowledge of small farm
units is even less complete, since the great mass of peasants were illiterate,
and no accounts for small-holdings (were any compiled) appear to have
survived. In spite of these various difficulties, however, it is still possible
to comment usefully on the cost-structure of farming in the Tudor and
early Stuart periods and to give some consideration to the question of
profitability.[2]

2. Arable farming

Most farming enterprises in the sixteenth and seventeenth centuries
were of a mixed character. Cereal growers needed livestock to maintain
the fertility of their soil, while transport difficulties compelled many

[1] D. Oschinsky, 'Medieval Treatises on Estate Accounting', EcHR, XVII, 1947,
pp. 52–7; Simpson, op. cit., pp. 3–9; Kent AO, U 269, A 421; U 269, A 423; BM
Add. MS 33147.
[2] Lodge, op. cit., BM Add. MS 34162; 34163; 34166; Robert Loder's Farm Accounts;
Lincs. AO, H 97, 22, 2, 3; C. B. Robinson, (ed.), Rural Economy in Yorkshire in 1641,
being the Farming and Account Books of Henry Best of Elmeswell in the East Riding of the
County of York, Surtees Soc., XXXIII, Durham, 1857.

pasture farmers to grow their own food and forage crops, apart from hay. For the purposes of this section of our study, however, we will endeavour to treat each of the main branches of agriculture separately.

Once we turn to a consideration of arable production it becomes apparent that the principal factor determining the farmer's livelihood was his crop yield. This in turn depended upon the efficiency of the farmer, the fertility of his land, and the influence of the climate, though not necessarily in that order. Crop yields varied greatly, not only from one farm to another but from one year to the next. On the demesne lands of the manor of Grantchester, which supplied King's College, Cambridge, with produce in the mid-fifteenth century, the yield of wheat in the years 1455–66 varied between 9·0 and 17·7 bushels per acre, averaging 13·6 bushels over the whole period. On newly enclosed lands at East Peckham in the Weald of Kent the yield in several years between 1639 and 1651 ranged from 11.7 to 14·6 bushels. A questionnaire survey conducted by the Royal Society in 1664–5 revealed even wider differences. On the lighter soils of Devon and Cornwall, for example, the average yield of wheat was stated to range between 10 and 25 bushels per acre according to the character of the season, while on marl land, which was better suited to the cultivation of oats than of other cereals, an average wheat yield of between 5 and 12 bushels was cited as normal. Variations in the size of the crop appear just as marked when measured in terms of the productivity of seed. At Grantchester, in the years already mentioned, the yield of wheat per bushel of seed sown varied between 2·56 and 5·22 bushels. On Robert Loder's farm at Harwell, Berks., in 1612–20, wheat yields ranged between five times and fifteen times, with an average return over the whole period of 10·2 bushels per bushel sown. Some years later, Sir Roger Twysden, who had estates at Great Chart and Romney Marsh, in Kent, was less fortunate. His notes on yields, covering the period 1639–56, suggest that in only one year (1654) did he obtain a return of seed which approximated to the average achieved by Loder in the second decade of the century: in most years his wheat crop showed only a threefold to sixfold increase on seed.[1]

Sufficient has been said for it to be apparent that the yield of wheat was extremely variable, and the same was also true of other grains. This great variability in yield, both from area to area and from year to

[1] J. Saltmarsh, 'A College Home-Farm in the Fifteenth Century', *Econ. Hist.* III, 1936, pp. 156, 165–8; Lord Beveridge, 'The Yield and Price of Corn in the Middle Ages', *Econ. Hist.*, I, 1927, p. 162; R. Lennard 'English Agriculture under Charles II: The Evidence of the Royal Society's "Enquiries"', *EcHR*, IV, 1932, pp. 39–41; *Robert Loder's Farm Accounts*, p. xvii; BM Add. MS 34162.

year, cautions us against placing any great reliance on fragmentary documentary evidence in appraising the average level and trend of crop yields in the country as a whole. M. K. Bennett, who was faced with this problem of unsatisfactory source-material, discarded the use of farm accounts altogether in estimating the yield of wheat in our period, basing his conclusions instead upon an analysis of Gregory King's statistical estimates of national income and output, published in 1695. As a result of his calculations, Bennett concluded that the average British wheat yield per acre increased by about 30 per cent between 1450 and 1650, rising from 8½ bushels to 11 bushels. A consideration of individual farm accounts and other relevant data tends to confirm an increase of the order suggested by Bennett, though his estimates of actual wheat yields, both in 1450 and 1650, may be slightly on the low side.[1]

In order to illustrate the importance of high crop yields to the arable farmer, and the nature of the expenditure incurred by him, we may construct a schedule of costs and output for a hypothetical farm of, say, 30 acres, which we will assume was in existence in the early years of the seventeenth century (see Table 25). For the purposes of our example, we will further assume that the farmer was of average efficiency, that the land which he occupied was moderately fertile, and that weather conditions during the harvest year in question were fair. Under such circumstances a crop yield of 12 bushels per acre for wheat and 16 bushels per acre for barley would have been reasonable. At the level of prices ruling in the early seventeenth century, we may estimate the total market value of the year's crop at £42 10s. 0d.

On the side of expenditure, we may note first of all, that a holding of 30 acres was generally too small to require hired workers. No entry is therefore made for labour costs, our farmer and his family working the land without outside assistance. It will be apparent from Table 25 that a major item of expenditure for the cereal grower was the cost of seed. Even if, as was often the case, the farmer used seed saved from his previous crop, this was a cost to him, and must be entered on the debit side of his account. In respect of the amount of seed used, contemporary practice varied considerably, depending upon the farmer's resources and prejudices and the type of soil. Examples have been found of wheat seed being sown at the rate of 2 bushels to the acre, while occasionally, as at Heighton St Clair in Sussex in 1562, as much as 4 bushels per acre were used. Our figure of 2½ bushels probably represents the most common practice. Similarly with barley—a crop which, like oats, was normally sown more thickly than wheat—sowing rates varied between about 3½ and 8 bushels to the acre. The latter figure was

[1] Bennett, op. cit., pp. 12–29.

Table 25. *Expenditure and output of hypothetical arable farm of 30 acres, c. 1600–20*

	Total cost £ s. d.	Cost per acre s.		Total output £ s. d.	Output per acre s.
Seed:			10 acres fallow	—	—
25 bushels wheat @ 3s. 9d.	4 13 9 }	6·46	10 acres wheat: 120 bushels @ 3s. 9d.	22 10 0	15·00
40 bushels barley @ 2s. 6d.	5 0 0 }		10 acres barley: 160 bushels @ 2s. 6d.	20 0 0	13·33
Rent: 30 acres @ 4s. 0d.	6 0 0	4·00			
Manure	1 2 6	0·75			
Feed for oxen	2 12 0	1·73			
Interest and capital depreciation:					
Onstock	2 18 2	1·94			
On equipment	19 4	0·64			
Miscellaneous (e.g. veterinary, marketing)	10 0 0	0·33			
Totals	23 15 9	15·86	Totals	42 10 0	28·33
			Tithes	4 5 0	2·83
				38 5 0	25·50
			Net Profit	14 9 3	9·64

exceptional; and the rate we have adopted for our farmer, of 4 bushels per acre, was probably close to the norm.[1]

A second major item of expenditure incurred by the arable farmer—assuming payment of the full current market value—was rent. The subject of rent will be discussed in detail later on, but for our present purpose we will assume that land is paid for at the rate of 4s. per acre, this being approximately the commercial rent which moderately good common-field land commanded in the early years of the seventeenth century. We will further assume that the rent paid by our farmer includes interest on the landlord's investment in buildings and improvements, and that the repair and maintenance of fixed capital on the holding is the landlord's responsibility.

In our example, it will be noted that the combined expenditure on rent and seed accounts for approximately two thirds of the farmer's outgoings. This proportion is extremely high by modern standards, and reflects the very uneconomical use of seed and land in earlier times. Other expenditures, which nowadays figure much more prominently in arable-farming costs, were less heavy. The cost of manure to the small cultivator in early Stuart times is difficult to estimate since we know practically nothing about the quantity used or its price. Information relating to later in the seventeenth century suggests that, over a period of years, some farmers with enclosed arable land spread an annual average of about three loads of manure on every acre, apart from other dressings. At this rate, 90 loads of dung would be required for 30 acres. An early seventeenth-century pamphleteer cites a price for manure of 6d. per load, and on this basis the annual cost of dunging 30 acres of enclosed land would amount to £2 5s. 0d. Our farmer, however, occupies common-field land, which would be used during part of the year for grazing the livestock of the village. We will therefore assume that he obtains half of his manure free of charge, and purchases the remainder at a cost of £1 2s. 6d. No allowance is made for other dressings, such as lime and marl, since it seems unlikely that small cultivators in early Stuart times could afford to apply them in worthwhile quantities.[2]

Many peasants who occupied arable land also possessed sheep, from

[1] See sources listed in notes   , pp.   above; Warw. RO, B 13, 998; Worcs. RO, 705, 24, 857; PRO E 133, 1625, Eliz. I; Fitzherbert, *The Boke of Husbondrie*, ed. W. W. Skeat, 1882, pp. 23, 40; J. Blagrave, *The Epitomie of the Art of Husbandry*, London, 1669, pp. 22–7; E. Kerridge, 'The Notebook of a Wiltshire Farmer in the Early Seventeenth Century', *Wilts. Arch. & Nat. Hist. Mag.*, LIV, 1951–2, pp. 417–19; Cornwall, *thesis*, pp. 116–17, 119.

[2] Lennard, EcHR, IV, 1932, pp. 32–4; Edward Maxey, *A New Instruction of Plowing and Setting the Corne, Handled in Manner of a Dialogue betweene a Ploughman and a Scholler*, London, 1601.

which an income was derived by means of the sale of wool, mutton, and pelts. In order to save unnecessary complication, the only livestock which we assume our farmer to posses sare four oxen for draught purposes. This appears to have been the minimum number necessary for the plough team. Many farmers, of course, used horses for draught; but where physical conditions were suitable, small men often preferred to employ oxen, since they were less costly to feed in winter, were cheaper to equip, and depreciated less in value. In calculating the cost of feed for our four oxen, it has been assumed that free pasturage on common land, supplemented by straw threshed from the farmer's crop, sufficed to maintain his stock during the spring and summer months, while our estimate of the cost of keep during the remainder of the year has been based on data relating to the amounts paid for agistment—i.e. a practice whereby a man took in some one else's stock to feed in return for a money payment or a share in the progeny of the stock. The amounts charged for this service varied, depending upon the type of animal, the current price of hay, and whether the object was to fatten or merely to keep alive. For oxen, agistment charges in the early seventeenth century appear to have generally ranged between about 4d. and 9d. a week per beast, though occasionally as much as 2s. was charged. Our figure of £2 12s. 0d. for the cost of feed is based on a weekly expenditure of 6d. per beast for 26 weeks. In order to calculate the depreciation on stock, we have assumed that oxen were purchased at £3 10s. 0d. each, and after five years of toil were re-sold at £2 apiece. Thus, we put the total original outlay at £14 and loss of value over the five-year period at £6. By discounting capital at the statutory rate of 10 per cent, we therefore arrive at a figure of £2 18s. 2d. for interest and depreciation on stock. If we add this amount to the expenditure on feed, we find that the farmer's four oxen were costing him £5 10s. 7d. a year: a substantial sum for a husbandman's very limited resources. This cost was evidently too much for many small peasant cultivators, who of necessity had to share a plough team, for we find inventories that list "halfe the teame" among the dead man's possessions.[1]

The sum which we have entered in Table 25 for interest and depreciation on equipment will appear exceedingly small to the eyes of a present-day arable farmer, for whom the operation, repair, and replacement of machinery is a major item of expenditure. The agricultural appliances of Tudor and Stuart times, however, were few, simple and

---

[1] Markham, *op. cit.*, pp. 146–7; J. Blagrave, *op. cit.*, pp. 9–10; Gloucs. RO, D 621, M 18; Lancs. RO, Derby MS. 1553, 51; Kent AO U 269, A 418/3, 5; BM Add. MS 34166, fo. 43ᵛ; Kerridge, *op. cit.*, p. 427; Trow-Smith, *op. cit.*, pp. 239–40; Hoskins, *op. cit.*, p. 149.

cheap. In sixteenth-century Leicestershire, Dr Hoskins found that the average farmer above the poorest possessed a plough, one or two carts, and two or three harrows, apart from such implements as spades, scythes, and rakes. Wagons and rollers were uncommon, even in the early seventeenth century. The farm gear of small cultivators was made mainly from wood, since equipment which used iron was very much more expensive. Many husbandmen probably fashioned some of their implements themselves, using timber to which they may have been entitled under the terms of their tenancy. In any case, the cost of construction by country carpenters and smiths was not high. The most expensive part of the arable farmer's equipment was the cart or wain, and the cost of this depended very largely upon whether the wheels were iron-shod or bare. In 1610, for example, King's College paid 15s. for a pair of new wheels, and 42s. 2d. for the tire of them. It seems very unlikely that small farmers would be able or willing to incur the latter expense. Other agricultural appliances were much cheaper. It was possible to buy a new plough for 1s. 8d. in Staffordshire in 1582, and for 3s. in Norfolk in 1621.[1] Altogether, it seems doubtful whether the small arable farmer's equipment in the early seventeenth century was worth more than about £3, and this is the figure which we have adopted for our calculations. We have further assumed that appliances were replaced every five years and have discounted capital at the same rate of interest as before. On the basis of these assumptions we find that only 4 per cent of our farmer's total expenditure was attributable to the cost of equipment. Clearly, this fact had considerable significance for the pattern of farming in our period; and the small capital outlay needed to equip the typical arable farm must have played an important part in deciding the majority of peasant cultivators to concentrate upon tillage or mixed farming rather than upon livestock husbandry, where total capital requirements were much greater.

Apart from the main items of cost already analysed, our hypothetical arable farmer was likely to be faced with some small expenses of an occasional nature. If his oxen fell sick he might find it necessary to purchase medicaments or have the cattle blooded. He might also incur some small marketing charges when purchasing supplies or disposing of produce. We have allocated an arbitrary sum of 10s. per year to cover these incidental outgoings. Since we have assumed our farmer to be paying a full market-value rent, we have made no estimate for the

[1] Hoskins, op. cit., pp. 149–50, 154; R. E. Prothero (Lord Ernle), English Farming Past and Present, London, 1912, pp. 91–2; C. M. L. Bouch and G. P. Jones, A Short Economic and Social History of the Lake Counties, 1500–1830, Manchester, 1961, p. 104. Rogers, Agriculture and Prices, v, p. 676; W. Salt Lib., D 1734, 118; Norwich Pub. Lib., Townshend Coll. 88, MS 1505, fo. 15; BM Add. MS 33147, fo. 17ᵛ.

payment of local rates and taxes. This was a burden which landlords sometimes passed on to tenants occupying under-rented holdings.[1]

In Table 25 the total value of the farmer's crop is estimated at £42 10s. 0d. After deduction of tithes, assuming that these were paid at the full rate, the profit remaining after all farming expenses have been met is £14 9s. 3d. Not unexpectedly, this sum compares favourably with the income of the agricultural wage-earner in the early years of the seventeenth century. At the prevailing ordinary wage-rate of 8d. per day, and excluding the payment of higher rates for special tasks, the maximum annual earnings of an agricultural labourer in southern England at this time could not have exceeded £10 8s. 0d. This figure makes no allowance for public holidays or unemployment, and if these factors are taken into account, it is doubtful whether the wage-earnings of even the fullest employed agricultural labourers were more than about £9 per annum. Ignoring possible subsidiary sources of livelihood open to both cottagers and peasant cultivators, this means that, in a normal year, the income of an arable farmer with a holding of 30 acres may have been some 60–70 per cent higher than that of a better-off agricultural wage-earner. This suggests that, in times of moderate plenty, a net farming profit of £14–£15 per annum made possible a tolerable, though by no means easy, existence. If we accept eighteenth-century estimates, the average size of a working-class family was six (mother, father, and four children), while the consumption of breadcorn per head totalled six bushels a year. Expenditure on farinaceous products seems to have amounted to about 50 per cent of total essential personal expenditure. On the basis of these figures, the family of a farmer with a small-holding of 30 acres in the early decades of the seventeenth century could have subsisted in years of moderate harvest on an annual income of about £11 5s. if wheaten and barley bread were consumed in equal proportions, and on somewhat less if only inferior bread were eaten. In such years, our small arable farmer would therefore have a margin of about £3–£5 to spend on raising the standard of life of his family above the bare minimum. This margin was small and could easily disappear in times of crop failure: a point which is illustrated by Table 26.[2]

Referring to this table, it will be seen that, even though we assume a substantial increase in the market value of the farmer's produce when his crop was poor (because of the inelasticity of demand for grain), the value of corn remaining for sale after all other commitments have

[1] Oxford RO, Garsington Estate Accounts, 1625–98, temp. no. 41, fo. 1; see also *infra*, pp.   .

[2] Lipson, *op. cit.*, III, pp. 392–3, 501; Phelps Brown and Hopkins, *Economica*, NS XXVI, 1959, p. 29.

Table 26. *Effect of change in crop yield on income of small farmer*

	Moderate crop £ s. d.	Poor crop £ s. d.
Value of output:		
120 bushels wheat @ 3s. 9d.	22 10 0	
160 bushels barley @ 2s. 6d.	20 0 0	
70 bushels wheat @ 7s. 6d.		26 5 0
100 bushels barley @ 5s. 0d.		25 0 0
Tithes	4 5 0	5 2 6
Home consumption of grain:		
18 bushels wheat @ 3s. 9d.	3 7 0	
18 bushels barley @ 2s. 6d.	2 5 0	
18 bushels wheat @ 7s. 6d.		6 15 0
18 bushels barley @ 5s. 0d.		4 10 0
Required for next year's crop:		
25 bushels wheat seed @ 3s. 9d.	4 13 9	
40 bushels barley seed @ 2s. 6d.	5 0 0	
25 bushels wheat seed @ 7s. 6d.		9 7 6
40 bushels barley seed @ 5s. 0d.		10 0 0
Other farm expenses	14 2 0	14 2 0
	33 13 3	49 17 0
Remaining	8 16 9	1 8 0

been met is insufficient to cover the full cost of the succeeding year's farm expenses and also provide an adequate income for the absolute minimum of personal expenditure (say, £5) on non-farinaceous products. In the event, unless capital had been put aside in other years, both the home and the farm were likely to suffer, and the payment of rent, in particular—since this was the least essential expense from the farmer's point of view—to fall into arrears. Several such bad harvests in succession could hardly fail to bring complete ruin to many small cultivators. This prospect diminished as farms became larger, until a point was reached, at probably somewhere between about 50 and 100 acres, when a general crop failure meant an increase in net income for the producer. With very large arable farms the gain would be considerable. The main reason for these differences in fortune was that the larger farmer, even if he were no more efficient than the small producer, had a proportionately greater marketable surplus. A smaller proportion of his output would be retained for domestic consumption, since the farmer with 300 acres could not easily consume ten times as much bread as the cultivator with 30 acres. Moreover, the assumption about equal efficiency is questionable, and although the large grower may have sown seed in the same quantities per acre as the subsistence farmer, there seems good reason to think that his yield per bushel of seed was in some cases much higher.

There is little information to guide us on the respective profit-margins per unit of output of the large and small arable enterprise. It appears likely, however, that the big farmer obtained a higher yield at a greater cost per unit of land. There was probably little difference between the large and small farm in the cost of seed per acre, since there is no evidence to invalidate our suggestion that sowing rates were roughly similar. On the other hand, the acreage rent (or value) of land occupied by the large producer was likely to be greater than for a small-holding, since it would more probably be enclosed or otherwise improved by the farmer or his landlord. In some cases, part, at least, of this enhanced value could be attributed to a comparatively large expenditure on manures and other dressings, though there is little evidence of such expenditure before the last quarter of the sixteenth century. In 1600 James Bankes of Winstanley, in Lancashire, advised his son to marl the lands which he would eventually inherit, informing him that "the charg of the marlying of an acare wyll stand you in fyfe markes [i.e. £3 6s. 8d.] so that therby you shall in cres your Rentes in good sort." At Chute, in Wiltshire, during the reign of James I, Francis Golding, yeoman, claimed to have spent £100 about "the scyleinge, manuringe, marlinge and betteringe" the land of Escott farm, improving the annual value by £30. In Sussex, in the

42-2

1630's, Sir Thomas Pelham laid out considerable sums on denshiring and liming land. In 1634 he spent over £21 on such work: more than the value of many a farmer's stock. It was cheaper to apply raw chalk than lime, but even this was generally too expensive for the husbandman, since to be effective it required 20 or 30 tons to the acre. Some years ago Sir William Ashley suggested that the expense of marling land encouraged small cultivators to grow rye instead of wheat, but there is no real evidence in support of this view. In sixteenth-century Leicestershire Dr Hoskins found that, as a general rule, it was the large farmers, rather than the small, who grew some rye; and it seems reasonable to suppose that peasant cultivators, with a limited acreage and no labour costs but their own, would prefer whenever possible to grow the more highly valued wheat. In some districts, of course, this was out of the question owing to the unsuitability of physical conditions; but where the nature of the soil was such that wheat was an uncertain proposition, a compromise solution which was sometimes adopted was the sowing of a blend of wheat and rye, termed maslin.[1]

If the large farmer generally spent more on soil dressings and rent per acre than the husbandman, the reverse probably applied to outlays on stock and equipment. In regard to these costs the small farmer suffered from the economic problem of 'indivisibility'—i.e. he still required a full plough-team and an adequate range of appliances with which to cultivate his land, no matter how limited its acreage. Unless his team and implements were hired out to his neighbours or otherwise shared, they would often be under-utilized and would be relatively expensive in terms of output or land. Up to a certain point the size of farm could be increased with little or no additional expenditure on these items. In the chalk districts of Wiltshire, for example, Dr Kerridge found that a ploughteam of three or four horses was normally used to work an arable area of up to 60 acres. On his farm in Suffolk in 1630–1, Paul D'Ewes, Esq., had seven horses and geldings "with their furniture for plough and carte" (valued in all at £30), to cultivate a total arable area which probably amounted to between about 100 and 150 acres, since his autumn-sown land, alone, consisted of seven acres of wheat and 31 acres of rye (valued, in this period of scarcity, at £3 10s. and £2 per acre respectively, after deduction of rent).[2]

[1] Joyce Bankes (ed.), *The Memoranda Book of James Bankes, 1586–1617*, Inverness, 1935, p. 8; E. W. J. Kerridge, *The Agrarian Development of Wiltshire, 1540–1640*, University of London Ph.D. thesis, 1951, pp. 133, 181–2; Cornwall, *thesis*, pp. 117, 178, 212–13; BM Add. MS 33147; Ashley, *The Bread of Our Forefathers*, Oxford, 1928, pp. 137–42; Hoskins, *op. cit.*, p. 163; J. Blagrave, *op. cit.*, p. 24.

[1] Kerridge, *thesis*, pp. 165, 443–4, 551, BM Harl. MS 7657.

With fewer draught animals in relation to acreage than the small cultivator, the large arable farmer was also likely to have a proportionately lower feed bill, in spite of the fact that his horses and oxen were probably better fed; and though he may have invested in higher-quality stock and equipment than the husbandman, this was by no means a dis-economy, since the life of these assets would presumably be longer than in the case of the average small farm.

A major item in the costs of the large arable enterprise, which scarcely affected the typical unit of peasant agriculture, was the cost of hiring labour. The relative importance of labour costs varied with the size and efficiency of the undertaking, the level of wages, and the type of crops cultivated. In general, it appears that a single-plough farm could be managed by the occupier and his family with little need of wage-labour; but a two-plough farm of between, say, 60 and 120 acres, would probably provide fairly regular employment for one, two, or three labourers, plus additional workers at harvest time. On very large arable farms as many as twenty workers, including a bailiff and various specialists, might be employed. Some of these would be boarded farm servants, hired perhaps on a yearly basis at one of the local hiring fairs, and receiving a large part of their wages in kind—e.g. grain, pasturage for stock, and, occasionally, their employer's discarded clothes and boots! Other workers, many of whom had small plots of their own to cultivate, were engaged irregularly on a day or piece-rate basis. Wages were graded according to the character of the work; but in some instances relatively high rates, especially at harvest time, reflected the seasonal demand for labour, rather than any peculiar differences in skill.[1]

When we come to consider more closely the labour costs incurred by the large arable farmer, we are again faced with problems posed by the inadequate and unsystematic nature of contemporary accounts, and it once more becomes necessary to visualize the position as it might apply to a hypothetical producer. In order to facilitate comparison with our earlier example relating to the 30-acre farm, we will assume, first of all, that the acreage of land, the total of non-wage expenditure, the yield of crops, and the value of produce are as previously set out in Table 25. Given these assumptions, and basing our estimates of wage-expenditure on piecemeal data gleaned from various estate accounts, we conclude that the annual labour costs involved in the cultivation of an arable area of 30 acres in the early years of the seventeenth century were not markedly dissimilar to those indicated in Table 27.

[1] Kerridge, *thesis*, pp. 441–5, 561; W. Hasbach, *A History of the English Agricultural Labourer*, London, 1908, pp. 67, 83–4, 86; Cornwall, *thesis*, p. 390; Robinson, *op. cit.*, *passim*; Saltmarsh, *Econ. Hist.*, III, 1936, pp. 160–1.

Table 27. *Estimated annual labour costs on 30 acres of*
arable land, 1600–1620

	£	s.	d.
Ploughing 30 acres twice @ 2s. per acre	6	0	0
Harrowing and sowing 20 acres at 2s. per acre	2	0	0
Weeding 20 acres @ 4d. per acre		6	8
Reaping and binding 10 acres of wheat @ 3s. per acre	1	10	0
Mowing and raking 10 acres of barley @ 1s. 7d. per acre		15	10
Threshing 120 bushels of wheat @ 1s. 6d. per quarter	1	2	6
Threshing 160 bushels of barley @ 1s. 0d. per quarter	1	0	0
Miscellaneous (dunging, carting, etc.)		10	0
Total labour costs	13	5	0
Other costs	23	15	9
Total costs	37	0	9
Value of crop after deduction of tithes	38	5	0
Net profit	1	4	3

It will be noted that the most important single item of expenditure related to ploughing. Normally, land (including fallow) was ploughed at least twice a year; and where soils were heavy, three and even four ploughings might be given. The cost of weeding was negligible, since many farmers appear to have attached little importance to the practice, and it was usually undertaken by female workers at about half the ordinary daily wage for men. At harvest time, when piece-rate incentives were often used, some workers were able to double their normal daily earnings, but the cost, in wages, of gathering the harvest was not especially high, amounting, in our example, to only 17 per cent of total labour costs. Wheat was a more expensive crop to gather than barley and it was also dearer to thresh. The cost per acre of harvesting oats was about the same as for barley, but owing to the higher yield normally obtainable, the cost per unit of output was often well below that for other grains. Threshing costs (at 8d. per quarter in the early seventeenth century) were also less. Thus, on the lands of Sir Charles Morison at Cassiobury in Hertfordshire, in 1609, the yield of oats—the major crop in terms of output—amounted to 29·4 bushels per acre, as against 16·6 bushels for barley and 12·8 bushels for wheat. The average cost of harvesting and threshing oats amounted to 1·09s. per quarter, as compared with 1·76s. for barley and 3·37s. for wheat. The task of threshing a large grain crop was a formidable one, and on a big estate might employ several workers well into the following year.[1]

It will be evident from Table 27 that wages constituted a major element in the cost-structure of the large arable farm: in our example they account for 36 per cent of total costs, and exceed expenditure on either seed or rent. It will also be evident that the income remaining to the farmer after all outgoings had been met would be quite inadequate to permit a reasonable standard of living, unless the enterprise were very large indeed. In other words, in the conditions of the early seventeenth century, the large farmer who paid a full market-value rent on moderately good arable land, could not make a livelihood from yields of 12 bushels per acre of wheat and 16 bushels per acre of barley. Either he had to grow other, more profitable, crops, if this were possible, or he had to increase productivity. The difference which higher productivity could make to the farmer's position may be illustrated if we assume that his crop yields per acre averaged 16 bushels of wheat and 20 bushels of barley. At the level of prices previously stipulated—viz., 30s. per quarter for wheat and 20s. for barley—the value of produce grown on 30 acres of land (10 being fallow) would amount to £55. If this were achieved with no addition to total costs, net profit would amount to £12 9s. 3d.: almost as much as the income of our small peasant cultivator employing no hired labour. The assumption about total costs remaining unchanged is, of course, unrealistic, since any significant rise in productivity would probably have been impossible without some additional outlay. This, however, need not have been large in relation to the returns achieved; and it seems probable that the big arable farmer in circumstances such as those described would have a good margin on which to operate, except in years when the price of grain was very low.

3. *Pasture farming*

The business of pasture farming in the Tudor and early Stuart periods is relatively better documented than that of tillage, partly because rearing and grazing were more likely to attract the attention of large landowners, and it is mainly in relation to the conduct of large estates that accounts have survived. In their existing form, however, contemporary accounts

[1] Norwich Pub. Lib., Townshend Coll. 88, MS. 1505, ff. 1–5; Maxey, *op. cit.*, *passim;* Lennard, EcHR, IV, 1932, pp. 31–2; Essex RO, D, DP, A 18; A 22; F. Hull, *Agriculture and Rural Society in Essex, 1560–1640,* University of London, Ph.D. thesis, 1950, pp. 88, 498–500, 536–51; Lodge, *op. cit., passim;* W. Salt. Lib., D 1734, 22; 38; BM Add. MS 28242; 33147; 34166; Kent AO, U 269, A 417; A 418; *Robert Loder's Farm Accounts, passim;* Herts. RO, 6604, 6718.

of sheep and cattle-farming enterprises give a very misleading impression of profitability, since certain costs are generally taken for granted or otherwise omitted, including the most vital costs of all—those of pasture and feed. To obtain an insight into the income and cost-structure of the pastoral undertaking, therefore, it again becomes necessary to construct a model based as closely as our information permits on the conditions of the period. In Table 28 we have set down the possible expenditures and receipts of a sheep farm consisting of 400 acres of good pasture and 100 acres of rich meadowland in the early years of the seventeenth century. A problem arises in connection with the form which our enterprise is to take, since sheep were kept for a number of reasons and for varying lengths of time. For example, many farmers concerned themselves primarily with the production of wool, breeding their own stock and selling animals which were mainly old, inferior, or diseased. On the other hand, farmers with good fattening pastures might do little or no breeding, buying in stock in order to sell again at a higher price later on. At Dogsthorpe, near Peterborough, where Fitzwilliam had a mixed pastoral enterprise, beasts were generally kept for only a short time before resale. Most of the sheep were bought between Lady Day and May Day and were sold before the following Michaelmas, having been clipped in the intervening period. The principal purchases were of couples of ewes and lambs bought in the spring and sold separately in the autumn.[1] In enterprises where the production of mutton was a major aim of sheep-farming activity, mainly wethers would probably be kept, perhaps for a few months, possibly for a year or longer, depending upon the age and condition of the stock and the movement of market prices.

The farm which is envisaged in Table 28 combines most of the elements mentioned above. Wethers are purchased in the spring at 12s. each, and after clipping and fattening are sold the following spring for 16s. 6d. Ewes cost 10s. each, and after three years of bearing lambs and providing wool are completely replaced, being sold at 8s. 6d. apiece. All lambs are marketed at an average price of 6s. without being sheared. Rams, which like other stud animals did not normally command very high prices at this time, are purchased at 15s. and sold three years later at 12s. 6d. All these prices are based upon the transactions of Toke's sheep-farming enterprise in the late 1610's. In order to save unnecessary complication, it is assumed that all farm output (apart from hay) is sold, and that interest charges on credit purchases and sales cancel out. A more difficult problem concerns the number of stock which our sheep farm of 500 acres could maintain. At the present day, stocking rates vary between about one ewe to every five acres on the mountains to

[1] Finch, *op. cit.*, p. 122; Northants, RO, F. (M) Misc. vol. 52.

Table 28. *Expenditure and output of hypothetical sheep farm of 500 acres, 1600–1620*

	Expenditure £ s. d.	Cost per acre s.		Output £ s. d.	Income per acre s.
Rent:					
400 acres pasture @ 12s.	240 0 0 }				
100 acres meadow @ 18s.	90 0 0 }	13·20	Wool: ewes and rams, 4133½ lb. @ 1s.	206 13 6 }	
			wethers, 4500 lb @ 1s.	225 0 0 }	17·27
Feed:					
For sheep	130 0 0 }				
For oxen	5 4 0 }	5·41	Lambs: 1029 @ 6s.	308 14 0	12·35
Interest and capital depreciation:			Gross profit of 4s. 6d. each on sale		
On equipment	9 13 3	0·39	of 957 wethers	215 6 6	8·61
On oxen	5 16 4 }				
On ewes and rams	96 7 4 }	7·26			
On wethers	79 7 0 }				
Materials: tar, pitch, ruddle, grease	5 7 3	0·21			
Marketing expenses: driving charges, tolls, grass	20 10 11	0·82			
Labour:					
Shepherds' wages	48 0 0 }				
Shearing time	7 10 0 }				
Haymaking @ 4s. per acre	20 0 0 }	3·42			
Miscellaneous	10 0 0 }				
	767 16 1	30·71		955 14 0	38·23
			Tithes	74 0 9	2·96
				881 13 3	35·27
			Net profit	113 17 2	4·55

sold, out of the original total of 1,000 calls for explanation. This twelve sheep to the acre on the best fattening pastures on Romney Marsh. We have assumed that the grassland in our example is of high quality and that it is supplemented by a generous allowance of meadow-land and purchased winter feed. Under such circumstances a stocking rate of five to six sheep per acre of pasture may not be unrealistic, and gains some support from other evidence. We have therefore assumed that our sheep farm supports 1,000 wethers, 1,143 ewes, and 38 rams, the original outlay on sheep amounting to £1,200. The ratio of rams to ewes is 1:30, which accords with the advice given by Henry Best and the practice followed by some large sheep farmers during our period.[1]

The income of our farmer is assumed to be derived from the sale of wool, lambs, and fattened wethers. Any significant fall in the price of one of these commodities (especially wool) could substantially affect the level of profits and might even lead to a net loss. In order to calculate the value of wool sales it is necessary to make assumptions about fleece weights and wool prices. We have estimated the average weight of a wether's fleece at 4½ lb. and of other fleeces at 3½ lb. Such weights were not uncommon on good-quality enclosed pasture at this time, and in some Midland districts fleeces weighing 6-7 lb. were obtained. The price of wool is assumed to be 28s. per tod (i.e. 1s. per lb.), which was the price received by Sir Thomas Temple of Stowe for several wool clips marketed in the early years of the seventeenth century. In Table 28 the total value of wool sold by our farmer is given as £431 13s. 6d., this accounting for 45 per cent of the gross value of output.[2]

The income derived from the sale of lambs depended not only on their price but on the ewes' fertility. Nowadays, lambing rates in Britain seldom fall below 1·0 and sometimes rise to 2·0 lambs per ewe per annum. In Tudor and Stuart England lambing rates varied a great deal from flock to flock and from year to year, but seldom, if ever, reached an average of 1·0. On a large well-managed sheep farm, such as that owned by the Bacon family at Culford in west Suffolk at the beginning of the seventeenth century, a lambing rate of approximately 0·9 was normally achieved, and this is the figure which we have adopted in our calculations. Our 1,143 ewes are therefore assumed to produce an average of 1,029 lambs per year.[3]

The fact that only 957 wethers are recorded in Table 28 as being

[1] Lodge, *op. cit., passim;* R. Dexter and D. Barber, *Farming for Profits,* London, 1961, p. 44; PRO E 133, 657 East. 28 Eliz. I; Robinson, *op. cit.,* pp. 2, 4; Bowden, *op. cit.,* p. 21.

[2] Bowden, *op. cit.,* pp. 30–3; Henry E. Huntington Library, ST.48.

[3] Bowden, *op. cit.,* p. 22; Simpson, *op. cit.,* pp. 185, 190–1.

adjustment has been made in order to allow for casualties among the farmer's flock. The casualty rate among sheep could be very high in years when rot was prevalent; and even in comparatively favourable years common-field farmers may have suffered quite severe losses. In normal years, however, and on large enclosed farms, losses seem to have averaged between about 1 per cent and $3\frac{1}{2}$ per cent each year. In our example we have assumed a casualty rate of 2 per cent, which gives us a figure of forty-three sheep lost by virtue of accident or disease. In practice, of course, not all casualties could have been of wether sheep, but it makes our example less involved if we make this assumption and if we also assume that all losses occured after shearing time. Dead sheep, however, did not represent a complete loss to their owner, since their fells and carcases were of some value and could be sold. We have assumed that for every dead wether our farmer received 3s., thereby losing 9s. on sheep which originally cost 12s. This loss has been taken into account by including a sum of £19 7s. 0d. on the expenditure side under the heading of interest and capital depreciation on wethers. The total of this charge is given as £79 7s. 0d., the remaining £60 representing one year's interest at 10 per cent on the original price of £600 paid for 1,000 wethers.[1]

Turning more specifically to the expenses incurred by the large sheep farmer, it will be at once apparent from Table 28 that the major part of expenditure was associated with the provision of pasture and other feed for stock. If we include haymaking costs, our farmer's outlay on rent and fodder crops (whether purchased or grown at home) accounts for almost exactly two thirds of total expenditure Other costs, apart from interest foregone and capital depreciation on sheep, were very much less important. At the same time, the view, which owes much to Sir Thomas More, that a sheep farm could be run by a shepherd and his dog, oversimplifies the position, since draught animals, equipment, and additional labour were also required, if not continuously, at least from time to time. Oxen and carts, together with their owners, were sometimes hired at the busy haymaking season, but the possession of transport facilities was also likely to be essential on other occasions. We have therefore assumed that our farmer owned eight oxen, which made him self-supporting in this respect. Our figures for interest and capital depreciation on oxen, and the cost of their feed, are based on similar assumptions to those made in connection with Table 25. The value of the sheep-farmer's appliances and other equipment is difficult to assess.

[1] *Supra*, p.   ; W. Salt Lib., D 1734/22, 24, 38, 56, 2–4 Edward VI (not numbered), 4–5 Edward VI (not numbered); Kent AO, U 269, A 418, 1; U 269, A 419, 1; U 269, A 421, 1–5; U 269, A 423; Northants. RO, F. (M) Misc. vol. 52; BM Harl. MS 129; BM Add. MS 39836; Bowden, *op. cit.*, pp. 15–17.

A large flockmaster would almost certainly possess a number of carts or wains, as well as the usual range of small agricultural implements. Additionally, he would need to invest in specialized equipment, such as hurdles and pens. We have assumed that the total cost of all these assets is £30, and that they are written off over five years. Their annual charge on the enterprise would thus be comparatively insignificant. The same may be said of purchased materials—tar, pitch, ruddle, and grease—used for marking and veterinary purposes. Our figure for the cost of such materials is based on the accounts of William Wickham's farm at Garsington, Oxon., for the period 1625–30, which enable us to calculate expenditure on materials as 1·26 per cent of receipts from the sale of wool.[1]

A somewhat more substantial charge on the sheep-farming enterprise was the expense involved in the marketing of stock. Toll payments and other costs were incurred, both at markets and fairs and on the roads to and from them. Drivers and other helpers had to be hired, and both they and their charges required overnight accommodation and food if on the roads for more than one day. In practice, the total expense involved in despatching or collecting sheep normally varied between about one half and two per cent of the value of the animals concerned, depending primarily upon the distance between the points of departure and destination. The figure in our table assumes an average marketing charge of one per cent on purchases and sales.[2]

A more constant and important element in the costs of sheep farming was that of labour. In common-field villages common shepherds were employed to tend sheep and guard them against thieves and wool pluckers. In large specialized undertakings shepherds were quite often the only permanent employees, though in very big enterprises a sheep-reeve was also usually appointed to exercise general supervision. The number of shepherds employed by large sheep farmers varied with the size of flocks and the nature and geographical distribution of pastures. Obviously, it would not have been economically sensible to employ a shepherd to look after a few sheep, while there were limits to the size of the flock which one man could effectively manage alone. On well-stocked and compact pastures a good shepherd could probably handle up to 600 sheep quite competently, requiring assistance only on special occasions; but if the sheep farm were scattered and the terrain difficult, a larger permanent labour force would be required. In the case of the

---

[1] Kent AO, U 269, A 417; U 269, A 418, 5; Lincs. AO, H 97, 22, 2; Allison, *thesis*, pp. xxix–lxii; Simpson, *op. cit.*, p. 186; Oxford RO, Garsington Estate Accounts 1625–98, temp. no. 41.

[2] Kent AO, U 269, A 417; U 269, A 418, 2; Lincs. AO, H 97, 22, 1; Lord Dormer's Papers, 1600–30; W. Salt Lib., D 1734, 22 etc.

sheep farm in our example, we will assume that four full-time shepherds are employed, each receiving money wages and allowances to the value of £12 per annum.[1]

Apart from shepherds' wages, the substantial sheep farmer also incurred other labour charges. Additional workers were required for a variety of purposes during the year, but above all they were needed to gather in the hay crop and to assist at shearing time. On large undertakings the former task was often spread over several weeks and involved considerable expenditure. In 1631 it cost the earl of Middlesex £102 3s. 1d. in wages and other hiring charges to have the hay growing on his West Midland estates mown, transported, and stacked. Without it, the 6,000 or so sheep and other stock which he possessed at this time would have spent a very hungry winter. The expense of gathering the hay crop depended not only upon the local level of wage-rates, but also upon the yield of grass and the distance over which it had to be transported. In 1629 it cost Sir Roger Twysden £2 7s. 0d. before hay, growing on 9 acres of land in Romney Marsh, was home and literally dry. Bearing in mind the probable abundance of the crop, this outlay by Twysden, which averages out at 5s. 2¾d. per acre, may not have been unduly high. However, we have based our estimate of hay-making charges on an average expenditure of 4s. per acre, which allows for the rather lower level of wages at the beginning of the century and is more in line with evidence from other sources. Even so, it will be noted that the labour costs of our farmer in connection with his hay crop were almost half the annual wages he paid to his shepherds.[2]

Less substantial than either of these changes were the costs incurred at shearing time. In this connection, the main expenditures on labour related to the washing and clipping of sheep and the winding of wool. Other payments were made to helpers who performed such tasks as rounding up sheep and gathering locks. The principal expense was that of shearing. In arriving at the figure given in Table 28, we have assumed that clippers were paid at the same rates as those employed by Sir Richard Townshend in 1626—viz., 3s. for every 100 ewes and rams sheared, and 3s. 4d. for every 100 wethers. This gives us a total of £3 8s. 9d. for shearing, while a further £1 14s. 5d. has been allowed for the driving and washing of sheep. The usual rate of payment for winding wool in the early Stuart period was 4d. per score of fleeces, which puts the cost of this operation at £1 16s. 4d. The remaining sum in our example is made up of 6d. for the gathering of locks and 10s.

---

[1] Bowden, *op. cit.*, pp. 18–19; Allison, EcHR, 2nd Ser., XI, 1958, p. 110; Lodge, *op. cit.*, pp. xxxvi–xxxvii.

[2] Kent AO, U 269, A 423; BM Add. MS 34166, fo. 42; 33147, ff. 7–7ᵛ; Norwich Pub. Lib., Townshend Coll. 88, MS 1505, fo. 3.

to cover the cost of any food and drink which may have been provided by the farmer.[1]

The sum of £10 allowed in Table 28 for miscellaneous labour charges is quite arbitrary, but may not be too wide of the mark. On the large pasture farm there were a variety of tasks which required additional or specialized labour at different times of the year. Among the sheep-farming accounts of the period one finds references to payments for gelding lambs, greasing hoggs, and assisting at lambing time. At Misterton, in the severe winter of 1550–1, helpers were engaged to look for sheep in the snow, watch for foxes, and trap dogs which had been worrying stock. Some sheep farmers paid to have water-furrows ploughed in their pastures and manure spread in their meadows. Hedges and ditches needed to be kept in good repair, since animals could otherwise escape. The extent to which tenants assumed the burden of such repairs depended upon the terms of their tenancy. On most large pasture farms a vigorous battle was waged against moles and mole hills "for encreyce of grasse and meadow grounde to make the graysse gyner grayne." Many accounts record periodic payments for dead moles; and on the earl of Middlesex's estates in the 1630's a "mole taker" was a permanent member of the labour force.[2]

Turning to the overall position on our sheep farm, we find that total expenditure amounts to £767 16s. 1d., while the value of output after deduction of tithes is £881 13s. 3d. The net profit of the enterprise is thus £113 17s. 2d., which averages 4·55s. per acre, or 1·04s. per sheep. These figures are not, of course, absolutely reliable, since in order to arrive at them a certain amount of guesswork has been necessary, but they are much more realistic than the figures of alleged profitability put forward by Professor A. Simpson in connection with certain sheep-farming enterprises in Norfolk during our period. The "profits" of Professor Simpson's study are not, in fact, profits at all, but some form of gross return which contains within itself the rental value of land and interest on capital invested; no allowance is made in respect of depreciation and the maintenance of stock, nor for the value of feed. In fact, all the major elements of the sheep-farmer's expenditure are taken for granted. It follows that Professor Simpson's estimates of changes in the profitability of sheep farming in Norfolk during Tudor and early Stuart times are not very meaningful.[3]

[1] Bowden, op. cit., pp. 22–4; Allison, thesis, pp. 223–4; Kent AO, U 269, A 417, A 418, 5, ff. 50–1; Lincs. AO, H 97, 22, 1, 2; Lodge, op. cit., p. xxxvi; BM Add. MS 39836.

[2] Allison, EcHR, 2nd Ser., XI, 1958, p. 110; W. Salt. Lib., D 1734, 24; Essex RO, D, DP, A 18, A 22; Hull, thesis, pp. 87, 536–7; BM Add. MS 33147; 34166; Lincs. AO, H 97, 22, 1 and 2; Kent AO, U 269, A 418, 5, fo. 29ᵛ.

[3] Simpson, op. cit., pp. 186–96.

Our own figures clearly show why the specialist sheep farmer was unlikely to be a man with less than 50 acres of pasture at his disposal. Compared to tillage, the amount of labour required for sheep farming was small: in Table 28, wages constitute only 11 per cent of total expenditure, compared with our previous estimate of 36 per cent for a large arable undertaking. A small sheep venture was therefore unlikely to keep a peasant farmer fully occupied. More important was the fact that considerable outlay on stock, rent, and feed was required before an adequate income could be secured. In Table 25 we estimated the annual net profit of our small arable cultivator at £14 9s. 3d. or 9·64s. per acre of land. The comparable figure for our large sheep farmer is 4·55s. per acre. If, in the latter case, wage costs are completely excluded, on the assumption that the occupier provides all the labour himself, we obtain a net profit of 7·98s. per acre, or 1·83s. per sheep. On the basis of these figures, we may calculate that it would require 158 sheep (costing between £80 and £90) and 36 acres of good enclosed pasture to make the same net profit of £14 9s. 3d. achieved by our peasant cultivator with 30 acres of common-field land and a much smaller capital outlay. Clearly, these sort of requirements put specialization upon sheep farming out of reach of many small producers, and while most peasants with more than a few acres owned some sheep, it was probably only in districts where pasture land was unusually cheap or common grazing exceptionally abundant that the comparatively small specialized sheep enterprise was able to make significant impression. Moreover, we need look no further for an explanation as to why the small farmer in pastoral areas, as well as in mixed farming districts, strained every effort to increase his acreage under the plough. On the other hand, since the business of sheep farming could be carried on with a minimum of technical organization, it was well suited to the large landowner who desired to participate in commercialized agriculture but did not wish to become too directly involved with matters of detail.

Much of what has been said about sheep farming applies also to cattle grazing. Indeed, sheep and cattle were often combined in the same undertaking, if for no other reason than because of the broadly similar pattern of routine and the complementary feeding habits of the two kinds of stock. As with sheep farming, the main costs of beef production were those of pasture, feed, and interest on capital invested in livestock. Comparatively little was tied up in fixed assets. Marketing expenses may have been somewhat higher, on average, than for sheep, since longer journeys to market were often involved, but labour charges and casualties were probably less. The economics of buying, feeding, and selling cattle during our period are obscure, for few detailed cattle-farming records have survived. An entry in Toke's account book, dated 8 April 1620, notes the sale to a Londoner of seventeen northern oxen for £148 which had cost £83 at St Bartholomew's Fair the previous year, "soe for feedinge £65." This gives a gross return of nearly £4 a head. The net figures would have been very much less by the time all costs had been taken into account. The winter stall-feeding of an ox in order to bring it to prime condition was likely to have required a total ration of at least 40 cwt of hay spread over a period of twenty weeks. At the local level of hay prices in 1619–20, this item alone would have cost Toke between £1 10s. and £3 per beast. According to Lisle, who wrote at the beginning of the eighteenth century, steers would not beef until they were four or five years old, although a heifer would make "very pretty beef" at three. Other considerations apart, this fact alone is sufficient to explain why cattle grazing exercised little attraction for small farmers, who needed a more rapid turnover on capital in order to survive. Small men often engaged in cattle-breeding, but partly, if not mainly, as a complement to dairying, where quick returns could be obtained. Doubtless, the majority of husbandmen and cottagers followed the advice of a contemporary pamphleteer, and disposed of their calves before winter because of the high cost of feed.[1]

Of all the major branches of livestock husbandry, dairy farming was the one best calculated to suit the particular needs of the small producer. Dairying required much more labour than either sheep farming or beef production, not only because cows demanded regular milking, but also because the inadequacies of the transportation system meant that much milk had to be converted into butter and cheese before it could be sold. The sale of dairy produce brought the farmer a regular income, at least during part of the year, while the necessary utensils—the milking pails, sieves, butter churns, cheese tubs, and presses—cost little. Even in a large buttery the value of equipment in the latter part of our period was unlikely to exceed a few pounds. These considerations, though of major importance to the small farmer who possessed little besides his ability to work, carried less weight with the large producer. Moreover, dairy farming necessitated a routine and labour force which did not dovetail neatly into the organization of the specialist sheep venture or cattle-fattening enterprise, and this doubtless helps to explain why, in some instances, even substantial graziers and flockmasters, such as Hatcher of Careby, in Lincolnshire, produced insufficient quantities of butter and cheese to meet ordinary domestic requirements. This was not, of course, always the case. Sir William

[1] Thirsk, op. cit., pp. 175–6; Lord Dormer's Papers, 1600–30; Lodge, op. cit., p. 489; Lisle, Observations in Husbandry, 1757, II, pp. 5–6, 9; J. Blagrave, op. cit., pp. 85–9.

Fitzwilliam kept milch kine, as well as most other types of stock, at Dogsthorpe. Between Michaelmas 1585 and 1594 the values of milk, butter, and cheese produced there averaged £12 7s. 7d. per year, all of which was apparently consumed at home. In Berkshire Robert Loder also kept dairy cattle to supply produce for the needs of the household, rather than for sale. In 1618 his twelve milkers yielded a daily average of one gallon per cow during the 129 days between weaning and drying off. This suggests a whole lactation yield of the order of 200–220 gallons, achieved on downland pasture of not very high quality. At this time milk was priced at about 2½d. per gallon, and Loder believed his kine to be among his most profitable livestock assets, calculating the profit per cow at £1 16s. 8d. Experience of other contemporary accounts, however, leads us to question the reliability of this figure.

Information about the remaining branches of livestock husbandry is, if anything, less precise. It seems clear, however, that the breeding and rearing of horses required more capital than other kinds of stock farming, not only because of the larger initial outlay but also because of the comparatively high cost of feed and slow rate of capital turnover. Obviously, these considerations would preclude the small man from concentrating attention upon the raising of horses. Better suited to the limited resources of the small producer was the keeping of pigs and poultry. The organization of pig production on a commercial basis, however, seems to have been limited largely to forest and dairy farming districts where feed was especially cheap. Elsewhere most pig-keepers appear to have aimed primarily at catering for domestic consumption or utilizing the waste of the farmstead. There is even less evidence of specialization upon poultry-farming, except in East Anglia, though regular sales of eggs and occasional sales of birds probably enabled many small cultivators to eke out a bare existence. On most large farms pigs and poultry appear to have been of little significance, partly it may be suspected, because of the attention which these stock required. To some extent this gap might be filled, in the case of landowners, by the receipt of produce rents in the form of hens, eggs, and the like. Even so, the household accounts of many large landed families indicate the expenditure of substantial sums on the purchase of 'white meats'. It is difficult to escape the conclusion that pig-keeping and poultry farming, like dairying, were mainly the concern of the small producer.[1]

[1] G. E. Fussell and Constance Goodman, 'The Eighteenth-century Traffic in Milk Products', *Econ. Hist.*, III, 1937, p. 380; Val Cheke, *op. cit.*, pp. 87, 90; G. D. Ramsay (ed.), *John Isham, Mercer and Merchant Adventurer: Two Account Books of a London Merchant in the Reign of Elizabeth I*, Northants. Rec. Soc. XXI, 1962, Gateshead, pp. 161, 162; Thirsk, *op. cit.*, pp. 175–6; Northants, RO, F (M) Misc. vol. 52; *Robert Loder's Farm Accounts*, pp. 153–6; Trow-Smith, *op. cit.*, pp. 185–6, 237–8, 250–5.

4. *The landlord*

The gross income of the landlord, who had no other source of livelihood but receipts from tenants, depended upon the size of his rent-roll.
Out of this sum he had to finance the expenses of estate management
and—where these burdens were not passed on to tenants—the costs
of the repair and renewal of fixed capital and other charges on land.
The economic changes of Tudor and early Stuart times affected the
landlord, both in his capacity as a *rentier* and as a consumer. Various
factors served to increase the demand for land, and with it the landlord's potential income. In an age of mansion-building, when the
possession of a landed estate was the principal indication of social
status, the non-pecuniary advantages of farming were becoming more
highly regarded. Moreover, during the sixteenth and early seventeenth
centuries rural population was growing faster than opportunities for
industrial employment, and this was bound to lead to strong competition for farms and an upward pressure on rents. More important than
either of these two considerations, however, was the rise in the general
profitability of farming during our period. On the demand side, the
growth of population was reflected in the rising trend of farm produce
prices, which benefited agriculturalists as against other sections of the
community. On the side of supply, the real costs of agricultural
production were tending to decrease, owing to greater productivity
and a fall in factor costs (measured in terms of the value of output).
In respect of costs, we have already noted that agricultural wages
lagged behind commodity prices during much of the period under
review, while in the early decades of the seventeenth century capital
seems to have become available on easier terms. The net effect of
these various changes was to widen the margin between agricultural
prices and non-rent costs (including adequate remuneration to the
farmer of average efficiency). This margin, or surplus, was potentially
available to the landlord as rent, though in practice all or part of it
might be retained by the tenant. It was not, however, necessary for the
landlord to take the entire surplus, or even all that part of it attributable
to the rise in agricultural prices, in order to maintain his standard of
life, since a substantial proportion of his expenditure would presumably
have been on non-agricultural commodities and services, whose prices
increased less markedly than those of farm produce.[1]

The extent to which Tudor and early Stuart landlords were in
practice able to benefit from the general rise in land values depended

[1] For a discussion of factors affecting the rent of land, see R. Turvey, *The Economics
of Real Property: an analysis of property values and patterns of use*, 1957, pp. 55–66;
G. Hallett, *The Economics of Agricultural Land Tenure*, London, 1960, *passim*.

largely upon the terms of tenancy by which their lands were let; and here custom played no small part. Nowadays, many farms are occupied by tenants under leases terminable by either landlord or tenant at twelve months' notice. Such leases permit rents to be frequently adjusted, if necessary, in line with changes in the market value of land. The tenures inherited by Tudor landlords from an earlier period of land surfeit, in which all the bargaining power had rested with tenants, were, in general, much less flexible. Demesne lands were sometimes leased on a short-term basis, and thus provided the best opportunity for rent revision. But tradition conferred a high degree of security of tenure in the case of many customary holdings, especially the copyholds of inheritance. Leasehold and other forms of tenure were often for lives or for long periods of time. Changes of tenancy might thus be at infrequent intervals, and even then to raise rent on much copyhold land was difficult, if not impossible.

Even under such circumstances as these, however, it did not necessarily follow that the landlord was bound to suffer a decline in real income. The assumption made earlier, that rent was the landlord's only source of revenue, does not, in fact, represent the true position. Landlords' receipts in the sixteenth and seventeenth centuries came from a variety of sources. Most landlords probably engaged in direct farming to cater for the needs of the household, if not for the market. The interest in commercial agriculture varied, as we have seen, according to the pull of economic forces; and the early sheep-enclosure movement clearly showed that, given sufficient incentive, not only demesne land might be farmed, but a covetous eye also cast upon common land and tenants' holdings. The great majority, if not all, of the farmers whose activities have been singled out for special mention in the earlier pages of this study, were landlords as well as cultivators, deriving their income from rents as well as from the sale of produce. In the first few years of the seventeenth century the total revenue from the estates of Sir Thomas Temple of Stowe amounted to some £2,500–£2,600 per annum. Of this amount, revenue from rents, including not only rents from land and borough tenements, but also from tithes, mills, and manorial dues, did not account for more than about £500 or £600 a year. The remaining £2,000 came from Temple's own farming enterprise. On the west Midland estates of the first earl of Middlesex in the two years ending 1 November 1631 rents accounted for only 13 per cent of total gross receipts, the bulk of income being derived from sales of wool, livestock, and corn. With the decline of Cranfield's direct farming interests the relative importance of revenue from rents increased, and in the sixteen-month period ending 27 February 1637 some 51 per cent of gross income was obtained from this source. Almost half a century earlier, in the 1590's, the rent-roll of Sir Thomas Tresham of Rushton, Northants., amounted to approximately £1,000 per annum. More than half of Tresham's gross income in this decade, however, came from the sale of farm produce, especially wool and sheep, but most other kinds of livestock were also sold, as well as corn, hops, cheeses, hides, timber, and lime. A substantial income was obtained from the sale of rabbits, this being a business which many large landowners found profitable. At Misterton, in the mid-sixteenth century, the cony warren was a highly-valued asset, its commercial exploitation providing permanent employment for a warrener and a net knitter who made and repaired the nets used for snares. Other workers were engaged on an occasional basis. In the year ending Michaelmas 1551, total expenditure in connection with the warren on wages and materials (including meat and milk for the ferrets) amounted to about £10, while proceeds from the sale of rabbits came to £130 13s. 2d. Total demesne receipts in the same year amounted to £587 10s. 5d., of which wool accounted for £170, while rents from tenanted holdings totalled £206 18s. 8½d. The demesne figure is of gross receipts from sales at Misterton, and makes no allowance for the value of produce consumed by the Paget household at Drayton in Middlesex, nor of receipts arising from the sale of kitchen by-products, notably hides, fells, and tallow. Most substantial landowners, whether they farmed for the market or not, probably obtained some income from the sale of such products, and in large households the receipts were sometimes considerable. Thus, in the year ending Michaelmas 1616, Lord Dormer sold 884 fells for £62 12s., while debts outstanding on wool sold the previous year brought in £773. On the earl of Northampton's estates at Compton, War., hides and fells sold in the eight-month period ending 26 March 1631 fetched £70 15s. 1½d., while the sale of tallow realized £55 2s. 9d. The diet of wealthy seventeenth-century landowners may have been deficient in vitamins, but certainly not in proteins ! For the landlord who retained in his own possession more grazing land than his livestock required, agistment charges frequently provided a useful supplementary source of income. Alternatively, grass or hay could be sold locally; and since hay was very costly to transport, its scale was also sometimes favoured by the stock-grazing landowner whose properties were widely dispersed. In the late 1590's Thomas Grantham, Esq., who possessed a large scattered estate in Lincolnshire, was selling more than 170 acres of grass each year, despite the fact that he himself owned some 1500–2700 sheep and perhaps 100–200 head of cattle. In 1598 hay and grass sold by Grantham's bailiff at St Katherine's (now part of Lincoln city) brought in £94 16s., while barley—the main arable crop—fetched £119 16s. 2d. The hay was sold unmown at 10s. per acre: a practice which relieved the land-owner of the costs and responsibilities of hay making and marketing.[1]

Apart from rent income and the proceeds of direct farming, how-ever, by far the most important source of receipts for the majority of landlords was timber. In many contemporary estate accounts, especially those relating to the early seventeenth century, references frequently occur to sales of fallen wood or standing timber; and though tenants were occasionally required to plant so many trees of specified kinds, there is little evidence of afforestation by the majority of landowners. It thus appears that in early Stuart times, at any rate, many landlords were living partly on their capital, though how far this was forced upon them by a rigidity in other sources of income in a period of inflation, and how far it was motivated by a desire to benefit from the rising demand for timber, cannot be precisely determined. The largest sales of wood and woodland were, of course, made by the Crown, but comprehensive accounts are few and data are both confused and widely dispersed. The last comprehensive general account to be found for the sixteenth century relates to 1546, when sales of timber brought in gross receipts of about £2,000. By the years 1606–9 this figure had risen to an average of £8,645 per annum, of which something like a quarter to a half may have been swallowed up by costs of administra-tion. In spite of a threefold to fourfold increase in the market price of timber in the intervening period, the receipts for 1606–9 probably represented only a small proportion of the true commercial value of sales; and there seems little doubt that the Crown was making greater inroads into its reserves of woodland in the early seventeenth century than it had done sixty years previously. However, these reserves still remained very large, an estimate made in 1612 putting the value of all royal woods at £403,000. During the years that followed, depletion continued at a more rapid rate, but commercial exploitation was severely restricted by limitations of the transportation system. While, therefore, Crown receipts from wood sales showed a marked increase in districts such as the Forest of Dean, which were relatively densely populated or in close proximity to industrial consumers, royal woods situated in remote and isolated localities were largely unaffected by the rising demand for fuel. The same factor of transport possibilities doubtless played an important part in determining the exploitation of woodland resources by other landowners. Much also depended, of course, upon the extent of such resources, since some regions had been

[1] Gay, *op. cit.*, pp. 421–2; Kent AO, U 269, A 423; Finch, *op. cit.*, pp. 74–5; W. Salt Lib., D 1734, 24; Lord Dormer's Papers, 1600–30; BM Add. MS 33417; Bowden, *op. cit.*, pp. 12–13; Warwick. RO, CR 556, 5, fo. 22; Gloucs. RO, D 621, M 18; Lincs. AO, And. 1; Thirsk, *op. cit.*, pp. 90–1.

largely cleared of trees by Tudor times or had never possessed a great abundance of forest. In the arable districts of East Anglia, for example, wood sales by landlords in the sixteenth and early seventeenth centuries appear to have seldom made more than a minor contribution to revenue. Southern and central England, on the other hand, were still well-wooded in many districts at the beginning of Elizabeth's reign, and most extant records of substantial wood sales by private landowners relate to these regions of relatively dense settlement. The Cromwell family of Ramsey, Hunts., was selling several hundred pounds-worth of timber annually towards the end of the sixteenth century. Near by, at Leighton Buzzard in Bedfordshire, sales of spires, bark, underwood, and faggots between 1611 and 1614 brought Sir Thomas Leigh gross receipts averaging £130 4s. 3d. per annum. At Finchampstead, Berks., Sir Richard Harrison raised a total of £1,760 17s. 3d. by similar sales in the twenty-five years ending September 1637. On the Oxfordshire and Buckinghamshire estates of Sir Henry Lee, one of the king's wards, receipts for wood sold in the year September 1640–1 amounted to £601 11s. 6d., while sales over the whole 11-year period 1639–50 realized almost £3,000. To the west, in Warwickshire, a single wood, 'Coldoak Coppice', yielded the earl of Northampton £538 14s. 6d. in 1630–1. Further north, on Brudenell's Northamptonshire estate, sales of underwood, oaks, and bark between 1606 and 1635 brought in average gross receipts of £222 13s. 4d. per annum, out of a total estate revenue which varied between about £2,500 and £4,600. In the same county Brudenell's contemporary, Sir William Fitzwilliam, drew more heavily upon his timber supplies. Accounts for the five years 1603–8 show that Fitzwilliam's gross annual receipts from wood sales ranged between £572 0s. 3d. and £691 15s. 10d., while the total yearly revenue from his estate amounted to about £2,500. There seems little doubt that Fitzwilliam, like many other landowners of the period, was utilizing his woodland in order to live beyond his income, but there is no evidence of long-term indebtedness on his part. For the landlord in financial difficulties, depletion of timber reserves was an obvious means of attaining temporary solvency. The earl of Northumberland, for example, sold wood worth almost £2,000 from his Petworth estate in Sussex between 1585 and 1595 in order to satisfy his creditors, and this was not the end of his depredations. From the standpoint of the landowner, particularly if he lacked capital as well as foresight, one of the main attractions which the commercial exploitation of woodland possessed over direct farming, was the smaller outlay incurred in relation to receipts. Expenditure varied, depending not only upon the acreage and location of woodland, but also upon whether sales were made of standing timber or felled wood. In either case, coppices had to be fenced, guarded, and tended; woodwards' wages had to be paid and hedges maintained. But these costs were comparatively small. Thomas Grantham, who possessed at least four separate woods, paid out £14 16s. in woodwards' wages in 1594-5, while hedging and allied charges totalled £8 12s. 1d. Grantham's annual gross receipts from timber sales in the period 1594-8 averaged £130 11s. 3d., which exceeded the value of either barley or hay sales, and accounted for about 10 per cent of total gross revenue. Many landowners sold wood in small quantities to local inhabitants, and in this way disposed of old or fallen timber. Large wood dealers and industrial consumers, however, relied less on casual sales than on purchasing or leasing areas of woodland, paying the landowner a specified annual 'rent' per acre and assuming full responsibility for felling and carriage. Many minute parcels of coppice were also sold in this way, local men buying an interest in perhaps a quarter or half acre of woodland. The 'rents' charged in these transactions varied enormously—the value of the timber, the location of the wood, and the business instincts of the landowner, all playing a part. The average 'rent' received by the Crown for coppices leased in eleven counties in the years 1604-12 worked out at 2s. 3d. an acre. At the other end of the scale, Sir George Heneage of Hainton, in Lincolnshire, was receiving as much as £10 per acre for certain parcels of coppice in the 1630's. The woods in question must have been exceptionally well-stocked, even allowing for the enhanced value of woodland since the beginning of the seventeenth century.[1]

Clearly, as the preceding discussion indicates, to consider the landlord's economic position solely from the standpoint of farm rents may be to ignore other, more important, sources of income. The standard of living of many substantial landowners, however, depended primarily upon their rent receipts, and the ability to adjust these in an age of rising prices afforded a major protection against inflation. One way in which rent revenues could be increased, of course, was by charging more for existing holdings; and much has been written concerning the conflict between landlord and tenant over the "unearned increment" (i.e. the economic rent) of land resulting from its rise in value. The point is obviously a very valid one; but probably no less important to some landowners was the additional revenue derived from the creation

[1] Hull, *thesis*, p. 324; G. Hammersley, 'The Crown Woods and their Exploitation in the Sixteenth and Seventeenth Centuries', *Bull.* IHR, xxx, 1957, pp. 137-59; Simpson, *op. cit.*, *passim;* BM Add. MS 33458, 9; Beds. RO, DD. KK. 739; BM Add. MS 34302; Oxford RO, DIL. XVIII, M, 121; Warwick. RO, CR 556, 5, fo. 36; Finch, *op. cit.*, pp. 129, 163; Cornwall, *thesis*, pp. 127-33; Lincs. AO, And. 1; Hen. 3, 2; Kent AO, U 269, A 421, 3; Norwich Pub. Lib., MS 20449; PRO E 133, 465, East. 20 Eliz. I.

of new holdings and farm extensions by intakes from the adjoining forest or waste. Not only were such intakes normally let for market-value rents, but, with growing land hunger, the cultivated area on many manors was greatly increased.[1] On some estates, especially in districts of rapidly expanding population, the income acquired by additions to the acreage of productive land must have largely, if not completely, offset any rise in the landlord's cost of living.

Moreover, an improvement in net rent receipts did not necessarily have to take the form of increased money payments by tenants. The landlord's disposable income depended upon costs of estate administration and maintenance as well as upon rents. If the former charges could be reduced, net estate revenue would rise. In some cases, economies in administration were effected by the sale of outlying properties and the concentration of lands into more compact and easily manageable units. In other instances, part of the burden of estate administration was placed upon tenants in lieu of higher rent charges. This development was not in itself novel, since under the system of feudal agriculture much of the work of manorial administration, as well as the cultivation of the lord's demesne, had been undertaken by customary tenants; indeed, in spite of the widespread commutation of labour services which preceded the Tudor age, vestiges of villein tenure still survived in the occasional boonworks and other obligations exacted on some manors as late as the mid-seventeenth century. These services, however, formed part of a long-established, though greatly weakened tradition, and affected customary tenants rather than other occupiers. The main departure, as far as the period covered by our study is concerned, was the imposition of new services on leaseholders. A feature of the leases granted by Sir William Petre after 1550 was the obligation on lessees to occupy manorial offices, such as those of bailiff collector, and reeve. Annual surveys of the Petre lands were compiled from terriers drawn up by tenants and completed by an outside surveyor.[2]

While costs of administration might thus be reduced, expenditure on estate maintenance suggested greater possibilities of economy, especially in connection with small under-rented holdings whose upkeep was the landlord's responsibility. Contemporary complaints concerning the

[1] W. G. Hoskins, 'The Reclamation of the waste in Devon', EcHR, XIII, 1943, pp. 85–9; E. Kerridge, 'The Movement of Rent, 1540–1640', EcHR, 2nd Ser., VI, 1953, pp. 24–31; E. Hopkins, The Bridgewater Estates in North Shropshire in the First Half of the Seventeenth Century, University of London M.A. thesis, 1956, pp. 53–63.

[2] Finch, op. cit., p. 44; Kerridge, EcHR, 2nd Ser., VI, 1953, pp. 17–18; Hull, thesis, pp. 340–2; M. Campbell, The English Yeoman Under Elizabeth and the Early Stuarts, New Haven, 1942, pp. 142–3; Salop. RO, 123, 1, p. 35; Lancs. RO, DDF, 75, fo. 11; Emerson, thesis, pp. 134–5, 285.

"decay" and engrossing of farms reflect the widespread nature of this problem and indicate two of the principal solutions which recommended themselves to landowners. In the one case, the landlord allowed the farmstead to "decay," that is, he neglected his obligations on the ground that the rent received scarcely covered the value of the timber used for maintenance. In the other case, small-holdings were thrown together to create large farms, thereby effecting a saving in the cost of repairs. Nor were these the only possibilities. On many holdings, responsibility for the upkeep of buildings, generally assumed by the landlord at the beginning of the Tudor period, was increasingly placed on the tenant; so also was the maintenance of hedges, fences, and ditches. For these purposes timber was normally supplied by the landlord, either as a specific allowance or, more generally, in the common terminology of housebote, hedgebote, firebote, ploughbote, and cartbote. Occasionally an upper limit was placed on the cost of repairs for which the tenant was liable, but this was not usual. Moreover, the tenant's responsibility in regard to repairs was sometimes extended beyond the holding which he occupied. He might, for example, be required as a condition of his tenancy to repair and maintain the lord's swinehouse, or any mills, weirs, or fisheries on the manor. In localities where there was a danger of flooding, as in parts of south-east England or Lincolnshire, the repair of sea-walls and dikes, or the payment of "scots" in lieu, was often delegated, in whole or in part, to the occupier. In addition, various other public charges, such as maintenance of bridges and highways and the relief of the poor, were sometimes placed on the tenant, so also was responsibility for the payment of any fee-farm or quit-rent issuing out of the property, together with taxation charges, fifteenths being specifically referred to in certain leases.[1]

Even the cost of estate improvement was sometimes borne by the tenant, although this was not the usual practice. One does, however, find instances, as at Kilpeck in Herefordshire in the 1530's, where long-term leaseholders were required to clear land and bear the costs of its enclosure. Just over a century later, at Ayston in Rutland, tenants had to meet all or most of the costs of enclosure on land belonging to Brudenell of Deene. On Petre's Essex estate in the late sixteenth century several leaseholders were required to put in certain specified buildings

[1] J. Thirsk, *Tudor Enclosures* (Historical Association Pamphlet, General Series: G. 41), 1959, pp. 10–13; Hasbach, *op. cit.*, p. 384; Rogers, *Agriculture and Prices*, IV, p. 62; Hull, *thesis*, pp. 319–22; Emerson, *thesis*, pp. 133–4; Northants. RO, Westmorland-Apethorpe Coll. 4, XVI, 5; Herts. RO. X. C. 7. A, fo. 31; Lancs. RO, DDCL, 1660–1685; BM Add. MS 34163, ff. 21–21^v, 46^v; 34166, fo. 25; PRO E 133, 481, Trin. 20 Eliz. I; PRO E 133, 1223, Mich. 37–8 Eliz. I; Lumley MS 2305 (in possession of the Earl of Scarbrough).

or other capital improvements on their holdings within a stipulated
time of having entered them. At Wrexham, and possibly a number of
other places, local custom ruled that landlords should compensate
outgoing tenants for the costs of any improvements effected, but
legislation provided the occupier with no general protection of this
nature. Thus the progressive tenant who improved the value of his
holding was as likely to be rack-rented as compensated. The existence
of such conditions inevitably tended to act as a brake on agricultural
progress, and, particularly towards the end of his tenancy, the occupier
must have been tempted to over-crop or under-manure his holding.
The husbandry clauses which are to be found in some leases endeavoured
to prevent this situation by, for example, stipulating the proportion of
arable to pasture or fallow, and by specifying the application of quantities
of manure and other dressings.[1]

If a reduction in the burden of estate expenditure enabled some landowners to ride out the worst effects of inflation, additional protection
against the fall in the value of money might be obtained by levying
rents in kind. Sometimes such provision rents were sold on the open
market; but not uncommonly they were used, along with demesne
yields and receipts from tithes, if any, to furnish the landlord's household and to provide feed for his stock. Produce rents were not new;
indeed, cottagers had long rendered part-payment for their small
properties in capons, hens, eggs, and the like, and in the sixteenth and
early seventeenth centuries many continued to do so. It was, however,
in connection with a different class of tenant and a wider range of
agricultural produce that rents in kind began to assume greater significance in the Tudor period. From the early sixteenth century onwards
an increasingly common feature of leasehold tenure on many estates
was the obligation laid on tenants to pay all or part of their rents in
corn or other produce. In the case of stock-and-land leases, whereby
the landlord supplied capital apart from land and buildings, such
arrangements were normal. Many leases of this type were similar to
that renewed by Bacon at Ingham in Suffolk in 1562, which provided
for a rent of £93 and 133 combs of barley and rye with an option to
pay 5s. a comb. But apart from tenancies of this nature, the payment of
rent wholly or partly in the form of produce was frequently stipulated
in leases of demesne lands, as, for example, at Wilton in Wiltshire,
where leaseholders were required to pay large rents in wheat, barley,

---

[1] Nat. Lib. Wales, Pye of the Mynd Coll. Nos. 65, 73; Kent Church Court Coll.
No. 320; Finch, *op. cit.*, p. 161; Emerson, pp. 252–4; PRO E 133, 223, 16–17 Eliz. I;
W. Blith, *The English Improver Improved or the Survey of Husbandry Surveyed*, London,
1652, preface; G. Plattes, *A Discovery of Infinite Treasure Hidden Since the World's
Beginning*, London, 1639, p. 16; Salop. RO, 320, 5, p. 13.

malt, oats, poultry, and rabbits. Moreover, institutional landowners, as well as private landlords, were affected by this development. In 1576 an Act of Parliament (18 Eliz. I, c. 6) empowered the colleges of Oxford and Cambridge and the schools of Eton and Winchester to take one third of their leasehold rents in corn or its maximum current market value. Even before this act was passed, however, produce rent, at fictitious prices, had for some time been customary at King's College, Cambridge, and had figured in occasional collegiate leases granted elsewhere. In the years immediately preceding the Dissolution many monastic houses were deriving a considerable revenue from rents in kind, chiefly from leased-out portions of the demesne. At St Augustine's Canterbury, in 1535, almost one fifth of total gross income (£309 out of £1,684) took the form of produce rents, but this proportion was exceptional. On ecclesiastical lands in the seventeenth century, rents in kind were, if anything, more important than in early Tudor times, and generally constituted a major element in annual rent receipts. Together with tithes—where these were not leased out or otherwise commuted for fixed money payments—such rents must have provided the clergy with a comforting wind-break against inflation. On the other hand, provision rents, tithes, and other payments in kind were an encumbrance to the Crown, and those arising on former monastic properties were quickly farmed out, exchanged, or commuted.[1] One such payment was heriot: a charge most commonly levied at the death of a tenant, but sometimes additionally demanded on the surrender or alienation of land. Despite its feudal origin, this payment, which normally took the form of the tenant's best beast or chattel (or a money sum in lieu), was a widespread feature of copyhold tenure throughout our period, and it was not in the least unusual for it to be charged against leasehold or freehold land. Heriot was claimed on many of the estates belonging to private landowners, the Church, and the Crown. In the latter case, it features in two fifths of the leases for lives granted in the final decade of Elizabeth's reign—but as a fixed money payment, and not as a levy in kind.[2]

In spite of provision rents and similar charges, however, it was principally to larger money payments that the majority of landlords looked for an improvement in their rent-rolls. The extent to which such payments could be exacted from tenants depended primarily

[1] Herts. RO, 6604; 6718; Simpson, op. cit., pp. 81–2; Kerridge, EcHR, 2nd Ser., VI, 1958, p. 18; Finch, op. cit., p. 122; Emerson, thesis, pp. 136–49, 154; Bury and W. Suff. RO, E 3, 15.51, 2, 2; D. Knowles, The Religious Orders in England: The Tudor Age, Cambridge, 1959, p. 251; Hereford Dean & Chapter Lib., 3 A; 3 E; 5096; Norwich Dean and Chapter Lib., Parliamentary Survey of Lands (1649).

[2] Campbell, op. cit., pp. 116–17, 126–7; Hull, thesis, pp. 343–5; Cornwall, thesis, pp. 270, 284; CSPD, 1591–1603, passim.

upon the type of land tenure, and this could vary greatly, not only from estate to estate, but also from one property to another. In the case of freehold land, frequently held "by fealty only" or in return for small token payments, rents were fixed and could not be increased. Even at the beginning of the Tudor period such rents had often added little to the landlord's income, and with the fall in the value of money they became less and less significant. Thus, by the middle of the seventeenth century many freeholders had ceased to make any payments whatever, and freehold had almost achieved its modern meaning.[1]

On customary land, tenures at will provided the landlord with the best opportunity to adjust rents in line with rising land values, and it is sometimes claimed that the sixteenth and early seventeenth centuries witnessed the spread of tenancies of this type. Examples of this process can certainly be found; but, on balance, the evidence appears rather more suggestive of a development away from tenures at will in favour of longer-term leaseholds for years or lives. From the landlord's point of view there were disadvantages as well as advantages in the tenancy at will, and flexibility in the matter of rent adjustment was not everything. The tenant who occupied a holding for an uncertain term and was liable to be dispossessed at short notice had little incentive to improve his land, and was not chargeable at law with reparations. Moreover, since the period of tenure was indefinite, the payment of an entry fine, i.e. a premium, on admittance was not practicable. At a time when estate improvement was often financed to a large extent out of fines and receipts from the sale of timber, this could be a big drawback to the progressive but penurious landlord, as well as to the debtor or spendthrift. Thus, on the Ellesmere estate of the financially embarrassed earl of Bridgewater, in north Shropshire, in the years 1637–40, annual lettings at rack-rents were regarded as a poor second choice to long-term leases, and were considered only in the case of tenants who were unable or unwilling to pay the comparatively heavy entry fines demanded for the latter.[2]

Conditions governing the exaction of such fines were of decisive influence in determining the movement of rent on copyhold land, where the occupier paid a premium on admittance and low annual reserved rent. As a general, though by no means universal, rule, the copyholder of inheritance paid a fixed fine, which normally amounted to the equivalent of one or two years' annual rent, depending on the custom of the manor. With holdings of this type there was little

[1] Campbell, op. cit., pp. 114–15; R. H. Tawney, The Agrarian Problem in the Sixteenth Century, 1912, p. 30.
[2] Finch, op. cit., pp. 150, 159, 161; Aaron Rathbone, The Surveyor in Foure Bookes, London, 1616, p. 180; Hopkins, thesis, pp. 68–72, 155–60.

prospect of rent increase unless the landlord could successfully prove that at some date variable fines had been imposed, or unless he could persuade tenants to exchange copies for leases. Since, by the end of the sixteenth century, rising prices had given the copyholder of inheritance an almost freehold interest in his land, there was no advantage to him in the latter course. Indeed, as in more recent times of inflation, rent restriction helped to pave the way to outright purchase, and we find many instances of copyholders of inheritance enfranchising their holdings on highly favourable terms. In general, the copyholders for lives—who in Tudor times possibly outnumbered those of inheritance by about two to one—were less fortunate. In the first place, their copies were normally granted for not more than three lives, at the end of which the natural heir had no guarantee of succession to a property, but only the right of first refusal. Moreover, the entry fine in this class of tenure was usually arbitrary, and could in practice, as well as in theory, vary from a penny to scores of pounds, according to the size and value of the holding and the amount of the reserved rent. Thus, on the manor of Rivers Hall in Boxted, Essex, copyhold fines in 1620 amounted to £136 2s. 9d., compared with copyhold annual rents of £11 6s. 2d. Where the prospective copyholder lacked capital resources, a high entry fine could preclude occupation of a holding, and the land-lord was free, if he wished, to put in a more substantial tenant, or to throw several such properties together in order to create a large leasehold farm. The extent to which this happened is unknown. There is no doubt that on many manors the acreage under lease was growing at the expense of copyhold, but the change of tenure did not necessarily imply a change of tenant. In most parts of England at the end of the sixteenth century copyholders still outnumbered leaseholders, though the latter may well have occupied a larger area of land. Moreover, even arbitrary fines were sometimes regulated by custom, as on certain Norfolk and Suffolk manors in early Stuart times, where premiums on entry varied from a few pence above to a few pence below the sum of 2s. per acre.[1]

It is generally assumed that the entry fine formed an increasingly important element in the rent paid by the leaseholder in the sixteenth and early seventeenth centuries, and on many estates this was un-doubtedly so. Information on this score for early Tudor times, however, is piecemeal, but such evidence as there is suggests that, in the matter of

[1] Kerridge, EcHR, 2nd Ser., VI, 1953, pp. 18–19; Campbell, *op. cit.*, pp. 134–5 144–5; Cornwall, *thesis*, pp. 264 ff., 297, 331; Tawney, *op. cit., passim;* Hull, *thesis*, pp. 333, 347, 350–1; Finch, *op. cit.*, pp. 73, 117, 149–50; J. Spratt, *Agrarian Conditions in Norfolk and Suffolk, 1600–1650,* University of London M.A. thesis, pp. 115–17.

fines, the leaseholders' position at the beginning of the sixteenth century differed little from that of the copyholder, i.e. he paid a premium on the grant or renewal of lease, and this sum was generally equivalent to one or two years' reserved rent. By the Elizabethan period, when our data became more plentiful, this was no longer necessarily the case, and one finds numerous instances of the landlord's interest being asserted by heavy entrance fines combined with low annual rents. Thus, to give but one example of such a "beneficial" lease: in 1571 James Brodribbe (who also possessed 22 acres of freehold land) secured the renewal of a lease for twenty-one years of eight acres of enclosed pasture on the manor of Pylle, five miles north-west of Bristol, in return for a fine of £10 and an annual rent of 10s. If we wish to calculate the true rent cost of this holding, we must make allowance, as contemporaries did, for the interest forgone by the tenant on his advance premium payment—i.e. we must discount the amount of the fine at the current rate of interest over the whole of the period of tenure. At 10 per cent compound interest (the maximum statutory rate), Brodribbe's £10 fine would have cost him, on average, £3 10s. 6d. per annum. Added to the reserved annual rent, this gives a total yearly charge of £4 0s. 6d. for the whole holding, or 10s. 1d. per acre. How far the easing of credit facilities in early Stuart times affected this type of tenure is uncertain, but by the mid-seventeenth century there was a growing tendency for the entry fine to be dispensed with altogether, and for the landlord's claim on the lessee to be limited to the annual rent; in other words, leasehold and copyhold were parting company, and the former was assuming its modern shape. Thus, on some leaseholds in Northamptonshire in the early seventeenth century, beneficial leases were superseded by lettings at commercial rents. In Sussex and Yorkshire during the same period, premiums were not usually demanded for leasehold land except where an improvident gentleman or nobleman wanted to raise large sums quickly. One such was Josias Lambert of Carlton, father of the parliamentary general, who granted leases for 3,000 and 6,000 years at negligible annual rents and for fines which were almost equivalent to the freehold value of the lands concerned.[1]

The terms of the leases granted by Lambert were, of course, highly exceptional; but there were probably many estates in the early decades

[1] Somerset RO, X, WLM, O, 822, fo. 10^v; T. Clay, *Briefe, Easie and Necessary Tables, of Interest and Rents Forborne*, London, 1624; Anon., *Tables of Leases and Interest ...*, London, 1628; Kerridge, EcHR, 2nd Ser., VI, 1953, pp. 19–24; Finch, *op. cit.*, pp. 49; Cornwall, *thesis*, pp. 290–2; J. T. Cliffe, *The Yorkshire Gentry on the Eve of the Civil War*, University of London Ph.D. thesis, 1960, pp. 111, 143–4.

of the sixteenth century, where leases for forty years and upwards predominated over those for shorter periods. Thus, a survey made in 1590 of the former monastic property of Brillie, Hereford, reveals that the majority of tenants were still holding under indentures for ninety-nine years granted between 1491 and 1535. The rents received at the time of the survey were far below the commercial letting value of the land, and a memorandum noted that, in future, leases were to be limited to a maximum term of three years. In Devon the lease for three lives, coupled with a definite term of ninety-nine years, remained the predominant form of tenure until the late eighteenth century. Elsewhere in the west of England, and in parts of the north, long leases were also common. In general, however, the tendency was towards shorter terms; and by the end of Elizabeth's reign the lease for twenty-one years had been widely adopted in many places with the lease for three lives next in frequency. How far the prevalence of these terms was the result of the various enabling and restraining statutes is difficult to determine. But the Act of Leases (32 Hen. VIII, c. 28) disallowed reversions of more than twenty-one years or three lives, while legislation passed in Elizabeth's reign (13 Eliz. I, c. 10; 14 Eliz. I, c. 14; 18 Eliz. I, c. 11) limited ecclesiastical and collegiate leases to similar terms. Thus we find, for example, that church leases of land in the Durham Palatinate in the period 1610–31 employed these two terms in roughly equal proportions. Among Crown leases granted in the years 1591–1601 approximately two fifths were for twenty-one years and one quarter for three lives. The same predilection for a term of twenty-one years is to be noted in the records of many private landowners, with a tendency on some estates in favour of even shorter periods in the early seventeenth century.[1]

It will be apparent, however, that, whatever the term of tenure, the lessee benefited from any rise in the value of land between the grant of a lease and its renewal. But on each renewal it was possible for the landlord to adjust rent so that, temporarily at least, it reflected the enhanced value of the land. Such rent adjustments might be very large: indeed, in the conditions of the sixteenth and early seventeenth centuries the *proportionate* increase in rent could be much greater than the rise in the value of land, or in the price of agricultural produce which mainly contributed to it, without reducing farm profits to an unremunerative

[1] Hereford City Lib., L. C. Deeds 6581; W. G. Hoskins and H. P. R. Finberg *Devonshire Studies*, London, 1952, pp. 84, 337; Campbell, *op. cit.*, pp. 82–4; Hull, *thesis*, pp. 317–8; Cornwall, *thesis*, pp. 31–3; Finch, *op. cit., passim;* R.T. Gent., *Tenants' Law, or The Laws Concerning Landlords, Tenants and Farmers*, London, 1666, pp. 58–61; Prior's Kitchen, Durham, 220,194; 220,240; CSPD, 1591–1601, *passim;* HMC, Seventh Report, p. 530 a.

level. In order to appreciate the full significance of this argument, we should recall that rent is essentially a residual payment, and in a perfectly competitive market for agricultural land represents the difference between farm costs (including tenant's 'fair' remuneration) and the value of farm output. A simple example may make the position clear.

Table 29. *Effect of change in the value of land on rent and tenant's remuneration*

| | Before rise in value of land | After rise in value of land | |
		Money rent unchanged	Tenant's real income unchanged
	£	£	£
Landlord's Rent	10	10	225
Other farm costs	60	240	240
Value of produce	100	600	600
Tenant's remuneration	30	350	135
	Index number of real income		
Landlord	100	22	500
Tenant	100	259	100

In Table 29 we assume the existence of a large arable holding worked by hired wage labour. No claim is made for the accuracy of the figures contained in the table, but the changes which are shown are broadly representative of those which occurred between the beginning and end of the sixteenth century—viz., a sixfold increase in the value of farm output, due mainly to higher prices and partly to improved productivity; a fourfold increase in farm costs, particular allowance being made for the lag of agricultural wages behind prices; and a rise of 450 per cent in the cost of living. On the basis of these assumptions, it can be seen that if rent remains unchanged in spite of a rise in the value of land, the tenant's net income in our example is increased almost twelvefold in money terms, and more than two and a half times in real terms. At the same time, the purchasing power of the landlord's gross income from the holding declines to between one quarter and one fifth of its former level. In the second instance, where it is assumed that the entire economic surplus arising from the holding is taken by the landlord and the tenant's real income remains unchanged, it appears that the landlord's real income increases fivefold, while his money income rises by 2,250 per cent. The *proportionate* increase in rent is thus almost four times greater than the stipulated rise in the value of farm output.

In the context of the sixteenth and early seventeenth centuries, the contrast in the two situations illustrated by Table 29 has more than theoretical significance. On the majority of estates at this time long leases and customary tenures restricted the rent of some holdings far below the level of that obtainable on new commercial lettings. The predominant tendency, therefore, was for the range of rents, as between different holdings, to widen. On Petre's Essex lands in 1566 the range of leasehold rents was about 10:1, from the highest to the lowest rented properties on the estate; by 1590 this range had been increased to 24:1, from the Dairy House farm at East Thorndon, renting at 12s. per acre, to Westlands farm in Mountnessing, which was still at the old rent of about 6d. per acre set under the terms of a 1528 monastic lease. This situation was not in any way exceptional, and many similar examples could be cited. In general, it was the large leasehold farm operated on commercial principles by the capitalist farmer which provided the best opportunity for high rent; and the landlord whose estate consisted partly of such properties coming up for periodic revision of rents had little to fear from inflation, even though receipts from other holdings might remain inflexible. The rent of small farm units was often restricted by custom; but even where this was not the case, the economic surplus which the landlord could tap was generally smaller, in relation to size, than with large farm undertakings; for not only was productivity on the small-holding usually lower than on the large, but the subsistence cultivator in some instances supplemented his income by wage earning, and so was more likely to suffer than benefit from the relative fall in agricultural wage costs. Thus, apart from economies in expenditure on estate maintenance, there were positive advantages to the landlord in replacing small farmsteads by large holdings. However, security of tenure and artificially low rents doubtless enabled many small tenants to continue in possession who would otherwise have been squeezed out in favour of more efficient producers. Moreover, since the demand for land was rising, tenants who occupied under-rented holdings were well placed to sub-let all or part of their property at enhanced rents; and in many districts there appears to have been a tendency for the number of share-croppers and other undertenants to increase. The rents which figure in manorial surveys and leases, therefore, were not always the rents paid by the ultimate cultivators of the soil.[1]

[1] Emerson, *thesis*, pp. 128, 250, 286; Hull, *thesis*, pp. 354, 369; *Kerridge, thesis*, pp. 385–402; Cornwall, *thesis*, pp. 69, 298–301; Hopkins, *thesis*, p. 61.

When we turn to a detailed analysis of rent data, it becomes apparent that the general movement of rent in Tudor and early Stuart times cannot be measured with any degree of statistical exactness. Most of the relevant material which has come down to us is insufficiently detailed and too unreliable to justify statistical manipulation. But even if this were not the case, the range of rents was so wide that averages calculated from an unrepresentative sample of estates would not be very meaningful. Dr Kerridge has shown how, given a series of comprehensive manorial surveys, it is possible to calculate, for individual estates, the movement of rent on new lettings.[1] But if this enables us to determine the trend of rents, it tells us little about their general level, even on individual estates, since new lettings in any one year would seldom account for more than a small proportion of the total area of tenant-occupied land. Thus, one would expect the curve of total rent receipts to have followed a different course to that of rents on new takings, at first rising more slowly and then more rapidly as old leases fell in and customary rent restrictions were eased in some instances.

The date at which rents generally commenced to rise cannot be fixed with any certainty, and much must obviously have depended upon the type and geographical location of land. It may be suspected that in some pastoral districts rents showed a tendency to increase in the late fifteenth century, but, in general, there is no evidence of a sharp upward movement in arable rents before the 1520's. Thereafter, complaints about the exaction of high entry fines, or *gressums*, abound, and the rack-renting activities of "covetous" landlords become a subject of severe censure by moralists and churchmen. This, however, cannot be taken as evidence of a universal rise in rents; and on the majority of estates the disparity between rent receipts and rent potential widened as old tenancies proceeded to the completion of their terms. For many landowners, a wholesale revision of rents was delayed until the 1570's and 1580's; but from then onward, with land values continuing to rise, rent-rolls on estate after estate doubled, trebled, and quadrupled in a matter of decades. Thus, on manors belonging to the Seymour family in Wiltshire, while rents per acre for new takings approximately doubled, total rent receipts increased from £475 12s. 5½d. in 1575–6 to £1,429 11s. 0d. in 1639–40, and to £3,203 19s. 4d. in 1649–50. On Petre's Essex estate, properties producing annual rents of £1,400 in 1572 were renting for £2,450 in 1595, and for at least £4,200 in 1640. Between 1572 and 1640 the rents on many large leasehold farms on the estate were increased between five and tenfold. In little more than thirty years (1619–51) the rents on twelve Yorkshire

[1] Kerridge, EcHR, 2nd Ser., VI, 1953, pp. 16–34.

manors in the possession of the Saviles of Thornhill were increased by more than 400 per cent, the result of a major change in leasing policy. On the estates of other landed families in Yorkshire, Northampton-shire, East Anglia, and elsewhere, a doubling or trebling of rent receipts in the half century or so preceding the Civil War was by no means exceptional.[1]

Thus, in the late sixteenth and early seventeenth centuries there is evidence of a marked increase in rents on the estates of many private landowners. The same, however, cannot be said of Crown lands, which—thanks to the pressures of inflation and political uncertainty— were regarded less as long-term income-yielding investments than as a means of raising capital and rewarding allegiance. In Wiltshire rents per acre for new takings on lands of the duchies of Lancaster and Corn-wall increased about threefold in the course of the sixteenth century. By comparison, similar rents on the Seymour manors increased almost ninefold. Administration of the Crown estates appears to have been generally inefficient and corrupt. Surveys made in 1608 show that tenants on royal manors in Somerset, Devon, Dorset, and Wiltshire paid rents of £506 for land worth £7,500 per annum; in Cumberland, Westmorland, and the West Riding rents amounting to £2,206 were paid for properties valued at £9,294. These surveys were undertaken as part of a policy, instituted by Salisbury, of raising Crown rents to an economic level. But the policy, at first pushed with vigour, was later allowed to lapse, and the surveys were never completed. In consequence, although some quite sharp rent increases occurred under James I, many traditional rents were allowed to persist unaltered until after the Civil War. On ecclesiastical estates—where not only land but also manorial rights were sometimes farmed out—rents were generally at a less remunerative level than on private properties, though the disparity was not so marked as with Crown lands. On the estates of both the Crown and the Church, lessees—who included many substantial landowners in their own right—were often able to make high profits from direct farming or by sub-letting to undertenants. In 1633 the earl of Pembroke paid the bishop of Salisbury just over £118 rent for manors that he sublet for an upper rent of nearly £206. In 1616 the estate of Sir Timothy Hulton of Marske, whose father had been

[1] *Ibid.;* TED III, pp. 20–1, 39–43, 489, 57, 59, 61–3, 71–2, 337–8; Lamond, *op. cit.,* pp. 17–20, 38–9, 40–1, 104, 186–7; A. E. Bland, P. A. Brown and R. H. Tawney, *English Economic History: Select Documents,* London, 1914, p. 249; LP XII, pt. I, pp. 71, 72, 136, 226, 274, 415; LP XVIII, pt. I, pp. 444–5; LP XX, pt. II, pp. 342–3; Emerson, *thesis,* pp. 232, 236; Cliffe, *thesis,* pp. 112–14; G. R. Batho, 'The Finances of an Elizabethan Nobleman: Henry Percy, Ninth Earl of Northumberland', EcHR, 2nd Ser., IX, 1957, pp. 439, 442; Simpson, *op. cit.,* pp. 196–216; Finch, *op. cit.,* pp. 129, 163.

archbishop of York, was valued at £1,449 per annum, of which no
less than £573 was derived from church leases. Also in Yorkshire, at
about the same time, the Alfords of Meaux held the Crown property
of Meaux Abbey on a lease worth some £320 per annum more than
the yearly rent.[1]

It is clear that in Tudor and early Stuart times tenurial relationships
played a significant part in the determination of rent; and differences
in the system of land tenure and in the disposition of the landlord
could lead to wide variations in the rents charged for holdings of
essentially similar land. In a perfect market these considerations would
cease to exercise any effect, and the determination of rent would
depend upon the location of land and the size of the economic surplus
arising from it. Whilst the influence of these latter factors is not always
easily discernible among the complexities and inconsistences of Tudor
and Stuart land tenure, they nevertheless played a significant part in the
determination of rent during our period.

Rents, generally, were highest in the London region and in other
districts, such as the south-west, where major groupings of population
provided the farmer with an easily accessible market for his produce.
In Essex, for example, land on manors furthest away from London was
valued at the lowest rates. In most areas the shortage and high cost of
transporting hay led to a high premium being placed on meadowland,
which frequently commanded two or three times the rent of common-
field arable and was usually more expensive than pasture. In marshland
districts, however, hay was exceptionally plentiful, and pasture normally fetched the highest rents. Thus, at Trusthorpe and Sutton in
Lincolnshire in the early seventeenth century, pasture was worth
9s.–10s. per acre, compared with 7s. for meadow and 5s. for arable.
In such areas rent often depended partly upon the state of the drainage
works and the expenses needed to keep them efficient. In general,
meadowland was highly rented because its economic surplus was large.
Unlike arable, which normally lay fallow for one year in three, meadow
was cropped annually and was cultivated at low factor cost, apart from
rent. The same considerations, applied with rather less force, resulted
in higher rents being generally charged for pasture than for arable. The
fertility of the soil, whether due to its inherent qualities or man-made
improvements, had an important bearing on rent, though high yields
and high rents do not inevitably go together. Thus, enclosed arable
normally rented at higher rates than common-field land, while good
grassland was much dearer than rough grazing. For example, in

[1] Kerridge, EcHR, 2nd Ser., VI, 1953, pp. 29–34; F. C. Dietz, *English Public
Finance, 1558–1641*, New York, 1932, pp. 297–8; Norwich Dean and Chapter Lib.,
Parliamentary Survey of Lands (1649); Cliffe, *thesis* pp. 104–5.

Northamptonshire in the mid-seventeenth century, high-quality pasture rented for up to 26s. 8d. per acre, while in the north of England rough grazing could be had for a few pence.[1]

Over the Tudor and early Stuart periods as a whole, one of the most significant features in the long-term movement of rent was the narrowing of the differential between rates charged for poorer and better qualities of land. As a corollary of this, the rent of arable increased to a greater extent than that of pasture or meadow. Thus, between 1556 and 1648 the rents of certain lands in Warwick increased by 1031 per cent, while the rents of better lands in the same place increased by 833 per cent. On one Derbyshire estate between 1543 and 1584 a more than fourfold increase in the rent of meadowland was accompanied by an even greater rise in arable rents. In parts of Norfolk and Suffolk the rent of arable land increased from 4s. per acre in the first decade of the seventeenth century to 10s. the acre in 1640–50; pasture rose from 5s. 11d. to 12s. in the same period, and meadow from 10s. in 1600–10 to 11s. 8d. in 1630–40.[2] The proportionately large increase in arable rents is not unexpected, since the long-term rise in the price of cereals exceeded that for other farm products, while arable production afforded the greatest scope for raising yields and lowering costs in terms of output.

Over shorter periods, also, one might expect to find disparities in the movement of rent on different categories of land, in accordance with changes in the relative profitability of arable and livestock husbandry. In our analysis, made earlier, of trends in the agrarian economy, we indicated alternate phases in which grain prices were either rising or falling in sympathy with the prices of pastoral products, and it seems reasonable to suppose that the movement of rents on arable and grassland also tended to alternate in sympathy with prices. In the case of lands subject to inflexible tenures any such relationship is difficult to discern, though it appears to emerge fairly clearly on new lettings at commercial rents. Thus, while rents on new (predominantly) arable takings in Wiltshire doubled in the 1530's, when harvests were generally poor, pasture rents changed little. In the succeeding decade rents on new arable takings remained almost static while, according to literary evidence, grassland rents sharply increased. We should note, however, that while land is by no means homogeneous, a considerable degree of substitution between different categories exists, and in

[1] TED III, p. 341; Hull, *thesis*, p. 373; Thirsk, *English Peasant Farming*, pp. 60–2; Spratt, *thesis*, pp. 215–7; Finch, *op. cit.*, pp. 48, 157; R. Lennard, *Rural Northamptonshire Under the Commonwealth*, Oxford Studies in Social and Legal History, V, 1916, p. 53; Prior's Kitchen, Durham, M. 80.

[2] Campbell, *op. cit.*, pp. 84–5; VCH *Derby*, II, p. 176; Spratt, *thesis*, p. 216; Hull, *thesis*, p. 376; Blith, *op. cit.*, p. 82.

periods of major economic upheaval all land values tend to react sympathetically. Thus, the severe structural adjustments of the 1550's and '60's and 1620's and '30's, which left most large arable farmers better off than before, led to a general slowing down, and even temporary reversal, in the upward movement of arable rents, as well as those on pasture.[1] Clearly, the main explanation for this situation is to be found in a temporary surplus of untenanted land—at ruling levels of rent—attributable to the reduced profitability of pasture farming, and the throwing up of small-holdings by peasant cultivators following adverse harvest conditions.

D. CONCLUSION

The inflation of Tudor and early Stuart times is generally believed to have confronted English landowners with serious problems: problems which derived from the inelasticity of tenures, and which, so it is argued, could only be overcome by the adoption of rational techniques of estate management, or—according to another school of thought— by and injection of income from the proceeds of office or business. Under the influence of these conceptions, historians have envisaged major shifts in the balance of economic, social, and political power in the century preceding the Civil War.[2] If such theories carry great scholarship behind them, they also seem in the light of present evidence to be built on very uncertain foundations. In the first place, our own study suggests that the basic premise of landlord embarrassment has been seriously overstated. Rent was not the landlord's only source of estate revenue, and proceeds from direct farming—not to mention timber sales and other receipts—were sometimes of much greater importance. Moreover, in spite of rigidities due to the prevailing system of land tenure, there were probably few estates where rental revenues remained inflexible for any length of time. In most districts, pressure of population created a constant need for additions to the cultivated area, while on demesne lands, if not on customary holdings, tenancies could be periodically renewed at greatly enhanced rents in money or in

[1] See sources listed in note 1, p. 691 *supra*; Kerridge, EcHR, 2nd Ser., VI, 1953, pp. 24–31; Hull, *thesis*, pp. 371, 380; Spratt, *thesis*, p. 216; Cliffe, *thesis*, p. 112; Finch, *op. cit.*, pp. 130, 157.

[2] R. H. Tawney, 'The Rise of the Gentry, 1558–1640', EcHR, XI, 1941, pp. 1–38; 'The Rise of the Gentry; A Postcript', EcHR, 2nd Ser., VII, 1954, pp. 91–7; L. Stone, 'The Anatomy of the Elizabethan Aristocracy', EcHR, XVIII, 1948, pp. 1–53; 'The Elizabethan Aristocracy: A Restatement', EcHR, 2nd Ser., IV, 1952, pp. 302–21; H. R. Trevor-Roper, 'The Elizabethan Aristocracy: An Anatomy Anatomised', EcHR, 2nd Ser., III, 1951, pp. 279–98; *The Gentry, 1540–1640*, EcHR, supplement No. 1. (1953); J. P. Cooper, 'The Counting of Manors', EcHR, 2nd Ser., VIII, 1956, pp. 377–89; Finch, *op. cit.*, pp. xi–xix; Simpson, *op. cit.*, pp. 179–80, 210–16.

kind. On many properties, as we have seen, much of the burden of estate expenditure was placed upon the tenant; and in some instances, large, highly-rented leasehold farms were created out of small holdings. Whatever doubts may linger about the landowner's position in the years before 1580, few can remain in connection with the succeeding period up to 1620, which saw a massive redistribution of income in favour of the landed class: a redistribution which, in the final analysis, was as much at the expense of the agricultural wage-earner and consumer as of the tenant farmer. Even after 1620 the rent-rolls of many landlords continued to increase, though on some estates rents on new commercial lettings, particularly of pasture land, remained stationary or declined. Not all landowners, of course, stayed prosperous, even under the highly favourable conditions of the late sixteenth and early seventeenth centuries; but not every landed family which declined did so because of poor estate management or because agricultural income failed to rise. Where these factors were operative, however, it may be suspected that the social class of the landowner—whether gentry or aristocracy—was of seldom more than marginal significance. In general, given the level of personal expenditure, the prosperity of the landowner in Tudor and early Stuart times must have depended much less upon his social origins than upon the nature of the land which constituted his estate and its sensitivity to economic change.

CHAPTER X

RURAL HOUSING IN ENGLAND[1]

A. INTRODUCTION

Rural buildings in the English countryside can be divided into two classes. First, there are those designed primarily for a single family and as a farming centre. Second, there are those houses which, though their owners might be involved in the local economy, had to accommodate a larger number of persons, the majority of whom were not engaged in agriculture. The former class, which is vastly the more numerous, will engage most attention in this chapter. The second class, which includes castles, larger manor houses, and the new mansions of the Tudor and early Jacobean periods, are the proper subject of the architectural historian, and much has already been written about them. Even so, the literature consists mainly of accounts of individual houses with emphasis on their family history, and the essential data for a study of the great house in the sixteenth century, as a social rather than an architectural product, have yet to be gathered together. Nevertheless, an account of rural building must start at the top of the social scale, if only because ideas of comfort and convenience percolated downwards more rapidly in this period than at any earlier time, under the stimulus of rising standards.

The two classes of house had distinct origins which can be separated even in Anglo-Saxon times. The ancestry of the farmhouse lies in a single building which provided shelter for the family and its livestock and storage space for the products of husbandry. The study of farmhouses has made very rapid progress in recent years, thanks to two branches of archaeology. Excavations have begun to reveal Anglo-Saxon and medieval peasant houses in this country and their relation with continental houses of the migration period and earlier. The examination of surviving houses has begun to reveal the remarkable wealth of England and Wales in houses older than the eighteenth century, and the complexity of the cultural and technological develop-

[1] Acknowledgement is made to those individuals and institutions whose photographs are reproduced, and to those who have generously allowed their plans of houses, (most of them hitherto unpublished) to be used (see Lists of Plates and Figures). Mr N. Summers has redrawn the plan of Audley End from Winstanley's survey, and the plans of Raynham Hall from the Survey of 1671 in the R.I.B.A. Library. The staff of the National Monuments Record (formerly the N.B.R.) has been most helpful in procuring illustrative material.

ments that they incorporate. This type of research can only be conducted on a regional basis. One exempary study has reached print:
Monmouthshire Houses, by Sir Cyril Fox and Lord Raglan. A study of
north Oxfordshire has been published and others have been completed
in thesis form; still more are in progress, but there remain a number of
counties whose farmhouses are almost completely unknown. The
most striking result of these regional studies so far is to emphasize the
difference between the highland and lowland zones (see below pp.
and   ); further work will certainly elaborate and define these
contrasts, and put the relations of the zones on a clearer cultural and
chronological basis.[1]

As the excavation of King Edwin's palace at Yeavering in Northum-
bria has already shown, the development of the great house starts from
the fact that the needs of the king and his peers could only be met by
erecting a number of buildings for distinct purposes. The great household must be seen as an institution, and the evolution of its buildings
linked with those of other institutions such as the monastery and the
college. That evolution was determined by the desire for an efficient
relationship between the hall, the kitchen, and other rooms connected
with it and the sleeping accommodation required for persons of all
ranks—over which considerations of defence might impose themselves.
Architectural historians have tended to concentrate their interest on
those parts of the great house, such as the hall, on which most care was
lavished; precisely how retainers and household servants were accommodated has only recently been noticed.[2] The relations between
different parts of a monastic or collegiate institution were formalized
during the Middle Ages, and the relations between buildings round a
cloister or quadrangle became remarkably uniform. By contrast, the
needs of any great household were so much less constant and the
conditions imposed by defensive walls so varied, that a formal and
standard layout, round one courtyard or more, is a less significant

[1] Fox and Raglan, *Monmouthshire Houses*, 3 vols., 1951–4; J. T. Smith, in *Arch. J.*,
CXII, 1955, and CXV, 1958. Further references may be found in M. W. Barley, *The
English Farmhouse and Cottage*, 1961. R. B. Wood-Jones, *Traditional Domestic Architecture in the Banbury Region*, 1963, appeared too recently for advantage to be taken of its
evidence and conclusions. For a map showing the relation between highland and
lowland zones in terms of roof types, see R. A. Cordingley in *Trans. Ancient. Mon.
Soc.* IX, 1961, p. 74.

[2] Apart from accounts of individual houses, especially in *Country Life*, see the various
volumes of J. A. Gotch, such as *Early Renaissance Architecture in England* (various
editions), *The Growth of the English House*, n.d., c. 1909, and J. Summerson, *Architecture
in Britain 1530–1830*, 1953, Part I. For accommodation for servants in medieval
houses, see W. A. Pantin, 'Chantry Priests' Houses and other medieval Lodgings'
Med. Arch., III, 1959, pp. 243–58.

feature of surviving great houses of this class. Formality began to be imposed in the Elizabethan age and later, under the influence of Renaissance ideas to which social needs were subordinate.

B. THE GREAT HOUSE

The noble household of the sixteenth century was still organized, as it had been for centuries, on lines which differed only in scale and not in character from those of the royal household. Both depended on a hierarchy of staff ranging from those of good birth who served the family at table, in the chamber and abroad, to the porter at the gate: a range of gentlemen, yeomen, grooms, and others in which every man knew his place, his salary, and his allowances. How large it might be, and how costly to maintain, we learn when a nobleman, such as the earl of Northumberland early in the sixteenth century, or the earls of Huntingdon a hundred years later, tried to check extravagance and rivalry by setting down the whole household and its working in a paper scheme. The numbers might amount to nearly 150 persons in the case of the earl of Northumberland, or sixty-eight in the service of the earl of Huntingdon in 1609; even the household of the Saviles at Rufford, Nottinghamshire, and Thornhill, Yorkshire, a not particularly wealthy or ambitious family, rose from about forty to sixty in the twenty years before the Civil War. Apart from its cost—the wages bill of the earls of Northumberland rose from about £150 per annum in the 1590's to £600 in 1632—such a household called for buildings in which large quantities of food could be stored and prepared, and where living and sleeping accommodation of great variety had to be provided.[1]

Let us take first the needs of the kitchen. In 1611 a treatise on the provision of supplies was drawn up at Belvoir Castle. In it the annual needs of the household were stated to be seventy cattle, four hundred sheep, forty lambs, thirty pigs, and 1,200 couples of rabbits, and in addition great quantities of sea fish, bought at Kings Lynn, and freshwater fish from local ponds and rivers.[2] It was for catering on such a scale that the ancient tradition of the kitchen as a detached building lived on through this period, to be incorporated in the more formally planned great houses of the eighteenth century. The danger of fire was slight in houses of stone or brick, but the kitchen was a large and busy element within the household, and it could not be merged conveniently with the living quarters of the family.

[1] *The Regulations and Establishment of the Household of Henry Algernon Percy, 5th Earl of Northumberland...*, ed. Bishop Percy, 1770; J. Nichols, *History and Antiquities of Leicestershire*, 1811, III, ii, p. 594.   [2] H.M.C. *Rutland*, IV, pp. 480–6.

For the accommodation of the lower ranks of the household, the outer courtyard no doubt served, as did the outer bailey in earlier castles. In the later Middle Ages the practice of maintaining liveried retainers, many of them of gentle origin, had set the great feudatories the problem of providing large numbers of rooms, of comfortable and uniform standard. The north court of Dartington Hall, Devon, built at the end of the fourteenth century, shows how it was solved. The west side of the court consisted of a two-storey range comprising single rooms, each with its window, fireplace, and garderobe. The east side, now demolished, may have had stabling, but part of it certainly consisted of more lodgings of the same kind. The north side of the court was taken up with a barn, a gatehouse, and another range of simpler lodgings. At South Wingfield Manor, Derbyshire, built in the middle of the fifteenth century, the outer court was surrounded by a barn and by other buildings such as stables which may have had chambers for retainers or domestic servants over them. Thornbury Castle, Gloucestershire, built in the later years of Henry VII by the duke of Buckingham, has in its north court one of the most complete surviving examples of a range of stables with chambers over, approached as at Dartington by outside stairs. These were no doubt for servants, rather than retainers, for the rooms were large and must have been shared. Petworth House, Sussex, had in 1574 an outer court surrounded by three barns and a stable. The latter had "a lodging in the end for horsekeepers;" there were five other lodgings in the outer gatehouse and twelve more in the range between the inner and outer courts.[1]

The principal innovation of the fifteenth century, which reached fullest expression in the sixteenth, was the lofty gatehouse which, besides the dignity it gave to the house, provided large numbers of lodging chambers for servants. At Layer Marney, Essex, the original design cannot be recovered, since it was not completed, and what was built has been much altered, especially by making the gatehouse into the principal part of the residence, but there are in all thirty-nine chambers in the gatehouse, most of them small and without fireplaces (Plate V). The stables flanked the gatehouse to one side, and they were of two storeys, but the first floor, instead of being divided into chambers, consisted of a long dormitory where other servants slept.[2] The remaining building erected by Lord Marnay before his death in 1523 was a large brick barn. This and the buildings in the outer courtyard at South Wingfield Manor have been loosely called farm buildings, but

[1] A. Emery, 'Dartington Hall, Devonshire', *Arch. J.*, cxv, 1958, pp. 190–3; 'A View of Petworth', 1574, in Alnwick MSS., L. and P., iii fo. 32. I am indebted to Mr C. R. Batho for this and other information about the Percy household.

[2] *Country Life*, 21 February 1914.

the great house of the sixteenth century was not a farm. It had stables for riding horses and barns for fodder, but not cowsheds or wagon houses; a yard where fuel was stacked and cut up, but not for wintering cattle. The variety of service buildings is well recorded in the survey of Audley End, Essex, prepared by Henry Winstanley (Fig. 18). The distinction between the Manor House as the residence of the lord of the manor and the Manor Farm from which the demesne was worked goes back in origin to the practice of leasing the demesne. Although economic conditions in the sixteenth century would have made direct participation in farming very profitable to the aristocratic classes, social conventions were against it. Only rising families with more ambition than pride, such as the Brudenells of Northamptonshire, were content to give time and thought to farming.

The few new buildings of size in the first half of the sixteenth century are confined to the south-eastern half of England. They are in the main either royal palaces, such as Richmond Palace at Sheen, or buildings which were meant to mark the success of the men about the court (Plate VI a). The latter range from Layer Marney, started by Henry Lord Marney, "a scant well born gentleman of no great land," or Little Leighs, Essex, and Kirtling Hall, Cambridge, both built by chancellors of the Court of Augmentations, to West Stow Hall, Suffolk, built by Sir John Croftes, a local squire connected with court circles; the gatehouse at West Stow is a miniature version of Layer Marney. Apart from successful court servants, the other builders of large mansions were really City merchants turning country gentlemen —already familiar figures in English society, who were to become more numerous in this period. Sir William Fitzwilliam, alderman and merchant tailor of London, was building at Milton, Northamptonshire, by 1530. Thomas Kytson, citizen and mercer of London, built Hengrave Hall, Suffolk, in the years 1521–38. It had a principal court with a hall at the further side from the gatehouse; the kitchen and service buildings made a second court on the east side, and the stables and other offices were in a third court outside the area of the moat.[1]

Within the traditional plan for these larger houses one significant development in the later Middle Ages, apart from the storeyed gatehouse, was the addition of more parlours. The parlour began to take the place of the great chamber or solar in the life of the aristocratic household. This change began in the fourteenth but appears to have taken place mainly in the fifteenth century, though more field work

[1] For Layer Marney and Milton see A. Tipping, *English Houses*, II, p. xx; for Hengrave Hall, A. J. Gotch, *Early Renaissance Architecture in England*, pp. 57–60 (the kitchen court was demolished in 1775, and the published plan shows the stable court).

is required on this subject.[1] For instance at Gainsborough Old Hall, Lincolnshire, built in the 1480's by Lord Burgh, there was in 1625 a Little Dining Parlour at the upper end of the hall and within the hall block, a Little Side Parlour beyond it (no more than a passage), and two others, the Garden Parlour and the Great Parlour, in the east wing.[2] The Great Chamber was over the Great Parlour and was used as the principal bedroom. The Dining and Great Parlour served as dining- and drawing-room respectively, but the other parlours were lodging parlours or bedrooms. It is commonly said that such houses had a winter and a summer parlour, but there is no evidence that these terms, or the practice or changing by season from one parlour to another, were in general use. The earliest usage was no doubt for the family to take meals apart, and a separate room for sitting, as distinct from dining, follows somewhat later.[3]

It has often been said that while the desire for privacy and seclusion for the family and its immediate circle led to the abandonment of the hall, the place of the latter was taken by the gallery, a spacious room where social intercourse need not be interrupted by the traffic of domestics. Certainly some social prestige must have been attached to having a gallery, to judge from its scale in many of the great houses of 1575–1640, but inventories show that it was not always the handsome and dignified feature portrayed in Nash's nineteenth-century drawings. The Saviles of Rufford, Nottinghamshire, used it as a store for bedding and linen—it held twenty feather beds, twenty-five feather bolsters, thirty pairs of blankets, and twenty rugs—and an examination of inventories of Lancashire gentry gives the impression that it served as "a general store place, not to say junk room." An inventory of Red Hall, Bourne, Lincolnshire (Fig. 20, p.   ), made in 1633 not long after the house was built, the "high gallery" contained spare beds, cheese and butter.[4] Another very similar innovation was the loggia, a gallery

[1] Solar or great chamber was used in the Middle Ages only of a room on the first floor; the parlour was invariably a ground-floor room. Chamber alone, may, in some parts of England, indicate a room on either floor. For definitions, based on contemporary evidence, of these and other terms, see M. W. Barley's 'Glossary of Names for Rooms in Houses of the Sixteenth and Seventeenth Centuries', in I. Ll. Foster and J. Alcock (eds.) *Culture and Environment*, 1963, p. 479.

[2] Inventory of Sir William Hickman, 1625, Lincs. AO Inv. 130, 228, reprinted as a pamphlet, with a plan of the house, by J. Hodson and M. Whitworth for the Friends of the Old Hall Association, entitled *The Contents of Gainsborough Old Hall*, 1625.

[3] E.g., Smithell's Hall, Lancashire, a timber house of the first half of the sixteenth century, had one parlour in the original design; a better parlour or withdrawing room, with fine wainscotting, was added not long after. Tipping, *loc. cit.*, pp. 226–9.

[4] J. Summerson, *Architecture in Britain 1530–1830*, pp. 3, 11; 'An Inventory of goods left at Rufford Abbey taken 20th September 1642', in Notts. RO, DDSR 215/15; O. Ashmore, 'Household Inventories of Lancashire Gentry', *Hist. Soc. of*

or arcade on the ground floor with one side open to the air. In a great many instances the openings of these loggias in Elizabethan and Jacobean houses were filled in at a later time because the English climate made such an open arcade useless.

The rising standards of comfort and convenience in the century before 1530 can best be seen in the lodging which some medieval abbots built for themselves. The provision of a guest house adequate to the rank of those visitors for whose hospitality the abbot himself was responsible was an important element in the monastic plan by the thirteenth century. By the Dissolution, richer houses had usually a group of buildings, often still on the west side of the cloister range, in which the abbot had both a hall for superior guests and a range of private rooms for his own use, as well as a separate kitchen. At Chester, Gloucester, and Peterborough, the old abbot's house became the new bishop's palace without any considerable alteration. Others survived without alteration because they could serve equally well for the laymen who acquired them; they were new and convenient, and sometimes splendid by contemporary standards. At Notley Abbey, Buckinghamshire, a new wing to the abbot's house contained "larger and more elaborate private apartments of the abbot," which were not more than a generation old at the Dissolution. At Thame Park, Oxfordshire, the range of buildings put up by Robert King, the last head of the Cistercian house there, included on the first floor of the tower a particularly fine parlour, with panelling and an internal porch. Abbot Chard's hall and tower at Forde Abbey, Dorset, built in the years before 1539, became the great hall and parlours of a private house. The prior's lodging at Much Wenlock, Salop, was taken over untouched by the Lawley family, but the monastic infirmary was added to the residence to increase the accommodation. At Watton Priory in the East Riding, the fifteenth-century prior's lodging survived as a farmhouse. It consisted of a ground floor hall with an oriel, a dining chamber over the hall, and a solar in an attached wing. The medieval kitchen has gone. Lord Darcy, who had been Master of Ordnance to Henry VIII and acquired in 1553 the former St Osyth's Priory, Essex, retained the fine gatehouse of c. 1450 and the lodgings built by Abbot Vintoner in 1527.[1]

In general, monastic buildings suffered every kind of vicissitude, from complete demolition and the re-use of their material for other

---

Lancs. and Cheshire, CX, 1958, p. 63; Joan Varley, 'New Light on the Red Hall, Bourne', in Lincs. Historian, 2 (12), 1965, p. 18.

[1] Arch. J., LXXXIII, 1923, pp. 139–66, and LXXXVI, 1929, pp. 59–68; Oxoniensia, VI, 1941, p. 39; Hist. Mon. Comm., West Dorset, pp. 240, 244–5, and Essex, III, p. 198.

buildings or even for local road repairs, to adaptation with the minimum of change. The larger the house and the property with which it was associated, the less likely it was to survive (Plate VI (b)). The cloister court could be turned with ease into the focus of a private house, as it was at Newstead, Nottinghamshire, or Hinchinbrooke, Huntingdonshire. Where the principal monastic buildings were on the first floor, over vaulted undercrofts, the popularity of the first-floor house among the aristocracy might ensure their survival.[1] The monastic church itself rarely survived, though at Buckland Abbey, Devon, the nave of the church became the hall and parlour of the private house, and only the transepts have disappeared.

By the 1570's the new pattern of social and political power emerging from the Reformation had become stable enough to express itself in new building. It was centred even more strongly than before on the royal court, in that the buildings, at their most lavish, were intended primarily to satisfy what has been called the cult of the sovereign.[2] Their new architectural quality was a symmetry directed outwards, not into a courtyard, though the latter remains, in the largest houses, an essential feature. Planning within was unchanged, and symmetry meant that a kitchen or storeroom might have as large a window as a parlour. The fact that the finest houses were built to receive the queen and the large numbers of her entourage placed a new importance on the provision of lodgings for guests. The best instance is Kirby Hall, Northamptonshire, begun in 1570 by Sir Humphrey Stafford, but mainly the work of Sir Christopher Hatton, captain of the queen's bodyguard and later lord chancellor. The inner court has on its two flanks a series of heated rooms of uniform scale; the long gallery was over the west range, and there were more lodgings over the gateway and loggia.[3] The outer court had no more than a circular drive of the kind which now became fashionable; as carriages swept round to the gateway the visitor had time to look at the north front.

There is plenty of evidence of the expense and trouble to which the aristocracy was prepared to go to provide a suitable setting for a royal progress. Hatton died in 1591, heavily in debt to the queen herself, without every having had a chance to entertain her there. At Ashby de la Zouch, Leicestershire, a set of rooms said to have been built by the earl of Huntingdon for James I's visit in 1617 is shown in eighteenth-century prints of the castle.[4] When James visited Belvoir Castle in 1603 on his first progress southwards, there was no time for building,

[1] See, for instance, Buck's view of Battle Abbey, Sussex.
[2] Summerson, *op. cit.*, ch. IV.
[3] H.M.S.O., *Kirby Hall* (Official Guide).
[4] H.M.S.O., *Ashby de la Zouch Castle* (Official Guide).

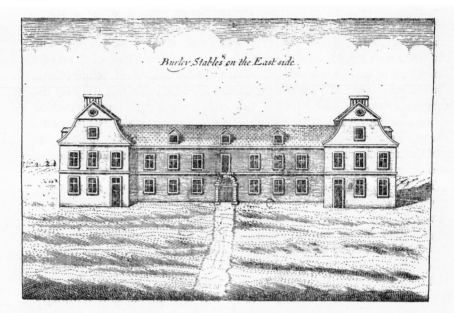

Burley Stables on the East side.

Fig. 17. The stables at Burley on the Hill, Rutland, built *c.* 1625 by
Charles Villiers, duke of Buckingham.

and so distinguished visitors had to bring their tents and bedding, but
windows were repaired, ovens and ranges built in the open air, and
plate borrowed in neighbouring towns.[1]

Along with this change in the scale and purpose of the great house
went a development in the stables. They were commonly placed in a
separate court, which rarely formed a closed group of buildings. The
first duke of Buckingham, George Villiers, put up at Burley-on-the-
Hill, Rutland, a stable block described later as "the noblest Building
of this kind in England." It consisted of a long range, in stone, with
central entrance and wings, symmetrically treated (Fig. 17). The stables
had vaulted ceilings, to reduce fire risk, and galleries or dormitories for
servants on the first floor. It was typical in all respects except in the
vaulted ceiling of the ground floor.[2] The views in Kip's *Britannia
Illustrata* (published in 1714 and 1715, but including a number of houses
built before 1640) show that stables were invariably of either one and a
half storeys, with dormer windows in the roof, or of two storeys.
The dormer window, which had been evolved in the Middle Ages for

[1] H.M.C., *Rutland*, IV, p. 440.
[2] J. Wright, *History and Antiquities of Rutland*, 1684, p. 32; P. Finch, *History of
Burley on the Hill*, 1901, I, pp. 6, 102.

providing places (not necessarily lighted) for beds in the roof space with its sloping sides, no doubt served its proper purpose in such a stable building. The inventory of Sir Anthony Drewrie, knight, of Besthorpe, Norfolk, who died in 1638, after reciting the contents of the house proper, lists the contents of outbuildings, including the first, second, third, and fourth chamber over the stables. Each contained a bed. Whichever servants slept there, they were superior to the husbandmen, or resident farmworkers, who shared a room with several beds, reached by "a great ladder to go up to the men."[1] Such chambers were not usually heated. The stables at Audley End built during Elizabeth's reign were exceptional in having two storeys and garrets as well (Fig. 18). At Hatfield House the stables are also exceptional for another reason; they consist of the main range of the palace built by Morton, bishop of Ely c. 1480, and converted by the earl of Salisbury. Over the woodwork of the boxes is the open roof of Morton's great hall and great chamber, while the service rooms at the north end were turned into harness rooms.[2]

By the first half of the seventeenth century the fashion for symmetry had spread from the house itself to the stables and coach houses, and even to the other buildings. Instead of stables isolated or in their own court, they were now frequently placed on one or both flanks of the forecourt, framing the visitor's first view of the house. They were often treated with as much care as the house, though on a simpler scale: a symmetrical range with central pediment, and above it a cupola holding a bell, with no doubt a clock below. Behind the stables on one side or the other was a small paddock or yard, with a barn or barns for fodder and the stack of timber for fuel.

Within the house proper, the most significant development of the later Middle Ages was the incorporation of the kitchen in the main structure. The most common arrangement in larger houses, and one which had evolved in the thirteenth century, had an open hall flanked by storeyed ranges at either end, the lower or service end being divided into two rooms, traditionally pantry and buttery. Sometimes these two rooms were separated by a passage leading to the kitchen beyond. Whether there was such a passage or not depended on the siting of the kitchen, which was a detached building, and might in some cases be reached equally conveniently from the screens passage at the lower end of the hall. In the great house the kitchen, because of the scale of operations there carried on, the storage space required for a large household, and the number of servants engaged about it, could never become part of the principal arrangement of rooms about a single court. It had and

[1] Norwich Diocesan Records, Inv. 1638, 147.
[2] *Hist. Mon. Commission, Herts.*, pp. 53–61.

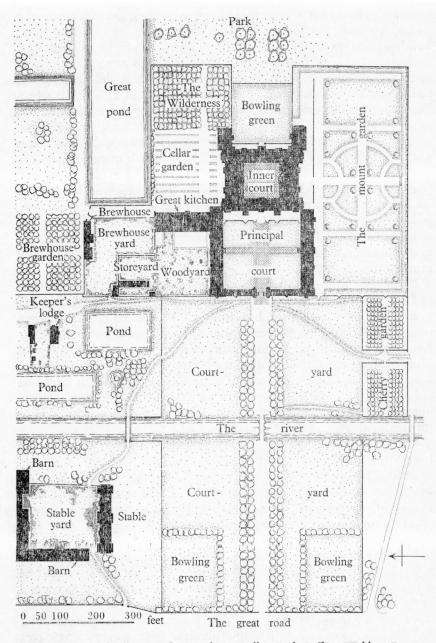

Fig. 18. Plan of the house and grounds at Audley End, Saffron Walden, Essex, as given in the survey of 1688 by Henry Winstanley, and showing the relation of the house to its grounds and ancillary buildings.

continued to have its own court, providing separate ingress for food supplies and domestic staff. In the later seventeenth century the rigorous application of symmetrical planning to the house led to the kitchen being placed on one limb of an extended design, and linked with the principal block (and the dining parlour) by a covered way or even an underground passage.

In somewhat smaller houses, of manor house status and below, the service wing, instead of being used merely for serving and storing food and drink, became the kitchen. This was made possible by the extension of the wing to contain several rooms in a range at right angles to the hall and so reasonably accessible from it. This often involved making the kitchen the front room of the wing, balancing the parlour in the other wing and with it flanking the entrance to a house of H or U plan. This arrangement is found at Barrington Court, Somerset, a large manor house built, perhaps before 1530, by Henry Daubney, a friend of Henry VIII, and important in architectural history as a symmetrical exercise in Tudor Gothic style. It is also found at Horham Hall, Essex, by 1540. In the freer planning of Hardwick Hall, Derbyshire, the kitchen has a place on the principal front, showing that Hardwick belongs in scale of conception to the tradition of the manor house rather than the great house.[1]

Several great houses of *c.* 1575 onwards contained a revolutionary element in their design. For the sake of a more compact plan, the service rooms were placed in a semi-basement, and servants were relegated to those conditions of half darkness from which social changes have rescued their few descendants only in this century. This arrangement was particularly convenient on a sloping site, such as that chosen in 1588 by Thomas Cecil, Burghley's son, for Wimbledon House, Surrey. It was for the same reason adopted for Fountains Hall, Yorkshire (1610), and Weston Hall, Staffordshire (*c.* 1630). The earliest great houses with basement services are, however, Longleat, Wiltshire (1567–75), Wollaton Hall, Nottinghamshire (1588), and Hardwick Hall, Derbyshire (1597), in all of which Robert Smythson was involved as mason. The basement also appears at Barlborough Hall, Derbyshire (1583), in which there are other reasons for suspecting Smythson's hand, and at Wootton Lodge, Staffordshire (Plate XIV), also his work. This new type of design was specifically French in origin. The chateau of Montceux-en-Brie, begun in 1547, has its service rooms in a basement and this arrangement was recommended by Philibert de l'Orme, writing in 1567. At a time when interest in French architecture was strong, both among patrons like John Thynne and in the masons they

[1] Summerson, *op. cit.*, pp. 14, 34, 36; J. A. Gotch, *The Growth of the English House*, p. 128.

employed, the idea of basement services may well have been picked up by Robert Smythson while at Longleat, where French craftsmen were engaged. The idea found favour very rapidly. Sir Thomas Tresham used it at Lyveden New Build, which he designed himself about 1600. John Thorpe's plan of Nottingham House, Kensington, built for Sir George Coppin *c.* 1605, has the note "All Offices and Cellars underground;" Inigo Jones placed them there in Wilton House and Sir Roger Pratt in Coleshill, for the semi-basement fitted the Renaissance mansion even more properly than it did the sham castle like Wollaton. It also aided the designing of a house on a restricted urban site, and so became particularly a feature of town houses after 1660.[1] The design is illustrated here from Raynham Hall, Norfolk, begun in 1622 and completed at the latest in the 1650's (Fig. 19).

The architectural development of the great house up to 1640 thus expressed radical changes in the social relations which existed within it. Although the great hall, once the focal point of household life, lost little of its architectural importance, its social use declined with the installation of a dining parlour and of a long gallery. The family used the ground floor parlours and the first floor chambers. The domestic staff worked on both those floors and in the basement, and slept in the garrets. In a household which used several floors in a consistent and organized fashion, the staircase assumed a new importance. None of the houses in Thorpe's collection of drawings has less than two staircases, of the new framed design. Often they formed architectural features, obtruded in the angles of an H or U plan, or forming balancing wings on either side of a square block. Such staircases usually went right up to the garrets, and sometimes (as at Wollaton) down to the basement.[2]

[1] See Summerson, *passim*, especially plates 14, 16, 19, 22a, 46, 48a, 51a. The plan of Wollaton Hall reproduced there (p. 34) from Thorpe shows kitchen, buttery, and pantry on the west side of the ground floor, but indicates no fireplaces in the kitchen, and in this respect is inaccurate. The original staircase to the basement and other features of the service arrangements have survived eighteenth-century alteration. There are brick-lined water conduits and sewers cut in the sandstone on which the house is built. For the French origin of the basement with service rooms, see Philibert de l'Orme, *Livre d'Architecture*, 1567, II, ch. 1, p. 52. I am indebted to Mrs Rosalind Coope for drawing attention to this evidence and to that of French châteaux prior to 1570 which have this feature. She has also shown reasons for thinking that French examples are not dependent in their turn on Italian models. It might be possible to link this French development with the tradition of the first-floor-hall house of the Middle Ages.

[2] See Thorpe drawings (Soane Museum), pp. 27, 38, 44 (H plan); 110, 121 (square plan). The well design of staircase ascending round an open square or rectangle, and the dog-leg design, ascending half a storey before turning on itself, seem to have been used indifferently.

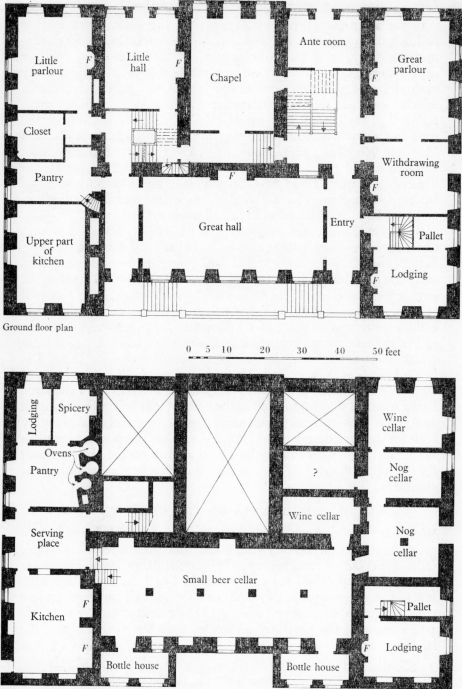

Ground floor plan

0 5 10   20   30   40   50 feet

Basement plan

Fig. 19. Plans of the ground floor and basement of Raynham Hall, Norfolk, designed in the 1620's. The names for rooms are taken from a survey of 1671, to show the working of basement services.

In the south-eastern quarter of England, the use of brick in new building often indicates, if not the work of a courtier, that of a gentleman whose vision of a new house was not limited to what a village craftsman could build for him. The south-eastern counties have many examples of houses, now often reduced in size or largely rebuilt, which lie outside the local vernacular style because of their materials rather than their size.[1] This use of brick was largely confined at the time to regions where brick-making was already traditional. Halstead Hall near Woodhall Spa, Lincolnshire, is a fragment of a large house of 1500–50 with a fine brick barn, and stands not far from brick-built Tattershall Castle. These new brick houses are invariably storeyed throughout, and must have played an important part in the displacement of the medieval fashion for a hall open to the roof.

If the landowner, and especially one with newly acquired wealth, chose an entirely new site for a house, he usually had in mind a hunting lodge (Plate XIV b). Such lodges had originally been conceived as temporary buildings with the minimum of comforts; building or paying for their erection had sometimes been an obligation of manorial tenants. The concept of the lodge is probably the source of the Elizabethan gentleman's choice of a hilltop site for a new house; by the end of the seventeenth century lodges sometimes had a flat roof from which game could be espied and women could watch the chase. The house known as Beckley Park, Oxfordshire, was built c. 1540 by Lord Williams of Thame, a commissioner for the dissolution of monastic lands, who did well for himself in the county, and built a fine mansion at Rycote. It is of brick, with three tall storeys, and was probably built for the accommodation of hunting parties. The plan is basically a simple rectangle with hall, parlour, and kitchen on the ground floor; the two upper floors must have contained numerous good chambers for guests.[2]

C. THE HOUSES OF THE GENTRY

We now turn to the houses of those who reckoned themselves of gentle blood but carried on farming as a principal source of livelihood. Of all the classes of rural society the gentry contained men of the most varied condition. The houses they inherited or built in this age have suffered many changes at the hands of later owners, and their present state reflects, as does every building in the countryside, not only the achievement of the years 1500–1640 but also the vicissitudes of the landed gentry and of agriculture in later centuries. Those houses whose

[1] E.g. Gosfield Hall, Essex, c. 1550 (H. Mon. C., *Essex*, I, p. 104); Panfield Hall, c. 1500 (*ibid.*, p. 207); the manor house at Chenies, Buckinghamshire, built c. 1530 by John, Lord Russell (*Bucks.*, I, p. 90).   [2] *Country Life*, 23 March 1929.

owners' fortunes were higher in the Tudor and early Stuart period than later preserve intact the domestic standards and achievements of that time. Sometimes, on the other hand, it is precisely the manor house divided into tenements before 1640, because the manor was split up by sale or was leased, which has been least altered.[1]

We have seen that the rebuilding of great houses received its impetus from the court and was much accelerated after 1570. When we turn to the upper crust of the classes involved in agriculture, we find that in the counties with richest soil and the best access to markets, a steady advance in wealth and standards of domestic life had begun long before Elizabeth's reign. Essex is of the greatest importance in this development, and it is unlikely that the significance of its wealth of houses will be much diminished by further field work in other counties. An Essex parish may contain as many as nine houses on medieval moated sites, every one rebuilt between 1500 and 1640 along with their outbuildings. All these houses were built on a unitary plan, under one roof, rather than on the compound plan of the great house built round one courtyard or more. The focus of the design was the farmyard, surrounded by house, barns, and other farm buildings. The largest of the new houses of early Tudor times were storeyed throughout, like the great house, and this applies equally whether they were of the traditional H plan with cross-wings, or of the simplest rectangular plan. The former plan made it possible to have two parlours in one wing and a convenient range of service rooms in the other. Each design incorporated a passage through the hall at its lower end, a feature which was common to all but the smallest house through most of this period. The fireplaces were all on external walls, another medieval feature, and the main staircase was circular, rising from the parlour to the chamber above it. This position for the principal staircase was completely in the medieval tradition. The wings were separated at first floor level by the open hall and so necessarily had separate access to the chambers.[2]

The most substantial of the buildings belonging to the manor house were its barns, and Essex is remarkable for their number and size, a key to the scale of arable farming. Throughout this period they

---

[1] E. Kerridge, *Survey of the Manors of Philip, First Earl of Pembroke, 1631–2*, 1953, pp. 86–8 (manor house at Wylie); *Hist. Mon. Commission, Essex*, I, pp. 184–5 (Harper's Farm and Old Bell Cottages, Little Maplestead).

[2] Finchingfield, Hist. Mon. Commission, *Essex*, I, p. 90; Lambourne, VCH *Essex*, IV, p. 78; Gatehouse Farm, Felstead, Hist. Mon. Commission, *Essex*, II, p. 77 (a medieval layout still intact); storeyed houses, Cust Hall, Toppesfield, *c.* 1500 *ibid.*, I, p. 324; St Aylott's, Saffron Walden, *c.* 1500, p. 142; Eastbury House, Barking, "a complete example of a mid-sixteenth century mansion" with two contemporary barns, II, pp, 9–10.

continued to be built with nave and aisles, a method which goes back at least to the Anglo-Saxon settlement, and which is explicitly recorded in twelfth-century leases. John Browne of Abess Roding, who held two manors in Henry VIII's time, one of which was Rookwood *alias* Brownes in that parish, rebuilt both his houses and at Rookwood also put up two very fine aisled barns, each of eight bays.[1]

Outside these south-eastern counties where proximity to London—the home of the court, as well as an insatiable market for grain and foodstuffs—prompted a steady flow of money and new ideas into the countryside, there is no sign, before the reign of Elizabeth, of any change in the medieval scale and pace of new building. Since later rebuilding was so widespread, manor houses of the period 1500 to 1570 are not easy to find in unaltered condition. The counties which have been surveyed sytematically, such as Herefordshire, can produce enough examples to show that the medieval design of an open hall with storeyed wings was still current in the middle of the Tudor period. Eyton Court preserves a two-storeyed wing built of timber with close studding and jettying on two adjacent sides. In south-west Herefordshire, where building in stone had always been more common, Old Court, Whitchurch, has an open hall range with storeyed wings, all in proportions no different from a house of a century earlier. In Herefordshire and Devon, which had larger areas of rich soil than any other counties of the highland zone, there is in consequence much more variety in scale and opulence among the houses of the gentry. There is a great contrast between the modest manor house at Hareston, Devon, built by John Wood in the early years of Henry VIII, and Cadhay, of which the earlier part was built shortly before 1500.[2] In Lancashire, on the other hand, it is now much more difficult to find examples of small manor houses, to bridge the gap between splendid and ostentatious houses such as Rufford Old Hall or Bramall Hall, and those of yeomen farmers. Rufford belonged to a family which owned two manors and other property in sixty or more townships in north-western England. Bramall Hall is described in an inventory of 1480 and has seen only minor additions since that time. The inventory shows that the pewter was kept in the screen-passage of the hall, and the service wing had a kitchen and half a dozen other rooms. At the upper end of the hall the wing contained a parlour and a chapel. There were ten chambers in all—in the two wings, over the gatehouse, and over the building round the courtyard at the rear.[3]

---

[1] *Domesday of St Paul's*, Camden Soc., 1858, pp. 123, 129, etc.; VCH *Essex*, IV, pp. 192–3.   [2] For Cadhay, see *Arch. J.*, CXIV, 1957, pp. 159–63.

[3] *Lancs. and Cheshire Wills and Inventories*, ed. Rev. G. J. Piccope, Chetham Soc., XXXIII, 1857, pp. 76–81.

We have already seen that the one innovation in the later medieval house was the introduction of a parlour, a ground floor room at the upper end of the hall, for the reception of private visitors. There was one such parlour at Bramall Hall. In the houses of the lesser gentry of the north, we find, even at the beginning of our period, that there was more than one parlour. The boundary between the southern zone in which no house had more than two parlours, and the northern zone, where the large house even at the beginning of our period might have three or more parlours, appears to run from the Wash due westwards. The house at Stillington in the vale of York which had belonged in 1526 to an archdeacon of Richmond consisted of a hall, three parlours, a chapel, and a kitchen on the ground floor, with four chambers (including the great chamber) and two over parlours upstairs. A house at Brotherton belonging in 1562 to John Tyndall, esquire, had in all five parlours as well as five chambers with beds in them. Apart from Tyndall's own "bed parlour" there was one for maid-servants and another for the man servants about the house. The farm servants slept in the oxhouse and the stable.[1] This practice of extending the sleeping accommodation by adding parlours downstairs was common to the higher clergy, the lesser gentry, and the yeomen of the north; class habits within the village community were less differentiated than further south, and the tradition of the single-storey house endowed ground-floor rooms with an importance which was remarkably pertinacious.

From Elizabethan times onwards there are plenty of domestic inventories to show the style of life of the lesser gentry; it was of course indistinguishable from that of wealthier yeomen. John Aiscough, esquire, farmed at Tadwell in the Isle of Sheppey before his death in 1603. He had a two-storey house with a useable garret in the roof. The ground floor comprised a hall, one parlour, and a kitchen with pantry and pastry near it. Somewhere—perhaps at the rear of the kitchen wing—there was a larder, a brewhouse, and a milkhouse. His bed-chamber was downstairs, with a maid-servants' chamber next to it. There were other chambers over the porch and over the kitchen wing. Farm servants slept in a chamber over the outbuildings. William Kent, esquire, of Hartlip near Chatham, who died in 1631, occupied a house which illustrates even better the similarity between a gentleman's way of life and that of a wealthy yeoman. It also illustrates a striking development of larger farmhouses in the first half of the seventeenth century: namely, a much more elaborate and extensive provision for

---

[1] LP, IV, pt. i, pp. 874–6; York Probate Registry, Dean and Chapter, T General. This reference to "over parlours" is the only one known to the writer to parlours presumably on the first floor.

storing and processing farm produce, a necessary consequence of the engrossing of land. Kent's house was somewhat larger than Aiscough's, and had two parlours, one of them containing a closet. The service end of the house contained two butteries, kitchen, milk cellar, brewhouse, and boulting house. There were five chambers, upstairs and down, furnished for sleeping, but five more were used for storing farm produce. The cheese loft contained twenty-four cheeses and twenty quarters of hemp, the wool chamber twenty fleeces, the apple loft thirty bushels of apples (on 30 December); the wheat and oat lofts seem to have been empty. The first two and the oat loft seem to have been in the house, the others in outbuildings.[1]

The inventory of Owen Brown, gentleman, of Kelsall, Suffolk, who died in 1587, presents a similar picture. His house had two storeys throughout, and a garret. He had only one parlour, and the service end of the house had a kitchen, a buttery, a dairy, and a cellar, with a bakehouse and storehouse as well. There were seven chambers, including one for servants and a corn chamber. Part of the roof space was used for sleeping, no doubt for servants as well: the "chamber in the vannse roof" contained a bed and various oddments. Occasionally an inventory refers specifically to additions to the house. Thomas Gawsell, gentleman of Denver, Norfolk (d. 1587), had two parlours, one of them called the New Parlour.

Berden Hall, Essex, built c. 1580, is a good example of the type of new house built by men of this class. It was of brick, on a U plan, with two full storeys and garrets lighted by windows in the three gables on the front and sides. Although the main form of the front was symmetrical, there were in effect four bays of openings below the three gables. The entrance was central, and gave on a cross passage leading to the handsome well-type staircase which filled the space between the rear wings.[2] Toseland Hall, Huntingdonshire, was also of brick, built c. 1600, with the proportions and arrangements of its symmetrical front properly managed; the three gables matched the window and door openings on the two principal floors. Toseland Hall and Berden Hall represent very clearly stages in the evolution of the manor house from medieval tradition to the new ideas of Elizabethan builders, worked out first in great houses like Haddon. Berden Hall presents the fashionable appearance of rows of uniform gables on three sides of the house, but its ground plan is the traditional U plan; the elevations of Toseland Hall are identical in outline (though not in detail), but the plan is square, with two roofs in parallel. The result is a more compact plan, and presumably a roof of this design appeared to builder and

[1] Kent RO, PRC 10, 30; 10, 64.
[2] Hist. Mon. C., *Essex*, I, pl. facing p. xxiv. The sketch-plan on p. 24 is inaccurate.

patron to present no problem. This is in fact one of the earliest surviving examples of the square house or "double pile" which by the middle of the seventeenth century began to have a distinct vogue which lasted for another hundred years (compare Fig. 20). By 1640 all the elements of this design—two storeys with gables in a symmetrical elevation— except for the double plan were to be found in a small number of houses throughout most of the counties of England. The variations reflect the degree to which what one must call Renaissance ideas were absorbed. For instance Turton Old Hall, Staffordshire, built of brick with stone quoins, has a symmetrical façade with small mullioned windows and gabled dormers (instead of gables proper), but the chimney stacks are in the traditional place at the gable ends, not on a roof axis, and the plan is U shaped. A house even of that degree of Renaissance design is much more rare in the west Midlands before 1640 than in the counties to the east. In general it is to be found most frequently in stone, more rarely in brick (compare Fig. 21), and very seldom in timber. An unusual example in timber is Preston Court near the Herefordshire border of Gloucestershire. The house has a lofty façade which would look much more at home in a Ledbury street, and a U plan with staircases in the inner angles. The large garret space was designed for storage, most probably of wool, for it still contains a timber hoist with wooden pulley wheels. Dowsby Hall, Lincolnshire, built in very good local ashlar and of similar proportions but square plan, also has an opening in a gable through which wool is still hoisted into a garret.

More commonly, new manor houses adhered to the traditional design of a hall range with one or two cross wings and two storeys with garrets; the façade was symmetrical and its ends gabled, whether or not they projected at the front and were of equal projection at the rear (Fig. 21). Within this more customary framework, variations in proportion and detail were a matter of regional fashion. Even if no cross-wing proper was required at one end or the other, the gable provided more headroom in the garret, although in some cases it was not lighted.[1] By the early seventeenth century it must have been unusual for garrets not to have lighting from such gables. Wimberley Hall in the Lincolnshire fenland parish of Weston is a good example of a symmetrical H plan in brick with mullioned windows of stone. It has no through passage, for that feature seems not to have been a strong element in the Lincolnshire tradition; the entrance at the lower or service end of the central range gives on to a small lobby at the side of the chimney stack placed on the axis of the house and taking the flues

[1] Hist. Mon. C., *Essex*, II, pl. facing p. 111, for several examples carried out in timber.

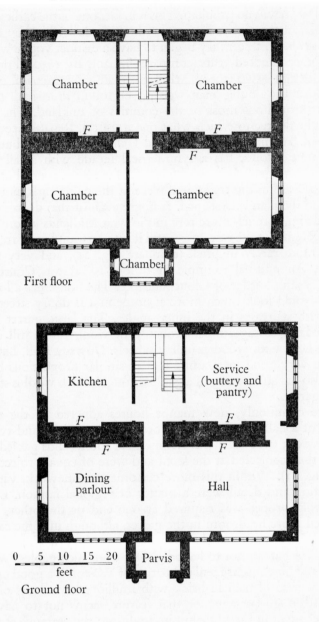

First floor

Kitchen

Service
(buttery and
pantry)

Dining
parlour

Hall

0 5 10 15 20
feet

Parvis

Ground floor

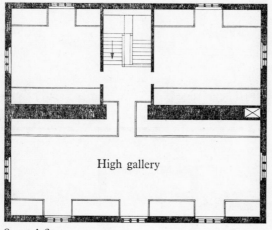

Second floor

Fig. 20. Red Hall, Bourne, Lincolnshire, built by Gilbert Fisher who died *c.* 1633, having secured local recognition as a 'gentleman'. This small mansion is an early example of the 'double pile', with rooms two deep. The names for rooms are taken from Fisher's inventory of 1633. There were also outbuildings containing an 'out kitchen', brewhouse, dairy house, etc.

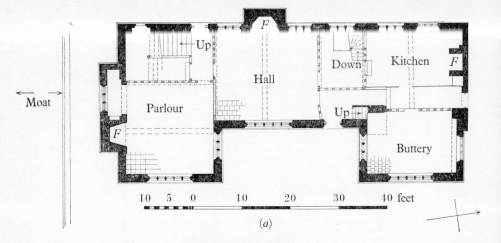

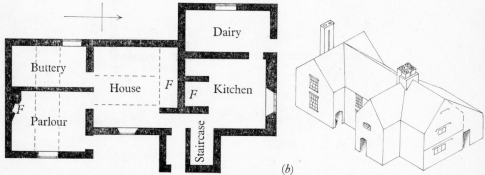

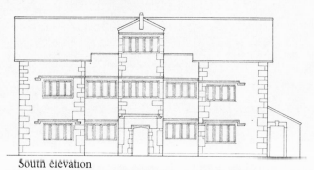

South elevation

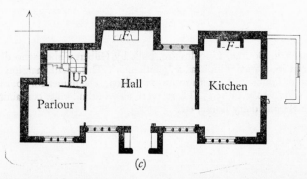

from hall and kitchen fireplaces. Further west two manor houses in stone may be compared. Manor Farm, Orton Waterville, Huntingdon-shire, was rebuilt in 1571, with the same H plan. The central range is low, its chambers being half in the roof and lit by dormers; there is a through passage at the lower end of the hall with a fireplace backing on it. In both these respects it belongs to the vernacular tradition of the limestone belt. Manor Farm, Clipsham, Rutland, was built in 1639. It is of two full storeys, with lofty and well lighted garrets in the wings. There is no through passage, but the same arrangement of rooms and fireplaces as at Wimberley Hall.[1]

In the west Midlands the small manor house of the years 1580–1640 was commonly built with one cross-wing only, and examples can be found all the way from Derbyshire to Herefordshire. Old Hall Farm, Youlgreave, Derbyshire, built in 1631, and Ballingham Hall, Hereford-shire, built by William Scudemore in 1602, are examples in stone. Many examples in timber are to be seen in Cheshire, Staffordshire, and Shropshire, reflecting the standards of the lesser gentry (and no doubt the wealthier yeomanry) of the region. The plan is quite uniform. The houses are of two storeys throughout; the entrance is either in the centre of the hall range, opposite an axial stack between hall and kitchen, or, in the smaller examples, in the angle between hall range and cross wing. The latter sometimes has its own axial stack, between two parlours, but at Haughton Manor, Staffordshire, built at the end of our period in timber, there is no original fireplace in the wing. Here, as at Youlgreave, the main staircase is at the rear of the wing, the remainder of the further half being a buttery. The parlour, still used only as the best bedroom and not as a sitting room, has no original fireplace in either of these houses. We shall find that these two features —an unheated parlour, and a buttery at the parlour end of the house rather than at the service end—are common among midland farm-houses of this age.[2]

[1] M. W. Barley, *The English Farmhouse and Cottage* pp. 105, 159, pl. viii a.
[2] *Ibid.*, pp. 97, 170.

Fig. 21. Manor houses with a basically medieval plan (hall and one or two cross-wings) but without screens passages and possessing some novel elements. (a) Morley Old Hall, Norfolk (now demolished), rebuilt in brick under Elizabeth on a moated site, was of two tall storeys and garrets. (b) Sowerby Hall, Lancashire, built in the early seventeenth century in brick—an unusual material—has one wing with parlour and buttery, clearly designed for entertaining; the other wing combines porch with staircase. The dairy was added later. (c) Carr House, Bretherton, Lancashire, built in brick in 1613, has a porch of three storeys and wings which project so slightly that the whole house has a continuous range of roof; a well-type staircase is housed in a projecting turret.

We turn now to houses which the gentry enlarged or improved in some fashion without complete rebuilding. William Harrison's comment, in 1577, that timber building was giving way to stone, is broadly borne out. The evidence naturally comes most plainly from houses which were only partially rebuilt. The rising price of timber was no doubt responsible for the use of stone extending to the margins of the limestone belt, in for instance north-west Huntingdonshire, though it is very doubtful whether timber building had been usual in upland villages of the Cotswolds. The west Riding of Yorkshire has produced the most explicit instances of rebuilding of timber houses in stone. Rectory Hall at Guiseley, a manor house which became the parsonage house in the middle ages, was rebuilt by the rector in 1601, but its plan and surviving woodwork within show that the earlier house was an aisled hall with one aisle. Pennine roofs are in any case low pitched, which makes for a wide span, and this, together with the persistent influence of the aisled hall tradition, explains the northern development in the seventeenth century of a plan two rooms deep under a single span roof. It emerged independently of the influence of the southern "double pile" under a double span roof.[1]

In the south-east of England, where standards of medieval building had been highest, many small manor houses, of medieval origin, were brought up to date at this time (Fig. 23). They required, first and foremost, more chambers, both for storage of expanding farm produce and for sleeping accommodation. The first way to improve both the amount of accommodation upstairs and the access to it was to insert a chamber over the open hall (Plate IX b). This necessarily meant building a chimney stack in the hall, to replace the open hearth which had been a common feature in old houses of all sorts. Opportunity was also taken to build a framed staircase, either within the hall range or adjacent to it; from the staircase both storeyed wings could easily be reached. No misgiving was felt at the necessity of using chambers as passage rooms leading to other parts of the upper floor. The chamber over the hall was often used only for storage either of grain or linen, since the hall chimney made it dry; moreover, being the latest addition to the house, it had no customary place in the pattern of home life. The position of the fireplace varied. In the Midlands it might well be built at the lower end of the hall, backing on the cross-passage; this had been the customary disposition in medieval houses in the highland zone, and the new stone fireplaces and chimneys of this age were only an improvement on their timber and daub predecessors. In the south-eastern counties it was

---

[1] [M. W. Barley, *The English Farmhouse and Cottage* pp. 115–16. See also L. Ambler, *Old Halls and Manor Houses of Yorkshire*, pl. xlix (Nunnery, Arthington), lxiv (Linthwaite Hall).

most commonly at the upper end of the hall, but naturally the traditional arrangement of a fireplace on a lateral wall still persisted. The other novel arrangement was to sacrifice the through passage by placing the chimney stack in it, perhaps under the influence of the idea of the axial stack. There are many instances where these improvements can be ascribed to the period 1560–1640 by explicit evidence such as a date on a chimney stack, on the dormer window to a hall chamber, or on the new doorway into the hall; more often they are dated by the character of the mouldings to the beams of the new hall ceiling, or to the new hall fireplace. The framed staircase was not a necessary part of such a modernization, and so may often be found added somewhat later.[1]

Within their houses, the gentry began more often to incorporate features which added to the comfort and the style of their home life. Moveable hangings, such as tapestries and even glazed window casements, which could be carted from one house to another in the train of a rich household, were replaced by wooden panelling for walls, ornamental plaster work for overmantels, friezes, and ceilings, and fixed glazing for windows. The parlour and the best bed chambers were the rooms most commonly panelled or 'wainscotted', because the basic purpose of such ornamentation was to exclude draughts and damp, as is shown by the fact that the internal porch is another improvement of this time. The fashion for ornamental plaster work had started under Renaissance influence in the buildings of the court. It spread throughout the country and eventually had its widest acceptance and its most enduring vogue in the counties most distant from London. By 1600 it was found not only in large houses of the West Country and Yorkshire, but also in small manor houses of a size in which it is never found in, say, the home counties.[2] Plaster work in farmhouses in Devonshire and the Lake District belongs mainly to the years after 1660.

The subsidiary parts of a manor house, as of any farmhouse, are in the nature of things much less easily dated than the principal structure. They were not given those details of finish, such as mouldings to ceiling beams, which provide dating criteria, and they have also suffered more structural alteration and change of use. Documentary evidence, principally that of probate inventories, is difficult to use, because the larger the house, the more dangerous is any assumption

[1] E.g., Kite Manor, Monk's Horton, Kent (Barley, *loc. cit.*, pl. iii a); The Savoy, Denham (Hist. Mon. Commission, *Bucks., South*, pp. 116–17) Shelley Manor, Shelley (VCH *Essex*, IV, p. 206). Walker's Manor House, Farnham, a timber framed house of *c.* 1560, had a staircase wing added at the rear early in the next century. Hist. Mon. Commission, *Essex*, I, p. 85.

[2] Mapperton Manor House (Hist. Mon. Commission, *West Dorset*, p. 154); Bradfield House, Uffcombe, and Cehvithorne Barton, Devon (*Arch. J.*, CXIV, 1957, pp. 142, 144); Lower Hall, Norland, Halifax (Ambler, *op. cit.*, pl. xc, fig. 68).

TAH

that the rooms of a house are listed in a significant order and that none are omitted because they were empty at the time the inventory was taken. Neither kind of evidence can therefore answer clearly a particular question which ought to be asked: how commonly did such houses possess a detached kitchen, and at what period did it cease to be built and used? But for the explicit evidence about parsonage houses in many counties (*infra*, p.   ) and the discovery by Fox and Raglan of such a kitchen still in use in Monmouthshire farmhouses in 1950, the question would not appear to be worth asking.[1] Many examples have been noticed of an outbuilding with a fireplace (and an upper floor) and some may well have been built as kitchens, even in the sixteenth century or later, but without the confirmation of current or recent usage, it is impossible to distinguish between a kitchen and a brewhouse or kilnhouse. Walton's at Bartlow End, Essex, is a brick house of the first half of the sixteenth century. It has two ranges of outhouses, both of two storeys, built a century later. One of them has an axial chimney stack with flues to two ground-floor rooms, one of which must have been a kitchen. The other range may have been stables. At Rickling Hall, Essex, a farmhouse was built *c.* 1500 within the bailey of the castle, and it consisted originally of a gatehouse block and a hall block, while a third building, called by the investigators a 'cottage', may well have been the kitchen.[2] Other examples can be found in the Royal Commission's inventories for the counties of Essex, Huntingdon, and Hereford, variously described as cottages, brewhouses, washhouses, dairies, or merely as outbuildings, but sometimes explicitly said to contain an open fireplace[3]. The washhouse is undoubtedly a London innovation; it appears only in Kent and Essex inventories of the seventeenth century. The wellhouse at Berden Priory, Essex, with its large tread wheel, is also seventeenth century in date.

Although the lesser gentry were dependent on farming for a livelihood, they began to separate the house and its particular amenities from the farmyard. The medieval fashion for a gatehouse controlling access to the house and all its dependent buildings lingered on only in more remote counties.[4]

At Place Farm, Tisbury, Somerset, a medieval grange of Shaftesbury, the gatehouse gave on a large court, flanked on one side by the residence, with its own internal gatehouse, and on the other by a tithe barn of

[1] See *Monmouthshire Houses*, III, pp. 50–2.

[2] Hist. Mon. Commission, *Essex*, I, pp. 13–14, 222.

[3] Hist. Mon. Commission, *Essex*, I, pp. 17 (3), 126–7 (4), 77 (7); *Hunts.*, pp. 121–2 (4) 197 (3); *Hereford, East*, p. 194 (3); *West Dorset*, pp. 54 (4), 270 (3).

[4] E.g., at King's Pyon (*Hereford, South-west*, plates 118, 119); Burnside Hall, Strickland Roger (*Westmorland*, p. 223, pl. 154). The former is ornamental, since the gateway is not wide enough for a cart.

thirteen bays. The medieval buildings still stand, but at some time since the first half of the sixteenth century the court has been divided into a farmyard and a clean forecourt to the house. Along with such rearrangements goes the layout of a garden, walled for shelter and for fruit growing, with perhaps a summerhouse in it.[1] The manor house at Cold Aston, Gloucestershire, probably built by a Bristol merchant turned country gentleman, shows in the layout of house, gardens, and farmyard the ideas which such a man might adopt.[2]

The farm buildings belonging to manor houses exemplify variations in types of agriculture and in vernacular building traditions. In the south-eastern quarter of England the aisled barn in timber continued to be built to the end of our period, together with a growing number of brick barns (Plate X). Where arable farming predominated there were often two or even more barns, one for each kind of grain, strikingly impressive in size and construction. The Grange, Takeley, Essex has four barns, all of the seventeenth century, and Colchester Hall in the same parish has three, one of them aisled. Paul's Hall in Belchamp St Paul's has an aisled barn of seven bays, of the same date. In the east Midlands barns must have been of inferior construction—mud and stud, with poorer timberwork—for very few have survived from this period. West of the jurassic ridge, where arable crops were less important, the cruck tradition imposed a limitation on the height and width of barns (Plate XI a) which few landowners had an incentive to break down until the sixteenth century, though some medieval tithe barns show that it was possible to do so. Even in Herefordshire a manor house might have two barns, or occasionally three, but one alone is normal, and they were never aisled, but constructed (whether of timber or of stone) with a tie beam roof, principal trusses having raking struts or queen posts. With the numerous barns of eastern England went a cart house, an open-fronted building, and an oxhouse or stable for draught animals, sometimes with corn chambers over. In pastoral country, a cow byre took the place of the oxhouse. Amberley Court, Marden, Herefordshire, a remarkably complete fourteenth-century manor house which its Tudor owners left unaltered, possessed two barns, each of five bays, and a cowhouse of three bays, all built towards the end of this period.[3] The dovecote, mark of a manorial monopoly which was abandoned towards the end of this period, was usually built in one of the home closes a short distance from the house.

[1] For Place Farm, see A. R. Dufty in *Arch. J.*, CIV, 1947, p. 168; summerhouse, *Essex*, I, p. 121; garden walls, *Bucks., North*, pp. 94–5; *Hereford, East*, p. 211; *Hunts.*, p. 253.

[2] A. Tipping, *English Houses*, Period III, II, p. 133.

[3] *Essex*, I, pp. 17, 300–1; *Hereford, East*, pp. 137, 169–70, *South-west*, p. 22.

This period, then, witnessed so much new domestic building by the aristocracy and the gentry that the Elizabethan and Jacobean country-house have become, along with the medieval castle and the Georgian mansion, a characteristic sight of the English countryside. Houses of the right scale and style could now confer a prestige on their owners which required completely new building, not the piecemeal enlargement or improvement of the old. For that reason, the medieval house with a hall and two cross-wings, typical of the gentry rather than the aristocracy of the Middle Ages, was the starting-point of most new designs (Fig. 21), and by 1640 it had undergone considerable modification. The roof, especially in stone houses, often had a continuous range of gables. In areas of timber building, the front sometimes had a continuous jetty at first floor level, with small frieze windows between those normal size in upper rooms, and Renaissance ornament to the woodwork—urban fashions finding their way into the country. Inside, convenient staircases linked the two floors. The hall was no longer the focal room and the solar upstairs was no longer the best private chamber; their place had been taken, for the family, by one or more parlours on the ground floor. The needs of guests and household staff left an even more obvious mark on the design of secondary parts of the house, such as a gatehouse tower or a range of stabling, than had the needs of retainers in the earlier age of what has been called bastard feudalism. By 1640 a beginning had been made in the organizing of the whole complex of building, and not merely the domestic nucleus of it, in the symmetrical form required by a growing knowledge of classical concepts of architecture.

D. THE HOUSES OF THE PAROCHIAL CLERGY

The parsonage house is the best documented of the houses in the village, and so serves as a valuable key to domestic standards, as well as to building traditions. The parochial clergy varied greatly in wealth, and their dwellings invite comparison with the houses of men of all sorts, from lesser gentry at one extreme to poorer husbandmen, if not labourers, at the other. Since they were usually engaged in cultivation of glebe land, or at least dependent on tithes for a part of their income, their vicissitudes of fortune in this period ought to reflect those of the majority of the rural community. Their personal condition changed radically when the Elizabethan settlement gave them licence to marry, but it appears that this had less effect on the parsonage house than might be assumed. The houses of the wealthier clergy were already large enough, for they had been built for numerous occupants—the rector or vicar, the chaplains, deacons, clerks, servants, and guests.

The poor parson no doubt took in a wife without necessarily working out the likely consequences beforehand, but her aid in managing the dairy and that of sons in working the glebe may help to explain the improvement in the living standard of the Elizabethan parson which certainly took place.[1] Although we shall find that many parsonage houses were no better than cottages, they tend as a class to reflect a higher standard of living than could be maintained on the income of a single living. One reason must be that pluralism was so widespread. The fortuitous and temporary combination of two or more livings in one parson's cure often left a legacy of a new or an enlarged house in one of his parishes, and the combination of livings might be changed in the next generation with similar consequences. These variations apart, it must be remembered that documentary information only becomes plentiful from late Tudor times onwards, and is then very uneven in its distribution, since for some counties neither of our main sources—probate inventories and parsonage terriers—is available.[2]

Although the size of a parsonage house might not exactly reflect the wealth of the living in question, it was invariably built in the local vernacular, so that contemporary descriptions of these houses are a reliable clue to the materials used. To the east of the limestone belt many parsons lived in houses whose walls they described as of mud, clay, earth, loam, daub, or witchert. They made no reference in their terriers to timber in the walling, though it is clear in some instances— for example in Lincolnshire—that the clay was carried over the face of timber uprights, concealing them from all but an observant eye. In most instances, then, these phrases indicate an inferior version of timber-frame building. It is found in a region which extends south-wards from Seamer on the margin of the Cleveland Hills, and includes the East Riding and the counties east of a line from the Yorkshire Ouse to Southampton, though references to clay walls are most common in the east midlands and East Yorkshire, where timber was scarcest. In that region the shortage of timber is also shown by the fact that many houses had upper floors also of earth—that is of puddled clay laid on reeds or straw spread across the joists—or else of gypsum or lime plaster.

In parts of the highland zone, parsons used the same phrases—"walls of earth" or "mud"—to indicate that different technique which is now known as cob walling. In such houses walls were 2ft. 6 in. or more in thickness, instead of the 9 in. or so in the east Midlands, and were built

[1] W. A. Pantin, 'Medieval Priests' Houses in South-west England', *Med. Arch.*, I, 1957, pp. 118–21; F. W. Brooks, 'The Social Position of the Parson in the Sixteenth Century', in *J. Brit. Arch. Ass.*, x, 1945–7, p. 37.

[2] For the whereabouts of inventories and their value, see Barley, *op. cit., passim.*

up without any timber frame. Terriers of the seventeenth century refer to such building in parts of Devon and Cornwall, and of course it is known from observation in Somerset. Mud or cob walling was also used in west Lancashire and in the Lake District. It was thought inferior to stone, the material of a large minority of Devonshire parsonage houses in the seventeenth century. Hence the house was sometimes of stone and its outhouses of cob.[1]

In the counties south-east of a line from the Wash to Southampton Water and in the west Midlands, the two regions which had long had the finest tradition in timber building, the use of brick made only slight inroads before the end of our period. Until 1600 new houses of brick were confined to a few small areas, such as the neighbourhood of Boston, Lincolnshire, where bricks had already been made and used for centuries and where the shortage of timber was most acute (Plate VII). Although the use of brick for chimney stacks was well established, not a single parsonage house built of brick in this period was noted by the Royal Commission for Historical Monuments in the counties of Essex, Buckingham, or Huntingdon. The fine brick parsonage at Great Snoring, Norfolk, built in the early years of this period, is quite exceptional. The gentry, as we have seen, had family connections, property interests, and personal ambition which might lead them to abandon the local vernacular style and the local builder who maintained it, in favour of some outsider who could build in brick. The parson on the other hand had no such inclination, and this fixes his social position as a member of the village community rather than a poor member of the gentry class. The Buckinghamshire parsonage house, then, except in the north-west of the county, was "built of timber and covered with tile." At Milton Keynes the house was "built partly with stone and partly with timber...covered with tile and slate;" no doubt the variation represented work of different periods. Occasionally a parson described the infilling of a timber frame: Aylesbury was "built with timber of oak with rods and plastering for the walls."[2] In most of eastern England rods sprung into grooves in the timber frame, rather than woven wattle work, provided the usual base for clay infilling.

The change from building in timber to brick construction, and even the replacement of clay infilling with brick, belongs to the years after 1660, rather than earlier. The terriers are not of a nature to throw light on any change from timber to stone, but there is nothing in them to

[1] Terriers for Creed, 1688 (Cornwall RO); Alphington c. 1679 (Devon RO); Childwall (Preston RO, DRL, 3) and Coniston (ibid., DRB, 3); R. S. Ferguson, *Miscellany Accounts of the Diocese of Carlisle*, 1877, pp. 17, 18; R. W. Brunskill, 'The Clay Houses of Cumberland' in *Trans. Ancient Mon. Soc.*, 10, 1962, p. 57.
[2] Lincs. AO, Terriers 17, 19.

contradict Harrison's assertion that it began in his time. Those houses, mainly on the margins of the jurassic zone, which were said to be built of timber and stone may have had stone foundations, stone filling for a timber frame, or even ground floor walls of stone with timber first floor.

Within the house, earth floors were almost universal; even if suitable stone was available locally for flagging the hall, the service rooms still had earth floors throughout this period. In the west country such a floor was usually described as of 'lime ashes', the material from the bottom of the lime kiln. A smooth earth floor must have been nearly as clean as stone flagging and was easily repaired. If suitable cobbles could be found, they were used in service rooms. The use of brick for paving, as for infilling, belongs to the period after 1660. Although an earth floor could be reasonably smooth and clean, it was cold and damp and must have turned somewhat muddy if a change of temperature caused condensation. For that reason many parsons laid a boarded floor in the parlour. It is not possible from terriers for the diocese of Lincoln to tell how far that process had gone by 1640, and in the diocese of Exeter the terriers of 1679 give the earliest indications of "planched" floors, but it is likely that this improvement began in the early seventeenth century.

For the floors of chambers upstairs local timber was obtainable at a price, or imported Irish oak and Scandinavian deal, at, no doubt, a higher price. It was convenient, especially when the chamber was used for storage, not to fasten either the joists or the floor boards laid across them, so that they could be moved to get sacks of wool or other bulky goods into the chamber. Occasional evidence of loose floors can be detected in the wording of terriers, and the fact that floors were sometimes valued with furniture in inventories of this age shows that chambers were in those cases a new improvement to a house and were regarded as tenants' fixtures. In the east Midlands two thirds of the chamber floors were made either of gypsum or lime plaster, or of earth. The first explicit comment on such floors, by Bess of Hardwick c. 1556, suggests that she thought most of their smooth finish.[1] They were made by laying reeds or straw across the joists, and over that a layer, as much as three inches thick, of plaster which had been burnt in a kiln with some addition of clay (or pounded brick) and ashes. Such floors by eventual carbonation of the lime mortars become a limestone, and their only fault is that their weight may eventually cause joists to sag and the floor to crack. Where neither gypsum nor lime was easily available, mud floors were laid in exactly the same fashion, though in

[1] Bess of Hardwick instructed her steward to "cause the floor of my bedchamber to be made even either with plaster, clay, or lime." *Archaeologia*, LXVIII, 1912–13, p. 351.

the course of the seventeenth century imported deal boards largely took their place.

Internal partitions were usually of the same material as the outer walls, except in parts of the highland zone where timber was plentiful and some care was given to the making of timber partitions, with vertical (and often moulded) studs at close intervals and plank filling between. In the Lake District the fashion for a large cupboard built into the partition between hall and parlour belongs mainly to the years after 1675, but a few earlier examples can be found.

The minimum information given in a terrier was the size of the house in bays, but since the length of that unit varied from one region to another, and was difficult to apply exactly to a stone house, the parson's return cannot be used to infer variations in housing standards between one diocese and another. In Elizabethan Lincolnshire, the commonest type of parsonage house was one of three to four bays, with between four and nine rooms, and it ranked in size and commodity with houses of the wealthier yeomen. That generalization covers rather more than half the houses in the diocese of Lincoln; of the rest, most were larger, but one in ten was of two bays only, the usual minimum for all but the poorest cottages. The parson's official residence varied, then, from the size of the manor house to something indistinguishable from the small husbandman's home.[1]

A very few parsons of the sixteenth century inherited a medieval house which was well enough built to require little improvement. The rectory at Therfield, Hertfordshire, was a large house of fifteenth-century date. By 1625 the parson had added "one other little new built parlour" to the east wing, making three parlours in all. The service wing to the west of the hall contained "one little lower chamber, a cellar, a kitchen, a larder, a scullery," but there was also "without, on the south side, one little walking cloister, one other kitchen, a brew-house, a bolting house, a dairy house, a coal house, a little garden plot." Since only the fifteenth-century parlour wing survives, we have no evidence for the date of the service rooms, whether in the house or detached from it, but the kitchen indoors and some of the detached service rooms are likely to be sixteenth-century improvements.[2] A few parsonage houses stood on moated sites, and others still possessed a gatehouse. The rector of Belleau, Lincolnshire, charged in 1607 with taking down "a very fair gatehouse of freestone and timber," answered that a gatehouse and portal were not now necessary.[3] In the border counties the medieval pele tower was certainly regarded as still useful,

---

[1] Barley, op. cit., pp. 92–4.
[2] Lincs. AO, Terriers 14; Hist. Mon. Commission, Herts., p. 218.
[3] Lincs. AO, Faculties, 19, 123.

but, as at Asby, Westmorland, the adjacent living range was commonly rebuilt.[1] At Market Deeping, Lincolnshire, the rectory still possesses a fine open hall of the fifteenth century. In contrast, the most striking feature of some of the west country houses of medieval date is that surviving examples commonly have a chamber over the hall (Fig. 22). They are perhaps best explained as local derivatives from the earlier tradition of the first-floor hall among the lesser gentry, franklins, and wealthier parsons. One of them, the stone house at Dunchideock, had a two-storey outbuilding of cob, containing a kitchen, which has now vanished. The service end of the main house contained in 1679 only a buttery and ground-floor cellars.[2]

The comfortable standard of living indicated by these large medieval houses of the west country is also illustrated by inventories from Leicestershire and Lincolnshire. The richer parson at the time of the Reformation could afford to have resident servants. Thomas Glover of Narborough, Leicestershire, referred in his will to "Margaret my housekeeper" and "Ame my servant."[3] John Facy's inventory for the parsonage at Colsterworth, Lincolnshire, in 1540 mentions "the woman's chamber" and "the manservants chamber." At Bassingham, Lincolnshire, the house had two parlours in 1538–40, a feature which became common among yeomen of Elizabethan times. They were usually both furnished as bedrooms, and did not differ from the room described in the inventory of Robert Butler, vicar of Swinstead, Lincolnshire, as "the chamber behind the dais." On the other hand, the rectory at Harston, Leicestershire, consisted in 1519 of only two rooms, the hall living room and the parlour bedroom.[4] These differences persisted throughout our period, though in the seventeenth century parsons were increasingly unwilling to take a living which had no better house than a labourer's. Such livings tended to remain vacant for long periods, or were held in plurality and the house let to "Mechanicks and Labourers," as a nineteenth-century parson described the tenants from "time immemorial" of the house at Ancaster. The vicar of Kirmington c. 1664 said that the parsonage house there "may rather be called an Hospital because it is the receptacle of such as have collection (i.e. poor relief) and cannot provide themselves better."[5]

[1] Hist. Mon. Commission, *Westmorland*, p. 15 (4).

[2] W. A. Pantin in *Med. Arch.*, I, 1957, pp. 124–8. Cellar is the only known name for the storeroom under the solar.

[3] W. G. Hoskins, 'The Leicestershire Country Parson in the Sixteenth Century', in *Essays in Leics. History*, 1950, p. 7. Lincolnshire inventories at Lincs. AO are now indexed under personal names, and hence no reference numbers will be quoted.

[4] Hoskins, *op. cit.*, pp. 3–4.

[5] See Hist. Mon. Commission, *Hereford, East*, 24 (5); *West*, p. 149 (10), *South-west*, p. 135 (2), for parsonage houses built in this period and now described as cottages.

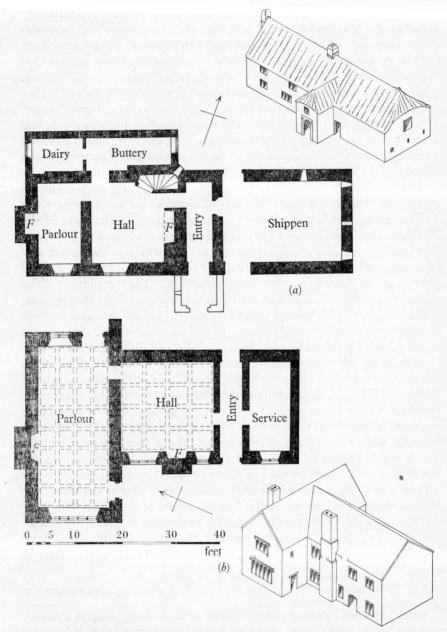

Fig. 22. Two Devonshire houses of traditional design. (*a*) Higher Tor, Widecombe in the Moor, is a long house, with the refinement of an entrance for cattle into the byre separate from the cross passage. (*b*) The Old Rectory, Sampford Peverel (early sixteenth century) of two full storeys in the west country tradition for parsonage houses, has unusually small service accommodation and ample space for the rector and his guests. Both the hall and the very large parlour have fine panelled ceilings.

Nevertheless, about one parson in ten, as we have seen, had to put up with a small and incommodious house. It was made more tolerable when it was chambered over, for this doubled the accommodation. Out of about two hundred Lincolnshire terriers for 1606, only one, from Alkborough, describes a house with no chambers. It had three bays, containing hall, parlour, and kitchen, and by 1709 it was no longer used by the parson. The vicar of Queniborough, Leicestershire, had in 1598 a house with a hall, a lodging parlour, one chamber, and a study. It is not clear whether his study was upstairs (as were most parsons' studies if they had one) or whether he had appropriated what would have been the buttery or kitchen in a husbandman's house. Apart from the two bedrooms, all that the family needed for daily life was crowded into the hall—two framed tables, two chairs, four stools, and two benches or forms; the pots and pans for cooking, pewter for the table, and even churns, pails, and various wooden vessels used for milk.[1] The vicarage at Calceby, Lincolnshire, was said in 1606 to be built of wood and thatched, with three bays, chambered over, and containing hall, parlour, and kitchen. Before Christopher Dinis, the vicar, died in 1620, he had made a second parlour, perhaps by dividing one room into two. Although he was comfortably off he did not use the chambers for anything but "implements," and he had no study, though he possessed books worth £4. In almost every case where it is possible to compare a Lincolnshire terrier of 1606 with an inventory made during the ensuing generation, there is evidence of small improvements, but very little to suggest wholesale rebuilding of parsonage houses.

The parsonage house at Sherrington near Olney, Buckinghamshire, said in 1625 to have been "newly built by the incumbent now living" and still standing today, shows that his ideas were identical with those of the richer yeomen of his time. He built in stone, doubtless replacing a timber house. The new one has an H plan with two storeys, and five bays—i.e. one bay for the hall and two for each wing. The ground-floor rooms comprised hall, parlour, kitchen, buttery, and boulting house (i.e. bakehouse) "with chambers over entry room well and sufficiently boarded." Probably it had parlour and buttery in one wing (where there remains one original fireplace only) and kitchen and boulting house in the other; if this is correct, the boulting house has since been turned into a study and the buttery into a dining room.[2]

Inventories from other parts of England reveal the country parson as sharing the way of life of his parishioners. John Pearne, rector of Ford-

---

[1] Leics. RO, A.63.

[2] Lincs. AO, Terriers 8; Hist. Mon. Commission, *Bucks, North*, p. 261 (5). An inscribed stone in the south wall shows that it was built by John Martin in 1607, not T.M. as the Commission stated.

ley, Suffolk (d. 1633), had a house of fourteen rooms, including outbuildings. The hall was still used as the living room, and cooking seems
to have been done in the backhouse, a general service room common
in East Anglia; he had a dairy, and a quern-house in which malt was
ground and horse harness kept. At the other end of the hall a parlour
and two other chambers on the ground floor were all furnished with
beds, but the parlour was also used as a sitting room. This continued
use of the word chamber for ground floor room is common in the
southern half of England. His study, comfortably furnished with a
cushioned chair, a desk, a looking glass, and books, was at the same end
of the house, probably downstairs. The only other ground-floor room
was a buttery where beer, drinking vessels, and the like were kept. Of
the rooms upstairs, only one, over the buttery, had a bed in it, probably
for a servant. That over the parlour held the linen (which suggests
that the parlour always had a fire in it and so was used as a sitting room);
that over the hall held wheat, malt, and bacon; the chamber over the
backhouse held barley and feathers; and a "little upper chamber"
contained scales and a beam, as if for wool.[1]

Devonshire parsons, in describing their houses in 1613, were either
terse or somewhat incoherent, and their phrases are much less informative than those of 1679–80. Nevertheless, they reveal a quite different
domestic tradition. One aspect of it, the antiquity and importance of
the chamber over the hall, has already been referred to. The traditional
open hall was also to be found: in 1680 the rector of Bigbury spoke of
"one hall excellently well timbered," and the rector of Church-
staunton had "a great hall floored with earth, no chamber over it."
In Somerset, for which there are informative terriers of the period
1606–40, Combe Florey, Crowcombe, and Wedmore certainly had
parsonage houses with open halls. Some Devonshire parsonage houses
appear to have consisted of distinct ranges of building round a small
court. The parson of Alphington wrote in 1601: "there are 4 houses:
hall and parlour under one roof, kitchen and malthouse under another,
the third a barn, the fourth a shippon with a new stable and a corn
chamber which I have built." Sometimes such phrases were used to
describe what was really only a H or U plan, with cross wings. The
rectory at Street, Somerset, had three ranges of building: the first
contained hall, two parlours, two butteries, and chambers over,
amounting to six or seven 'fields' or bays; the second contained one
other lower room of two 'fields', and the third had a kitchen, brewhouse, larder, and two chambers, of five to six 'fields'.

Some west country parsons suggest by their phrases that the kitchen
was detached from the house proper, though here again their words

[1] Norwich Diocesan Records, Inv. 1633.

may indicate only that the kitchen was not conceived as part of the house. The name kitchen was, in western counties as elsewhere, sometimes given to a brewhouse or a bakehouse; the term must have meant merely a room with a particular type of hearth and equipment rather than one specifically for cooking and the preparation of food. Phrases like "a dwelling house with an old kitchen" (Berrow, Somerset), "a dwelling house with a kitchen near adjoining" (Curry Mallet), may carry more than one interpretation. Malthouses were nearly as common in Devonshire and Somerset as in the eastern counties. The parsonage house at Awliscombe, Devon, had "a kitchen with a dry" or malt kiln. Such an arrangement, which occurs in a substantial minority of parsonage houses from Somerset westwards, certainly implies outside access to the kitchen, as well as to other service rooms. Sometimes the court round which they lay had an open-fronted building or linhay on one side, as at Beer Ferrers, Devon ("a gallery supported with posts of timber"), Coleridge ("a back court between hall and kitchen, enclosed, with a convenient linney in the same") or Heathfield, Somerset ("a close court on the north side with a pump and a hanging house over it"). These West Country houses thus reveal the medieval courtyard plan at a lower social level than we have met it elsewhere. This concept of the house as a loosely organized group of distinct buildings presents a sharp contrast with the more highly organized plan favoured in south-eastern England. The same ancient features—the survival of the detached kitchen and the gatehouse, the lack of interest in an integrated plan when new building was designed— can be observed in Monmouthshire and to a less extent in the southern half of the jurassic zone.[1] No doubt the danger of fire was a good reason for keeping the brewhouse at a distance. The terrier of St Just, Cornwall, made c. 1601, has a sketch-map, showing among other things "the kill or dry House 60 paces from the parsonage house foregate—the house has been casually burnt drying malt." Nevertheless the west country concept of the house belonged to a different world from the dawning fashion in the south-east for the double house with all the rooms and services under two joined roofs.

From the northern counties there is enough evidence of parsonage houses only to show that their occupants shared the simple standards of northern farmers. John Allen, who was minister at Great Longstone, Derbyshire, until 1637, seems to have had a house of only five rooms. They comprised the living room (known to the appraisers, as to most people in the north-midland and northern counties, as the "house"), kitchen, and milkhouse, with two chambers. One of them was the

[1] Fox and Raglan, *Monmouthshire Houses*, II, figs. 37, 38; III, figs. 26, 36; Barley *op. cit.*, pl. iv.

minister's lodging chamber; the other had a bed in it but also contained[1] linen yarn and other stores. Both rooms were most probably on the first floor. Robert Murrow, vicar of Pittington, Durham, was a wealthy man when he died in 1594, but his house had no more than six (or possibly seven) rooms. Much of his wealth lay in flocks of sheep grazing at Sherborne and Witton as well as in his own parish. He had a "hall house" (another common northern expression), a kitchen, one or possibly two parlours, a study, one bedchamber, and a loft full of malt, corn, and wool.[1]

The parsonage house thus reflects, in its materials and in the disposition and use of its rooms, the region to which it belongs. The farm buildings belonging to it are rarely of architectural interest, because few parsons took any special interest in their glebe. One thing alone distinguished the parson from the yeomen and husbandmen of his parish: the possession of books and a study. Not every parsonage house had a study, but it was certainly more common at the end of our period than at the beginning, and was usually upstairs. It was clearly a small room, rarely heated; in a house with an 'entry' or cross passage, the chamber over it was often so used; alternatively the storeyed porch, increasingly fashionable in this period, provided a chamber which served the purpose.

E. THE HOUSES OF YEOMEN AND HUSBANDMEN

We now turn to what may be termed the ordinary farmhouses, occupied by men who called themselves yeomen or husbandmen, for the designation farmer was still rarely used in 1640. Although both classes are to be found in every county, there were significant regional variations in the proportions of one to the other. The yeoman was much commoner in Kent than the husbandman, and by 1640 the local probate courts there had little other business, among country folk, than proving yeomens' wills. In the northern counties too the yeoman class occupies the forefront of the picture. Husbandmen were a larger class in midland England and reflect the greater importance there of copyhold tenure.

This group which we have chosen to consider as one is naturally as diversified in its standards and attainments as any already discussed. It includes yeomen who lived as well as the lesser gentry, who might indeed be descended from families of gentle blood or be in process of lifting themselves by their own boot-straps to the status of gentlemen. In some regions too the opportunity of advancement lay not only in farming but also in trade or in the processing of farm products; for

---

[1] John Allen's inventory, Lichfield Peculiar Probate Records (now deposited at Lichfield), A 1562–1709; Robert Marrow, Durham RO, bundle 1594.

example, in malting and brewing in East Anglia. There is no doubt
that yeomen were normally wealthier than husbandmen as well as
enjoying a superior social status, and that the class contained many
members who by efficient farming, on conventional lines, or by enterprise in new directions, were able in this period to put a greater distance
between themselves and the rank and file of the farming community.
In many regions, local types of farmhouse appropriate to one or other
of these classes can be distinguished.

In Kent and parts of Surrey and Sussex, the Wealden type of house
is best regarded as a status symbol of yeomen living on the richest soil
that Kent or its adjacent counties could provide.[1] The house had an
open hall, sometimes only one bay in length, with either one or two
storeyed wings; men who chose to build such a farmhouse, either in a
village street or away from others in a lonely valley, had been numerous
enough in the middle ages to leave a more substantial legacy of well-
built houses than in most other regions. New houses of this design
were being built after 1500, and all they needed eventually to bring
them up to date was a chamber over the hall, a brick fireplace and
chimney to replace the open fire of the hall, a framed staircase, and
glazed windows (Fig. 23). Close studding remained fashionable in
timber building until the end of Elizabeth's reign, and then gave way,
under the impact of rising prices, to large rectangular panelling.
Although the fine quality of the building of the fifteenth century
deserves emphasis, and the use of glass may well have come into fashion
earlier here than in more remote parts, there was a degree of conservatism among rural classes which spread structural improvements over
the whole of this period and even longer. Alexander Paramore of
Reculver, who died in 1568, is an example of a small Kentish yeoman
who had not yet been moved to adopt (as far as we can judge from his
inventory) any of these modern devices. His house had an open hall
with a storeyed wing at each side; the one contained a parlour and
another chamber downstairs and a loft over them, the other a kitchen
also with a loft above. John Bromley, yeoman, of Bedgar, died in
a similar house in 1600. It had a hall with a parlour, a buttery, and an
'entry' (probably a through passage), but no kitchen. The chamber
over the buttery was furnished as a bedroom, but the loft over the
parlour was a storeroom for apples, hemp, wheat, and various small
things. Bromley was a farmer, but also had a "wheeler's shop."

These two inventories illustrate a good many features of yeoman's
houses of their age and locality. The kitchen was not yet a necessary part
of a farmhouse of modest size. Bromley had none, and Paramore had

[1] For the distribution and date of Wealden houses see S. E. Rigold in *Culture and
Environment*, pp. 352–4.

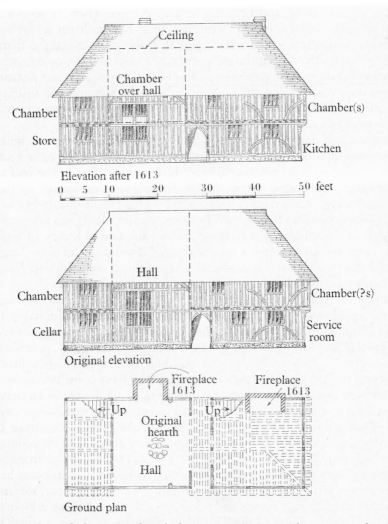

Fig. 23. Plan and elevations of Durlock Grange, Minster in Thanet, Kent, showing how an early fifteenth-century house of Wealden type was modernized in this period. Before this insertion of the side fireplace in the hall and a chamber over, smoke from the open hearth escaped between specially curved tiles on the hall roof.

one because his wife wanted to brew at home as well as to remove cooking gear from the hall. Where the parlour end of the house had two rooms, as it commonly did, the second room in counties south of the Thames was called a chamber, and of course each contained a bed. One or more of the upper rooms might be used as a bedroom, but at least one was simply a store and in these counties upper rooms were more likely to be called lofts than chambers. A chamber was reached by a staircase, a loft by a ladder only. There is no trace in such houses of the tradition of using the first-floor room at the superior end of the hall as the best bedroom or calling it the solar. Before 1640 certain developments can be discerned, especially in the houses of wealthier yeomen. Chambers are mentioned more often and lofts less so, which must indicate the gradual spread of two-storey building, instead of houses of one storey only with lofts in the roof space. Indeed a few rich yeomen found it necessary to use the garret or roof space of a two-storey house, a practice which probably spread from the towns. The inventory of Henry Binge of Acrise (1631) included a "garret or corn loft." Such men used first-floor chambers either as bedrooms for the family and for servants living in—Henry Binge's house included "the Folks' Chamber"—or as special store-rooms for corn, apples, and the like. Before 1660 Kentish yeomen with farm workers or domestic servants living in remained a small minority, but it was a growing one. The other distinct development, especially after 1600, was the multiplication of service rooms: a brewhouse as well as a kitchen; a boulting house where bread was prepared, and a wash house. The last seems to have come out of London.

The Kentish husbandman's house was more modest in all respects than that of the yeoman. In two out of three cases, even at the end of our period, the hall was still used for cooking, and the one or two service rooms were more likely to be used as milkhouse or buttery than as kitchen (Fig. 26, p. 753). Not every husbandman had come to describe his bedroom, alongside the hall, as the parlour; a few still called it the lower chamber, or simply the chamber. Some still had no upper chamber at all, and it was rare to find more than one. In west Sussex standards were even simpler. It was not until the eve of the Civil War that a few wealthy husbandmen began to speak of having a parlour. Upper rooms were usually called lofts, and in these small houses, the one upper room was more likely to be over the hall than over the chamber, no doubt because it would be drier for storage. The coastal zone of Sussex today is poor in vernacular building of this age, and this reflects not so much a poverty in materials, though inferior materials such as flint and cobbles were those principally used, as of a more highly manorialized society, yielding only moderate wealth to its yeomen and husbandmen. The greater freedom and independence of Wealden society, and the greater wealth of some of its members, is still memorialized in good stone houses of this age.

In the counties north and north-east of London members of the yeoman class have left more traces of their enterprise in this period than in any other part of England. Reference has already been made to

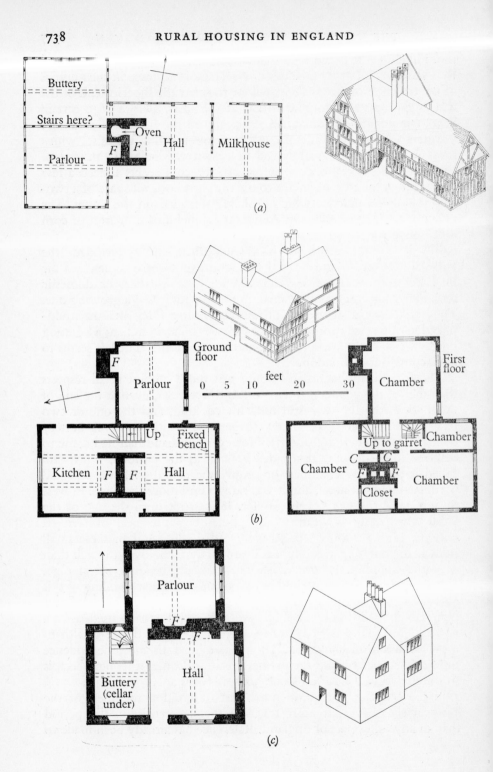

the remarkable number of farmhouses in some Essex parishes which stand within a medieval moat and were rebuilt or improved between 1550 and 1640. Some were no doubt occupied by men of gentle origin, but the majority must have been homes of yeomen. They seldom rebuilt their houses in a new material, though the use of brick for foundations and chimney stacks became general. The fact that there are a few farmhouses in Essex named 'Brick House' or 'Brickhouse Farm' show that the material was rare enough to be distinctive, and they belong mainly to the years 1600-40. Timber was more expensive and the housewright had to be content with inferior quality and less quantity; the practice of plastering over the exterior must have begun before 1640, though its more ornate form belongs to the years after 1660.[1] The jettied upper floor became rare in new houses built after 1600. Apart from these minor modifications in building technique, the principal changes were in the adoption of storeyed building in the form which the gentry had made fashionable, but with modifications to suit more modest needs.

The principal innovation, widely adopted in new houses of lesser yeomen and husbandmen, was to build a chimney stack on the axis of the house (Plate XV b), with, most commonly, two flues for adjacent rooms (though occasionally with one alone for the hall), and to combine with it the principal staircase (Fig. 24). In medieval houses the new chimney stack was sometimes placed in the through passage, and the axial stack combined with staircase was typically placed opposite the entrance to the house, so that the passage through the house at the lower end of the hall ceased to be a normal feature.[2] It

[1] For brick farmhouses in Essex, see Hist. Mon. Commission, Essex, IV, index; for economy in timber, see R. Reyce, Suffolk in the Seventeenth Century, 1902, p. 51.

[2] It has been suggested that in Hatfield, Hertfordshire, the vogue for this design lasted only through the first quarter of the seventeenth century, and that in the Banbury region masons did not adopt it for new stone houses until the later part of the century. B. Hutton, Hatfield and its People, Part 10, February 1963, pp. 13–19; Wood-Jones, op. cit., p. 153.

Fig. 24. Three variants on the hall and cross-wing, or T plan. (a) Keys Farm, Bentley, Worcestershire, represents a Severn valley type, with back-to-back fireplaces at the junction of the arms and the main entrance in the angle, giving on a tiny lobby. (b) At Woodroffe's, Marchington, Staffordshire, a yeoman's house of the early seventeenth century, the rich quality of the building (close studded walls, jettying on the gable ends, panelled rooms) contrasts with the relatively modest amount of accommodation. The lateral fireplace to the parlour is traditional; the axial stack for the hall and kitchen fireplaces, with a lobby entrance is an innovation. (c) The Garage, Little Milton, Oxfordshire, is a more modest yeomans house in the Cotswold vernacular. Compared with Woodroffe's, it lacks a kitchen and has only one entrance. The chambers over hall and parlour have fireplaces, and the garrets provide ample storage room.

may well be that this change reflected the change from a medieval habit of building the farmhouse parallel to the road (so that the passage was required for convenient access to the farmyard) to a new practice of building with a gable end to the road. Too little is yet known of the layout of medieval villages to prove this hypothesis, but the best explanation of the commonly observed fact that houses of this age often stand at right angles to the village street may be that they mark the effect of the major increase in population which certainly took place in the sixteenth century. Such filling in of closes and crofts with new houses would provide more housing without encroaching on farm land.

There was not room in the width of the house for a lobby entrance, a chimney stack, and a framed staircase as well. Such staircases are rare in farmhouses before 1625, and the problem was solved in less ambitious fashion, by building a newel stair of traditional form, turning through two right angles between ground and first floor. With minor regional variations this arrangement spread from the northern home counties to the Midlands by 1640. In the home counties the staircase is often placed between the entrance and the stack: elsewhere, it is more often next to the further or back wall of the house. The rapid spread of this innovation shows how marked a need it fulfilled. It served at least as much to satisfy the demand for storage as for sleeping accommodation, although, since eastern farmers did not multiply their parlour-bedrooms as did northern men, they naturally used more upper rooms for sleeping. The notion that the 'solar' was always a bedroom of superior quality on the upper floor is exploded by numerous East Anglian references to grain "on the soller."

The conservatism which retained the medieval term solar also explains the name backhouse for a service room used for cooking, brewing, baking, and similar general purposes. In Elizabethan times that name was used more often than kitchen, but by 1640 the latter had virtually supplanted it. Backhouse also occurs in the coastal zone of Lincolnshire, and seems to be identical with the Yorkshire nether house; it was used later in Devon. Like the term firehouse for the hall, which also survived in East Anglia and Yorkshire at lower social levels, it had not been borrowed from the gentry; both terms must belong to an older peasant society. This usage raises the question of whether in lowland England the houses of the lesser peasantry at this time owed anything in their plan to the longhouse or byrehouse: that is, to a structure with house and byre under one continuous roof. The evidence of excavation, of surviving buildings and of documents cannot yet be integrated; nor has agreement been reached even within any of these fields of study, let alone between them. It has been inferred from excavations (not yet published in detail) that the byrehouse was widespread in lowland England down to *c.* 1500. Possibly the backhouse of eastern England, Yorkshire and Devon was originally a byre for which conservative peasants had not adopted any specialized term, such as kitchen or buttery, because it had traditionally been available for domestic purposes only in summer while livestock were out of doors. In the present state of knowledge, the onus lies on students of vernacular building to consider how far the concept of the medieval byrehouse in the highland zone, on which agreement is being reached, can be extended to the jurassic uplands and other parts of lowland England.

By Elizabethan times in many homes of wealthier yeomen and husbandmen the backhouse was only one of several service rooms. John Browne of Raydon, Suffolk, husbandman, had a house with eight rooms and a stable and a barn. The two ground-floor chambers were both bedrooms. At the other end were a buttery, a kitchen, and a backhouse. A chamber over the hall and a solar over the buttery were both used for storage. The difference between them—whether of age, or construction—is not clear from his inventory. William Myles, a wealthy yeoman of Sutton, Suffolk, had three service rooms (buttery, backhouse, and cheesehouse) but no kitchen.[1] In these houses the backhouse may have been the second of two service rooms traditionally found below the cross passage of a medieval house: that is, the equivalent of the pantry, a term which is never used at this social level.

In eastern England, the multiplication of service rooms in the yeoman's house was the most striking development in the first half of the seventeenth century. Partly as a result of the increased bulk of foodstuffs requiring processing within the house, partly because of a rise in standards, men and their families wished to have some rooms for family use not cluttered with churns, tubs, and other utensils. Richer yeomen commonly had two butteries by 1640, one of them serving the parlour-sitting room, the other the kitchen.[2] Such men also had one or two chambers for farm servants living in, but in most yeomen's houses resident servants of either sex were very much more rare before 1640 than they were to become in the years after 1660. These same wealthier yeomen were also beginning to use the attic space for storage. The home of Robert Glamefield of Hoxne epitomizes the East Anglian yeoman's way of life in the last years of Elizabeth's reign. His house was probably built on an **H** plan, with two and a half storeys throughout. The hall was still used for cooking. One wing contained a parlour with a bed and some sitting-room furniture, and "the Chamber by the Hall where he lay." The other wing contained buttery, dairy, and cellar. If the cellar was below ground level,

[1] See Suffolk inventories (Ipswich Public Library), bundle 1582–4, nos. 32, 91.
[2] F. W. Steer, *Farmhouse and Cottage Inventories of Mid-Essex*, 1950, nos. 7, 19.

it was a novel feature at this time. Some of the chambers over hall, parlour, buttery, and dairy were furnished for sleeping, while the vance roof over them contained rye, maslin, and corn measures. Some yeomen who like Glamefield were content to do without a separate kitchen (because the backhouse served some of its purposes) began before 1640 to call the hall the kitchen, because by now their betters were turning the hall into a formal entrance room. This left them with no other suitable name for the one room in which food was cooked. It is curious that the medieval name 'hall' should begin to disappear first from the vocabulary of a conservative folk, but this change must have followed from the existence of another room serving some of the purposes of a kitchen.

The large and collectively wealthy villages on the margin of the Wash contained in Elizabeth's later years a large number of farmers, mostly calling themselves husbandmen but occasionally yeomen, whose small holdings of rich soil supported a way of life much more primitive than that of East Anglia. The commonest type of farmhouse had only four rooms: a hall living room, a parlour bedroom, one service room (called more or less indifferently kitchen, milkhouse, or buttery) and one chamber upstairs, used both for storage and, among large families, for a bedroom. This type of house must have been originally a two-roomed dwelling, with living and sleeping parts, rather than the hall-and-cross-wing plan of more advanced regions. By the end of our period a four-roomed house, evolved from this two-roomed type, was commonly found over a large part of the north-east Midlands, especially in the clay valleys. The two inventories surviving from Bedfordshire in James I's reign present a similar picture, of simple houses undergoing rapid improvement. One yeoman built a new parlour with a chamber over it, his old parlour having only a loft above. A poor husbandman was living in a house with hall, chamber downstairs for sleeping, and over them a loft newly put in to store barley and rye.[1]

Such improvements in copyhold farms led the Crown and some estate owners to order surveys covering not only land but buildings as well. Ralph Treswell's survey of the Lincolnshire manors of the duchy of Lancaster,[2] dated 1608, gives a vivid cross-section of Lincolnshire society which can be supplemented by inventories of some of the husbandmen in it. It includes men of every rank from gentleman downwards, since any might be found as tenants of copyhold land. Houses on the limestone were larger, as we should expect, than those

[1] F. G. Emmison, 'Jacobean Household Inventories', *Beds. Hist. Record Soc.*, xx, 1938, pp. 50–143; nos. 175, 155.
[2] PRO, DL 42/119. The contents are analysed in Barley, *op. cit.*, pp. 87–9.

in the fen and marshland. William Pitman of Waddington was called a yeoman by his neighbours when he died in 1624. In 1608 he held a messuage with a 'garth' (the usual Lincolnshire and northern word for a yard) and one oxgang of arable. His house consisted of hall, parlour, and kitchen, all chambered over. There are minor discrepancies between the further details of the house in 1608 and 1624—a kilnhouse and malthouse are mentioned in 1608 but not later, and a buttery, an entry, and a long chamber at the later date. All the rooms upstairs were furnished as bedrooms. William Caborne, yeoman, lived in the marshland village of Tetney and in 1608 held only a toft with a croft, a garth of three acres and two closes of pasture. The house had only two rooms, hall and parlour. Whether or not he died on the same holding he had much improved his position, for his goods were worth £254 and included a large farm stock. His house now had two parlours, a new and an old, with chambers over both and over the hall, as well as three service rooms, kitchen, buttery, and brewhouse. Some of the husbandmen who formed the majority of the duchy's tenants were also able to better themselves in a small way. John Osborne of Donington on Bain was in 1608 tenant of a cottage containing the usual two rooms, hall and parlour, and a garth of twenty poles. When he died in 1615 he possessed seventeen sheep and two kine, and his goods were worth only £12, but he had built a chamber over his parlour. On the other hand John Wright of Belchford who also held a two-roomed cottage in 1608 was still only a very poor husbandman twenty years later, with three cattle, six "rotten sheep," hay and corn in the yard, and household goods amounting in all to only £8 8s. clear.

The scarcity of timber in Lincolnshire and the consequent low standard of house carpentry have left very few unaltered houses of this period, but it is clear that only the richest yeomen can have aspired to the fully developed derivative of the medieval house: that is, a building with hall and two cross-wings, storeyed throughout. One example can be seen in the Trent valley, in the hamlet of Little Carlton, two or three miles north of Newark. The parish in which it lies (South Muskham) was enclosed early, probably during this period, and the house indicates the changing social conditions which accompanied such agrarian change. It is in marked contrast with the village of Norwell, three miles further north, where all the land was copyhold and the tenants of Southwell Minster were rather poor husbandmen. Surviving houses emphasize the distinction between the three-unit house (with or without cross-wings) with its cross-passage, and the house with axial stack and lobby entrance which had originally only two units. From the latter most houses of lesser yeomen and husbandmen in the east Midlands were derived.

Farm buildings of this period display as marked regional characteristics as do the houses; the building traditions of each area were adapted to climatic, agrarian, and social conditions. In eastern England, arable farming on a large scale required two or even more barns on rich yeomen's holdings. While many such men enlarged or modernized their medieval houses, the barns they inherited were often perfectly adequate. Aisled barns continued to be built during the whole of this period, and can be found throughout the region south of the Fens and east of the limestone belt. Barns elsewhere in England, except those required to store tithes, were never so commodious (Plates X, XI a).

In common-field England there is evidence of another type of structure for storage, especially among small husbandmen. In Northamptonshire and parts of Nottinghamshire and Lincolnshire, few farmyards were without a hovel or two, and inventories show that it was not a mere shed, but a granary with raised floor to keep unthreshed corn, peas, or hay off the ground. Lincolnshire inventories occasionally refer to peas *on* the hovel. An inventory from E. Drayton, Nottinghamshire, describes "a bound hovel with overlyers and pales and a door with hecks with certain peas and ling lying upon the same." Lincolnshire folk sometimes called such a structure a belfry: "beans unthreshed upon a belfray." North of the Humber it was called a helm: "a hovel or helm with the overlyers" (Market Weighton, 1613). Henry Best of Elmswell had two helms: "the Great Helm in the stack garth held 43 loads, the Helm in the fore garth held 23 loads." The name *helm* is of Scandinavian origin, and on the Continent, both in Scandinavia and in the Germanic lands, the essential feature of the helm was a roof which could be adjusted to the height of its contents. Granaries supported on substantial posts, arranged in a square, a rectangle, or a polygon are a regular feature of Germanic villages in the migration period and later; the adjustable roof is shown in manuscripts of the later middle ages. In English inventories the only technical term used is 'overliers', which presumably refers to the floor rather than the roof. There is no positive evidence that the English helm had an adjustable roof, but that seems more than likely. Continental examples had come to the notice of English writers by the end of Elizabeth's reign, and the scattered examples in this country dating from the eighteenth century and later seem to belong to large estates and are imitations, taken from books, of continental practice.[1]

[1] Inventories, Lincs. AO, Francis Collingwood, labourer, N. Cockerington, 1618; Peterborough Diocesan Records, Richard Small of Grafton Underwood, Henry Hills of Waldgrave, both 1660; York Probate Registry, Dean and Chapter, Elizabeth Marshall of East Drayton, Nottinghamshire, Edmund Gleadall of Market Weighton, Yorkshire, 1613; Henry Best, *Rural Economy in Yorkshire in 1641*, Surtees Soc.,

The farmhouses of the south-eastern half of England bear witness, then, to a revolution in housing standards during the course of this period. How much emphasis ought to be placed on new building, and how much on the improving of substantially built old houses, only further research will show. Historians have tended to draw attention to the evidence for new building, while archaeologists have added immensely to the known number of medieval houses, as well as to understanding of their plan and structure. It seems likely that in some parts building in the century prior to 1550 was as important as that of the century after. No contemporary commented on new building or improvements in Kent in the period 1575 onwards, as Carew did on Cornwall and King on Cheshire, although rebuilding seems to have been very vigorous in the Weald in the late sixteenth century. Field observation has confirmed the words of another contemporary, William Harrison, in so far as timber building now ceased within the jurassic zone, and new stone houses appeared in those villages on its margins which were reasonably near to quarries. Elsewhere, the replacement of timber by brick made little headway before 1640.

The new standards sprang in part from the greater wealth of the yeomen and husbandmen, and manifested themselves in a great increase in material comforts: glazed windows (often with curtains), chairs and cushions, pewter on the table, and feather beds in the parlour. They also sprang from the great need felt by more efficient farmers for better facilities for processing and storing farm produce. Both comfort and convenience could be obtained by modifying the traditional design of the lowland farmhouse. The only element in the medieval plan which had, by 1640, lost its popularity was the through passage. Otherwise the usual arrangement of a hall, flanked by service rooms on one side and sleeping rooms on the other remained unchanged, but only poor husbandmen did not aspire to a house of two storeys throughout. Better access was required to rooms upstairs, whether they were used for sleeping or for storing farm produce. Nevertheless, traditional ways of using ground-floor rooms were beginning to lose their hold. Some yeomen used a parlour as a sitting room, and those husbandmen whose wives still cooked in the hall were beginning to call it the kitchen.

In terms of planning, the idea of a chimney stack on the axis of the house, with back to back fireplaces on the ground floor, and sometimes on the first floor as well, acted as a solvent of traditional notions. Its

XXXIII, 1857, p. 58. For the helm on the continent, see Shetelig, Falk, and Gordon, *Scandinavian Archaeology*, p. 326; E. van Giffen in *Germania*, XXXVI, 1958, pp. 67–9; G. E. Fussell, 'Low Countries Influence on English Farming', EHR, LXXIV, 1959, p. 621. Fussell shows that Dutch barns with adjustable roofs were known to Barnaby Googe and Sir Hugh Plat.

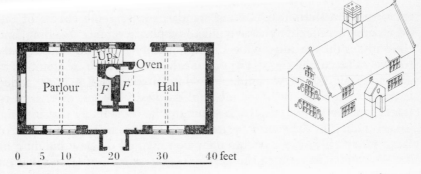

Fig. 25. Haunt House, Weldon, Northamptonshire, built *c*. 1636 by a local master-mason, Humphrey Frisbey. Buildings of this plan and scale are not uncommon and represent the lowest level of thorough innovation in house design before 1640.

most striking exemplification is the type of house illustrated in Fig. 25 (Haunt House, Weldon, Northamptonshire, built at the very end of the period) and Plate XV *b* (Rectory Farm, Britford, Wiltshire, of the same date or a little later). This plan, which combines symmetry of design with an inconvenient simplicity of arrangement—every one of the four principal rooms was later subdivided—seems to imitate the compactness of the 'double pile'. It soon lost its appeal to those who wanted houses of this size, but remained popular later for cottages.

An understanding of the character of farmhouses in the northern and western half of England requires awareness not only of climatic and agrarian contrasts with the other half, but also of the cultural relations between highland and lowland zone which have long been evident to archaeologists. Rural society in the highland zone had never ceased to take over and adapt elements of material domestic culture from the lowland zone. Some of the aisled halls which have recently been discovered in the upland townships of the parish of Halifax must be of sixteenth-century date, though that type of construction is thought to have gone out of fashion more than a century earlier in the south-east. Alongside such relatively novel forms of house design, much older forms persisted, such as cruck construction, and underwent development of a kind which showed that highland culture was strong enough to borrow from the lowlands without merely copying. The material culture of the highland zone consisted therefore, of an amalgam of features of varying age, the more ancient once common to both zones, the more recent originating in other and more prosperous regions. The frontier between the two zones is hard to define, because the boundaries of agrarian regions do not coincide with those of different building materials, such as stone and timber, and in any case, timber was largely replaced by stone during this period. Between highland and zones was an intermediate zone which can now be defined and in which the traditions of the two zones were blended. For this reason the limestone belt, from Kesteven south westwards, belongs in this context as much to the highland as to the lowland zone, and farmhouses of common-field Nottinghamshire and Leicestershire, for instance, have affinities with the Pennine region.[1]

In the highland zone of England the characteristic feature of farmhouse planning was the persistence of the cross passage. The plan is found in south Nottinghamshire as well as in the highlands proper: indeed, it is characteristic of medium sized farmhouses of the seventeenth century in the Cotswolds and north Somerset, in contrast to the three-unit, axial stack plan, without passage, of south Lincolnshire stone houses. The Cotswolds and Somerset examples almost invariably faced the street, and may reflect not only the conservatism of stone masons but also the fact that on the limestone uplands land was less valuable than in the clay vales and the lowland pasture regions. These houses were of one and a half or two storeys, and the staircase was usually alongside the hall entrance from the passage, within the width of the house, and not built out on the rear wall as in the highland zone proper. Though stone building was already an ancient tradition in these upland regions, a distinct regional style began to take shape by the later years of Elizabeth. The transition from timber to stone can be observed in villages such as Longleat in Wiltshire, situated in the valleys and on the margins of the limestone belt, and detailed study of them may throw light on the ancestry of what became by Stuart times the characteristic plan. The local stone quarries, such as Ancaster in Lincolnshire, Hornton near Banbury in north Oxfordshire, or Ham Hill in Somerset, must have been the meeting place of masons from which local styles were disseminated. After 1660, and possibly earlier, masons could here buy components such as doorways and mullioned windows ready cut.

The improvements to their houses which copyhold tenants everywhere were making by the first third of the seventeenth century led the earl of Pembroke to arrange for the same kind of survey of his manors in Wiltshire as Treswell had carried out in Lincolnshire for the duchy of Lancaster. Another such survey of manors in west Somerset was made in 1619.[2] The south Wiltshire villages consisted of houses

---

[1] C. Fox, *Personality of Britain*, 1947, and R. A. Cordingley in *Trans. Ancient Mon. Soc.*, 9, 1961, p. 74; for lowland forms of building in the highland zone, *Yorks. Arch. J.*, CLVIII, 1960, p. 192.

[2] E. Kerridge, *Surveys of the Manors of Philip, First Earl of Pembroke*, 1631–2, 1953; Somerset RO, DD, WO.

built in the timber vernacular of the southern counties such as Sussex and Berkshire; they were simple rectangular structures, with, most commonly, three "ground rooms," "lofted over." The survey speaks of "lofts" rather than chambers; they were no doubt made within the roof space, lighted at best by dormers and reached by a ladder; the house of two full storeys with a staircase was still a rarity. Outshots, or 'cuts' as the local term went, were also very rare; that particular way of adding to accommodation belongs everywhere in the lowlands to the eighteenth and nineteenth centuries rather than earlier. The Somerset survey is more informative, though it does not describe so many houses. They belong to the south-western cob tradition. The whole complex of buildings commonly consisted of a house with between three and six rooms, usually with chambers, though sometimes with lofts over them, and outhouses and farm buildings round a court or yard, often with a linhay or some covered accommodation in it, and occasionally still entered by a gatehouse.

As for the house itself, the most striking development in the region stretching from north-west Somerset into Cornwall was the emergence of a new type with two full storeys and a chimney stack making an ornamental feature on the front of the house. It is found both in stone and in cob, and, beginning c. 1580, the fashion lasted throughout the next century. This type of house usually stood facing the street, not at right angles to it, and there was invariably a passage alongside the stack from which the hall, the room which contains the principal if not the only ground floor fireplace, was entered. This plan confirms the impression that the medieval through-passage, which was losing its place in eastern houses of the early seventeenth century, lasted a hundred years longer in the west. The front chimney stack usually contained two flues, one for the hall and one for the chamber above it, which was thereby designated as a room of high standing. With this arrangement went sometimes a parlour on the other side of the passage, in a room which had once been used either for storing food or for cattle. At the other side of the hall was a room sometimes used as a bed chamber, sometimes as a buttery.[1] These houses had developed out of diverse elements of a tradition entirely different from any so far observed: that is by taking over one feature, storeyed building, from the lesser gentry and wealthier parsons, and adapting it to the traditional peasant design containing a hall with a storeroom to one side and a through passage with a shippon beyond it. A parlour was incorporated either by converting the buttery or milkhouse within the hall, or the

[1] "The Inner Chamber" with John Letherer, Winkleigh, 1646 (Devon RO); "the chamber within the hall" in the Nettlecombe Survey and in inventories of John Collins, husbandman, N. Curry, 1590, etc.

service rooms across the passage. The chamber over the hall, instead of being merely a storeroom, as it was in many eastern houses, was occasionally called "the Parlour Chamber over the Hall" as in the inventory of Hugh Upcott of Witheridge, 1645. The staircase in such houses was usually at the rear of the block, projecting in its own round or square wing from the back wall of the hall. The builders of these new houses had, by the seventeenth century, modified the cruck method to suit the greater height of storeyed construction by making their cruck blades in two pieces, jointed together, instead of in one. Devonshire still possesses a great wealth of houses of this age, exhibiting all the features here mentioned as well as further improvements of the eighteenth century, such as the addition of a kitchen. The great variety of plans shows that as much rebuilding was going on in the West Country in this age as to any part of England. Piecemeal improvement is indicated by phrases in inventories like "the glass in the windows with boards and joists for a chamber" (John Collins, North Curry, Somerset, husbandman, 1590) or "all the moveable boards in the two lofts" (John Willey, Old Cleeve, Somerset, husbandman, 1634). It seems that glazing and wainscotting both begin *c.* 1570 in Devonshire.

In Devonshire, in parts of Herefordshire and in the Lake District the tradition of the byre house, with human and animals under one roof, is still evident in new houses of the sixteenth and seventeenth centuries (Fig. 21). The living part consisted of a hall, used for all purposes, with a small store room or dairy beyond. The byre was at least as long as the rest of the dwelling. They were built on sloping sites, like the medieval platform houses noted in Wales, whether or not the low end was to be used as a byre. The opposed entrances were slightly staggered, as if to facilitate the separation of humans and animals within the building. The cross-walk was turned into a wide cross-passage by dividing it from the byre. The fact that many surviving byre houses are evidently not of one build shows that farmers felt increasingly that, although conjoined, the byre was an inferior part of the house, to be treated differently: its rebuilding was deferred, or done in cheaper material.[1] The dairy or storeroom within the hall was sometimes turned into a sleeping chamber, or parlour and service rooms added in an outshot at the rear. Additional sleeping room might be contrived by inserting a chamber over the hall, which usually served as a cooking as well as a living room. It is not as yet possible to determine how far such changes, and particularly the conversion of the byre into a service room of some kind, had proceeded by 1640, but they were certainly under way. Cooking was from first to last done in the hall.

[1] These sentences are based on the work of S. R. Jones and J. T. Smith in papers unpublished) to the Vernacular Architecture Group.

In wealthier parts of the county, while the same practice may have held, the yeoman and husbandman sometimes had a detached building called either a kitchen or (more commonly in west Somerset, according to the Nettlecombe Survey) a bakehouse. The latter term no doubt implied that it contained the claom or earthenware oven for bread which was still manufactured until recently at Truro. No doubt it had also the bacon-curing chamber which has sometimes been labelled a smuggler's hide. The curing chamber consisted of a circular aperture, perhaps 5 feet in diameter, alongside a fireplace in a gable end, with an opening at low level from the fireplace and a return flue from the corbelled roof into the chimney. Though such a structure cannot easily be dated, there is no doubt that its development belongs to this age of increasing food production and the elaboration of storage and processing facilities. The west-country farmer, just as much as his eastern counterpart, needed one or more chambers within the house for storing apples, cheese, corn, or wool. Brewing was at least as common as cider making, judging from references to a brewhouse, a 'dry' (kiln) or a 'dry hair', the horsehair cloth on which malt was spread in the kiln.[1]

In the seventeenth century a new type of cow house began to appear in Devon and Somerset farmyards: the linhay, an open-fronted structure with a hay loft over. Its adoption in Devon may have been provoked by the declining hold of the byre house tradition, but the main stimulus was no doubt increasing dairy production. The earliest linhays were built entirely of timber, in a manner derived from the cruck technique.[2] In the northern part of the highland zone farmers also evolved—from what source cannot yet be discerned—a storeyed building sheltering cattle on the ground floor with a hay loft over them. These northern buildings, which belong mainly to the period after 1660 but probably appeared earlier, were fully enclosed, and were built on a slope so that hay wagons could be driven straight into the barn or loft.

In the west country no radical change in building techniques took place, though the use of stone may have gained ground at the expense of cob. In the west Midlands and the Severn valley builders were compelled, as they were to the east of the limestone, to adjust their methods to the increased cost of timber. The ordinary yeoman did not aspire to a brick house, though he certainly wanted an improved fireplace, and from the early Elizabethan period brick began to be used

[1] Barley, op. cit., p. 168; inventory of Faith Knight of Whimpole, 1643 (Devon RO).
[2] N. W. Alcock, 'Devonshire Linhays: a Vernacular Tradition', Trans. Devonshire Ass., xcv, 1963, pp. 117–30.

for chimney stacks. Many medieval houses in Staffordshire had upper floors and chimney stacks inserted at this time, though the open-hall house had not disappeared, to judge from references in inventories to "bacon at the roof." In one of the commonest Staffordshire and Cheshire house designs the stack was placed at the junction of hall and cross-wing, with an entrance in the angle facing the stack (Fig. 24). Further south and west, on both sides of the Severn valley, the same plan usually had stone stacks built outside the line of gable walls. For the walling, timber remained the principal material until the later years of the seventeenth century, and the customary right of a tenant to take timber from the hedgerow for house repairs probably lingered longer in the west Midlands than in any other part of the country.[1] The housewright never adopted the eastern practice of rendering external walls to protect (and conceal) inferior framing, for suitable timber was more abundant than in the east. But the prodigal method of close studding eventually gave way to a system of panel framing which became remarkably uniform in the last phase of timber building after 1660. The transition was as slow as in any part of England; a house at Madeley, Staffordshire, with close studding and jettied first and attic floors bore the inscription "Walk knave: what look'st at?" and the date 1647.[2] Within such houses, timber was used as generously as for main walls: partitions were framed in timber and ceilings divided into square panels by substantial beams. For the upper rooms which so many more houses now possessed, the term solar continued in use. John Hall of Bennetts in the parish of Suckley, Worcestershire, who died in 1614, had a "soller over the parlor" and a "soller over the Buttery." The inventory of William Windle of Camborne, Warwickshire (1614), refers to "the room or soller over the chamber." Robert Leadon a wealthy farmer at Great Comberton, Worcestershire, had a "soller over the hall" which held linen, onions and garlic, malt, barley, wheat, wool, hops, apples, and various oddments, including a mousetrap. The solar over the buttery held five spinning-wheels, hemp, and yarn, and a bed; both it and the chamber solar were used not only as bedrooms but also as storerooms for food, farm produce, or articles not in regular use downstairs. The reference to a chamber solar shows that, as elsewhere in the south of England, a ground-floor bedroom was not always called a parlour.[3]

The inventory of one Worcestershire husbandman, Roger Noxton

[1] See VCH *Staffs.*, IV, pp. 136–8; T. Cave and R. A. Wilson, *Parliamentary Survey of Worcester, 1649*, Worcs. Hist. Soc., 1929, pp. 15, 60, 112, 136.

[2] M. W. Barley, *House and Home*, 1962, plate 46.

[3] Birmingham Probate Registry, Worcester Consistory, bundle 1613–14, nos. 3271, 3278, 3289.

of Kingston, who died in 1613, may serve as a reminder that not all farmers were able to better themselves in these times. His goods were worth only £5 15s. 2d., of which the corn in the barn amounted to £2 10s. He seems to have had two rooms, a hall and a chamber. The hall had a framed table, a form and a fixed bench, and two chairs; the chamber three bedsteads, one press, and one coffer. His remaining goods make a brief list: spits, cobirons, links, and pothooks about the fire; a frying pan and a gridiron; two small spinning wheels and a malt mill, and then the brass, pewter, coopery, and treen ware. The only item not strictly utilitarian was the painted cloths on the walls.[1]

Extremes of wealth and poverty, such as we have already had glimpses of in the lowland zone, were a much more noticeable feature of northern society; great contrasts in living conditions were to remain characteristic, and indeed can still be seen. In Lancashire both highland and lowland, observers of the past and the present have commented on the extreme simplicity of building methods and living standards.[2] Although the West and North Ridings were a good deal wealthier than Lancashire, a similar simplicity characterized housing standards of all but the rising members of the yeoman class. Between the four northern counties of Cumberland, Westmorland, Northumberland, and Durham on the one hand and East Anglia on the other, the contrast in wealth and domestic manners can scarcely be exaggerated. In terms of building technique this meant that the cruck method of construction was still practised throughout the period (Fig. 26). This is inseparable from the persistent tradition of single-storey housing, which was little shaken among the poorer peasantry until after 1660. There is no doubt that byrehouses were still to be seen. Daniel King, writing during the Commonwealth, stated that Cheshire farmers until the early seventeenth century "had their fire in the midst of the house, against a hob of clay, and their Oxen also under the same roof."[3]

Within the building, the formal and functional divisions long current in the lowland zone were, until the seventeenth century, of much less significance. Yorkshire inventories often speak of the netherhouse, the nether end of the house or the low end; it was a service room with no distinctive use, and its significance has already been discussed (p. above). The hall-living room is commonly called the fire-house, though before 1640 that name had already begun to be replaced by forehouse, as the other rooms, reached through the living room, came into greater use. In the West Riding and further north, climate required

[1] Ibid., no. 3251.
[2] T. D. Whitaker, History of Whalley, 4th ed., 1876, II, p. 574; R. Watson in Lancs. and Cheshire Hist. Soc., CIX, 1957, pp. 61–6.
[3] Daniel King, The Vale-Royall of England, 1656, p. 19.

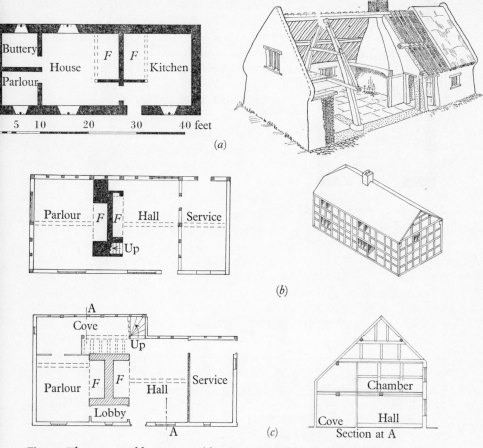

Fig. 26. Three-roomed houses, possibly appropriate to husbandmen or lesser yeomen. (*a*) Ivy Cottage, Bispham, Lancashire cruck built with mud walls, has only one entrance, on to a lobby by the side of back to back fireplaces. (*b*) Townland Cottages, Billingshurst, Sussex, timber framed with a brick chimney stack, has the entrance at the lower end of the hall. (*c*) Warner's Cottage, Nutfield, Surrey, of similar plan and also timber-framed, has an outshot or cove, in the local tradition, used in this case to house the staircase.

that the hearth should be a room within a room. Hence the "ingle nook" of lowland Scotland and the border counties. It has been observed that in the West Riding, the hall fireplace, backing in the cross-passage, had a great hood supported by a beam spanning the hall and even by an upright post in the middle of the floor. It has been suggested that the space under the hood was the firehouse, but inventories do not support this distinction. Beyond the firehouse was a

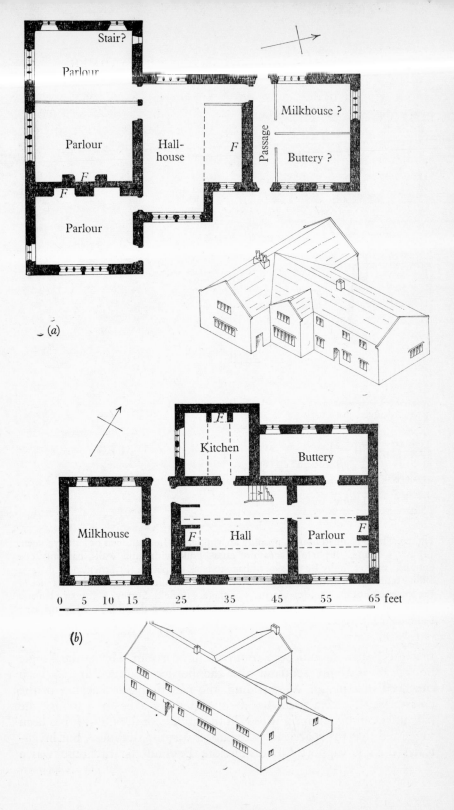

Stair?

Parlour

Parlour

Hall-house

F

Passage

Milkhouse ?

Buttery ?

F

F

Parlour

Parlour

(a)

F

Kitchen

Buttery

Milkhouse

F

Hall

Parlour

F

0   5   10   15   25   35   45   55   65 feet

(b)

room which Cumberland folk still called the bower.[1] Elsewhere that ancient term had gone out of use, in favour of either chamber or parlour, both ground-floor rooms. Rooms added to the rear of the house, in an outshot, were more common than in the south, because that technique derived from the aisled hall tradition. More than one Lancashire house was said to consist of so many bays with 'aisling'. Lofts or first-floor chambers must have been rare before 1640 except in houses of wealthier yeomen. In a survey of houses in Cracoe and Silsden, West Yorkshire, most of which were cruck-built, only one had a "chamber over the wall plate."[2]

Before 1640 ideas of betterment were largely confined to a small element of the yeoman class, and spread mainly in regions where the textile industry put more money into farmers' pockets: rebuilding timber houses in stone began only c. 1600 in the West Riding, and houses with open halls were still being built at the end of our period. The period from 1575 to 1660 probably saw greater contrasts than either before or after among the farmhouses of the north. The yeomen father of Adam Martindale of Prescot, Lancashire, built a new house beside his old one some time before 1613, in order to have more comfort and more "stowage for corn."[3] The house has since been rebuilt, but we may guess that it was of two storeys, with a kitchen as well as a house-living room, two or even more parlours, and two or three service rooms. When a house like that of Arnold Kirk, a successful yeoman of Martinside in the parish of Chapel-en-le-Frith, is said in 1640 to have had four parlours, it is difficult to believe that they were all ground-floor rooms, but there is no evidence that rooms upstairs were so called. Certainly the multiplication of parlour bedrooms is one of the characteristics of northern yeomen's houses of 1600 onwards. A surviving example is Dean House, Allerton, in the parish of Bradford, built in the early seventeenth century by Robert Deane, yeoman. It had a **U** plan, with two parlours in one wing, and in the other the

[1] E.g., Carlisle Diocesan Records, Cumberland inventories: Thomas Broomsfeilde the Elder of Hameshill in Bridekirk, 1631; Hugh Marshall of Brockellbank in Westwood, 1637.

[2] Lancs. RO, DDF, 52, survey of Worden, Lancs., 1569; Yorks., Arch. Soc. Library, Leeds, DDI, 21, 31.

[3] *The Life of Adam Martindale*, ed. R. Parkinson, Chetham Soc., IV, 1845, pp. 1–2.

Fig. 27. Two yeomen's houses in Hebden Royd, an upland township in the parish of Halifax. (*a*) High Hurst built in late Elizabethan times and altered in 1629 (the date on a plaster frieze in the hall) has three parlours in the cross wing. A hood over the hall fireplace covered a large part of the area of the hall. The original staircases have disappeared and the rooms in the service end were much altered late in the seventeenth century. (*b*) Stannery End (1629) has the novelties of a kitchen behind the hall, a buttery next to the parlour and chambers or lofts over each ground-floor room.

third parlour and two service rooms (kitchen and milkhouse) behind, and the 'house body' or hall between.[1] The space between the wings at the rear is now filled with additional service rooms in a lean-to, and comparison with other houses of this age in the Halifax area suggests that the kitchen was often placed behind the hall in the main range, for this had the advantage of leaving space for both wings for parlours (Fig. 27). Robert Deane had probably been engaged in the textile industry, though the only evidence in the inventory taken at his death in 1636 was a cushion loom, probably no longer used, in one of the chambers upstairs. It is impossible to explain the great wealth of substantial stone houses in the West Riding except on the assumption that the combination of agriculture with cloth production—mainly of kerseys, but including such local specialisms as cushion cloths in the Bradford area—gave the local farmer a particular advantage (Plate IX a). Only the poorest class, of labourers and poor husbandmen, did not possess a loom. This local boom led many medieval timber houses to be rebuilt in stone, and recent field work has shown that a substantial proportion of the older houses had been aisled halls.[2] Not all local industries of the north had such evident effect on the prosperity of a region. In Derbyshire, although many yeomen and husbandmen were engaged in lead mining, and others in more localized crafts such as millstone making, the standard of life was distinctly lower than in the West Riding (Fig. 28: Staden Farm), and the largest farmhouses belonged to upland farmers with large pastoral interests.

In County Durham, the few inventories which reveal details of living arrangements show a simplicity comparable only with houses of a century earlier in the south-east, and Durham wills of the Elizabethan age, with their bequests of livestock rather than items of furniture or clothing, have the same old-fashioned flavour. John Carter of Shincliffe, yeoman, whose goods, when he died in 1598, were worth the respectable sum of £128, had no more than two or three rooms. The standards of some of the gentry were no more elaborate than those of modest yeomen in the south: Ralph Billingham of Crook Hall, Brancepeth, had a hall, a parlour, two service rooms (buttery and milkhouse), and a high chamber. Houses which were so simply planned could hold, by contemporary standards, only a minimum of furniture. Richard Eltringham of Auckland St Andrew, farmer, had a forehouse or hall with only one chair, one table, two cupboards, along with brass and

[1] *Wills proved in...Crosley*, Bradford Ant. Soc. Local Record Series, I, 1929, pp. 83–9; W. B. Crump 'The Yeoman Clothier of the Seventeenth Century', in *Bradford Antiquary*, VII, 1933, pp. 222–6.

[2] See F. C. Stell, *Vernacular Architecture in a Pennine Region* (unpublished thesis, Liverpool 1960).

pewter; a parlour with a standing bed and a clothes press; a low house used as a second bedroom, and a high chamber which contained a standing bed and some rye.

The inference that these northern counties were as yet largely untouched by the new ideas of comfort and convenience which had flooded over the lowland zone of England is confirmed by various studies of vernacular building in Cumberland and Westmorland. Parallels to Elizabethan and early Stuart rebuilding and enlargement by southern farmers are to be found only in houses of the period 1660–1720. Building in stone then began to replace the common technique of 'clay daubing'; before that, stone was used only in houses of the gentry and prosperous yeomen.[1] Where stone is plentiful these clay houses have vanished completely; the rare survivors are confined to north-west Cumberland. Lamonby, in the parish of Burgh by Sands, consists of a very long range of buildings with clay walls on stone footings, comprising now two small houses and a barn. The roof throughout is of cruck construction, though not all of one date, and both houses have chambers of the simplest kind in the roof space.[2]

In Westmorland and Cumberland, both the fell and the lowland parishes carried a large population of small farmers whose tenure was customary in name but who enjoyed almost as much security as freeholders. Inventories are uninformative and few in number, so that it is impossible from direct evidence to generalize about their houses, beyond the fact that personal possessions were very few, and that single-storey building, usually with cruck framing, must have been usual. Increasing wealth and security of tenure eventually produced, in the period after 1660, a great rebuilding of statesmen's houses which, although it is difficult to find one rebuilt in a single operation, are remarkably stereotyped in plan and in details of construction. They had three units with a through passage in the manner common throughout the highland zone: a hall entered from the passage (or hallan), with the large fireplace occupying as much as a third of the hall and backing on the cross-passage; the parlour or bower, beyond the hall and divided from it by a wooden partition; the third room, beyond the passage, known as the down house, the backhouse, or the house end, was used for one of several domestic or farming purposes. The staircase, of stone, was built against the back wall of the hall. The plan corresponds exactly to the commonest type in other parts of the highland zone, and the variations in the function of the third room are

[1] W. M. Williams, 'Farmhouses of south-west Cumberland' in *Cumberland and Westmorland Arch. and Ant. Soc.*, LIX, 1954, pp. 256–7.

[2] K. S. Hodgson, C. M. C. Bouch, and C. G. Bulman, 'Lamonby Farm: a Clay House at Burgh-by-Sands', *ibid.*, LIII, 1955, pp. 149–59.

particularly characteristic. Although this plan, in the houses of customary tenants, belongs essentially to the Restoration period and later, its prototype already existed in some of the houses of the lesser gentry, such as Barwise Hall, Hoff, dated 1579. A few examples earlier than 1640 can also be found of the fitted cupboards and other conveniences typical of the later houses. Other essential features of upland building, which are best seen at a later date, must also have had their origins in this period. One common practice was to place farm buildings on a slope so that the byre and hayloft over it could both be entered from the ground. The spinning galleries which a few Lakeland houses still possess are a result of the same practice of building on a sloping site.[1]

The farmhouses of that part of England north and west of a line from Scarborough through York and Oxford to Lyme Regis shared, then, a common tenacity of tradition, displayed particularly in the persistence of the plan comprising three rooms and a cross-passage, with a uniform disposition of hall fireplace. In one of the poorest and most remote parts of that zone, Dartmoor, the ancestry of that plan is evident in the survival of long houses from which the plan derived. The common tradition developed, in the age of new building which began in the sixteenth century, at a pace which varied according to the economic resources of regions within the highland zone, and in a manner dependent partly on materials and craftsmen, partly on local differences in the tradition. Such variants included the aisled hall plan in Lancashire and Yorkshire, a recent import from the south which led

[1] Hist. Mon. Commission, *Westmorland*, *passim*, R. W. McDowall, 'The Westmorland Vernacular' in *Studies in Architectural History*, ed. W. A. Singleton, II, 1956, pp. 131–2; J. Walton in *Antiquity*, xxx, 1956, pp. 142–7; H. S. Cowper, *Hawkshead, in the northernmost parish of Lancashire*, 1899, pp. 144–57. R. W. Brunskill in *Trans. Ancient Mon. Soc.* 10, 1962, p. 57.

Fig. 28. Two-roomed houses. Very few houses of this size survive from the period before 1640, and it is difficult to date such simple structures; hence some examples of later date have been included, to illustrate the variety of construction and plan originating before 1640. None of these has more than one entrance. (*a*) Vesey Cottage, High Heath, Sutton Coldfield, Warwickshire, with one room on each of two floors and a garret in the roof, represents the smallest type among the houses erected by Bishop Vesey (1462–1554) in his birthplace. (*b*) Higher Spargo, Mabe, Cornwall, though very modest, represents the new standards which began to pervade Cornwall from late Elizabethan times: granite walls and thatched roof; few windows; no parlour, but a fireplace in the single chamber over the whole house. (*c*) No. 6 Corby Road, Weldon, Northamptonshire, has stone walls and a roof with upper crucks; the entrance is in the gable end. (*d*) Albutt's Cottage, Hanbury, Worcestershire, has a large stone chimney, built out from the gable-end of a timber-framed house. (*e*) Staden Farm, near Buxton, Derbyshire, possibly *c*. 1700 or even later, has the entrance alongside the gable-end fireplace.

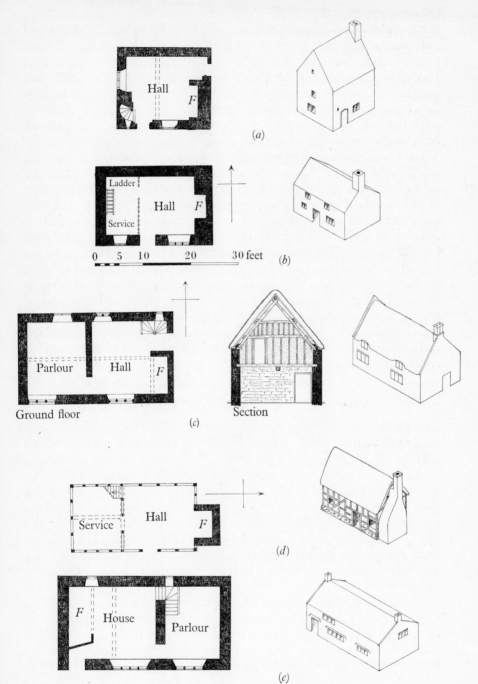

Hall

F

(a)

Ladder

Hall   F

Service

0   5   10   20   30 feet   *(b)*

Parlour   Hall   F

Ground floor   Section   *(c)*

Service   Hall   F

(d)

F   House   Parlour

(e)

to the appearance there before 1640 of houses two rooms deep which were of independent, northern, origin. The habit of building houses of only one storey was more persistent in the north than in the west country, and was not extinct, in small farmhouses, even in 1640. Devonshire farmhouses displayed remarkable variety in this and succeeding periods; the forms which can still be observed include developed long houses; two-storey houses with a superior chamber over the hall, and houses where the room beyond the hall may still be a storeroom rather than a parlour. In building construction, the West Country developed its own derivative of cruck construction, the jointed cruck. All in all, Devonshire farmhouses demonstrate better than those of any other English county not only the conservatism of the highland zone, owing to remoteness and poverty, but also the capacity of richer areas and classes within it to absorb, and to develop in their own fashion, elements of lowland culture (Fig. 28: Higher Spargo). The immense power of lowland influences, and the opportunities which at this time were open even in a remote county, are shown by Richard Carew's description of the condition of Cornish husbandmen in his time, the 1580's: "walles of earth, low thatched roofes, few partitions, no planchings or glass windowes, and scarcely any chimnies. . . but now most of these fashions are universally banished, and the Cornish husbandman conformeth himself with a better supplied civilitie to the Easterne pattern. . ."[1]

F. THE HOUSES OF DOMESTIC CRAFTSMEN

Every village contained men who were not dependent solely on agriculture for a livelihood, and a few of them carried on pursuits which affected their living arrangements. The wealthier entrepreneur—an Essex clothier, a Sussex ironmaster, a Norfolk brewer, a tanner—was usually a farmer as well, and his trade merely led him to add a shop and other special outbuildings to his farmyard. The village craftsmen working in wood or iron—carpenters, wheelwrights, ploughwrights—had both a workshop and a stake in the land. Others used equipment or raw materials which were neither bulky nor expensive, and carried on their trade within the home. The most numerous of these were weavers and tailors.

The tailor worked in the hall-living room of his house, since he was no purveyor of material but made up the cloth brought to him by the customer. Where the weaver carried on his craft depended on the scale of his operations. He most commonly had two looms, and certainly when he had more than one his weaving was usually done in

[1] *Survey of Cornwall*, 1769, p. 66 b.

a shop—that is a room or building additional to his house. Occasionally poor weavers with only one loom worked in the living room of their house, or else in what would otherwise have been the parlour or downstairs chamber. On the other hand, the installation of the loom in an upstairs room, which was to become the characteristic feature of domestic industry, had begun before 1640; this was one of the various uses to which the new chambers in early Stuart houses could be put. Among surviving inventories for the period 1599–1642 from a group of West Riding townships, two show weavers with a loom in the house or the parlour; four others had a weaving shop, and five carried on their work in an upstairs chamber.[1]

G. THE HOUSES OF VILLAGE LABOURERS

We have already seen that there was no simple equation between house type and social class, and this is as true of the labourer as of the gentleman. The labourer's cottage included a wide range of types. Mobility was common in this expanding agrarian economy, and some labourers must have managed by good fortune and hard work to raise themselves to the level of husbandmen. On the other hand, the engrossing of land must have degraded many farmhouses to cottages, and this may explain some of the instances in which labourer's holdings had more or larger outbuildings than might be expected. A major increase in population in the second half of the sixteenth century led to a growth of the practice of adapting farm buildings as dwellings, dividing large houses, and of building cottages on the waste, either with or without permission. The manor house at Wylie, Wiltshire, was divided into eight tenements in 1631, each family having two or three rooms. A petition to the lord of the manor to build a cottage on the common at Fornham All Saints was supported by those who would lose common rights on the half rood of land in question because the cottage was for a ploughwright who would be an asset to the village. Between 1581 and 1616 numerous appeals were addressed by villagers on the Pelham estate in Sussex for leave for widows or aged labourers to build cottages for themselves on the lord's waste, and the Parliamentary Surveys contain many references to cottages recently built on the waste.[2]

The rural scene included cottages of every condition, especially in parishes where there was much waste, and on land recently disforested.

[1] *Wills proved in...Crosley...*; see inventories of John Hudson, William Birkinshaw, John Cosin, Edward Tennants, etc.

[2] E. Kerridge, *Surveys of the Manors of Philip, First Earl of Pembroke*, 1953, pp. 86–8; Barley, *The English Farmhouse and Cottage*, p. 271; VCH *Sussex*, II, p. 193; *Gwerin* III, 1961, p. 7; T. Cave and R. A. Wilson, *Parliamentary Survey of Worcester*, 1929, pp. 108–10, PRO, Parliamentary Surveys, E 317 (Derbyshire), fos. 12, 19, 20, 30.

The distinction between permanent homes and the temporary shelters made by migrant workers such as charcoal makers was less marked than in the nineteenth century, when the traditions of those workers finally disappeared. A deposition of 1604 describes a "sorry cote pitched into a nook of a rock of stone" in Charnwood Forest, and states that it "hath been a dwelling house, upon the want and necessity of another house, of a poor man, a wisket (basket) maker, that for his own succour made the same of sticks and turves, but paid no rent or fine."[1] The distinction between such a primitive structure and a permanent dwelling is one between a house constructed by its occupant and one built by a craftsman, whether mason or house carpenter. Surviving houses of this age are certainly all the work of craftsmen, and historical records fail to make clear how often, if at all, the yeoman or the husbandman was able to repair or to enlarge his dwelling without calling in a craftsman. The husbandman certainly still valued the right to take 'housebote' from the hedgerow and woodland trees from the manor. On the other hand in normal circumstances the lord of the manor accepted responsibility for building and for rebuilding when necessary (as distinct from repairing) the cottages of his tenants, as medieval manorial accounts occasionally show. In default of evidence of surviving buildings—and no houses which would certainly have ranked as cottages originally have survived from a date earlier than about 1700—it would be wrong to equate the average Tudor cottage with the charcoal-burner's hut. It must usually have had vertical walls, and by 1640 rarely had less than two rooms.[2]

Surveys show that the term cottage was almost as useless in the seventeenth century as it is today as an indication of the size of a dwelling. The survey made in 1631-2 of the Wiltshire manors of the earl of Pembroke includes 322 houses and forty-two cottages. The proportion of cottages—i.e. of dwellings with no more than a garden attached to them—is low enough to show that much of the wage labour on larger farms must have been provided by men who had not entirely lost their own stake in the land. One of the cottages had only a single room; it was held by Joan Taylor, aged 22, and her younger sisters; it had been built on the waste but since 1630 a rent of 6d. a year had been paid for it. An ancient cottager's holding consisted of "a little dwelling house of 1 ground room lofted over," with six acres

[1] G. H. Farnham, 'Charnwood Forest, the Charnwood Manors', Leics. Arch. Soc., xv, 1927-8, p. 248.
[2] For cottages with vertical walls shown in the Bayeux Tapestry, see Barley, The House and Home, plate 4. Temporary shelters of migrant workers are illustrated in Cumb. and Westm. and Ant. Soc., I, 1901, pp. 141-3; Somerset Arch. and Natural Hist. Soc., LV, 1910, pp. 175-80.

of arable and common rights. The commonest type of cottage on these manors had a hall-living room, a chamber-bedroom alongside, and a storage loft over one of the ground-floor rooms. A survey of duchy of Lancaster manors in Lincolnshire, made in 1608, includes 185 houses and sixty-four cottages. It covers manors in the limestone uplands, the coastal marshland, and the fens, and cottages are distinctly more rare in the fens than elsewhere, because on that rich soil the poorer peasants seem to have enjoyed greater comforts than elsewhere. Of the sixty-four cottages, exactly half comprised two rooms, house-living room and parlour-bedroom. A quarter had a service room (buttery or milkhouse) as well, but only three were identical with the commonest Wiltshire type in having a chamber over one of the two ground-floor rooms. This contrast emphasizes the distinction already made between the south, where storeyed building was already popular, and the north-midlands and north, where the single-storey tradition lasted much longer. The standard Lincolnshire cottage was in fact the commonest single type of dwelling of any kind in the country at the date of the survey, for exactly half the 'messuages' were of that size.[1]

A survey of Toynton All Saints, a village on the southern fringe of the Lincolnshire Wolds which included some fenland, gives similar results. Out of thirty-nine tenants, seventeen had cottages, and of those eight consisted of two rooms, hall and parlour, and were of two bays. Two of them are distinctly said to consist only of a hall of one bay. Four of them had in addition to the two rooms, an "outend" or "back-end." These terms were not in widespread use, but obviously indicated further building at the end or the rear of a house; one of the husband-men's tenements in the village had a "backend kitchen built in the yard;" another had a "milkhouse at the backend of the hall with a chamber over it." No doubt the cottager's backend or outend also held his few tools or implements.[2]

In the northern counties it is impossible to isolate the cottage as a type of dwelling because the term was not used by surveyors; they distinguished only buildings containing a hearth, and so used as dwellings, from those used for other purposes. Any dwelling was therefore a firehouse, as distinct from a hay house, a kiln house, or a turf house. The firehouses usually ranged in size from two bays to four bays, and many of the smaller ones, regarded later as cottages, consisted only of "single apartments, without chambers, open to their thatched roofs, and supported upon crucks."[3]

[1] E. Kerridge, op. cit., passim; PRO, DL 49/119, passim.　　[2] Lincs. AO, 5 Anc. 4a.
[3] T. D. Whitaker, History of Whalley, 1876, II, p. 574; Yorks Arch. Soc. Library, Leeds, DD 121, 31. The survey of Sheffield dated 1611, published by S. O. Addy, Evolution of the English House, 1905, pp. 207–10, includes thirty houses and only two cottages.

The use of the term labourer was as localized in distribution as was the word cottage. It is not found in Yorkshire, except in the East Riding and the Vale of York. In the wold villages of the East Riding, the labourer whose common rights were an important source of his livelihood was known as a grassman. Inventories of labourers are most numerous in Lincolnshire, Nottinghamshire, and Bedfordshire, much less so in East Anglia, and very rare in Kent and Sussex. In west Sussex for instance, there appear to be none earlier than *c.* 1670. Jervice Verser of Wittersham, Kent, who died in 1632, was called a labourer, yet he left goods worth £87, lived in a five-roomed house, and had a sizeable farm stock; it is difficult to see why a man of his substance, so genteelly christened, should have been so called. It appears that a labouring class, so called, was a feature of common-field England. Elsewhere, rural society scarcely bothered to distinguish between one husbandman who had enough land to maintain his family and another who was compelled regularly to seek employment for wages to eke out what he could get from his own few acres. The common-field labourer was not necessarily poorer—Lincolnshire and Nottinghamshire inventories show that he too often had some arable of his own—and in any case, as Professor Tawney has pointed out *á propos* of Gloucestershire at this time, any picture of social classes in rural England is superimposed on "a system of family farms worked with the aid of relatives and only to a small extent with hired labour."[1]

Many labourers' inventories, even in the counties where they are most numerous, fail to mention the names of the rooms in the house. Occasional inventories of men of every class have that defect, and in some counties, particularly of the north-west, only a very small proportion of inventories earlier than 1640 are arranged under specified rooms. In the east midlands this appears to be more than a casual shortcoming of the records (or of the local appraisers who made them), for the number of such inventories declines significantly in the period 1580 and 1630, and they rarely occur after 1660. Taken in conjunction with other evidence, this leads to the conclusion that before 1580 the single-roomed cottage was not uncommon among labourers and other poor members of the village community, and that many of them were able to take advantage of favourable economic conditions between 1580 and 1640 to improve their domestic condition. This they did by

[1] A. J. and R. H. Tawney, 'An Occupational Census of the Seventeenth Century,' EcHR, v, 1934–5, p. 53. Labourers formed 24 per cent of the total of yeomen, husbandmen, and labourers in Gloucestershire in 1608, compared with 4 per cent in Bedfordshire in 1617–18 (F. G. Emmison, 'Jacobean Household Inventories' in *Beds. Record Soc.*, xx, 1938), and 44 per cent in inventories of five Trent valley villages, 1565–1640. The Gloucestershire proportion rises to 37 per cent if servants of yeomen and husbandmen are included.

making a structural division between the living half and the sleeping half of the house. To judge from later two-unit houses in the east Midlands, which invariably have an axial stack between the two rooms, the simpler dwelling must have had a hearth in the centre, opposite an entrance in the middle of the side wall. In the map accompanying the 1614 survey of Toynton already described, widow Pinder's "cottage at the fenside," said to consist of two bays with hall and parlour, can be picked out as a dwelling of this type. The origin and diffusion of this two-unit dwelling with axial hearth, and the determination of the kind of fireplace it had, are among the outstanding archaeological problems of the medieval and sub-medieval periods.

The single-unit dwelling developed in more than one direction. It might be chambered over, to provide sleeping room upstairs. Cottages consisting of a house or hall and a chamber occur in Lincolnshire, and a common type of fenland cottage, of eighteenth-century and later date, consists of a living room, a bedroom over it, and a small kitchen or scullery, usually in an outshot. Such outshots are rare before 1640, except in Yorkshire, and this fenland type is a modern elaboration of a sixteenth- and seventeenth-century type. The single-unit cottage of that period is also the ancestor of the rows of cottages built for farm labourers in the eighteenth and nineteenth centuries with a single living room, an outshot scullery, and a bedroom upstairs. A few examples have also been recorded of free-standing cottages with a single living room and a tiny buttery or storeroom made by screening off part of the living room, as well as a chamber above. Such simple dwellings are by their nature very difficult to date closely, and are not likely to be earlier than 1660. Two such cottages were found by Fox and Raglan in their Monmouthshire survey. However, the antiquity of this type—the single-cell chambered over—is carried back to the early sixteenth century by the fact that it is found among the houses (fifty-one in number, according to Leland) built in the parish of Sutton Coldfield, Warwickshire, by Bishop Vesey. The seven surviving houses have been too much altered to permit generalization about their plan, beyond the fact that all were chambered over and had stone newel stairs. Vesey Cottage, Little Sutton, has two rooms below and above, but Vesey Cottage, High Heath (Fig. 28), has only one room with a stone staircase to the chamber.[1]

The one common feature of these single-cell houses, especially those in the western half of England is their gable-end fireplace, and most have an entrance at the end by the side of the fireplace. There is also in the southern part of the jurassic zone, and in stone areas to the west

[1] P. B. Chatwin and E. G. Harcourt, 'The Bishop Vesey Houses and other Old Buildings in Sutton Coldfield', in *Birm. Arch. Soc.*, LXIV, 1941–2, pp. 1–20.

of it, a great number of two-roomed houses with fireplace and entrance in that position. This plan is indistinguishable from that of the byre-house, *minus* its byre. It is difficult to evade the conclusion that these cottages share an ancestry with the byrehouse of the lesser peasantry of the Middle Ages, but this view has yet to be substantiated by field work. The single-roomed cottage with gable end fireplace is also found among early buildings in New England, to which emigrants from the south-eastern counties took not only the building techniques they were skilled in, but also the types of house they knew.[1]

While the exigencies of their new life made some New England settlers content with such a home, in the old country only the very poor had to put up with it. They included the aged, who either managed to find a place by their own efforts, or moved gratefully into one of the almshouses which the well-to-do were beginning to erect in the later part of our period. Although these almshouses have not been systematically surveyed from the point of view of housing standards, their provision appears to have ranged, like the cottages described, from one room only to a living room with a buttery and chamber, depending mainly on whether they were designed for single persons or for couples. The appearance of the village almshouse, together with the survival of the single-roomed cottage, is a significant aspect of the effect of economic development on housing conditions in this period. The essential change from 1500 to 1640 lay not in planning, for new houses were rarely more than improved versions of medieval types. Nor did it lie in the materials used, for more important developments in that respect came after 1660. It lay in the increasing divergence between the standards of accommodation provided in the farmhouse and in the cottage. This reflected the much greater gulf which by Charles I's time divided the successful and ambitious farmer from the poor commoner.

[1] W. G. Davie and E. G. Dawber, *Old Cottages, Farmhouses...in the Cotswold District*, 1905, p. 11, fig. 1; R. Nevill, *Old Cottages and Domestic Architecture in South-West Surrey*, 1891, p. 10; Fox and Raglan, *Monmouthshire Houses*, III, 1954, pp. 120 5; A. Garvan, *Architecture and Town Planning in Colonial Connecticut*, 1951, pp. 105–6.

CHAPTER XI

RURAL HOUSING IN WALES[1]

A. INTRODUCTION

The first half of the sixteenth century saw the formal incorporation of Wales in the English kingdom. It is an appropriate period at which to review Welsh architecture and to consider what may be derived from native traditions and what from English influences.

In their distribution the homesteads of the sixteenth century reflect what has been traditionally regarded as the Celtic pattern of dispersed settlement. Although hitherto unsuspected elements of nucleation have been detected in the medieval countryside, which tended to disappear with the decline of tribal society, the Welsh settlement was basically dispersed compared with that of midland and south-eastern England. In parts of Oxfordshire, for example, it is rare to find a house built before 1700 outside a village. In Wales, only in areas of Anglo-Norman colonization, mainly the vale of Glamorgan and Pembrokeshire, is the large ancient nucleated village to be found (Fig. 30). Comparing the English parts of the latter county with the Welsh, the Elizabethan antiquary, George Owen, says, "their buildings are English like in townreddes and villages and not in several and lone houses." In Welsh Wales the people lived, as Leland noted, *sparsim* rather than *vicatim*, and the ancient houses are to be found not in the village street, but alone in the fields and on the mountainside (Fig. 29).[2]

[1] I must express my especial thanks to Mr M. Bevan-Evans, Mr Peter Hayes, Mr Ffrangcon Lloyd, Mr C. E. V. Owen, Mrs Sunter Harrison, and Miss M. Vernon who have made a very substantial contribution to this work. Most of the houses in Flintshire, Denbighshire, and Montgomeryshire were visited at their suggestion and surveyed with their help. From Mr Griffith Jones, Miss J. Harding, and the late Miss E. M. Gardner I have also received invaluable assistance as also from Mr T. B. Pugh who read the paper through and saved me from two historical errors.

I must also place on record the help I have had from the recording of Breconshire houses instigated by Mr Deiniol Williams and the Breconshire Education Committee, and carried out by Mr S. R. Jones and Mr J. T. Smith with the help of Breconshire teachers. I have to thank the Committee and Mr S. R. Jones for permission to base drawings on Figs. 34, 41, and 51 on plans prepared for this survey.

I must also thank my wife for reading the proofs.

[2] T. Jones-Pierce, 'Clennenau Letters and Papers', *Nat. Library of Wales J. Supplement*, 1947, pp. v–xxi; G. R. J. Jones, 'The Tribal System in Wales', *Welsh Hist. Rev.*, II, 1961, pp. 111–62; J. G. Thomas, 'Settlement Patterns—Rural and Urban' in *Wales a Physical Historical and Regional Geography*, Ed. E. G. Bowen, 1957, pp. 141–57; R. B. Wood-Jones, 'The Banbury Region', *Ancient Monuments Soc.*, NS, IV, 1956, p. 133; H. J. Randall, *The Vale of Glamorgan*, p. 25, quoting Owen's 'Description of Pembrokeshire; J. Leland, *Itinerary in Wales*, ed. Toulmin Smith, 1906, p. 94.

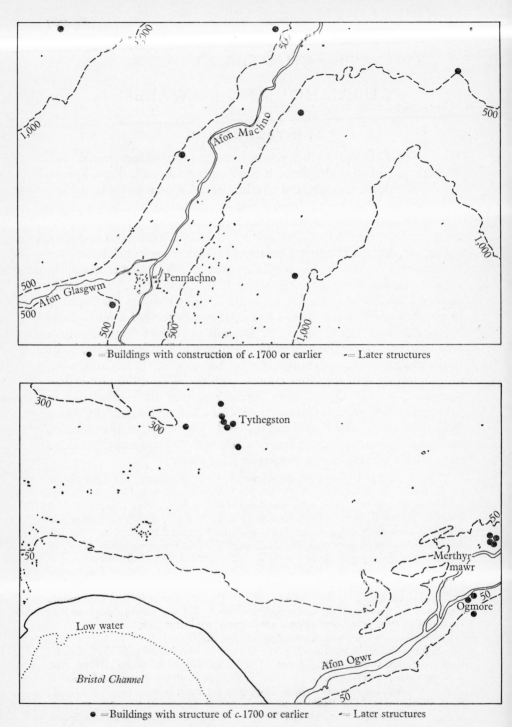

Fig. 29. (*a*) Scattered settlement, Penmachno, Caerns. (*b*) Village settlement, Tythegston and Merthyr-mawr, Glam. (*a* based on O.S. Caerns, 24 SW, *b* on O.S. Glam. 40 SW, with acknowledgements.)

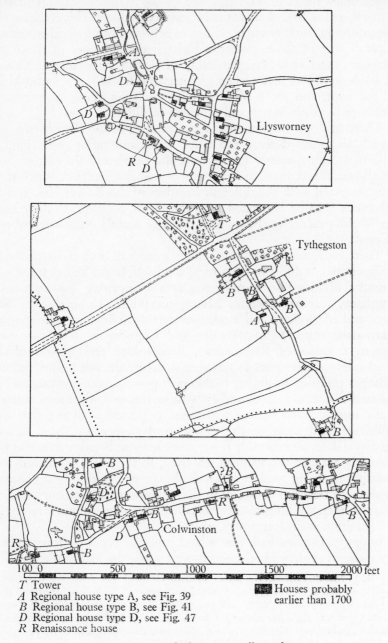

T Tower
A Regional house type A, see Fig. 39
B Regional house type B, see Fig. 41
D Regional house type D, see Fig. 47
R Renaissance house

Houses probably
earlier than 1700

Fig. 30. Types of Glamorgan village plan.

The quest for origins is hampered by the meagreness of architectural remains dating from before the Norman Conquest. This contrasts with the numerous early stone buildings in Scotland and Ireland constructed before either of those countries had felt the influence of the Anglo-Norman state. However, the study of British vernacular architecture as a whole shows that certain architectural features are found mainly in the west, and some of these have been conjecturally ascribed to Celtic rather than Saxon and Norman traditions.

There are two fundamental types of roof in the British Isles from which all others derive: the cruck truss, and rafter roof (Fig. 31). The first occurs mainly in the west and north and the second in the south-east. It is difficult to escape the conclusion that these types of roof are connected with the different invaders of the British Isles, and that the cruck is to be associated with the Celtic peoples.[1] In their houses the Welsh practically always used cruck or mainly cruck-derived types of roof.

There are however also marked differences in both construction and design between different parts of Wales itself. In the broadest terms the country divides into a northern area comprising the counties of Anglesey, Caernarvonshire, Montgomeryshire, Denbighshire, Flintshire and Merioneth, and a south-western province of Cardiganshire, Carmarthenshire, Pembrokeshire and Glamorgan, with the south-eastern counties of Radnorshire, Breconshire and Monmouthshire as an intermediate zone. In terms of structure the north shows a much stronger tradition of timber building. It possesses the great majority of the half-timbered houses, and even those houses with stone containing walls usually have timber partitions. It possesses all the few aisled buildings, and most of the ornate roofs, especially those of post-medieval date. Significantly it has more half-timbered towns, and these formerly reached the western seaboard. In the south black-and-white building in towns made a much shallower penetration being confined to the south-eastern counties. In the south-west the masonry tradition was stronger, vaulting commoner, the containing walls invariably, and the partition walls frequently, of stone.

In design the first hall, tower, and 'upland' types of storeyed house are more in evidence in the south-west while the hall-house and 'low-

---

[1] R. T. Mason, 'Medieval Timber Framed Houses,' *The Illustrated Carpenter and Builder*, 1 Nov. 1957, pp. 3552-3; 8 Nov., pp. 3636-7; J. T. Smith, 'Medieval Roofs: A Classification', *Arch. J.*, cxv, 1958, pp. 111-49; R. A. Cordingley 'British Historical Roof-Types and their Members: a Classification' (typescript prepared for the Vernacular Architecture Group), *Ancient Monuments Soc.*, NS, IX, 1961, pp. 73-117; T. L. Marsden, 'A Timber-framed Town House in Manchester', *Ancient Monuments Soc.*, VI, 1958, pp. 110-14; W. A. Singleton, 'Traditional Domestic Architecture in Lancashire and Cheshire', *Lancashire and Cheshire Antiq. Soc.*, LXV, 1955, pp. 33-47.

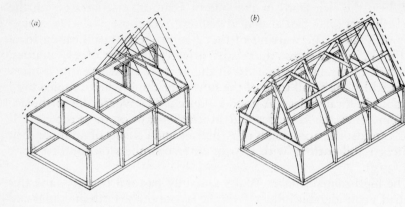

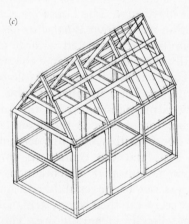

Fig. 31. Types of roof and frame. (*a*) Lowland and south-eastern: box-frame and crown-post rafter roof. (*b*) Highland and north-western (i): cruck truss. (*c*) Highland and north-western (ii): box-frame, collar and tie-beam truss. (*a* and *b* after R. A. Cordingley, 'British Historical Roof-Types and their Members: a Classification', *Ancient Mont. Soc. Trans.*, NS IX, 1961, p. 91.)

land' types of storeyed house are more conspicuous in the north which appears the more advanced generally of the two provinces in spite of its more mountainous terrain and later incorporation in the Angevin Kingdom. The north has much in common with the west midlands, while the south has closer parallels not surprisingly with the Devonian Peninsula and the Cotswolds but also with the far north-west of England.

Until the coming of major industries, a country's houses reflect the productivity of its agriculture. The numbers of well-built houses reared on the rich lands of the vale of Glamorgan contrast with the much thinner scatter of ancient dwellings over most of the remaining parts of Wales. The waiving of the £20 property qualification for a Welsh J.P. in 1536 shows the relative poverty of many Welsh counties. This lack of means was marked in the north-west where one is often surprised by the small scale of the houses of those who occupied high positions in local society. A good instance is Maesygarnedd, birthplace of John Jones the regicide, and brother-in-law of the Protector. It stands amidst the stony fields of Ardudwy and consists of no more than a kitchen and parlour with two or three chambers on the first floor (Fig. 39 g).

The high rainfall makes Wales a mainly pastoral country, and this has had a considerable influence on the layout of the farm buildings and in some areas on the farmhouse itself. An aspect of Welsh pastoralism was transhumance. Noted in the "Laws" as early as the tenth century, it survived into the nineteenth. The house erected in the uplands for this summer migration was known as *hafod* or *hafoty* (summer house). The *hafod* was a primitive structure and without architectural significance, but occasionally the old *hafod* became the permanent home of a new branch of the family who left the *hendre* (old house) for good. The survival of the name *hafod* in a number of substantial sixteenth- and seventeenth-century farmhouses illustrates this process involving the more intensive occupation of difficult mountain land.[1]

The majority of houses with which this account is concerned were not only country seats and the centres of small estates but also working farms. The notion that a gentleman should not directly cultivate the soil was yet to be established, and only the greatest in the land lived entirely off their rents, fees, and court perquisites, and did not engage directly in agriculture. The majority of houses of 1500–1640 have all the appurtenances, barns, and beast-houses, of a farm.

In our period much of the land in Wales was in the hands of fairly small landowners, and in some parts we have a picture of a landscape "so densely packed with *tai cyfrifol*,....or 'gentlemen's seats,'...that we wonder where room could be found for the tenantry who provided for their upkeep."[2] However, the adoption of the English custom of primogeniture in place of the native partible inheritance assisted in the creation of great estates which became a characteristic part of the

[1] Melville Richards 'Hafod and Hafoty in Welsh Place-names', *Mont. Coll.*, LVI, part I, 1959, pp. 13–20; 'Meifod, cynaeafdy, and hendre in Welsh Place-names', *Mont. Coll.*, LVI, part II, pp. 177–183.

[2] R. T. Jenkins, 'Some Pages in the History of Pant Glas, Ysbyty-Ifan', *Caerns. Hist. Soc.*, X, 1949, p. 16.

Welsh scene by the eighteenth century. The process is reflected in the farmhouses. The house of the sixteenth and seventeenth century was often built with much beautiful detail. By the eighteenth century fine detail was largely confined to larger houses. The descendants of the small sixteenth-century proprietor, who lavished money on decorating his house, had by the eighteenth century often become tenants. Though the small, tenanted farm continued to reflect improved standards of accommodation and comfort, it was not built with such attention to detail by a remote landlord, as it would in an earlier generation have received from a freeholding yeoman or gentleman-owner.

Houses surviving from the sixteenth century are more numerous than from any earlier period. Houses dating from the late Middle Ages are comparatively rare, and from before the fourteenth century, unknown. This suggests that the art of erecting permanent dwellings was a comparatively late achievement and our earliest surviving houses were in fact the earliest dwellings of a permanent nature to be erected. Although the amenity of a permanent dwelling spread downwards from the well-to-do, most of the surviving houses from our period were in fact those of a small upper class who alone could afford to employ tradesmen to build houses substantial enough to last till our own day. A large number of the people must have continued to live in hovels built by themselves which could not in the nature of things last more than a few generations. As a result, the homes of the small-holders or crofters, which today form such a conspicuous feature of the Welsh countryside, particularly in the west, cannot be studied in detail in this chapter, for it is unlikely that any of them survive from as early as our period. Writing about 1773 Pennant described the "houses of the common people" in Llŷn, Caernarvonshire, as being "made of clay, thatched, and destitute of chimneys." Most cottages today are structurally more advanced and presumably later than the buildings described by Pennant, and represent the emergence of the poor in the late eighteenth century from the temporary hovel to the dignity of a permanent dwelling, an advance the wealthy had achieved centuries earlier. It is likely that the houses of many of the poor in the sixteenth century had improved little on the "small huts made of boughs of trees twisted together, constructed with little labour and expense and sufficient to endure throughout the year" described by Giraldus Cambrensis. Even when their poverty of construction did not result in an early dissolution, it was natural that they should be destroyed or abandoned as standards improved, while the houses of the well-to-do were still considered suitable for those lower in the social scale than their original owners. Thus often the seventeenth century home of a sixteen survives today as the abode of a tenant farmer. As a result much more is known about this type of house than the largely vanished cottages of the poor.[1]

B. THE HOUSE IN RELATION TO ITS OUTBUILDINGS

The ancient Welsh poetic use of the plural *tai* (houses) rather than *tŷ* (house) recalls the early medieval house as a collection of separate buildings which only gradually coalesced into a single multicellular structure.[2] One of the last of the detached elements to be united with the house was the kitchen.

Seventeenth-century detached kitchens were noted in Monmouthshire, and a licence to repair the parsonage at St Florence, Pembrokeshire, dated 1733, refers to a "separate Building Seventeen foot square formerly a kitchin." The kitchen of a house of about 1900 near Aberystwyth, Cardiganshire, briefly occupied by the writer, could not be reached without going into the open.

Detached bake-houses (*tŷ-ffwrn*, *tŷ popty*) should be distinguished from kitchens. They are mainly late and have been found near houses already provided with kitchens. They represent the introduction of the wall-oven to houses previously ovenless. The Welsh cottage had no oven, and the baking was done in a cooking-pot on an open fire outside.

It is suggested that the cooking-pot is the native tradition, and the wall-oven is an English intrusion. However, the latter occurs occasionally in small Welsh houses from about 1600, which is as early as its appearance in its small English contemporary. These ovens, built in the jamb of the hall-fireplace, suggest another tradition, that of cooking inside the house using the hall as a kitchen, and may explain why there is no sign of an outside kitchen near many ancient houses. The practice of cooking inside and outside the house must have co-existed over a long period as did the cooking-pot and wall-oven.[3]

The 'unit system' is another example of the dispersed layout, whereby two or more separate houses were built round the same farmyard.[4] Instead of adding a wing to the additional house for a younger family, a new house was built, but the farm continued to be worked as one.

[1] Thomas Pennant, *Tours in Wales*, ed. Rhys, II, p. 374; Giraldus Cambrensis, *Descriptio Cambriae*, ed. Thos. Wright, p. 205.

[2] I. C. Peate, *The Welsh House*, 1944, p. 113.

[3] Sir Cyril Fox and Lord Raglan, *Monmouthshire Houses*, III, 1954, pp. 115–19; *Register of the Bishop of St David's*, IV, 1705–58, p. 218 (*ex inf.* D. E. Williams); I. C. Peate, 'The Pot-oven in Wales', *Man*, XLIII, 1943, pp. 9–11.

[4] W. J. Hemp and Colin Gresham, 'Park, Llanfrothen and the Unit System', *Arch. Camb.*, XCVIII, 1943, pp. 98–112.

At Plasnewydd, Llanfrothen, Merioneth, the earlier, probably sixteenth-century, house has two late seventeenth-century houses built at each corner, neither intercommunicating with it. The system may be associated with Welsh traditions of partible inheritance and clearly had considerable advantages in avoiding friction between successive generations of the same family.

In contrast to these examples of detached planning, the linking of the house with certain outbuildings is a characteristic of the highland zone and seems to have been noted by William Harrison as early as the sixteenth century. In his *Description of England*, published in 1577, it is stated: "the mansion howses of our countrie townes and villages are builded in such sort generallie, as that they have neither dairie, stable, nor bruehouse annexed unto them under the same roofe (as in manie places beyond the sea & some of the north parts of our countrie)."[1]

It is claimed that literary references show that the poorer Welsh peasants of medieval and later times were living in 'byre-houses' consisting of a single oblong cell with men at one end and cattle at the other. Hardly any of such dwellings have survived to the present day, but there are a large number of farms in which house and byre are built end to end in what might be called a house-and-byre homestead. Two interpretations of this relationship have been put forward. The first is that the house-and-byre homestead is the direct descendant of such byre-houses, its layout determined in an evolutionary fashion by a byre-house ancestor. The second interpretation is that the house-and-byre homestead is to quote R. A. Cordingley merely "a poor man's house," its design determined by the local types of gentry house and the byre placed alongside for reasons of economy. Much of the argument turns on a particular type of house-and-byre homestead, the long-house of south-west Wales in which the house is entered through the adjoining byre (Fig. 42, Plate XIX *b*). The interpretation of this house has to take into account the large number of houses similar in their main layout except that the adjoining room is not a byre but a kitchen or service room (Fig. 41, Plate XIX *a*). These are later described as the type B regional house. According to the positive view the long-house, originally byre-house, is the primary form of the plan, and in many type B houses where now stands the kitchen once stood the byre. According to the eclectic view the long-house is merely a poor version of the type B gentry house on these three grounds. The first, and by far the most important, is that a number of the earliest type B houses such as 'The Hospice' Bridgend (Fig. 43) have clearly never been associated with a byre. It is difficult to believe that this house could have been built in imitation of poor peasant byre-houses of the moun-

[1] Quoted by H. M. Colvin in *Medieval England*, ed. A. L. Poole, 1, 1958, p. 89.

tain interior especially as these would at the time have had neither stairs nor chimneys. The second ground for scepticism is that in many long-houses the house-and-byre are not structurally continuous. The third is that if the long-house arose from the division of a byre-house the division does not take the form that one would expect, namely a chimney or division wall inserted between continuous containing walls.

The eclectic theory would explain why this long-house plan does not feature in North Wales where the type B gentry-house did not gain favour, while in South Wales eighteenth and nineteenth-century long-house versions of the type B plan are extremely numerous (Fig. 44). The core of the type B plan seems to be the uplands of the English midlands, and until such houses round Banbury for example, can be proven to have originated as long-houses, the eclectic interpretation has much in its favour. The decisive battle of the long-house will be fought not on the fells of Westmorland or in the valleys of South Wales but on this classical English battlefield.[1]

C. THE EARLY SIXTEENTH CENTURY

At the opening of the sixteenth century domestic architecture was still essentially medieval. The main types of medieval dwelling, the castle, the tower-house, the first-floor open-hall, and the ground-floor open-hall, the latter henceforward called the hall-house, continued to be inhabited and indeed built.

Many of the great magnates were living in their castles at the beginning of the century and continued to do so, gradually modifying their defensive character and increasing their comfort. A good example of sixteenth-century modernization is the suite with large glazed windows built by Sir John Perrot along the north curtain of Carew Castle, Pembrokeshire. The process of demilitarization had not gone so far that the castles were not defensible in the civil war. Not till then did many a castle come to the end of its useful life. The castle slighted, the owner built a house nearby, as Lord Cherbury built Lymore after the destruction of Montgomery Castle. Raglan, which had been rebuilt in the middle of the fifteenth century, continued to be modified and embellished by the addition of such features as a long gallery in the

---

[1] Sir Lleufer Thomas in *Report of the Royal Commission on Land in Wales*, 1896, pp. 693–7; Peate, *op. cit.*, pp. 51–84; J. T. Smith, 'The Long-house in Monmouthshire', *Culture and Environment*, 1963, P. Smith, 'The Long-house and the Laithehouse', *Culture and Environment*, 1963; I. C. Peate, 'The Welsh Long-House' *Culture and Environment*, 1963; A. D. Rees, *Life in a Welsh Countryside*, 1951, pp. 47–59; R. B. Wood-Jones, *Traditional Domestic Architecture of the Banbury Region*, 1963.

Elizabethan period, and to receive adornments till the civil war. Its fall was followed by sacking and slighting, and it was not reoccupied. Powys Castle, originally a thirteenth-century structure, was modified in the sixteenth and seventeenth century and has continued to be inhabited, as have many others, such as Picton in Pembrokeshire or Chirk near Wrexham, to the present day.

Fortification in Wales was largely a monopoly of the king and the marcher lords. Tower-houses, the diminutive castles of the small chieftain, and the normal dwellings of the Scottish and Irish upper classes from the fifteenth to the middle of the seventeenth century, were few. The whole Principality contains probably not more than a dozen compared, for example, with no less than four hundred in County Limerick alone.[1] The moated house, too, was uncommon except in English Maelor, where the high water-table was particularly favourable to its construction.

The rarity of tower and moat is important archaeological evidence for social conditions. It is likely that the building of towers in the turbulent fifteenth century was effectively discouraged by penal legislation following Glyndŵr's revolt. In our period, however, their absence is attributable to the peaceful conditions resulting from the Welsh acceptance of the Tudors and the success of their government. The disasters of the sixteenth and seventeenth century, which perpetuated the tower-house in Scotland and Ireland, for the most part passed Wales by. As a result the Welsh were able to build dwellings appropriate to a peaceful society.

Most of the few Welsh towers were built in the south, mainly Pembrokeshire, but also in Glamorgan where Candleston Castle (Plate XVII) shows the complete layout of vaulted tower, hall alongside, and fortified enclosure. 'The Tower', near Mold in Flintshire built in 1445, with two lower rooms vaulted, was enough of a rarity for its name to be distinctive. The early block at Gwydir, Caernarvonshire (Fig. 32 b, Plate XVII) probably built about 1520 was unvaulted, and not primarily a defensive structure, but its builder, Maredudd ap Ieuan, a man with many enemies, needed a house that could be defended in an emergency. The house has four storeys with a heated room on each floor.[2]

The tower-house was a modification of the first-floor hall, having as its primary accommodation an open-hall on the first-floor over a basement or undercroft. Several medieval examples with barrel-vaulted undercrofts survive in south Pembrokeshire built by the descendants of the Anglo-Norman settlers. Of the few in north Wales the finest is

[1] H. G. Leask, *Irish Castles*, 1951, p. 75.
[2] R.C.A.M., *Caerns.*, I, 1957, No. 656.

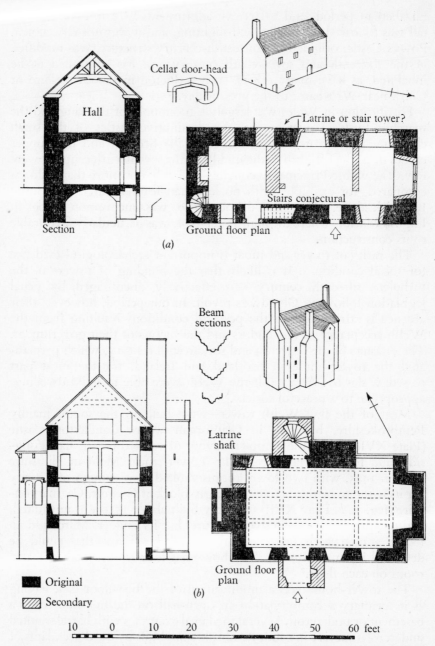

Hall

Cellar door-head

Latrine or stair tower?

Section

Ground floor plan

Stairs conjectural

(a)

Beam sections

Latrine shaft

Ground floor plan

■ Original

▨ Secondary

(b)

10   0   10   20   30   40   50   60 feet

Fig. 32. First-floor hall and tower-house. (a) Llyseurgain, Northop, Flint. Late fifteenth century. (b) Gwydir, Trewydir, Caerns. c. 1510. (b after R.C.A.M., *Caerns.*, 1, p. 182.)

Llyseurgain, Northop, Flint (Fig. 32 a), probably the work of Howel ap Dafydd ap Ithel Fychan, clearly a man of unimpeachable Welsh ancestry. It consists of an open hall over two vaulted rooms, one at ground-floor level running the full length of the building, the other a basement occupying only the south end. The ground-floor room was heated, indicating that it was losing its subordinate status, and anticipating the sixteenth-century type of storeyed house.[1] The first-floor hall is one ancestor of the storeyed house which sometimes has as much the appearance of a first-floor hall descending as a hall-house rising.

Far more usual than the 'first-floor hall' was the 'hall-house', the commonest type of medieval dwelling, and one that remained in favour for much of the sixteenth century. By hall-house is meant a structure whose primary accommodation is a single open room or hall standing on the ground and occupying the full height of the building (Fig. 36).

The hall-house was usually only one room wide, and the only important variations are the curious houses with lateral outshuts noted near St David's north Pembrokeshire, and lately in Gower.[2]

When built on a hillside the house was sited up and down rather than along the slope so that the upper end stood on excavated ground and the lower end was embanked. But the site works sufficed only to reduce the slope and not to eliminate it, as revealed in the steps from room to room. The traditional arrangement preferred the service rooms, or byre if a long-house, downhill, and the private rooms at the higher end. It has been held that this up-and-downhill siting was to present as little a front as possible to surface water running down the hill which would also be diverted by the mound of excavated material at the upper end. An alternative explanation is that it was to drain the cows' part of the byre-house away from the living quarters. The siting however is found in many early houses without a trace of the byre-house or long-house plan, which suggests the former reason is the more likely.

The medieval hall-house, pivoted on the entrance passage (Fig.) which is also found in many of the storeyed houses of the sixteenth and seventeenth centuries (Figs. 33, 35, 39, 41). It is a puzzling facet of the medieval plan for which none of the explanations put forward carry entire conviction. These are either that it arose in the village house to allow a passage through the house on the street to the farm buildings at

[1] I am indebted to Mr George Lloyd for drawing my attention to this hitherto unnoted structure and to Mr P. Hayes for discovering its probable builder. See also E. Bachelery, *L'Oeuvre Poétique de Gutun Owain*, 1951, II, p. 306.

[2] J. Romilly Allen, 'Old Farmhouses with Round Chimneys near St David's', *Arch. Camb.*, II, 1902, pp. 124–43.

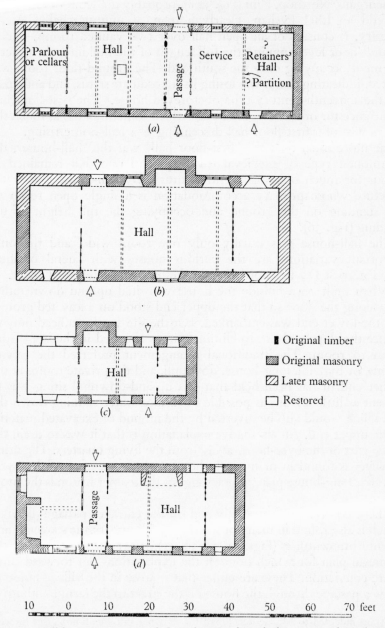

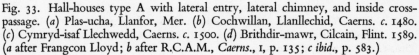

Fig. 33. Hall-houses type A with lateral entry, lateral chimney, and inside cross-passage. (a) Plas-ucha, Llanfor, Mer. (b) Cochwillan, Llanllechid, Caerns. c. 1480. (c) Cymryd-isaf Llechwedd, Caerns. c. 1500. (d) Brithdir-mawr, Cilcain, Flint. 1589. (a after Frangcon Lloyd; b after R.C.A.M., Caerns., 1, p. 135; c ibid., p. 583.)

Fig. 34. A sixteenth-century cruck-framed hall-house type A, based on Leeswood
Green, Mold Rural, Flint. (With acknowledgements to S. R. Jones.)

the rear, or that it originated in the great house to give access from one
courtyard to another. A recent suggestion that where the two opposed
doorways are not in line it was to give alternate entry to men and
cattle, fails on an examination of the structural evidence. The non-
alignment in the houses quoted is either non-existent or greatly exaggerated by errors of survey. The mis-alignment of the doors of the
great house Cochwillan (Fig. 33), certainly no long-house, is in fact
no greater than in the houses for which this explanation has been put
forward.

The classical medieval house was in three major units, the open hall
and entrance passage, a service room below the passage and a retiring
room beyond the hall (Fig. 51 a). But in several houses the room beyond
the hall is too small to be other than a storeroom, while the room
below the passage is quite sizeable. It has been suggested that in such
cases the lower room was a byre, but there are houses with secondary
rooms of these proportions such as Plas-ucha and Brithdir-mawr
(Fig. 33 a, d) or Gadlys (Fig. 39 g) where such an explanation cannot
hold.[1]

Most halls were originally chimneyless but where a chimney was

[1] Fox and Raglan, op. cit., II, 1952, p. 105. J. T. Smith, 'Long-house in Monmouthshire', Culture and Environment, 1963, pp. 392–3; S. R. Jones and J. T. Smith 'The
Houses of Breconshire', Brycheiniog, X, 1964, pp. 115–16.

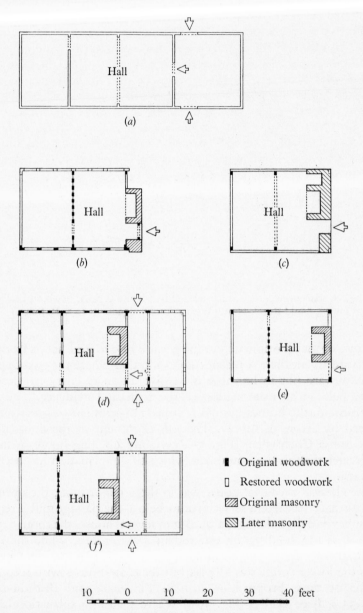

10   0   10   20   30   40 feet

Fig. 35. Hall-houses type B with end entry or outside cross-passage, late fifteenth to sixteenth century. (a) Early form of outside cross-passage house. (b) Pool Farm, Llangattock-vibon-avel, Mon. (c) The Pant, Raglan, Mon. (d) Pit Cottage, Llanarth, Mon. (e) Newland, Dingestow, Mon. (f) Pwll, Tregarc, Mon. (b after Sir Cyril Fox and Lord Raglan, *Mon. Houses*, I, p. 18; *c ibid.*, p. 45; *d ibid.*, facing p. 56; *e ibid.*, p. 30; *f ibid.*, p. 28.)

provided or later added it was placed either along the lateral wall (type A, Fig. 33) or between the hall and the entrance passage (type B, Fig. 35). Many of the type B houses now consist of two units, the hall and upper room only, but whether this was the original nucleus of the house, or whether it is a mere fragment of a three-unit house whose original lower room has been destroyed or rebuilt is debatable.

The second group has a southern distribution in Wales which persisted, and in fact became more marked with the storeyed development of the plan in the late sixteenth century. In England this group tends to be highland and western. The predominance of the first group in North Wales and its proportionately lesser importance in South Wales is difficult to account for, but may indicate to some major difference between the two districts either in social evolution or farming methods.

It is not certain whether the third common type of plan, that is a central chimney standing opposite an entrance lobby and between hall and parlour existed before the coming of the storeyed house. Abernodwydd, formerly at Llangadfan, Montgomeryshire, and now at St Fagan's Museum, is a good instance of a small timber-framed hall house, but it is contended that the central chimney opposite the entry was an addition made when a loft was inserted some time after the house was built.[1]

The windows of the hall-house were usually unglazed and consisted of a series of closely-spaced diagonally-set wooden mullions (Plate XVII). A surviving piece of horn-like membrane in one of the windows at Brithdir-mawr, Cilcian, Flint., suggests that a thin semi-transparent sheet was stretched across the mullions.[2] The windows were also shuttered and placed on opposite lateral walls so that the shutters could be closed against the prevailing wind, and the light still admitted from the windows opposite on the lea. Only a few wealthy houses enjoyed the luxury of a glazed window and most of these were small.

Few stairs in hall-houses have survived *in situ* or intact. The straight-flight stair with solid treads housed in heavy closed strings at Brithdir-mawr was probably typical of many (Fig. 33 *d*). In many of the smaller hall-houses a ladder had to suffice as at Leeswood Green, Mold Rural, Flint. (Fig. 34) where two trimmed openings at each end of the house had headroom only for a ladder. The winding stone newel stair in the thickness of the wall, or in a projecting turret, though common enough in medieval tower or castle, was rarely provided in domestic work before the storeyed houses of the late sixteenth century, and in Anglesey,

---

[1] M. F. H. Lloyd, 'Abernodwydd', *Mont. Coll.*, LXIV, 1935–6; I. C. Peate, *op. cit.*, p. 52; I. C, Peate, *Mont. Coll.*, LIII, part I, 1953, pp. 34–38.
[2] Brithdir Mawr, *ex inf.* E. Topley, M. Bevan-Evans.

apart from two medieval fragments, no stairs earlier than the mid-seventeenth century have been recorded.[1]

The majority of hall-houses were without chimneyed fireplaces, at least in the hall, which was heated by an open hearth in the middle of the floor (Fig. 36). This was not the result of unfamiliarity with the advantages of fireplaces for these heated castle and tower-house, and often the storeyed parts of the hall-house itself. The open hearth was part of a way of life. The preference for an open fire as against an enclosed stove is one of the features distinguishing the folk culture of the Atlantic seaboard from eastern Europe.[2] The traditional Welsh fireplace up to 8 feet wide and 4 feet deep kept as much of the character of the old open hearth as possible.

The coming of the fireplace preceded the disappearance of the open-hall as is clear from the lateral fireplace in the great hall of Cochwillan of c. 1480 (Fig. 33 b). But its use did not become general until the storeyed house made it a necessity. When the substantial hall, Brithdir-mawr, was built in 1589, probably among the latest of hall-houses, it was without a fireplace, a defect not remedied until its reconstruction in the seventeenth century (Fig. 33 d).

The great glory of the hall-house was its roof (Figs. 34, 36, 37). Even in the smaller examples it was customary to introduce a note of elaboration at this point. The central truss over the hall was usually made more elaborate than the other trusses, often having cusping at the apex. The better surface of the timber faced the upper end, and struts and other pieces of lesser scantling were made flush with the main truss on the side facing the dais. Once the central truss of the hall has been identified, the rest of the building, however mutilated, begins to fall into place. The average hall is not often a very striking building viewed from the outside. Once within, however, if the roof survives to view, the visitor can be agreeably surprised by its beauty and refinement.

At the opening of the sixteenth century two main types of walling were in use: the framed wall of timber, and the solid wall of stone or cob.

The former consisted of a wooden framework with panels filled in with wattle-and-daub usually laid out in broad squares. This type of wall was common in eastern Wales, particularly in the lowland and valley areas, and could have been found in most of the towns except in the south-west.

Domestic masonry may be derived either from the castle-builder or

[1] R.C.A.M., *Anglesey*, 1937, p. clvii.
[2] A. Campbell, 'Irish Fields and Houses', *Bealoideas*, v, 1935, p. 70.

Fig. 36. Hall-house interior, Plas-ucha, Llangar, Mer., showing open hearth, louvre truss, cruck main truss, spere partition truss, and unglazed shuttered windows.

from the peasant and farmworker. Masonry of the former class was used for domestic work in Anglesey, Caernarvonshire, Pembrokeshire and probably Glamorgan by the fourteenth century. Pembrokeshire, in particular, is noted for the fine quality of its late medieval stone building. There alone in Wales are vaulted ceilings extensively to be found. Describing his native county George Owen explains "most houses of any accompt were builded with vaultes verye stronglie and substanciallye wrought."[1] The vault had probably only recently fallen into disuse. The peasant type of wall is less well built and shorter lived but represents an ancient tradition. This walling in Cardiganshire and Carmarthenshire is used in conjunction with a roof-framework of jointed crucks. In the same counties, the best part of Wales for the study of purely peasant building, there survive a few houses with round quoins, such as Glynmiherin, Llanwenog, Cardiganshire. These were also revealed by the spade at Beili Bedw, St Harmon, Radnorshire, and at a house discovered on St Tudwals Island, Caernarvonshire. The round quoin is easier to construct than the square, a product of comparative sophistication, and may derive from the stone building and round huts of the Iron Age Celt. A matter of some interest is the fact that in most parts of Wales the internal partition walls were timber framed even where the containing walls were of masonry. Only in parts of the south-west, and were the partitions usually of the same masonry as the containing walls. Elsewhere the house is, as it were a stone shell only.[2]

The Welsh house, whether walled with stone or timber, had roof trusses in the cruck tradition (Figs. 31, 34, 37). The use of this type of roof, as indicated earlier, is one of the salient features of the domestic architecture of west Britain. Briefly, the western cruck is structurally distinct from the rafters it supports while the eastern trussed-rafter roof is formed by stiffening and latterly enlarging rafters themselves at suitable intervals. The cruck consists of a curved blade springing from below the wall-plate and rising to the ridge. This peculiarity has preoccupied most students, and it has only recently been realised that the cruck, and the western collar-beam or tie-beam roof, are essentially of the same development having an evolution distinct from the eastern roof. The cruck-type roof impresses by massiveness and weight, and though it is not easy to arrive at a comprehensive distinction between the two classes, an example of one is immediately recognizable and not to be confused with the other (Fig. 31).

Most crucks survive in barns and cottages, and because of this, were first thought of as a rather primitive folk-technique. However it is now clear that the cruck was once general for houses of wealth and distinction and the earliest examples were in large upper-class dwellings in Wales and the Welsh border. The famous hall at Stokesay Castle, Shropshire, seems originally to have had a cruck roof, while Bryndraenog, Bugeildy, Radnorshire, and Plas Cadwgan, Esclusham Below,

[1] George Owen, *Description of Pembrokeshire*, 1892, ed. Henry Owen, I, p. 77.
[2] Sir Cyril Fox, 'Three Rounded-gable Houses in Carmarthenshire', *Arch. Camb.*, CI, 1951, pp. 106–12; Glynmiherin, *ex inf.* T. Jacob-Davies; Beili-Bedw, *ex inf.* L. Alcock; St Tuchvals *ex inf.* D. B. Hague.

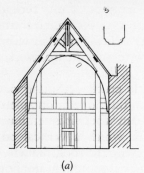

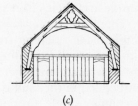

(a)   (b)   (c)

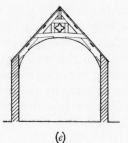
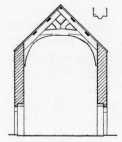

(d)   (e)   (f)

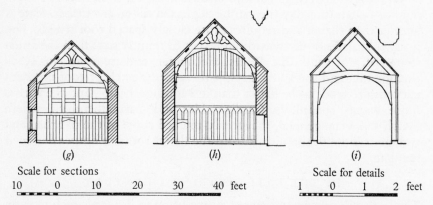

(g)   (h)   (i)

Scale for sections   Scale for details

10   0   10   20   30   40 feet   1   0   1   2 feet

Fig. 37. Hall-houses in section showing types of through-purlin (cruck-tradition) roof truss. The profiles to the top right of *a, b, d, f, h, i* represent the moulding on the blade and soffit of the arch. (*a*) Plas Cadwgan, Eclusham Below, Denbs. Fourteenth century. (*b*) Tŷ-draw, Llanarmon Mynnydd Mawr, Denbs. Fifteenth century. (*c*) Hafod Ysbyty, Llanffestiniog, Mer. *c.* 1500. (*d*) Bryndraenog, Bugeildy, Radnors. *c.* 1460. (*e*) Plas-Onn, Nerquis, Flint. Fifteenth century. (*f*) Plas-uchaf, Llanfair Dyffryn Clwyd, Denbs. Sixteenth century. (*g*) Brithdir-mawr, Cilcain, Flint. 1589. (*h*) Gloddaeth, Penrhyn, Caerns. Early sixteenth century. (*i*) Lower Berse, Bersham, Denbs. Fourteenth century?

Denbighshire, will contain excellent early examples of this type of construction.[1] At the former, the crucks are used in conjunction with perpendicular-style detail of refinement, the apex being filled in with a fretwork of late-gothic tracery; at the latter, the crucks are massive and simple and their effect is monumental (Fig. 37 *a*, *b*).

There are three types of cruck: the simple cruck consisting of a single blade reaching from near the ground to the ridge in one piece; the base-cruck extending as far as the collar-beam where it is continued by a separate member; the jointed-cruck, in which a vertical post embedded in the wall is scarfed to a blade carrying the roof, the whole forming a single structural unit. The base-cruck is most commonly to be encountered in great houses, the jointed-cruck in the small houses of Cardiganshire and Carmarthenshire.

The cruck was eventually replaced by the collar-beam or collar-and-tie-beam roof truss. These bore the same relationship to the other roof members as the cruck, carrying the rafters by means of ridge and through-purlins, but resting on the wall top, not below it. In those areas where good load-bearing masonry developed early the cruck had given way to the collar-beam truss by the opening our period except for cottage and farm buildings. For this reason crucks are rare in Caernarvonshire and Anglesey, and none have so far been reported from Pembrokeshire.

Welsh roof coverings fall into two main types: some form of stone slate or thatch (the clay tile can be neglected till recent times). Slate is heavier than thatch and requires more closely spaced roof trusses. The easily split slates of Gwynedd can be cut to thinner sizes than the sandstone slates of south-east Wales, are lighter, and fit more closely to exclude rain and snow. As a result the average pitch of roof in Caernarvonshire tends to be flatter than in Monmouthshire, and the trusses more widely spaced. In Cardiganshire and Carmathenshire, where thatch was very general, the steeply-pitched roofs of the old thatched cottages can be distinguished from the flatter roofs of houses designed for slate.

D. THE LATE SIXTEENTH CENTURY

The sixteenth century witnessed a revolution in domestic architecture. The tower-house and castle ceased to be built, the first-floor hall and hall-house became obsolete. A house of two main storeys became the normal type, with masonry fireplaces, chimneys, and a permanent stair. The change took place gradually, gaining momentum after the middle of the century. It was part of the 'great rebuilding' which occurred over large parts of England between 1550 and 1640. The

[1] Stokesay Castle, *ex inf*. Prof. R. A. Cordingley.

rebuilding seems to have been more marked in some areas than others. There seems, for example, to be much less domestic architecture of this period in south Pembrokeshire, than in the vale of Glamorgan. In Monmouthshire it is believed that there was much building activity from 1550 until the outbreak of the civil war, after which the pace in the later seventeenth century slackened. In the upper Severn valley, on the other hand, many of the half-timbered houses certainly date from after the Restoration. There the great rebuilding was late Stuart and early Georgian.[1]

The change to the storeyed house coincided with major developments in building construction. The first was the decline of the cruck and the spread of the 'box-frame' within the half-timbered technique. The box-frame, a structure of upright posts joined by tie-beams, was the traditional wall construction of south-eastern England. Although occasionally found in the Welsh hall-house from the fourteenth century, it did not displace the cruck extensively until the late sixteenth century when the headroom it afforded gave it a notable advantage over its rival in the construction of the storeyed house (Figs. 31, 46). The native tradition survived, however, in the through-purlin collar-beam truss which roofed the new box-framed houses. Structurally the Welsh half-timbered house had become a hybrid (Fig. 31).

In its box-frame form, the half-timbered house remained popular in most of Montgomeryshire until well on in the eighteenth century, and lasted beyond the end of our period in parts of lowland Flintshire, Denbighshire, and also in many of the towns. Indeed, it is in the seventeenth century that it achieved its greatest measure of external elaboration and ornament. It may even have gained on the stone house in some localities, and so may explain George Owen's puzzling quotation: "Gwaith vaeth Maen saer, gwell well pren saer, which is that masons shall get worse and worse and carpenters better and better."[2]

While the timber-walled house was being transformed in certain parts of Wales, it was being abandoned altogether in others, where the stone wall was becoming the normal method of enclosing the house and in most cases supporting the roof. This happened in Monmouthshire, and in the upland districts of Flintshire and Denbighshire.

The reason for the development of the timber house in some areas,

[1] W. G. Hoskins, 'The Rebuilding of Rural England', *Past and Present*, IV, Nov. 1953, pp. 44–59; Sir Cyril Fox and Lord Raglan, *Monmouthshire Houses*, III, 1954, p. 139; P. Smith and C. E. V. Owen, 'Traditional and Renaissance Elements in some Late Stuart and Early Georgian Half-timbered Houses in Arwystli', *Mont. Coll.*, LV, 1958, p. 119.

[2] Owen, *op. cit.*, I, p. 76.

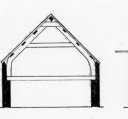
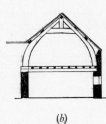
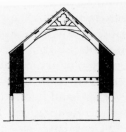

(a)   (b)   (c)

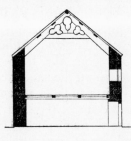
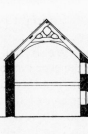
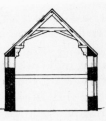

(d)   (e)   (f)

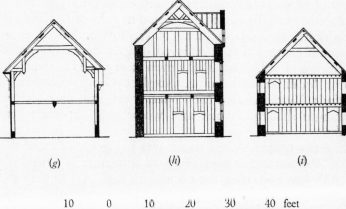

(g)   (h)   (i)

10   0   10   20   30   40 feet

Fig. 38. Storeyed houses in section, showing types of through-purlin. (a) Nant-gau-isaf, Mynnydislwyn, Mon. (b) Glynmiherin, Llanwenog, Cards. (c) Tŷ-mawr, Llandwrog, Caerns. Early sixteenth century. (d) Plas-du, Llanarmon, Caerns. Early sixteenth century. (e) Maes-y-groes, Cilcain, Flint. Seventeenth century. (f) Coed-y-cra, Halkyn, Flint. 1636. (g) The Walks, Penrhos, Mon. c. 1600. (h) Plas-mawr, Conway, Caerns, 1585. (i) Upper Wern-hir Llanbadoc, Mon. Late sixteenth century. (a after Mon. Houses, II, p. 65; g ibid., p. 97; i ibid., p. 23; c R.C.A.M., Caerns., II, p. 184; d ibid., p. 114; h ibid., I, p. 60.)

and for its obsolescence in others, is far from clear. It is likely that cultural influences were as important as natural causes such as the abundance or lack of suitable building material. The massive scantling of the oak used for floors, roofs, and partitions, in many stone-walled houses hardly suggests a shortage of timber in the districts in which such houses were built.

Generally speaking the Welsh carpenter did more finished work than the Welsh mason, for good oak was abundant while good freestone was rare. In many districts stone suitable for carving had to be imported so that ornamental work was often confined to the wooden members of stone houses. This was conspiciously the case in Monmouthshire.[1]

The second half of the sixteenth century saw the introduction of brick building. Its earliest dated use is at Bachegraig, a house built by the London merchant, Sir Richard Clough in 1567 in the Flintshire part of the vale of Clwyd. This house is said to have been copied from a Dutch model with bricks imported from Holland. However that may be, brick building became fairly common in this area with bricks of local manufacture. Bachegraig was built with walls of load-bearing brick. The alternative use of brick as an infilling for the panels of a timber-framed house occurs in the late sixteenth-century Bryn, Halghton, Maelor, at the eastern end of the county. Here the bricks had nibs fitting into grooves in the timber frame. In Maelor, too, the seventeenth century saw a fair amount of brick building.[2]

This early use of brick in the north-east is a reminder that this area was the most influenced by advanced techniques. However the brick wings at Bodwrda c. 1621 long remained unique in Caernarvonshire, where the use of brick was confined to small details such as flues.

The new storeyed house clearly derived from the old hall-house and first-floor hall. The first was no doubt the major influence and indeed many new storeyed houses are no more than the local hall-house with the hall floored over, and a permanent stair and fireplace as standard rather than occasional features. However, the influence of the flirst-floor hall cannot be entirely neglected as the chamber over the hall was often a room of importance. In fact it is difficult to decide whether such a house as Plas-du, Llanarmon, Caernarvonshire, is to be regarded as a late medieval first-floor hall, or an early storeyed house (Fig. 38 d).[3]

The characteristic open roof of the hall-house or first-floor hall continued in use in the new storeyed houses, though the roof ceiled at the tie had made its appearance by about 1570. The open roof often

[1] Fox and Raglan, *op. cit.*, III, p. 46.
[2] Bachegraig, *ex inf.* M. Bevan-Evans; The Bryn, *ex inf.* D. B. Hague.
[3] R.C.A.M., *Caerns*, II, 1959, no. 1091.

retained the medieval decorative features, the cusped struts, arched braces, and sometimes diminutive cusped windbraces as well (Figs. 38, 40). The retention of medieval ornamental roof details in storeyed houses is much more noticeable in the northern and eastern counties, than in the south where roofs are more utilitarian.

The characteristic medieval plan, that is a longish house, one room wide, sited up and down the slope, persisted, the houses being built as before in two or three main units (Figs. 39–47). They continued to be classifiable according to the position of the entry. Indeed, the classification moves onto firmer ground because fireplaces and stairs were built as original features and their siting fits into the general scheme of classification. The first group type A (Figs. 39, 40; Plate XVIII) is characterized by a lateral entry, and a fireplace and stair on a lateral or upper end wall. This group has a wide distribution but is predominant only in the north, the lateral fireplace in the north-east and Anglesey, the upper end-wall fireplace in Caernarvonshire and Merioneth. The second group the 'end-entry' type B (Figs. 35, 41; Plate XIX) has the entry in the lower end wall of the hall, from an entrance passage outside the hall in the three-unit type. The main fireplace thus backs on the entry. The relationship of type B to the long-house has previously been discussed. Between the two emerged the "central chimney" type C (Figs. 45, 46; Plates XX, XXIV). In houses of this plan, nearly all of timber-framed construction the entry is opposite the back-to-back fireplace and chimney standing between the hall and a parlour at the lower end of the house, the service rooms being at the upper end. This class is common in the Severn valley. The fourth common type of Welsh regional house type D (Fig. 47) also has a central chimney, opposite the entry, but its second chimney is on the end gable wall. It thus has some similarity to both B and C, but as it is found mainly alongside B particularly in Glamorgan where it is the commonest type of large regional house, it is more likely to be related to B than C.

There can be no reasonable doubt about the basically regional distribution of these plan types. At least forty three-unit type B houses are cited in *Monmouthshire Houses* from the late Middle Ages to the seventeenth century. Not one example was recorded in Anglesey and only two very doubtful examples, the outside cross-passage resulting from reconstruction, in Caernarvonshire. Both these counties were very thoroughly explored. In contrast, a brief exploration of Carmarthenshire led to the rapid discovery of a dozen type B houses, mainly of the long-house type. Prolonged searches in Flintshire have in comparison produced one certain and two doubtful examples of the three-unit type B house. The two-unit house makes a similar contrast. In Monmouthshire, two-unit end-entry houses outnumber the two-unit

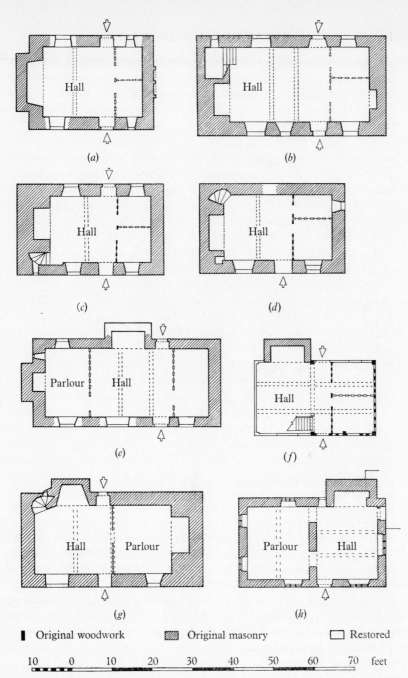

■ Original woodwork   ▨ Original masonry   ☐ Restored

10   0   10   20   30   40   50   60   70   feet

Fig. 39. Regional houses type A, with lateral entry, end or lateral chimney, and inside cross-passage, sixteenth and seventeenth century. (*a*) Garreg-fawr, Waunfawr, Caerns. (*b*) Tŷ-mawr, Llandwrog, Caerns. (*c*) Coed-mawr, Llanbedr, Mer. (*d*) Llan-nerch, Caerhun, Caerns. *c.* 1590. (*e*) Llwyn Erddyn, Brynford, Flint. (*f*) Colomendy, Llanrhaeadr yng Nghinmeirch, Denbs. (*g*) Maesygarnedd, Llanbedr, Mer. (*h*) Llystyn, Llanasa, Flint. (*a* after R.C.A.M., *Caerns.*, II, p. 253; *b ibid.*, p. 184; *d ibid.*, I, p. 25.)

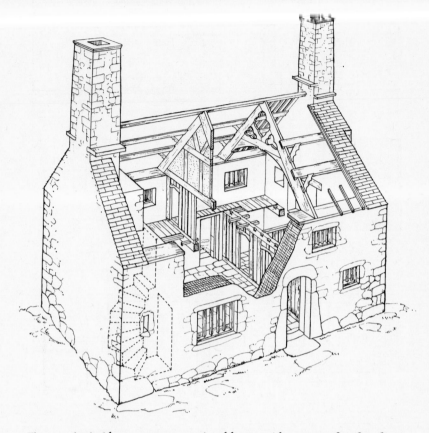

Fig. 40. An inside cross-passage regional house with open roof to first floor.
(Based on various houses in Caernarvonshire and Merioneth.)

houses with a lateral entry by about two-to-one. Compare this with
one certain and one doubtful end-entry house in Caernarvonshire, one
so far in Flintshire, and none in Anglesey, of all those houses investigated
whose original entry could be established with certainty (Fig. 44).

These regional houses all have English parallels, the end-entry
type B being a very common upland type occurring widely in Northamptonshire, the Cotswolds, the Banbury area and the north-west and
south-west of England with long-house derivatives in the highland
extremities of Devonshire and Westmorland. The central chimney
type C is a common lowland plan developed in Kent and Essex as early
as c. 1560. In other areas, for example Worcester, the inside cross-
passage house with chimneys on the peripheral walls, lateral or gable,
is common, a type resembling in general plan the inside cross-passage

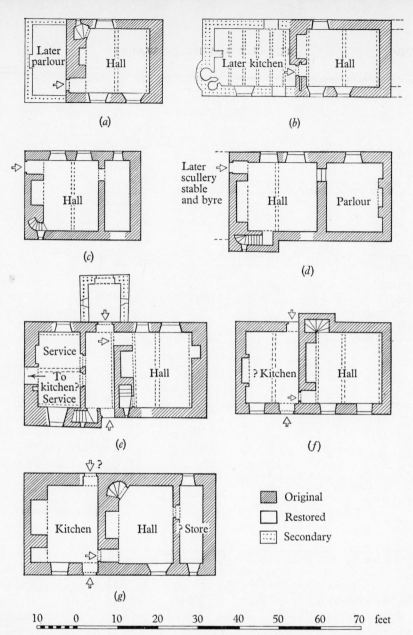

Fig. 41. Regional houses type B, with end entry to the hall through lower room, and outside cross-passage. *a* and *b* originally single-unit (hall only); *c* and *d* two-unit, hall with inner room; *e* and *f* two-unit, hall with outer room; *g* three-unit, hall between inner and outer room. (*a*) House on Cowbridge Road, Llantwit Major, Glam. (*b*) Cottage, Lampha, Ewenny, Glam. (*c*) Pentre-hwnt, Lampha, Ewenny, Glam. (*d*) Clements Farm, Tythegston, Glam. (*e*) Church House, Newcastle Hill, Bridgend, Glam. (*f*) The Bush Inn, St Hilary, Glam. (*g*) Gadlys, Llanmaes, Glam. (*e* after C. N. Johns.)

All the above houses are in Glamorgan. A similar sheet could, however, easily be assembled for Breconshire and Monmouthshire. Their similarity in plan to the long-houses in Fig. 42 is apparent.

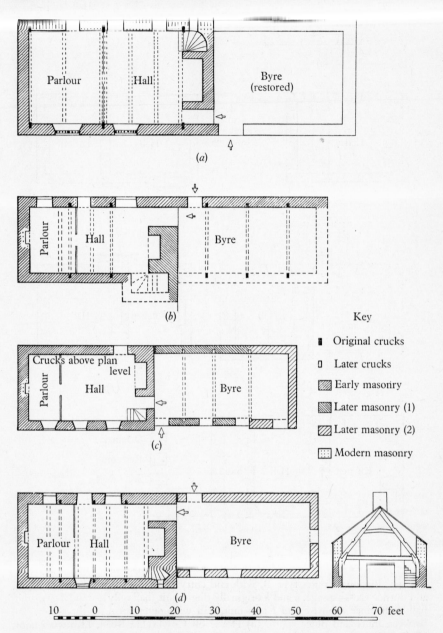

Fig. 42. Long-houses. In *a* and *b*, house and byre are apparently of a single build; in *c* and *d* the byre is an addition. (*a*) Nannerth-canol, Llansantffraid-Cwmteuddwr, Radnors. (*b*) Maes-y-rhiw, Llansadwrn, Carms. (*c*) Ty'r Celyn, Llandeilo, Carms. (*d*) Cwm Eilath, Llansadwrn, Carms.

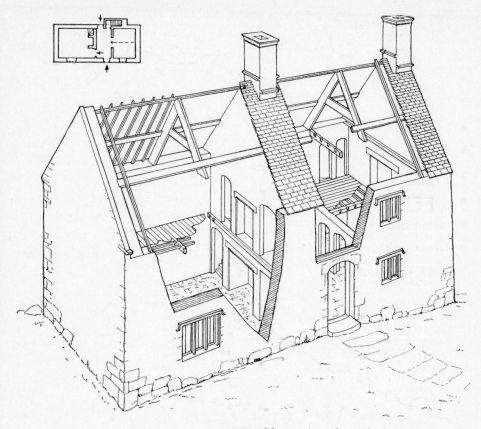

Fig. 43. An outside cross-passage regional house. (Based on The Hospice, Bridgend, Glam.)

house (type A) predominant in North Wales. These different plans must reflect differences in English society at the time of their development. It is possible however that they reflect not only differences in Welsh society, but also the different parts of England with which the particular Welsh region was most closely associated. The strength of the central chimney type plan, essentially a lowland type, in the uplands of Montgomeryshire is as likely to arise from ideas transmitted along the upper Severn valley, as from a type of society materially different from Breconshire where the end entry type B predominates. This end entry type is presumably associated with similar houses in Monmouthshire, Glamorgan, Gloucestershire, Devonshire, and Cornwall. Regional house types also seem to cross Wales like the main railway lines from east to west, rather than to spring from centres within the country.

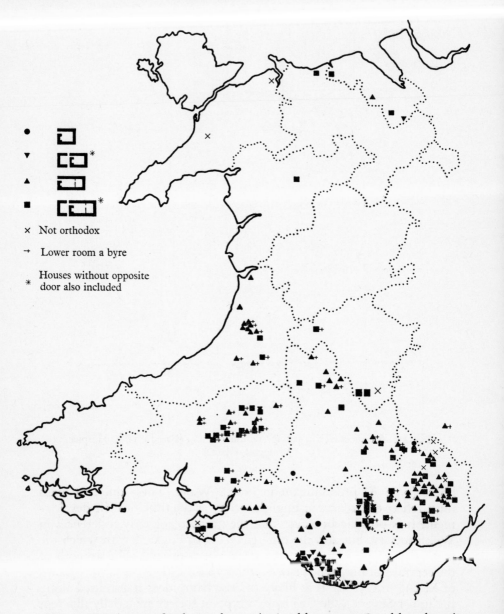

Fig. 44. Distribution of end-entry houses (regional house type B and long-house). This map is not complete, but for those areas which have been thoroughly searched, namely Anglesey, Caernarvonshire and Flintshire in north Wales, and Glamorgan, Breconshire and most of Monmouthshire in south Wales it is probably fairly reliable.

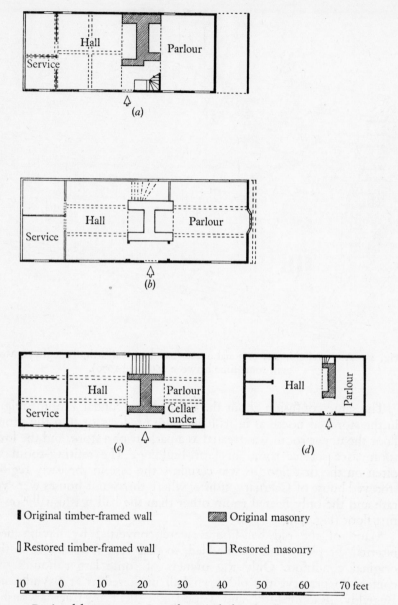

Fig. 45. Regional houses type C, with central chimney between hall and parlour opposite the entry. (a) The Old Packhorse Inn, Welshpool, Mont. ?1576. (b) Talgarth, Trefeglwys, Mont. 1660–70. (c) Hiriarth, Llanidloes, Mont. 1722. (d) The Little House, Llandinam, Mont. 1696. (a after D. B. Hague, Mont. Coll., LV, 1958, facing p. 26.)

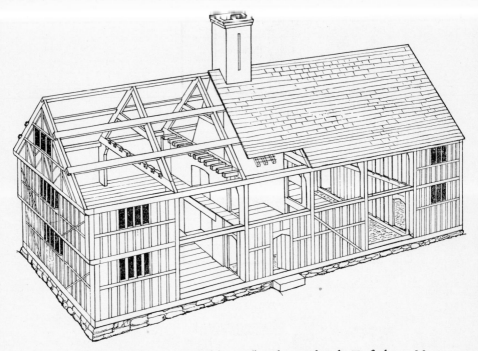

Fig. 46. A central-chimney regional house (based on Talgarth, Trefeglwys, Mont.,
built some time between 1660 and 1670).

The same confusion about the use of the secondary rooms reigned
in the storeyed house as in its hall-house predecessor. On the ground
floor the upper room was treated as a parlour or a store, and the lower
room as a service room or farm-building. The retiring-room was
often on the first floor as was certainly the case in the early regional
storeyed house of Caernarvonshire, where three-unit houses were very
rare and the only heated room other than the hall was usually on the
first floor (Fig. 40).

Many of the old hall-houses were converted by having floors
inserted, fireplaces and stairs added, so that very few survive in their
original condition. Only the owners of some larger houses were
content to preserve the old open hall unaltered as at Bryndraenog,
Bugeildy, Radnorshire, and Gloddaeth, Penryn, Caernarvonshire,
because the hall was suitable to a mode of life requiring much entertaining, and because they did not feel the need to make additional floor space
in the most economical manner.[1]

[1] Gloddaeth, R.C.A.M., *Caerns*, I, 1956, no. 649.

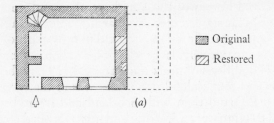

Original
Restored

(a)

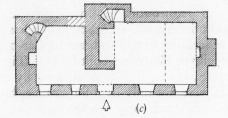

(b)

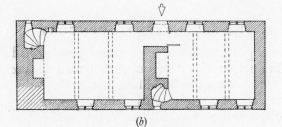

(c)

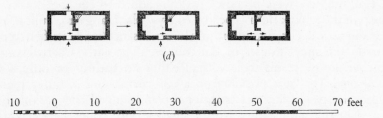

(d)

10   0   10   20   30   40   50   60   70 feet

Fig. 47. Central-chimney houses type D, with main chimney opposite entry but secondary chimney on end wall. (a) Duffryn-maelog Llysworney, Glam. (b) Walterston-fawr, Walterston, Glam. (c) Limpert, Gileston, Glam. (d) Possible origin of central-chimney house type D from type B.

The small storeyed houses of the Welsh yeomen and minor gentry are historically of great significance. Similar in size, scale, and quality, to houses of the same type of men to be found in most parts of England, they indicate a comparatively large class of small independent proprietors living in conditions of peace and prosperity. They show that in social conditions and material culture Wales was in many ways more comparable with England than with Scotland and Ireland where the tower continued to reign over a warring and impoverished countryside.

E. THE SEVENTEENTH CENTURY

The basic regional plans, which in the sixteenth century had developed from the traditional medieval layouts, continued in use until the eighteenth century with a few modifications, perhaps the first being the disappearance of the opposite entries and cross-passage.

The ornate open-roof remained till the end of our period at least in the north. The latest dated open-roof with arched braces is in a house of otherwise purely renaissance character, Henblas, Llanasa, Flintshire, built in 1645. The medieval open-roof had already been combined with renaissance detail in the through-purlin hammerbeam truss at "The Walks," Penrhos, Monmouthshire, and an example of a less ambitious treatment, the addition of scroll brackets to a braced collar-beam roof occurs at Coed-y-Cra, Halkyn, Flintshire, built in 1636 (Fig. 38 f).[1]

Many houses, in contrast, obtained additional space by ceiling the first floor. The new lofts were not only used for storage, but also for servants' quarters. Many advanced early seventeenth-century houses had three storeys besides the loft, and were tall in proportion to their length.

The main increase in accommodation however was in the parlour and the kitchen. "Parlour" is used here in its original sense, that is a retiring room, or bedroom on the ground floor. In Monmouthshire several instances were noted of parlours added to existing houses, and it was in the new parlour block of Allt-y-Bela, Llangwm, built in 1599, that the new decorative idiom of the renaissance made its first appearance in the small houses of the county.[2] The early Caernarvonshire storeyed house seems to have had either no parlour or only a very small one. This was provided in a few seventeenth-century regional houses, by modifying the traditional plan, the hall and parlour being placed in the same range with a small service room between them. This plan is found elsewhere though it is interesting to note the entry

[1] The Walks, Fox and Raglan, op. cit., II, 1953, pp. 96–7; Coed-y-Cra, ex inf. P. Hayes.
[2] Fox and Raglan, op. cit., III, 1954, pp. 19–24.

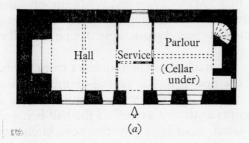

(a)

(b)

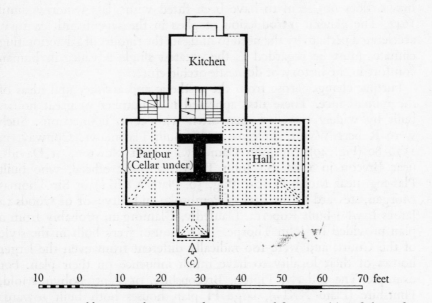

(c)

Fig. 48. Regional houses with seventeenth-century modifications. (a) Hafod Lwyfog, Beddgelert, Caerns. 1638. (b) Ty-mawr, Dingestow, Mon. 1690. (c) Plasau-duon, Carno, Mont. c. 1640. (a after R.C.A.M., *Caerns.*, II, p. 20; b after *Mon. Houses*, III, p. 51.)

on the end wall in T I Mawr, Dingestow, Monmouthshire, as an instance of the persistence of local usage (Fig. 48 b). The addition or enlargement of the parlour in this type of layout suggests that the hall was developing into a kitchen.

Alternatively an attached kitchen, distinct from the hall, was placed at the back of the house. In the central-chimney house this addition was combined with a significant modification of the local plan, the small service rooms at the upper end of the hall being dropped, when they were rendered superfluous by the new kitchen (Fig. 48, Plate XXIV).

The reversal of the sequence of rooms in relation to the slope was a further seventeenth-century innovation, the parlour being placed downhill on a boarded floor over the cellar (in one instance, with direct access between the two), and the service rooms being sited uphill (Fig. 45).[1]

There was no glass in the windows of the smaller sixteenth-century storeyed houses, which were fitted with closely spaced, diagonally set, mullions as had been the hall-houses. Glass began to be introduced from about 1590 but spread slowly as the Flintshire hall, Brithdir-mawr, does not seem to have been fitted with glass windows until 1642. The general introduction of glass in the seventeenth century, accelerated perhaps by the need to mitigate the rigours of a deteriorating climate, must be regarded as the greatest single advance in human comfort in the history of domestic architecture.[2]

Further changes arose from the aesthetic and architectural ideas of the rennaissance. These first appeared in a number of great houses built by widely travelled men often with court connections. Such were Robert Wynn, diplomat, who built Plas-mawr, Conway, in 1576–80 (Fig. 49), Sir John Games who built Newton, St Davids, near Brecon in 1582, Sir John Trevor, a court official, who built Plas-teg, near Mold, in 1610 (Fig. 50, Plate XXIII b) or Sir Thomas Morgan, steward to the Earl of Pembroke and surveyor of woods to James I, who built Ruperra, Llanfedw, Glamorgan, probably from a plan provided by John Thorpe. These houses were built in the style of the Court, and were too radically different from even the larger houses of their locality to have much influence on their plan. For example The Dderw, Pipton, Breconshire, or Pentrehobyn, Mold, Flintshire (Plate XXI a), large **H** plan houses both built towards 1640, have plans which show no trace of the influences evident in these mansions of the renaissance. They still retained the off-centred entry

[1] Smith and Owen, *op. cit.*, p. 114.
[2] For climatic changes see, H. H. Lamb, 'The World's Changing Climate', *The Listener*, LXIII, 7 April 1960, pp. 613–4.

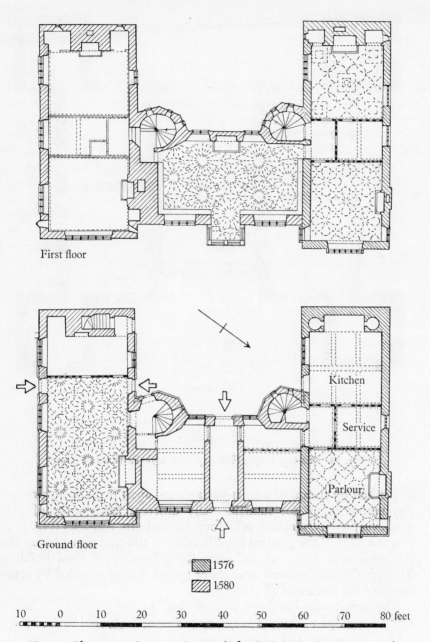

First floor

Ground floor

1576

1580

10   0   10   20   30   40   50   60   70   80 feet

Fig. 49. Plas-mawr, Conway, Caerns. (After R.C.A.M., *Caerns.*, I, p. 59.)

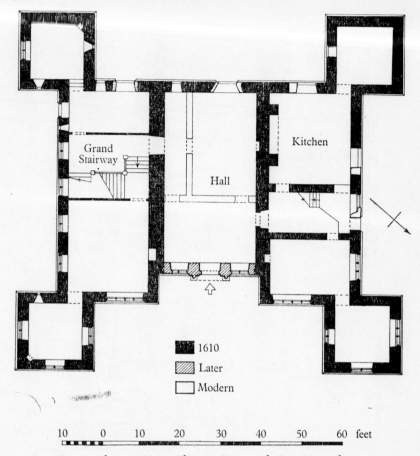

Grand
Stairway

Kitchen

Hall

■ 1610

▨ Later

□ Modern

10   0   10   20   30   40   50   60 feet

Fig. 50. Plas-teg, Hope, Flint., a Court-style Renaissance house.

to the hall by means of a cross-passage, and apart from being storeyed
throughout were not fundamentally different from some of their
medieval predecessors such as Hafoty, Llansadwrn, Anglesey (Fig. 51 *a*).
It was rather in the gradual modification of the traditional house that
the renaissance began to influence the generality of rural building.
Though the architectural renaissance spread slowly it ended by transforming the houses of all classes.[1]

The renaissance has been termed the "age of display."[2] Care in
siting is needed to show a house to advantage. The old siting up and

[1] Plas Mawr, R.C.A.M., *Caerns*, I, 1956, no. 185; Plas Teg, *Flints. Hist. Soc.*,
XVIII, 1960, pp. 157–62. See also E. Mercer, 'The Houses of the Gentry', *Past and
Present*, V, May 1954, pp. 11–32; Ruperra *ex inf.* C. N. Johns.

[2] Fox and Raglan, *op. cit.*, III, 1954, p. 17.

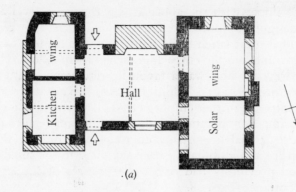

.(a)

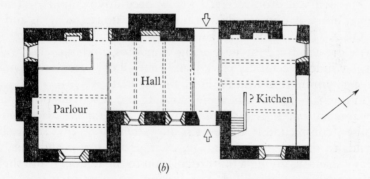

(b)

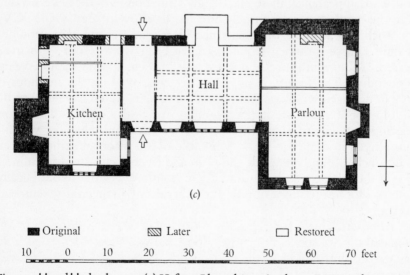

(c)

Fig. 51. H and U plan houses. (a) Hafoty, Llansadwrn, Anglesey. Fourteenth century.
(b) The Dderw, Pipton, Brecons. Seventeenth century. (c) Pentrehobyn, Mold Rural,
Flint. ?1640. (a after R.C.A.M., *Anglesey*, p. 111; b after S. R. Jones by kind permission
of the Breconshire Education Committee.)

down the slope, with the approach on the same level as the entry, was not designed to impress. Under the influence of the renaissance the house tended more often to be built along the contour with the front facing downhill and the entry approached from below.

The storeyed porch was a favourite renaissance feature, built primarily for display, as the additional useful space afforded was small. The porch gave a further emphasis to the entry, and was evidence of a new conscious consideration of the outward appearance of the house and gave a special importance to the front. Indeed, the idea of a prestige front and a utilitarian back was new to the small rural house, which had previously had opposite entrances of similar design and equal importance (Figs. 48, 52, 54).

The end walls too received a new decorative emphasis. The traditional house had its windows on the opposite lateral walls and (Plates XXII, XXIV) the end walls had been unfenestrated. The advent of glass gave greater freedom in placing windows, and the end walls had large windows centrally placed, and centred over each other, making a strong symmetrical feature (Figs. 52, 54; Plate XX).

In the half-timbered houses increasing use was made of jettying and ornamentation. It is perhaps in the timber-framed black-and-white houses, conspicuously those of Montgomeryshire, that show the new trends to the greatest advantage, their jettied fronts and ends casting heavy shadows giving a fine articulation to the building, and the gables and first-floor walls filled with various patterns of raking studs. In outward appearance, these black-and-white houses of the Severn valley are the handsomest the Principality has to show (Plates XX, XXIV).

With the advance of renaissance ideas came changes in moulded details. These moulded sequences have been worked out with great care in Monmouthshire, and as far as is known, apply to South Wales generally.[1] The first type of moulding employed on the mullions of the new glazed windows was the sunk chamfer, which gave way to the ovolo about 1625, the latter moulding for both beams and mullions lasting until about 1670. In North Wales the sunk chamfer was not employed in domestic work, while the ovolo made an earlier appearance, being found alongside the plain and hollow chamfer for mullions from the late sixteenth century. As in South Wales the ovolo became general for beams, door frames, and other details in the mid-seventeenth century.

Another vehicle for renaissance ornament was the doorhead. The normal type of sixteenth-century doorhead was a plain depressed four-centred pointed arch. In the seventeenth century this was varied with ogee and even more fanciful profiles.[2]

[1] Fox and Raglan, *op. cit.*, III, pp. 20–47.   [2] Fox and Raglan, *op. cit.*, III, p. 46.

The sixteenth-century fashion of the great of displaying a shield of arms spread to lesser houses, and one is often surprised by the small size of the house whose owner was yet armigerous. To the poorer gentleman of Wales these concrete tokens of gentility were particularly precious. Though his acres might be unproductive, and his tenants few, this shield, bearing the totems of remote ancestors, showed that he was yet descended from a noble or a royal tribe, and had good claim to kindship with much wealthier landowners. Had not Sir John Wynn observed: "a great temporall blessing it is, and a greate heart's ease to a man to find that he is well descended"?[1]

These developments, the new siting, the kitchen, the porch, the fenestrated ends, the new mouldings and decorative details, could be incorporated in houses without affecting the fundamentals of the traditional plan. While these changes were being assimilated however, the renaissance was ushering in more sweeping innovations leading to the creation of the compact, centrally planned, symmetrical, and completely compartmentalized house, in place of the old elongated, largely open plan, of tradition (Fig. 52). The houses built under the influence of these major changes show comparatively slight regional variation. The uniformity of plan, which the seventeenth century was ushering in, was to be completed by the unifromity of materials of the present day.

The most important change lay in the siting and construction of the stair. The traditional plan had a winding stair, inconspicuous in the recess by the hall fireplace. In the earlier examples of the new houses the winding stair round a wooden newel was sometimes retained, but it was put in a central position near the entry, usually in a projecting rear turret, or sometimes in the porch, so that all parts of the house could be reached much more directly. All forms of winding stair soon gave way to a framed stair in straight flights. Such a stair was much easier to use than the old stair which must have caused many a tumble. Placed in a conspicuous position, the new framed stair was often richly decorated, and from being an obscure and utilitarian feature, was transformed into the show-piece of the house (Fig. 52).

A break was also made with the traditional siting of the chimneys, which were often now placed to gain a certain external effect, and if possible, though this seems to have been less important, in such a way as to make the arrangement of the interior easier. The siting of the two chimneys on the rear lateral wall flanking the stair turret, as at Upper Dyffryn, and Kingsfield, both at Grosmont, Monmouthshire, was a considerable departure from their traditional position in that area.[2]

[1] Sir John Wynn, *History of the Gwydir Family*, ed. 1878, p. 57.
[2] Fox and Raglan, *op. cit.*, III, pp. 49, 29.

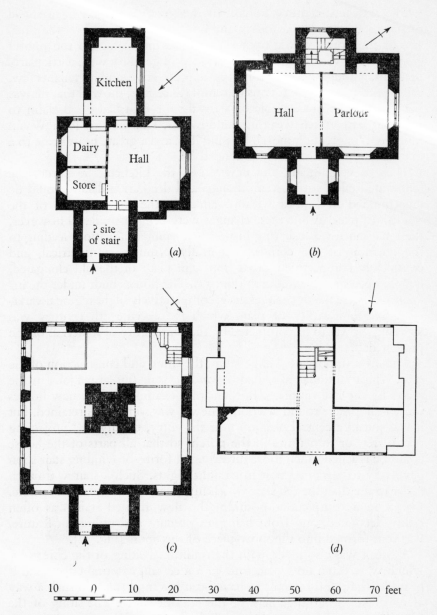

Fig. 52. Renaissance Houses. (*a*) Nant-y-Bannw, Llantrissent, Mon. 1625. (*b*) Upper Dyffryn, Grosmont, Mon. Early seventeenth century. (*c*) Trimley Hall, Llanfynnydd, Flint. 1653. (*d*) Plas Newydd, Carno, Mont. Late seventeenth century. (*a* after *Mon. Houses*, III, p. 26; *b ibid.*, p. 49.)

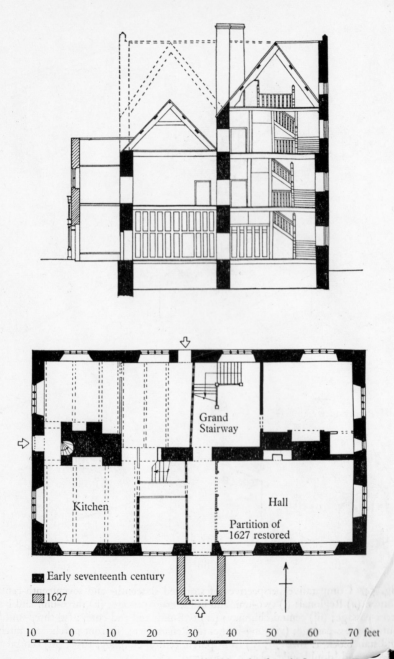

Fig. 53. Treowen, Wonastow, Mon., a double-pile plan. (After G. H. D...

■ Early seventeenth century

▨ 1627

Grand Stairway

Kitchen

Hall

Partition of 1627 restored

10   0   10   20   30   40   50   60   70 feet

(a) Regional

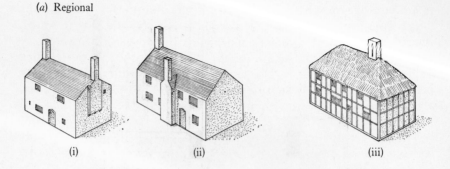

(i)   (ii)   (iii)

(iv)   (v)   (vi)

(b) Renaissance

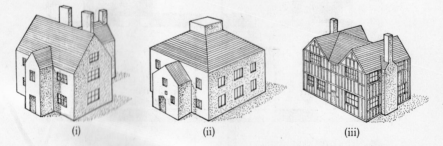

(i)   (ii)   (iii)

Fig. 54. Comparative perspectives of storeyed sixteenth- and seventeenth-century houses. (a) Regional: (i) two-unit and inside cross-passage; (ii) three-unit and inside cross-passage; (iii) central-chimney; (iv) two-unit and end-entry; (v) three-unit and outside cross-passage; (vi) long-house. (b) Renaissance: (i) front porch, rear kitchen, and stair block, c. 1620–70; (ii) front porch, central chimney, 1653; (iii) central stair sage and 'double-pile' plan, c. 1670–1720.

A type of plan that became popular after the restoration, the double-pile house, was another seventeenth-century innovation. To have the house two rooms wide instead of the customary one was the most economical way of increasing the size of the house. However, very few houses of this plan had appeared in Wales before 1640, though one large example, Treowen, Wonastow, Monmouthshire, built shortly before 1627, combined the traditional hall, cross-passage, kitchen, and service rooms, with the double-pile plan and well-stair (Fig. 53, Plate XXIII *a*).[1]

Though renaissance changes led in the end to more comfortably laid-out houses, the early builders did not always achieve happy results, building in a style they little understood. Sometimes the attempt to achieve symmetry produced a house that was odd outside and inconvenient within. Such was a very peculiar Flintshire house Trimley Hall, Llanfynnydd, built in 1653, in which the whole house was grouped round one single vast central chimney (Figs. 52, 54). The long low informal traditional house is often more pleasing than the squat tall house of the early renaissance with its sometimes awkwardly contrived symmetry.

Even by 1640 the renaissance had still affected comparatively few houses. The great majority were still being built according to the traditional plan of the neighbourhood, only fitted with such amenities as glass. A number still adhered to basic elements of the old plan, but had a number of the newer ideas incorporated in them. A few only, those of higher members of the gentry, showed a complete breakaway from the old layout, and the adoption of the new.

[1] I have to thank Mr A. L. Socket and Mr K. Kissack for telling me about Treowen, and Mr R. A. Wheelock for lending me his plan.

814

STATISTICAL APPENDIX

A. PRICE OF AGRICULTURAL COMMODITIES:
ANNUAL AVERAGES

1450–1499 = 100

Table I. *Price of arable crops*

INDEX NUMBER

Harvest year	Grains					Hay	Other arable crops				Average—all arable crops
	Wheat	Barley	Oats	Rye	Average—all grains		Straw	Peas	Beans	Average—all other arable crops	
1450	116	116	100	142	119	95	116	86	148	111	115
1451	112	100	94	121	107	108	112	73	98	98	102
1452	99	97	97	110	101	120	111	84	90	101	101
1453	87	116	106	68	94	105	100	109	97	103	99
1454	73	92	91	74	83	121	115	88	—	108	93
1455	94	102	102	—	99	—	—	55	—	55	88
1456	89	77	91	46	76	116	89	86	90	95	86
1457	116	99	94	103	103	87	118	81	90	94	99
1458	105	105	95	118	106	92	67	74	—	78	94
1459	93	100	100	84	94	146	116	104	104	118	106
1460	132	124	105	128	122	102	—	125	—	114	119
1461	138	115	120	—	124	108	102	108	—	106	115
1462	74	81	86	114	89	64	—	88	97	83	86
1463	60	70	79	59	67	59	69	53	92	68	68
1464	74	106	127	74	95	131	195	146	107	145	120
1465	83	130	106	96	104	95	122	106	110	108	106
1466	92	102	94	80	92	96	81	92	89	90	91
1467	106	97	88	109	98	129	86	94	104	103	101
1468	114	88	88	100	98	104	102	77	82	91	94
1469	114	80	103	121	105	110	105	113	97	106	105
1470	121	95	98	141	114	93	106	120	—	106	111
1471	112	112	109	99	108	84	102	111	—	99	104
1472	79	99	98	74	88	107	72	78	—	86	87

Table I (cont.)

Harvest year	Grains					Other arable crops					Average—all arable crops
	Wheat	Barley	Oats	Rye	Average—all grains	Hay	Straw	Peas	Beans	Average—all other arable crops	
1473	79	93	113	62	87	85	102	107	104	100	93
1474	82	72	90	74	80	88	102	92	—	94	86
1475	89	71	90	95	86	107	102	86	97	98	92
1476	89	72	93	74	82	97	102	126	71	99	91
1477	122	78	89	—	96	123	102	—	—	113	103
1478	130	90	97	101	105	152	—	109	97	119	111
1479	92	95	79	84	88	85	76	110	97	92	90
1480	94	95	79	98	92	76	—	—	119	98	94
1481	132	163	130	117	136	95	80	149	136	115	125
1482	177	184	116	196	168	98	65	220	—	128	151
1483	132	141	90	—	121	74	105	—	—	90	108
1484	98	105	102	96	100	74	110	120	97	100	100
1485	86	82	89	82	85	72	65	99	—	79	82
1486	96	109	103	160	117	75	87	104	—	89	105
1487	108	95	105	133	110	79	81	88	—	83	98
1488	106	113	144	102	116	104	105	103	148	115	116
1489	91	95	90	84	90	113	87	82	102	96	93
1490	127	86	98	168	120	85	86	119	—	97	110
1491	100	116	98	74	97	105	92	95	85	94	96
1492	89	117	143	102	113	85	81	—	—	83	103
1493	81	88	90	97	89	85	81	78	69	78	84
1494	70	77	87	71	76	99	105	73	77	89	82
1495	70	59	93	102	81	106	125	126	106	116	98
1496	103	79	101	124	102	108	106	82	85	95	99
1497	102	113	104	99	105	128	106	55	74	91	98
1498	99	114	134	74	105	135	151	121	124	133	119

1499	72	100	97	74	86	96	95	103	115	102	94
1500	126	113	104	136	120	91	96	—	100	96	109
1501	128	113	119	135	124	95	94	119	101	102	113
1502	147	109	111	184	138	96	89	—	75	87	116
1503	130	117	105	141	123	115	118	121	98	113	118
1504	98	152	127	110	122	110	121	102	—	111	117
1505	99	116	104	149	117	57	94	115	82	87	102
1506	98	95	95	102	98	78	88	106	91	91	94
1507	113	88	104	121	107	93	96	112	102	101	104
1508	85	102	105	83	94	84	118	89	83	94	94
1509	69	77	94	67	77	115	85	86	97	96	86
1510	81	82	97	88	87	100	83	72	69	81	84
1511	111	99	103	112	106	112	91	95	83	95	101
1512	144	93	108	109	114	99	111	90	89	97	105
1513	121	104	101	100	107	123	104	117	—	115	110
1514	102	127	121	132	121	90	102	96	—	96	110
1515	127	112	115	96	113	102	103	105	107	104	108
1516	105	106	124	108	111	113	125	137	145	130	120
1517	109	132	178	97	129	117	152	151	176	149	139
1518	97	114	121	120	113	121	157	159	128	141	127
1519	140	154	127	156	144	160	138	188	279	191	168
1520	191	175	170	235	193	97	181	251	132	165	179
1521	166	176	153	236	183	88	126	162	132	127	155
1522	104	124	121	—	116	94	93	140	136	116	116
1523	109	77	135	118	110	96	99	97	—	97	105
1524	99	121	142	101	116	126	114	132	113	121	119
1525	95	116	129	101	110	115	80	157	156	127	119
1526	110	168	146	—	141	102	135	177	195	152	148
1527	227	121	207	236	198	125	174	239	231	192	195
1528	175	146	138	269	182	89	81	—	158	109	151
1529	165	—	134	269	189	106	87	152	118	116	147
1530	130	160	129	172	148	85	124	115	127	113	130
1531	162	232	152	236	196	117	122	—	107	115	161
1532	150	162	173	267	188	97	173	173	146	147	168

Table I (*cont.*)

Harvest year	Grains					Other arable crops					Average—all arable crops
	Wheat	Barley	Oats	Rye	Average—all grains	Hay	Straw	Peas	Beans	Average—all other arable crops	
1533	133	127	156	202	155	120	127	160	153	140	147
1534	116	106	145	225	148	113	99	150	122	121	135
1535	213	199	184	303	225	133	118	164	169	146	185
1536	156	124	182	154	154	121	124	149	133	132	143
1537	108	151	139	93	123	81	146	—	119	115	120
1538	113	136	144	102	124	95	144	112	163	129	126
1539	116	184	144	149	148	103	122	112	133	118	133
1540	122	201	140	—	154	111	111	—	143	122	138
1541	146	166	147	—	153	145	108	165	175	148	150
1542	139	239	147	—	175	126	105	—	140	124	149
1543	185	—	143	—	164	120	105	—	154	126	141
1544	192	—	192	—	192	138	119	199	178	145	164
1545	288	319	251	—	286	115	116	—	—	143	215
1546	139	142	200	—	160	131	119	—	166	139	150
1547	99	118	172	—	130	133	121	168	150	143	137
1548	138	—	186	—	162	197	133	—	—	165	164
1549	265	—	330	—	298	181	147	—	256	195	236
1550	294	—	411	—	353	259	212	—	469	313	329
1551	329	—	297	—	313	—	252	—	—	252	293
1552	204	302	337	—	281	277	255	—	332	288	285
1553	179	377	282	—	279	171	250	—	147	190	234
1554	267	—	413	—	340	328	304	—	171	268	297
1555	383	805	374	—	521	327	143	389	461	330	412
1556	528	582	564	—	558	164	184	454	469	318	421
1557	194	237	275	—	235	198	200	226	—	208	222
1558	179	402	270	—	284	160	168	—	256	195	239

Year											
1559	275	250	231	—	260	259	314	—	336	—	291
1560	290	242	—	224	225	278	337	—	331	340	339
1561	305	313	338	—	283	319	296	—	356	260	271
1562	361	350	394	316	472	185	372	—	358	331	426
1563	353	360	410	211	345	370	343	—	317	436	275
1564	244	233	211	232	253	257	258	—	247	283	244
1565	260	268	287	244	259	294	335	—	313	298	394
1566	265	264	242	332	267	303	267	281	302	252	247
1567	328	334	372	265	273	360	321	395	313	455	235
1568	339	318	—	241	307	383	355	—	378	393	252
1569	262	255	279	239	241	260	277	345	310	—	243
1570	271	244	220	198	248	267	299	406	291	296	265
1571	270	235	221	269	255	266	305	531	272	252	288
1572	328	287	248	388	283	349	368	639	298	343	301
1573	419	360	495	346	271	285	478	399	417	427	427
1574	332	330	396	235	234	342	334	—	285	323	328
1575	310	259	214	294	263	322	378	—	319	467	348
1576	320	301	326	265	280	302	359	426	306	—	411
1577	324	275	302	269	263	268	391	470	375	428	369
1578	324	276	222	321	261	353	372	456	407	345	309
1579	361	308	—	304	324	280	414	483	461	—	310
1580	376	308	310	300	296	321	444	531	405	537	379
1581	361	306	325	323	302	298	434	365	439	—	381
1582	371	320	316	277	300	340	422	213	396	429	333
1583	348	325	350	364	293	379	370	777	406	394	316
1584	316	308	307	449	286	274	324	703	374	409	299
1585	460	364	481	500	281	244	556	—	472	547	427
1586	552	420	594	370	285	299	684	—	709	697	626
1587	333	309	325	435	242	300	365	652	403	361	331
1588	350	307	312	328	206	276	407	—	502	399	320
1589	421	312	351	592	254	315	531	—	465	568	437
1590	550	496	541	—	405	444	624	—	757	720	394
1591	394	346	383	—	349	306	443	—	573	451	304
1592	319	343	317	298	365	391	296	210	392	287	295

Table I (cont.)

Harvest year	Grains					Other arable crops					Average—all arable crops
	Wheat	Barley	Oats	Rye	Average—all grains	Hay	Straw	Peas	Beans	Average—all other arable crops	
1593	388	379	417	216	350	434	423	322	371	388	369
1594	578	520	765	—	621	343	504	506	412	441	518
1595	607	740	574	801	681	489	414	443	487	458	569
1596	811	971	1148	1227	1039	352	436	788	816	598	819
1597	746	779	718	869	778	337	400	585	615	484	631
1598	462	545	535	531	518	323	310	376	356	341	430
1599	407	676	498	706	557	428	403	366	347	386	472
1600	485	876	962	808	768	556	449	548	537	523	645
1601	416	583	526	693	555	504	360	387	525	444	499
1602	432	677	419	450	480	431	323	381	337	368	424
1603	391	358	502	450	420	492	388	357	372	402	411
1604	434	487	581	—	501	510	338	369	450	417	453
1605	401	629	589	—	543	521	529	369	444	466	499
1606	447	506	523	—	492	488	409	385	346	407	443
1607	571	571	519	—	554	658	438	428	479	501	523
1608	715	527	721	—	654	581	448	493	601	531	584
1609	493	759	648	—	633	477	493	530	441	485	549
1610	495	534	633	—	554	561	422	432	440	464	502
1611	545	668	853	—	699	541	663	577	619	600	642
1612	606	752	810	—	736	504	742	593	831	668	697
1613	667	788	721	—	725	466	431	565	—	487	606
1614	504	752	695	—	650	568	504	436	540	512	571
1615	574	749	924	—	749	950	660	592	769	743	745
1616	590	664	717	—	657	529	532	698	469	557	600
1617	647	624	616	747	659	561	519	465	419	491	575
1618	517	565	603	659	586	509	547	412	389	464	525

Year											
1619	450	493	661	—	535	589	545	492	461	522	527
1620	366	391	539	—	432	667	548	427	461	526	486
1621	598	670	730	—	666	466	580	513	512	518	581
1622	763	886	596	845	773	634	532	499	528	548	660
1623	573	648	599	845	666	564	502	424	538	507	587
1624	625	614	607	690	634	672	520	524	552	567	601
1625	637	745	768	764	729	535	494	621	751	600	664
1626	521	577	517	798	603	579	494	325	472	468	535
1627	427	443	532	615	504	481	507	388	478	464	484
1628	525	690	667	889	693	—	551	515	717	594	651
1629	609	825	741	717	723	659	674	688	632	663	693
1630	881	1277	1034	—	1064	610	603	873	—	695	880
1631	630	689	639	1031	653	489	517	430	820	564	602
1632	684	795	663	1024	793	651	531	459	769	602	698
1633	686	812	754	902	819	549	575	574	—	566	711
1634	668	862	745	331	794	1454	574	563	—	864	824
1635	645	792	900	720	667	643	612	582	—	612	644
1636	645	817	824	1146	752	631	668	741	819	715	733
1637	750	1225	1004	808	1031	905	687	842	1189	906	909
1638	575	899	764	—	762	549	529	556	—	545	669
1639	507	602	597	—	569	725	488	393	—	535	552
1640	615	728	781	—	708	568	567	536	—	557	633
1641	574	657	717	—	649	684	542	435	513	544	589
1642	616	637	666	—	640	811	547	576	487	605	620
1643	542	582	571	—	565	710	638	412	—	587	576
1644	546	574	680	—	600	539	640	515	614	577	587
1645	590	634	764	—	663	573	512	502	413	500	570
1646	804	736	1000	—	847	571	650	582	922	681	752
1647	997	1191	1085	—	1091	864	596	822	—	761	926
1648	943	1135	1140	—	1073	1250	668	839	—	919	996
1649	942	1097	1030	—	1023	1106	756	998	774	909	958

Table II. *Price of cattle and sheep*
INDEX NUMBER

Harvest year	Cattle				Sheep			
	Oxen	Cows and heifers	Calves	Average—all cattle	Wethers	Type unspecified	Lambs	Average—all sheep
1450	105	—	99	102	106	—	75	91
1451	124	—	70	97	67	—	—	67
1452	112	79	106	99	80	—	—	80
1453	107	69	77	84	68	—	120	94
1454	100	90	73	88	74	79	87	80
1455	111	94	—	103	83	—	101	92
1456	122	87	106	105	81	108	91	93
1457	101	82	111	98	71	56	87	71
1458	115	95	106	105	91	99	85	92
1459	106	93	108	102	88	—	77	83
1460	103	118	61	94	96	—	82	89
1461	108	—	102	105	101	—	—	101
1462	63	98	98	86	84	—	81	83
1463	112	88	101	100	110	—	110	110
1464	92	115	93	100	109	—	135	122
1465	104	113	105	107	98	105	116	106
1466	115	109	95	106	90	113	101	101
1467	105	136	136	126	67	130	109	102
1468	73	113	117	101	—	91	115	103
1469	82	102	113	99	—	103	127	115
1470	127	107	122	119	—	—	104	104
1471	92	113	132	112	—	—	—	—
1472	104	—	125	115	—	104	121	113

1473	115	109	95	106	133	97	132	121
1474	124	—	—	124	91	—	—	91
1475	109	114	88	112	105	—	—	105
1476	97	115	—	100	80	87	108	92
1477	92	—	101	92	84	—	40	62
1478	109	110	—	107	93	91	118	101
1479	97	81	—	89	—	—	57	57
1480	85	—	111	85	63	—	53	58
1481	107	95	92	104	120	108	93	107
1482	85	103	133	93	210	128	134	151
1483	115	129	124	126	147	—	80	118
1484	—	156	—	140	126	—	80	103
1485	—	115	—	115	98	—	80	89
1486	113	—	100	113	113	—	168	141
1487	80	97	99	92	103	—	138	121
1488	98	90	74	96	99	—	131	115
1489	90	—	111	82	116	—	98	107
1490	72	82	—	88	112	—	201	157
1491	113	—	59	113	114	—	—	114
1492	88	80	—	76	101	—	90	96
1493	—	97	111	97	—	—	101	101
1494	75	—	55	93	116	—	—	116
1495	128	67	63	83	113	—	72	93
1496	76	80	96	73	112	—	64	88
1497	91	80	135	89	92	—	120	106
1498	74	101	—	103	101	—	50	76
1499	87	—	66	87	92	—	70	81
1500	99	89	68	85	109	75	—	92
1501	100	104	100	91	104	—	63	84
1502	93	82	77	92	114	103	47	88
1503	120	—	—	99	63	97	84	81
1504	107	96	—	102	98	—	65	82
1505	108	110	—	109	100	—	76	88
1506	—	88	116	102	92	101	128	107

Table II (cont.)

Harvest year	Cattle				Sheep			
	Oxen	Cows and heifers	Calves	Average—all cattle	Wethers	Type unspecified	Lambs	Average—all sheep
1507	121	64	115	100	116	103	105	108
1508	141	—	—	141	130	99	105	111
1509	137	75	102	105	113	107	105	108
1510	103	75	91	90	121	108	105	111
1511	102	79	125	102	138	—	105	122
1512	—	71	139	105	138	—	161	150
1513	—	87	—	87	131	—	85	108
1514	—	107	—	107	165	—	122	144
1515	97	87	170	118	146	—	105	126
1516	94	—	197	146	155	—	136	146
1517	138	—	156	147	142	106	136	128
1518	162	92	150	135	126	—	122	124
1519	159	162	148	156	141	123	105	123
1520	158	—	—	158	152	213	156	174
1521	156	126	97	126	144	—	—	144
1522	163	—	—	163	143	—	—	143
1523	154	—	—	154	130	—	—	130
1524	140	95	112	116	139	103	132	125
1525	108	—	123	116	121	—	—	121
1526	126	—	—	126	151	106	150	136
1527	140	—	161	151	131	—	—	131
1528	153	—	168	161	137	—	—	137
1529	149	—	173	161	151	117	—	134
1530	153	149	109	137	178	159	169	169
1531	181	161	164	169	180	196	175	184
1532	164	142	—	153	139	—	159	149
1533	103	147	108	119	144	138	172	151

Table III (*cont.*)

Harvest year	Capons and hens	Geese and ducks	Average—all poultry	Rabbits	Average—poultry and rabbits
1620	443	519	481	389	450
1621	409	534	472	420	454
1622	502	444	473	443	463
1623	782	489	636	450	574
1624	737	429	583	435	534
1625	611	498	555	397	502
1626	705	—	705	374	540
1627	695	—	695	443	569
1628	802	381	592	344	509
1629	718	—	718	389	554
1630	—	—	—	321	321
1631	852	—	852	427	640
1632	701	—	701	—	701
1633	785	—	785	—	785
1634	805	—	805	—	805
1635	762	—	762	—	762
1636	782	—	782	519	651
1637	—	—	—	—	—
1638	768	874	821	427	690
1639	782	—	782	—	782
1640	579	599	589	466	548
1641	662	646	654	389	566
1642	609	851	730	504	655
1643	702	806	754	458	655
1644	745	637	691	443	608
1645	601	941	771	466	669
1646	—	—	—	—	—
1647	—	—	—	—	—
1648	—	—	—	—	—
1649	—	—	—	519	519

Table IV. Price of livestock

INDEX NUMBER

Harvest year	Sheep	Cattle	Horses	Pigs	Poultry and rabbits	Average—all livestock
1450	91	102	101	91	101	97
1451	67	97	98	100	101	93
1452	80	99	148	96	101	105
1453	94	84	113	98	101	98
1454	80	88	86	95	101	90
1455	92	103	97	95	100	97
1456	93	105	109	77	100	97
1457	71	98	81	93	100	89
1458	92	105	97	88	107	98
1459	83	102	113	105	101	101
1460	89	94	78	96	101	92
1461	101	105	64	115	112	99
1462	83	86	196	103	105	115
1463	110	100	—	100	101	103
1464	122	100	—	89	103	104
1465	106	107	58	105	102	96
1466	101	106	73	105	100	97
1467	102	126	135	102	92	111
1468	103	101	77	110	100	98
1469	115	99	—	107	101	106
1470	104	119	70	113	101	101
1471	—	112	94	102	101	102
1472	113	115	143	109	101	116
1473	121	106	86	114	100	105
1474	91	124	86	86	113	100
1475	105	112	102	84	100	101
1476	92	100	59	90	101	88
1477	62	92	—	98	101	88
1478	101	107	69	96	109	96
1479	57	89	69	109	105	86
1480	58	85	96	112	99	90
1481	107	104	111	123	103	110
1482	151	93	157	115	102	124
1483	118	126	72	—	—	105
1484	103	140	149	100	100	118
1485	89	115	84	80	92	92
1486	141	113	73	106	104	107
1487	121	92	77	106	95	98
1488	115	96	133	100	102	109
1489	107	82	104	93	—	97
1490	157	88	123	117	99	117
1491	114	113	115	110	—	113

Table IV (*cont.*)

Harvest year	Sheep	Cattle	Horses	Pigs	Poultry and rabbits	Average— all livestock
1492	96	76	84	112	98	93
1493	101	97	128	—	101	107
1494	116	93	—	86	—	98
1495	93	83	112	117	97	100
1496	88	73	72	82	94	82
1497	106	89	86	109	82	94
1498	76	103	102	61	99	88
1499	81	87	115	118	88	98
1500	92	85	83	92	110	92
1501	84	91	107	114	84	96
1502	88	92	99	99	95	95
1503	81	99	78	80	140	96
1504	82	102	89	125	225	125
1505	88	109	109	149	161	123
1506	107	102	139	142	143	127
1507	108	100	127	118	106	112
1508	111	141	148	99	—	125
1509	108	105	162	96	125	119
1510	111	90	94	91	91	95
1511	122	102	70	122	72	98
1512	150	105	117	128	94	119
1513	108	87	101	153	87	107
1514	144	107	100	158	94	121
1515	126	118	138	121	87	118
1516	146	146	144	110	94	128
1517	128	147	110	163	92	128
1518	124	135	101	144	90	119
1519	123	156	111	161	108	132
1520	174	158	151	127	101	142
1521	144	126	138	178	109	139
1522	143	163	153	197	109	153
1523	130	154	150	118	—	138
1524	125	116	103	121	—	116
1525	121	116	133	142	—	128
1526	136	126	142	146	—	138
1527	131	151	110	138	—	133
1528	137	161	—	157	—	152
1529	134	161	153	114	131	139
1530	169	137	105	126	112	130
1531	184	169	157	117	107	147
1532	149	153	121	140	153	143
1533	151	119	97	134	138	128
1534	179	151	197	127	—	164
1535	148	139	118	133	103	128

Table IV (cont.)

Harvest year	Sheep	Cattle	Horses	Pigs	Poultry and rabbits	Average— all livestock
1536	160	157	—	144	—	154
1537	167	155	174	103	—	150
1538	141	153	148	94	—	134
1539	133	140	154	126	180	147
1540	190	152	88	130	195	151
1541	165	163	196	139	188	170
1542	201	156	180	141	157	167
1543	195	171	154	144	153	163
1544	198	160	—	—	244	201
1545	196	175	169	146	196	176
1546	240	143	167	138	192	176
1547	244	204	196	164	216	205
1548	239	215	293	164	239	230
1549	228	198	209	169	263	213
1550	315	259	280	184	250	258
1551	279	264	307	292	235	275
1552	222	244	206	352	—	256
1553	227	223	193	219	209	214
1554	204	212	258	243	326	249
1555	258	258	225	228	288	251
1556	293	339	216	447	192	297
1557	285	277	293	220	299	275
1558	255	282	271	256	220	257
1559	292	305	241	140	297	255
1560	303	257	259	382	273	295
1561	309	310	243	171	267	260
1562	349	295	283	216	283	285
1563	361	281	277	—	252	293
1564	316	300	279	170	274	268
1565	261	283	237	197	263	248
1566	319	292	220	394	265	298
1567	285	285	273	309	221	275
1568	313	293	287	317	267	295
1569	299	308	306	—	244	289
1570	364	289	299	373	214	308
1571	355	334	276	244	291	300
1572	372	338	329	231	358	326
1573	386	364	304	307	330	338
1574	407	402	343	292	391	367
1575	379	398	329	296	327	346
1576	388	339	412	238	320	339
1577	393	379	334	285	310	340
1578	362	399	382	428	310	376
1579	397	338	253	279	344	322

Table IV (cont.)

Harvest year	Sheep	Cattle	Horses	Pigs	Poultry and rabbits	Average— all livestock
1580	427	359	346	302	310	349
1581	446	364	392	—	305	377
1582	346	337	539	235	276	347
1583	379	391	331	242	290	327
1584	376	370	342	275	292	331
1585	345	437	380	261	307	346
1586	388	413	350	258	328	347
1587	401	429	371	284	347	366
1588	396	382	441	269	289	355
1589	415	409	450	292	316	376
1590	504	399	398	267	316	377
1591	519	400	415	266	312	382
1592	533	446	399	263	311	390
1593	456	435	389	264	367	382
1594	424	489	461	—	374	437
1595	429	483	481	289	414	419
1596	473	502	401	298	359	407
1597	424	540	490	390	374	444
1598	470	510	548	381	378	457
1599	474	441	454	368	475	442
1600	577	469	486	415	423	474
1601	464	447	468	361	432	434
1602	476	478	395	363	430	428
1603	503	484	396	349	397	426
1604	503	448	411	347	403	422
1605	475	485	409	407	287	413
1606	538	523	478	441	347	465
1607	448	525	524	361	401	452
1608	481	537	485	390	469	472
1609	485	497	605	498	517	520
1610	459	533	473	431	427	465
1611	464	528	615	430	499	507
1612	527	502	520	397	484	486
1613	531	559	539	448	502	516
1614	489	605	561	439	516	522
1615	544	545	593	534	442	532
1616	508	530	435	487	523	497
1617	569	581	460	494	431	507
1618	580	587	548	449	488	530
1619	574	555	455	486	450	504
1620	452	521	526	426	450	475
1621	515	487	544	468	454	494
1622	546	496	539	436	463	496
1623	487	514	578	387	574	508

Table IV (cont.)

Harvest year	Sheep	Cattle	Horses	Pigs	Poultry and rabbits	Average— all livestock
1624	557	494	577	384	534	509
1625	544	601	665	368	502	536
1626	615	604	618	531	540	582
1627	614	593	523	445	569	549
1628	615	565	558	389	509	527
1629	624	578	587	499	554	568
1630	628	590	702	511	321	550
1631	613	594	623	596	640	613
1632	535	621	714	567	701	628
1633	562	673	566	572	785	632
1634	577	627	638	598	805	649
1635	590	693	676	661	762	676
1636	607	671	711	582	651	644
1637	572	676	656	602	—	627
1638	604	696	668	605	690	653
1639	577	622	569	600	782	630
1640	574	592	682	589	548	597
1641	656	536	669	587	566	603
1642	636	800	691	581	655	673
1643	563	592	507	611	655	586
1644	621	635	442	598	608	581
1645	764	731	648	510	669	664
1646	701	852	771	—	—	775
1647	807	837	703	591	—	735
1648	761	841	724	—	—	775
1649	727	711	918	534	519	682

Table V. *Price of animal products*

INDEX NUMBER

Harvest year	Dairy products and eggs						Wool, fells and hides				Average—all animal products
	Milk and cream	Butter	Cheese	Average—all dairy products	Eggs	Average—all dairy products and eggs	Wool	Sheepskins and wool fells	Cattle hides	Average—wool, fells and hides	
1450	59	—	—	59	101	80	91	83	74	83	82
1451	—	—	—	—	101	101	70	54	58	61	81
1452	59	106	—	83	101	89	71	77	94	81	85
1453	—	106	—	106	101	104	71	63	106	80	92
1454	59	106	—	83	101	89	80	94	100	91	90
1455	—	106	—	106	101	104	80	60	151	97	101
1456	—	—	—	—	101	101	95	89	105	96	99
1457	—	—	—	—	—	—	85	80	103	89	89
1458	—	—	—	—	—	—	89	76	114	93	93
1459	—	106	—	106	—	106	91	71	104	89	98
1460	—	—	—	—	101	101	84	67	106	86	94
1461	—	—	—	—	—	—	99	—	—	99	99
1462	—	—	91	91	—	91	102	—	—	102	97
1463	—	—	91	91	101	96	152	—	—	152	124
1464	—	—	91	91	101	96	118	—	43	81	89
1465	—	—	—	—	101	101	115	—	111	113	107
1466	—	—	91	91	101	96	118	148	94	120	108
1467	—	—	—	—	101	101	116	161	99	125	113
1468	—	—	—	—	101	101	100	122	114	112	107
1469	—	—	—	—	101	101	89	130	118	112	107
1470	—	—	—	—	101	101	97	—	—	97	99
1471	—	—	—	—	101	101	104	—	—	104	103
1472	—	—	—	—	101	101	109	95	104	103	102

Table V (cont.)

Harvest year	Dairy products and eggs						Wool, fells and hides				Average—all animal products
	Milk and cream	Butter	Cheese	Average—all dairy products	Eggs	Average—all dairy products and eggs	Wool	Sheepskins and wool fells	Cattle hides	Average—wool, fells and hides	
1473	—	—	—	—	101	101	109	129	—	119	110
1474	—	—	—	—	101	101	99	108	—	104	103
1475	—	—	—	—	101	101	97	116	99	104	103
1476	—	—	—	—	101	101	99	82	—	91	96
1477	—	—	—	—	101	101	92	103	—	98	100
1478	—	—	105	105	101	103	99	103	65	89	96
1479	—	—	—	—	101	101	84	118	—	101	101
1480	—	—	—	—	101	101	88	—	—	88	95
1481	—	108	—	108	101	105	107	—	103	105	105
1482	—	98	111	105	101	103	122	—	—	122	111
1483	—	98	111	105	—	105	128	—	73	101	101
1484	—	98	111	105	—	105	132	—	—	132	111
1485	—	98	111	105	—	105	117	—	—	117	111
1486	—	98	111	105	—	105	116	90	—	103	104
1487	—	94	111	103	89	98	104	—	—	104	101
1488	118	98	93	96	—	96	101	140	87	109	103
1489	—	100	111	110	—	110	112	159	93	121	110
1490	—	95	83	89	—	89	88	—	—	88	89
1491	—	98	111	105	—	105	100	—	—	100	103
1492	—	—	—	—	96	96	83	—	132	108	102
1493	—	—	—	—	96	96	97	—	—	97	97
1494	—	85	—	85	—	85	101	—	114	108	97
1495	—	103	—	103	96	100	101	—	—	101	101
1496	167	104	—	136	—	136	99	90	—	95	116
1497	138	94	—	116	—	116	101	—	138	120	118

Year											
1498	97	95	—	—	95	99	96	102	—	102	—
1499	87	93	—	95	91	81	—	81	64	98	—
1500	104	115	179	75	92	92	92	—	—	—	102
1501	107	107	134	96	90	106	96	109	93	131	—
1502	98	104	123	101	87	92	93	91	91	—	—
1503	100	104	117	97	97	96	96	—	—	—	—
1504	109	111	139	95	98	106	—	106	—	106	62
1505	92	102	128	95	83	82	96	75	—	88	106
1506	101	104	116	115	81	97	96	97	—	88	72
1507	97	107	121	110	91	86	96	82	—	91	—
1508	104	113	121	116	101	94	—	94	—	94	—
1509	104	114	139	97	107	94	98	90	—	90	—
1510	107	116	119	120	109	97	98	95	—	95	—
1511	108	111	116	114	103	104	119	88	—	88	—
1512	112	109	—	—	109	115	142	88	86	88	—
1513	113	118	—	129	107	107	126	88	—	88	—
1514	108	119	169	—	119	97	117	87	—	88	—
1515	128	152	192	142	135	103	117	88	—	88	—
1516	134	154	—	—	129	113	117	108	102	108	—
1517	122	141	171	—	141	103	117	88	125	88	107
1518	123	142	171	—	113	104	117	98	107	88	107
1519	127	149	—	108	126	104	117	99	62	88	107
1520	112	117	—	—	117	107	—	107	—	88	102
1521	103	106	—	—	103	99	—	99	97	88	107
1522	104	122	—	—	122	86	—	86	86	89	—
1523	85	94	—	—	94	75	—	75	—	75	105
1524	97	96	162	—	96	97	—	97	122	88	—
1525	119	141	162	—	119	96	—	96	105	106	59
1526	111	144	—	—	126	77	—	77	81	94	118
1527	111	110	—	—	110	112	—	112	99	95	—
1528	112	121	—	—	121	102	—	102	97	98	—
1529	97	102	—	125	102	92	—	92	—	102	—
1530	102	106	—	—	87	97	—	97	—	94	—
1531	108	116	—	—	116	99	—	99	—	101	—

Table V (*cont.*)

Harvest year	Dairy products and eggs						Wool, fells and hides				Average—all animal products
	Milk and cream	Butter	Cheese	Average—all dairy products	Eggs	Average—all dairy products and eggs	Wool	Sheepskins and wool fells	Cattle hides	Average—wool, fells and hides	
1532	166	91	—	129	136	131	131	—	—	131	131
1533	145	91	—	118	136	124	146	—	215	181	153
1534	—	88	—	88	—	88	136	—	—	136	112
1535	—	88	115	102	193	132	121	—	227	174	153
1536	—	133	126	130	193	151	150	—	—	150	151
1537	145	88	—	117	—	117	117	—	—	117	117
1538	—	101	—	101	—	101	108	—	—	108	105
1539	—	—	—	—	—	—	112	—	163	138	138
1540	—	—	—	—	—	—	190	—	166	178	178
1541	—	—	—	—	—	—	155	—	180	168	168
1542	—	—	—	—	—	—	—	103	160	132	132
1543	—	—	—	—	—	—	150	122	208	160	160
1544	—	—	—	—	—	—	141	—	—	141	141
1545	—	—	—	—	—	—	180	—	—	180	180
1546	—	—	136	135	—	135	126	86	—	106	121
1547	—	133	—	118	224	171	120	125	225	157	164
1548	—	118	143	147	—	147	—	144	246	195	171
1549	—	151	162	157	—	157	168	165	254	196	177
1550	—	151	—	—	—	—	281	181	234	232	232
1551	—	—	—	—	—	—	268	121	169	186	186
1552	—	—	—	—	—	—	192	105	280	192	192
1553	—	—	—	—	—	—	124	131	197	151	151
1554	—	—	—	—	—	—	166	—	207	187	187
1555	—	212	—	212	288	250	160	77	—	119	185
1556	—	—	—	—	—	—	262	—	354	308	308

Year											
1557	206	188	—	103	272	224	—	224	224	—	—
1558	224	238	410	160	143	209	188	220	228	211	—
1559	254	299	410	—	187	209	—	209	174	208	246
1560	196	153	—	—	153	239	286	216	—	276	155
1561	248	220	—	—	220	276	—	276	205	276	—
1562	184	150	—	213	150	217	—	217	242	228	—
1563	220	193	246	254	172	246	728	246	179	249	259
1564	294	220	253	310	160	367	337	247	201	303	248
1565	243	219	267	290	219	266	—	242	189	276	—
1566	236	282	265	262	—	189	—	189	197	—	—
1567	237	277	262	205	273	197	561	197	208	—	155
1568	231	253	248	167	231	208	—	208	177	313	—
1569	268	233	325	238	233	302	365	215	197	276	207
1570	199	200	372	214	184	197	—	197	188	293	—
1571	263	266	336	350	234	259	550	224	172	253	207
1572	217	261	295	272	197	172	—	172	234	294	—
1573	314	302	388	303	219	326	—	251	184	276	207
1574	223	261	304	315	226	184	—	184	232	289	—
1575	264	296	319	303	229	231	—	231	230	253	207
1576	274	286	319	383	251	262	—	262	192	276	—
1577	260	296	319	405	254	223	—	223	207	—	207
1578	272	295	319	—	262	248	—	248	211	293	—
1579	284	327	319	339	280	241	—	241	208	240	259
1580	287	327	319	289	257	247	—	247	213	264	257
1581	252	290	346	312	234	213	365	213	215	286	284
1582	310	331	390	312	265	289	366	264	193	330	284
1583	288	304	390	195	234	271	—	239	217	326	284
1584	283	310	408	256	211	255	—	255	—	313	278
1585	298	314	417	318	214	282	—	282	265	316	—
1586	277	255	390	—	179	298	—	298	224	323	284
1587	310	268	361	—	187	351	568	278	197	—	—
1588	332	313	404	—	217	350	539	255	230	—	284
1589	317	333	415	—	250	300	371	277	260	—	284
1590	350	351	390	—	311	349	516	294	—	—	298

Table V (cont.)

Harvest year	Dairy products and eggs						Wool, fells and hides				Average— all animal products
	Milk and cream	Butter	Cheese	Average— all dairy products	Eggs	Average— all dairy products and eggs	Wool	Sheepskins and wool fells	Cattle hides	Average— wool, fells and hides	
1591	310	300	—	305	433	348	322	—	397	360	354
1592	310	299	—	305	580	396	334	348	390	357	377
1593	325	304	158	262	334	280	344	377	392	371	326
1594	—	255	224	290	389	323	346	392	375	371	347
1595	284	349	—	317	593	409	325	—	431	378	394
1596	313	344	315	324	500	368	324	418	429	390	379
1597	284	358	331	324	588	390	279	502	420	400	395
1598	—	357	—	357	562	460	289	442	408	380	420
1599	—	353	—	353	371	362	276	476	425	392	377
1600	292	330	—	341	638	440	296	476	461	411	426
1601	—	435	331	398	—	398	318	468	341	376	387
1602	283	397	241	277	488	330	370	391	362	374	352
1603	227	308	364	300	352	313	412	508	373	431	372
1604	—	326	232	279	—	279	371	537	408	439	359
1605	—	406	199	303	518	374	362	458	432	417	396
1606	—	373	265	319	454	364	356	486	430	424	394
1607	310	354	265	323	475	361	364	529	458	450	406
1608	310	413	298	340	536	389	334	433	460	409	399
1609	407	391	245	348	—	348	297	508	425	410	379
1610	—	385	331	359	726	481	271	454	459	395	438
1611	384	405	331	373	536	414	300	431	481	404	409
1612	341	391	298	343	585	404	286	465	507	419	412
1613	341	413	—	380	481	413	310	—	503	407	410
1614	341	400	430	390	593	441	344	665	489	499	470
1615	341	396	—	369	682	473	371	—	495	433	453

1616	458	531	510	662	420	385	536	335	275	389	341
1617	488	552	540	717	400	424	542	385	397	416	341
1618	472	547	533	680	428	397	476	370	397	372	341
1619	473	528	521	659	403	417	519	383	397	412	341
1620	427	466	537	524	338	387	460	362	364	382	341
1621	406	430	504	469	316	381	463	354	331	390	341
1622	406	383	493	389	267	428	642	321	298	344	—
1623	419	414	486	439	316	424	562	355	—	369	341
1624	420	441	520	478	326	399	476	360	—	379	341
1625	396	451	511	464	378	340	—	340	331	349	—
1626	409	472	553	485	377	345	—	345	305	384	—
1627	440	498	549	529	417	381	497	343	298	389	341
1628	444	510	588	534	407	378	429	353	362	343	341
1629	490	552	597	506	—	427	494	404	397	475	341
1630	403	485	553	508	393	320	—	320	331	309	—
1631	471	488	516	542	405	454	628	367	—	393	341
1632	483	483	561	—	405	—	—	—	—	—	—
1633	424	485	554	500	401	363	—	363	319	406	—
1634	472	505	547	544	425	439	579	393	405	432	341
1635	471	508	585	512	428	433	588	382	371	433	341
1636	475	489	578	466	424	460	515	441	552	430	341
1637	481	507	585	518	419	455	—	455	401	508	—
1638	435	476	552	474	403	394	—	394	340	448	—
1639	434	437	582	357	371	431	519	387	—	426	348
1640	421	431	621	324	348	410	466	382	—	422	341
1641	405	421	587	338	337	388	458	364	331	420	341
1642	400	406	557	254	—	394	493	361	323	418	341
1643	393	375	457	327	340	411	528	372	342	433	341
1644	429	465	486	443	—	392	427	381	363	438	341
1645	473	556	554	558	—	390	481	359	310	426	341
1646	470	455	578	359	427	485	—	485	—	485	—
1647	549	502	640	370	497	596	—	596	644	548	—
1648	521	473	620	372	427	569	—	569	563	574	—
1649	519	519	665	372	—	518	—	518	644	625	284

Table VI. *Price of all agricultural products and timber*
INDEX NUMBER

Harvest year	Grains	Other arable crops	Livestock	Animal products	Average—all agricultural products	Timber
1450	119	111	97	82	102	83
1451	107	98	93	81	95	100
1452	101	101	105	85	98	115
1453	94	103	98	92	97	124
1454	83	108	90	90	93	107
1455	99	55	97	101	91	124
1456	76	95	97	99	92	82
1457	103	94	89	89	94	—
1458	106	78	98	93	94	93
1459	94	118	101	98	103	124
1460	122	114	92	94	106	124
1461	124	106	99	99	107	100
1462	89	83	115	97	96	—
1463	67	68	103	124	91	—
1464	95	145	104	89	108	88
1465	104	108	96	107	104	97
1466	92	90	97	108	97	94
1467	98	103	111	113	106	89
1468	98	91	98	107	99	92
1469	105	106	106	107	106	100
1470	114	106	101	99	105	87
1471	108	99	102	103	103	—
1472	88	86	116	102	98	—
1473	87	100	105	110	101	—
1474	80	94	100	103	94	—
1475	86	98	101	103	97	—
1476	82	99	88	96	91	94
1477	96	113	88	100	99	—
1478	105	119	96	96	104	96
1479	88	92	86	101	92	96
1480	92	98	90	95	94	96
1481	136	115	110	105	117	104
1482	168	128	124	113	133	136
1483	121	90	105	103	105	125
1484	100	100	118	119	109	104
1485	85	79	92	111	92	—
1486	117	89	107	104	104	—
1487	110	83	98	101	98	—
1488	116	115	109	103	111	98
1489	90	96	97	116	100	99
1490	120	97	117	89	106	—

Table VI (*cont.*)

Harvest year	Grains	Other arable crops	Livestock	Animal products	Average—all agricultural products	Timber
1491	97	94	113	103	102	100
1492	113	83	93	102	98	88
1493	89	78	107	97	93	83
1494	76	89	98	97	90	99
1495	81	116	100	101	100	—
1496	102	95	82	116	99	83
1497	105	91	94	118	102	83
1498	105	133	88	97	106	93
1499	89	102	98	87	93	98
1500	120	96	92	104	103	—
1501	124	102	96	107	107	89
1502	138	87	95	98	105	—
1503	123	113	96	100	108	84
1504	122	111	125	109	117	—
1505	117	87	123	92	105	92
1506	98	91	127	101	104	82
1507	107	101	112	97	104	85
1508	94	94	125	104	104	85
1509	77	96	119	104	99	79
1510	87	81	95	107	93	81
1511	106	95	98	108	102	—
1512	114	97	119	112	111	—
1513	107	115	107	113	111	—
1514	121	96	121	108	112	—
1515	113	104	118	128	116	105
1516	111	130	128	134	126	—
1517	129	149	128	122	132	—
1518	113	141	119	123	124	100
1519	144	191	132	127	149	104
1520	193	165	142	112	153	99
1521	183	127	137	103	138	99
1522	116	116	153	104	122	101
1523	110	97	138	85	108	94
1524	116	121	116	97	113	98
1525	110	127	128	119	121	83
1526	141	152	138	111	136	99
1527	198	192	133	111	159	108
1528	182	109	152	112	139	102
1529	189	116	139	97	135	97
1530	148	113	130	102	123	134
1531	196	115	147	108	142	84
1532	188	147	143	131	151	101
1533	155	140	128	153	144	84

Table VI (cont.)

Harvest year	Grains	Other arable crops	Livestock	Animal products	Average—all agricultural products	Timber
1534	148	121	164	112	136	100
1535	225	146	128	153	163	99
1536	154	132	154	151	148	102
1537	123	115	150	117	126	99
1538	124	129	134	105	123	106
1539	148	118	147	138	138	87
1540	154	122	151	178	151	105
1541	153	148	170	168	160	102
1542	175	124	167	132	150	108
1543	164	126	163	160	153	106
1544	192	145	201	141	170	122
1545	286	143	176	180	196	126
1546	160	139	176	121	149	86
1547	130	143	205	164	161	118
1548	162	165	230	171	182	127
1549	298	195	213	177	221	145
1550	353	313	258	232	289	151
1551	313	252	275	186	257	153
1552	281	288	256	192	254	173
1553	279	190	214	151	209	160
1554	340	268	249	187	261	184
1555	521	330	251	185	322	181
1556	558	318	297	308	370	156
1557	235	208	275	206	231	174
1558	284	195	257	224	240	220
1559	314	250	255	254	268	193
1560	337	242	295	196	268	199
1561	296	313	260	248	279	136
1562	372	350	285	184	298	144
1563	343	360	293	220	304	181
1564	258	233	268	294	263	176
1565	335	268	248	243	274	196
1566	267	264	298	236	266	190
1567	321	334	275	237	292	166
1568	355	318	295	231	300	194
1569	277	255	289	268	272	195
1570	299	244	308	199	263	194
1571	305	235	300	263	276	206
1572	368	287	326	217	300	195
1573	478	360	338	314	373	182
1574	334	330	367	223	314	217
1575	378	259	346	264	312	186
1576	359	301	339	274	318	238

Table VI (*cont.*)

Harvest year	Grains	Other arable crops	Livestock	Animal products	Average—all agricultural products	Timber
1577	391	275	340	260	317	226
1578	372	276	376	272	324	190
1579	414	308	322	284	332	228
1580	444	308	349	287	347	265
1581	434	306	377	252	342	206
1582	422	320	347	310	350	240
1583	370	325	327	288	328	230
1584	324	308	331	283	312	257
1585	556	364	346	298	391	254
1586	684	420	347	277	432	253
1587	365	309	366	310	338	273
1588	407	307	355	332	350	239
1589	531	312	376	317	384	251
1590	624	496	377	350	462	255
1591	443	346	382	354	381	285
1592	296	343	390	377	352	261
1593	350	388	382	326	362	287
1594	621	441	437	347	462	281
1595	681	458	419	394	488	299
1596	1039	598	407	379	606	314
1597	778	484	444	395	525	300
1598	518	341	457	420	434	312
1599	557	386	442	377	441	299
1600	768	523	474	426	548	280
1601	555	444	434	387	455	323
1602	480	368	428	352	407	324
1603	420	402	426	372	405	299
1604	501	417	422	359	425	362
1605	543	466	413	396	455	317
1606	492	407	465	394	440	345
1607	554	501	452	409	478	347
1608	654	531	472	399	514	370
1609	633	485	520	379	504	382
1610	554	464	465	438	480	381
1611	699	600	507	409	554	404
1612	736	668	486	412	576	304
1613	725	487	516	410	535	397
1614	650	512	522	470	539	403
1615	749	743	532	453	619	359
1616	657	557	497	458	542	378
1617	659	491	507	488	536	425
1618	586	464	530	472	513	467
1619	535	522	504	473	509	454

Table VI (cont.)

Harvest year	Grains	Other arable crops	Livestock	Animal products	Average—all agricultural products	Timber
1620	432	526	475	427	465	447
1621	666	518	494	406	521	413
1622	773	548	496	406	556	493
1623	666	507	508	419	525	392
1624	634	567	509	420	533	404
1625	729	600	536	396	565	460
1626	603	468	582	409	516	433
1627	504	464	549	440	489	483
1628	693	594	527	444	565	582
1629	723	663	568	490	611	395
1630	1064	695	550	403	678	445
1631	653	564	613	471	575	428
1632	793	602	628	483	627	503
1633	819	566	632	424	610	449
1634	794	864	649	472	695	429
1635	667	612	676	471	607	429
1636	752	715	644	475	647	538
1637	1031	906	627	481	761	485
1638	762	545	653	435	599	534
1639	569	535	630	434	542	510
1640	708	557	597	421	571	580
1641	649	544	603	405	550	545
1642	640	605	673	400	580	549
1643	565	587	586	393	533	582
1644	600	577	581	429	547	468
1645	663	500	664	473	575	420
1646	847	681	775	470	693	501
1647	1091	761	735	549	784	548
1648	1073	919	775	521	822	504
1649	1023	909	682	519	783	549

Table VII. *Price of wheat in England and western Europe*

Harvest year	Index number	
	England	Western Europe
1450	116	66
1451	112	64
1452	99	68
1453	87	65
1454	73	70
1455	94	130
1456	89	123
1457	116	121
1458	105	76
1459	93	111
1460	132	90
1461	138	69
1462	74	52
1463	60	42
1464	74	48
1465	83	67
1466	92	72
1467	106	67
1468	114	72
1469	114	70
1470	121	71
1471	112	69
1472	79	76
1473	79	88
1474	82	94
1475	89	71
1476	89	70
1477	122	134
1478	130	144
1479	92	115
1480	94	136
1481	132	273
1482	177	254
1483	132	85
1484	98	72
1485	86	97
1486	96	161
1487	108	170
1488	106	181
1489	91	122
1490	127	137
1491	100	163

Table VII (cont.)

Harvest year	Index number	
	England	Western Europe
1492	89	140
1493	81	81
1494	70	64
1495	70	59
1496	103	78
1497	102	109
1498	99	92
1499	72	51
1500	126	85
1501	128	126
1502	147	139
1503	130	102
1504	98	97
1505	99	100
1506	98	101
1507	113	103
1508	85	117
1509	69	100
1510	81	142
1511	111	153
1512	144	166
1513	121	144
1514	102	134
1515	127	152
1516	105	178
1517	109	149
1518	97	99
1519	140	113
1520	191	159
1521	166	196
1522	104	109
1523	109	136
1524	99	168
1525	95	109
1526	110	128
1527	227	175
1528	175	218
1529	165	222
1530	130	221
1531	162	236
1532	150	161
1533	133	146

Table VII (*cont.*)

Harvest year	Index number	
	England	Western Europe
1534	116	128
1535	213	157
1536	156	153
1537	108	120
1538	113	160
1539	116	133
1540	122	133
1541	146	142
1542	139	148
1543	185	195
1544	192	234
1545	288	270
1546	139	153
1547	99	118
1548	138	137
1549	265	181
1550	294	184
1551	329	247
1552	204	228
1553	179	207
1554	267	181
1555	383	250
1556	528	333
1557	194	186
1558	179	201
1559	291	230
1560	339	229
1561	271	290
1562	426	352
1563	275	243
1564	244	256
1565	394	418
1566	247	335
1567	235	317
1568	252	281
1569	243	291
1570	265	378
1571	288	489
1572	301	582
1573	427	658
1574	328	510
1575	348	410

Table VII (cont.)

| Harvest year | Index number | |
	England	Western Europe
1576	411	360
1577	369	370
1578	309	355
1579	310	428
1580	379	437
1581	381	431
1582	333	437
1583	316	451
1584	299	411
1585	427	598
1586	626	904
1587	331	588
1588	320	507
1589	437	596
1590	394	675
1591	304	612
1592	295	652
1593	388	561
1594	578	626
1595	607	711
1596	811	720
1597	746	728
1598	462	602
1599	407	549
1600	485	565
1601	416	497
1602	432	528
1603	391	539
1604	434	457
1605	401	453
1606	447	478
1607	571	582
1608	715	616
1609	493	582
1610	495	590
1611	545	619
1612	606	567
1613	667	566
1614	504	584
1615	574	528
1616	590	559
1617	647	616

Table VII (*cont.*)

Harvest year	Index number	
	England	Western Europe
1618	517	515
1619	450	519
1620	366	585
1621	598	657
1622	763	767
1623	573	726
1624	625	686
1625	637	843
1626	521	779
1627	427	713
1628	525	711
1629	609	794
1630	881	1096
1631	630	810
1632	684	764
1633	686	670
1634	668	669
1635	645	715
1636	645	725
1637	750	802
1638	575	784
1639	507	740
1640	615	760
1641	574	761
1642	616	858
1643	542	891
1644	546	761
1645	590	622
1646	804	597
1647	997	783
1648	943	808
1649	942	1022

B. PRICE OF AGRICULTURAL COMMODITIES
DECENNIAL AVERAGES
1450–99 = 100

Table VIII. *Price of arable crops*

INDEX NUMBER

Decade	Grains					Other arable crops					Average—all arable crops
	Wheat	Barley	Oats	Rye	Average—all grains	Hay	Straw	Peas	Beans	Average—all other arable crops	
1450–9	98	100	97	96	98	110	105	84	102	96	98
1460–9	99	99	100	98	99	100	108	100	97	101	101
1470–9	100	88	96	89	93	102	96	104	94	101	97
1480–9	112	118	105	118	114	86	87	121	121	99	107
1490–9	91	95	104	99	97	103	103	95	92	98	98
1500–9	109	108	107	123	112	93	100	106	92	98	105
1510–9	114	112	119	112	115	114	117	121	134	120	117
1520–9	144	136	148	195	154	104	117	167	152	132	143
1530–9	140	158	155	190	161	106	130	142	137	128	145
1540–9	171	197	191	—	187	140	118	177	170	145	164
1550–9	285	450	356	—	348	238	223	356	317	261	301
1560–9	293	338	322	338	316	301	293	258	317	294	301
1570–9	336	360	343	459	370	303	268	282	294	288	326
1580–9	385	482	457	523	454	305	274	365	367	328	389
1590–9	499	600	638	651	590	385	401	475	464	428	507
1600–9	479	583	599	600	560	522	418	425	453	454	503
1610–9	560	665	723	703	655	578	557	526	548	551	599
1620–9	564	648	630	770	642	584	540	492	564	546	594
1630–9	667	876	792	852	790	721	578	601	899	660	728
1640–9	717	796	843	—	786	768	612	622	620	664	721

Table IX. *Price of cattle and sheep*
INDEX NUMBER

Decade	Cattle				Sheep			
	Oxen	Cows and heifers	Calves	Average—all cattle	Wethers	Type unspecified	Lambs	Average—all sheep
1450–9	110	86	95	98	81	86	90	84
1460–9	96	110	102	102	95	108	108	102
1470–9	107	107	110	108	98	95	97	9—
1480–9	97	112	105	105	120	118	106	11
1490–9	89	84	90	90	106	—	96	10—
1500–9	114	89	92	103	104	98	86	9—
1510–9	122	95	147	119	140	112	118	128
1520–9	144	110	139	143	140	135	146	138
1530–9	154	146	133	147	162	148	161	158
1540–9	195	171	155	174	207	221	203	210
1550–9	293	273	239	266	312	232	242	263
1560–9	279	292	304	290	325	292	313	312
1570–9	331	431	353	358	396	343	432	380
1580–9	362	444	377	389	385	393	388	392
1590–9	428	517	449	465	460	492	458	471
1600–9	450	561	484	489	589	498	489	495
1610–9	516	624	527	553	555	537	507	525
1620–9	508	590	549	545	622	557	522	557
1630–9	555	744	629	646	650	566	542	587
1640–9	600	823	733	713	740	587	684	681

Table X. *Price of poultry and rabbits*
INDEX NUMBER

Decade	Capons and hens	Geese and ducks	Average— all poultry	Rabbits	Average— poultry and rabbits
1450–9	102	99	101	111	101
1460–9	102	101	102	95	102
1470–9	101	106	103	111	103
1480–9	99	99	100	98	100
1490–9	95	91	94	96	95
1500–9	136	120	134	95	132
1510–9	98	86	93	92	91
1520–9	113	—	113	—	113
1530–9	127	131	127	122	132
1540–9	239	206	220	174	204
1550–9	343	249	311	193	257
1560–9	328	275	304	219	261
1570–9	383	331	361	273	320
1580–9	330	288	309	302	306
1590–9	387	405	400	314	368
1600–9	493	405	441	353	411
1610–9	503	490	495	446	476
1620–9	640	471	591	408	515
1630–9	780	874	786	424	682
1640–9	650	747	698	463	603

Table XI. *Price of livestock*

INDEX NUMBER

Decade	Sheep	Cattle	Horses	Pigs	Poultry and rabbits	Average—all livestock
1450–9	84	98	104	94	101	97
1460–9	103	102	98	103	102	102
1470–9	94	108	87	100	103	98
1480–9	111	105	106	104	100	105
1490–9	103	90	104	101	95	99
1500–9	95	103	114	111	132	111
1510–9	128	119	108	135	91	117
1520–9	138	143	137	144	113	138
1530–9	158	147	141	124	132	143
1540–9	210	174	184	148	204	185
1550–9	263	266	249	258	257	259
1560–9	312	290	266	270	261	281
1570–9	380	358	326	297	320	336
1580–9	392	389	394	269	306	352
1590–9	471	465	444	310	368	414
1600–9	495	489	466	393	411	451
1610–9	525	553	520	460	476	507
1620–9	557	545	572	433	515	524
1630–9	587	646	652	589	682	630
1640–9	681	713	675	575	603·	667

Table XII. *Price of animal products*
INDEX NUMBER

Decade	Dairy products and eggs						Wool, fells and hides				Average—all animal products
	Milk and cream	Butter	Cheese	Average—all dairy products	Eggs	Average—all dairy products and eggs	Wool	Sheepskins and wool fells	Cattle hides	Average—wool, fells and hides	
1450–9	59	106	—	91	101	97	82	75	101	86	91
1460–9	—	—	91	91	101	98	109	126	98	110	105
1470–9	—	—	105	105	101	101	99	107	89	101	101
1480–9	118	99	109	105	98	103	113	130	89	110	107
1490–9	152	97	86	102	96	100	96	93	128	101	101
1500–9	86	99	92	93	96	95	93	100	132	108	102
1510–9	107	91	94	93	119	105	119	126	156	131	118
1520–9	100	92	98	94	—	94	111	108	162	115	105
1530–9	152	97	109	109	165	116	122	125	202	136	127
1540–9	—	138	147	139	224	153	153	124	206	161	159
1550–9	246	210	208	216	238	223	206	126	283	210	213
1560–9	204	274	200	225	478	251	205	256	258	220	236
1570–9	217	275	207	223	458	234	234	283	323	279	257
1580–9	279	294	218	261	442	286	225	303	384	305	295
1590–9	303	334	257	313	487	369	315	422	406	375	372
1600–9	305	377	271	323	494	360	348	479	415	414	387
1610–9	346	398	357	369	568	425	353	592	504	472	448
1620–9	341	380	336	354	503	389	354	482	534	462	426
1630–9	342	421	389	389	566	417	407	491	561	486	455
1640–9	333	479	440	439	500	455	396	372	577	460	458

Table XIII. Price of all agricultural products, timber and industrial products

INDEX NUMBER

Decade	Grains	Other arable crops	Livestock	Animal products	Average—all agricultural products	Timber	Industrial products	Agricultural/Industrial × 100
1450–9	98	96	97	91	96	106	99	97
1460–9	99	101	102	105	102	98	103	99
1470–9	93	101	98	101	98	93	100	98
1480–9	114	99	105	107	106	109	103	103
1490–9	97	98	99	101	99	91	97	102
1500–9	112	98	111	102	106	85	98	108
1510–9	115	120	117	118	118	97	102	116
1520–9	154	132	138	105	132	98	110	120
1530–9	161	128	143	127	139	100	110	126
1540–9	187	145	185	159	169	115	127	133
1550–9	348	261	259	213	270	174	186	145
1560–9	316	294	281	236	282	178	218	129
1570–9	370	288	336	257	313	206	223	140
1580–9	454	328	352	295	357	247	230	155
1590–9	590	428	414	372	451	289	238	189
1600–9	560	454	451	387	463	335	256	181
1610–9	655	551	507	448	540	397	274	197
1620–9	642	546	524	426	535	450	264	203
1630–9	790	660	630	455	634	475	281	226
1640–9	786	664	667	458	644	524	306	210

Table XIV. *Price of wheat in England and western Europe*

INDEX NUMBER

Decade	England	Western Europe
1450–9	98	89
1460–9	99	65
1470–9	100	93
1480–9	112	155
1490–9	91	97
1500–9	109	107
1510–9	114	143
1520–9	144	162
1530–9	140	161
1540–9	171	171
1550–9	285	225
1560–9	293	301
1570–9	336	407
1580–9	385	536
1590–9	499	644
1600–9	479	483
1610–9	560	566
1620–9	564	726
1630–9	667	778
1640–9	717	786

Table XV. *Agricultural day wage rates[a] in southern England*

Decade	Oxford	Cambridge	Eton College	Average	Index number
	d.	d.	d.	d.	
1450–9	4	4	—	4·00	101
1460–9	4	4	—	4·00	101
1470–9	4	4	4	4·00	101
1480–9	4	—	3½	3·75	95
1490–9	4	—	4	4·00	101
1500–9	4	4	4	4·00	101
1510–9	4	4	4	4·00	101
1520–9	4	4	4½	4·17	106
1530–9	4	4	5	4·33	110
1540–9	4	5	5	4·66	118
1550–9	6	6	7	6·33	160
1560–9	8	5	8	7·00	177
1570–9	8	7½	9	8·17	207
1580–9	8	8	8	8·00	203
1590–9	8	10	8	8·66	219
1600–9	8	10	8	8·66	219
1610–9	8	10	9	9·00	228
1620–9	10	10	10	10·00	253
1630–9	10	12	12	11·33	287
1640–9	12	12	12	12·00	304

[a] These are median wage rates for ordinary day-to-day agricultural operations performed by male workers—e.g. hedging, ditching, spreading dung. Seasonal tasks, such as mowing and haymaking, normally paid at higher rates, are not included. Also excluded are rates supplemented by payments in kind.

Table XVI. *Wage rates in southern England and their purchasing power*

INDEX NUMBER

	Agricultural labourer			Building craftsman
Decade	Money wage rate[a]	'Cost of living'[b]	Purchasing power of wage rate	Purchasing power of wage rate[c]
1450–9	101	96	105	104
1460–9	101	101	100	100
1470–9	101	97	104	103
1480–9	95	111	86	93
1490–9	101	97	104	103
1500–9	101	104	97	96
1510–9	101	114	89	88
1520–9	106	133	80	76
1530–9	110	138	80	68
1540–9	118	167	71	70
1550–9	160	271	59	51
1560–9	177	269	66	62
1570–9	207	298	69	64
1580–9	203	354	57	57
1590–9	219	443	49	47
1600–9	219	439	50	46
1610–9	228	514	44	39
1620–9	253	511	50	39
1630–9	287	609	47	—
1640–9	304	609	50	49

[a] Data taken from Table 15.

[b] Based on the preceding price tables, using the following weights: Arable crops, excluding hay and straw (5), animal products (2), livestock (1), timber (1), industrial products (1).

[c] Re-calculated from figures given by E. H. Phelps Brown and Sheila V. Hopkins in 'Seven Centuries of the Prices of Consumables, compared with Builders' Wage-rates', *Economica*, NS XXIII (1956), 312.

C. NOTE ON STATISTICAL SOURCES AND METHODS

The principal sources of data used in the compilation of our price indices have been J. E. T. Rogers, *A History of Agriculture and Prices in England*, vols. III and VI; W. Beveridge *et al.*, *Prices and Wages in England from the Twelfth to the Nineteenth Century*, vol. I; and unpublished statistics forming part of the Beveridge Collection of Price Material at the Institute of Historical Research. These sources contain many different series of price quotations of varying degrees of usefulness. The series which have been utilized in this study, together with the relevant agricultural commodities, are listed below.

In order to save space, the following abbreviations for commodities are used:

B	= Barley	G	= Geese or ducks	Pe	= Peas
Be	= Beans	H	= Hens	R	= Rye
Bu	= Butter	Ha	= Hay	Ra	= Rabbits
C	= Capons	Hi	= Hides	S	= Straw
Ca	= Calves	Ho	= Horses	T	= Timber
Ch	= Cheese	L	= Lambs	V	= Various: six or
Co	= Cows or heifers	O	= Oats		more commodities
E	= Eggs	Ox	= Oxen	W	= Wool
F	= Fells or skins	P	= Pigs	We	= Wethers
				Wh	= Wheat

Rogers, *History of Agriculture and Prices*

Alciston (C, Co, G)
Alton Barnes (C)
Apuldram (V)
Balneth (E)
Bardney (Bu, Ca, Ch, Co)
Barking (H)
Battle (Co, G)
Beeding (H, T)
Biggin (O, Pe)
[1]Cambridge Colleges (V)
Canterbury (P, T, Wh)
Castor (B, P)
Chatham (Hi)
Colchester (C)
Coleshill (V)
D'Ewes Accounts (Ch, Co, H, O)
Downham (V)
Durham Cells:
  Finchale
  Jarrow   } (V)
  Wearmouth
Durham Obedientiary (V)
Ellsworth (C)
Elmswell (B, O, R)
[1]Eton College (V)
Fountains Abbey (V)
Gawthorp (V)
Guyton (C, E, H)
Hardwick (Be, R)
Harling (V)
Harting (Hi, We)
Hawkesbury (E)
Heightredbury (H)
Heyford (O, Wh)

Hickling (V)
Hinton (B, R)
Honden (C)
Hornchurch (C, H, O, Wh)
Houghton (E)
Howard Accounts (Ca, Hi, L)
Hunstanton (R, W)
Ipswich (R)
Kirkby Stephen (C)
Kirtling (V)
Laughton (V)
Le Strange A/c's (R, W)
Lewes (B, Hi, Ox)
Loders (G, H, R, Wh)
London (Ha, O, R, T)
Lullington (B, Ox, P, Wh)
Mendham (V)
Metingham College (F, Hi, We)
Newton Longville (C)
Norwich (V)
Ormsby (V)
Osney (Co, F, Hi, L)
Otterton (Be, G)
[1]Oxford Colleges (V)
Oxford City (V)
Portsmouth (Hi)
Radcliffe (G, P)
Rochester (Hi)
Rotherham (R)
Royden (Ca)
Ruislip (Be)
St Osyth (Ca, F, Hi, Ho)
Selborne (C, P)
Sion and Isleworth (V)

[1] Sources of data for wage tables.

Skidmore Upton (C)
Spitling (B, C)
Stamford (S)
Stoke (Co, G, Ha, Hi, O)
Sutton-at-Hone (F, Hi, Ox, We)
Takley (C, Co, H, O)
Theydon Garnon (V)
Wardrobe (V)
Winchester College (V)
Worksop (V)

Wormsleighton (V)
Writtle (C, G, P)
Wye (V)
Wykenholt (E)
Wymondham (V)
Wythingham (C, E, H)
Yartcombe (C)
Yeovil (B, Be, O, R)
Yotes Court (Be)

Beveridge, *Institute of Historical Research*

Cambridge Colleges (V)
Dover Assize (Wh)
Durham Cells (V)
Durham Obedientiary (V)
Ely (Wh)
[1]Eton College (V)
[2]Exeter Assize (Wh)
Hungerford (V)
Lambeth Palace (Be)
Laughton (V)
[3]Loder's A/c's (V)
London Assize (Wh)
London City Cos. (Wh)
Norwich Assize (Wh)
Norwich Obedientiary (V)
Nottingham (Wh)
Oxford Colleges (V)

Penshurst and Robertsbridge (V)
[1]Sandwich (Bu, Ch, F, Ha)
Shrewsbury (Co, Ho, Ox, We, Wh)
Tattershall (V)
Taunton (Wh)
[1]Victually Contracts (Bu, Ch, Hi,
  T, Wh)
Western Europe:
  France ⎫
  Germany ⎬ (Wh)
  Low Countries ⎭
[1]Westminster School and Abbey
  (T, Wh)
[1]Winchester College (V)
Winchester Manor (R, Wh)
York (Wh)

Other sources of price material which have been drawn upon are as follows:

K. J. Allison, *thesis*, Appendix Five: Norfolk Sheep and Wool Prices.

P. J. Bowden, 'Movements in Wool Prices, 1490–1610', *Yorks. Bull.*, IV, 1952, pp. 109–24.

Durham Parish Books: Churchwarden's Accounts of Pittington and Other Parishes in the Diocese of Durham from A.D. 1580 to 1700, Surtees Soc., LXXXIV, Durham, 1888, *passim:* Wool Prices.

Finch, *op. cit.*, p. 19: John Isham's Wool Sales.

Hill, *op. cit.*, Appendix III: Corn Prices returned by Leet Juries, 1513–1712, Lincoln.

Lodge, *op. cit.*, *passim:* Toke's Purchases and Sales of Livestock.

Henry E. Huntington Library, California, U.S.A., ST. 48: Sir Thomas Temple's Account Book on Wool Sales, 1592–1626.

Kent A O, A 423, Cranfield Family Estate Accounts: Sheep, Wool and Fell Prices.

[1] Published, in whole or in part, in Beveridge, *Prices and Wages in England.*

[2] Published in W. H. Beveridge, 'A Statistical Crime of the Seventeen Century', *Journ. Econ. + Bus. Hist.*, 1929.

[3] See *Robert Loder's Farm Accounts, 1610–1620*, ed. G. E. Fussell, Camden Soc., 3rd Ser., LIII, 1936.

Lincoln, A O, H. 97/22, John Hatcher's Estate Accounts: Livestock and Animal Product Prices.

Lincoln A O, HEN. 3/2, Account Book of Sir George Heneage: Wool and Wether Prices.

Lumley MS. 2305, Estate Accounts of Sir Nicholas Saunderson: Wool Prices.

Northants. RO, F(M) Misc. Vol. 52, Fitzwilliam's Dogsthorpe 'Cattle Book': Livestock Transactions.

Oxford A O, DIL III/6/2, Lee Family Wool Sales.

William Salt Library, D 1734, Misterton Manorial Accounts: Livestock and Animal Product Prices.

The main problem confronting the sixteenth- and seventeenth-century price historian is the lack of adequate statistical data. For many commodities long series of observations from the same source are not available, and wheat is the only product for which several series exist covering all or most of the period treated in our study. It is therefore necessary to rely to a considerable extent upon scattered observations covering comparatively short terms of years and derived from a variety of sources. For a number of reasons data from such sources are unlikely to be strictly comparable; for example, there are likely to be differences in local demand and supply conditions; there may be variations in local standards of weights and measures, about which we know little; while there may be differences in the quality of the product or in the conditions of sale. Obviously, there is a risk of serious distortion if scattered observations are simply lumped together indiscriminately. This has been avoided by treating sources separately; and where information has been available, separate price series have been distinguished for each source according to the type of transaction and the narrowest possible definition of product. For example, purchases have been differentiated from sales, and livestock have been distinguished by age as well as by kind. On the other hand, owing to the inadequacy of the data, no attempt has been made to adjust for seasonal price movements. Suspect prices have been discarded.

The statistical procedure used in the compilation of price indices can probably best be illustrated with reference to a specific product, say wheat. The first step was to select a series of wheat prices against which other series of wheat prices could be measured. The Exeter series extended throughout the whole period and so was well suited for this purpose. The next stage was to adjust prices from the remaining thirty-four series to the price of wheat in Exeter. The total price of each series in the years for which quotations were obtained was compared with the total of Exeter wheat prices in the same years, and the ratio between the two totals established. Each individual price quotation was then multiplied by the ratio of the total Exeter price to the total price of the wheat series to which it was related. For example, the total price of wheat in Cambridge was found to be 0·822 times that of wheat in Exeter in the same years. Each Cambridge wheat price was, therefore multiplied by a factor of 1·217, or $\frac{1}{0\cdot822}$. After each wheat series had been treated in this way, simple arithmetical averages were obtained of each year's adjusted prices. Finally, these averages were expressed in the form of an index, with the average price ruling in the period 1450–99 as base.

Essentially the same procedure was followed with all other commodities. Where, as was sometimes the case, it was not possible to establish a direct relationship between a series and the series selected as the standard, an indirect relationship was established through some third overlapping series the ratio of whose total price to the total price of the basic series was known. Yearly averages and indices were calculated as for wheat. Throughout, calculations have been based on harvest years (beginning Michaelmas) and not on calendar years, since, as we have seen, the size of the harvest exercised a major influence on agricultural prices. Thus, harvest year 1620, for example, relates to the period 29 September 1620 to 28 September 1621.

The standard series and base price for each commodity are listed below:

Commodity	Standard Series	Base price (average 1450–99)
Wheat	Exeter	6·32s. per qtr.
Barley	Cambridge	2·82s. per qtr.
Oats	Cambridge	1·92s. per qtr.
Rye	Loders	3·97s. per qtr.
Hay	Cambridge	3·17s. per load
Straw	Cambridge	1·63s. per load
Peas	Cambridge	3·72s. per qtr.
Beans	Oxford	3·90s. per qtr.
Oxen	Cambridge	13·77s. each
Cows (and heifers)	Shrewsbury	8·50s. each
Calves	Cambridge	2·21s. each
Wethers	Wardrobe	1·72s. each
Unspecified sheep	Cambridge	1·84s. each
Lambs	Eton College	1·32s. each
Capons (and hens)	Cambridge	0·30s. each
Geese (and ducks)	Oxford	0·33s. each
Rabbits	Winchester	0·13s. each
Horses	Oxford	33·93s. each
Pigs	Cambridge	8·46s. each (boars)
Cream (and milk)	Cambridge	3·52s. per doz. gall.
Butter	Cambridge	1·30s. per doz. lb.
Cheese	Sandwich	0·76s. per doz. lb. (Suffolk Cheese)
Eggs	Cambridge	0·67s. per 120
Wool	Durham	2·30s. per stone
Sheepskins and wool fells	Sandwich (1st qtr)	0·47s. each
Cattle hides	Eton College	2·82s. each
Timber	Cambridge	7·99s. per 100 faggots

In calculating average price indices for each group of commodities (e.g. grains, cattle), no attempt has been made to weight products according to their relative importance, since the necessary information is lacking. In years where all products in a group are not represented, simple arithmetical averages have taken in respect of those commodities for which data exist. Similarly the indices for 'all agricultural commodities' are simple unweighted averages of indices of major groups of products.

The unorthodox method of treatment which has been adopted can be criticized on theoretical grounds, but the nature of the material is such that the use of refined techniques is obviously out of the question. Theoretically, there is the possibility that the long-term trend of prices for individual commodities will be misrepresented if the trend of the standard series is markedly different from that of other series, especially if the total number of observations is small. This possibility has been kept in mind as far as practicable in the selection of basic series, and while there may be some distortion from this cause, in most cases it is not likely to be of more than slight significance. As for the shorter term movement of prices, it will be evident that the measurement of year-to-year variations is, in general, less reliable than that for rather longer periods, though the unreliability is more likely to be a matter of degree than of direction. It will be recognized, of course, that the concept of an average price level is an abstraction, and that in the conditions of Tudor and early Stuart times prices might vary widely from one local market to another.

SELECT BIBLIOGRAPHY

Alcock, L. and Foster, I. LL. (eds.). *Culture and Environment.* London, 1963.

Allan, D. G. C. *Agrarian Discontent under the early Stuarts and during the last Decade of Elizabeth.* University of London M.Sc. (Econ.) thesis, 1950.

—— 'The Rising in the West, 1628–31', EcHR, 2nd Ser., V, 1952.

Allen, J. Romilly. 'Old Farmhouses with Round Chimneys near St David's', *Arch. Camb.*, II, 1902.

Allison, K. J. 'Flock Management in the Sixteenth and Seventeenth Centuries', EcHR, 2nd Ser., XI, 1958.

—— 'The Sheep-Corn Husbandry of Norfolk in the Sixteenth and Seventeenth Centuries', AHR, V, 1957.

—— *The Wool Supply and the Worsted Cloth Industry in Norfolk in the Sixteenth and Seventeenth Centuries,* University of Leeds Ph.D. thesis, 1955.

Ambler, L. *Old Halls and Manor Houses of Yorkshire.* London, 1913.

Ascoli, Georges. *La Grande-Bretagne devant L'Oopinion Française au XVIIe Siècle.* Travaux et Mémoires de l'Université de Lille, NS, Fascicule 13, 1, Paris, 1930.

Ashley, Sir William J. *The Bread of our Forefathers.* Oxford, 1928.

Ashton, T. S. *An Economic History of England: the Eighteenth Century,* London, 1955.

—— *Economic Fluctuations in England, 1700–1800,* Oxford, 1959.

Aylmer, G. E. *The King's Servants.* London, 1961.

—— 'The Last Years of Purveyance, 1610–1660', EcHR, 2nd Ser., X, i, 1957.

Bacon, Nathaniel. *Annalls of Ipswiche.* Ipswich, 1884.

Bailey, J. and Culley, G. *General View of the Agriculture of the County of Northumberland.* London, 1813.

Bankes, Joyce (ed.). *The Memoranda Book of James Bankes, 1586–1617.* Inverness, 1935.

Barley, M. W. *The English Farmhouse and Cottage.* London, 1961.

Barnes, D. G. *A History of the English Corn Laws from 1660 to 1846.* London, 1930.

Barnes, T. G. *Somerset Assize Orders, 1629–1640,* Som. Rec. Soc., LXV, 1959.

Bates, E. H. *The Particular Description of the County of Somerset, 1633,* Somerset Rec. Soc., XV, 1900.

Batho, G. R. 'The Finances of an Elizabethan Nobleman: Henry Percy, Ninth Earl of Northumberland', EcHR, 2nd Ser., IX, 1957.

—— *The Household Papers of Henry Percy, ninth Earl of Northumberland,* Camden Soc., XCIII, 1962.

Beale, John. *Herefordshire Orchards, a Pattern for all England.* London, 1657.

Bean, J. M. W. *The Estates of the Percy Family, 1416–1537.* London, 1958.

Bell, H. E. *An Introduction to the History and Records of the Court of Wards and Liveries.* Cambridge, 1953.

Bennett, M. K. 'British Wheat Yield Per Acre for Seven Centuries', *Economic History,* III, 1935.

Beresford, M. W. 'Glebe Terriers and Open-Field Buckinghamshire', *Records of Bucks.*, XVI, 1953–4.

—— 'Habitation versus Improvement. The Debate on Enclosure by Agreement', *Essays in the Economic and Social History of Tudor and Stuart England,* ed. F. J. Fisher. Cambridge, 1961.

—— 'A Journey to Elizabethan Market Places', chapter VI in *History on the Ground.* London, 1957.

Beresford, M. W. *The Lost Villages of England*. London, 1954.
—— 'The Lost Villages of Medieval England', *Geog. J.*, CXVII, 1951.
—— 'The Lost Villages of Yorkshire', *Yorks. Arch. J.*, XXXVIII, 1952.
Best, Henry. *Rural Economy in Yorkshire in 1641, being the Farming and Account Books of Henry Best of Elmeswell in the East Riding*, ed. C. B. Robinson. Surtees Soc., XXXIII, 1857.
Beveridge, Lord. 'British Exports and the Barometer', *Economic J.*, XXX, 1920.
—— 'The Yield and Price of Corn in the Middle Ages', *Economic History*, II, 1927.
—— 'Wages in the Winchester Manors', *EcHR*, VII, 1936–7.
—— 'Weather and Harvest Cycles', *Economic J.*, XXXI, 1921.
Beveridge, Lord, and others. *Prices and Wages in England from the Twelfth to the Nineteenth Century*. London, 1939.
Bickley, W. B. *Abstract of the Bailiffs' Accounts of Monastic and other Estates in the County of Warwick*. Dugdale Soc., II, 1923.
Bindoff, S. T. *Ket's Rebellion, 1549*. Hist. Assoc. Pamphlet, General Series 12, 1949.
—— *Tudor England*. London, 1950.
Birch, Walter de Gray. *A Descriptive Catalogue of Penrice and Margam Manuscripts*, Series I–IV. London, 1893–5.
Blagrave, J. *The Epitomie of the Art of Husbandry*. London, 1669.
Blake, W. T. 'Hooker's Synopsis Chorographical of Devonshire', *Devon Assoc.*, XLVII, 1915.
Bland, A. E., Brown, P. A., and Tawney, R. H. *English Economic History. Select Documents*. London, 1914.
Blith, Walter. *The English Improver Improved*. London, 1652.
Blome, Richard. *Britannia*. London, 1673.
Bouch, C. M. L., and Jones, G. P. *The Lake Counties, 1500–1830*. Manchester, 1961.
Bourne, George. *The Bettesworth Book. Talks with a Surrey Peasant*. London, 1920.
—— *Memoirs of a Surrey Labourer: a record of the last years of Frederick Bettesworth*. London, 1911.
Bowden, P. J. 'The Home Market in Wool, 1500–1700', *Yorks. Bull. of Econ. and Soc. Research*, VIII, ii, 1956.
—— *The internal Wool Trade in England during the Sixteenth and Seventeenth Centuries*. University of Leeds Ph.D. thesis, 1952.
—— 'Movements in Wool Prices, 1490–1610', *Yorks. Bull. of Econ. and Soc. Research*, IV, 1952.
—— *The Wool Trade in Tudor and Stuart England*. London, 1962.
Brace, H. W. *History of Seed Crushing in Great Britain*. London, 1960.
Bradley, Harriet. *The Enclosures in England—an Economic Reconstruction*. New York, 1918.
Brenner, Y. S. 'The Inflation of Prices in Early Sixteenth Century England', *EcHR*, 2nd Ser., XIV, 1961.
—— 'The Inflation of Prices in England, 1551–1650', *EcHR*, 2nd Ser., XV, 1962.
Brett-James, N. G. *The Growth of Stuart London*. London, 1935.
Brown, E. H. Phelps and Hopkins, Sheila V. 'Seven Centuries of Building Wages', *Economica*, NS, XXII, 1955.
—— 'Wage-rates and Prices: Evidence for Population Pressure in the Sixteenth Century', *Economica*, NS, XXIV, 1957.
—— 'Builders' Wage-rates, Prices and Population: Some Further Evidence', *Economica*, NS, XXVI, 1959.
Browning, Andrew (ed.). *English Historical Documents, 1660–1714*. London, 1953.
Brunskill, R. W. 'An Appreciation of Monmouthshire Houses', *Mont. Coll.*, LIII, ii, 1954.

Brydson, A. P. *Some Records of two Lakeland Townships—Blawith and Nibthwaite— chiefly from original documents.* Ulverston, 1908.

Burton, William. *The Description of Leicestershire.* London, 1622.

Caley, J. and Hunter, J. (eds.). *Valor Ecclesiasticus temp. Hen. VIII . . .*, (6 vols.) London, 1810–34.

Camden, W. *Britannia,* trans. R. Gough. 3 vols., London, 1789.

Campbell, Mildred. *The English Yeoman Under Elizabeth and the Early Stuarts.* New Haven, 1942.

Carew, Richard. *The Survey of Cornwall.* London, 1602.

Carpenter, H. J. 'Furse of Morhead', *Devon Assoc.,* XXVI, 1894.

Cave, T. and Wilson, R. A. (eds.). *The Parliamentary Survey of the Lands and Possessions of the Dean and Chapter of Worcester.* Worcs. Hist. Soc., 1924.

Chalklin, C. W. 'The Compton Census of 1676: the dioceses of Canterbury and Rochester', *A Seventeenth Century Miscellany.* Kent Arch. Soc., Records Publication Committee, XVII, 1960.

—— 'The Rural Economy of a Kentish Wealden Parish, 1650–1750', AHR, x, 1962.

Charles, B. G. 'The Second Book of George Owen's Description of Pembrokeshire', *Nat. Lib. Wales J.,* v, 1947–8.

Charman, D. 'Wealth and Trade in Leicester in the early Sixteenth Century', *Leics. Arch. Soc.,* XXV, 1949.

Cheke, Val. *The Story of Cheese-making in Britain.* London, 1959.

Chippindall, C. L. W. H. (ed.). *A Sixteenth-century Survey and Year's Account of the Estates of Hornby Castle, Lancashire.* Chetham Soc., NS, CII, 1939.

Cipolla, C. M. 'La prétendue "révolution des prix". Réflexions sur l'expérience italienne', *Annales E.S.C.,* 10e année, 4, 1955.

Clapham, Sir J. *A Concise Economic History of Britain from the Earliest Times to 1750.* Cambridge, 1949.

Clark, G. N. *The Wealth of England from 1496 to 1760.* Oxford, 1947.

Clarkson, L. A. 'The Organization of the English Leather Industry in the Late Sixteenth and Seventeenth Centuries', EcHR, 2nd Ser., XIII, 1960.

Clay, J. M. *Yorkshire Monasteries: Suppression Papers.* Yorks. Arch. Soc. Rec. Ser., XLVIII, 1912.

Clay, T. *Briefe, Easie and Necessary Tables of Interest and Rents Forborne.* London, 1624.

Cliffe, J. T. *The Yorkshire Gentry on the Eve of the Civil War.* University of London Ph.D. thesis, 1960.

Cobbett, William. *Rural Rides.* Everyman edn., London, 1957.

Coleman, D. C. 'Industrial Growth and Industrial Revolutions', *Economica,* NS, XXIII, 1956.

—— 'Labour in the English Economy of the Seventeenth Century', EcHR, 2nd Ser., VIII, 1955–6.

Collier, C. V. 'Burton Agnes Courts, Miscellanea II', *Yorks. Arch. Soc., Rec. Ser.,* LXXIV, 1929.

Collis, I. P. 'Leases for Term of Years, determinable with Lives', *J. Soc. Archivists,* I, 1957.

Considerations Touching Trade, with the Advance of the King's Revenue . . ., 1641.

Cooper, J. P. 'The Counting of Manors', EcHR 2nd Ser., VIII, 1956. 'The fortune of Thomas Wentworth, Earl of Strafford', EcHR 2nd Ser., XI, 1958.

Cordingley, R. A. 'British Historical Roof Types and their Members', *Ancient Monuments Soc.,* NS, IX, 1961.

—— 'Stokesay Castle, Shropshire: The Chronology of its Buildings', *The Art Bulletin* (U.S.), XLV (2), 1963.

Cornwall, J. C. K. *The Agrarian History of Sussex, 1560–1640.* University of London M.A. thesis, 1953.

Cornwall, J. C. K. 'English Country Towns in the Fifteen Twenties', EcHR, 2nd Ser., xv, i, 1962.

—— 'Farming in Sussex, 1560–1640', Sussex Arch. Coll., xcii, 1954.

Cox, J. C. (ed.). The Records of the Borough of Northampton, ii. Northampton, 1898.

Craig, Sir J. The Mint. A History of the London Mint from A.D. 287 to 1948. Cambridge, 1953.

Cramer, J. A. (ed.). The Second Book of the Travels of Nicander Nucius of Corcyra. Camden Soc., xvii, 1841.

CREIGHTON, C. A History of Epidemics in Britain from A.D. 664 to the Extinction of Plague. Cambridge, 1891.

Crook, Barbara. 'Newnham Priory: Rental of Manor at Biddenham, 1505–6', Beds. Hist. Rec. Soc., xxv, 1947.

Cross, M. Claire, 'An Exchange of Lands with the Crown, 1587–8', Bull. IHR, xxxiv, 1961.

Cunningham, W. The Growth of English Industry and Commerce in Modern Times, ii, Cambridge, 1919.

Daniel-Tyssen, J. R. 'The Parliamentary Surveys of the County of Sussex', Sussex Arch. Coll., xxiii, 1871.

Darby, H. C. The Draining of the Fens. Cambridge, 1940.

—— (ed.). Historical Geography of England before A.D. 1800. Cambridge, 1936.

Darby, H. C. and Saltmarsh, J. 'The Infield-Outfield System on a Norfolk Manor', Economic History, iii, 1935.

Davies, D. J. The Economic History of South Wales prior to 1800. Cardiff, 1933.

Davies, Elwyn. (ed.). Celtic Studies in Wales. Cardiff, 1963.

Deane, Phyllis and Cole, W. A. British Economic Growth. 1688–1959. Cambridge 1962.

Defoe, Daniel. A Tour through England and Wales. Everyman edn., London, 1959.

Dendy, F. W. 'The Ancient Farms of Northumberland', Archaeologia Aeliana, 2nd Ser., xvi, 1894.

Denney, A. H. The Sibton Abbey Estates: Select Documents, 1325–1509. Suffolk Rec. Soc., ii, 1960.

Dexter, R. and Barber, D. Farming for Profits. London, 1961.

Dickens, A. G. 'Estate and Household Management in Bedfordshire, c. 1540', Beds. Hist. Rec. Soc., xxxvi, 1956.

—— The Register or Chronicle of Butley Priory, Suffolk, 1510–35. Winchester, 1951.

Dietz, F. C. English Government Finance, 1485–1558. University of Illinois, Studies in the Social Sciences, ix, 3, Urbana, 1920.

—— English Public Finance, 1558–1641. New York, 1932.

Dodd, A. H. Studies in Stuart Wales. Cardiff, 1952.

Edwards, Ifan Ab Owen (ed.). A Catalogue of Star Chamber Proceedings relating to Wales. Cardiff, 1929.

Eland, G. (ed.). Thomas Wotton's Letter-Book, 1574–1586. London, 1960.

Ellis, Sir Henry (ed.). Speculi Britanniae Pars: an Historical and Chorographical Description of the County of Essex by John Norden, 1594. Camden Soc., ix, 1840.

Elsas, M. J. 'Price Data from Munich, 1500–1700', Economic History, iii, 1935.

—— Umriss einer Geschichte der Preise und Löhne in Deutschland vom ausgehenden Mittelalter bis zum Beginn des Neunzehnten Jahrhunderts, i, ii. Leiden, 1936–49.

Elton, G. R. The Tudor Constitution. Cambridge, 1960.

—— The Tudor Revolution in Government. Cambridge, 1953.

Emerson, W. R. The Economic Development of the Estates of the Petre Family in Essex in the Sixteenth and Seventeenth Centuries, University of Oxford D.Phil. thesis, 1951.

Emery, F. V. 'West Glamorgan farming circa 1580–1620', Nat. Lib. Wales J., ix, x, 1955–6, 1957–8.

Emmison, F. G. *Tudor Secretary: Sir William Petre at Court and Home.* London, 1961.

Ernle, Lord. *English Farming Past and Present.* London, 1912.

Evans, A. 'Battle Abbey at the Dissolution', *Huntington Lib. Qutrly.*, IV, 1941–2.

Evans, Elwyn. 'Two Machynlleth Toll-Books', *Nat. Lib. Wales J.*, VI, 1949–50.

Evans, G. Ewart. *The Horse in the Furrow.* London, 1960.

Everitt, Alan. *The County Committee of Kent in the Civil War.* Leicester, Dept. of English Local History, Occasional Papers, 9, 1957.

—— *Kent and its Gentry, 1640–1660: a political Study.* University of London Ph.D. thesis, 1957.

—— *Suffolk and the Great Rebellion.* Suffolk Rec. Soc., III, 1961.

Farrer, W. *Chartulary of Cockersand Abbey*, III, iii, Chetham Soc., NS, LXIV, 1909.

Feaveryear, A. E. *The Pound Sterling. A History of English Money.* Oxford, 1933.

Felix, D. 'Profit Inflation and Industrial Growth', *Qutrly. J. of Economics*, LXX, 1956.

Fiennes, Celia. *The Journeys of Celia Fiennes.* ed. C. Morris. London, 1947.

Finberg, H. P. R. 'An Early Reference to the Welsh Cattle Trade', AHR, II, 1954.

—— *Gloucestershire Studies.* Leicester, 1957.

—— 'The Gostwicks of Willington', *Beds. Hist. Rec. Soc.*, XXXVI, 1956.

—— *Tavistock Abbey.* Cambridge, 1951.

Finch, Mary. *The Wealth of Five Northamptonshire Families, 1540–1640.* Northants. Rec. Soc., XIX, 1956.

Fisher, F. J. 'Commercial Trends and Policy in Sixteenth Century England', EcHR, X, 1939–40.

—— 'The Development of the London Food Market, 1540–1640', EcHR, V, 1935.

—— 'London's Export Trade in the Early Seventeenth Century', EcHR, 2nd Ser., III, 1950.

Fisher, H. A. L. *The History of England, 1485–1547.* London, 1906.

Fishwick, H. (ed.). *The Survey of the Manor of Rochdale.* Chetham Soc., NS, LXXI, 1913.

Folkingham, W. *Feudigraphia: The Synopsis or Epitome of Surveying Methodized.* London, 1610.

Foster, I. L., *see under* Alcock, L.

Fowler, J. T. *The Coucher Book of Selby Abbey, II.* Yorks. Arch. Soc., Rec. Ser., XIII, 1893.

Fowler, R. C. 'Inventories of Essex Monasteries in 1536', *Essex Arch. Soc.*, NS, X, 1909.

Fox, Sir Cyril. *A Country House of the Elizabethan Period in Wales: Six Wells, Llantwit Major, Glamorganshire.* Cardiff, 1941.

—— 'The Round-chimneyed Farm-houses of Northern Pembrokeshire', *Aspects of Archaeology in Britain and Beyond, Essays presented to O. G. S. Crawford*, ed. W. F. Grimes. London, 1951.

—— 'Three Rounded Gable Houses in Carmarthenshire', *Arch. Camb.*, 1951.

Fox, Sir C. and Raglan, Lord. *Monmouthshire Houses: A Study of Building Techniques and Smaller House-Plans in the Fifteenth to Seventeenth Centuries.* 3 vols. Cardiff, 1951–4.

Fussell, G. E. 'Adventures with Clover', *Agriculture*, LXII, 7, 1955.

—— 'Cornish Farming, A.D. 1500–1910', *Amateur Historian*, IV, 8. 1960.

—— *The English Rural Labourer.* London, 1949.

—— 'Four Centuries of Cheshire Farming Systems, 1500–1900', *Hist. Soc. Lancs. & Cheshire*, CVI, 1954.

—— 'Four Centuries of Farming Systems in Derbyshire, 1500–1900', *Derbyshire Arch. & Nat. Hist. Soc.*, LXXI, 1951.

—— 'Four Centuries of Farming Systems in Dorset, 1500–1900', *Dorset Nat. Hist. & Arch. Soc.*, LXXIII, 1952.

—— 'Four Centuries of Farming Systems in Hampshire, 1500–1900', *Hants. Field Club & Arch. Soc.*, XVII, iii, 1949.

Fussell, G. E. 'Four Centuries of Farming Systems in Shropshire, 1500–1900', *Salop Arch. Soc.*, LIV, i, 1951–2.

—— 'Four Centuries of Nottinghamshire Farming', *Notts. Countryside*, XVII, 2, 1956.

—— History of Cole (*Brassica* Sp.)', *Nature*, 4471 (9 July), CLXXVI, 1955.

—— *Robert Loder's Farm Accounts, 1610–1620*. Camden Soc., 3rd Ser., LIII, 1936.

Fussell, G. E. and Goodman, Constance. 'The Eighteenth-century Traffic in Milk Products', *Economic History*, III, 1937.

Gardiner, Dorothy (ed.). *The Oxinden Letters, 1607–1642*. London, 1933.

Gardiner, S. R. (ed.). *The Constitutional Documents of the Puritan Revolution, 1625–1660*. 1906 edn., Oxford.

Gay, E. F. 'Inclosures in England in the Sixteenth Century', *Qutrly J. of Economics*, XVII, 1903.

—— 'Inquisitions of Depopulation in 1517 and the Domesday of Inclosures', RHS, NS, XIV, 1900.

—— 'The Midland Revolt and the Inquisitions of Depopulation of 1607', RHS, XVIII, 1904.

—— 'The Rise of an English Country Family: Peter and John Temple, to 1603', *Huntington Lib. Qutrly*, I, 1938.

—— 'The Temples of Stowe and Their Debts: Sir Thomas Temple and Sir Peter Temple, 1603–1653', *Huntington Lib. Qutrly*, II, 1938–9.

Glass, D. V. 'Gregory King's Estimates of the Population of England and Wales, 1695', *Population Studies*, III, 1950.

Gough, R. (ed.). *Description des Royaulmes d'Angleterre et d'Escosse composé par Etienne Perlin, Paris 1558*. London, 1775.

Gould, J. D. 'Mr Beresford and the Lost Villages: a Comment', AHR, III, 1955.

—— 'The Inquisition of Depopulation of 1607 in Lincolnshire', EHR, LXVII, 1952.

Grafton, Richard. *A little Treatise conteyning many proper Tables and Rules, very necessary for the use of all men*. 1602 edn., London.

Gras, N. S. B. *The Evolution of the English Corn Market...*, Cambridge, Mass., 1926.

Gray, H. L. *English Field Systems*. Harvard Historical Studies, XXII, 1915.

Green, Mrs J. R. *Town Life in the Fifteenth Century*. London, 1894.

Habakkuk, H. J. 'The Long-term Rate of Interest and the Price of Land in the Seventeenth Century', EcHR, 2nd Ser., V, 1952.

—— 'The Market for Monastic Property, 1539–1603', EcHR, 2nd Ser., X, 3, 1958.

Haldane, A. R. B. *The Drove Roads of Scotland*. London, 1952.

Hallam, H. E. 'Some Thirteenth-century Censuses', EcHR, 2nd Ser., X, 3, 1958.

Hallett, G. *The Economics of Agricultural Land Tenure*. London, 1960.

Hamilton, E. J. 'American Treasure and Andalusian Prices, 1503–1660', *J. Econ. & Bus. Hist.*, I, 1928–9.

—— *American Treasure and the Price Revolution in Spain, 1501–1650*. Harvard, 1934.

—— *Money, Prices, and Wages in Valencia, Aragon, and Navarre, 1351–1500*. Harvard, 1936.

—— 'The Decline of Spain', EcHR, VIII, 1938.

Hammarström, D. I. 'The Price Revolution of the Sixteenth Century: Some Swedish Evidence', *Scand. Econ. Hist. Rev.*, V, 1957.

Hammersley, G. 'The Crown Woods and their Exploitation in the Sixteenth and Seventeenth Centuries', *Bull. IHR*, XXX, 1957.

Harland, John (ed.). *The House and Farm Accounts of the Shuttleworths of Gawthorpe Hall...*, Parts I and II. Chetham Soc., XXXV, XLI, 1856.

Harris, A. 'The Agriculture of the East Riding of Yorkshire before the Parliamentary Enclosures', *Yorks. Arch. J.*, CLVII, 1959.

Harrison, William. *Harrison's Description of England in Shakespeare's Youth*, ed. F. J. Furnivall, New Shakespere Soc., 6th Ser. I and VIII. London 1877 and 1881.

Hartlib, Samuel. *Samuel Hartlib his Legacie*. London, 1652.

Harvey, N. 'Farm and Estate under Elizabeth the First', *Agriculture*, LX, 1953.

Hasbach, W. *A History of the English Agricultural Labourer*. London, 1908.

Hasted, Edward. *History of Kent*. Canterbury, 1797–1801.

Havinden, M. 'Agricultural Progress in Open-field Oxfordshire', AHR, IX, 1961.

Hembry, P. M. *The Bishops of Bath and Wells, 1535–1647: a social and economic study*. London University Ph.D. thesis, 1956.

Hemp, W. J. and Gresham, Colin. 'Park, Llanfrothen and the Unit System', *Arch. Camb.*, XCVII, 1942.

Henman, W. N. 'Newnham Priory: a Bedford Rental, 1506–7', *Beds. Hist. Rec. Soc.*, XXV, 1947.

Hervey, Lord Francis (ed.). *Suffolk in the Seventeenth Century. The Breviary of Suffolk by Robert Reyce, 1618*. London, 1902.

Hexter, J. H. *Reappraisals in History*. London, 1961.

—— 'Storm over the Gentry', *Encounter*, X, 1958.

Heylyn, Peter. *A Help to English History*. 1709 edn., London.

Hill, C. *Economic Problems of the Church, from Archbishop Whitgift to the Long Parliament*. Oxford, 1956.

Hill, J. W. F. *Tudor and Stuart Lincoln*. Cambridge, 1956.

Hilton, R. H. *The Social Structure of Rural Warwickshire*. Dugdale Soc. Occasional Paper, 9, 1950.

—— 'Winchcombe Abbey and the Manor of Sherborne', *Gloucestershire Studies*, ed. H. P. R. Finberg. Leicester, 1957.

Hirst, L. F. *The Conquest of Plague*. Oxford, 1953.

Hobsbawm, E. 'The General Crisis of the European Economy in the Seventeenth Century', *Past and Present*, V, VI, 1954.

Holdsworth, W. S. *An Historical Introduction to the Land Law*. Oxford, 1927.

Hopkins, E. *The Bridgewater Estates in North Shropshire in the First Half of the Seventeenth Century*. University of London M.A. thesis, 1956.

Hoskins, W. G. *Devon*. London, 1954.

—— 'English Provincial Towns in the early Sixteenth Century', RHS, 5th Ser., VI, 1956.

—— *Essays in Leicestershire History*. Liverpool, 1950.

—— 'Harvest Fluctuations and English Economic History, 1480–1619', AHR, XII, 1964.

—— *Industry, Trade, and People in Exeter, 1688–1800*. Manchester, 1935.

—— *The Midland Peasant*. London, 1957.

—— 'The Reclamation of the Waste in Devon', EcHR, XIII, 1943.

—— *Two Thousand Years in Exeter*. Exeter, 1960.

Hoskins, W. G. and Finberg, H. P. R. *Devonshire Studies*. London, 1952.

Howells, B. E. 'Pembrokeshire Farming *circa* 1580–1620', *Nat. Lib. Wales J.*, IX, 1955–6.

Hudson, W. H. *A Shepherd's Life*. Everyman edn. London, 1949.

Hughes, H. 'Notes on the Architecture of some old houses in the neighbourhood of Llansilin, Denbighshire', *Arch. Camb.*, XV (5th Ser.), 1898.

Hughes, H. and North, H. L. *The Old Cottages of Snowdonia*. Bangor, 1908.

Hulbert, N. F. 'A Survey of the Somerset Fairs', *Som. Arch. and Nat. Hist. Soc.*, LXXXII, 1937.

Hull, F. *Agriculture and Rural Society in Essex, 1560–1640*. University of London Ph.D. thesis, 1950.

Hurstfield, J. 'Corruption and Reform under Edward VI and Mary: the Example of Wardship', EHR, LXVIII, 1953.

—— 'The Greenwich Tenures of the Reign of Edward VI', *Law Qutrly Rev.* LXV, 1949.

—— 'Lord Burghley as Master of the Court of Wards', RHS, 4th Ser., XXXI, 1949.

—— 'The Profits of Fiscal Feudalism', EcHR, 2nd Ser., VIII, 1955.

—— *The Queen's Wards, Wardship and marriage under Elizabeth I*. London, 1958.

Jackson, J. N. 'Some Observations upon the Herefordshire Environment of the Seventeenth and Eighteenth Centuries', *Woolhope Nat.* Field Club, XXXVI, i, 1958.

James, M. E. *Estate Accounts of the Earls of Northumberland, 1562–1637*. Surtees Soc., CLXIII, 1955.

Jefferies, Richard. *Field and Hedgerow. Being the Last Essays of Richard Jefferies*. London, 1904.

—— *The Toilers of the Field*. London and New York. 1892.

Jevons, W. S. *Investigations in Currency and Finance*, 2nd edn., London, 1909.

Jevons, H. S. *The Causes of Unemployment, The Sun's Heat, and Trade Activity*. London, 1910.

—— 'Trade Fluctuations and Solar Activity', *Contemporary Rev.*, August, 1909.

Johnson, A. H. *The Disappearance of the Small Landowner*. Oxford, 1909.

Jones, Emyr G. (ed.). *Exchequer Proceedings (Equity) concerning Wales, Henry VIII–Elizabeth*. Cardiff, 1939.

Jones, E. L. 'Eighteenth-century Changes in Hampshire Chalkland Farming', AHR VIII, 1960.

Jones, Francis. 'An Approach to Welsh Genealogy', *Trans. Cymmrodorion Soc.*, 1948.

Jones, S. R. and Smith, J. T. 'The Houses of Breconshire, Part I', *Brycheiniog*, 1963.

Jones, T. I. Jeffreys. (ed.). *Exchequer Proceedings concerning Wales in Tempore James I*. Cardiff, 1955.

Kennedy, J. *The Dissolution of the Monasteries in Hampshire and the Isle of Wight*. London University M.A. thesis, 1953.

Kenyon, G. H. 'Petworth Town and Trades, 1610–1760: Part I', *Sussex Arch. Coll.*, XCVI, 1958.

Kerridge, E. 'Agriculture, *c.* 1500–*c.* 1793', VCH *Wilts.*, IV, 1959.

—— *The Agrarian Development of Wiltshire, 1540–1640*, University of London Ph.D. thesis, 1951.

—— 'The Floating of the Wiltshire Watermeadows', *Wilts. Arch. Nat. Hist. Mag.*, CXCIX, 1953.

—— 'The Movement of Rent 1540–1640', EcHR, 2nd Ser., VI, 1953.

—— 'The Notebook of a Wiltshire Farmer in the early seventeenth century', *Wilts. Arch. & Nat. Hist. Mag.*, LIV (CXCVII), 1952.

—— 'A Reconsideration of some Former Husbandry Practices', AHR, III, 1955.

—— 'The Returns of the Inquisitions of Depopulation', EHR, LXX, 1955.

—— 'The Revolts in Wiltshire against Charles I', *Wilts. Arch. & Nat. Hist. Mag.*, LVII, 1958–9.

—— 'Ridge and Furrow and Agrarian History', EcHR, 2nd Ser., IV, 1951.

—— 'The Sheepfold in Wiltshire and the Floating of the Watermeadows', EcHR, 2nd Ser., VI, 1954.

—— 'Social and Economic History of Leicester', VCH *Leics.* IV, 1958.

—— *Surveys of the Manors of Philip, First Earl of Pembroke, 1631–2*. Wilts. Arch. and Nat. Hist. Soc., Records Branch, IX, 1953.

King, G. *Natural and Political Observations and Conclusions upon the State and Condition of England*. 1696.

Klotz, E. L. and Davies, G. 'The Wealth of Royalist Peers and Baronets during the Puritan Revolution', EHR, LVIII, 1943.

Knocker, H. W. 'Sevenoaks: the Manor, Church and Market', *Arch. Cant.*, XXXVII, 1926.

Knowles, D. *The Religious Orders in England*, III. Cambridge, 1959.

Knox, Ronald. *Enthusiasm: a Chapter in the History of Religion*. Oxford, 1950.

Koenigsberger, H. G. 'Property and the Price Revolution (Hainault, 1474–1573)', EcHR, 2nd Ser. IX, 1956.

Lambarde, William. *A Perambulation of Kent*. 1826 edn., Chatham.

Lamond, E. (ed.). *A Discourse of the Common Weal of this Realm of England*. Cambridge, 1954.

Laslett, T. P. R. 'The Gentry of Kent in 1640', *Canb. Hist. J.*, IX, 1948.

Leadam, I. S. *The Domesday of Inclosures, 1517–18*. 2 vols. RHS, 1897.

Le Hardy, W. *County of Buckingham: Calendar to the Sessions Records, I, 1678–1694*. Aylesbury, 1933.

Leland, J. *Itinerary in England*, ed. L. Toulmin Smith. 5 vols. London, 1906–8.

Lennard, R. 'The Alleged Exhaustion of the Soil in Medieval England', *Econ. J.*, CXXXV, 1922.

—— 'English Agriculture under Charles II: The Evidence of the Royal Society's "Enquiries"', EcHR, IV, 1932.

—— *Rural Northamptonshire Under the Commonwealth*. Oxford Studies in Social and Legal History, V, 1916.

Leonard, E. M. 'The Inclosure of Common Fields in the Seventeenth Century', RHS, NS, XIX, 1905.

—— 'The Relief of the Poor by the State Regulation of Wages', EHR, XIII, 1898.

Lewis, E. A. (ed.). *An Inventory of the Early Chancery Proceedings concerning Wales*. Cardiff, 1937.

—— 'The Toll-Books of some North Pembrokeshire Fairs (1599–1603)', *Bull. BCS*, VII, 1934.

Lewis, E. A. and Davies, J. Conway. (eds.). *Records of the Court of Augmentations relating to Wales and Monmouthshire*. Cardiff, 1954.

Lipson, E. *The Economic History of England*, III. London, 1947.

Lisle, E. *Observations in Husbandry*, II, London, 1757.

Lister, J. 'Some Local Star Chamber Cases', *Halifax Antiq. Soc.*, 1927.

—— *Yorkshire Star Chamber Proceedings*, IV, Yorks. Arch. Soc., Rec. Ser., LXX, 1927.

Lloyd, Nathaniel. *A History of the English House from primitive times to the Victorian Period*. London, 1931.

Lodge, E. C. *The Account Book of a Kentish Estate, 1616–1704*. Records of the Social and Economic History of England and Wales, VI. London, 1927.

Low, David. *On the Domesticated Animals of the British Islands*. London, 1845.

Lyte, Henry. *A Niewe Herbal or Historie of Plantes...translated out of French by H.L.* London, 1578.

McGrath, P. V. *The Marketing of Food, Fodder, and Livestock in the London Area in the Seventeenth Century*. University of London M.A. thesis, 1948.

Malfatti, C. V. *Two Italian Accounts of Tudor England*. Barcelona, 1953.

Markham, Gervase. *Cheape and Good Husbandry*. 1623.

—— *Markham's Farewell to Husbandry*. London, 1625.

Marshall, William. *The Rural Economy of Norfolk*. London, 1787.

—— *The Rural Economy of the Southern Counties*. 2 vols., London, 1798.

Mascall, L. *The Government of Cattell...*, London, 1620.

Matthews, C. M. 'Annals of the Poor: taken from the Records of a Hertfordshire Village', *History Today*, V, 1955.

Maxey, E. *A New Instruction of Plowing and Setting of Corne, Handled in Manner of a Dialogue betweene a Ploughman and a Scholler*. London, 1601.

Meekings, C. A. F. *Dorset Hearth Tax Assessments, 1662–1664*. Dorset Nat. Hist. and Arch. Soc., Occasional Publications, Dorchester, 1951.

Mercer, E. 'The Houses of the Gentry', *Past and Present*, 5, 1954.

Miller, H. 'The Early Tudor Peerage' (thesis summary), *Bull*. IHR, XXIV, 1951.

—— 'Subsidy Assessments of the Peerage in the Sixteenth Century', *Bull*. IHR, XXVIII, 1955.

Minchinton, W. 'Bristol—Metropolis of the West in the Eighteenth Century', RHS, 5th Ser., IV, 1954.

Moore, H. L. *Economic Cycles: their Law and Cause*. New York, 1914.

—— *Generating Economic Cycles*. New York, 1923.

More, Sir Thomas. *The Utopia of Sir Thomas More*, ed. J. H. Lupton. Oxford, 1895.

Morton, J. *The Natural History of Northamptonshire*. London, 1712.

Mousley, J. E. 'The Fortunes of Some Gentry Families of Elizabethan Sussex', EcHR, 2nd Ser., XI, 1959.

Mortimer, J. *The Whole Art of Husbandry*. London, 1707.

Munby, L. *Hertfordshire Population Statistics, 1563–1801*. Hitchin, 1964.

Nalson, John. *An impartial Collection of the great Affairs of State*. I. London, 1682.

Nef, J. U. 'A Comparison of Industrial Growth in France and England, 1540–1640', EcHR, VII, 1937.

—— 'Mining and Metallurgy in Medieval Civilisation', *The Cambridge Economic History of Europe*, ed. M. Postan and E. E. Rich, II, Cambridge, 1952.

—— 'Silver Production in Central Europe', *J. Polit. Econ.*, XLIX, 1941.

—— *The Rise of the British Coal Industry*. London, 1932.

—— 'The Progress of Technology and the Growth of Large-scale Industry in Great Britain, 1540–1640', EcHR, V, 1934.

Norden, John. *Speculum Britanniae. An Historical and Chorographical Description of Middlesex and Hertfordshire*. London, 1723.

—— *The Surveyors Dialogue*. London, 1607.

Notestein, W., Relf, F. H. and Simpson, H. (eds.). *Commons Debates, 1621*. 8 vols. New Haven, 1935.

Oschinsky, D. 'Medieval Treatises on Estate Accounting', EcHR, XVII, 1947.

Owen, George. *Description of Pembrokeshire*, 2 vols. ed. H. Owen. London, 1892.

—— *The Taylors Cussion*, ed. E. M. Pritchard. London, 1906.

Owen, G. Dyfnallt. *Elizabethan Wales. The Social Scene*. Cardiff, 1962.

Owen, L. 'The Population of Wales in the Sixteenth and Seventeenth Centuries', *Hon. Soc. Cymmrodorion*, 1959.

Page, F. M. *Wellingborough Manorial Accounts, A.D. 1258–1323*. Northants. Rec. Soc., VIII, 1936.

Palmer, A. N. *History of Ancient Tenures of Land in the Marches of North Wales*. Wrexham, 1883. Second edition in Collaboration with Edward Owen, 1910.

Parenti, G. *Prime ricerche sulla rivoluzione dei prezzi in Firenze*. Florence, 1939.

Parker, L. A. 'The Agrarian Revolution at Cotesbach, 1501–1612', *Studies in Leicestershire Agrarian History*, Leics. Arch. Soc., XXIV, 1948.

—— 'The Depopulation Returns for Leicestershire in 1607', *Leics. Arch. Soc.*, XXIII, 1947.

—— *Enclosure in Leicestershire, 1485–1607*. University of London Ph.D. thesis, 1948.

Parliament. House of Commons. *Journals*, I, II, 1547–1642.

Pearce, Brian. 'The Elizabethan Food Policy and the Armed Forces', EcHR, XII, 1942.

Peate, I. C. *The Welsh House, A Study in Folk Culture*. Liverpool, 1944.

Pelc, J. *Ceny w Krakowie w latach 1369–1600, Badania z dziejóu spolecznych i gospodarczych*. Lwow, 1935.

Pierce, T. Jones (ed.). 'An Anglesey Crown Rental of the Sixteenth Century', *Bull. Board of Celtic Studies*, X, 1940.

Pierce, T. Jones (ed.). *A Calendar of Clenennau Letters and Papers*. Aberystwyth, 1947.
—— 'The Law of Wales—the last Phase', *Trans. Cymmrodorion Soc.*, 1963.
—— 'Notes on the History of Rural Caernarvonshire in the Reign of Elizabeth', *Trans. Caernarvons. Hist. Soc.*, 1940.
—— 'Pastoral and Agricultural Settlements in Early Wales', *Geografiska Annaler*, XLIII, 1961.
Platt, Sir Hugh. *The Jewell House of Art and Nature*..., London, 1594.
Plattes, G. *A Discovery of Infinite Treasure Hidden Since the World's Beginning*. London, 1639.
Plot, R. *The Natural History of Oxfordshire*..., Oxford, 1677.
Plymley, Joseph. *General View of the Agriculture of Shropshire*. London, 1803.
Pollard, A. F. and Blatcher, M. 'Hayward Townshend's Journals', *Bull.* IHR, XII, 1934–5.
Postan, M. M. 'Some Economic Evidence of Declining Population in the later Middle Ages', EcHR 2nd Ser. II, 1950.
—— 'The Chronology of Labour Services', RHS, 4th Ser., XX, 1937.
—— 'The Fifteenth Century', EcHR, IX, 1939.
Pribram, A. F. *Materialien zur Geschichte der Preise und Löhne in Österreich*. Vienna, 1938.
Pringle, A. *General view of the Agriculture of the County of Westmorland*. London, 1813.
Public Record Office, London. *Acts of the Privy Council, New Series, 1542–1630*.
Pugh, R. B. *Antrobus Deeds before 1625*. Wilts. Arch. & Nat. Hist. Soc., Records Branch, III, 1947.
—— *The Crown Estate, An Historical Essay*. London, 1960.
Pugh, T. B. (ed.). *The Marcher Lordships of South Wales, 1415–1536*. Cardiff, 1963.
Purvis, J. S. 'A Note on Sixteenth-century Farming in Yorkshire', *Yorks. Arch. J.*, XXXVI, 1944.
—— *A Selection of Monastic Records and Dissolution Papers*. Yorks. Arch. Soc., Rec. Ser., LXXX, 1931.
Ramsay, G. D. (ed.). *John Isham, Mercer and Merchant Adventurer: Two Account Books of a London Merchant in the Reign of Elizabeth I*. Northants. Rec. Soc., XXI, 1962.
Rathbone, A. *The Surveyor in Foure Bookes*. London, 1616.
Rea, W. F. 'The Rental and Accounts of Sir Richard Shireburn, 1571–77', *Lancs. & Ches. Hist. Soc.*, CX, 1959.
Rees, W. *A Survey of the Duchy of Lancaster Lordships in Wales, 1609–13*. Cardiff, 1953.
Reid, Rachel R. *The King's Council in the North*. London, 1921.
Rew, R. H. *An Agricultural Faggot. A Collection of Papers on Agricultural Subjects*. Westminster, 1913.
Richards, Thomas. *A History of the Puritan Movement in Wales, 1639–53*. London, 1920.
Richardson, H. *Medieval Fairs and Markets of York*. St Anthony's Hall Publications, 20, York, 1961.
Richardson, W. C. *History of the Court of Augmentations, 1536–1554*. Baton Rouge, 1961.
—— *Tudor Chamber Administration, 1485–1547*. Baton Rouge, 1952.
Robinson, Thomas. *The Common Law of Kent; or, the Customs of Gavelkind. With an Appendix concerning Borough English*. London, 1822.
Rodgers, H. B. 'Land Use in Tudor Lancashire: the Evidence of the Final Concords, 1450–1558', *Inst. British Geographers*, XXI, 1955.
—— 'The Market Area of Preston in the Sixteenth and Seventeenth Centuries', *Geographical Studies*, III, 1, 1956.
Rogers, J. E. T. *A History of Agriculture and Prices in England*. Oxford, 1866–1900.
—— *Six Centuries of Work and Wages*, London, 1894.

Rogers, P. G. *Battle in Bossenden Wood*. London, 1961.

Rowse, A. L. *The England of Elizabeth*. London, 1950.

—— *Tudor Cornwall: Portrait of a Society*. London, 1941.

Royal Commission on Ancient Monuments in Wales and Monmouthshire. *Anglesey Inventory*. London, 1937.

—— *Caernarvonshire Inventory*, 3 vols. London, 1956–64.

Royal Commission on Historical Monuments. *Monuments threatened or destroyed: a Select List*. London, 1963.

Royal Commission on Land in Wales and Monmouthshire. *Report*. London, 1896.

Royce, D. (ed.). *Landboc sive Registrum Monasterii . . . de Winchelcumba . . .*, II, Exoniae, 1903.

Russell, J. C. *British Medieval Population*. Albuquerque, 1948.

Rye, W. B. *England as seen by Foreigners*. London, 1865.

Sabin, A. *Some Manorial Accounts of Saint Augustine's Abbey, Bristol*. Bristol Rec. Soc., XXII, 1960.

Salter, E. Gurney. *Tudor England through Venetian Eyes*. London, 1930.

Salter, H. E. *Cartulary of Oseney Abbey*, VI. Oxford Hist. Soc., CI, 1936.

Saltmarsh, J. 'A College Home-farm in the Fifteenth Century', *Economic History*, III, 1936.

—— 'Plague and Economic Decline in England', *Camb. Hist. J.*, VII, 1941.

Savine, A. 'Bondmen under the Tudors', RHS, NS, XVII, 1903.

—— *English Monasteries on the eve of the Dissolution*. Oxford Studies in Social and Legal History, ed. P. Vinogradoff, I, 1909.

Sayce, R. U. 'The Old Summer Pastures Pt II', *Mont. Coll.*, LV, i, 1958.

Schenk, W. *The Concern for Social Justice in the Puritan Revolution*. London, 1948.

Scott, W. D. Robson. *German Travellers in England, 1400–1800*. Oxford, 1953.

Simiand, F. *Recherches anciennes et nouvelles sur le mouvement général des prix du XVIᵉ au XIXᵉ siècle*. Paris, 1932.

Simpson, A. *The Wealth of the Gentry, 1540–1660: East Anglian Studies*. Cambridge, 1961.

Skeat, Rev. W. W. (ed.). *The Book of Husbandry by Master Fitzherbert*. English Dialect Soc., 1882.

Skeel, Caroline. 'The Cattle Trade between Wales and England . . .', RHS 4th Ser., IX, 1926.

Slack, W. J. *The Lordship of Oswestry, 1393–1607*. Shrewsbury, 1951.

Smith, J. T. 'The Long-house in Monmouthshire: a Reappraisal', *Culture and Environment*, ed. Alcock & Foster, 1963.

—— 'Medieval Roofs: A Classification', *Arch. J.*, CXV, 1958.

Smith, P. 'The Long-house and the Laithe-house', *Culture and Environment*, ed. Alcock & Foster, 1963.

—— 'Plas Teg', *J. Flints. Hist. Soc.*, XVIII, 1960.

Smith, P. and Gardner, E. M. 'Two Farmhouses in Llanbedr', *J. Merioneth Hist. and Rec. Soc.*, III (iii), 1959.

Smith, P. and Owen, C. E. V. 'Traditional and Renaissance Elements in some late Stuart and early Georgian Half-timbered Houses in Arwystli', *Mont. Coll.*, LV, 1958.

Smith, R. A. L. *Canterbury Cathedral Priory, A Study in Monastic Administration*. Cambridge, 1943.

Smith, W. J. (ed.). *Calendar of Salusbury Correspondence, 1553–1700*. Cardiff, 1954.

Somerville, R. *History of the Duchy of Lancaster*, I, 1265–1603. London, 1953.

Speed, Adolphus. *Adam out of Eden . . .*, London, 1659.

Speed, Aldolphus. *The Husbandman, Farmer and Grazier's…Instructor…or Country-man's Guide*. London, [1705 or later].

Spratt, J. *Agrarian Conditions in Norfolk and Suffolk, 1600–1650*. Univ. of London M.A. thesis, 1935.

Steer, F. W. (ed.). *Farm and Cottage Inventories of Mid-Essex, 1635–1749*. Chelmsford, 1950.

Stone, L. 'The Anatomy of the Elizabethan Aristocracy', EcHR, XVIII, 1948.

—— 'The Elizabethan aristocracy—a Restatement', EcHR, 2nd Ser., IV, 1952.

—— 'Elizabethan Overseas Trade', EcHR, 2nd Ser., II, 1949.

—— 'The Fruits of Office: The Case of Robert Cecil, first Earl of Salisbury, 1596–1612', in *Essays in the Economic and Social History of Tudor and Stuart England*, ed. F. J. Fisher, Cambridge, 1961.

—— 'The Nobility in Business, 1540–1640', *The Entrepreneur*, Harvard University, 1957.

—— 'State Control in Sixteenth-century England', EcHR, XVII, 1947.

Straker, E. 'Ashdown Forest and its Inclosures', *Sussex Arch. Coll.*, LXXXI, 1940.

Straton, C. R. *Survey of the lands of William, first earl of Pembroke*. Roxburghe Club, 2 vols., 1909.

Summerson, Sir J. N. *Architecture in Britain 1530 to 1830*. London, 1953.

Supple, B. E. *Commercial Crisis and Change in England, 1600–1642*. Cambridge, 1959.

Sylvester, D. 'The Open Fields of Cheshire', *Hist. Soc. Lancs. & Cheshire*, CVIII, 1956.

Sylvester, D. and Nulty, G. *The Historical Atlas of Cheshire*. Chester, 1958.

T., R., Gent. *The Tenants' Law, or the Laws Concerning Landlords, Tenants and Farmers*. London, 1666.

—— *Tables of Leases and Interest…*; London, 1628.

Tawney, R. H. *The Agrarian Problem in the Sixteenth Century*. London, 1912.

—— *Business and Politics under James I: Lionel Cranfield as Merchant and Minister*. Cambridge, 1958.

—— 'The Rise of the Gentry, 1558–1640', EcHR, XI, 1941.

—— 'The Rise of the Gentry: A Postcript', EcHR, 2nd Ser., VII, 1954.

Tawney, A. J. and R. H. 'An Occupational Census of the Seventeenth Century', EcHR, V, 1934–5.

Tawney, R. H. and Power, Eileen (eds.). *Tudor Economic Documents*, 3 vols. London, 1924.

Taylor, H. *Old Halls of Lancashire and Cheshire*. Manchester, 1884.

Thirsk, Joan. *English Peasant Farming*. London, 1957.

—— 'Industries in the Countryside', *Essays in the Economic and Social History of Tudor and Stuart England*, ed. F. J. Fisher. Cambridge, 1961.

—— 'The Isle of Axholme before Vermuyden', AHR, I, 1953.

—— *Tudor Enclosures*. Hist. Assoc. Pamphlet, General Ser. 41, 1959.

Thomas, D. R. *The History of the Diocese of Saint Asaph*. 3 vols. Oswestry, 1908.

Thomas, Lawrence. *The Reformation in the Old Diocese of Llandaff*. Cardiff, 1930.

Thompson, Flora. *Lark Rise to Candleford*. 1957 edn., London.

Thorpe, S. M. *The Monastic Lands in Leicestershire on and after the Dissolution*. University of Oxford B.Litt. thesis, 1961.

Topographer and Genealogist, I. London, 1846.

Torr, Cecil. *Small Talk at Wreyland*. 1926 edn., Cambridge.

Trevor-Roper, H. R. 'The Elizabethan Aristocracy: an anatomy anatomized', EcHR, 2nd Ser., III, 1951.

—— *The Gentry, 1540–1640*, EcHR Supplement, I, 1953.

Trow-Smith, R. *A History of British Livestock Husbandry to 1700*. London, 1957.

Tupling, G. H. 'An Alphabetical List of the Markets and Fairs of Lancashire recorded before the Year 1701', *Lancs. and Ches. Antiq. Soc.*, LI, 1936.

—— *The Economic History of Rossendale*. Chetham Soc., NS LXXXVI, 1927.

—— 'Lancashire Markets in the Sixteenth and Seventeenth Centuries', *Lancs. and Ches. Antiq. Soc.*, LVIII, 1947.

—— 'The Origin of Markets and Fairs in Medieval Lancashire', *Lancs. and Ches. Antiq. Soc.*, XLIX, 1933.

Tyack, N. C. P. *Migration from East Anglia to New England before 1660*. University of London Ph.D. thesis, 1951.

Upton, A. F. *Sir Arthur Ingram c. 1565–1642*. London, 1961.

Utterström, G. 'Climatic Fluctuations and Population Problems in Early Modern History', *Scand. Econ. Hist. Rev.*, III, 1955.

Verlinden, C. and Others. 'Mouvements des prix et des salaires en Belgique au XVIe siecle', *Annales E.S.C.*, 1955.

Wales, . A Bibliography of the History of. . . . Cardiff, 1962. *See also* Supplement I, Bull. Board of Celtic Studies, 1963.

Walford, Cornelius. *Fairs, Past and Present: a chapter in the History of Commerce*. London, 1883.

Walker, F. *Historical Geography of South-West Lancashire before the Industrial Revolution*. Chetham Soc., NS, CIII, 1939.

Wallen, W. C. 'Tilty Abbey', *Essex Arch. Soc.*, NS, IX, 1904–5.

Watkin, Dom Aelred. 'Glastonbury 1538–9 as shown by its account rolls', *Downside Review*, LXVII, 1949.

Wedgwood, C. V. *The Great Rebellion: II, The King's War, 1641–1647*. London, 1958.

West, T. *The Antiquities of Furness*. Ulverston, 1805.

Westcote, Thomas. *A View of Devonshire in MDCXXX*. Exeter, 1845.

Westerfield, R. B. *Middlemen in English Business, particularly between 1660 and 1760*. Transactions Connecticut Academy of Arts and Sciences, XIX, Connecticut, 1915.

White, Gilbert. *The Natural History of Selborne*. Everyman edn. London, 1945.

Wiebe, G. *Zur Geschichte der Preisrevolution des XVI und XVII Jahrhunderts*. Leipzig, 1895.

Willan, T. S. *The English Coasting Trade, 1600–1750*. Manchester Economic History Series, XII. Manchester, 1938.

—— *River Navigation in England, 1600–1750*. London, 1936.

Willan, T. S. and Crossley, E. W. (eds.). *Three Seventeenth-Century Yorkshire Surveys*. Yorks. Arch. Soc. Rec. Ser., CIV, 1941.

Williams, Clare. *Thomas Platter's Travels in England, 1599*. London, 1937.

Williams, Glanmor. *The Welsh Church from Conquest to Reformation*. Cardiff, 1962.

Williams, N. J. *The Maritime Trade of East Anglian Ports, 1550–1590*. University of Oxford D.Phil. thesis, 1952.

—— 'Sessions of the Clerk of the Market of the Household in Middlesex', *London and Middlesex Arch. Soc.*, XIX, ii, 1957.

—— *Tradesmen in Early-Stuart Wiltshire*. Wilts. Arch. and Nat. Hist. Soc., Records Branch, XV, 1960.

Williams, W. Ogwen. *Calendar of the Caernarvonshire Quarter Sessions Records*. Cardiff, 1956.

Wilson, Rev. J. M. (ed.). *Accounts of the Priory of Worcester for the year 13–14 Hen. VIII, A.D. 1521–2*. Worcs. Hist. Soc., 1907.

Winchester, Barbara. *Tudor Family Portrait*. London, 1955.

Wolffe, B.P. 'The Management of English Royal Estates under the Yorkist Kings', *EHR*, LXXI, 1956.

Wood, E. B. (ed.). *Rowland Vaughan, His Booke.* London, 1897.

Wood-Jones, R. B. *Traditional Domestic Architecture in the Banbury Region.* Manchester, 1963.

Woodward, G. W. O. *The Benedictines and Cistercians in Yorkshire in the sixteenth century.* Trin. Coll., Dublin, Ph.D. thesis, 1955.

Woodworth, Allegra. 'Purveyance for the Royal Household in the Reign of Queen Elizabeth', *American Philosophical Soc.,* NS, XXXV, 1946.

Worlidge, John. *Systema Agriculturae; the Mystery of Husbandry discovered: . . . 2nd edn. with additions by the author.* London, 1675.

Wright, T. *Three Chapters of Letters relating to the Suppression of the Monasteries.* Camden Soc., 1843.

Wynn, Sir John. *History of the Gwydir Family.* Cardiff, 1927.

Wynn of Gwydir. *Calendar of Wynn of Gwydir Papers, 1515–1690.* Aberystwyth, 1926.

Youings, J. A. *Devon Monastic Lands: Calendar of Particulars for Grants, 1536–58.* Devon and Cornwall Rec. Soc., NS I, 1955.

—— 'The Terms of the Disposal of the Devon Monastic Lands, 1536–58' EHR, LXIX, 1954.

Young, F. Brett. *Portrait of a Village.* London, 1937.

SELECT BIBLIOGRAPHY